Choose the Right Word

A Modern Guide to Synonyms

Formerly titled Modern Guide to Synonyms

S.I.Hayakawa

PERENNIAL LIBRARY

Harper & Row, Publishers, New York
Cambridge, Philadelphia, San Francisco, Washington
London, Mexico City, São Paulo, Singapore, Sydney

This work was originally published in hardcover by Funk & Wagnalls under the title *Modern Guide to Synonyms and Related Words*.

First PERENNIAL LIBRARY edition published 1987

Library of Congress Cataloging-in-Publication Data

Hayakawa, S. I. (Samuel Ichiyé), 1906–
  Choose the right word.

  Rev. ed. of: Funk & Wagnalls modern guide to synonyms and related words. 1968.
  Includes index.
  1. English language—Synonyms and antonyms.
I. Funk & Wagnalls modern guide to synonyms and related words.
II. Title.
PE1591.F8   1987   423′.1   86-46071
ISBN 0-06-055080-5   87 88 89 90 91 RRD 10 9 8 7 6 5 4 3 2 1
ISBN 0-06-091393-2 (pbk.)   87 88 89 90 91 RRD 10 9 8 7 6 5 4 3 2 1

CONTENTS

EDITORIAL STAFF

INTRODUCTION

by S. I. Hayakawa

English has the largest vocabulary and the most synonyms of any language in the world. This richness is due to the fact that the English language has grown over the centuries by constantly incorporating words from other languages. Even before the Norman Conquest, the Anglo-Saxon vocabulary included words borrowed from Latin (*street, mile*, the suffix *-chester* in the names of towns), Greek (*priest, bishop*), Celtic (*crag, bin*), and Scandinavian (*law, fellow, egg, thrall*). After the Norman Conquest, the English vocabulary was virtually doubled by the addition of French words, especially those reflecting a higher standard of living and a more complex social life: for example, words connected with food (*sugar, vinegar, boil, fry, roast*), clothing (*garment, robe, mantle, gown*), law (*plaintiff, perjury, legacy*), religion (*convent, hermitage, chaplain, cardinal*), and social rank and organization (*prince, duke, count, vassal, mayor, constable*).

While much of the new French vocabulary described new ideas and activities, much of it duplicated the pre-existing Anglo-Saxon vocabulary, giving the writer or speaker a choice of synonyms: *cure* (French) or *heal* (Anglo-Saxon), *table* or *board*, *poignant* or *sharp*, *labor* or *work*, *mirror* or *glass*, *assemble* or *meet*, *power* or *might*. Sometimes the duplication of vocabulary was used to make distinctions: *ox, swine, calf*, and *deer* were called, when killed and prepared for cooking, *beef, pork, veal*, and *venison; hitting, striking, stealing*, and *robbing* became, when viewed through the eyes of French law, *assault, battery, larceny*, and *burglary*.

With the enormous expansion of classical learning in the Renaissance, there was a great influx of words of Latin and Greek origin into the language, dictated by the demands of an enriched intellectual and cultural life. Also, the larger world discovered through travel (from the Crusades onward) and exploration (especially in the Elizabethan period) was a great stimulus to culture and language. There also arose in the sixteenth century a fashion of ornamenting one's discourse with what were then called "aureate" or "inkhorn" terms drawn from Greek and Latin. Shakespeare's "multitudinous seas incarnadine" is a famous example, and what happened to these particular words is typical of the fate of this new vocabulary: *multitudinous* stayed in the language as one of several synonyms for *many*, while *incarnadine* is not heard any more except in this context. In brief, many words of classical origin introduced into the language during the Renaissance became permanent additions, but most were soon forgotten or were relegated to special technical contexts, like *hebdemodary* (weekly) and *gressorial* (having to do with walking).

The adventures of English-speaking people as they traded and fought and traveled around the world in modern times—in Europe, North America, India, Australia, Africa—also expanded the vocabulary. Words were borrowed from Dutch (*tub, spool, deck*), Spanish (*sherry, armada, grenade*), American Indian (*squash, toboggan, hickory*), East Indian (*cashmere, punch, shampoo*), Afrikaans (*veld, trek*), Italian (*soprano, casino, macaroni*), Mexican (*chocolate, tomato*), Australian (*kangaroo, billabong*), Japanese (*kimono, ricksha*), Malay (*amok, ketchup*), and many others.

Furthermore, the United States, as a separate nation with its own life and character and institutions, added vastly to the English vocabulary, beginning in Colonial times. With the rise of the United States to a position of world influence in politics, science, industry, trade, and the popular arts, American words and phrases have gained recognition and prestige everywhere. *Ice cream, jeep,* and *rock-and-roll* are internationally known terms, as are *containment, DEW-line,* and *nuclear deterrence.* Moreover, American terminology for many things exists side by side with an English terminology, placing another whole group of synonyms at our service: *help* (American) and *servant* (British), *sidewalk* and *pavement, billboard* and *hoarding, movies* and *flicks, druggist* and *chemist, installment plan* and *hire-purchase system, water-heater* and *geyser, checkers* and *draughts, soft drinks* and *mineral waters,* and so on through an almost interminable list.

Synonyms in English are therefore of many kinds. Some groups of synonyms, like *foreword* (English), *preface* (French), *introduction* (Latin), and *prolegomenon* (Greek), seem like a simple embarrassment of riches. Some, like *plain* (French), *steppe* (Russian), *pampas* (Spanish, from South American Indian), *prairie* (French voyageur), *savannah* (Spanish), *tundra* (Russian, from Lappish), refer to geographical variants of the same kind of thing. Others, like *teach, educate, indoctrinate, instruct, school, tutor,* differ from each other principally in degrees of abstraction: *teach* is certainly the most general word of this group, while the others are more specialized in application. Some words of quite similar meaning make distinctions at the concrete, descriptive level: *tip, cant, careen, heel, list, slant, slope, tilt; screech, scream, clamor, yammer, howl.* These are truly synonyms only if translated into more general form, the former group into *incline,* the latter into *outcry.*

It can be argued that there really are no exact synonyms—no exact equivalences of meaning. Such a position can be upheld if by "meaning" we refer to the total range of contexts in which a word may be used. Certainly there are no two words that are interchangeable in all the contexts in which either might appear. But within a given context, there is often exact synonymy: I *mislaid* my wallet; I *misplaced* my wallet. In a slightly different context, however, the two words are not interchangeable: it would not be idiomatic to say, I *mislaid* my suitcase —all of which may suggest that while *misplace* is applicable to both small objects and large, *mislay* applies only to small. Also, one may suffer disappointment because of *misplaced,* but never *mislaid,* trust. This example shows again that words which are synonymous in *one* of their meanings may differ considerably in their *other* meanings.

Some groups of words describe the same actions, but imply different relationships among the parties concerned. We *accompany* our equals; we *attend* or *follow* those to whom we are subordinate; we *conduct* those who need guidance, *escort* those who need protection, and *chaperone* those who need supervision; merchant ships are *convoyed* in time of war.

Feminine, effeminate, womanly, and *womanish* are much alike in referring to female characteristics, but the second applies only to males, and then in a derogatory sense.

Some differences in locution reveal differences in the degree of formality of the occasions described: a *luncheon* as distinguished from a *lunch.* Sometimes different locutions reveal differences not in the situations described but in the formality of discourse about them: *He went to bed,* for instance, as compared to *He hit the sack.*

Semanticists and linguistic scholars continue to remind us that words change in meaning according to time and place and circumstance. Their warnings are certainly not to be ignored. The *democracy* of Sweden is not identical with that which bears the same name in England, Japan, or the German Democratic Republic; and the *democracy* of any of these nations changes from decade to decade, from year to year.

Yet, with all the changes that go on both in language and in the world described by language, there are remarkable elements of stability in a vocabulary with as rich a literary and cultural history as English. The distinctions between *bravery* and *foolhardiness,* between *weeping* and *whining,* between *fury* and *rage,* between *thought* and *deliberation,* between *desolate* and *disconsolate,* remain remarkably constant through Shakespeare to Swift to Jane Austen to Mark Twain to the present-day English or American (or Canadian or Australian) writer. It is gratifying to call the reader's attention to the many new words—even fad words—and new meanings discussed in the present volume. But I like to think that the reader will find equal pleasure—perhaps more—in the continuities and constancies in the meanings of English words that persist despite changes of time and changes of scene.

Nothing is so important to clear and accurate expression as the ability to distinguish between words of similar, but not identical, meaning. There are occasions in which we have to make choices between *transient* and *transitory, mutual* and *reciprocal, gaudy* and *garish, inherent* and *intrinsic, speculate* and *ruminate, pinnacle* and *summit,* because in a given context one is certain to be more appropriate than the other. To choose wrongly is to leave the hearer or reader with a fuzzy or mistaken impression. To choose well is to give both illumination and delight. The study of synonyms will help the reader come closer to saying what he really wants to say.

HOW TO USE THIS BOOK

Using the Index. To find a word you want, turn first to the Index, beginning on p. 701. If the word is printed in small capital letters, as in the case of COURAGE, for example, that word appears as the head word of an essay. The page number on which that essay begins appears to the right of the word. You may then turn directly to the indicated page in the main section of the book. You will find COURAGE, for example, as the head word of an essay comparing *backbone, fortitude, grit, guts, nerve, pluck*, and *resolution* beginning on page 133. More often, however, the word you are interested in will *not* be a head word, but will appear in an essay listed under another word. In that event the Index will cross-refer you to the head word, printed in small capital letters, under which the word you are seeking will appear. Suppose you want to find *indigent*. In the Index you will find: indigent PENNILESS 433. This means that *indigent* is discussed in an essay under the head word PENNILESS beginning on page 433.

Some words, like *good*, have so many important meanings that they must be included in several essays that discuss different aspects of meaning. In such cases the nature of the head word will suggest which meaning is discussed. For example:

> good BENEFICIAL 45
> good OBEDIENT 402

Head words are always identified by part of speech when ambiguity would otherwise result. For example:

> ACT (n) 5
> deluge FLOOD (v) 224
> DEMAND (v) 151
> retreat ESCAPE (v) 197

In a few cases the same word appears as the head word of more than one essay; the Index distinguishes between such essays by listing either the part of speech or, if both are of the same part of speech, by the alphabetically-first word discussed in each essay after the head word. For example:

> PLAIN (n) 445
> PLAIN (adj) 446
> REQUEST (n) 504
> REQUEST (v) 505
> STOP (arrest) 592
> STOP (cease) 593

Finding the Word You Want. To aid you in locating the word you want, the head word of each essay is printed in large, boldface type in the margin beside the point where its essay begins. The other words discussed are printed in large, lightface type in the margins below their respective head words. Whenever there is not room to list all the words on the first page of an essay, the head word is repeated on the following page with the word *continued* in parentheses, with the remaining words treated in the essay listed below. In addition, the first paragraph of each essay begins without indentation to mark off even more clearly where each essay starts.

As a further aid in finding the word you want, the first occurrence of each word discussed within each essay appears in prominent boldface type, subsequent occurrences in italic type. Thus if you are looking for a particular word, for example *perennial* in the essay PERMANENT, you needn't read about *lasting, enduring, perpetual,* and *durable*—all discussed first—in order to get to it. Just scan the boldface words until you find what you are looking for. Of course, we hope you will more often want to read the entire essay, but we have made this guide to synonyms flexible enough to be useful for quick reference as well.

Cross-References. Cross-references at the end of essays, as in the Index, are always made to head words which, as stated above, always appear in small capital letters. We have used cross-references liberally in the hope of stimulating the reader's interest to turn to other related essays and learn more about the complicated but fascinating interrelationships that exist between clusters of meaning in English. Cross-references, therefore, do not necessarily refer to a word of the same part of speech as the head word of the essay under which they appear. For instance, under SARCASTIC, an adjective, cross-references are made to CONTEMPTUOUS (an adjective), RIDICULE (a noun), SCOFF (a verb), and SOUR (an adjective). Cross-references are thus not intended to refer you to other synonyms or near-synonyms, but are used as a means of suggesting relationships that may interest you. Sometimes these relationships are close enough to approximate synonymy, as in the cross-reference to CLEAN from SANITARY; at other times, the relationship is one of nuance or similarity of usual context and is very far removed from synonymy, as in the cross-reference to MOUNTAIN and STEEP from ROUGH. In this way we hope to enlarge the reader's grasp of vocabulary and meaning, to lure him on, so to speak, into making more extensive inquiries than he perhaps originally intended, and thereby to help him discover how richly and subtly intertwined are the many elements of the English vocabulary.

Antonyms. Not every essay suggests a set of antonyms, and we have not attempted to force lists of antonyms into positions where they do not fit. Essays like CHARACTERISTIC, ROTATE, and SAMPLE can have no antonyms. Antonyms are listed at the end of those essays to which they apply following the indented word *Antonyms.* The antonym lists serve a different function from that of the cross-references, and the treatment accorded them is therefore different. Antonym lists are commonly used by people searching for a word rather than a meaning. Antonym lists should therefore be of the same part of speech as that of the words discussed in the essay under which they appear. You will note that some antonyms are listed in italic type whereas others are listed in small capital letters: for example, the antonyms of SAVORY are listed as BLAND, *insipid, tasteless.* Words listed in small capital letters are head words, and rather than repeat every word discussed in the essay designated, we refer the reader to the essay itself. The antonyms printed in italic type are either not included in the work or are not included in a sense antonymic to that of the head word under which they appear. For example, *graceful* and *sure* are listed in italic type among the antonyms of CLUMSY, even though *graceful* is discussed under EXQUISITE and *sure* is a head word in its own right. But since all the words discussed at EXQUISITE and SURE are not antonyms to CLUMSY, we cannot fairly refer the reader to these essays. Thus whenever an antonym appears in small capital letters, you can be sure that each word discussed under that head word is also an antonym.

We have tried to make this work accurate, clear, and as easy to use as possible, but we are only too well aware of our fallibility. If the reader has any suggestions on how the book might be improved—by the correction of existing essays, by rearranging the present groups of synonyms, or by the addition of other essays not now included—he is most cordially invited to write to: Harper & Row, Publishers, 10 East 53rd Street, New York, N.Y. 10022.

A

These words, all relatively formal, indicate the taking in of one thing by another. **Absorb** is slightly more informal than the others and has, perhaps, the widest range of uses. In its most restricted sense, it suggests the taking in or soaking up specifically of liquids: the ink *absorbed* by the blotter. In more general uses, it may imply the thoroughness of the action: not merely to read the chapter, but to *absorb* its meaning. Or it may stress the complete disappearance of the thing taken in within the encompassing medium: once-lovely countryside *absorbed* by urban sprawl. **Ingest** refers literally to the action of taking into the mouth, as food or drugs, for later absorption by the body. Figuratively it designates any taking in, and suggests the receptivity necessary for such a process: too tired to *ingest* even one more idea from the complicated philosophical essay he was reading. To **digest** is to alter food chemically in the digestive tract so that it can be *absorbed* into the bloodstream. In other uses, *digest* is like *absorb* in stressing thoroughness, but is even more emphatic. [You may completely *absorb* a stirring play in one evening, but you will be months *digesting* it.]

Assimilate is even more emphatic about the thoroughness of the taking in than either *absorb* or *digest*—in both its specific physiological and general uses. Physiologically, food is first *digested*, then *absorbed* by the bloodstream, and then *assimilated* bit by bit in each cell the blood passes. In more general uses, *assimilate*, unlike previous words, often implies a third agent beside the absorber and the absorbed—an agent that directs this process: the architect who *assimilates* his building to its environment. The process, furthermore, often implies the complete transformation of the absorbed into the absorbing medium. *Assimilate* also suggests a much slower process than *digest* and certainly than *absorb*, which can be nearly instantaneous: It would take the city generations to *assimilate* the newcomers into the patterns of a strange life.

Incorporate is the only word here that does not have a specific use pertaining to the taking in of liquids or of food, meaning literally "to embody." It compares to that aspect of *assimilate* which stresses the loss of separate identity for the absorbed quantity: *incorporating* your proposals into a new system that will satisfy everyone. It is unlike *assimilate* in lacking that word's suggestion of necessarily careful, time-consuming thoroughness.

Imbibe, while capable of uses comparable to those for *assimilate*, is mainly rooted still to its specific use for the taking in of liquids. Even this use, and certainly any others, now sound slightly archaic and excessively formal: Do you *imbibe* alcoholic beverages? See EAT.

Antonyms: disgorge, disperse, dissipate, eject, emit, exude.

absorb

assimilate
digest
imbibe
incorporate
ingest

abstain

forbear
refrain

Abstain means to withhold oneself from an action or self-indulgence. [There were six votes in favor, two against, and two *abstaining*; He *abstained* from drinking.] **Refrain** has to do with withholding an action temporarily, or checking a momentary desire: She *refrained* from scolding her child until the company left. To **forbear**, in its intransitive sense, is to exercise self-control, often out of motives of patience or charity. [Though impatient, the customer *forbore* to upbraid the harried sales clerk; The teacher *forbore* to report Johnnie's misbehavior to his parents.] See FORGO, FORSWEAR.

Antonyms: BEGIN, PERMIT.

absurd

farcical
foolish
irrational
ludicrous
preposterous
ridiculous
senseless
silly
unreasonable

Absurd means opposed to reason or truth, and may be applied to that which is grossly, and sometimes grotesquely, inconsistent with common sense or experience. **Preposterous** denotes a great contrariness to nature, reason, or common sense, and is used to describe that which is outrageously *absurd*. **Ridiculous** refers to that which is *absurd* in a way that invites ridicule or mockery. [It is *absurd* to predict that the sun will not rise tomorrow; It is *preposterous* that virtue should go unrewarded while vice goes unpunished; It is *ridiculous* to judge a foreign culture by its plumbing.]

Farcical and **ludicrous** are applied to that which is *absurd* in an amusing way. *Farcical* indicates a humorous distortion of fact, convention, or reason. *Ludicrous* implies playful absurdity, but may also be synonymous with *ridiculous* in describing something that is greeted with scorn or derision. [The *farcical* introduction of a talking horse gave the play its flavor; The *ludicrous* antics of the harlequins delighted the audience; The speaker made a series of *ludicrous* mistakes which were rewarded with hoots and catcalls.]

Foolish, **senseless**, and **silly** add a suggestion of folly or even of a trivial intellect to their synonymity with *absurd*. [To buy stocks in an unlisted gold-brick enterprise is a *foolish* investment; To beat a dead horse is *senseless*; To make unsupportable claims is *silly* affectation.]

Unreasonable and **irrational** mean contrary to reason, the difference between them being the fact that *unreasonable* implies a bias or intent to go wrong and *irrational* suggests an uncontrollable lack of understanding. [It is *unreasonable* to maintain a geocentric theory of the universe; It is *irrational* to expect an adult reaction from a child.] See HUMOROUS.

Antonyms: consistent, logical, rational, reasonable, sagacious, SENSIBLE.

accompany

attend
chaperon
conduct
convoy
escort

Accompany and **attend** are alike in meaning to go with, but each suggests a different relationship between persons. We *accompany* our equals, and *attend* those to whom we would show courtesy or to whom we are subordinate. When they refer to things, *accompany* and *attend* mean to be present with as a result of. [A sense of accomplishment often *accompanies* hard effort; A feeling of depression *attends* many illnesses.]

Escort and **convoy** are closely related, but *escort* is the broader term. To *convoy* means to *accompany* ships or vehicles for protection, while to *escort* is to go with them, or with persons, either for the purpose of guarding or as a mark of courtesy. Militarily, a land movement is *escorted*, a sea movement *convoyed*. During World War II, merchant ships were *convoyed* across the Atlantic by the Navy. A troop march may be *escorted* by armed vehicles. As a mark of courtesy, a ship making its maiden voyage is *escorted* by other craft in or out of the harbor. A boy is expected to *escort* his date to the door.

Chaperon means to *accompany*, but carries the implication of guidance or supervision in the interests of protection or propriety. A young girl may be *chaperoned* by her aunt while traveling abroad; a college instructor may be asked to *chaperon* a basketball dance.

Conduct, like *chaperon*, suggests guidance as part of *accompanying*, but here the interest is merely to physically lead: Let's hire a guide to *conduct* us through the old section of town. See GUIDE.

Antonyms: LEAVE.

Accomplice and **confederate** both denote a person who is associated with another in the perpetration of a crime, whether that association is limited to the planning stages or is extended to the entire execution of the wrongdoing. Thus, an *accomplice* or *confederate* may, but need not necessarily, be present at the scene of the crime. [The role of the murderer's *accomplice* was that of weapon procurer; Although Fredericks planned the theft, it was one of his *confederates* who actually entered the house and stole the jewels.]

An **abettor** is an *accomplice* or *confederate* who is present and who participates in the execution of a crime. A look-out is an *abettor* in a bank robbery.

Accessory is the legal term for an *accomplice* who helps a felon without being present at the scene of the crime. If he helps the felon's preparations, he is an *accessory* before the fact; if he helps the felon to escape punishment once the crime has been committed, he is an *accessory* after the fact.

Conspirator and **plotter** refer to persons who are involved in a secret or underhanded agreement to do some evil act. *Conspirators* are those who take part in a *conspiracy*, which is a legal term denoting an intention to violate the law; in general use, it is applied to major crimes and even more particularly to treason. *Plotters* are implicated in an activity which has a sinister purpose, but which, even though it is difficult to plan and execute, may be petty in scope. See ASSISTANT, ASSOCIATE, HELP.

Antonyms: OPPONENT.

accomplice

abettor
accessory
confederate
conspirator
plotter

Accumulate and **amass** both mean to pile up by successive addition. To *accumulate* is to heap or pile up or bring together by degrees or by regular additions; to *amass* is to bring together a great quantity and usually suggests great value. A housewife may *accumulate* trading stamps. A speculator may try to *amass* great wealth; an army may *amass* armaments for a final push. **Collect** and **gather** are interchangeable in the sense of bringing together into one place or into a group. *Collect*, however, suggests discriminating selection in a way that *gather* does not: to *collect* stamps as a hobby but with the idea of reselling them later at a profit; to *gather* a large bunch of wildflowers along a country road. **Hoard** means to *gather* and store for the sake of accumulation. It always connotes a selfish desire to keep permanently or for future use and suggests secrecy in the process. [A miser *hoards* his money; In wartime, individuals may *hoard* scarce items.] See PILE.

Antonyms: disperse, dissipate, scatter, spend, squander, waste.

accumulate

amass
collect
gather
hoard

All these words, as here considered, mean a mass of things that come or are brought together. They all imply that the things are neither merged with one another nor united organically in the resultant mass. **Accumulation** means that the things have come together by a series of

accumulation

aggregation

accumulation
(*continued*)

collection
conglomeration

additions rather than all at once. It often implies that the things are of the same kind, such as the *accumulation* of dust on surfaces, or of money in banks, and does not imply any coherence or organization in the mass gathered.

Collection and *accumulation* are often used interchangeably, but *collection* frequently implies a high degree of selection and organization in the mass collected: An *accumulation* of many specimens is needed when one is preparing a scientific *collection*.

Aggregation always denotes a mass brought together that forms, in some sense, a coherent whole, but one that has a lesser degree of organization than does a *collection*: An industrial empire is often an *aggregation* of unrelated enterprises.

Conglomeration implies that many different and sometimes even incongruous things are brought together from widely scattered sources or regions: The population of New York City is a *conglomeration* of many different kinds of people from various countries and cultures. See PILE.

accurate

correct
exact
nice
precise
right
true

Accurate, exact, precise, and true, as here considered, agree in implying close conformity to an objective standard. *Accurate* suggests that there are degrees of conformity to such a standard and stresses the painstaking care necessary for the attainment of fidelity to truth or fact: It took a week of investigation to get an even reasonably *accurate* account of the accident. *Exact* emphasizes extreme accuracy in measurable quantities and qualities: The *exact* wave length assigned to a transmitting station must always be maintained. *Precise* stresses great accuracy in regard to minute details: The assembling of the parts of a watch must be *precise*. *True*, as here considered, implies absolute accuracy, particularly in reproductions of an original: a *true* copy of a birth certificate.

Correct suggests the absence of error or fault and a conformity to some standard. It is more general than the other words in this group because it applies to such things as taste and fashion as well as to truth or fact: the *correct* dress for a formal dinner. Right is largely interchangeable with *correct*, but often adds a hint of moral approval: the *right* course of action.

Nice, in this sense, meaning a high or even an inordinate degree of precision or exactness, is passing out of usage, but it is still encountered in formal writing. See DUPLICATE, GENUINE.

Antonyms: erroneous, false, inaccurate, incorrect, inexact, wrong.

accuse

arraign
charge
impeach
incriminate
indict

These words all mean to declare a person to be guilty of some offense or shortcoming. Accuse is the most general word, and may be used in formal or informal, official or personal, contexts. An investigating committee may *accuse* an officeholder of wrongdoing; a neighbor may *accuse* a man of playing his radio too loud.

Charge, in this context, means to *accuse* formally, usually before a court; by extension, it means to *accuse* informally of a violation of some accepted standard. [The police *charged* the driver with reckless driving; The candidate *charged* his opponent with evasion of the basic issues.]

Incriminate means to *charge* a person with a crime directly, or to involve him in a crime by damaging testimony. In popular use, the latter is the more usual meaning: He was *incriminated* by an eye witness who placed him at the scene of the crime.

Indict and arraign are legal terms. *Indict* is to *charge* officially and to make subject to an appearance before a jury or judge. In an extended sense, *indict* is to *charge* unofficially but publicly: to *indict* a school of writing or painting as being obscurantist. To *arraign*, legally, is to call an *indicted* person before a court for trial; by extension, to *arraign* is to call publicly but unofficially a person or a movement to stand judgment before public opinion or some other standard.

Technically, **impeach** means to *arraign* a public official before a competent tribunal on a charge of malfeasance in office. In the United States, the House of Representatives *impeaches* federal officeholders, and the Senate sits as the court. [In February, 1868, President Andrew Johnson was *impeached* by the House; in May of that year he was acquitted by the Senate by a margin of one vote.] In extended use, to *impeach* is to discredit or to call into question: to *impeach* a witness; to *impeach* a person's motives. See DISAPPROVAL, REBUKE.
Antonyms: EXONERATE, PARDON.

These words agree in meaning to accept openly, though with some reluctance, the truth or existence of a fact, condition, etc. One **acknowledges** something embarrassing or awkward, and usually not voluntarily; more often, the acknowledgment is extracted from one more or less unwillingly: The general *acknowledged* that the war had not been going as well as expected, but he affirmed that a shift in strategy would enhance the prospects of victory.

Admit is a bold acknowledgment of implication in something one has formerly tended to deny or to equivocate about: He *admitted* under questioning that he was in the service of a foreign power, but denied that he was guilty of espionage. One **concedes**, usually because of overwhelming evidence, something which he has been very reluctant to *admit*. [He had no choice but to *concede* that he had been guilty of bad judgment; In the face of the disastrous military battle, they *conceded* that victory was no longer attainable, and agreed to a negotiated surrender.] **Confess** is to *admit* guilt, as to a crime, or to *admit* to a shortcoming: to *confess* that he was an accomplice of the robbery; He *confessed* that he had never read *Lady Chatterley's Lover.* See ASSERT.
Antonyms: CONTRADICT, FORSWEAR.

An **act**, in the sense considered here, is something that is done. The *act* may be done by a person, a group, or an impersonal entity, and is not limited by motive, nature, or result. Thus, an *act* of God is a violent outbreak of nature; the *act* of a maniac may endanger the community; the *act* of a philanthropist may enrich it. While *act* refers to something that is accomplished, **action** refers to the accomplishing of it or the process by which it is accomplished: the *action* of acid on metal.

Deed, while sometimes used to connote any *act*, good or bad, big or small, is usually synonymous with **exploit** and **feat** in meaning an achievement of great courage, nobility, intelligence, strength, or skill. An *exploit* is often a physical *act*; discovering a continent, scaling a high mountain, rocketing to a distant planet, and descending to the ocean floor are all *exploits*. A *feat* may also be a physical *act*, but it applies to mental *acts* as well. [Formulating the General Theory of Relativity was a prodigious mental *feat*; Playing several chess games simultaneously while blindfolded is a remarkable and impressive *feat*.] A *deed* is generally an *act* that is noteworthy for its difficulty or nobility. [The labors of Hercules were *deeds* of courage and ingenuity; A good *deed* may range from endowing a university to helping an old lady cross the street.]

acknowledge

admit
concede
confess

act

action
deed
exploit
feat
operation
performance

Operation and **performance** in this context can be synonymous with *act* or *action*, but are usually considered to be combinations of *acts* or the manner in which they are carried out. A military *operation* is a series of coordinated individual and group *acts*; the *performance* of an employee is the manner in which he carries out the *acts* that are part of his job's routine. See METHOD, PERFORM.

activity

bustle
commotion
stir
to-do

Activity means the state of being in motion, or the expenditure of energy. *Activity* is a broad word, applicable to physical or mental exertions or pursuits by a person or a group, and is often used to convey the idea of a number of separate simultaneous or successive operations: the *activity* of the heart; a busy week filled with social *activities*.

Bustle, commotion, stir, and **to-do** all mean a feverish, noisy, or excited *activity* by either an individual or a group. *Bustle* suggests busyness, *activity* with a purpose: the *bustle* on the floor of the stock exchange. *Commotion* suggests excitement and noisy disorganization: the *commotion* in a schoolroom during the teacher's absence. *Stir* suggests excited or lively movement: the *stir* aroused in the stands by a brilliant play on the field. *To-do* hints at unnecessary or uncalled-for excitement: the *to-do* generated by the new secretary coming to work in slacks and loafers. See ACT.

Antonyms: inactivity, inertia, inertness, laziness, SLOTH.

acumen

acuity
insight
perception

These words all refer to a highly developed mental ability to see or understand what is not obvious. **Acumen** has to do with keenness of intellect, and implies an uncommon quickness and discrimination of mind. It requires *acumen* to solve an intricate problem in human relationships, or to emerge unscathed from a venture into the stock market.

Insight and **perception** mean the power to recognize the hidden springs of behavior or the true nature or cause of a situation or condition: A psychiatrist's *insight* into human behavior may uncover the underlying cause of a boy's delinquency; a doctor's *perception* may recognize a patient's complaints as symptoms of a psychic disorder. *Perception* in its basic sense applies to anything recognized or understood by the senses, and in its extended sense to anything recognized or understood by the mind, thus suggesting a likeness between mind and the senses. *Perception* therefore suggests a view of the mind as a keenly receptive but nonetheless passive instrument, sensitive to very slight stimuli. *Insight*, on the other hand, is consistent with a view of the mind as an active agent, seeking and sifting ideas and probabilities as well as the evidence of sensations. In most contexts *insight* implies a more profound use of intellect and wisdom than does *perception*; *insight* suggests a knowledge of the inner character or essence of a thing, whereas *perception* relies primarily on the sharpness or **acuity** of one's senses.

Acuity means sharpness or keenness, and is applied exclusively to *perception*: visual *acuity*; The intelligence test was used as a basis for judging his mental *acuity*. See KEEN, SENSATION, VISION, WISDOM.

Antonyms: bluntness, dullness, obtuseness, stupidity.

adapt

accommodate
adjust

Adapt and **adjust** mean to change someone or something to suit new circumstances or a different environment. *Adapt* involves considerable change to meet new requirements, while *adjust* implies a minor change, as in the alignment of parts: to *adapt* a novel for the stage; to *adjust* a motor; to *adjust* the differences between two parties in a dispute. *Adapt* emphasizes the purpose for which the change must be made: The shrewd politician *adapts* his speech to suit the interests of his audience. *Adjust* is also used to mean to *adapt* oneself to a changed environment: Astronauts in flight must *adjust* to weightlessness.

Conform as here considered, means to correspond to a model or pattern: The building must *conform* to the blueprints. In a commonly used extended sense, *conform* means to adhere or *adjust* to conventional behavior: When traveling in a foreign country, it is wise to *conform* to the habits of the natives. This last example may also be recast reflexively: to *conform* oneself to the habits of the natives. To *fit* something is to *adapt* it to a purpose or use: A prudent man *fits* his standard of living to his budget.

Accommodate and **reconcile** are similar to *adapt* in meaning to change something or oneself in acknowledgement of an external condition. [An American visitor to the Far East must *accommodate* himself to habits of life that may seem very strange to him; A man following a military career must *reconcile* himself to long absences from his family.] *Reconcile* implies an *accommodation* not without misgivings or resentment; one *reconciles* oneself to certain conditions because the alternatives are even less palatable. *Accommodate*, on the other hand, conveys no such connotation, but suggests that the adjustment will make one's own lot easier because it will gratify others. See CHANGE.

Antonyms: derange, disarrange, discompose, disjoin, dislocate, displace, dissent, misfit, resist.

These words suggest the ease with which something will respond to an external force without breaking. **Adaptable** is the most general and the most abstract, suggesting the favorable quality of an ingenious or practical ability to alter habit as a response to changed circumstances: The ice ages exterminated many less *adaptable* species. **Yielding** is nearly as abstract as *adaptable* but more readily suggests an unfavorable passivity or unassertiveness than a favorable ability to improvise responses to challenges: the familiar stereotype that makes all women out to be helpless and *yielding*.

Flexible and **elastic** have concrete applications to physical objects, in which case they suggest something with spring to it or something that will quickly resume its shape after being distorted. *Elastic* suggests stretching, as of a band or membrane; *flexible* suggests bending, as of a rod or tube. **Adjustable** is applied to objects that can be manually altered to suit different uses or purposes: An *adjustable* automobile seat slides backwards or forwards to accommodate the driver.

Used in the sense of *adaptable*, *elastic* suggests the ability to recover quickly in the face of a threat or upset: a man who was amazingly *elastic* and imperturbable under pressure. *Elastic* can also refer to a projected set of requirements, rules, or figures when they are open to revision in the light of experience: an *elastic* budget that allows for unexpected outlays for new equipment; *elastic*, sensible rules drawn up by the students themselves. *Flexible*, in this context, is closer in meaning to *adaptable* than any other word here. It does not, however, necessarily suggest a permanent adjustment to change but rather momentary shifts of position to maintain balance: a society so *flexible* in the face of new influences as to lack unity or purpose. As in this example, *flexible* may suggest low standards or a chameleonic nature, whereas *adaptable* can suggest a slow, hard-won process of decisive movement in a new direction. See MALLEABLE, SUPPLE.

Antonyms: CLUMSY, dilatory, fixed, inflexible, rigid, set, sluggish.

add

affix
annex
append
attach

Add, the most general word in this group, means to join or unite so as to increase the importance, size, quantity, or scope of something: to *add* a new line of merchandise to one's goods; to *add* a new wing to a building; to *add* five new salesmen to a staff; to *add* a touch of levity to an otherwise solemn speech.

Attach, as here considered, means to connect or join on as a part, and is close in some contexts to **append**: to *attach* a stipulation to a contract; to *append* a query to a manuscript. *Append* emphasizes that the addition is subordinate or minor in relation to the original work. Both words are formal, but *attach* has a legalistic ring to it lacking in *append*: to *attach* a rider to a bill; to *append* a footnote. Note that *add* could be used in place of either of these words, but would make the tone less formal and therefore less impressive.

Affix means to fix or attach to: to *affix* a seal to document. *Affix* is appropriate only in very formal contexts, as in the description of state affairs: The president solemnly *affixed* his signature to the bill regulating nuclear disarmament.

Annex means to add something supplemental. It implies not only that the addition is a subordinate part, but often that the addition remains distinct: to *annex* an adjoining territory; to *annex* a building to an older one. See ENLARGE.

Antonyms: abstract, deduct, LESSEN, REDUCE, *subtract.*

addition

accessory
adjunct
appendage
appendix
appurtenance
attachment
supplement

These words all refer to parts of a whole, either integral or incidental. **Addition** and **supplement** share one sense in which the part and whole being joined are alike in kind, so that only an increase in quantity results. [The new members will be a welcome *addition* to the club; A vitamin *supplement* is not necessary for the average diet.] Both words have uses, on the other hand, in which the part remains distinguishable from and subordinate to the whole. [What a charming *addition* the sunporch makes to your house; The paper-covered book of quizzes was a *supplement* to the class's mathematics textbook.] A *supplement* can also be a standard or special section of a newspaper: the Sunday *supplement* on the fall fashions. **Appendix**, like *supplement*, can refer to a part of a book, but is more often bound with the book itself. Neither of these are essential to the book's completeness, although both would offer additional details on given material.

Appendage refers to a more integral part of a whole than do any of the other terms. It is especially used in the life sciences to indicate the limbs or extremities of a plant or animal. No one except such a scientist, however, is likely — even in the most formal of contexts — to use *appendage* in preference to limb, branch, arm, leg, tail, or whatever. Biologists themselves, in fact, can be every bit as exact and certainly more succinct in speaking of a monkey's *tail* rather than its caudal *appendage*. In other uses of this word, the subordination of the part to the whole is emphasized. Such uses may be rather stiff except when a note of mockery is conveyed. [It was apparent to everyone that the husband had become a mere *appendage* to his wealthy wife.]

Appurtenance and **adjunct** both refer to a part that becomes a valuable *addition* to a whole, though not essential to it. *Appurtenance* has a specific legal sense of an incidental property right that goes along with a major right, such as the right of way to a building. The sense of a gratuitous advantage pervades its other meanings as well: He was unusual in considering her beauty as an *appurtenance* to her vigorous mind, and not vice versa. In *adjunct*, the separateness of the added part is stressed: Memorization is only an *adjunct* to real education, not its staple.

Attachment and **accessory** refer to parts that are neither essential to nor fused with the whole they complement. An *attachment* increases the usability of the original whole for which it is specifically designed, although its use is optional: If we had a flash-bulb *attachment*, we could also take pictures at night. One meaning of *accessory* is identical to that of *attachment*, as in automobile *accessories*. Another sense of *accessory* points to its enhancing of the beauty, rather than the usefulness, of the whole to which it is added: the tastefully chosen *accessories* that dramatize the simplest dress or suit. See EXTRANEOUS.

Antonyms: abstraction, deletion, omission, subtraction.

These words mean equal to what is required or expected, but not exceeding it by much. **Adequate** means suitable to the case or occasion: an *adequate* supply of fuel for the winter months. Like **satisfactory**, *adequate* may apply to quality as well as quantity: an *adequate* performance, but nothing to rave about; His knowledge of French was *adequate* for the job, although he was not fluent in the language. *Satisfactory* implies a standard to which something is being compared or against which it is being tested. [The child's reading ability was *satisfactory* for his age level; The response to our call for financial contributions was wholly *satisfactory*, exceeding our goal by several thousand dollars.]

Enough is in some contexts interchangeable with *adequate*, but is used only to indicate amount or degree, not quality. Moreover, unlike *adequate*, *enough* is not used after an article and before a noun. One can say *an adequate fuel* but not *an enough fuel*. (Note that *adequate fuel* can mean either *enough fuel* or *fuel of acceptably high quality*, whereas *an adequate fuel* can refer only to quality.) *Enough* modifies either plural nouns or nouns denoting something that is measurable or of which there can be a quantity: *enough* salesmen; *enough* time; *enough* air — but not: *enough* supply; *enough* house.

Sufficient implies a quantity or number *adequate* for a particular need or to fulfill a particular purpose: Our military response to the aggressive act was limited but *sufficient* to show our determination. Unlike *satisfactory*, it does not imply measuring up to a standard. It emphasizes instead the end being sought; the degree to which something contributes to the achievement of that end is what makes it *sufficient* or insufficient. See PLENTIFUL.

Antonyms: DEFICIENT, *inadequate, insufficient, unqualified, unsuitable.*

Advice and **counsel** mean an opinion or a judgment given by one person to another urging him either to do something or not to do it. *Advice*, the more general term, may be given on serious matters or relatively trivial ones, but *counsel* suggests solemn *advice* given in an official or authoritative capacity about a matter of some importance, at least to the person seeking it: to give *advice* to one's son on the choice of a career; a woman seeking *advice* on hair styling; a young intern who profited from the *counsel* of an experienced surgeon. *Advice*, unless qualified by an adjective suggesting otherwise, often implies that the adviser has a direct and more or less personal interest in the person advised; the subject of *advice* is thus often personal in nature. *Counsel*, on the other hand, suggests a detached, impersonal view on the part of the person giving it; and the subject of *counsel* is often of a business nature.

Recommendation, in this sense, suggests *advice* given on the basis of one's own experience, and expresses a stronger, more positive endorsement of a particular course than *advice*. One's *advice* may be to choose the lesser of two evils; a *recommendation* implies that one course is distinctly favorable and ought to be pursued on its own merits: to read a new book on the *recommendation* of a friend. See HELP.

afraid

aghast
alarmed
anxious
apprehensive
fearful
frightened
scared
terror-stricken

Afraid means showing fear. When used by itself, no particular degree of fear is indicated. [She's *afraid* of dogs, even of puppies; We are *afraid* to walk in the park at night since the woman was killed there.] In most uses, being *afraid* is personal, and the fear has to do with bodily harm. *Afraid* is also used in polite discourse to indicate nothing more than mild concern: I'm *afraid* I'm a bit late for my appointment. Sometimes this use conceals great fear: If our present policy is continued, I am *afraid* that war is inevitable.

Frightened and **scared** often suggest fear of bodily harm, but not invariably; both may be used to describe vague fears of unknown source. [When the lights went out I got *scared*; She's always *frightened* when she's alone in the house.] *Frightened* has a more genteel sound than *scared*, but both apply strictly to physically felt fear, even if the causes are emotional or imaginary.

Anxious means tense and worried. **Fearful** may mean full of terror or dread, but more often means merely **apprehensive** — that is, anticipating danger, failure, or trouble. In the latter sense, *fearful* shares with *anxious* the suggestion that the worry stems from inner concern without much relevance to external conditions, and is in this sense unreasonable. *Apprehensive* suggests awareness of impending danger caused by circumstances, and does not depend so much on one's peculiar nature or habitual state of mind. [She was *anxious* about her daughter being out so late at night; The playwright was *fearful* that his first opening would be a failure; an investor who was *apprehensive* about his holdings during the recession; We are frankly *fearful* of another depression unless the economy improves radically in the next few months.]

Aghast, **alarmed**, and **terror-stricken** are applied to strong feelings of fear or fright. *Aghast* means *afraid* or *frightened* to the point of shock. A man waking up in a burning house will be *aghast* at the thought that his family may be in grave danger. *Alarmed* means suddenly and sharply *afraid* or *frightened*. Parents will be *alarmed* by a sudden outbreak of polio in their community. *Terror-stricken* is the strongest word in this list, and suggests fear so strong that normal reactions are suppressed. A *terror-stricken* person who is drowning may in panic resist the efforts of someone who is trying to save him. See FEAR, FRIGHTEN, INTIMIDATE.

Antonyms: audacious, BRAVE, *calm, confident, unafraid.*

aggression

assault
attack
offensive

All these words refer to actions initiated against other persons or groups, especially in wars. **Aggression** means unprovoked belligerent action, as by one nation upon the territory of another. An **attack** is aimed at injuring or destroying others, often by catching them off guard and unprepared. An **assault** is a violent *attack*, so violent that it often implies personal abuse motivated by envy, malice, and the like. Both *attack* and *assault* can be applied to any violent conflict, verbal as well as physical: a personal *assault* on the character of the president; a vigorous *attack* on the farm policy of the present administration.

[We will continue to resist *aggression* because tyranny must be resisted; The *attack* came just before dawn; The final *assaults* were designed to clear the last remnants of enemy resistance.] *Aggression*, as the above example illustrates, is now widely used among diplomats to describe a variety of actions contrary or hostile to the interests of their own countries; *aggression* is thus a linguistic casualty of the cold war, and has lost much of its meaning. *Assault* suggests perhaps more than *attack* the element of suddenness and surprise, as evidenced by the expression "surprise *attack*"; such emphasis is unnecessary with *assault*. In psychoanalytic usage *aggression* is a tendency toward hostile action. This sense has led to a number of analogous popular usages: He's just taking out his *aggressions* on me!

An **offensive** is a movement or position of offense or *attack*. In some contexts it is interchangeable with *attack*, but in others it applies to a large-scale coordinated military campaign of men and materiel: a major new *offensive* was launched in the western front. In recent diplomatic language, *offensive* is sometimes used synonymously with *initiative*: a peace *offensive* in the form of a 3-point offer to negotiate an end to the war. See ATTACK, FIGHT.

Antonyms: defense, repulsion, retreat, surrender, withdrawal.

These words refer to a person who habitually drinks alcoholic beverages to excess. **Alcoholic** and **drunkard** are the most general of these, the first being the more formal and neutral of the two. *Drunkard* carries a tone of condemnation and can apply justly only to someone who frequently drinks past the point of sobriety: Anyone can see he's a common *drunkard* the way he staggers home night after night. *Alcoholic* was at one time simply a medical description for someone who could not moderate his intake after the first drink. It has since become so popular as a general term that it appears often in informal contexts as well. Even informally, the word lacks the tone of disapproval implicit in *drunkard*. It should be noted, however, that an *alcoholic*, unlike a *drunkard*, may have abstained from alcohol completely for years: He used to be a *drunkard*, but now he refuses drinks at parties by saying, "Sorry, but I'm an *alcoholic*."

Inebriate and **dipsomaniac** are technical terms to describe an excessive drinker, but *alcoholic* has so widely displaced them that both terms now seem antiquated or fusty. An *inebriate*, strictly speaking, is a person who is intoxicated at the moment of being described. *Dipsomaniac*, once the word for a chronic *alcoholic* (one whose steady intake does not disrupt his living patterns), now might be primarily jocose.

The rest of these words are either extremely informal or slang. A **boozer** might denote an acute *alcoholic*, one who alternates between periods of sobriety and intoxication in a pattern disruptive of his normal life. On the other hand, *boozer* can be used almost admiringly to describe a person who drinks a great deal without losing control of himself. [He was the most unbelievable *boozer* I ever saw; he could down six straight shots of bourbon and never bat an eye.]

Drunk is, of course, a shortening of *drunkard*, having greater informality than the latter and a tone of even greater contempt. A **sot** is one who is drunk most of the time; the word would strike most Americans as being British in flavor. A **lush** may mean only a habitual drinker; sometimes it is used, however, for the drinker who enjoys the showy spending of money or who claims to drink strictly for the "glow" liquor gives him.

alcoholic

boozer
dipsomaniac
drunk
drunkard
inebriate
lush
sot
tippler
wino

Tippler and **wino** both refer to specific kinds of drinkers. A *tippler* drinks small amounts at frequent intervals over long periods of time. The word is often used for the secret or private drinker: No one would have guessed that the headmistress was a *tippler* except the man who carried away the empty bottles. *Wino* is usually applied to a hobo or bum whose addiction to alcohol is satisfied by drinking inexpensive fortified wines. It is also used for any heavy drinker whose intake is primarily of wine.

Antonyms: abstainer, nondrinker, teetotaler.

allegiance

fealty
fidelity
loyalty

Allegiance refers to the obligation of faithfulness, i.e. of **fidelity**, that a citizen owes his country or his sovereign in return for the benefits and privileges he receives by virtue of his citizenship. *Allegiance* is now widely used to refer to any similar obligation a person feels, as to a principle or a political leader. [In the Declaration of Independence, the colonists renounced their *allegiance* to the British Crown; a lasting *allegiance* to the Democratic Party.] **Fealty** is used specifically of the feudal obligation a vassal owed his lord. The oath of *fealty* expressed both *allegiance* and *fidelity*.

Fidelity implies a strong and faithful dedication; His *fidelity* to the principles of justice never wavered. **Loyalty** is more often associated with personal relationships than is *fidelity*. Where *fidelity* suggests adherence, *loyalty* points to devotion. It emphasizes a profoundly personal commitment. [His judgment was frequently faulty, but his *loyalty* to the nation could not be questioned; Company *loyalty* made him turn down many attractive job offers.] See TRUST.

Antonyms: disaffection, disloyalty, rebellion, sedition, treachery, treason.

allegory

fable
parable

These words all denote a story told about fictional persons and events to teach or illustrate a moral principle. In an **allegory** or **parable** the moral is not stated, but is left to the hearer to discover. An *allegory* is usually long and elaborate, with many characters and incidents; a *parable* is brief, and typically shows the application of a moral precept to a familiar situation. A **fable** usually states the moral at the end, and is told in terms of animals that speak and reflect the nature of human beings. [Dante's *Divine Comedy* is an *allegory* based on the struggle between the city-states of what is now Italy; The *fable* of the tortoise and the hare drives home the moral that steady, persistent application is more rewarding in the end than arrogant, unstable brilliance; The *parables* of the New Testament make abstract moral principles concrete and vivid.] See NARRATIVE.

aloof

detached
reserved

These words are comparable when applied to persons who are, or seem to be, emotionally distant from others. **Aloof** is applied to persons who are distant in manner or interest, as from a reluctance to associate with those whom they regard as intellectual or social inferiors, or because of habitual shyness or idiosyncrasy. [She held herself *aloof* from society, preferring to spend her days and nights dwelling on her memories; She always affected a grand, *aloof* manner with us poor middle-class people who work for a living.] **Detached** means free from emotional or intellectual involvement, and often suggests the neutral attitude of the impartial observer: the doctor's *detached* approach to pain. *Detached* may also mean inwardly distracted, emotionally untouchable. [He always seems so *detached* about everything; you just can't reach him at all.] **Reserved** implies reluctance to express one's feelings or thoughts.

Where *reserved* emphasizes manner, *detached* stresses attitude. Both *reserved* and *detached* can be associated with attractive qualities, whereas *aloof* is seldom so considered. [He was a diffident, scholarly fellow with a *reserved* but genial manner; He looked about him with a very *detached* air, and announced to no one in particular that he was about to be sick.] See DISTANT.

Antonyms: communicative, GREGARIOUS, *neighborly*, *sociable*, TALKATIVE.

These words are applied to a person who has some knowledge or proficiency in a certain area, but who is not an expert. **Amateur** usually means a person who pursues an interest, study, or skill as a hobby or avocation rather than as a profession. Thus, a physician who plays the violin in his spare time is an *amateur* in music, even if his playing is skillful. However, the word is sometimes used disparagingly to stress that a person's skill, being nonprofessional, is not as good as it could be. If a man can't fix a leaky faucet, his wife may chide him by saying, "Oh well, you're just an *amateur!*"

Dilettante means literally taking delight in and was originally applied to a person who was a lover of the arts. The word has in recent years, however, come to be associated with frivolousness and shallowness. A *dilettante* is a person who, though he shows interest in a field of knowlege or in an artistic skill, pursues it chiefly for enjoyment or ostentation, thus never attaining more than a superficial knowledge of it.

Dabbler is an even more disparaging term than *dilettante* and denotes a person who merely dips into something without serious intent or perseverance.

Antonyms: connoisseur, expert, professional, specialist.

amateur

dabbler
dilettante

These words all denote a diplomatic representative of a head of state or of a government. An **ambassador** is a diplomatic officer of the highest rank, appointed as the representative of one government to another. An *ambassador extraordinary* is one sent on a special mission, as distinguished from one, called an *ambassador ordinary*, who resides permanently in the country to which he is assigned.

A **minister** is a diplomatic representative of lower rank than an *ambassador*. A *minister* sent on a special mission is called an **envoy**. **Nuncio** and **legate** are diplomatic representatives of the Holy See, or Vatican State. A *nuncio* is an accredited ambassador of the Pope in a foreign country; a *legate* is a papal *envoy*, i.e. a diplomatic representative of the Pope dispatched to a country on a special mission.

A **plenipotentiary** describes any person fully empowered to represent a government, whether he be an *ambassador*, *minister*, or *envoy*. The term is most commonly applied to *ministers plenipotentiary*, who, though ranking below *ambassadors*, are nevertheless invested with full authority to conduct important matters of state in the name of their government.

ambassador

envoy
legate
minister
nuncio
plenipotentiary

These words all refer either to a general distrust of centralized government or to specific ideologies and their techniques for deliberately disrupting the fabric of an existing society in order to gain a stated set of goals.

Anarchism has general, philosophical, and historical senses. Most generally, the word can refer merely to a situation of utter disorganization: Unless we find a better way of working together, sheer *anarchism* will result. In a philosophic framework, the word refers to a tendency

anarchism

Bakuninism
Gandhism

anarchism
(continued)

nonviolence
pacifism
syndicalism

that sees individual freedom threatened by any trend toward collectivism in government: Thoreau's very personal *anarchism* stemmed from an absolute dislike for all institutions in general. Most specifically, the word refers to a historical movement of the nineteenth and twentieth centuries that held all existing societies to be corrupt and proposed to destroy them. Some strains of *anarchism* proposed single acts of symbolic, pointless violence, which gave rise in the popular imagination of the 1890's to the figure of the bearded, bomb-throwing anarchist. One strain of militant *anarchism* was called **Bakuninism** after the Russian theorist who deeply influenced the development of Marxism. Another strain, known as **syndicalism**, foresaw a worldwide shutdown of industry by workers in order to cause the collapse of capitalism. After this "general strike," comparable to the worldwide revolution foreseen by Marx, workers would govern society directly through the trade-union structure. [The Industrial Workers of the World, known as Wobblies, were a curious group who sometimes appeared to advocate *syndicalism*, sometimes merely isolated acts of violent *anarchism*, and sometimes a systematic socialism.]

   Pacifism is a strain of *anarchism* sharply distinguished from others by its total disavowal of violence. Often called *pacifist anarchism*, it applies especially, but not exclusively, to those who wish to abolish war and who agitate against any military solution of international problems. Mahatma Gandhi, an adherent of *pacifism* and admittedly inspired by Thoreau's philosophical *anarchism*, founded **Gandhism** (or *satyagraha*), a specific method of civil disobedience that successfully used nonviolent techniques to free India of British rule.

   Civil rights workers in America, agitating against the segregation of Negroes, deliberately adopted philosophical *anarchism* and the techniques of *pacifism* and *Gandhism* to win their goals. The phrase first used to describe this fusion of theory and method was *passive resistance*, but unwanted overtones in the phrase, implying helpless passivity, caused it to be rejected in favor of **nonviolence**, a word now used by pacifists, nonviolent anarchists, and integrationists alike to describe their methods. *Nonviolence* implies active resistance to an unjust law or custom by such acts as demonstrations, boycotts, and disruptions of the normal functioning of society. See LAWLESSNESS, SOCIALISM.

ancestor

forebear
forefather
progenitor

The words in this list are very close in meaning, each being most strictly applied to a person from whom one is descended. **Ancestor**, **forebear**, and **forefather** are hardly ever applied to parents or grandparents, whereas **progenitor** is sometimes applied to them as well as to more remote *ancestors*. [Although Napoleon and his immediate *progenitors* were Corsicans, he is considered by most modern Frenchmen to have been as French as their own *ancestors*.]

   Ancestor and *progenitor* are often applied to things other than people. [Eohippus is an *ancestor* of the horse; The *progenitors* of Italian lyric verse forms were those used by the troubadours of Provence.] *Progenitor*, in this sense, points to an early form that created, caused, or led to the development of a newer one; *ancestor*, even in this extended sense, retains the idea of historical evolution, the course of which is determined by forces over which man has no control and little knowledge. [The impressionist movement was one of the *ancestors* of abstract art; Johnson's dictionary was the *progenitor* of many others that followed its style and treatment of the language.]

   Forefather and *forebear* are usually used in the plural. *Forefathers* is

most often used in a poetical context and frequently connotes strong
family or racial feeling, or continuing habitation in one place, whereas
forebears has such connotations to a much smaller degree. See DESCENT.
   Antonyms: descendant, offspring, progeny.

Ancient means existing or occurring in times long past: *ancient*
rituals; *ancient* coins. As applied to history, *ancient* refers to the period
beginning with the earliest times and ending about the time of the fall of
the Roman Empire in A.D. 476. **Old**, a more general word, must be
qualified to avoid ambiguity. It may mean *ancient*: cowrie shells and
other *old* forms of currency; or aged: Oxford is an *old* university; or it
can be used as a substitute in some contexts for any of the other words
in this group.
   Antique is applied to that which has survived from the past, either
from ancient times or from some less remote period. As used in describing furniture or other objects, *antique* may indicate an age of no more
than several generations: an *antique* shop specializing in turn-of-the-
century merchandise. **Immemorial** is applied to that which is so
ancient that its origins are beyond all memory: *immemorial* customs.
The word is often used in the phrase *since time immemorial.* Otherwise
its use tends to sound grand and affected. **Hoary**, which literally means
white, gray, or having white or gray hair, is applied figuratively to things
surviving from the distant past: *hoary* relics of *ancient* civilizations.
See OLD.
   Antonyms: fresh, MODERN, *new, novel, recent, up-to-date.*

These words denote, in varying degrees, feelings of strong displeasure
or antagonism directed against the causes of an assumed wrong or
injury. **Anger,** the most general word of this group, provides no clue as
to the direction of this feeling or its means of expression. One may feel
anger at an unfortunate turn of events, at oneself, or at another person.
Rage often implies a loss of self-control, and **fury**, the strongest word
in the group, suggests a *rage* so violent that it may approach madness.
[The surly insolence of the waiters drove him into a *rage,* and he flung his
napkin to the floor and stalked out of the restaurant; The *fury* of a
woman scorned, according to Congreve, is unmatched in hell; Mad with
fury, he pounded his fists on the wall and beat his breast.]
   Indignation denotes *anger* based on a moral condemnation of something felt to be disgraceful or ignoble: Abolitionists viewed the institution of slavery with *indignation.* **Wrath**, now limited in use to literature
and figures of speech, suggests a strong *anger* directed at some specific
person or thing. The source of *wrath* is always impressive, sometimes
divine; hence it traditionally inspires awe and fear: the *wrath* of the
gods. **Ire**, meaning *anger* or *indignation*, is no longer encountered
except in poetry and period literature: His *ire* was strongly provoked by
the discourtesy of the host in failing to address him by his proper title.
See RESENTMENT.
   *Antonyms: amiability, calmness, clemency, docility, forbearance, gentleness,
leniency, placidity, tranquility.*

These words refer to living things other than plants. **Animal** may
refer to all such beings, as in biological terminology where life is divided
into two groups, plants and *animals*. In common use, however, the
word is more specifically applied to all such beings with the exception of
humans: man and the *animals* he lives among. The contexts of some uses

ancient

antique
hoary
immemorial
old

anger

fury
indignation
ire
rage
wrath

animal

beast

animal
(continued)

brute
creature

furthermore, make it clear that birds, fish, and insects are also not included in the term. At its most restricted, the word can even refer strictly only to domestic quadrupeds: hogs, sheep, cattle, and other *animals*. When the word is applied to a human being in other than a scientific context, the emphasis is on depravity or amorality: a disgusting *animal* who cared for no one but himself. **Creature** does not have this range of possibility in meaning; it refers invariably to all living beings other than plants: all God's *creatures*. When a human being is referred to by this word, however, pity or contempt is usually present: the poor little *creature*; what a vile *creature*.

Beast and **brute** both restrict themselves to *animals* other than man, but especially to the higher mammals: lions, tigers, and other *beasts* of the veldt; such *beasts* of burden as the donkey and the horse. While *beast*, thus, has a neutrally descriptive possibility, *brute* is charged with an emphasis on supposedly nonhuman qualities like wildness, viciousness, or stupidity: the jungle rule of *brute* versus *brute*. More commonly, *brute* is used to describe a strong, cruel, or stupid human being: a nasty *brute* of a man. *Beast* can also be applied to a human being, but unlike *brute*, it stresses mostly degradation and extreme inhumanity: the woman who was called the *Beast* of Belsen. In this use, *beast* is more pejorative than *brute*, but both are more negative than *animal* when it is used in this way.

answer

rejoinder
reply
response
retort
riposte

These words apply primarily to something said or written to satisfy or acknowledge a question, call, request, charge, etc. **Answer** is the most general word in this list, and though all the words here considered may be used figuratively of actions as well as words, *answer* is more variously used than any of them. When a question is asked, any words or actions in return may be called an *answer*: a prompt *answer* to a letter; His *answer* was an uppercut to the jaw. Indeed, any satisfactory conclusion may be styled an *answer*: He had hoped that divorce would be the *answer* to all his problems. An *answer* in the form of a statement appropriate to the question is a **reply**: General McAuliffe's famous *reply* to the German call to surrender in World War II was "Nuts!"

A **response** is the reaction to a stimulus: Pavlov's experiments proved that a conditioned *response* to a given stimulus could be induced in rats by the learned association of the right *response* with satisfaction and of the wrong *response* with pain. In more general use *response* refers to any *answer* to an urgent question or appeal, or to a set question: a *response* to a cry for help; the *responses* of a litany. A *reply* to a *reply* is a **rejoinder**, often in the form of a second question or demand; this word is particularly applicable to the give-and-take of a debate: a telling *rejoinder* which left his opponent momentarily speechless. **Riposte**, from the Italian word for *answer*, first meant a return thrust in fencing. By extension, it came to be applied to a verbal duel, meaning a quick, clever, retaliatory *reply*: a brilliant, if somewhat savage, *riposte*. A **retort** is a sharp *answer*, as to an accusation or criticism: The libelous accusation provoked a bitter *retort*.

Antonyms: QUESTION (n.).

anxiety

angst
apprehension

These words describe troubled states of mind in which a person feels frustrated and helpless concerning his present situation, or in which he fears that some harmful event will occur in the future. **Anxiety**, the most general of these words, can relate on one hand to those words here that describe a fearful state of mind concerning the future: *anxiety* about the outcome of the election. Unlike any of these other words, however, it can refer to a fear of the future per se and not just of a single hazard. This meaning is particularly used by psychiatrists to refer to patients who are immobilized by such a feeling without being able to explain what it is they fear: The boy had been so mistreated that he faced each day with a vast, uncomprehending *anxiety*.

Anxiety also relates, on the other hand, to words of this group that are not necessarily tied to fear of the future. Existential philosophers developed this meaning to refer to the helpless, all-encompassing frustration of the human condition when confronted with the inexplicability of life. Recently this kind of *anxiety* is often referred to by the word **angst**, from the Danish of the philosopher Soren Kierkegaard: In the Age of Anxiety, W. H. Auden claims that our fear of the future is really a fear of ourselves and our own irrepressible *angst*.

Dread, apprehension, and **foreboding** emphasize the fear of something that has yet to happen. *Dread* is the most intense of any of the words listed here, with overtones of helplessness in the face of something as inevitable as it is terrible. The thing *dreaded* may be a specific occurrence or a less well-defined evil that is nonetheless terrifying to consider. [During the missile crises even the diplomats were filled with the *dread* of nuclear war; She did not know what to expect on the dark road ahead, but every shadow filled her with *dread*.] The word can, of course, be used hyperbolically for more trivial occasions: I *dread* the rush-hour traffic so much that I often avoid it by coming late to work. *Apprehension* is more formal than either *dread* or *anxiety*, less intense in feeling, and applies to vaguer fears of a future happening. It is not so much a harmful inevitability that is foreseen as an uncertain outcome that keeps one in suspense: No matter how perfect the weather, she never conquered the *apprehension* with which she saw him off at the airport. Like *anxiety*, *foreboding* is midway between *dread* and *apprehension* in its formality, its intensity, and its conviction of certain or possible harm. What sets this word aside is its aura of superstitiousness: Because it rained on her wedding day, she spent the rest of the week in gloomy *foreboding*. The word can be used without this overtone, however, in which case it points to a more general nagging doubt about the future: He carried his report card home with a sharp *foreboding* of the nasty scene he should face that evening.

Worry is far less formal than the previous words and implies an obsessive concern for far more mundane matters. It frequently appears in the plural. [Forget your *worries* and relax.] It is often used as an abstraction for a habit of mind that compulsively frets about the future without real result: *Worry* never makes up for what hard work could have accomplished.

Misgiving is doubt about the outcome of an action, or a feeling of *apprehension* provoked by such doubt: He had some *misgivings* about investing in the stock, and when he saw the company's annual report he knew at once they were justified. **Uneasiness** and **disquiet**, unlike *misgiving*, do not necessarily apply to fear about the future. Both suggest that actual physical discomfort or restlessness accompanies the apprehensive or fearful state, *uneasiness* most strongly so. *Disquiet* refers to a more subtle *uneasiness* over an often ill-defined danger. [What had at first been merely a faint *disquiet* as the minutes passed became at last outright *uneasiness* that set him to pacing about the hospital's waiting room.] See AFRAID, FEAR.

Antonyms: assurance, calmness, composure, CONFIDENCE, *ease, equability, equanimity, nonchalance, placidity, quietude, security.*

anxiety
(continued)

disquiet
dread
foreboding
misgiving
uneasiness
worry

appearance

aspect
look
semblance

These words are all used to denote visual impressions of the way a person or thing is or seems. **Appearance**, in the sense here considered, is the most neutral of these terms, making only a flat assertion of what one perceives. [It had the *appearance* of an eighteenth century church; He had the rugged *appearance* of an athlete.] *Appearance*, however, like the other words, can be used to accent the contrast between what seems to be so and what is the fact of the matter: a despot who assumes the *appearance* of a benefactor.

Look usually applies to facial expression or demeanor rather than to other forms of *appearance*, such as dress, although it may—implying an analogy with a person's face—be used to describe things as well: a Renaissance *look* to a building. Compare these two phrases: the *appearance* of a snob; the *look* of a snob. The former suggests dandyish clothes and a too-elegant manner; the latter suggests, along with other qualities, a supercilious expression.

Aspect is often interchangeable with *look*, but suggests more strongly the changing nature of *appearance* as it confronts the beholder: the pleasant *aspect* of a lake; an artist who had the *aspect* of a prizefighter. *Aspect* implies that the perception is a quality inherent in the thing perceived, a quality that is drawn out — into focus, as it were — by the eye of the beholder.

Semblance is almost invariably used to contrast *appearance* with reality: a doubtful assertion that has the *semblance* of truth; an enemy who cloaks his threats with the *semblance* of civility. It may, however, be used to mean outward *appearance* without any suggestion of falseness: The faceless person in his dreams began to acquire the *semblance* of his dead brother.

applause

acclaim
acclamation
plaudit

These words refer to simultaneous expressions of approval or praise by a number of persons. **Applause** may be given by voice or by clapping the hands. The word does not suggest any particular degree of enthusiasm, and depends on context or qualifying adjectives to indicate the intensity or sincerity of the approval. [At the end of the concert, the pianist was greeted with a smattering of *applause* and a few whistles; The crowd rose as one with a great roar of *applause*.] **Acclaim** and **acclamation** are more formal terms, and refer specifically to vocal expressions of praise or approval. In parliamentary bodies, a measure adopted by *acclamation* is one adopted by shouts of approval and *applause* rather than by individual votes; *by acclamation* can therefore be taken to mean by enthusiastic endorsement of the assembly. *Acclaim* need not refer particularly to actual cries of approval, but is perhaps more commonly used nowadays to express figurative *applause*: Einstein's achievements earned him the *acclaim* of the entire scientific community. **Plaudit**, also a formal term, means a burst of *applause*, but like *acclaim*, is often used figuratively, commonly in the plural: to receive the *plaudits* of one's fellow musicians for an outstanding performance. See APPROVAL.

Antonyms: abuse, booing, censure, disapprobation, disapproval, execration, hissing, jeering, obloquy, reproof, vituperation.

appoint

assign

The situation that unites these words is one in which a person is being chosen to fulfill a given function by someone else. Unlike other ways of matching people to tasks, these words imply an official situation — in an office, club, or government — in which the choice is made by means other than an elective process. **Appoint** indicates that the selection is made by someone officially charged with this duty, although the actual selection itself may be arbitrary or judicious: Some city officials are elected to their posts, while others are *appointed* by the mayor or the political bosses. Of this set, **name** is the most informal and tells least about the chooser or the method of choice adopted: Since no one has volunteered, I hereby *name* the following to serve on the credentials committee. Sometimes the word, thus, stresses outcome rather than process: a judge *named* to the Supreme Court.

Designate is the most formal of all these terms, even to the point of stiffness. It can be useful, however, to distinguish from *appoint* a process of selection that is only quasi-official in nature: The candidate *designated* as his running mate the man who had been his main opponent in the primaries.

Assign differs from the other words here in that it most often refers, not to the picking of a person for a task, but to the delegation of a task to one or more members of a group. It has an overtone, not invariably present, of arbitrariness, possibly a survival of some early resentment on our part for the teacher who *assigned* us "too much" homework. It is occasionally used of people rather than of the task; in this case, the person being *assigned* usually joins others already *designated* in a common task: Jones is *assigned* to KP, Smith is *assigned* to guard duty, and Anderson is *assigned* to the laundry detail. See NAME.

Antonyms: discharge, fire, let go, suspend, withdraw.

These words are used for the formal assent given to a proposed undertaking or for the official honor given upon the successful completion of a task. **Approval** is the most general and least formal of these. In the official context, it usually means the giving of permission to undertake a task. [We can't introduce our bill on the floor without first getting the committee's *approval*; Would you initial this requisition as a sign of your *approval*?] It can also simply mean concurrence in opinion: Your suggestion met with the president's highest *approval*.

Approbation, the most formal of these, refers to the giving of authoritative *approval*, especially in an ecclesiastical context. It carries overtones of warmth and congeniality in a more general context, but its use — even in many official situations — might be thought unnecessarily pretentious: His controversial report gained the hearty *approbation* of other experts in his field.

Commendation and **sanction**, more formal than *approval*, are both limited almost exclusively to an official context. *Commendation* is further restricted, within this context, to formal recognition for a task well done: a *commendation* for your brilliant sales record. The word can also refer to the written document of *commendation*: He framed his *commendation* for bravery and hung it on the wall. *Sanction* can mean either before-the-act *approval* or after-the-act *commendation*. [I'm sure you can get the committee's *sanction* to proceed with your project; Only after the crisis did he get the president's *sanction* for the way he had acted.] Caution must be observed in the use of this word, however, for it can also mean, confusingly enough, official restrictive measures taken against a proposed act, a group of people, or a group's behavior: The civil rights group said it would post *sanctions* against those businesses that still discriminated. See ENDORSE.

Antonyms: censure, disapprobation, DISAPPROVAL, *dissatisfaction.*

These words all mean within some degree of exactness or closeness, as in distance, time, amount, etc. **Approximately** implies an accuracy

approximately
(continued)

about
around
roughly

so near to a standard that the difference is virtually negligible. [It was *approximately* 100° in the shade; π is *approximately* 3.1415.]

About is often used interchangeably with *approximately*, but it does not stress the closeness to accuracy that *approximately* does: a hat costing *about* five dollars; reaching home at *about* dinner time. **Around** sometimes appears in informal contexts in place of *approximately* or *about*: to go to bed *around* midnight; to invite *around* fifteen people to a picnic.

Roughly is often used in place of *approximately* or *about* when there is no real attempt to be exact. [The cost of the car repairs was estimated at *roughly* fifty dollars; The population of Delaware is *roughly* 450,000.] *Roughly* also carries a suggestion of casualness or haste, which the other words do not convey. [The books were shelved *roughly* in alphabetical order; *Roughly* speaking, I would guess that we are headed for a depression.]

argue

debate
discuss
dispute
reason

All these words mean to talk with others in order to reach an agreement, to persuade, or to settle a question of fact. **Argue**, the most general in the list, may refer to a reasoned presentation of views or to a heated exchange of opinion amounting to a quarrel. [The Senator *argued* his position with such cogency and wit that even his adversaries were impressed; They *argued* vociferously over who should pay the bill.] **Debate** means to argue formally, usually under the control of a referee and according to a set of regulations: The House of Representatives *debated* the proposal for three weeks. Any argument in which each person has strongly held opinions, however, can be styled a *debate*. *Debate* is also used less formally to mean to consider or think about alternatives: They *debated* about which train to take.

Discuss means to talk over, usually in an informal, friendly way. It implies that the participants have less intensely held opinions than in a *debate*, and emphasizes their common desire to resolve the question satisfactorily: a committee appointed to *discuss* and formulate recommendations on how to improve job opportunities for the underprivileged. *Discuss* points to the elucidation of an issue rather than to the narrow presentation of one's own view.

Reason means to *argue* or *discuss* in a careful and painstaking manner in order to persuade or explore a subject in depth: Supreme Court justices *reasoning* with each other in interpreting the Constitution.

Dispute, in this context, means to *argue* with more passion than logic, often from a factional point of view: Adherents of rival candidates at a convention frequently fall to *disputing* about subtle rules of procedure. See CONTROVERSY.

Antonyms: CONSENT.

arise

emanate
emerge
issue
originate
result
stem

These words refer to the development of one thing out of another. **Arise** suggests a chain of causality, possibly from simple to complex: new social organizations *arising* from the industrial revolution. **Emerge** suggests a gradual process that stresses simple change more than causality: a parliamentary system *emerging* slowly from the old order of absolute monarchy. **Originate** stresses the starting point for change: egalitarian sentiments that *originated* in contract theories of government. **Result**, by contrast, stresses the end product of change: contract theories of government that *resulted* in the growth of egalitarian sentiments.

Stem is closely related to *originate* in stressing the beginning of

change, and like *arise* in stressing direct causation; it usually appears
with *from*: civil rights laws that *stemmed* from national indignation over
the brutal suppression of the protest marchers. **Issue** is similar in force
to *stem* but is considerably more formal in tone: a sense of freedom
issuing from more than a decade of experimentation in the arts. **Emanate**, the most formal of these words so far, stresses the point of origin
like *originate*, *stem*, and *issue*, but it might be thought too formal for
many contexts. It can, however, suggest a less clearly defined pattern of
causation to which many imponderable factors may have contributed:
a new sense of security *emanating* from greater prosperity and a lessening
of the cold war. See BEGIN, BEGINNING.

    Antonyms: DECREASE, FINISH, STOP.

These words pertain to the guns and other military equipment used
in fighting wars. **Arms** and **weapons** are general terms, nearly interchangeable, for the instruments of combat. A bow-and-arrow, sword,
or rifle are all *arms* or *weapons*. Of the two terms, *arms* is more
frequently restricted in use to those *weapons* that an individual soldier can wield,
whereas *weapons* are anything used in the fight, from chance sticks and
stones to hydrogen bombs. In its most general sense, *arms* can also refer
to the whole military capability of a country: Both nations bankrupted
themselves in their foolish race to manufacture *arms*.

    Armament is similar in meaning to this last sense of *arms*, but it is
much clearer in that it points without confusion both to the *weapons* and
the military equipment used to wage war: The country's *armament*
includes the most versatile planes, the fastest ships, and the most rugged
tanks in the world. *Armament* may also be used to refer to the total
weapons available to a military vehicle: The destroyer's *armament*
consists of several small cannon, two torpedo bays, and a number of anti-
aircraft guns. **Ordnance** may be used, like *armament*, for the total
military effort of a country, but much more commonly refers specifically
to heavy firearms, mounted cannon or mortars, and other heavy artillery.

    Materiel and **munitions** both refer to equipment rather than to
weapons. *Materiel* suggests all the supportive equipment and supplies
necessary to combat, while *munitions* most commonly suggests ammunition only: Dry socks are as important an item of *materiel* as *munitions*.

    Arsenal and **deterrent** have come into fairly recent use to refer to a
country's nuclear *arms*. *Arsenal* previously meant simply a place where
weapons are stored, but in this specific instance it indicates a stockpile of
nuclear warheads. *Deterrent* is an almost euphemistic word for a nuclear
arsenal: The atomic *arsenal* of either nation alone could lay waste to the
entire planet, yet each emerging country clamors to build its own *deterrent* as well. See FLEET, TROOPS.

arms

armament
arsenal
deterrent
materiel
munitions
ordnance
weapons

Artificial may be applied to anything made by human beings in
imitation of something natural: *artificial* flowers; an *artificial* leg.
Synthetic is synonymous with *artificial* in this sense, but there is a
connotation in *synthetic* of production by chemical combinations or
similar techniques: *synthetic* rubber. **False** and **ersatz** both suggest
a substitute made because of the costliness or lack of the original item:
false teeth; the proliferation of *ersatz* goods during periods of war and
inflation. *False* often implies the presenting of a misleading appearance
when it refers to a function-masking decorative detail: *false* drawers that
were actually a single door concealing stereo equipment. *Ersatz* commonly describes a cheap or inferior copy that can fool no one: bowls of

artificial

ersatz
false
synthetic

wax fruit and a dusty collection of *ersatz* flowers in brass-plated planters. See MAKE, SHAM.

Antonyms: GENUINE, *natural.*

artisan

artificer
craftsman
creator
designer
executor
workman

These words all refer to makers or constructors of products at some level below that of artistic creation. An **artisan** falls midway between the full-scale artist who creates single inimitable works and the mere worker who turns out identical, anonymous products: Italian *artisans* were imported to New York expressly to hand-carve the masonry on the brownstone buildings of the 1890's. *Artisan* was once much closer in meaning to artist, however, as witness the stained-glass windows of a medieval cathedral. These were created by anonymous *artisans*, but they are often great works of art nonetheless. **Artificer** still can suggest its earliest meaning of a worker who possesses mechanical facility: the *artificer* in an infantry company who cares for and repairs its weapons. In other uses *artificer* had begun to sound fusty until James Joyce reintroduced the word in *Portrait of the Artist as a Young Man* to stand for the artist as creator and controller of art and life. It has sometimes been used since in this highest sense.

Craftsman has risen somewhat in the scale to the artist end of the spectrum since the advent of machine-made objects in the nineteenth century: Replaced by factories, the furniture-maker, the bookbinder, the dyer, and the weaver were all skilled *craftsmen* whose century-old secrets were lost during the industrial revolution. *Craftsman* is now a common term to describe a worker in the minor arts; a ceramist or a pottery-maker would not feel insulted to be called a *craftsman*. In the other arts, the word is used of an artist unusually adept in the technical aspects of his art: The young poet was an extraordinary *craftsman* simply from the standpoint of the variety of poetic forms that he could command effectively.

Creator and **designer** in the minor arts are parallel terms and imply the existence of a subordinate **executor** who carries a plan or design into effect. The person named on the playbill as the *creator* of a play's costumes conceived and sketched them; someone else probably *executed* them. A fashion, book, or automobile *designer* plans the physical appearance of the completed product down to the smallest detail, but others are the *executors* of these designs.

Workman implies someone who has more craftsmanship than a worker would possess but far less than an *artisan*. [We called in an *artisan* to repair the broken pane in our Tiffany shade; At the same time, *workmen* arrived to fix our leaky roof.] See ARTIST, LABORER.

artist

craftsman
creator
painter
stylist
virtuoso

These words refer to people who produce works of art. **Artist,** in one of its uses, is the most general and all-inclusive of these, indicating a practitioner of any one of the fine or applied arts: *artists* who paint, compose music, or write novels. Its main usefulness lies in the fact that it can refer equally well as a group word to workers in diverse fields: a section of the city where all kinds of *artists* lived. By extension, the word is often used of someone who shows unusual taste or discrimination in other tasks: a real *artist* when it came to planning and giving interesting parties. When the word is not clearly a group word, however, it can often be taken to apply more strictly to the visual arts, especially to painting: a gathering place for *artists* and writers. **Painter** thus specifically emphasizes one of the possible meanings of *artist*, to the exclusion of all others. In general, *artist* can be replaced to advantage by the more specific term whenever appropriate: gatherings of *painters*, sculptors, novelists, poets, and composers.

The remaining words all relate to *artist*, rather than *painter*, in grouping a variety of specific roles under one general heading. **Creator** emphasizes the origination of artistic ideas by a single person; it may or may not imply that others bring the idea to its realization: the *creator* of huge canvases teeming with scenes of Venetian life; a man credited as the *creator* of a film on which many had collaborated. The word also has a use to refer to an *artist* who works in a number of media: the *creator* of frescoes, architectural designs, and sonnets. The word is also used in the applied arts, sometimes to lend esthetic appeal to a business: the *creator* of a new line of fall fashions.

Craftsman, stylist, and **virtuoso** are general words that emphasize technical skill or flair when substituted for *artist*. In this context, *craftsman* suggests any *artist* who lavishes painstaking care on the construction of his work and is consciously concerned with fine details: a real *craftsman* in his ability to shape dialogue toward natural and inevitable climaxes. *Stylist* suggests an *artist* unusually gifted with a flair for working in one or a number of demanding modes: those rare, truly innovating *stylists* of the short story. The word can also be used of lesser or applied arts to suggest singularity or professionality: hair *stylist*; a unique song *stylist*. *Virtuoso* originally applied to a musical performer who was able to execute difficult passages with apparent ease and bravura. Now it may refer to any *artist*, as well, who shows unique mastery of technical difficulties or is especially given to displays of technical facility: a *virtuoso* in the sonnet form; a *virtuoso* who, for all his technique, remains a shallow and superficial *artist*. See CREATE.

These words describe qualities in a work of art, its creator, or its appreciator. **Artistic** and **esthetic** are closely related; most simply, the *artistic* instinct belongs to the creator, the *esthetic* instinct to the beholder: *artistic* skill; *esthetic* pleasure. In another sense, however, the *esthetic* attitude might be taken as generic, the *artistic* attitude as a specific but by no means exhaustive example of the more general term. In this distinction, the *esthetic* instinct expresses itself in all areas of life where taste, discrimination, style, and balance are desirable: an *esthetic* flower arrangement; an *esthetic* flair for matching the right wine to the right entrée. In yet another sense, *esthetic* describes specifically those discriminations sorted out by estheticians; one connotation here may be unnecessary refinement or passivity as opposed to the boldness and activity of the *artistic* attitude: too bogged down in *esthetic* distinctions to have any *artistic* spontaneity. In describing a work of art rather than an attitude, *esthetic* would be largely irrelevant, *artistic* inane or tautological. Both may be used to praise creations not commonly thought of as works of art: an *artistic* grouping of furniture.

Arty and **mannered** both refer to attitudes that tend toward parody of the *artistic* sensibility. *Arty*, the more strongly negative of the two, is also the most informal of any of these words. It suggests the phoniness of the poseur or artist manqué, stressing particularly that exaggerated and affected behavior that may be totally unrelated to the creation of works of art: the *arty* bohemian crowd in Greenwich Village. *Mannered* is more formal and more restrained in its disapproval. It suggests behavior that is contrived and unnatural: the *mannered*, fey look of her costume. The word can also refer to the work of art itself, suggesting the same qualities of contrived artificiality.

artistic

artificial
arty
esthetic
harmonious
mannered
precious
stylized
tasteful

Artificial most often refers only to the work, suggesting a lack of spontaneity and of naturalness. It is more negative in tone than *mannered*. The latter may suggest worthwhile content that has been harmed by unnecessary stylistic manipulation. *Artificial*, on the other hand, suggests a lack of content that a pretentious style is struggling to conceal. **Stylized** is like *mannered* and *artificial* in suggesting an emphasis on mode as opposed to content, but it contrasts with them in ranging from a neutral to an approving tone: the *stylized* patterns of the kabuki dances. It emphasizes the ordering of the artist's raw materials into significant, if unrealistic, designs.

Precious is the most negative in tone of any word here and is the most free-wheeling in range, applying to the work, the artist, or to someone who is not artistic in any way. It points to a taste for the genteel and overelegant, especially when these qualities are as far removed as possible from reality or normality. It suggests a complaisant attempt to be different and striking, and typically results in over*stylized* affectation — "cute" in the worst sense of the word: a *precious* writer of the Mauve Decade; a beauty queen who underlined her *precious* way of speaking with coy gestures and an exaggerated simper.

Tasteful and **harmonious** refer to *esthetic* qualities that may be found in *artistic* works. *Tasteful* is extremely subjective in referring to what is in accordance with the canons of taste; what is *tasteful* to one person, such as a pink and purple Christmas tree, might be thought vulgar by another. *Harmonious* is more objective in pointing to a smooth, well-balanced relation of parts: a *harmonious* ordering of the room's spatial relationships. On the other hand, what one age thought chaotic or cacophonous, another finds simple, *tasteful*, and *harmonious*. All words in this area are ultimately subjective. See FORMAL.

Antonyms: displeasing, distasteful, GAUDY, inartistic, shoddy, tasteless, unesthetic.

assert

affirm
allege
asseverate
aver
avouch
avow
maintain
testify

These verbs all mean to state positively, as though anticipating or countering argument or skepticism. Whereas **assert** means to state with some force or conviction, **allege** means to state without offering proof: It was *alleged* that he was present at the scene of the crime, but he *asserted* that he was in Europe at the time. Whatever one *asserts* he would defend in argument, but whether anyone believes something *alleged* is beside the point; the aim of *alleging* is to learn the truth by proving or disproving the claim made.

Affirm means to declare or state positively that something is true; it indicates firm belief or unshakable conviction: to *affirm* one's faith in God. **Asseverate** is nearly synonymous with *assert* but even more positive; the word is uncommon even in formal writing. **Testify** means to bear witness, as in a court of law, or declare solemnly to be true: to *testify* on behalf of the defendant; I can *testify* to this man's veracity and good character.

Maintain, as here considered, means to *assert* something in the face of evidence or arguments to the contrary: In spite of circumstantial evidence pointing to his guilt, the accused *maintained* that he was innocent. *Maintain* almost always involves controversy or disagreement; it presupposes a prior statement to which one is adhering, and in this sense is a reaffirming of one's position.

Aver means to declare confidently as fact. **Avouch** means to vouch for or affirm positively. **Avow** means to declare openly: to *avow* one's guilt. None of these words is common in contemporary writing; all

occur only in formal writing, and *avouch* seldom even there. See DE-
CLARE, UTTER.
    Antonyms: CONTRADICT, *controvert, demur, dispute,* DOUBT, *refute.*

These words apply to a person who contributes to the accomplishment
of a task. **Assistant** and **helper** are nearly identical except for the
latter's greater informality. Because of this difference, *helper* may seem
warmer in tone, implying affection, whereas *assistant* remains coolly objective. [She had to admit that her husband was a good *helper* around
the house; It is not unusual for a woman executive to have a man as
her *assistant.*] Furthermore, one might become someone else's *helper* out
of generosity, whereas *assistant* usually implies a paid position. On the
other hand, *helper* is frequently used in the area of manual labor, while
assistant implies a position within a profession and is sometimes part of
an official title: plumber's *helper*; *assistant* to the vice-president in
charge of sales.
    Subordinate emphasizes the inferiority of a *helper* or *assistant*, and
its greater formality does not always mitigate an overtone of condescension, sometimes extending even to contempt. [The first sergeant treated
the second lieutenants in the company as though they were merely his
subordinates.] *Subordinate* can, however, be neutral in tone, merely
describing an unequal relationship: a trusted *subordinate*. **Adjutant**
and **aide** are drawn from military life to describe the administrative
assistant or *subordinate* of a superior officer. *Aide*, because of its brevity,
has come to be used by journalists and especially headline writers to
describe any government administrator. See ACCOMPLICE, ASSOCIATE.

The words in this set refer to professional, business, or work relationships between people. **Associate** is the least specific of these; its formality would suggest a business or professional context. While it implies
close connection, the relationship might be the result of choice, chance,
or necessity: a man's business *associates*. In a more specific use,
associate is a component of some professional titles, denoting the second
of three ranks: an *associate* editor; an *associate* professor. It is also
used specifically to indicate less than full membership in a group: A
member pays $200 annually in dues, but you can become an *associate*
for $50. In this sense, *associate* may refer either to a person or to a
group within a larger group. **Affiliate** compares with this use of *associate* in being now mostly used of a group related to another group:
the television *affiliate* of the town's daily newspaper. It is frequently
used to relate a small group to a national or international parent group:
the local *affiliate* of the American Medical Association. The word suggests that two *affiliates* are coequal in a loose relationship of autonomous
groups, even when a smaller-to-larger hierarchy is involved. This contrasts with *associate* in its suggestion of subordinate membership in a
group.
    Ally and **partner** may apply either to individuals or to groups. *Ally*
always suggests a relationship of choice. One's *allies* unite with one in
a common cause and most often against a common enemy. *Allies* are
not necessarily friends outside the cause that jointly concerns them:
The two senators were enemies on questions of domestic affairs, but
allies on foreign policy. *Ally* is chiefly used in reference to nations that
are on the same side in an international war: England and Russia were
our *allies* in World War II. *Partner*, like *ally*, may apply to one nation
joined with another in a common cause: France and England were *part-*

assistant

adjutant
aide
helper
subordinate

associate

affiliate
ally
colleague
co-worker
fellow
partner

ners in an atomic power project. But *partner* often indicates a closer or a contractual relationship. It is the legal term for one of the co-owners of a business: He was made a *partner* in the firm. And it may also refer to a much more personal association: marriage *partners*. Unlike the other words in this group, *partner* sometimes points to a one-to-one relationship involving a couple or a pair: his dancing *partner*; to draw for *partners* in playing bridge.

The remaining words refer exclusively to person-to-person relationships, as does *associate* in its more general sense. **Co-worker** is the least formal of these and applies as readily to manual labor as to more highly skilled occupations: his *co-workers* in the factory; his *co-worker* on the government's man-in-space project. *Co-worker* is distinctly neutral in tone, implying neither animosity nor the cordiality that may be suggested by *associate*. **Colleague** is restricted almost solely in use to professional association. It is formal in tone, but may range in feeling from neutrality to an expression of respect or approbation: my *colleagues* in the philosophy department. **Fellow**, as here considered, is now seldom used except as a title or component. In an academic context, it may mean a graduate student on a fellowship grant, but it may also be used of certain faculty positions, especially in England: a Fulbright *fellow* at Padua; a *fellow* of All Souls College, Oxford. See ACCOMPLICE, ASSISTANT, FRIEND.

Antonyms: OPPONENT.

assure

guarantee
insure
promise

These words mean to make or attempt to make something certain or secure by removing doubt. **Assure** can mean either to make certain or to cause to feel certain. [The doctor *assured* him that his child would recover from the illness; The fact that the hospital had a good reputation *assured* him that his child would be well taken care of.] **Insure**, or, as it is also spelled, *ensure*, means to make certain as the consequence of some action or agent: To *insure* the child's quick recovery, the doctor gave him an antibiotic. *Insure* also means to make safe, to protect against harm: to *insure* freedom against tyranny.

Guarantee means to assume responsibility for the quality of a product or for the performance of a service or obligation. One who *guarantees* a debt *assures* the creditor that he will be paid.

Promise, like *assure*, is often designed to make someone feel certain, but hardly *guarantees* that the outcome will measure up to one's expectations. *Promise* implies intention, not obligation, and every child knows that not all promises are kept: to *promise* someone a raise in pay; to *promise* to keep an appointment. In another sense, *promise* simply indicates grounds for favorable expectation. An invalid's renewed appetite may be deemed a *promising* sign. See PLEDGE.

Antonyms: imperil, jeopardize, renege, warn.

attack

assail
assault
besiege

These words all mean to set upon violently or to do battle with. **Attack**, the most general term of this group, may be applied to any offensive action, but more narrowly means to begin hostilities: to *attack* an enemy encampment; The watchdog *attacked* a would-be burglar and drove him off. *Attack*, like all these words, is also used figuratively: The senator *attacked* the views of a colleague.

Assail and **assault** have the same etymological origins but differ in meaning. *Assail* means to *attack* violently and repeatedly, implying that victory depends not so much on the force or effectiveness of one's attack but on one's persistence and pertinacity. To be *assailed* is to be worn down, to have no respite: a man *assailed* by doubts. *Assault* typically suggests close physical contact and extreme violence, especially against one or a few people. *Assault* may be used as a euphemism for rape. [They were *assaulted* by a gang of hoodlums not two blocks from their home; The noise of car horns, jet planes, jackhammers, ambulance sirens, fire engines, subways, and helicopters *assaults* the ears of city dwellers.]

Charge and **storm** both suggest a forceful *assault* on a fixed position. To *charge* is to make a violent onslaught or attack upon an enemy: The cavalry *charged* the hostile fort. But *charge* in this sense is most often used imperatively as a command. *Storm* means to take or try to take by force, with all the rush and fury of a storm: Seasoned veterans were picked to *storm* the difficult enemy position. *Storm* often conveys a feeling of desperation, an all-out effort to avert defeat and disaster.

Besiege means to surround or beset with an armed force in order to capture: to *besiege* a fortified city. In its figurative uses it is close to *assail*, but retains some of its basic sense of being hemmed in or enclosed rather than punished repeatedly: *Besieged* with fears, he decided to seek the aid of a psychiatrist.

Bombard means to *assail* with missiles, or, in figurative senses, with abusive words. [The TV station was *bombarded* with complaints against a tasteless program; A prominent clergyman *assailed* the executives who had permitted it to be shown, and in the state legislature an assemblyman *attacked* federal laxity in enforcing government regulations.] See AGGRESSION, FIGHT.

Antonyms: aid, PROTECT, UPHOLD.

These words, as here considered, refer to a capability resulting, at least in part, from conscious effort. All are frequently used in the plural. **Attainment** is the loftiest term. It implies a fully developed talent which leads to eminence in the arts, in science, or in some comparable field of endeavor: Bertrand Russell is not only a distinguished philosopher but also a man of high literary *attainments*. **Accomplishment**, in this sense, refers to any ability or manner acquired from practice or experience; specifically, *accomplishments* are social graces meant to please or entertain. [In the nineteenth century, a young woman of many *accomplishments* might sing, play the piano, and paint; Skill in dancing and the ability to make small talk are *accomplishments* considered desirable by most American adolescents.]

An **acquirement** is a skill gained by study or practice rather than through natural talent. Where *accomplishments* may be showy and impressive, *acquirements* are substantial and useful: The ability to read Sanskrit is an *acquirement* rarely found even among scholars. **Acquisition** usually refers to a newly obtained material possession, especially one of intrinsic value that is regarded as a sought-after prize: A library takes pride in its rare-book *acquisitions*. *Acquisition* may also apply to the *attainment* of a quality, skill, or body of knowledge that is valuable in itself: Self-discipline is an invaluable *acquisition*. See GENIUS, SKILL.

Attraction refers to the power or quality that draws a person to another person, an idea, or a thing. An **affinity** is a natural or instinctive *attraction* or inclination: an *affinity* among children of the same age. *Attraction* means the power to attract. If a woman has an *attraction* for a man, he is attracted or has an *affinity* for her; nothing is implied about the woman's feelings toward the man. *Affinity* is also used to refer to any individual preference or liking that is presumed to be deep-seated or stem from one's nature or background: an *affinity* for Italian movies; an *affinity* for mystery novels.

Sympathy, as here considered, refers to an agreement of affections, inclinations, or temperaments that makes people agreeable to one another. Two people are in *sympathy* if they have like *affinities* — for example, if they share the same tastes in art, recreation, or food. See LOVE.

Antonyms: antagonism, antipathy, aversion, discord, estrangement, repugnance, repulsion.

attribute

ascribe
credit
impute

Attribute means to consider one thing as belonging to or stemming from something else. [Some scientists *attribute* intelligence to ants; others say that the complex organizational life of ants should be *attributed* to instinct.]

Ascribe means to assign or *attribute* a cause, quality, source, etc., to something as a property or as being characteristic of it: to *ascribe* good (or bad) motives to someone; to *ascribe* an unsigned painting to Picasso; to *ascribe* an artifact to the Paleolithic era.

Credit, as here considered, means to *attribute* or *ascribe* in a favorable sense: to *credit* a scientist with a major discovery; to *credit* a seemingly trivial skirmish with being the turning point of a war.

Impute means to attribute a fault, crime, etc., to a person: to *impute* nepotism to the senator because of his decision to give a lucrative government contract to his brother-in-law. *Impute*, however, is not invariably associated with derogatory contexts. It may also be used to mean simply to consider as the source or cause of: to *impute* one's happiness to modest ambitions. See PRESCRIBE.

Antonyms: deny, dissociate, separate.

authoritarian

autocratic
despotic
dictatorial
fascistic
oligarchic
paternalistic
plutocratic
totalitarian
tyrannical

These words refer to the wielding of power by a single person or a small group of people, usually without the consent of the governed. **Authoritarian**, the most general of these, is also the most objectively descriptive and least disapproving in tone, although any of these words will have negative implications for the citizens of a democracy. *Authoritarian* may describe any form of rule — from a monarchy to a democracy — in which unquestioning obedience to those in power is expected or demanded: the military junta that instituted such *authoritarian* measures as censorship of the press; children whose upbringing was neither permissive nor *authoritarian*. **Paternalistic** refers to an *authoritarian* tendency that sees a populace as childlike and unable to govern itself. The word may suggest either benevolent rule or a style of government determined to keep the governed helpless and dependent: the *paternalistic* stance of most banana republics; the *paternalistic* attitude of most postbellum whites toward the recently freed Negro. **Oligarchic** refers to the rule of an elite, but does not suggest what grounds are used to determine who is a member of this ruling group: the *oligarchic* power of the English nobility before the rise of the monarchy. **Plutocratic** suggests an *oligarchic* rule based specifically on wealth: the first *plutocratic* industrial giants of the nineteenth century.

The remaining words are all much harsher in tone than the foregoing. Of these, **autocratic** is the mildest, though stronger than *authoritarian*. It suggests the absolute rule of a single person, but such a rule may be as repressive or benevolent as the person chooses: *autocratic* rulers as different as Queen Elizabeth I and Louis XIV; the rare husband who still insists on *autocratic* control over his family.

Totalitarian is perhaps the least exact of these words in its implications. It suggests the concentration of power in the hands of the few;
it also suggests the context of a modern collectivist state. A *totalitarian*
government is certainly *authoritarian*, but may or may not be *oligarchic*,
plutocratic, *paternalistic*, or *autocratic*. Such a state would certainly
suppress civil liberties, but might still have a benevolent notion, however misguided, of its duties to the people. On the other hand, it might
be based exclusively on the self-aggrandizement and greed of a ruling
class: the Puritans of the New World who, out of self-defense, constructed what amounted to a *totalitarian* state; a Stalinist regime that
was more *totalitarian* than those that preceded or followed it.

Dictatorial and **tyrannical** both may be simply descriptive of
autocratic rule, but more often suggest strong disapproval for repressive
tactics. *Dictatorial*, at its most neutral, specifically refers to leaders
other than hereditary rulers such as kings. At its most negative, it
suggests repressive harshness: Cromwell, who was less *dictatorial* than
many kings; family life embittered by her *dictatorial* momism; corporations no longer *dictatorial* toward their employees. *Tyrannical* may once
have been most appropriate to describe the power of a king, but now it
applies more generally to any arbitrary, almost whimsical one-man rule:
the *tyrannical* head of the congressional committee; his *tyrannical*
outburst against his son's disobedience.

Fascistic and **despotic** are the most harshly negative of all these
words. *Fascistic* in its narrowest sense applies to a strongly nationalistic
and militaristic right-wing regime that suppresses civil liberties and
attacks selected minorities: the *fascistic* tendencies of many anti-Sem-
ites. The word, however, is often used loosely as pure invective for any
authoritarian stand: *fascistic* gangsters who took control of the neighborhood. *Despotic* could once be applied less negatively to any absolute,
autocratic rule, but now it would be more often understood as indicating
a fiercely cruel and savagely repressive ruler or government: the rapidly
disappearing *despotic* family head; a government so *despotic* that citizens
could be shot without a trial.

Antonyms: compliant, constitutional, democratic, free, lenient, liberal, limited,
permissive.

auxiliary

ancillary
contributory
secondary
subsidiary

Auxiliary, like the rest of these words, refers to something that gives
additional help or support. The help given is usually similar to but less
important than the main effort being made: The *auxiliary* police are
called in only when the main force has been overtaxed. Sometimes the
word can refer simply to additional or supplementary resources: an oil
firm with *auxiliary* investments in shipbuilding and auto parts. Sometimes the word seems to be used almost euphemistically to avoid any
suggestion of subordination or inferiority to the main item: the ladies'
auxiliary club.

Like *auxiliary*, **ancillary** may refer to something useful that may or
may not be called into action. The *ancillary* item, however, may be
dissimilar though closely related to what it supports: psychology as
ancillary to the study of literature. In other instances, *ancillary*, more
than any of the other words, may suggest a dependence of the main
thing on the *ancillary* thing, almost as if the latter were its prerequisite,
or preceded it in time: Counterpoint and harmony are certainly *ancillary*
to serious composition.

Contributory suggests a definite cause-and-effect relationship unique
among these words, indicating one of several factors that result in a

particular effect. The *contributory* cause, however, only accompanies a major cause: *Underground sabotage was a contributory factor in the German retreat before the Allied onslaught.* Unlike *ancillary* or *auxiliary* items, something that is *contributory* exists only if actually called into action; it cannot be held in abeyance and still be *contributory*. Also, a *contributory* factor may be part of a destructive as well as a constructive result: *Cigarette smoking may be regarded as a contributory cause of cancer in his case.*

Secondary and **subsidiary** both clearly state the subordination or inferiority of the added factor. *Secondary* relates to *contributory* in having a cause-and-effect meaning but, unlike *contributory*, can refer to both causes and effects. A *contributory* cause, for example, may result only in a *secondary* effect. *Secondary* may be applied in any context where comparison is made between primary values, goals, benefits and less important or gratuitous ones. In this respect, *subsidiary* is more specific, meaning all the attached ramifications that may exist along with a primary situation: *an author's subsidiary rights in the stage and film versions of his novel; a main store's subsidiary branches. Subsidiary,* in this sense, is most like *auxiliary* in suggesting a similar but less important aspect of a larger whole. See ADDITION, ASSISTANT, SUBORDINATE.

avoid

elude
escape
eschew
evade
shun

Avoid means to keep away from or keep at a distance, either by design or as the automatic or accidental consequence of an action. [*He drove home over the bridge to avoid the traffic congestion at the tunnel; By driving home over the bridge he unknowingly avoided the tunnel congestion.*]

Escape in its basic sense refers similarly to a deliberate or accidental keeping clear of something. A criminal may adopt a ruse to *escape* detection, or he may *escape* apprehension by the death of the only witness. *Escape* is also used with the sense of to manage to *avoid,* or to remain untouched or uninfluenced by something evil or harmful: *to escape from being injured by the falling debris.*

To **elude** is to *avoid* or *escape* by the use of dexterity or artifice. A quarterback may *elude* tacklers by a feint; a fugitive may *elude* pursuers by planting false clues. **Evade** may sometimes be used in place of *elude,* but often carries the connotation of avoidance of duty or obligation by underhanded methods: *a taxpayer who evaded taxes by falsifying his accounts* — a punishable offense — although he might legally have *avoided* a portion of the tax by taking advantage of allowable deductions; *a soldier who evades hazardous duty by malingering.*

Shun and **eschew** are to *avoid* with repugnance or distaste, or for reasons of morality or prudence. [*A virtuous man will shun evil companions and practices; A man on a diet may shun or eschew rich foods.*] *Eschew* is restricted to formal contexts, and is narrower in application than *shun.* Whereas *eschew* points to abstention, *shun* may indicate either abstention or physical withdrawal; one can *shun* people as well as things. [*During his illness he shunned all society, and in particular those who had been his dearest friends.*]

Antonyms: catch, encounter, face, MEET, *seek, solicit.*

award

bounty

These words involve the showing of favor either out of generosity or out of respect for achievement. **Award** and **prize** are now nearly identical in meaning, although *prize* is less formal in tone. Both refer to a tribute given for some outstanding accomplishment. Both may or may not imply the giving of a sum of money. [The Olympic winner was offered only a crown of olive as an *award*; An *award* of ten thousand dollars accompanied the *prize* for the best novel of the year.] *Prize* may also signify the objective or attainment of a struggle. [The company took the hill after an all-night battle, but it was a costly *prize*; Although he had not guessed it when he proposed, his wife turned out to be quite a *prize*.]

Honor is more general than the foregoing. Whereas *award* and *prize* may suggest an official ceremony of recognition, *honor* may share this implication or depart from it to indicate simply private, unofficial respect. [The visiting head of state was given the *honor* of a twenty-one gun salute; It is an *honor* to hear you speak so highly of me.]

Premium is most specific in meaning, referring to an additional value beyond an agreed-on sum, the *premium* being given when a further condition has been met: They gave him a *premium* for selling the most insurance that month. More generally, the word may simply mean a high valuation, like *honor*: I put a high *premium* on the truth.

Bounty may mean generosity in general, or the gift given as a favor, a rather formal use: The land's *bounty* passed all expectation. *Bounty* is also used specifically to mean a sum of money given by a government for killing a predatory animal: the *bounty* offered for killing a mountain lion. See APPROVAL.

Antonyms: forfeit, penalty.

award
(continued)

honor
premium
prize

These words mean to have knowledge of the existence or fact of something. **Aware** is the broadest term, and may mean having knowledge of something inside oneself or of some external fact or condition. Such knowledge may be based on the evidence of one's senses or on the intellect: to be *aware* of hunger pangs; *aware* of a sharp drop in temperature; *aware* of a new trend in public opinion.

Conscious at its most restricted is close to *aware* in indicating the mind's registering of a sensation, perception, or state of affairs: *conscious* of how dim the room had grown as the twilight deepened; *conscious* of what the other students thought of her. Even on this level, however, the word may suggest the minimal registering of a perception, whereas *aware* more often implies a keener response or greater alertness that may encompass evaluation or rational judgment: People had been *conscious* of the problem before, but the new book made them *aware* of its magnitude. *Conscious*, furthermore, can apply as *aware* cannot to the waking state in general, as opposed to a sleeping or comatose state: a local anesthetic under which a person remains *conscious* throughout the operation. In a psychological context, the word can apply to those contents of the psyche that are present or available to the ego: a *conscious* hatred of his mother; slowly becoming *conscious* of his long-buried feelings of inferiority. Less technically, the word can refer to a deliberate or voluntary judgment: urged to make a *conscious* choice before events decided the question for them.

Cognizant implies knowledge of a more public character than the other words here considered. To say that one was *cognizant* of a breeze would be absurdly pretentious, but one may without fear of ridicule claim to be *cognizant* of new methods in the teaching of foreign languages. [A Congressman ought to be *cognizant* of the attitudes and opinions of his electorate.] *Cognizant* thus suggests a deliberate effort to know, and the things known are usually of some public importance. **Mindful**, like *cognizant* a rather formal word, emphasizes the giving of

aware

cognizant
conscious
mindful
on to

attention more than the acquisition of knowledge. [Because I am always *mindful* of my own mistakes, I am tolerant of the mistakes of others; *Mindful* of the strong opinions of his electorate, the Congressman voted against the measure.] **On to** is a colloquial expression meaning *aware of*, especially of something involving deception or skulduggery. It usually expresses a good deal of indignation, if not outright hostility. [I'm *on to* you and your fancy ideas about how I should spend my money; you're nothing but a crook!] See INFORM.

Antonyms: blind, HEEDLESS, *ignorant, insensible, unaware, unmindful.*

B

backcountry

backwoods
boondocks
inland
interior
midlands
sticks

These words refer to the inner portions of a country, to rural regions, or to those remote from cosmopolitan or urban centers. Many of these nouns also function attributively as adjectives. **Backcountry** is the most general of these and can apply to any of the three situations listed above; its connotations imply a provincial, backward, and rude area that is sparsely settled or unimportant: tourists who stop over in the country's main port but seldom visit the *backcountry*; a *backcountry* doctor. **Backwoods** restricts the possibilities of *backcountry* to the notion of an out-of-the-way forested region: the *backwoods* of Maine. The note of provinciality is even clearer here: rednecks from the *backwoods*.

Interior and **inland** are restricted in reference to the inner portions of a country, rural or urban, both words having fewer connotations than the previous pair. *Inland* may suggest the greater remoteness of these two words: the *inland* of the continent; the *interior* of the island. *Interior* can, however, suggest greater inaccessibility: an *inland* lake; the first expeditions to the *interior* of Africa. **Midlands** can also function neutrally but is used mostly to refer to *inland* regions of England: the great industrial cities of the *midlands*. Neither remoteness nor inaccessibility is implied here, although provinciality may be indicated.

Boondocks, which comes from a Filipino word for mountain, can refer to any stretch of rough country filled with dense brush or jungle: the *boondocks* of Luzon; headquarters personnel who are isolated from actual field conditions of troops in the *boondocks*. More recently, the word may refer informally to any rural or noncosmopolitan *backcountry*, especially with reference to its provincial isolation: a college town in the *boondocks*. **Sticks** is even more informal in concentrating exclusively on this last possibility of *boondocks*, pertaining to rural areas or provincial centers that are unsophisticated or backward. It is always somewhat derogatory or disparaging in tone: a hick from the *sticks*; like so many young men who left the *sticks* to seek his fortune in the big city. See PLAIN.

Antonyms: CITY.

backward

depressed

These adjectives are applied to countries, areas, or peoples that need to advance economically if they are to compete in the modern world. **Backward** is a purely negative word, expressing an unfavorable comparison. A *backward* land is one that lags far behind other nations in its development. Its failure to progress stems from what it lacks —

adequate income, education, industry, technology: the impoverished, illiterate people of a *backward* mountain region. At best, *backward* is bluntly descriptive. At worst, it is pejorative, implying inferiority as well as ignorance and suggesting a blameworthy lack of initiative. **Primitive**, by contrast, simply indicates an early stage in the development of civilization, a stage prior to industrialization. A *primitive* society has no written language and no advanced technology or system of production. Its economy and material culture are simple and unsophisticated: a *backward* land where farming methods have not changed for hundreds of years; a *primitive* land of huntsmen and food gatherers. *Primitive* may also refer to anything that is crude and simple because it is in a rudimentary stage or form: *primitive* agriculture.

Depressed designates an area that is economically underprivileged — a place of unequal opportunity, marked by widespread unemployment and a low standard of living. It implies a contrast with previous or surrounding conditions, often indicating a severe economic decline or a pocket of poverty in a prosperous land: a once-thriving coal-mining region that is now a *depressed* area full of ghost towns; volunteers teaching preschool children in *depressed* neighborhoods.

Underdeveloped marks a shift in emphasis, focusing on potential. It may be used as a euphemism for *backward*, since it stresses the presence of untapped resources. Or it may be used in conjunction with *backward*, describing a land that is *backward* in some respects or to some degree. [The most *backward* of the *underdeveloped* countries are those that have the fewest outside contacts with the modern world.] The fact that a country or region is *underdeveloped* may be due to insufficient investment capital, technical *backwardness*, or a deep-rooted resistance to progress and change. A **developing** country, by contrast, is committed to progress, trying to catch up with the prosperous nations so as to share in the world's wealth: foreign aid for the *developing* countries; the *developing* nations of Africa and Latin America. But a *developing* country may be subject to growing pains — the problems arising during a period of rapid growth or change: *developing* nations that are saddled with heavy debts, their resources taxed by a burgeoning population.

Emerging and **emergent** are the most positive of all these words. *Emerging* implies a national self-consciousness that propels a land toward political as well as economic independence. An *emerging* country is typically moving from the subordinate status of a colony, protectorate, or dependency to the status of a nation among nations: nationalist movements in the *emerging* countries. *Emergent* is a more pretentious word than *emerging*, smacking of bureaucratic jargon. Nevertheless, it has favorable connotations, being applied to newly independent nations that are coming forth to take their place on the international scene: *emergent* African nations joining the U.N.

These words describe qualities or situations that arouse feelings of displeasure or dislike, but usually not of strong aversion. **Bad**, the most general word of this group, may be a weak synonym for any of the other terms, indicating an unfavorable or undesirable quality. *Bad* government usually means corrupt government; a *bad* typist is an incompetent typist; a *bad* odor is often a disgusting or offensive odor; a *bad* child is a troublesome child; a *bad* situation may be either an unhappy or a dangerous situation.

Unpleasant is also a general word, but with a more limited application than *bad*. *Unpleasant* simply means not pleasant, failing to please:

backward
(continued)

developing
emergent
emerging
primitive
underdeveloped

bad

disagreeable
distasteful
objectionable
unpleasant

an *unpleasant* evening spent listening to a bore. However, *unpleasant* is often used as is *bad* to describe things that are displeasing or painful in various degrees of intensity. An *unpleasant* operation may be a polite description of a painful operation; an *unpleasant* day may be a tiring day or a stormy day; an *unpleasant* person may be a selfish, quarrelsome, or dirty person; an *unpleasant* taste may be a bitter or rancid taste.

Disagreeable and **distasteful** are stronger and more specific terms than *bad* and *unpleasant*. That which is *disagreeable* offends the senses, the feelings, or the opinions: the *disagreeable* taste of sour milk; to find the attentions of an unwanted suitor *disagreeable*; to find expressions of bigotry not only *disagreeable* to listen to, but almost impossible to eradicate. That which is *distasteful* is something which one finds *disagreeable* or shuns, not because it is inherently *bad* or undesirable, but because it goes against one's tastes or nature. [Some people find hard work *distasteful*; Asking a favor from anyone was *distasteful* to my mother.] *Distasteful* is now only rarely applied to food or drink that is poorly prepared or has a *disagreeable* taste.

Objectionable carries strong overtones of disapproval and moral indignation: The censors declared the love scenes in the book to be *objectionable*. *Objectionable* may also apply to that which is counter to one's sense of what is proper, fitting, or aesthetically pleasing. [Sentimentality is *objectionable* to critical, informed lovers of art; The Japanese, with their love of simplicity and order, find cluttered interiors *objectionable*.] See FLAW, MISCHIEVOUS, PROFLIGATE, REPULSIVE, SIN, WEAK.

Antonyms: acceptable, desirable, good, pleasant, PLEASING, *satisfactory, unobjectionable.*

banal

fatuous
inane
insipid
jejune
vapid

These words refer to what is offensive to good taste because of its want of sense, significance, or freshness. **Banal**, most strictly, refers to something that is so commonplace that it lacks freshness: *banal* jokes, hoary-headed with age. But the word has gathered connotations that go beyond this strict meaning, referring to an odious or deplorable lack of taste: another season of *banal* television programs.

Both **insipid** and **vapid**, like the Latin words from which they come, can literally refer to foods that lack savor. In applying to what is tasteless or gauche, both words also point to staleness, flatness, or want of spirit. They are often thought to be interchangeable, but subtle differences between them can be felt. *Insipid* is especially pertinent for describing instances of expression or behavior suggesting weakness or feebleness; this contrasts it with *banal*, which suggests outrageous bad taste: choosing between the *insipid* dullness of a drawing-room comedy and the *banal* brashness of a musical extravaganza. *Vapid*, on the other hand, might be thought more pertinent to describing a whole personality, one of limited mentality: a *vapid* starlet who kept making *insipid* remarks about the weather. *Vapid*, when it describes behavior rather than character, often suggests patent insincerity: thanking him with a *vapid* smile.

Unlike the foregoing, **jejune** and **inane** are less concerned with something that has lost its freshness than with something that reveals a total lack of substance to begin with. *Jejune* derives from a Latin word meaning hungry and applies emphatically to what is worthless and uninteresting. [This play cannot be called *banal*, considering its novelty, nor *insipid*, considering its liveliness, nor *vapid*, considering its sensitivity; nevertheless, it is utterly unstimulating and *jejune* in every particular.]

Inane derives from a word meaning empty and refers to something that is regarded as worthless because it lacks sense to the point of becoming foolish or silly: attempts at flattery that would be laughable if they weren't so *inane*. *Jejune* can also suggest an enduring state of mental exhaustion or emptiness: grimly resigning herself to the *jejune* patterns of suburban living. Because of confusion with *jeune*, the French word for *young*, the word is also used disapprovingly to indicate immaturity or naiveté: *jejune* teen-age fads. **Fatuous** is an intensification of *inane* in that it adds a suggestion of self-contented smugness to the silliness suggested by *inane*: a *fatuous* grin that revealed how witty she imagined her *inane* remark to be. See MONOTONOUS, SENTIMENTAL, SUPERFICIAL, TRITE, TRUISM.

Antonyms: meaningful, SIGNIFICANT.

These words refer to public places in which alcoholic drinks are served. **Bar** is now the general U.S. word for any place where the serving and drinking of liquor is in itself the primary concern. **Pub** is the comparable British term. **Saloon** has a much more complicated set of meanings. In Britain, it indicates a partitioned section of a *pub* where the furnishings are more luxurious and the drinks are more costly. Drawn from the French *salon*, the word can also indicate the main gathering place of a passenger ship, reflecting its earliest use pertaining to the room in a home where people gathered for conversation. In any case, *saloon* originally suggested an elegantly appointed place, one both sumptuous and respectable. As such, it was taken over in America to confer respectability on public drinking places, but with the Prohibition era, the word lost favor and came to indicate any sordid, low-life *bar*, a connotation from which the word, in America, has never recovered. After Prohibition, an attempt to replace *saloon* with **tavern** was made, but this word soon achieved the disesteem of *saloon*, and nowadays may suggest the same sort of sordid or tawdry place.

Cocktail lounge does indicate the elegant surroundings once suggested by *saloon*. Typically, such a place might be spacious and well-upholstered; it would offer a menu of food and possibly a singer or pianist for entertainment, though most likely it would not accommodate social dancing. The main function, here, is still that of serving liquor. **Nightclub** suggests a more lavish setting than *cocktail lounge*, indicating a place where eating and entertainment are as important as drinking itself. Whereas one could frequent a *cocktail lounge* in the afternoon or early evening, *nightclub* specifically indicates late hours; furthermore, the entertainment typically includes social dancing, a band (or "combo") of musicians, often with a singer, and the performances of one or more comedians. The entertainment may be on a far more lavish scale, involving an orchestra, chorus girls, etc.

Cabaret also indicates a place offering entertainment as well as liquor. It suggests smaller, more intimate surroundings, however, where singing or dancing acts are presented, though social dancing may not be involved. Recently, satirical revues and even serious plays have been presented in *cabarets*. At its inception, the recent word **discothèque** referred to a place where the new forms of social dancing were done to recorded music. Now the word is also used of places where modern social dancing is done to live music. *Discothèque* is the one word here that need not imply the serving of alcoholic drinks, since some of these places cater particularly to teen-agers to whom alcohol may not be sold. See RESTAURANT.

bar

cabaret
cocktail lounge
discothèque
nightclub
pub
saloon
tavern

bare

naked
nude
stripped

These words mean devoid of clothing or of a usual covering. **Bare**, when applied to objects, means without covering or ornament: a *bare* outcropping of rock; a tree *bare* of leaves. When used of a person, *bare* usually applies to a part of the body rather than to the entire body: *bare* knees; *bare* arms and legs. By extension, it is also used to indicate the omission of fancy trappings or nonessential adjuncts: Just give us the *bare* facts, without embellishment.

Naked, when applied to a person, means completely devoid of clothing. *Naked* is often invested with moral or emotional connotations, and may suggest sexual excitation or exhibitionism. [The hotel fire caught them both *naked*; She couldn't wear bikinis because they made her feel *naked*.] In other contexts, *naked* may suggest purity or innocence or simply be a neutral description: *naked* nymphs; *naked* children frolicking in the streets; The body was *naked* when discovered. In the sense of *bare*, *naked* is also used about physical objects or forces, generally for poetic effect or for emphasis: *naked* boughs; *naked* power; the *naked* truth.

Nude applies only to persons and may be neutral in connotation by itself, but its context — sexual interest being what it is in modern society — often makes it highly charged with emotional feeling. The noun *nude* denotes an unclothed figure in painting or sculpture, and the association of the word with esthetic appreciation often invests it with a kind of glamorous appeal lacking in *naked*. *Nude* has a more respectable tone than *naked*; thus fashion writers can advertise some feminine clothing as having a *nude* look, but dare not call it *naked*. For the same reason one speaks of sleeping in the *nude*, never *naked*.

Stripped literally means having been rendered *bare*, *naked*, or *nude* by some outside agency, but it is often used figuratively to mean deprived: *stripped* of his medals for disobeying a commanding officer; *stripped* of all his rights pending his appeal to the higher court.

Antonyms: clothed, covered, dressed.

barter

exchange
swap
trade

These words are alike in referring, most specifically, to a bargaining for goods or services that is conducted without the use of money.

Barter is the most formal and most specific of these. In the most primitive economic system, one gives the product he has made or grown in return for someone else's product — with no intermediary devices to assess abstract value. A farmer, in such a system, might *barter* several sacks of fodder for a pair of boots made by a shoemaker who happens to need feed for his horse. *Barter* in this strict definition does not involve middlemen; a person *barters* only for what he needs and intends to use. If the shoemaker, however, didn't need fodder at the exact moment of his bargain, he might still take the fodder, planning to **trade** it with someone else for something he could use. In any but the most primitive societies, of course, *bartering* as such, except among children, is almost unknown, but many kinds of *trading* may exist. A person may *trade* merely for sustenance, as with *barter*, but more commonly in order to sell what he gets for a profit; *trading*, thus, can be an occupation or livelihood: a record number of shares *traded* at the stock exchange. In senses other than the economic, *barter* has fewer uses than *trade*, and would strike most ears as needlessly formal: diplomats who *bartered* for peace. *Trade*, more informal, also has a wider range of general application: *trading* compliments; *trading* glances in the crowded bar.

In *bartering* and *trading*, a person must **exchange** one item for another. *Exchange* is not limited to the economic sense, however, applying to any reciprocal giving and receiving. In some uses, the things given and received may be equally valued: *exchanging* partners at a dance. Or the value may not be an important aspect: *exchanging* gifts at Christmas; *exchanging* letters. Perhaps more often, *exchange* implies the divesting of something unsuitable or unsatisfactory for something better: *exchanging* jobs; *exchanging* merchandise damaged in delivery.

Swap, most specifically, is like *barter*, except for its extreme informality. [The prospector *swapped* his gold dust for a jug of whiskey; I'll *swap* my slingshot for your caterpillar.] In some cases it may enter formal speech or writing when descriptive of a specific phenomenon: The sociologist did research on housewives who *swapped* husbands at Saturday night parties.

basic

These words are concerned with concepts of totality and completeness or of necessity. **Basic** and **fundamental** suggest first principles that underlie more complex considerations. *Fundamental* is the more formal of the two and is more natural in a philosophical context when applied to the principles themselves: a *fundamental* truth. In an educational context, it strongly suggests something that is indispensable or a prerequisite to more advanced development: reading as a *fundamental* skill. While *fundamental* often points to what is ideally necessary, *basic* may point to what is actually the case. [Lacking the *fundamental* ability to make distinctions, their *basic* vocabulary was greatly reduced.] *Basic* also has a wider range of application: the *basic* black of women's evening dress; a *basic* distrust of strangers. In these cases, the word may suggest not what is necessary but what is accepted or standard.

absolute
categorical
fundamental
ultimate
unlimited

Absolute in one sense is used simply as an intensification of *basic*: an *absolute* dislike of women. *Absolute*, however, relates philosophically to **ultimate** and **categorical** in another sense. Here, it refers to totality of power. Where *fundamental* indicates an initial necessity, *absolute* suggests final and conclusive authority: The child's *fundamental* instinct toward cooperation was overruled by the *absolute* value the tribe placed upon competition. *Ultimate* also suggests the highest or final authority: the *ultimate* court of appeal. Unlike *absolute*, it carries an implication of something worked through in time: What our *ultimate* view of the universe will be no one can say. **Unlimited**, while suggesting totality, contrasts with *ultimate* in relating more often to quantity than to time: *unlimited* profits. It compares to *absolute* in suggesting less a highest authority than one to which no opposition exists. [The king's powers were *absolute* but hardly *unlimited*, considering the strictures of canon and common law.] *Categorical* in its philosophical sense refers to something, usually a principle, which is inescapable, undeniable, and universal. Like *fundamental*, it suggests an ideal necessity; like *absolute*, it suggests finality and totality. [The *categorical* imperative of Kant was a moral truth that the structure of the universe made inevitable.] See CENTER, KERNEL, SPECIFIC.

Antonyms: circumscribed, MARGINAL, *peripheral*, PROVISIONAL, *tangent*, TRIVIAL.

basis

These words all refer to something upon which something else rests or depends. **Basis** differs from **base** in being more often used in metaphorical senses: The *basis* of his argument was that the victory was unattainable without seriously jeopardizing our domestic programs. *Base*, on the other hand, normally refers to physical objects that form the lowest or supporting part of anything: the *base* of a statue. It can,

base

basis
(continued)

foundation
ground

however, be used metaphorically as well: the *base* of a theory. In this sense *basis* and *base* are practically synonymous; *base*, however, more often suggests the idea of an underlying **foundation**, whereas *basis* is broader in application and may suggest the idea of a central or fundamental part as well as that of an underlying principle. [Axioms are the *base* of geometry; the *basis* of his decision; On what *basis* do you propose to pay me?]

Foundation can mean the *base* on which something rests: the *foundation* of a building. *Foundation* suggests a more imposing, solid structure than *base*, which can apply to the bottom part of anything: the *base* of a lamp; the *foundation* of an ancient city. *Foundation* also means that on which anything is founded, and in this sense is close to *basis*: The *foundation* of democracy is the will of the people to preserve liberty. It should perhaps be noted that *foundation* is now used commercially to refer to a variety of feminine accouterments that supply an underlying *basis* or that give support, such as facial makeup applied beneath other makeup and certain undergarments that hold in vital parts of the body so that outergarments do not reveal their actual shape.

Ground, as here considered, means a *foundation* or *basis* for a decision, argument, or relationship. It is often used in the plural in this sense, and when plural, it may be construed as singular. [The *grounds* for his decision was never clearly stated; Absenteeism constitutes *grounds* for dismissal.] *Grounds* implies the underpinnings of reason: Leverrier's mathematical computations were the *grounds* for his theory that there was a planet beyond Uranus. See CENTER, KERNEL.

Antonyms: superstructure, top.

beat

flagellate
flog
scourge
spank
thrash
whip

These words refer to physical punishment meted out by means of blows administered primarily by hand or by some instrument held in the hand. **Beat** is the most general of these and the least specific. It perhaps most strongly suggests a pummeling with the fists; this may be the result of spur-of-the-moment anger between opponents: ruffians who *beat* him up after school. But the word can also suggest a more deliberate inflicting of punishment on an inferior by a superior: a psychotic mother who *beat* her children unmercifully. In these latter cases, some sort of instrument may well be used: *beating* the dog with a rolled-up newspaper. **Thrash** is more likely to be restricted to the first situation, expressing spontaneous anger between opponents. Although fisticuffs might be the main element of the attack, the word suggests a general sort of knocking about by any means whatsoever. *Thrash* may have a euphemistic flavor in that it seems to imply a less serious or cruel infliction of injury than *beat,* and may be an attempt to make light of the intent behind the act; but it can, despite this, indicate a more thorough or methodical act than *beat* and often suggests an act motivated by the wish to reprove someone for insolence or misbehavior: threatening to *thrash* him within an inch of his life unless he took back the insult.

Spank is very much more specific than either *beat* or *thrash* in its application. It refers unambiguously to the corrective or salutary punishment meted out by a parent on a child, with no intent to inflict actual harm. The action specifically involves hitting the child's buttocks with the open hand, often with the child laid face-down across the parent's knees. [G. B. Shaw wondered how parents could wait until their anger had cooled in order to *spank* their children in cold blood.] The remaining words all relate to punishment meted out by means of some instrument, usually one held in the hand.

The following words specifically stress the inflicting of physical injury to a degree that is not a necessary implication of the words discussed so far. **Whip** suggests the beating of someone usually by means of a flexible cord or series of cords expressly designed for this use, made of leather, metal, or rope and attached to a handle: *whipping* the horse into a quicker pace; ordering that the mutinous soldiers be put in irons and *whipped*. The word, less specifically, can refer to any act of *beating* done by means of any sort of instrument, whether flexible or rigid, whether improvised or designed for the occasion: known to *whip* prisoners in his charge with a razor strop or a metal ruler; claiming that his interrogators had pistol-*whipped* him. **Scourge** is often used metaphorically for any calamity or harsh attack; but most concretely, it refers specifically to beating with a many-tongued or many-thonged whip. In this sense, however, it is less often used except in reference to the Biblical account of Christ's being *scourged*.

Flog may specifically suggest *whipping*, especially with a many-tongued lash, but it can also indicate *beating* with any sort of instrument, flexible or rigid: suspected informers who were *flogged* with chains before being killed. A historical context unique to this word is the nautical one in which this sort of set punishment was inflicted upon sailors for certain infractions of orders. The word might also apply in this way to military or penal situations. **Flagellate**, most strictly, has a religious or psychosexual context. In either case the sheer infliction of pain is emphasized and is carried out by means of whip, lash, or other cord-like instrument, often many-tongued, knotted, barbed, or nettled, although this may be applied by oneself or by others, especially (as with *flog*) across the back. Religious zealots engaged in this activity to punish the flesh for its inherent sinfulness, and sado-masochistic neurotics may engage in flagellation for the sexual stimulation it affords them.

These words refer to pleasing facial appearances. **Beautiful** indicates a strikingly desirable or attractive face, suggesting symmetry of features or perfection of proportion, although ultimately the word is dependent on the subjective taste of the user. Because of this it is extremely unspecific in reference, although it would most often be used of a woman's face. **Good-looking** is equally as weak in specificity, but it can be used appropriately of both men and women: a *good-looking* couple.

Handsome and **pretty** are complementary terms in that *handsome* usually applies to men and *pretty* even more exclusively to women. *Pretty*, however, indicates a less elevated or more superficial appeal than *beautiful*: the rare woman who is truly *beautiful* as opposed to the many who are merely *pretty*. In this opposition, *pretty* might suggest vivacity and sweetness, while *beautiful* might suggest elegance and nobility. *Handsome*, used of men, is comparable to *beautiful*, used of women, suggesting regularity of features and a sturdy manliness. Sometimes *handsome* may be used of women as well, in which case it does not, strangely enough, suggest an epicene mannishness, but a radiant force of almost animal good health and vividness: insisting that Garbo was not merely *beautiful*, but breathtakingly *handsome*. *Handsome* in this sense would be used only of mature women, never of girls. *Pretty* would never be used of a man, except pejoratively to suggest effeminacy. *Beautiful* may rarely be used of a man without negative effect; in this case the face is usually regarded in an artistic light or as redolent of some special attribute: a man with *beautiful* features; a *beautiful* and expressive face that spoke both of strength and of suffering.

beautiful

comely
cute
good-looking
gorgeous
handsome
pretty

Because **comely** may now sound outdated, it is sometimes used to suggest earthy or rustic good looks in women: the *comely* milkmaid in a Constable painting. Once its particular emphasis, however, was on freedom from blemish, as in the Song of Solomon: "I am black, but *comely.*" **Cute** is an informal word for good looks in women that suggest cheerfulness and wholesomeness; the word thus gives less praise than *pretty* and far less than *beautiful*. *Cute* may also be used by women to describe men who may not be *handsome* but who are boyish or sweet-tempered. **Gorgeous** is sometimes used hyperbolically to refer to someone extremely *beautiful* or *handsome*; like many hyperboles its extravagance has tended to strip it of meaning. See CHARMING, PLEASING.

Antonyms: UGLY, uncomely.

begin

commence
inaugurate
initiate
institute
launch
start

These words refer to the earliest period in a thing's existence. **Begin**, the broadest term of this group, means to take the first step or do the first act or part of something: to *begin* a course of study leading to a doctorate; to *begin* to understand one's past mistakes. In many contexts **start** is interchangeable with *begin*: The engine *started* (or *began*) smoking. But *start* places more emphasis on the fact of making a beginning, the mere act of setting out, whereas *begin* often suggests the start of a process in fulfillment of a purpose. The relationship between *start* and *begin* is not unlike that between *speed* and *velocity*; the second word in both sets implies direction. [He was *beginning* to think of himself as an old man; She *started* (or *began*) skiing last winter; The train *started* with a lurch.]

Commence is a more formal word for *begin*. There are practically no contexts in which *begin* will not serve very well in place of *commence*, but *commence*, and sometimes **institute**, is preferred in some contexts, especially legal, where *begin* is felt to be insufficiently formal, too much an everyday word, to dignify the proceedings. Thus legal action is *instituted*, rarely *begun*, and judicial sessions *commence*, seldom *begin*. *Commence* is sometimes used vulgarly or humorously in other than solemn contexts: We *commenced* to drink our beer. *Institute* in other senses means to *begin* with a view toward setting up or putting into operation: to *institute* needed reforms in the ministry. *Institute* suggests a great deal of enterprise, and frequently foresight as well: to *institute* new management methods that saved millions of dollars.

Initiate is close to *institute* in pointing to the motivating force or creator that starts something, but does not, like *institute*, convey the idea of carrying through what one has started to the point of seeing it in operation: to *initiate* legislation; He *initiated* the reforms, but the state agency *instituted* them.

Inaugurate means to *begin* formally or officially. Thus to *inaugurate* a new policy or legislation suggests some ceremony or traditional observance to commemorate it. [Once the president is *inaugurated*, he begins his term of office; The ball was *inaugurated* by the introduction to society of several young debutantes.] The word is also used for *begin* in historical contexts implying great scope or import: The Industrial Revolution *inaugurated* a new era.

Launch is a related word, but means to *begin* not so much with ceremony as with fanfare and publicity. [The Treasury is *launching* a new bond drive; The advertising agency will *launch* a campaign to introduce a new soap.] This sense doubtless derives from the fanfare attached to the *launching* of large sea-going vessels. See CREATE, ORIGIN.

Antonyms: FINISH, STOP.

These words refer to someone who has not yet acquired the skills and experience that are required to qualify him in a given field. **Beginner** is the most informal of these words and is the least negative in tone, suggesting someone who has already started to acquire the necessary abilities but has not worked long enough to master them; the word may imply a young person, but this is not necessarily so: a ballet class for adult *beginners*; piano lessons for children and *beginners*. **Apprentice** most concretely refers to a young person taken on by a master to be taught the skills of a trade; this practice, more common in the past, is still reflected in the titles given by some trade unions in accordance with a person's amount of experience: the *apprentice* who becomes a journeyman and at last a master. In broader uses, the word refers to any *beginner*, often with an emphasis on his low or menial position or lack of polish: a writer whose first book reveals him to be an *apprentice* rather than a mature artist.

Both **novice** and **neophyte**, but especially the former, may refer to a newly introduced member of a religious order. In broader contexts, both are less factual and more uncomplimentary. *Novice* in this case may suggest clumsiness due to lack of training or even to an amateurish lack of discipline or application: light meters made so that even the rankest *novice* can use them; a *novice* whose canvases show the lowest possible standards and the worst set of influences. *Neophyte* may be used somewhat less negatively than *novice*, especially since it implies an eagerness to learn and a humble respect for and seeking out of knowledgeable authority: the *neophytes* who clustered around the established poet in hopes of catching some pearl of wisdom he seemed always on the verge of dropping.

Tyro is perhaps the most negative of these words in that it refers to an inexperienced and amateurish approach to a complicated field, suggesting a raw or young recruit who has yet to begin the task of mastering his craft: the *tyro* who has taken one or two survey courses in literature and proceeds to write critical reviews for his school paper. See AMATEUR.

Antonyms: connoisseur, expert, old hand, old-timer, veteran, virtuoso.

These words are used to refer to things that are in the initial or early stage of existence or to things that are unformed, undeveloped, or elementary in character. **Beginning**, the most general of the five, can mean either first or early. The *beginning* chapter of a book is its first chapter; the *beginning* section of the same book would embrace the first chapter but would also include several of the other early chapters. In another sense, *beginning* describes something that deals with elementary principles, skills, or routines: The *beginning* course in physics will not be offered this term.

Incipient shares with *beginning* the meaning of just coming into existence: The *incipient* stage of a urinary infection is often marked by high fever. **Inchoate**, like *beginning* and *incipient*, can describe a condition or activity that has just recently come into existence or operation. It more often, however, suggests the absence of order, form, or coherence: an *inchoate* plan, badly organized and full of contradictions. One of the general meanings of *inchoate*, that referring to a lack of completion or perfection, is part of the specialized terminology of the legal profession. An *inchoate* contract is one that has not been executed by all the parties involved.

Rudimentary, which means fundamental or elementary, is often

beginner

apprentice
neophyte
novice
tyro

beginning

inchoate
incipient
primeval
rudimentary

used to express a limitation: He had only a *rudimentary* knowledge of chemistry. It also can characterize something as primitive, undeveloped, or imperfectly developed. [Their dwelling place was *rudimentary* in nature, rather more like a hut than a house; A pair of *rudimentary* hind legs are part of the skeleton of the boa constrictor.]

Primeval refers to the earliest ages of the world, particularly to that time before the appearance of man on earth: the *primeval* hills of Appalachia. It is applied by extension to things that are very old and have existed since time immemorial: *primeval* forests. See BEGIN.

Antonyms: closing, developed, ending, late, MATURE.

behavior

conduct
demeanor
deportment
manners

These words refer to the characteristic ways that people reveal themselves in their actions. **Behavior** is the most general of these; at its most technical, it refers to all activity of people, singly or collectively, that might be studied by psychologists, sociologists, or anthropologists: paranoid *behavior*; peer-group *behavior* in preschool children; mating *behavior* in New Guinea. In everyday use, the word more frequently refers to positive or negative social activity: promising to be on my best *behavior*; such incredibly rude *behavior*. **Conduct** can also refer to individual or group activity, but in a less technical sense than *behavior*; it also may be categorized positively or negatively. It does suggest a narrower range of activity than *behavior*, implying the breaking or following of prescribed rules: a bad *conduct* discharge from the army; a prison sentence commuted for good *conduct*. The word is distinct from these other words because it may suggest an ethical or moral basis for measuring *behavior*: *conduct* befitting an honest man.

Manners refers not so much to adherence to ethical standards as to the arbitrary forms by which a social group has traditionally acted. Here a positive or negative evaluation may depend on subjective taste as much as anything else: the vulgar *manners* of the nouveau riche; the easy, natural *manners* that were second nature to her. The word most often refers to individuals, but can sometimes apply collectively to a whole social group: the affected *manners* of our debased age.

Deportment is a more formal synonym for *conduct*, but the set of rules that measure *deportment* may be arbitrary choices to facilitate a goal or may be superimposed from above, instigated especially to instill a respect for authority. Its most common use is to describe the *behavior* of pupils in school: sending home remarks critical of his uncooperative *deportment*; measures to improve the *deportment* of her class. **Demeanor** is distinct from all these words in that it almost exclusively refers to the way a particular person acts at a particular time, and suggests an assessment of the person's dress, bearing, attitude, and expression: a habitually quiet man who had never shown such an agitated *demeanor*; a supervisor known for her invariably soft-spoken and relaxed *demeanor*. See ACT.

beleaguer

bait
heckle

These words mean to harass or torment another person so persistently as to disturb his peace of mind or undermine his self-confidence. **Beleaguer**, from its literal meaning of surrounding and shutting in an enemy force with one's own army, carries the implication of a hemming in on all sides by a multitude, so that escape is virtually impossible: a landlord *beleaguered* by complaining tenants; a man *beleaguered* by worries; a countryside *beleaguered* by a plague of locusts.

Hound strongly suggests the relentless and unflagging pursuit of a hunting dog on the scent: an escaped criminal *hounded* from state to state by the police. By extension, *hound* also implies repeated urging and nagging, especially to the point where the victim can do little except submit: to be *hounded* by bill collectors; a teacher *hounded* from his job because of his political views.

The literal meaning of **bait** is to set dogs for sport on a chained or penned animal, especially a bear or a bull. Figuratively, *bait* implies malicious pleasure in tormenting another by teasing and ridicule, especially when retaliation is difficult: *baited* by the other boys at school for his poor showing in sports; to *bait* an old man whose ideas are not in agreement with yours. *Bait* may also mean to tease or twit in a more or less amiable way: He *baited* his wife for spending so much time talking on the telephone.

Ride, which is chiefly colloquial, evokes the action of urging a mount on to greater speed by the use of spurs or a whip. Therefore, *ride* may imply driving or goading someone to reach a goal (not necessarily an undesirable one), but often suggests mischievous or malicious intent. [Parents complain that the fifth-grade teacher *rides* her brighter pupils too hard; The boys at the office are always *riding* me because my wife calls me at five o'clock sharp every day to make sure I'm coming straight home; The old-timers *rode* the rookie shortstop unmercifully, calling him "Junior" and shouting, "Hey, you want a security blanket?" and similar remarks.]

Heckle emphasizes the harassing of a speaker in public by means of taunts, questions, and other interruptions in order to confuse or intimidate him or to ferret out the weaknesses in his argument: to *heckle* a candidate for political office; to *heckle* the leader of an antiwar demonstration.

Hector strongly suggests bullying and browbeating by scolding, nagging, or derision: an authoritarian father who *hectors* his children instead of trying to understand them; a warden who keeps order by *hectoring* his prisoners. See INTIMIDATE.

Antonyms: ENCOURAGE.

These words all mean capable of being believed or worthy of being accepted as real, true, or trustworthy. **Believable** is the most general term and describes anything that is possible, probable, or acceptable either because it is in accordance with one's everyday experience and observation or because it is not directly contrary to fact. [He gave us a frightening, but *believable*, account of his childhood in the slums; The boy's tale of meeting a pirate on the deserted beach is simply not *believable*.]

Credible is sometimes used interchangeably with *believable*: a *believable* excuse for his lateness; a *credible* explanation for having failed to finish his work. However, *credible* goes a step beyond *believable* in that something that is *credible* merits belief and is supported by known facts: a *credible* account of the causes of World War II. *Credible* is now rarely used of persons except in the expression *credible witness* — that is, a witness who is reliable and trustworthy in giving accurate testimony.

Something that is **convincing** is *believable* because it overcomes any doubt, uncertainty, or hesitancy in accepting it. A *convincing* argument compels one's belief in its soundness because it satisfies the sense of logic or fitness.

The earlier meaning of **plausible** adhered closely to its etymology, "worthy of applause" — that is, commendable or capable of winning favorable acceptance by the mind. It now carries a strong implication

beleaguer
(continued)

hector
hound
ride

believable

convincing
credible
plausible

of deception and speciousness. A *plausible* statement will very likely be one that appears to be *convincing* or *believable* on the surface, but which, upon closer examination, is not so. See ACCURATE, GENUINE, TRUTHFUL.

Antonyms: DOUBTFUL, *implausible, incredible, suspect, unbelievable, unreliable.*

belittle

deprecate
depreciate
detract
discredit
disparage
minimize

These words refer to criticism designed to diminish the worth of something. **Belittle** is the most general and informal of these; it may suggest a deliberately fault-finding attitude: *belittling* every practical suggestion she came up with. It may imply an attitude that simply cannot tolerate excellence or effort in others: *belittling* those who had continued to work on the project after he had given up. It may also suggest a cumulatively telling process of slight or trivial attempts to undermine another's position: constantly *belittling* everything he believed in.

Minimize is a more formal substitute for *belittle*; it refers specifically to the attempt to set a lower value on something than it commonly carries or deserves: *minimizing* the worth of civil defense measures previously in force. In contrast to *belittle*, any note of spiteful censoriousness may be absent from this word, which by its formality may emphasize, instead, a judicious or reasoned reassessment: *minimizing* the effect of Augustine on later medieval thought. The sense of animus, by contrast, is definitely present in **detract**, even to a greater degree than in *belittle*. Where *belittle*, furthermore, may suggest a sniping at trivial failings, *detract* suggests an attempt at a more drastic lowering of esteem: a fiercely argued view that sought to *detract* from the usefulness of the earlier study.

Disparage and **deprecate** contrast with the foregoing words by suggesting a general effort to make something seem without worth or value. *Disparage* suggests the animus of *detract*, but may imply a seizing of any faults, small or large, to prove a judgment already formed: caustically *disparaging* each new production as further proof of the playwright's worthlessness. While *deprecate* may sometimes suggest only an attempt to devalue rather than to reject something utterly, its effect is strengthened by the amused, scornful, or sarcastic consideration it implies: *deprecating* the notion of integration with a weary laugh. Some purists assert that **depreciate** and not *deprecate* should be used in the sense of lowering or underestimating the value or worth of: the tendency of people who are not talented to *depreciate* those who are. Many excellent writers, however, use *deprecate* in this sense, and it can only be considered a well-established usage today.

Discredit is the most severe of these words, exclusively suggesting criticism designed to demolish a position or accomplishment utterly, often by unfair means: attempting to *discredit* his opponent by glancing and suggestive references to his personal life. See DISAPPROVAL.

Antonyms: credit, ENCOURAGE, *enhance, exaggerate.*

bend

bow
lean

These verbs are applied to bodily movements and denote a shift from a straight, natural, or fixed position. **Bend** implies a folding movement of the head or body or an angular movement at a joint: to *bend* from the waist; to *bend* the elbow. **Lean** refers to a sloping movement away from an erect position. It implies a slant in a certain direction or a propping against a support. The *leaning* body or part, itself, is straight or only slightly curved, though at an angle. [*Lean* back and relax; *Lean* your head on my shoulder; He *leaned* against the wall.] When *bend* and *lean* are close in meaning, *bend* suggests a more marked downward shift and implies greater effort, force, or concentration. [The clerk *leaned* over the counter; The student *bent* over his books.]

To **bow** is to *bend* the head or upper body forward and down: to *bend* over backwards; to *lean* sideways; to *bow* before the king. *Bowing* is a formal action, done for a symbolic rather than a practical purpose. [*Bend* down and pick it up; *Bow* down and worship.] One may *bow* to show reverence, respect, humility, or submission: to *bow* before an altar; to *bow* the head and *bend* the knee in prayer. Or one may *bow* as a matter of custom, formal courtesy, or protocol: to *bow* to one's audience after performing; a *bowing* headwaiter; *bowing* diplomats. In *bending* over, *leaning* down, or *bowing* from the waist, one lowers the body by *bending* the back. To **stoop** is to lower the body by *bending* the knees: He *stooped* down to talk to the child on the child's own level. Posture experts prefer *stooping* to *bending* because in *stooping*, the head and torso remain upright and no strain is put on the back. In another sense, however, *stoop* indicates poor posture, describing a habitual forward inclination of the head and shoulders: *stooped* shoulders.

Turn means to shift or swing part way around. It implies rotation of the head or body and refers to a change in direction. [*Turn* to the left; He *turned* his head to look behind him; She *turned* to face me; *Turn* over; *Turn* around; They *turned* the patient on his side.] In a special sense, *turn* may describe a sudden inward collapse or outward wrenching of the ankle that results in a strain or sprain: She stumbled at the curb and *turned* her ankle. **Twist** indicates a strained, contorted, or violent *turning* of part of the body. It suggests the muscular tension set up when one part of the body changes position while the rest remains in place. [She *twisted* around in her seat, craning backward; He *twisted* my arm.] *Twisting* may also involve a sinuous *bending* or winding: to *twist* one's legs around a chair. Or it may suggest a constant, restless *turning* or squirming: He *twisted* and *turned* all night.

All of these words may be used in figurative senses. *Bend* stresses force or flexibility, the power to subdue or the facility to yield, adapt, or change: stern and *unbending*. [They *bent* to his wishes; He *bent* (or *bowed*) them to his will.] *Bow* may imply a submissive yielding suggestive of a broken or servile spirit: *bowed* down by heavy sorrows; bloody but *unbowed*; to *bow* and scrape. *Stoop* emphasizes the idea of lowering oneself by doing something that one deems degrading: I would not *stoop* to such methods. *Lean* stresses the idea of inclination, a sympathy of views that draws one in a certain direction: a moderate who *leans* toward conservatism. *Turn* calls to mind a whirling rotation. It may be used of something that makes a person giddy or that causes him to lose his sense of proportion: Compliments *turned* her head. *Twist* implies a violent *turning* out of the natural course and may connote distortion or deformity: to *twist* someone's words; a *twisted* mind. See ROTATE.

Antonyms: rise, straighten.

These words describe conditions that are positive in their effect on health or financial well-being. **Beneficial** is general and relatively formal. While it can refer to financial well-being, it more naturally applies to things conducive to mental or physical health: government programs *beneficial* to the poor; a sunny day's *beneficial* influence on my darkest moods; milk and vegetables *beneficial* to a growing child. In one sense, it suggests something that is an added help, but is not strictly necessary: a friendship *beneficial* to both of them. **Good** is, of course, the most

beneficial

(continued)

profitable
salubrious
salutary
wholesome

general word here and the least formal; it has a multitude of uses in pointing to what promotes financial or physical strength: a *good* climate; *good* circulation; a *good* business proposal; a *good* stock. Its very generality invites the substitution of a more precise synonym.

Advantageous and **profitable** are words which carry overtones of financial well-being. *Advantageous* can, of course, refer to anything chosen for its desirability or to improve one's situation: a more *advantageous* view of the sunset; resorts *advantageous* to the husband-hunting secretary. More often, an actual monetary gain is present or implied: an *advantageous* position in his firm. *Profitable* is even clearer on this score: a *profitable* business in a *profitable* location; Good looks are a more *profitable* commodity in Hollywood than talent and hard work. In Victorian times, *profitable* was often used for something *beneficial* to the development of character: a *profitable* book to read for spiritual guidance. This use is less frequent today.

The rest of these words relate more specifically to the promoting of health. **Healthful**, the most general, should be distinguished from healthy. The first refers to what will give health, the second to the state of having it. The ill, rather than the healthy, are most concerned with seeking out *healthful* climates. Both, however, may enjoy what is *healthful*: *healthful* exercise; *healthful* meals; the *healthful* sport of mountain-climbing. **Wholesome** suggests less the promoting of well-being than the inherently *good* or *healthful* situation in and for itself. It also carries a tone of moral uplift and is as often used of mental as of physical health: a *wholesome* movie for the whole family; *wholesome* food; *wholesome* good looks. Its Pollyanna overtones become clear when one considers that some *healthful* activities might decidedly not be considered *wholesome* in many situations.

Salutary suggests the correcting of a physical or mental lack: a *salutary* diet for anemia; sea breezes *salutary* to insomniacs; an editorial *salutary* in its fierce honesty and forthright proposals. **Salubrious** is comparable to but more intense than *salutary*, suggesting a positive physical or mental enrichment, without suggesting any previous impoverishment. It also describes any invigorating or stimulating experience: the *salubrious* mineral waters of the spa; the *salubrious* effects of a long ocean voyage; a *salubrious* shock to the complacent middle-classes. See FAVORABLE.

Antonyms: bad, detrimental, disadvantageous, harmful, injurious, insalubrious, ruinous, unhealthful, unhelpful, unprofitable, unwholesome.

benefit

advantage
favor
gain
profit

These words refer to some desirable good that can be given, acquired, or earned. **Benefit** is the most general of these, referring to any kind of good, however acquired, material or otherwise: lessons designed to be of *benefit* to growing minds; the *benefits* accorded to one of his lofty position. **Advantage** is narrower in scope than *benefit*, since it can suggest more strictly either material *benefits* or things won in competition against an opponent: all the *advantages* of suburban living; a naturally fortified hill that would give them the *advantage* over the enemy. The word, of course, can function more abstractly and without any implication of depriving someone else of the same benefit: all equally free to take *advantage* of our tradition of free speech and respect for dissent. **Favor** may suggest being given the *advantage* in a competition: ruling in *favor* of the plaintiff; unequal odds that made the battle sure to come out in the aggressor's *favor*. The word, however, most often refers to *benefits* that result from securing the approval of others: a new product

seeking *favor* in the marketplace; audiences that looked with *favor* on
his plays. The word can also be used to indicate narrow self-interest:
acting only in his own *favor*.

Like *benefit*, **gain** can suggest an intangible good given or acquired at
no one's expense: a law that resulted in a clear *gain* for civil liberties;
a *gain* in technical competence over his last work. More commonly,
however, the word suggests material acquisition: capital *gains*; greedy
for *gain*. **Profit** is even more restricted to material or monetary acquisition: realizing a ten percent *profit* on each sale; speculators eager for a
quick *profit*. Sometimes, however, the word can refer to *gains* outside
the context of money-making: a book anyone can read with *profit*. See
HELP, IMPROVE.

Antonyms: disadvantage, harm, loss.

These words refer to a well-wishing friendliness or concern for the
needs and desires of other people. **Benevolence** has the widest range
of any of these words, suggesting an expansive and good-humored tolerance and sympathy for others: brimming over with a feeling of sunny
benevolence toward everyone he encountered. Sometimes the word implies the sympathy of a superior toward a subordinate, an implication
strengthened by the word's formality: working conditions sought as a
right, not as a *benevolence* of their employer. **Generosity** is more informal and focuses exclusively on the aspect of giving, referring to an
unstintingly helpful act or habit: the *generosity* with which he shared
his toys with other children. In contrast to *benevolence*, which may remain an unacted-upon feeling, *generosity* is measured by actual behavior:
a plantation owner who looked on his slaves with *benevolence* but could
hardly be accused of treating them with *generosity*.

At a level of greater informality, **good will** and **kindness** are related
somewhat like the previous pair, with *good will* referring primarily to
feeling and *kindness* to action. *Good will* may refer to an open, charitable
attitude, without reservation or bitterness: Christmas carollers full of
merriment and *good will*. The word may also refer to a willingness to be
fair-minded or impartial: both sides bargaining in *good will*. *Kindness*
may suggest thoughtful or courteous consideration for the feelings of
others: neighbors who were always the soul of *kindness*. Often, however,
the word specifically points to the help one person gives to someone less
fortunate, less well, or less able than himself: a nurse who treated the
sick and wounded with almost reverent *kindness*. This word, consequently, can sometimes have a patronizing flavor, like *benevolence*: insisting that he wanted only her *good will*, not her *kindness*.

Unselfishness and **altruism** both point to a *generosity* that is based
on a lack of self-concern. Where *generosity* may emphasize the quantity
given, possibly for ostentatious reasons, *unselfishness* stresses the effacing
personal sacrifice required — even if a lesser amount is given: It was
the tax deduction involved, rather than *unselfishness*, that prompted his
generosity to the charity drive. While *unselfishness* is most often used to
indicate a personal trait, the more formal *altruism* is usually reserved to
indicate a moral or ethical principle. The word refers to the setting aside
of all special or personal interests in determining which course of action
will most benefit the group welfare. This makes the word a more specific
and exact synonym for one possibility in *good will*: Peace Corps volunteers, searching for a way to put their youthful *altruism* into practice.
See GENEROUS, HUMANE.

Antonyms: EGOISM, MALICE, *miserliness, stinginess.*

benevolence

altruism
generosity
good will
kindness
unselfishness

bequest

endowment
legacy

A **bequest** is something given or left to a person or an institution by the will of a benefactor. A **legacy** is something given or passed on by an ancestor, a predecessor, or an earlier era, and may be contained in a will or transmitted informally or automatically: to receive a *legacy* of a million dollars from the estate of a deceased aunt; to be heir to a *legacy* of good will through his father's reputation. [The United Nations was left a *legacy* of unsolved problems by the League of Nations.]

An **endowment** is something settled or bestowed on a person or institution, and is not necessarily a posthumous gift. A philanthropist may, during his lifetime, establish an *endowment* for scholarships at a university, or may bestow upon a deserving student an *endowment* for paying the costs of his education. See PRESENT.

between

amid
amidst
among
amongst
betwixt

Between, as here considered, means flanked by two objects, one on either side. [Continental United States lies *between* Canada and Mexico; *between* the devil and the deep blue sea]

When *between* and **among** are used by extension to indicate a sharing, *between* is normally used when two objects are involved and *among* when more than two are involved: an inheritance divided *between* two heirs and shared *among* three heirs. Occasionally *between* is used to express such a relationship involving more than two objects, particularly if the relation involves each object individually or if it involves relationships between pairs of objects within the larger group: A political dispute involving six nations may be settled by an agreement *between* them.

Amid means surrounded by either separate objects or an undifferentiated mass or quantity. [A church stands *amid* skyscrapers; A reaper works *amid* the grain; A man may keep calm *amid* confusion.]

Among, as here considered, means surrounded by or included in a group of separate but similar objects. [Augustus Caesar was called *princeps* — chief *among* equals; A diary was *among* the effects left by a deceased.]

Amidst, **amongst**, and **betwixt** are variants of *amid*, *among*, and *between*. *Amongst* and *betwixt* are generally avoided as archaic, except when used poetically or rhetorically. *Amidst* is more common in Great Britain than in the United States.

biased

one-sided
partial
partisan
prejudiced
slanted
subjective

These words refer to a lack of fairness in judging or reporting because of the favoritism given to one way of viewing a subject. **Biased** suggests that someone judging or reporting a controversy is already disposed for or against one of the contending sides: He insisted that the jury was already *biased* by improper remarks made by the prosecution; an education that gave him a *biased* view of cultures different from his own; a *biased* account referring to civil rights workers as carpetbaggers. **Prejudiced** in this context suggests a mind already disposed specifically against one view of something at issue; it also pertains more to judging something than to reporting it: The fairness of the trial was *prejudiced* by undue publicity; people who become *prejudiced*, however subtly, by the constant stereotyping of minority groups. **Subjective** refers to an inability to put personal interests aside in order to view a situation without preconceptions; it is a relative word in that the most conscientious attempt at objectivity cannot wholly overcome one's innately *subjective* perspective: a *subjective* account of the war, overstressing the importance of those things the author happened to see first hand.

Slanted and **one-sided** pertain mostly to reports rather than to judgments. *Slanted* suggests the deliberate suppression of some facts and expansion of others either to flatter the *biased* minds of readers or to convince them that the *biased* attitudes of the writer or publisher are correct: a news story that was *slanted* to make the incumbent candidate appear certain of reelection. *One-sided* suggests a far more extreme position than *slanted* in that only facts supporting a particular attitude are presented: a *one-sided* history of the conflict that made it appear to be a struggle between angels and monsters.

Partial and **partisan** suggest different degrees of alignment with a cause. *Partial* may suggest either an unconscious or conscious favoring of a particular stand: countries that claimed to be neutral but were actually *partial* to the West; frankly admitting that he was *partial* to the union's set of arguments. *Partisan* suggests wholehearted and unashamed commitment to and advocacy of a cause: to give equal time to *partisan* statements on the value of the proposed legislation. A *partisan* view of a matter is not necessarily unfair, provided the person is an advocate of that view and is not set up to judge between that view and another. One may even be *partisan* without being *one-sided*, if one is attentive to and considerate of other viewpoints. See BIGOTRY.

Antonyms: DISINTERESTED, *open-minded, unbiased.*

bigotry

bias
intolerance
narrow-mindedness
prejudice

These words refer to an unfair, irrational, or unexamined attitude toward issues or people based on blanket preconceptions. **Bigotry** now refers almost exclusively to an intense dislike or even violent hatred for a particular group, race, or religion. The comparable use of **prejudice** would indicate a similar but far less intense predisposition against such a group. *Bigotry* almost surely would be evidenced in unashamed public utterance or behavior, whereas *prejudice* might remain largely unexpressed — or even unknown to the person so afflicted: easier to cope with the outright *bigotry* of the Ku Klux Klan than the invisible walls of *prejudice* in the north. *Prejudice*, also, can apply to any preconception: an abhorrence for the maltreatment of animals that would make him unable to hear the case without *prejudice*.

Intolerance is now less commonly used in these senses than the previous pair, possibly because it sounds odd to pose these concerns in terms of whether or not one can tolerate — or put up with — a group of people; the question now is more often seen in terms of a genuine equalizing acceptance or lack of it. The word is used widely outside the context of racial, religious, or ethnic *prejudice*, however, when it indicates an inability to give a fair hearing to ideas at variance with one's own: She looked with *intolerance* on the weird music preferred by her teen-age daughter. **Bias** is unique among these words, since it can point to a predisposition either for or against something: He admitted that he had a sentimental *bias* for anything pertaining to Ireland; a strong *bias* in ghettos against policemen. Where *prejudice* can indicate a fixed, inflexible attitude, *bias* might suggest only a tendency to take a given view. Yet even such a mild predisposition could be disastrous where strict impartiality is required, as in a judge or juror: The lawyer argued that the judge's *bias* had affected the conduct of the case.

Narrow-mindedness points to a rigidity of preconceived attitudes, but specifically sees them as stemming from inexperience or a lack of exposure to a broader scale of values: the typical *narrow-mindedness* of people who stay in one rut without ever getting out of it to see how other people live. The word often suggests habitual insularity, backwardness, provinciality, and lack of sophistication, but might be evidenced by an uneventful passivity or withdrawal rather than the hostile taking of stands suggested by the first pair: She was prevented from going to movies or dances by the *narrow-mindedness* of her parents. But the word can apply to any dogmatic rigidity of view: Permissive parents are often guilty of as much *narrow-mindedness* as those who are belabored for their authoritarian views on child-rearing. The word frequently points specifically to a prudish or puritan attitude toward sex or pleasure: He accused her of *narrow-mindedness* for refusing to have dinner with him in his apartment. Obviously, the word is extremely relative and can be used by someone to refer to any behavior, however tolerant, that he may not find sufficiently acquiescent. See BIASED.

Antonyms: impartiality, objectivity, open-mindedness, tolerance.

bisexual

androgynous
epicene
hermaphroditic
polymor-
    phous perverse

These words refer to the uniting of both sexes in one individual, either in a biological or psychological sense. **Bisexual** is the most general of these, having the widest range of possible meaning. In a biological sense, it can refer to any living organism in which both male and female organs are present. For many forms of life, this is normal: *bisexual* flowers; *bisexual* angleworms. Thus, as a generic term, the word can group together all normally double-sexed plants and animals. In its reference to people, however, the word would never refer to those rare individuals who are abnormally born with both male and female organs. On the contrary, it refers to those people who, physiologically normal, are psychologically responsive to both sexes: that transitional phase when adolescents are *bisexual* in their sympathies and loyalties. This responsiveness may extend to erotic attraction or to sexual activity. Many psychologists view every individual as being normally *bisexual* in make-up, although only those men and women who have both homosexual and heterosexual relations can be called actively *bisexual*. The word is not likely to be used to describe someone whose appearance combines both male and female characteristics.

Hermaphroditic and **androgynous** are more clear-cut in their reference to biological description. *Hermaphroditic* refers most specifically as a zoological term to animals in which the organs of both sexes appear normally in each individual, whereas *androgynous* applies as a botanical term to such double-sexed plants: viewing the volvox either as a colony of cells or as a *hermaphroditic* organism; effecting the hybridizing of corn by the sexual polarization of a normally *androgynous* species. Among such sexually polarized species as man, of course, a *hermaphroditic* individual may rarely occur as a biological abnormality, but the word would be strictly reserved for those cases in which both male and female sexual organs are anatomically present. Sometimes *hermaphroditic* is used less technically to refer to general appearance that partakes of both sexes. In this case, the word carries a tone of hyperbolic disapproval or amusement: The hair styles of young people grow more and more *hermaphroditic*. *Androgynous* has a more formal ring even in its strict biological use, and can sound abstruse or curious when it applies more generally; here, it is not so likely to be confused with reference to biological structure, however: cultures in which sexual role-playing is relatively *androgynous* outside such biological functions as child-bearing.

Epicene has no relevance to biological classification whatever, referring strictly to someone who in appearance or attitudes unites qualities of both sexes: a large, puffy face with soft features that were strikingly *epicene* in appearance. The word usually carries a disapproving or at least negative tone. Unlike *bisexual*, *epicene* may not refer to activity at all and may in fact suggest someone who appears sexless or is marked by no strong characteristics of either sex. In a culture that places a high value on manliness, *epicene* can often refer to effeminacy in men or even to neurasthenic male qualities: cultural stereotypes of the virile warrior and the *epicene* intellectual.

Polymorphous perverse is currently a fad phrase that oddly enough can carry an approving tone. It refers to sexual behavior that not only may be *bisexual* but guiltlessly pregenital in gaining satisfaction from other erogenous zones. The phrase, coined by Freud to describe the nonpolarized sexuality normal to the child, is now used loosely to describe a whole range of experimental adult sexual behavior: distinguishing between "normal" foreplay that is *polymorphous perverse* and a sole concentration on such acts. See FEMININE, MASCULINE.

These words refer to a caustic, sharp, or rancorous temper or manner. **Bitterness** can indicate, most generally, a gloomy, dour, or cold disposition, but its special connotations suggest a deep-seated rage directed inward more than an anger directed at others, with disillusion or a conviction of injustice as its possible source and a smoldering cynicism as its possible result: lifelong *bitterness* at losing the woman he loved. **Sourness** is less intense than *bitterness* but suggests somewhat the same dour manner with an inward-directed disillusion as its source: What was *sourness* in Hamlet's view of the world has deepened to *bitterness* in Timon's. On the other hand, *sourness*, unlike *bitterness*, might suggest an external appearance only: a cheerful disposition that belied the *sourness* of her wrinkled face. **Harshness** relates more to manner than to disposition, suggesting not so much rancor as cruelty, either deliberate or unintentional: a teacher who met every infraction of the rules with *harshness*. *Harshness*, however, might merely be employed as a tactic: trying to soften his will first with wheedling, then with *harshness*.

The remaining words have a greater degree of formality than the foregoing. **Acerbity** relates most closely to *sourness*, suggesting an acidity of attitude that might, however, be expressed by a more directly sharp manner than with *sourness*: the abrupt *acerbity* with which he countered our every attempt at a casual conversation. **Asperity** relates most closely to *harshness*, with special emphasis on roughness or severity of treatment, implying even an arbitrary unevenness of disposition: the bewildering *asperity* of a governess who first ignored his questions and then punished him for asking them. **Acrimony** relates most closely to *bitterness*, but with a more outwardly directed rancor implied, even to the point of biting, irritating, and enraged actions: trying to make peace in a charged atmosphere clouded by *acrimony*. See SOUR, VINDICTIVE.

Antonyms: blandness, mildness, sweetness.

bitterness

acerbity
acrimony
asperity
harshness
sourness

These words refer to anything that is thought extremely strange, eccentric, unusual, abnormal, ugly, or deformed. **Bizarre** points to the strange and unusual when they cause shock or surprise because of the unexpected, incongruous, or sensational forms they assume: skyscrapers that were as *bizarre* to him as his village of mud huts would have been to us; the flamboyant gothic style in which the stonework of the arches and windows took on *bizarre* convoluted designs. **Grotesque** suggests more readily the eccentric or deformed when seen as a comic or horrible caricature of some norm: Falstaff and the other *grotesque* cronies of the young prince; children with *grotesque*, cadaverous bodies, blighted by disease and malnutrition.

bizarre

fantastic
far-out
grotesque
outlandish
weird

Fantastic is more general and less concrete than the previous words. It can be used of anything that is fanciful or dreamlike or that appears as a departure from common-sense reality: the *fantastic* nightmare world of Hieronymous Bosch; a *fantastic* tower made of concrete, bottles, hubcaps, and cans. The word is overused as a hyperbole for anything pleasant, good, or out of the ordinary. **Weird** is similar to *fantastic* in suggesting a sharp break from ordinary reality: a *weird* feeling that time was standing still as the car hurtled down the cliff; *weird* forms of ocean life that live where sunlight never reaches them. This word, too, is overused as a hyperbole for anything mildly unusual. **Outlandish** once suggested behavior typical of people on the periphery of a cultural center; now it more commonly suggests anything that is unusual to the point of shock or outrage: the *outlandish* look of the four boy singers.

Far-out is currently a fad word for anything that represents a sharp departure from the norm. Most often, the word is used as an approving hyperbole for anything out of the ordinary: a marvelous, *far-out* party. The word is often used in descriptions of avant-garde art or the rebellious nonconformity of young people. See QUEER, UNUSUAL.

Antonyms: NORMAL, *unexceptional.*

bland

dull
gentle
mild
moderate
soothing

These words refer to taste, odors, and other sensations that are unassertive in character. **Bland** is the most specific of these, referring most appropriately to food that has not been heavily spiced: The doctor recommended a *bland*, salt-free diet for the patient. In other uses, the word may refer similarly to something of even disposition, without extremes, or lacking in tension: the *bland* domestic atmosphere in the house, free of argument or petty bickering; a *bland*, hazy spring day, neither too warm nor too cool. While these uses give a positive connotation, the word can become negative in tone when it suggests a lack of desirable excitement, flavor, or interest: the *bland*, anonymous cooking of the English; a *bland* novel that I began but couldn't finish; the *bland* attitudes of many college students during the McCarthy era.

Moderate is more neutral in tone than *bland*, being simply descriptive of a middle ground between extremes, without necessarily suggesting a positive or negative evaluation: a *moderate* winter and summer; a *moderate* conservative. Juxtaposed with a bad extreme, however, the word can give an approving tone: a reign that was thought *moderate* and tolerant after the blood-baths of the previous ruler. Both **gentle** and **mild** suggest an avoidance of extremes, but with a more forthrightly approving tone than *moderate* has. *Gentle* suggests a slight use of force to gain a result or a tender consideration for someone else: a *gentle* breeze off the patio; a *gentle* way of reprimanding her son. Unlike *gentle*, *mild* does not point to restrained power or considerate behavior so much as it indicates something thoroughly without harshness by its very nature: *mild* fall weather; *mild* suburban faces. Like *bland*, however, *mild* can suggest something so toned-down as to be uninteresting or unexciting: a comedy that offers only *mild* amusement; disclosures that were *mild* compared to those still forthcoming. The negative tone here is still far less intense or thoroughgoing than is true for *bland*.

Soothing is the most positive in tone of all these words. Something might be *gentle* or *mild* and still not necessarily beneficial. By contrast, *soothing* suggests sensations that are positively comforting, helpful, or healing, either by the removal of irritation or by the application of something to overcome it: listening to the *soothing* silence; *soothing* music; a cloudless, sunny day that was *soothing* to the spirits; a *soothing* ointment to relieve her sunburn. **Dull** compares strikingly with *soothing* in suggesting the complete absence of anything pleasurable. As such, it almost exclusively stresses, and with greater force, possibilities inherent in *bland* or *mild*: a *dull* evening playing cards with the neighbors; *dull* meals completely lacking in zest. *Dull* may of course apply more descriptively, like *moderate*, to low-key sensations: a *dull* gray sky; an artist who tended to use a palette of *dull*, subtly shaded colors. See MONOTONOUS, TRANQUIL.

Antonyms: *exciting, harsh*, KEEN, SOUR.

These words refer to people or things that look wasted or inhospitable. **Bleak** is the most general of these and can apply equally well to people or things, especially landscapes or houses. It suggests a bare or unpleasant prospect: the *bleak*, ice-incrusted mountains of the Andes; the *bleak*, unpainted house that seemed almost uninhabitable. Used of people, it suggests a facial expression that is unhappy or unfriendly: She gave her husband a *bleak*, unsatisfied look. It can, of course, suggest anything unhopeful or unpromising: their one *bleak* hope for survival.

Gaunt and **haggard** are more closely tied to the physical appearance of people. *Gaunt* stresses leanness but it may or may not suggest a wasted or shrunken appearance: the sailor's *gaunt*, weather-beaten face. *Haggard*, however, insists on emaciation or at very least suggests a drawn expression resulting from strain or shock: the *haggard* faces of the prisoners in the concentration camp; a face *haggard* with grief. *Gaunt* can also apply to things or landscapes, in which case it suggests a harsh or bare scene: the *gaunt* moors of the Brontë country. In this context, *bleak* is more intense than *gaunt*: grateful for even the *gaunt* prairies of the Midwest after the *bleak* deserts of Death Valley. *Haggard* would sound less natural in describing anything other than people, but used metaphorically, it might suggest a worn, run-down appearance: the rows of *haggard* houses that testified to poverty and neglect.

Desolate and **barren** refer to uninhabitable or unfeatured landscape. *Desolate* suggests an underpopulated starkness, *barren* a complete absence of life: only a few farmhouses strung out over the *desolate* countryside; *barren* rocks where the smallest shrub could find no foothold. *Desolate* can, however, also suggest solitariness or friendlessness: a *desolate* pine or two struggling for life above the timber line; a girl left *desolate* in the strange city. *Barren*, like *bleak*, can suggest an unpromising outlook: a plan *barren* of practical remedies. *Barren*, in the sense discussed here, could not be applied to people. See DISMAL, GLOOMY.

Antonyms: CHEERFUL, COMFORTABLE, HEALTHY, *luxurious*.

These words refer to a pleasant, warm, cheerful, or high-spirited disposition or manner. **Blithe** indicates an attitude that is cheerful, mirthful, joyous, or gay: *blithe* crowds enjoying the sunny weather in the park. The word can have a less favorable application to a manner that is casual, indifferent, or airy, particularly when directed toward something that should be taken seriously: listening to my grievance with a *blithe* lack of concern.

Genial points to a more low-key or long-term good-humored attitude that is exhibited in a kindly, pleasant, or warm manner; it suggests an unruffled or even temper and an ability to put people at ease: an extremely *genial* host. **Light-hearted** is closer in tone to *blithe*, since it suggests an absence of care or a positive state of buoyant delight: *light-hearted* youngsters singing as they hiked through the woods. A contrast

bleak

barren
desolate
gaunt
haggard

blithe

convivial
ebullient
elated
genial
jovial
light-hearted

with *genial* is apparent in that one may behave in a *genial* way regardless of how one feels, whereas the very essence of *light-hearted* is its suggestion of a spontaneous welling up of high spirits. *Genial*, furthermore, suggests friendly relationships with others; *light-hearted* may pertain to someone completely alone.

Convivial serves as an intensification of *genial*, suggesting jolly sociability and warm fellow-feeling; its Latin root pertains to a feast or banquet and this is often reflected in the English use of the word: *convivial* merrymakers at Mardi Gras. **Jovial** may suggest sociability, but it is less specific in indicating any sort of good-natured amiability. The word is very often used to describe a jolly but dignified fat man, so much so that the word is sometimes taken to specify this situation. Similarly, *blithe* sometimes suggests a spry, elfin, or fey person, particularly a woman. Although neither of these associations is invariable, it would seem odd to speak of a *jovial* wisp of a girl or a *blithe* Santa Claus.

Elated and **ebullient** both refer, like *light-hearted*, to a welling up of high spirits. *Elated*, however, can often refer to a response to some external occurrence or news, whereas *ebullient* suggests the same spontaneity as *light-hearted*. *Ebullient* stems from the root of a Latin word meaning to boil out, and the English word reflects this in pointing to a bubbling over with enthusiasm, excitement, or exuberance: fans that were *elated* when the team scored another touchdown; an *ebullient* personality that always seemed to overflow with vivacity and zest. See PLEASURE.

Antonyms: DISMAL, GLOOMY, *ill-humored, melancholic, morose,* SAD, *sullen,* TRANQUIL.

blockhead

boob
chump
dolt
dunce
fool
nincompoop
ninny

These words are all informal pejoratives for people who behave in stupid or foolish ways. **Blockhead**, **dolt**, and **dunce** suggest foolish behavior that results from a lack of intelligence. *Blockhead* suggests a dense, slow-witted person who predictably misunderstands information or is filled with exasperatingly obvious ideas or attitudes: a party at which he talked with one insufferable *blockhead* after another. *Dolt* specifically suggests a lack of flair, imagination, or perception that results from cloddish conventionality: *dolts* in the audience who liked her medley of show-tunes better than her group of Schubert songs. *Dunce* may suggest a momentary failure of intelligence rather than a permanent lack of it: He made a *dunce* of himself by forgetting the name of the guest of honor.

Fool and **chump** need not suggest a lack of intelligence at all. Both can suggest silly or ridiculous behavior that arises from any number of causes: letting the woman make a *fool* of him. *Chump*, besides being a much more informal substitute for *fool*, can indicate somebody who allows himself to become the butt of a joke or confidence game: looking for *chumps* who could be lured into buying worthless stock certificates. *Chump* can also be a severely contemptuous term for any sort of unsophisticated or ordinary person: *chumps* dumb enough to be taken in by sensational journalism.

The remaining group of words relates to this last suggestion of *chump* in indicating contempt for ordinary or simple people. When it is not an informal substitute for *fool*, **boob** suggests a person crippled by middle-class values: H. L. Mencken used the term booboisie to refer to class rule of, by, and for *boobs*. **Nincompoop** has particular relevance in describing a foolish man, suggesting a weakling afflicted by timidity and passivity: situation comedies that stereotype husbands as bumbling *nincompoops.* **Ninny** can apply to either sex, but may be particularly useful in reference to foolish women, suggesting silly, precious, or prissy behavior: a *ninny* who wrote saccharine poems about butterflies and daffodils. See MORON.

Antonyms: sage, savant, wise man.

These words refer to the spilling of blood or to an attitude that delights in bloodshed. **Bloody** suggests freshly spilled blood or conflict that results in heavy casualties: the *bloody* hands of the suspect; the *bloody*, four-day battle. It is also frequently used as an epithet for someone or something responsible for wanton slaughter: the *bloody* Stalinist purges; Hitler's *bloody* henchmen; *Bloody* Mary. In Britain, *bloody* can be used as a curse word for anything displeasing. This use was once taken as a blasphemous reference to Christ's blood, but overuse has weakened its force: He cursed the *bloody* tricycle he had tripped over in the dark. **Gory**, by contrast, suggests clotted or dried blood: newsmen photographing the *gory* icepick. It may also refer to any production that revels in giving extremely detailed accounts of gruesome accidents or murders: a *gory* detective story. This use also appears in the cliché, *the gory details*, which suggests the loving and minute description of anything unpleasant.

The remaining words apply primarily to an eagerness to let blood, either literally or figuratively. **Bloodthirsty** is most specific here, suggesting a delight in inflicting harm on others, especially in armed combat: *bloodthirsty* generals who urged the king to declare war; *bloodthirsty* nightriders intent on terrorizing Negro sharecroppers. The word can also be used figuratively to describe people who enjoy reading or seeing accounts of *bloody* happenings: *bloodthirsty* audiences who dote on *gory* television dramas.

Sanguinary is considerably more formal than these other words, giving a literary, almost euphemistic substitute for *bloody* or *bloodthirsty*: the *sanguinary* oppression of the conquered nation. It may also be used merely to refer to someone in a foul temper or ugly frame of mind: a *sanguinary* disposition. See GRUESOME.

Antonyms: bloodless, HUMANE, *merciful.*

These nouns denote various ways of hitting with the hand. **Blow** is the inclusive term. In a generic sense, it may be applied to any forceful impact of a hand, implement, or weapon against another object: a *blow* with the flat of the hand; a hammer *blow*; a *blow* with a blunt object. In specific comparison with the other words, a *blow* is a forceful hit with the fist: The fighter felled his opponent with a mighty *blow*. **Punch** is a more informal word than *blow*; and, unlike *blow*, it is limited in application. A *punch* is a quick, short *blow* or jab with the fist, typically aimed at a particular target: a *punch* in the eye. *Punch* is a boxing term: to throw a *punch*; to land a *punch*; to roll with a *punch*. A boxer dazed by repeated *blows* to the head is referred to as *punch*-drunk. Outside the ring, *punch* often suggests a belligerent attitude, the desire to pick a fight: I'm going to give you a *punch* in the nose.

A **slap** is a sharp *blow* delivered with the open hand or with something flat. A *slap* in the face stings or smarts and is often intended to be a rebuke; Her blind date started to get fresh and she gave him a *slap*. In earlier days, a *slap* on the cheek with a glove was a calculated insult whereby one man challenged another to a duel. But a *slap* in the face may be given to shock someone out of hysteria. And a *slap* on the back

bloody

bloodthirsty
gory
sanguinary

blow

box
cuff
knock
punch
rap
slap

is a hearty, friendly, man-to-man form of greeting or congratulations.

Cuff once could mean a *blow* with the fist, a usage that survives in the word *fisticuffs*; but now a *cuff* is usually a sidelong *blow* with the open hand or a cushioned *slap* with a paw: The mother cat gave her kitten a *cuff*. A **box** may be struck with the palm or fist, but where *cuff* stresses the type of *blow*, *box* emphasizes the part of the body that is hit — the ear, cheek, or side of the head. Both *box* and *cuff* are specifically applied to a *slap* on the ear, a punishment that was part of the schoolhouse discipline of an earlier era: to give an unruly boy a *cuff* (or a *box*) on the ear.

A **rap** is a sharp, quick *blow* and a **knock** is a harder, heavier one. Both may be made with the knuckles, and both make sounds that signal a person's presence: an insistent *knock* at the door; a light *rap* on the window pane. But a *rap* may also be administered with an implement as a mild form of punishment, and in this case the knuckles may receive the *blow* rather than striking it: The teacher gave him a *rap* on the knuckles with her ruler. *Knock* as a noun suggests the physical punishment of a fight only in a figurative sense: the school of hard *knocks*. *Blow*, *punch*, and *slap* are also used figuratively. A *slap* in the face is an insult, rebuke, or slur. An editorial with *punch* has vitality and force. A *blow* is a calamity that hits the emotions with a sudden, forceful impact: His tragic death was a *blow* from which she never fully recovered. See BEAT, FIGHT.

Antonyms: caress, touch.

blush

color
flush
redden

All of these words have uses to describe the change in a person's facial appearance when he is embarrassed or under a strain. **Blush** is specifically restricted to the rushing of blood into the face of someone who is shocked or embarrassed: She *blushed* easily at any talk of bodily functions. It is more commonly used to describe a woman; a man who *blushes* might be thought effeminate. **Color** is a less precise, almost euphemistic synonym for *blush*: the girl who *colored* under his glance. When applied to a man, it might suggest an attempt to avoid the effeminacy implied in *blush*. In any case, because *color* has so many other uses and can sound confusing in this context, it might best be avoided altogether.

Flush, like *color*, might be used in place of *blush* to avoid any note of effeminacy: his face *flushing* at the mere mention of her name. It is more commonly used, however, to refer to a feverish condition, either from illness, exertion, or exposure: their faces *flushed* from hours of drill and calisthenics. *Flush* can also indicate emotional seizures other than embarrassment: a face *flushed* with anger; a crowd *flushed* with excitement.

Redden, like *color*, can substitute for *blush*, but in being specific about the physical change involved, it sounds less euphemistic than *color*. It also, like *flush*, can result from other emotional seizures: a scowl *reddened* by rage. Both *redden* and *color* can, of course, describe skin changes outside the present context: a face *reddened* by long exposure to sun and wind; the skin slowly *coloring* from the sharp blow. See COLOR.

Antonyms: blanch, PALE, whiten.

boast

brag

These words refer to feelings of self-congratulation. **Boast** may suggest justifiable self-satisfaction: a college that *boasts* an unusually high number of distinguished alumni. More often, however, the word suggests a self-important and tasteless pointing out of one's own

boast
(continued)

crow
gloat
pride
strut
vaunt

successes: He monopolized the conversation by *boasting* of his own prowess at hunting and fishing; continually *boasting* and blowing his own horn. Occasionally the word can refer to self-congratulation for a victory not yet won: He *boasted* that he would finish off the challenger in the first round. **Pride** is close to the justified self-satisfaction possible for *boast*, but it more often specifically suggests private self-regard rather than a public expression of it; it is usually reflexive: He secretly *prided* himself on a life of absolute honesty. The word can suggest a stiff-necked self-righteousness, however, or a faulty estimate of one's own virtues: *Priding* himself on tolerance, he nevertheless signed a restrictive housing clause.

Brag intensifies the note of tastelessness in *boast*, suggesting limitless conceit and, possibly, inaccuracy of the claims being made: *bragging* about his imaginary exploits in the last war; *bragging* about his son's success at college as a way of patting himself on the back. **Crow** suggests noisy or vociferous *bragging* of an extremely offensive kind: publicly *crowing* about the landslide defeat of his opponent. **Gloat** is an intensification of *crow*, although it need not be verbal and sometimes suggests taunting someone that one has bested: rubbing his hands in secret and *gloating* over the way he had made the other applicants look foolish; *gloating* openly and lording it over those who had not won a weekend pass.

Strut suggests less animus than *gloat* but it is similar in not necessarily being verbal. It invariably suggests, however, an act done as a matter of public display: so puffed up and smug over his recent successes that he could not keep from *strutting* about and preening himself before his fewer and fewer friends. **Vaunt** is considerably more formal than the other words here; it compares to the understandable self-satisfaction suggested by *boast*, but it is a shade more self-righteous, possibly suggesting a claim that cannot be substantiated. It differs from *pride* in usually implying a public expression of self-esteem: *vaunting* far and wide the cultural opportunities lying in wait for visitors to their small town. See CONCEITED, CONFIDENCE, EGOISM.

Antonyms: BELITTLE, *minimize, underrate.*

boil

braise
fry
pan-broil
poach
sauté
simmer
steam
stew

These words all refer to methods of cooking by direct heat or flame, especially on top of a range. **Boil** implies rapid cooking in more or less large quantities of water heated to the point (212° at sea level) where bubbles escape at the surface: to *boil* potatoes; to *boil* an egg.

Simmer means to cook slowly in a hot liquid just below the boiling point, and usually for a long time.

To **steam** food is to cook it by direct exposure to steam or by using heat generated by steam, as in a double boiler. Direct *steaming* is usually accomplished by placing a metal rack above the level of the boiling water in a pot so that the food does not touch the water: to *steam* corn; to *steam* clams.

Poach implies a method of cooking a few foods, such as eggs without their shells, or pieces of chicken or fish, by dropping them into hot water, milk, or stock and *simmering* until done.

Stew is a close synonym of *simmer* in that both mean to cook slowly in liquid over low heat: to *stew* prunes. However, to most people, *stew* strongly suggests the familiar dish that is cooked in this way — meat or fish combined with vegetables in a gravy or sauce. *Stewing* always involves *simmering*, but one may *simmer* (not *stew*) soups, vegetables, sauces, etc.

When cooks speak of *stewing* meat, they usually mean to **braise** it. *Braise* implies the browning of meat (and often of accompanying vegetables) in a small amount of fat prior to adding a stock or other liquid and *simmering* in a covered pan.

Fry and **sauté** are closely related in that the food is cooked in hot fat. *Sautéing* is done very quickly with a minimum amount of fat and may or may not imply browning. Meat is usually *sautéed* before it is *braised*. *Frying* suggests cooking in greater amounts of fat than that used in *sautéing*, and may be done in a pan containing up to one or two inches of fat or in a pot designed for deep *frying*, in which large amounts of fat are used. Foods, especially potatoes, cooked in deep fat until crisp are often called "French-*fried*."

The cooking of chops, small steaks, fish, etc., on the top of the stove in a dry pan with little or no fat is preferably referred to as **pan-broiling** rather than *frying*. See GRILL.

bold

aggressive
forward
pushing

These words share the connotation of self-assertive, confident, and energetic dispositions, with or without a disregard for the rights of others. **Bold** shares with **aggressive** the implication of a vigorous attack on a problem or prosecution of one's aims, and in this sense carries no derogatory connotation. An *aggressive* or *bold* entrepreneur will seek success farther afield and will risk more in this search than will his more timid competitor. *Bold* does, however, have a wider range of application than *aggressive*. In some contexts *bold* suggests impudence or sauciness, although this use is certainly less common now than it once was: The *bold* fellow simply put out his hand and asked for more money. In other contexts it suggests commendable enterprise: a *bold* new venture in space science. *Aggressive* typically describes one who has a more lively sense of his own destiny than of other people's feelings.

Aggressive shares with **forward** and **pushing** a derogatory connotation of callousness in seeking one's ends. A *forward* or *pushing* social climber may resort to gossip, slander, and back-biting. *Pushing* may also be used in the less derogatory sense of *aggressive* to mean enterprising and energetic. See OPPORTUNISTIC, RECKLESS.

Antonyms: AFRAID, COWARDLY, MODEST, TIMID.

bombastic

orotund
purple
turgid

These words are used to describe styles of speaking or writing. **Bombastic** and **turgid** are alike in designating a lack of restraint and discipline that so inflates the language used in a piece of writing or in a speech that its style and content are thrown out of balance. *Bombastic* is derived from the noun *bombast* which originally denoted the kind of cotton, wool, or other soft material which is used for padding and stuffing. The suggestion of padding is very much present in any reference to a *bombastic* style which, though it does not always connote the complete absence of thought, certainly indicates an imbalance between the thought and the manner used to express it: For so trivial a topic, his speech was *bombastic* and cheaply theatrical. *Turgid* literally means swollen or distended, as by contained air or liquid: a healthy, *turgid* muscle; a leg *turgid* with infection. Like *bombastic*, *turgid* carries over a suggestion of its literal meaning into its figurative referral to style: a tiny idea which the author has blown up into this *turgid*, trying novel. **Orotund** is used positively to describe a full, clear, round, and resonant tone of voice. The figurative sense of the word, however, is pejorative in its synonymity with *bombastic*. *Orotund* can apply to pompous, inflated speech or writing, but, because of its particular reference to sound, it is most often used to describe the spoken word: a speech so *orotund* as to cause yawns and whispers all over the auditorium. **Purple**, in the sense being compared here, means ornate or flowery. It is pejorative in its suggestion of too much color and showiness: a good playwright who ruined some of his most dramatic moments with passages of bad poetry and *purple* prose. It also has come to refer to the erotic, the lurid, the vulgar, or the profane: a TV emcee whose interviews led to such *purple* exchanges that a sponsor demanded his dismissal. See FORMAL.

Antonyms: brief, precise, quiet, simple, TERSE.

These adjectives refer to extreme thinness in which the underlying bones are evident. **Bony** is the most general word and is relatively free of connotations. It simply indicates a prominent bone structure, whether this is deemed a sign of attractiveness, asceticism, chronic undernourishment, or near-starvation: a crooner's *bony*, boyish face; a waiflike actress with *bony* shoulders and big eyes; a *bony* Indian fakir; a *bony*, sway-backed nag. *Bony* is frequently applied to a single part of the body: long, *bony* fingers; *bony* knees. And it may sometimes emphasize attributes of bone that are not seen but felt, such as hardness or sharpness: She jabbed me with a *bony* elbow.

Gaunt implies a paucity of flesh and prominence of bone. It comes from the Old Norse word for a tall, thin person, and it indicates an angular leanness: the tall, *gaunt* figure of Don Quixote. Specifically, *gaunt* often calls to mind the haggard look of the hungry, anguished, ill, or old. It suggests the weariness of long suffering or constant strain, describing one who seems to have been worn down to the bone: the *gaunt*, ascetic figure of a saint; a *gaunt* old man, hollow-eyed, with prominent cheekbones and attenuated limbs.

Wasted implies a loss of flesh, stressing the cause of *bony* thinness. A *wasted* body is one that has been gradually consumed — reduced to skin and bone by the ravages of time, grief, hunger, or disease: *wasted* away by tuberculosis; a pallid face and *wasted* frame. Hence *wasted* implies physical weakness and frailty: the *wasted* form of a 100-year-old woman; a body *wasted* by disease.

Emaciated focuses on both the cause and the fact of abnormal leanness. It indicates a previous wasting away, implying the depletion of the body by grave illness, great suffering, or terrible deprivation. **Skeletal** is the most extreme of all these words, pointing to the deathlike dominance of bone. Both *skeletal* and *emaciated* may suggest the leanness of living men who look like skeletons, their ribs and sharp bones showing through the skin: *emaciated* (or *skeletal*) survivors of a Nazi concentration camp. But *skeletal* has about it the further suggestion of something lifeless or unreal, not fully human or alive: a painting of *skeletal* men and women in a barren future world; a novelist whose characters seem to be *skeletal* symbols, thoroughly analyzed but not fleshed out and never really brought to life. *Emaciated*, by contrast, is often expressive of human pity or horror at a *skeletal* appearance: the awful sight of *emaciated* children with distended bellies and glazed expressions. See LANKY, PALE, THIN, WEAKEN.

Antonyms: FAT, *nourished, well-fed.*

These words all refer to persons who are in authority over others. **Boss** is a colloquial word that originated in the United States and in its strictest sense applies to an employer, foreman, or manager of a group

bony

emaciated
gaunt
skeletal
wasted

boss

chief

boss
(continued)

commander
head
leader
maestro
master

of workmen. By extension it has also become a popular term for any executive, supervisor, or immediate superior: the *boss* of the payroll department; my *boss*, the pharmacist; the *boss* of a large clothing store. *Boss* may also apply to any person who is in control of things, whether by prerogative or by tyrannical behavior. [A horse must understand who is *boss*; Many parents discover that a spoiled child has become *boss* of the household.] In another sense, a *boss* is a professional politician who controls a party organization: William M. Tweed was the *boss* of New York City politics right after the Civil War.

Chief, the most comprehensive of these words, can be applied to anyone who occupies the position of highest authority over a group, large or small: the editor in *chief* of a newspaper; the *chief* architect of the housing project. However, *chief* is more commonly used of the supervisor of some department of established government: a *chief* of staff; the *chief* of police; a fire *chief*. *Chief* and *boss* are sometimes used interchangeably: I need my *chief's* (or *boss's*) signature on these contracts. In its original sense, a *chief* is the ruler of a primitive or nomadic tribe.

Head, like chief, is also a general term, but it is usually used of people who hold a more subordinate position than does a *chief*: the *head* of the telegraph office; the *head* of a boys' school; to be the *head* of one's class.

A **leader** is one who is voluntarily followed because of an ability to guide and control others or because he has been chosen by a group or party to be its *head*. One tends to think of a *leader's* having arrived at his position chiefly because of his talent for influencing others and for acting as a guiding force: the *leader* of the German Reich; a *leader* in the fashion world; the *leader* of a labor movement.

In its commonest sense a **master** is a person who has been given the authority to enforce obedience, but the word does not suggest the innate ability of the *leader* to guide and influence others. A *master* may be one who employs servants, is a male teacher at a boys' private school, or owns an animal, such as a dog, who can be trained to obey him. *Master* is also the formal title for the captain of a merchant ship. A teacher or *leader* in philosophy, religion, etc., who has followers or disciples is often called a *master*, as is Jesus by many Christians. *Master* is also applied to people of exceptional skill or artistic ability: a *master* plumber; the old *masters* of Renaissance painting; a *master* of the keyboard.

Commander is narrower in its meaning than are the other words of this group. Originally, it meant one who commands, as a *leader*, *chief*, etc.; now it applies almost exclusively to highly placed personnel in the armed forces. In the Navy, a *commander* is an officer ranking next below a captain. The officer in charge of a military post is also called a *commander*, or *commanding* officer. The person holding supreme command of all the armed forces of a nation (as the President of the United States) is called a *commander* in chief, as is any high-ranking officer in charge of a fleet or a major force.

Maestro (from the Italian for *master*) is used of a person who is highly proficient in an artistic field; but it is now most often used of an eminent conductor, composer, or performer in music. *Maestro* sometimes carries overtones of affectionate veneration, as in its application to the late Arturo Toscanini.

Antonyms: ASSISTANT, *dependent, follower, servant, subordinate, underling.*

bother

disturb

These words imply one of two situations: either one in which a person is actively annoying another, or to a situation in which a person is upset by something not necessarily the actions of someone else. Some of these

bother
(continued)

harass
pester
plague
trouble
worry

words can carry either the active or passive implication; others are mainly restricted to one sense or the other.

Bother, disturb, and **plague** are often used in both active and passive senses. On the passive scale, *bother* usually indicates a minor complaint that may come and go: frequently *bothered* by a slight stiffness in his joints. *Disturb* is more intense, suggesting specifically, at its most extreme, mental derangement: the mentally *disturbed* delinquent. In milder uses, *disturb* points to a state of upset more thoroughgoing than that of *bother*: I was *bothered* by the lack of news at first, but now, after a month, I am really *disturbed*. *Plague*, in its passive sense, is perhaps the most intense of all these words, but suggests a specific kind of upset, one that repeatedly hammers inside the mind without letup. The person who is *plagued* — by thoughts or by conditions around him — is by implication in control neither of the things that hound or harry him nor of their recurrence within his possibly unstable mind: *plagued* by constant recollections of his long-dead wife; *plagued* by the odor in the packing plant; *plagued* by a continual lack of money.

These same three words — *bother, disturb,* and *plague* — give a somewhat different scale of effects in their active senses. In this case, *disturb* is the weakest in intensity. One person, for example, may *disturb* another unintentionally by actions not directed specifically to the latter: Did my whistling *disturb* you? *Bother*, here, is stronger than *disturb*, since an implication is present that the action may be done intentionally to *disturb*: Just pay the bill and I'll stop *bothering* you. *Plague* is even stronger in the active voice than in the passive, suggesting repeated, deliberate annoyances that may have an almost demoniacal insistence: The bill collector *plagued* us with unrelenting phone calls, visits, and threats.

Trouble and **worry** are largely confined to the passive implication of being upset about something. [I am *troubled* by the doctor's report; I'm *worried* that I'll fail the exam.] Both words are more forceful than the passive use of *bother* but less so than the same use of *disturb*. *Trouble* is slightly more formal than *worry* and suggests a definite cause for alarm; *worry* suggests less clear-cut reasons for uneasiness, specifically implying suspense over the outcome of something. *Trouble* is also more inclusive; one may be *troubled* without indulging in the helpless wasted motions of thought implied by *worry*.

In contrast, **pester** and **harass** are almost exclusively restricted to the active sense of someone annoying another person. [The platoon sergeant constantly *harassed* his men in ingeniously excruciating ways; Stop *pestering* me!] Both words are more forceful than the active use of *disturb* and even of *bother*. *Pester* is like the active use of *plague* in suggesting repeated and deliberate annoyances that interrupt someone else, but remains restricted mainly to trivial matters. *Harass* is considerably stronger, even carrying the possibility of physical punishment or worse: guerrillas nightly *harassing* the border villages. *Harass* may even be stronger than *plague* in this case, since the latter stops short of any implication of physical violence. See ANGER, ENRAGE, UPSET.

Antonyms: comfort, console, placate, solace.

All of these words describe ways in which the direction of a moving object can be radically changed. **Bounce,** the most general term, can be applied to virtually any missile that rebounds, such as a ball, stone, penny, apple, etc. [He didn't see me toss him the book; it *bounced* off his chest and fell to the floor.] But *bounce* commonly emphasizes re-

bounce
(continued)

deflect
ricochet

siliency. [The basketball *bounced* high in the air; My little girl loves to *bounce* up and down on her bed.]

Carom is a curious word, because the noun refers to a highly skillful and carefully controlled billiards shot, whereas the verb often implies lack of control and recklessness. In billiards, a *carom* is a shot in which the cue ball strikes against two other balls in succession. As a verb, *carom* means to hit and rebound, often in a context that implies that the rebound is uncontrolled and damaging. [The car *caromed* off the telephone pole and hurtled into a parked mail truck.]

Deflect means to turn aside or cause something to swerve from its course. **Ricochet** means to glance from a surface in the fashion of a stone thrown over the surface of water, making a series of skips or bounds. Thus *ricochet* in practice means to *bounce* away fast, with little loss of speed, whereas *deflect* stresses the change in direction of a moving object. Compare these two examples. [The bullet *ricocheted* off the sidewalk and shattered the window glass; The arrow, *deflected* by strong winds, missed its target completely.] In some contexts *ricochet* and *carom* are interchangeable, but *carom* emphasizes collision and the force of the rebound whereas *ricochet* emphasizes the speed of the deflection. *Bounce* can substitute in most contexts for *carom* and *ricochet*, but not for *deflect; deflect* differs essentially from the other words in not involving the actions of bounding away or collision. It means what the others only imply: a change in the direction of movement of an object.

boundary

border
bounds
confines
frontier
limit

These words denote a line that marks the outermost part of an area, or a division between areas. **Boundary** is used chiefly of territory, and suggests a definite demarcation, such as a line or mark that can be precisely located on a map. **Bounds** are less definite, and may be used figuratively of behavior: His impudence exceeds all *bounds*. The colloquial expression *out of bounds*, derived from its use in various sports, is commonly used with the meaning of unfair, improper, or indecent: Holding hands was *out of bounds*, and as for kissing — that was unthinkable.

Whereas *boundary* points to an outermost limit, **border** emphasizes the division between two areas: the *border* between the U.S.S.R. and Finland. [He crossed the *border* into Belgium; By international agreement the *boundary* of each nation fronting a body of water extends exactly three miles from the coastline.] *Border* often suggests a territorial feature, such as a river or mountain range, and hence is not as precise as *boundary*. *Boundaries* may be changed by treaties, i.e. on paper; *borders* may change by the changing course of a river or by military action.

Limit is the most general term of this group, and can be applied to any outermost extent, range, demarcation, etc. As here considered, the term is usually plural: to pass beyond the city *limits*. In military usage *off limits* serves to notify military personnel not to enter the building or area so stigmatized. **Frontier** may refer to the part of a nation's territory lying along the *border* of another country; it thus describes the *border* region of a country from an interior perspective. *Frontier* also means the part of a settled region lying along the *border* of an unsettled region; this sense is surely familiar to all Americans. *Frontier* is often used in extended senses: beyond the *frontier* of knowledge; at the *frontier* of space exploration.

Confines, like *bounds*, define the extent of an area without reference to what lies beyond, but *confines* is less consistently restricted to the description of geographical *limits:* He was not permitted to pass beyond the *confines* of his room. *Confines*, like *bounds*, is commonly used figuratively: His genius soared beyond the narrow *confines* of his education; beyond all *bounds* of decency or common sense. See CIRCUMSCRIBE, EDGE, PERIMETER.

These words can all be used to describe commercial names, commodities, and services, and are in this sense related; but they are not synonyms, and there are important distinctions of fact to be made between them. **Brand** is generally understood to mean a definite, usually well-known and advertised type of commodity: the Lipton *brand* of tea; a popular *brand* of cigarettes. By extension, *brand name* identifies a whole group of products made or sold by the same enterprise: Westinghouse is the *brand name* of a line of electrical appliances.

Trademark (sometimes hyphenated as *trade-mark*) comes closest to having a definite legal status, especially when formally registered with the appropriate government agency. By federal law a *trademark* is "any word, symbol, or device or any combination thereof adopted and used by a manufacturer or merchant to identify his goods and distinguish them from those manufactured and sold by others." Of the thousands in active use most take the form of words, as *Kodak, Vaseline, Technicolor, Coca-Cola, Dacron*, etc. It will be noted that such words are spelled with an initial capital letter, a practice strongly recommended by their owners as a means of emphasizing exclusive rights to the good will and equity inherent in their commercial use.

Service mark extends this form of identification to enterprises engaged in providing a specified line of services under some slogan, monogram, title, etc.: Blue Cross is the *service mark* of the Associated Hospital Service of New York. **Trade name**, though used as a variant of *trademark*, is legally synonymous with the commercial name under which a firm, enterprise, corporation, association, etc., conducts its business. [*Dupont* is both the *trade name* and *service mark* of a manufacturer of chemical products, many of which carry *trademarks*.]

A **logotype** is any single piece of type containing several letters, a word, or words. In advertising, *logotype* applies specifically to a particular design or style used to represent the name of a company or a *trademark* so as to make it more readily identifiable and emphasize its protected status in the public mind. Thus there are *logotypes* — or **logos**, as they are called for short — for many well-known *trademarks*.

A **colophon** was formerly an inscription placed at the end of a book, showing the title, the printer's name, date, and other information, such as the style and size of type used. Now the word is more commonly used to refer to a design or emblem adopted by a publisher to represent a particular line of books or the publishing house as a whole; the *colophon* is usually printed on the title page of books.

brand

colophon
logo
logotype
service mark
trademark
trade name

These words are synonyms when they mean to move something rapidly back and forth or in circles. **Brandish** means to wave or shake a weapon, especially in public, so as to threaten or intimidate someone: The drunk at the bar suddenly *brandished* a gun, and everybody scrambled for cover. **Flourish** implies a display of self-confidence, triumph, or merely high spirits: The victorious army *flourished* a captured flag. **Swing**, in this sense, means to move rhythmically to and fro or backward and forward, like the pendulum of a clock or the clapper of a

brandish

flourish
swing
wield

bell. It may imply a wide, sweeping motion, even rotation: to *swing* an ax; Huckleberry Finn recommended *swinging* a dead cat over one's head to cure warts. **Wield** emphasizes the command one has over the use of a weapon or instrument: to *wield* a hammer and chisel; to *wield* forceps with consummate skill. Sometimes *wield* approaches *brandish* in meaning: He turned toward me and suddenly *wielded* a short, ugly knife.

Antonyms: arrest, hang, suspend.

brashness

brass
cheek
chutzpah
gall
nerve
sauciness

These words describe shameless, bold, or arrogantly brusque behavior. **Brashness** indicates a decisive, insistently aggressive, or come-what-may attitude. When the word is approving, it expresses wonder or admiration for someone's audacity and zest; more commonly, it is used to criticize a rash lack of judgment or a lack of consideration for others: the *brashness* of such a small country in successfully defending itself against its enemies; a foolhardy *brashness* that often tempted him to tackle situations he knew nothing about; the *brashness* with which he pushed his way to the top of the heap, injuring the feelings of everyone else in the office. The word can also point to a garish vulgarity of taste: The *brashness* of his sports clothes almost made my eyeballs ache. **Sauciness** suggests, instead, an imperious, insouciant, and haughty manner, often exhibited in an inferior or in someone replying sharply or out of turn: the *sauciness* of that impertinent little salesgirl; the indignant *sauciness* with which he refused to take his nap. Often, the word can be used humorously or affectionately to describe the spirited display of someone who is weak or powerless: the roguish *sauciness* of a small kitten; the boy's *sauciness* in grandly declining to play house with his older sister. **Chutzpah** is a U.S. slang word, derived from Yiddish, for brazen insolence or self-seeking: her *chutzpah* in demanding the best table in the restaurant. Like *brashness*, this word can be approving for someone's audacity or disapproving for someone's effrontery: Give me someone who knows what he wants and has the *chutzpah* to go after it without shilly-shallying; a woman who had the *chutzpah* to charge into the doctor's office ahead of everyone else in the waiting room.

The remaining words are all extremely informal words for the same idea expressed by *chutzpah*. Of these, however, only **nerve** can function with either positive or negative force. When approving, the word points to cool self-possession and courage in acting against odds: It took *nerve* for him to stand up for his rights in an atmosphere thick with recrimination and threats of reprisal. In disapproval, *nerve* suggests a shameless disregard for good taste or manners: Imagine the *nerve* of him asking her to stay with him for the night! **Brass** and **cheek** both indicate an insistent and insolent self-assurance. *Brass* is the more disapproving of the two, suggesting a coarse or ingrained lack of sensitivity to the feelings of others: Not even the prosecutor had the *brass* to ignore the tears of the woman on the witness stand. *Cheek* is milder in suggesting a smug or simpering self-regard that prompts uncritical, brazen, or tasteless behavior: the *cheek* to ask for a raise after a week on his new job. Like *sauciness*, the word can be used humorously or affectionately for a cute forwardness in one's inferiors: the *cheek* of the boy in asking for another helping of dessert. **Gall** is the most severely disapproving of all these words, suggesting shameless acts of unwarranted discourtesy: the *gall* to invite himself to tea. But the word is very general, applying to any act one dislikes. See CONCEITED, EFFRONTERY, OVERBEARING.

Antonyms: civility, meekness, politeness, self-effacement.

These words indicate a readiness to face danger, difficulty, or even death when called upon by circumstance to do so. **Brave** is the most general word. It indicates the showing of one's mettle under stress, implying self-possession and resolution. **Courageous**, like *brave*, may focus on response to a situation, but it often implies firmness arising from strong moral convictions. Both words imply a willingness to proceed with the necessary in spite of external deterrents or internal misgivings. A *brave* or *courageous* soldier carries out a dangerous mission, not without fear, but without letting fear prevent him from doing his duty.

Dauntless and **undaunted** indicate bravery under exceptionally trying circumstances. Both imply a refusal to be disheartened, intimidated, or otherwise discouraged from going on. [Scientists pursue their experiments with *dauntless* determination, despite repeated failures and disappointments; Stalemated negotiators must resume their talks each day with *undaunted* optimism.] **Fearless** and **intrepid** imply a resolute freedom from fear or a cool, unshakable determination. [A *fearless*, crusading newspaper exposes corruption in high places without being deterred by the danger of reprisal; The *intrepid* pioneers traveled west in spite of hardships and the constant danger of Indian attack.]

Valiant and **valorous** are applied to persons and actions that exhibit the kind of courage and fortitude associated with knighthood. *Valiant* may suggest bravery shown in a worthy cause, against impossible odds, or with commendable consequences. *Valorous* is usually applied to the spirit or deeds of the *valiant*. A *valiant* fireman may save persons trapped in a burning building by a *valorous* disregard of his own safety. A dying man may put up a *valiant*, but hopeless, fight for life.

Heroic and **gallant** imply outstanding bravery coupled with nobility of motive or selfless dedication. *Heroic* stresses exceptional courage, fortitude, or enterprise, especially in time of war or danger. It implies a willingness to risk or sacrifice one's own life to save another or others. *Gallant* implies inner nobility that is manifested in chivalrous action. [The defense of the Alamo was a *heroic* action of *gallant* men.]

Plucky is a somewhat informal word, usually applied to contenders who persist against unfavorable odds. A *plucky* prize fighter does his best to hold his own against a heavier, more skillful opponent. **Bold** indicates an actively *brave* nature or a confident audacity. The *bold* man is daring and is undeterred by fear of consequences: Washington's *bold* crossing of the Delaware caught the enemy by surprise and resulted in the fall of Trenton. See BOLD, DARING, RECKLESS.

Antonyms: AFRAID, COWARDLY, *daunted*, *intimidated*, TIMID.

brave

bold
courageous
dauntless
fearless
gallant
heroic
intrepid
plucky
undaunted
valiant
valorous

These words refer to intervals during which some activity stops or slackens. **Break** stresses the idea of interruption. It indicates a temporary time-out, as from work, for rest, refreshment, recreation, or other purpose: a coffee *break*. **Pause** is less abrupt and drastic, indicating a brief rest or a momentary suspension of action: the *pause* that refreshes. A scheduled interruption of a radio or TV program that is called a station *break* at the studio is referred to in milder terms on the air as a *pause* for station identification. *Pause* is also used to stress the temporary nature of a cease-fire: a *pause* in the bombing; Government sources said there would be no prolonged *pause* in the war. **Respite** is a much more formal synonym for *break*. A *respite* is an interval of relief, as from some source of strain: ceaseless toil that knows no *respite;* The holiday truce was a welcome *respite* for the front-line troops. One takes

break

interlude
intermission
letup
lull
pause
recess
respite

a *break* but is granted a *respite:* The workmen took a *break* so we enjoyed a brief *respite* from the noise.

A **recess** is an interval between the sessions of a school, court, legislature, or the like. It implies a formal adjournment for a limited time, with a temporary suspension of business: the university's spring *recess;* a legislative *recess* before elections. A *recess* may be as brief as a *break* or as long as a vacation, but it presupposes some sort of official authorization. [The cast decided to take a *break;* The judge declared a two-hour *recess.*] In grammar school, a *recess* is a free period between classroom sessions during which the children may play, relax, or get something to eat: boys shooting marbles at *recess.*

An **interlude** is a period or episode that occurs in the course of a longer process and breaks its continuity: noise with *interludes* of quiet. By nature, an *interlude* contrasts with the activity it interrupts or the events it comes between — often occurring as an interval of calm, a time of content, or a touch of comic relief: *interludes* of lucidity in his delirium; a humorous *interlude* in a sober history; Their honeymoon was an idyllic *interlude.* An **intermission** is a scheduled *recess* between the acts of a play or the parts of a performance: to go out for a smoke during *intermission. Interlude,* on the other hand, may apply to an entertainment of a different kind that fills a *break* between the acts, as a brief, farcical comedy or a short, transitional passage of music: an orchestral *interlude.* In another sense, *intermission* may apply to any temporary cessation: The noise went on without *intermission.*

Letup is an informal word and is usually used negatively after *no* or *without.* It often indicates abatement rather than cessation, pointing to a lessening of force, a slackening of pace, or a reduction in number or intensity. [The rain poured down without *letup;* We've worked two hours without *letup;* There has been no *letup* in the stream of complaints.] **Lull** designates an interval of stillness or calm that contrasts with prior and subsequent noise or confusion: a *lull* in a storm. *Lull* may also refer to a falling off of activity, implying a loss of momentum and suggesting the sluggishness of a slack period: a *lull* in business; a *lull* in the conversation.

break

burst
crack
crush
fracture
shatter
shiver
smash

These words refer to the forcible destruction, breaching, or injury of something. **Break** is the most general word. It most often suggests the separation of a rigid body into pieces, implying either partial or total destruction of a whole: *breaking* the firewood in two for easier burning; *breaking* a vase by accident. *Break* may also indicate a temporary injury, as to a bone: *breaking* a leg in a fall. And it may involve getting free from some restraint or enclosure: to *break* out of jail; buds *breaking* open. **Burst** is close to *break* in this latter sense but involves much greater violence. It is a highly specific word, suggesting a forceful *breaking* open that is due to internal pressure: squeezing a pimple until it *bursts* open; a dam so weakened by floods that it finally *burst;* blowing up a balloon until it *bursts.*

Crack usually means to *break* without separation of parts. It suggests the *breaking* out across a surface of slitlike openings or hairline ruptures, either because of wear, age, or pressure: a window that he *cracked* by leaning against it; a *cracked* cup; linoleum that had faded and *cracked.* In other uses, however, *crack* may mean to *break* apart or *break* into pieces: *cracking* open the walnut without *breaking* the meat. **Fracture** can suggest a deeper, more thorough, but also more localized *breaking* than *crack: fracturing* the bone in two places; boulders *frac-*

tured by continual freezing and thawing; old habit patterns *fractured* by changing technology.

Shatter and **shiver** most often suggest a total *breaking* up of a thin surface. *Shatter* is the more general of the two, implying the *breaking* of such a surface into sharp pieces or jagged fragments: heavy enough to *shatter* the melting ice; a well-aimed stone that *shattered* the already *cracked* window. The word can, however, refer to the *breaking* of any brittle object, in which case, it suggests reduction to many fairly small pieces: a marble statue that had been completely *shattered* in the earthquake. *Shiver*, by contrast, is more closely restricted to glass or glass-like surfaces, suggesting a reduction into long, narrow shards or slivers: *shivering* the mirror. The word might now seem outdated except as a noun.

Crush and **smash** suggest forceful action taken to destroy or *break* something. *Crush* points to the effect of great external pressure; it suggests squeezing something out of shape: *crushing* the empty cigarette pack in one hand; eggs that had been *crushed* by canned goods placed on top of them in the carton. *Smash* describes the kind of complete deformation resulting from a heavy, noisy blow. This word suggests the *shattering* of something brittle either by throwing it or by throwing something against it: *smashing* the window with his bare fist; He *smashed* the bottle to smithereens against the rocks. See CRACK, DESTROY, EXPLODE.

Antonyms: CONNECT, REPAIR, *weld*.

bright

beaming
brilliant
effulgent
glowing
incandescent
radiant
resplendent
shining

All these words refer most specifically to the intense, steady light emitted from a source, rather than to wavering or reflected light. **Bright** is the most general of these, stressing chiefly the intensity of the light: the *bright* stars. It is more useful than the other words as a comparative: the *brighter* of the two neon signs. In its very generality, *bright* permits reference to wavering or reflected light, but only to emphasize intensity: a *bright*, cheerful fire; sun-*bright* ripples. **Brilliant** lends itself to the same uses as *bright*, but suggests even greater intensity: *brilliant* headlights. *Brilliant* can have a lyrical quality absent in the more matter-of-fact *bright*, and consequently it can imply excellence or beauty: the *brilliant*, cloudless day.

Incandescent suggests light created specifically by combustion, and it may or may not carry overtones of emitted warmth as well as light. *Incandescent* may simply refer technically to a white-hot light: an *incandescent* lamp. In other uses it suggests fierceness or intense whiteness rather than the excellence or beauty of *brilliant*: the *incandescent* glare of the streetlights.

Resplendent is in every way an intensification of *brilliant;* though more formal, it is even more lyrical, stressing vivid brightness and dazzling splendor: the *resplendent* sun; a sky *resplendent* with stars. *Resplendent* can refer to sources of reflected light as well, but with the same lyrical force and implication of luster: bedecked with diamonds and *resplendent* in her jeweled gown. **Effulgent** is like *resplendent* in lyricism and formality except that it is more precisely restricted to sources of light. Also, its extreme formality may make its use seem inflated or pretentious: *effulgent* rays streaming through the thunderhead.

While far less formal than *resplendent* or *effulgent*, **shining** as an adjective has been so overworked when used with lyrical intent that it may now strike one as a cliché in most contexts: a knight in *shining* armor.

Shining may escape this liability when it is merely descriptive: the *shining* beacon far out at sea. Used in such a way, it contrasts with all the foregoing words by describing light that need not necessarily be intense. **Glowing** and **radiant**, similarly, do not emphasize intensity. *Glowing* suggests a slow burning or the last stages of burning; it implies warmth as well, but faintness of both light and warmth may be the point of its use: the *glowing* remains of a fire. *Radiant* suggests the emission of light in all directions; it carries a unique connotation of mild, gentle warmth: a *radiant* June day, so unlike those of *incandescent* July. **Beaming** refers specifically to light sent out in long arms, either stationary or sweeping: the *beaming* searchlight.

All of these words can refer figuratively to qualities of personality, intelligence, or passion. Indeed, their metaphorical use has been extensive in describing all that is good or desirable in human nature — perhaps a comment on the high value man has continued to place on light. In brief, *bright* refers to intelligence, but more as potential than as accomplishment: a *bright* student. *Brilliant* goes beyond *bright* to indicate great intellect or talent. It may also refer to a highly admired accomplishment or illustrious achievement: a *brilliant* novel. *Resplendent* may suggest the blaze and brilliance of triumph or majesty: soldiers *resplendent* in victory. *Effulgent* may describe something that seems to radiate outward like light: her *effulgent* loveliness. *Glowing* suggests a being possessed by warm or passionate emotions; *radiant* suggests their satisfaction — or a being possessed by calmer, gentler feelings: eyes *glowing* with desire; a face *radiant* with tenderness. *Beaming* suggests pleasure or self-satisfaction, while *shining* in most of its figurative uses is decidedly trite. See LUMINOUS, SPARKLING.

Antonyms: dim, dull, GLOOMY, OBSCURE, *opaque.*

brusque

abrupt
bluff
blunt
curt
gruff
surly

All of these words point to a shortness or discourtesy of manner in a person's treatment of others. **Brusque** derives from an Italian word meaning rude. It is applied to a noticeably short, brisk, or terse manner that may or may not be rude, depending on intent and circumstance. [A no-nonsense woman, the governess gave her employer a *brusque* handshake; Being in a hurry, he made an unintentionally *brusque* reply.] At worst, *brusque* may imply incivility, ungracious sharpness, or undue severity: a *brusque* dismissal. **Bluff**, by contrast, is not at all negative in tone but implies a hearty frankness — an openness that may lack finesse but does not intend discourtesy. *Bluff* is used almost exclusively to describe men. The *bluff* man talks and laughs loudly and freely, says and does whatever he pleases with fearless good nature, and with no thought of annoying or giving pain to others: A *bluff*, beefy man, he didn't mince his words, but there was a twinkle in his eye. **Blunt** is fairly close to *bluff* at one extreme, though it can imply only a well-meaning directness. Unlike *bluff*, however, *blunt* more often suggests a flat-footed forthrightness that verges on discourtesy. It may describe a manner of speech as well as a person. [Shall I lie politely to you, or shall I be *blunt*? Be as *blunt* as you like — I won't mind your rudeness if you tell me the truth.] At the other extreme, *blunt* may indicate a tactless frankness that is inconsiderate or needlessly cruel. The *blunt* man may say things which he is perfectly aware are disagreeable, either from a defiant indifference to others' feelings or from the pleasure of tormenting.

Abrupt and **curt** both suggest an uncooperative terseness, especially in reply to a question or appeal for help: His laconic answers to my repeated requests for directions were both unfriendly and *abrupt*.

Abrupt may also imply a disconcerting directness: an *abrupt* refusal. *Curt* is stronger than *abrupt*, implying hardness or coldness of manner as well as a willful intent to be unpleasant: a *curt* rejoinder. [I can understand being a little *abrupt* if one is really busy, but she's always *curt* even when she's just wasting her time.]

Gruff and **surly** suggest bad-tempered or rude behavior; but they need not imply either straightforwardness, as in *bluff* and *blunt*, nor undue brevity of response, as in *abrupt* and *curt*. Of the two words, *gruff* is more appropriately applied to a man and is most applicable to disposition. It describes one who is *brusque*, rough, and crusty in manner or hoarse and guttural in speech. [He'll grumble for minutes at a time when he's *gruff* and grouchy, but don't expect a straight answer from him then.] *Surly* suggests extreme discourtesy and may be applied to either sex. It implies not so much a sour frame of mind as an abiding attitude of hostility to people — a crabbed, churlish disposition evident in both speech and manner: a *surly*, insubordinate servant. [Give me the *gruffest* clerk in the world and I won't complain — just so long as I don't have to put up with that *surly* woman in the lingerie department. I'll even take the *blunt* remarks about my figure from the woman in the dress department or the *curt* answers of the credit manager when I ask to pay by check. Believe me, a *surly* salesclerk is far worse.] See CANDID, TERSE.

Antonyms: diplomatic, gracious, mannerly, POLITE, *tactful, unctuous,* URBANE.

bug

arachnid
arthropod
beetle
crustacean
insect
spider

These words relate to a large and varied division of invertebrate animals. **Bug** is a name loosely applied to any very small creeping, crawling, jumping, or flying creature that is generally thought of as a nuisance. Sometimes, in informal usage, *bug* is even applied to the completely unrelated bacteria and viruses that cause disease. *Bug* is the least specific word in the group, but **arthropod** is the inclusive, zoological term. *Arthropods* have no backbone; they are characterized by jointed legs or appendages, segmented body parts, and usually, hard outer coverings. The true *bugs* belong to a special order of *arthropods* whose members have biting or sucking mouth parts, such as bedbugs, water bugs, and plant bugs. **Beetles** also have biting mouth parts and have hard, horny forewings that cover and protect their hind wings. *Bugs* and *beetles* form part of the largest class of *arthropods*, the **insects**. There are close to a million kinds of *insects*, all having bodies divided into three sections, each of which carries a pair of legs, making six legs in all. This characteristic distinguishes *insects* from **spiders**, which have eight legs and which, with scorpions, mites, and ticks, are placed in another, separate class of *arthropods*, the **arachnids**. The class of **crustaceans** includes shrimps, crabs, lobsters, barnacles, and crayfish, living mostly in or near water. *Crustaceans* are characterized by tough outer shells that are shed by molting as they grow larger. See VIRUS.

build

construct
erect
fabricate

These verbs all indicate the assembling and fitting together of materials into a structure. **Build**, the most general and least formal word, has the widest range of uses, from the most concrete and specific to the highly figurative and abstract. [Carpenters *build* houses and birds *build* nests; Cavemen *built* fires at the mouths of their caves; The Wall Street broker hoped to *build* a business empire; Nations *built* their hopes for peace on the fear of nuclear war.] **Construct** has a much more limited range of application. It emphasizes the intricate or complex nature of a *building* process, where *build* may focus on the assembling of separate parts and the resulting connection: to *build* a bookcase; to *construct* an office building. The phrase *to build a bridge* stresses the act of creation and the link created. The phrase *to construct a bridge* emphasizes engineering problems and the workmen and equipment involved. The same distinctions hold with reference to mental activities — *build* pointing to gradual, step-by-step creation through continued efforts. [Philosophers *construct* complicated systems for describing existence; Neurotics may be unable to *build* healthy relationships.] If substituted for *build* in the last example, *construct* would have an unfortunate overtone of artificiality.

Like *build*, **erect** may involve the assembling of parts. A child *builds* with blocks but may also play with an *erector* set. *Erect*, however, chiefly stresses height and vertical position, meaning to put or set something up: to *erect* a skyscraper; to *erect* a monument; They finally *built* a road up the Acrocorinth to the tower that had been *erected* centuries before. *Erect* also has figurative uses: to *erect* a tariff wall; to *erect* a trade barrier.

Fabricate has least the sense of building a structure on its intended location. In suggesting the assembly and fitting together of parts, it implies more the standardized manufacturing of smaller items in a factory: to *fabricate* parts for do-it-yourself furniture-making kits. Recent techniques of house-building have, of course, perfected the prefabrication of all units, which are then shipped and assembled on the spot. Unless this type of building or construction is meant, however, one would still not use *fabricate* of house or bridge building. In other uses, the word has taken on a strong negative overtone of artificiality or falsity: a friend who *fabricates* flimsy stories to conceal his irresponsibility. See CREATE, MAKE.

Antonyms: DESTROY, *devastate*.

bum

beachcomber
beggar
gold-brick
loafer
panhandler
scavenger
tramp

These words refer to a chronically lazy or unemployed person. **Bum** and **tramp** both refer to unemployed men who live outside respectable society and survive by means of handouts or short-term manual labor. Both typically suggest ill-kempt, poorly dressed, and prematurely old men. *Tramp* would be the term used by a person of rural background to describe someone who roams the countryside and lives by his wits and, occasionally, day-labor. *Bum* would be used by a city person to describe an unemployed, often homeless man who drifts about the city. *Bum* might be substituted for *tramp*, but not as often vice-versa. By extension, *bum* can be applied disapprovingly to any man who is thought to be worthless: her no-good *bum* of a husband. *Tramp* can be applied disapprovingly to a sexually promiscuous woman: accusing her of being nothing but a cheap *tramp*. It should be noted that *bum* is not used in this sense in Britain, since there the word is a slang expression referring to the buttocks.

Beggar and **panhandler** indicate people who survive by seeking money, food, or other goods from strangers or passers-by. *Panhandler* is the more informal term, specifically suggesting a *bum* who stops people on the street and asks for money, often telling a hard-luck story: the *panhandler's* pitch about having just lost his wallet. *Beggar*, besides being more formal, is much more general. It can apply to any *bum* or *tramp* who asks for handouts; on the other hand, it can refer to someone who is licensed to ask money for some token object he has to offer in exchange: the *beggar* selling pencils on the streetcorner. In other cultures, the word can even apply to venerated holy men: Buddhist monks who live as itinerant *beggars*. At its most general, the word can refer to anyone impoverished: Businessmen were made *beggars* overnight by the stock market crash. *Panhandler* almost exclusively suggests a man; this is true of *beggar* only when it occurs unmodified in the singular: the family of *beggars;* a *beggarwoman*.

Scavenger and **beachcomber** specifically point to *bums* or *tramps* who live by collecting flotsam or refuse and using or selling it. *Beachcomber* suggests a seaside wanderer, a man who lives on what he can find or beg, especially in the ports of South Sea islands. *Scavenger* is much more general in pointing to anyone who lives off the leavings of others, or who searches refuse for usable material: *scavengers* who dig through garbage cans and litter baskets for old magazines and soda bottles. The word can take on a more ominous or disapproving tone by reflecting its use as a generic word for birds and animals that feed on carrion, as jackals and vultures: gossip columnists who act as *scavengers*, living off tidbits of scandals.

Gold-brick and **loafer** shift the emphasis to laziness; rather than referring to *bums, tramps,* or someone unemployed, both words can indicate someone who has a job but gives it minimal attention. *Gold-brick* is army slang for a shirker, usually one who scrapes by without incurring reprimand. *Loafer*, aside from being more general, is distinct in not indicating the person's success at scanting his duties: *gold-bricks* who sat out the war in the quartermaster corps; a boss who was absolutely savage about clock-watchers and *loafers*. Both of these words are used jocularly among friends or intimates, especially *gold-brick*, which almost always is accompanied by a humorous, half-indulgent quality. See WANDERER.

Burn, the general word, means to effect a change in an object through the action of heat or fire. The object may be changed only slightly, or it may be totally destroyed. [A cigarette *burned* the finish on the table; A fire *burned* the house down.] Although it usually connotes some degree of destruction, *burning* may accomplish a useful purpose. A householder *burns* fuel to heat the house. In autumn, a gardener *burns* leaves to dispose of them. Not only heat but also extreme cold, corrosive chemicals, gases, electricity, radiation, friction, and the like may cause the kind of surface change or stinging sensation associated with a *burn*. Hence, acid is said to *burn* the skin, and a cutting wind may make the cheeks *burn*. *Burn* can also mean to cause a feeling of heat in a part of the body: The hot spices *burned* his mouth and tongue.

To **scald** is to *burn* with a very hot liquid or steam. Thus, the careless cook may *scald* herself if she spills hot soup or boiling water.

Singe, scorch, and **char** are related in that they mean to *burn* partially, slightly, or superficially. To *singe* is to *burn* the surface or ends of something: The fire *singed* his eyebrows. *Singeing* is sometimes done deliberately, as to remove bristles or to keep hair from splitting. A cook may *singe* a plucked chicken to remove pinfeathers by passing the fowl through an open flame. To *scorch* is to *burn* something to the point of discoloration, usually by hot metal: She *scorched* the dress by setting the iron too high for the fabric. *Char* may imply a more advanced stage of combustion. It means to reduce a substance to carbon, either completely, as in charcoal, or partially: Pieces of *charred* wood remained after the campfire had burned out; the *charred* remains of a burned-down house.

burn

brand
cauterize
char
scald
scorch
sear
singe

Sear, brand, and **cauterize** all connote deliberate *burning* to achieve a definite purpose. All are also used of flesh. Of the three, *sear* is the most general word, as it can mean both *brand* and *cauterize*. *Searing* involves the subjecting of a surface to intense heat for a very short time. This may have the effect of hardening, sealing, drying up, destroying tissue, or leaving an ineradicable imprint. [Before stewing the beef, the cook *seared* it over high heat to seal the juices in.] To *brand* is to *sear* with a hot iron, burning a mark into the flesh, as to signify ownership. A rancher *brands* his cattle so that he can identify them if they stray or are stolen. To *cauterize* is to *sear* tissue with a caustic agent or heated iron for curative purposes. A doctor may *cauterize* a wound to prevent infection. See COMBUSTIBLE, HOT, PASSIONATE, STIGMA.

busy

active
engaged
engrossed
occupied

These adjectives all refer to activity or involvement. **Busy** is the least formal word. It may indicate nothing more than that a person is working on or doing something, or that a thing is in use. [Mr. Brown is *busy* right now; The line is *busy*.] Or it may imply constant, concentrated involvement in business, or intensive and varied activity of any kind: a *busy* man; a *busy* day; a *busy* market place; a *busy* legislative session. The effort involved in being or staying *busy* may be, by implication, valuable or productive: Get *busy* and get something done. But in some cases, the word gives a special overtone of empty fuss and hollow results: *busy* work to keep the troops out of trouble; kept *busy* half the day by peddling neighborhood gossip. Another special use refers disapprovingly to a distracting elaborateness of design: such a *busy* pattern for a skirt.

Active stresses action, operation, or involvement as opposed to passivity or dormancy: an *active* man; an *active* life; an *active* listing. *Active* accounts are productive, and *active* investments yield interest. An *active* volcano is not extinct but may erupt, though it seldom does. Used of persons, *active* often points to actual work or participation as contrasted with mere approval or association: *active* on behalf of civil rights; *active* in community affairs; an *active* church member as opposed to a mere name on the rolls. A soldier on *active* duty is involved in military service on a full-time basis, but he may not be *busy* all the time. *Active* may also mean brisk or lively, suggesting a heaviness of traffic or transactions: a day of *active* trading.

Occupied shares with *busy* and *active* a simple contrast with idle. When used of a person, it suggests his involvement with a specific task: *occupied* with sweeping out the fireplace. When used of an object, it suggests its physical use at that moment. A telephone line can be *busy* but cannot be *occupied*. Conversely, a telephone booth can be *occupied* but cannot be *busy*. *Occupied*, when used of someone's mental state, means absorbed in thought, either purposive or idle: *occupied* in adding the figures before him; She *occupies* herself with trifles. In either case, it can suggest concentration to the point of distraction: so *occupied* in thought that he did not see the speeding car. **Engrossed** compares closely with this special use of *occupied*, implying even greater concentration, but with the added suggestion of pleasurable, willing, or fascinated involvement: *engrossed* in a good mystery story; *engrossed* in his work.

Engaged suggests involvement, like *busy*, but implies concentration on a specific task, like *occupied*. It also has a special sense of coming to grips with a situation: The *engaged* artist struggles to state the dilemmas facing his society. It has a military use for units involved in a hostile encounter: The *engaged* patrol was cut off from its own front line. It also refers to a man and woman in the formalized period of courtship just before marriage: an *engaged* couple. See ACTIVITY, DILIGENT, FIGHT, HIRE, OVERT, PREOCCUPIED.

Antonyms: idle, inactive, inert, passive, relaxed, unoccupied.

C

These words refer to the revealing or expressing of one's true thoughts or feelings. **Candid** can refer generally to a forthright manner or statement, but the word has been heavily influenced by its related use to refer to impromptu or unposed photographs; a *candid* camera is one suitable for taking such pictures. Consequently, the word has acquired overtones pertaining to natural, informal, and unrehearsed statements, as well: He agreed to give his *candid* opinion if his name weren't mentioned in the news story. **Frank** can also apply in a general way, but it is most often used to describe statements: a *frank* admission of guilt. In positive use, it can indicate an admirable openness and sincerity, but sometimes it can apply less favorably to someone who is unnecessarily blunt or flat-footed about things, despite other people's feelings: her *frank* disapproval of the way they had furnished their living room.

Bluff indicates a direct manner or blunt statements that may show little consciousness of or consideration for the vulnerabilities of other people, but that are usually without malicious intent: a *bluff* first sergeant who enjoyed ribbing his men about their misadventures with women. The word can also convey, more favorably, a hearty candidness: a lovable, *bluff* old curmudgeon.

Ingenuous can refer descriptively to a lack of guile, but more often it can also suggest a person who is simple or unaware to the point of gullibility: She gave *ingenuous* answers to all of the stranger's questions. The word frequently applies more to manner or disposition than to individual statements. See BRUSQUE, OUTSPOKEN, SINCERE, TRUTHFUL.

Antonyms: insincere, MISLEADING, sly, subtle, tricky, wily.

These verbs all mean to seize and to take captive. **Capture** is the strongest word. It implies the use of force or stratagem in overcoming active resistance: to *capture* an enemy fort; to *capture* an armed robber. **Catch** is the most general word. It suggests the seizure or detection of something fugitive or elusive — often implying active pursuit, clever entrapment, or a taking by surprise: to *catch* a runaway horse; to *catch* a thief.

Arrest is applied only to persons and always carries the implication of a legal offense. It means to take into custody by legal authority and often involves detention in jail: An officer *caught* him fleeing the scene of the crime and *arrested* him as a suspect. **Apprehend** is a more formal word for *arrest*, involving the seizure of someone in the name of the law: He was *apprehended* five hours after his escape. *Apprehend* is the sort of word used in official documents and reports; it seems stilted or pretentious in everyday contexts. **Nab** is an informal synonym for *catch*

candid

bluff
frank
ingenuous

capture

apprehend
arrest
bag
catch
nab
trap

or *arrest.* It stresses the suddenness of the seizure, often implying a rough grabbing: Police *nabbed* him as he ran out of the raided nightclub.

In extended senses, *catch* and *capture* may mean to seize something fleeting, to grasp something hard to get hold of. *Capture* implies the greater difficulty and achievement: to *catch* a likeness in a sketch; an artist who *captures* a fleeting expression. Both words may also mean to captivate or enthrall. [The song *caught* her fancy; The book *captured* his imagination.]

Four of these verbs are used of the seizure of animals in hunting. *Capture* is applied to wild animals brought back alive, as for exhibition in a zoo or training by an animal tamer: to *capture* lions and tigers. *Catch* is applied to small or harmless animals that are enticed by a bait or fooled by camouflage: to *catch* fish; to *catch* a mouse in a trap; to *catch* a bird in a snare. **Trap** focuses on the use of a trap, snare, or pitfall to *catch* unsuspecting animals: to *trap* fur-bearing animals for their pelts. Persons may be *trapped* like animals by being *caught* in a cul-de-sac, cut off from all escape routes: *trapped* in a burning building; *trapped* in a dull job and a bad marriage. **Bag** is expressive of the hunter's satisfaction at having his quarry literally in the bag: to *bag* an elk. In a figurative sense, *bag* stresses the triumph of the successful hunt, the bringing home of some sought-after prize: She *bagged* a minor poet for her salon. See GRASP, HUNT.

Antonyms: free, let go, liberate, release.

careful

conscientious
meticulous
punctilious
scrupulous

These words are all used to describe people in reference to the care they exercise in their general behavior, in the performance of duties and in attention to detail. **Careful** is the most general word in the list. It can mean thorough or painstaking, and in this sense suggests the avoidance of error by virtue of the care exercised: a *careful* secretary who always checked her work twice. It can mean concerned or mindful: *careful* about his manners at the party. It can mean cautious or watchful: Be *careful* when you drive on icy roads.

Conscientious and **scrupulous** agree in connoting a painstaking carefulness based on an ethical, logical, moral or other standard. [A *conscientious* researcher, through a highly developed regard for the truth, is *careful* to avoid error or omission; A *scrupulous* juror, out of a dedication to justice, is *careful* to weigh all the evidence and excludes all personal feelings.]

Meticulous and **punctilious** denote a very strict or even an excessive attention to details or standards. *Meticulous* suggests an almost finicky concern, often about trivial matters, based on a fear of making an error: A *meticulous* dresser is *careful* to avoid all violations of the canons of fashion. *Punctilious* implies an exaggerated regard for the fine points of the rules and forms prescribed by law or custom, as in etiquette: a *punctilious* social climber who was so *careful* about doing everybody else's "right thing" that he never developed any standards of his own. See CAUTIOUS.

Antonyms: HEEDLESS, *neglectful, negligent, remiss, sloppy.*

caress

cuddle
dandle

These words refer to the pleasurable, desirous, or affectionate holding or stroking of something. **Caress** indicates a brief, gentle, or embracing motion expressive of love or desire: tenderly *caressing* her once more before boarding the train. **Fondle** may stress desire more than love, but carries the same connotations of gentleness as *caress.* Whereas *caress* might be done with the arms and body, however, *fondle* might more

caress
(continued)

fondle
hug
neck
pet
smooch

typically be done solely with the hands and so suggest a greater possible distance than *caress*: *fondling* the nape of his neck with her open palm. **Cuddle** is more informal than the foregoing; it specifically suggests body-to-body contact, but not necessarily to imply desire at all so much as affectionate pleasure: sleeping kittens *cuddled* next to their watchful mother. **Hug** emphasizes one possibility in *caress*, specifically suggesting an armclasp expressive of affection or desire. Being much more informal than *caress* or *fondle*, and even than *cuddle*, *hug* seems better suited to indicate earthier emotions, although it contrasts with all the foregoing by stressing intensity of feeling rather than gentleness: desperately *hugging* her injured child; turning to *hug* each other as soon as they were in a secluded part of the park. **Dandle** is perhaps the most specific of all these words, restricting itself most concretely to the bouncing or rocking of a child in one's lap or on one's knee: gently *dandling* the child as she sang a lively nursery rhyme.

Pet, in its oldest sense, is close to *fondle* in indicating the stroking of a body with one's hand: *petting* the purring cat. In a more recent quasi-slang sense, the word relates to *caress* and *fondle*, but more specifically suggests intense sexual play between lovers that stops short of intercourse: teen-agers who find that *petting* in the back seats of automobiles only intensifies their natural frustrations. **Neck** is a slang term that exclusively pertains to this last sense of *pet*, but usually suggests kissing, and may imply greater restraint than *pet*: couples who sat in the balcony of the theater and spent more time *necking* than watching the movie. **Smooch**, also a slang term, is similar in meaning to *neck*, but often suggests the loud, almost slobbery kind of kiss that has comic rather than serious or sexual overtones: the sometimes amusing, sometimes maddening spectacle of two teenagers *smooching* and munching popcorn. Unlike *pet* and *neck*, *smooch* has connotations of mutual affection; it is sometimes used in contexts meant to suggest physical displays of affection without any implication of sexual satisfaction: We've been married thirty-odd years and we still love to *smooch*. See EMOTION, LOVE, YEARN.

Antonyms: BLOW.

caricature

burlesque
mimicry
parody
take-off
travesty

These words refer to an exaggerated rendering of the recognizable features of something in order to mock or poke fun at it. **Caricature**, most specifically, refers to a drawing or cartoon of someone in which salient features are distorted or overemphasized for comic effect. This may be done in good-humored fun or in an attempt at character assassination: a room filled with *caricatures* of Broadway stars; a *caricature* that represented the distinguished statesman as a masked gangster. The word can be used more widely of any production that deliberately distorts the recognizable features of something for whatever purpose: a novel that presents us with stereotyped *caricatures* rather than living human beings. **Take-off** is the most informal and general of any of these words, alluding to any exaggerated imitation designed to hold up its original to ridicule: a skit that was a *take-off* on the absurdities of several reigning Broadway musicals; an imaginary transcript of a press conference that was a biting *take-off* on the real thing.

Mimicry, most specifically, suggests the exaggerated acting out of another person's mannerisms and speech patterns; as with *caricature*, this may be done out of good humor or malice: his whining *mimicry* of the professor's voice; a series of impersonations in which his keen sense for *mimicry* is expertly displayed. This word also is frequently used for a wider range of exaggerated imitations: his devastating *mimicry* of the worst features of Lawrence's prose style. Sometimes the word can be used for inept imitation of an admired figure or style: his pitiful *mimicry* of upper-class manners.

Burlesque suggests a rowdy or zany reduction to the absurd of the content or style of some production or work, especially where the original is afflicted with pomposity or excessive solemnity: a revue that was a *burlesque* of the typically woebegone naturalistic play. Sometimes, like *caricature* or *mimicry*, the word can indicate specifically the satirizing of the characteristics or mannerisms of a particular person: a figure in the novel that was clearly a *burlesque* of a well-known feminist of that day. **Parody** most specifically suggests the ridiculing of a literary work by an exaggerated imitation of its style: a howling *parody* of Longfellow's "Evangeline"; a virtuoso *parody* of the author's endlessly tortuous sentence structure. Where *burlesque* may imply broad, slashing strokes applied slapdash, *parody*, by contrast, more often suggests an extremely skillful and understated imitation that is all the more effective for so cleverly catching the style of its original. Sometimes *parodies* have been done so consummately as to be mistakenly admired as a serious effort; this could almost never happen with a *burlesque*.

Travesty was once and is still rarely used, like *burlesque* or *parody*, to suggest a broad or skillful mocking of someone else's style. It is now more often used to suggest an utterly inept or totally depraved debasement of something admirable; a shocking *travesty* of impartial judicial procedures. Sometimes, in its most hyperbolical uses, the standard to which something is compared is not even indicated: The whole concert was simply a *travesty*. See IMITATE, RIDICULE.

carry

bear
bring
convey
take
transport

These words are alike in referring to the moving of objects or people through space. **Carry** and **bear** both suggest the supporting of a load, but of the two only *carry* necessarily implies movement from place to place. A donkey can *bear* a heavy load simply by standing still, but *carrying* the load implies moving it somewhere: The bridge was designed to *bear* the heaviest load any train could *carry*. *Bear*, of course, can suggest movement as well, in which case a dignity of comportment and style is suggested: the royal carriage *bearing* the queen and her consort. *Carry*, on the other hand, need not necessarily emphasize the heaviness of the thing being moved: *carrying* only a small handbag and a pair of gloves. *Bear* has an additional connotation of suffering not implied by *carry*: He *bore* with him all his life the memory of her painful death.

Transport is more formal and technical than these and is normally restricted to the shipment of goods or people considered as freight: ships to *transport* troops to the battlefield. *Transport*, more than *carry*, emphasizes movement to a goal or destination. It contrasts with the style implied in *bear* by stressing the mere physical event of shipment as a problem in logistics.

Bring and **take** are the most informal of all these; *bring* refers to movement toward the speaker, *take* to movement away from the speaker. Both are often used imperatively: *Take* away this ghastly veal cutlet and *bring* me my slippers. In actual usage, the *to* or *from* distinction is not always observed; both may also imply an accompanied or guided movement rather than one in which one thing *carries* another. [*Take* me to the nearest hospital; The ski lift will *bring* you within a few feet of the mountaintop.]

Convey was in Shakespeare's time a simple synonym for *bring* or *take*. In this sense it is now extremely formal and is mainly used in referring to the transmitting of a message through an intermediary. [*Convey* my best wishes to the rest of your family; The ambassador personally *conveyed* the president's message to the premier.] *Convey* does not necessarily imply actual movement. [If my letter *conveyed* the impression that I was indifferent, please forgive me; His tone *conveyed* his real feelings more truly than his words.] See MOVE, POSSESS.

Antonyms: LEAVE.

These words refer to misfortunes that result in grave loss or heavy casualties. **Catastrophe** is equally appropriate for a personal or public misfortune: taking along a first-aid kit to cope with unexpected *catastrophes*; air pollution that has reached the proportions of a *catastrophe*. In personal application, the word is often used hyperbolically of minor incidents: how to deal with the *catastrophe* of a large, visible run in her stocking. In reference to a general event, the word may refer to the negative effect on a particular group rather than to the public as a whole: a land reform program that benefited the poor but was a *catastrophe* for rich landowners. **Cataclysm** is most sharply in contrast with these possibilities of *catastrophe* in allowing little use for personal misfortune and in restricting itself to severe mishaps that have negative results for everyone; it stresses, furthermore, a momentous disruption that results in severe damage and loss: a hairbreadth escape from nuclear *cataclysm*. More than these other words, *cataclysm* is especially suggestive of a natural upheaval: The extinct volcano's eruption would mean a *cataclysm* for the city.

Disaster is the most general of these words, referring both to personal and public misfortunes in a wide range of possibilities: household *disasters*; a country afflicted with the twin *disasters* of food shortages and an exploding population. Like *cataclysm*, the word can refer to natural upheavals, but without the implications of total destruction present in *cataclysm*: a flood that was the worst *disaster* the city had ever faced. *Disaster* compares with *catastrophe* by stressing the actual harm done: They were glad they had survived the *catastrophe* and had met with no *disaster*. The word can, of course, be used hyperbolically, like *catastrophe*, for minor misfortunes: a party that turned out to be a complete *disaster*.

Calamity is similar to *catastrophe*, but at a reduced level of intensity. It may also now sound more formal than these other words, or at least a shade outdated. It is more often used for a personal misfortune, seriously or hyperbolically, but it can also be used of public misfortunes on occasion, in which case it functions more abstractly or subjectively than *disaster*: a little *calamity* that happened on his way to school; a *calamity* that wiped out his savings; arguing that the bill's passage would result in a *calamity* for the whole country. **Debacle** once referred specifically to a serious disruption or natural upheaval, as of a flood, especially when severe damage or failure results: the *debacle* of the Children's Crusade; a stock market *debacle*. Now, the word more often refers to an attempt that is ridiculously inept or that results in humiliating defeat: a high-level conference that was nothing short of a *debacle*. See DESTROY, FIRE.

Antonyms: BENEFIT, *blessing, boon, comfort, success.*

These words refer to thoughtful restraint in behavior. **Cautious** is the most general of these, suggesting a careful holding back from action until all possibilities have been considered: a *cautious* attitude toward buying into his company. The word can, as well, suggest careful action,

catastrophe

calamity
cataclysm
debacle
disaster

cautious

cautious
(continued)

circumspect
discreet
guarded
prudent
wary

in which case it suggests a slow, tentative, or even timid manner: his *cautious* crossing of the rickety bridge. **Wary** is an intensification of all the implications of *cautious*, stressing an extremely hesitant manner that sees every course of action fairly bristling with dangers: giving a *wary* reply to the enigmatic comment of the stranger; asking the campers to be particularly *wary* of starting a forest fire during the dry season.

Guarded also intensifies the implications of *cautious*, but puts special stress on a *wary* manner in social interchanges that is marked by a reluctance to reveal too much about oneself or give too much of oneself except to people with whom one is thoroughly familiar: a *guarded*, non-committal answer to the interviewer's blunt questions. It may also suggest a deliberate suppression of one's feelings for fear of having them proved wrong: a *guarded* optimism about the outcome of the election. Whereas the former words point to restrained behavior that might result from fear, unfamiliarity, or uneasiness, **prudent** suggests action that is the outcome of wisdom gained by experience. Such action need not be *cautious* or *wary* at all; these words might, in fact, suggest the opposite of *prudent* when no real cause for fear exists: It was not *prudent* to be so *cautious* in climbing the slope, because it put her in constant danger of losing her balance.

Circumspect and **discreet** both refer primarily to social behavior. *Circumspect* indicates a strict adherence to social proprieties. [A *prudent* politician must perforce lead a rigorously *circumspect* life; if he cannot, he had best be *cautious* as to which temptations he permits himself to surrender to.] *Discreet* refers to a different kind of social propriety than *circumspect*, indicating an ability to keep the confidences of other people and to be extremely *guarded* about entrusting personal details to others: wondering how *discreet* her friend could be about what he knew of her past life. In a less specific use, *discreet* approaches the meaning of *circumspect*, suggesting a *prudent* choice of inoffensive behavior or an ability, to handle difficult matters with tact and delicacy. In this same sense the word nevertheless contrasts with *circumspect* in suggesting a more intuitive, less rigid approach to social behavior. See AFRAID, PRUDENCE.

Antonyms: BOLD, BRAVE, *confident*, DARING, *reckless*.

cave

burrow
cavern
grotto
tunnel

These words refer to a hollow or opening in the earth, either natural or artificial. **Cave** is least specific and can be applied to any hollowed-out area in the earth, usually one that occurs in the side of a mountain, cliff, or hill. The cliff dwellers found that natural *caves* gave them warmth and protection during the Ice Age. Bears, for similar reasons, hibernate in *caves* during the winter.

Cavern, when used in place of *cave*, tends to sound inflated in diction. It can be used accurately, however, to refer to a more extensive subterranean *cave* or set of *caves* indefinite in extent, especially when it suggests a natural chamber such as one formed in limestone by running water. In this case, the sense of an opening into the slanted face of a hill is not necessarily maintained. One or more mouths of the *cavern* may open onto relatively level ground: The tourists clutched the guide-rail and hurried along the shelf of the *cavern*, oppressed by its airlessness and lack of light. *Cavern* may also be used metaphorically for any obscure recess: the dark *caverns* of his mind.

Grotto is the most specific of these terms, though it can refer either to an artificial or natural hollow. When artificial, it is a cavelike, man-made structure built as a recreational retreat or shrine: The towns-people placed a Christmas tree within their quaintly decorated *grotto* and sang carols there throughout the holidays. When natural, a *grotto* is typically picturesque, often forming a recess in a *cavern*, one that may be filled with odd-shaped stalagmites and stalactites: Daylight has never touched the cave paintings in the *grotto* at Lascaux.

Burrow and **tunnel** are alike in suggesting an artificial opening in the earth and often implying a linear shape as contrasted with the roughly spherical hollow most typical of a *cave*. *Burrow* refers to the hollow dug by some animal such as a gopher or a rabbit: The *burrow* of a gopher usually has two openings a considerable distance away from each other. *Tunnel* can refer to a hollow in the earth dug by an animal, but it is used most frequently to refer to one dug by man. If its purpose is to permit movement from one point to another, as in a subway system, a *tunnel* would be mainly horizontal over most of its course. If dug for purposes of mining, a *tunnel* would usually slant sharply downward into the depths of the earth: The miners were trapped in the *tunnel* by a cave-in along the passage just behind them. See HOLE.

These words refer to joyful gatherings of people. **Celebration** and **party** are both general, suggesting any coming together of a number of people to rejoice over some happy event. *Celebrations* and *parties* can be large or small, public or private, formal or informal; but *celebration* usually connotes a large gathering and *party* a more intimate group, often of persons who are close friends or at least acquainted: the candidate's victory *celebration* that drew nearly a thousand people; He felt fortunate to be a guest at one of her small, select dinner *parties*. **Ball** implies an official or stately occasion, and suggests a scrupulously selected guest list and formal attire: the debutante's coming out *ball*; the President's inaugural *ball*.

Festival suggests the *celebration* of a whole community either periodically at a significant time of the year or on some important occasion: the town's annual harvest *festival*. It is frequently applied to a planned series of cultural events: Lincoln Center's Bach *festival*; such lures for summer tourists as the Salzburg and Spoleto *festivals*. It is also used to describe annual religious ceremonies: the *festival* of Trinity Sunday. **Feast**, like *festival*, has a religious connotation: the *feast* of Palm Sunday. But in wider applications, it suggests a single *celebration* at which a great deal of food is eaten: all the knights and ladies gathering for a sumptuous *feast*. Outside a religious or historical context, the word may sound outmoded now, except in metaphorical or hyperbolical uses: That dinner you gave was a real *feast*. **Banquet**, in fact, has almost replaced *feast* in the sense of a formal or official dinner; it suggests the honoring of a special event or guest or the observing of an important occasion: After the wedding *banquet*, there will be a formal *ball*.

Festivity is vaguer in reference than most of these related words. It now might sound like inflated diction when it replaces *festival* or, especially, *party*: promising to look in later on the *festivities*. It is still viable, however, in suggesting a mood of convivial merry-making: the air of *festivity* that even the smallest town takes on during Christmas. See RITE.

These words refer to a position equidistant from the extremities or periphery, or to the vital part of something. **Center**, most concretely, indicates such a point within the circumference of a circle or a sphere: the *center* of the earth. It can, of course, suggest an approximate location of this sort within any configuration: at the *center* of the intersection.

celebration

ball
banquet
feast
festival
festivity
party

center

center
(continued)

core
heart
hub
middle
midst

Used metaphorically, it suggests a place of extreme density or importance: a metropolitan *center*; at the very *center* of his philosophy.
Middle, most typically, indicates a point equidistant from the two ends
of something: folding the paper down the *middle*. It can be used more
loosely, as an informal substitute for *center*, especially when an approximation is intended: right in the *middle* of the ocean. It is better used
for a moment of time than *center*: in the *middle* of the day. It can also
indicate a point or moment that occurs in the thick of things: in the
middle of our other troubles. Here, it suggests passivity as compared
with *center*: the man who was at the *center* of the controversy. **Midst**
is now mostly used in this last sense of *middle* but without the implication
of passivity; even here it might sound excessively formal except in some
standard expressions: in the *midst* of battle.

Core specifically suggests the *center* of a solid figure: an apple *core*;
the hollow *core* of the building. Metaphorically, it has a wide range of
uses suggesting the irreducible minimum or quintessence of something
that may in its fullness be extensive and manifold: The *core* of our appeal is freedom of speech; the *core* of his argument. **Heart**, at its most
concrete, contrasts with all these other words in referring to a vital organ
rather than to an exact or approximate *center*. In metaphorical uses,
however, it may refer to the vital *center* of something: the very *heart* of
the city. It may also, like *middle*, refer approximately to the point of
greatest density: in the *heart* of the jungle. In more abstract uses, it
relates most closely to *core* in suggesting the sine qua non of something,
although in this case the irreducible *core* is also seen as animating
principle. [The Bill of Rights is not a superfluous addendum to the
Constitution; it is the *heart* of our democracy.]

Hub, most concretely, refers to the *center* of a wheel; in metaphorical
uses, it may refer to the psychological *center* of a city, even one laid out
on a grid system: the *hub* of business activity in lower Manhattan. The
word seems more exactly used when a network with radiating arms is
suggested: the *hub* of the cocktail party around whom the lesser known
spread out in diminishing rank. See KERNEL.

Antonyms: BOUNDARY, EDGE, PERIMETER.

chance

accidental
adventitious
contingent
fortuitous
incidental

These words refer to what occurs either unexpectedly or without prearrangement or plan. **Chance** is the least formal of these. On one hand
it can indicate coincidence: a *chance* meeting in the street. On the other,
it can suggest an occurrence that is governed by no known physical laws:
the development of quantum theory to explain seemingly *chance* shifts
in atomic particles. **Accidental** stresses the lack of intention or forethought, but is now strongly influenced by accident, meaning mishap,
to suggest an error that brings undesirable or even disastrous results:
an *accidental* misreading of her bank balance; the specter of an *accidental* nuclear holocaust. **Fortuitous** can point to something that is apparently without cause or design, but it often suggests a good or desirable
occurrence, an overtone that puts the word in the strongest possible
contrast with *accidental*: a *fortuitous* change of plan that kept them out
of the city during the *accidental* blackout.

Contingent can refer, most simply, to what is unexpected or unforeseen: a *contingent* thunderstorm that scattered the marchers. More
often, the word points to something that is dependent on an uncertain
event or condition; in this case the word is used with *on* or *upon*: an
increase in your allowance that is *contingent upon* how well you do in
your studies.

Incidental points to something occurring without design or regularity: an *incidental* shrub or two beside the path. Thus, the word can refer to something unplanned or unexpected, but usually of value, however slight, especially when this is a concomitant or side benefit gained in the pursuit of some other goal: an *incidental* knowledge of Nigerian folksongs gained during his stint in the Peace Corps. **Adventitious** can be a much more formal substitute for *incidental*, pointing to a *fortuitous* acquisition or coming together: *adventitious* circumstances that encouraged the rise of capitalism. Like *incidental*, the word can also indicate something that is not inherent, particularly something that is extrinsic to a primary consideration: *adventitious* flaws that did not detract from the power of the time-battered piece of sculpture. See MARGINAL, PROVISIONAL, RANDOM.

Antonyms: CONCLUSIVE, INEVITABLE, INEXORABLE.

These words all refer to the process of making something over or making it different. **Change**, the most general and least formal, can mean any process of differentiation, slight or great, in appearance or essence, in quality or quantity: *changing* the desert into farmland; *changing* his mind; *changing* the way she wore her hair.

Alter, convert, and **modify** suggest relatively slight revisions of something, generally in appearance or use. Each also has a use with somewhat different effect for a change in attitude or belief. As listed, these words move from the slightly to the highly formal, with perhaps a similar progression in implication, from lesser to greater change. *Alter*, most commonly, refers to *changing* the fit of clothes, either making them looser or tighter by letting out or taking in seams: the seamstress who *altered* the hemline of the skirt. It also commonly refers to the redecoration of buildings: workmen *altering* the drugstore into a paperback bookstore. In both of these uses, *alter* implies that the basic structure is worked with and around rather than contravened, although no value judgment is present concerning the result. *Alter*, more than any of the sewords except *change*, has a wide range of application. [He *altered* his stand on birth control; She *altered* the mistake on the price-tag.] *Convert* suggests the adaptation of an object by a specially designed addition that will increase its usefulness: an attachment that *converts* your vacuum cleaner into a paint sprayer. When used of attitudes or beliefs, *convert* suggests a far more drastic change than *alter*: the man who *converted* to Buddhism. *Modify*, when used of objects, suggests more basic changes than *alter* or *convert*, in which function more importantly than appearance is *changed*: car aerials *modified* by teenagers into lethal weapons. When applied to attitudes, however, *modify* implies less change than either *alter* or *convert*. It often has a special overtone of making less extreme. [He didn't *alter* his position so much as *modify* its severity; in any case, you could hardly say he was *converted* by the arguments of the opposition.]

The remaining words suggest more drastic changes than the preceding, changes so profound that an entirely new entity may appear to have taken the place of the old. **Transmute** emphasizes an elemental change in the inner structure of a material, often implying a shift from a lower to a higher state: coal *transmuted* to diamonds by eons of intense pressure; alchemists vainly trying to *transmute* lead into gold. Change of this magnitude, obviously, is not accomplished by revision, as in *alter*, or by addition, as in *convert*. **Transform** suggests change equally as profound, but in concentrating on outward form or appearance, it is

change

alter
convert
modify
transfigure
transform
transmogrify
transmute

perhaps slightly less intense than *transmute* and certainly more general. *Transform* may suggest change in a person or a definite entity, *transmute* in a less well-defined quantity; *transmute* also tends to suggest a slow, analyzable or scientific process, *transform* a sudden or mystical change: the frog that was *transformed* into a prince; plans that were *transformed* overnight into reality. *Transform* also lends itself to hyperbole, perhaps overused: lit candles that *transformed* the oak table into an elegant dining table.

Transfigure intensifies the mystical element in *transform*, adding a note of supernatural or religious rapture: the statue of St. Teresa *transfigured* by ecstasy. When used hyperbolically of more common circumstances, a positive or joyful change is indicated: her plain features *transfigured* with tenderness. **Transmogrify**, on the other hand, always stresses negative change, bizarre or ugly: the peasant lad *transmogrified* into a dragon. In more usual circumstances, the effect is comic: the graceful child *transmogrified* into a gangling adolescent. See ADDITION, BUILD, DEVISE.

Antonyms: maintain, stabilize, sustain.

characteristic

attribute
feature
mark
peculiarity
quality
trait

These words all refer to an aspect that is an identifiable part of a person, place, mood, or object. **Characteristic** may imply neutral description in referring to any aspect of something, without evaluating its relative importance to the whole: a psychological report that lists every possible *characteristic* of the person being studied. More often, however, the word suggests an aspect of the whole that is regarded as typical: a town that had all the *characteristics* usual to any sea-side resort; the preponderance of *characteristics* that supported the diagnosis of alcoholism. The word has many scientific or technical uses in this sense, but may be overused in other contexts where a less formal word is available.

Attribute may escape the charge of inflated diction or imprecise jargon when used in place of *characteristic* for nontechnical situations. It also may be used to refer to something typical, but leans perhaps to greater neutrality in suggesting one of many possible aspects that make up a whole: eagerness to learn, an often overlooked *attribute* in small children. **Peculiarity**, on the other hand, is far from neutral in suggesting an unpleasant *attribute* that is quite noticeable: a *peculiarity* in his shuffling walk; a *peculiarity* of mind that insisted on an exact order in doing even the smallest task; a *peculiarity* of the northern climate.

Feature and **mark**, like *peculiarity*, refer to something quite noticeable, but *feature* most readily suggests something positive, while *mark* may suggest either positive or negative aspects. *Feature* most specifically refers to physical appearance: an aquiline nose that was her best *feature*. In more general uses, it may refer to an unusual or outstanding aspect of something: the siesta that is a distinguishing *feature* of life in Mexico. In the entertainment or advertising worlds, the word is used to refer to a special or added attraction: the *feature* of the evening's entertainment; the new model's compactness as an added *feature*. *Mark* is stronger than *feature* in suggesting something that sets its possessor apart: generosity as the *mark* of a civilized man. But it has negative uses that compare with *peculiarity*: the sadism that is the disfiguring *mark* of all fascistic regimes. In this use, *mark* differs from *peculiarity* in suggesting an intrinsic rather than accidental or external departure from the norm.

Trait and **quality** refer to more abstract *attributes* than *peculiarity*, *feature*, or *mark*. *Trait*, most specifically, is used to describe abiding behavior patterns, rather than single or monetary actions: a *trait* of suspiciousness that underlay all his relationships with people; *traits* of fortitude and industry that spelled survival for the settlers of a new world. *Quality* is more general than any of the other words here; it may suggest a momentary aspect or an abiding one; it may suggest positive or negative *attributes*. It may imply measurable, concrete aspects, but is often used, contrarily, to suggest a vague or subtle gathering of impressions: a *quality* of despair in her drawn face; a strange *quality* of light in the room; *qualities* of exuberance and spontaneity that made the people easy to live with. See TEMPERAMENT.

All of these words are superlatives used mainly to describe the pleasing manner of an attractive person, usually a woman. **Charming** emphasizes gracious behavior or elegance of manner, especially in social situations: Her *charming* considerateness made everyone feel at ease. It applies readily to feminine accomplishments or apparel: a *charming* table setting; a *charming* gown. Used of men, it suggests sophistication and suavity: the *charming* man with the slight French accent. Originally it suggested being put under a magic charm; the force of this original meaning is still felt, perhaps, when the word refers to a beautiful scene or landscape: the *charming* mountain views we glimpsed through the windows of our train.

Bewitching, **enchanting**, and **entrancing** also once suggested being put under a magic spell. Now, used to describe an attractive woman, they do not suggest social grace so much as qualities of freshness, strangeness, or exotic allure, all considerably less innocuous than anything implied by *charming*. One might call the girl next door *charming*, for all her simplicity, but one would think twice about calling her *bewitching* — unless one lived in a rather unusual neighborhood. *Bewitching* most strongly suggests this exotic quality; *enchanting*, through overuse, is more innocuous than its two companions — shading off toward *charming*. *Entrancing* still has some of its freshness left, suggesting an ability to command an onlooker's stunned, almost hypnotized attention: stupidly staring back at every *entrancing* smile she gave him. The same scale of forces for these three prevails when they are used to describe scenery. None of them would be a likely description for a man.

Captivating and **winning** suggest a different and fainter submerged metaphor — of military conquest. They might both be most precisely used to imply an initial resistance on the part of the onlooker. *Winning*, however, suggests warm-hearted sunniness of disposition, whereas *captivating* carries an overtone of sexual allure and vivacity. *Winning*, also, might pertain to a single act, while *captivating* might apply more easily to a whole manner of behavior: her *winning* appeal to him for help; his fading resistance to the *captivating* figure she made, standing alone and silent on the moonlit piazza. Both of these words may describe men, in which case an attempted conquest of a woman is implied, *winning* referring to an ingratiating pleasantness of manner and *captivating* to a rakish insouciance. [She forgot his *winning* courtesy and consideration in a twinkling when she saw the *captivating* smile of the man who rode by in the white convertible.] *Winning* would have little use in describing scenery, but *captivating* might suggest a collection of fanciful qualities that sweeps one away in spite of one's distrust for the strange or unusual: one of thousands who surrendered whole-heartedly to the *captivating* uniqueness of Venice.

charming

bewitching
captivating
enchanting
entrancing
fascinating
winning

Fascinating has perhaps suffered less from overuse as a superlative than these other words. Although more general in application, it still can suggest, like *entrancing*, a prospect that is almost hypnotic in its inviting quality. It applies to men as well as to women, to any attractive scene or view, or to any idea or thing that is extremely interesting. In all cases it is like *captivating* and *winning* in suggesting the ability to overcome resistance, however strong: Against his will, he found himself caught up again and again in the life of this most *fascinating* of peoples. See BEAUTIFUL, LIVELY, PLEASING.

Antonyms: dull, REPULSIVE, *tedious,* UGLY.

chaste

continent
pure
virtuous

These words refer to the abstinence from immoral thoughts and actions, especially those of a sexual nature. **Chaste** is most often taken to mean a strict abstinence from sexual activity of any sort: men who date promiscuous women but insist on marrying one who has been *chaste*. The word has a wider range of use, however: *chaste* in thought, word, and deed. It can also refer to a married person who refrains from committing adultery: a *chaste* wife; Her husband had remained *chaste* largely through lack of opportunity. While humorous, the last example indicates that *chaste* can be taken as indicating mere lack of activity. Generally speaking, where action is concerned, self-restraint or self-denial is, in fact, usually implied as necessary in maintaining *chaste* behavior. But *chaste* thoughts would be those completely and naturally free of sensual or sexual desire. *Chaste* can also refer to whatever is self-restrained, free of frivolity, and spare or severe in effect: a *chaste* prose style that was striking in its simplicity and clarity.

Pure emphasizes what has never been adulterated by immoral or sexual strivings. In this it is like *chaste* as it applies to thought, but here, *pure* can apply to the whole range of possibilities with this emphasis: the *pure* in spirit; He insisted that even the *purest* infant had already been tainted with original sin. **Virtuous** is much milder in its force than either *pure* or *chaste*, pointing to someone who refrains from immoral actions. With this word, the stress is less exclusively on sexual behavior, indicating a generally moral or decent behavior: the *virtuous* citizens of his home town; those who are blessed with a *virtuous* husband or wife.

Continent refers strictly to refraining from acting upon desires or needs. Where sexuality is concerned, a person might not be *pure* in feeling or *chaste* in his imaginings and yet be *continent* if he successfully resists actual physical activity: She insisted that they remain *continent* until they were engaged to be married. In addition to sexuality, resistance to other appetites may be indicated by the word; here moderation rather than abstinence may be the point of its use: the alcoholic who found it impossible to be *continent* at a cocktail party; Thanksgiving dinners at which few remain *continent*. The aspect of control is especially evident in a related use, pertaining to the ability to retain bodily discharges: devices to help bed-wetters become *continent*. See INNOCENT, MORAL.

Antonyms: DIRTY, *immoral, impure,* INDECENT, LEWD, *tainted.*

chatter

babble

These words all refer to confused, rapid, incoherent, or worthless talk. **Chatter** is the most general of these; it may refer to quick rambling talk that is light, idle, or inconsequential, or it may refer to a din of voices all speaking at once: the man who pretended to listen silently as his wife *chattered* on and on; the women *chattering* in the back yard like a flock of magpies. The word is perhaps most appropriate to describe women's voices, since a high-pitched quality of speech is usually implied. **Babble** suggests the almost idiotically meandering talk of a person or group of persons, without reference to sex: the drunkard who *babbled* out his life history to everyone in the crowded bar; the senators in the cloakroom whose combined voices *babbled* in one continuous uproar.

Jabber is a jocose, slangy way of referring to rapid interchanges of a conversation one doesn't understand or considers trivial: two merchants *jabbering* away in their bargaining for the sheer delight of hearing their own voices. The suggestion is even stronger in this word of a frenetic pace without let up. **Gibber**, however, is more strongly pejorative than *jabber* when applied to people. It suggests that the sounds produced are literally meaningless: dancers who *gibbered* in grunts and groans that kept time with the music. The word may be purely descriptive when applied to animals: monkeys *gibbering* back and forth in the branches overhead. **Prattle** shares with *jabber* and *gibber* suggestions of unintelligible sounds, but if confined to children or sounds in nature, the result is not pejorative: a baby *prattling* contentedly in his crib; a lazy waterfall that *prattled* to itself all day. If used of adult speech, of course, the word suggests stupidity or childishness: the old man who *prattled* to himself on the park bench.

In **prate**, the suggestion of frenetically paced group speech present in *chatter* and *babble* is absent, as well as the unintelligibility present in those words grouped with *babble*. *Prate*, on the contrary, most readily suggests a tedious, long-winded monologue full of the speaker's self-importance: a teacher who *prates* on disconnectedly but relentlessly about everything that comes into his head. **Yak** is a slang word for conversation that is neither necessarily hectic nor unintelligible; it suggests, instead, a contented, relaxed flow of talk that is idle or trivial: His favorite pastime at college was *yakking* with his friends at all-night bull sessions. The word can also carry a pejorative implication, in which case constant, frenetic, and noisy talk may be indicated: He was nearly driven mad by the way his wife *yakked* at him without letup. See CONVERSATION, CRY, LAUGH, RAILLERY, SAY, TALKATIVE.

These words refer to deliberate attempts to gain something from another by unfair or dishonest scheming or dissembling. **Cheat** is relatively informal and **victimize** relatively formal, but both are general in their application, indicating any situation where one person preys upon someone else. *Cheat*, in its transitive use, always implies a victim, although the act indicated may range from the mildly unfair to the outrageously unjust or heinous: The boy *cheated* his friend out of the apple by insisting that it was rotten, if not poisonous; a real estate agent who *cheated* the widow out of the land on which oil had been discovered. As can be seen, deception is usually implied by *cheat*; *victimize* does not specify the means used to prey on the other person. The word can, in fact, apply to situations where nothing is to be gained but sadistic pleasure: a bully who *victimized* the other children after school. The word does stress the harm done to the victim and is consequently the harshest word here in its disapproval, whether or not tangible gain is implied: gangsters who *victimized* a whole city with their ten-year reign of terror.

Swindle more specifically points to a scheme, often complicated, by which someone is *cheated*: a famous stock market racket that *swindled* investors by means of forged stock certificates. Often, the word points to the *cheating* of gullible people who are persuaded to part with their

chatter
(continued)

gibber
jabber
prate
prattle
yak

cheat

con
defraud
fleece
swindle
victimize

valuables by trickery or deception or by appeals to their cupidity: confidence men who *swindle* unsuspecting investors with get-rich-quick propositions spun out of whole cloth. **Defraud** suggests the use of less complex stratagems to divest someone of his valuables; the word can more often suggest a quick or one-time action accomplished through simple misrepresentation or lying: door-to-door salesmen who *defraud* housewives by taking orders for vacuum cleaners that they never intend to deliver.

Fleece and **con** are both extremely informal words for *cheat* or *swindle*. *Fleece* suggests the same kind of complicated scheme as is indicated by *swindle*; by implication, the victim here is seen to be naive and innocent as a lamb: an avid art collector who was *fleeced* of a million dollars by a ring that sold counterfeit paintings attributed to Impressionist masters. The word can be reduced in force to apply to any outrageous price obtained for cheap goods or services: tourist attractions set up to *fleece* the unwary sightseer. **Con** is a slang term that derives from confidence game, in which someone is *swindled* by gaining his trust. The word applies to situations in which the victimizer has a smooth line and a sympathetic manner that wins the confidence of his victim: a man who would *con* his own mother out of her last dollar. The word has become a fad word for any sort of insincerity that is put on to persuade or win the sympathy of someone else, even where no ostensible gain is in the offing: a drunkard who tried to *con* all his friends into pitying the hard luck he had met with in his life. See DECEPTION, MISLEADING, ROB, THIEF, TRICK.

cheer

encourage
exhilarate
gladden
warm

These words refer to the raising of someone's morale or to the creating of a positive or lively frame of mind. **Cheer** suggests, most concretely, that some occurrence has given a boost to an otherwise despondent outlook: We were *cheered* that the sun had finally come out and would at least dry our damp, clammy clothing; *cheered* by news that one helicopter had sighted a feeble fire further up the mountain slope. **Encourage**, like *cheer*, may refer to a raising of morale; as such it implies a resulting frame of mind that is less hopeful than with *cheer*: *encouraged* to look back on the considerable distance they had come, but still uneasy about the distance they had yet to cross. In another context, *encourage* may suggest the awakening of interest in someone else through sympathetic concern: He had been *encouraged* by his teacher to take his writing seriously.

Gladden may suggest the same situation as *cheer*, but like *encourage* it can function in its own context, without reference to the raising of a flagging morale: *gladdened* by their success at building a fire big enough to be seen a good distance off; *gladdened* by the news that he had become the grandfather of twins. *Gladden* can sometimes, however, sound faintly outdated or a shade too formal when compared with *cheer* and especially with *encourage*. **Warm** may refer to a revival of morale or to a simple intensity of emotion, deeper than that implied by *cheer* or *gladden*: *warmed* by the ease at which they had cleaned up what had seemed the hopeless mess before them; *warmed* to know that her savings would go toward seeing her nephew through college.

Exhilarate is unique among these words in suggesting a situation in which one is filled with a bracing exuberance and zest: He felt listless until the sea breeze *exhilarated* him and steadied his nerves. See ENCOURAGE, JOYOUS, LIVELY, MERRIMENT.

Antonyms: chill, depress, DISCOURAGE, *dispirit*, RIDICULE, sadden.

These words refer to positive frames of mind or to a brightly optimistic disposition. **Cheerful** suggests an extroverted and open manner
that is warm, pleasant, and contented: She smiled back at the *cheerful*
faces of her students; the *cheerful* vacationers at the resort. **Cheery**,
by contrast, can suggest a *cheerful* manner that is forced or intrusive in
its attempts to make others feel better: the *cheery* nurses in the hospital
who proved to be such a grating nuisance. The word can sometimes be
less unpleasant in tone: giving me a *cheery* wink as I passed by.

Happy suggests an inward state of contentment that does not necessarily show itself in any outward bustle such as *cheerful* or *cheery* may
indicate: so *happy* at the news that tears gathered silently in her eyes
and ran down her cheeks. **Sunny** refers particularly to an untroubled
disposition that is warm and friendly: a *sunny* laughter that rang out
from the kitchen; the *sunny* expressions of children at a circus.

Both **blithe** and **winsome** suggest a light lack of seriousness in
manner. *Blithe* particularly indicates an almost reckless insouciance or
indomitable light-headedness: a *blithe* way of stuffing unpaid bills in a
drawer, as though that would take care of them; a *blithe* willingness to
try anything on impulse. *Winsome* contrasts with *blithe* by suggesting
an almost staid sweetness or delicacy of manner, warm but subdued; it
is most often applied to women: a *winsome* smile that in the next minute
turned into an embarrassed blush. See BLITHE, JOYOUS, LIVELY, OPTI-
MISTIC.

Antonyms: downcast, GLOOMY, MISERABLE, SAD, *woebegone.*

These words all refer to young human beings who are not yet adults.
Child is the most inclusive word and has a wide, general application:
when he was a *child* of three; trying to explain the meaning of death
to a *child*; the delighted cries of *children* playing in the surf. A *child*
usually ranges in age from that of a small baby to a boy or girl entering
puberty. Occasionally adults speak of adolescents as *children*: high-
school *children*. *Child* also means an offspring or descendant of any age.
[Most young men want to marry and raise *children*; Lincoln was the
child of a Kentucky pioneer; The Jews are sometimes called the *Children* of Israel.]

Baby and **infant** both designate a newborn or very young child who
is still in arms. *Baby* is the everyday word, while *infant* tends to sound
impersonal or medical. *Baby* has a more personal quality about it, and
is richly connotative of endearment and affection. One would say that
a woman is about to give birth to a *baby* or to a *child,* but it would sound
stilted if she were said to be about to bear an *infant. Baby* is also the
more general term, being used of the last born of two or more brothers
or sisters or of the youngest member of a group: the *baby* of a large
family; the *baby* of the graduating class. In law, an *infant* is a person
who has not yet attained the age of legal majority, usually 21.

A **toddler** is a *child* between about the ages of one and two years,
who is just emerging from *infancy* or *babyhood. Toddler* is a pleasant,
homely word, vividly suggesting the short, unsteady steps taken by a
child of this age in learning to walk.

Little boy and **little girl** are applied to young *children* generally
between the ages of two and six when they are no longer *babies* but
still regard their parents, rather than other *children,* as the center of
their world. Because *son* and *daughter* have become rather formal — to
some even old-fashioned — *little boy* or *girl* have probably become the
commonest way parents use, especially in speech, to refer to *children* of

baby
infant
little boy
little girl
preschooler
toddler
youngster

this age. The *little* does not mean *small*; *small boy* and *small girl* refer to size, whereas *little boy* and *little girl* refer to age, and must now be considered compounds with distinct meanings and connotations not conveyed by the parts of which they are composed.

Preschooler, a fairly recent term, is applied to a *child* between the ages of two and five years who is too young to enter elementary school but who may be attending a nursery school or kindergarten. *Preschooler* is often used in contradistinction to "school-age *child*" and has the ring of pedagogic jargon.

Youngster may refer to a *child* or adolescent of any age. It is used mainly by older people, and it carries a suggestion of the liveliness and vigor of youth rather than its helplessness or dependency. Hence, it is applied more frequently to a boy than a girl.

childish

childlike
immature
infantile
juvenile
puerile

These words refer to behavior unbecoming to an adult. **Childish** suggests lack of control or restraint and carries possible connotations of petulance, irrationality, impatience, and self-preoccupation: a *childish* insistence that everyone listen to him; a *childish* terror of insects. The word is so negative in tone that it is seldom now used to describe a young person, or even his understandable limitations. **Childlike** is also not used to describe the young, since it would be obviously tautological. Used of adults, however, it gives a tone in strong contrast to *childish*. It suggests having the freshness, curiosity, or honesty of the young; it gives possible connotations of innocence, lack of inhibition, zest, or eagerness: a *childlike* ability to look at paintings unhampered by preconceptions; He felt an almost *childlike* wonder at the beauty of the forest. In uses where it is least positive, it still suggests a touching lack of experience or sham: her *childlike* naiveté in agreeing to go to his hotel room for a nightcap; a *childlike* unconcern for the rank and title of his assembled guests.

Unlike the foregoing **immature** and **juvenile** may be used in factual reference to the young or things pertaining to them: an *immature* seedling; a *juvenile* court. In this case, *immature* is more general since it can refer to any living thing not fully developed, whereas *juvenile* refers specifically to young human beings. In reference to adults, both words are disapproving in tone, *juvenile* somewhat less and *immature* considerably less than *childish*. [I suppose we are all a little *immature*, but while I have been guilty of *juvenile* behavior from time to time, he is downright *childish*.] *Juvenile* indicates behavior typical of a young person nearing adulthood, and thus may suggest intemperance, extremism, laziness, excessive zeal or idealism, or thoughtless inconsiderateness: a *juvenile* inability to compromise; a *juvenile* habit of seeing everything in black and white; *juvenile* snap judgments. In recent usage, *immature* has become a fad word for any failing in rationality or lack of understanding in group relations. As such it would be inclusive of behavior suggested by *childish* or *juvenile*, except that overuse has made it milder sounding, since almost any failing can be considered *immature*: an *immature* wish to get divorced at the first sign of friction; an *immature* dependence on others for his opinions. Also, the word might specifically refer to behavior that falls short of that appropriate to a person's chronological age: *immature* of him to go off courting as though he were still a young man.

Infantile and **puerile** are the most disapproving of all these words. From their construction, both might be thought capable of neutral description, but *puerile* is almost never used in this way, and *infantile* only when used as a technical word; even in such contexts *infant* is often preferred: *infantile* paralysis; *infantile* (or *infant*) behavior. Similarly one would refer to a boy's *boyhood* (not *puerile*) dreams. *Infantile*, when applied to other than infants, is in fact an intensification of *childish* and suggests complete self-absorption and helplessness: his wife's *infantile* tantrums. The most formal of these words, *puerile* is also more vague in its condemnation. It can suggest anything callow, weak, stupid, or inept. At its most vague, it can mean simply worthless: *puerile* efforts to negotiate; the pianist's *puerile* performance. See GULLI-BLE.

Antonyms: experienced, MATURE, *sophisticated.*

Choose, pick, and **select** mean to take one or more from a number of things available — usually a matter of preference. They may be used as exact synonyms: a man buying a lawn mower *chooses* (or *picks* or *selects*) the one best suited to his needs. However, these words have separate shades of meaning that may make one or another of them more appropriate in a particular context. In the word *choose*, for example, the emphasis is on the act of will exercised in making the decision and, sometimes, on the finality of the decision. When we say that a young man *chooses* a career, we imply that he is making a voluntary decision and that he will probably pursue that career for the rest of his working life. To *select* is to *choose* from several things (we *choose*, never *select*, one of two alternatives), and it suggests discrimination and a careful weighing of the reasons for the choice: At the beginning of the trail, a great deal of time was spent *selecting* the jurors. *Pick* is less precise in meaning than the other two words and can be used to cover situations in which neither decision-making nor discrimination is required: A housewife in a supermarket, confronted by twenty cans of tomatoes of identical size and quality, will often *pick* the one nearest to her.

Elect usually connotes choosing from a limited number of alternatives. In its usual sense, it means to *choose* a person for office by a majority or plurality of votes. [The high-school class *elected* him treasurer; The American people *elect* a president every four years.]

Cull means to *pick* the good from the bad or, conversely, the bad from the good: A chef who is about to cook dried beans usually *culls* them first to remove discolored beans. See DECIDE, DISCRIMINATE.

Antonyms: FORSWEAR, REJECT.

These words indicate a roundabout way of expressing ideas or of referring to something. **Circumlocution**, derived from Latin roots that mean speaking around, is quite formal. **Periphrasis**, derived from comparable Greek roots, is even more formal and more technical in tone. Both pertain to the substitution of lengthy phraseology for more simple expressions: the *circumlocutions* of a candidate who wished to win friends on both sides of every issue; judicial rulings that are clogged with *periphrasis*, peppered with whereases, and understandable by no one. *Circumlocution*, being slightly more common, has gathered more connotations to it; the word can suggest the avoidance of direct statement out of squeamishness, insincerity, self-interest, or a misplaced desire for elegance: the emphasis of diplomatic protocol on its own strange set of polite *circumlocutions*. *Periphrasis*, by contrast, is more restricted to a grammatical context and is perhaps more neutral in simply indicating the choice of a longer rather than a shorter expression of comparable function. "In order to" is sometimes a needless *periphrasis* for "to."

choose

cull
elect
pick
select

circumlocution

euphemism
euphuism
indirectness
periphrasis

Indirectness, of course, is a much less formal, much more general, and much clearer synonym for the previous pair of words. It refers to the avoidance of simple or forceful expressions for whatever reason: an *indirectness* of style that stems from his reliance on the passive voice and his constant reference to himself as "one." By contrast, **euphuism** is highly specific. This word comes from the name of a literary character, *Euphues*, subject of two Elizabethan works of fiction by John Lyly. It refers to a ridiculous straining after an elegant prose style by clothing a paucity of thought in orotund parallelisms, flowery similes, and other verbal frills.

Euphemism, sometimes confused with *euphuism*, comes from Greek roots meaning to speak well. It refers to a specific tendency in speech or writing which involves the substituting of a mild, inexact, or technical-sounding term for a more forceful, clear, or blunt term when the latter is thought capable of giving offense. *Euphemisms* are commonly substituted for words pertaining to parts of the body, death, sex, and bodily functions. "Limb" was a Victorian *euphemism* for "leg." Some use the *euphemism* "pass away" instead of saying "die." "The departed" is often used as a *euphemism* for "the dead." See TALKATIVE, VERBOSE.

Antonyms: brevity, conciseness, condensation, directness, succinctness, terseness.

circumscribe

bound
contain
encircle
enclose
encompass
envelop
surround

These words refer to something that lies on all or many sides of something else. **Circumscribe** is the most formal of these words but the most precise in reference, specifically indicating the drawing of a line around a plane figure so as to touch as many points of the figure as possible: a square *circumscribed* by a circle. Used to describe geographical situations, it need not adhere to this strict geometrical definition, but it still suggests something hedged in on all sides: a small country completely *circumscribed* by mountains. In other uses, the point of the word is an emphasis on the restriction of something within set limits: severely *circumscribing* the freedom to dissent in time of war. **Encompass** means to take in or embrace. Like *circumscribe*, it may refer to a line drawn around a figure, but it more particularly indicates something set within a circle. It may, furthermore, suggest a setting of limits, but it more often implies a measuring of natural capacities: a view that *encompassed* the whole of the campus; a mind that could *encompass* only a few obvious truths; an erudition that *encompassed* amazing expanses of abstruse knowledge.

Bound almost exclusively pertains to the setting of limits found in *circumscribe*. It may not, however, necessarily suggest a total hedging in on all sides by the same medium: a city accessible to motorists from the North, although *bounded* on the South and East by jungle, and on the West by desert. **Surround**, by contrast, suggests something hedged in on all sides by the same thing, and thus it might be thought a more informal substitute for *circumscribe*. *Surround*, however, very often emphasizes an undesirable, hostile, or dangerous *circumscribing*: a cabin *surrounded* by the wilderness; decimated troops *surrounded* by Indians; watching the wolves *surround* the injured elk. The word can, of course, be used without negative implications: *surrounded* by the smiling faces of his friends. **Encircle** is closest to *surround* in its generality, but it does specifically suggest a tighter cluster about a central object and most often indicates a deliberate grouping for a definite reason: Oppressed serfs throughout the *surrounding* countryside joined together to *encircle* the castle.

While the previous words suggest, in simplest terms, a two-dimensional *encircling*, the remaining words all may indicate a three-dimensional gathering of one thing about another. **Envelop** refers most strictly to such a situation. It suggests the total *surrounding* of something, especially by folds or layers, so as to cover up or obscure the thing within: a porcelain vase *enveloped* in cotton; an airplane *enveloped* in fog; He *enveloped* her in the folds of his cloak. In more metaphorical uses, it may refer to a pervasive atmosphere or a totally preoccupied state of mind: *enveloped* by a sense of warm, sleepy contentment. It may also have overtones of protectiveness or secrecy: the overarching love with which she *enveloped* her son; an episode *enveloped* in mystery. **Enclose** is similar to *envelop* except that the latter often suggests an amorphous material in which something else may become lost or blurred, whereas *enclose* may suggest a hollowed solid or anything especially designed to fit around something else: a clock *enclosed* by a glass bell. *Enclose* suggests specifically a difficulty of access and often carries overtones of imprisonment or protectiveness: radioactive substances *enclosed* in heavy lead containers; housewives *enclosed* in a world of drab routine; a sleeping child *enclosed* in its mother's arms. **Contain** may refer to the mere presence of one thing inside another: plants that *contain* potassium; the safe that *contained* the jewels. But it may more specifically suggest the resistance of the thing *contained*: measures that might *contain* the vandalism of the students. It has also become a recent fad word in the terminology of power politics: the deployment of missile bases to *contain* the aggressor. See BOUNDARY, CONFINE.

These words are concerned with the presentation of supporting evidence in discussion, analysis, or argument. **Cite** is a highly specific word, precisely directed to this concept. To *cite* an example is to bring it forward as proof or illustration of a point. *Cite* almost always suggests a backing up of assertions by authoritative investigation or knowledge, rather than a mere hazarding of guesses. In particular, *cite* often implies a collection or repository of sources or examples that any other investigator could easily go to for corroboration: The bibliography *cited* more than a hundred source books that the author had consulted. *Cite* may also suggest that a complete and detailed presentation of an argument is being given: to *cite* the reasons behind Roosevelt's abstention from war prior to the Japanese attack.

Of all these words, **refer** is the least definite in suggesting how much or how little corroborating evidence will be presented. A treatise might merely *refer* to well-known facts in passing, on the assumption that they will be familiar to everyone. On the other hand, especially in verbal discussions, *refer* may imply the looking up of authoritative information about the point in question: to *refer* to the dictionary; turning to the Bible in order to *refer* to the exact wording of a disputed quotation.

Adduce means to bring forward for proof or consideration, and may refer to an example, argument, or item of evidence. It suggests a succinct listing of the details that support a case, although each detail might be sketched rather than developed in full: *adducing* reasons why the United States should have entered the war in 1939. One might *refer* to definitive proof that the world is round, but one would have to be more specific in order to *adduce* the reasons why this is known to be true. In other instances, *adduce* may be closely synonymous with the other words in this set; but it is much more formal and may seem unduly erudite or stuffy in tone.

cite

adduce
quote
refer

Quote refers to an exact, word-for-word citation of one's sources. If one *cites* another person's arguments, one may be paraphrasing them. But if one claims to be *quoting* those arguments, then one is responsible for reproducing them exactly as they appear in the source. [The President had his aides pass out typescripts of his speech, since he was all too familiar with the inability of journalists to *quote* his remarks accurately.] See QUOTATION.

city

megalopolis
metropolis
suburb
town
village

All of these terms denote a geographically or politically defined area and the population it contains. A **city** is a municipality of the first class with definite boundaries and with various legal powers derived from a charter granted by the state. The ordinary **village**, which is thought of as being the smallest area in the group, is a collection of buildings in a rural district; the number of buildings and the population they house is more often than not a small one. A **town** is generally an area with a more considerable collection of buildings than a *village*. It is interesting to note that although one generally thinks in terms of area progression from *village* to *town* to *city*, a *city* need not necessarily be the largest unit in any given set of three. A *village*, for example, can be larger than either a *town* or *city*. Some large *villages* could, indeed, change their political status if the population of the *village* acceded to the legislative measures necessary for such a change. But, although incorporation of a *village* into a municipality gives the area certain rights and privileges, it can also carry with it certain liabilities, as, for example, a larger tax burden. Hence a potential *town* or *city* may maintain its unincorporated status and its designation as a *village*.

In conversation and informal prose, the distinction between *village*, *town*, and *city* is often overlooked. Small *towns* are often described as "lovely little *villages*." People ask "What *town* were you born in?" and one gives an answer without adding that the "*town*" is really a *city*. It is perhaps in instances like these that the connotation of the three words takes precedence over the denotation. *Villages* are thought of as small rural districts, *cities* as large metropolitan areas, and *towns* as the great bulk of communities in between.

When *towns* and *villages* are primarily residential areas adjacent to or close to a large city, they are known as **suburbs**. A single such *town* or *village* is a *suburb* or suburban community. The kind of *city* around which suburban communities spring up is often referred to as a **metropolis**. The *metropolis* might be a capital *city*, or a center of trade or culture. It is, in any event, one of the most important *cities* of the state or country in which it is located.

A word with which *metropolis* is sometimes confused because of sound and spelling is **megalopolis**. A *megalopolis* is an urban complex made up of several major *cities*. Such a complex is the one which is bounded by Boston on the north and Washington on the south, with New York as its center. *Megalopolis* is a Greek word which means great *city*. The Greek *megalopolis* was a large *city* with a population made up of people who moved there from surrounding *villages*.

claim

perquisite

These words are concerned with establishing ownership or possession of land, money, or other valuables. A **claim** may be an actual document that permits one to possess land formerly in the public domain — or it may be the land itself: a *claim* of only a few acres that seemed worthless until gold was discovered nearby. In a more general sense, a *claim* may be an assertion of one's legal or moral entitlement to something that is held, withheld, or owed to one by another: the drama coach who made a *claim* on the estate of the deceased actress; the Negro's *claim* to full equality; an injured workman's *claim* to compensation. **Title**, like *claim*, may also refer to an actual document that gives one possession of land or real estate. But unlike a *claim* that one may earn or come to possess by following a certain set of procedures, a *title* cannot usually be had except by purchase or inheritance. [The prospector staked, then filed, his *claim*; Her uncle's will gave her *title* to the town-house.]

A **perquisite** is now more often called a "fringe benefit." In any case, it is something that accrues to one as an added advantage of one's usual job or position: *perquisites* that included free room and board. It may suggest a monetary consideration in the form of a tip or bonus; and it may be specified in writing, as in a union contract, or may be simply an unwritten understanding between employer and employee.

A **right** is the most general of these terms and might substitute for any of them. In its narrowest sense, it may imply a legal proof of ownership, or a contractual agreement that has been put into writing. In its larger sense, it may refer to those things to which someone feels entitled without actually possessing them; such a *right* may be a moral, ethical, emotional, or tactical one: a *right* to ten percent of all proceeds from the book's sales; a child's *right* to love and understanding; the inalienable *rights* of life, liberty, and the pursuit of happiness. See RIGHT.

These words refer to attempts at removing confusion or making something understandable. **Clarify** usually pertains to words or actions that are introduced to make clear an earlier event, situation, statement, or state of affairs: a position paper released to *clarify* his voting record on past legislation; contradictory answers that he made no attempt to *clarify*; adding details to the sketch that would *clarify* the spatial relationships; a plot structure that needed *clarifying*. **Elucidate** is a more formal substitute for *clarify*. While the root of *clarify* refers literally to clearness, the root of *elucidate* refers to light. To *elucidate* something is to throw light on it. The word's use reflects this in indicating any enlightening process that puts an end to confusion: searching for the clues that would *elucidate* the mystery; psychological theories drawn up to *elucidate* human behavior. Thus *elucidate* in its very formality has a wider range of application than *clarify*. **Explicate** is more restricted and specific in use than the foregoing. It refers to a point-by-point discussion of a complex matter, especially as in the paraphrase and analysis of a literary text: asking each student to *explicate* the difficult poem; popular books that attempt to *explicate* Einstein's theories.

Explain and **interpret** are far less formal than the previous words and have wider ranges of use. A person may *explain* a thing by describing its form or structure, tracing its origins and development, showing its operation or use, or citing its reasons and the relations of its parts. Hence an expert might *elucidate* one detail of a complex matter without *explaining* the whole. In its most informal sense, *explain* suggests a verbal attempt to justify actions or to make them understood: trying to *explain* why he had stayed out so late. When it is closer in meaning to *elucidate*, it may suggest a total falling into place of a causal sequence: experiments designed to *explain* the mechanics of heredity; the discovery of several notes that *explained* his homicidal outburst. *Interpret* is like *explicate* in suggesting a point-by-point treatment of an earlier situation, pronouncement, or event so that it can be understood; it is like *elucidate* in implying the use of knowledge or insight to cast light on some baffling problem or puzzle, though it differs in stressing personal judgment or understanding: to *interpret* a symbolic dream; to *interpret* an obscure piece of writing. In a limited sense, *interpret* may refer to oral translation from one language to another: A skilled linguist was needed to *interpret* the statements of the visiting head of state. Less specifically, the word may imply any sort of after-the-fact analysis, in which case it may point to a less exhaustive or technical approach than *explicate*: a journalist who *interpreted* economic trends for the layman. See EXPLANATION, IN-FORM.

Antonyms: *becloud, bedim, befog, complicate,* CONFUSE, *obfuscate, obscure.*

class

caste
estate
order

These words, as here considered, refer to groupings in, or divisions of, a stratified society. **Class** is the most general word. It refers primarily to a social division of society, as the middle *class*; but a *class* may also be an economic division, as the working *class*; a functional division, as the managerial *class*; or a division embracing persons with other common characteristics, as the educated *class*. *Classes* are based on such things as lineage, income, and occupation. A **caste**, by contrast, is a strictly hereditary division of society — especially one of the four Hindu social *classes* in India. The highest of these is the Brahman, or priestly, *caste*. A member of the lowest *caste* was formerly called an untouchable, his touch having been counted as pollution by Hindus of higher station. A person is able to move from one *class* to another; but where a rigid *caste* system is in effect, he cannot escape from his *caste*.

An **estate** is a *class* of people with a distinct political or social status, having in common special duties, privileges, powers, or limitations with respect to government. An *estate* was originally one of the three *classes* of feudal society in Europe — the *Estates* of the Realm being the clergy, the nobility, and the common people. The political power of the press later caused the journalistic fraternity to be dubbed the fourth *estate*. In a general sense, *estate*, like *class*, may be used to indicate rank, position, or social standing: a lady of high *estate*. *Class* is also applied to things or services as a measure of quality: first-*class* as opposed to tourist-*class* accommodations.

In one sense, **order** is close to *class* in indicating a stratum of society or a cohesive social or professional group: the scorn of the aristocracy for the lower *orders*. Specifically, *order* often refers to the rank or position of an ordained Christian clergyman—a bishop being in the highest *order* of the ministry, a priest in the second, and a deacon in the third. In traditional angelology, *order* designates one of the nine grades or choirs of angels, which are, in ascending rank, angels, archangels, principalities, powers, virtues, dominations or dominions, thrones, cherubim, and seraphim. *Order* may also refer to an honorary society to which members are named by a sovereign as a mark of the highest distinction: The *Order* of the Garter is the highest *order* of knighthood in Great Britain. See CLUB, POSITION (rank).

clean

cleanse
dust

These words refer to the removing of dirt, disorder, or unwanted matter. **Clean** is the most general of these, referring to any methods whatever by which something is freed of grime, refurbished, or made pure: *cleaning* her nails with a fingernail file; *cleaning* the mud from his boots with a brush; *cleaning* the cutting board with soap and water; a machine to *clean* and recirculate the air. **Cleanse**, when substituted for *clean* in any of these examples, gives an odd or inappropriately formal tone.

In other uses, it may suggest an especially thorough *cleaning* or immersion in water. At its most specific, it indicates a careful bathing action: *cleansing* the wound of infected matter. It is also appropriately used metaphorically when *clean* might be ludicrous or too concrete: *cleansing* the administration of graft and corruption; the breaking through of sunlight to *cleanse* the day of its sullen shadows. The word also has special pertinence with reference to the removal of pollution or the washing away of evil or sin: *cleansing* our rivers of poisonous wastes; *cleansing* the soul of every impure thought.

The remaining words concentrate, more mundanely, on some specific aspect inherent in the general suggestions of *clean*. **Dust**, most specifically, suggests rubbing, brushing, or swabbing to free a surface of loosely accumulated particles: *dusting* the furniture with an oily cloth. **Sweep** suggests the same action done specifically with a broom, usually to clean floors of loose dirt: *sweeping* up the sawdust; *sweeping* out the kitchen. **Wipe** specifically suggests a light rubbing or swabbing action, sometimes involving a cloth or rag that may or may not be moistened with water or a cleanser: *wiping* the dishes with a dry towel; *wiping* down the steps with a soapy rag; *wiping* the sweat from his forehead. **Tidy** suggests the removal of disorder by returning things to their proper place: offering to *tidy* up after the party. When a housewife *cleans* house, she scrubs, mops, *sweeps*, and *dusts*, and also *tidies* up. But *tidy*, in contrast to *clean*, may sound overly coy or precious in some contexts: going to the powder room to *tidy* up. See ORDERLY.

Antonyms: befoul, besmear, POLLUTE, SOIL, stain.

These words refer to anything that is unsoiled by use or neglect or that is untainted by dirt or grime. **Clean** emphasizes freedom from dirt, grime, or stain. A thing may be *clean* because it is new, unused, or unmarked: a *clean* sheet of paper. More often, the word suggests that something has been freed of soil or the marks of use in order to be used again: *clean* dishes; *clean* sheets. Less concretely, *clean* can refer to an absence of fault or failing which combines in some uses with its reference to the absence of marks, implying a place where faults might otherwise be marked down in a list: a *clean* slate; a *clean* record. The word's implications of purity further extend to the moral sense, referring to that which is innocent, especially of sexual impropriety: a *clean* mind; *clean* jokes. *Clean* can, however, refer simply to what is well-meaning and harmless: good *clean* fun.

Fresh is often used in apposition with *clean* to emphasize newness or lack of use as well as purity: *fresh, clean* snow; a *fresh, clean* shirt. It may also suggest something revivifying in its purity: *fresh* air. Used in reference to failings, it suggests, not an absence of faults, but the putting aside of past mistakes: a *fresh* start; *fresh* approaches. **Spotless** refers to an actual absence of marks or blemishes. It is, however, more emphatic than *clean*, and carries implications of neatness and tidiness as well: a *spotless* room. Otherwise, the word may simply be a hyperbolic substitute for *clean*, though it may differ in describing something never sullied: a *spotless* record.

Stainless may be used in a way closely resembling *spotless*. Much more often now, however, it indicates something that cannot be stained, especially something designed with this quality in mind: *stainless* steel dinnerware. In this sense, something that is *stainless* need not necessarily be *clean*. **Immaculate**, the most formal of these words, can function like *spotless* as a hyperbole for *clean* in all situations: an *immaculate*

clean
(continued)

sweep
tidy
wipe

clean

fresh
immaculate
spotless
stainless

suit. On this level, it reflects its Latin root which means literally without spot. But the word also has a wider range of application to moral propriety and is particularly relevant in a religious context, meaning sinless: hermits who strove to lead *immaculate* lives. The doctrine of the *Immaculate* Conception holds that the Virgin Mary was conceived untainted by original sin. See CHASTE, INNOCENT, PERFECT, SANITARY.

Antonyms: *adulterated, contaminated,* DIRTY, *grimy, impure, marked, polluted, stained, sullied, tainted.*

clear

definite
distinct
unmistakable

These words refer to something that stands out in vivid or sharp relief from its surroundings. **Clear** is the most general and informal of these words. It suggests something that is not the least bit confused, vague, or fuzzy and therefore easy to understand or perceive: *clear* directions on how to reach the resort; the *clear* lettering of the handmade poster. Where *clear* may emphasize lack of confusion or ambiguity, **distinct** is restricted to sharpness of impression or lack of blur: instructions that were *clear* enough if only she had spoken in a more *distinct* voice. *Distinct* can also suggest well-defined outlines: the right focus for getting a *distinct* image. Or it can suggest something that stands out noticeably: the *distinct* note of annoyance in her voice.

Definite relates to the lack of ambiguity implied by *clear* and to the sharpness of outline or impression implied by *distinct*: setting up *definite* rules of procedure; a *definite* litmus reaction that proved the presence of acidity. **Unmistakable** intensifies the implication of *distinct* and suggests a noticeable forcefulness not to be overlooked; the word emphasizes the presence of evidence that removes all possibility for doubt: an *unmistakable* nod of her head; the *unmistakable* wail of a siren. See DEFINITE, SPECIFIC, SURE.

Antonyms: *blurred, confused,* DOUBTFUL, FOGGY, *fuzzy, muddled,* OBSCURE, *unclear, unintelligible,* VAGUE.

clergyman

cleric
divine
ecclesiastic
prelate
religious
theologian

These words refer to those members of a religion that are set apart from its ordinary followers either by the responsibilities of leadership or by other duties. **Clergyman** is the generic term for all men set apart in this way; it applies equally well to leaders of Catholic, Protestant, and Jewish faiths: cardinals, bishops, and other *clergymen* who met at the Second Vatican Ecumenical Council in Rome; a conference of Lutheran, Presbyterian, and Methodist *clergymen*; a study group composed of Jewish seminarians and *clergymen*. Just as clergy contrasts with laity, so *clergyman* contrasts with layman to distinguish authorized leaders from ordinary members: a closer relationship between *clergymen* and laymen. In Christian faiths, the word more specifically indicates someone set apart by ordination, someone who is regularly authorized to preach the gospel and administer sacraments; in addition, it can include in Catholic, Orthodox, and Anglican usage anyone who lives in holy orders: priests, monks, and other *clergymen*. At its most general, *clergyman* may be applied to the leaders of other religions at least when no more appropriate term from that religion suggests itself: Buddhist *clergymen*.

Cleric may refer, like *clergyman*, to any member of the clergy, but its use is restricted to the more ritualized or hierarchic faiths. Most specifically it refers to someone distinguished by a tonsure, although it now can suggest any *clergyman* whose ordination is symbolized by clothing markedly different from that of a layman: a procession of *clerics* in their colorful regalia. Unlike *clergyman*, *cleric* may sometimes give a contemptuous tone when used in criticism, not so much of a church itself, but of church leaders regarded as corrupt: *clerics* who flout their duties and ignore the needs of the faithful.

Theologian represents a much more specific concept, referring to anyone who formulates or clarifies the doctrines and thinking of a religion; the word may occasionally be applied to members of other than the Western religions: the Hindu *theologian* Shankara. In any case, the word suggests a learned, philosophical, or well-reasoned approach. Theoretically, *theologian* can apply to anyone accomplished in such technical discussion, male or female, *clergyman* or layman. In practice, a *theologian* has most often been a *clergyman* of the religion his thinking deals with: the Jewish *theologian* Maimonides who influenced the thought of St. Thomas Aquinas. While the word suggests an official or orthodox approach, this is not always necessarily implied in practice: the *theologian* Arius whose doctrines were declared heretical in the fourth century A.D.; recent *theologians* who formulated the controversial "God-is-dead" theory. While **divine** may refer in a general way to a *clergyman*, particularly one highly placed, the word at its most specific refers to a *theologian* whose doctrines are accepted and honored by his religion: church *divines* of the early centuries whose main task was to combat such heresies as Arianism and Manicheanism.

Ecclesiastic refers to any *clergyman* in a church with an emphasis on a clergy arranged in a ranked and structured hierarchy, thus applying particularly to Catholic, Orthodox, and such Protestant churches as the Anglican: an *ecclesiastic* in the Church of England. **Prelate** more specifically refers to an *ecclesiastic* of superior rank and authority, as a bishop or cardinal, or to a dignitary of a particular church. This word, even more than *cleric*, can be given a negative ring by someone critical of the clergy: *prelates* who grow fat and rich while the people starve.

While **religious** is restricted in reference to someone living in holy orders, usually in the context of the more formalized faiths, the word is unique here in that it applies equally well both to a man or woman in such orders: a girl who wished to become a *religious* and retire to the sheltered life of the convent. [Not always mandatory for parish priests, celibacy nevertheless was always in force for the *religious*, both monks and nuns.] See MINISTER.

Upward movement is indicated by all these words. **Climb** suggests most strongly a laborious or tortuous moving upward: the men who *climbed* Everest; a car slowly *climbing* the steep hill; an erratic market *climbing* to new highs; the airplane *climbing* to get above the cloudbank. **Scale** is closely related to *climb* in suggesting effort-filled upward movement, but it is more often restricted to the actual physical effort required for someone to surmount an obstacle. It also suggests a skillful dexterity or thoughtful effort: those who would *scale* the heights; *scaling* the wall to get word to his compatriots. **Mount** relates to *scale* and *climb* in that it can suggest a step-by-step process: slowly *mounting* the look-out point for a view of the bay; *mounting* the stairs. By contrast, it can suggest upward movement by a single leap or by an increase in the volume of something: *mounting* his horse; tidewater slowly *mounting* the sloping beach.

Ascend and **rise**, unlike the foregoing, need not suggest laborious movement up an incline, but may refer instead to perpendicular movement through water or air: the moon *ascending* a cloudless sky; smoke *rising* from chimneys. *Ascend*, when it is used for movement up an

climb

ascend
mount
rise
scale

incline, is more formal and less vivid than *climb*: *ascending* the steep
face of the mountain. In metaphorical uses, the word can affect a
religious or spiritual overtone: a prayer for peace *ascending* from the
hearts of all men. *Rise* is even less colorful than *ascend*; because of its
openness to implications provided by context, it has a wide range of
abstract uses: if prices *rise*. See ARISE.

    Antonyms: DESCEND, *fall*.

clique

circle
coterie
group
set

These words refer to a small cluster of friends that excludes outsiders
and confers status on those who belong. Of these, **clique** is the most
pejorative in tone and points to the fewest members. It also most
strongly suggests both secrecy and snobbishness; in its quasi-official
rigidity, in fact, it may all but resemble a social club: a clearly defined
clique of teen-age girls who set style and fashion for their whole high
school; a *clique* of conservative officers within the War Ministry. No
person would describe his closest friends and himself as a *clique* — except
to disparage them and himself. **Circle**, by contrast, carries no pejorative
judgment and could be used descriptively either by an outsider or by a
member of a social cluster: a *circle* of impressionist painters in the 1890's;
my *circle* of friends. The word implies less intimacy than *clique*, but does
suggest mutuality of interests, frequency of gathering, and, possibly,
decorous civility carried out on a more formal social scale than *clique*:
Mme. de Staël and her *circle* of intelligentsia.

    Coterie, although more formal than either, more closely resembles
clique than *circle*. It is not necessarily so pejorative as *clique*, however,
and points to a larger cluster of friends with perhaps wider interests, less
exclusive status, and with the possibility of greater social fluidity. While
every member of a *clique* or *circle*, for example, would be well acquainted
with every other member, the members of a *coterie* might be more on a
more personal or familiar basis. Also, a *clique* or *circle* might point more
strictly to sociability as a motivating factor, while *coterie* may more often
suggest some uniting ideal or purpose beyond mere camaraderie: the
coterie of Fabian socialists whose ideals were ultimately embodied in the
Labor Party.

    Group and **set** are much less restricted in meaning than these other
words. *Group*, when referring to social clusters, may range in suggestiveness from the intense intimacy of *clique* to a much vaguer casualness that
includes all the friends and acquaintances one happens to have: my
group at college; a *group* of young mothers who met in the park over
their baby carriages. *Set* indicates a much larger *group* of members than
any of these other words; while it may be used pejoratively to point to
snobbishness, like *clique*, it may be used more neutrally to indicate a
particular social *group* that can be classified as to status and similar
interests. Where *clique* all but suggests a club, *set* all but implies a class
or caste of people. Most important, members of a *set* need not even know
each other: modish dress that obviously indicated they were members
of the fast-living, world-traveling jet *set*. *Set*, used of a smaller *group*, is
even more emphatic about status, although this need not approach the
snobbishness implicit in *clique*: falling in with a *set* of young executives
who spend their weekends in the Hamptons. See CLUB.

club

association

These words all apply to organized groups of people or things. A **club**
suggests intimacy and informality as well as good fellowship. *Clubs* may
be designed for a variety of purposes, but social *clubs* are usually of an
exclusive nature; membership depends upon the personal judgment,

feelings, or prejudices of the established members rather than upon any objective qualification. Political *clubs*, of course, are less exclusive, but the payment of dues and the attendance of periodic meetings of a more or less social nature characterize all *clubs*. The word *club* has lately become popular in commercial enterprises because of its pleasant connotations of comfort, relaxation, and fellowship; thus we find it used in *book club*, which is simply an **association** of potential book buyers for the purpose of obtaining a limited number of books at reduced prices. *Association*, then, applies to more formal and businesslike relationships that may obtain between organizations as well as individuals: the American Automobile *Association*; the American *Association* of University Professors; an *association* of law schools.

Federation applies especially to a cooperative organization of states or semi-independent groups for a specific, mutual purpose, as to conduct foreign affairs, or, as in the case of the American *Federation* of Labor, to strengthen the bargaining position of each of its member **unions**. The most common sense of *union* refers to the labor *union*, an organization of workers that represents the collective interest of its members in dealing with their employer. In another sense *union* is close to **league**. A *union* or *league* is a combining of forces for some common end: the American Civil Liberties *Union*; the *League* of Nations. But *union* sometimes signifies a closer and more enduring relationship than *league*: The United States is often called the *Union*.

Fraternity may refer to a fraternal society such as the Freemasons or to a Greek-letter *fraternity* of college students. The latter are usually social and are run very much like *clubs*; but some *fraternities* are devoted to service, and others, like Phi Beta Kappa, have an intellectual basis for membership. A **lodge** is a local branch of a secret or fraternal society. **Order** denotes a society with common aims and obligations, as a fraternal *order* or a religious *order*: The *Order* of the Odd Fellows; the Masonic *order*; the Franciscan *order*. A religious *order* is an organization of monks, nuns, or priests who have taken vows pledging themselves to live under a certain discipline or to perform certain social or religious duties. See CLIQUE.

These words refer to actions lacking in skill or grace or to the faulty results of such actions. **Clumsy** indicates halting or imprecise movement, a propensity for making mistakes, or to results that reflect these things: a *clumsy* walk; her *clumsy* attempt to match the colors of the original; a *clumsy* sweep of his hand that sent the vase toppling; the *clumsy* dialogue of the play. While the defects suggested by *clumsy* result from lack of muscular coordination, skill, talent, or training, **awkward** suggests similar but less serious defects that stem from misproportion or more especially from an unnerved state of mind: an *awkward* build; an *awkward* grammatical construction; a mutual suspicion that made for *awkward* silences in their talk; shyness that left her flustered and *awkward*. [One student's work is sensitive but still *awkward*; the others are without exception hopelessly *clumsy*.] **Bungling** specifically stresses a propensity for making mistakes, and to an even greater degree than is true for *clumsy*. It also focuses on the inexpert handling of delicate matters rather than a *clumsy* physical carriage: his *bungling* mismanagement of the whole affair. Similarly, **inept** refers less to physical movement than to an abject and total failure to accomplish a desired result: a completely *inept* attempt at humor; an *inept* movie.

club
(continued)

federation
fraternity
league
lodge
order
union

clumsy

awkward
bungling
gawky
inept
lumbering
ungainly

Ungainly specifically suggests a lack of grace that may or may not result, like *awkward*, from some innate misproportion: an *ungainly* attempt to retrieve the fallen napkin; an *ungainly* body incapable of agile movement. **Gawky** is much more emphatic about the physical basis for *awkward* or *ungainly* action; it may specifically suggest long, thin, or attenuated limbs: the usual *gawky* adolescent. **Lumbering**, by contrast, suggests ungraceful physical misproportion that stems from an overly heavy or outsized build: the big brute who *lumbered* after me down the stairs; the slow pace of the *lumbering* play. See GAUCHE.

Antonyms: adroit, clever, dexterous, graceful, handy, skillful, sure.

clutter

chaos
confusion
disarray
disorder

All these words mean a lack of order and arrangement. **Clutter** implies that objects are jumbled together in heaps, while **disorder** means that they are not in their normal places. *Clutter* emphasizes the miscellaneous or various nature of the mess, whereas *disorder* points to the lack of proper arrangement of the individual objects, and thus usually refers to spatial relationships within an area. [Finding a particular book amidst the *clutter* of papers and books on his desk was indeed a challenge; to find a rare clock in the *clutter* of an antique shop; Burglars left the apartment in a state of *disorder* — the contents of every bureau and desk drawer scattered about the floors.] *Disorder* may of course refer to any lack of order: riots and civil *disorder*. **Disarray** refers specifically to the lack of orderly arrangement, and may apply to people, especially if usually in a disciplined arrangement, as well as to things. [The troops retreated in *disarray*; The office, usually so neat, was in complete *disarray* after we moved.] *Disarray* may also be used of one's clothing or person. [Her hair was in *disarray*; Jarred and shaken from his fall, he began to adjust his clothing, which was in a state of *disarray*.] *Disarray* is a rather formal or literary word and would be out of place in any informal context; it is seldom used in speech.

Confusion, as here considered, suggests that things are so disordered that it is difficult to identify the individual objects in the general *clutter*: Burglars left things scattered in such *confusion* that it was days before we knew what had been stolen. **Chaos** implies both extreme *disorder* and nearly total *confusion*: After the bombing attack, the city was in a state of *chaos*. See JUMBLE.

Antonyms: METHOD, *neatness, order,* SEQUENCE.

coincide

agree
correspond
jibe
tally

These words all refer to close similarity in relationship between separate things. **Coincide, correspond,** and **tally** are related in their application to two or more things that conform to one another or share certain characteristics. *Coincide* means to conform exactly — to have identical elements. [The birthdays of twins usually *coincide*; It is fortunate when a young man's career goals and the wishes of his parents for him *coincide*.] To *correspond* is to have comparable elements. A national dish may *correspond* to one in the cuisine of another culture; evidence given in court should *correspond* with the facts in the case. *Tally* means to *correspond* in the sense of being consistent with. [The calculations of two scientists working on the same problem *tallied* exactly; Saying that the earth is flat does not *tally* with scientific observations.] **Jibe** is a colloquial term which, like *tally*, emphasizes the accordance or consistency of facts, elements, relations, etc.: His version of the accident should *jibe* with that of the other witnesses. *Jibe* thus points to fitting into an overall consistent pattern rather than a point-by-point correspondence between two separate things.

Agree is the most general word in this list, and in this context stresses the sharing of like characteristics, attitudes, or elements. It can be used in place of each of the other words in this list in many constructions. [His version of the accident should *agree* (*jibe, correspond*) with that of the other witnesses; plans *agree* (or *coincide*); figures *agree* (or *tally*)] *Agree* can indicate any degree of likeness, from a slight similarity to virtual identity. See ADAPT.

Antonyms: CONTRADICT, DISAGREE.

These words refer to a relatively low temperature or to an unexcited, disconcerted, or unfriendly attitude. In reference to temperature, **cold** may refer to something desirably low-key: a *cold* drink on a hot day. Aside from this situation, however, the word more often connotes an unpleasantly low temperature: *cold* weather; a *cold* wind; numbed through in the *cold* rooms. **Frigid** and **frosty** are intensifications of *cold*, specifically referring to a temperature below freezing. *Frigid* factually stresses something that has been frozen solid or a temperature permitting this: *frigid* cuts of meat in the freezer; a week of absolutely *frigid* weather. *Frosty* may suggest a slightly warmer temperature, one at which frost first begins to form or breath vapor can be seen: windows turning *frosty* overnight; *frosty* winter gales. Like *frigid*, **gelid** and **icy** imply a temperature *cold* enough to result in the production of ice: a *gelid* mass of hailstones; a clear but *icy* day. *Icy* may also be merely a hyperbole for *cold*: *icy* waters.

In reference to temperature, **cool** often suggests something pleasant or mildly low-key: a heat wave followed by *cool* weather; a winter that was *cool* but not *cold*; moving from the direct sun into the *cool* shade. **Chilled** refers to someone who has become *cold* or something that has been caused to turn *cool*: *chilled* to the bone; *chilled* wine. **Chilly**, by contrast, refers more often to air or weather midway between *cool* and *cold*: a *chilly* autumn wind; a *chilly* house. The word, in fact, may suggest an erratic coming and going of *cold* winds: *chilly* gusts.

When these words refer to emotional states, their interrelations differ. *Cold* may refer to an unresponsive attitude or, more drastically, to hostility: a book he remained *cold* to from beginning to end; giving him a *cold* look. In their greater intensity, *frosty* and *icy* usually stress the hostility implicit in *cold*: replying to her with *frosty* disdain; moving with an *icy* anger. *Frigid*, however, is now so often used specifically of sexual unresponsiveness in women that it may sound odd or comic in any other emotional context: psychotherapy for the *frigid* woman.

Cool suggests reserve based on shyness, lack of enthusiasm, or disapproval: a *cool* response to all his proposals; curt answers filled with a *cool* contempt. The word may also suggest an ability to remain objective or impartial or to avoid anger or panic: sorting out the arguments with a *cool* objectivity; keeping a *cool* head during the crisis. *Chilly* suggests manners that are stand-offish or openly hostile: bidding a *chilly* goodnight to the guests who had overstayed. *Chilled*, by contrast, pertains mostly to a discouraged or horrified reaction to something else: *chilled* to see our dwindling store of ammunition; *chilled* to see a trail of blood leading into the bedroom.

Gelid has a rather literary tone and connotes the kind of *cold* numbness produced by unfriendliness, hostility, fear, or horror: nervous laughter that turned into *gelid* silence when she realized his murderous intent. See ALOOF, DISTANT, IMPERTURBABLE.

Antonyms: *balmy*, HOT, PASSIONATE, WARM.

cold

chilled
chilly
cool
frigid
frosty
gelid
icy

color

dye
paint
stain
tinge
tint

All these words mean to impart color to something. To **color** is the most general of these words, and stipulates neither the extent of the process nor the materials used nor the object *colored*.

To **dye** means to permanently change the color of something, as fabric or hair, by impregnating it with a *coloring* agent: to *dye* a white dress red by soaking it for several hours in a *dyeing* solution.

To **stain** means either to *color* an object chemically, as to *stain* wood, or to impart to an object a color foreign to it through use, negligence, or the like, as to *stain* one's clothing with spilled soup.

To **paint** is to apply color to an object or a surface for the purpose of decorating it, as to *paint* a chair or a wall. The substance used in *painting* is usually a durable one that preserves as well as decorates.

To **tint** and to **tinge** mean to *color* something slightly. To *tint* is to impart a light or pastel color for decorative purposes; to *tinge* is to modify the basic color of something slightly or superficially, as to *tinge* ivory yellow by frequent handling. See DISCOLOR.

Antonyms: bleach.

combustible

burnable
flammable
inflammable

These words are all used to describe material that can catch fire. **Combustible** is the most formal term here and also the most neutral in simply denoting material that will burn easily: *Combustible* building materials such as laths are slowly being replaced by such noncombustible materials as asbestos plasterboard.

Burnable is at the other end of the scale from *combustible* in its relaxed, almost slangy tone. It is also less neutral in pointing to a desired or desirable quality: Cub Scouts scouring the woods for every *burnable* stick of firewood.

Inflammable and **flammable** are identical in meaning and are frequently used as warning signs to label hazardous materials that may result in unwanted fires unless handled with caution: Highly *combustible* substances such as confetti must not be shipped without *"flammable"* clearly written across the carton. Recently, *flammable* has almost completely replaced *inflammable* as the word of warning, primarily because too many people confused *inflammable* with its opposite, nonflammable. See BURN.

Antonyms: incombustible, nonflammable.

come

arrive
gain
reach

These words refer to movement toward a goal. **Come** is the most informal and general of these words. Its emphasis is on movement toward the observer or movement seen from the perspective of the intended or likely goal: the man *coming* toward me; trains *coming* into and leaving the station. The word can indicate the actual appearance of something at the goal, but it can also indicate mere movement toward something without suggesting that it is or will be achieved: He was *coming* home from work when the accident occurred.

With the remaining words, there is no suggestion of movement either toward or away from the observer. In contrast to *come*, **arrive** stresses the actual achievement of a goal: If he were *coming*, he would have *arrived* by now — unless something happened to him along the way. The word is otherwise neutral in its overtones, suggesting in itself neither ease nor effort of movement. At its most neutral, **reach** can suggest a midway point or stop in an ongoing movement: having *reached* the third chapter before realizing what the author was getting at; hoping to *reach* Milan by nightfall and Venice the next day. When the word applies to the achievement of a final goal, however, it often suggests the culmination of a slow, painstaking, or methodical process: *reaching* the summit of Everest after years of planning and countless failures. At any rate, the word can suggest more effort than *arrive* or possibly the working through of a devious or uncertain course: *reaching* the address after picking his way through a maze of sinuous streets. **Gain** intensifies the implications of effort inherent in *reach*. Successful struggle against odds or in the face of peril or uncertainty can be suggested by the word: *gaining* the embattled city after heavy casualties. Often, the word specifically suggests upward movement: *gaining* a precarious perch from which to view the parade. See REACH.

Antonyms: GO, LEAVE.

comfort

ease
leisure
relaxation
relief
repose
rest

These words refer to a feeling or situation of pleasurable serenity. **Comfort** suggests the possession of complete peace of mind and physical contentment, either through the satisfaction of all needs and desires or through the elimination of anything unpleasant or disturbing: airlines that vie with each other over details of passenger *comfort*; prescribing a pill that would allow him to sleep in *comfort*; beachgoers seeking *comfort* from the heat wave. **Relief** is specifically restricted to this last possibility of *comfort*, stressing the removal of unpleasant or painful stimuli. Even here, *relief* is more restricted to expressing the mere absence of negative elements, whereas *comfort* might suggest replacing them with something positive: a medication for *relief* of sunburn; finding *relief* from his doubts but little *comfort* in the new doctrine.

Ease and **relaxation** refer exclusively to positive states and so relate to a side of *comfort* in contrast to simple *relief*. *Ease* has the widest range of any of these words, referring to things that make for contentment, like *comfort*, but going beyond this word to suggest utter naturalness, lack of tension, or profound mental and physical peacefulness: taking our *ease* in the cool of the garden; the *ease* with which she made the arrangements; a smile that put us immediately at *ease*; never having felt so full of *ease* in his life. *Relaxation* is much more limited in reference than *ease*; it refers particularly to a state of freedom from or dwindling away of tension: a secluded corner where he could work with complete *relaxation*; a *relaxation* of hostilities; arm muscles paired in a continual opposition of tension and *relaxation*. The word also has a special informal use to pertain to recreation: asking him what he did for *relaxation*. **Leisure** is the most restricted of these words in relating exclusively to this last use of *relaxation*. *Leisure* refers, most specifically, to one's free time after work, regardless of how the time is spent: having the *leisure* to pursue a new hobby; executives who carry office tensions to the *leisure* of the golf course.

Rest and **repose** are an intensification of possibilities for *ease*, suggesting an extreme peacefulness and a quiescence approaching sleep. *Rest*, in fact, may be used synonymously with sleep, or as a group word to include both waking and sleeping *relaxation*: recommending plenty of *rest* for the patient following the operation. As this example shows, *rest* may be used like *relief* to suggest a restorative process. *Repose* is the most formal of these words here and gives a lyrical tone. It suggests an utter stillness or lack of movement, implying a complete cessation of both desire and tension. Where *relaxation* can suggest a noisy letting off of steam, *repose* always suggests a profound quiet, as of contemplation: a *repose* so deep that he didn't hear the conductor asking for his ticket; the town's old-world sense of decorum and *repose*. See RETIRE.

Antonyms: agitation, nervousness, restlessness, unrest.

comfortable

cozy
restful
snug

These words mean feeling or conducing to a feeling of contentment, relief, or well-being. **Comfortable** is the most general word in the group and can apply to a variety of personal feelings and to anything that contributes to those feelings. [I feel very *comfortable* in this chair; The house is not *comfortable* tonight because our air conditioner is not working; He makes no more than a barely *comfortable* income; The patient complained that he had not spent a *comfortable* night.]

Cozy and **snug** are suggestive of the kind of comfort that comes from warmth, a compact shelter, security, and an easy friendliness: to spend a *cozy* evening in front of a fireplace; a *snug* summer house that's just big enough, and isn't too much of a housekeeping burden for my wife; a *snug* job that keeps his family well provided for; a *cozy* dinner party with a few dear old friends.

Restful implies the comfort that comes from being quiet, at rest, or in repose. It also describes anything that induces such comfort. [It was *restful* to sit on the beach, watching and listening to the gentle lapping of the waves; The marketplace was strangely *restful* at night since no one lived there even though thousands worked in it by day.] See CONTENTED, PLEASING.

Antonyms: DISMAL, *uncomfortable.*

command

direction
directive
injunction
instruction
order

These words pertain either to an authoritative statement that someone is to do something or to the giving of knowledgeable advice or guidance. **Command** and **order** are the least formal of these words referring to the stated demand of a superior. Of these, *command* is the more formal and more general; it may pertain to an overall plan that is to be executed, whereas *order* might pertain more to a limited action or to a detailed part of such a plan: They received headquarters' *command* to attack at dawn, along with the special *orders* each unit was to follow. In addition, *command* is more forceful, peremptory, and less impersonal: Your wish is my *command*; a standing *order* to remain in uniform during off-duty hours. But *command* can refer to a position of control: the general's ten-year *command* of the infantry division.

Directive and **injunction** are considerably more formal than the foregoing and are much more limited and specific in their application. *Injunction* now pertains mostly to a legal context, where it indicates a court *order* which is backed by the threat of strenuous punishment for disobedience. An *injunction* often takes the form of a *command* to refrain from a specified action: an *injunction* that prevented the union from following through on the strike. *Directive* refers to *orders*, often detailed at length, which those in *command* send down through channels to gain the compliance of all affected personnel. Where the previous words can suggest either oral or written statements, *directive* most often suggests written guidelines for action. The word can seem to apply, euphemistically, to advice that carries no explicit threat of punishment for disobedience; but the rulings of a *directive* are usually mandatory and beyond appeal: a *directive* issued to all executives concerning a step-up in production during the next quarter; a battalion's *directive* on changes in the dress uniform; the dean's *directive* on admissions procedure.

Direction and **instruction** both have applications referring to *orders* that may not be contravened; in this sense both are extremely formal. *Direction* would suggest a less detailed verbal or written statement than *directive*; it is also less forceful and more euphemistic in tone: a *direction* on hiring practices that was sent down to the personnel department.

Often it can apply to informative but mandatory guidelines: the company's *directions* concerning the issuance of new stock certificates. In the context of *orders*, *instruction* stresses that a desired action cannot be done without including the necessary information as part of the *command*: junior officers awaiting the *instructions* of the company commander; the judge's *instructions* to the jurors; She left detailed *instructions* to the maid about preparations for the party. When the giving of information is not suggested by the word, it can be even more euphemistic than *direction*: the first sergeant's *instruction* to fall out for reveille.

The last pair pertain more often and less formally to the giving of knowledgeable advice or guidance. In the plural, both can indicate a programmatic or diagrammatic plan for a relatively complicated action that one wishes or chooses to perform. *Directions* would be more appropriate for a one-time action, *instructions* for an action one may wish to learn by heart or perform more than once: printed *directions* for assembling the components of the sound system; *instructions* for using the electric frying pan. *Direction* can apply, of course, to information about reaching a place: She asked for *directions* to get to the railway station. *Instruction* most commonly relates to an entirely separate context pertaining to teaching and learning. See DEMAND, LAW, REQUEST, REQUIRE, TEACH.

Antonyms: CONSENT.

These words are concerned with carrying out an action. **Commit**, in this sense, is used mostly in reference to acts which are looked on with disapproval or disfavor: *committing* a crime; *committing* suicide. **Perpetrate** is even more restricted than *commit* to negative senses, meaning to be guilty of, to perform atrociously, or to act deceitfully: to *perpetrate* a miscarriage of justice; to *perpetrate* such an inexcusably bad piece of writing; *perpetrating* a secret plot against the king.

Dispatch and **discharge** contrast with *commit* and *perpetrate* by mainly emphasizing approval for the manner in which a task is done. *Dispatch* suggests efficiency or speed of performance: *dispatching* the unpleasant job with extreme care. *Discharge* suggests the able or faultless performance of a duty or obligation: *discharging* his promise to work directly with the poor. Sometimes, however, *discharge* can suggest a literal or minimal rather than an inspired performance: *discharging* the responsibilities of his job only listlessly and reluctantly.

Do is the least formal and most general of these words and carries no implications whatever about how a task is carried out: *doing* the job brilliantly; *doing* greater harm as a private citizen than he had as prime minister. See PERFORM.

commit

discharge
dispatch
do
perpetrate

These words are used to describe diseases. **Communicable** and **contagious** are synonymous in designating that kind of disease which is conveyed by direct contact with an affected person or animal, or by contact with a secretion or discharge or by some article touched by him or it. Measles can be called either a *communicable* or a *contagious* disease. *Communicable* is a broader term than *contagious* in that it is also applied to diseases which are transmitted by some intermediary agent such as an insect. Malaria and yellow fever are examples of such *communicable* diseases. **Infectious** refers to a disease which is caused by the invasion into the body and the resulting growth and action of pathogenic microorganisms, especially bacteria and protozoa. Botulism and wound infections are *infectious* diseases. **Catching** is an informal

communicable

catching
contagious
infectious

word used in place of all three of the other terms but more often as a substitute for *communicable* and *contagious* than for *infectious*. See VIRUS.

Antonyms: noncommunicable.

compact

compressed
concise
condensed
constricted
dense
solid
miniaturized

These words refers to confinement or weightiness in a relatively small space. **Compact** in its most general use suggests a physique that is small but firm and shapely. In a more specific and technical sense, *compact* suggests that the essentials of something useful have been reduced to a smaller scale for convenience: a *compact* automobile; *compact* luggage for air travel. An intensification of this trend toward utilitarian smallness is designated by the fairly recent **miniaturized**, which refers to the making of smaller and smaller electronic equipment through the use of transistors; this makes the inclusion of more equipment feasible in situations where bulk and weight are critical, as in space travel: the *miniaturized* computer; the *miniaturized* radio.

Solid and **dense** emphasize weightiness, but *solid* does not necessarily suggest reduction to a small space, only the rigidity or firmness of a material. In reference to a physique, it suggests one without fat or flabbiness: *solid* muscle. *Dense* suggests the crowding of a heavy substance into a confined space; it may, unlike *solid*, refer to gasses or liquids as well as solids: *dense* fog; a *dense* forest.

Concise, **condensed**, and **compressed** suggest progressively greater confinement in space; one use of this progression is to suggest brevity in writing or a lack of wordiness. *Concise* suggests the use of exactly as many words as are required to express something and no more; it would apply more usually to technical, factual work, but may apply to imaginative prose: a *concise* report; the *concise* sentences of Hemingway. *Condensed* suggests the boiling down of a longer piece of writing to its rudiments: a *condensed* book. *Compressed* suggests extreme concision, but not necessarily that something longer has been shortened: a *compressed* statement that will explain the already *condensed* report. *Condensed* and *compressed* also have specific uses in the physical sciences. *Condensed* refers to the heating of a liquid so that water is driven off and a *denser* or semi*solid* substance remains: *condensed* milk. *Compressed* in this context refers to the putting of a gas under pressure to make it occupy less space: *compressed* air.

Constricted suggests extreme confinement in general, with an added note of uncomfortable limitation: *constricted* movement in the crowded subway car. See MINUTE, SHORTEN, SMALL, TERSE.

Antonyms: extended, loose, VERBOSE.

compare

approach
approximate
correspond
parallel
resemble
savor of
smack of

These words refer to things that are roughly similar but not exactly alike. **Compare** suggests that one thing is like another in some significant way, however unlike in others: a war that *compares* to the Korean conflict in its evident stalemate of constructive alternatives. In the imperative, the word may also be an invitation to regard two things side by side in order to note their differences as well as their similarities: *Compare* these examples of Rembrandt's early and late styles. **Resemble** is not readily used in the imperative, but otherwise it is closely related to *compare*. Its stress, however, is on a closer likeness, indicating that one thing *compares* in a number of ways to something else. Also, the word carries a stronger visual suggestion than *compare*: children who *resemble* their mother; a girl who *resembled* someone I used to know; an argument that *resembles* an earlier but now discredited theory.

In many uses, **correspond** is a more formal word for ideas suggested by *resemble*: an activist movement that *corresponds* to similar movements in the 1930's. The word has its own area of meaning, however, in suggesting things that are alike in that they match or complement each other: an availability of funds that seldom *corresponds* to the needs of units at work in the field. **Parallel** can also be used as a more formal substitute for *resemble*, but most often it suggests the separateness of two similar things: projects in the North that would *parallel* those underway in the deep South; proposals that not only *paralleled* but actually preceded Darwin's.

With **approximate**, the emphasis is on the roughness of the likeness: a bill that only *approximated* the demands of the lobbyists. The word may also suggest that one thing falls short of matching another in obvious ways: designs that desperately attempted to *approximate* the latest Paris fashions. **Approach** is like *approximate* in suggesting that one thing cannot measure up to something with which it is *compared*; the special emphasis here, however, is on quantity or volume: stock market levels that only *approached* previous highs. Often, the word emphasizes a lower level: a book that *approaches* his others in quality.

Savor of suggests that one thing only vaguely *compares* to another in some almost elusive way. Thus the amount of similarity suggested is even less than for *approximate* and *approach*: a novel that *savors of* a feeble attempt to mimic Joyce; a northern port that nevertheless somehow *savored of* the Mediterranean in its whitewashed houses and tiled roofs. While *savor of* can suggest equally well an advantageous or unfortunate likeness, the more pungent and colloquial **smack of** almost exclusively suggests an undesirable similarity: an offer that *smacks of* bribery. Both words tend to relate a single example to a larger category of things which it *resembles*, however distantly. See COUNTERPART, DUPLICATE, SIMILAR.

Antonyms: contrast, oppose.

compel

coerce
constrain
force
necessitate
oblige

These words all denote the urging or driving of a person to do something or the obtaining of the performance of some action, all by the use of irresistible physical or moral force. **Compel** may have as its agent a person, an impersonal entity, a law, an action, or a set of conditions, and its object may be a person or an action. A parent may *compel* his child to do his lessons by threatening to suspend his allowance; the government *compels* young men to perform military service; the law *compels* one to report one's income on pain of penalty; an attack *compels* one to defend oneself; a recession may *compel* an employer to lay off many of his employees; the government may take steps to *compel* compliance with the law.

Force suggests an actual physical process, the use of power, energy, or strength to accomplish something or to subdue resistance: to *force* a confession out of someone; to *force* the enemy back; to *force* a lock; to *force* someone to change an opinion; to *force* a smile. **Coerce** can imply the actual use of *force* but very often suggests its potential in an attempt to secure the surrender of the will: A child may be *coerced* into obedience by physical punishment or by the threat of it.

Constrain has connotations of repression, restriction, confinement, or limitation. It means to *compel*, but often suggests that the action being prompted or urged is in a negative direction or at least away from that which one may consider positive or pleasant: a man who was *constrained* by his weak heart to give up all forms of strenuous exercise.

To **necessitate** and to **oblige**, as here considered, mean to make an action necessary by the imposition of conditions that must be reacted to. There is often a suggestion of urgency about these words. [Reduction of income *necessitates* a curtailment of spending; Courtesy *obliges* a man to respond to an invitation.] See IMPEL, INDUCE, PROPEL.

compete

contend
oppose
rival
vie

These words refer to two or more people or factions struggling against each other to win a given objective. **Compete** is the most general of these, applying to the widest range of situations: pianists *competing* in the contest; baseball teams *competing* for the championship; candidates *competing* for the office; armies *competing* for victory in the battle; businesses *competing* for the biggest slice of the market. As can be seen, the objective implied by this word can be, most concretely, a prize or award that is won by a single confrontation, or, more abstractly, a share in something that falls to one side for its continuing effort: television programs *competing* throughout the season for the largest share of the audience.

Contend and **vie** suggest, more strictly, the moment of direct confrontation, and thus are narrowed to one possibility for *compete*. *Contend*, however, adds a note of actual hostility or serious disagreement, where *compete* may suggest none; furthermore, the word often suggests a dispute carried on verbally, as in a debate: speakers who fell to *contending* about the least important points in the proposal. Even when the verbal implication is not present, the animus often remains: forces *contending* bitterly to win the uncommitted delegates. The implications of *vie* stress a series of countering maneuvers in an ongoing struggle: neighbors continually *vying* with each other as to who could display the greater number of status symbols. The word is, however, more like *compete* than *contend* in lacking overtones of hostility.

Oppose may often, by implication, restrict the competing sides to two: extroversion, as *opposed* to introversion; primary elections in which many *compete* for the right to *oppose* the other party's choice in the main election. This narrowing of sides to two is not always present in the word: a debate in which many factions *opposed* each other. In any case, *oppose* does stress the choosing of clearly defined sides and suggests a greater rigidity of position than any of these words. It may suggest hostility, like *contend*, or at least a serious discrepancy of views not easily compromised: attitudes toward drug addiction that were sharply *opposed* to each other. **Rival** can be specifically used to suggest a struggle of two or more sides to outdo each other: candidates who *rival* each other in popularity; dresses that *rival* each other in vulgarity. Even more specifically, the word may suggest that one performance nearly matches another: domestic wines that *rival* the best French imports; a role in which she *rivals* the best acting she has previously shown us. These special applications of the word, in this context, make it the most restricted in meaning of words grouped here. See ARGUE, CONTROVERSY, FIGHT, OPPONENT.

Antonyms: COINCIDE, *collaborate, cooperate.*

competent

able
capable

These words are applied to persons who exhibit more than average acquired or native skill in the performance of some act or operation. **Competent** attributes to the subject the ability to carry out the requirements of a specific task. By implication, the completed task is one that can be rated objectively as being either satisfactory or unsatisfactory: No *competent* tax accountant could possibly have made such egregious errors in making out your return. Thus, while *competent* can suggest expertise in a complicated field, adequacy rather than excellence may be indicated by the word. A performing artist, for example, might be insulted if described by this word: *competent* piano-playing that nevertheless lacked inspiration and nuance.

Able and **capable** at their most neutral may indicate the practicable or possible: an infant barely *able* to walk. *Capable* is stronger here in indicating potential, possibly unsuspected, whether for good or ill: a husband *capable* of more tenderness than his wife had ever allowed him to express; totalitarian governments *capable* of the most unspeakable enormities. Where the words approach *competent* in referring to above-average skill, *able* suggests versatility and resourcefulness and *capable* a practical, problem-solving approach: an *able* architect; a *capable* stenographer. *Capable* stresses trained proficiency for a specific task, whereas *able* suggests a wider perspective or potential: *capable* lawyers, well-schooled in the intricacies of corporation law; *able* children, eager for knowledge, though thwarted by a lack of training in the fundamentals of reading. Also, *capable* can be applied to things as well as animals: an electronic computer *capable* of storing millions of bits of information; a shipyard *capable* of producing two nuclear submarines a month. *Able*, on the other hand, applies only to creatures *capable* of performing an action.

Qualified stresses the possession of required skills, and is generally applied to professions or trades for which a minimum of schooling or training is required. A *qualified* teacher has completed the academic training prescribed, but is not necessarily *competent*.

Efficient adds to *competent* the idea of a skill in making the most of the time and material available. A mechanic who is *competent* and *efficient* will perform a repair job more quickly and cheaply than a mechanic who is merely *competent*.

Fit and **good** are general words often used in place of the other words in this list. *Fit* is usually used predicatively: the manager is not *fit* for his position (meaning not *qualified*, not *competent*, not *efficient*). The specific meaning of *good*, when used in this sense, is indicated by the context. A *good* teacher is both *qualified* and *competent*; a *good* manager is both *competent* and *efficient*. See ADEQUATE, EXCELLENT, GENIUS, SKILL.

Antonyms: DEFICIENT, *incompetent, inefficient, unfit.*

These words refer to the act of finding fault with one's circumstances. **Complain** is the most general and also the most neutral of these, suggesting either justified or unjustified dissatisfaction with one's situation: They *complained* about the terrible brutality with which they were treated; *complaining* about imaginary slights from the neighbor ladies. **Bewail** was once similar to *complain* in its neutrality, but its archaic flavor now makes it suitable only for the unsympathetic satire of *complaining* that is motivated by self-pity, especially when the subject is a woman: like a tedious Puccini heroine *bewailing* her sad fate. **Grumble** suggests an habitual ill-humor, especially of a man, that does not quite expect to be taken seriously: husbands who *grumble* every summer as they dutifully pack the car for the family vacation; prisoners *grumbling* over the poor quality of institutional food. **Whine** implies a high-pitched, self-pitying tone, often used for a continually *complaining* or nagging woman or for a petulant child; its use suggests complete lack of sympathy for the subject: The patient *whined* on and on about how unfairly her psychoanalyst had treated her. If applied to a man, it

competent
(continued)

efficient
fit
good
qualified

complain

beef
bellyache
bewail
bitch
gripe
grouse
grumble
whine

suggests weak or cowardly behavior: He *whined* about his bad luck while others put out the fire.

The rest of these words range from the extremely informal to slang. They also range, in the order of their discussion, toward less and less sympathy for the subject. **Gripe** can be used for any fruitless expression of dissatisfaction, but is especially pertinent to military life: The officers were told to beware of soldiers who have nothing to *gripe* about. This context has emphasized the word as a normal everyday *complaining* about trivial things; it would not be used for outraged indignation or even serious dissatisfaction. **Grouse** implies a greater animus than *gripe* and may suggest a more pointed lashing out in accusation or insult: *grousing* about the food only when the mess sergeant could overhear them. **Beef** works as an intensification of *gripe* but does not necessarily suggest the bitterness of *grouse*; it can suggest an unjustified *complaining*: They *beefed* about mistreatment only to get front-page treatment in the newspapers. **Bellyache** suggests *complaining* that is interminable, tiresome, and completely without justification: continually *bellyaching* no matter how his roommates tried to shut him up. The slang word **bitch** is extremely general in its reference to *complaining*; it can range in application from the fruitless dissatisfaction indicated by *gripe* to the bitterness of *grouse*: He *bitched* about the weather, the food, and anything else that crossed his mind; They *bitched* about the favoritism the teacher showed to the daughter of the superintendent. See DEPLORE, DISAPPROVAL, UPSET.

Antonyms: applaud, approve, PRAISE.

compliant

agreeable
broad-minded
complaisant
obliging
suggestible
willing

These words refer to a pleasant or tolerant manner, open to other people's demands or desires. **Compliant** suggests a passive nature readily molded to conform to the wishes of others, one easily persuaded with little effort: meekly *compliant* to even his harshest expectations. **Suggestible** is a less formal word for the same idea, but it has an additional implication indicating a naive or unguarded sensibility that can be influenced even by subtle or indirect methods: They disapproved of giving such violence-ridden fare to *suggestible* children.

Willing stresses a more conscious decision to do something and does not, unlike *compliant* or *suggestible*, suggest an innately weak or conforming nature: informing her that he would be *willing* to run the errand for her; *willing*, eager students. On the other hand, **obliging** refers not to a conscious choice but to a nature that is cheerfully ready to assist or that will permit someone else to satisfy a wish: an *obliging* stewardess; teen-age girls who feel they must be *obliging* on dates or become unpopular. **Agreeable** stresses the cheerful side of *obliging*: an *agreeable* personality. It may also suggest anything that is simply pleasurable: an *agreeable* climate. But the word, in another use, can suggest an even more *willing* and open attitude than *obliging*: finding that she was *agreeable* to anything he suggested.

Complaisant in one of its uses is simply a more formal term for *agreeable*, but with a greater stress on the conforming character suggested by *compliant*: her *complaisant* eagerness to please. The word has a special use, however, to suggest a cheerful or hypocritical indifference to strict moral standards, either in others or oneself: parents who are permissive and *complaisant* about their children's behavior; a *complaisant* lover. **Broad-minded** is in some ways a more informal substitute for *complaisant* in this context; it suggests a lax regard for moral standards, although it does not necessarily imply a cheerful attitude. In other contexts the word might suggest an admirable ability to see all sides of a question. Here, by contrast, it suggests, almost euphemistically, an ability to accept the misbehavior of others without protest: parties that put a strain on the most *broad-minded* of her older friends. See ADAPTABLE, LENIENT, MALLEABLE.

Antonyms: narrow-minded, STUBBORN, UNWILLING, WILLFUL.

These words all refer to parts of a whole. **Component** refers to a part that functions in association with other parts but that can easily be detached from them; this is in contrast to an organic whole in which the parts are fused or have lost their individual identity within the larger entity. In choosing hi-fi equipment, for example, one can buy separate *components*, such as speakers, turntable, and amplifier, and wire them together oneself. Or one can buy a prepackaged console, designed as a single unit. The word can suggest a more intimate relationship, as in chemistry, where it refers to a substance that in varying degrees is present in a mixture without being chemically integrated into it; in this case, a change in appearance or apparent loss of identity may be indicated: Salt is a *component* of sea water. **Ingredient** is a more general word, referring equally well to the unaltered substances mixed together in an amorphous mass and to the fused or transformed parts of an entity or organic whole: Turmeric is an *ingredient* of curry powder; a novel that contains all the *ingredients* of a good mystery story.

Element and **constituent** both refer more strictly to essential, necessary, or intrinsic parts of a whole. *Element* comes from a Latin root meaning first principle; this is reflected in its use to indicate the rudiments of a subject: the *elements* of good writing. As in this example, the word's stress is often on simple or basic parts of a more complex whole. In chemistry, the word refers to those basic substances, such as oxygen, mercury, and copper, that are irreducible by ordinary chemical means and that are the building blocks of all matter. *Constituent* refers more generally to a part that is necessary to the functioning of a whole. Such a part often loses its individual identity completely in contributing to the new entity; conversely, withdrawing it from the whole would drastically change the larger entity: The *element* hydrogen is a *constituent* of water. See ADDITION, PART.

Antonyms: entity, WHOLE.

These words refer to pieces of nonfiction writing. **Composition** indicates a formal exercise that is planned in advance rather than improvisatory in character. It is used to refer to any sort of writing assignment in school, often on a set subject, with an emphasis on grammar and style rather than on research or factual presentation: The teacher asked them to describe their summer vacations in the first class *composition*. **Theme** is a less formal word and is restricted in reference to such an assigned piece of writing in school. The word emphasizes organization around a single topic, may suggest briefer treatment, and is even less likely than *composition* to require factual research: a class *theme* of three hundred words. The word may also refer to the dominant idea of any piece of writing: the *theme* of alienation in his study of middle-class culture.

Essay is a much more general word than the previous pair. While it may be used in place of either to refer to a writing assignment in school, the word more widely indicates any sort of nonfiction writing shorter than book-length, whether scholarly, humorous, propagandistic, or

component

constituent
element
ingredient

composition

article
dissertation
essay
paper
theme
thesis
treatise

reflective. The word, moreover, may suggest any approach from the extremely informal and personal to the solemn, stately, or stylized: the refreshing irreverence of Addison's chatty *essays*; the Ciceronian elegance that Carlyle attempted in his early *essays*; howlingly funny *essays* about the perils of suburban living. **Article** is restricted to any piece of nonfiction that has appeared in a newspaper, magazine, or journal; it ranges in reference from the briefest and most utilitarian news release through all the possibilities inherent in *essay*, including the most abstruse scholarly or scientific study: an *article* giving up-to-the-minute election returns; an *article* treating the effects of radiation on arthropods.

Paper has two areas of relevance. One relates to *composition* and *theme* in referring to a written assignment, usually in high school and college: term *papers* due the last day of the term. In this use, the word may suggest any sort of approach, from a demonstration of writing ability to the presentation of factual research. The word's other use refers to a scholarly *essay* read to one's colleagues, or to a scholarly *article* published in a learned journal: a *paper* on disturbances in the earth's magnetic field. **Treatise** indicates an exclusively scholarly context, referring to any presentation from *essay*- to book-length in which conclusions are drawn from a body of data in a formal and systematic way: a *treatise* on the development of the Gregorian chant.

The remaining pair of words also is restricted to a scholarly or academic context. **Thesis** may suggest briefer or less exhaustive treatment than *treatise*, pointing to the establishing and defending of a principle: a *thesis* in which he corroborates Keynes's theory of deficit spending. Like *theme*, *thesis* may also refer to the dominant idea or contention of a piece of writing, although it pertains mainly to argumentative nonfiction: a collection of *essays* each of which illustrates his *thesis* that American novelists are unable to create memorable women characters. Most concretely, *thesis* refers to the extended paper, possibly of book-length, that is sometimes required of candidates for a Master's degree. **Dissertation** is the most formal of these words and suggests the most formal sort of writing, as well. It may refer to any reasoned treatment, like *treatise*, but most concretely it indicates such a work, usually of book-length, when it is a requirement for a Ph.D. or other doctoral degree: a *dissertation* analyzing cold-war strategies. The word may sometimes be used pejoratively for any long-winded and pompous piece of exposition: giving us another dreary *dissertation* on the evils of imperialism. See REPORT, WRITE.

compulsory

binding
de rigueur
imperative
mandatory
obligatory

These words describe actions that are judged to be inescapably necessary. **Compulsory** suggests that someone in authority has imposed a course of action that may not be departed from: *compulsory* attendance of classes. It may further suggest that the *compulsory* ruling will be enforced, by coercion if necessary, and that violators will be punished: *compulsory* blacklisting. **Mandatory** is like *compulsory* in suggesting an imposed rule: *mandatory* silence in the library. In contrast, it is milder than *compulsory* in that it stops short of suggesting coercion and punishment as methods of enforcing the ruling.

Binding also describes a ruling handed down by an authority, but it may specifically suggest a one-time decision concerning a specific dispute between two parties who agree beforehand to abide by the results: *binding* arbitration. It may also suggest that earlier, more tentative rulings have been appealed to a final authority. [The teacher's *compulsory* ruling against wearing Bermuda shorts to class was appealed to the principal, whose decision would be *binding*.]

Obligatory is like *binding* in its legal sense. In a more general use, however, it suggests something expected or made necessary by morality or conscience, rather than by a higher authority as in the previous words: the *obligatory* chaperone at teen-age parties. As such, its force is more what should be done than what is or must be done: notions of *obligatory* timidity she could not subscribe to. **Imperative** refers to a necessity dictated by circumstances rather than by an authority or a code of morality: *imperative* to get food and water before sundown. If used to refer to an imposed rule, it is more like *mandatory* than *compulsory*.

De rigueur is close to *obligatory*, but is milder in referring to those acts or observances considered necessary according to etiquette or required by good form; it usually appears only as a predicate adjective: an unwritten rule that made evening dress *de rigueur* for attending her soirées. See INEVITABLE, REQUIRE, SURE.

Antonyms: LENIENT, *optional, unnecessary.*

These words refer to a person who is afflicted with unwarranted self-admiration or a feeling of his own superiority. **Conceited** pertains to an excessive affection for oneself that may be revealed by an uncritical smugness and aloofness from others: *conceited* girls who walk home from school with their noses in the air. More specifically, the word may point to a person who becomes swell-headed because of a particular accomplishment or occurrence, often a trivial one: She became unbearably *conceited* after the football captain asked her out on a date. **Vain** suggests a person who is extremely concerned about his personal appearance or the impression he makes on others. A *conceited* person might feel that his superiority is self-evident, whereas a *vain* person would more likely strive constantly to impress others or improve his appearance: The typical dandy of old was so *vain* about his appearance that he spent almost as much time primping before a mirror as his female counterpart.

Egotistical need not suggest an outward show, like *vain*, so much as an extreme self-preoccupation and lack of interest in the feelings or affairs of others. On the other hand, where *conceited* usually suggests that someone is self-admiring for clearly defined reasons, however specious, *egotistical* may suggest a more unconscious, narcissistic habit of mind: an *egotistical* snob who thought the world began and ended on Park Avenue. Sometimes, however, the word can point to the habit of calling attention to oneself and one's accomplishments, while ignoring the interests of others: the *egotistical* artist who monopolized the conversation with talk of his work in progress.

Boastful and **vainglorious** concentrate on this last possibility of *egotistical*, both referring to self-praise and attention-seeking in public. *Boastful* emphasizes unsubtle and even boorish public displays of vocal self-approval: After a few drinks, he always became *boastful* about his sexual exploits and conquests. *Vainglorious* focuses more exclusively on hollow show, not necessarily verbal at all. The attempt may be more subtle than *boastful* self-praise, but conspicuous displays of status symbols are often involved: *vainglorious* dowagers dripping minks and diamonds.

Proud can, of course, indicate legitimate satisfaction at accomplishing a goal or honor: *proud* of his high score on the examination. It can also apply to things invested with real dignity: a *proud* history; *proud* mountains silhouetted in the sunset. When the word takes on a dis-

conceited

boastful
egotistical
proud
vain
vainglorious

approving tone, it suggests a stiff-necked and unrealistic lack of humility: too *proud* to admit that he had been grossly in error. See BOAST, CONFIDENCE, EGOISM, OVERBEARING.

Antonyms: deferent, humble, MODEST, TIMID.

conclusive

decisive
definitive
determining

These words are concerned with those moments in a sequence of events that are crucial to bringing about a given result. **Conclusive** suggests a final act that settles questions at issue in a previous course of action: the bombing of Hiroshima as the *conclusive* event of World War II. The word may be used in another sense to refer, not to the events themselves, but to a later analysis of them. In this sense, *conclusive* refers to an incontrovertible interpretation of these events as a whole: *conclusive* proof that Richard II was not the villain Shakespeare made him out to be. A **decisive** event differs from a *conclusive* event in that it need not necessarily be the last one in a given sequence. Indeed, it may be a situation present almost at the outset, with the whole following course of action merely corroborating it. [The South's lack of industrial development was *decisive* to its defeat, long before a single shot was fired.]

Determining, like *decisive*, may refer to something that comes early or late in a course of action. *Decisive* may be more suitable in describing a single overt act of choice, while *determining* might better describe underlying factors that are inherent in a situation and prejudice the outcome. [No matter how many *decisive* victories Justinian won, the split of East and West into two alien cultures was the *determining* factor in his ultimate failure to reunite the Roman Empire.]

Definitive, when referring to an act, combines the meanings of both *conclusive* and *decisive*. It applies when a sequence of events has been in doubt until the very last act, which irrevocably settles things: Elizabeth's *definitive* victory over the Armada settled the question of British naval superiority for centuries. When the word refers to a later analysis of events, it takes in all that is implied by *conclusive* in this sense, but adds to it implications of authoritative accuracy and incontestable interpretation not to be surpassed. In this sense, *definitive*, unlike *conclusive*, need not suggest the settling of controversy or the proposing of any thesis whatsoever; it simply suggests finality of examination and analysis: the *definitive* history of the Boer War; the *definitive* biography of Byron that strips away all myth and conjecture to show us the actual man as he was. See FINAL, OUTSTANDING, SIGNIFICANT.

Antonyms: inconclusive, indeterminate, PROVISIONAL, *tentative.*

condescend

deign
patronize
stoop
tolerate
unbend

These words refer to the treating of another person as one's inferior. **Condescend** suggests particularly the awareness of a social or class distinction, false or real, which one person bridges in dealing or speaking to someone beneath him. The person who *condescends*, however, calls attention to the difference and does not wish it forgotten. Once, this word was simply descriptive: Her Highness *condescends* to recognize the foreign ambassador. Nowadays, in our egalitarian world, the word has an almost exclusively negative implication: tourists who *condescend* to the "natives." **Deign** emphasizes choice; it implies that one could very well have chosen an opposite, perhaps more appropriate, course. It is not necessarily restricted solely to dealing with one's inferiors: He didn't *deign* to reply to his colleague's accusation. The word's extreme formality limits its use today, except for satirical effect: the saleswoman who actually *deigned* to wait on me.

Stoop was earlier like *condescend* in emphasizing social station and like *deign* in suggesting choice; but it now has uses mostly relating to a discreditable moral act: statesmen who *stoop* to exchanging political favors. *Condescend* might suggest a generally grand, arch, or pompous behavior; *stoop* suggests single questionable acts. Unbend is more like *condescend* on this score, but its overtone, in contrast, is one of approval for a stuffy person who learns to relax or act less officiously. [Why does she have to *condescend* to me all the time? Can't she *unbend* a little and treat me like anyone else?]

Patronize, even more than *condescend*, suggests haughtiness of bearing and an overtone of looking down on someone: a teacher who *patronized* his students by oversimplifying everything he taught them. Tolerate, in this context, has gone through several shifts in usage. It has meant and can still mean simply to accept: society women who will *tolerate* eccentric guests so long as they are artists. The word at one point took on a note of reconciliation: learning to *tolerate* minority groups. Now this last use is avoided as resembling *patronize* or *condescend* too closely: Negroes who wish to be accepted, not merely *tolerated*. See OVERBEARING.

Antonyms: accept, respect, REVERE.

These words refer to a psychological trait that involves a conviction of one's own worth or an unselfconscious certainty of succeeding at whatever is attempted, unhampered by doubt, hesitation, or fear. Confidence stresses a general optimism that all is or will be well: able to face the future with *confidence*. The word may also suggest fearless trust, whether well- or ill-advised: talking to the unsavory people in the bar with effortless *confidence*. Self-confidence restricts these possibilities to a general optimism concerning one's own capacities and accomplishment, suggesting a complete absence of timidity and, less positively, an aggressive bearing: social clubs set up to promote *self-confidence* in teen-agers; a garish costume that matched the *self-confidence* with which she plowed her way through the startled members of the receiving line.

Aplomb and self-possession stress the ability to keep oneself under firm control. *Self-possession* suggests the restraining of conflicting impulses or the brushing aside of distractions, accompanied by a cool unemotional approach even in trying situations: calmly working her way through the customs inspection with unflustered *self-possession*. *Aplomb*, by contrast, emphasizes a total lack of self-doubt and may suggest a carefree or uncritical exuberance: Although he had never dueled before, he faced his opponent with *aplomb*.

Poise stresses steadiness and balance and, somewhat like *self-possession*, suggests a calm sureness of manner able to cope courteously with any contingency: a shy and awkward adolescent who had turned overnight into a young woman amply endowed with grace and *poise*. With its emphasis on a mastery of social properties, savoir faire relates closely to *poise* in stressing an intuitive ability to do the right thing socially and to get on well with other people whatever the situation: a *savoir faire* that never deserted him whether he found himself among first-nighters at the opera or among bohemians in a Greenwich Village coffee house.

Self-assurance and smugness stress an extreme conviction of one's own worth, ability, or superiority. *Self-assurance* can be used either positively or negatively, but *smugness* is exclusively disapproving: an astonishing *self-assurance* in whizzing through an exam which he had

confidence

aplomb
poise
savoir faire
self-assurance
self-confidence
self-possession
smugness

spent only a few hours preparing for; insisting with unblushing *self-assurance* that even the stupidest native would understand her English if only she spoke loudly and clearly enough. *Smugness* suggests an uncritical vanity or pride in one's own privileged position and a failure to see things from other people's point of view. This puts it in strong contrast to *savoir faire* which stresses a sensing of what people will find pleasant and apt: the *smugness* with which she chose to stay at American hotels throughout Europe in order to avoid unscrupulous foreigners. See EGOISM, JAUNTY, OVERBEARING, ZEST.

Antonyms: ANXIETY, *diffidence,* DOUBT, *hesitation, shyness, timidity.*

confine

imprison
incarcerate
intern
jail

These words refer to the shutting up, usually of people, in a particular place. **Confine** is the most general of these and indicates a reduction of mobility for whatever reason: He felt *confined* and claustrophobic in a big city; *confined* by ill-health to her bed. More pertinent to this context, the word suggests removing someone to a prison or mental hospital, usually against the person's will: a sentence *confining* him to life imprisonment; a court order *confining* him indefinitely to a sanatorium for the criminally insane.

The directness and informality of **jail** makes *confine* sound euphemistic by comparison when it refers to shutting someone up in prison: *jailed* on a disorderly conduct charge. Although identical in meaning to *jail,* **imprison** gives a more formal tone without sounding euphemistic like *confine*: a regime that *imprisoned* anyone suspected of dissent. The one possible difference between *jail* and *imprison* is that *jail* might be used for a relatively short stay: *jailed* overnight because he had trouble raising bail; *imprisoned* for ten years in the Bastille. **Incarcerate** is the most formal of all these words; while close in meaning to *imprison*, it may suggest the initial act of *imprisoning*: He was *incarcerated* in Sing Sing to begin the serving out of his sentence. *Incarcerate* is sometimes used to suggest a harsh, punitive, or brutal *imprisoning* under inhumane conditions: They *incarcerated* him in a windowless basement cell. The word, furthermore, can refer like *confine* to the shutting up of the mentally ill; here the emphasis may be on inhumane treatment: The family *incarcerated* the wretch in a concealed, airless room in the attic.

Intern, like aspects of *confine* and *incarcerate*, may refer to hospitalization, but in this case a hospital of any sort may be implied, and the *interning* may be voluntary or involuntary: Hospitals no longer *intern* women for extended periods following childbirth; *interned* in a mental hospital whose "open door" policy permitted weekend leaves. As in the last example, the sense of constricted movement may be lessened, as compared with *confine*. The use that makes the word unique among this group, however, pertains to the impounding of people or even equipment, as during war: the policy of *interning* American citizens of Japanese descent during the war. The word, furthermore, contrasts sharply with the punitive possibilities of *jail, imprison,* and *incarcerate*, in that the *interning* can conceivably be done for the internee's own good: They *interned* the demonstrators to protect them from the fury of the mob. See CIRCUMSCRIBE.

Antonyms: emancipate, free, liberate, release.

confuse

bewilder

These words refer to a disordered emotional response to complex or puzzling experiences or events. **Confuse** is the most general of these and suggests the mildest disorientation: detailed directions that only served to *confuse* me further; *confused* by his sudden pendulum swings between exuberance and depression. The word may suggest only a temporary lack of equilibrium or resilience. **Bewilder** deepens the suggestions of *confuse* and adds a note of harried emotional discomfort: completely *bewildered* by the crossfire of conflicting commands shouted at him by his parents. The word suggests a disorientation that is longer lasting than *confuse* and that may paralyze one's ability to choose or act coherently: She was so *bewildered* by his accusations that she sat down and cried. **Confound** suggests a complete and possibly intentional undoing of someone by contravening them at every point or by exposing them to unfriendly scrutiny or ridicule: an appeal for help that was utterly *confounded* by red tape and bureaucratic double talk.

Dumbfound and **nonplus** are closely related, both suggesting a momentary astonishment at some sudden occurrence or sharp retort. *Dumbfound* implies an acute emotional shock that leaves one speechless; *nonplus* suggests a more intellectual surprise at some irrational incongruence, leaving one unable to think clearly for a moment: He was *dumbfounded* at her insistence that he explain where every penny of his allowance had gone; *nonplused* by the strange costumes he saw everywhere in the bohemian section of the city. See DOUBT.

Antonyms: CLARIFY, ENCOURAGE, *hearten*, HELP, *reassure*.

connect

attach
couple
join
link
unite

These verbs apply to things that are brought or fastened together. **Connect** is used of things that come into contact at some point while clearly remaining separate. Things may be directly *connected* or, as is often the case, *connected* by some intervening means or agency: *connecting* rooms in a hotel, with a bath between them; two large land masses *connected* by an isthmus. *Connect* also may suggest a contact that results in the transfer of power from a source to a receiver. One *connects* a radio by inserting its plug into an electrical outlet. A switchboard operator can *connect* two people over the telephone by *connecting* the proper electric circuits. A baseball player who hits the ball solidly is said to *connect*. **Attach** is applied to things that are or that may be *connected* securely but that retain their separate identities and are separable. *Attaching* implies the fastening on of a part to a whole, of a lesser thing to a greater, or of something movable to something fixed. Hence one may *attach* a flash gun to a camera, a pin to a dress, or a hose to a hydrant. A barnacle *attaches* itself to a ship. A door is *attached* to the doorpost by hinges. Applied to persons, *connect* may suggest an indefinite relationship, while *attach* may imply a specific but temporary association. [He is *connected* with the government in some capacity; An attaché is a person officially *attached* to a diplomatic mission.]

Link suggests a connection like that of loops in a chain. When things brought directly together are *linked*, they are interlocked: to *link* arms. But things not in contact may also be *linked* by something that forms a bond between them. A *linking* verb is one that serves to *connect* the subject of a sentence with the predicate. *Link* may also mean to find or point out a connection between things: to *link* cigarette smoking to cancer. **Couple** stresses pairing. To *couple* is to *connect* two things, often by means of a *linking* device: to *couple* railroad cars. To *couple* electric circuits is to *connect* them magnetically or directly, permitting transfer of power from one to the other.

Join and **unite** are applied to things that come together closely or combine. *Join* stresses the previous, and possibly the future, separateness of the parts, while *unite* emphasizes the new whole that is formed. Two or more things may *join* through mutual action or adjacent location, or may be *joined* by being fitted or *linked* together. [The two groups *joined* forces against a common enemy; *Join* hands and form a circle.] Also, a lesser thing may *join* a greater or a single person may *join* a group, each becoming a part of the whole: to *join* a club. [*Join* us at our table; The Ohio and the Missouri Rivers *join* the Mississippi.] To *unite* is to *join* together so as to form one integral whole. Two or more things that *unite* give up all or part of their separateness in order to exist or act as one: to *unite* two ingredients in a mixture or compound; The states *united* to form a nation.

All of these words may be applied to interpersonal relationships. *Attach* suggests personal ties of affection: He grew *attached* to her. *Link* may imply a coupling: Their names were *linked* in the gossip columns. *Couple* may mean to copulate. *Join* and *unite* are applied to marriage, while *connect* indicates a looser, much less intimate association: to *join* a man and a woman in holy matrimony. [They were *united* in marriage; Their families are now *connected* by marriage.] See ADAPT, ADD, COMPONENT, MIXTURE.

Antonyms: alienate, dissociate, SEPARATE, SEVER.

consent

acquiesce
agree
assent
concur
subscribe

These words refer to a positive response or to a congruence between or among things. **Consent** is restricted to the giving of permission or the accepting of a proposal or request. [The first sergeant *consented* to the corporal's request for an emergency leave; She *consented* to his proposal of marriage.] *Consent* always implies the power not to *consent*: The king gave willing *consent* to his son's marriage to a princess, and reluctant *consent* to his daughter's marriage to a commoner. Where *consent* often implies the permission of a superior, **assent** can indicate the approval of an equal. The word, furthermore, is most often limited to an affirmative response to a statement or opinion: She *assented* to the doctor's assertion that her son was ill, but would not *consent* to having him hospitalized. **Acquiesce** suggests either lukewarm or minimal compliance or a compliance compelled by outside force or circumstances: With a shrug, she *acquiesced* in his proposal that they go to the baseball game together; a spontaneous uprising that forced the government to *acquiesce* to the demands of its citizens. In the latter case, the word does not suggest the uncompromised freedom to choose that is inherent in the previous words.

Agree is much wider in its application than the previous words. It can apply, like *consent*, to a positive response: After hearing his prepared statement, many on the committee *agreed* with his stand. But the word can also indicate congruence of opinion that does not involve statement and response, or even previous negotiation or discussion: I met the new manager today and found that we *agree* on basic policies. In its widest use, the word can indicate things that are alike: Both husband and wife were surprised to find that the balances in their separate checkbooks *agreed* to the penny. **Concur** is restricted to statements, findings, or opinions, but otherwise can indicate, like *agree*, positions that are found to be alike: The two scientists, working separately and unknown to each other, had reached conclusions that *concurred*. More often, however, the word refers to a common position reached by serious deliberation or negotiation: Each member of the committee finally *concurred* as to what position they should take on the controversial matter. The word can also indicate *agreeing* to a position already taken by another or others: One Supreme Court justice wrote a separate but *concurring* opinion.

Subscribe indicates wholehearted approval for an already formulated position. The word's root suggests the signing of one's name beneath a statement; the word may sometimes suggest this situation, but much more often it indicates only a comparable willingness to support and defend a position: a public-opinion poll that proved that the voters *subscribed* to administration policy. Sometimes the notion of a public avowal is completely absent: They *subscribed* in secret to discriminatory hiring practices. See APPROVAL, COINCIDE, ENDORSE, SUBMIT.

Antonyms: CONTRADICT, DEMUR, DISAGREE.

conserve

hoard
maintain
preserve
save
store

These words are concerned with attempts to keep something intact or to possess it in greater quantities. **Conserve** pertains to the wise use of a valuable item that one already has, with the suggestion that it will be difficult to replace once it has been used up: leaflets requesting citizens to *conserve* water during the drought; efforts to *conserve* forest land from the incursions of timber speculators. **Preserve**, on the other hand, emphasizes keeping something that is valuable exactly as it is, without change and, in some cases, even without using it at all. It suggests greater urgency and, in contrast to *conserve*, may suggest that the item in question is literally impossible to replace, once it is gone: proposals to *preserve* the house as it was when Poe lived in it; He was in favor of *preserving* the Bill of Rights without stricture or modification.

Maintain and **save** relate somewhat like *conserve* and *preserve*. *Maintain* emphasizes careful use and replenishment of a quantity, like *conserve*, but it suggests that a steady routine of work will be enough to keep the item in its present state. *Maintain*, also, does not necessarily suggest something of great value; it can pertain to anything one wishes to keep in good working condition: We can *maintain* essential services by insuring a steady flow of revenue; *maintaining* a house in good shape by an almost predictable annual outlay of time, effort, and money. *Save*, on the other hand, is somewhat more like *preserve*, suggesting greater urgency and the irreplaceability of what might otherwise be lost. If anything, it is more urgent (and certainly more informal) than *preserve*, especially in its sense of rescue: action that narrowly *saved* the country from defeat. In an informal context, however, it can function exactly like the more formal *conserve*: *saving* water during the crisis. Where it is distinct from all the words so far discussed is in suggesting the accumulating of a quantity. Both *conserve* and *preserve* concentrate on what one already has; *maintain* emphasizes the taking in and giving out to keep an unchanging balance. *Save*, however, can suggest the adding of new quantities to what already exists: He was *saving* up money for a college education; As she grew older she took to *saving* bits of string she found in the street.

Store and **hoard** relate to this last meaning of *save*. *Store* suggests the piling up of goods that may be bulkier than those suggested by *save*; but, as with *save*, the *stored* item may be valuable or worthless, may be *stored* for future use — or for no purpose whatsoever: reservoirs with which to *store* water against periods of slight rainfall; *storing* his books with friends until he returned from Europe; She stored every flotsam relic of her life without ever looking at it again. *Hoard* gives an unpleasant picture of someone *saving* or *storing* valuables out of fear, greed, or mental derangement: Everyone *hoarded* food during the famine; *hoarding* his money while living like a beggar. See POSSESS, RECOVER, REPAIR.

Antonyms: disperse, dissipate, scatter, spend, squander, waste.

consider

count
deem
reckon
regard

These words refer to a belief that something is the case. **Consider** can indicate a belief reached after thoughtful deliberation or intimate experience. [All the critics *considered* the book a masterpiece; Most of the soldiers *considered* the guerrilla force to be a formidable opponent.] A favorable verdict is not always necessary: Scientists of that day *considered* his experiments to be without merit. **Regard** comes from a French word meaning to look at. Compared with *consider*, *regard* often reflects its derivation by suggesting a more external assessment or, sometimes, a visual one: He *regarded* his wife as a beauty, though others found her plain. Again, a positive judgment is not inevitable, despite the word's related use referring to approval: They *regarded* him as a harmless fool.

Count and **reckon** can refer literally to numbering or to figuring sums; in the present context, they seldom carry this sense over, though they do refer to the forming of a judgment. Here, *count* is most often restricted to stock phrases: *counting* himself lucky; *counting* the day well spent. *Reckon* suggests the weighing of evidence on all sides: He was *reckoned* by everyone to be an honest man. But the word has lost ground to its informal or dialect use, meaning to suppose or guess: I *reckon* it's time to go. This use has been popularized by Western movies and television programs.

Deem is now somewhat formal and occurs perhaps more often in legal contexts than in other contexts. It refers more to opinion than belief, but to opinion arrived at after deliberation; if the opinion is that of a judge, it may well be as firm or binding as the belief implied by *consider* and *regard*: The judge *deemed* it inadvisable to hear the appeal. *Deem* almost always carries with it a note of authority: He was *deemed* a traitor by his own people. See STUDY, THINK.

considerate

attentive
diplomatic
helpful
tactful
thoughtful

These adjectives describe persons or actions that show a kind or courteous concern for other people. **Considerate** and **thoughtful** emphasize the unselfish spirit behind the act, the generous thought that prompts the deed. A *considerate* person is mindful of other people's feelings, aware of their circumstances, and responsive to their needs. He considers consequences before he acts, feeling that he should spare others needless annoyance, difficulty, or distress. A *thoughtful* person is *considerate*, but in a more positive way, having an active regard for others that leads him to anticipate their needs. He thinks of benefits he might bestow and then he acts, hoping to help others or to please them: *thoughtful* friends who offer to buy groceries for a shut-in; *considerate* neighbors who try not to disturb a convalescent with their noise. Both *considerate* and *thoughtful* are often followed by *of* plus an object. [He is *considerate of* older people; It was *thoughtful of* you to remember my birthday.] *Thoughtful* is also used for its connotations to describe a welcome remembrance: a very *thoughtful* gift.

Attentive emphasizes constant acts of courtesy, indicating an apparent thoughtfulness or devotion that may or may not be real. An *attentive* escort opens doors for his date, offers her his arm, helps her with her coat, lights her cigarette. But he may be either gentleman or gigolo, either genuinely *thoughtful* and *considerate* or anxious to seem so for selfish reasons. [She was *attentive* to her sick sister, whom she loved; He became very *attentive* to his aunt when he learned the old lady was rich.]

Helpful is a matter-of-fact, workaday word, stressing a practical motive or result. A person or thing can be *helpful* by meeting a specific need — providing useful service or assistance: a *helpful* salesclerk; a *helpful* hint. [He is very *attentive* in public but not very *helpful* around the house.] *Helpful* may at times imply little more than a willingness to assist, so it is sometimes used to claim or give credit for good intentions. [I wasn't meddling; I was only trying to be *helpful*.]

Tactful and **diplomatic** emphasize method, an ability to handle sensitive people and situations gracefully, without causing hurt or angry feelings. A *tactful* person is *considerate* of others and is careful not to embarrass, upset, or offend them. He senses instinctively what to say and what to leave unsaid, often practicing restraint or taking a roundabout approach in order to be kind: a *tactful* suggestion that another hair style might be more becoming; He knew it was a sore subject, and being *tactful*, he did not bring it up. *Diplomatic* is a more formal term than *tactful* and suggests a deliberate rather than an intuitive courtesy. It presupposes the special tact required of a diplomat — skill in handling delicate or explosive situations, in mediating disputes, and in resolving differences through conciliation and compromise: a situation that requires *diplomatic* handling, not angry ultimatums; He was very *diplomatic* in dealing with customer complaints. See BENEVOLENCE, GENEROUS, HUMANE, KIND.

Antonyms: GAUCHE, HEEDLESS, *inattentive, negligent.*

These words refer to the assuaging of unhappiness or grief. **Console** suggests the effort of one person to mitigate the serious grief felt by another: on hand to *console* him through the whole of his mourning. The word may specifically suggest the attempt to make up for a loss by offering something in its place: They tried to *console* him for losing the prize by taking him to a movie. This making up for a loss may occur within the loser's mind: She was *consoled* to think that she at least had an understanding husband to turn to. **Condole**, by contrast, is a great deal more formal than *console*, almost to the point of sounding fusty and pompous; it does, however, give the specific meaning of actively grieving along with someone else: parents who *condoled* with each other over the loss of their child. The word has now been adopted for standard or formal expressions of regret: His fellow workers sent him a note *condoling* with him in his grief. This accounts for the word's tendency to sound officious and insincere.

Comfort and **cheer up** are less formal than *condole* and even than *console*; they also can apply to less serious unhappinesses. *Comfort*, of the two, has the wider range of use; it suggests a tactful and understanding ministering to someone who is unhappy: She *comforted* the grieving child with a tight embrace. This word can also refer to thoughts within the mourner's mind that mitigate grief: *comforted* to know that everything had been carried out exactly as his friend would have wished. *Cheer up* is decidedly limited to active attempts to ease someone's mind over a less extreme unhappiness: She knew that if he failed to get the job she would have to exert every wile she possessed in order to *cheer* him *up*; a bubbling manner that *cheered up* the most despondent men in the ward.

Solace is almost as formal as *condole* and might sound precious as a substitute for the more direct *comfort*; the word can suggest a tender intensity of fellow-feeling: Whitman's attempts to *solace* the wounded and dying during the Civil War. **Sympathize** in this context suggests an understanding and attentive manner to the needs of the grief-stricken. The word implies a more passive role than these other words: *sympathizing* silently with the patient's rambling accounts of his many ills;

console

cheer up
comfort
condole
solace
sympathize

all those who *sympathized* with us in our bereavement. See CHEER, ENCOURAGE.

Antonyms: aggravate, GRIEVE, HURT, *sadden*, UPSET.

conspiracy

cabal
junta

These words refer to a group of people who have joined forces for some secret purpose which is looked upon as evil and often has to do with the displacement or discrediting of an established authority or government. **Conspiracy** is the most general term; it can apply to any combination of persons united for the accomplishment of an unlawful or reprehensible end: a *conspiracy* of gangsters who were forcing nightclub owners to pay protection under the threat of personal harm; a *conspiracy* of businessmen who were trying to wrest control of a large company from its legal owners; the *conspiracy* which assassinated Caesar. **Cabal** suggests a small, well-organized group of highly placed people intent on a clearly defined goal; this usually involves an attempt to bring about a power shift in some governmental structure or to overthrow someone in a position of great authority: a *cabal* of cabinet ministers seeking to overthrow the president and turn the republic into a fascist state. **Junta** is the most specific of these words in that it almost always denotes a group of people united for political intrigue: a shaky regime that was ripe for seizure by a military *junta*. The word also may carry the implication of a temporary government during a crisis or of an emergency governing structure set up after a revolution: broadcasts by the *junta* promising free elections once the dissidents had been purged. See INTRIGUE.

consult

confer
negotiate
parley

These words refer to discussions held to clarify a question or reach an agreement. **Consult** emphasizes clarification as the motive, without necessarily suggesting ultimate agreement: The President *consulted* with his Cabinet on a variety of questions. Often the word may suggest the seeking out of an authority: *Consult* your dictionary when unsure of your spelling. Similarly, the word can suggest the applying of an inferior to a superior: The salesgirl said she would have to *consult* with the floor manager about the matter. Sometimes, the word points to a secret or private discussion: Have you thought of *consulting* a psychiatrist? **Confer** also emphasizes clarification more than agreement, but here the notion of inferior and superior is less often present. What is stressed is the exchanging of views: union meetings at which members could *confer* with each other about work problems. The word may suggest intimate and informal but not necessarily secret discussion: The coach sat up front *conferring* with the trainer.

Negotiate and **parley** are restricted to situations in which the main motive is the attempt to reach agreement between opposing sides or positions. Both words suggest formal meetings. *Parley* comes from a French word, meaning to speak, and applies to actual enemies attempting to resolve differences through words rather than force: Representatives of the French and English kings *parleyed* on the battlefield. The word calls to mind the vanished world of warring European kingdoms and is less often used for comparable contemporary situations. The preferred word now is *negotiate*; it applies to any formal meeting of opposing sides to settle their differences through compromise rather than through force or some other form of direct action or confrontation. [Labor and management finally *negotiated* a settlement after two weeks of grueling bargaining, thus averting a strike; The Secretary General urged both sides to *negotiate* a settlement to the bloody war.] See ADVICE, ARGUE, CONVERSATION, INFORM.

These words refer to people, acts, or things that are unworthy, immoral, or intensely disapproved of because of bad behavior, bad execution, or bad taste. **Contemptible** indicates that something merits disapproval because it patently falls short of even minimal standards of worth or adequacy. The standard implied here is usually one pertaining to morals or conduct: the candidate's *contemptible* appeal to greed and prejudice; her *contemptible* rudeness to the guest of honor. But it can extend to any evaluating process: The concerto was a *contemptible* piece of trash. **Execrable** can apply through a comparably wide range, but in actual use it applies more often to bad taste or conduct than to immoral acts: dressed in *execrable* taste; an *execrable* lack of concern for the feelings of others. Because of this distinction, *contemptible* is the stronger word, even though it suggests something worthy of scorn, whereas *execrable* suggests something worthy of hearty condemnation.

Despicable and **detestable** are both stronger than the preceding pair, pointing to something worthy of hatred or intense revulsion. *Despicable* can sometimes apply to work or conduct that one finds utterly worthless: a *despicable* painting; a *despicable* bore. But these uses shade off, with weakened force, into hyperbole. At its most intense, the word suggests a fiercely negative judgment of immoral character or action: Few criminals, even the most vicious, are so *despicable* as those gangsters who traffic in narcotics and prostitution; a *despicable* dictator who sentenced thousands to prison and death. While *despicable* can be used less forcefully to register a personal opinion, *detestable* is more readily used in this way, since it can suggest an extreme aversion rather than moral outrage: He found early Italian opera utterly *detestable*. Even when its reference is to morals, this note of personal distaste may be present: He was amazed that no one else seemed to notice the *detestable* cruelty with which she treated her children. See DEPRAVED, REPREHENSIBLE, REPULSIVE.

Antonyms: admirable, EXCELLENT, MORAL.

Contemptuous, the strongest word in this list, means viewing something or someone as mean, vile, or worthless, and actively showing or expressing that view. Attributively, *contemptuous* is applied to a person's words or actions; predicatively it may be used to describe the person. A man may utter a *contemptuous* remark; he may be *contemptuous* of his associates.

Scornful and **disdainful** agree in their application to persons feeling or expressing contempt based on pride or a sense of superiority. The expression of contempt is often limited to the dismissal of the object as unworthy of attention. Like *contemptuous*, these words are used attributively with expressions of contempt, and predicatively with the person expressing it: a *scornful* glance; a *disdainful* rejection; The nobles were *disdainful* of the peasants. *Scornful* differs from *disdainful* in indicating greater emotional hostility to whatever is being condemned; *disdainful*, in comparison, may more readily suggest archness or haughtiness based on a sense of social superiority: a *scornful* attack by his enraged opponent; dismissing her maid with a *disdainful* nod. *Scornful* and *contemptuous* are closer in tone, but *contemptuous* suggests negative evaluation that may be expressed in ironic ways. *Scornful* points more to reaction than evaluation and might apply to more direct expression: a *contemptuous* look that suggested how worthless he found her proposal to be; a *scornful* outburst.

Insolent intensifies aspects implicit in *disdainful*, suggesting an

contemptible

despicable
detestable
execrable

contemptuous

audacious
disdainful
insolent
scornful
supercilious

arrogant or impudent pride that is expressed in rude behavior: the prima donna's *insolent* remarks about the director's ineptness. Where someone might be justified in feeling *contemptuous* or *scornful* of something — or even *disdainful* — *insolent* always indicates a peremptory or overweening grandiosity. **Audacious** applies to reckless behavior that is conspicuous and outrageous: His *audacious* manners are an effrontery to good taste.

Supercilious indicates a haughty or affected manner that is so excessive or unfounded as to become pompous or ridiculous: *supercilious* flattery; a plain-spoken man who was *contemptuous* of her *supercilious* airs and grand gestures. The word comes from the Latin for eyebrow; raised eyebrows are often characteristic of a *supercilious* expression. See CONCEITED, HOSTILE, OVERBEARING.

Antonyms: considerate, humble, POLITE, *respectful, reverent.*

contented

content
gratified
pleased
satisfied

These words refer to the appeasement of need or desire. **Contented** refers to the fulfilling of requirements to the point of satiation: *contented* cows; She pampered him so that he would feel thoroughly *contented*. By contrast, **content** almost exclusively appears as a predicate adjective and suggests, not the full or complete filling of needs or desire, but the willingness to accept a modest or reasonable amount: peasants who were thought to be *content* with their humble station in life; The reporter tried to feel *content* with the brief interview he was granted.

Satisfied is closer to *contented* than to *content* in suggesting complete appeasement of need or desire: gorging himself until he felt almost uncomfortably *satisfied*. The word contrasts with *contented* in that the latter may more often refer to a state of mind akin to complacency, whereas *satisfied* more often suggests the filling of a particular need: dull, *contented* faces; *satisfied* about his score on on the exam.

Gratified suggests unambiguous joy in the fulfilling of a need or desire; in this it is more intense than either *satisfied* or *contented*: a longing for excitement that was only fully *gratified* when he moved to the big city. *Gratified* can also function in a wider range than the other words, suggesting happiness at a well-executed task, role, or duty: *gratified* at the way her students took up the challenges she laid down for them. **Pleased** is less intense than *gratified* and is the vaguest of these words; it may suggest less demanding needs or desires to begin with: *pleased* with the refreshing simplicity of her light snack. It would seldom suggest, in fact, that a question of satiation exists, and may have more to do with the expression of mild approval: She was *pleased* at the courteous way in which he addressed her. See CHEERFUL, COMFORT, JOYOUS.

Antonyms: discontent, frustrated, malcontent, MISERABLE.

contradict

contravene
controvert
deny
disprove

These words refer to the rejection of a previous statement by argument or evidence. **Contradict** may indicate no more than disagreement with a statement: He flatly *contradicted* her assertion that he was too lazy to mow the lawn. In this case, no attempt at proof may be involved. The word also applies to an obvious discrepancy between statements or things, where no proof is necessary: parents who *contradict* each other when giving orders to their children. [The findings of the two studies *contradict* each other; His voting record *contradicts* his claim to be a liberal.] In its widest application, **deny** can point to something refused or withheld: *denying* his request for a weekend pass; Substandard schools *deny* children the chance to learn. In the context of disputes, *deny* often suggests the specific situation of giving a negative answer to a charge or accusation: The treasurer hotly *denied* any misappropriation of funds.

contradict
(continued)

Gainsay is a more formal word that is now rarely used in speech; it does suggest that someone gives vocal dissent to an opinion or accusation, perhaps arbitrarily, tersely, or abruptly, without supporting arguments: her habit of *gainsaying* anything he suggested. The word most often appears now with a negative: arguments for an appeal that not even the most cautious judge could *gainsay*; new evidence that simply could not be *gainsaid*. Here, something is presented as so convincing or conclusive that an arbitrary rejection is not possible. **Oppose** is far less formal in tone than *gainsay* and applies widely beyond the context of dispute or argument. It can suggest unreasoning enmity to a position, with no attempt to argue or present evidence: They still *opposed* the new theory despite all the corroborating facts mustered in its defense. *Oppose* can also suggest reasoned disagreement: the superior skill that Lincoln revealed in *opposing* Douglas's arguments.

gainsay
oppose
refute

Contravene can function like *contradict* when it points to a discrepancy between statements or things, especially where one entity conflicts with another: No law can stand that *contravenes* the Bill of Rights. In terms of argument, the word may point to an attempt to overthrow a whole trend of thought by making telling points: a speech in which he marshaled every available argument that might help him to *contravene* the objections to the bill's passage.

The previous words are mainly concerned with situations in which one statement is at odds with another. The remaining words all can indicate the situation in which a statement or position is demolished by facts or evidence. **Disprove** is the most forceful of these, indicating that a statement, proposition, theory, or even something accepted as a fact has been demonstrated as untrue by countering evidence: explorers who *disproved* the notion that the world was flat; He *denied* her assertion, but couldn't *disprove* it. When two scientific theories *contradict* each other, for example, further investigation will *disprove* one or the other or both, whether in whole or in part. **Controvert**, a more formal word, points to someone who *opposes* a given view and wishes to *disprove* it by offering evidence: His opponents searched the data given in his report, hoping to find inconsistencies by which they could *controvert* his findings. When contrasted with *contravene*, the emphasis of *controvert* falls more heavily on proof: However much they *contravened* his conclusions, they could not *controvert* them. **Refute** can suggest the successful demolishing of an argument by reasoning alone, but it applies even more forcefully when supporting evidence is suggested: They *refuted* his claim of innocence with eyewitness testimony. See COMPETE.

Antonyms: affirm, agree, corroborate, maintain, UPHOLD.

These words describe statements, opinions, concepts, methods, or emotions that are incompatible. The term **contradictory** refers to things that mutually exclude each other, so that both cannot exist in the same object at the same time, as life and death. In formal logic, two statements are *contradictory* if they cannot both be true and cannot both be false. In other words, the statements are so related that if one is true the other must be false, as *I am an American* and *I am not an American*. **Contrary** statements, on the other hand, cannot both be true, but they can both be false, as *I am an Italian* and *I am a Frenchman*. The falsity of either *contrary* proves nothing about the other, but the truth of one establishes the falsity of the other. In a general sense, *contrary* points to

contradictory

conflicting
contrary
opposed
opposite

a basic difference in essence or disagreement in purpose or aim: a *contrary* viewpoint. Things are *contrary* when the highest degree of both cannot exist in the same object at the same time, but where a middle term is possible, partaking of the qualities of both. Thus wisdom and folly are *contrary*, for the perfection of either excludes any trace of the other; yet most human acts and statements partake of both.

Loosely, *contradictory* may mean no more than differing significantly: *contradictory* versions of an accident. In this sense, *contradictory* and **conflicting** are often interchangeable. *Conflicting* means clashing and stresses discord, implying mutual antagonism, as of interests, feelings, or ideas: *conflicting* opinions as to the best location for the new school; The prospect of a return to his home town filled him with *conflicting* emotions.

Opposite comes close to *contradictory* in referring to things that are diametrically different in tendency, character, or point of view: *opposite* opinions; the *opposite* sex. But *opposite* is more likely to be applied to difference in direction, position, or condition than to mutually exclusive statements. [The condition *opposite* to cold is heat; The direction *opposite* to north is south; Black and white are often said to be *opposite*.] Where *opposite* refers to position, tendency, or the like, **opposed** is chiefly used of feeling and intent. People who live on *opposite* sides of a fence may or may not be *opposed*. *Contrary* and *opposed* are often used interchangeably to mean differing from in any way: to do something that is *contrary* (or *opposed*) to another person's wishes. In other uses, *contrary* suggests active opposition, and *opposed* implies passive contrariness. A person holding a *contrary* point of view may suggest that a different line of action should be taken. But a person may be *opposed* to a line of action without proposing any alternative. Both *contradictory* and *contrary* may be used to describe persons who perversely beg to differ at every possible opportunity. See CONTROVERSY, DISPARATE, OPPOSED.

Antonyms: accordant, acquiescent, agreeing, compatible, concordant, consenting, consistent, consonant, corresponding, harmonious.

control

administer
direct
govern
manage
regulate
rule
supervise

To **control** is to exercise a restraining or dominating influence over a person or thing. **Regulate** means to order or *control* by rule, method, or established mode. A major stockholder may *control* a large block of shares in a company. The police may attempt to *control* an unruly mob. The Securities and Exchange Commission *regulates* stock-exchange activity. A government may *regulate* its balance-of-trade payments by *controlling* exports.

Direct stresses guidance and refers to the exercise of leadership: to *direct* a play. *Direct* may refer specifically to the control or conduct of affairs: to *direct* a large corporation. In this sense, it is close to **manage**, which emphasizes operational control: to *manage* a hotel; to *manage* a campaign. Of the two verbs, however, *direct* implies a stronger, overall control, while *manage* often refers to the actual running or handling of specific affairs, and may imply delegated authority. The President *directs* the nation's foreign policy. A person may be hired to *manage* a business for the owner.

The verb **administer** implies official management and direction of affairs: a well-*administered* state government. It indicates the performing of executive functions and may be used of government or institutional officials. The chief of a government agency *administers* the funds allotted to his agency. The chancellor or president of a university may *administer* the school's financial affairs. In a strictly legal sense, *administer* means to act as an executor or trustee in settling or *managing* an estate: to *administer* the estate of a deceased or incompetent person. To **supervise** an operation or an employee is to be in charge of assigning, *directing*, and inspecting the work done. Like *direct*, *supervise* involves overseeing and guidance; but it indicates a more personal control than *administer*, and, like *manage*, may imply the exercise either of personal or of delegated authority: to act as a group leader and *supervise* a dozen workers. A housewife may *supervise* the work done by her maid. An office manager may *supervise* the work of several departments.

To **govern** is to *control* by authority, arbitrarily or constitutionally. *Govern* implies the exercise of knowledge and judgment as well as power, and usually involves systematic administration. To **rule** is more autocratic than to *govern*, implying the exercise of absolute or dictatorial power and the imposition of arbitrary commands. In a democracy, an administration *governs* with the consent of the majority. A dictator, by contrast, may *rule* (or *govern*) with an iron hand. In a less specific sense, *govern* often refers to the exerting of any *controlling* influence: What motives *governed* his actions? It may also mean to keep in check, and in this sense it may serve as a more formal synonym for *control*: unable to *govern* (or *control*) his temper. See COMMAND, GUIDE, POSSESS, SUBDUE.

Controversy, discord, and **dissension** mean a prolonged disagreement expressed in terms ranging from reasonable to belligerent. *Controversy* is generally applied to disagreements between groups, such as nations, political parties, or religious sects. Internationally one speaks of the *controversy* over disarmament; politically, of the *controversy* over federal versus state power; and religiously, of the *controversy* over priestly celibacy. *Discord* is *controversy* carried to unpleasant lengths, and implies an unlikelihood of easy resolution. *Discord* between branches of a family often lasts for generations. *Dissension* is factional *discord*, and is often expressed in voluble protests or accusations: *Dissension* among the rank and file of the labor union forced a change in leadership.

Argument, debate, and **dispute** mean verbal expressions of disagreement. An *argument* is usually between individuals, and suggests a combined appeal to reason and to the emotions. It may or may not result in a resolution of the disagreement. [An *argument* between parents regarding the rearing of their children often goes on for years; The umpire always wins the *argument* about a close play in baseball.] A *debate* is an *argument* between selected individuals or groups, and is carefully controlled and monitored; it is normally limited to an appeal to reason, and is usually an attempt to arrive at the truth rather than to overpower by tricks of oratory: A Congressional *debate* on a piece of proposed legislation is designed to bring out all the relevant facts to enable Congressmen to vote on the merits of the bill. A *dispute* is an *argument* carried on over a long period of time and is often marked by heated clashes: The *dispute* over an international boundary produced a long exchange of strong allegations couched in diplomatic language.

Contention, friction, conflict, and **strife** mean disagreement carried so far as to be marked by ill will and sometimes by hostile actions. *Contention* is usually limited to verbal *discord* carried to extreme lengths, and implies vying for a contested goal. *Contention* between rival camps at a political convention is often acrimonious. *Friction* implies a steady and continuous disagreement between individuals or groups, and is characterized by frequent clashes. *Friction* between labor and management can result in mutual recriminations, strikes, and lockouts. *Conflict*

controversy

argument
bickering
conflict
contention
debate
discord
dispute
dissension
friction
quarrel
strife
wrangle

implies a disagreement so violent that resolution by action other than verbal must be resorted to: The *conflict* between Guelphs and Ghibellines in medieval Italy passed from *controversy* over papal authority to petty wars between city-states. *Strife* implies a *conflict* so basic and contestants so implacable that it is characterized by continuous hostility and an uncompromising attitude: The tactics of the cold war are resorted to in the *strife* between contending power blocs.

Bickering, **quarrel**, and **wrangle** mean *argument* about petty matters, usually carried on in a petulant manner. These words may be applied to individuals or groups, and carry a suggestion of opprobrium. *Bickering* suggests a prolonged exchange of ill-tempered remarks: *bickering* about who should be first in line. *Quarrel* is more general in application; it is usually highly personal and can range from a mild verbal *dispute* to a violent *argument*: a *quarrel* between neighbors about a borrowed lawn mower; violent *quarrels* in which she hurled pots and pans at him and he knocked her about like a rag doll. A *wrangle* is an angry or noisy *quarrel;* the suggestion of petulant intransigence is especially strong, and the word often implies an unwillingness to listen to reason or to be understanding of the other person's point of view: a long *wrangle* over who should pay the bill. See DISAGREE.

Antonyms: agreement, coincidence, consensus, unanimity.

conversation

chat
colloquy
dialogue
discussion
talk
tête-à-tête

These words refer to formal or informal vocal exchanges. **Conversation** and **discussion** are the most general of these, the former applying mainly to an informal social situation, the latter applying often but not exclusively to a formal or official situation. *Conversation*, of course, can and does take place at extremely formal affairs, but in this case the word points to incidental exchanges that are not usually the main point of such a gathering. Much more often the tone of the word suggests a relaxed, informal atmosphere, either festive or intimate: a party at which the *conversation* flowed like wine; a long *conversation* between the two of them over nightcaps of brandy. Any situation, however, in which two or more people speak to each other at some length can constitute a *conversation*: He warned her against getting into *conversations* with other passengers on the train. When *discussion* indicates formal or arranged situations, it still suggests a rambling or free-wheeling meeting in which people express their views or sentiments to each other: asking the committee to hold open *discussions* on the housing project. The word can specifically point to a period that follows some sort of one-sided presentation, one during which audience reaction is heard: a *discussion* that was to take place after the play; the general *discussion* following his speech. When *discussion* suggests an even more informal situation, the word still differs from *conversation* in indicating a purposeful approach that limits itself to a given theme, possibly to arrive at conclusions or determine a course of action: family *discussions* in which each member can openly present his grievances; an innocuous *conversation* that turned into a heated *discussion* on police brutality.

Dialogue and **colloquy** are more formal than the previous words, particularly the latter. *Dialogue* can refer to speeches in a play or to essays in play form. In the context of *conversation*, it strictly suggests a two-person exchange, yet this distinction is commonly ignored. The word has recently come to mean arranged *discussions* among people of dissimilar views: a new *dialogue* among the Protestant denominations and the Catholic church; a year-round *dialogue* between labor and management. *Colloquy* is an extremely formal substitute for *discussion*, and is typically used of formal situations: an extended *colloquy* between the witness and the defense attorney. It may refer to a high-level prearranged conference: a continuing *colloquy* on disarmament at the ambassadorial level. It might also be used humorously to suggest guarded verbal exchanges: my tense *colloquy* with the customs inspector.

Talk is both relatively informal and very general. It can serve as an informal substitute for *conversation*, with greater emphasis on intimacy, sincerity, and frankness: looking forward to having a good long *talk* with all his old friends; feeling relieved after their heart-to-heart *talk*. It can also refer to the substance of *conversations* or *discussions*: soirées where the people were interesting and the *talk* scintillating. The word can also refer informally to a one-sided presentation, as a speech or a lecture: a *talk* on the poverty program. Sometimes, the word is a more general substitute for gossip: indiscreet behavior that caused *talk* among the neighbors.

Chat and **tête-à-tête** are emphatic about the informality and intimacy of the conversation they point to. But *chat*, most informal of all these words, can refer to two or more people and most strongly suggests light, pleasant, and rambling *talk* in which personal matters, if touched on, are pursued without great intensity: an hour's *chat* about the doings of their mutual friends; a *chat* between mother and daughter about the girl's dating problems. By contrast, *tête-à-tête* specifically indicates a talk between two people (literally, head-to-head), in which the emphasis is on sincerity and frankness of a confidential, romantic, or even conspiratorial sort: seen having a *tête-à-tête* with her husband's employer; a courtship that consisted of long *tête-à-têtes* in dimly lit restaurants; a *tête-à-tête* between representatives of the two deadlocked candidates. See ARGUE, CHATTER, PATTER, SPEECH.

convulsion

fit
paroxysm
seizure
spasm

These words all refer to involuntary upheavals that disrupt normal processes. **Convulsion**, most specifically, suggests a violent contraction of muscles, as when the body is struggling to throw off a poison; since these contractions come in a series, the plural is often used in this physiological sense: a case of ptomaine poisoning that resulted in fatal *convulsions*. **Spasm** refers to any involuntary convulsive muscular contraction. When manifested by alternate contractions and relaxations it is a *clonic spasm;* when persistent and steady, it is a *tonic spasm*. Like *convulsion*, *spasm* can be used to refer figuratively to any sudden, violent change or burst of feverish activity: a *spasm* of fear every time she recalled the accident; *spasms* of active trading on the exchange; The market was thrown into a series of *convulsions* due to the abrupt rise in tariffs. *Convulsion*, both in its figurative and physiological senses, suggests involuntary movement of greater intensity and severity than *spasm*.

Fit is more informal than *convulsion* and suggests a malfunction of psychological or physiological processes rather than the attempt to reject a poison. It is still commonly used to describe an attack of epilepsy: an epileptic *fit*. But the word may sound outdated when applied to a psychological malfunction: a *fit* of madness. It is, however, frequently used jocosely to describe being overcome by any extremely intense emotion that has physical manifestations: a *fit* of anger; a *fit* of laughter that left us weak; a *fit* of hiccups.

Seizure, like *convulsion*, can apply in a number of contexts. It can be used in conjunction with *convulsion* and as a more formal substitute for *fit*. It emphasizes the involuntary nature of the affliction: a *seizure* of *convulsions*; an epileptic *seizure*. In the latter case, the substitution might once have seemed euphemistic; now, however, it is merely more dispassionate and objective than *fit*, which when used in this sense evokes the pre-Freudian era when epileptics were considered accursed. *Seizure* can apply to other intense physical or emotional upheavals: a *seizure* of coughing; a psychotic *seizure*. It can also refer to group responses: a nation paralyzed by a *seizure* of terror following the assassination.

Paroxysm may pertain to a physiological situation, referring to one of a series: *convulsions* in which each *paroxysm* was more prolonged than the one before. More commonly, however, it is used in the plural to refer to an acute emotional attack. In this case, it is like *seizure* in avoiding the jocose overtones of *fit*, but is more intense than either, even to the point of hyperbole: *paroxysms* of anger; *paroxysms* of grief. See HEART ATTACK.

copy

duplicate
facsimile
model
replica
reproduction

These words refer to an exact or approximate rendering of an original. **Copy** is the most general of these, applying both to exact and inexact renderings: a carbon *copy* of the letter; a Roman *copy* of the original Greek statue; manufacturers who mass-produce *copies* of Paris fashions; a poorly executed counterfeit *copy*. **Duplicate** and **replica**, by contrast, specifically stress the exactness of the *copy*. *Duplicate* may suggest an exact and valid replacement: applying for a *duplicate* of his lost passport. It may even refer more particularly to one of two identical things: sorting through his library for *duplicates*; a frieze that is the *duplicate* of one on the front of the building. In less precise usage, the word may shade off in reference merely to things that resemble each other, or to an accurate *copy*: an obelisk that is the *duplicate* of several in Egypt; a *duplicate* of the bill of lading. *Replica*, most precisely, refers to a *copy* made by the creator of the original: Rodin's habit of making a number of *replicas* each time he cast a statue. As in this example, any sense of original and *copy* is obliterated. More loosely, however, the word is simply a more formal substitute for *copy*; it may even be popularly understood to mean a rough approximation: a *replica* of what an Elizabethan theater must have looked like.

Though more formal, **facsimile** is almost as general as *copy*, since the degree of exactness is not specified. Often the word is used to indicate only a schematic approximation of an original: a contest anyone can enter by sending in a candy wrapper or a reasonable *facsimile* thereof. Even in other uses, the word always suggests easily noticeable differences between original and the *copy*. **Reproduction** is also vague about the degree of accuracy implied. Sometimes the stress is on a close resemblance to the original: a remarkably skillful *reproduction* of the original painting. Often, however, the word may be used to suggest a simplified or less expensive version of a prototype: applauding hand-sewn showpieces that will deluge the country as machine-stitched *reproductions*. **Model** is unique among these words in specifically indicating an approximate rendering; the word suggests a schematic approximation, often of reduced scale, that may precede the construction of the original: a desk-top *model* of the proposed supersonic transport plane; a working *model* of the new turbine. The word, in any case, seldom suggests the kind of *copy* that could be mistaken for the original; a functional or illustrative mock-up is more often indicated: using a *model* of the space capsules to show the maneuvering involved in docking. See COUNTERPART, DUPLICATE, SAMPLE.

Antonyms: PROTOTYPE.

These words refer to a dead person or animal. **Corpse** is the most general term here, applying to any physical specimen that is not alive. It is neutral in tone and is equally suitable in common, medical, or criminological parlance: identifying a *corpse* in the morgue; the *corpse* being wheeled into the autopsy room. **Body** is substituted for *corpse* in common speech when the latter is felt to be brutally blunt. Because *body* is both simple and factual, however, it does not give a euphemistic tone. One would certainly speak to someone bereaved about the *body*, not about the *corpse*. Where considerations for the feelings of others is not an issue, *corpse* is more exact, since *body* can, of course, refer to the living as well as the dead. In this neutral context, on the other hand, *body* might still be more appropriate for the recently dead than *corpse*.

Cadaver, most specifically, refers to a *corpse* used for medical education or research, excluding those examined in an autopsy merely to determine the cause of death. *Cadaver* may be used of nonhuman animals slated for medical dissection as well as of human *bodies*. Outside this medical context, *cadaver* would have overtones of grisliness or gallows-humor.

Remains, in one context, is a euphemism used by undertakers who evidently consider *body* too indelicate to mention. This use intends, perhaps, to distinguish between the surviving soul or spirit and the physical part it leaves behind. The word is more accurately descriptive of a *corpse* that has been partially destroyed — as in an explosion or other catastrophe. This possibility makes its use as a euphemism for *body* somewhat risky, and would strike some ears as vulgar and tasteless.

Stiff is a slang word for *corpse*, and has a bizarrely humorous quality owing to its association with gangland movies in the past two or three decades. Today it sounds a little dated. [Hey, Charlie, where'll we put the *stiff*?] One can imagine anyone using the term, however, who becomes so familiar with handling *corpses* that he begins to regard them utterly dispassionately as objects. In this context, use of the word by medical students or police officers may not betoken any lack of respect for life, but only represent a necessary pose of jocularity to make their close association with death more bearable.

These words refer to something that resembles, completes, or corresponds to another thing. **Counterpart**, the most general, can function in all these ways, though it specifically suggests a close relationship between the two things considered. In reference to resemblance, it suggests a precise or near likeness: the very *counterpart* of his father. In reference to completion, it suggests two things that form an entity: finding that he had the first volume of the work but lacked its *counterpart*. In reference to correspondence, the word particularly suggests one of a matching pair of things that are alike but opposite: a coffee table that separated one piece of the sectional sofa from its *counterpart*. In this last sense **opposite number** is sometimes used, but unlike *counterpart* it need indicate no likeness in appearance, only in function. An *opposite number* is a person or thing that corresponds to another in terms of each's relation to the sets of which they are part. In some instances *opposite numbers* may be physically opposed, as linemen in a football game; in others they may simply play similar roles, as third basemen of two opposing teams. Two account executives of different advertising agencies competing for the same account may be called *opposite numbers* or *counterparts*. It is to be noted that when the opposition becomes more a matter of role than of physical position, *counter-*

part comes into play as a synonym for *opposite number*. But *counterpart* is in any event more elevated in tone.

Correlate indicates a much closer relationship than *counterpart*, but need not imply likeness at all. It indicates instead interdependence or reciprocity, with or without the suggestion that one of two things is a cause of the other: the anomie that is an inevitable *correlate* of ghetto life. The word can, however, suggest one of two similar things, each existing in mutually exclusive areas; in this case any notion of causality is distinctly absent: tales of the Samurai that have their *correlate* in European Arthurian legends. **Parallel** is related to this last sense of *correlate*, but, in this case, a slighter resemblance may be suggested; again, no causality is implied. [The current birth-control controversy has a *parallel* in the similar dispute about usury in medieval times.] *Parallel* can point to a more essential likeness, correspondence, or match, but the word's clear reference to the geometric situation of lines that run equidistant to each other gives strong implications of kinship but not of close contact or causality. *Parallel*, however, is the one word here that readily suggests similarity between several things, rather than just two: a plot line that has innumerable *parallels* in the detective novels of the past decade.

Of all the words here, **complement** puts the least stress on likeness and similarity; none at all, in fact, need be suggested by the word. Instead, the word points to one of two things that together make up a whole. These two things, furthermore, need not be equal halves or mirror images as is the case with *counterpart*: a woman in whom intelligence and femininity were not antagonists but *complements* to each other; a year-end bonus that was a small but by no means negligible *complement* to his annual earnings. The word should not, of course, be confused with compliment, which refers to praise or flattery given by one person to another. See COPY, DUPLICATE, SIMILAR.

Antonyms: antithesis, contradiction, contrast, opposite.

countless

immeasurable
incalculable
innumerable

These words refer to quantities or sizes that are great, infinite, or difficult to determine. **Countless** refers to large amounts that are difficult or impossible to total either because of their vastness or because their full extent is not known or unknowable: *countless* grains of sand scattered by the wind. Though the visible stars in the sky are often hyperbolically referred to as *countless*, they have in fact been counted, as well as those studied by other means. In the strictest sense, only those that may exist beyond any observation are *countless*, though these may be few or great or even infinite in number. Similarly, *countless* may refer to large quantities that cannot now be totaled: the *countless* numbers who died of malaria before the discovery of quinine. While *countless* may sometimes refer to instances in time and **innumerable** may refer to quantities in space, the latter is particularly used for occurrences that cannot be totaled because of frequency or lack of record: *innumerable* instances in the past when a new idea was found dangerous to the established order. The word is frequently used merely as a hyperbole for many: *innumerable* occasions on which he had stayed out all night carousing.

Immeasurable refers more strictly to spatial size or to dimensions that are either infinite or completely impossible to determine. Thus, unlike *countless* and *innumerable*, the word is less likely to be used hyperbolically, whether to refer to greatness or difficulty of reckoning: distances that in an infinite universe would be literally *immeasurable*;

immeasurable quantities of natural resources that were lost forever through misuse. **Incalculable** most strictly resembles the first pair of words in referring to large amounts difficult to total. The word may also be used like *immeasurable* for large volumes, but in this case the size may be hard to determine because of its uncertain dimensions: a deep trough on the sea floor, one of *incalculable* size. More commonly, however, the word refers particularly to the effects something has, when these are difficult or impossible to determine or can never be known: the *incalculable* effects of Luther's break with Rome, effects that still have not run their course; the *incalculable* benefits that ripple outward from even the most trivial act of kindness; aware that he was taking an *incalculable* risk. See INFINITE, MASSIVE.

Antonyms: calculable, limitary, measurable, numbered.

These words refer to a bold and determined attitude that is undaunted by difficulties and fearless in the face of danger. **Courage** is the most general word, embracing all the rest. It indicates a dauntless spirit and the ability to act bravely under stress or to endure in times of adversity: the *courage* of the fighting men; the rocklike *courage* of a mother who lost three sons in the war. A person may show *courage* in response to circumstances, doing what is necessary despite the personal risk involved. But *courage* may also imply a firmness that arises from a strong belief in the moral rightness of a position or course of action: He has the *courage* of his convictions.

Fortitude is the most formal of these words, indicating firmness or strength of mind. It emphasizes the facing of obstacles with brave and unwavering resourcefulness: an ordeal that required every ounce of *fortitude* he possessed; the *fortitude* of a Daniel in the lions' den. **Resolution** is far less inclusive than *fortitude*. It implies a determination to be firm in conviction, faithful in allegiance, unswerving in course, or unwavering in devotion to a task. *Resolution* does not necessarily suggest fearlessness but emphasizes the firm pushing aside of any mental reservations or qualms about attaining an objective: the *resolution* with which he ran into the burning house despite the terror that possessed him.

Nerve may be compared to *fortitude* and **pluck** to *resolution*, although both of these words are considerably more informal than the previous pair. *Nerve* is particularly emphatic in stressing the unflustered, cool, and steady daring with which someone takes calculated risks to win an objective: the *nerve* with which he drew himself, hand over hand, along the last cable of the broken rope bridge. Sometimes, even more informally, the word suggests brashness or rudeness in a social situation. [He had a lot of *nerve* to ask her the day before the dance; You've got some *nerve* coming in here without knocking.] *Pluck*, like *resolution*, need not suggest the fearlessness of *fortitude* and *nerve*, but it does suggest a jaunty willingness to try anything, whether out of high spirits, conviction, or the zealous eagerness of the good sport: Any lowering of morale could endanger the *pluck* of our fighting forces; a stripling who showed more *pluck* on the march than many a seasoned scout.

The remaining words are more informal still, with less clearly defined spheres of separate meanings, all being colorful substitutes for *courage*. **Backbone** may suggest strength of character or stubborn determination, while **grit** may refer to a resolute spirit or a tenacious enduring power: having the *backbone* to endure ridicule for his unpopular views;

courage

backbone
fortitude
grit
guts
nerve
pluck
resolution

showing his *grit* by taking every indignity the drill sergeant foisted upon him. **Guts**, a slang word, may imply a brash, hearty boldness or a presumptuous audacity: having the *guts* to ask his boss for a raise after his first month on the job. But *guts* more often indicates an admirable display of *courage* when it really counts, and is in this sense synonymous with the cliché *intestinal fortitude*: the cop who showed real *guts* in a running gunfight with bank robbers; It took *guts* to stand up against the mob. See BRAVE, EFFRONTERY, OPPORTUNISTIC.

Antonyms: cowardice, cowardliness, FEAR, *pusillanimity, timidity, timorousness.*

covenant

agreement
compact
concordat
contract

These words denote promises or understandings made between two or more parties as to a course of action.

Covenant carries strong overtones of obligation and responsibility. A *covenant* is often a solemn pledge made by members of a religious or other dedicated group to maintain and promote a body of doctrine or a set of principles: the *Covenant* of the Liberty of Worship drawn up in Scotland in 1557; the *Covenant* of the League of Nations.

Agreement is the most general and most positive term, suggesting that a settlement has already been reached. *Agreements* range in importance from those made informally between persons to those drawn up between countries or states. [By tacit *agreement*, Clark's friends all avoided any mention of his mentally ill wife; During the course of history, many *agreements* have been made between France and England.]

A **contract** is a formal *agreement* almost always in written form and enforceable by law. *Contracts* may be drawn up for the performance of work at a fixed rate and within a given period: a *contract* to deliver military supplies to the government; a *contract* signed by a teacher for the coming academic year. Or it may be a binding, legalized *agreement* between persons: a marriage *contract*.

Compact carries the idea of a solemn *agreement* between persons or between political groups or states. A *compact* may or may not be in written form, but the chief guarantee of its being carried out is that each party is under strong pressures of obligation and mutual trust. [The two brothers made a *compact* that the family business would always be handed down to their descendants; Faust made a *compact* with Satan; The seven nations made a *compact* to regulate tariffs.]

Concordat is confined to formal *agreements* between the papacy and a national government to terminate or avert dissension between the Roman Catholic Church and civil power. See TREATY.

cowardly

craven
pusillanimous

These words mean lacking courage to a degree that arouses disapproval and disgust. **Cowardly** is the most common word of the three, and is applied opprobriously to persons who are unwilling or unable to prevent their fear or timidity from influencing their actions unduly; it can also refer to the actions themselves: In frontier days, shooting a man in the back was considered *cowardly*; too *cowardly* to stand up and fight.

Craven and **pusillanimous** are formal words encountered mainly in writing. *Craven* is applied to persons or conduct that is outrageously or abjectly *cowardly*, and that flagrantly violates the prevailing cultural standards of courage: The *craven* captive groveled at our feet, begging for mercy. *Pusillanimous* differs from the other terms in pointing more strongly to temperamental timidity than to fear as the basis of the resulting action or inaction. *Pusillanimous* represents a contemptible moral squeamishness rather than a physical cowardliness, although it is quite possible for the same person to be both *pusillanimous* and *cowardly*. What chiefly distinguishes the *pusillanimous* person, however, is his unwillingness to press for his rights: His *pusillanimous* reaction was to sigh and say, "Well, it really won't do to raise a fuss." See AFRAID, TIMID.

Antonyms: BOLD, BRAVE.

These words refer to a small gap or opening in a surface. **Crack** suggests an opening longer than wide, and may refer to a normal opening or to one formed by force, violence, or some malfunction: the *crack* under the door; faint *cracks* running through the whole base of the pillar; putting his eye to a *crack* in the partition. While *crack* may or may not suggest an opening through which light or air might pass, **chink** invariably suggests such an opening: the unfilled *chinks* between the logs forming the cabin wall; a *chink* in the dike through which water had begun to seep. **Breach** suggests a gap in something that might impair its functioning and made, usually, by wear or some sundering force: a *breach* cut by the enemy through our front lines, leaving headquarters vulnerable to attack. It may, however, refer as well to any natural gap of any size or shape in the distribution of items forming a group: a *breach* in the row of trees that widened out finally into a path. **Cleft**, by contrast, most commonly suggests a natural indentation in something: a *cleft* in his chin; in the *cleft* of a tree. It may also suggest something formed by wear or force: a bird perching where the lightning had made a *cleft* in the rock. In no case does the word suggest an opening clear through to the other side of something, as is true of *chink*. **Crevice** and **fissure** both usually refer to long *cracks* formed by natural forces at work in a terrain. *Crevice* most commonly suggests a *crack* in an incline or hillside: a mountaineer moving sure-footedly from *crevice* to *crevice* in the mountain face. *Fissure*, by contrast, suggests a long slitlike opening in a more level surface: *fissures* in the ground formed by the earthquake; stretches of snow that tremored and broke open in *fissures* at every step he took. *Crevice* can also be applied outside this context: *crevices* between the bricks deep enough for him to gain a toe-hold in the wall; using plaster of Paris to fill the *crevices* in the flaking paint and spackle to seal up the smaller *cracks*. See HOLE.

These words are all concerned with the act of bringing something into being that did not exist before. **Create** may suggest conscious intention, esthetic discrimination, power, control, or all of these. It is most appropriate for situations in which the raw materials and the finished product are very different from each other: a Supreme Being who *creates* the universe out of darkness and chaos; the novelist who *creates* a unique view of life by using everyday language; statesmen attempting to *create* world order out of the discords of warring nations. The word is also frequently used as a status word for far less significant pursuits: the fashion czar *creating* a new line of spring dresses. **Design** and **compose** are like *create* in referring to esthetic acts, but are more specific in their application. Someone who *designs* dresses, cars, or stage sets may simply execute the plans for these products, leaving their actual construction to lesser craftsmen. Thus *design* emphasizes conception rather than building. Also, it suggests a less profound change from raw material to finished product than *create*: We can *design* tech-

crack

breach
chink
cleft
crevice
fissure

create

compose
design
invent
make
produce

niques to prevent urban sprawl, but we can hardly *create* utopias from scratch at this late date. *Compose*, most specifically, refers to musical composition: to *compose* a symphony or a popular song. In this sense, it is more like *create* than *design*. In its passive use, however, the esthetic implications disappear and the word refers to the possibly arbitrary constituents of a group or object: a city *composed* of many ethnic strains.

Make, the most general of these words, is pivotal in that it may apply to esthetic or scientific acts on the one hand, or on the other to mere production of any kind: artists who *make* sculptures; biologists who *make* new species through hybridization; nations that *make* atom bombs; factories that *make* detergents. Because of the word's wide range of possibility, a more specific word is sometimes preferable.

Invent in a scientific or technological context is parallel to *design* in its esthetic context. The person who *invents* a product plans and tests a new concept, though he may leave its production to others. Just as *create* has more status than *design* in the arts, so discover, as the highest goal of the sciences, has more scientific status than *invent*: Franklin discovered electricity, but Edison *invented* the light bulb.

Produce refers mostly to the mere turning out of work: the last years of his life in which Shakespeare *produced* no new plays. In another sense, however, the work implied by *produce* may be done by people who had no part in *creating*, *designing*, or *inventing* the product: theatrical technicians who *produce* what the playwright *creates*; seamstresses who *produce* the gowns fashion experts *design*; factories that *produce* the light bulbs based on the one Edison *invented*. See BUILD, CHANGE, DEVISE, FIND, MAKE, MOLD.

Antonyms: BREAK, DESTROY, KILL, *obliterate*

creative

imaginative
ingenious
inventive
original
resourceful

These words apply to the active, exploratory mind and to its products, describing creators or creations that employ ordinary materials in extraordinary ways. **Creative** suggests the entire process whereby things that did not exist before are conceived, given form, and brought to being. **Original** is more limited in scope and more specific, pointing to the creator not as maker but as source. The *original* mind, slipping free of the conventional and the commonplace, comes up with things no one else has thought of—the new idea, the different approach: an *original* insight; a highly *original* poet. The *creative* mind goes further, combining the fruits of experience and imagination in an *original* way to re-create reality in a new form: the *creative* process; a mind in *creative* ferment.

Where *creative* and *original* describe the mind, *creative* and **imaginative** have to do with the imagination. Great literary works are produced by the *creative* imagination; but the creators of such works and the works themselves are called *imaginative*, not *creative*: *imaginative* writers; *imaginative* literature. *Creative*, when applied to people and what they do, makes an elementary distinction. The *creative* people in an advertising agency are the artists and writers, as distinguished from the bookkeepers and businessmen. *Creative* writing is the writing of fiction or poetry, as distinguished from the writing of fact or opinion. But the word *creative* is also used pretentiously in advertising lingo to mean novel, new, or different: *creative* hair styling.

Imaginative and **inventive** are alike in indicating an active fancy, a nimble exercise of mind; and both words apply to works that are strikingly *original*. But where the *imaginative* person may visualize things very different from reality, the *inventive* person figures out how to put things together in a new way so that they will work. Inventiveness is a practical kind of creativity. It calls into play analytical qualities of mind, often in the service of a common-sense idea of what is needed.

The **resourceful** mind solves its problems despite limitations, finding whatever means are available and adapting them to its ends. Where an *inventive* mind poses its own problems, a *resourceful* mind copes with externally imposed problems. [The *resourceful* Scarlett O'Hara made a ball gown from her draperies.] An *imaginative* child may express himself by drawing. An *inventive* child may do wonders with an erector set. A *resourceful* child may drape an old sheet over a card table to make his own private playhouse. Imposed limitations are not always implied by the word, however. Faced with the same abundance of toys, one child still might become easily bored; a *resourceful* child, by contrast might soon begin to develop new games, using untried combinations of these elements.

The **ingenious** person is both *inventive* and *resourceful*; but above all, he is brilliantly clever. *Ingenious* may, in fact, sometimes suggest a superficial cleverness indulged in for its own sake, without a cause. But the word is more often complimentary, an expression of admiring surprise at the ability to solve a problem neatly in a highly *original* way. Applied to products themselves, *ingenious* may indicate something unusually complex or intricate: an *ingenious* water clock. It can also suggest something deliberately devised to trick or mislead: an *ingenious* way of coping with absentees; an *ingenious* method for cheating on exams. See ARTISTIC, IMAGINATION.

Antonyms: BANAL, *dull, helpless, mindless, myopic, witless.*

creed

doctrine
dogma
tenet

These words refer to the articles of faith on which a group of adherents, as to a religion, are agreed. **Creed** most specifically refers to a concise statement of the essential points to which all believers must subscribe: the Athanasian *creed*. **Doctrine** suggests a particular stand that may be briefly summarized but which usually can involve complex or extensive theological discussion for full treatment: the easily affirmed *doctrine* of the Trinity to which so many church fathers devoted at least a volume of explanation. The word may also refer to any item that makes up a *creed*: the *doctrine* of the Resurrection. By extension, the word can also sometimes refer, in other fields, to views generally subscribed to: the Keynesian economic *doctrine* of stimulating growth through the unbalanced budget.

Dogma refers to an authoritative stand or a bundle of such stands that all believers must accept as correct. A *dogma*, however, need not be of such first-rank importance as to be part of a religion's *creed*; it best suggests, in fact, an accretion of moral stands that have become institutionlized by time into an inflexible set of rules for the living of life: the shattering of worn-out *dogma* during the Reformation and Counter Reformation. By extension, the word refers to any set of unquestioned assertions or attitudes in any field: Maoist *dogma* that branded the Soviet Union as a betrayer of the revolution. **Tenet** refers to an attitude, principle, or precept that may or may not be part of a body of *dogma* or *doctrine*. In any case, *tenet* suggests something more provisional in nature than these other words and thus more susceptible to change: holding to the *tenet* that the best officers are those who come up through the ranks. See IDEA, OPINION, RELIGION.

crime

felony
misdemeanor
offense
treason
violation

These words pertain to the breaking of a law. **Crime** refers specifically to serious misconduct, **violation** specifically to lesser breaches of regulation; **offense** generically includes both kinds of law-breaking: slums rife with theft, murder, and other *crimes*; a traffic *violation*; a scofflaw who repeats the minor *offense* of illegal parking and, by ignoring the tickets, becomes guilty of a major *offense*; a light sentence because it was a first *offense*. *Crime* may be used as an abstract noun to suggest all illegal activity: a mogul of organized *crime*. It may be used hyperbolically to mean any misjudgment: It's a *crime* to waste your money on such a movie. It may also imply a breach of moral standards: a *crime* against nature; a *crime* against humanity. Outside the legal context, *violation* may suggest a breaking of faith or the rape or desecration of something held sacred: the *violation* of a confidence; a *violation* of the test-ban treaty; soldiers responsible for the widespread *violation* of the captured city's women; the *violation* of holy relics. *Offense*, outside the legal context, may suggest extremely bad taste or injury to someone's sensibility: a film so ribald as to give *offense*.

Crime is commonly subdivided into two categories — **misdemeanors**, the less serious, and **felonies**, the more serious *offenses*. The line between *misdemeanor* and *felony* is arbitrarily set by tradition or law. Thefts up to a certain monetary value, for example, are *misdemeanors*; over that value, they become *felonies*. Severity of sentence may also be a determining factor. **Treason** is distinct in kind rather than degree from *misdemeanor* and *felony*; it involves a deliberate betrayal of one's country to an enemy, whether in peace or war. Of these three words, only *treason* is occasionally used in other than its legal sense. In this case it refers to some monstrous desecration or ethical violation: Nazi doctors whose experiments constituted moral *treason* against our most deeply ingrained human instincts. During periods of heated political controversy, *treason* is often used loosely to describe any act deemed unpatriotic or damaging to the national interest: In my book, burning our flag is an act of *treason*. See MISCHIEVOUS, SIN.

Antonyms: benefaction, good deed, mitzvah, service.

crucial

acute
critical
pressing
urgent

These words refer to the growing lack or need of something vital or to the turning point in an emergency or crisis. **Crucial** is the most general of these words in that it can refer to either of these situations equally well: a *crucial* battle that would determine the outcome of the whole war. By contrast, **acute** usually refers to a lack or need that has intensified to crisis proportions: an *acute* water shortage; an *acute* lack of lower-income housing. Less frequently, the word refers to other emergencies: the *acute* problem of air pollution in cities. In medical terminology, *acute* means grave or severe: an *acute* attack of bronchitis.

Critical is very similar to *crucial* in the way it refers either to an extreme lack or to a turning point: a *critical* absence of safety features in the new models; a *critical* showdown vote on the proposed legislation. The word differs from *crucial* in often suggesting a more exact measurement of the lack, especially when even a slight decline could have far-reaching consequences: Another minute's lack of oxygen could be *critical*. The greater seriousness of *critical* as compared to *crucial* is also present when the reference is to a turning point. Where *crucial* may emphasize the absolute necessity that something happen in order to achieve a satisfactory result, *critical* more often suggests a balance between positive and negative outcomes that is beyond our power to influence: a decision that was to prove *crucial* to the great victory won that day; helpless to combat the *critical* weakening of the body's defenses. *Critical* can also be used to imply that something is scarce but vital: a list of *critical* materials.

Pressing and **urgent** are milder than the rest of these words. *Pressing* is especially so, since it can refer to a serious lack that is chronic rather than *acute*: a *pressing* need for changes that are not likely to be accomplished soon. *Urgent* suggests a nearer approach to crisis, but the lack it points to might be one among many, without necessarily being the decisive one: faced with so many *urgent* needs that they had to decide which of them were the *critical* ones and which could wait a little longer. Both *pressing* and *urgent*, moreover, can refer to an emergency without necessarily referring to its turning point: a *pressing* matter; an *urgent* conference between heads of state. Both words can refer to appeals rather than to the lack itself: a *pressing* request for funds; an *urgent* appeal for help. In all the various possibilities, however, *urgent* maintains its greater intensity when compared to *pressing*.

These words pertain to harsh or harmful acts that inflict pain on others or to inhumane temperaments and attitudes that are lacking in sensitivity or compassion. **Cruel** can apply to both the act and the attitude: the *cruel* way he mistreated the helpless child; *cruel* and vicious prison guards. While the word can suggest the gratuitous or unmotivated infliction of pain, *cruel* is also used to describe situations where punishment may be deserved or thought desirable, but is meted out unjustly or excessively: a constitutional ban on *cruel* and unusual punishment; a *cruel* and repressive regime. But the word can also apply to anything that causes pain or harm, even where all intent to hurt or punish is absent: the *cruel* sea; the *cruel*, inexorable forces of nature. By contrast, **sadistic** always implies a deliberate wish to cause pain and even more specifically focuses on inflicting it for its own sake rather than out of necessity or as punishment. The word suggests a warped mind that gets pleasure from seeing or causing other living things to suffer: the disturbed child who tore butterflies apart with *sadistic* gusto; a *sadistic* man who got sexual release only from flogging his female partner. Such pleasure often masquerades itself in the guise of meting out necessary discipline or authorized punishment.

Brutal and **bestial** both compare *cruel* behavior to that of animals. *Brutal* emphasizes a lack of sensitivity or compassion and can suggest a gross and unintelligent person given to the use of excessive and indiscriminate force in attaining his objective: Many a movie mogul reached the top by trampling on others in the most *brutal* way. By contrast, it is possible to be both clever and *cruel*; also, the *sadistic* mentality may contrive intricate ways of inflicting pain. *Brutal* alone stresses sheer, savage force. Because of this, *brutal*, like *cruel*, can be used to refer to nonhuman actions, especially those that are harsh or energetic: The ship was beleaguered by the *brutal* pounding of the violent storm. *Bestial* is applied exclusively to humans; it does not point solely to forcefulness as does *brutal* nor necessarily to the inflicting of pain like the first pair. It indicates, instead, any sort of behavior that is thought unworthy of a human being because of its depravity, degeneracy, or viciousness: the *bestial* society that gave rise to Auschwitz and Treblinka. In a related use, the word can apply to unrestrained or unnatural appetite of any sort: the *bestial* lust he felt for his own daughter. As Mark Twain pointed out, it may well be inaccurate to call *cruel* behavior *bestial*, since most animals inflict pain only out of such necessities as hunger and self-

cruel

bestial
brutal
nasty
sadistic

defense, whereas man has often been known to do so gratuitously.

Nasty is the mildest of these words; at its most informal it can describe anything that is severe, serious, or harmful: a *nasty* cut. Used of behavior, it points to extreme unkindness or callousness and not necessarily to inflicting physical pain at all: She told him that she wouldn't put up with his *nasty* remarks any longer. In describing personality, it can point to an extremely disagreeable temperament or to a habitual mistreatment of others: He woke up in a *nasty* frame of mind; a *nasty* man who treated other people like dirt. See DEPRAVED, HOSTILE.

Antonyms: gentle, HUMANE, *kind, merciful.*

cry

bellow
outcry
roar
scream
shout
shriek
yell

These words all refer to a voice raised in excitement or urgency. Although each word suggests most readily a particular emotion, all have been used interchangeably to pertain to any expression of intense feeling: joy, anger, pain, grief, despair, amazement, resentment, and many others. All of them, furthermore, pertain to one person's tone of voice, but are commonly used for groups of people when one wishes to suggest that the group responds almost unanimously to some event with a single reaction.

Cry, shout, and **yell** are the most general, emphasizing mainly the loudness of a voice or voices: a *cry* of delight; a tortured *cry*; a *shout* of approval that rang through the hall; a *yell* for help. *Cry* particularly suggests a surprised or involuntary response. In an informal context, however, *cry* is especially associated with emotions that result in tears: the woman who sat down and had a good *cry*. This informal use is sometimes present as an overtone in other uses of the word: watching him leave and *crying* for him to come back. *Yell* is especially relevant to a situation in which someone is calling for help: hoping their *yells* would carry far enough to be heard. *Yell* also has a particular use for *cries* of enthusiasm at sports events, either spontaneous or planned: cheerleaders who led the spectators in a school *yell*; *yells* of "Murder him" that echoed above the boxing ring. *Shout* can relate to the situation of seeking help, but it also pertains particularly to the emotion of anger: an apoplectic *shout* from her husband that rang through the cafe.

Bellow and **roar** relate to this aspect of *shout* in being most appropriate for angry *cries*. *Bellow* suggests deepness of voice as well as loudness and thus implies a man's voice or a group dominated by men; it is also used for enraged animals, such as an angered bull: the platoon sergeant's *bellow* of disgust; a furious *bellow* from the wounded bull. *Roar* also suggests anger when it refers to a single person, but it is especially appropriate for describing the reaction of a crowd. In the latter case, the emotion need not necessarily be that of unanimous anger, but of a mingling of diverse emotions: the *roar* of praise and disapproval that swelled through the theater. *Roar* can, of course, also refer to any loud mingling of noises, neither human nor animal: the *roar* of the printing presses.

Shriek and **scream** refer most appropriately to *cries* of pain, terror, or surprise: the *shriek* of a woman trapped under piles of debris. In sharp contrast to *bellow*, *shriek* suggests high-pitched sound, discordant, grating, or whining: The woman's *shriek* of terror carried further than the man's enraged *bellow*. Because of this implication, *shriek* is sometimes used of birds: the *shriek* of gulls above the harbor. It can also be used for any grating sound: the *shriek* of chalk against the blackboard. Like *shriek*, *scream* often implies a high-pitched, piercing sound: the *scream* of a siren. But it emphasizes loudness more than pitch, and more often than *shriek* may apply to hysterical or panicky shouts of men as well as women: Clutching his crushed foot, he let out a *scream* of pain. Both *shriek* and *scream* may be used hyperbolically in situations suggesting intense surprise: When she opened the present she gave a little *shriek* of joy; a *scream* of delight. And both are commonly used to describe the *shouts* of children.

Outcry relates to *shriek* as it pertains to *cries* of pain. But its most specific use is for an outburst of indignation, usually from a group of people: neighbors who watched the murder but made no *outcry*. The sense of protest is present even in metaphorical uses: newspaper editorials that cause a public *outcry* against such indifference. See CHATTER, SAY, SQUEAL.

These words refer to the denouncing of something or the calling down of evil on someone. **Curse** is the only relatively informal word here and the one most widely used in a variety of ways. Most informally, it can refer to any blasphemous oath or example of profanity, but more pertinent here, it suggests the denunciation of someone in whatever terms: *cursing* her for being an unfaithful wife. Behind this use lies the more specific situation of appealing to a supernatural power to punish a wrongdoer or enemy: King Lear's calling upon the gods to *curse* his ungrateful daughters. The word can also pertain to any condition seen as a handicap or misfortune: the *curse* of being a woman in a man's world. Behind this use lies the more specific situation of seeing the occurrence of some affliction as a punishment sent by fate: arguing that his misfortunes were a *curse* for his inconstancy.

Execration and **imprecation** are more formal substitutes for *curse* in the sense of denouncing or calling down harm upon someone. Of the two, *execration* is the more intense, suggesting greater violence and loathing: his *execration* of his son's misbehavior before the whole family. The word can also refer to the denunciations themselves: the columnist's predictable *execrations* of the party in power. *Imprecation* derives from a Latin word meaning to pray and this was reflected in a now obsolete use of the word for any sort of praying. More recently, the word points exclusively to the expressing of wishes or hopes that someone will meet with misfortune. This may be expressed verbally or in thought only, but the word suggests a private, even guarded expression to oneself of ill wishes, rather than the face-to-face denunciation of the person involved, as suggested by *execration*: muttering *imprecations* to himself against his mother-in-law; voodoo *imprecations* conducted in secret and employing wax dolls through which pins are stuck.

Malediction and **anathema** are the most formal of these words. Where *execration* can refer to a face-to-face attack and *imprecation* to a completely solitary expression of ill-will, both of these words refer most often to public denunciation expressed to arouse general disapproval. *Malediction* compares with its opposite, benediction, and may similarly suggest a formalized, ritual, or clerical denunciation: priestly *maledictions* against heresy within the church; a full-page ad taken by university professors to present their *malediction* against the administration's foreign policy. Its public nature can be seen in that the word is sometimes used as a synonym for slander: spreading unfounded *maledictions* that amounted to a character assassination of his ex-colleague. *Anathema* at its most specific refers to a formal ecclesiastical ban or *curse*, in which a person is excommunicated or a book or idea is condemned: pronouncing an *anathema* against the teachings of psychoanalysis. More generally,

curse

anathema
execration
imprecation
malediction

the word can refer to anything disliked or detested by anyone: explaining that his old crony was now *anathema* to him. See PROFANITY.

Antonyms: benediction, blessing.

cursory

careless
hasty
scant
slapdash
superficial

These words refer to giving less than full attention or effort to a demanding task. **Cursory**, the most formal of these words, is also both the most specific and most inclusive, as well, referring to a deliberately rushed or shallow treatment: rejecting the manuscript after a *cursory* glance at it; only a *cursory* attempt to keep in mind the requirements of his clients. The other words here all emphasize one aspect of *cursory*. **Careless** suggests that the poor performance results from sloppiness and inattention to details: so *careless* as to render her best efforts *cursory*. **Hasty**, by contrast, emphasizes a refusal or inability to spend the time necessary to a more adequate performance: after a *hasty* thumbing through the pamphlet of instructions; a *hasty* consideration of the merits of the case. **Slapdash** approaches *cursory* in inclusiveness since it combines the implications of both *careless* and *hasty*, suggesting a sloppy, rushed performance: trying to work from a *slapdash* sketch instead of a painstakingly executed blueprint.

Superficial limits *cursory* to a refusal or inability to look into the deeper meanings or complexities of something: a *superficial* analysis of the poem; *superficial* competence that could hardly face any serious challenge. *Superficial* is in sharp contrast to *careless* and *hasty*, since one might give adequate care and time to an effort and still come up with a *superficial* result. Most often, in fact, *superficial* suggests an inability to do better and thus contrasts to all these words when they imply a deliberate refusal to meet the demands of something. **Scant**, in this context, refers specifically to brevity of effort: paying *scant* attention to his class assignments. This word differs from *hasty*, however, in emphasizing a short amount of time rather than work done too rapidly. One might have a great deal of time and still do *hasty* work; conversely, one might work methodically in the *scant* time allotted a task. Only in *cursory* are both the tendencies necessarily combined. See NEGLECT.

Antonyms: CAREFUL, *minute, painstaking, profound, searching, thorough.*

cut

gash
incision
slash
slit

All these words mean openings or separations of parts by edged or pointed instruments. A **cut** may be of any size and may be produced by any kind of instrument, intended for cutting or not. A bulldozer may produce a *cut* in a mound; the edge of a piece of paper may produce a *cut* on the finger. An **incision** is a *cut* made for the purpose of gaining entry. The word is mostly used in surgery: an abdominal *incision* to expose an inflamed appendix. A **gash** is a long and broad *cut*, usually accidentally produced: Flying windshield glass produced a *gash* on the face of a witness to the automobile accident. A **slash** is a long, often deep *cut*, usually administered with intent to injure with some sharp instrument like a sword or a knife, and is produced by a long, swinging motion. A **slit** is a long, thin *cut* or *incision*. Some surgical *incisions* are mere *slits*; a letter-opener produces a *slit* in an envelope.

Gash often suggests a jagged, ugly wound, whereas *slash* stresses the length and depth of the wound, which may have been cleanly made; *slit* describes a more precisely made and usually narrower *cut*. [The *gash* on his leg from the barbed wire took thirteen stitches to close; The *slash* from the saber extended from his shoulder to his forearm; The *slit* in the patient's throat enabled the surgeon to insert a tube to assist his breathing.] See HARM, WOUND.

D

These words refer to things that are commonplace or that occur every twenty-four hours or during daylight. **Daily** and **everyday** are the most informal of these. *Daily* refers most specifically to something that occurs once every twenty-four hours: a *daily* newspaper; a tantrum that was almost a *daily* occurrence. It may also refer to things that inevitably occur each day, regardless of number: Give us this day our *daily* bread. It may even suggest things accounted for by the day or things that differ from one day to the next: a *daily* record of expenditures; restaurants that have *daily* menus. *Everyday*, by contrast, refers almost exclusively to anything usual or ordinary, whether or not it can be strictly said to occur once every twenty-four hours: the *everyday* life of the town. More specifically it refers to things appropriate for ordinary, humble occasions rather than for special events: *everyday* clothes. It can even suggest that something is plain or drab: *everyday* routine.

Quotidian and **diurnal** are much more formal. *Quotidian* is the more inclusive of the two in referring to aspects both of *daily* and *everyday*. It can indicate something that occurs *daily*: a *quotidian* fever. *Diurnal* suggests something that goes through its cycle of changes once every twenty-four hours: the *diurnal* motion of the stars. See TEMPORARY, USUAL.

Antonyms: nightly, nocturnal, UNPARALLELED, UNUSUAL.

These words refer to the possibility of harm or destruction. **Danger**, the most general of these, can refer to any situation that confronts one with an undesirable or injurious eventuality: He had stayed up so late that he was in *danger* of oversleeping and being late for work; discussions to reduce the *danger* of a military confrontation between the two nations. The word is a familiar warning on road signs. [*Danger*. Winding road ahead.] As in the last example, *danger* often suggests a difficulty that can still be avoided through forethought. By contrast, **peril** exclusively points only to grave dangers and may sometimes suggest a worsening situation that can no longer be averted by the use of forethought alone: Many species are already in *peril* of extinction because of our destruction of their natural habitat. More broadly, the word can suggest the unpredictable *danger* that must be faced in pursuing a course of action: the great *perils* that the earliest Arctic explorers confronted.

Risk is related to this last use of *peril*, but is more general and can indicate less extreme or imminent *danger*. At its most specific, it indicates the chance of misfortune that accompanies an act undertaken in hope of gain or benefit: a business insured against the *risk* of failure. Here, the negative possibilities can to some extent be foreseen and weighed against the possibility of success: a calculated *risk*. **Hazard** can function as a more formal substitute for *risk*, though it may suggest that greater *danger* attends the action. In this, it combines the gravity of *danger* suggested by *peril* with the weighing or taking of chances suggested by *risk*: the *hazards* of mountain climbing. The word can also function as a hyperbole for the predictable liabilities in any situation: He braced himself for the *hazards* of an evening spent with his mother-in-law. It is also commonly used to refer to taking an unwise *risk*: Storing newspapers in the attic is a fire *hazard*. **Jeopardy** can substitute for *risk* at an even greater level of formality than *hazard*. It now mainly appears in the phrase *in jeopardy*: Such a gamble against odds would put their whole venture *in jeopardy*. The word frequently appears in a legal context, where it indicates the *risk* of being convicted and sentenced; the phrase *double jeopardy* refers to the situation, barred by the Constitution, of standing trial twice for the same crime.

Threat and **menace** can both refer not to *danger* inevitably accompanying an act but to a malevolent or coercive *danger* independent or external to oneself: an escaped psychopath who became a *menace* to the community. *Menace* suggests the possibility of violence or destruction and points to a graver *danger* than any of these words except *peril*. The word can also refer more emphatically than *hazard* to something that represents an unwise *risk*: a rickety stairway that was a *menace* to life and limb. *Threat* is milder than *menace* and much more general. Most concretely, it can indicate an expressed intention to harm: a *threat* against the senator's life; a *threat* to expose him unless he continued to work for the gang. More generally, the word can indicate a situation or act that puts something in *danger*: provocations that were a *threat* to peace. See FEAR, PRECARIOUS.

Antonyms: defense, PROTECTION, *safeguard, safety, security.*

daring

adventurous
venturesome
venturous

These words refer to a fearless willingness to take risks. **Daring** stresses bold, decisive, forceful, or startling acts that set the performer apart and that may be viewed with awe or fear: a *daring* trapezist. Usually, the word implies admirable fortitude, cool-headed proficiency in the face of danger, or an unusual or original approach: a *daring* foray into enemy territory; a *daring* proposal to eliminate urban blight. Often the word is favorable and implies the successful execution of an action: a *daring* novel brilliantly executed. Sometimes the word is used as a euphemism for risqué or salacious: *daring* photos of nude models. **Adventurous** indicates a habit of mind that is interested in exploring the new or untried, but the word gives fewer implications about the manner of execution. In this it is more general, being as applicable to a more relaxed or casual approach as to the decisive forcefulness indicated by *daring*: an *adventurous* mind that could painstakingly digest vast areas of new knowledge. Also, *daring* more often implies a single or specific goal, whereas *adventurous* can point to a general curiosity or zest for exploration: a *daring* maneuver; *adventurous* students out on a lark and ready to try anything.

Venturesome also concentrates more on single or specific goals, but is otherwise less rich than *daring* in its implication. It can suggest a canny — even prudent — weighing of odds before action, however unconventional the action itself may be: a *venturesome* gamble with fledgling stocks that paid off on the market largely because of the investor's shrewdness. **Venturous** is now less common in use, pointing to the taking of risks, but with no necessary implications of shrewdness or decisiveness: a *venturous* fellow who had at least learned to roll with the blows. See BOLD, BRAVE, OPPORTUNISTIC, RECKLESS.

Antonyms: CAUTIOUS, COWARDLY, TIMID.

dead

deceased

These words refer to something that is no longer in existence. **Dead** refers, most concretely, to any once-living thing that has died: his *dead* father; a *dead* rabbit; a *dead* tree. It can even refer to anything that no longer functions: a *dead* battery. By contrast, **deceased** and **departed**

are exclusively restricted in reference to *dead* people. *Deceased* is a legal
term that seems euphemistic in any other context, although it sometimes
appears in ordinary use. *Departed*, by contrast, would strike many as a
euphemism for *dead*; it is meant to be delicate by suggesting that the
dead person has gone to a better world. Compared to *departed*, *dead* is
simple, dignified, and universally unoffending.

Defunct and **extinct** contrast with the foregoing by not referring to
the death of a living individual at all (except for comic effect). Although
defunct could with all seriousness once be used of a *dead* person, it now
applies mainly to the lapsing or closing down of nonliving things: a *defunct*
literary magazine; an anthropomorphic attitude that is now *defunct* in
the biological sciences; a *defunct* restaurant. *Extinct* refers to the lapsing
of a whole species or line of individuals: when the brontosaurus became
extinct; a family name that became *extinct* when the only heir died without issue.

Lifeless has a wide range of uses from the literal to the lyrical: *lifeless* inorganic compounds; dawn lighting the *lifeless* streets of the city.
When used of someone *dead*, the implication may be of a recent death:
staring down at his *lifeless* face on the pillow. See CORPSE, DIE.

Antonyms: existent, LIVING.

dead
(continued)

defunct
departed
extinct
lifeless

These words pertain to the use of misrepresentation to win the trust
or approval of others. **Deception** has the widest range of uses; at its
mildest, the word can suggest a necessary or inconsequential misrepresentation: She referred to the pills as candy, a harmless *deception* that
made it easier to administer them to the child. At its most disapproving,
the word can point to selfish dishonesty: a candidate who practiced all
kinds of *deception* on the voters to win their confidence. **Deceit**, which
is wholly negative in tone, is considerably harsher than *deception* in its
disapproval. It can suggest a habitual liar or schemer or refer to an involved plan to take advantage of someone else: the flagrant *deceit* by
which he kept his wife from knowing about the affair. Where *deceit* often
stresses the dishonesty of one person to another, **fraud** more often
points to a complex, more impersonal system for cheating all comers or
the public at large. It often suggests official dishonesty or financial
malfeasance: a land-development *fraud* that bankrupted a dozen elderly
couples. Sometimes the word is used hyperbolically for anything one
finds utterly worthless: That movie was a total *fraud*.

Equivocation is most closely related to the mildest sense of *deception*,
but can be even less severe, since it need indicate no intent to deceive.
Instead, it points to an evasive or pussyfooting approach: Her *equivoca-
tions* sometimes seemed to be nothing more than a reluctance to give him
a straight yes or no answer. In some cases, the word is used as a mere
euphemism for a lie: He denied having lied to her, although he admitted
that he had been guilty of an *equivocation* or two. **Trickery** points less
to verbal misrepresentation alone than to the deliberate giving of false
appearances. It is milder in its disapproval than *deceit* and *fraud*, although it can apply to either personal or public behavior. *Trickery* is a
harsher term than *deception*, however, in suggesting the selfish seeking
of gain, often by means of a systematic scheme: the *trickery* they
practiced on their fair-weather friends in order to seem richer and more
famous than they were; He had gained control of the corporation by
trickery in manipulating the proxy votes entrusted to him. While **chicanery** suggests less serious offenses than do *trickery* or *fraud*, the word
adds a note of disgust for trivial or shoddy methods or goals: Press

deception

chicanery
deceit
equivocation
fraud
trickery

agents for movie stars will stoop to any kind of *chicanery* to get their clients publicity. See CHEAT, GUILE, TRICK.

Antonyms: candor, frankness, honesty, sincerity, veracity.

decide

determine
resolve
settle

These words pertain to the reaching of conclusions. **Decide** stresses the making of a choice, regardless of how it is arrived at: jurors who have already *decided* what to think before hearing a shred of evidence; an investigative committee that took months to sift testimony and *decide* if new legislation should be drafted. Sometimes a conclusive factor may be the subject: Above all, it was his earnestness that *decided* her. Using a passive construction is often thought to make the conclusion seem more objective, impassive, and official: It was *decided* at our meeting to abolish the honor system during exam week.

Settle is considerably more forceful than *decide*, pointing exclusively to the reaching of a definite or final choice after a period of indecision or dispute: a new hearing to *settle* the question once and for all; He had considered a number of jobs before *settling* on a career in advertising. With *for*, the word can indicate a reluctant or compromise choice: They had wanted to spend a week in Rome, but *settled for* a few days. A related context for **determine** pertains to investigation or discovery; here, in reference to choice, the word still implies thoughtful or searching consideration: She asked him for help in *determining* where to hang the pictures in her new apartment. The force of the word changes considerably when it is used as a past participle to express a decisive choice, purpose, or conviction: He was *determined* to win the game. **Resolve** is closely related in meaning to this one sense of *determine*, referring to an even greater conviction or purpose with which something is *decided*. [He *resolved* to clear his father's name; She was *resolved* to become a ballet dancer.] The word can also refer to the *settling* of a question by a group, most often after debate: The student group *resolved* that draft deferments should be rescinded. More generally, the word can refer, like one use of *decide*, to something that is conclusive: means to *resolve* the questions surrounding the assassination. See CONSIDER, FIND, JUDGE.

Antonyms: fluctuate, HESITATE.

declare

advertise
announce
broadcast
enunciate
proclaim
publish

These words refer to the releasing of information or rulings in official or public ways. More informally, **declare** can relate simply to forceful or direct assertion: She *declared* that she didn't want to see him again. This possible implication of forcefulness may or may not be present when the word applies to official rulings. [The judges *declared* the contest a tie; The military police *declared* the tavern off-limits.] In any case, the word here emphasizes an authoritative utterance.

Announce pertains almost exclusively to public or official statements, but these can be declared in any medium and they may be informative as well as authoritative decisions. [He called a press conference to *announce* his candidacy; They *announced* to the assembled guests that they were engaged to be married; The officials *announced* new rules to cover the championship bout.] On an informal level, **proclaim** can indicate the *declaring* of a considered and definite decision or judgment: She *proclaimed* the dress to be too daring for her personality. Pertaining to official utterance, the word stresses extreme formality: the ceremony at which he would officially be *proclaimed* archbishop. The word can also indicate resolute conviction: We *proclaim* these truths to be self-evident. **Enunciate** carries over its reference to clear speech when it applies to official statements, since here it stresses the careful but authoritative spelling out of detailed rules or doctrine: the pope who first *enunciated* the doctrine of the Assumption of the Virgin.

The remaining words all now pertain primarily to the dissemination of information through various communication media. **Publish** pertains to books, magazines, newspapers, and other printed media. **Broadcast** once referred merely to making something known far and wide, but more often now it pertains to anything programmed on radio or television or announced over a public-address system. **Advertise** now indicates a paid presentation to win popularity for a product or candidate. Unlike *publish* and *broadcast*, however, *advertise* can suggest every conceivable medium in which paid messages can appear. A company may *advertise* its products by means of newspapers, magazines, television, billboards, and even skywriting. See ASSERT, SLOGAN.

Antonyms: censor, conceal, withhold.

These words refer to a lessening in numbers, intensity, or volume. **Decrease** and **dwindle** can both be applied widely but are particularly pertinent to a reduction in numbers. Of the two, *decrease* is the more general and has fewer connotations. [In winter, the number of arrests generally *decreases*; The number of nations allied with us *decreased* as the war continued.] Where *decrease* can apply as well to a reduction in undesirable things, *dwindle* usually suggests a loss of something valuable; the word often gives a lyrical or elegiac tone and can suggest a wasting process. [Sanctuaries for wildlife have *dwindled* alarmingly in the last decade; His health *dwindled* slowly day by day.]

Abate and **subside** both point to a slow reduction in intensity: The ferocity of the enemy's counterattack *abated* after the first few hours. *Subside* can in particular suggest a return to calm or repose after agitation: a violent struggle after which he *subsided* into a feverish sleep. Like one possibility for *dwindle*, both of these words are often applied to a slow loss of strength or health.

Decline and **sink** are particularly relevant to a reduction in volume. *Decline* is more neutral and factual, whereas *sink* can give a lyrical or elegiac tone. While both can apply to illness, both also can refer factually to the gradual reduction in the measurable level of something: The volume of stocks traded *declined* as prices continued to *sink* throughout the day. Both refer metaphorically to downward movement, but *sink* is more graphic here and can suggest a more drastic or quicker shift: daylight that *declined* almost infinitesimally at first and then *sunk* away rapidly when the sun had set. *Sink* is relatively informal when compared to the previous words.

Drop and **fall** both concentrate on a sudden shift downward or a reduction in numbers, intensity, or volume. Both, like *sink*, are relatively informal. A possible distinction between the two exists in that *drop* might more naturally describe a desired reduction and *fall* an unfortunate one. [The incidence of malaria *dropped* dramatically following the eradication program; The national dialogue *fell* to a new low, with name-calling and denunciation replacing rational discourse.] When *fall* is used with *off*, the word applies more generally to any *decline*, slow or rapid, good or bad: Unemployment continued to *fall off* in the third quarter. See REDUCE, WANE, WEAKEN.

Antonyms: CLIMB, ENLARGE, ESCALATE, grow, strengthen, wax.

These words refer to a resolute commitment or a bestowing of honor, credit, reverence, or respect. **Dedicate** can pertain to a formal or public

decrease

abate
decline
drop
dwindle
fall
sink
subside

dedicate

dedicate

(continued)

consecrate
devote
hallow

act in which something is metaphorically assigned to the honor or credit of someone who is not its immediate creator: He *dedicated* the book to his wife; a holiday *dedicated* to the memory of those who died in the nation's battles. Parallel to this, a person may *dedicate* himself to a particular goal; in this case, the word stresses resolution and conviction: He *dedicated* his life to the abolition of slavery. **Devote** relates almost exclusively to this last sense of *dedicate*, but the word puts less stress on an idealistic commitment and more on something pursued out of warmth, affection, or personal inclination: a man *devoted* to his wife; a loner *devoted* to a life of pleasure-seeking. Even where the word approaches *dedicate* in use, a more intimate or personal note is felt: She was to *devote* herself to a simple life in the service of others.

    Consecrate and **hallow**, both relatively formal, are specifically religious in tone; at their most restricted, they suggest a ritual in which something is set aside for a sacred purpose: *consecrated* ground; *hallowed* be Thy name. Both apply outside the religious context to any extreme or solemn commitment, although here, *consecrate* possibly applies more widely: a truly great President who *consecrated* himself to seeking and upholding the public good; a day set aside to *hallow* the founding of the country. See AWARD, ENTRUST, RESPECT.

    Antonyms: desecrate, dishonor, profane.

defeat

beat
best
drub
lick

These words agree when they mean to overcome an opponent in a competition or struggle. **Defeat**, the most general of these terms, has a wide range of applications, but does not itself connote any particular margin of victory or the ease with which it has been effected: barely *defeated* after a long, fiercely waged struggle; utterly and humiliatingly *defeated* and put to rout. Sports writers have adopted *defeat* and the other terms to their own use: Reds *defeat* Giants, 3–0.

    Best implies merely that one gets the better of his opponent: Jefferson was *bested* by Hamilton in the controversy over the relative strength of federal versus state power. *Best* has a more formal tone to it than *defeat*. **Beat**, unlike *defeat*, implies that one's opponent is completely overcome: Achilles *beat* Hector. *Beat*, though quite often used in formal contexts, is equally at home in informal contexts, and can be used to describe any competition, however far removed from the field of physical combat: to *beat* someone at checkers. *Defeat* would sound a little pretentious in this context unless the checkers match were part of a formal competition.

    Lick, a colloquial term meaning to *beat* badly, now sounds a little quaint, if not old-fashioned. It still has the ring of adolescent speech to it, but not of today's adolescents. It is often used as a challenge: I can *lick* you at table tennis. In more serious contexts it now sounds misplaced: The Allied armies *licked* the Nazis in World War II. **Drub** implies that the defeated party has been so badly beaten that the competition was no contest; the score was lopsided, the loser humiliated. *Drub* and *lick* both have meanings of to *beat* physically, and both retain connotations of severe punishment, suggesting satisfaction in the administration of a sound beating. See SUBJUGATE, VANQUISH.

    Antonyms: give up, surrender.

deficient

inadequate

These words refer to what is substandard or low in quality. **Deficient** is by far the most specific and exact in meaning. The word points to a lack of something that is required to accomplish a given goal or purpose: a check returned because of *deficient* funds; Rickets can result from a

diet *deficient* in vitamin D. Usually the word does not suggest a lack that
is a matter of degree but one, whether small or large, that fails to meet
a minimum level of need below which something cannot function at all.
Applied to aspects of character, the word suggests a flaw or failing,
whether correctable or not, that makes someone unable to perform some
activity: an armchair theorist *deficient* in practical experience.

Poor, the least specific and most wide-ranging of all these words,
applies in this context to a matter of degree rather than to a cut-off
point at which something ceases to function: *poor* eating habits that,
miraculously, did not result in a vitamin deficiency; anemia that resulted
from a diet *poor* in iron. **Inadequate** relates more closely to *deficient*
in indicating a failure to meet minimal standards. *Deficient*, however,
often points to a minimum that can be objectively measured, whereas
inadequate can point to a more subjective evaluation: *deficient* by two
votes of passing the proposed legislation; a pianist whose technique
seemed *inadequate* to the demands of the pieces he had chosen to play.
But *inadequate* can indicate lacks that are a matter of fact rather than of
taste: a water supply *inadequate* to the needs of the city. By contrast,
unsatisfactory stresses the first sense of *inadequate*, pointing more to
subjective evaluation than to measurable lack: The teacher informed
him that he was making *unsatisfactory* progress in his studies. It can
also indicate a matter of degree, like *poor*: many brilliant scenes in a
play that on the whole was *unsatisfactory*. As in the last example, the
word at its most literal can refer to a failure to give satisfaction or
pleasure. See SCANTY, WEAK.

Antonyms: ADEQUATE, good.

These words may all describe statements that are flat, clear-cut, and
direct. **Definite** and **unequivocal** both refer to expressions unclouded
by any ambiguity. *Definite* is unique in suggesting decisiveness of
choice; a *definite* answer would be one that is conclusive and perhaps
binding. *Unequivocal*, in contrast, is more concerned with truthfulness
and with expressions free of misleading possibilities. A *definite* agreement
made in bad faith would not be *unequivocal*.

Categorical, **unqualified**, and **unconditional** refer to expressions
reduced to the simplest statement possible, without reservations of any
kind. *Categorical* suggests that possibilities for reply have been sorted out
into a very few categories in advance: a *categorical* yes-or-no answer; a
categorical denial of the charges. *Unqualified* is similar to but more
sweeping than *categorical* in suggesting that the statement will hold true
regardless of any limitations or restrictions that might be brought to
bear. If a critic gives his *unqualified* approval to a play, it means he
found every aspect of it worthwhile — the acting, staging, sets, costumes,
and dialogue — whether or not he mentions these things item by item in
his review. Because of this suggestion that details need not be given,
unqualified sometimes suggests a rashness of judgment: *Unqualified*
views are unwarranted in such a complex situation. *Unconditional* is
more apposite to agreements or the making of bargains. It suggests that
one's stand is not dependent upon provisos: *unconditional* surrender;
an *unconditional* guarantee.

Explicit, **specific**, and **express** emphasize that the statement is
spelled out, in all its details if necessary. This emphasis contrasts
sharply with *unqualified*, and with the necessary brevity implied in
categorical. In suggesting a stated rather than assumed situation, they
are more like *definite*. The latter, however, is more concerned with

clarity than with detail. One might infer what is *definite*, but *explicit* implies an actual putting into words. [It was *definite* that he was to be a passenger on the boat, though he would not be *explicit* about his destination.] *Explicit* often tends to suggest the stating of choice among alternatives, while *specific* may simply emphasize accurate description without evaluation. *Specific*, more than *explicit*, also suggests full treatment in giving particulars: a *specific* block-by-block report on the city's housing needs. *Express* is slightly more formal than *explicit* or *specific* and means expressing in plain words what might already be implied. [An *express* agreement among honest men is seldom necessary.] See AB-SOLUTE, CANDID, CLEAR, OVERT.

Antonyms: *ambiguous*, IMPLICIT, OBSCURE, *tentative*, VAGUE.

delay

detain
hold
keep
retard

These words refer to any actions that prevent something from pursuing its natural or intended course forward. **Delay** may suggest either a slowing down of movement or a temporary but full stop in a forward motion. **Detain**, in contrast, suggests a longer, possibly permanent halt. **Retard**, in distinction from both, suggests a considerable slowing down of movement but not necessarily a halt at all; it is also more formal than *delay* or *detain*. [I was *delayed* several times on my walk by people seeking my name on various petitions; I was *detained* from keeping our appointment by a business conference that lasted most of the day; Economic progress in Latin America has been consistently *retarded* by a high birth rate.]

Hold and **keep** are more informal than the previous words of this group. *Hold* can be used with *back* or *up* and generally suggests a direct or personal intervention, with the possible implication of physical contact: a man who would have joined the fight but for two friends who *held* him *back*; a flight that was *held up* for several hours because of poor visibility. As can be seen, *hold* suggests the temporary full stop possible for *delay*. *Keep* also shares this suggestion; it often appears with *out* and *back* and suggests the imposition of a barrier, not necessarily physical, that must be removed before progress can be resumed. [He was *kept* from crossing the bridge by a large force of deputies; She was *kept* from speaking out by her innate distaste for unpleasant scenes; They were *kept out* of the square by the large demonstration that was under way; Traffic was *kept back* by hastily erected barricades.] See HINDER, THWART.

Antonyms: FURTHER, QUICKEN, SEND, SPEED.

delusion

fantasy
hallucination
illusion
mirage

These words refer to mental experiences that appear realistic or believable but have, despite their vividness, no objective reality. **Delusion** refers to the most extreme and inclusive form of this mental phenomenon, since it may combine vivid sensory imagery with complex notions or conceits; in the psychotic person, these *delusions* are totally mistaken for reality and are not voluntarily called up: a *delusion* that he heard voices urging him to kill; a *delusion* that he was Abraham Lincoln; the final stages of alcoholism in which *delusions* are commonplace. The phrase *delusions of grandeur* is actually a clinical term but is often used commonly for anyone with inflated self-regard.

Fantasy and **illusion** are considerably less extreme than *delusion*, referring to mental activity that everyone, not just a psychotic person, has commonly experienced. *Fantasy* applies mostly to an imaginary scene, such as that in a daydream, whether called up voluntarily or not, which is acted out mentally with vivid sensory imagery, but which is not, except in the mentally ill, mistaken for reality. The word may emphasize a general tendency of imagination toward the fanciful, whimsical, surreal, or grotesque: a *fantasy* in which he watched his parents mourning over his coffin; a delightful element of *fantasy* that makes his ghost stories chilling but also convincing. *Illusion* can refer to an ideational cluster of notions that everyone experiences, voluntarily or not, but which do not correspond to any objective view of things: under the *illusion* that he could accomplish the whole job without the help of his co-workers. Two related, but milder, uses of this word exist; one refers to the bundle of ideals or necessary lies each person maintains to buoy up his ego: an *illusion* that the society in which he lived was very near perfect; an *illusion* that he was well liked by his fellow workers. Another use of *illusion* refers to confused optical phenomena that trick the eye into seeing a situation as other than it is: Heavy fog had created an optical *illusion* that made the opposite shore seem closer than it was. **Mirage** is specifically restricted to this last sense of *illusion*: a *mirage* that made the highway ahead seem to be flooded with water. When a person is under extreme stress, however, his inward mental disturbance may cooperate with deceptive optical clues to create something more similar to a full-blown *delusion*: Gasping through lips cracked by the desert sun, he claimed that he saw a silver palace just over the next dune, unaware that the whole vision was nothing but a *mirage*.

Hallucination is mainly restricted to vivid sensory experience, like *fantasy*, but in its intensity a *hallucination* approaches the believability of a *delusion*. This experience would tend to occur involuntarily to any person under certain extreme circumstances, as during a long-term fever, after heavy dosages of painkiller or other drugs, during delirium tremens, or in connection with certain physical illnesses such as brain tumors. In this sense, a *hallucination* might be most typically fleeting, like a waking dream. In other uses, however, the word may point to nervous malfunction expressive of a deep-seated mental imbalance, in which case it indicates one possible constituent of a psychotic *delusion*. See IMAGINATION, MISLEADING.

Antonyms: actuality, fact, reality, truth, verity.

demand

ask
claim
exact
order
request
require

These verbs all refer to rather forceful communications between a speaker and another person. **Demand** most commonly suggests a speaker in authority who bluntly insists upon being obeyed and does not intend to be contradicted: *demanding* your compliance with all our regulations. Its forcefulness may be weakened in some uses to a less blunt insistence: a book that *demands* your full attention; to be surrendered when the bearer *demands* payment. **Request** is considerably weaker than any sense of *demand*; it suggests a courteous statement of desire: *requesting* the orchestra to play her favorite tune. The word has a special relevance here, however, in that it is more and more used as a euphemism for *demand* in order to disguise the latter's harshness: The vice president firmly *requested* the manager's resignation. **Require** may suggest a stated set of rules listing necessary conduct: employers who *require* perfect punctuality and flawless performance. *Require* is like *demand* in suggesting authority and insistence, but unlike the latter in that it stresses need and may suggest an impartial code drawn up in advance. [No rational person would *require* such constant reassurances as she *demanded*.]

Ask is like *request* in depending on context for whatever overtone of harshness or force it may suggest: *asking* timidly if he might see a menu;

political parties that *ask* for the complete surrender of all individuality. By contrast, **order** is like *demand* in its peremptoriness, suggesting power and authority on the part of the person who directs someone else to do something. It is further removed than *demand*, however, from any suggestion of anger; it may be, like *require*, quite impersonal, especially in a military context. [I'm not *asking* you to fall out for drill, I'm *ordering* you.]

Claim and **exact** involve a slightly different situation than these other words. *Claim* suggests that a right is being asserted: *claiming* this land in the name of the queen; unions that *claimed* a right to share in the company's profits. *Exact* is stronger than *claim* in suggesting someone with enough authority to back up his *claim*, possibly with force, if necessary: a dictator who *exacts* grotesque extremes of obedience from his underlings. In this, it is similar to but stronger than some uses of *require*. In other uses, the word shades off, like *require*, into impersonality, with less suggestion of force: states that *exact* tolls on newly built highways. See CLAIM, REQUEST (v.), REQUEST (n.), REQUIRE.

Antonyms: FORGO, RELINQUISH.

demur

balk
boggle
recoil
scruple
shirk
shrink
shy

These words refer to the act of hanging back from full participation or full assent. **Demur** suggests mild dissent or personal objection, possibly in reply to a direct request: gently *demurring* to her notion of leaving the party early. It may also imply hesitation prompted by doubt or indecision: Though urged to stay to dinner, she still politely *demurred*. *Demur*, in comparison with the other words in this set, might now seem too stiffly formal. **Scruple**, closely related to *demur* and only a little less formal, points specifically to hesitation or objection on moral or ethical grounds. [A single girl of that era often *scrupled* about being left alone with a gentleman; He did not *scruple* to tell lies when it served his interests.] The verb *scruple* might now especially apply to overly fussy or niggling ethical distinctions. The note of propriety present in *scruple* is absent from **shy**. *Shy* emphasizes instead a skittish starting aside or squeamish holding back out of fear, doubt, or caution. It thus suggests a more intense negation than *demur* or *scruple*, pointing to a reaction based less on reflection than on instinct. [The horse *shied* at the first hiss of the snake; The girl *shied* away from looking the strange man in the eye.]

Recoil and **shrink** relate more closely to *shy* than to *demur* or *scruple*. *Recoil* suggests a sudden springing back out of surprise, distaste, or fear. *Shrink* does not carry the implication of suddenness but emphasizes an indecisive cringing from something ominous, frightening, or even disgusting. [She *shrank* from entering the grimy tavern with him but once inside, she *recoiled* at every depraved face that met her gaze.] *Shrink* may also suggest excessive timidity: a *shrinking* violet.

Balk suggests a holding back that is more determined than *shrink*, but not necessarily sudden, as with *recoil* and *shy*. The determination implied by *balk*, in fact, extends to downright stubbornness: workers who simply *balked* at the poor conditions in the factory. The word also has a special overtone implying that the subject has gone along with a situation as long as possible, but now stops short, calling a halt out of weariness or anger. [They *balked* at going another step until their guide agreed to name a fee for his services; The donkey *balked* at climbing the next hill until he had food and water.] **Boggle**, by contrast, suggests a refusal at the outset, triggered by disbelief, shock, or amazement. In one sense, it is an intensification of *recoil*: senators who *boggled* at the President's astonishing proposal.

Shirk has a special sense that separates it sharply from these other words. The holding back, here, is simply an expression of laziness or unwillingness to cooperate: teachers who *shirk* the responsibilities they have to their students. See DISAGREE, HESITATE.

Antonyms: accede, accept, CONSENT.

These words designate bodies of believers who are united in a common faith and form of worship. By derivation, the word **denomination** is precisely directed to this concept. It comes from the Latin word for name, and applies to a religious group adhering to a particular creed under a distinctive name. In its broadest sense, *denomination* may refer to any such group: State aid to *denominations* is forbidden by the Constitution. The adjectival form, *denominational*, is often used in this sense as a synonym for parochial: *denominational* schools. But in a restricted sense, the noun *denomination* is commonly reserved for specific Protestant communions: Representatives of several Protestant *denominations* were present — Baptists, Methodists, Presbyterians. **Church** is interchangeable with *denomination* in this sense. The Methodist *denomination*, for example, is more often referred to as the Methodist *Church*. But *church* has a much wider range of application than *denomination*. In its broadest sense, it may refer to ecclesiastical organization and authority, as distinguished from secular authority: the separation of *church* and state. In the context of Christianity, it may designate all, or a major part, of Christendom. [All Christians are members of the universal *Church*; The Pope is the head of the Roman Catholic *Church*; The Archbishop of Canterbury is the highest prelate of the *Church* of England.] In its most strictly limited sense, it may refer to an individual congregation or to the building in which that congregation worships. [Which *church* do you belong to?; My *church* (or the First Presbyterian *Church*) is on 10th Street.] Also, where *church* stresses the union of believers in one body, *denomination* emphasizes separateness. Hence, in an ecumenical age of interdenominational activity, the word *denomination* is less often used in its religious context than formerly.

Religion is a general word embracing all systems of religious belief. It can be used to refer to the major faiths or to their larger subdivisions: the Christian *religion*; the *religion* of the Mormons; the Jewish *religion*; the *religion* of the Essenes; Islam is the *religion* of the Moslems. Like *denomination*, *religion* may sometimes emphasize differences in belief, and in this sense it is often used with reference to Catholicism, Protestantism, and Judaism: to marry outside one's *religion*.

Sect may designate a smaller group within a *denomination*, especially one that differs from the larger body in a particular matter of faith or worship. *Sect* is also used derogatorily of a relatively small, unorthodox *denomination*, to stress its separateness or peculiarity: odd *sects* that spring up and bank on emotional appeal. The word *sect* acquired this derogatory connotation as a result of the many historical instances when *sects* were formed by groups that had split from their parent *religion* because of doctrinal discontent: the *sects* of the Gnostics.

The term **cult** is often applied to the forms or followers of a religious system that is looked on with suspicion or disfavor: The *cult* of Dionysus inspired orgiastic revelry during the celebrations of the Eleusinian mysteries. It also denotes a kind of worship or veneration that is not theistic in principle and is sometimes faddish in practice: the *cult* of nature; teen-age worship that found momentary expression in the *cult* of James Dean. See FACTION, RELIGION.

denomination

church
cult
religion
sect

deplore

bemoan
bewail
lament
mourn

These words refer either to sincere or censorious disapproval or to an aggrieved or regretful feeling of loss. **Deplore** often suggests a feeling of righteous indignation. It refers to disapproval that is thoroughgoing and is called up by some affront to decency, taste, propriety, or morality: to *deplore* a statesman's vacillating policies; *deploring* the book's bad writing; *deploring* the man's boorish manners.

Bemoan and **bewail** are often used in tandem to suggest a *deploring* attitude that is overly solemn, hypocritical, or censorious: *bemoaning* and *bewailing* their capture as though they were innocent victims. Both words once were used with serious intent, but now they are mostly restricted to pejorative or satirical uses. While both words indicate a verbal display of sorrow or grief, *bemoan* might suggest a greater incoherence, one more nearly reduced to wordless sounds; *bewail*, by contrast, might suggest a self-indulgent rush of sanctimonious or hypocritical rhetoric. Often no distinction can be seen between the two in actual usage: *bemoaning* the effort he had to make to support his family; loudly *bewailing* her husband's treatment of her to the neighbors.

Lament can also be used pejoratively or satirically, like *bemoan* and *bewail*; it more specifically suggests, in this case, a hypocritical or self-pitying expression of bereavement or loss: *lamenting* the passing of the good old days. The word still has legitimate serious uses, however, to indicate sincere grief or remorse: *lamenting* the fact that it was her own lack of concern that had driven the boy from the house that night. **Mourn** has pejorative possibilities, but it is much more commonly used to refer to serious expressions of deep loss: a whole nation unashamedly *mourning* the loss of their leader. See COMPLAIN, GRIEVE.

Antonyms: applaud, approve, cheer, commend, PRAISE.

depraved

corrupt
degenerate
evil
heinous
infamous
nefarious
vicious
vile
villainous
wicked

These adjectives describe persons, qualities, or actions that are morally base, malicious, or malevolent. **Depraved** is perhaps the most sinister word. It points to utter perversion, meaning, by derivation, completely bad or totally immoral. In its most common use, it suggests a compulsive or willful turning away from the good, indicating a warped character or a twisted mind: a *depraved* sadist; *depraved* tastes. Where *depraved* tends to be absolute, **degenerate** is relative, implying a descent from a higher state or better condition. It may indicate moral, physical, or mental deterioration from a standard or norm: the *degenerate* heir to a fortune; the decline of a *degenerate* empire; a *degenerate* dope addict. Since *degenerate* focuses on the results of degradation, however, it is commonly applied to persons or things that may never have been normal to start with: a sexual *degenerate*; *degenerate* habits. **Corrupt** is clearer than *degenerate* in its implication of a lapse from a better condition, even when the resulting adulteration has totally vitiated any positive values that may originally have been present. But where *degenerate* is applied to very low specimens of humanity, *corrupt* is often used of persons in high positions whose moral decay may not be apparent on the surface: a *corrupt* government, shot through with graft, vice, and venality; a *corrupt* official who was always receptive to a bribe.

Wicked and **evil** are both general words with wide application. *Evil* means morally bad: *evil* practices; *evil* companions. In an abstract sense, it is the polar opposite of good and can suggest utter and insidious malevolence: the eternal struggle between good and *evil* forces in the moral universe. Hence *evil* can be a much stronger word than *wicked*, which implies sinfulness and may sound downright old-fashioned: a *wicked* and unrepentant old reprobate. *Wicked* is now often used in a humorous, tongue-in-cheek, or even admiring way: a tennis player with a *wicked* serve.

Vile suggests something noxious or loathsome in its depravity, something utterly despicable or repulsive. A *corrupt* official might present a pleasant or attractive appearance, but *vile* indicates disgusting qualities that are readily apparent: a *vile* mass of putrescence. *Vile* may, however, be used in a looser sense as a colorful intensive of awful or terrible. [What *vile* weather!; She's in a *vile* mood; Don't use such *vile* language.] **Villainous** suggests egregious wickedness and can be applied disapprovingly to anyone thought guilty of *evil* behavior: a *villainous* traitor. Even more than *wicked*, however, *villainous* now imparts an old-fashioned, melodramatic flavor to a denunciation: The *villainous* scoundrel absconded with her life's savings; a *villainous* deed.

Unlike the other words in this set, **infamous** refers to notoriety and ill fame, indicating a *vile* reputation. It points to *evil* that has gained wide publicity or that deserves universal condemnation, and it may apply to a person, action, or place: the *infamous* commandant of Auschwitz; the *infamous* Nazi concentration camps; his *infamous* act of treason. **Nefarious** is the most formal word in the group and the word least often encountered. It may suggest a glaring disregard for law or accepted morality, or a shocking disrespect for things that are worthy of reverence. It often has implications of premeditated group activity that is clandestine and underhand: a *nefarious* dope ring; a *nefarious* scheme. **Vicious** calls to mind a mean, snarling animal baring its fangs and preparing to attack. It is used to describe persons, things, or ways of acting that are cruel or brutal, whether or not an *evil* act is intended: a *vicious* dog; a *vicious* gunman. *Vicious* may also mean spiteful or malicious, as in a *vicious* lie; *evil* or *depraved*, as in *vicious* associates; or morally injurious, as in *vicious* habits. **Heinous** comes from an Old French word meaning to hate. It is applied to something so atrocious as to inspire hatred, horror, or outrage: Jack the Ripper's *heinous* crimes. The word *heinous*, however, is distinctly high-flown or old-fashioned in flavor. See DIRTY, POLLUTE, PROFLIGATE.

Antonyms: CHASTE, HONEST, INNOCENT, MORAL, PIOUS.

These words refer to downward movement. **Descend** suggests slow or gradual movement, often down an incline: mountain climbers *descending* from their overnight camp near the peak's summit; an airplane *descending* for a landing. **Drop** and **fall**, by contrast, suggest a sudden and sharp downward movement. *Fall* may refer to any such movement regardless of how it is caused; *drop* most strictly suggests something released or set free at a height: a misstep that sent him *falling* down the stairs; *dropping* food by parachute to the stranded survivors. This distinction is not always adhered to, however, in the case of *drop*: Prices *dropped* drastically during the last hour of heavy trading.

Sink refers to direct downward movement through water or air rather than along an incline. The word often suggests a relatively slow or gradual fall, although this is not always the case: watching the boat fill with water and finally *sink*; The sun *sinks* in the West; cold air *sinking* into the low-lying valley; lead pipes that *sank* quickly without a bubble. *Sink* may also suggest the fading away of energy or consciousness or a gradual decrease in volume: She *sank* into a coma; the tide *sinking* back along the beach. **Decline** is exclusively concerned with this last sense of *sink*, specifically pointing to a dying down or running out of some-

descend

decline
drop
fall
sink

thing: wondering how long it would be before the fever began to *decline*; a recession in which prices slowly *declined*. *Decline* would most appropriately suggest a gradual lessening, failing, or waning. If a sharp or sudden downward course were indicated, *drop* or *fall* would render this meaning less ambiguously. See DECREASE.

Antonyms: CLIMB, *increase, lift, soar*.

descent

ancestry
lineage
pedigree

These words may designate, collectively, those from whom one is descended, or may indicate characteristics inherited from them. **Descent** is the most general word. It is frequently used to refer to the nationality, race, or ethnic characteristics of one's immediate forebears: a woman of Swedish *descent*. **Ancestry** refers most strictly to all of one's progenitors on both sides: He could trace his *ancestry* all the way back to William the Conqueror. It may also, like *descent*, mean ancestral derivation, of whatever kind: a youth of royal *ancestry*; a mongrel of dubious *ancestry*. Unlike *descent*, however, *ancestry* sometimes points specifically to noble or distinguished forebears: He thought he was better than other people because of his *ancestry*. **Lineage** emphasizes a direct line of *descent* from a particular ancestor. It may embrace in one family, for purposes of genealogy, all of the descendants of such a progenitor: St. Joseph was of the house and *lineage* of David. *Lineage*, however, excludes all other branchings of the family tree. Many people are of the *lineage* of William the Conqueror, but the rest of their *ancestry* varies so greatly that their being of William's *lineage* has relatively little significance in accounting for their individual characteristics.

Pedigree stresses notable *ancestry* that is documented in detail and that usually includes many outstanding forebears. It may also refer to a list or table of *descent*, often a genealogical register of an animal. [A *pedigreed* pet is one of pure breed; Many dog owners are prouder of their pets' *pedigrees* than they are of their own.] See ANCESTOR, KIN.

desecration

debasement
defilement
profanation
sacrilege
violation

These words all refer to irreverent or improper acts. **Desecration** is the opposite of consecration. It indicates the dishonoring of something sacred by wrongful use or irreverent treatment, and it commonly implies a conscious or intentional act. Specifically, the word often points to the deliberate degrading, damaging, or destroying of a religious building or place: The stabling of horses in a church would be a *desecration*; the *desecration* of Jewish synagogues and cemeteries by the Nazis. Outside a religious context, *desecration* may suggest the contemptuous abuse of anything that is held dear or regarded as sacred: a *desecration* of the American flag. **Profanation** is a milder word than *desecration* and is less commonly used. It may or may not involve physical abuse of a sacred place, but focuses on a lack of proper respect or a callous or shocking act of irreverence: the *profanation* of a shrine by thoughtless sightseers; a cult that considered it a *profanation* to visit its temple without a full day of fasting. Literally, *profanation* suggests a reduction of something sacred to the level of the secular; but the word has few general uses outside the religious context. **Sacrilege** comes from a Latin word meaning temple robber. In a theological sense, it may imply the improper use of a sacrament, as by one unfit to give or receive it. In a broader sense, it often points to an irreligious or taboo act that profanes the sacred character of a person, place, or thing in a shocking way: The primitive tribe considered it a *sacrilege* to utter the sacred name. *Sacrilege* is even less concrete than *profanation*, though, since the irreverence involved can consist of a thought as well as an act and need not occur within religious surroundings: It was deemed a *sacrilege* to question the witch doctor's teachings even for a moment.

Defilement suggests the dirtying or *profanation* of something that should be cherished or kept pure. In a religious sense, it may indicate the act of rendering something ceremonially (though not literally) unclean: the *defilement* of the temple by the presence in it of infidels. In a broader sense, it may indicate either a physical or spiritual sullying: the *defilement* of justice by prejudiced and corrupt officials. **Debasement** is less often used in a religious sense and does not suggest befouling or pollution. Instead, it focuses on a lowering in character, quality, or worth: determined to tolerate no *debasement*, however slight, of the club's standards. Applied to persons, *debasement* may indicate a public humiliation, as through verbal attack: The accusations he shouted at her during the formal dinner made his *debasement* of her complete.

Like *desecration* and *profanation*, **violation** may apply to the irreverent treatment of a sacred thing or holy place: the *violation* of the shrine by souvenir hunters; the vandals' *violation* of the sanctuary. But this word more often carries legal connotations than religious ones, suggesting the breaking of a law or a failure to abide by the terms of a binding contract: a *violation* of the tenure clause. Outside this specific context, it can be used of a sexual attack: medical tests to determine if there had been a sexual *violation* of the woman. In its most general sense, it can refer to any outrage of decency: a *violation* of his sense of fair play. See CRIME, DIRTY, DISGRACE, POLLUTE, WORLDLY.

Antonyms: consecration, purification, sanctification.

These words refer to a defeated, pessimistic attitude. **Despair** is the most general and informal of these. It implies the loss or abandonment of hope and may suggest a permanent state of mind or a momentary one brought about by some calamity: lives doomed to want and uncreative *despair*; their silent *despair* at having lost the election. It may also refer specifically to pessimism about the future, whether momentary or permanent: a growing *despair* of ever getting through college. **Hopelessness** relates exclusively to this last possibility of *despair*, implying a pessimism more deep-seated and long lasting: the utter *hopelessness* with which she regarded her narrow range of choices. The word may also suggest that someone's present position is extremely imperiled, with or without his realizing it: They were not yet aware of the *hopelessness* of their situation, given the lack of fresh water on the lifeboat.

Discouragement is a much milder word than the others of this group. It restricts itself to one possibility of *despair* in that it pertains almost exclusively to a feeling of letdown at some misfortune or rebuff: the understandable *discouragement* with which he took the rejection of his application. The word most often suggests a response to the thwarting or frustration of an ongoing process of effort; it can be momentary (as above), gradual, or total: growing *discouragement* to see everyone in the office promoted except him; a general *discouragement* with his life that he couldn't even explain or analyze. **Despondency** also pertains to a thwarted or frustrated feeling of letdown, but it is more intense than *discouragement* in suggesting more strictly a sense of total defeat that is expressed in lethargy, introversion, and apathy: days of *despondency* in which he hardly bothered to get out of bed; a long period of *despondency* before the first suicide attempt. This word relates tangentially to *hopelessness* in that such thoroughgoing defeat as the word suggests usually implies, as well, a feeling that the future will not improve one's situation.

despair

desperation
despondency
discouragement
hopelessness

Desperation is unique among these words in suggesting such an intensity of *despair* that one may easily be goaded into wild, blind, or reckless action as a last resort. Thus the word contrasts drastically with *despondency* and its implications of lethargy: fighting back at his tormentors with the *desperation* of a cornered rat; willing to risk anything in his seizure of *desperation*. See MISERABLE, MISERY, SAD.

Antonyms: CONFIDENCE, *encouragement,* EXPECTATION, *hope, hopefulness, optimism.*

despise

abhor
disdain
loathe
scorn

These words refer to a strong contempt or revulsion toward something. **Despise** indicates intense aversion or moral disapproval: I *despise* situation comedies; those of us who *despise* bigotry. **Loathe** focuses mainly on aversion or dislike: Her husband simply *loathed* her cooking. **Abhor**, by contrast, is stronger in suggesting outright hatred and hence extends to moral opprobrium better than *loathe*, which has been weakened by its extensive use for simple distaste: *abhorring* the smug, priggish suburbanite and his moral hypocrisy.

Disdain suggests a feeling of superiority toward something or someone else; consequently, the word can suggest an unwarranted self-righteousness in addition to its reference to distaste: an airy *disdain* for all those less well-educated than she was. **Scorn** is a much stronger substitute for *disdain*, suggesting a haughty rejection or denunciation: *scorning* his proposal as though nothing could have been more repugnant to her. See CONTEMPTUOUS, ENMITY, REPULSIVE.

Antonyms: admire, adore, appreciate, like, LOVE, RESPECT.

despotic

autocratic
dictatorial
tyrannical
tyrannous

These words suggest repressive rule by a single person or group. **Despotic** is the clearest of these words in its disapproving indication of repressiveness and unrestrained power. Once, this was not always true, as the phrase benevolent despotism indicates. Now it more uniformly suggests a harsh and cruel wielding of power: *despotic* parents; a *despotic* president. **Dictatorial** refers more neutrally to unrestrained power, usually in the hands of a single person, and can apply whether this power is used fairly or harshly: a *dictatorial* regime that took over from the corrupt democracy that preceded it. The word does, of course, often carry the same disapproval as *despotic* and can imply the same harshness of rule: the reign of terror during Stalin's *dictatorial* leadership of the Soviet Union.

Tyrannical can suggest the arbitrary and abusive exercise of power concentrated in the hands of a single person; it is now less used to refer to government than to any mishandling of authority: a *tyrannical* office manager; a *tyrannical* union leader. **Tyrannous** is less commonly used than *tyrannical*, except for rhetorical flourish; it might refer to a whole situation, rather than to a person: *tyrannous* laws.

Autocratic is the most neutral of these words, indicating one-person rule and referring descriptively to such a person's absolute power rather than to how he exercises it: an *autocratic* father. Context can, of course, give the word a disapproving flavor: an arrogant and *autocratic* foreign secretary. See AUTHORITARIAN, CRUEL, OVERBEARING.

Antonyms: COMPLIANT, *conciliatory, democratic,* LAWFUL, *representative.*

destiny

fate

These words refer to a situation or outcome as though it were fixed or predetermined. **Destiny** is the most general and least specific of these. It can suggest an occult prearrangement of the future: No man can escape his *destiny*. At the other extreme, it can refer simply to a result, without suggesting any forces at work beyond cause and effect: Congressmen meeting to decide the *destiny* of the abortion reform law. **Fate,** by contrast, is much stronger in implications of a deterministic pattern. Where *destiny* might point to a desired goal without rejecting the notion of free will, *fate* points to an outcome, good or bad, as though choice, chance, or cause and effect played no part in its working out: Oriental religions that advise man to accept his *fate* without bitterness. Even when weakened by use to refer merely to result, the word often suggests an unpleasant outcome: mountain-climbers who met a disastrous *fate*.

Fortune suggests a future determined by luck or chance. By contrast with *fate*, it often indicates good luck or a pleasant outcome, especially when personified: hoping that *fortune* would smile on their efforts. A related use refers to a favorable future goal toward which one can work or struggle: going off to seek wealth and *fortune*. **Lot** once suggested a *fate* or *fortune* that befell one by chance; now, however, it refers mainly to one's station in life, however arrived at: peasants whose *lot* in life was hard and bitter; Each person must learn how to bear his *lot*. See CHANCE.

Antonyms: choice, freedom, free will, will.

destroy

annihilate
demolish
eradicate
exterminate
extinguish
extirpate
raze
ruin
uproot
wreck

These words refer to the complete and usually forcible breaking up or damaging of something so that it is no longer recognizable or effective. **Destroy** is a general word with few overtones beyond its emphasis on force and thoroughness: the tornado that *destroyed* dozens of houses in the town. **Ruin** is even more general, pointing only to the thoroughness of the damage; force, however, may not be involved and a single destructive act may not be at issue: manuscripts *ruined* by long exposure in the cold, damp cellar. **Wreck** suggests a battering action that breaks something up into an unusable mass or heap of fragments: companies that specialize in *wrecking* buildings. These three words, particularly, have a wide range of use beyond actual physical destruction. Here, *destroy* may suggest malevolent action that makes something impossible: escalation that *destroyed* all hopes for a negotiated peace. *Ruin* points to anything that spoils or mars something good or desirable: a thunderstorm that *ruined* our picnic. *Wreck* suggests the breaking down of some cohesive unity: the constant squabbling that finally *wrecked* their marriage.

Demolish and **raze** are generally applied to big or substantial things, such as buildings or other edifices. A building is *demolished* if smashed to pieces, and *razed* if leveled to the ground. *Demolish*, unlike *raze*, is often used figuratively of the reduction of any complex whole to ruins: to *demolish* a theory with a few incisive comments. *Raze* is used almost invariably of buildings or their remains: to *raze* the upright timbers left in the aftermath of the fire.

Annihilate is the most extreme word in this list, and literally means to reduce to nothingness. As more commonly used, however, it denotes a severe degree of damage to a thing or person. An army may *annihilate* an enemy force by so damaging it as to render it incapable of further offensive or defensive action, but without literally removing all traces of its existence. A debater may be said to *annihilate* his opponent if he defeats him decisively.

Eradicate and **uproot** are etymological equivalents, but differ in their applications. To *eradicate* weeds is not only to *destroy* their visible parts but to pull them out by the roots and thus prevent their reappearance. *Eradicate* can mean simply to eliminate completely: The new vaccine *eradicated* all traces of the disease within three months. *Uproot* means to pull up by the roots, and is used figuratively as well as literally: trees *uprooted* by the hurricane; a family *uprooted* by the decision to build a highway through its property.

Exterminate, **extinguish**, and **extirpate** often mean to destroy purposefully. *Exterminate* means to wipe out or kill in great numbers: to *exterminate* insects by spraying with DDT. *Extinguish* means to put out, as a fire; the word is also used metaphorically as a synonym for die, thus implying a comparison between life and a spark or flame: His life was finally *extinguished* by the onset of pneumonia. *Extirpate* refers to the rooting out or utter destruction of something: to *extirpate* a disease by destroying the organisms that cause it; to *extirpate* heresy within the church. See BREAK, HARM, REMOVE, VANQUISH.

Antonyms: BUILD, CREATE, DEVISE, *establish*, REPAIR.

devise

conceive
contrive
formulate
invent

These words are concerned with the development of plans for solving a particular problem. **Devise** and **contrive** both stress the actual working out of the plan, detail by detail. *Devise* is neutral in tone, making no comment on the value of the plan or its objective; it also emphasizes the tentative nature of the proceedings, suggesting that many possibilities are entertained, used, rejected, or revised: *devising* proposals to deal with air pollution; *devising* a strategy that could win the battle. *Contrive* is similar in most respects to *devise* except for its tone, which may now suggest a conspiratorial or illicit plotting toward unworthy ends: *contriving* a fool-proof scheme for robbing the bank. In a different but also negative sense, *contrive* may suggest unrealistic planning, needless complication, or artificial devices that avoid the problem rather than solve it: a law so *contrived* that the average person could not possibly understand or obey it.

Conceive refers to a point in the planning process that must precede *devising* or *contriving*. The word suggests the first ideas that form themselves in a person's mind when faced with a problem, but before these ideas have necessarily been tested by the process implied in *devise*. He *conceived* of a hundred answers to his dilemma, but none helped him to *devise* an escape from it. **Formulate**, by contrast, refers to an act that follows *devising*, in which the rough plan is spelled out, formalized, or put into words. Each step of the whole planning process may be evaluated separately. [The proposed law, while brilliantly *conceived*, has been poorly *devised* to do the job at hand; even worse, it is so vaguely *formulated* that it invites misinterpretation.]

Invent is a word much larger in scope than the others here. It includes the whole planning process — *conceiving*, *devising*, and *formulating*. Also, its product is more often an actual object than simply a set of procedural techniques: *inventing* new synthetic fibers; *inventing* new techniques for coping with juvenile delinquency. See CREATE, INTEND, SUPPOSE.

die

bite the dust
depart
die with one's boots
    on

Die is the simplest word in this group, the most straightforward and direct way of saying to stop living, to experience the permanent cessation of all vital functions. It is used figuratively in reference to anything that ceases to exist. [The smile *died* on his lips; The flames in the fireplace *died* slowly, keeping the room warm for an hour or more.] To **die with one's boots on** originally designated the end of a person who *died* violently, especially in battle and in the kind of battle dress which included boots. Today a person who *dies with his boots on* is one who *dies* while engaged in some activity, as his work, profession, etc., not during a period of prolonged illness or retirement. **Expire** means to breathe out air from the lungs. This sense is extended somewhat euphemistically to a breathing out of one's last breath and so is synonymous with *die*: The old man *expired* only after he'd made a final confession and been administered extreme unction. It is also used figuratively of things that cease to exist by reaching a natural limit: My lease will *expire* on September 30th of this year. To **perish** is to *die* untimely or in a violent way: Hundreds of settlers *perished* that year because of drought and famine. *Perish* is a rather literary word and is often used to denote complete destruction and decay: a civilization that *perished* of greed and decadence. **Depart** is a euphemism suggestive of the soul's leaving this plane of existence at the time of death and going on to another life elsewhere. **Pass away, pass on**, and **pass over** all are like *depart* in their implication of moving to an afterlife, while **go to meet one's Maker** is even more explicit in its designation of the terminal point of the soul's journey. **Bite the dust** and **kick the bucket** are both slang expressions for *die*. The former once pertained especially to death on the battlefield where one literally *bit the dust* in a fall from a horse when wounded. Today it applies not only to actual death but to the figurative death that is caused by failure or ruin: Another small business *bit the dust* this week. *Kick the bucket* is thought to be derived from the last act of a person who hangs himself by fixing around his neck a noose which is attached to the ceiling and then kicking away an upturned bucket on which he has been standing. See CORPSE, DEAD, FATAL, KILL.

Antonyms: EXIST, PERSIST, *survive*.

die
(continued)

expire
go to meet one's
Maker
kick the bucket
pass away
pass on
pass over
perish

These words describe the continual painstaking exertion of intense care and effort. **Diligent** suggests the accomplishment of work that is well-done and that demands the worker's alertness and dedication to the task: his *diligent* efforts to vindicate his father's name. There is also an implication of wary watchfulness and the making of extremely fine distinctions: inspectors *diligent* enough to catch the slightest lowering of standards. **Sedulous** is considerably more formal than *diligent* but also stresses attentiveness, with a special overtone of unwearying application to an exhausting task: a teacher who proceeded so rapidly that only the most *sedulous* student could follow him. **Assiduous** is only slightly less formal than *sedulous*; it emphasizes the ability to do quantities of sheer hard work. There is less implication that the work is well-done as in *diligent* or that it is extremely taxing as in *sedulous*. It does suggest dogged determination and an energetic approach: an *assiduous* struggle against the untamed land that every year brought forth more and more crops. [A poorly edited book requires the reader's *sedulous* attention to make up for the lack of *diligent* copy editing and *assiduous* proofreading.] **Persevering** has an area of meaning that sets it more clearly apart from the foregoing words; it refers to an unremitting effort that is not weakened by momentary failures: to watch the *persevering* spider attempt to build her web time and time again. *Persevering* clearly indicates nothing about the quality or quantity of the work done, only about the unflagging nature of the effort: *persevering* in the typing assignment despite her exhaustion and her loss of accuracy and speed. **Industrious** also makes no comment upon the quality of the work accomplished, but it does stress constancy or speed of execution. It also suggests a cheerful or good-humored bustle: *industrious* clerks who turned out mountains

diligent

assiduous
industrious
persevering
sedulous

of filing and paper work in just a few hours. See BUSY, CAREFUL.

Antonyms: FLIPPANT, HEEDLESS, *impatient,* JAUNTY, *lazy, negligent, procrastinating,* SLOW.

dirty

filthy
foul
soiled
sordid
squalid
unclean

These words refer to things impure, defiled, adulterated, or layered with foreign matter. **Dirty** can refer to a lack of cleanliness that comes about through normal use: making a pile of *dirty* clothes to be sent to the laundry. It can also suggest an unusual or more extreme cause: a dust storm that had left everything in the house *dirty*. The word has more force in reference to impure morals: *dirty* stories; a *dirty* old man. **Soiled** concentrates mostly on things made *dirty* through normal use: a *soiled* apron; hands *soiled* from working in the garden. The word can suggest a layering over of something with dirt or soil. In the moral context, the word is even more forceful than *dirty*: a *soiled* reputation.

On the literal level, neither of the previous words need suggest disapproval for what may be a natural process. **Filthy**, however, suggests something extremely *dirty* and, possibly, disgusting or noxious: an unkempt bum whose clothing was *filthy*. Morally, the word serves as an intensification of *dirty*, but the specific context is even more likely to be sexual in nature: lewd and *filthy* acts; pornography that included *filthy* pictures. **Squalid** adds to the implications of *filthy* a sense of disarray, disorder, and distasteful rankness: *squalid* slums. In reference to morals, the word suggests habits and patterns considerably outside the norm: hippies who live *squalid* fly-by-night lives.

Foul now is largely restricted to what is morally reprehensible; its disapproval is vague, attaching to anything the user may deplore: a *foul* traitor. Language that includes so-called *dirty* words is often called *foul*. **Unclean** can be used neutrally for anything *soiled*, but oddly enough it is particularly suggestive of a moral or religious context: *unclean* in mind and spirit. **Sordid**, more than any of the other words here, fuses together references to both physical and moral uncleanliness: *sordid* crimes committed in a *sordid* environment. See LEWD, REPULSIVE, VULGAR.

Antonyms: CLEAN, *pure, unsoiled, unsullied, virginal.*

disagree

bicker
cavil
differ
dissent
object
quibble

These words refer to an expressed lack of concurrence between the ideas of two people. **Disagree** may refer to any verbalized discord, whether trivial or fundamental, whether arising out of a dispute over facts or simply out of a contest of wills: *disagreeing* over which road to take; *disagreeing* as to when Shakespeare was born; those who *disagree* merely for the sake of controversy. **Differ** is milder than *disagree*; it might sound excessively formal to some ears, except in the common phrase, "I beg to *differ* with you." As a substitution for *disagree*, it can even sound euphemistic: urging them not to *differ* over so slight a matter. It has a real use, however, when one wishes to suggest lack of agreement that does not arise from hostility: *differing* on the causes of poverty but agreeing on steps to eradicate it. The word, also, can suggest mere factual discrepancy from which no conclusions have yet been drawn: the detective who asked us why our versions of the accident *differed*.

Object and **dissent** are more intense than either *disagree* or *differ* and suggest a more thoroughgoing dispute. *Object* most appropriately pertains to a single point of disagreement: *objecting* vehemently to his last inference. *Dissent*, on the other hand, would suggest the complete rejection of someone else's case, both formulated in detail. [A radical does not merely *object* to a few scattered instances of injustice; he *dissents* from a whole way of life.]

Cavil and **quibble** pertain to the raising of petty objections to a line of thought. *Cavil* is the harsher of the two, with its implications of ill-tempered hostility: frowning negotiators who *caviled* at every new proposal simply to prolong the deadlock. *Quibble* may suggest the bad humor of *cavil* or it may refer only to a super-solemn, over-refined attention to detail that is sophistical in its nit-picking: scholastics *quibbling* over the number of angels that could dance on the head of a pin. *Quibble*, when it suggests contention, still stresses an almost legalistic pettiness: *quibbling* for hours about which candidate had the stronger platform. **Bicker** is an intensification of this sense of *quibble*, suggesting more hostility between the arguers, but with no lessening of the triviality inherent in the argument. Name-calling and groundless assertions, however, may be included as techniques of dispute: *bickering* about who should get up and bar the door. See CONTRADICT, DEMUR.

Antonyms: CONSENT.

These words refer to negative judgments or attitudes toward something. **Disapproval** is the most general of these; it may refer to a fixed, irrational dislike of a person or to a specific instance of reasoned, analytic rejection of an idea or a way of behaving: meeting his efforts at friendliness with ever harsher signs of her icy *disapproval*; attempting to demonstrate her *disapproval* of such a solution to their problems. **Criticism** is more exclusively restricted to this last possibility of *disapproval*, usually suggesting an expressed rejection of a specific thing because of its failure to meet certain standards: his constant *criticism* of her way of dressing; fierce *criticism* of every weakness in the debater's argument. The word, as commonly understood, most often suggests *disapproval*, although in more formal use it can suggest neutral analysis or even approving evaluation: the first work of *criticism* to claim greatness for a certain contemporary author. **Blame** does not suggest a measuring of something against standards; it stresses, on the contrary, an attempt to determine who is at fault for some failure or catastrophe that has already occurred. Thus the word most specifically suggests the assigning of guilt or responsibility: fixing *blame* on the police for their handling of the riot; taking the *blame* for the failure of their marriage.

The remaining words are considerably more formal than the foregoing and also suggest a much greater severity of *disapproval*. **Animadversion** is censure of a high, authoritative, and somewhat formal kind. It may suggest a single point in a more extensive *criticism*, especially one motivated by hostility: his expected *animadversion* upon the book's risqué language; a discussion that was nothing but a string of bilious *animadversions*. **Aspersion** suggests an even greater fierceness of attack than *animadversion*; its special emphasis is on ill-founded or reckless accusation of a defamatory nature, with the implication that such *criticism* is rendered in a sneering or self-righteous manner: unfounded *aspersion* of the petitioner's good faith; taunting her and casting *aspersions* on her truthfulness. **Reprehension**, unlike *animadversion* or *aspersion*, does not imply prejudiced or unjustified *criticism* but rather indicates a stern rebuke, reproof, censure, or reprimand directed against something blameworthy. *Reprehension* is supposed to be calm and just, motivated by good intentions; it is therefore a serious matter, even when mild, and is capable of great force, as expressed in the phrase *severe reprehension*. [He spoke out in *reprehension* of bossism; bigotry deserving of *reprehension*.] See DISCIPLINE, MALIGN, REBUKE, REPREHENSIBLE.

Antonyms: APPROVAL, *credit, endorsement, praise.*

disapproval

animadversion
aspersion
blame
criticism
reprehension

discard

junk
scrap
shed

These words all mean to get rid of something that is no longer needed or wanted. **Discard**, when applied to physical objects, emphasizes the action of casting aside or throwing out: to *discard* an old pair of shoes. It stresses the worthlessness of the object so disposed of, and thus when applied by extension to a person, conveys a large measure of contempt. When applied to ideas, *discard* suggests a strong and usually permanent rejection: The recommendation that nuclear weapons be used was *discarded* as reckless and uncalled-for.

Junk, an informal term, means to *discard* as trash: to *junk* an old car. It implies that the thing *discarded* can no longer be used for its original purpose, but that its materials may still be used. The metal and some parts of a *junked* car, for instance, can be re-used. **Scrap** is similar to *junk* in suggesting that the materials of something no longer serviceable can be re-used, but *scrap* is used almost exclusively of metal things, and usually of large structures: to *scrap* an old World War II battleship. *Scrap* does not necessarily imply that the object *discarded* is worn out; it may simply be obsolete: The supersonic VT-705 jet fighter plane was *scrapped* in favor of a still faster and more maneuverable model. Unlike *junk*, *scrap* often suggests that the thing *discarded* will or might be replaced by something else, or that the putting aside is a temporary expedient: The plan for slum clearance had to be *scrapped* for lack of funds, but it is hoped the next legislature will restore the necessary funds.

Shed means to cast off by a natural process, as hair, skin, etc.: Snakes *shed* their skins periodically; trees *shedding* their leaves in autumn. The idea of a protective covering is retained when the word is applied figuratively to human beings: to *shed* warm clothing when summer arrives; to *shed* one's inhibitions after a few drinks. It here suggests getting rid of something unwanted, but the thing rejected is often of such a nature that it cannot be *discarded* entirely or permanently. See REJECT.

Antonyms: keep, maintain, preserve, retain, save.

discipline

castigate
chasten
chastise
correct
punish

These words refer to acts taken by someone in authority to restrain or rectify the behavior of someone in his charge. **Discipline** in this context suggests remedial measures, harsh or mild, that are taken to cause an improvement in conduct; they are usually imposed in the form of precise regulations to govern misbehavior: strictly *disciplining* his class for every departure from the rules; *disciplining* her child unmercifully even when it had done no wrong. **Correct** and **punish**, in their greater informality, can make *discipline* sound almost euphemistic by comparison. *Correct* refers specifically to the pointing out of error; this, of course, can be done as a help, but in this context it suggests some sort of imposed remedial measure: *correcting* his tardiness by making him stay after class. Both *discipline* and *correct* seem to imply that an obedience to imposed rules alone will "improve" behavior. *Punish* is considerably more honest in its frankness, at least, by referring directly to the imposing of a penalty for undesirable performance: *punishing* her daughter by denying her a week's allowance; arguing that prisons should rehabilitate rather than *punish* lawbreakers.

Chasten is extremely formal but may range in suggestion from actual physical mistreatment to the imposing of any pain or affliction that leaves someone humble or tractable: the *chastening* of his careless ways by her withdrawn and bitter mood. It might particularly suggest the administering of harsh verbal reproaches: choosing a formal meeting of the board to *chasten* the office manager for his ill-advised policies. **Chastise** would now strike most ears as an outdated euphemism for physically *punishing* an inferior: a hickory stick on the desk with which to *chastise* unruly students.

Castigate suggests, as does one aspect of *chasten*, a caustically severe verbal reprimand: *castigating* the secretaries for their sloppy job of filing; The inspector was *castigated* for having failed to check the electrical wiring as he was supposed to. See REBUKE.

Antonyms: applaud, ENCOURAGE, PRAISE, *reward*.

Discolor, stain, and **tarnish** all mean to change the color of something for the worse. *Discolor* shares with *stain* the specific meaning of changing something to a different color, *stain* emphasizing that this change is caused by foreign matter. Thus, after a fight, one's clothes are likely to be *discolored*, especially if they are *stained* with sweat, dirt, and blood.

Discolor shares with *tarnish* the specific meaning of depriving of color, or of dulling. *Discolor* is used in this sense when fading, streaking, or the like are referred to: curtains *discolored* by the action of sunlight. *Tarnish* is used to refer to the dulling of luster by action of air, dirt, water, or the like: silverware *tarnished* by the action of sulfur compounds in the atmosphere and in such foods as eggs. See DISFIGURE.

Antonyms: CLEAN, COLOR.

discolor

stain
tarnish

These words all refer to an intent to alter the actions or plans of another person by means of some kind of persuasion. **Discourage** suggests an attempt to prevent or repress an action by dulling a person's enthusiasm for it or by weakening his sense of purpose: The dean *discouraged* the student from enrolling for an extra course because the student was already overworked. *Discourage* often presents a proposed action in an unfavorable light: I *discouraged* him from taking a position with that unknown and possibly unreliable insurance company. *Discourage* may also refer to actual, physical obstacles that make an action difficult if not impossible: Low hedges around lawns *discourage* people from walking on the grass.

Deter is a stronger word than *discourage*. To *deter* is to prevent from acting or proceeding by the consideration of danger, difficulty, or uncertainty which might countervail the motive for action. [Few penologists believe that the death penalty *deters* the committing of murder; Fear of the snarling watchdog *deterred* the salesman from entering the house.]

When you **dissuade** someone from doing something, you try gently to bring him around to your point of view by giving tactful advice or perhaps even by appealing to his better nature. *Discourage* and *deter* often involve stronger means of persuasion, even to the extent of browbeating, while *dissuade* refers to a milder method that is not always as successful. [When he became furious with his boss, I *dissuaded* him from rushing in to submit his resignation; Overweight people may be *dissuaded* from eating too much by friendly reminders that they will both feel and look better after they have lost some weight.]

To **divert** is to turn another person's mind from one concern or occupation to another. *Divert* does not involve as much actual persuading as it does distracting the attention and offering an acceptable substitute. If you wish to *divert* a small child from littering the livingroom with his toys, you may suggest to him that it would be fun if he would help

discourage

deter
dissuade
divert

you unpack canned goods in the kitchen instead. See QUELL, SUBDUE.
Antonyms: ENCOURAGE, *persuade.*

discriminate

differentiate
discern
distinguish

These words refer to an ability for making fine distinctions, or to the possession of qualities that set the subject apart from others of its kind. **Discriminate** pertains mostly to someone perceiving and evaluating differences among very similar things: *discriminating* the real antique from the hoked-up fraud; the connoisseur who can *discriminate* among several equally fine wines. **Discern** relates closely to *discriminate* but is somewhat more general in stressing any intense or accurate perception, without necessarily implying that it is a sorting out of closely related items: *discerning* clearly the faint trail of clues that led to the identity of the murderer.

   Distinguish, by contrast, can refer either to an ability of the perceiver or to the differences actually perceived. In the former case, it suggests the making of even finer distinctions than *discriminate* and making them among things even more closely resembling each other. The word, consequently, stresses the skill needed for the mere detection of differences and does not emphasize, like *discriminate*, esthetic evaluation as a part of the process. [She was unable to *distinguish* the gray shadow she made from all the other shadows in the garden; Anyone can learn to *distinguish* a Goya from a Velásquez, but only a real student of the period can *discriminate* between their stylistic tendencies.] *Distinguish*, however, when it refers to characteristics of a thing perceived, is quite the opposite; in this case, it suggests drastically different and often superior qualities: amazing agility that *distinguishes* him from all other dancers.

   Differentiate, in referring to qualities in something perceived, contrasts sharply with *distinguish*, suggesting slighter differences and ones seldom the result of excellence. [The yellows used to paint the sun were only faintly *differentiated* from the other yellows used throughout the whole sky; it took a sharp eye to *distinguish* one shade from the other.] *Differentiate* in the sense of making distinctions is most appropriate to a technical context: the entomologist who had *differentiated* sixty separate species of insect. See FIND, PERCEIVE.
   Antonyms: blur, CONFUSE, JUMBLE.

disfigure

blemish
deface
deform
mar

These words agree in meaning to inflict injury or damage that spoils the appearance of a person or thing. **Disfigure** and **mar**, as here considered, imply comparatively permanent injury or damage; a person's face may be *disfigured* by scars, or the surface of a desk may be *marred* by deep scratches. The two words differ in that *disfigure* suggests a change in outlines or lineaments, whereas *mar* may suggest random nicks and scratches that do not substantially change appearance but may hamper effectiveness or functioning. [The church was *disfigured* by the half-built steeple; The record was so *marred* that it was almost impossible to listen to.]

   Deface and **blemish** are often used interchangeably with *disfigure* and *mar*, but often imply less permanent damage or injury; a wall may be *defaced* by pencil markings, or a person's face may be *blemished* by pimples. *Deface* nearly always suggests flaws introduced into something originally not *disfigured*; deliberate malice is often suggested as the motive: campaign posters *defaced* by graffiti. Something may be *blemished* by inherent defects, however: a program *blemished* from the outset by a lack of funds.

Deform implies a lasting change for the worse or deviation from the normal in the structure or form of something: a baby *deformed* by congenital abnormalities; *deformed* by a serious accident. See FLAW, HARM, STIGMA.

Antonyms: adorn, beautify, CONSERVE, *restore.*

disgrace

abase
debase
degrade
demean
humble
humiliate

These words indicate the act of stripping someone of pride, self-respect, rank, or reputation. **Disgrace** points to lowering someone in other people's estimation: a scandal that *disgraced* both husband and wife. **Degrade** may or may not refer to a literal demotion: a sergeant *degraded* to the rank of private first class. More often, the word suggests disgusting or immoral habits or behavior that destroys a person's character or publicly *disgraces* him: a fine mind *degraded* and dulled by dope addiction; accusations intended to *degrade* him and destroy his reputation. **Humiliate** can refer to any inner feeling or outward act that robs someone of his self-respect: a husband who enjoyed *humiliating* his wife in public; She felt thoroughly *humiliated* at her own lack of insight.

Debase suggests an action that reduces the intrinsic value of something: currency *debased* by inflationary measures; political discussion *debased* by an atmosphere of hysteria. As can be seen, *debase* may be more factual or descriptive than *degrade*, which suggests a more thorough but more subjective or moral sort of depredation.

The remaining words all concentrate on what one does to oneself. **Abase** can suggest sycophantic groveling or merely a ceremonial showing of respect: *abasing* himself before the hardened criminals he had been confined with; The vassal *abased* himself before the throne of his liege at the beginning of every audience. **Demean** suggests any lowering of oneself by unworthy motives or behavior: *demeaning* himself in his eagerness to meet the famous author. This word can refer to a hostile act toward someone else: attempting to *demean* the witness by asking all sorts of extraneous questions about his personal life. **Humble** can refer to an awesome experience: feeling small and *humble* as he stood gazing up at the Sistine murals. When not reflexive, the word functions as a milder substitute for *humiliate*: trying to *humble* her husband by making him ask for every penny he spent. See IGNOBLE, REDUCE, SHAMEFUL.

Antonyms: compliment, exalt, praise, raise, RESPECT.

disinterested

dispassionate
fair
impartial
neutral
objective
unbiased
unprejudiced

These words refer to a willingness to listen to all sides of a case without prejudging it. **Disinterested** does not imply a lack of interest, as is sometimes mistakenly thought, but a receptive interest that does not take sides in a dispute, at least until the truth can be discovered: *disinterested* judges and jurors on which a just trial depends. To be *disinterested*, in fact, requires attentiveness to detail and an evenness of temper, though it by no means implies coldness or lack of feeling. **Fair** is much more informal than *disinterested*, and would be more appropriate to describe a decision or a decision-maker once a verdict has been rendered: I could tell by the *disinterested* attitude of the judge that he would give a *fair* verdict. Also, where *disinterested* stresses keeping an open mind, *fair* suggests the taking of a stand, based on ethical considerations: striving to remain *disinterested* until he could arrive at a *fair* solution to the problem.

Impartial and **unbiased** are more closely related to *disinterested* than to *fair* in emphasizing open-mindedness. *Impartial* suggests literally taking no one's part; it implies, perhaps, a greater impersonality than *disinterested*: a judge free of all political pressures and thus aloof enough to remain *impartial*. While very closely related, *unbiased* suggests someone who is inherently free of any predispositions toward conflicting sides or parties. A person who has such predispositions might still, by putting them aside, succeed in being *impartial*, but being *unbiased* suggests he has none to start with: a lack of contact with minorities that left him completely *unbiased* for or against them. In reference to reporting, *impartial* might suggest uninvolvement, while *unbiased* would suggest a *fair* treatment of all sides, even though a definite point of view emerges: I don't ask a newspaper to be *impartial*, but I do expect it to be *unbiased* at least to the extent of distinguishing between fact and opinion.

Dispassionate and **unprejudiced** both emphasize the control of emotions rather than of thoughts. *Dispassionate* suggests someone unswayed by extraneous appeals designed to excite sympathy or indignation: remaining *dispassionate* amidst wild accusations of treason and favoritism. It is even more strikingly different from *disinterested*, however, in being applicable not only to an *impartial* judge, but to an involved contender who remains low-keyed, even-tempered, and factual in argument: countering the hysteria of his opponent with a *dispassionate* presentation of the evidence. *Unprejudiced*, in this emotional context, relates most closely to *unbiased*, but *unprejudiced* seems more fundamental and thoroughgoing, more inclusive in stressing the absence of any irrational, deeply ingrained emotional blind spot. *Unprejudiced*, furthermore, might suggest an inward state, while *unbiased* would suggest the result or proof of this state in action. One could learn to behave in an *unbiased* way even though he were not wholly *unprejudiced*: a new law that requires *unbiased* hiring practices, whether the owners of a business are *unprejudiced* or not.

Neutral and **objective** both suggest an even greater distance than any of the foregoing words. *Neutral* emphasizes the taking of no sides even to the point of rendering no final judgment whatsoever: jury trials in which the judge may remain *neutral* to the very end; *neutral* countries that refuse to be drawn into the cold war. *Objective* suggests an interest only in cold fact as distinct from belief, opinion, or attitude; unlike *disinterested*, it may also suggest lack of feeling: the *objective* attitude of scientists that would be fatal if extended to the sphere of human responsibilities. Some writers would argue that *objective* is necessarily a relative rather than an absolute quality: No one can argue he is wholly *objective* about anything. Most of these words, furthermore, are approving in tone — but only within the context of weighing and judging. They could all describe a moral weakness in other situations. [Who but a depraved person could remain unmoved and *objective* at the thought of a third world war?] See ALOOF, UNINVOLVED.

Antonyms: BIASED, *prejudiced, unfair.*

dislike

antipathy
aversion
distaste

These words are alike in pointing to a negative emotional response to someone or something. **Dislike**, the most general of these words, has a wide variety of applications, and can be substituted in most contexts for any of the other words here considered. It can be applied to both people and things: a *dislike* of crowds; His *dislike* for his work was matched by his enjoyment of his salary.

Distaste implies a mild *dislike*, usually stemming from temperamental or constitutional inclination. It suggests, not always accurately, that one's taste or esthetic sensibility has been offended by exposure to something: a *distaste* for controversy; a *distaste* for broad hats. Apart from intentionally jocular or comical contexts, *distaste* almost always describes things rather than people. It is commonly used with *for*.

Aversion is *dislike* that impels one to take steps to avoid the thing that offends; like *distaste*, it usually applies to things or animals rather than people. In formal contexts it more often suggests strong *dislike* amounting to a virtually uncontrollable desire to avoid: an *aversion* to snakes; an *aversion* to bloodshed. In less formal contexts, however, it often applies to mildly irritating things: an *aversion* to sweet wine. *Aversion* is commonly used with *to*.

Antipathy, whose etymological meaning is to feel against, refers to an instinctive *dislike*. An *antipathy* is not so much irrational as nonrational — it is simply not thought out, only felt, and may incidentally be quite supportable on rational or ethical grounds: an *antipathy* to Nazism; a natural *antipathy* to politicians. See ENMITY, REPULSIVE.

Antonyms: like, LOVE, *penchant, predilection.*

These words refer to appearances or prospects that are cold, unfriendly, or unpromising. **Dismal** suggests woebegone low spirits: the *dismal* sobbing of hungry children. Or it may suggest a course of action that portends utterly unfavorable consequences: a chance for survival that was at best *dismal*. It can also suggest extremely uncomfortable or unpleasant surroundings: a room so squalidly *dismal* as to make her faintly sick to her stomach. **Grim** can be used in the same way as *dismal*. Once it might have added a note of horror to each of the situations discussed above, but it has been used hyperbolically so often that it may have lost much of its force. Its full seriousness can sometimes be recaptured: the *grim* efficiency of the firing squad; the *grim* leer of the psychopath. In more informal uses it has less force than *dismal*: the *grim* look the wife gave her husband; an exam that was really *grim*.

Depressing, which refers to a lowering of the spirits, has also been overused — so much so that it can apply very inexactly to any unwelcome situation: a *depressing* incident on my way to work; *depressing* weather; a *depressing* motion picture; her *depressing* gaiety. A more exact choice of word is often possible.

Cheerless and **dour** are milder than *dismal* but still refer to unpleasant appearances. *Cheerless* most readily suggests a prospect that promises to be drab and unrelieved: a *cheerless* apartment that could be brightened considerably with a little effort. *Dour* most appropriately suggests ill humor: a *dour* glance that fully expressed her long-suffering pessimism. In describing a person, *cheerless* might suggest someone overly solemn: unable to tolerate the *cheerless* way she lived her life. *Dour* has a suggestion of sternness and, unlike *cheerless*, is seldom applied to anything but people or human qualities: A *dour* look was all the answer I got on how he liked the weather; a *cheerless* day, overcast and drizzling.

Forbidding suggests an ominous appearance that promises to be unfriendly or threatening on closer acquaintance: the dank walls and barred windows of the *forbidding* castle. See BLEAK, GLOOMY.

Antonyms: bright, cheerful, gay, JOYOUS, OPTIMISTIC, *promising, uplifting.*

These words are used to describe people or things that are dissimilar, or which do not agree or go together. **Disparate** means unlike or unequal, as in kind, quality, character, or amount. It usually refers to

dismal

cheerless
depressing
dour
forbidding
grim

disparate

disparate

(continued)

discordant
incompatible
incongruous

differences that are so extreme as to make the compared people or things totally distinct: such *disparate* art forms as sculpture and the oratorio; The two facets of his personality were *disparate* enough to recall Dr. Jekyll and Mr. Hyde.

Discordant suggests the unpleasant effect which is the result of an association of two or more musical sounds that are not in harmony or concord: a modern orchestral work that was so advanced in melodic structure as to seem not merely dissonant but *discordant*. In general application *discordant* can refer to anything that is not in agreement with any other thing, but most often it is reserved for situations which imply the presence of opposition or conflict: Our chairman's ideas about the projected expenditures were so *discordant* with those of the rest of the committee that our meeting ended in a stalemate. When people are described as *discordant* it is because they exist in a disagreeable, quarrelsome atmosphere: a *discordant* family whose children all left home to get away from their parents' constant bickering. Such people may be called **incompatible** — that is, unable to exist or get along with each other in a pleasant or friendly way. In one way *incompatible* is a milder word than *discordant*; it does not necessarily imply the open clash or opposition that *discordant* does. It would be possible, for example, for two people to work together in a small office without open disagreement and yet be called *incompatible* because one is so much more talkative than the other that he disturbs the quiet person's working habits. In another way, however, *incompatible* is stronger than *discordant* since the incompatibility of two persons or things often implies the impossibility of their coexistence. Two *discordant* people might stay on in a place of employment, or as part of a family unit, continually fighting but nonetheless existing together. But *incompatible* strongly suggests the inability to remain together. Thus the word is often used to describe couples whose marriage has gone on the rocks or whose contemplated marriage is thought of as unworkable. When *incompatible* is used in reference to things rather than people, there is the same suggestion of an incapability of mutual existence because of a basic difference in nature: the idea that matter and spirit are *incompatible*; the use of *incompatible* colors in a painting.

Incongruous designates that which is not in agreement or is not suitable, reasonable, or harmonious: his *incongruous* behavior at his father's funeral; the *incongruous* proportions of a building. It also suggests a lack of conformity, a being at odds with some accepted standard: a plan *incongruous* with reason. *Incongruous* sometimes has a connotation of the ludicrous or the absurd in the lack of agreement, harmony, conformity, etc., which it describes: the *incongruous* combination of a formal gown and tennis shoes. See ABSURD, HETEROGENEOUS.

Antonyms: consistent, consonant, harmonious, identical, SIMILAR.

distant

faraway
inaccessible
remote

These words refer to places considerably removed in space or time. **Distant** suggests that space is a barrier to easy contact: a country very *distant* from our own. **Remote** takes up the suggestion of mere space as a barrier, but adds to it overtones implying isolation that results from being out of the way or off the beaten track: the *remote* interior that is harder to reach than many more *distant* places. **Inaccessible** almost exclusively emphasizes barriers other than sheer space itself: a short cut through the mountain that is, however, extremely *inaccessible* in winter. **Faraway** suggests a *distant* place that might also be exotic or picturesque: *faraway* islands where people live on coconuts and bask all day in the sun.

Distant and *remote* also can refer to separation by time: ruins that once were palaces in the *distant* past; a vanished culture *remote* from ours. In these uses, *remote* is an intensification of the lack of contact suggested by *distant*. In reference to future possibilities, *distant* suggests sheer time as the barrier, *remote* other added difficulties that make for an unlikely prospect. [Real disarmament is a *distant* possibility; The chances for negotiation are *remote*.]

In reference to attitudes, *distant* suggests a wandering mind: a *distant* look in his eye. *Faraway* suggests absorption in possibly pleasant fantasies of another kind of life: a *faraway* hint of wanderlust in his expression. *Remote*, however, stresses coldness of manner: the woman who held herself rigid and *remote* in a chill silence. See ALOOF, DISINTERESTED.

Antonyms: accessible, close, near, near-by, proximal, proximate.

These words indicate various degrees of caution, doubt, or fear that lead to a lack of faith in something or an embittered outlook. **Distrustful** refers to seemingly well-grounded suspicions of undependability or disloyalty that make one unwilling to give credence to something: inaccuracies in the report that made him *distrustful* of its conclusions; *distrustful* of adults who always spoke of how much harder they had worked when they were young. **Mistrustful** suggests a much less clear-cut suspicion, one which might amount to no more than a growing uncertainty mingled with an indefinable uneasiness and possibly even fear: more and more *mistrustful* of her companion as he led her deeper into the dense forest. *Distrustful* may suggest detached or informed judgment that guards one from taking a false step; *mistrustful* may suggest an anxious vulnerability that might already be exposed to or involved in danger because of a previous misstep.

Chary is more closely aligned with *mistrustful* in indicating a cautious, fussy, or grudging attitude, whether it is the result of natural timidity or painful past experience. The word suggests the same uneasiness or fear as *mistrustful*, but implies a hanging back from rather than involvement in a situation: *chary* of strangers; *chary* of eating undercooked food even after the epidemic was over. **Disillusioned** specifically suggests a posture of detachment or bitterness born of past experience that has subverted one's hopes or ideals. [Had she been more *distrustful* of his extravagant promises, she wouldn't be so *disillusioned* now; She travels with a group of teen-agers who try to appear *disillusioned* and blasé about life.]

Cynical indicates a *disillusioned* attitude that has hardened into extreme bitterness, although this may be leavened with resignation: She was *cynical* about her husband's vow to quit drinking. The word can also point to a readiness to be *distrustful* on the basis of little or no evidence: *cynical* about any account of the altruism and idealism of people younger than he.

Jaundiced is a more informal and colorful substitute for *cynical*, suggesting a hard-bitten skeptic who prefers to look at something or at everything from a negative point of view: He had a *jaundiced* attitude toward all proposals for slum clearance that differed in the slightest from his own; a man who was content to look at life with a *jaundiced* eye. See ANXIETY, CAUTIOUS, DOUBT, SKEPTIC, TIMID.

Antonyms: confident, SURE, trusting.

distrustful

chary
cynical
disillusioned
jaundiced
mistrustful

diversify

variegate
vary

These words mean to give unlike characteristics or appearances to the members of a group of things. To **diversify** one's reading is to read about a number of different subjects; to *diversify* one's investments is to buy equities in different kinds of business enterprises.

To **vary** is to make different the successive elements of a series of related things. To *vary* one's diet is to eat different kinds of food at successive meals; to *vary* one's work routine is to break up one's day into segments devoted to various aspects of one's job rather than to concentrate on one aspect of it over a long period of time.

To **variegate** is to impart variety to a group of similar things by giving them different colors, shapes, sizes, and the like. Easter eggs are *variegated* by coloring, bouquets by arrangement, books by jacket design or choice of type. See DIVIDE, MIXTURE, RANDOM.

Antonyms: solidify, unify.

divide

allocate
allot
apportion
assign
distribute
prorate
ration

This group is concerned with the parceling out of a quantity, such as money or goods, among the members of a group. **Divide** is the most general of these and says the least about what means are used in the process. When two people or groups are to share in the quantity, the word carries implications of an equal division: Even though I put up more capital than you, let's *divide* the profits between us. This is not invariably true, however, and when more than two shares are involved, the implication of equality disappears completely: Thieves and pirates, according to legend, often *divide* their spoils unfairly.

Assign, **allot**, and **allocate** also carry no implication of a fair or equal division, but all three words suggest that someone in authority has determined how the quantity is to be divided among the group he represents or controls. Of these, *assign* is the least and *allocate* the most formal. *Assign* carries the strongest implication of arbitrariness on the part of the one who *assigns*. The quantity being parceled out, furthermore, is more often tasks or roles than goods or money: How many chapters did the professor *assign*? *Allot* implies the matching of items on one list to those on another: I've *allotted* six dollars a month for carfare and twenty dollars a month for lunches. *Allocate*, as well as being the most formal of these three, is the most specific. It is most often used of a governing body's action in setting aside a fixed sum of money for a government program. Outside this governmental context, the word would seem forced and stiff. [Congress *allocated* $3 million for highway improvement.]

Distribute is most used for the dispersing of a quantity in space or among the scattered members of a group. [The paperback edition of a book is usually more widely *distributed* than the hardcover version; This year, the corporation decided not to *distribute* dividends to its shareholders.]

The three remaining terms all imply a process of division that is equal, fair, or judicious — based on some fixed plan or equitable rule. **Ration** is specifically used for a method of sharing or *distributing* some scarce commodity when demand exceeds supply. It usually but not necessarily suggests a method of distribution based on need. [In wartime, meat and gasoline are often *rationed*.] **Prorate** refers to the sorting out of a quantity into different sizes, based on some prescribed variable: Since you worked twice as long as I on the project, we should *prorate* two-thirds of the fee to you. To **apportion** is to determine the composition of a smaller group in proportion to a larger group. It most strongly suggests a just and fair parceling out, based on some objective standard: The

Supreme Court ruled unconstitutional those state legislatures *apportioned* on any other basis than population. See DIVERSIFY, SEVER.

Antonyms: commingle, CONNECT, *fuse, unify.*

These words refer to a willingness to be managed, led, taught, or trained. **Docile** stresses a complete lack of unruliness that makes for easy handling; the word comes from a Latin root meaning teachable and it often appears in the context of education: *docile* pupils. **Amenable**, by contrast, suggests most strongly a good-willed openness to suggestions or recommendations, but the word does not imply the built-in acquiescent temperament of *docile*: Teen-agers may not be the most *docile* creatures imaginable, but they are more *amenable* to sympathetic guidance than most parents think.

Tractable suggests manageability to an even greater degree than *docile*. It comes from a Latin word meaning to handle; this is reflected in its use applying to the willingness of people to be led: a *tractable* audience that was willing to listen as long as the speaker had voice to exhort them with. The word can give a tone that is not very flattering to the people it describes, since it can seem to discuss human beings as though they were a material or inanimate substance to be manipulated, a substance having no will of its own.

Tame and **submissive** point to the greatest amount of servility suggested by any of these words. With *tame*, the servility may be innate or ingrained, as with domesticated animals: a *tame* horse. A *tame* animal may, however, be far from *docile* in temperament. *Submissive* at its mildest can indicate nothing more than meek humility before one's superiors, but in any case it suggests an extremely responsive attitude toward the needs, desires, or whims of another, sometimes to the point of humiliating abjectness: the ideally *submissive* wife of the Victorian era. See ADAPTABLE, COMPLIANT, MALLEABLE, OBEDIENT.

Antonyms: aggressive, inflexible, STUBBORN, UNRULY, WILD, WILLFUL.

docile

amenable
submissive
tame
tractable

These words all denote persons engaged in treating sick or injured people. **Doctor, physician,** and **surgeon** are all licensed practitioners of medicine and have one or more degrees from an accredited medical school. *Doctor* is the most general term and it may also apply to specialists in related branches of medicine, such as psychiatrists, dentists, and veterinarians. A *physician* is a *doctor* who is engaged in general practice or in one of its many specialties, while a *surgeon* is primarily concerned with diseased conditions or injuries that require operative procedures. However, since in recent years medical knowledge has become such a vast field, more and more *doctors* are taking postgraduate training and are restricting their practice to pediatrics, gynecology, obstetrics, urology, and other specialties. As a result, many of these specialists are not only *physicians* but are often qualified *surgeons*. *Doctor* is the correct title for all of them and is a reference to their having earned the appropriate *doctor's* degree, as M.D. (*doctor* of medicine), D.D.Sc. (*doctor* of dental science), D.V.M. (*doctor* of veterinary medicine). Psychiatrists have earned an M.D. previous to their psychiatric training, whereas psychologists have not. Psychologists, however, like those pursuing any discipline in the arts and sciences, may earn a Ph.D. (*doctor* of philosophy), but this would not permit them to practice medicine.

An **osteopath** is a practitioner of a school of healing known as osteopathy, which stresses the importance of the musculoskeletal system and

doctor

chiropractor
medic
osteopath
physician
surgeon

its proper functioning as a basis for health. An *osteopath* is a *doctor* by virtue of having earned a D.O. (*doctor* of osteopathy) and is now widely permitted by law to practice medicine, prescribe drugs, or undertake surgery when qualified. Often, his preferred method of treatment is manipulation of the muscles and bones, especially the backbone. A **chiropractor** puts a similar emphasis on the spinal area as basic to health and treats patients by the manual adjustment and manipulation of this and related areas. Unlike the *osteopath*, however, the *chiropractor* does not practice internal medicine or surgery and is not trained to do so. Thus, his right to be addressed as *doctor* is disputed by some.

In its narrowest sense, **medic** refers to an enlisted man in the armed forces who is trained to assist *doctors* with medical duties in service hospitals or to work with the sick or wounded in combat areas. Such a person would not, of course, be himself a *doctor* nor would he be addressed as such. At its most informal, *medic* can be used in a more general or imprecise way to refer to any *physician*, *surgeon*, or hospital intern. See DRUG, HEALTHY, SICKNESS.

doubt

dubiety
skepticism
suspicion
uncertainty

These words refer to a lack of conviction that results in a reluctance to believe something or an inability to decide. **Doubt** is the most general of these and has the widest application. It can indicate dissent from a proposition because of evidence to the contrary, though this evidence falls short of being conclusive: There were growing *doubts* about the victory statement, based on scattered reports coming in from remote battle stations. More often, the word indicates a lack of full assent to a proposition that evidence alone can neither confirm nor deny: He expressed considerable *doubt* that man was innately good. In this sense, a lack of faith or trust may be indicated by the word: *doubt* about the existence of God; the first *doubts* concerning her husband's affection for her. The phrase *in doubt* refers to something still unsettled or in question: The result of the election remained *in doubt* until the next morning. The word, used alone, can also reflect this lack of decisiveness: Tormented by *doubt*, he stood at the intersection of the two paths, not knowing which to take.

Dubiety can function as a considerably more formal substitute for *doubt*. The word may impart the notion of actively calling something into question rather than simply being passively unsure: a touch of *dubiety* in his voice as he asked her to repeat her outrageous accusation. On the other hand, the word can suggest a wavering between conclusions.

This last possibility for *dubiety* makes it a more formal substitute for **uncertainty**, which stresses wavering indecision for whatever reason, particularly as it relates to choice or outcome: She expressed *uncertainty* about which man she should marry. **Suspicion** more often concentrates on a single possibility, rather than on alternatives, and indicates a questioning *uncertainty* that something is what it purports to be: the first *suspicions* that their marriage would fail.

Skepticism is considerably more decisive in tone than the other words here, pointing to an unwavering posture of *doubt* until faced with undeniable proof: He greeted her protestations of innocence with amused *skepticism*. Often, the word suggests a rationalistic or scientific attitude — or an irreverent attitude toward the claims of religion or the occult: the necessary *skepticism* of science toward new scientific theories; Talking to the medium had only increased his *skepticism* about spiritualism. See UNBELIEF.

Antonyms: assurance, certainty, confidence, conviction.

These words relate to suspicion, indecision, or a lack of clarity. **Doubtful** can function in all three of these areas. [She was *doubtful* of his good intentions; still *doubtful* about which plane to take; The outcome of his appeal is still *doubtful*.] The word can also be used as an indefinite way to impugn the worth or value of something: a man of *doubtful* habits; a book of *doubtful* merit. **Dubious** is closely related to this last use of *doubtful*, but it carries a greater air of veiled insinuation and, relating to morals, may have more sinister overtones: a *dubious* person. The phrase, a *doubtful* person, by contrast, would pertain to someone who did not know what to do. Similarly, an outcome that was *doubtful* would be one not yet decided; a *dubious* outcome would be an undesirable one. Referring to hesitation, the word may suggest less basis on which to choose, but this may be accompanied by a sense of greater suspicion, wariness, or even danger: She was beginning to be *dubious* about the man's claim to be a window-washer. **Questionable** can be used euphemistically in reference to immorality: a house where *questionable* activities were conducted. In other uses, it points to something genuinely open to doubt, analysis, or criticism: a *questionable* foreign policy.

Uncertain can refer, most simply, to an inability to choose: *uncertain* about which dress to wear. The word also applies to a lack of clarity or evidence or to an unforeseeable outcome: an *uncertain* legend on the rusted sign; an *uncertain* dating of the new fossil discoveries; these *uncertain* times, in which there is little to be hoped for and much to be feared. **Problematic** emphasizes one aspect of *uncertain*, referring to something that cannot be definitely established by the available evidence: The ultimate origins of the Aztec and Mayan cultures are likely to remain *problematic*. The word can also pertain to results that are endangered or unclear because of an attendant pattern of complex causality: Multilateral approval on each item of a nuclear-control agreement tends to make disarmament *problematic*.

Both **ambiguous** and **equivocal** concentrate on a lack of clarity. *Ambiguous* can refer to either an intentional or unintentional failure to be precise or definite. [He kept making *ambiguous* remarks instead of straightforward yes-or-no replies; In explaining his stand, he only made everything more *ambiguous* than it had been to begin with.] *Equivocal* stresses an intentional wish to remain unclear; the word can, in fact, suggest deliberate deception or the saying of one thing while meaning another. [She kept putting him off half-heartedly with *equivocal* replies to his proposal.] At its strongest, the word suggests something that might be thought of as morally compromising: They advised their daughter against putting herself in *equivocal* situations when she was out on dates. But the word can also apply to what is merely *uncertain*, unprovable, or of *doubtful* validity, even when *dubious* motives are absent: statistical factors that make even the most scrupulous public-opinion polls *equivocal* in their findings. See CONFUSE, UNWISE, VAGUE.

Antonyms: CLEAR, *confident, decided,* DEFINITE, SURE.

Drawing shares with other words in this list the meaning of a representation by lines or shadings. A **sketch** is a *drawing* usually showing only the chief features of the object depicted; *sketches* are often rough or incomplete *drawings* and are sometimes used as bases for later elaboration into finished paintings or the like. Portrait painters often draw several *sketches* of their subjects before beginning a portrait in oils.

Cartoon is popularly known as a *drawing* appearing in a newspaper

doubtful

ambiguous
dubious
equivocal
problematic
questionable
uncertain

drawing

cartoon
diagram

drawing
(continued)

illustration
sketch

or other periodical and often having humorous or satirical intent. However, the word also refers to a full-size *sketch* for a fresco, mural, or the like, and is often quite detailed and elaborate. *Cartoons* are much prized by art historians and collectors as records of the plans and progress of famous works, as well as for their own beauty.

A **diagram** is either a generalized *drawing* made for scientific, mathematical, technological, or similar purposes, such as the *diagrams* in a geometry book; or a design in the form of a *drawing* which represents certain relationships by analogy rather than by literal depiction of objects, such as graphs, charts, and the like.

Illustration is applied to any *drawing*, whether a depiction or a *diagram*, which helps make clear the subject matter of a book or article, aids the telling of a story, or decorates a publication. More widely, the word can indicate any graphic material or art work that accompanies a printed text: the well-known photographer who did the book's *illustrations*. See ARTIST, COLOR, PORTRAY.

dress

apparel
attire
clothes
clothing
costume
garb
garments

These words all refer to coverings worn on the body. **Dress** is the outer covering for both men and women, especially when suitable for a formal occasion: evening *dress*; court *dress*. *Dress* may be used specifically to mean the skirt and waist, usually in one piece, worn by women and girls.

Clothes and **clothing** are more general terms. *Clothing* denotes the entire covering taken as a whole. [In winter children need warm *clothing*; Aborigines in hot climates tend to wear little or no *clothing*.] *Clothing* need not be limited to the persons wearing it, but may suggest the manufacturer or dealer: a factory that makes children's *clothing*; a second-hand *clothing* store; a sale of winter *clothing*. *Clothes* and **garments**, on the other hand, suggest that coverings worn on the body are made up of separate parts. When one speaks admiringly of a woman as having beautiful *clothes*, one means that everything she wears — coats, dresses, suits, shoes, hats, etc. — is in excellent taste and of high quality and is also very becoming to the wearer. *Clothes* may also be designed especially for various activities or for persons in a certain conditon or time of life: sports *clothes*; school *clothes*; maternity *clothes*; baby *clothes*. A *garment* is an article of *clothing*, especially of outer *clothing*, but it may also be a piece of underclothing with a distinct function: a foundation *garment*. *Garment* may also apply as an attributive to *clothing* in general, and especially to its manufacture: the *garment* industry.

A **costume** is the characteristic *clothing* worn by the people of a given region, time, or group: the national *costume* of Bavaria; Elizabethan *costume*; cowboy *costume*. In this sense, *dress* is sometimes used interchangeably with *costume*: T. E. Lawrence often wore Arab *dress* in the desert. In its second sense, *costume* can also refer to the *clothing* worn by an actor during the playing of a role or by a person posing as an imaginary character in any situation. [As Hamlet, Booth wore a *costume* of black velvet and a long gold chain around his neck; My cousin went to the party in a pirate *costume*.] **Garb**, a rather literary word, is used chiefly with reference to the *clothing* characteristic of a profession or rank: the *garb* of a priest; kingly *garb*.

Apparel and **attire** are chiefly used of complete and elegant outer *clothing*, although *dress* has largely supplanted them in this sense. *Apparel* (which is often rendered as *wearing apparel*) is a somewhat formal word for both *clothing* and *clothes*. It carries more of the suggestion of a collection of separate *garments* in which a person is clad than does *attire. Attire* often stresses the impression that one's *clothes* may make upon others: the rich *attire* of a Renaissance pope; the strange *attire* of the eccentric old woman. See STYLISH, VOGUE.

These words relate to substances, natural or synthetic, that are intended to aid in the diagnosis, prevention, treatment, or cure of physical and mental disorders.

drug

biological
medicament
medication
medicinal
medicine
narcotic
pharmaceutical
remedy
specific

Drug is the most general, being applicable to any substance serving those purposes. [The doctor prescribed a new *drug* for his patient; Many *drugs* have been used in the treatment of malaria.] The plural form carries an added suggestion of improper or excessive use: an addiction to *drugs*. **Medicine** and **remedy** are close synonyms for *drug*, but both may be extended to other agencies or procedures supposedly conducive to health. [Sunshine and rest are good *medicine* for convalescents; The best *remedy* for overweight is careful dieting.] **Medicament** is a learned variant of *medicine*, seldom used nowadays. **Medicinal**, known chiefly as an adjective, is preferred by commercial enterprises concerned with the manufacture and marketing of *drugs*: the export of *medicinals* to South America.

Biological, generally used in the plural, denotes a class of *drugs* prepared from living animal sources and usually administered under medical supervision; serums, vaccines, and hormone products are *biologicals*. **Pharmaceutical** is a semiofficial term referring to all medical preparations made by *drug* firms, especially those meeting certain standards of quality and obtainable from pharmacists only on prescription: cosmetics, *drugs*, and *pharmaceuticals* sold here.

Narcotic, in the medical sense of the word, is a *drug* that has a limited, often variable capacity to relieve pain or induce sleep; morphine, codeine, and certain other opium derivatives are *narcotics*. It is this power, together with a strong habit-forming tendency, that has led to their widespread abuse and given both the *drug* and the word a bad name: the traffic in *narcotics; narcotic* addiction. **Specific**, as the word implies, refers to any *drug* or *medicinal* that is adapted for the treatment, alleviation, or cure of some clearly identified abnormal condition. [Digitalis is a *specific* for many kinds of heart disease; The best *specific* for the control of diabetes mellitus is insulin.]

Medication has become popular as a generic term for anything that is given or administered to a patient undergoing therapy. This eliminates the possible unpleasantness of *drug* when it might be mistaken as applying to *narcotic* addiction rather than to prescribed treatment: nurses responsible for giving each patient the *medication* specified by his doctor; a new *medication* to combat *drug* addiction. It can apply widely from the simplest *remedies*, such as aspirin, to the most complex. Also, it refers less harshly to the tranquilizers and other *drugs* used to control the symptoms of mental disorder, where a cure is not possible or pragmatic: hospital bed-space freed by handling many of the mentally ill as outpatients who can be maintained by a program of regular *medication*. See DOCTOR, HEALTHY, SICKNESS.

These words refer to things lacking in moisture. **Dry** is the most general, being equally suitable for describing solids, atmospheres, or climates: She wiped the dish until it was *dry; dry*, hot air in the sauna; New Mexico's *dry* climate. The remaining words all stress that something containing moisture has been rendered *dry*. **Dried** is commonly used to describe foods from which moisture has been partially or totally

dry

crisp
dehumidified

dry
(continued)

dehydrated
desiccated
dried
parched

removed as a way of preserving them: *dried* beef; *dried* peas; *dried* apricots. In some cases, preparation involves restoring water to the product, as with peas; in other cases, the food is used as it is. **Dehydrated** is a more formal and technical term for the same idea, although it more often applies, in this sense, to foods that have not only been *dried*, but powdered as well: *dehydrated* milk; *dehydrated* eggs. In other senses, the word can indicate an unwanted loss of moisture: a fever that had caused his body to become dangerously *dehydrated*. **Parched** is a much less formal term that concentrates exclusively on this last possibility of *dehydrated*, referring to an undesirable or uncomfortable lack of or need for water: the *parched*, drought-stricken countryside; He had gulped down the last of the water in his canteen, but still felt *parched* with thirst.

Crisp applies almost exclusively to brittle or shriveled solids, particularly those in thin sheets or layers. Also, the word suggests that this *dry*, brittle state has been arrived at by heating or cooking: *crisp* potato chips; the steak she had burned to a *crisp*. This is not always true, however: *crisp* autumn leaves. **Dehumidified** is comparable to *dehydrated* in formality and would seem identical in meaning, but whereas *dehydrated* applies to solids, *dehumidified* most often applies exclusively to atmosphere: the amount of *dehumidified* air that an air conditioner can put out. **Desiccated** can function as a much more formal substitute for *dried: desiccated* yeast. Here, it compares to *dehydrated* in suggesting a powdered substance. Much more often, however, the word is used in metaphorical ways, suggesting something wasted, old, dried-up, lifeless, or dull: the *desiccated* old fuddy-duddy. *Dry* and *crisp* also have metaphorical uses. *Crisp* can suggest a brusque, sharp, or efficient manner: She rejected his proposal with a *crisp* remark; the *crisp* smile of the airline stewardess. *Dry* has an extremely wide range of metaphorical uses. It can indicate anything droll, boring, or lacking in humor: a *dry* remark, given with a deadpan expression; a *dry* book. The word can also refer to an alcoholic drink that is free of sweetness: a *dry* martini. See HOT, STERILE.

Antonyms: damp, deliquescent, moist, soggy, wet.

duplicate

congruent
exact
identical
true

These adjectives refer to copies that are replicas of one another or reproductions of an original. **Duplicate** designates a copy that is just like another or others. It may indicate two corresponding copies, one of which is a second or extra copy: *duplicate* receipts, the original retained by the bank, the carbon returned to the depositor. Or it may apply to multiple copies that look exactly alike: a dozen *duplicate* prints of a photograph. A *duplicate* copy may be made with or from an original, as by use of carbon paper or a duplicating machine; or it may be made from a pattern, as a stencil, negative, or engraved metal plate: *duplicate* copies of a letter; *duplicate* copies of a book. At one extreme, *duplicate* designates a replica that is virtually indistinguishable from the original: a *duplicate* key. At the other extreme, it may indicate simply an accurate copy made at the same time or in the same form as the first: a *duplicate* copy of an income-tax report, kept for the taxpayer's personal records.

Like a *duplicate* copy, an **exact** copy or **true** copy is made from an original. But *exact* and *true* stress strict substantive accuracy and may or may not indicate correspondence in form. *Exact* implies a precise reproduction of all details in a standard or model. [Writing painstakingly in longhand, the student made an *exact* copy of the printed poem;

By means of the photocopying process, one can make an *exact* reproduction of the printed page.] *True* indicates absolute accuracy in reproduction, conformity to fact, and consequent validity. It stresses content rather than form. [The college registrar certified the transcript as a *true* copy of the student's record; The Director of Vital Statistics certified that the birth registration card was a *true* copy of facts recorded on the birth record.]

Identical is applied to copies that are just like one another or that seem to be exactly alike. It is the strongest of these words and implies correspondence in every detail. [So far as an untrained eye could tell, the reproduction was *identical* to the designer's original.] Where a *duplicate* copy is clearly secondary, though it may be *exact*, *identical* implies equality, indicating mutual likeness: two women wearing *identical* dresses; *identical* prints made from a woodblock; Your pen is *identical* to mine. In plane geometry, **congruent** refers to figures that are *identical* in shape and size, filling exactly the same space. Triangles are *congruent* if every point of one can be brought into correspondence with every point of the other in space, so that the flat figures would coincide exactly if they were superimposed. See ACCURATE, COPY.

Antonyms: contrasted, different, dissimilar, faulty.

E

These words refer to a state of extreme readiness and interest in some prospective action or subject, suggesting one's willingness to become involved in it. **Eager** may suggest a general thirst for experience of all kinds or an intense interest of a more specific nature: young, *eager* students ready to take on the world; *eager* for his first look around Paris. While the word most often suggests a period before involvement is possible, it may also describe the intensity of involvement itself: an *eager* lover. **Intent** relates to this last possibility of *eager*, suggesting an undivided concentration on the activity itself: *intent* on the book he was reading. It may also suggest a purposeful and determined search for something that interests one: *intent* on finding the café he had read about in magazines.

Avid and **desirous** both pertain mostly to the period before involvement. Both may refer to an intense longing or craving, but *desirous* might now seem old-fashioned or archaic-sounding to many: *desirous* of her hand in marriage. *Avid* still retains its forcefulness as an intensification of *eager*, suggesting a craving on the point of desperation: *avid* for news of the city; the *avid* reader of pornography. Like *eager*, it may also describe actual involvement, but again with greater intensity: He dispatched the meal with a series of *avid* gulps.

Keen and **enthusiastic** both may suggest an extreme liking for or approval of something. *Keen* best describes *eager* involvement: children who watched the clowns with *keen* delight. Much more informally, the word indicates a special liking or appetite for something: *keen* on mystery stories. *Enthusiastic* is unique among these words in applying mostly to participation rather than expectation, or to a favorable verdict on something already experienced or proposed. For example, a person

eager

avid
desirous
enthusiastic
intent
keen

can be *eager* for a vacation and *enthusiastic* about the plans he has made, but he cannot be *enthusiastic* about the vacation itself until it is underway or over. Thus the word pertains to activity undertaken with gusto, verve, and exuberance, or to an extremely favorable judgment that contains few reservations: an *enthusiastic* group of mountain-climbers; *enthusiastic* reviews of his book. See PASSIONATE, PREOCCUPIED.

Antonyms: deadbeat, IMPASSIVE, *indifferent, listless, uninterested,* UNINVOLVED.

eat

consume
devour
dine
gobble
gorge
sup
wolf

These words refer to the partaking of food. **Eat** is the most general, applying equally well to man or animal: the woman *eating* a hot dog; horses *eating* fodder. Only context can give further details: slowly *eating* his breakfast of hot chocolate and croissants; *eating* his bowl of soup almost in one gulp. **Dine** and **sup** are relatively formal; both specifically refer to *eating* done by people. *Dine* can point to the day's main meal: She *ate* a light lunch so that she would be able to *dine* later without a guilty conscience. Or the word can refer to any formal or special meal: She asked her husband's employer to *dine* with them next week. *Sup* now sounds archaic and, worse, pretentious, though once it could refer to an evening or late evening meal: They had a nightcap and *supped* on leftovers once the guests were gone.

Unlike the preceding pair, **consume** can refer to either man or animal, but its point in either case is the thoroughness of the *eating*, suggesting the utter and avid taking in of a food: a pack of lions able to *consume* the whole carcass of an impala in a single night; The hungry boy *consumed* every last scrap on his plate. Thus, the word can apply to any process that involves total destruction and in which one thing can be seen as feeding off another: the raging fever that was *consuming* her body. **Gorge** compares to *consume*, but stresses *eating* or even overeating to the point of satiety or possibly discomfort, suggesting the gluttonous and indiscriminate stuffing down of food: the sleepy hounds lying about *gorged* with food; the fat man who *gorged* himself constantly with mountainous desserts.

Gobble emphasizes rapid *eating* rather than the thoroughness indicated by *consume* or the excessiveness possible for *gorge*: chickens who *gobbled* down the scattered breadcrumbs in a twinkling; He warned the girl that she'd get sick if she *gobbled* her food that way. **Wolf** also emphasizes quickness, but it indicates a ravenous ferocity or desperation, as well. Since its obvious metaphor pertaining to one animal might make the word tautological in that instance and inappropriate in others, the main point of the word is to describe human *eating* in terms of a wolf's swift and rapacious feeding: *wolfing* down one canape after another as though he were starving; a movie that depicted Henry VIII *wolfing* down an incredible array of viands.

Devour can apply equally well to animals or men, though it is more general in its implications than the preceding, suggesting either the total consumption of something or the rapidity with which it is eaten: kittens that *devoured* the whole plate of catfood before the dozing mother cat could stir; hungry soldiers who *devoured* the tasteless creamed beef ladled out to them by the mess sergeant. Like *consume*, this word can have metaphorical uses, referring in this case to eager or enthusiastic taking in or, possibly, to the predatory destruction of something. [She *devoured* her French lessons so that she would be proficient by the time of her first trip abroad; All their assets were *devoured* by an unscrupulous loan shark.] See ABSORB.

These words all denote an aspect or peculiarity of a person's character or manner. **Eccentricity** is used to identify a characteristic, action, practice, or habit that differs in some way from what is usual or expected; the word suggests a strangeness or irregularity that may be harmless but that is an ingrained part of the personality. [Smoking cigars was part of the old lady's *eccentricity*; One of his *eccentricities* was a stubborn reluctance to entrust his savings to a bank.] By contrast, **quirk** is the most general of this group and suggests little as to the nature or the trait involved; *quirks* can be pleasant or unpleasant, amusing or irritating: Knuckle-cracking was his most annoying *quirk*. The word originally referred to a kind of verbal trick or conceit. Bright retorts, plays on words, subtle evasions, all were described as *quirks*. Although the term can be and still is used in this way, it more often now designates a distinctive trait of behavior rather than of speech. In any case, the word can suggest a slight slip, flaw, or distortion: a keen mind, but one full of *quirks*. **Idiosyncrasies** are like *eccentricities* in that they are strange in nature, but the word implies less a divergence from the general than an emphasis on the individual. *Eccentricities* are often an indication of mental aberration, *idiosyncrasies* the evidence of a strongly independent personality: His refusal to wear a tie at work in the summer is one of my uncle's most admirable *idiosyncrasies*. **Oddity** is interchangeable with *eccentricity* because of its suggestion of the aberrant and peculiar. However, the word is more often used to designate an odd or unique person or thing than a quality or trait. [What a collection of *oddities* he invited to his party!; A bargain is an *oddity* in that store; all their merchandise is overpriced.] See CHARACTERISTIC, FLAW, TEMPERAMENT.

Antonyms: commonness, conventionality, normality, ordinariness, typicality.

These words refer to the bounding line or outline of something. **Edge** refers to the thin line along one side of a thing: the south *edge* of the terrace. Or it may refer to the line between two sides or planes: the *edge* of an ax. In either case the word refers to a line that does not circumscribe a figure but may form part of its perimeter. As such, it can refer to any sort of boundary: the ragged *edge* of the forest. Unqualified, however, the word often suggests a straight or sharp line: He tested the *edge* of the knife with one finger. Metaphorically, the word may indicate the sharp line between two contrasting qualities or states or, particularly, the line delimiting an undesirable state: nations drifting closer to the *edge* of disaster.

Brink also indicates a line that is not circumscribing, but the word's stress is on an abrupt division between high and low ground: the *brink* of the cliff; the *brink* of a valley. **Verge** once could refer literally either to a dividing or circumscribing line in as general a way as *edge*, but now it is almost completely limited to metaphorical uses. Here, it suggests the imminence or nearness of an abrupt shift to some other condition, good or bad: on the *verge* of succeeding at last; on the *verge* of a nervous breakdown. *Brink* functions similarly in a metaphorical way, except that it almost exclusively applies to the imminence of something undesirable: on the *brink* of war. It may also suggest speed, inevitability, and possible destruction such as would be true in falling over a literal chasm: In international affairs, brinkmanship is the tactic of risking nuclear confrontation in the hope that one can stop short in time without plummeting headlong over the *brink*.

All the remaining words can refer to a circumscribing outline. **Border** and **margin**, furthermore, most often refer to plane figures. *Border*

eccentricity

idiosyncrasy
oddity
quirk

edge

border
brim
brink
margin
rim
verge

can indicate the area of such a figure that is nearest to its outside *edges*: They walked about the *border* of the park. The word can also refer to a circumscribing boundary that contrasts distinctly with what it encloses and thus sets off or frames the contained area: a black *border* around the portrait of the dead president; a modest *border* of lawn around the house. In this sense, the word may imply an added, decorative *edge*: the lace *border* of her handkerchief. *Border* can, however, refer like *edge* to a dividing line, as in its common use for the boundary between two countries: the *border* between Canada and the United States. *Margin* emphasizes exclusively one aspect of *border*, pointing to the outer area circumscribing something, an area that is often distinct in appearance from what it encloses. Unlike *border*, however, *margin* more frequently refers to the emptiness, blankness, or lack of decoration that sets off and surrounds something: Typescript looks best when at least an inch of *margin* is left on all four sides of the page. To this implication of space left unused can be added the notion of its being saved for an emergency: *margin* for error.

Rim and **brim** also refer to a circumscribing outline, in this case that of a circle. *Rim* refers most specifically to the open lip of a cylindrical or rounded shape: She tested the *rim* of the glass to see if it was nicked; on the *rim* of the volcano. *Brim* can refer to the same open lip, but is most often associated with a situation in which a container is completely filled: a teacup filled to the *brim*. This use extends to shapes that are not rounded: boxcars filled to the *brim* with grain. But *brim* has at least one use where it functions more like *border* or *margin*: the *brim* of a hat. See BOUNDARY, CIRCUMSCRIBE, PERIMETER.

Antonyms: CENTER, *interior*.

effect

cause
produce
realize

These words pertain to the accomplishing of results. **Effect** can refer to the successful accomplishment of an intended action: The pilot *effected* a take-off despite the bomb-pocked runway. As in this example, the point of this use is often the overcoming of difficulty or a previous uncertainty as to outcome. The word can also indicate putting into practice a previously formulated goal: We *effected* the plan with a minimum of fuss. No sense of difficulty or uncertainty need be implied here. When *effect* applies, however, to the formulating of a plan, goal, or solution, rather than to putting one into action, the word takes on a different set of overtones: a board of mediators to *effect* a compromise in the newspaper strike. While initial resistance is implied, the goal reached is not necessarily known at the outset, but is arrived at through experiment, innovation, and improvisation. Also, the word sometimes suggests a rough-and-ready or expedient result, if not a jerrybuilt one: ready to *effect* a solution to the problem by any means available.

By contrast, the desired objective implied by **realize** is always seen in advance, at least in the sense pertinent here: to *realize* a long-standing dream. The stress of the word, in fact, is on making actual or real something that has previously existed only as a plan or desire. **Produce** can also emphasize visible or actual results, but can apply to intentional or unintentional as well as to both good or bad results: a plan that *produced* concrete improvements in its first year of operation; proposals that *produced* fiery outbursts on the floor of the Senate. At its most literal, the word can apply to the bearing of fruit or the creation of something: countries that *produced* bumper crops while the famine raged; factories that *produce* war materiel. At its most neutral, the word merely assigns actions or results to the factors or agents that brought them about: Penicillin can *produce* an extreme allergic reaction in some people.

Cause is most closely related to this last sense of *produce*, stressing the relationship between a result and the factors responsible for it. [A stroke can *cause* permanent paralysis; Continual conflict among city-states *caused* the eventual decline of Greek civilization.] On this neutral level, the word points to the dispassionate or scientific tracing of a train of causality, often from the philosophical viewpoint of determinism. More informally, the word can apply to the laying of blame: parents who *cause* their children to grow up warped and apathetic. But a stress on inadvertence rather than on blame can be the point of the word in this use: He had unwittingly *caused* the accident by misreading a road sign. See CREATE, DECIDE, PERFORM, REACH.

Antonyms: DESTROY, *deter*, HINDER, PREVENT, STOP.

These words pertain to the physical or mental application that is devoted to achieving a result. At its mildest, **effort** can be used in reference to measuring the amount of application a given task requires. [How much *effort* will it take to get the requisitions out on time?; It only takes a little *effort* to keep your shoes shined.] With a slight increase in force, it can stress a more than ordinary attentiveness or thoughtfulness: students who make an *effort* to catch their own spelling errors; She decided to make a special *effort* to please him. When the word points specifically to a great outlay of energy, a challenging, difficult, or unpleasant task is implied: a real *effort* to win the race; a crisis that will require all our will and *effort* to survive; What an *effort* it took to endure the blabbering old busybody without insulting her.

Exertion more readily suggests a considerable or exhausting outlay of *effort*: He stood gasping with *exertion* after reaching the summit of the hill; the mental *exertion* it took to make the accounts balance. Unqualified, the word is more likely to apply to physical *effort*, but not always: Students on probation are expected to show greater *exertion* in their studies. **Pains** and **trouble** would also seem to stress outlay of *effort* in the face of difficulty or resistance, but both words are used idiomatically to indicate, instead, thoughtfulness or carefulness without necessarily suggesting great *exertion*. [She took whatever *pains* necessary to put her guests at ease; He'd be a good worker if he'd only take the *trouble* to get to work on time.] *Trouble* in particular can be used ironically to suggest a small *effort*, whereas *pains* can as easily be used for exacting *effort*: taking great *pains* with every detail of the program.

Struggle is the one word here that almost exclusively points to extreme *efforts*, those called up not only by the difficulty of the task or the external resistance to its achievement but by the determination, will, or zeal of the actor as well: his heroic *struggle* to overcome all obstacles in a situation where it would have been a *struggle* merely to stay alive. When qualified, however, the word need not always be so positive or approving: a feeble *struggle* to extricate himself; a hopeless *struggle* to escape his just punishment. See LABOR.

Antonyms: ease, facility, rest, SLOTH.

These words refer to aggressive rudeness born of crude vulgarity or unashamed egotism. **Effrontery** indicates an insult to good manners by someone who is pushy or conceited: the *effrontery* to ask the woman how she felt when she first got word of the accident; the *effrontery* to ask the distinguished guests if they had read his book. As in these examples, the

effort

exertion
pains
struggle
trouble

effrontery

churlishness

effrontery
(*continued*)

impertinence
impudence

word often suggests offensive behavior that comes as a shock or surprise, but this is not always the case: I knew what he wanted and was only waiting to see if he would have the *effrontery* to put it into words. **Impertinence** is a shade milder than *effrontery*, suggesting an offense to good manners that results from action that is out of place or from an uncalled-for remark: his *impertinence* in coming to the party uninvited; her *impertinence* in asking about details of our private life. As in the last example, the word can sometimes point to a prying busybody who meddles in the affairs of others. In this case the stress is on aggressiveness rather than on arrogance. At its mildest the word can point to a mere lack of relevance: It is an *impertinence* in scholarly work to insist on assigning blame rather than analyzing actual conditions in an objective way. Usually, however, the word does suggest impropriety or a lack of breeding.

Churlishness emphasizes this last possibility of *impertinence*, concentrating on grossly ill-mannered behavior that is the result of a crude, coarse, or vulgar background. This use reflects the word's derivation from a root referring to a low born man or one of the lowest rank. In addition, *churlishness* is the most extreme and disapproving of these words, implying an accompanying manner that is surly, contentious, hostile, and drastically inconsiderate: Both his constant quarrels with the neighbors and his chronic mistreatment of his children attested amply to his inescapable *churlishness*. Ill breeding may sometimes be absent as an implication: the brazen *churlishness* of the woman in the complaint department. **Impudence** relates more closely to *effrontery*, pointing to aggressive behavior that is not restrained by considerations of taste or courtesy. The word's special stress, however, is on a contemptuous or obnoxious arrogance: the *impudence* to suggest that his Ivy League background made him better qualified for the job than applicants from the state university. As can be seen, *impudence* and *churlishness* contrast strongly in that *churlishness* can indicate a low or coarse background whereas *impudence* can indicate a supposedly superior background. *Impudence* contrasts with *effrontery* and *impertinence* in that this pair often points to specific acts; furthermore, these acts could conceivably be inadvertent. *Impudence*, however, points to an insufferable manner that is reflected in deliberate insolence: an *impertinence* that resulted mostly from sheer ignorance rather than from outright *impudence*. See BRASHNESS, CONTEMPTUOUS, OVERBEARING, RUDE.

Antonyms: civility, courtesy, kindness, meekness, politeness, timidity.

egoism

conceit
egotism
narcissism
self-importance
selfishness
solipsism
vanity

These words refer to a preoccupation and concern only for oneself. **Egoism** and **egotism** are a related pair with a fine distinction in meaning. *Egotism* is disapproving in tone, suggesting someone with an inflated or unrealistic view of his own worth because of extreme self-preoccupation: the typical *egotism* of those who think the world owes them a living. *Egoism*, on the other hand, is a more ambiguous term. It might apply to someone who does not necessarily consider himself superior but who nevertheless remains preoccupied exclusively with himself: the *egoism* of the young office executive seeking advancement. The word has been given a new slant of meaning, furthermore, by psychological theorists of the last half-century. Theories that stress the importance of a strong ego (or "positive self-concept") as a key to mental stability have made it possible for *egoism* to suggest healthy self-interest coupled with a solid sense of identity: the *egoism* normal to a small infant; activities that will develop a healthy *egoism* in young adolescents.

Conceit and **vanity** stress the sense of inflated worth that is involved in *egotism*. *Conceit* suggests a general state of being puffed-up about one's own imagined superiority to others, so extreme as to rule out any self-assessment or self-criticism whatsoever: a fathomless *conceit* that prevents him from working hard enough to perfect his real but unformed talents. *Vanity* suggests self-pride that is based not so much on a feeling of superiority to others as on an unrealistic admiration and love for oneself: the actress who requires constant obeisance and flattery to satisfy her *vanity*. *Conceit* no longer sounds as extremely informal as it once may have, but *vanity* is still the slightly more formal of the two words. **Self-importance** is closely related to *conceit* and *vanity* but is more neutral and descriptive: diplomats who bustled about in a display of their own *self-importance*. Sometimes, the word can suggest considerations of status or involvement in serious or worthwhile affairs rather than a strictly personal *conceit*. [She spends hours before her mirror feeding her *vanity*, but is that any worse than your tedious concern with office protocol simply as a way of insuring your own *self-importance*?]

Narcissism and **solipsism** may once have been technical terms drawn respectively from psychology and philosophy, but they have now gained a wider currency, even in normal conversation, for the cluster of meanings discussed here. *Narcissism* in a strict psychological sense refers to an extreme withdrawal into self-preoccupation and self-love. It has come to be used more loosely to substitute for *egotism*: the star system in the theater that is responsible for a most pernicious form of *narcissism* among actors. *Solipsism* in a strict philosophical context refers to a disbelief in the existence of anything beyond the self; it now extends pejoratively to anyone completely wrapped up in a private world of his own: the *solipsism* of those avant-garde writers who do not even attempt to communicate with their audiences.

Selfishness need not suggest an inflated sense of worth at all or even extreme self-preoccupation. Its main connotation is that of grasping greediness without concern for others: the *selfishness* of those lobbyists who press for legislation beneficial to special interests but harmful to the general public. Under certain circumstances, however, it need not be wholly pejorative; in this it may approach some uses of *egoism*: the natural *selfishness* of the three-year-old. See BOAST, BRASHNESS, CONFIDENCE, OVERBEARING.

Antonyms: altruism, humility, meekness, modesty, shyness.

These words refer to what is highly fashionable or formal in style and is costly, detailed, or lavish, as well. **Elegant** is the most general but least concrete of these, being an approving word that refers to what is striking for its taste and value: a set of books with *elegant* bindings. It may suggest rarity as well as refinement, but may or may not suggest a piling up of great or costly masses of detail: the heavy gold scrolls of the *elegant* picture frame; a room *elegant* in its bareness, being sparsely furnished with a few pieces of modern furniture.

Elaborate and **ornate** both specifically indicate great detailing, but neither necessarily carries the built-in approving tone of *elegant*. *Elaborate* indicates a full-scale working out of something with painstaking care and thought: an *elaborate* epic poem with an amazing amount of themes and interrelated strands of imagery; *elaborate* costume balls that bored him silly; an *elaborate* hoax. The word can also apply to argument or reasoning that is methodical, lengthy, and abstruse: an *elaborate* hypothesis. *Ornate* is more restricted to decoration, suggesting a denseness that

elegant

deluxe
elaborate
grandiose
luxurious
ornate
sumptuous

is not so much orderly as sensual: *ornate* verbal imagery. The word stresses the finished effect more than the care or work that went into it. Sometimes richness or costliness of the result is implied: an *ornate* piece of jewelry studded with several different kinds of precious stones.

Luxurious and **sumptuous** specifically stress the sparing of no expense to create something fashionably lavish. These words may or may not point to the tastefulness suggested by *elegant* or the amassing of detail emphasized by the previous pair, but they do point to a showiness of general effect. *Luxurious* often suggests, as well, a setting arranged for comfort and convenience: the *luxurious* hotel; a *luxurious* car complete with air conditioning, telephone, and bar. The word need not be approving; a *luxurious* airport that was in the most garish and banal taste possible. Often, however, the word is applied approvingly to things in nature, eliminating any notion of costliness but emphasizing denseness, beauty, or richness, as of visual effect: the *luxurious* plumage of the peacock; a *luxurious* forest floor of interlaced pine needles. *Sumptuous* is more likely to be restricted to man-made things; its root refers to expenditure and this emphasis on costliness is frequently present in the word's use: a *sumptuous* Gobelin tapestry; critics who judged the car complete with air conditioning, telephone, and bar. The word need *sumptuous* new opera house to be an esthetic disaster. Used more loosely, the word may indicate something well turned out, tasteful, or lavish, without necessarily implying expenditure: the only woman on the beach with a really *sumptuous* figure.

Deluxe comes from the French phrase that means *of luxury*. Thus it might function identically to *luxurious*. *Deluxe*, however, very often refers to special accommodations: a *deluxe* compartment on the train; a *deluxe* hotel suite. In these and other cases, it can refer to added benefits, comforts, or value that costs more than the ordinary version: a *deluxe* leatherbound edition of the encyclopedia. Since the word has become chiefly a merchandizing term, it is often used to be deliberately deceptive: proof that the canned mushrooms labeled *deluxe* were not significantly different in quality from the regular grade.

Grandiose is the one word here that specifically and exclusively stresses a pretentious, inflated, or pompous striving for the *elegant* or *sumptuous*: a *grandiose* speech filled with empty rhetoric. In this sense, it has a wider, more general range of applications than other words here: a *grandiose* symphony that ran on for more than two hours; the *grandiose* delusions of some schizophrenics. See EXCELLENT, EXQUISITE.

Antonyms: inexpensive, MEDIOCRE, *plain, simple, unadorned,* USUAL, VULGAR.

embarrassment

chagrin
discomposure
humiliation
mortification
shame

These words refer to a disconcerted state of mind brought on by the broaching or exposing of an impropriety or by some blow to the ego. At its mildest, **embarrassment** may refer merely to social uneasiness: her *embarrassment* at having to introduce her fiancé. Or it may refer to a cringing from indelicacy: her *embarrassment* at overhearing the coarse talk of some soldiers. More to the point, however, it refers strongly to alarm at any public exposure of one's own ineptness or impropriety: his *embarrassment* at not remembering the name of his distinguished guest; the *embarrassment* of being discovered by her parents in the arms of the strange man. **Discomposure** is more formal and is restricted to the milder sense of *embarrassment*, usually suggesting a social uneasiness for any reason whatever: greeting his unexpected guests without being able to conceal his *discomposure*. **Chagrin** concentrates specifically on *em-*

barrassment because of a blow to the ego: She looked down with *chagrin* at her own unstylish dress.

The remaining words all point to more severe states of *embarrassment* than the foregoing words. **Shame** suggests a guilty disgust for one's own actions: looking back with *shame* on his night's escapades; boiling with *shame* at having failed the examination. **Humiliation** suggests a public loss of self-respect or the respect of others; this can result through a person's own failure or through someone else's malicious attempt to discredit him: the *humiliation* of having to ask the dean for reinstatement in his classes; those who regard receiving welfare checks as a *humiliation*; false accusations that resulted in his public *humiliation*. **Mortification** derives from a word meaning to kill and reflects this root in referring hyperbolically to someone almost destroyed by *shame* or *embarrassment*: her *mortification* at learning she had given all her money to confidence men. It is the most intense of all these words, except that frequent hyperbolical use has weakened its force considerably. See ANXIETY, TIMID, UNSETTLE, UPSET.

Antonyms: BRASHNESS, *composure,* CONFIDENCE, *contentment, exaltation, temerity.*

These words refer to subjective or affective states of mind rather than to objective or rational attitudes. **Emotion** is the most general and neutral, including all states of mind from the slightest shift in mood to the most intense or violent seizures: a wistful *emotion* that briefly clouded her eyes; a struggle within him of *emotions* so intense he could hardly speak. **Feeling** is similar to but more informal than *emotion*. It too can refer both to weak or intense states: a faint *feeling* of disgust at his proposition; Violent *feelings* broke out into full, ungovernable expression. *Feeling*, however, has a specific use to refer to a state of intense receptivity or expressivity: jurors who listened to her story with evident *feeling*; trying to play the piano piece with more *feeling*. While *emotion* might occasionally be used in this way, it sounds less natural in such a context than *feeling*.

Passion may once have been used in a fairly neutral way to describe strong *emotions* of all varieties; now, however, it is more strictly limited to sexual *feeling* or obsessive *emotions*: a *passion* for his wife undimmed by the years; an absolute *passion* for seeking out the untraveled byways of a country. In the sense of obsessive preoccupation, the word has so frequently been used hyperbolically that its force has been somewhat dulled and made trivial: a *passion* for garlic pickles. In its sense of sexual *feeling*, it can seem antiquated or euphemistic: an unholy *passion* for the fair sex. **Desire** is now the preferred word for suggesting sexual *feeling*, but it can also refer to any *feeling* of wanting or needing something: a *desire* for the opposite sex that is first expressed by hair-pulling and practical jokes; a strong *desire* to see his native country once more before he died. In contexts where *passion* escapes the charge of fustiness, it would suggest a greater potential for action than *desire*. [He was aware of the *desire* that had led him to call on her again, but he was surprised at the overwhelming *passion* he felt at seeing her face smiling up at his.]

Sentiment may specifically suggest a fixed attitude that is an abiding part of one's personality and that can be called up afresh as *feeling* by some external catalyst: politicians appealing to *sentiments* as safe as love of God, home, and mother. In a more general use, it can, like *feeling*, suggest any of a variety of strong *emotions*. It also has a special use,

emotion

affect
desire
feeling
passion
sentiment

referring to the expression of an emotional stand: He expressed his *sentiments* about the war with great eloquence. **Affect** is the most formal and
technical of all these words; it is used in psychiatric parlance to refer to
an emotional state in its discernible psychological rather than physiological aspect. [The excessive *affect* with which she reacted to several of
the inkblots was also reflected in changes in her pulse and respiration;
He was still in a state of shock and thus able to speak of his recent ordeal
without *affect*; the typical catatonic's total loss of *affect*] See ATTRAC-
TION, IMAGINATION, PASSIONATE, PREOCCUPIED.
  Antonyms: indifference, insensibility, rationality, reason.

encourage

embolden
foster
hearten
inspire
promote
support

These words all refer to the giving of help, hope, or succor. **Encourage** is the most general term, and means to give hope, confidence, or
spirit, or to give active help: to *encourage* a young writer with praise;
to *encourage* new industry by granting it tax abatements; a teacher who
encourages his students to form their own opinions.

To **embolden** is to give someone confidence to undertake something.
Success with a short story may *embolden* (or *encourage*) someone to try
his hand at a novel. To **hearten** is to renew someone's spirit, especially
to the point of giving him fresh courage to pursue his course of action:
a victory that *heartened* the weary army; a visiting dignitary *heartened*
by the unexpectedly warm reception he was accorded. To **inspire**,
literally to breathe in, is to infuse with confidence or resolution, or to
fire with enthusiasm, as though a new and vibrant spirit were breathed
into one's being: The example set by their valiant commander *inspired*
the troops to take the hill despite heavy enemy fire.

To **foster** is, literally, to nurture, and by extension has come to mean
to *encourage* by extending aid: to *foster* (or *encourage*) growth in the
economy by lowering taxes. But even in extended senses, *foster* often
retains the idea of gradual cultivation: Too rigid parental control *fosters*
rebellion in children. In this sense *foster* is often used in contexts suggesting an unwise or at least controversial kind of help, and is sometimes
akin to cherish, at other times to instigate: to *foster* the illusion that
peace can be preserved by preparing for war; overzealous arguments
that only *fostered* dissent and division.

Support, more than any of these words, implies that without the
assistance offered the thing helped might founder and fail. It depends
on the help given to survive or grow: to *support* a dying industry by
granting it government subsidies. In another sense *support* means to
back up or endorse: a lawyer's opinion that *supported* a litigant's claim.
Or *support* may mean simply to do what one can to help: to *support* the
war effort by buying bonds.

To **promote** is to *encourage* the growth or success of something: tariff
revision that served to *promote* world trade; a good example serving to
promote good manners in the young. *Promote* implies an aggressive and
deliberate kind of assistance, often with a specific aim in mind: to *promote* one's own welfare at the expense of others. See ENDORSE, HELP, IM-
PLANT, INCITE, STIMULATE.
  Antonyms: abash, DISCOURAGE, *dishearten,* HINDER, THWART.

encroach

infringe

These words refer to an unwelcome advance, usually upon someone
else's territory or privacy. **Encroach** emphasizes the slowness or subtlety of an advance that may at first have proceeded without a countering complaint only to be recognized finally as a threat: powers of the
executive branch that have gradually *encroached* on the rights of the

encroach
(continued)

intrude
invade
trespass
violate

other branches; a mother-in-law whose attentions are not meant to *encroach* on the privacy of the newly married couple; urban sprawl that *encroaches* on unspoiled countryside.

Intrude is more often limited to overstepping of personal privacy than to territorial expansion. It suggests a situation in which a person or group has deliberately withdrawn in order to escape interruption — but without success: parents who *intrude* on the secrecies of childhood. Unlike *encroach*, however, *intrude* may more often be unintentional or sudden: embarrassed at finding that he had *intruded* on the young lovers. It can sometimes be used more generally, but the note of a personal situation is still retained: newspapers that attempt to *intrude* on the decision-making process.

Invade and **violate** are much harsher terms; they would never suggest unintentional acts, like *intrude*, nor gradual acts, like *encroach*. They may, in fact, suggest savagery and violence. *Invade* most readily brings to mind a military attack by one nation on another: the day Hitler *invaded* Poland. In other uses this context of military conquest is usually present as a negative connotation: forests *invaded* by timber speculators. *Violate* has both a sexual and a legal context: a woman *violated* by her attacker; a court ruling that basic constitutional rights had been *violated*. In more general uses, it can express outrage at unethical tactics: discrimination that *violates* the very ideals most citizens hold sacred.

Infringe and **trespass** are mainly restricted to a legal context and are consequently less intensely negative in tone than *invade* or *violate*. *Infringe* most appropriately refers to the *violation* of a principle or a legal right, while *trespass* most appropriately refers to the illegal use of or *encroachment* on someone else's property: laws that *infringe* on free speech; *infringing* on a copyright; hunters who *trespass* on a farmer's land. *Infringe*, thus, compares with *intrude*, but does not have the personal tone of the latter. *Trespass*, similarly, compares with *invade*, but need not imply a concerted attack. Both *infringe* and *trespass*, of course, have wider applications, although they carry with them connotations from these most specific uses. See INSERT, MEDDLESOME.

Antonyms: desist, observe, respect, withdraw.

endorse

accredit
approve
confirm
O.K.
ratify
sanction

These words are alike in suggesting favorable judgment or support given someone or something. **Endorse** means literally to write on the back of: to *endorse* a check. In its figurative sense, *endorse* means to give approval and support to. [Local officials have *endorsed* changes intended to modernize the building code; a TV commercial in which a well-known actor *endorses* a brand of cigarettes; to *endorse* a political candidate]

To **accredit** is to furnish someone with credentials or to invest with authority. *Accredit* suggests either formal acceptance of or the meeting of official standards: to *accredit* an ambassador; a school *accredited* by a professional association.

Approve is the most general term in this group of words, and may indicate anything from mild acquiescence to enthusiastic support; moreover, it may refer to official endorsement or to a wholly personal reaction: to *approve* a subordinate's expense account; to *approve* one's daughter's marriage. [The Congress *approved* unanimously the new stamp in honor of President Kennedy; He had no choice but to *approve* the application for membership.]

Confirm, **sanction**, and **ratify** share with *endorse* the meaning of making legal or effective by *approving*. To *sanction*, the strongest of these terms, is to *approve* authoritatively or to make valid. Like *endorse*, it couples support with approval: a church that refused to *sanction* racial discrimination; Public opinion *sanctioned* a more liberal view on divorce. *Ratify* always suggests formal approval in an official and authoritative setting. [The Senate *ratified* the nuclear test-ban treaty; The Constitution was *ratified* by the original states.] *Confirm* is not as strong as either *ratify* or *sanction*, though it is sometimes used interchangeably with *ratify*. To *confirm* is to make valid or binding by approval or acceptance: The Senate was asked to *confirm* a Presidential selection for Secretary of State; a government arbitrator who *confirmed* an agreement reached between labor and management.

O.K. is an informal term that often implies a written expression of approval, as a signature or initials: The editor *O.K.'d* the manuscript for publication; a bank official who *O.K.'d* a shipment of gold bars. See ACKNOWLEDGE, CONSENT, ENCOURAGE.

Antonyms: censure, condemn, disapprove, discredit, REJECT, *reprehend,* VOID.

enlarge

**amplify
augment
expand
increase
magnify**

These words are comparable when they mean to make something larger or greater. **Enlarge** points to size or dimension: to *enlarge* a photograph; to *enlarge* a house by adding a new wing; to *enlarge* a staff by hiring three new people. **Increase** may point to quantity or intensity as well as size: to *increase* one's stock of food during wartime. [Melting snow *increases* the flow of water in many streams during spring thaws; The safety of automobiles was *increased* by the addition of seat belts and collapsible steering columns.] In other senses, *increase* may mean to grow in number: May your tribe *increase*. Or to step up or accelerate: to *increase* the rate of productivity.

Expand may mean to *increase* in range, scope, or volume as well as in size: to *expand* the economy by introducing government spending on a broad scale. *Expand* conveys the idea of a general *enlarging* in all dimensions rather than one, and suggests an unfolding or opening out: to *expand* one's operation to include all aspects of the clothing business. *Expand* also can refer to the filling in or development of details: to *expand* a speech; to *expand* an equation. **Amplify** can also refer to the filling in of details, but stresses the addition of material for the sake of completeness, as by illustration. [The President was asked to *amplify* his statement that our goal was nothing less than total victory; to *amplify* a comment by providing reporters with background information] As the contexts of these illustrations indicate, *amplify* is most often used of formal situations. In its more basic sense, *amplify* is nowadays used almost exclusively to refer to the increase in the strength of sound or of the electromagnetic waves that produce it: to *amplify* sound with the use of microphones.

Augment means to add to, and is in some contexts interchangeable with *increase* or *enlarge*: to *augment* (or *increase* or *enlarge*) a sales force. *Augment*, however, emphasizes the action of addition more than the increase in size, and often suggests that the addition is a temporary expedient rather than a permanent or structural increase: to *augment* a besieged infantry regiment with fresh troops. *Augment* may refer to intensity as well as amount: to *augment* an electrical signal by *increasing* the power, thus *amplifying* the sound.

Magnify means to make something larger or greater either in fact or in appearance: A microscope *magnifies* objects by making them appear larger even though it does not *increase* their actual sizes. Sometimes *magnify* implies exaggeration — that is, making something appear to be larger or more important than it really is: to *magnify* a relatively trivial loss. See ESCALATE, EXTEND, SWELL.

Antonyms: condense, contract, decrease, narrow, REDUCE, SHORTEN.

These words are alike in denoting feelings of ill will or active dislike. **Enmity** is the quality or feeling that characterizes an enemy; it may be personal or impersonal, overt or hidden, but it is usually the result of a long-standing argument or of a prolonged series of conflicts, and hence is profoundly felt and not easily eradicated: The *enmity* between Arabs and Israelis threatened to break into open war at any time. **Hostility** embraces the actions by which *enmity* is displayed; it is often used in the plural: The *hostilities* were marked by brief periods of savage fighting. *Hostility* also refers to the state of being hostile, i.e. of feeling unfriendly or ill-disposed toward, often to the point of menace: The *hostility* between the pro-war demonstrators and anti-war picketers was marked by several scuffles; the *hostility* with which the middle-class mothers in the park regarded the group of guitar-playing hippies.

Hatred is an intense dislike coupled with a strong desire to harm the object of one's feeling. *Hatred* is deep-seated and malicious, and may be the end result of *enmity* or of prolonged *hostility*: the *hatred* felt for the Nazis by concentration camp survivors; Discrimination and persecution have created an atmosphere of *hatred* between Negro and white in some parts of the country. *Hatred*, however, can also be applied to things and conditions, and may depend on instinct or temperamental aversion: a cat's *hatred* of water.

Antagonism emphasizes mutuality of ill will between persons or groups, and often implies temperamental incompatibility. Unlike *hostility*, *antagonism* seldom implies that harmful actions will result: Actors sometimes resent too specific guidance from their directors, and a feeling of *antagonism* may spring up between them. **Animus** implies a feeling of ill will or antipathy so deep-rooted and intertwined with character and background that a coherent explanation of its cause is seldom possible: to harbor an *animus* against boys who wear their hair long; an *animus* against intellectuals in government.

Animosity and **rancor** are stronger than *enmity*, but often less enduring; *animosity* suggests vindictive anger, and *rancor*, bitter resentment. [He nourished a feeling of *animosity* for his penny-pinching boss; a sergeant who felt *rancor* at being passed over for promotion by his commanding officer] *Rancor* is intensely bitter *enmity* or *hatred*, often coupled with malice or even malevolence: *Rancor* over his party's humiliating defeat at the polls led him to organize a military coup with the aim of completely destroying the party in power. See DESPISE, DISLIKE.

Antonyms: amity, camaraderie, fellowship, friendship, harmony, LOVE, *sympathy.*

These verbs all mean to arouse extreme displeasure, and usually antagonism, in a person or animal. **Enrage** means to throw into a rage — in other words, to put someone in such a state of frustration, anger, or annoyance that he is beside himself and may react compulsively or violently. *Enrage* always implies strong provocation: to *enrage* a wounded bull by taunting him with a cape; He was *enraged* by the policeman's rough treatment of his wife.

Anger, a more general term, may apply to mild as well as severe displeasure: What *angered* him most was the lack of writing paper in his

enmity

animosity
animus
antagonism
hatred
hostility
rancor

enrage

anger
incense
infuriate

hotel room. *Anger* is often used as a participle to describe one's disposition: a diplomat not easily *angered* or flustered; He was always capable of being *angered* by trifles.

Incense means literally to set on fire, and thus emphasizes the volatility and heat of anger. It need not, however, imply a long-standing or profound feeling, only one of great intensity: The mayor, *incensed* over the filthy condition of the hallways of the slum building he was inspecting, ordered an immediate investigation. *Incense* often implies sharp indignation resulting from a slight or incivility: He was *incensed* by the curt refusal of the headwaiter to seat him at the table of his choice.

Infuriate is the strongest term of this group, implying a reaction so intense that one virtually loses control of one's actions. That which *infuriates* is felt to be unbearably offensive. [While the display of luxury by the French aristocracy of the eighteenth century *incensed* the poor of Paris, Marie Antoinette's suggestion that they eat cake when they had no food positively *infuriated* them.] *Infuriate* is often used hyperbolically in less formal contexts to indicate any degree of anger: She was simply *infuriated* by her husband's nasty remark about her new dress. See ANGER, BOTHER, FRANTIC, OUTRAGE, UPSET.

Antonyms: mollify, pacify, placate, quiet, soothe, tranquilize.

entertain

amuse
divert
interest

These words have to do with activity that draws the attention and makes time pass agreeably. To **entertain**, either oneself or others, is to provide some occupation that will afford pleasure or relieve monotony or boredom. *Entertainment* may be simple and personal at one extreme, or formal and public at the other, ranging from short-term distraction and private hospitality to large parties and theatrical performances: a child *entertaining* himself with his building blocks; to *entertain* out-of-town guests; a comedian and his traveling troupe *entertaining* servicemen overseas. *Entertaining* someone implies the putting forth of active effort: Let me *entertain* you; an *entertaining* show. **Amuse,** by contrast, focuses on response: an *amusing* book; The Queen is not *amused.* To *amuse* a person is to affect him in such a way that he is put or kept in a pleasant mood. In a nonspecific sense, *amuse* can suggest any form of distraction that contents the mind: Try to keep the child *amused.* Specifically, *amusement* emphasizes light *entertainment*, pointing to something that brings a smile or laugh or that is thought of as fun. A person may be *amused* by a clever thought of his own, a bizarre sight, a game, a story, an evening's *entertainment.* But a performance of a Greek tragedy, which can *entertain* an audience by holding their attention and affording them esthetic satisfaction, would not be said to *amuse.*

Divert is close to *amuse* but stresses the fact that the *amusement* is not constant but is a temporary form of escapism. To *divert* is to draw the mind away from serious thoughts or pursuits, distracting the attention from work, worry, pain, or commonplace concerns and focusing it on pleasure: a *diverting* comedy. [An evening out may *divert* an overworked housewife; The students set aside one night a week for *diversion.*]

Interest is the most general of these words. To *interest* someone is to excite or hold his curiosity or attention, for whatever reason. [A psychopath *interests* a psychologist; The student found the lecture *interesting.*] But the specific sense in which *interest* compares with the other words in this set involves an awakening of attention by some *entertaining* expedient: The showing of slides *interested* the dozing student, and he sat up and took notice. See HOBBY.

Antonyms: annoy, bore, tire.

entire

complete
full
intact
total
whole

These words refer to things of which no part is missing, damaged, omitted, empty, or imperfect. **Entire** may apply both in concrete and in abstract senses, referring to a physical, numerical, temporal, or qualitative entity. [The *entire* continent was covered with snow; The *entire* cast was present for dress rehearsal; The *entire* day was ruined; His concern as a doctor was for the *entire* man, not just for the body.] **Whole** is more informal and more general than *entire* but is very close to it in meaning and may be substituted for it in the examples above. Both words apply to that which is unbroken or undivided, but sometimes one or the other is used exclusively in a certain context. [When the Venus de Milo was *entire* (or *whole*), there were arms on the statue; A *whole* number is distinguished from a fraction.] *Whole* differs from *entire* in suggesting a moral or physical perfection that can be lost and recovered, as by the regaining of health: Your faith has made you *whole*. Here, *entire* is closer to **intact**, which refers to something that has remained in its original condition. [The second generation kept the family fortune *entire*; The heiress kept her father's art collection *intact*.] A thing is said to be *intact* if it has successfully resisted attempts made on its integrity, or if it has been subjected to destructive influences or forces and has come through unscathed. [She escaped from his clutches with her virtue *intact*; Few buildings in the bombed city remained *intact*; Though subjected to brainwashing, the prisoner of war emerged with his integrity *intact*.]

Complete focuses on the presence of all needed or normal parts, while **total** simply implies a measurable aggregate. Both words may describe a collective entity: a *complete* set of dishes; the *complete* works of Shakespeare; his *total* earnings for 1967. *Total*, however, involves a precise determination of the size of an existent *whole*; and whether a *total* amount or number is added to or subtracted from, it still remains a sum *total* so long as it is inclusive and accurate. *Complete*, by contrast, means finished or perfected, implying the meeting of a standard or fulfillment of a goal. [The *total* number of jurors selected so far is nine, but the jury is not yet *complete*.] In an abstract sense the two words are much more closely synonymous, describing that which covers everything without exception or reservation: *total* (or *complete*) destruction; a *total* (or *complete*) commitment. Both are also sometimes interchangeable with *entire*: He has *entire* (or *total* or *complete*) control of the business.

Full stresses content. In its most concrete sense, it implies that a receptacle contains as much as it can hold: to drink a *full* (or a *whole*) cup of coffee; a glass *full* of water. Like *complete*, it may stress the presence of all belonging parts: a *full* dozen. It may also describe something that is maximum in size, extent, degree, or the like: a *full* moon as opposed to a crescent; a *full* load; *full* speed ahead. *Full* is close to *whole*, *entire*, and *complete* in implying that a thing is not deficient or that nothing is being omitted or withheld. To take a *full* course of study is to take a *complete* course or a *whole* course. But the other words are stronger and more forceful in referring to something that is absolute and unlimited. [You have my *entire* confidence; I have *complete* (or *total* or *full*) confidence in you.]

All of the words in this set, with the sole exception of *intact*, may be used as intensives: You've missed the *whole* point; It took us an *entire* week; a *full* four years; *complete* contempt; *total* abstinence. See FINISH, TOTAL.

Antonyms: broken, damaged, destroyed, divided, empty, imperfect, incomplete, limited, partial.

entrust

commit
confide
consign
delegate

These words involve the transfer of responsibility to someone else. **Entrust** stresses safety and reliance. A person may be *entrusted* with authority or with a specific task: to *entrust* an agent with power of attorney. A thing *entrusted* may be a specialized task or an object that needs to be protected: *entrusting* all jewelry and important documents to a safety-deposit box; *entrusting* the canvassing of voters to a public-relations firm. **Confide** gives intenser overtones of safety, caution, or discretion: *confiding* the enforcement of the new legislation to the federal courts. In this sense, it is more formal than *entrust* and has been overshadowed by other meanings of *confide* not directly related here.

Commit and **consign** are less personal than *entrust* and are more formal in this context. At its most general, *commit* means to place a person or thing in someone else's charge: *committing* the child to a nurse's care. Specifically, it may involve the placing of a person in protective custody: to *commit* someone to a mental hospital. The word often carries an undertone of giving something up for better or worse to forces beyond one's control: *committing* their chances for survival to the prospect of being sighted by a passing ship or plane. *Consign* suggests great impersonality and has a legalistic or commercial flavor: *consigning* the shipment to another railroad. In other cases, the word may suggest criticism for a lack of concern that allows power to fall into the wrong hands: *consigning* our most basic rights to the hazards of a kangaroo court. Both *commit* and *consign* may also sometimes focus on the fact of getting rid of a thing for good and all: to *commit* a paper to the flames; a critic airily *consigning* an author to oblivion.

Delegate is the most neutral word of this group, implying neither the security and confidence of some, nor the impersonality of others. Its tone is one of mere description without evaluation. It suggests a bureaucratic context in which a leading executive is responsible for work he must none the less allow others to execute: the fatal flaw of being unable to *delegate* authority; *delegating* all but the most serious matters to a crack team of assistants. See APPOINT, REPRESENTATIVE, TRUST.

equip

furnish
outfit
supply

These words refer to the act of providing things necessary for function or use. **Equip** may give a technical flavor, but the provisions involved may apply to a person, a device, or a place: soldiers *equipped* with rocket launchers; a car *equipped* with air conditioning; a phonograph *equipped* with stereo speakers; a laboratory *equipped* for atomic research. **Outfit** suggests the same range of possibilities, but is considerably more informal than *equip*: a battalion *outfitted* for tropical warfare; campers *outfitted* for mountain climbing; a conference room *outfitted* with tape recorders and sales charts. When applied to people, the word usually suggests wearing apparel, whereas *equip* might suggest more specialized accessories: vacationers *outfitted* for all kinds of weather and *equipped* with fishing tackle and snorkels.

Furnish applies especially to making rooms livable by the addition of furniture: *furnishing* the living room with modern chairs and sofas from Denmark. Although the word most appropriately suggests this general or basic context, it can be used for more specialized circumstances: a space capsule *furnished* with all the materials necessary for an eight-day flight. It may also, in an abstract sense, mean to provide: activities that *furnish* an outlet for student opinion.

Supply is much more general than any of these other words. It can be used to suggest the addition of any provision under any circumstances: paintings that *supplied* the stark room with notes of warmth and color;

supplying an infantry rifle company with all the clothing and equipment to make it battle-ready. The word, in reference to a person, would not suggest clothes worn at the moment, but might suggest their procurement. [She was *outfitted* to go sightseeing in the mild spring weather; She had *supplied* herself with many changes of clothing to meet any possible contingency.] See ADDITION.

Antonyms: denude, divest, strip.

These words refer to the removal of markings from a surface, possibly so that they can be replaced by other markings. **Erase** is the least formal and most general of these, referring to symbols removed by any wiping or rubbing action: asking each child to *erase* his work from the blackboard; *erasing* the penciled guidelines after the lettering had been inked in. **Eradicate** is the most formal of these words. Aside from its etymological reference to rooting out, it applies here to the *erasing* of ink markings by a specially prepared chemical: revisions made in washable ink so that the editor could *eradicate* them if he chose.

Cancel and **delete** are less clear than the foregoing about the means used to cause the removal of markings. *Cancel* once pointed specifically to the crossing out of something: *canceling* every entry that was out of date. By extension, it may mean to rescind or terminate: *Cancel* my subscription. *Cancel* also refers to overmarkings on postage stamps or to action that reduces the effectiveness of something: erratic behavior that *canceled* out the good impression he had made previously. *Delete* still chiefly refers to the editing of a text by removing unwanted expressions; this may be done by crossing out, *erasing*, *eradicating*, or covering the thing to be *deleted*: using red ink to *delete* objectionable phrases from the manuscript.

Efface is also vague about the means of removal, but it may often suggest that markings have become partially or wholly indistinct, not by design but by time and attrition: weathering that had *effaced* the inscription on the tombstone; ideas whose vividness has been *effaced* by use. **Expunge** and **obliterate** refer to forceful and total removal, whether by design or not. *Expunge* compares to the less formal *delete*, but may suggest the total removal of a larger body of material by whatever means: *expunging* from the diaries all reference to people still living, and *deleting* a few remarks about figures out of the recent past. In any case, *expunge* suggests an uncompromising removal and the total disappearance of such material. *Obliterate* suggests even more force than *expunge*, even to the possible extent of damaging the surface or material on which the markings appear. Otherwise, the word compares to *efface* in sometimes suggesting indistinctness that results, not by design, but from the action of natural forces: fire damage that had *obliterated* many passages in the manuscript; erosion that had nearly *obliterated* all trace of the earliest Minoan settlements. See DESTROY, VOID.

Antonyms: impress, imprint, INSERT.

These words refer to a state of being filled with sexual feelings or to things designed to call up such feelings. **Erotic**, stemming from a root meaning love, stresses none the less a specifically sexual love. The word can refer either to such feelings or to things eliciting these feelings: aware of his own *erotic* impulses; an *erotic* movie. **Sensual** can also refer to either situation, but it refers to sexual desire only by implication. Theoretically, it should indicate someone given to a life of the senses or something appealing to the senses, but the word has been used suggestively,

erase

cancel
delete
efface
eradicate
expunge
obliterate

erotic

amorous
arousing
concupiscent

erotic
(continued)

desirous
passionate
sensual
sexy

perhaps euphemistically, so often that sexual desire is inevitably a part of its reference, although not so strongly insisted upon as in the case of *erotic*: a *sensual* appetite for exotic women; *sensual* music to which veiled women danced.

Concupiscent is a learned synonym for lustful, coming from Latin roots meaning to desire intensely. It focuses on fleshly desire that seeks its own gratification, as contrasted with unselfish love, and it carries the implication of original sin: a *concupiscent* husband, unfaithful to his wife; the *concupiscent* elements in human character.

Desirous, amorous, and **passionate** refer exclusively to someone filled with *erotic* feeling. *Desirous* may suggest a vague longing or lack, without an object in view, or it may suggest a specific sexual wish for a particular object: *desirous* of a kind of woman he had never met; He became more and more *desirous* and she seemed more and more desirable the more she rebuffed his advances. In the latter case, *desirous* suggests a distinction between sexual eagerness and love. *Amorous* is consequently warmer in feeling, since it can suggest an affectionate desire for love-making or sex play: a wife smiling back at her *amorous* husband. *Passionate* is more intense than either *desirous* or *amorous*, but it may or may not be divorced in its intensity from notions of affectionate love: a nymphomaniac making *passionate* advances to a strange man; proposals of marriage that grew more and more *passionate*.

Sexy is the most informal of all these words. It may be applied to any person or thing that seems to project, radiate, or intensify sex appeal: a very *sexy* girl; a *sexy* walk; a *sexy*, form-fitting sweater. Used of books, plays, movies, and the like, the word points to a titillating preoccupation with sex: a *sexy* novel. **Arousing** refers solely to those things that call up sexual desire: a coy manner deliberately designed to be *arousing*. See EAGER, EMOTION, HOT, LEWD, PASSIONATE, STIMULATE.
Antonyms: COLD, *sexless.*

escalate

increase
intensify
step up

These words refer to the heightening of something in scale, as pressure, tension, pay, or military activity. **Escalate** is a new word for such build-ups; it can imply either a gradual process or a series of sudden or surprise spurts. It is most often used for rising prices and pay rates or for military activity: factors causing the cost of living to *escalate* during the third quarter; a built-in clause that would *escalate* their weekly pay to keep pace with rising prices; They *escalated* the war by mining the enemy's harbors. As in the second example, the word can suggest two scales rising reciprocally, or one of these rising in response or anticipation of the other: any aggressive act that would *escalate* the war to a new level of intensity on both sides. The word's faddish appeal can be seen in the way it replaces simpler words in a wide range of contexts: We *escalated* our efforts to get the cabin built before summer.

Step up, by contrast, might more logically suggest a series of spurts with level intervals between them: businesses that must *step up* production during periods of seasonal demand. This notion is by no means held to, however, and the word can be used for any single or even gradual act of heightening: immigration quotas that were *stepped up* by the new law; directors who inevitably *step up* their pressure on the actors as opening night approaches.

Increase is a much more general word than the foregoing and can often replace either to advantage, with a possible gain in simplicity and clarity. While the word can apply to any build-up, its particular point is sometimes to indicate a gain in amount. [The number of people browsing in the bookstore *increases* sharply during lunch hour.] **Intensify** is of comparable generality, but it is often directed toward a heightening of pressure, tension, or insistence: floods that *intensified* the force with which the river battered against the weakening levees; the introduction of a plot device to *intensify* the movie's suspense; arrogant behavior that only caused the union leaders to *intensify* their demands. See ENLARGE, EXTEND, SWELL.

Antonyms: DECREASE, LESSEN, REDUCE, WEAKEN.

These words refer to a withdrawal from danger or from an unpleasant situation. **Escape** is the most general of these, applying to any sort of withdrawal. The word does, however, carry connotations of urgency, though not necessarily of haste. [He lay perfectly still and played dead to *escape* capture by the enemy; She rushed down the stairs to *escape* her enraged pursuer.] **Run away** is the most informal of these expressions; unlike *escape*, it specifically indicates swift movement and is most often restricted to actual physical action; on the other hand, it need not imply urgency: children who *run away* from home for no observable reason; those burglars who will *run away* if caught in the act. Sometimes the phrase is used without the physical implication: candidates who try to *run away* from controversial issues.

Retreat may suggest both urgency and haste, but unlike the previous words, it need not necessarily suggest either. It is common to a military context, but is used widely outside this specific area: orders to *retreat* only in a desperate situation and then in an orderly, well-planned way. [They *retreated* in frantic, disorganized haste; the decision to *retreat* before any threat of confrontation arose; He *retreated* slowly and quietly to his room before he could be seen.] **Abscond** also pertains to a specific context but unlike *retreat* is almost exclusively restricted to it. It refers to embezzlement or theft in which property is illegally seized and carried off: the club's last treasurer, who had *absconded* with the funds. It is sometimes used jocosely for less serious situations: warning her not to *abscond* with the book if he lent it to her.

Flee and **fly** both refer to a hasty escape and usually imply urgency as well: those who *fled* the burning hotel; those Trojans who are always depicted as *flying* from the courageous Greeks. The only effective difference between these words, now, is that *fly* is much more formal than *flee* and, in fact, would sound archaic to most ears. Furthermore, the word's other and more common meaning, pertaining to travel through the air, can make its use in this sense seem confusing or, sometimes, comical: a child who *flew* from his kidnappers; refugees who have *flown* from persecution in other lands. *Fled* would seem preferable in both these circumstances. See AVOID, LEAVE (depart), RUN.

Antonyms: confront, face, give up, REMAIN, SUBMIT, surrender.

These words all refer to what has no beginning or no end, or to what exists outside or beyond time. **Everlasting** stresses something that endures through time, particularly something that will never cease to exist, once created. **Eternal** contrasts with this by admitting the implication that the thing described has always existed in the past, as well, and thus has neither beginning nor end. [In Christian theology, the soul of each newborn infant is a fresh creation that is immortal and consequently *everlasting*; In Hinduism, the soul has no beginning and need never end and is consequently *eternal*.] *Everlasting* can also function as a negative hyperbole for a continual or constant annoyance or even

escape

abscond
flee
fly
retreat
run away

everlasting

endless
eternal

everlasting

(continued)

interminable
never-ending
timeless
unending

for something that seems to take forever and has worn out one's patience or tolerance: his *everlasting* boasting; this *everlasting* war. When negative, *eternal* is used more loosely, less specifically, and with less force: her *eternal* carping.

Timeless may refer more informally than *eternal* to something without beginning or end: the *timeless* laws of the universe. Even when used less literally, the word is mainly positive in its effect, referring in this case to something that does not go out of date but seems to be always fresh or relevant: the *timeless* poetry of Shakespeare. *Timeless* can also refer to something outside time or to a situation in which time seems to have stopped: It is possible to conceive of a *timeless* universe, but not one without space; the *timeless* moment of satori, or enlightenment. **Unending** refers more informally and exclusively than *everlasting* to something that has no end: the *unending* torment of souls condemned to hell; the philosophical view of the universe as being in an *unending* state of flux. Used less exactly, the word can be either an approving or disapproving hyperbole. In approval, it often suggests what is boundless as well as lasting: She gave her son *unending* love. In disapproval, a failure to get to the point may be implied: *unending* negotiations while the fighting continued.

Never-ending can point, perhaps more emphatically than *unending*, to what endures forever: the *never-ending* omniscience of God. As a loose hyperbole, the word can be positive, with a tone approaching that of *timeless* in this use, but with an additional suggestion of recurrent or continually renewed freshness: fairy tales that have been a *never-ending* delight for many generations of children. Used negatively, the word may have greater force, suggesting a tiresome refusal to come to a halt: a *never-ending* bore.

Endless is the most informal of these words, has the widest range of uses, and is most open to the demands of context. It can refer to something without an end in time: the *endless* convolutions of matter and energy. But since it can also suggest something that continues without end through space, it can be ambiguous: a theory holding that the universe was *endless*. As a hyperbole, it can be approving, with implications like those for *unending*: *endless* admiration; a lovely afternoon that seemed *endless*. More often, it is loosely used as a harsh negative: *endless* delays during registration week. **Interminable** is the one word here that is almost exclusively limited in use as a negative hyperbole for something that is long-lasting. It is more formal than *endless* but is less ambiguous than the latter in referring solely to time. It is also the most harshly disapproving of these words: *interminable* filibusters that disrupt the orderly functioning of the legislature. See IMMORTAL, INFINITE, MONOTONOUS, PERMANENT, PERSISTENT.

Antonyms: finite, TEMPORARY.

examine

audit
inspect
investigate
scan
scrutinize

All these words mean to look something over or inquire into it, usually for a definite purpose. **Examine** is the general word; it can refer to a cursory look or a thorough study of all details. **Investigate**, **scrutinize**, and **inspect** mean to *examine* thoroughly, but their connotations vary. To *investigate* is to make a methodical, searching inquiry into a complex situation in an effort to uncover the facts. *Scrutinize* suggests *examining* critically and with painstaking attention to detail: a printer *scrutinizing* a photographic transparency for specks of dust or imperfections in the type. *Inspect* usually implies that the object of one's attention is being critically compared to a standard of excellence, quality, or the like, with a view toward noting discrepancies or deficiencies in the former: firemen *inspecting* an abandoned warehouse for potential fire hazards; a sergeant *inspecting* the rifles of his men. One may *examine, scrutinize,* or *inspect* a person, an inanimate object, or a situation; *investigate* is usually applied to situations or events, except in the case of formal inquiries into the lives or actions of a person, as because he is suspected of a crime or because he has applied for a job of a particularly sensitive nature: to *investigate* the background of a potential member of the secret service. [The detective *investigating* the murder case *examined* the body, *inspected* the scene of the crime, and *scrutinized* the weapon for clues.]

To **audit** is to *examine* accounts or records. Thus, to justify an increase in advertising rates, a magazine publisher may have an outside firm *audit* the circulation figures.

Scan is a word that is undergoing a complete reversal of meaning. Its former meaning — to *examine* closely and analytically — is still valid but is now applied chiefly to analysis of poetic meter: to *scan* Virgil. More frequently now, *scan* means to glance quickly at something to get the gist of it: to *scan* a newspaper by glancing at the headlines. See HUNT, STUDY.

These words refer to something rated as being among the best of its kind. **Excellent** points literally to something that excels other things. As such, it is often used to designate the highest class in a grading, rating, or ranking system: an eating guide that rated many restaurants as good or very good, but only a few as *excellent*. Often, however, as with most superlatives, *excellent* is not thought to be high enough in its praise and it takes second place to some other word: a debating team disappointed at getting an *Excellent* instead of a Superior rating.

Neither **first-class** nor **first-rate** admit of this sort of devaluation; one thing cannot be more *first-rate* than another. Both indicate the topmost category in a ranking system. *First-class* can suggest a military or paramilitary system: a *first-class* scout; a *first-class* marksman. Even outside this context the word would suggest a set of clear categories into which things can be placed by objective evaluation: designating as *first-class* those cities with populations over 500,000; *first-class* mail; a *first-class* permit. As can be seen, any notion of excellence may well be absent from this word's meaning. Used more loosely and subjectively, the word can describe anything one likes or approves of: a *first-class* fellow; a *first-class* movie. *First-rate* may sometimes suggest careful evaluation based more on imponderables than on objective categorization: feeling in *first-rate* health; a *first-rate* analysis of current political tendencies. But while inherent worth is usually indicated by the word, it can sometimes point to something consequential rather than *excellent*: a *first-rate* world power. This word is even more open than *first-class* to uses indicating mere subjective approval: a *first-rate* girl friend; a *first-rate* party. Both words can also indicate something that is thought to be supremely bad; *first-class* may lend itself more readily to this use, but in any case, it can give a more informal tone and may have comic force: a *first-class* heel; a *first-class* bore; a *first-rate* disaster.

Most specifically, **prime** indicates, under the grading system of the U.S. Department of Agriculture, the highest grade of beef or lamb; **choice** indicates a grade between *prime* and good. In other contexts, *prime* can refer to something of first significance, urgency, or value: television programs that appear in *prime* time; the *prime* need being to get the combatants to the conference table. *Prime* can also refer to any-

excellent

choice
first-class
first-rate
prime
select

thing that is excellent, best, most typical, or at its peak: *prime* theatrical fare; a *prime* example; inductees in *prime* condition. More neutrally, it can suggest the main part of something or what comes first: our *prime* reason for deciding to approve the bill; her *prime* concern being for the safety of her children. *Choice,* by contrast, refers to what has been winnowed out because it fulfills high and discriminating standards. Oddly enough, *choice* often seems the stronger of the two words in other contexts than the grading of meat. By implication, what is *prime* may be overlooked or easily available, whereas *choice* suggests the successful discrimination of what is both rare and *excellent*: their *choicest* wine from a vast stock that contained nothing of less than *prime* quality.

Select can refer to lumber that is by and large free of blemish or knots. More generally, *select* compares with *choice* by stressing discrimination, but differs in often referring to a mere sampling of *excellent* things that cannot be presented in full: *select* highlights from ten Broadway musicals; only *select* programs listed in the television run-down. A weakening of the word's force may result by analogy with selected, which may indicate arbitrary compression or subjective sampling. See ELEGANT, EXQUISITE.

Antonyms: bad, faulty, imperfect, MEDIOCRE, *poor, second-class.*

excuse

alibi
apologia
apology

These words are comparable when they refer to causes, circumstances, or motivations which are put forth in order to defend, explain, or extenuate an action, viewpoint, or the like. An **excuse** is an implicit admission of wrong, but it is offered as a full or partial justification of one's actions. By contrast, an **apology**, in current usage, is an open admission that one has done wrong and is sorry for it. Whereas an *excuse* is a means of avoiding or mitigating the responsibility for one's actions, an *apology* is the contrite recognition of that responsibility. [His *excuse* for being late was that his train was delayed; He could only offer a frank *apology* for having forgotten about our dinner engagement.]

Apology and **apologia** both originally implied the intent of clearly setting forth the grounds for some action, conviction, or the like, which others consider wrong or improper. *Apology* is now seldom used in this sense, *apologia* being preferred. [The purged Communist stoutly defended his revolutionary zeal and wrote a lengthy *apologia* in explanation of his allegedly counter-revolutionary ideas.]

Alibi, in common usage, implies that an *excuse* is plausible rather than true. In legal use, however, the word means a plea by an accused person that he was elsewhere when the crime was committed. Even in other contexts, *alibi* does not invariably suggest dubiety. [His *alibi* depended upon the eyewitness testimony of a taxicab driver; a desperate, last-minute *alibi* intended to save him from the wrath of his father.] See EXPLANATION, REASONING.

exile

banish
deport
expatriate
relegate

These words refer to the sending away or placing apart of a person, group of people, or thing. In some periods of history, a government could punish a citizen by **exiling** him, that is, by forcing him to leave the homeland. Although few if any modern nations have such a punishment now, the word has remained in the language as a metaphorical reference to any imposed or voluntary separation from one's home: Jazz Age writers who *exiled* themselves to Paris to learn the craft of writing; parents who *exile* their children to kindergartens simply to be rid of them. **Banish** has a history similar to *exile*, but its present-day uses permit a wider range of application, suggesting any forcible removal:

The judge ordered the hecklers *banished* from the courtroom; television commercials that promise that their product can *banish* washday drudgery, *banish* bad complexions, or *banish* acid indigestion in a twinkling. **Rusticate** means to send or *banish* to the country, and especially, in Great Britain, to punish a university student by suspending him and sending him away temporarily.

Relegate, in reference to people, suggests disposing of them without much concern for their welfare: *relegating* minority groups to second-class citizenship; *relegating* freshman senators to a role of watchful silence. In reference to other matters, *relegate* suggests their assignment to an unimportant place: *relegating* his fears to a corner of her mind reserved for the trivial and forgettable.

Deport and **expatriate** both have present-day technical uses like those that *exile* and *banish* once had. *Deport* refers to the official sending away of someone who is not a citizen: *deporting* the gangster who had entered the country illegally. *Expatriate* refers to the stripping of citizenship from someone, either by his own choice or by the nation's choice: a malcontent who *expatriated* himself to a country more to his liking; a law to *expatriate* those who serve in a foreign army.

Sequester means to place apart or separate. It differs from the other words here considered in emphasizing separation rather than the action of sending away: to *sequester* a construction area in which blasting is necessary. In a related sense, *sequester* applies to people and is often used reflexively with the meaning of making private or secret or of being secluded. [She lived a *sequestered* life in a mountain village; He *sequestered* himself for the summer in an oceanfront cottage to write his first novel.] The emphasis is still on placing apart, but additional stress is given to the motive — that of secrecy or seclusion. See IMPEL, PRIVACY, REMOVE.

Antonyms: GREET.

These words are alike in referring to conditions or things having actual presence or reality. **Exist** and **be** (here considered only as a substantive verb) are interchangeable when a flat assertion of reality is intended: God *exists*; God *is*. Of the two, *be* is the more forceful, carrying the weight of intense personal conviction; *exist* has a more detached connotation, more often suggesting that a record is simply being made of observable or otherwise known phenomena. In other senses *exist* and *be* are not commonly interchangeable. *Exist* can mean to continue to *be*: Animals cannot *exist* without oxygen. *Be* can be used to designate that something *exists* in a particular place or time: There *are* bears in the zoo.

Live means to have life, to function as an animate organism: The dazed survivor of the collision asked whether his brother was *living* or dead. *Live* is commonly used to mean to continue in existence, to remain alive, and in this sense is sometimes interchangeable with *exist*: Animals cannot *live* (or *exist*) without oxygen. But when it refers to a particular place or time, it parallels *be*. [Kangaroos *live* in Australia; There *are* kangaroos in Australia.]

Subsist, which has the etymological meaning of to stand under, means to maintain one's existence or manage to *live*, and often suggests a relation between existence or life and the conditions which support it: For three months the stranded sailors *subsisted* solely on indigenous plants and an occasional fish washed ashore. Although either *exist* or *live* could be used in the foregoing example, *subsist* emphasizes the dependence of life on the conditions described more strongly than either of

exile

(continued)

rusticate
sequester

exist

be
live
subsist

the other words. *Subsist* is less commonly and more formally used to-day to refer to anything that has existence or reality, or that continues to *exist*: beauty that *subsisted* in the brilliantly conceived concordance between color and form within the painting. Even here a contingent relation is suggested. See CREATE, FLOURISH.

Antonyms: DIE.

exonerate

absolve
acquit
exculpate
vindicate

These words all mean to clear of guilt or wrongdoing. **Exonerate** means to free from accusation or blame, and stresses freedom from future suspicion: The hearings before the subcommittee *exonerated* him from suspicion of complicity in the swindle. To **absolve** is to set free from obligation or penalty attaching to an act: The aircraft company was *absolved* from liability following the investigation of the disaster. To **acquit** is to set free from accusation, usually for lack of evidence, and often of a specific charge: to be *acquitted* of perjury in the first degree. [The motorist was *acquitted* of reckless driving; he was thereupon *absolved* from any claim for damages arising out of the collision.]

Vindicate means to clear completely through the examination of evidence. [The accused bookkeeper *vindicated* himself by producing bank statements; The testimony of witnesses *vindicated* the prisoner.] It may also refer to judgment which has been borne out by subsequent events: The justice's minority dissent was finally *vindicated* in later years when the majority endorsed his arguments and reversed its former decision. **Exculpate** means to free from blame or prove innocent of guilt or fault. Unlike *exonerate*, it does not necessarily imply that a formal charge was made nor that the blameworthy act was illegal or illicit. It may apply to any culpable action: Investigation *exculpated* the driver from the suspicion of having caused the accident. See INNOCENT, PARDON.

Antonyms: ACCUSE, *inculpate*.

expectation

anticipation
expectancy
hope
outlook
prospect

These words all point to the future, and the likelihood of certain events or conditions taking place. **Expectation** and **expectancy** are close synonyms meaning the waiting for something to happen, or the probability with which the awaited can be presumed to happen. [There had been no *expectation* of war among the general public when the Japanese attacked Pearl Harbor; Those who drop out of school must lower their *expectations* of success.] *Expectancy* is used to describe a state of tense *expectation*: There was an air of *expectancy* as the President was ushered to the podium to make a statement. It is also commonly encountered in the phrase *life expectancy*.

Anticipation, in this context, is a strong *expectation* based on fore-knowledge. [The *anticipation* of cold weather leads the householder to lay in fuel in the fall; building up the armed forces in *anticipation* of war]

Hope, as here considered, is *expectation* based on desire, with or without any likelihood that the hoped for will happen or materialize. [Parents have high *hopes* for their children; A man saves money in the *hope* that inflation will not wipe it out.]

Outlook and **prospect** refer to future probabilities based on present indications or analyses. [The employment *outlook* for the next year is based in part on contracts signed this year; The *outlook* for this weekend is good, with warm, sunny weather expected to hold up through Monday.] Whereas *outlook* may describe grim *expectations*, *prospect* is more often applied to *expectations* of success, profit, or comfort: The *outlook* was bleak; the *prospect* of taking off his shoes and settling down into an easy chair with a good book; good *prospects* for complete recovery from the illness. The association with pleasant *expectations* is, however, not invariable: The *prospect* of a bloody war was alarmingly increased. See FOREKNOWLEDGE, PREMONITION.

These words describe things that cost a lot, especially with reference to money. **Expensive** refers to things that cost a lot of money but that give pleasure and satisfaction because of their good looks or high quality: to live in an *expensive* apartment; to frequent *expensive* restaurants. *Expensive* also hints at a tendency to extravagance: to have *expensive* tastes in clothes or wines. Something that is *expensive* may cost more than the purchaser thinks it is worth to him, but it also may be more than he is able to pay — or thinks it practical to pay. [That is a beautiful coat, but it is too *expensive* for me; We really don't need such a big, *expensive* car.]

High-priced is the most general term and the least specific. That which is *high-priced* simply costs a lot of money, either in an absolute sense or in a relative one. The word carries little suggestion of real value, quality, or desirability.

Something that is **costly** is very *expensive*, but for the reason that it is rare, elegant, or of superior workmanship: a *costly* diamond necklace; *costly* Persian rugs. In another sense, *expensive* and *costly* may both have reference to something that demands unusual effort or time, or that taxes one's resources beyond a reasonable limit. [A long illness is an *expensive* misfortune for the average family; This is a *costly* war in terms of the number of men killed and wounded.]

Dear, now rather an old-fashioned or regional word except in Great Britain, is the direct opposite of cheap. Most people aspire to own *expensive* or *costly* things, but not those that are *dear* or *high-priced*. *Dear* is applied chiefly to ordinary commodities which have risen in price because they are temporarily in short supply. [In the middle of the summer, fresh oranges are *dear*, but in the winter months they are cheap; During World War II nylon stockings were very *dear* and hard to come by.]

Anything is **overpriced** when it is offered for sale at a price much higher than its actual value warrants: shops selling *overpriced* antiques on a fashionable street. Buyers will not be attracted to goods that are *overpriced* when they discover that they can obtain similar things elsewhere for less money or do without. Products that are *overpriced* are sometimes said to "price themselves off the market."

Antonyms: economical, INEXPENSIVE.

explanation

annotation
commentary
definition
description
exposition
interpretation

The words in this list all mean an undertaking to make the meaning of something clear to oneself or to someone else. **Explanation** is the broadest of these words, and is applied to ideas, utterances, actions, or operations. It is often used in place of many of the other words in the list.

A **definition** is, etymologically, a setting of limits or boundaries. In this context it is used to give the exact meaning of a word or phrase, or to delimit a problem or an undertaking. In a debate, one is often required to give a *definition* (or *explanation*) of technical terms to be used.

A **description** is a detailed account of the important aspects of something. A *description* may have as its object merely the pleasure of the listener or reader: a *description* of a sunset. As here considered, however, a *description* has a didactic purpose. Thus, to give a *description* of the parts of an intricate machine is to give an *explanation* of how it works.

An **exposition** is a long, detailed, often scholarly setting forth of all the salient points of an argument, proposal, theory, or the like: a theoretical physicist who published an *exposition* of his ideas in a scientific monograph. **Annotation** and **commentary** are *expositions* in the fields of law and theology, respectively, although both are also used in more general contexts as well. *Annotation* can apply to a single critical or explanatory note, whereas *commentary* applies to a series or body of notes or remarks.

Interpretation, in this context, is the application of imagination or insight to the *explanation* of a difficult passage in literature, a baffling problem, an action difficult to account for, a dream, or the like: a grave *interpretation* of the curt diplomatic message; a disputed *interpretation* of an obscure passage from Eliot's *The Wasteland*. See NARRATIVE, REPORT.

explode

burst
bust
erupt

These words all mean to break out, open, or apart in a sudden and violent way, as if from some internal force. **Explode** has specific reference to the physical phenomenon which occurs when any substance or mixture of substances react on impact or by ignition with a sudden expansion of gases and the liberation of relatively large amounts of thermal energy. *Explode*, in this sense of blowing up, suggests more violence and noise than any of the other words in this group. [The bomb *exploded* at a great distance from our observation point but with so much noise that I was deafened for several minutes.] The same kind of noisy breaking out is implied when *explode* is used figuratively to indicate the sudden release of an emotion: to *explode* with laughter; to *explode* with anger. Another figurative usage of *explode* is its designation of the destruction of something by disproving, refuting, or discrediting it: to *explode* an out-of-date theory; a tissue of lies which was *exploded* by an honest slip of the tongue. **Burst**, like *explode*, can mean to blow up: the sound of shells *bursting* over our heads. It has, however, more general applications than *explode* in the sense of breaking out or apart. Here, in a literal or figurative way it suggests the energy produced by a sudden release from confinement or the force generated by great tension: a dam that *burst* during a season of heavy floods; the feeling that one is about to *burst* from overeating; to die as a result of a blood vessel that *burst* in the brain. *Burst* is also used figuratively like *explode* to denote the expressing of an emotion: a man who was *bursting* with resentment. **Erupt**, which is also used literally and figuratively, means to *burst* forth or to break out. In this word, as in the one sense of *burst*, there is an implication that the *bursting* or breaking out is done from a restrictive place or condition. [Hot ashes and molten lava *erupted* from the volcano; Angry oaths suddenly *erupted* from the man who had been fighting to keep his temper under control.] **Bust**, in the sense pertinent to this comparison, means to break open or apart. It is a slang variant of *burst*: a couple of drunken guests who in seconds *busted* all the balloons it had taken me hours to blow up. See BREAK (v.), TEAR.

Antonyms: implode, suck in.

exquisite

fine
graceful

These words refer to what reflects rare beauty or delicacy in taste, fashion, or manners. **Exquisite** is extremely vague as a superlative used in any of these situations; to these notions it adds overtones of what is consummate in its execution, admirable in effect, and gives evidence of extreme sensitivity, discrimination, and fastidiousness: *exquisite* miniatures showing the greatest delicacy in their use of color; a ballet dancer of *exquisite* skill; an *exquisite* day, breathtaking in its beauty. The word

exquisite
(continued)

polished
raffiné
refined
soigné

can also refer to what is keen or acute: suffering the most *exquisite* torment.

Polished is metaphorical as it applies here, suggesting a correctness in manners and an elegance of grooming that has been carefully learned or inculcated: the *polished* society of the 1890's. The word can also refer to technical facility: a *polished* performance of the *exquisite* sonata. **Refined** extends the implications of *polished* to a larger range of uses. It can refer beyond manners to esthetic excellence or taste in the widest sense, often suggesting the arduous process of separating what is valuable from what is dross: *refined* manners; a *refined* style, free of flaw or eccentricity; observing that art was nothing more than life *refined*. Often, however, the word can refer to what has become too rigidly correct, mannered, lifeless, or genteel: a *refined* and bloodless prose style; *refined* taste that found the explosive complexities of Greek drama too rich for its palate.

Soigné and **raffiné**, borrowed from the French, both share an emphasis on good grooming. *Soigné* stresses elegance and modishness as well: the latest *soigné* fashions for women. *Raffiné* can indicate more general qualities of *refined* delicacy, subtlety, or cleverness: the *raffiné* wits of the mauve decade. Disapprovingly, *raffiné* can point to what is foppish, superelegant, or overrefined: new styles in men's clothing that give more than a hint of becoming dandified or *raffiné*.

Graceful most vividly suggests physical bearing or movement that is lithe, agile, and lyrical: a *graceful* walk. It can also indicate delicately smooth execution in the arts: a *graceful* modeling of the female nude. It can point as well to manners that show poise, calmness, and correctness: her *graceful* way of making introductions. **Fine**, in this context, can refer to minute, delicate, or perfectly executed ornamentation or detailing: the *fine* carving of the filigree scroll framing the bas-relief. It can also suggest something *refined* or of high merit: *fine* manners; the *fine* arts. Less strictly, of course, it can be a vague superlative for anything one regards favorably: a *fine* film; a *fine* painter; a *fine* friend. See ELEGANT, EXCELLENT, ORDERLY, URBANE.

Antonyms: CLUMSY, *coarse, common,* GAUCHE, ROUGH, *untutored,* VULGAR.

extend

draw out
elongate
lengthen
prolong
protract
stretch
widen

These words agree in meaning to increase in one or more dimension. **Extend**, as here considered, means to increase a thing's length, breadth, or duration. An army may *extend* its supply lines; a bird *extends* its wings when soaring; and a tedious preacher may *extend* his sermon beyond his congregation's span of attention.

Lengthen and **draw out** mean to *extend* a thing in length or in duration, but not in breadth. *Draw out* sometimes even implies a loss of breadth accompanying the increase in length; metal wires become both longer and thinner when they are *drawn out*. **Elongate** is used only to mean to *lengthen* spatially, not in time, and like *draw out*, sometimes implies to *extend* in length at the expense of breadth, but in any case suggests disproportionately great length: one of the sculptor Giacometti's mournful *elongated* figures.

Prolong and **protract** now usually refer to *extended* time, although *prolong* may also refer to space. *Prolong* implies an extension beyond natural or normal limits: to *prolong* the meeting until a quorum could be rounded up; to *prolong* a war by inept diplomacy and miscalculation of the enemy's aims. *Protract* means to *draw out* or *extend* greatly in time; it is often used adjectivally: *protracted* negotiations covering four months of serious discussions.

Stretch, as here considered, means to *extend* a thing in length, breadth, or in both dimensions: to *stretch* a rubber band; to *stretch* canvas; to *stretch* a sweater by pinning it while wet. *Stretch* is now also used as an adjective applied to articles of clothing made of synthetic fibers that can be *stretched* to fit a variety of sizes: *stretch* socks. **Widen** means to increase only a thing's breadth: to *widen* a highway by adding two lanes. *Widen*, like *extend*, may be used figuratively to apply to any broadening: to *widen* (or *extend*) one's interests to include the study of nature. See ENLARGE, ESCALATE, PERSIST.

Antonyms: contract, cut short, narrow, SHORTEN, *shrink, terminate, truncate.*

extenuate

gloss over
palliate
whitewash

These words all mean to make seem less wrong, evil, blameworthy, etc. **Extenuate** suggests the effort to lessen the blame incurred by an offense, while **palliate** implies concealment, as of the incriminating facts or the gravity of their consequences: to *extenuate* past neglect by present concern; to *palliate* the errors in a book. [Starvation may serve to *extenuate* an instance of theft; A doting parent may seek to *palliate* the excesses of an errant son.]

Gloss over stresses the disguising or misrepresentation of incriminating facts: to *gloss over* a mediocre academic record. To **whitewash** is to represent by completely false information or a dishonest judgment: The accused man went free, *whitewashed* by a packed board of investigation. See LESSEN, MISLEADING.

Antonyms: enhance, exaggerate, heighten, intensify.

extraneous

extrinsic
immaterial
inessential
irrelevant
superfluous

These words refer to whatever is not an inherent part of a given consideration or entity. **Extraneous** stresses something that is not necessary or has no bearing, but the word is otherwise very general in its implications. It does suggest a difference in kind: sorting out the hard-core facts from the *extraneous* interpretations. The unnecessary element referred to may, if not excluded, be either harmless or deleterious: *extraneous* substances that make the sunburn preparation smell pleasant but have no healing effect; *extraneous* minerals in the water supply that made it unsafe to drink. **Superfluous** is different in its effect, often pointing to simple excess, not a difference in kind: wiping away the *superfluous* oil with a clean rag. Even where the word shows a less clearcut contrast with *extraneous*, it still points to what is useless or redundant: a room cluttered with *superfluous* furniture.

By contrast, **extrinsic** functions as an intensification of *extraneous*, emphasizing that something is by its very nature completely unlike a given entity or completely outside the scope of some concern: pointing out that oxygen consumption might well be *extrinsic* to the life cycle as it may have developed in other parts of the universe; literary standards that are *extrinsic* to any understanding of popular media. **Inessential** is more like *extraneous* in referring to what may be present and tolerated but is in any case not needed and may therefore be excluded by choice or necessity: an editor who helped the novelist cut from his book those scenes that were *inessential* to the main theme; ordering the people in the lifeboat to throw overboard everything that was *inessential* to their survival.

Immaterial refers not to what is unnecessary, in excess, or unlike something else, but to what has no effect or makes no difference: She told him that it was *immaterial* to her whether he stayed or left. In the context of reasoning, the word may point to what contributes nothing to an objective proof and thus is unimportant: the judge's ruling that the political beliefs of the accused were *immaterial* to the question of his guilt. **Irrelevant** also indicates what is unimportant or inapplicable, in this case because it lacks any direct bearing on the concern at hand: proof that the mother's dreams were *irrelevant* to the development of the fetus. Most specifically, the word suggests a lack of logical relationship as in a non sequitur: injecting *irrelevant* details about the man's life into our consideration of his candidacy. See MARGINAL, TRIVIAL.

Antonyms: essential, intrinsic, material, relevant, SIGNIFICANT.

F

These words refer to a loose grouping of like-minded people within a larger aggregate. **Faction** suggests a relatively small grouping that coheres because of attitudes or objectives that are different from that of others in the larger whole. A *faction*, by implication, is more concerned with winning acceptance for its views than for the welfare or effectiveness of the parent group; rather than compromise these views a *faction* might leave the parent body and form a rival group. Thus, the word may have pejorative connotations ranging from stubbornness, disharmony, to outright disloyalty: He begged them to set party unity above the bickering of *factions*. A **splinter group** is an even more cohesive and well-defined unit that has already or is just about to break away from the larger parent group, usually because of doctrinal disagreement; it may be of doubtful stability or endurance: *splinter groups* that vote with their party in national elections but against it in local elections; a movement that was destroyed by its tendency to break into *splinter groups*. **Sect** is used primarily of religious groups that adhere to their own special doctrines and either remain loosely associated with a larger group or break away from it completely: the formation of a number of Protestant *sects*. The word may also be used for any identifiable groupings within a dogmatic aggregate: Maoist *sects* at work within de-Stalinized countries.

Bloc and **wing** refer to far larger groupings than the previous words. Both also refer to much looser allegiances. *Wing*, however, need not suggest actual membership in some organized parent group so much as a definable position within a spectrum of possibility: a rare agreement between the left and right *wings* of the country's political sentiment; disclosures that should be satisfying to gadflies of the right *wing*. More strictly, the word can apply within an organized group, but still with the notion of an extreme position on that group's scale of values: cooperation between the left *wing* of the Conservative Party and the right *wing* of the Labour Party. One could not, obviously, refer to middle-ground sentiment by using this word. *Bloc* is not restricted, like *wing*, to suggesting simple polarization along a scale of values. It refers to a practical alliance of strength and consequently need not stress ideological intransigence at all: a power *bloc* made up of several political shadings. The word suggests a joining of forces fostered by threatened security, rivalry, and the will to survive: African delegates that vote as a *bloc* in the UN Assembly. The word is sometimes like *wing*, however, in suggesting no parent group that overarches rival *blocs*: the neutralist *bloc* of nations;

faction

bloc
sect
splinter group
wing

the rival power *blocs* of East and West. See ADDITION, COMPONENT, DENOMINATION, PART.

faint

black out
collapse
pass out
swoon

These words mean to enter a state of unconsciousness, impairment of awareness, or extreme weakness. To **faint** is to lose consciousness suddenly because of a temporary deficiency of the blood supply to the brain. *Fainting* (for which the medical term is syncope) may be caused by emotional shock, pain, overexertion, or exposure to high temperatures. **Swoon** was once a synonym for *faint*, but is now obsolescent. *Swoon* appears widely in literature of the past, especially in the 19th century, where it often evokes the stock image of the delicate, vaporish lady of the Victorian period who habitually *faints* when under stress or in the grip of strong feelings: She *swooned* under the rain of his kisses; to *swoon* at the sight of blood.

Black out is used of airplane pilots experiencing partial or complete loss of vision and sometimes of consciousness, caused by rapid changes in velocity during flight. By extension, *black out* has come to mean any temporary memory lapse, usually without *fainting*, especially one resulting from emotional tension or the consumption of large amounts of alcohol. [The accused claimed that he had *blacked out* and did not remember strangling the murdered man; Jonathan was able to recall very little of what happened at the party because he *blacked out* early in the evening.]

Pass out is an informal term for *faint*: to *pass out* from the heat; to *pass out* from fright. Unlike *faint*, *pass out* carries a suggestion of humor with little or no medical connotation, especially in its most popular use to describe falling into the stuporous sleep that overtakes some people after they have had too much to drink: a derelict who had *passed out* in a doorway; She was able to down one cocktail after another without *passing out*.

Collapse is a much stronger term than the other words and may indicate grave illness. To *collapse* may also involve *fainting*, but the word, from its literal meaning of giving way or caving in, emphasizes a complete and sudden loss of vital strength or health, which may be either brief or prolonged: those who *collapse* into bed after an exhausting day; He *collapsed* from overwork; to *collapse* from nervous strain; to *collapse* with a heart attack. See SICKNESS, WEAKEN.

Antonyms: come to, rally, revive.

famous

celebrated
noted
notorious
renowned

These words refer to people or things that are widely known. **Famous** is the most general of these, the least formal, and the weakest in connotations. It refers simply to anything that has gained the attention of many people for whatever reason: a *famous* movie star; a country *famous* for its good cooking. While the word does carry a positive connotation, it may suggest popularity or general recognition rather than discriminating approval or inherent excellence: a meeting between the *famous* popularizer and the less well-known originator of the theory.

Celebrated and **renowned** are intensifications of *famous*, both specifically adding the note of wide approval for accomplishment. *Renowned* is the more formal of the two and might seem too precious in some uses; its emphasis is also on the wideness of the acclaim rather than on discrimination. It is most viable now, perhaps, for places or things rather than for people: a world-*renowned* castle on the Rhine. It may also suggest something that has become legendary or is no longer available for an objective evaluation and must be approached through admiring but second-hand reports: the *renowned* band of Spartans who held Thermopylae. *Celebrated* refers, more objectively, to someone or something that has been given acclaim or honored with awards or prizes: a *celebrated* Nobel Prize winner. It can, sometimes, function like *famous* in indicating a more popular or less critical approval: the most *celebrated* of the *famous* movie stars. Sometimes the word can be a less formal substitute for *renowned:* a cathedral *celebrated* in song and story.

Noted is unique among these words in specifically suggesting that accomplishment is singled out for notice because of its excellence. It is often used to describe a more intellectual kind of effort, indicating an authority or expert or their theories: a *noted* authority on bee-keeping; a *noted* critic of new fiction. Because of this use, *noted* points to a much more limited general recognition than these other words; a *noted* expert, while honored by others in his field, might not be known widely to the general public at all. **Notorious**, in sharp contrast to all these words, indicates someone or something that has become *famous* because of its undesirable or offensive behavior: the *notorious* immorality of Hollywood in its heyday; a *notorious* gangster. See GREAT, OUTSTANDING, SIGNIFICANT.

Antonyms: fugitive, inglorious, OBSCURE, *unknown.*

These words refer to the cultivation of plants or the raising of animals, either for food or as produce. **Farming** is the most informal of these words and can apply to the whole range of possibilities here or to a specialization: Wheat is the main product of *farming* in the Great Plains; chicken *farming*; cattle *farming*. **Agriculture** is more formal but just as all-embracing; it is widely used on all levels of speech. The word is the preferred term when used of educational institutions that teach *farming* as a science: courses in *agriculture* at the state agricultural college.

All the remaining words emphasize particular aspects of *farming*. **Husbandry** now appears most often in the formal phrase *animal husbandry*, referring to the care and raising of all kinds of animals as an occupation. The phrase *good husbandry* indicates the efficient and prudent management of the affairs of *farming* — or other concerns. [He had shown *good husbandry* in ordering seed when the prices were at their lowest; Young married couples often learn the *good husbandry* of their income only after bitter experience.] Unqualified, the word pertains in Britain to small-scale *farming*.

Tillage refers strictly to the planting, cultivating, and harvesting of crops, but is now less often used for this activity than *farming* itself. **Agrology** refers formally and specifically to the study of soil make-up and chemistry, often taught as a course in *agriculture*. **Agronomy**, also extremely formal, is more general; it includes *agrology* in its wider concern with the best possible conditions for maximum land use and crop output: the *agrology* of alkaline soils; sensible techniques of *agronomy*, based on crop rotation and soil fertilizers.

Gardening, like *tillage*, is exclusively restricted to the raising of plants. In contrast with *tillage*, the word is relatively informal and refers to the small-scale cultivation of fruits and vegetables for personal use or to the cultivation of trees and shrubs as a source of pleasure or beauty: Most families did some *gardening* in their backyards as a way of economizing on grocery bills during the summer and fall; horticultural hints for *gardening* enthusiasts; interested in the profession of landscape *gardening*.

farming

agriculture
agrology
agronomy
gardening
husbandry
tillage

farthest

extreme
furthest
outermost
ultimate
utmost
uttermost

These words, both as nouns and modifiers, refer to the greatest distance, the most inclusive boundary of something, the point of its greatest extension, or to anything at its most ample or serious. **Farthest** and **furthest** are the superlative forms of farther and further. *Farthest* applies strictly to the greatest distance, whereas *furthest* can not only apply identically, with no distinction in shading and meaning, but also to many other situations here, both literal and figurative, particularly where the notions of movement or progress are present. [Which of these cities are the *farthest* (or *furthest*) from us?; This line marks the *furthest* advance of the glacier; behavior reflecting the *furthest* departure from the norm] **Outermost** is like *farthest* in referring strictly to distance, but it is even more specific in suggesting the outside of a plane or solid figure: the *outermost* layer of skin; the *outermost* periphery of the Roman Empire's influence; the *outermost* planet.

Extreme and **ultimate** are considerably more general than the other words here; each, however, has an occasionally used area of specific reference. *Extreme* can apply like *farthest* and *outermost*: the *extreme* edge of the desert. When it refers more generally to great amounts, degrees, or intensities, it often suggests an unwise, excessive, or grave departure from the norm: the *extreme* left wing of the party; He always went to *extremes* with his drinking; an *extreme* illness. But the word can be compared and, hence, may not be as forceful as *furthest*: the more *extreme* of the two positions; Which of these *extreme* factions went *furthest* in its demands? *Ultimate* can refer to something that is last in space or either first or last in time: the *ultimate* island in the archipelago; the modern word's *ultimate* form in Indo-European; The mystery isn't unraveled until the *ultimate* chapter of the book. More commonly, the word refers to a final outcome: the *ultimate* results of our foreign policy. At its most general, *ultimate* functions more vaguely to indicate the most *extreme* or perfect form of something: the *ultimate* catastrophe; a hotel that was the *ultimate* in luxury.

Utmost and **uttermost** are the most formal of these words and can refer very generally to anything at its greatest, most *extreme*, or best. *Utmost* can apply like the last use of *ultimate*: the *utmost* in craftsmanship. An added suggestion here, as in its other uses, may be one of the *extreme* effort required to reach some goal: We will do our *utmost* to get it delivered on time. *Uttermost* can seem like an intensification of *utmost* in some uses: a crisis that will demand our *uttermost* in time and patience. Often, the word suggests something severe or final: the martyr's *uttermost* sacrifice of his life; his *uttermost* agony. At its most specific, the word, unlike *utmost*, can also apply more neutrally to distance: the *uttermost* tip of South America. See BOUNDARY, FINAL, HIGHEST, SUMMIT.

Antonyms: closest, initial, inmost, least, mildest, nearest.

fat

adipose
buxom
chubby
corpulent
obese

These words refer to a physique that is fleshy or overweight. **Fat** is the most informal and also the most concrete and direct of these words: a woman who was unbelievably *fat*. The word does, however, recognize degrees of this condition: a young man who already looked slightly *fat*. By contrast, both **corpulent** and **obese** refer to excessive states of overweight; they are also much more formal than *fat*. *Obese* is the clinical term used to describe this condition when it is considered medically rather than esthetically and with particular reference to its endangering of health; consequently an unequivocally extreme case is indicated: the incidence of heart failure in *obese* persons. *Corpulent* refers, literally, to fleshiness of physique and thus may suggest bulk or overall heaviness rather than a medically *obese* condition; it would thus not require so extreme a case to become applicable: a smiling, *corpulent* Buddha.

Portly and **stout** are both genteel euphemisms for *fat*, especially used to describe elderly people. *Portly* suggests dignity of bearing in a figure of great girth; *stout* suggests, somewhat like *corpulent*, a general heaviness of physique: the *portly* matrons who served tea after the recital; the *stout* innkeeper with the cherubic face.

Plump and **buxom** indicate the slightest degree of overweight suggested by any of these words; both can be approving rather than disapproving. *Plump* suggests a soft ripeness of figure that is thought attractive: Rubens' *plump* female figures that would today be considered *fat*; a *plump* baby. The word can, of course, be used euphemistically: the *plump*, potbellied scoutmaster and his scrawny charges. *Buxom* is restricted to describing a *plump* or well-developed woman, especially one radiating sturdy good health: *buxom* pioneer women. Both this use of the word and its use as a euphemism for *fat* have recently given way to its specific use for a sensual and, particularly, bosomy figure: *buxom* burlesque queens.

Chubby suggests a squareness of figure, filled out with fleshiness, that might be thought earthy or robust: the *chubby* little girl; the *chubby* man's twinkling eyes. The word sometimes has an aura of well-intended humor. **Adipose** is most strictly a biological term for fatty tissue itself; when used as a substitute for *fat*, the word has comic effect, sometimes less well-intentioned than *chubby*: *adipose* ladies and gentlemen who rush in droves to reducing salons. See HEALTHY, HUSKY, LARGE, MASSIVE.

Antonyms: emaciated, THIN.

Fatal is used to describe anything that is capable of causing or that actually has caused death; it carries a strong suggestion of the inevitability of fate: an illness which might not be serious for a young person, but which will almost certainly prove *fatal* to the old lady. **Deadly** is interchangeable with *fatal* in this sense: Leukemia is a *deadly* disease. *Deadly*, however, in a way that *fatal* cannot, can refer to a person who desires or seeks to cause the death of another person: The murdered man had many *deadly* enemies. **Mortal**, like *deadly*, can be applied both to things or people that cause, are capable of causing, or seek to cause someone's death. In its reference to things, *mortal* differs from *fatal* and *deadly* only in the fact that it is usually found in contexts which detail a death that has already occurred. [He was struck down by a *mortal* blow upon the head; Because of an ancient family feud, the two cousins had been *mortal* enemies from birth.] **Lethal** refers to something which, because of some intrinsic quality in its makeup is certain to cause death, and may indeed exist for the express purpose of causing death: Cyanide is a *lethal* poison.

With the exception of *lethal*, all of these words can be used to describe something that causes great fear, or discomfort, or that brings about disaster or ruin, but that does not lead to physical death: a *fatal* mistake; a *deadly* insult; in *mortal* terror. See DEAD, DIE.

Antonyms: enlivening, invigorating, life-giving.

These words refer to the attitude or act of disapproval that consists in attacking weaknesses, imagined or real, in someone else or in his behavior or achievements. **Faultfinding** is the most neutral of these words in that it can, conceivably, apply to a helpful or friendly ferreting out of actual weaknesses: giving his next-to-final draft to a friend who

fat
(continued)

plump
portly
stout

fatal

deadly
lethal
mortal

faultfinding

captious

faultfinding
(continued)

carping
caviling
censorious
hypercritical
nit-picking
pedantic

could always be counted on to be openly *faultfinding*. More often, it is true, the word suggests an eagerness to seek out weakness for its own sake, but even here the word is less severe in tone than the following words: certain that the inspecting officer would prove to be tediously *faultfinding*.

Hypercritical suggests a harsher attitude than that suggested by *faultfinding*, pointing to someone overly eager to disparage, possibly out of a reluctance to recognize or honor the good qualities in others: views so *hypercritical* that his companion wondered what on earth could possibly meet with his approval. In further contrast to *faultfinding*, a *hypercritical* person need not necessarily dwell on weaknesses in something at all; he may simply reject it wholesale as obviously inferior. **Censorious** is similar to *hypercritical* in allowing the possibility of a blanket rejection. It is even harsher in tone, however, suggesting an attitude that is exclusively negative in its judgments. Someone who is *hypercritical* might be expected to spell out his views in some detail and to have, at least, standards for measurement; someone *censorious*, however, might merely express his negative evaluation without explanation or without having such standards. The word, furthermore, has overtones of prissy or priggish ill will: easy for the contemplative man to be *censorious* of every attempt at acting out an ideal.

Captious suggests a further extreme than the foregoing words, but not so much toward a greater severity of judgment as toward a truly irresponsible or whimsical refusal to be pleased by the most meticulous effort. The word may suggest *faultfinding* that deliberately wishes to confuse rather than to enlighten, especially when this results in fruitless argument: an interviewer who made *captious* remarks in order to get "interesting responses" from his subjects.

Carping and **caviling** are better used to describe single acts of *faultfinding* rather than a *hypercritical* or *censorious* attitude. Both may suggest a zealous glee in scornfully condemning something on the basis of picayune considerations or niggling faults; some difference between them can be seen, however, by noting that *caviling* stems from words meaning jest, mock, or raillery, and *carping* from words meaning dispute or boast. *Carping* best suggests a pedantic railing at or making a mockery of something for small failures; *caviling* more often suggests strident or grating verbal attacks in which reasonable or generally acceptable propositions are imputed because of trivial lapses: a *carping* reviewer who thought a few split infinitives more important than the whole range and sweep of the work; the prosecution's *caviling* rebuttal that seemed to see in the defendant's nervous manner a proof of guilt.

Nit-picking is a colorful and informal word that specifically stresses an excessive concern with small or trivial faults or with making distinctions so fine as to be pointless; this concern may be either well-intentioned, though misguided, or deliberately hostile: diplomats busy at their *nit-picking* while the whole world was going up in flames; an opponent who could find nothing wrong with my program and so had to content himself with *nit-picking*. **Pedantic** is a word that is less directly related to the notion of disapproval. It emphasizes, instead, someone intent on needless displays of learning or petty points of scholarship: a *pedantic* dissertation, full of musty footnotes and gobbledygook. In the context of disapproval, it is a more formal alternative for *nit-picking*: *pedantic* objections to practical proposals. See DISAGREE, DISAPPROVAL.

Antonyms: approving, commendatory, complimentary, encouraging, flattering, laudatory.

These words refer to the gaining of benefit or advantage or to the promise of such an outcome. **Favorable** can refer to a present situation that exposes one to positive possibilities: *favorable* influences absent from most slum schools. More simply, the word may refer to approval: *favorable* reviews of the play. Most pertinent here, the word pertains to signs that suggest an advantageous result: *favorable* indications that the stock market would recover rapidly and reach new highs.

Auspicious and **propitious** are restricted to this last possibility of *favorable*. Both suggest the foretelling of a beneficial outcome from preceding omens. Of the two, *auspicious* may better suggest an abundance of beneficial indications or conditions, *propitious* the absence of negative or deleterious ones: *auspicious* signs that victory would be theirs by nightfall; *propitious* weather that promised a calm voyage. In another context, *auspicious* may be used to indicate a clairvoyant telling of the future: She tended to see *auspicious* rather than ominous portents in her customers' tea leaves. *Propitious*, by contrast, is more commonly used to indicate the promise or gaining of more practical advantages: a business contract that seemed *propitious* to both parties.

Strictly speaking, **providential** is a heightening of the supernatural possibility inherent in *auspicious*, suggesting divine intervention to bring about a *favorable* outcome: They saw the breaking of the storm as a *providential* blessing on their mission. Often, however, the force of the word is weakened to indicate anything that seems remarkably opportune: a *providential* escape from the avalanche. **Lucky** is a more informal synonym for this last meaning of *providential*, carrying no implication in current use of any divine or supernatural intervention. The word, instead, refers to a chance occurrence that proves to be beneficial: the *lucky* accident by which they met. In a less precise use, the word can also refer to any positive circumstance, with less emphasis on chance: *lucky* to be living in a free country.

Good, of course, is the least formal and, in its generality, the least precise of these words in referring to any positive circumstance: *good* results on the test. It can also refer to signs that augur a beneficial outcome: a *good* prognosis. **Fortunate** may once have implied a *favorable* augury; more often, now, it indicates present success or *good* circumstances: contributions to those less *fortunate* than oneself. This implication even overshadows a use that relates to *lucky* in stressing, more formally, benefits that result from chance: a *fortunate* throw of the dice. One use of **happy** relates it to these words, suggesting advantages that result, not from chance, but from a discriminating choice of means that later events corroborate: Hiring him proved to be a *happy* decision. Sometimes, however, the word suggests fortuitous benefit, in which case the emphasis is on the beneficial outcome rather than, as with *lucky*, on the overcoming of odds: a *happy* accident. See BENEFICIAL, OPPORTUNE.

Antonyms: adverse, bad, doomed, ill-fated, inauspicious, unfavorable, unlucky, untoward.

These words refer to seeking approval from others by praising them or behaving toward them in an obsequious or servile manner. **Fawn** can literally indicate the affectionate action of a dog toward his master, exhibited by licking him and sprawling before him, by tail-wagging, and by other forms of adoring behavior. Servile behavior of a comparable sort is suggested when a person acts in this way, although here the word becomes contemptuous, whether or not the obsequious display is sincere

favorable

auspicious
fortunate
good
happy
lucky
propitious
providential

fawn

butter up
compliment

fawn
(continued)

flatter
toady
truckle

or undertaken cynically for self-advancement. [Only an uxorious husband could *fawn* on a woman the way he does; She *fawned* over her famous guests, but sneered at them when they were gone.]

Truckle and **toady** are both harsher in their contempt than *fawn*, although both are less vivid and specific about the behavior they point to. *Truckle* indicates any sort of servility, whether exhibited because of necessity, cowardice, or self-interested obsequiousness: slaves who had to *truckle* to their harsh masters or be killed for insolence; He *truckled* to the repressive mores of his day for fear of being ostracized; people who bow and scrape and *truckle* to get ahead. As in the last example, the word can imply a stooped, humbled carriage. *Toady* gives no visual suggestions whatsoever about manner or bearing, but it does specifically suggest the attempt to curry favor with one's superiors by ingratiating actions: those who are willing to *toady* their way to success; an actress who needed an entourage of lickspittles and lackeys to *toady* to her.

The remaining words all emphasize verbal praise as the means of gaining approval. Of all these words, **compliment** alone can be used approvingly; the word can even indicate genuine admiration expressed for no ulterior motive: a teacher who was as ready to *compliment* deserving effort as she was to criticize slipshod work. But the word often applies to praise given insincerely as an empty formality or as a self-interested gesture; in this case, the tone of disapproval is much milder than that of any other word here. [He *complimented* her on her new dress without even looking at it; She refused to *compliment* the fatuous critic merely to win his approval.] **Flatter** concentrates exclusively on the paying of insincere compliments for whatever reason: She thought it could do no harm to *flatter* her escort a bit, at least on his taste in wines; a movie producer who expected to be *flattered* by the ambitious underlings that surrounded him. Sometimes the word can indicate a surprising but genuine interest that is taken by the recipient as a not wholly deserved honor: She *flattered* us by coming early and staying late; *flattered* by the sincerity of his concern for her.

Butter up is an informal phrase that suggests not only the obsequious behavior of *fawn*, *toady*, and *truckle* but also the insincere praise indicated by *flatter*. The word adds to these implications a completely cynical attitude behind the ingratiating acts and words and even a disrespectful or contemptuous attitude toward the person being courted: dropouts who claim to detest their middle-class parents but know how to *butter* them *up* when the need arises. See OBSEQUIOUS, PRAISE.

Antonyms: carp, condemn, criticize, dominate, insult, tyrannize.

fear

alarm
fright
horror
panic
terror

These words refer to an upsetting emotional response to something unpleasant or dangerous. **Fear** is the most general of these and the least intense; it may suggest a mildly troubled emotion as well as more extreme states: her *fear* that the rain would damage her new shoes; his *fear* of facing the enemy's mortar fire. It might also suggest mere timidity, or in another context, a vague state of psychological malaise: his *fear* of disagreeing with his boss; countless *fears* that leapt up whenever she had to face any new situation in life. **Fright** is more specific and more intense; it particularly suggests a sudden troubled reaction to some concrete external threat: filled with *fright* by the madman's first lunge at her. The word can, unlike fear, have a slightly outmoded sound in some uses, especially because it has been used informally to describe anything ugly or unpleasant: a ball gown that was simply a *fright*.

Alarm and **panic** are words that may now sound more natural than *fright* in the context of a sudden external threat. *Alarm*, however, is almost as general as *fear* in extending from a mild uncertainty or uneasiness to intense and excited responses: his growing *alarm* at her lack of taste; the *alarm* that shone in his face as he saw the bridge begin to give way. When the word describes a more intense state, it suggests an initial response to danger, possibly in the instant when the danger is first recognized but before protective action can be taken: paralyzed by *alarm* at the first news of the bombings. *Panic*, on the other hand, suggests the confused, hysterical actions that might follow the first feelings of *alarm*. It stresses ineffective action, especially of a group: the only one who did not lose his head in the general *panic* that filled the burning theater. When the word is used of a single individual, action is not stressed so much as a disabling *fear*: He flailed the water helplessly in his sudden *panic*.

Horror and **terror** are closely related words that suggest an intense emotional upheaval at being confronted with something disgusting or dangerous. *Horror* stresses revulsion from the ugly or grotesque or from ethical depravity: They stood in *horror* at the unsanitary methods used to prepare their breakfast. It also suggests intense *fear*, possibly when the threat to one's personal safety is unclear or absent: walking in *horror* through the snake room at the zoo; watching with *horror* as the tightrope walker struggled to regain his balance. *Terror* suggests a direct threat of personal danger; it is the most intense of all these words: He shook with *terror* as the door slammed shut and gas began to fill the room; huddled in *terror* along the walls of the air-raid shelter. When this pair of words refer to types of fiction, a fine distinction is often made between them. *Horror*, in this context, refers to a reliance on the grisly and macabre to gain a frightening effect: monsters, dungeons, open coffins — all the trappings of the usual tale of *horror*. In contrast, *terror* suggests a story in which danger and suspense predominate, or one in which *fear* is called up by frightening situations rather than by cruder displays of the shocking or disgusting: a tale of *terror* all the more chilling for being set in an ordinary living room. See ANXIETY.

Antonyms: calmness, COURAGE, equanimity.

feminine

effeminate
female
ladylike
womanish
womanly

These words refer to qualities that ideally or appropriately pertain to women. **Feminine** may carry a factual tone in indicating what pertains to women in general: the common *feminine* aversion toward violence in any form. The tone of the word changes drastically, however, when it is used to evaluate the degree to which a woman possesses characteristics thought to be the ideal attainments of women; in this case it is strongly positive: a hostess unashamedly *feminine* in her ability to put people at ease. When applied to men, the word carries a negative tone: advertising campaigns that encourage men to take a rather *feminine* interest in aftershave colognes and hair preparations; a man with an unfortunately *feminine* build.

Female may be used in simple classification, applying to any species with sexual polarization: a *female* gorilla; magazines that compete for the *female* market. Outside of factual classification, the word sounds flatfootedly brusque, if not derogatory, and often carries an emphasis on distinctive biological functions: arguing that her fears were just so much *female* silliness; advertisements that are supposedly discreet in referring to "*female* troubles." By contrast, **womanly** is wholly positive in restricting itself to desirable *feminine* qualities in women: dresses that showed off to advantage her lithe, *womanly* body. Changing cultural values have influenced the word; Victorians might have referred approvingly to a woman's shyness or self-effacement as *womanly*. Now, by contrast, the word is often used with a new frankness to refer favorably to sexual attractiveness or capability in women: wives who are unafraid of expressing a natural and *womanly* desire for their husbands. Thus, the word is comparable not only to *manly*, but has expanded to compare as well with *virile* (for which no corresponding *female* term exists — as though this area of concern were absent in women).

The remaining words all tend toward the pejorative in their different ways. **Ladylike** was once wholly favorable and may still be so used: teaching the girls in her charge how to behave in *ladylike* fashion. More often now, however, the word indicates over-haughty or prissy behavior in women: too *ladylike* to dream of working her way through college; career women who think it no betrayal of their *feminine* natures to dispense with any *ladylike* insistence on special treatment. The word is, of course, extremely derogatory in its rare use to describe a man's behavior: his comical, *ladylike* way of mincing at every step. **Womanish** applies disapprovingly to men, but also to women: his *womanish* habit of throwing up his hands whenever the office routine got the least bit hectic; breaking down into *womanish* fits of weeping at any imagined slight from her husband. **Effeminate**, by contrast, applies exclusively to men in a disapproving way; it may refer to physical or mental characteristics as well as behavior, unlike *ladylike* in this context: a man with an *effeminate* physique; an *effeminate* lisp that made him difficult to listen to. *Feminine* in this context compares to *effeminate* by having a more factually descriptive tone: The longer, more *feminine* hair styles of male singers are no longer regarded as *effeminate*.

Antonyms: MASCULINE.

fight

action
battle
bout
clash
engagement
fray
skirmish

These words refer to competition or conflict between two hostile forces. **Fight** is the most general of these, ranging from suggesting any struggle toward a goal by one or more people to suggesting actual physical combat between numbers of people: a *fight* for life against great odds; a desperate *fight* to win the tournament at all costs; a *fight* that broke out in the bar between two drunks and soon spread to the whole neighborhood. **Bout** very often suggests any sort of competition specifically between two people: a name-calling *bout* between the two senators; a drinking *bout*; the *bout* for the heavyweight championship. The word can, however, suggest the struggle of one person against some adversity: a *bout* with tuberculosis. And it can be used for larger groups, even including a military conflict, in which case it is mostly used for color: a shooting *bout* between the decimated guerrillas and the well-supplied invaders.

Clash clearly refers to a two-sided conflict between comparable forces: a *clash* of wills between student and teacher. When physical combat is referred to, a hasty or unexpected *fight* may be suggested: a *clash* that was over before the artillery could zero in on vulnerable enemy targets. **Fray** suggests a disorganized free-for-all or melee that involves a number of people: a *fray* that broke out on a side street of the ghetto. It may also refer to the very heart of a military conflict: medics unafraid of worming their way into the thick of the *fray*.

Battle refers most strongly to one specific *fight* that may be part of a larger or continuing war: a *battle* that resulted in heavier casualties than any other of the whole war. The word may, more abstractly, refer to some total war effort: our unceasing *battle* to drive the aggressor from these shores. *Battle* may also metaphorically describe *fights* or *bouts* outside the military context: a raging *battle* between the man and his wife.

The remaining words are all more formal than the foregoing and all apply more exclusively to military combat. **Skirmish** suggests a quickly organized or localized thrust against the enemy or a trivial, perhaps accidental, *clash* between the combatants: night patrols sent out to engage the enemy in a series of small *skirmishes*; lines held without incident except for a few *skirmishes*. **Action** and **engagement** are both rather formal and colorless words to describe a *battle*. *Action* may suggest a full-scale struggle or a sporadic flickering of hostilities: a mopping-up *action* that was decisive; enemy *action* that continued throughout the night. *Action* may also be used euphemistically to describe an actual war, usually for political convenience: a Soviet police *action* that really consisted of armed intervention in their deepening civil war. *Engagement* refers to a single *battle* in a war, suggesting that opposing armies in search of each other have met and are contending for victory: reporting an *engagement* of sizable forces east of the line of attack. See AGGRESSION, ATTACK.

Antonyms: détente, pacification, reconciliation.

These words all refer to the action that a liquid or gas undergoes in passing through another substance or medium. To **filter** means to pass (a liquid, air, etc.) through a porous substance such as paper or cloth, in order to extract certain impurities or essences. Papers folded into the shapes of cones and inserted in the mouths of test tubes or coffee-making devices are familiar uses of *filters*. Photographically, certain kinds of light or certain colors are *filtered* by means of specially colored and constructed glass or plastic lens coverings.

Percolate means to pass or cause to pass through fine openings or interstices. In coffee-making, as the hot water passes through a container of finely ground coffee, it extracts the essence of coffee and carries it along with it. *Percolate* emphasizes the process of passing through or permeating a substance; *filter* points to a particular means by which this process can take place. [Rainwater *percolates* through the soil to form an underground reservoir; To get red, you have to *filter* out the greens and blues; The spilled ink *filtered* through the blotter.]

Exude and **seep** mean to ooze or trickle out through pores or small openings. *Seep* suggests a gradual and often accidental or unwanted movement of a substance into or out of something. [Gas *seeped* into the room; Air *seeped* from the balloon; Blood *seeped* from his wound and reddened his bandages.] *Exude* is often used of natural or planned phenomena: to *exude* sweat; Gum *exuded* from the tree. It is also used figuratively with the sense of a powerful diffusion of any quality: to *exude* charm. See LEAK.

These words all pertain to the end or conclusion of something that can be considered sequential. **Final** simply means coming at the end: *final* exams. It often carries a strong note, however, of decisiveness or conclusiveness: a *final* chance to buy a property before it was sold to someone else. **Last** means coming after all the others in a series, i.e. *final* in order, sequence, or time: the *last* page of a book; the *last* day of summer; He waited until the *last* minute before jumping on the train. **Concluding** means bringing to an end, and usually conveys the suggestion of a *final* settlement or arrangement. A *concluding* chapter brings the narrative or text of a book to a close; the *last* chapter is simply the one after which there are no others; the *final* chapter is the one toward which all

filter

exude
percolate
seep

final

concluding
last
ultimate

those before it have been leading. Because of the implicit suggestion within *final* of progression or of a series of related events having direction, the word is more often used in figurative expressions than either *last* or *concluding*: a *final* chapter in a long and tempestuous career.

Ultimate, as here considered, means beyond which there is no other, and is denotatively synonymous with *last*: the *ultimate* (or *last*) stanza in a poem. *Ultimate* is, however, more formal in tone, and is often more emphatic in pointing to the *last* item in a series: his *ultimate* offer for an out-of-court settlement before instituting legal action. While *last* states the fact that something is the *concluding* item in a series, *ultimate* often conveys strong feeling and determination, and is in this sense sometimes interchangeable with *final*: That is our *ultimate* (or *final*) proposal, and no other changes will be considered. See CONCLUSIVE, FINISH.

Antonyms: BEGINNING, *first, initial, opening.*

find

ascertain
detect
determine
discover
learn
locate
unearth

These words share the implication that something already in existence is being newly brought to light. **Find** and **discover** can both be used for an accidental or gratuitous gaining of knowledge; of the two, *find* is the less formal. [Explorers in Australia *discovered* flora and fauna *found* nowhere else in the world.] Both can, of course, be used to describe an intentional effort; *find* in this case may imply either a search for something new or the discovering of something lost but previously possessed. [He finally *found* the missing keys in a jacket he had put in storage for the summer; We know there must be a law that governs the odd gravitational behavior of certain stars, but it may take us decades to *find* it.] *Discover*, when it implies an intentional search, always suggests the acquiring of something that already exists but is new to the discoverer: Mendel raised crop after crop of snapdragons to *discover* the laws governing heredity. It should be noted that this sense of *discover* contrasts sharply with invent, words often confused. [Franklin *discovered* electricity, but Edison invented the electric light bulb.]

Learn, unearth, and **detect** are equally able to suggest either intentional or accidental discovery, although they tend more strongly toward the former. Of the three, *learn* is the most general and informal, *detect* the most specific and formal. *Learn* in one sense can imply a minimum of effort in gaining unsought knowledge: It was only today I happened to *learn* the name of the song I'd been whistling for years. But the weight of usage here is on conscious, painstaking effort toward a predetermined goal: A pianist *learns* the secret of a major work only by practicing it intensively over a long period of time. *Unearth*, when referring to accidental discovery, implies the rediscovery of something lost or obscured by the passage of time: In his researches he was startled to *unearth* the manuscript of a major work by Boswell, never before published. Again, the suggestion of deliberate search is more frequently present, in which case digging deep into a subject is suggested: The district attorney swore he would *unearth* the real facts in the case if he had to grill everyone who had known the dead man. *Detect* is more rarely applicable to accidental discovery: To his surprise, he *detected* a bright red glow emanating from a crater in the moon. It most often suggests deliberate, deductive investigation and the making of extremely precise observations: Her pulse was so weak and erratic that the doctor could barely *detect* it. In one use, the word has a sharply negative sense that contrasts with a positive use of *discover*: It may take time for the public to *discover* your real worth as a writer, but fortunately the vapidity of his work has been quickly *detected*.

Determine, ascertain, and **locate** are almost exclusively suggestive of deliberate search and discovery. *Determine*, in fact, is charged with the suggestion of painstaking conscious effort, especially to resolve a controversy. [From the facts presented to them, the coroner's jury was able to *determine* conclusively that the death was not a suicide; No student may leave until he can *determine* the acidity or alkalinity of the chemical placed before him.] *Ascertain* implies that the searcher began with an awareness of his lack of knowledge on a given matter and worked to correct it; in this it is similar to but much more formal than *determine* — even to the point of pomposity, except in very technical, legal, or scientific writing. [We shall probably never be able to *ascertain* the exact nature of these subatomic particles; With careful research, it is possible to *ascertain* the often unspoken assumptions held by people of a particular historical era.] *Locate* is more specialized in meaning than either *determine* or *ascertain*, usually implying the fixing of an occurrence or thing in space. [All efforts have failed to *locate* decisively the birthplace of Columbus; From his directions, it shouldn't be difficult to *locate* the beach house, even though you've never been there before.] See CREATE, DEVISE.

Antonyms: FORGET, MISLAY, *miss.*

These words are alike in meaning to reach the end of a task or activity. **Finish** and **complete** mean to bring to an anticipated end by doing all things that are necessary or appropriate to achieving that end. Although the two words may be used as exact synonyms, *complete* suggests the fulfillment of an assigned task and is therefore not always an appropriate substitute for *finish*. An author may *complete* or *finish* his novel; a reader might *finish* it, but one would not say that he *completed* it unless he were reading it as a school assignment.

Close and **conclude** emphasize the final stages that *complete* an action. [The district attorney usually *closed* his case with a plea for conviction; The hymn sung by the congregation *concluded* the religious ceremony.]

End and **terminate** are more general in meaning. An action may be *ended* or *terminated* before it is *completed*. In addition, both of these words carry more of a sense of finality by suggesting a definite cut-off point. [Heckling from the audience *ended* the speech before the speaker had *concluded* his remarks; The truce *terminated* hostilities; If Congress refuses to appropriate funds, the foreign aid program might be *terminated*.]

Finalize has achieved currency, mainly in bureaucratic use, with the meaning of to bring to a conclusion something that has been worked on for a long time or that has been held in abeyance: to *finalize* a budget estimate. See FINAL.

Antonyms: BEGIN, *initiate, open.*

These words refer to the burning of something. **Fire** is the most general of these, referring both to slow or rapid burning, whether of small or great size: a wisp of tissue paper that caught *fire*, burned an instant, then went out; a forest *fire* that covered several miles at the peak of its intensity. **Flame** may refer to one isolated small *fire*: reading his watch by the *flame* of a match. Or it may refer to each momentary fork or tongue of a larger *fire*: watching the largest log on the *fire* finally burst into *flame*. In this case, the word is often used in the plural to express the multitude of such elements making up a *fire*, or to indicate their diversity of placement: staring for hours into the flickering *flames*; The

finish

close
complete
conclude
end
finalize
terminate

fire

blaze
conflagration
flame

fireman pointed to new *flames* licking through the roof and the second-story windows of the building.

Both **blaze** and **conflagration** stress intensity and rapidity of burning, with *blaze* functioning as an intensification of *fire* and *conflagration* as an intensification of *blaze*. In addition, *blaze* can give connotations of a controlled, cheerful warmth, while *conflagration* is more closely restricted to a widespread destructive or accidental burning: a comforting *blaze* roaring in the fireplace; a *conflagration* that destroyed the whole center of London. *Blaze* can, of course, be used in ways that approach the suggestions of *conflagration*: a *blaze* that took the lives of six inhabitants and one fireman. See CATASTROPHE.

flagrant

glaring
gross
rank

These words refer to extreme, obvious, or outrageous failures or offenses. At its mildest, **flagrant** may be used to indicate what is deplorably obvious: *flagrant* indifference to the suffering of the poor. More commonly, however, the word is more emphatic in suggesting the public flaunting of blatant incompetence or impropriety: the proofreader's *flagrant* disregard of even the simplest errors; the *flagrant* cynicism of politicians who work hand in glove with racketeers and gangsters. **Glaring** is even more emphatic about the obviousness of the failing, but is otherwise milder than *flagrant* in that it more often points to error, however inexcusable, than to unethical or immoral conduct: a play chock-full of *glaring* faults. The word might also suggest an annoyed rather than disgusted reaction: exasperated by his *glaring* bad manners. Occasionally, the word has the force of *flagrant*; even here, however, the misconduct that stands out is stressed: the *glaring* betrayal of a public trust.

With **gross** and **rank**, the emphasis shifts from the obviousness of faults to their extreme or offensive nature. *Gross* is often used simply to mean extreme: *gross* unfairness. More precisely, the word suggests coarse or callous insensitivity to correct or decent standards of behavior: *gross* mistreatment of a helpless child. Another reference of the word — to heaviness — is often implicated in this context, suggesting an almost immovable failing of great weight: an administration almost crippled by its own *gross* incompetence. *Gross* failings, however, need not be obvious: *gross* errors in the report that went completely unnoticed. *Rank* stresses disgusting offensiveness and tends to indicate moral corruption rather than simple error: the *rank* indecencies that occurred at the party. While the word does not necessarily suggest a public display, like *flagrant*, it does suggest corruption that would be obvious to anyone exposed to it: a book that brought the *rank* injustices of slavery to public attention. As with *gross*, other meanings of *rank* affect its shadings here, especially its references to things malodorous or overgrown: a *rank* system of payoffs that should have reeked of foul play to any impartial investigator; a tangled bureaucracy filled with *rank* inefficiency. See CLEAR, DEFINITE.
Antonyms: IMPLICIT, *mild, slight, venial.*

flaw

blemish
defect
failing

These words indicate a lack in something that prevents it from being complete, wholly effective, or desirable. **Flaw** is the most general of these words, suggesting the existence or presence of something that spoils an otherwise sound entity: a *flaw* in his ingenious theory; an admirable character cursed by the tragic *flaw* of pride. While *flaw* suggests something that detracts from completeness, effectiveness, or perfection, **fault** points to something that impairs excellence. A *flaw* can refer to something missing: The *flaw* in the weapon was its inability to

flaw
(continued)

fault
foible
imperfection
mar
shortcoming

fire rapidly. *Fault* usually refers to something present and to something inherent in the nature of a thing rather than external to it; *flaw* can refer to the superficial as well as to the profound. [The length of her white gloves was the only *flaw* in her appearance; a central *flaw* in his argument that invalidated his entire position; a *flaw* (or *fault*) in the marble near the base of the statue; Snobbishness was his main *fault*.] In connection with character, *flaw* is somewhat more elegant and dramatic than the more prosaic *fault*.

While *flaw* may or may not indicate something easily removed or overcome, **defect** often suggests a *flaw* so serious as to completely prevent functioning: a *defect* in the fuel lines that prevented the missile from blasting off. Since it is now often used of machines, its application to human personality sometimes indicates a judgmental or simplistic view of human nature, suggesting easily traceable explanations for malfunction: probing for the *defect* that had made him resort to violence. In other contexts *defect* may refer to an error or the lack of something needed for completion. [A *defect* in judgment led to the accident; The *defect* in the microphone caused a humming sound.]

Mar and **blemish** refer especially to marks or qualities that disfigure or make imperfect. *Blemish* applies particularly to *defects* of the skin: a facial *blemish*. *Mar* is more general, and may be used of any slight *defect*: a *mar* in the finish of a vase. Both words may be used figuratively: the first *blemish* on an otherwise spotless record; a *mar* on the good name and offices of this company.

Imperfection is closer to *flaw* than to *defect* in that it stresses malfunction less than incompleteness or lack of order: a slight *imperfection* in an otherwise beautiful design. Whereas *flaw*, however, points to a *mar* that is self-evident, *imperfection* points more often to a lack that may be a matter of opinion. Like *defect*, the word also implies a pre-established canon by which to judge something: stylistic advances in his art that were regarded as *imperfections* by his contemporaries. And as *defect* relates to function, *imperfection* relates to form, drawing the former toward a scientific context, the latter to an artistic one. With *imperfection*, however, the judgment remains relative since no completely perfect thing exists.

Failing, shortcoming, and **foible** are the mildest of these words, suggesting a specific lapse in an otherwise sound entity. All three words most commonly relate to personality, describing a characteristic way of behaving that is not desirable but does not vitiate goodness or overall effectiveness. *Foible* is perhaps the mildest of the three, suggesting a slight but ingrained eccentricity that may be easily recognized by others and allowed for without causing great difficulties. A *foible* may, in fact, be almost harmless and even endearing: a love that was strengthened rather than weakened by their acceptance of each other's *foibles*. *Failing* may suggest a more severe *shortcoming* that has more serious consequences: a lack of compassion that can be an insurmountable *failing* in either husband or wife. Sometimes the special point of the word is to indicate well-intentioned effort that does not succeed: the lack of convincing evidence that is the book's main *failing*. *Shortcoming*, like *failing*, may refer to failures or deficiencies in things as well as people, and in this sense compares with one sense of *flaw*: The weapon's chief *shortcoming* (or *flaw*) was its inability to fire rapidly. When applied to personality or character, it is milder than either *flaw* or *fault*, and is close to *failing* in meaning. [We all have our *shortcomings* — that man dotes on his wife, this one flirts with other women, a third flies into jealous rages at the drop of a hat.] See CHARACTERISTIC, DISFIGURE, ECCENTRICITY, LACK, MISTAKE, SIN, STIGMA.

Antonyms: MERIT, *perfection.*

fleet

armada
convoy
navy

These words all refer to organized groups of vessels. **Fleet** may refer to the entire number of ships of a government, including merchant vessels, whereas **navy** refers either to the warships of a country or to its entire military sea force, including servicemen, yards, and equipment. *Navy* always implies a military purpose, whereas *fleet* need not. *Fleet* is used, however, to mean all the ships under one command in a particular area, and the command may be a military one. [The U.S. Sixth *Fleet* was assigned to the war in southeast Asia; a Russian fishing *fleet* of trawlers] *Fleet* is also commonly used to refer to a group of vessels or vehicles organized or viewed as a unit, or belonging to one company: a *fleet* of taxicabs. [A *fleet* of buses brought the Boston hockey fans to New York; The company's *fleet* of tugboats was idled by the strike.]

Armada, the Spanish word for armed, means a *fleet* of warships. In this country the word is commonly associated with the disastrous experience of the Spanish (or Invincible) *Armada*, which sailed against England in 1588, was defeated, and was virtually destroyed by storms.

A **convoy** usually refers either to the protecting escort accompanying ships at sea, as in dangerous areas during wartime, or to the ships being so escorted. The word need not be restricted to ships, however; trains or trucks may also be considered *convoys*. *Convoy* is also applied to a group of military vehicles, such as trucks, personnel carriers, tanks, mounted guns, etc., traveling together in an organized way for protection, efficient movement, or to avoid impeding other traffic.

flimsy

frail
tenuous
unsubstantial

These words refer to anything slight, weak, thin, or sheer and thus either lacking in permanence or vulnerable to damage or criticism. **Flimsy** is the most general in embodying all these meanings, particularly emphasizing a lack of density that makes for limpness rather than rigidity: *flimsy* cloth that clung to the outlines of her body; a *flimsy* stalk that caused the flower to droop in its vase. Less concretely used, the word may refer to inferior materials, worthlessness, implausibility, or low standards: *flimsy* books that come apart in your hands; the *flimsy* reporting of tabloid newspapers; a *flimsy* excuse; a *flimsy*, meretricious movie. **Frail**, by contrast, concentrates more on slenderness, weakness, or enfeeblement; furthermore, it need not suggest limpness: the *frail* filaments used in light bulbs; the *frail* teacup of bone china; a disease that left him *frail* from loss of weight. *Flimsy*, also, suggests possible damage through tearing, *frail* through breaking or shattering. Used even more metaphorically, *frail* does not function with the same intensity of disapproval felt in *flimsy*, although it can give a negative tone: a grasp of orchestration too *frail* to give his symphonic ideas convincing weight. More often, however, the word can render a sharply contrasted connotation of pity: *frail* hopes long ago shattered by the brutal facts of ghetto life.

Tenuous can also emphasize, like *frail*, thinness, although in this case weakness is not necessarily involved: a heavy free-floating sculpture hung from *tenuous* wires that made it seem light and airy. The word's particular relevance, however, is to haziness: a *tenuous* fog that threatened to thicken by morning. Related to this possibility is its more metaphorical suggestion of vagueness or confusion: ideas too *tenuous* to result in a realistic research project. **Unsubstantial** is the most formal of these words and emphasizes a lack of density, firmness, permanence, or stability: building houses out of paper and other *unsubstantial* materials. Less specifically, the word points to something that is without basis in fact, cannot pass inspection, or that partakes of fancy or fantasy: *unsubstantial* theories; *unsubstantial* grounds for an appeal of the case; *unsubstantial* dreams of escaping her dreary existence. See TRANSLUCENT, TRANSPARENT, WEAK.

Antonyms: firm, rugged, solid, sturdy, substantial, tough.

These words refer to someone who shrinks from a person or action because of alarm, cowardice, or servility. **Flinch** indicates an involuntary and startled drawing back in the course of performing an action. [*Flinching* from the anticipated report of the rifle is the most common cause of poor marksmanship; She *flinched* as the doctor inserted the needle in her arm.] At its most concrete, as in these examples, the word suggests a convulsed recoil or muscular spasm. The word can function more abstractly to refer to any psychological reluctance or avoidance: He *flinched* from thinking about the wife and children he had left behind. While *flinch* most often suggests alarm or fear as the cause of the recoil, **wince** points to pain or discomfort as the motivating factor. The recoiling action, furthermore, may be a slighter, briefer, or less noticeable movement than that indicated by *flinch*: She gingerly touched her bruised shin and *winced* at the pain. The word can function less literally for any pained response: She *winced* and blinked under his withering attack. In this context, *flinch* better suggests initial aversion or reluctance, while *wince* is better suited to describing a discomfited response.

Cringe is more general than the preceding pair and can function in the place of either, referring to any recoil caused either by fear or pain. The action may not be so intense or sudden as those of *flinch* and *wince*, but it may be longer-lasting: left standing by the rail to *cringe* under a steady onslaught of sea spray. Also, spasmodic movement is not suggested here so much as a crouched or stooped posture. This is especially true when the word refers to servile, cowardly, or obsequious behavior: slaves who *cringed* under the wrath of their master; a candidate who *cringed* from direct confrontation with his opponent; disgusted by the way he *cringed* and fawned before his teacher in rapt self-abasement.

Cower and **grovel** both relate more closely to *cringe* than to the first pair of words, emphasizing stooped or sprawled postures adopted out of fear, servility, or obsequiousness. *Cower*, however, can also indicate a fearful and trembling recoil or drawing back from danger, pain, or extreme discomfort: He *cowered* in frozen panic as the horses stampeded toward him; oarsmen who *cowered* and groaned at each fall of the lash. In reference to obsequiousness, *cower* is now more specific, vivid, and disapproving than *cringe*, indicating someone who seeks approval by an extreme display of deferential humility: the sanctimonious remorse with which he *cowered* before the judge in hope of winning a lighter sentence. *Grovel* is the most extreme of all the words in any of the situations possible for this group; it specifically points to a sprawled or supine position, suggesting abject and incapacitating fear, loathsome servility, or self-abasing adoration: choked with sobs and *groveling* on the floor in terror as the two men fought over her; those who hope to influence policy by *groveling* before the policy-makers and flattering their sense of self-importance; He worshiped his wife so much that no amount of *groveling* seemed adequate to express his utter surrender to her. See ANXIETY, DEMUR, FAWN, FEAR.

Antonyms: brazen out, carry off, confront, face.

flinch

cower
cringe
grovel
wince

flippant

casual
flip
fresh
nonchalant
sassy
smart
wise

These words are all used to describe particular kinds of attitudes, speech, and behavior. **Flippant, flip, sassy,** and **fresh** are always unfavorable in connotation. They all imply impertinence or lack of respect; *flippant* and the colloquial *flip* also indicate an inappropriate levity in the face of something serious. The four can describe attitudes and actions, but very often relate to speech or writing. *Sassy* is distinctly dialectal in flavor. [She's a *sassy* little girl, disrespectful to her elders and peevish with her peers; His *flip* remark at the time of the accident was typical of his rudeness and bad taste; It is a *flippant* editorial, not at all in keeping with the importance of its theme; He was *fresh* when he was a child, and his manners have not improved with age.]

Unlike the foregoing words, **casual** and **nonchalant** can be neutral or even complimentary in tone. Both words indicate a lack of concern, interest, or excitement: a *casual* air; a *nonchalant* approach to business problems. *Nonchalant*, however, may suggest an attempt to be disciplined or detached: All during the meeting, Mr. Jessup maintained his *nonchalant* manner, even when the shouting and arguing were at their height.

Smart and the slang term **wise** are close in meaning to *sassy, flip, flippant,* and *fresh*. However, since other senses of *smart* and *wise* relate to the possession of intelligence or wisdom, there is sometimes a suggestion of those qualities present even when the words are used in criticism or disparagement. The intelligence and wisdom hinted at are perverted by arrogance or a nasty wit, but they can make the distinction between someone being *smart* or *wise* instead of *sassy* or *fresh*. [She was a good editor, but she kept making *smart* remarks to the department head and he finally had to fire her; The sergeant was court-martialed for being *wise* to his commanding officer.] When *smart* or *wise* is used in reference to a child, it describes someone who is unpleasantly assertive or forward. [The little boy was so *smart* to his mother that she sent him to bed without supper; A couple of *wise* kids broke the window of the new post office.] See CONTEMPTUOUS, SARCASTIC, UNINVOLVED.

Antonyms: POLITE, *serious, solemn.*

flood

deluge
engulf
inundate
overwhelm
swamp
whelm

These verbs mean to cover with water or other liquid, as by a downpour, wave, or overflow. **Flood** is the most general word. It indicates the submergence of something that is not normally under water: A leak in the plumbing *flooded* the basement. The noun *flood*, in its commonest meaning, refers to an overflowing of dry land by water, as when heavy, concentrated rainfall fills a stream beyond capacity. Hence the verb *flood* means to fill, overflow, drench, or submerge with water. [During spring rains the river *floods*; The river *flooded* extensive areas of the countryside; A calamitous storm tide *flooded* the coast; The hurricane *flooded* the beach cottage and did considerable water damage.] Figuratively, *flood* may refer to anything that seems to move in a full stream: Sunlight *flooded* the room. Or it may mean to supply with an excess or abundance of anything: to *flood* an engine with gasoline; They *flooded* him with advice.

Flood comes from an Old English word. Its collateral adjective, *diluvial*, and its closest synonym, **deluge**, derive from the Latin word for *flood*. *Deluge* may designate a worldwide *flood*, or one covering a considerable part of the earth's surface. Specifically, it applies to the rain of forty days and forty nights in the time of Noah — a cataclysm called either the *Deluge* or the *Flood*. In general use, however, where *flood* focuses on the rising flow of water in a swollen stream, *deluge* stresses the idea of an unremitting downpour. In a literal sense, the verb *deluge* may imply a drenching with torrents of water: Heavy monsoon rain *deluged* southern India, *flooding* the rivers. But the verb is most often used in a figurative sense, indicating any kind of profuse downpour or incessant stream: a candidate *deluged* with telegrams from well-wishers; an author *deluged* with offers of honorary degrees.

The verb **inundate** is synonymous with *flood* but is far more literary. *Inundate* goes back in derivation to the Latin word for wave. It is close to *deluge* in force and meaning, but it differs in its emphasis on a wave-like overflow. To *inundate* is to overrun with water and cover completely. [If the dikes of the Netherlands gave way, the sea would *inundate* the lowlands; A submarine earthquake caused a tidal wave that *inundated* the peninsula.] In a figurative sense, *inundate* points to an overflowing abundance: a bookstore *inundated* with orders for a best seller; a mail-box *inundated* with junk mail; a congressman *inundated* by requests from his constituents. *Inundate* may also mean to overpower like an onrushing wave: The work piled up and threatened to *inundate* him.

Swamp is close to *inundate* but is much more informal. Literally, it means to drench or submerge: The rampaging river *swamped* scores of villages during the *flood*. To *swamp* a boat is to sink it by filling it with water: The canoe was nearly *swamped* by the waves. In a colloquial sense, *swamp* means to overburden with an unmanageable number or amount of anything: an Ivy League college *swamped* with applications; I'm *swamped* with work. *Swamp* may also suggest utter defeat or a thoroughgoing rout: The home team *swamped* the opposition.

Where *inundate* implies standing water covering a surface, **overwhelm** may suggest liquid going over and under, around and through. *Overwhelm* comes from a Middle English word meaning to turn upside down. It calls to mind the overpowering force of a mighty wave that rolls over and buries everything in its path: Streams of lava *overwhelmed* the village at the foot of the volcano; a lost continent *overwhelmed* by the sea. *Overwhelm* is now more commonly used in figurative senses, often referring to abstractions: *overwhelmed* by grief; His foolhardy accusations opened the floodgates of suspicion, and unreason *overwhelmed* the land. **Whelm** is very close to *overwhelm* but sometimes conveys a greater sense of foreboding. It suggests a being enveloped on all sides by water or by something that covers and suffocates like water: A dust storm *whelmed* the wagon train; a town *whelmed* by an earthquake. *Whelm* is used with telling force by Gerard Manley Hopkins in *Spelt from Sibyl's Leaves:* "Our evening is over us; our night / *whelms, whelms,* and will end us." **Engulf** means to swallow up, as in an abyss or bottomless gulf. It suggests a being utterly *overwhelmed* by waters — enveloped and buried beyond any hope of escape: The legendary island of Atlantis was *engulfed* by the sea and disappeared without a trace. See MARSH, VANQUISH, WET.

Flourish is comparable with the other words listed in the sense of increasing toward or being in a very desirable condition, or one of maximum development. Thus, a farm is said to *flourish* when it is well tended and producing large crops, and a school of painters is said to have *flourished* at the time when most of its best paintings were produced. **Flower** means to be in the best condition or period of development: Keats' talent *flowered* in his early twenties.

Luxuriate means to grow or increase so abundantly as to reach or border upon excess: Dandelions *luxuriate* on untended lawns.

flourish

flower
luxuriate
prosper
thrive

Prosper is applied to persons or enterprises that do well or succeed financially. A man may *prosper* through effort and good fortune, or his farm may *prosper* through good management and an absence of drought.

Thrive is generally applied to living things that enjoy physical growth or well-being. [Tropical plants *thrive* in a greenhouse; Growing children *thrive* in summer camps.] *Thrive* is occasionally applied to non-living things that by extension are considered living: a *thriving* community. See MATURE (v.).

Antonyms: decline, die, WANE.

flow

gush
pour
run
spout
spurt
squirt
stream

These words refer to the movement of fluids or a mass of particles. **Flow** indicates continuous and free movement, and often suggests slow, steady, and untroubled passage: the broad river that *flowed* through my hometown; the prevailing air current that *flows* from west to east in the northern hemisphere; salt that gets damp and refuses to *flow*. *Flow* can have a lyrical tone: We watched the river as it *flowed* on under the bridge. By contrast, **run** is more matter-of-fact, although it is usually restricted to the movement of liquids. In this context, it is very general, suggesting any amount, channeled or unchanneled, moving in any direction: water *running* down the windshield; In which direction does the river *run*? In reference to streams or rivers, *run* may suggest faster movement than *flow*.

Pour most often suggests sharp downward movement: soot *poured* out over the city; water *pouring* over the dam. **Stream** can also apply to a movement both of fluids and of particles, but is otherwise like *run* in suggesting any amount moving in any direction. It usually suggests more rapid or more forceful movement, however: tears *streaming* down her face; smoke *streaming* from the chimney. As in the last example, movement in a narrow band or through a small aperture is often implied: water *streaming* through the irrigation ditches; cars *streaming* over the bridge.

Gush suggests surging, turbulent, or sudden movement, whether in a general upwelling or a rapid jet: blood *gushing* from his head; water *gushing* in a fine spray from the fountains. **Spout** more strictly refers to a continuous or intermittent jet: water *spouting* from the leaky pipe; Wounded to the quick, the whale began to *spout* blood.

Spurt can suggest small or intermittent jets: He squeezed the plunger of the hypodermic until the needle *spurted* out a few drops. **Squirt**, when distinct from *spurt*, may suggest a wider or more diffuse spray: water *squirting* from the fire hose. More commonly, the word is transitive: He *squirted* water at me. See FLOOD, LEAK, STREAM.

Antonyms: congeal, freeze, stagnate.

foggy

cloudy
murky
opaque
turbid

All of these words apply to what is obscure and confused or shows a lack of clarity. Even when used in an abstract way, the closely related **foggy** and **cloudy** can sometimes allude to distinctions between a fog and a cloud. The former is low-lying, enveloping, diffuse, and indefinite in configuration; the latter, partly because it is usually seen from a distance, is typically thought of as being a denser, more remote, and more clearly defined mass that may affect but does not impinge upon the viewer. Similarly, *foggy* can refer to an enveloping obscurity or confusion in a thinker's mind: *foggy* generalizations without any substantiation in fact. By contrast, *cloudy* can suggest remoteness, lack of relevance, or uncertainty that is external to the thinker or speaker: The prospect for passage of the bill was somewhat *cloudy*, in view of its evident unconstitutionality. As in this example, the word often refers to a future outcome; *foggy* is more apt for present confusion: *cloudy* eventualities; I haven't the *foggiest* notion what you're talking about. Both, of course, can serve as literal description: a *foggy* day; a *cloudy* day. *Cloudy* can also be used to describe milky or unclear liquids: *cloudy* tap water that clears after a few minutes.

Literally, **turbid** means muddy or unsettled, and applies particularly to suspensions of foreign particles within a liquid, such as particles of dirt in water. Whereas *cloudy* in this sense emphasizes a misty appearance, *turbid* stresses the presence of foreign material that pollutes, muddies, or unsettles the basic medium. *Turbid*, however, is probably more commonly used in figurative than literal senses. It may mean thick and dense, like heavy smoke or fog: a *turbid* smoke screen of deceitful hints and outright lies. It may mean confused or impure, suggesting a chaotic intermixture of incompatible elements: The stream-of-consciousness technique in fiction has been likened to a *turbid* confluence of fact, passion, and ratiocination.

Murky and **opaque** suggest lack of light. *Murky* can mean oppressively dark or, by extension, unclear and confused, as if seen through a mist. *Opaque*, which in its basic sense means impervious to light, suggests denseness and relative impenetrability: *opaque* writing, filled with erudite but inept allusions; a *murky* exegesis of an arcane work, full of dark, involuted clues to which only the author has the key. See OBSCURE, TRANSLUCENT, VAGUE.

Antonyms: bright, CLEAR, *sunny*, TRANSPARENT.

fold

crease
line
pleat
wrinkle

These words function as both nouns and verbs and apply to marks, grooves, ridges, or furrows made in a smooth surface. To **fold** something is to bend it over upon itself so that one part covers another: to *fold* a blanket; to *fold* a newspaper; to *fold* up a road map; Do not *fold*, spindle, or mutilate. Used intransitively, the verb *fold* means to close together with the parts touching or facing: A fan *folds*. The noun *fold* may designate a *folded* or *folding* part, piece, or layer: the *folds* of the bellows of an accordion. The eyelid is a movable *fold* of skin that smooths out when lowered over the eye. A double chin is a fatty *fold* of flesh under the chin. *Fold* may also apply to a mark made by *folding* or the hollow between two *folded* parts: to tear paper evenly along a *fold*; He enveloped her in the voluminous *folds* of his cloak.

A **line** is a long, straight, slender mark, as one crossing the brow: the *lines* in her pale, drawn face; a forehead *lined* by care. The *lines* in the palm of the hand indicate the flexional *folds* of the skin which make firm grasping possible. Palmists claim that the so-called life *line*, head *line*, and heart *line* are indicative of a person's fortune. A **crease** is a mark, ridge, or furrow made by *folding*. Like a *line*, a *crease* may indicate the place where something *folds;* but a *crease* is usually considered to be heavier than a *line* though shallower than a *fold*. Hence, when the hand is slowly closed, the *lines* in the palm first deepen into *creases*, then thicken into *folds*. *Crease* is also used of heavy *lines* about the mouth or eyes or on the forehead: A sullen scowl *creased* his brow. And it may indicate a line of soreness or tension that results from bending or twisting: The lumpy mattress put a painful *crease* in his back.

A **wrinkle** is a small *line*, *crease*, or *fold* in a smooth surface, as a furrow made in the forehead by raising the eyebrows. To *wrinkle* is to contract into alternate ridges and furrows: He *wrinkled* his brow in concentration. Permanent *wrinkles* in the skin may result from age, anxiety, or excessive exposure to the elements: a *wrinkled* crone. Applied to fabric, *wrinkle* indicates a temporary mark made by crushing or rumpling. The verbs *wrinkle* and *crease* are synonymous in this sense: Linen *wrinkles* (or *creases*) easily. The noun *crease*, however, may indicate a deliberate or permanent *line*, as one of the two sharp edges pressed into men's trouser legs. A **pleat** is a *fold* of cloth doubled on itself and pressed or sewn in place: a kick *pleat*; *pleated* draperies; a *pleated* skirt. *Pleat* may also indicate the way a thing is *creased* and *folded*: an accordion *pleat*. See CRACK.

Antonyms: smooth, straighten, unfold.

folk

nation
people
race
tribe

These words refer to ethnic groups or subcultures that can be identified by specific acts or shared traits, whether physical or cultural. **Folk** is the most vague of these words and applies better to periods of history before the Industrial Revolution. It refers to the common people or peasants of those eras and is based on a class rather than an ethnic distinction. It would, in any case, be rarely used except as a combining form, referring to the products of this class of people: *folk music, folk culture, folk tales.* It has a modern slang or informal use to refer to one's nearest relatives or to the community in which one may have grown up: the *folks* back home; I write regularly to my *folks.*

Nation can, of course, refer to any government, ancient or modern, but in this context, it refers more particularly to nomadic groups that maintain a common culture, despite their being widely scattered: the Indian *nations* of the far West; the gypsy *nation*; the Jewish *nation* that somehow survived despite its scattering during the Diaspora. **People** is a less confusing term to describe a group, whether scattered or not, that share a common ethnic and cultural background: a *people* as conscious of individual liberty as the Greeks; the *peoples* of the earth, each with a distinctive contribution to make toward defining mankind. **Tribe** is more specific than *people* or *nation* in referring exclusively to a closely knit primitive culture group: the *tribes* of Africa and the Pacific.

Race refers to those large divisions of humans into physical types that are determined solely by some combination of skin color, facial characteristics, and other imponderables. Physical anthropologists have concluded that all such attempts to define clear-cut *races* are inexact, subjective, and unscientific: the Caucasian or white *race*; the Negro *race*; the Oriental *races*. See KIN, MANKIND.

follow

chase
pursue
shadow
tag
tail
trail

These words refer to moving in the path of someone who has gone before. **Follow** is the most neutral of these, yielding the fewest overtones. The gap between leader and follower may be slight or great; the motives for *following* may range from admiring emulation to a desire to catch or kill the leader: soldiers who *followed* the platoon leader in single file at the interval of a few paces; an expedition to *follow* the path that Alexander must have taken to the Indian subcontinent centuries before; She *followed* after him with cries for help; armed detectives *following* the route taken by the escaped convict.

Shadow and **tail** are both extremely informal words that restrict themselves to the act of *following* out of unfriendly motives; they also suggest a wish to remain unobserved but to stay close to the person being *followed.* Of the two, *shadow* suggests a more relentless and short-range action: He assigned a plainclothes man to *shadow* the woman every second of the day. *Tail* may suggest a briefer involvement, one at a greater distance: *tailing* the car until it had driven beyond the city limits.

Chase and **pursue** both suggest swiftness or determination: a posse to *chase* the escaping cattle thieves. *Chase* may also suggest the actual driving away of an enemy: She *chased* the hooligans from her yard. But while *chase* often suggests unfriendliness, the act may also be done out of sportiveness or high spirits: The boy *chased* his playmate around the block. It may also suggest an eager, desiring search: a man who *chased* after women all his life. *Pursue*, except for its overtones of speed and determination, is almost as devoid of overtones as *follow*. No situation or motive is necessarily suggested by the word in itself: detectives who *pursued* the murderer across several state lines; She *pursued* the absent-minded man to give him back the briefcase he had left behind.

Tag suggests close surveillance, either secretively or with the leader's full knowledge. In the situation of secrecy, the word approaches the meanings suggested by *shadow* and *tail*: *tagging* the man to find out where he lived. In the situation of acknowledged pursuit, the word may suggest the admiring imitation of someone thought of as a model or superior: the child who *tagged* after his older brother wherever he went.

Trail may suggest a laggard and spiritless *following* after someone else: hikers who *trailed* into camp hours after the first ones had arrived. More often, however, it refers to a stealthy *pursuing* of someone after he has gone on his way, an action that is done by seeking clues as to which way he might have taken: Indian scouts expert at *trailing* someone with a day's head start; They used hounds to *trail* the escaped convicts. When the word pertains to a closer following, it approaches the meanings suggested by *tail* or *pursue*. See HUNT.

Antonyms: lead, precede.

foreigner

alien
immigrant
newcomer
outsider
stranger

These words pertain to someone who does not belong, either at all or as yet, to the group he finds himself in the midst of. **Foreigner** specifically indecates that someone is a native or citizen of a nation other than the one he is now living in or visiting. The word can theoretically be used in neutral description, but in the past it was so often used to express suspicion or disapproval that it is difficult to avoid this tone completely even in the most innocent use: the *foreigners* who moved in across the street from us. A *foreigner* who intends to remain permanently in his new country can be more neutrally referred to as an **immigrant**. Although this word, too, could once be used pejoratively, its use as a precise legal term has kept it more viable and neutral than *foreigner*: an *immigrant's* visa. Until an *immigrant* becomes a citizen of the new country, providing that is his intention, he is known legally as an **alien**, that is, someone who resides in a country but is not a member of it: All *aliens* must register annually with the immigration bureau. Once a citizen, such a person is no longer an *alien*, but he might still be regarded as an *immigrant* by others so long as his speech, clothes, or living habits reflect his country of origin and remain in contrast to the national norm. The xenophobic or unfriendly onlooker could, in fact, call such a naturalized citizen a *foreigner* to express his own intolerance for any departure from the norm.

The remaining words are all more general and wider ranging in their implications. **Stranger** can indicate anyone who is not known to someone else or who is not familiar with or accepted as part of some group: She hurried past the beckoning *stranger*; great excitement when *strangers* came to a frontier town. **Newcomer** can refer more informally to an *immigrant*, but applies more widely to a person only recently accepted into a group, yet still largely unfamiliar with it: a *newcomer* to New

York. The word can also suggest an initiate to any area of experience: a *newcomer* to poetry. Where *newcomer* suggests recent membership, **outsider** stresses alienation from or rejection by a group: backhills people who were wary of *outsiders*; a boy who didn't have many friends in his class but preferred to remain an *outsider*; Both labor and management refused to call in an *outsider* to mediate the dispute. See BEGINNER, EXILE, WANDERER.

Antonyms: citizen, inhabitant, native.

foreknowledge

farsightedness
foresight
forethought
prescience

All these words deal with a shrewd, prophetic, or mystical ability to anticipate, predict, or see into the future. **Foreknowledge** can refer to a supernatural faculty: Augustine's treatment of God's *foreknowledge* and man's free will; a medium who claimed to have *foreknowledge* of the future. **Prescience**, the most formal of these words, can also point to such a faculty, although it is less often attributed to people than to the Deity: God's *prescience* is only one aspect of his general omniscience. Both words, however, can apply without any suggestion of the mystical or supernatural. In this case, *foreknowledge* would refer to having information concerning something that has not yet occurred: attempts to gain the same *foreknowledge* of weather conditions that we now have of lunar and solar eclipses; She denied that she had any *foreknowledge* of the plot her husband was involved in. *Prescience* indicates not the simple ability to anticipate but an acute and intelligent ability to see what lies in store in the future: their *prescience* concerning the problems that would await them in the New World; his *prescience* in seeing the dangers of overpopulation.

Foresight is an informal alternative for the last meaning of *prescience*. But more simply, it can also indicate an ability to think ahead, prepare for eventualities, and take prudent precautions against any undesirable possibility: She had the *foresight* to lock all the windows, as well as the doors, before leaving on her vacation; the *foresight* to plan for the inevitable obsolescence of the automobile as a practical means of transportation. **Farsightedness** can refer both to an intelligent envisioning of the future, like *prescience*, or a practical tendency to plan ahead, like *foresight*. It adds to either situation, however, the specific ability to extend one's thinking and awareness to the distant rather than the near future: the *farsightedness* of those who framed our Constitution in allowing for the changing circumstances and needs of future generations. **Forethought** is close to *foresight* in meaning; but where *foresight* might be most aptly applied to envisioning circumstances that are independent of oneself, *forethought* suggests the careful planning out of something more completely within one's own control: He could have avoided the accident by using *forethought*; writers who have the *forethought* to plan the general outlines of their work well in advance of the actual writing. See EXPECTATION, PREDICT, PREMONITION.

Antonyms: heedlessness, hindsight, ignorance.

forget

neglect
omit
overlook

These words refer to oversights or failures to remember or act. **Forget** suggests a failure to keep something in mind, either because of its unimportance or complexity, or because of an unintentional lapse: She *forgot* all about the gossip as soon as she reported it; *forgetting* the way to the station; *forgetting* to water the plants as he had promised to do.

Overlook and **omit** are both more specific than *forget* in suggesting almost exclusively failures to act. The failure may be slight and excusable and may be either intentional or deliberate. *Overlook* concentrates on a failure to notice or check something: He had *overlooked* the fact that the back door was not locked; politicians who deliberately *overlook* the real needs of the city. The word might also refer to a conscious decision to excuse someone else's failing: He agreed to *overlook* her breach of confidence this once. *Omit* suggests a failure to act in a certain approved way. Extenuating circumstances may be implied for the reason of the failure, but conscious intention may also be a motivation: *omitting*, in my haste, to tell her where I was going; *omitting* to tell the doctor the whole story behind the child's injury. The word, in a related sense, can refer to the deletion of something, usually because it might be thought disadvantageous or unpleasant: They *omitted* from the report any mention of the program's difficulties. Except in this sense of deletion, *omit* is the one word here that might no longer sound fresh or natural in ordinary conversation.

Neglect may suggest an inadvertent failure to act, but more often its connotation is one of deliberate inattention: His secretary had *neglected* to double-check the correspondence file. [*Forgetting* one or two small details is one thing, but *neglecting* the major responsibilities of your job is something else again.] See CURSORY, NEGLECT.

Antonyms: FIND, REMEMBER.

These words indicate the surrendering of what one has had or is entitled to have. **Forgo** contrasts with **give up** because of its greater formality, but otherwise these two terms are alike in being very general. When *forgo* applies to abstaining from or relinquishing pleasure or benefit, the word usually implies a free choice based on principle: asked to *forgo* meat during Lent; actors who voluntarily *forwent* pay for the benefit performance. But the word may also refer to any missed opportunity, regardless of reason: a youngster who *forwent* a chance to go to college out of sheer laziness; an old refugee who had long ago *forgone* any hope of seeing his homeland again. *Give up* could be substituted in most of these instances, but whereas *forgo* usually implies relinquishing something in advance, *give up* often implies surrendering something that is already in one's possession: He *gave up* his seat on the bus to an old woman standing nearby; farmers who *gave up* their land to the government only after a struggle. As in the last example, *give up* is more apt than *forgo* for a reluctant yielding, or one based on necessity or defeat. Intransitively, the term can mean surrender: enemy soldiers who had *given up*; I *give up*!

Waive stresses the voluntary yielding possible for *forgo*, but it is exclusively focused on yielding in advance a right that one is technically entitled to. [The defense *waived* cross-examination of the witness; Both sides agreed to *waive* the arbitration clause in the contract.] Sometimes, the implication of voluntary choice masks what is in fact mandatory: a law that required state employees to *waive* immunity in grand jury investigations or lose their jobs. **Sacrifice** can indicate both the involuntary and voluntary relinquishing of something, but its special point is the hardship entailed in doing so. If a voluntary surrender is indicated, the word implies nobility or generosity in the actor; if an involuntary act is indicated, the word stresses difficulty or even suffering: soldiers willing to *sacrifice* their lives for their country; those who *sacrifice* part of their income to help the disadvantaged; parents who must scrimp and *sacrifice* to send their children to college; prison conditions under which inmates are forced to *sacrifice* the last vestiges of their humanity. In some uses, neither generosity nor difficulty may be present: blithely

forgo

give up
sacrifice
waive

sacrificing the lives of others to his own self-interest. See ABSTAIN, FOR-SWEAR, RELINQUISH, TEMPERANCE.

Antonyms: DEMAND, *keep, preserve.*

form

configuration
contour
figure
gestalt
outline
shape
structure

These words can refer to the whole pattern or ordering of something, its make-up or constitution, or its enclosing surfaces. **Form** is the most general of these, applying in all these ways: the sonnet *form*; Ice is water in solid *form*; rectangular in *form*. At one extreme, it can merely indicate external appearance: a *form*-fitting dress. At the other, it can contrast with *content* all the interrelated patterns and techniques that make of something an organic unity: The author's keen sense of *form* sustains him through a subject that could easily have gone awry.

Shape more readily suggests a three-dimensional bulk, but it is not restricted to this reference: the gnarled *shapes* of Monterey cypresses. The word can also apply to the enclosing surfaces of both a plane or solid object: an elliptical *shape*; a dress to show off her lovely *shape*. When *form* and *shape* are contrasted, *form* usually suggests a prescribed or typical pattern, whereas *shape* suggests the individual interrelationships that a specific thing exhibits: the startling variety of *shapes* with which the sculptor had fleshed out the human and animal *forms* he had chosen as his subjects.

When **outline** and **contour** are contrasted, *outline* may apply to the bounding edges of a plane figure, whereas *contour* pertains exclusively to the enclosing surface of a solid figure: a star-shaped *outline*; the graceful *contours* of a pear. *Outline*, however, can refer more generally to the containing perimeter of any *shape*, plane or solid; in the latter case, it suggests one of a solid's possible silhouettes: the jutting *outline* of his chin in profile.

Figure refers in plane geometry to any *form* enclosed by three or more lines: A trapezoid is a *figure* bounded by four lines. In other uses, the word may suggest something reduced to its diagrammatic essentials, or to the characteristic *form* or set of *outlines* by which something is recognizable: eyes peeled for the familiar hunched *figure* of an apple tree that marked the right path to the farmhouse. At the same time, however, the word can refer to the details that fill out and give body to a *form*: a slow movement memorable for a complex pizzicato *figure* that recurs in the violins. Like *shape*, the word can refer to the human body, but with a greater emphasis on the total impression made by the relationship of part to part: a trim, clean-cut *figure*; He cut an imposing *figure* in his new tuxedo. **Configuration** can refer like *contour* to the *outlines* of a solid *shape*, but whereas *contour* can sometimes suggest gentle or smooth undulations, *configuration* can apply to any sort of *shape*; it is particularly relevant to landscape: a house designed by the architect to exploit and fit into the dramatic *configuration* of the cliff. In more general uses, *configuration* suggests the exact disposition of all the observable details within a *form*, as well as its external *outlines*: the lacework *configurations* of a snowflake; a *configuration* of jagged *shapes* within the symmetrical *form* of each inkblot.

Structure concentrates on the disposition of details suggested by one use of *configuration*. But *structure* may refer in addition to an underlying *form* that is not necessarily observable by a glance at the *outlines* of something: excessive fat disguising what was basically a perfectly formed bone *structure*. Also, *structure* emphasizes the organic interrelatedness of a whole, seen from the perspective of function: the complicated *structure* of the executive branch of the government; the *structure* of the gasoline engine. **Gestalt** is the most inclusive of these words in pointing to the totality of details that go to make up a moment of experience, referring to all those factors that impinge on a single psychological state. The word is drawn from *gestalt* psychology, which theorizes that the unity of such a totality is greater than the sum of its parts. The word has since been applied more generally to anything that can be said to have organic *structure*: Each of the scenes in the novel contributed to an overall *gestalt* of guilt and redemption. See BOUNDARY, CIRCUMSCRIBE, PHYSICAL, PROTOTYPE, SIZE.

Antonyms: content, formlessness, shapelessness.

These words describe elaborate or precise modes of behavior. The crucial discrimination to be made among them concerns the positive or negative overtones the words carry. The positive overtone suggests admiration for the skillful carrying out of a beautiful but complicated pattern; the negative overtone suggests abhorrence for an inflexible lack of spontaneity, sincerity, or naturalness. The choice of word may tell more about the speaker than about the behavior described.

formal

affected
ceremonial
ceremonious
pompous
proper
punctilious
ritual

Formal and **proper** are often neutral terms of description pertaining to correctness of behavior. *Proper* is almost exclusively restricted to this sense: the *proper* way of addressing a duke or duchess. *Proper* may also simply indicate what is appropriate or customary in a specific situation: the *proper* dress for mountain-climbing. *Formal*, on the other hand, can only refer to highly stylized situations: the *formal*, white-tie dinner. *Formal* dress, for example, would not be *proper* at a rock 'n' roll party, whereas jeans and a T-shirt would be *proper* in this instance, though *formal* in none. Both *proper* and *formal* can sometimes suggest the negative side to all these words. [She would be more fun if she weren't so *proper*; They felt a lack of warmth in the overly *formal* congratulations he gave them.]

Ritual, **ceremonial**, and **ceremonious** are allied to *formal* in describing acts or manners that are stylized according to set rules. They describe behavior that is *proper* only to the most formalized ceremonies in society. *Ritual* is neutral or approving when it describes an act that is a part of such a ceremony, especially a religious one: the *ritual* procession of cardinals. It is more ambiguous when describing a *formal* gesture not part of such an occasion: He lit the candles with a *ritual* flourish. It can even suggest perfunctory, indifferent behavior: a *ritual* good-night kiss. *Ceremonious* is most often used to describe people or their stylized behavior, while *ceremonial* is often restricted to those acts or artifacts that are part of an actual ceremony: The Japanese are never more *ceremonious* than when they enact together the *ceremonial* patterns of the bonodori dances. *Ceremonious*, in being more general, can refer to any ritualizing of behavior. If the behavior is *proper* to the occasion, the word remains neutral; if not, the word can suggest officiousness or artificiality: Her *ceremonious* attentions to the guests made relaxed conversation impossible.

Affected, **pompous**, and **punctilious** deal almost exclusively in the negative side to these words. Only *punctilious* may suggest a positive value in fastidious concern for detail: the *punctilious* attention to protocol necessary in diplomatic circles. Where this word emphasizes the precise or over-precise carrying out of a code of behavior, *affected* is more likely to refer to an inappropriate pseudo-elegance of manner, especially of speech or gesture: his *affected* English accent; her *affected* bargain-basement idea of elegance. *Affected* behavior in a man suggests artiness or effeminacy; *affected* behavior in a woman suggests the inability to distinguish between a bad or cheap imitation and the real elegance she can only affect. *Pompous* refers mostly to inflated manners of a stuffy or officious kind, and tends to be used mostly in describing men. It would be used when super-solemn rather than effeminate behavior is indicated: the droning of the *pompous* judge. One must remember that what one observer might call *affected, pompous,* or *punctilious,* another might call *formal, ceremonious,* or *ritual.* The observer's choice depends on what he considers *proper* or appropriate to the situation before him. See ARTISTIC, CONCEITED, ELEGANT, SYSTEMATIC.

Antonyms: haphazard, improvisatory, informal, natural, SPONTANEOUS.

forswear

abjure
disavow
disclaim
disown
recant
retract
take back

These words apply when a person rejects something, gives up his past behavior, or withdraws from a previously stated stand or belief. **Forswear** indicates the renunciation of past behavior; once, it referred to taking an oath to this effect, but now it can suggest an emphatic willingness to give up something completely. Most often, the word suggests an open admission of guilt or fault arising out of such behavior: a country that *forswore* future military aggression as a result of its decisive defeat; no use asking alcoholics to make high-minded oaths *forswearing* drinking. Where *forswear* can suggest moral resolve or penitence, **abjure** is more forceful in sometimes implying an angry rejection; it also referred once to renunciation under oath, but less often applies in this way now: a union official who *abjured* mediation as a solution to the dispute, especially considering the unwillingness of management to negotiate; bitter disappointments that made him *abjure* marriage in favor of a series of affairs.

Disavow and **disclaim** are now most commonly used to deny complicity or responsibility; thus both contrast with *forswear,* where an admission of guilt is often implied. *Disavow* once could involve a formal oath; now it more often points to a refusal to acknowledge something as valid or an insistence that no connection exists between one's own stand and that of another. [The candidate *disavowed* completely the statement that had been attributed to him by newsmen; The board *disavowed* the action of the executive and denied that his promises were binding on the company.] *Disclaim* can also function as a denial of responsibility, but its special point is the giving up of a right or title that might be offered in one's own behalf. [He *disclaimed* all complicity in the assassination plot; The company *disclaimed* any interest in the disputed land, even though the oldest deeds bore its name.]

Disown at its most general can suggest any sort of abandonment: The bureau *disowned* the project after the poor showing it made during its first year in operation. The word is often used in a special way, however, referring to the total rejection of a disliked person, often a near relative: a father who *disowned* his son and wrote him out of his will.

The remaining words all deal with a retreat from previously stated positions. **Take back** is the most informal of all these words, applying to an apologetic withdrawal of anything one has said previously. [His friend kept him pinned to the floor until he *took back* the insult; She immediately *took back* her accusation once she saw how wrong she had been.] **Retract** can apply to the same situation, often indicating a formal, official, or public statement. [He threatened to sue unless his opponent *retracted* the libelous allegation; The defendant *retracted* his confession, claiming that it had been coerced.] **Recant** once indicated the solemn *retracting* of a heresy by a former adherent: Witches were required to *recant* publicly or be hanged. It still applies to the repudiation of doctrine or ideology and is more forceful than *retract* in suggesting a total *disavowing* or abject capitulation, including an admission of past guilt and an implied promise to *forswear* the error in the future: those who *recanted* Communism after the infamous nonaggression pact. See ABSTAIN, FORGO, RELINQUISH.

Antonyms: ACKNOWLEDGE, ASSERT, *claim, uphold.*

fragile

brittle
frail
frangible
friable

These words refer to things easily broken. **Fragile**, beyond this general meaning, may suggest weakness or delicacy as well: a *fragile* teacup; the shipping of *fragile* materials; her *fragile* health; a lovely, *fragile* embroidery of flower motifs. **Frail** carries its own implication of slenderness or enfeeblement, as well as of breakability or weakness: a *frail* scaffold; *frail* columns bearing the architrave; made *frail* by persisting bouts of malaria. The noun *frail* is a slang term for a young woman or girl, regarded as a member of the weaker sex.

Brittle, like *fragile*, need not suggest slightness or slenderness, and it is also less apt than either of the previous words to indicate weakness or delicacy of construction. It refers to any hard material that tends to shatter easily under a direct impact: Glass is *brittle*; choosing building stones less *brittle* than marble or granite. More metaphorically, it contrasts sharply with the softness that may be implied by *frail*, suggesting instead a hard, brusque manner or appearance: giving him a *brittle*, contemptuous reply.

The remaining pair of words are considerably more formal than the foregoing and are also much more specific in meaning. **Frangible** may be used only to indicate breakability; but more relevantly here, it is often applied to materials specifically designed to be broken: a *frangible* capsule of ammonia that is broken and held under the fainting person's nose. **Friable** is even more restricted in meaning, referring exclusively to materials that can be easily crumbled: sandstone slabs that are not *brittle* but tend to be *friable*. Occasionally the word can refer to anything vulnerable to being worn down: topsoil made less *friable* by the planting of trees. See BREAK (v.), FLIMSY, WEAK.

Antonyms: *elastic, flexible,* MALLEABLE, *strong,* SUPPLE, *tough.*

fragment

remnant
scrap
shred

These words refer to a small part or piece separated from a larger whole. **Fragment** stresses breakage. In a literal sense, a *fragment* is a broken piece or shard: Archeologists discovered *fragments* of a marble column; a prehistoric man imaginatively reconstructed from bone *fragments*. Where *fragment* is typically, though not always, used of a brittle substance, the other words in this set may all apply to bits and pieces of cloth or food. In a specific sense, a **remnant** is a piece of cloth left over, as from a bolt, after the final measured cutting: to buy carpet *remnants* on sale. In a general sense, it may refer to any remaining part or portion: the *remnants* of the unfinished meal. A **scrap** is a small, odd piece that has been cut, broken, or torn from a larger piece: a *scrap* of silk. *Scrap* may refer to paper as well as to cloth or food; and where *remnants* may be saved for future use, *scraps* are often disposed of. Like *scrap*, **shred** may apply to a variety of substances. A *shred* is a long and narrow piece or strip, as one torn, cut, or shaved off lengthwise: *shreds* of carrot in a salad; *shreds* of crepe paper. Used of fabric, the plural *shreds* suggests a reduction to rags and tatters: In the fight, his suit was torn to *shreds*. *Shred* may also refer to a stringlike piece of something, as food: *shredded* wheat.

All of these words have extended, metaphorical uses. *Fragment* may designate any part incomplete in itself, existing, considered, perceived, or treated apart from a larger, inclusive context. *Fragments* may be all that remain of the work of an ancient poet. On the other hand, a *fragment* of a novel may be a piece of writing going up to the point where the writer broke off, leaving the conceptual whole uncompleted. *Fragment* may also refer to an isolated bit or part of anything abstract or immaterial. [Even the greatest scholar knows only a *fragment* of all there is to know; He overheard *fragments* of their conversation.] In a broad sense, *remnant* may mean a remaining trace or vestige of anything: *remnants* of early Indian settlements; a penniless aristocrat jealously guarding the *remnants* of past glory. It may also refer to a small remaining number of people: the last tattered *remnants* of the defeated regiment. *Scrap* and *shred* may apply to any particle, or to the smallest amount: our last *shred* of hope; not a *shred* of evidence or *scrap* of proof. See DISCARD, PART.

Antonyms: totality, whole.

frantic

delirious
frenetic
frenzied
furious
hectic

These words refer to extreme states of confused and disordered action. **Frantic** is the most general in that it does not of itself suggest the reason for the extreme state: *frantic* with fear; a *frantic* dash for the departing train. The word does suggest desperation and ineffective haste; it also may stress action taken under extreme pressure: the *frantic* pace of the big cities. **Hectic** is specific in exclusively stressing this last sense of *frantic*. The note of desperation is not necessarily present, however, and the word may simply refer hyperbolically to a rush of events: those *hectic* days after the first discovery of gold; the *hectic* traffic during rush hours. **Frenetic** also relates to this sense of *frantic*; it may suggest, however, suspense and excitement rather than the desperation of *frantic* or the busy swiftness of *hectic*: the *frenetic* last minutes of the tied basketball game; the *frenetic* race against the printer's deadline.

Both *hectic* and *frenetic* have roots or older uses that refer to a feverish physical illness. Only **delirious**, however, would now be pertinent in this context, since it can literally suggest the confused mental state resulting from a fever. In other uses, it escapes the specific situation of physical illness, referring instead to wild excitement; but it still hyperbolically suggests a confused, helpless, or disordered mental state: the grandstand crowd that was flushed with victory and *delirious* with joy; the *delirious* new dances that emphasize self-isolation and dehumanizing incoherence. *Frantic*, used in a favorable sense, compares with *delirious* here. As a term of approbation, it may stress a wild aliveness or a joyfully giddy whirl: a *frantic* party; The music was *frantic*.

Frenzied intensifies the note of desperation in *frantic*; it suggests a person completely out of control, one who is goaded or driven by external or internal pressures to act in a completely disorganized way: the charging bull, *frenzied* by frequent woundings; the rioters shouting *frenzied* accusations. **Furious**, by contrast, suggests a fierceness of behavior stemming mainly from anger. The word is not nearly so intense, however, as these other words. A person might be *furious*, but not give the slightest sign of his emotional state; or he might give vent to his *furious* anger, but still remain in control of himself: his cold but *furious* summation to the jury. The word may also merely suggest haste, like *frantic* or *hectic*: fast and *furious*; the *furious* rapids above the waterfall. See ANGER, FRENZY, PSYCHOTIC.

Antonyms: IMPERTURBABLE, SLOW, TRANQUIL, *unhurried.*

These words refer to extreme states of mental agitation, craving, disorder, or abnormality. **Frenzy** is the most general of these in stressing extreme agitation of any sort for whatever reason: in a *frenzy* to meet his deadline. Usually, the word suggests an actual acting out of the mental state in rapid but possibly disordered movements: the *frenzy* with which they struggled to put out the fire raging through the building. Also, the word suggests a given spurt or seizure of emotion that goads one into action, rather than a steady or constant state: the *frenzy* of activity during harvest time. When the word refers to emotional imbalance rather than hyperbolically indicating frantic effort, the emotions suggested include hate, anger, terror, or other negative responses to externals: driven by a cold *frenzy* to kill his opponent. **Mania** in one of its particulars contrasts strongly with this suggestion of negative response in *frenzy*, since it can refer to an extreme liking or craving for something: a *mania* for collecting rare books. Furthermore, a *mania* may be present over a long period of time without necessarily being acted out: never having indulged his secret *mania* for camping outdoors. In a psychiatric context, the word is used more strictly to refer to a mental disorder in which one is pervaded with a sense of well-being but acts in excessive and deranged ways: the *mania* that alternates with melancholy in the typical manic-depressive.

Where *frenzy* may suggest angry outbursts and *mania* a continual craving, **hysteria** suggests emotional seizures of grief or fear as expressed by uncontrolled sobbing: the *hysteria* of many aboard the sinking ship. Uncontrolled laughter is also a possible result of *hysteria*, although such laughter would hardly stem from even an illusory happiness. Psychiatrically, the word refers to an abnormal condition that results from nervous malfunction or sexual repression and that is characterized by violent emotional paroxysms and disturbances in the sensory and motor functions: the crippled woman whose classic case of *hysteria* set Freud to devising his psychoanalytic theories.

Delirium indicates a deranged state that may be the by-product of fever, epilepsy, or alcoholism, or the primary effect of narcotic or psychedelic drugs. The word may suggest agitation like *frenzy*, but it does not necessarily suggest any physical activity whatsoever; it does indicate a rambling or hallucinating mind: a *delirium* in which he thought he had stepped out of his body and looked back on it. More loosely, the word can refer to any feverish state or nightmare-ridden sleep: a *delirium* of troubled dreams from which he awoke in a cold sweat. Hyperbolically, *delirium* is sometimes used to indicate uncontrollable excitement, wild emotion, or frenzied rapture: a *delirium* of joy. See DELUSION, FRANTIC, PSYCHOTIC, UPSET.

These words all refer to a close or informal relationship with another person, distinguished on one hand from formal business relationships and on the other from closer love or family relationships. **Friend** in Shakespearean England meant one's mistress. Now, of course, it has lost this sexual meaning completely and means simply a person one is fond of and chooses to associate with. A business associate, one's spouse, or a member of one's family all may or may not be one's *friend*, while a *friend*, conversely, may or may not be a person one would wish to work with or live with. An **acquaintance** is a person one has met and sees occasionally with cordiality but without intimacy: *acquaintances* who were destined never to become *friends*. **Companion** is ambiguous. It may suggest the closeness of *friend*: my constant *companion*. Or it may

frenzy

delirium
hysteria
mania

friend

acquaintance
buddy
companion
comrade

friend
(continued)

confidant
crony
intimate

suggest the casual association of *acquaintance*: my *companions* on the ocean liner. In either case, it stresses the physical presence of the person referred to; in the latter case, the relationship might be controlled strictly by chance or necessity, without even the implied cordiality of *acquaintance*.

The rest of these words relate to the closeness of *friend*, each with a unique overtone that implies its own particular kind of closeness. **Intimate** suggests inseparable and affectionate friendship; it is less frequently used in this sense now, however, because the sexual reference of the word in another context obtrudes here where no note of sexuality was originally intended. **Comrade** has also suffered because of the obtrusion of another meaning of the word. Originally used for a man's male *friend*, with jolliness and heartiness as overtones, it has lost out to its specific use as a form of address among members of the Communist Party: Prince Hal's bawdy *comrades*; his *comrades* on the revolutionary council that governed the country.

Crony is now a more widely used informal word for a close *friend* than either *intimate* or *comrade*, but it has a strong colloquial tang and implies the gossipy closeness of a clique: his *cronies* at the club. Its common form, "old *crony*," suggests a relationship of long standing based on reminiscence: old *cronies* who on Saturday nights relived the major battles of World War II. Many slang words exist to describe close *friends*; the most common word of the moment may be **buddy**, partially replacing such choices as mate, chum, and pal: my *buddy* at college. The frequency with which words for a male *friend* rise into and fall from favor perhaps suggests an embarrassment over the affectionate side of friendship and a continuing search for the referent whose neutral and casual tone will be considered uncompromising in its manliness.

Confidant compares with *crony* in suggesting an exchange of gossip as the staple of a friendship. Where *crony* more commonly refers to a man's male friend, however, *confidant* refers more often to a woman's female *companion*. A further implication suggests that the talk exchanged between *confidants* is not so much reminiscence as personal secrets. [Over the years, her cleaning woman became her most trusted *confidant*.] See ACCOMPLICE, ASSISTANT, ASSOCIATE.

Antonyms: antagonist, OPPONENT.

frighten

scare
startle
terrify

These words mean to fill with fear or apprehension. **Frighten** is the most general word, having the widest range of use. It often indicates a fear of physical harm, but it may also apply to fears rooted in emotion or arising from imagination. In an immediate sense, a person is *frightened* by a cause of fear addressed directly and suddenly to the senses. He may react physically in a number of negative ways — shivering, shuddering, freezing, fainting, screaming, running, hiding, having a heart attack. At one extreme, being *frightened* may involve only a brief pang or flutter of fear: *frightened* by a strange noise in the middle of the night. At the other extreme, it may imply dread or terror that paralyzes thought, motion, or response, leaving one in a state of shock: a pedestrian crossing absent-mindedly against the light, *frightened* into immobility by an onrushing car. *Frighten* is also used to indicate a fearful, apprehensive state of mind: The prospect of being deserted by her husband deeply *frightened* her.

Scare is close to *frighten* in that it can imply either sudden, unnerving fear or a fearful, uneasy state. Even more strongly than *frighten*, it stresses a reflex physical reaction, whether literal or figurative: *scared* stiff. But *scare* is a more informal word than *frighten* and may suggest a milder or more superficial form of fear. Unlike *frighten*, it is a child's word, and it emphasizes the immediacy of fear, whatever the cause. [He is *scared* of the dark; Our approach *scared* the rabbit and he ran.] *Scare* is also often used to suggest the deliberate stimulation of fear, as in games, teasing, initiation, practical jokes, or other forms of amusement, whether harmless or dangerous: a *scary* movie; to *scare* children with a ghost story. [I *scared* you, didn't I?; The stunt pilot *scared* his passenger half to death with his daredevil feats.]

Startle stresses the element of sudden surprise, usually involving an involuntary reaction to an unexpected stimulus. A *startled* person may gasp, jump, draw back, or make a quick, jerky movement and then freeze. [Oh! You *startled* me — I didn't see you come in; *startled* by a rabbit running across his path] In another sense, *startle* may simply indicate an inner, intellectual surprise at something unexpected: *startled* by their daughter's request but trying hard not to show it.

Terrify is the strongest of these words, suggesting extreme, overwhelming fear that is close to panic: The violence of the storm *terrified* the sailors. The word may be an intensification of *frighten* in the sense of fear that paralyzes all the faculties, physical and mental: too *terrified* to speak. But it may also suggest wild, frenzied activity aimed at escaping a threatening situation: *terrified* people trying to get out of a burning building. In a looser sense, *terrify* is sometimes used hyperbolically to imply intimidation or nervous agitation: *terrified* by the exam; *terrified* that she would be late. See AFRAID, FEAR, INTIMIDATE.

Antonyms: calm, comfort, quiet, soothe, tranquilize.

These words all refer to movement that is high-spirited, zestful, and exuberant. **Frisk** suggests quick, playful, eager movements: dogs *frisking* about in the courtyard; letting the children *frisk* and scramble all day on the beach. The emphasis of **frolic** is close to that of *frisk*, but it stresses even more a playful, joyous activity: a playground where children skip rope and roller-skate and generally *frolic* without a worry in the world. *Frolic*, furthermore, can apply to a whole series of actions marked by joy, whereas *frisk* tends to suggest specific individual movements.

Caper and **gambol** are like *frisk* in indicating certain kinds of movement. *Caper* is the most specific of these, suggesting a dancelike way of jumping or leaping with a lively, bounding motion: teenagers *capering* around their beach fire far into the night; a nanny goat and her *capering* kids. *Gambol* suggests an impulsive series of skipping, bounding, or jerking movements that may seem unsteady, uneven, or erratic: lambs *gamboling* in the meadow after their more sedate mother ewe. See PLAYFUL, SKIP.

Antonyms: mope, sulk.

These words, which are alike in being both nouns and verbs, are comparable in their denotation of the deliberate or involuntary distortion of a person's facial expression because of displeasure, annoyance, pain, or the like. **Frown** is the most familiar word. As visually perceived, a *frown* involves a knitting, contracting, or wrinkling of the brows. As an expression, a *frown* can be a conscious or unconscious indication of displeasure. [The instructor *frowned* with annoyance when a student fell asleep during his lecture.] Mostly, though, a facial *frown* is involuntary. It can be a simple reaction to strong light: Many people who cannot wear sunglasses develop deep creases in their foreheads from *frowning*.

frisk

caper
frolic
gambol

frown

grimace
pout
scowl

A *frown* can also be the result of deep concentration or thought. [The novel was very amusing, but it required so much attention that I often found myself *frowning* when I should have laughed.] In a figurative sense, however, *frowning* registers disapproval or distaste: to *frown* upon overindulgence in food or drink.

The word with the most extensive application is **grimace**. A *grimace* is a distortion of the features, either habitual or momentary, that is caused by some feeling or impulse. It is usually ugly and uncontrollable, as when it is caused by pain or annoyance. [The agonizing pain of arthritis gave his face a constant *grimace*; A *grimace* appeared on the storekeeper's face every time a child approached the shelf of fragile articles.] But a *grimace* can be a deliberate attempt to provoke laughter, as when someone "makes a face": When the comedian's lines fell flat, he resorted to *grimacing* to get laughter from his audience.

Although **pout** can refer to a general sullenness of behavior, it more often is like *frown* in its designation of a special facial expression. *Pout* means to push out the lips, as in displeasure or ill humor. It is sometimes used in describing adults, but usually *pout* suggests the behavior of a child. [The little girl *pouted* all afternoon because her mother had refused to buy her a new dress.] A **scowl** is a lowering of the brows, much like a *frown*. It can indicate the same kind of displeasure or annoyance that a *frown* does. But the emotions that generate a *scowl* are usually stronger than those that produce a *frown*. There is a strong suggestion of anger, a threatening quality, and certainly an air of sullenness in a *scowl*. [His *scowl* hinted at the menace that lay behind his carefully modulated voice and calm demeanor.] See FOLD.

Antonyms: SMILE.

full-fledged

finished
perfected
seasoned

These adjectives are comparable when applied to that which has reached maturity or completion. **Full-fledged** is the most colorful word. Its literal reference is to a bird whose wing feathers are fully grown, enabling it to fly. The noun *fledgling* is applied to a young bird that has just grown enough feathers for flight; and by extension, it designates a person who is inexperienced or immature. But *full-fledged* stresses accomplishment, implying that a training or developing period is past and that full, independent status has been attained: a *full-fledged* teacher as opposed to a teacher trainee; a *full-fledged* doctor as opposed to an intern; A *full-fledged* pilot is one who has finished his flight training and has won his wings.

Seasoned goes beyond *full-fledged*, suggesting not only qualification but maturity or experience. Applied to timber, it indicates a drying or hardening process whereby the wood is made more suitable for use. Used of persons, it implies the development of expert skills and professional reliability through long practice: a *seasoned* ball club; a *seasoned* trouper, able to go on with the show despite laryngitis; a drill sergeant who took raw recruits and turned them into *seasoned* troops. A *seasoned* politician is one who has become astute and adroit in practical politics through having weathered many campaigns.

Finished stresses polish and resulting elegance. *Finished* furniture has a stained and polished surface. An artist with a *finished* technique has polished his style to an ultimate degree. A *finished* musician, as contrasted with a merely competent one, has refined his skills and has achieved excellence. **Perfected** is close to *finished* but is more emphatic in stressing consummate mastery or faultless excellence: A *perfected* technique is the mark of a virtuoso. See ATTAINMENT, EXQUISITE, FINISH,

MATURE (adj.), PERFECT, REACH.
   Antonyms: apprentice, callow, fledgling, immature, inexperienced, raw, undeveloped, unfledged, unseasoned.

These words refer to acts that give impetus to something already under way. **Further** is the most neutral of these in indicating any sort of action or effect, intentional or not, whether stemming from the primary agent involved or from an outside person, force, or factor: needing a rich patron to *further* his career; a pleasant voice that, without his realizing it, *furthered* the good impression he made on other people. The word can as easily be applied to undesirable developments: crisis conditions that *furthered* the spreading of hysterical rumors. **Advance** has more force than *further* and thus is useful for stressing intentional and decisive effort to *further* something desirable: selfless patriots who *advance* the cause of freedom. Despite these positive overtones, the word can be used, with the same increase in force, for undesirable developments: malnutrition that only *advanced* the progress of the disease. Here, in fact, the word suggests the speeding up of a harmful process. *Advance* does not carry this added weight in some of its milder uses, where it simply indicates a moving forward, putting forward, or giving beforehand: armies *advancing* through the city; *advancing* his suggestion timidly; *advancing* part of next week's allowance.
   Contribute contrasts sharply with the foregoing by suggesting secondary factors that give helpful but not crucial assistance to something solidly under way. *Further* and *advance* can conceivably suggest aid without which no more forward movement would result. This is far less true of *contribute*: recalling the lucky accidents that had *contributed* to her hard-earned success. The secondary factors suggested by the word, however, may derive from intentional or fortuitous acts or from established characteristics of the subject involved, as well as from external causes: internal weaknesses that *contributed* to the empire's rapid decline. **Implement** is a fad word in governmental or sociological parlance for the act of making more effective those arrangements that exist in theory, though not always in fact: taking steps to *implement* the long-standing ban against press censorship. Sometimes, the word seems to suggest the putting into effect of newly established programs, or the enforcement of decisions that have been newly arrived at: *implementing* the new civil rights laws. See ENCOURAGE, GO, HELP.
   Antonyms: DELAY, HINDER, *prevent, sidetrack.*

further

advance
contribute
implement

G

These words all mean to come or bring together into an organized body or group. In their transitive uses, **gather** emphasizes the act of bringing widely scattered things to one place, and **collect** suggests discriminating selection: to *collect* stamps; to *gather* wildflowers. When used of people or animals, *gather*, and less frequently *collect*, suggest some degree of necessity or compulsion: to *gather* refugees into one place. In intransitive uses *gather* and *collect* are often used interchangeably. [Autograph seekers *gathered* (or *collected*) around the movie star wherever she went;

gather

assemble
collect
congregate

gather

(continued)

convene

mass

muster

After the stirring sermon, parishioners *collected* (or *gathered*) around the minister to congratulate him.] But *gather* suggests a group formed by a more random process than *collect*. *Collect* usually emphasizes a gradual process of accumulation, often one by one, whereas *gather* may be used to describe the spontaneous forming of a group. [A few homeless beggars *collected* around the blaze for warmth; A crowd immediately *gathered* around the man stricken on the sidewalk.]

Assemble refers to people or organizations and suggests their coming together for some joint purpose, though not necessarily a prearranged one: to *assemble* a convention to nominate a candidate; Congress *assembled* for a summer session to catch up on lagging legislation. **Congregate** suggests a more spontaneous or haphazard coming together. [People *congregated* on balconies to catch a glimpse of the passing celebrity; Students *congregated* under the dean's window to protest a school decision.]

To **convene** is to come together or meet in a body. It is a formal word and applies particularly to the *assembling* of a formally organized body of people: A scientific congress *convened* to discuss the effects of nuclear testing on human health.

Mass means to *assemble* in great numbers: troops *massed* for an attack; Britons *massing* in the streets on Coronation Day. **Muster** is generally restricted to military use, and is applied to parts or units of a force that come or are brought together. [Recruits *muster* for a roll call; a fighting force that *mustered* for a final attack] *Muster*, like *gather*, *collect*, and *assemble*, can be used of qualities or data as well as of things. [He could barely *muster* the strength to raise his head from the pillow; to *muster* facts; to *gather* impressions on a trip to Europe; to *collect* anecdotes in preparation for a speech; to *assemble* data for a legal presentation] See ACCUMULATE, SUMMON.

Antonyms: disband, SCATTER, *separate.*

gauche

boorish

maladroit

tactless

uncouth

unpolished

These words refer to a graceless mode of social behavior. **Gauche** refers to someone or his actions when they do not conform to the standards of the social group in which he finds himself; he may, consequently, be considered unsophisticated, vulgar, or ill-bred by the group: certain American mannerisms that would be thought *gauche* in England. The term may be used as a subjective evaluation of quite innocent or harmless but intentional behavior. In the case of **maladroit**, the questionable behavior is inadvertent but results in injured feelings or resentment because it is ill-timed or in offensive taste: wanting to bite his own tongue for having made such a *maladroit* remark. Also, *gauche* might more commonly describe the whole picture someone presents socially, whereas *maladroit* more often refers to some particular slip or breach of taste.

Tactless is closer to *maladroit* than to *gauche*, but it may refer not only to a momentary slip but to an ingrained habit of being thoughtless or inconsiderate of the feelings of others: a *tactless* reference to her recent divorce; a thoroughly *tactless* person who never knew when to keep still. **Unpolished** concentrates on *gauche* behavior that results specifically from a lack of good breeding or sophistication; the word, furthermore, is not necessarily negative in its evaluation: a man whose shoes and manners were both noticeably *unpolished*; an *unpolished* simplicity of speech that was refreshing after the affectations of his city friends. **Uncouth** stresses a total lack of social experience and sophistication, but with no mitigating possibilities for a positive evaluation. It also implies harsh, offensive, or rude behavior: The *uncouth* manners of the waiter distressed her. *Uncouth* has an old-fashioned ring to it nowadays, and is often used with an undertone of irony at the expense of the excessively sensitive or snobbish: She regarded all men as vaguely *uncouth*. **Boorish** is the harshest of all these words in its disapproval. The word makes no attempt to explain away disgusting or vile behavior in terms of inexperience; it simply condemns. The word suggests manners that are fawning, sycophantic, surly, or indelicate: a *boorish* lout who accosted her and insisted upon seeing her home. See CLUMSY, VULGAR.

Antonyms: adroit, CONSIDERATE, POLITE, URBANE.

These words refer to tasteless displays of overdone finery or decoration, or to brazen, flaunting behavior. Of these words, **gaudy** is the least negative in tone, but still points to excessive use of decoration or to any sort of vividness that approaches vulgarity: *gaudy* make-up; the *gaudy* neon signs of Times Square. The word may not imply disapproval at all in some circumstances, suggesting a wild or irresistible abandonment to spectacular designs: the *gaudy* lights of the carnival; the *gaudy* peacock. **Flashy** is an informal substitute for *gaudy*, referring to anything deliberately chosen out of exuberantly vulgar ostentation: *flashy* costume jewelry; a taste for *flashy* clothes that caused giggling fits among the other girls in the office. This word, too, can function without necessarily implying disapproval: a *flashy* sports car that was the envy of the whole neighborhood; *flashy* beachwear designed for uninhibited summer fun.

With **garish**, the emphasis is wholly on extremely distasteful ostentation and more especially on a chaotic esthetic effect resulting from the disharmony of elements in a total design: green eye shadow that would have been thought *garish* in a bordello; the *garish* combination of striped pants, plaid jacket, and a clashing print shirt. The word can also refer to loud, coarse manners: other patrons who left because of their *garish* behavior.

Meretricious and **tawdry** both emphasize decoration that is made of cheap or worthless materials. With *meretricious*, the stress is on overuse, especially of phony or trashy gimmicks: *meretricious* gewgaws that made the living room look like a junk shop. The word has a special use to refer to esthetic dishonesty or propaganda appeals: novels that make *meretricious* use of sex to boost sales; *meretricious* campaign promises. *Tawdry* may, most simply, suggest cheapness combined with showiness in taste: a *tawdry* plastic tablecloth; a *tawdry* flowered sofa already beginning to fall apart. Used less concretely, the word may suggest unsavoriness or such an extreme abasement of taste as to be degraded and degrading: *tawdry* taverns where soldiers on leave could find girls on the loose; *tawdry* magazines that peddle filth, scandal, and sleazy amusement to eager audiences. See INEXPENSIVE, SHOWY.

Antonyms: MODEST, plain, quiet, simple, tasteful.

A **gem** is a cut and polished piece of mineral substance, either precious or semiprecious in quality. These mineral pieces are called **stones**, a term used especially by jewelers and one which can be applied to the mineral pieces in either their original or cut and polished form. Diamonds, emeralds, and rubies are precious *stones*; jade, amethyst, and garnet are semiprecious. **Jewel** can be used interchangeably with *gem*, although it more often designates a precious than a semiprecious *stone*. *Jewels* are cut and polished and usually set into a brooch, necklace, or other article of personal adornment. The article itself can be referred to as a *jewel*, but is probably more often described as **jewelry**. *Jewelry*

gaudy

flashy
garish
meretricious
tawdry

gem

ice
jewel
jewelry
rock
stone

is an inclusive word that embraces not only *gems* and *jewels* that have been set but also those articles of small worth known as costume *jewelry*: rings, tiepins, etc., manufactured with inexpensive metals, plastic, or imitation *stones*.

Gem and *jewel* are both used figuratively and informally to describe a person or thing that is valuable or highly thought of. A *gem* is something which has intrinsic worth, a *jewel* something which one prizes for personal as well as objective reasons. [That Daumier is a *gem* of a lithograph; It's a *jewel* of a restaurant, the chef's salad is divine.] People characterized as *jewels* usually have done something to warrant the appellation. [My nursemaid is a *jewel*; she cares for the children as if they were her own.] People who are *gems* may be *jewels* as well, but they might be so named simply because of some prominent trait in their nature, even an eccentric one: Miss Skinner is a perfect *gem*, the prototype of the spinster schoolmarm.

Ice and **rock** are slang terms. *Ice* means diamonds, but is used loosely to mean valuable *jewelry* of any kind. A *rock* is a precious *stone*, especially a large diamond.

general

accepted
common
popular
public
universal

These words all imply wide appeal, use, influence, and the like. **General** means current among the majority of the persons, things, or class specified: the *general* opinion. A *general* favorite is one widely liked. **Common** applies to many or a large part; a *common* belief is one widely shared. **Universal** applies to all or to the whole of a class of things; a *universal* truth holds in all instances. [It may be said that good health is a *general* condition, that occasional sickness is *common*, and that death is *universal*.]

Accepted means commonly recognized, believed, or approved: Wearing a jacket and tie to a good restaurant is an *accepted* convention. While *accepted* emphasizes willing compliance and approval, **popular**, as here considered, points to its etymological meaning "of the people," i.e. the common people, and thus emphasizes source rather than extent of recognition: a *popular* myth that the bite of the tarantula causes madness; Watching TV is a *popular* pastime.

Public pertains to people at large or to the community. In its suggestion of an organized or quasi-organized body of people, *public* differs from the other words here considered. [*Public*-opinion polls indicate a *general* feeling among the people that *accepted* standards of behavior are being deliberately flouted by long-haired hippies and the like.] See NORMAL, PREVALENT, SINCERE, USUAL.

Antonyms: QUEER, SPECIFIC, *uncommon*, UNPARALLELED, UNUSUAL.

generous

bountiful
lavish
liberal
magnanimous

These words refer either to a considerate, tolerant person who readily gives of himself or his money or to large helpings or sizable offerings. **Generous**, the most general, suggests kind concern and willingness to help others in tangible ways: a teacher *generous* with the time he devotes to after-class conferences; the *generous* habit of sharing his money with less fortunate friends. It can also suggest tolerance rather than narrow fault-finding: *generous* in his estimates of the plays he reviews. When used of a helping of food or an offer of any kind, it suggests an amount more than the receiver might have expected: a *generous* slice of beef; a *generous* offer to take a lower down payment than usual. The word is sometimes used ironically to suggest its opposite: *generous* with his criticisms, frugal with his praise.

More formal than *generous*, **magnanimous** is more likely to refer to well-intentioned kindness than to monetary generosity. In this sense, it may suggest courteous consideration given equally to everyone as a matter of principle, whereas *generous* is more likely to suggest a spontaneous impulse to help a particular person not so much out of principle as out of fondness: so *magnanimous* that he tended to forget that not everyone in the club shared his own unselfish motives for belonging. *Magnanimous*, in fact, can sometimes suggest an unconscious condescension or paternalism toward inferiors: giving *magnanimous* approval to her hopeless efforts at balancing their checking account. *Magnanimous* would not be used to describe a *generous* serving, but when used of an offer, it suggests restrained formality, possibly involving better terms than the receiver deserves: a *magnanimous* offer to buy the painting in spite of its imperfections.

Bountiful is still more formal than *magnanimous* and in the sense of *generous* is now mostly reserved for references to the Deity: *Bountiful* Lord. It occurs in a satiric phrase referring to charity that is condescending, self-righteous, and smug: playing the lady *bountiful*. In more common uses, it suggests productivity, and is often used for rhetorical effect: a *bountiful* harvest; the *bountiful* land.

Liberal and **lavish** most often refer to large servings or offers or to sizable expenditures of money: a sundae with a *liberal* sprinkling of nuts; a *liberal* trade-in offer on your old car; a *liberal* spender. *Lavish* goes beyond *liberal* in suggesting an excessive or unduly large amount or degree. In some senses it can suggest an excessive generosity adopted pretentiously for show: *lavish* displays of affection. In the stricter sense of *generous*, *liberal* can be used of a person, but here it suggests a permissive, easygoing nature: a doctor who was *liberal* about breaking rules when it might buck up a patient's morale. Sometimes the word can even suggest carelessness or moral flabbiness: a *liberal* disregard for fine ethical distinctions. See BENEVOLENCE, PREVALENT.

Antonyms: chary, GREEDY, *niggardly, parsimonious, selfish, sparing, tight.*

These words all refer to innate or superior ability. **Genius**, the strongest word, is conceived as a mental power far beyond explanation in terms of heritage or education and manifests itself by exceptional originality and extraordinary intelligence, surpassing that of most intellectually superior people: the *genius* of Leonardo da Vinci, whose notebooks, written in the late 15th and early 16th centuries, include designs of flying machines, improvements in weaponry, and complicated labor-saving mechanical systems utilizing gears and pulleys, as well as detailed scientific observations in biology, geology, and other subjects. *Genius* may be applied particularly to one area: the artistic *genius* of a Picasso, whose unique achievement assures him of a dominant place in the history of modern art.

An **aptitude** is a natural or acquired ability to learn and become proficient, while a **faculty** is a particular mental skill or power. While *aptitude* suggests quickness in learning, often in gaining mastery of an academic discipline or artistic skill, *faculty* is at once more modest and more general in application, suggesting only an inhering attribute or skill. [He lacks completely the *faculty* of self-criticism; an early *aptitude* for mathematics; He demonstrated his *aptitude* for music by the ease with which he picked out melodies by ear.]

Talent is a particular and uncommon *aptitude* for some special work or activity; it is conceived of as an inborn resource that may or may not be developed. Whereas *genius* applies to general intellectual or artistic

genius

aptitude
bent
faculty
gift
instinct
knack
talent

superiority, *talent* is a specific natural endowment or **gift**: a *talent* for designing beautiful clothes for young women; a remarkable *talent* for staging and directing plays. *Genius* may also be used in the sense of special *aptitude*: to have a *genius* for turning a small investment into a successful business. *Gift* is akin to *genius* but on a lower plane: the *gift* of a poet's sensibility and verbal acumen. *Gift* emphasizes the inborn quality of a skill. Unlike *talent*, *gift* does not necessarily imply creative ability, nor even originality: a *gift* of intensely appreciating music; the *gift* of enjoying life. *Gift* may apply to any striking or remarkable personal ability or power.

Whereas *faculty* is most often used positively when applied to an interpersonal quality, *talent*, and especially *genius*, being progressively more exaggerated and figurative in such contexts, are often used negatively and emphatically, sometimes with comical effect. [He has the *faculty* of saying the right thing at the right time; He has a *talent* for saying the wrong thing at the wrong time; He has a positive *genius* for putting his foot in his mouth.]

An **instinct**, as here considered, is a natural *aptitude*, in which sense it is really an extension of its basic psychobiological meaning referring to an animal's innate tendency or response to act in ways that are essential to its development or preservation. *Instinct* usually implies innate disposition rather than *talent*. [Good salesmen know by *instinct* the best approach to take with a particular customer; He has the *instincts* of an athlete: he really goes all out to win.] *Instinct* can, however, be used of qualities that are not inborn but have been so thoroughly acquired that they seem as if they were: an *instinct* for making money; to develop an *instinct* for staying out of trouble. In this sense *instinct* is close to **knack**, which refers to an ability to do something readily and well; *knack* applies more often to social situations than to intellectual ones: a *knack* for knowing when to leave a party; Some people have the *knack* of being able to keep silent without making others feel ill at ease.

Bent refers to personal inclination or penchant; it does not necessarily imply an accompanying *aptitude*, but since it is human nature to like doing what one does well, *aptitude* and *bent* are often present in the same person. [My son has a mechanical *bent* — he's always tearing motors apart and putting them back together again; Politicians seldom have any esthetic *bent*; From his earliest years he had a literary *bent*, but never showed much *aptitude* for writing creatively.] *Bent* often suggests devotion and industry: He demonstrated his *bent* for music by practicing six hours a day. See ATTAINMENT, SKILL.

genuine

actual
authentic
real
true

These words all refer to the idea that something is in fact what it is represented to be. In this sense **genuine** is the most general of this group of words, and applies to anything having the origin, authorship, or character claimed for it: a *genuine* example of cuneiform inscription; a *genuine* painting by Goya; a *genuine* bargain. **Authentic** is often interchangeable with *genuine*: an *authentic* (or *genuine*) antique. But *authentic* emphasizes formal proof or documentation that an article is what it is claimed to be, whereas *genuine* simply asserts that the article is not spurious, adulterated, or counterfeit. [The geologists declared the fragment to be an *authentic* specimen of a rare fossil; an *authentic* Utrillo, verified by several prominent art connoisseurs; an *authentic* replica of the drawing; *genuine* silver, unmixed with baser metals]

Actual means existing in fact, not imaginary, and is synonymous with one sense of **real**: an *actual* (or *real*) event in history. *Actual*, however, need not refer to physically existent things, whereas *real* usually does in this sense: an *actual* change in the rules; It was a *real* person, not someone invented in a dream. *Real* also means being in accordance with appearance or claim, not artificial or counterfeit, and is in this sense often synonymous with *genuine*: a *real* (or *genuine*) alibi; *real* (or *genuine*) money. The emphasis on appearance, however, sometimes distinguishes *real* from *genuine*: a *real* feast (i.e. a meal having the aspect of a feast); a *real* lecher (i.e. a person having the appearance or manner of a lecher). *Genuine*, if used in these examples, would convey a more conspicuous sense of personal style and a greater degree of informality.

True means being *real* or natural: a *true* specimen; *true* gold. In many contexts it is interchangeable with *real*, and often with *genuine* as well: a *true* (or *real*) feast; a *true* (or *real* or *genuine*) solution to a problem. Note that *true* in some contexts, as in *a true alibi*, is ambiguous, in that it can mean either conforming to the facts of the matter (i.e. with the truth) or being in accordance with the appearance of a *genuine* alibi (i.e. not appearing spurious or contrived). Obviously, a *true* alibi in the latter sense may well be false in *actual* fact. See ACCURATE, EXIST, TRUTHFUL.

Antonyms: ARTIFICIAL, *fake, forged, imaginary*, SPURIOUS.

get

acquire
gain
obtain
procure

These words refer to coming into possession of something. **Get** is the most general of these, with a wide range of uses that includes every situation discussed here; it can apply as well to forceful seizure as to passive reception: The FBI always *get* their man; *getting* the joke after everyone else in the room was in hysterics. The use of *get* in idiomatic phrases is, of course, manifold and since some of these idioms may be informal, some feel the need to replace it wherever possible with **obtain**. *Obtain* is certainly more formal, but as a mere substitute for *get* it often may sound high-flown or pretentious: *getting* her to sign the paper; *obtaining* her signature on the paper; urging people over 40 to *get* a physical checkup at least once a year; recommending that mature persons *obtain* a physical examination annually if not more frequently. *Obtain* is more precisely used in formal contexts where the stress is on the seeking out of something; here, *get* might not indicate clearly enough this intended meaning: an unmanned spacecraft that could *obtain* soil samples from the moon and return to earth with them.

Gain goes beyond *obtain* to indicate greater effort in the seeking process; it can indicate forceful seizure, as in the military sense: *gaining* the victory after a bloody battle. The word can also suggest an increase in something already possessed, or a piece-by-piece process of *obtaining* something: *gaining* additional honors with each new book he published; *gaining* ground on the speeding car. **Acquire** points to a piecemeal process of possession that is continuous and often slow: *acquiring* a controlling interest in the company over several years of stock purchases; assiduously *acquiring* a fine collection of impressionist paintings. As in these cases, the word is often used in a context of financial transactions. *Acquire* can also suggest the effort or exposure required to gain less tangible things, as in the learning process: wishing to *acquire* a speaking knowledge of French; surprised that he had actually *acquired* a taste for artichokes.

Procure implies maneuvering to possess something, suggesting involved, contrived, or even shady dealings. Thus the word's tone ranges from neutrality to disapproval: the complicated requisition forms by which the Quartermaster Corps *procures* needed supplies; a system of *procuring* favors from party hacks and ward heelers. Most specifically, the word can pertain to the act of pimping or pandering, that is, *obtaining* women to gratify the lust of others: a man who *procured* prostitutes for sailors in waterfront bars. This meaning of the word is often present as an overtone in its other uses. See ACCUMULATE, COME, REACH.

Antonyms: give up, let go, lose, RELINQUISH.

ghost

apparition
phantom
shade
specter
spirit
spook
wraith

These words refer to supernatural manifestations or appearances. **Ghost** is the general word for the appearance of a dead person in the semblance of his living form: the *ghost* of Hamlet's father. Once, the word could refer more widely to the soul or any nonmaterial being, but this survives only in a few phrases: the Holy *Ghost*; give up the *ghost*. **Wraith** contrasts with *ghost* in specifically indicating the *ghost*like manifestation of a person still alive but about to die: The *wraith* of her husband, long missing in action, appeared to her in a dream. The word can, however, refer less precisely to other supernatural manifestations. Metaphorically, it can refer to someone who is thin or to anything faint: the *wraith* of a child who sat in the refugee hospital; a *wraith* of smoke lazing up from the chimney.

Shade now sounds either high-flown or affected, except in the humorous exclamation, *shades of*, suggesting that one thing is unfortunately reminiscent of another: "*Shades of* Cézanne!" she said with a yawn, after looking over her friend's new painting. **Spook** indicates downright cynicism, skepticism, or amusement at the notion that *ghosts* exist: old maids so thwarted by life that they begin seeing *spooks* just for excitement.

Spirit is the most general word among these in the sense of indicating any sort of nonmaterial existent being; this may include the souls of living things, the *ghosts* of dead things, the essence of bodiless forms that have never been born and never died, and, in fact, the godhead itself: *spirits* of unborn children; the *spirits* assigned by Hinduism to snakes, frogs, and water buffaloes; the angelic *spirits*; the creator *Spirit* of the universe. It can also, in another sense, contrast all nonmaterial or mental life with that of matter or body: living the life of the *spirit*; afflicted both in body and *spirit*. It can also refer less metaphysically to the essence of anything: the materialistic *spirit* of the age. **Apparition** can refer to any supernatural manifestation; often it suggests a detailed or narrative vision vouchsafed to someone: an *apparition* in which Joseph was warned to take his family and flee to Egypt. It can also refer to the form seen in a vision: an *apparition* that had wings, wore a halo, and streamed with divine light. The word's point may be a sudden appearance: an *apparition* that stopped them stock-still in the midst of their flight. Often the word suggests something pleasant or beautiful, which explains its usual metaphorical point: She was a veritable *apparition* of loveliness in her new ball gown.

Specter contrasts with *apparition* in suggesting any sort of terrifying supernatural manifestation: the gruesome demon or *specter* that tormented those in the castle. Metaphorically, the word can suggest any unpleasant threat or prospect: the *specters* of want, hunger, and disease that hung over the world at mid-century. **Phantom** can apply to any manifestation, pleasant or not. Its point may often be to raise the question of whether the appearance is real or illusory: Hamlet was unable to decide whether the *phantom* was really the *ghost* of his father or merely a guise worn by the Devil to secure his damnation. Metaphorically, the word can point to any illusion, misconception, or bugbear: amputees who experience what are known as *phantom* limb phenomena; enticing the masses with the *phantom* of a future Utopia; raising the *phantom* of worldwide defeat whenever negotiations were suggested.

These words all mean to hand over freely to another. To **give** is primarily to transfer to another's possession without compensation, but the word also has many extended senses; a boxer *gives* a blow, a clock *gives* time, a delinquent child *gives* trouble. *Give* is the most general word in this group and may be used interchangeably with any of the other words listed in most contexts.

give

accord
award
confer
grant

   Award usually implies that the thing *given* is deserved, and the giver is in some sense a judge. Thus prizes are *awarded* to those who win contests, and damages are *awarded* to those who win civil lawsuits.

   Accord implies that the thing *given* either is deserved or is proper or suitable to the receiver for some other reason. Thus one may *accord* praise to those who do good deeds, but may also *accord* respect to one's superiors merely because of their status.

   To **confer** is to *give* in approval or as a reward: to *confer* knighthood; to *confer* an honorary degree.

   Grant implies that one gives something out of generosity, mercy, or a sense of justice, often in response to supplication. *Grant* points strongly to the giver's discretion to do as he pleases, and to the would-be receiver as depending utterly on that discretion: a captain who *granted* his crew a shore leave; to *grant* a favor to a friend; to *grant* male students the privilege of entertaining women in their dormitory during certain hours of the day. See AWARD, OFFER, RELINQUISH.

   Antonyms: take back, withdraw, withhold.

These words refer to dimly lit, unpleasant places or to pessimistic frames of mind. **Gloomy** is the most general of these words. In reference to places, it can suggest poor lighting: *gloomy* hallways I had to grope my way through. But it more often, now, suggests drabness: three *gloomy*, narrow rooms without a stick of furniture anywhere. In reference to a mental state, the word suggests someone who sees the hopeless side of any problem: his *gloomy* comments on the troubles they should have in clearing customs. In this context, the word has an overtone of criticism that suggests unnecessary worry. **Dreary** most appropriately describes drab surroundings rather than states of mind: escaping from a *dreary*, small-town existence. Used more loosely, the word is often meant to convey disapproval of a situation both tedious and sordid: the *dreary* machinations of corrupt politicians.

gloomy

dark
dreary
gray
murky
somber

   Somber and **murky** may both describe dimly lit surroundings: a clouded moon that made the path *somber* and forbidding; London streets made *murky* by fog. *Somber*, however, is the one word here that may have positive overtones in suggesting a restrained despair or a subdued, stark simplicity of effect: his *somber* acceptance of the bad news that stood in such sharp contrast to her wild, hysterical cries of self-pity; the novel's *somber* purity that removed it so decidedly from the charge of fashionable nihilism. The special overtones of *murky* suggest something clouded in confusing obscurity: motives that must always remain *murky* no matter how we attempt to reconstruct the actions of the killer.

   Dark and **gray** suggest a literal dimness or a *gloomy* outlook: the *dark* house; the *dark* cast of his mind; another *gray* morning of mist and rain. In referring to states of mind, however, *gray* has a special overtone of dull, unrelieved sameness: the *gray* monotony of the days behind her, the *gray* stretch of days that still lay before her. See BLEAK, DISMAL. *Antonyms:* BRIGHT, CHEERFUL.

go

advance
move
proceed
progress
rise

These words are comparable when they mean to exhibit motion or other activity in a forward or upward direction or toward some specific goal. **Go** and **move** are the most general, and include among their implications the ideas of **advance** and **rise**. *Advance* is the most explicit in indicating a forward direction, and *rise* is the most explicit in indicating an upward direction. Thus, a platoon may be ordered to *go* or to *advance* to the top of the next hill. An army may get an order to *move* or *advance* at dawn. Prices may *advance* or *rise*; a stagnant economy may be made to *move* or *advance*. A stalled automobile may be made to *go* or *move*.

To **proceed** is to begin or continue to *go* or *advance* in an orderly fashion, especially when used in the imperative. [*Proceed* to the next order of business; *Proceed* to the next crossroad.]

Progress means to *advance* or *move* toward a definite goal. [A schoolboy *progresses* toward graduation; The moon *progresses* through its successive phases.] See CLIMB, LEAVE (depart).

Antonyms: STOP (cease).

gobbledygook

claptrap
garbage
gibberish
nonsense
officialese

These words all denote writing or speech that suffers from an overuse of obscure, ponderous, or meaningless words, or that is worthless and empty of significance.

Gobbledygook is confused or even unintelligible speech or writing, especially when it is used to express a simple idea. "Do not become involved in a colloquy with the bench, but proceed without undue delay to discharge your obligation for violation of the city ordinance," is *gobbledygook* for "Don't argue with the judge — pay the fine."

Officialese is the *gobbledygook* found in legal, governmental, educational, or other formal speech or writing. "There should be implementation to meet the unmet needs of that segment of society that is socially and economically oppressed and to provide motivation for mobility away from self-demeaning indigence and morale-destroying dependence," is *officialese* for "Let's get those people off the relief rolls who are able to work." Both *gobbledygook* and *officialese* make communication difficult and dull without making it more accurate.

Gibberish emphasizes the unintelligibility of difficult or esoteric expression which may sometimes be *gobbledygook* or sometimes a terminology or a language with which one is unfamiliar. [Higher mathematics is *gibberish* to most people; The Ainus of Japan speak a *gibberish* unrelated to any other language; Those who follow the stock market reports communicate in a *gibberish* all their own.]

In the context of this discussion **nonsense** stresses language that is absurd or that lacks meaning and common sense. *Nonsense* may suggest incorrect or irrelevant remarks arising from stupidity or ignorance: His comments in class are always *nonsense*. Or it may suggest deliberate playfulness in the use of language: Many children's rhymes and play songs are charming *nonsense*.

Claptrap is a form of expression designed to attract and win popular approval by the use of cheap sensationalism or artifice. It stresses worthlessness and showiness: a piece of *claptrap* passing for a serious study of working-class life; an impassioned political speech full of *claptrap*.

Garbage, a slang term, carries stronger opprobrium than either *nonsense* or *claptrap* in that it is written or spoken language that is not only without merit but often objectionable. [She talks a lot of sentimental *garbage* about her dog having a soul; Even the most intelligent child is apt to have read a certain amount of *garbage* before he grows up.] See SLANG.

goodness

integrity
morality
probity
purity
rectitude
righteousness
virtue

Goodness has the broadest meaning of the words in this list and, as here compared, stresses inherent qualities of moral excellence and an underlying compassion. *Goodness* is applied to the Deity, to saints, and to persons whose actions are characterized by a surpassing humanity or ethical commitment.

The other words in this list are examples of moral excellence that is acquired or striven for. Of these, **morality** is the broadest word, in that it may mean moral excellence based on religious teaching or on adherence to a code of ethics. **Righteousness** is limited mostly to religious use, and means either a strict fidelity to the divine law or a code of conduct based on it. **Purity**, in this sense, is also limited in its use. It is usually found in such contexts as a life of *purity*, *purity* of motives, and the like, and implies an absence of faults rather than a positive striving for moral excellence.

Virtue is a broad word meaning moral excellence based on a conscious effort to do the right thing. Found often in religious contexts, *virtue* is also applied in connection with worldly, day-to-day actions.

Integrity, **probity**, and **rectitude** all imply a strict adherence to a stern code of ethics. *Integrity* and *probity* are based on an undeviating honesty that imputes broad *virtue* to the subject. *Rectitude* is a strict adherence to rules of right, justice, and the like, and carries a strong suggestion of self-discipline. See BENEVOLENCE, FAVORABLE, HONEST, MORAL.

Antonyms: badness, depravity, evil, foulness, immorality, WRONGDOING.

gourmet

gastronome
glutton
gourmand

These words refer to people who have an intense interest in food. **Gourmet** indicates someone who is a connoisseur of good cooking and is knowledgeable and discriminating about the niceties of food preparation and serving. The word suggests a taste for elegance and a concern for all aspects of the ritual of dining, including the selection of foods and wines that are thought to harmonize with each other: as much a *gourmet* of Indian as of Mexican or Chinese cuisine; thinking to pass himself off as a *gourmet* by criticizing the modest rosé she had chosen to accompany their seafood dinner. **Gastronome** is a more formal substitute for *gourmet* but, if anything, suggests even more expertise about everything pertaining to food: expatiating like a true *gastronome* on the effect to be obtained by spicing the filet with marjoram instead of thyme.

Gourmand suggests someone for whom the eating of food itself is the primary interest. Although the *gourmand* appreciates good cooking, he judges this more by its taste than by the canon of rules and regulations the *gourmet* or *gastronome* may be privy to: wives who treat their husbands like *gourmets* only to find them responding like *gourmands*; A *gourmand* must have originated the notion that the proof of the pudding is in the eating. **Glutton** is in sharp contrast to all these words by suggesting a person totally indifferent to the fine points of cooking and perhaps even to the taste of the food he eats. The main emphasis here is on endless appetite and the devouring of food in quantities: food so tasteless and ill-prepared that it could appeal only to a starving man or a *glutton*. The word is often used with humorous intention to describe an insatiable craving for a particular food: hot spells that turn us into *gluttons* for ice cream and watermelon. See EAT.

graphic

pictorial
picturesque
vivid

These words refer to things that have visual impact or are dramatically appealing. **Graphic** may refer as neutral description to work that uses the elements and techniques of visual design: training in all phases of the *graphic* arts. It also extends metaphorically to anything having the clarity and power of written, printed, diagrammatic, or visualized illustration: a *graphic* lesson in the pitfalls of befriending strangers; photographs that not only illustrate the article but lend it *graphic* force; giving *graphic* examples of how the two theories conflict. **Vivid** is a much more general and less specific word than *graphic*. Most strictly it suggests forceful visual representation or the use of dramatic *graphic* elements, especially color: the *vivid* colors of the painting; a self-portrait that was a *vivid* study of the sag and breakdown of flesh in old age. *Vivid* is, of course, used widely outside the visual arts for anything that has a heightened or concentrated dramatic impact: a speech denouncing his opponent in *vivid* terms; her *vivid* portrayal of Lady Macbeth.

Pictorial is often restricted to the neutrally descriptive aspect of *graphic*, referring to elements of visual design or to the fact that something is represented visually or contains pictures: *pictorial* magazines; a film director strong in handling the *pictorial* elements but weak in giving his story line any sense of momentum. It may also refer to something that calls up visual images: a fiction writer with a flair for *pictorial* description. **Picturesque** is more closely related to *vivid* in stressing things having a dramatic visual impact. The special tone of the word often suggests that a scene is thought striking because it is panoramic, quaint, strange, or unusual in some other way: Uccello's *picturesque* battle tableaux; the *picturesque* minarets of Istanbul; a *picturesque* ride on the Staten Island ferry. See DRAWING, PORTRAY.

grasp

clasp
clutch
grab
grip
seize
snatch

These verbs express the action of laying hold of things with the hands. To **grasp** is to take hold of firmly: He reached out, *grasped* my hand, and shook it. To **seize** is to take hold of suddenly, with force. [The hawk *seized* its prey with its talons; He *seized* the reins of the runaway horse.] Both *seize* and *grasp* are general in application and may be used figuratively as well as literally. [I don't *grasp* your meaning; The army *seized* power.] **Grab** is more informal, suggesting roughness in *seizing* or undue haste in getting hold of something. [He *grabbed* her arm and pulled her out of the path of the car; You may have a piece of candy, but don't *grab*.] In some contexts, both *grab* and *grasp* may imply greed. [She was greedy and *grasping*; When her uncle died, she *grabbed* everything she could get her hands on.] To **snatch** is to *grab* abruptly, with a sudden jerk; but where one may sometimes *grab* with the arms in order to hold, one *snatches* with the hands in order to take away. [Instead of *grabbing* her, the thief *snatched* her purse and ran.] When both *snatch* and *grab* mean to take, *snatch* implies greater haste and violence, suggesting urgency or desperation: Ravenous, he *snatched* the food out of my hands. *Snatch* may express the *seizing* of something one has no right to, but this is not always the case. Still, the haste of a person who *snatches* is often prompted by fear of consequences, whether he acts from good motives or bad. [She *snatched* the matches away from the child; The fireman *snatched* up the baby and carried him out of the burning house.] Both *snatch* and *grab* are also used in a more informal sense, meaning to get in what little time is available: to *grab* a bite to eat before the show; to *snatch* a few hours of sleep between performances.

Where *grasp* and *grab* mean to take hold of, *grasp* and **grip** mean to hold. A person *grasps* with a firm but moderate closure of the whole

hand. He *grips* with the strongest muscular closure of the hand that he can exert. To *grasp* is to hold firmly; to *grip* is to hold tight. [He *gripped* my hand so tight it hurt; He *gripped* the railing to pull himself up.] **Clasp** may mean to *grasp* firmly in or with the hand: The children *clasped* hands and formed a circle. Or *clasp* may mean to hold in the arms in an encircling embrace: The child *clasped* her doll protectively. A person *clasps* or **clutches** something to prevent its escape or removal; but as *grip* implies a stronger *grasping*, so *clutch* implies a stronger *clasping*: She *clutched* the doll tenaciously. *Clutch* may mean simply to *grasp* and hold firmly: the roots that *clutch*. Or both *clutch* and *grasp*, when followed by *at*, may mean to try to get hold of. A drowning man *clutches* (or *grasps*) at straws. But *clutch* implies a greater eagerness or urgency than *grasp* and may suggest downright desperation. Whether holding tight or only trying for a firm hold, the person who *clutches* feels frighteningly insecure. [She *clutched* her purse tightly, fearing that a thief might *snatch* it; He *clutched* at my arm as he fell.] See CAPTURE, CARRY.
   Antonyms: abandon, loose, release, relinquish.

These words all indicate warm feelings or expressions of gratitude. **Grateful** and **thankful** are close in meaning, but one distinction is commonly observed in that *grateful* is used to describe our feelings of gratitude to another person, and *thankful* refers to similar feelings toward divine providence, fate, or some less immediate agency. One is *grateful* for a gift or a kind word, but *thankful* for good health or fair weather. **Appreciative**, more than the other two words, indicates a demonstration of the gratitude which a person feels: a secretary who was so *appreciative* of the opportunity for advancement which her employer had given her that she worked overtime even when she was not asked to do so. See APPROVAL, ENDORSE, PRAISE.
   Antonyms: indifferent, ungrateful.

grateful

appreciative
thankful

These words refer to the burial places of the dead. **Grave** is the most general, referring to any place where a body or bodies are buried, whether completely unmarked or set off by a lavish display of costly materials: the mass *grave* outside Auschwitz; the wooden white crosses on the *graves* in Flanders fields; pyramids that were the *graves* for kings. While *grave* can also commonly be thought of as the pit or opening in earth into which a body is placed, **tomb** usually suggests some sort of man-made enclosure, whether above or below ground, constructed to house the dead; it also very often implies the existence of some sort of monument that both contains the dead person and commemorates his existence.
   While **sepulcher** can be simply a more formal word for *grave* or *tomb*, it may also suggest an above-ground house or room in which the coffins of the dead are kept; such a chamber might adjoin or be part of a church. In any case, the word tends to suggest an architectural display greater than that suggested by *tomb*. Most specifically, the word may refer to the resting place for holy relics, especially when this is near or part of a church altar. A **mausoleum** specifically stresses the splendor and lavishness of a structure designed to hold one or more coffins. It would be a more exact term than *sepulcher* for such a building.
   Both **crypt** and **vault** refer to burial chambers either wholly or partly underground. *Vault* suggests that the roof of such a chamber is arched, but this is not necessarily the case. *Crypt* is commonly used specifically for a *vault* that lies under the main floor of a church. Both words suggest a place for more than one coffin, although *vault* can also refer to a

grave

cenotaph
crypt
mausoleum
sepulcher
tomb
vault

metal or concrete casing in which a coffin is placed before being lowered into a *grave*.

Although not a *grave* in the literal sense of being a burial place, **cenotaph** refers to a type of empty *tomb* or *mausoleum* erected in commemoration of the dead but not containing the remains, which either have been buried elsewhere or have never been found.

great

eminent
illustrious
notable
noteworthy
preeminent
reputable

These words refer to people distinguished either by social standing or by accomplishment. **Great** is the most general and informal of these words and has a wide range of uses outside this context. Here, it may refer to groups that possess wealth, influence, or position: the *great* families of Boston. Or it may refer to an accomplished person or his accomplishments: a *great* composer; Newton's *great* discovery. The word is more far-reaching in the latter sense, since it implies that accomplishment has been critically evaluated or tested by time in light of its contribution to art, knowledge, or human well-being. The social sense of the word, by contrast, merely implies the winning of status in a constricted or transitory sphere.

Reputable, while much more formal, functions like *great* in both ways. In either case, however, it may point to mere acceptance or absence of fault rather than the genuine brilliance of a person or his work in its own right: a *reputable* middle-class family of merchants; a *reputable* scholar, a bit on the dry side; a *reputable* but outdated work on the subject. The word implies approval by those in a position to know rather than far-reaching fame; this makes it the mildest of the words here. **Illustrious**, the strongest term here, shows the sharpest possible contrast with *reputable*, since it always suggests fame or glory. The word furthermore is mostly restricted to the accomplished or their accomplishments and may not necessarily indicate a *reputable* person at all: *illustrious* deeds; an *illustrious* poet who scandalized the *reputable* upper classes of his day. When used in the context of social standing, the word usually applies to people who have added brilliant accomplishments to wealth, status, or rank: an *illustrious* family that gave England some of its finest generals, statesmen, and thinkers over several centuries.

Notable and **noteworthy** are somewhat stronger in tone than *reputable*, but both apply more exclusively to accomplished people or to their accomplishments. Both words would seem to point to something that merits attention, but in practice *notable* indicates those people or things that are actually known, respected, or admired, whereas *noteworthy* indicates what is worthy of attention but may not yet have received it: several *notable* authors who are scheduled to publish books in the coming season; the only critic to single out the book as a *noteworthy* attempt despite its failure. Also, as can be seen, *notable* often suggests successful achievement, *noteworthy* a promising effort.

Eminent is considerably stronger in emphasis than all the preceding words but *illustrious*. Here, however, the word functions equally well in the contexts both of social status and of accomplishment: families *eminent* enough to be listed in the Social Register; an *eminent* scientist. The word has a dignified tone, suggesting solid, well-respected values, and points to the most admired members of a given class. This makes the word less pertinent to the arts than to the academic disciplines, the sciences, or the learned professions: an *illustrious* painter; an *eminent* critic; an *eminent* Supreme Court Justice. **Preeminent** is a superlative for *eminent*, indicating that person who is the most respected of an already admired group. It also tends to suggest a position of great power and authority: the *preeminent* molder of taste in his era. Neither of this pair is likely to be used in description of some accomplishment itself. Moreover, both words in emphasizing respectability do not approach *illustrious* in suggesting widespread renown. A person might be *eminent*, even *preeminent* in his field, and still not be in any way *illustrious*. See FAMOUS, OUTSTANDING, SIGNIFICANT.

Antonyms: obscure, unknown.

These words describe various kinds of insatiable desire for food, money, power, or material possessions. **Greedy** is the most general word and is less formal than some of the other terms in this group. Although *greedy* can refer to a desire for money, power, or property, it more commonly relates specifically to an inordinate desire for food. [She stuffed one chocolate after another into that *greedy* mouth of hers; *Greedy* for land, speculators laid waste the virgin forests throughout the West.] *Greedy* less readily suggests the use of unethical means in seeking satisfaction: Unless you discipline a *greedy* child, he may grow up to be a selfish adult.

Avaricious is a more formal term than *greedy* and suggests an unbalanced, almost fanatic desire for money or possessions: The *avaricious* child lost his toys as soon as he got them, but still cried for more. The overtones possible in *avaricious* relate it to three much more informal words, **gluttonous**, **stingy**, and **miserly**. *Gluttonous* puts the emphasis on consumption, most commonly of food. [His *gluttonous* appetite made short work of all the leftovers in the refrigerator.] *Stingy* emphasizes a lack of generosity, especially the reluctance to spend money. [She was so *stingy* that she never tipped the grocery boy.] *Miserly* refers more to the hoarding of money or property than to either the *gluttonous* consumption or the *stingy* use of it. [Their *miserly* piling up of wealth had not made up for their inability to have children.] An *avaricious* person may be either *gluttonous* or *miserly*, depending on whether he consumes or merely possesses his wealth. In either case, he may or may not be *stingy* when he does use it. Of these four words, however, *avaricious* perhaps carries the strongest suggestion of being willing to use unethical means to satisfy a given desire. [The *avaricious* stockbroker had cheated his own parents out of the title to their land.]

Acquisitive is considerably more neutral in tone than any of these words. It suggests the actual process of coming into the possession of goods whether by fair means or foul. In being more externally descriptive, it puts the emphasis on the act rather than on the desire. A poor person might desire possessions, but he is not actually *acquisitive* until, by some means, he begins to assemble them. [Thoreau argues that our *acquisitive* tendencies prevent us from living unburdened, joyous lives.] In contrast to the neutrality of *acquisitive*, **rapacious** is the most strongly negative of all these words. It blurs together desire and act, with overtones of brutality and violence. It emphasizes the taking of things against the will of others, by force or unethical means. [He was so *rapacious* in his lust for money that he impoverished whole families at a time.]

Envious and **covetous** are opposed to *avaricious* and especially to *acquisitive* in suggesting more the intense desire for something than the act of possessing it. The desired item, furthermore, must necessarily belong to someone else. *Envious* implies the greater passivity of the two, referring to a hostile or inverted admiration for the belongings of another. Sometimes the very impossibility of possessing them is the key. [She

greedy

acquisitive
avaricious
covetous
envious
gluttonous
miserly
rapacious
stingy

would always be *envious* of her sister's beauty.] *Covetous* is the more intense of the two and the less passive, shading off toward *avaricious* in its potential for being acted upon. [The ninth and tenth commandments are a sharp condemnation of the *covetous* person.] Both words can apply to a wider range of desired goods or qualities than the other words grouped here. See EAGER, OPPORTUNISTIC, YEARN.

Antonyms: GENEROUS.

greet

accost
address
hail
salute
welcome

These words all refer to the words or actions offered or exchanged in the first moments of a meeting. **Greet** can indicate any sign of recognition or acknowledgment; on first glance it might be thought to suggest a warm, friendly, or cheerful response: *greeting* the children with a whoop of delight. But this is far from invariable: *greeting* him with a stiff, strained silence. **Welcome** is more specific than *greet* in indicating that one person receives another into a given situation, either as a newcomer or as one returning to it. Here, the word may more often suggest a warm, official, or formal reception: *welcoming* him back into the household with a passionate embrace; a committee of sophomores to *welcome* the arriving freshmen; a ceremony *welcoming* the visiting dignitary to the city. But again, the word need not always carry this positive tone: *welcoming* him each night with sullen stares and a stream of fault-finding remarks.

Hail now has largely been reduced to the special situation of referring to the *welcoming* of someone as a high honor: a ticker-tape parade to *hail* the visiting astronauts. It can refer, in fact, to any ovation, without any notion of *welcoming* whatsoever. A related use pertains to calling out in order to attract someone's attention: *hailing* a taxicab; *hailing* an old friend on the street. Like *hail*, **salute** can indicate any act of celebrating or honoring someone: a benefit performance to *salute* the Oscar winners. It now functions in terms of meeting only in the military context, where it refers to the obligatory hand gestures presented in passing between officers or officers and enlisted men.

In the context of meetings, **address** may focus on the manner of *greeting* or the exact terms used: *addressing* him by his first name. It may also suggest approaching a stranger or speaking to bystanders in general or at random: *addressing* his question to one of the men in the crowd; *addressing* her plea for help to everyone in the restaurant. In a wider context, of course, the word refers to formal speech or planned discourse: *addressing* the convention with a seconding speech. **Accost** more clearly restricts itself to the situation of approaching or *addressing* a stranger, often in an unfriendly or threatening way: *accosting* one of the villagers and asking for directions; the ruffian who *accosted* me and demanded my purse. The word has been used euphemistically for a number of kinds of physical or sexual assault; hence, it can often suggest any sort of violent attack: *accosted* on a dark street and mugged. See MEET, MEETING.

gregarious

affable
amiable
cordial
friendly

These words all refer to inviting or complaisant attitudes toward other people, and are alike in suggesting either an openness or willingness to make the acquaintance of others. In its broadest sense, **gregarious** is applied to animals as well as people. It involves a basic tendency to associate with one's fellows, implying a natural disposition for group living: Men and sheep are both *gregarious* animals. In another sense, *gregarious* applies to people who actively seek the society of others, preferring company to solitude, but even in this sense the implication of wanting to be with others of one's own kind is present: students who are so *gregarious* they are unable to spend a single evening alone for the sake of their studies. The more dialectal or folksy term **sociable**, on the other hand, implies the seeking of a personal acquainceship, often in conformity with one of the prevailing cultural mores: In some parts of the United States people consider it *sociable* to drop in on one's neighbors for a brief unannounced visit. **Social** is more formal than *sociable*, and applies more often in this sense to an individual's temperament than to an event, often defining one aspect of a person: the *social* side of his character; She's become very *social* lately, giving at least one party a month. When applied to temperament, **outgoing** is akin to *social* but more often suggests a sociological context: an *outgoing* personality. *Outgoing* indicates a person who is not indrawn, inhibited, or shy, but on the contrary one who expresses himself openly and makes acquaints easily. Because such traits are attractive to most Americans, *outgoing* is often linked with other favorable terms: a sweet, *outgoing* child; a pleasant, warm, *outgoing* teacher.

Where the foregoing words focus on the active individual whose *social* antennae "go out" to other people, **affable** and **amiable** indicate receptivity or accessibility to the gestures of others. Etymologically *affable* means capable of being spoken to, i.e. easy to approach. It suggests a benign and courteous attitude rather than one actively seeking new friends: The easy, *affable* manner of Robert Frost endeared him to the audiences to which he "said" his poems. *Amiable* has more of a note of kindliness, and suggests an openness to friendship. Unlike *affable*, *amiable* may also refer to a disagreement or dispute that is free from antagonism or ill feeling: An *amiable* rivalry existed between the two old friends.

Friendly has a wide variety of applications. It may, like *amiable*, mean free from ill feeling: a *friendly* argument. It may mean acting as or typical of a friend: *friendly* advice; Inviting us to stay the night was a *friendly* and hospitable gesture. *Friendly* may suggest an openness to a personal or intimate relationship based on the individual natures or interests of the people concerned; in this sense it differs from the more impersonal *amiable* and *affable* and the less individually-oriented *gregarious*. [She was *gregarious* but not *friendly*; she liked to be surrounded by crowds of admirers but assiduously avoided personal relationships with any of them; He was an *amiable* sort — never said a harsh word about anyone — but no one ever got very *friendly* with him; Einstein had an *affable* nature, quick to appreciate wit and with considerable personal charm, but he was nevertheless known intimately by very few, and could not be called *friendly*.] But *friendly* is also used more broadly to refer to kindliness in people and to the absence of antagonism or menace in animals. [He was a *friendly* fellow, always ready to lend a helping hand when needed; The dog seemed *friendly* enough until I tried to pet him.]

Cordial means warm and hearty, and suggests sincerity of feeling as well; it is nowadays used most often of formal situations rather than personal ones involving the private lives of individuals: A *cordial* welcome was accorded the visiting minister of state; a *cordial* greeting. Its formal context and tone should not be interpreted as somehow vitiating the sincerity of feeling the word connotes; it simply suggests a formal but nonetheless genuine expression of feeling: a long and *cordial* relationship between the violinist and his protégé. See BLITHE, COMPLIANT, FRIEND, LOVING.

Antonyms: ALOOF, *antisocial*, HOSTILE, *introverted, retiring, unapproachable, unsociable*.

grieve

lament
mourn
sorrow

These words refer to the inward feeling or active expression of unhappiness at a bereavement, failure, or loss. **Grieve** has the widest range of expressiveness, concentrating on thought or feeling. It implies inner anguish that may or may not be openly expressed: giving no sign that he had spent the morning *grieving* over his failure to get a promotion; surprised at how many attended the funeral to *grieve* over the death of their friend. **Mourn** is similar to *grieve* but is more formal. In its most solemn sense, it implies deep emotion felt over a period of time: privately *mourning* his mother's death. But the word is often used for a public show of bereavement that may or may not be sincere but that is often ceremonial or ritualized: to wear black as a symbol of *mourning*.

Lament comes from the Latin word for wailing or weeping. It specifically suggests giving vocal or verbal expression to a sense of loss or bereavement: loudly *lamenting* the loss of his job; *lamenting* her husband's tragic death with uncontrolled seizures of hysterical weeping. The word is sometimes used in a less serious sense to indicate someone who tediously verbalizes trivial disappointments: *lamenting* to all his friends about how unfairly the teacher had treated him. **Sorrow** may suggest milder feelings or a less tragic loss than the foregoing words; it combines sadness with regret, contrasting with *lament* by suggesting *grieving* that is inward or, at most, quietly expressed: *sorrowing* over all their missed chances to get to know each other better. In some contexts, *sorrow* as a verb may sound faintly outdated. *Grieve* contrasts with *sorrow* and *lament* in that it may apply to a forlorn animal as well as to a human being: a man *sorrowing* for weeks over the death of his dog; a dog *grieving* over the death of its master. See DEPLORE, MISERABLE, WEEP.

Antonyms: exult, jubilate, rejoice.

grill

bake
barbecue
broil
roast

These words all mean to cook food by exposing it to dry heat. **Grill** and **broil** are synonymous in their reference to the rapid cooking of small pieces of food by intense, direct heat. Fish, fowl, meat, and some vegetables such as tomatoes and mushrooms are *grilled* or *broiled*. In *grilling* and *broiling*, one surface of the food is exposed to the heating source at a time. Because of the intensity of the heat these surfaces are sealed, allowing the meat, fish, etc., to retain its juices with their intrinsic flavor and nutritive value. The difference between these two methods of cooking is one of equipment. *Grilling* requires the use of a grill or gridiron, which is a metal grate set in a frame. The food to be cooked is placed on this grate; the heating source is below the grate: to *grill* a hamburger. *Broiling* may be done, as *grilling* is, over hot coals, but today *broiling* usually suggests exposure to the radiant heat of a gas flame or electrically heated metal coils; in this kind of *broiling*, the food is cooked under the heating unit: to *broil* steak.

Before the invention of the stove, **roast** meant to cook by exposure to the heat of an open fire or flame, and it usually referred to the cooking of a large piece of meat or even a whole animal or fowl: to *roast* a pig. *Roasting* was a slower process than *broiling* or *grilling*; the food to be cooked was often placed on a spit that could be turned in order to let all sides of the food be exposed to the source of heat. Today *roasting* is done in an oven where the food is cooked by radiant and reflected heat and, in addition, by heat that is transferred from the pan in which the food is being cooked. This kind of *roasting* is faster than the older method, but is still a slower process than *grilling* or *broiling*. *Roast* is also used to denote the placing of food in hot ashes, embers, stones, etc., and the

keeping of it there long enough for it to be cooked. And it may mean to
dry and parch under the action of heat: to *roast* coffee; *roasted* peanuts.

Bake is like *roast* in that it refers to cooking by dry, continuous heat
in an oven or similar enclosed unit. There is no difference between these
two terms as far as the method of cooking is concerned. The difference
between *roast* and *bake* is that the former is used almost exclusively in
reference to large pieces of meat or fowl, while the latter can be applied
to anything else that is cooked in an oven: to *bake* a cake; to *bake* fish;
to *bake* a casserole of ham and beans; *baked* potatoes. To **barbecue** is
to *broil*, *grill*, or *roast* meat (usually beef, pork, or chicken) either on a
spit or gridiron or else over a trench called a *barbecue* pit. One may
barbecue meat over coals or an open fire. A modern *barbecuing* device is
the small, portable rotisserie which has an electrical heating unit. *Barbecued* food often consists of a whole animal or large pieces of one. In
most cases the meat is marinated and basted with some kind of highly
seasoned sauce: *barbecued* spareribs. As a noun, *barbecue* is a meat dish
consisting of stringy slivers of minced pork or beef prepared in a seasoned
sauce.

Applied to human beings, *broil* and *roast* mean to get or be extremely
hot and sweaty: travelers *broiling* in the sun as they cross the desert;
passengers *roasting* in a hot car during a traffic jam. *Bake* may mean to
tan in the sun, as while sunbathing; and *barbecue*, to get sunburned:
They got *barbecued* at the beach. In a more informal sense, *roast* and
barbecue may also mean to criticize or ridicule severely, whether in earnest or as a form of good-humored raillery. [I was *barbecued* at the conference — really raked over the coals; a club that *roasts* its members at
testimonial dinners] See BOIL, HOT, QUESTION (v.).

grind

champ
chew
chomp
gnash
masticate

These words all refer to the action of working the jaws and rubbing the
teeth together. **Grind** is the most general word in the group. It means
to pulverize, to reduce to fine particles, as by crushing or friction: *Grinding* bones helps keep a dog's teeth clean. *Grind* also means to rub together with a harsh or grating sound: The noise of his teeth *grinding*
kept his wife awake all night. To *grind* one's teeth in this way as a result
of rage, pain, or anguish is to **gnash**. *Gnash* more than *grind* sounds
like the action it denotes, but it is often used idiomatically rather than
in a literal sense: Their eviction was marked by much weeping and wailing and *gnashing* of teeth. *Gnash* also means to bite by *grinding* the
teeth: a hungry lion, *gnashing* his kill.

Chew and **masticate** are synonymous in designating a crushing or
grinding with the teeth. The difference between the two words is that
masticate, in addition to being more formal than *chew*, is only used in
reference to food that is swallowed after the crushing or *grinding* action.
One speaks, for example, of *chewing* tobacco or gum but never of *masti-
cating* them.

Champ and its variant **chomp** mean to crush and *chew* noisily. Like
gnash they are colorful words which summon up lifelike mental images.
[The young ranch hand *chomped* his dinner with as much gusto as he
displayed when roping a steer.] *Champ* and *chomp* are also used idiomatically to refer to a restless biting action, and by figurative extension, to
restlessness or impatience shown in any way: a horse *champing* the bit;
a convalescent *champing* at the bit in his eagerness to return to work.

group

These words refer to gatherings of people. **Group** is so general that it
may be used for small or relatively large gatherings that have come about

group

(continued)

band
body
company
gang
party
troop
troupe

by accident or intention: the *group* of people who happened to be waiting for the plane's arrival; a study *group* formed to keep track of the opposition's proposals. While these examples suggest relatively small gatherings, the word may be used, especially in statistical contexts, for a large number of people: the thousands of people still in the undecided *group*.

Body is nearly as general as *group*, but considerably more vague; it may refer to organized *groups*: a legislative *body*; a Protestant *body*; a *body* of foot soldiers. It may also suggest dedicated followers or a majority: a solid *body* of James Bond fanciers; the *body* of citizens who favor fair play. Except in standard expressions, such as student *body*, it might be effectively avoided in favor of a more concrete word for *group*.

Troupe and **company** both can refer to a traveling group of performing artists. *Troupe* has mostly gone out of use, however, except for such specialized *groups* as ballet, mime, or circus performers: a dance *troupe* setting out on a world tour; the carnival *troupe* that straggled into town late in the week. *Company* is now the preferred word for plays or musicals on tour; the word also suggests a legal or formal organization: the national touring *company* of the Broadway hit play. *Company*, unlike *troupe*, can also refer to performing groups that do not necessarily tour: a summer stock *company*; a repertory *company*. The word, furthermore, has a wider range of uses for various kinds of organized *groups*, such as military units or private businesses. It can also suggest a less well-defined array of like-minded people: a *company* of dissolute beatniks.

Troop, like *company*, can refer to a military *body*, but while *company* refers to a specific unit with a definite structure, *troop* is now seldom used in this sense. In the plural, however, it refers to soldiers in general: dispatching *troops* to the front.

Band and **party** both may have military uses. In this context, *band* would suggest a small *group* of soldiers who have perhaps accidentally fallen together during battle: the ragged *band* of survivors. The word, whatever its context, suggests a close working cooperation among the members: a *band* of crack experts on slum clearance. It may also suggest a furtive *group*, working secretly or illegally: a guerrilla *band*; a *band* of gangsters. *Party*, in its military context, suggests a detachment deployed for a specific purpose: the landing *party*. This suggestion of subdividing a larger *body* may be present in other uses: the *group* of canvassers being divided into smaller *parties*. The word may also refer to one side in a struggle or contract: a battle in which both *parties* received heavy casualties; both *parties* to the arbitration; a system of government based on two political *parties*.

Gang is the only word in this set with mainly negative connotations, suggesting a *group* whose purpose is the performance of illegal, violent, or hostile activities: a narcotics *gang*; a teen-age *gang*. But it can, informally, refer to one's cronies: the old *gang* who used to drop in at the neighborhood bar. It can also refer to a select *group* of laborers: the section *gang* on the railroad. See GATHER, MEETING.

gruesome

ghastly
grim

These words refer to what is repellently ugly or extremely distasteful. **Gruesome** may be used as a hyperbole for anything evoking such a response: a woman dressed in simply *gruesome* taste. More precisely, however, the word refers to spectacles of physical violence, or an unhealthy interest in such things: the *gruesome* atrocities committed by both sides in the tribal wars; *gruesome* murders that suggested a psychopathic killer; the *gruesome* delight with which some newspapers played

gruesome
(continued)

grisly
hideous
lurid
macabre

up the tragedy. **Grisly** is very close to *gruesome*, but is more intense in suggesting destructive violence that springs from a brutally sadistic or abnormal mind. It would, thus, apply less to impersonal destruction on a mass scale, such as might result in war: *grisly* indications that he had played cat and mouse with his victims before dispatching them; the *grisly* detachment with which unspeakable experiments were performed on human subjects; a *grisly* interest in descriptions of deviant sexual behavior. The word can have comic force in referring to excessively labored or vivid accounts of a clandestine nature: eager to tell everyone the *grisly* details of her neighbor's divorce.

Hideous, ghastly, and **grim** are much less specific than the previous pair. Each is popularly used as a hyperbole. *Hideous*, however, often has reference to extreme deformation or ugliness and *ghastly* to something frightening or filled with horror: a car accident that left *hideous* scars on his face; the *ghastly* realization that she had lost her way in the forest. *Ghastly* has a more specific reference, however, to a ghostlike or deathlike pallor, or one resulting from fear: a *ghastly* face that spoke of the harrowing experience she had suffered. *Grim* suggests something stern or forbidding, even to the point of being terrifying: the *grim* aftermath of a bloody Civil War battle.

Lurid, like *ghastly*, may suggest an extremely pale appearance: a face *lurid* with fear and shock. Paradoxically, the word also suggests redness such as produced by a smoky fire: the *lurid* torches of the enraged townsmen gathering in the courtyard. More generally, the word refers to anything *hideous* in its vividness: the *lurid* marks of the whip across his back. The word has special use to refer to *gruesome* or sensational verbal descriptions or pictorial treatment: *lurid* accounts of the carnage left by the two-day battle; *lurid* photographs of the airplane crash. **Macabre** refers specifically to horror-inspiring ideas or spectacles of any kind, without necessarily pointing to physical destruction of any sort: the *macabre* sexual exploits attributed to witches. *Macabre* is derived etymologically from danse *macabre*, dance of death, and suggests a *gruesome* and frequently bizarre interest in or connection with death: *macabre* tales of blood-sucking vampires, zombies, and other supernatural phenomena; the routine but nonetheless *macabre* preparation of a condemned prisoner for electrocution. See BIZARRE, REPULSIVE.

Antonyms: CHARMING, *delightful*, PLEASING.

guide

conduct
direct
lead
navigate
pilot
steer

These words all refer to the action of showing the way to something or someone. **Guide** and **conduct** mean to accompany in order to show the way to a destination. *Guide* usually indicates a close or personal relationship or a joint effort between the two parties, whereas *conduct* stresses the fact of escorting and the unequal relationship between the two parties; *conduct* may even imply helplessness or coercion. [The policeman *conducted* the suspect to the station house; The Coast Guard vessel *conducted* the damaged freighter to harbor for repairs.] *Guide* is much more general than *conduct*, and may apply to any direction given one's behavior, manner of life, etc. [He was always *guided* by his principles of honesty and fair play in his business life; *Guided* by the knowledge that he had only a year to live, he sold his business and went to Monte Carlo.]

To **direct** is to indicate a course without actually *guiding*: to *direct* a stranger in town to the railroad station. To **lead** is to *guide* by going ahead of. An usher *leads* playgoers to their seats; an officer *leads* his men into combat.

To **navigate** and to **pilot** are to determine and *direct* the course of a

ship or airplane. To **steer** is to *guide* in a desired direction by a rudder
or other means. *Pilot* and *steer* are also often used rhetorically to indicate
guiding through difficulties or intricacies of any kind: to *steer* the ship
of state through troubled waters. See ACCOMPANY, CONTROL.

guile

craft
cunning
duplicity

These words refer to the clever or perceptive manipulation of facts, appearances, or people in order to attain a goal. **Guile** suggests a wily and
shrewd person who uses subterfuge and stratagems to get his way: Don't
try to match your inexperience with the *guile* of an unscrupulous antique
dealer. At its mildest, the word can indicate approval, if not admiration,
for a clever person who has learned that indirect means are the only
effective ones in some complex situation: the old prospector's *guile* in
eluding those who tried to trail him back to the spot where he had discovered gold. When **cunning** is used with approval, it puts a greater
stress on intellectual prowess than on subtlety born of experience: The
detective had used all the *cunning* at his command to arrive at the murderer's identity. When it is negative, *cunning* is a harsher word than
guile; in this case its stress is on ferocity or single-minded obsessiveness.
It is often used, literally or metaphorically, in reference to animals:
sheer animal *cunning*; a man who had the *cunning* of a wolf.

    Duplicity is less ambiguous in its application; it is always negative
and refers either to underhanded double-dealing or to outright lying, in
which case it may have a euphemistic flavor: price fixers who practice
duplicity to cheat the public; She admitted that she had been guilty
of *duplicity* in saying she had another engagement that evening. **Craft**
is most like *guile* in suggesting someone practiced in using indirect means
to get his way. But the word is less often used than the first pair, except
in phrases that link it with one or the other: a man capable of incredible
craft and *cunning*; The best poker players are those for whom *craft* and
guile seem to be almost second nature. See CHEAT, DECEPTION, TRICK
(n.), TRICK (v.).

    Antonyms: artlessness, candor, ingenuousness.

gullible

credulous
naive
trusting

These words refer to a readiness to believe what one is told. **Gullible**
emphasizes that a person can be easily tricked or cheated; **credulous**
is less intense, suggesting simply a willingness to believe on slight evidence, without implying the presence of trickery in presenting the evidence. *Gullible* might suggest the greedy hope of getting something for
nothing, so easily exploited by confidence men. *Credulous* might more
appropriately suggest religious or superstitious persuasion that does not
necessarily result in material gain for either the persuader or persuaded.
A *credulous* person, furthermore, might be brought to believe something
without acting upon it to his own harm, whereas a *gullible* person's belief,
by implication, causes him to act in a foolish way that injures himself or
others. [Hamlet fears being *credulous* of the ghost's story — he must
corroborate it; Shakespeare's audience saw Othello less as a jealous man
than as a *gullible* one, easily duped by Iago's machinations.]

    Trusting suggests the same willingness to believe as *gullible* or *credu-
lous*, but ranges from neutrality of tone to one of approval: a *trusting*
girl alone in the big city; a people so *trusting* in the guarantees of a future
life as to be unshakably free from all temptation. **Naive**, on the other
hand, suggests an inexperienced optimism, an unawareness of the compromises life entails. A *naive* person is certainly *trusting*; he is also
likely to be *credulous*; he would, furthermore, be thought *gullible* by the
sophisticate. *Naive*, however, suggests an untried or untested person

rather than one necessarily *gullible*. Only when the *naive* person has actually made a fool of himself by permitting himself to be tricked does he actually become *gullible*. See NAIVE.

Antonyms: critical, disbelieving, doubtful, dubious, questioning, skeptical.

H

happen

befall

occur

take place

transpire

These words all mean to come about or come to pass. **Happen** is a general term and is very widely used to mean to come to pass, especially by chance. [It *happened* to snow that day.] It also means to chance upon or to come or go by chance. [We *happened* to be in town on the night of the concert; We *happened* on their country house by pure luck; I *happened* into the bank just at the very moment the robbery was taking place.] **Befall** is like *happen* in meaning to come about, but while *happen* can be used in speaking about pleasant or unpleasant things, *befall* is almost always used in reference to something unpleasant. [Disaster *befell* them when they were caught in Germany at the beginning of World War II.] *Befall*, too, is considered literary in tone, and much more than *happen* suggests that destiny or fate has played a part in the situation described. [Bad luck and ill health *befell* him throughout his life.] **Occur** and **take place** are both equivalent to *happen* in the sense of to come to pass, but while *occur* can refer to something accidental or something planned, *take place* most often suggests the presence of design. [The accident *occurred* despite all the precautions that had been taken to prevent it; The hearing is scheduled to *take place* tomorrow morning at eleven.] **Transpire** is sometimes used as a synonym for *happen, occur,* or *take place* in the sense of to come to pass: He told me what had *transpired* at the court hearing. Although widely used in this sense, *transpire* tends to sound stilted and affected. This usage has been considered erroneous by many people.

happiness

beatitude

blessedness

bliss

felicity

gladness

These words refer to states of well-being or to the pleasurable satisfaction that accompanies such states. **Happiness** is the most general term and may imply any degree of well-being from that of mere contentment or absence of sorrow to the most intense joy and sense of fulfillment. **Felicity** is a more formal and less often used term for great and sustained *happiness*: All men by nature seek ease of mind, but few can hope for unending *felicity*. The word is most often used of a pertinent or effective manner or style: a *felicity* of poetic expression.

Gladness is overflowing *happiness* and suggests an emotional reaction to a pleasant event, rather than a sustained state of mind: Her *gladness* at seeing us again was most touching.

Bliss in its commonest meaning points to complete, ecstatic *happiness* or to great contentment: the *bliss* of a young couple in love; the *bliss* experienced by a cat stretching in the sun. In the religious sense, *bliss* is a state of absolute *felicity* brought about by the submergence of the self into a divine infinity, as in the state of nirvana in Buddhism.

Blessedness and **beatitude** usually refer to intense spiritual *bliss*. *Blessedness* implies a *happiness* so profound as to be attributed to a deity or to unusually favorable fortune. *Beatitude*, a more formal and literary word, is supreme *blessedness* that approaches the transcendent. Its most familiar use is its application to the eight declarations of *blessedness* (the *Beatitudes*) occurring in the Sermon on the Mount in the New Testament. See JOYOUS, PLEASURE.

Antonyms: grief, MISERY, *sadness, sorrow, unhappiness.*

hard

arduous
difficult
laborious
perplexing
troublesome
trying

These words refer to efforts not easily made or to problems not easily solved. **Hard** is the most general and informal of these, with a wide range of possible use: *hard* labor; a *hard* assignment; a *hard* struggle. As with the rest of these words, *hard* does not suggest impossibility of success so much as the extremes of effort that will be required to attain it. **Difficult** is slightly more formal and somewhat more restricted in range as compared to *hard*. Where *hard* might suggest that a burdensome exertion alone is required, *difficult* frequently stresses a more complex task that may demand control or skill: the *hard* work of unloading the boxes and the *difficult* job of weighing and inspecting them. *Hard*, furthermore, might suggest a firm or unmerciful stand, whereas *difficult* again stresses complexity, often of a puzzling kind: a *hard* master; a *difficult* employer; taking a *hard* line on these *difficult* problems.

Laborious and **arduous** are both more formal than the preceding pair, but are otherwise more closely related to *hard* than to *difficult*. *Laborious* is more restricted than *hard* in applying almost exclusively to the use of sheer effort or exertion in accomplishing a task, with few suggestions of the skill that might be required and no reference to the complexity of a problem: the *laborious* job of digging new foxholes overnight. *Arduous* is even more formal than *laborious* and less restricted in suggesting burdensome effort or almost unmerciful firmness of stand: our *arduous* struggle to lay the carpet before the guests arrived; *arduous* regulations that applied to all enlisted men.

Perplexing relates closely to *difficult*, but is more exclusively restricted to describing a task or requirement that is *difficult* to understand. Thus, while *laborious* stresses effort, often of a physical kind, *perplexing* most often suggests the intellectual demands made by a task; it would not be appropriate, on the other hand, to describe effort of any sort: the *perplexing* job of finding the ten-cent discrepancy in the day's accounts.

Troublesome and **trying** also pertain mostly to *difficult* tasks rather than to the effort required to solve them. *Troublesome* suggests confusion or disorder or even unpleasant resistance; this contrasts with the intellectual demands made by a *perplexing* task: the *troublesome* job of interviewing every one of the suspicious neighbors. *Trying*, by contrast, is much less specific concerning the kind of resistance it points to; it may suggest any kind of obstacle that taxes the worker's patience, skill, or mental equanimity: too *trying* to be a baby sitter for such a spoiled child. The word goes beyond *perplexing* and *troublesome* in being applicable to effort as well, in which case it suggests the sapping of energy or will: finding the struggle to sit up too *trying* in her weakened condition. See LABOR, OBSTACLE, PUZZLE, STRESS.

Antonyms: SIMPLE.

harm

damage
disable

These words all mean to affect a person or thing in such a way as to lessen health, strength, value, beauty, etc. **Harm** and **damage** are both wide in application. *Harm* refers to living things and, occasionally, to inanimate objects: afraid that in his fury he would *harm* the child; worried that her belongings might have been *harmed*. The point of the word, however, is that it can suggest any sort of negative outcome, and thus is widely used in an abstract way, especially when an immoral or unethical impairment is at issue: those who unwittingly *harm* the cause of peace. *Damage* stresses impairment of value or function and, while it can be applied to living things, is more commonly used to refer to inanimate objects. [Her heart was slightly *damaged* as a result of her long illness; The gale *damaged* several houses; The mayor *damaged* his chances for reelection by a very poorly run campaign.]

Hurt, the most informal of the group, is mainly, but not wholly, restricted to living things, and is general in applying to both a severe or minor impairment: a puppy that had been *hurt* by the tomcat; a few scratches, proving that children are bound to get *hurt* when they play; badly *hurt* in the car crash; a reputation *hurt* by an enemy's vicious lies. **Injure** is a slightly formal substitute for *hurt*. But while *hurt* concentrates more on the registering of a pain that need not override usefulness, *injure* often indicates at least a temporary loss of some function: continuing to type as fast as ever, though she had *hurt* her finger while manicuring her nails; a bird that hopped about helplessly as if one of its wings had been *injured*.

Disable and **incapacitate** both intensify suggestions of *injure* in pointing more definitely to a temporary or permanent loss of function. Of the two, *disable* is more likely to suggest a partial impairment, perhaps permanent, but one that need not affect usefulness: serving as president, though *disabled* by polio. *Incapacitate*, by contrast, is more formal and tends to suggest a total loss of function or effectiveness: the tragedy of a very active man who had been *incapacitated* by a stroke. Both words, however, go beyond the previous pair in their application to inanimate things: its retro-rockets *disabled* by a misfire during blast-off; snow-clogged roads that would *incapacitate* any car without tire chains. See HURT, WEAK, WOUND.

Antonyms: REPAIR, TREAT.

healthy

hale
hearty
robust
sound
strong
vigorous
well

These words refer to a good or superlative physical or mental state. **Healthy** at its most neutral may refer to an absence of illness; at its most positive it refers to normal or excellent functioning: a recovery that left him perfectly *healthy* provided he doesn't overexert himself; *healthy* minds in *healthy* bodies. **Well** and *healthy* are the most common of these words, if not the most informal, but *well* is more nearly restricted to the neutral implications of *healthy* rather than its positive ones: asking the doctor when she would be *well* again. **Sound** is much more positive in feel, although strictly speaking it can refer simply to an absence of illness or defect, like *well*: an alertness and liveliness that marked the baby from the beginning as having an unusually *sound* constitution. **Strong** takes a different slant than the previous word, emphasizing powerfulness of physique or forcefulness of mind, although these qualities may be possessed by someone who is not *healthy* or *well*: *strong* athletes laid low by polio; Ruskin's *strong* mind becoming increasingly shadowed by mental illness.

The remaining words all stress exclusively the side of *healthy* that refers to excellent functioning. **Robust** adds to the emphasis of *strong* implications of positive health as well: *robust* warriors who were never sick a day in their lives; a *robust* personality able to triumph over every adversity. The word also has overtones of full-bodied zestfulness, manly eagerness, and ampleness of appetite: the *robust* and sometimes ribald songs of sailors; a *robust* interest in the opposite sex. **Hearty** concentrates mostly on these last aspects of *robust*, indicating an active expression of high spirits and the satisfaction of desire: a *hearty* appetite; living to a *hearty* old age. Here, a sexual connotation possible for *robust* is more clearly present, although the word is more often restricted to refer to men: the *hearty* camaraderie of most stag parties.

Vigorous refers to forcefulness, like *strong*, adding to this a note of positive well-being: rosy cheeks and sparkling eyes that spoke of *vigorous* good health; a closely reasoned theory that revealed a *vigorous* mind at work. The word, however, is completely lacking in those connotations of *robust* and *hearty* that refer to masculine appetite: the *vigorous* skill with which her poems are written. **Hale** would suggest excellent functioning, although strictly it pertains to absence of illness or defect. The word sounds, in any case, archaic, and except in stock expressions is not now often used: *hale* and *hearty*. See BENEFICIAL.

Antonyms: ill, sick, sickly, unhealthy, WEAK, *weakly.*

heart attack

arteriosclerosis
atherosclerosis
coronary
embolism
heart failure
hypertension
hypotension
stroke
thrombosis

This set of related words all pertains to disorders or malfunctions of the circulatory system. Serious confusion can result from treating any one of them as a synonym for any other. **Heart attack** refers to a sudden interference with or stoppage of the heart's pumping action for whatever reason; such a seizure may cause death, but one may also recover from it, with or without functional impairment. In common usage, **heart failure** may suggest a permanent stoppage of a weak or overtaxed heart, as in exertion or old age. Medically speaking, *heart failure* refers instead to a condition in which the heart cannot beat rapidly enough or pump a sufficient supply of blood to the body; this condition need not occur as a sudden seizure but can manifest itself by a gradual worsening. When it is not fatal, impairment may result. A **coronary** is *heart failure* in which the *coronary* arteries cannot supply enough blood to nourish the heart muscle, whether because of blockage or narrowing of arterial passages. Congestive *heart failure* occurs when the blood returned to the heart by the veins cannot be pumped back to the body in sufficient amounts.

Arteriosclerosis is a general term for any hardening or thickening of the artery walls, which results in a narrowing of arterial passages. This can be one cause of a *coronary*. **Atherosclerosis** is a specific form of *arteriosclerosis* in which the narrowing and hardening is caused by fatty deposits on the inside walls of the arteries; this also can be the cause of a *coronary*. **Hypertension** and **hypotension** are simply technical terms for high and low blood pressure. Both these conditions can ultimately lead to a *heart attack* or to *heart failure*.

Because damage to the brain is a frequent result of any nonfatal *heart attack* or *heart failure*, a **stroke** is often confused with these two conditions. A *stroke* results when an artery supplying blood to the brain is ruptured or blocked in such a way as to cause brain damage. An abrupt loss of consciousness occurs, followed by some degree of mental impairment or physical paralysis should the person survive. Thus, while the heart itself is not involved, circulatory malfunction is present and there is a resemblance to *heart attack* or *failure* in onset and outcome. A *stroke* can result either from an arterial hemorrhage in the brain, such as might be caused by *hypertension*, or from an arterial obstruction. **Thrombosis** and **embolism** both refer to such obstructions in any blood vessel anywhere in the body. *Thrombosis* pertains to the growth of a blood clot (thrombus) in a blood vessel when it remains attached to its original site; the resulting obstruction can cause a *coronary*, a *heart attack*, or a *stroke*. An *embolism* is an obstruction that can cause similar damage, but it results from the lodging of an abnormal body (embolus) circulating in the blood, such as a clot or an air bubble. Thus, a clot formed by a *thrombosis* elsewhere in the body can detach itself and, as an embolus, circulate to the heart or brain, where it may lodge, cause an *embolism*, and possibly result in a *heart attack* or *stroke*.

These words refer to a member of a religion or culture outside one's own. In the early stages of Christianity's growth, both **heathen** and **pagan** could refer indiscriminately to an adherent of a religion other than Judaism or Christianity, especially those unexposed or resistant to Christianization. Both suggested someone who belonged to a preexisting culture that was alien and therefore inferior to that of the speaker: Chinese *heathens*; Teutonic *pagans*; Moslem *heathens*. By the 19th century, a difference in the use of the word was clear. *Pagan* could refer, less disapprovingly, to the ancient Greek or Roman who worshiped a polytheistic pantheon of gods before the advent of Christianity. By contrast, *heathen* referred more specifically to an adherent of an existing religion subscribed to by a primitive culture or one remote from Christianity. In practice, those peoples were called *heathens* who were actually being proselytized by Christian missionaries in the field. Thus, adherents of Islam might no longer be so described, even though members of sophisticated cultures like the Japanese and Chinese were still thought of as *heathens*. The word often was used, in fact, as though it were synonymous with savage: African *heathens*; the cannibalistic *heathens* of New Guinea. In this century, a growing respect for the integrity of other cultures and religions has made any use of *heathen* suspect and out-of-date. *Pagan*, however, can be used for any individual, even within one's own culture, who rejects metaphysical speculation and values a life of the intellect and, particularly, of the senses.

Barbarian comes from a Greek root that means foreign, rude, or ignorant. It was in these terms that a sophisticated Greek viewed people from cultures other than his own. Historically, the word often refers to the Germanic peoples who overran the Roman Empire and later uses reflect this in carrying implications of ruthlessness, cruelty, illiteracy, and lack of civilized standards. Thus the word contrasts with others of this group in registering cultural rather than religious disapproval of an alien group. Except in historical reference, the word is seldom used except as a pejorative hyperbole for a crude, vulgar, or violent person: educators who see the current contempt for knowledge and scholarship as fostering a new generation of *barbarians*. **Infidel**, like *heathen*, once emphasized disapproval for an established non-Christian religion. But *infidel* was harsher in tone and was most often used for religions, such as Islam, that were aggressively resistant to Christian conversion or expansion: a crusade called to wipe out the Saracen *infidel* in the Holy Land. The word is often used to refer to what was a corresponding Islamic attitude toward Christians: sultans who contributed to the war against the invading Christian *infidel*. More recently, the word could refer to any individual unbeliever, but even this use is now dated.

Gentile is the one word here that can currently be used in exact and neutral classification. Its most widely understood reference is to anyone not an adherent to Judaism: European *gentiles* who assisted Jews in escaping from the Nazis; a new spirit of tolerance between Jews and *gentiles*. In New Testament usage, the word can refer to someone both non-Jewish and non-Christian: Paul's missions to convert the *Gentiles* to Christianity. See HERETIC, RENEGADE, SKEPTIC.

heathen

barbarian
gentile
infidel
pagan

heavy

burdensome
crushing
onerous
oppressive

These words refer to weight or pressure so severe that it is difficult to bear. **Heavy** is the most informal and the least intense of these words, indicating something of relative weightiness. [He wondered if the floor could support the *heavy* piano; She insisted that the package was not very *heavy*.] Metaphorically, the word suggests something difficult or unpleasant: a *heavy* duty; He went to meet her with a *heavy* heart. The word need not, of course, suggest the idea of a carried weight at all. **Burdensome**, by contrast, specifically refers to something that is *heavy* and must be carried or supported; it is also more formal and more frequently used in an abstract way: a *burdensome* obligation; the *burdensome* post of chief administrator. The implication is that while the weight or task is difficult it can, with effort, be supported.

Onerous is thus an intensification of *burdensome*, being at the same time still more formal than the previous words. It is almost exclusively used abstractly for describing such things as supremely trying tasks or duties: the *onerous* job of correcting one hundred themes a week. The word gives an implication of an unfair or unjust assignment of duties: class assignments that in one case were reasonable and in another, extremely *onerous*. **Oppressive** relates to this last possibility for *onerous*, suggesting harsh or cruel demands that can scarcely be borne: an *oppressive* taskmaster; *oppressive* registration requirements applied to deny the vote to minority groups. **Crushing** is the most intense of all these words and may suggest, both literally and metaphorically, a weight or force that cannot be borne at all: the *crushing* impact of the plummeting airplane that buckled and destroyed the bridge; poverty so *crushing* as to completely immobilize whole segments of society. See MASSIVE, SIZE.

Antonyms: easy, light, mild, TRIVIAL.

heedless

careless
incautious
inconsiderate
insensitive
thoughtless

These words refer to a lack of awareness that produces slipshod, dangerous, or offensive results. **Heedless** most strongly indicates inattentiveness, with disapproving suggestions of self-preoccupation, stubbornness, or indifference to the feelings or safety of others. [*Heedless* of everything but the striking impression she was making; *heedless* of his parents' sound advice; He kept making caustic remarks, *heedless* of whom he might offend; They let out sail, *heedless* of the gathering storm clouds.] **Thoughtless** is less disapproving in tone, suggesting a lapse or failure, possibly unintentional, rather than the determined disregarding indicated by *heedless*: a *thoughtless* mistake; He apologized for having been so *thoughtless* of her feelings. Consequently, it can be used euphemistically for *heedless*, although it occasionally expresses disapproval in its own right: the typically *thoughtless* and irresponsible behavior of teen-agers.

Inconsiderate relates most closely to *heedless*, and **insensitive** to *thoughtless*. Both words, however, concentrate more on doing injury to the feelings of others. *Inconsiderate* expresses almost as much disapproval as *heedless* in pointing to conscious, if not deliberate, discourtesy toward others: his *inconsiderate* insistence on playing the phonograph when his roommates were trying to study. *Insensitive* may suggest that the discourtesy is unintentional in that it stems from a lack of understanding for other people's needs: *insensitive* to how much they disapproved of his dropping in on them unannounced. The word also suggests a lack of awareness for finer shadings of meanings than any other word here: *insensitive* to the nuances of diplomatic protocol.

Careless is the most general of these words and can substitute, with a loss of preciseness, for any of them, regardless of the area of meaning involved. Most commonly, however, it is closest to **incautious** in indicating a *heedless* attitude to standards of accuracy or safety; laziness, indifference, or preoccupation may be suggested as possible reasons for the inaccurate or dangerous act: too industrious to be *careless* about her housekeeping; a sense of false safety that made them *careless* about locking their door at night; so rushed that he grew *careless* in adding up the last column of figures. *Incautious* is most specifically restricted to a *heedless* attitude toward safety, with the suggestion that this results from a *thoughtless* or *insensitive* recklessness: *incautious* about letting the children play out in the street. See IMPETUOUS, OBLIVIOUS, RECKLESS, RUDE.

Antonyms: careful, CONSIDERATE, OBSERVANT.

help

aid
assistance
relief
service
support

These words refer to an act that one person performs for another. Of these, **help** is the most informal; it is also sharply separated from most of the others in implying a more desperately needed item than they suggest. **Assistance** and **aid** only contribute to what one can do for himself, but a person in need of *help* may be literally helpless, that is, in danger or trouble. *Help* also necessarily connotes generosity or charity, something given out of kindness or pity, whereas *assistance* can be something purchased. [I was flat broke in a strange town with nowhere to turn for *help*; To the very last days of the siege, they never gave up hope that *help* would soon be arriving.] The element of urgency in this use is not, however, invariably present in other uses. *Help* may, for example, merely refer to the lesser part of a shared task: While she did most of the cooking, her daughters were of some *help*, however small. In this use, it approaches the meanings most commonly implied in *aid* or *assistance*.

Aid is slightly more formal than *help*, *assistance* more formal still. *Aid* is particularly used in combination: federal *aid* to education; foreign *aid*; first *aid*; visual *aid*; ladies *aid*. It can also be used for situations of emergency or danger: The stricken ship sent an SOS for immediate *aid*. In some cases where the use of *help* suggests itself, *aid* might sound unnecessarily stiff: Thank you for your *aid*. *Assistance*, unlike *aid*, would more rarely be used for urgently needed *help*, but it is an acceptable and more formal substitute for *help* when referring to the subordinate part of a shared task: A surgeon's success depends on the expert *assistance* of every nurse and orderly who attends him.

The relationship between **support** and **service** is somewhat like that between *help* and *aid*. Both may imply a subordinate task, but *support* suggests one more vitally needed, *service* one that may give added comfort but remains optional in nature. *Support* may suggest an advisory role, one primarily of giving encouragement, or one that consists of standing behind and defending someone in danger. [I don't know how to fix a flat tire, but I can give you moral *support*; The Quartermaster Corps gives front-line *support* to the infantry; Though a husband and wife have separated, he is still legally responsible for her *support*.] *Service* often implies a convenience that may be purchased: domestic *service*; telephone answering *service*; laundry *service*. On the other hand, it may suggest a gratuitous benefit gained with the purchase of something else: We offer free parking as still another *service* to our patrons.

Relief has more in common with *support* than with *service*, but it perhaps connotes more urgency than any of these words: If he could only stay afloat another day, he was certain that *relief* would be in sight.

It is also used to refer to government *aid* for the indigent: If you can't *support* your family, you can at least apply for *relief*. See BENEVOLENCE, COMFORT.

Antonyms: exacerbation, harm, hindrance.

heretic

dissenter
nonconformist
schismatic
sectarian

These words pertain to people who espouse independent or antiauthoritarian views in opposition to the doctrines of a religion or ideology. **Heretic** refers to a believer who willfully espouses a tenet that his church has officially declared to be anathema. Taking a stand on an issue the church has not ruled on would not make a person a *heretic*. And while the church may punish a *heretic* by ejecting him or, at one time, putting him to death, a *heretic's* aim need not be to separate from the church but possibly to stay within and reform it. A **schismatic**, by contrast, may or may not have serious doctrinal objections to church teachings, but his avowed aim is to establish a separatist faction or competing religious body. A *schismatic*, furthermore, would most likely be one of a group or its leader, whereas a *heretic* can be a single individual with or without followers: The early Protestants expected to be condemned as *heretics*, but didn't foresee that this would inevitably result in their becoming *schismatics*.

Dissenter and **nonconformist** both originally pertained to people who in some way opposed the established Church of England. A *dissenter* was someone who rejected a particular doctrine without leaving the church, while a *nonconformist* was anyone who would not give to the established church the loyalty required by law. Roughly speaking, a *dissenter* criticized from within the Church of England, the *nonconformist* resisted from without. **Sectarian** once referred to a *schismatic* who founded or advocated the founding of a denomination independent of the original church. Later, it could simply indicate a member of any denomination or sect. More recently, the word is avoided altogether because it can imply a superior-inferior relationship between the original church and the later formation.

Dissenter and *nonconformist* are widely used outside the context of religion. In this case, *dissenter* usually implies someone who is extremely critical of some established order and wishes to reform it: youthful *dissenters* who were organizing a protest march. *Nonconformist*, by contrast, more often refers to someone who is idiosyncratic in his personal behavior and appearance in such a way as to exhibit a sharp departure from custom; the word, thus, need not suggest the advocacy of any formulated ideological stand whatsoever: long-haired *nonconformists* who were little more than pleasure-seeking exhibitionists and had no political commitment of any kind. *Heretic* and *schismatic* can occasionally be used of people carrying on doctrinal disputes about an authoritarian ideology; in this case, the words often have a humorous or ironic note: those Communists that Stalin decided to condemn as *heretics*; the infighting common among Trotskyite *schismatics*. See DENOMINATION, FACTION, HEATHEN, RENEGADE, SKEPTIC.

Antonyms: adherent, compatriot, conformist, follower, SUPPORTER.

hesitate

falter
flounder

These words refer to indecisive actions. **Hesitate** suggests a momentary stopping of activity because of uncertainty, reluctance, or a conflict of emotions: She *hesitated* fearfully between accepting him and denying him; the secretary who *hesitates* to interrupt her boss when he is in conference. The act of *hesitating*, of course, may imply a completely mental weighing of alternatives, or an initial immobility before a decision has been made. This contrasts strongly with **pause**, which can only imply an interruption of motion already under way. *Pause* is also the most neutral of all these words in referring to a temporary halt; while all the other words suggest uneasiness, however faintly, *pause* may suggest a preconceived plan and indicate no irresoluteness whatsoever: They *paused* for six counts between each pirouette. The point of the word may be brevity: He *paused* before each painting only long enough to note the painter's name. Or its point may be to stress the mere fact of the halt, without ascribing motive: uncertain whether she *paused* at the door out of fear or fascination.

Falter has a much clearer emotional overtone than *hesitate* or *pause*. It suggests either intense doubt, helplessness, awkwardness, or incompetence: She *faltered* midway in her denunciation as she saw new reasons to detest him; pedestrians *faltering* across the dangerously icy street; an actor so drunk that he *faltered* through most of his lines. *Falter*, like *pause*, may suggest an interruption, but it can also suggest an extremely slow or faulty performance, as in the last example above. In this sense, **flounder** is an intensification of *falter*, referring to a bungled motion that continues erratically because of panic or disablement: obviously unprepared from the way he *floundered* through the recitation; the sudden cramp that caused him to *flounder* desperately in the deep water.

Waver and **vacillate**, by contrast, return to the milder uneasiness of *hesitate*, although both may suggest a poorly continued motion rather than a temporary halt or initial moment of indecision. Both, in fact, suggest a motion that goes back and forth between two alternatives. *Vacillate* would be more appropriate to describe mental activity that veers between extremes. Where *hesitate* in such a context might suggest a suspension of will, *vacillate* suggests wild swings of choice. [While she *hesitated*, he *vacillated* between taking back his offer and urging her to accept.] *Waver* would be more appropriate to describe a physical act that reveals uncertainty. In this context, it is close to *hesitate*; one who *hesitates* may not move at all, however, whereas *waver* suggests slight, indecisive gestures and uneasy movement. [She *hesitated* so long on the stair that at last he came *wavering* up to her.] *Waver*, when it refers to mental activity, suggests less violent swings than *vacillate*, and between less clearly defined positions: He stood *wavering* among a thousand dimly imagined possibilities. See DEMUR, INCONSTANT.

Antonyms: ascertain, CHOOSE, *continue*, DECIDE.

These words are used to characterize a collection or group of things or people that are not all alike, or are used to describe a mass made up of different elements. **Heterogeneous** emphasizes most strongly the differences among individuals or elements closely connected but not necessarily unified. [New York City has a *heterogeneous* population; The former tenants had left behind a *heterogeneous* pile of rubbish; Porphyry is a *heterogeneous* rock.]

Miscellaneous emphasizes diversity arising from lack of any unifying principle in selections and suggests things that have been brought together casually or by chance. [A small boy's pockets are likely to contain a *miscellaneous* collection of objects; Politicians tend to be on a first-name basis with hundreds of *miscellaneous* people.]

Mixed, as considered here, is often used interchangeably with the other words discussed. Specifically it suggests dissimilarity among elements or individuals in a group or mass, but seldom a diversity as extreme or fortuitous as that suggested by *miscellaneous*. [When you buy a can of *mixed* nuts, you get peanuts, cashews, Brazil nuts, almonds, and filberts; A *mixed* social gathering is made up of people of both sexes.]

Motley means literally having a variety of colors, but in this context it describes persons or things that are strongly contrasted or even discordant. Unlike *heterogeneous*, *miscellaneous*, and *mixed*, *motley* has a derogatory connotation. [Accidents always draw a *motley* crowd of onlookers; Being self-educated, he has read indiscriminately and absorbed a *motley* set of conflicting facts and concepts.] See DISPARATE, JUMBLE.
Antonyms: homogeneous, identical, pure, uniform.

hew

  chop
  cut
  hack

These words mean to penetrate and divide something by means of an instrument with a sharp edge. **Hew** usually means to make or shape by means of heavy blows of a tool such as an axe or by wielding a chisel or adz: to *hew* logs into short lengths; to *hew* stones into proper shapes for building a wall. *Hew* may also indicate a destructive act, although in this sense it tends to sound high-flown and literary: to *hew* down a mighty oak; to *hew* one's adversary to pieces.

Chop means to divide into two or many pieces or to make by a blow, or a series of blows, with a hatchet, cleaver, knife, etc.: to *chop* onions into small pieces; to *chop* open a coconut husk; to *chop* a hole in the ice.

Hack means to *chop* at something or to mangle or slash it away entirely by irregular and clumsy blows of a tool. [The firemen were forced to *hack* down the door to rescue the children; The vandals had *hacked* all the office furniture with knives; The little girl *hacked* off her long hair.]

Cut has a much wider application than the other words and may be a loose synonym for any of them. Frequently an adverb must be added to make the meaning of the action clear: to *cut* up meat for a stew; to *cut* off a hangnail; to *cut* down a dead bush. In many instances *cut* suggests care and forethought in what one is doing. [It takes years for a butcher's apprentice to learn to *cut* meat; The first step in making a dress is to *cut* out the pieces according to the pattern.]

high

  elevated
  lofty
  tall
  towering

These words refer to something of a relatively sizable vertical dimension or to something found or placed at considerable altitude. **High** functions in both these ways: *high* buildings; a little cabin *high* up in the hills. **Tall**, by contrast, is restricted to the first situation: a *tall* man; a child *tall* for her age. Because of this, *tall* is preferred over *high* in more formal contexts to indicate vertical height: *tall* buildings. But the informal use of *high* in this sense remains secure: climb the *highest* mountain. *High*, in general, does tend to suggest altitude, *tall* relative dimension. *High*, furthermore, is used metaphorically to refer to mobility or intensity: *high* moral purpose; *high* spirits. *Tall* has fewer metaphorical uses, one of them being in reference to masculinity: *tall* in the saddle.

Elevated, considerably more formal than the foregoing, is like *high* in referring both to vertical dimension and placement at an altitude: an apartment house *elevated* several dozen floors above its neighbors; an *elevated* railway. The word has a special use to indicate anything that has been raised above something else: an *elevated* walkway for pedestrians; the *elevated* tiers of a rice paddy that ran halfway up the mountain. Metaphorically, the word emphasizes nobility, dignity, or profundity: an *elevated* discussion of final causes. But the word can suggest pretentious pomposity or inflated self-esteem: considering herself too *elevated* to eat with the common horde in the dining room; *elevated* diction.

Towering, by contrast, is restricted like *tall* to refer to things of a considerable height, although it is an intensification of *tall*, almost to the point of hyperbole: the *towering* giant of a man who was walking toward us; the *towering* redwoods in Mill Valley; *towering* skyscrapers. Metaphorically, the word is vaguer than *high* or *elevated*, making a hyperbolic plea that something be regarded as greatly important or valuable: our *towering* need for solutions to present-day problems; a *towering* figure in world literature.

Lofty may refer, like *high*, either to stature or placement at an altitude: the *lofty* oak; the *lofty* mountain pass. Both of these concrete uses may seem less than natural now, however, having a ring that would sound too pretentious in many situations. The word, like *elevated*, once was used metaphorically to indicate nobility and profundity, but this use, too, could be thought dangerously affected: the *lofty* efforts of our Founding Fathers. The word does have a specific use to suggest a sense of superiority that causes someone to withdraw and act in a cold or remote manner; the word is, in this case, disapproving or pejorative in tone: the *lofty* arrogance of the white suburbs; a *lofty* indifference of some writers to the pressing problems of their times. See OUTSTANDING, POSITION, STEEP, SUMMIT.

Antonyms: base, degraded, low, short.

These words refer to things that in some way stand over or above their surroundings or above similar things, either in a literal or a figurative sense. **Highest** is the most general word. It may mean located at the greatest elevation: the *highest* story of a building; the *highest* peak in the mountain range. *Highest* also refers to something of the greatest importance: the *highest* law of the land; the *highest* good. In reference to degree, amount, or size, *highest* is frequently used. [We pay the *highest* prices for old gold; The tide is *highest* at eleven o'clock; Yuma, Arizona, has the *highest* temperatures in the United States; We have the *highest* regard for his opinions.]

The other words in this group emphasize one or more of the meanings of *highest*. **Supreme** is applied especially to persons or things that are not only *highest* in rank, quality, or importance, but are also considered unequaled: the *Supreme* Court; Zeus, the *supreme* deity of the ancient Greeks. [The *supreme* moment of a gambler's life is when he breaks the bank at Monte Carlo.]

Topmost may refer to a person who has the *highest* position in a specific situation: the *topmost* executive of the company. But it is more likely to be applied to something located at the greatest elevation: the *topmost* shelf of a closet; the *topmost* twigs of a fir tree.

Uppermost is often used interchangeably with *topmost*, but it tends to be used more often to describe people or things which have the *highest* and most important position or which receive the greatest amount of attention: the *uppermost* faction in a political party; those thoughts which are *uppermost* in his mind. See FARTHEST, STEEP, SUMMIT.

Antonyms: bottom, deepest, lowest, undermost.

highest

supreme
topmost
uppermost

These words mean to put difficulties or obstacles in the way or progress of. **Hinder** is the most general term and the least strong in meaning. Specifically, to *hinder* is to delay or slow down a person or thing, and it may imply either active interference or an accidental action or condition. [The child's hysterical crying *hindered* the doctor from completing his examination; Bad weather *hindered* the military operation; Overcrowded schoolrooms *hinder* the education of our children.]

hinder

encumber
hamper

hinder
(continued)

impede
obstruct

Impede is to delay by a deliberate act, and it retains much of its original meaning of fettering the feet. *Impede* suggests stronger obstacles than does *hinder* and implies a forcible slowing down that is frustrating and even painful. [The crowds at the scene of the accident *impeded* the arrival of the ambulance; Many a man is *impeded* in his career by a lack of belief in himself.]

Hamper means to *impede* by placing restraints of any sort which make action burdensome and difficult. [*Hampered* by four small whining children, the young mother had difficulty in getting on the bus; Too strong a sense of duty *hampered* him from enjoying life.]

Encumber, like *hamper*, suggests a *hindering* of action or motion by outside forces. However, in the case of *encumber*, the *hindering* comes about by the placing of a burden rather than by that of a restraint. [The little burro was so *encumbered* with produce for market that he could scarcely walk; Debts *encumbered* the young family while the children were small.]

Obstruct is the strongest term in this group. It implies not only a delay in action or movement, but often a complete halt by the placing of large, immovable objects in one's path. [The excavation has *obstructed* all traffic in this street for the past week; The bully *obstructed* the path of the small boy who was hurrying home.] See STOP (arrest), STOP (cease), THWART, UNWILLING, WITHSTAND.

Antonyms: ENCOURAGE, IMPEL, QUICKEN, *spur*.

hint

implication
innuendo
insinuation
intimation
suggestion

These words refer to signs or evidence, indirectly given or covertly present, from which certain meanings may be inferred. **Hint** is the most informal of these words and most often refers to a sign intentionally given to alert someone else to something that might otherwise be overlooked: giving him a *hint* that she wouldn't mind being asked for a date. The word may also refer to clues unintentionally given: inadvertent behavior that was a *hint* of some deeper emotional disturbance. At an even further remove, the word may suggest a sign inherent in any set of data: a campsite that gave *hints* of recent use; a *hint* of fall in the air.

Suggestion differs from *hint* in that it may refer to more directly presented statements; even here, however, the emphasis is on a tactful presentation that stops short of insistence or flat recommendation: her *suggestion* that he try thinning the paint with more benzine. Less commonly than with *hint*, the word may refer to inadvertent clues or to signs inherent in data: a *suggestion* of nervousness in the way he kept running his hand through his hair; a city that teemed with *suggestions* concerning the fast-paced life of its inhabitants.

Implication may, like *hint*, refer to an intentionally given sign, although greater indirection is stressed: He backed up her *suggestion* that the child get ready for bed, with a broad *hint* about a bedtime snack and an unspoken *implication* that the child might be punished for not obeying. More often, however, the word is restricted to indicate indirect evidence of any sort from which meaning can be inferred: arguing that the development of an inconsiderate selfishness was one *implication* of the permissive rearing of children; an *implication* of disapproval that underlay the author's seemingly objective treatment of his major character.

Intimation is alone among these words in stressing the gaining of an insight into the future: an *intimation* from the outset that he would not find his new job a pleasant one. Sometimes the word may suggest a vague feeling or suspicion arrived at without evidence of any kind, either by intuitive or supernatural processes: an *intimation* that he would one day ask her to marry him; an *intimation* that the world would come to an end on Friday. The word may also refer to intuitions or suspicions that do not pertain to futurity: getting any number of *intimations* that his friend's childhood had been unusually bleak and forbidding.

Innuendo and **insinuation** are closely related; both are set apart from these other words by concentrating mainly on intentionally given signs that bristle with unpleasant or hostile meanings. *Innuendo* can be seen as a negative *implication*; *insinuation* as a negative *suggestion*: making a thinly veiled *innuendo* that reflected on the morality of his opponent; a barrage of slight but mounting *insinuations* that he should perhaps give up trying to be a playwright. *Innuendo*, in addition, implies an unsupported or unsupportable personal attack that is never spelled out; *insinuation* may imply a process of worming one's way into someone's favor by obsequious methods in order to harm that person or someone else: Cassius's *innuendoes* to Brutus about Caesar's untrustworthiness; Iago's *insinuations* concerning Desdemona's virtue. See PREMONITION, SYMPTOM.

Antonyms: affirmation, assertion, declaration.

These words refer to people, usually young and sometimes artistic or quasi-artistic in bent, who as a group rebel against middle-class standards and choose to live a spontaneous, impoverished life characterized by eccentric dress, amoral behavior, and an anarchic, solipsistic, or leftist philosophy. **Hippie** refers to a member of the most clearly defined such group to emerge in the late 1960's. *Hippies*, most typically, were under thirty, were interested in psychedelic drugs, rock music, communal living, and an apolitical oriental philosophy based on universal love. Historically, **bohemian** can refer to a member of the earliest such group to gain notice, emerging in Paris around the turn of the century; a romanticized version of their life was the subject of Puccini's opera *La Bohème*. Unlike *hippies*, *bohemians* were more often struggling young artists whose poverty was involuntary, stemming from the neglect of their work by the public. The word was taken up and extended to any group of artists who congregated in certain sections of big cities: the *bohemians* who gathered in Greenwich Village during the depression. While the word is thus more general, it can now sound dated except in historical usage.

In the 1950's, **hipster** (earlier, *hepster*) referred to a member of a coterie that doted on avant-garde jazz and adopted a "cool" or uninvolved life-style that was a protest against what they saw as a dehumanizing society. At first, a *hipster* might have been most typically a Negro musician, but the word widened out to include anyone who modeled his life on such jazz heroes as Charlie Parker. Inspired in part by the *hipster*, a literary movement arose in this period whose practitioners were called **beatniks**. Forerunner of the 1960's *hippie*, the *beatnik* dressed in jeans and T-shirt, wore his hair long, advocated unconventional or undisciplined literary forms, and valued jazz, motorcyclists, aimless travels about the country, and the drug experience. In their extreme alienation from society, *beatniks* were often pessimistic in outlook, whereas the later *hippie* was often optimistic in that he saw himself as the opening wedge of a profound generational upsurge toward a more open and positive way of life. Also, the *hippie* was less often an artist, whether real or imagined.

Teenybopper was developed in the 1960's to refer to teen-age aspirants to the cult of the *hippie*. At first, *teenybopper* applied particularly

hippie

beatnik
bohemian
drop-out
head
hipster
provo
teenybopper

to a young girl who came to the big city and affected the dress and manner of the full-time and somewhat older *hippie*. Later applied to both sexes, *teenybopper* implies an intense devotion to rock music as well as an interest in psychedelic drugs and sexual experimentation. **Provo** refers to a member of a movement that emerged in the 1960's, one that paralleled and overlapped the cult of the *hippie*. *Provo*, short for *provocateur*, was first used by young people in Amsterdam to describe themselves and their interest in high-spirited acts of anarchism by which they confronted and challenged the established political order. With many of the same values as espoused by *hippies*, *provos* were more consciously political in orientation, although their activism did not rest on any coherently formulated ideology. *Provo* now refers to activist *hippies* in any big city who wish to grapple with what they see as the evils of society rather than to withdraw from them.

Head can refer to any *beatnik, hippie,* or other person who is fixated on some psychedelic drug as his main pleasure and interest: a close-knit group of *heads* who turned on together at least once a week. The word is sometimes a combining form, used in connection with a specific psychedelic: *pothead* (marijuana), *acidhead* (LSD), *A-head* (amphetamines). **Drop-out** refers to a *hippie* or a *head* who has completely withdrawn from society into a world of personal consciousness defined for him and heightened by the use of psychedelics. When used by members of the in-group, *drop-out* is not pejorative, since the act of withdrawing is considered necessary to full personal realization. A conflicting use confuses this sense, however, since the word can also refer to young people who do not continue in high school and thus are in danger of becoming unemployables living on the edge of society in the dehumanizing culture of poverty: a government program to train *drop-outs* and, if possible, return them to school. See ARTIST, BUM, WANDERER.

hire

draft
employ
engage
enlist
recruit

These words refer to taking on someone to fill a job. **Hire** is the most informal of these and, because of this, may apply most naturally to a wage-earning rather than a salaried worker: *hiring* three new waitresses. The word, however, is often used of more exalted positions: *hiring* a new managing editor. Sometimes, the word suggests taking on someone for a specific or one-time job: *hiring* a plumber to install the new dryer; *hired* to kill the rival ganglord. The word's brevity allows its use, as well, to refer to the general practice of filling vacancies: a department set up to take care of *hiring* and firing. **Employ** is a more formal substitute for *hire* and is sometimes used for positions of greater prestige: *employing* him as guidance counselor. In governmental and official terminology, the word universally replaces *hire*: urging businesses to *employ* the handicapped. The word goes beyond *hire*, however, in referring not just to the initial taking on of someone but to his continued use. Thus, *employ*, which is euphemistic for other senses of use and often for the simple act of *hiring*, is free of such a tone in this case: an operation that *employed* a staff of two hundred people; asking when he was last *employed*.

Engage seems unnecessarily indirect when used as a substitute for *hire* or *employ* in their most common senses. The word has pertinence, however, in referring to a specific or one-time contracting for someone's services, especially when these are of a professional nature: *engaging* a gardener to cut her lawn once a month; *engaging* a lawyer to argue his case in court. The word, like *employ*, may also refer to someone actually at work, especially in fields where work comes in spurts: *engaging* extra summer help; an actress who was not *engaged* for the coming season.

Draft, enlist, and **recruit** have special relevance to serving in the armed forces, but all of them are used widely outside this context. *Draft* always carries the implication of service that is compulsory or involuntary: *drafting* college students into the army at the completion of their studies; *drafting* several club members to hand out ballots during the voting. As in the last example, this word need not suggest working for pay, unlike the usual implications of the preceding words. *Recruit* contrasts sharply with *draft* in indicating an appeal for volunteers to undertake a task or position, not necessarily for pay: special training programs that made it easy to *recruit* young men into the air force; *recruiting* neighbors to help put out the fire. Used transitively, *enlist* is a more general substitute for *recruit*; it may suggest seeking monetary or moral support as well as the actual acquiring of someone's services: *enlisting* college graduates in the long-term government project; *enlisting* your help in the coming election. Used intransitively, the word indicates volunteering for an assignment: *enlisting* in the navy rather than waiting to be *drafted*. A confusion sometimes results because new arrivals or trainees in the armed forces, whether *recruited* or *drafted*, are called *recruits*; similarly, all noncommissioned personnel are called *enlisted* men (or women), though not all may have volunteered their service. See LABOR, LEASE, PROFESSION, USE.

Antonyms: buy, discharge, fire, purchase, retire.

These words denote a systematic record of past events. A **history** is a narrative that recounts events with attention to their importance, their mutual relations, causes, and consequences; it is therefore highly selective: Herodotus' famous *history* of the Persian wars; to commission an author to write a *history* of a company. A **chronicle** is a record of events in order of time; **annals** are similar but are divided year by year. Neither *chronicles* nor *annals* attempt to interpret events. A historian, for instance, might scan the *annals* of a political party before writing a *history* of its creation and growth; a magazine article might include a *chronicle* of the major political events of the last fifty years. See NARRATIVE, REPORT.

history

annals
chronicle

These words refer to play, leisure-time activities, or side interests pursued for amusement or pleasure. **Hobby** indicates an activity that may involve the development of intricate knowledge or expertise about a limited field. It particularly implies collecting or tinkering activities, often done by oneself at home and seldom involving physical exercise for its own sake: a lifelong *hobby* of stamp collecting.

Avocation is more formal than *hobby* and may suggest a more dedicated pursuit of something with cultural or social value: a doctor whose *avocation* was playing cello in an amateur string quartet. But more generally, the word can group together the whole range of activities considered here, since its only restriction is its emphasis on something that is secondary to a person's livelihood, career, or central concern. **Recreation** is comparable in its generality to *avocation*. While it doesn't emphasize the distinction between main and secondary interests, it does suggest pleasure-giving relaxation and low-key activity that would not be found in most vocations. The word's stress is on play or games. Thus, unlike *hobby*, it can more often suggest activity that is done in groups and that includes physical exercise: camps offering a variety of *recreations* that included folk dancing, handicrafts, swimming, and boating.

Pastime is closer to *hobby* than the previous pair, indicating any-

hobby

avocation
pastime
recreation
sport

thing done to occupy one's leisure; by implication, the word suggests busywork of little intrinsic worth: insisting that his painting was merely a *pastime* that kept him from being bored. This deprecatory note can be even more pronounced: few *pastimes* more foolish than autograph collecting. **Sport** is the one word here that points to a *recreation* or *pastime* that is primarily a matter of physical exercise, and suggests especially competitive group or individual activity: We enjoyed playing baseball, football, and other *sports*. Unlike all the other words here, *sport* can indicate an activity pursued as a money-making vocation: He had performed so brilliantly on his college's tennis team that he took up the *sport* as a full-time professional player. See PLEASURE.

Antonyms: business, calling, LABOR, *livelihood,* PROFESSION.

hole

cavity
excavation
hollow
pit

These words are compared as they denote an unfilled space within a solid body. **Hole** is the most general word, and also the most ambiguous; a *hole* in a stocking goes through it, a *hole* in a piece of timber may or may not go through, a *hole* in the ground does not go through the earth, but may be narrow or wide, shallow or very deep. **Hollow** and **cavity** refer to an empty space within something otherwise solid or filled; of the two, *cavity* is somewhat more learned or formal except for its popular use to describe a *hole* in a tooth: the pleural *cavity* in which the lungs are situated; the abdominal *cavity*. *Hollow* is frequently used of any depression or concavity in a surface: the *hollows* of the sea. **Pit** denotes primarily certain large natural *cavities*, especially in the ground; it is also used figuratively to suggest an abysmal depth, and is sometimes used to mean hell. **Excavation** is a man-made *cavity* or *pit*, as for the foundations of a building. See PIERCE.

Antonyms: bump, projection, protrusion.

home

abode
domicile
habitation
household
hovel
residence

These words refer to places or buildings in which people live, or to the people themselves. **Home** is the most general term, but it often means more than simply an occupied house or other dwelling. Specifically *home* refers to a place where one lives on a more or less permanent basis and with which one has strong personal ties of affection and loyalty. [In our *home*, Sunday dinner in the middle of the day has always been the custom; Loving parents tend to provide secure *homes* for children; The young soldier kept dreaming of *home*.] *Home* may also refer to a region or country in which one was born, brought up, or now resides. [Latvia is the *home* of the Letts; Although I have lived in California for five years, my *home* is Columbus, Ohio.] By extension, the natural habitats of animals or the places in which they seek shelter for the raising of their young are often spoken of as *homes*: the wolf's *home* in the rocky cave; the whale's *home* in the depths of the sea.

Residence is a more formal word for *home* and has the suggestion of an imposing or pretentious dwelling: the mayor's *residence*; the *residence* of the bank president. *Residence* may be used to distinguish a person's place of business or professional activity from his *home*: The doctor has his office in the city, but his *residence* is in the suburbs. A residential neighborhood is one made up largely of *homes* or *residences* rather than of commercial establishments. *Residence* is sometimes applied to housing provided by an educational or other institution for its students or staff members: a nurses' *residence*; a *residence* for graduate students; the *residence* of the Dean of Men. In a legal sense, a person may be said to have *residence* in the state of Massachusetts (that is, he is registered to vote there, owns property there, registers his automobile there, etc.) although he temporarily lives and works in another region or country.

Abode is a somewhat high-flown, literary term for *home* and has a wide application, for it does not in any way connote the actual character of a *home*. *Abode* can also refer to a place, such as a hotel, camp, cottage by the sea, etc., in which one stays only temporarily.

A **hovel** is a small, wretched *home* and suggests squalor and poverty. [Medieval serfs lived in *hovels* on their lord's estate; Over the years, the neglected little Tudor cottage became a *hovel*.]

Habitation is a generic term and is chiefly applied to the dwellings of people who have settled, permanent *homes*, in contradistinction to nomads or gypsies, who habitually shift their *abodes* to find food, pasturage, or work.

Except in a legal sense, **domicile** is rarely used. *Domicile* denotes a *home* or *residence* over which the owner has certain rights and responsibilities by law and in which he intends to reside indefinitely.

Household refers to a domestic establishment — that is, to the persons dwelling together under one roof as a social unit, and not to any actual structure. It may include not only the members of a family or other organized group, but servants and retainers as well. A *household* may also consist of a single person living alone. When the Bureau of Internal Revenue speaks of a "head of *household*" it is referring to the person in a family who pays the bills of maintaining the *home*, such as rent, mortgage payments, taxes, utilities, etc. See HOUSE, LODGINGS.

homonym

homograph
homophone

Homonym is used with a variety of meanings. It is commonly used to mean one of two or more words pronounced alike but having different spellings and meanings, such as *fair* and *fare*. In more precise contexts such words are called **homophones**, from the Greek *homos* same + *phōnē* sound. *Homonym* is also sometimes used to mean one of two or more words that are spelled alike but differ in origin and meaning and sometimes in pronunciation, such as *wind* (a breeze) and *wind* (to coil). Again, in more precise contexts such words are called **homographs**, from the Greek *homos* same + *graphein* to write. *Homonym*, in precise usage, means a word identical with another in spelling and pronunciation but differing from it in origin and meaning, such as *bear* (the animal) and *bear* (to carry).

Unfortunately or not, *homonym* is well established in each of these senses, and is perhaps most commonly used synonymously with *homophone* — that is, to refer to one of two or more words that sound alike but otherwise differ, such as *read* and *reed* or *whole* and *hole*.

hope

anticipate
await
dream
expect
foresee
wish

These words pertain to the attitude of looking forward to something that is to occur in the future. **Hope** suggests looking forward exclusively to some positive or favorable outcome; it may be well-founded in probability or completely beyond the pale of the possible: *hoping* that his extra effort on the theme would bring him a higher mark; still *hoping*, despite the driving rain, that it would be sunny when they reached the beach. **Wish** suggests something considerably less plausible or likely than *hope*: *wishing* that he could suddenly be made into a millionaire. Where *hope* may be part of an ennobling or heroic attitude, *wish* gives off a flavor of idle childishness that is unwilling to take a realistic stand: *wishing* for the good things of life rather than working for them full of confidence and *hope*. **Dream** suggests an even more tenuous basis for looking forward than *wish*, implying a complete, if momentary, retreat from reality: *dreaming* of the day when her husband would be acclaimed as a great writer. Unlike *wish*, *dream* can be used in a way that parallels the noble sense of *hope*: A person ceases to be human when he ceases to *dream*. Furthermore, both *dream* and *wish* are not necessarily restricted, as with *hope*, to future possibilities: *wishing* she had been born a princess; *dreaming* of a happier life on some other planet.

Anticipate is closer to *hope* in being restricted to thoughts of the future: *anticipating* the fast approach of Christmas and the presents she would at last be able to open. But while the word is frequently connected to thoughts of a pleasant outcome, it can also be used for imagining an unpleasant one: *anticipating* the eventual defeat of all his troops. **Expect** suggests looking forward either to a positive or to a negative outcome, but the point of this word is that it concerns itself with supposed certainties: *expecting* any minute to hear her husband climbing the stairs, home from work; fully *expecting* the rush of abuse that followed his unpleasant revelation. **Await** stresses a certain passiveness of attitude while watching for something imminent to occur, whether positive or negative, whether *expected* or not: *awaiting* her answer without the slightest clue as to what she would say; *awaiting* his passionately *hoped*-for return; grimly *awaiting* the fall of the guillotine blade.

Foresee introduces another aspect of looking forward to the future; it suggests an attempt to infer or guess what the future might be, rather than imagining an outcome either in accord with what is *hoped* or opposed to it: *foreseeing* by every sign that it would rain before morning. See PREDICT, SUPPOSE.

Antonyms: despair, despond.

horse

cob
colt
filly
foal
gelding
hunter
mare
nag
plug
pony
stallion
steed
stud

These words denote types, ages, and sexes of animals of the equine group, but especially of domestic **horses** of all sizes and breeds. *Horse* is the generic term. In its specific sense it refers to the full-grown male, whether a **gelding** or a **stallion**, as contrasted with the full-grown female, or **mare**. *Gelding* refers to an adult male *horse* that has been castrated, while a *stallion* is a full-grown male *horse* that has not been castrated. When kept for breeding purposes, a *stallion* is often referred to as a **stud**, or *stud horse*. *Mare* refers to any female *horse*, but correctly to one at least three or four years of age that may be bred.

A **colt** is any young *horse* under the age of four years, but the word is applied especially to a male. **Filly** is the term used of the female *horse* of the same age. Both of these words denote race *horses* in the two-year-old group.

A **foal** is a newborn *colt* or *filly*, usually up to the age of two weeks. *Foal* is also the verb used when a *mare* gives birth.

Originally, a **nag** was a small *horse* used for riding, but the word now emphasizes an old, ill, or broken-down animal. *Nag* is also used humorously of any *horse*.

Plug, like *nag*, is often applied to an old, broken-down *horse* and is also a humorous term. Specifically, it means a slow animal that is unwilling to exert itself: a livery-stable *plug*.

Pony customarily refers to any of several breeds of very small *horse*, usually under 14 hands (about 56 inches) at the shoulder. Breeds such as the Shetland *pony* and the Welsh *pony* are usually ridden by small children or used to draw carts. The word is also a regional name in the West for the *horses* that are used by cowboys while herding cattle or, in the past, for the *horses* ridden by Indians.

A **cob** is a short-legged, stocky little *horse*, of considerable strength, used either for riding or for pulling a light carriage.

A **hunter** is a *horse* that has been trained to carry a person of any weight, as in a fox hunt. He must have great endurance, as a *hunter* runs for long distances over rough terrain and has to be able to jump fences, streams, etc., with ease.

Steed is a literary term for a spirited war *horse* or one ridden on occasions of state and display: a knight on his richly caparisoned *steed*; Queen Elizabeth on a coal-black *steed*. As in the case of *nag* and *plug*, *steed* may also be applied to any mount, especially one of dubious ancestry or ridiculous aspect: The farm boy's *steed* was a lop-eared old mule with one eye.

Horse, *colt*, and *filly* are sometimes used figuratively of human beings. *Horse* suggests clumsiness, lack of delicacy, and even gluttony: to stamp up the stairs like a *horse*; to sweat like a *horse*; to eat like a *horse*. *Colt* and its adjective *coltish* convey the awkward, fresh charm of the older child or young adolescent who is having difficulty in coordinating his rapidly growing limbs. When applied to a girl or young woman, *filly* emphasizes abundant energy and wantonness as contrasted with the sedateness of maturity: an old fool in his sixties trying to make dates with twenty-year-old *fillies*. See ANIMAL.

Hostile is the strongest word in this group, and connotes an attitude of intense ill will and a course of action based on that attitude: *hostile* intentions of the enemy; the malicious barbs of a *hostile* critic.

Unfriendly, as here considered, **bellicose**, and **belligerent** imply an aggressive readiness to fight and an attitude that is usually careless of the object of its ill will. [A *bellicose* nation is a warlike nation that tends to resort to arms with little or no cause; a *belligerent* tavern brawler who picked a fight for the sake of fighting; an *unfriendly* tribe that attacked all interlopers without regard for their intent] See ENMITY, VINDICTIVE.

Antonyms: cordial, friendly, tolerant, warm.

hostile

bellicose
belligerent
unfriendly

These words refer to relatively high temperatures. **Hot** is the most general and the most relative, depending on context for preciseness: weather *hot* enough to begin melting off the snowdrifts; *hot* water; Even the coolest star is unimaginably *hot* by human standards. **Burning**, **scorching**, and **sizzling** are more specific in referring to temperatures that resemble or are the result of fire. Of these, *burning* is the most general; it is often used hyperbolically for anything *hot* or metaphorically for anything high-key: a *burning* sirocco; *burning* issues. *Scorching* is particularly relevant to a *hot*, dry atmosphere, although the implication of dryness is not always present: the *scorching* heat of a sauna as compared to the mugginess of a steam bath; humid, *scorching* weather. Metaphorically, it suggests anger: *scorching* disdain. *Sizzling* suggests, often hyperbolically, a *burning* that gives off sparks or spatters or that can sear upon contact: a pan of *sizzling* fat; sunbathers lying on the *sizzling* sand; *sizzling* weather. Metaphorically, it suggests luridness or arousal: *sizzling* pictures of half-clothed women.

Sultry, sweltering, and **torrid** concentrate more exclusively on one implication of the previous group, the one pertaining to weather. *Sultry* specifically suggests humid heat: in for another *sultry* summer. *Sweltering* is an intensification of *sultry*, suggesting an oppressive heat associated with heavy sweating or fainting: the customary siesta, made

hot

burning
feverish
scorching
sizzling
sultry
sweltering
torrid

necessary by the *sweltering* noonday heat. *Torrid* is more matter-of-fact than the preceding pair, referring more to climate than to weather: the *torrid* zone; the Congo's *torrid* season. Of this group, both *sultry* and *torrid* have metaphorical uses referring to emotional excitement. *Sultry* suggests passionate moodiness or intensity, *torrid* a more specifically sexual context: the *sultry* beauties in his harem; a *torrid* affair.

Feverish, most literally, refers to a high body temperature: He felt faint and *feverish*. Metaphorically, it can refer to haste and confusion: *feverish* attempts to meet the deadline. See HUMID, PASSIONATE, WARM.

Antonyms: COLD.

hotel

hostel
inn
motel

These words refer to buildings or groups of buildings that are set up to provide living quarters for customers, especially on a temporary basis. **Hotel** usually refers to a single building, large or small, in which rooms or suites are rented out on a fixed basis: *hotels* jammed by those pouring into town for the convention. Although the word most often suggests accommodations for travelers or transients, it may also apply to more permanent arrangements: She had lived in the resident *hotel* for a decade. **Hostel** represents an older borrowing from the same source word as *hotel* and once meant the same thing. Now it almost universally refers to one of a chain of lodging houses for young people on cycling or hiking tours: He planned his itinerary so that each night would put him near a different *hostel*.

Motel is a portmanteau word for motor *hotel*; it refers to a roadside building or, often, a group of buildings, such as a cluster of cabins, where people traveling by car may obtain lodgings: an attempt to choose among several *motels* that lay strung out along the highway. **Inn** also refers to a roadside *hotel*, but suggests a much more rustic setting than *motel* and is a place where travelers may obtain either food or lodgings, or both. Since the word has an archaic and convivial quality, it is often used pretentiously to refer to any sort of mere restaurant: your country *inn* in the heart of the city. Sometimes it serves as a genteel substitute for *motel*: a motor *inn*. See HOUSE, LODGINGS.

hound

pointer
retriever
setter
terrier

These words all refer to dogs used in hunting or tracking a quarry. **Hound** is by far the most general of these. Used loosely, it can merely be a more formal substitute for dog itself, giving an archaic or pretentious tone; used specifically, it can refer to a grouping of specific breeds. Between these two extremes, the word would most often be understood as referring to dogs that track quarry by scent or sight: They brought out *hounds* to track down the escaped convict; the packs of *hounds* used in fox hunting. Metaphorically, the word can suggest someone fixated on the pursuit of something: an autograph *hound*.

The remaining words are restricted to describing ways that hunting or sporting dogs track or capture their quarry. More specifically, of course, each may indicate a precise breed of dog or groups of such breeds. **Pointer** refers to a dog that signals the presence of quarry, such as birds, by fixing its body with tail uplifted and nose directed toward the prey. The **setter** acts similarly, but adopts a sitting position in indicating its prey. A **retriever** is any dog that brings back shot or killed animals to its master, whether over land or water. **Terrier** refers to a dog that digs up burrowing prey, such as gophers or moles. But this word has become more and more attached to particular breeds, valued as pets, without indicating this hunting activity at all. See ANIMAL.

These words refer to structures in which people live or work. **House** refers generally to any sort of structure meant for living in. Though it may classically call up an image of a free-standing, one-family structure of moderate size, it can apply to a whole spectrum of habitations, from those considerably more to those considerably less extensive than this midpoint: the baronet's fifty-room country *house*; They bought a one-story semi-detached *house* in the new development; a rickety one-room *house* built of unchinked logs; rows of grimy tenement *houses*. In informal use, the word frequently refers to the place one lives, even though it is a room or apartment or some other division of a larger structure: She takes the elevator to the tenth floor whenever she goes to play in Janie's *house*.

Dwelling is a more formal substitute for *house* and has fewer connotations, referring solely to any structure (or less often, to part of one) where people live. Its formality, however, makes it sound odd in other contexts than sociological discussion or the parlance of the construction industry: a study that compared children who lived in two-family *dwellings* with those in apartment *houses*; contractors who are equipped to mass-produce middle-income *dwellings* on a vast scale. Even in these uses, the word may sound like an unnecessarily inflated evasion of *house*. The word also can have an aura of faded lyricism or religiosity, in imitation of its valid use in the King James Bible: the simple *dwellings* of upright men.

Roof and **shelter** are more informal and more colorful substitutes for *house* than *dwelling*, both stressing the minimal factors of utility or protection given by any sort of structure. *Roof* is a synecdoche for the whole *house*: two families sharing the same *roof*. But it may suggest temporary accommodations rather than permanent living quarters: anxious to get a *roof* over their heads by nightfall. *Shelter* is useful as a general word with which to group together all living structures, permanent or temporary: man's basic needs of food, clothing, and *shelter*. It may even refer to any sort of protective retreat: a tree that provided *shelter* from the rain; to take *shelter*. Used as a specific reference to a particular structure, it is likely to suggest something rude or improvised: They collected driftwood to build a beach *shelter*. **Housing** is a general word referring to the supplying of or demand for living space of any sort: open *housing*; legislation in the areas of *housing* and education.

Building refers concretely to an actual structure, but it is not restricted, like *house*, to those designed or used as living space: farm *buildings* that included the farmhouse, a barn, and a silo. **Premises** is a technical term in insurance, legal, or criminological parlances. It may refer to a tract of land with *buildings* on it; to a *house*, *building*, or part of a *house*; or to the space occupied by a business: a policy insuring the *premises* against fire; suspicious characters seen on the *premises*. Sometimes it is used outside these contexts with comic effect: He got his golf clubs from the closet in the hope of getting off the *premises* without being seen. See HOME, HOTEL, LODGINGS.

These words are comparable in the broad sense of having an interest in or concern for the welfare and happiness of others. **Humane**, the most comprehensive of them, implies considerateness in our dealings not only with people but with all living creatures and in situations involving either: a *humane* judge; a *humane* treatment of animals; a *humane* management policy. **Benign** carries the suggestion of a mild, sometimes faintly condescending gentleness and tolerance, with a secondary mean-

humane

(continued)

compassionate
human
humanitarian
philanthropic
sympathetic

ing of harmlessness: a *benign* attitude toward the follies of others; a *benign* tumor.

Etymologically, **sympathetic** and **compassionate** mean the same thing: feeling or suffering, usually with another person. But *sympathetic*, from the Greek has a wider, frequently more generalized and impersonal range than the Latin *compassionate*. One can be *sympathetic* with a point of view, a philosophy, belief, or way of life, or feel sympathy for the hardships of a fictional character; but *compassionate* implies a stronger and more directly personal feeling for suffering and misfortune at the individual level: His own experiences had taught him to be *compassionate* toward lonely and misunderstood children.

Charitable, humanitarian, and **philanthropic** all suggest a sense of obligation to aspects of life that are, or are regarded as, worthy of generous understanding and practical help. A *charitable* person is disposed to show a kindly and merciful attitude toward people in distress and to help them when and where possible. A *humanitarian* will generalize his interest in mankind along philosophic and often vaguely sentimental lines that disregard the individual in favor of the mass. A *philanthropic* person may be *charitable* and *humanitarian*, but has both the capacity and desire to be useful by giving large sums of money to specific causes, institutions, foundations, colleges, etc.

In all these distinctions the word **human** is a rock-bottom term that can be used wherever men are thought of apart from animals and inanimate nature and are regarded as capable of concern for and communication with others: a drop of *human* kindness. *Human* and *humane* are very different in their implications, however. *Humane* can suggest an attitude of impersonal high-mindedness, whereas *human* can often gloss over weakness or failings as being all too common and, therefore, forgivable. [It is *human* to err; little foibles that made the great man more *human*; After all, it was only *human* to do everything he could to win the prize.] But the word can also suggest a flexible and tolerant attitude toward the imperfections of others: if he'd only stop moralizing all the time and be a little bit *human*. See BENEVOLENCE, CONSIDERATE, GENEROUS, LENIENT.

Antonyms: CRUEL, *hardhearted, parsimonious, selfish, stingy, unkind.*

humid

close
oppressive
sticky

These words are comparable in that they all are used to describe a condition of the weather. **Humid,** which means containing water or vapor, is the most specific term in the group because it refers to a measurable physical phenomenon called relative humidity. Relative humidity is the ratio, expressed as a percentage, of the amount of water vapor actually in the air at a specific time to the total amount which could be present at the same temperature. *Humid,* therefore, alone or with a qualifying adverb can designate any state of atmospheric dampness: It was not *humid* yesterday, but it is very *humid* today and the weather bureau predicts that it will be even more *humid* tomorrow.

The other words in this group are less precise in meaning but distinctly more colorful in tone. **Close** can refer to the weather or to a place. When one thinks of a *close* day it is in terms of being choked or suffocated by weather that is heavy, hot, and airless. A room described as *close* has probably not been ventilated for some time; its unmoving air has grown stale and thick so that it induces an uncomfortable feeling of confinement. **Oppressive** is the most general of these words; it can apply to any kind of harsh weather that causes depression or discomfort. A *close* day with a thunderstorm lurking and no breeze stirring is cer-

tainly *oppressive*. But so, too, is a day on which the wind never stops
blowing, whether it be hot or cold, rainy or dry. It is true that *oppressive*
is mostly used in reference to hot, sultry weather, but any climatic
condition that produces a state of oppression can be characterized by
this word: The mild Christmas season was followed by two weeks of
oppressive, icy weather that kept even the hardiest souls indoors.

In this context, **sticky** refers to sweatiness caused by an *oppressive*
and *humid* warmth that does not permit evaporation; this may result
from weather, an unventilated atmosphere, or from exertion. An implication pertaining to the adhesiveness between layers, as of cloth to
sweaty skin, may also be present: a *sticky* day; an overcrowded room
that soon became damp and *sticky*; He stripped off his *sticky* gym clothes.
See HOT, WARM.

Antonyms: arid, DRY, *parched.*

These words refer to what causes or is intended to cause amusement or
laughter. **Humorous** is most often restricted to successful attempts to
amuse or to people who succeed in such attempts: a *humorous* story;
a *humorous* fellow, full of diverting remarks. Less often, the word can
refer only to the attempt: His *humorous* essays are not half so amusing
as those of Thurber. The word seldom refers to what is unintentionally
laughable. *Humorous*, like humor, often refers to a warmhearted,
sympathetic, or good-natured treatment of small failings or ironies, those
that prompt smiles rather than laughter or derision.

Comic and **comical** relate instead to comedy, which can include the
humorous but is a more general category, including slapstick, parody, or
even caustic satire. *Comic* is a neutral word by which to refer to this
category: *comic* writers. *Comic*, in fact, is now often used as a noun to
refer to any comedian: stand-up *comics*. *Comical*, by contrast, can refer
to anything or anyone whose effect is amusing, laughable, or absurd,
whether such an effect is intentional or not: a *comical* misunderstanding
that delighted the spectators but caused the embarrassed delegates to
call for a recess; He cut a *comical* figure in his pretentious finery. These
distinctions are not always observed in the use of the two words.

Funny is the most general of these words and the most informal, but
it is focused mainly on whatever results in laughter: a comedian whose
jokes weren't really very *funny*; a howlingly *funny* slip of the tongue.
When something or someone is inadvertently *funny*, it may be because
of oddness, unfamiliarity, abnormality, or inappropriateness: the *funny*
old man with the *funny* walk. This shades off into a description of anything strange or suspicious: His wife gave him a *funny* look. On the
other hand, the word can categorize an attempt, like *comic*: professional
funny men; *funny* business that was tedious and overdone. **Facetious**
once could be approving, but now is exclusively an unfavorable description of silly or ill-timed attempts at the *humorous*: a *facetious* ass who
always forgot the punch lines to the jokes he told; *facetious* remarks that
kept sidetracking any serious discussion of the problem.

Jocose and **jocular** are the most formal words here and closely related in meaning. Both come from Latin roots meaning jest or joke and
both can apply to a person given to jesting or to the amusement caused
by such remarks. *Jocose* can sometimes function as a milder substitute
for *facetious*, pointing to feeble attempts at humor, especially when they
are heavy-handed or pompous: *jocose* inanities that were stuffy and old-
hat. *Jocular* may imply a constant resort to jokes or wisecracks in the
hope of cheering up or amusing others: *jocular* comments on the bad

humorous

comic
comical
droll
facetious
funny
jocose
jocular
waggish
witty

food and worse weather. It may sometimes apply to the deliberate turning away of a serious question by a light answer: the *jocular* anecdote with which he disposed of the young man's objection.

Droll compares with one aspect of *funny* in pointing to someone who is whimsical or odd: the *droll* old curmudgeon. It can also refer to a *comic* impulse that is clever, deadpan, or laconic: the *droll* understatement of the British. It can also refer to *comic* work that is in a mordant or sardonic vein: Balzac's *Droll Stories*. **Waggish** can also indicate humor that is clever, but the word also suggests a playful irreverence in someone given to in-jokes or sly rejoinders: *waggish* remarks about the poor lady's grotesque and *comical* evening gown. **Witty** is more inclusive than *droll* or *waggish* in pointing to a brilliant or surprising play of intelligence in the delivery of amusing and trenchant observations on human foibles or follies: Oscar Wilde's *witty* repartee; a *witty* parody of television commercials. *Witty* can apply as well to the light and good-natured, like *humorous*, as to the caustic and withering: *witty* conundrums about trivialities; *witty* aspersions that cast doubt on the sincerity and competence of the playwright. See ABSURD, JOKE, LAUGH, RIDICULE.

Antonyms: dull, GLOOMY, SEDATE.

hunt

comb
explore
ransack
scour
search
seek
sleuth
track

These words indicate any effort at finding, catching, following, or examining something. **Hunt** at its most specific can refer to the specific activity of pursuing and killing animals, whether for food, profit, or sport: tribes that *hunted* buffalo for food; on a safari to *hunt* game. More generally, the word can indicate an uncertain groping for something needed: He *hunted* for the light switch along the wall of the dark room. It can also indicate an urgent following: She *hunted* everywhere in the neighborhood for the tardy child. And it can point to any act of looking for something lost or missing: *hunting* for the missing book.

Track and **sleuth** relate closely to the aspect of *hunt* pertaining to following a quarry. *Track* can indicate the ability to detect a trail of clues: Indians skilled at *tracking* the spoor of a wounded animal. It can also apply more widely for *hunting* anything fugitive or difficult to find: determined to *track* down every suspicious item in the expense account submitted to him. *Sleuth* compares such action to detective work and can apply as widely. But here the word refers more often to the search for clues itself, particularly where the quarry is not yet known: They *sleuthed* out every angle, however slight, that could lead them to the killer; clinicians to *sleuth* down symptoms that might help diagnose the strange illness.

Search and **seek** are considerably more general than the previous pair. *Search* may indicate the act of looking for a lost object or for an object presumed to exist: navigators *searching* for a western route to the East Indies. The word may also apply to mere activity without clearly stated goals: young people *searching* for a cause that would give meaning to their lives. *Hunt*, by comparison to *search*, might suggest a more informed, purposive, focused, or relentless activity: They blocked off the canyon and methodically *hunted* down the trapped desperados. *Seek* can give a more archaic flavor than *search*, except in set phrases: *seek* and find; *seek* and destroy; *seeking* out directions, a place, or a person. The word can also indicate vague desires or high-minded aspirations: negotiators *seeking* the good of all mankind; peacemakers who have always *sought* for an end to war.

Explore is like the aspect of *search* pertaining to activity that does not or cannot have a precisely stated goal in advance. *Explore* is much more clear-cut about this, however, since it always implies an attempt to learn more about an unknown: missionaries who were the first to *explore* the upper Mississippi; the thrill of *exploring* the streets of a strange city; an operation to *explore* the tissue surrounding the tumor for any signs of malignancy. The action indicated by *explore* can, of course, have a stated general goal, but some sense of newness or unfamiliarity is always present in the word.

The remaining words all involve the notion of a thorough or meticulous search of an area for evidence or for something lost or presumed to exist: **Comb** indicates a methodical, careful, minute, and orderly covering of possibilities, often giving a tone of desperation and sometimes implying a group search: a *searching* party that *combed* the hills for the missing campers. **Scour** compares to *comb* in thoroughness, but may suggest greater effort or intensity: They *scoured* the grounds for the missing keys. Although these words can be used interchangeably, *comb* might be more appropriate for small areas, since *scour* here can confusingly suggest the literal action of abrasion. **Ransack** indicates a strikingly different action, comparable in thoroughness, but implying a hasty, careless, or disorderly search: They had broken in and *ransacked* the darkroom for the incriminating roll of film, leaving the place a total mess. The word most often suggests the search of an interior, such as a house or room, and can often point to a furtive or illegal action. See EXAMINE, FIND, FOLLOW.

hurt

afflict
aggrieve
distress
pain

These words are used in referring to acts or situations that cause someone to feel emotionally upset or mentally injured. **Hurt** is the most general and informal of these words; it suggests a small mental injury: accusations designed to *hurt* and frighten her. **Pain**, in this context, now tends to sound archaic: *pained* by his constant references to her past. Because the word may sound unnatural or forced, it can sometimes give an unsympathetic tone: easily *pained* by the smallest slight. **Distress** has an extremely formal sound in most of its uses as a verb and can give a prissy or euphemistic tone: the manager who claimed to be greatly *distressed* by his secretary's long lunch hours. It may seem more natural in describing a subjective state of mind: *distressed* by vague longings and poorly defined fears. **Aggrieve** has become so fusty-sounding that its only possible use is in the passive voice, for distraught states of mind: a parent deeply *aggrieved* by his children's disobedience. **Afflict** suggests a condition that is extremely uncomfortable or upsetting, and further hints that the condition is one of long duration: *afflicted* by tensions that drove him to suicide. See HARM, WRONG.

Antonyms: benefit, comfort, console, soothe.

husky

beefy
brawny
burly

These words refer to strong, heavy, powerfully built, or masculine physiques. **Husky** refers to masculine muscularity. It derives from husk, referring to the tough covering shell of a seed; also its other uses pertaining to dryness, roughness, or hoarseness give connotations here. While the word suggests largeness of frame, it is more emphatic about the strength or muscular density of physique, particularly of the torso, with suggestions of coarseness or toughness. Thus, it serves as an antonym to lithe or supple and implies instead a possibly slower-moving but more powerful body: the lithe physique best for runners and tennis players as compared to the *husky* builds required for wrestling or shot-put.

husky
(continued)

hulking
stocky
strapping

Brawny and **burly** both intensify the emphasis of *husky* on massive or dense muscular development, suggesting in these cases a grossness of build beyond that of any well-proportioned and cleanly defined athletic ideal. *Burly* may carry connotations over from another word, identical in form, that refers to the knots and burls of a tree, in this case suggesting a thick bunching of muscles that may verge on the grotesque; an overall thickness of frame, at any rate, is implied, with suggestions of coarse or crude power that are even stronger than those for *husky*: the *burly*, lumbering stevedore with the thick bullneck and barrel-shaped chest. *Brawny* is less extreme in its implications than *burly*, emphasizing instead the sheer power inherent in muscular development. Where *husky* may particularly point to a developed torso, *brawny* suggests general muscular density, such as acquired by hard physical labor: a *brawny* lumberjack.

Beefy points to muscular masses but, unlike the previous words, need not indicate power or density. The word can in fact suggest a fleshy grossness that may be repellent or flabby: the nightclub's *beefy* bouncer. **Hulking** and **stocky** both suggest sheer size or largeness of frame rather than pointing primarily to muscular development. *Hulking* particularly indicates a tall or looming male build: a *hulking* basketball player. *Stocky*, by contrast, emphasizes largeness rather than tallness of frame: a *stocky* plumber almost as wide as he was tall. Even more than *husky*, this word can be used euphemistically for a fat or heavy body: a reducing clinic for *stocky* executives. **Strapping** combines the suggestions of sheer size in the last pair with the stress on muscular development in the first group. The word is often used to indicate precocious growth and development in boys or young men: a *strapping*, tow-headed farmboy. See MASCULINE, PHYSICAL.

Antonyms: THIN.

I

idea

concept
conception
impression
notion
thought

All of these words denote something that exists in the mind during the processes of perceiving, thinking, or willing. **Idea** is the most general term, applicable to almost any part or aspect of mental activity. [The *idea* of death is frightening to some people; I had no *idea* of going to the party; She has a general *idea* of the cost of the repair job.] A **concept** is an *idea* of a category or kind that has been generalized from particular instances. Thus, the *concept* of "horse" arises from the many horses we see. *Concept* also refers to a widely held *idea* of what something is or should be: The *concept* of government of many small nations has been influenced by the democratic institutions of the United States. The meaning of **conception** is much like this second sense of *concept*, but differs in that the *idea* of what a thing is or should be is here held by an individual or small group and is often colored by imagination and feeling: A child's *conception* of the universe is formed by his limited experience and his own fancies. A **thought** is an *idea* based on intellectual activity, and is not directly attributable to a sense impression: He has many *thoughts* on the matter. A **notion** is a vague or capricious *idea*, often without any sound basis: to have a *notion* that the stock market will rise. An **impression** is an *idea* that arises from something external. It suggests either a half-formed mental picture or a superficial view or conclusion. [An infant may have the *impression* that its father is a giant; My *impression* is that he was lying.] See OPINION.

These words are alike in describing persons or actions regarded as being far below common worth or dignity. **Ignoble** and **mean** originally meant of low birth but they are seldom used today to refer to social status. *Ignoble* denotes a lack or loss of noble or praiseworthy qualities, and frequently implies a failure to meet ordinarily accepted standards of worth or excellence: the *ignoble* betrayal of a trust. *Mean* suggests a contemptible smallness of mind, or a petty, ungenerous nature: to repeat *mean* gossip. **Beggarly, cheap,** and **shabby** are close to *mean* in connotation, each suggesting the same nasty, sordid vulgarity. While *ignoble* could possibly describe the act of a person from whom we might expect a better sort of conduct, *mean, beggarly, cheap,* and *shabby* describe persons or actions for which we feel only scorn and disdain: a miserly landlord's *beggarly* treatment of an indigent tenant; the *cheap* quarreling of two brothers whose father had died intestate; the *shabby* charges and countercharges of rival political bosses. **Base** and **low** are alike in being strong words used to condemn that which is openly evil, selfish, dishonorable, or otherwise unmoral. As with *mean, beggarly,* or *cheap,* the character or action which is described as *base* or *low* is worthy only of contempt: a soldier guilty of *base* cowardice; a petty crook who was *low* enough to swindle a sick widow out of her life's savings. See CONTEMPTIBLE, SHAMEFUL.
    Antonyms: MORAL, *noble.*

These words refer to the mind's power to call up images, to picture or conceive things that are not actually before the eye or within the experience. At one time, **imagination** and **fancy** could be used interchangeably, but now the two terms are sharply distinguished both in application and in scope. Used in the broad sense of a basic mental faculty, *imagination* encompasses *fancy; fancy* is a playful or whimsical sort of *imagination.* Used in a restricted sense, *imagination* contrasts with *fancy; imagination* applies to the higher, creative faculty and *fancy* is limited to a capriciously inventive play of mind. More serious in purpose than the *fancy,* the higher *imagination* creates a new form of reality, bodying forth things unknown or new by recombining the products of past experience. The *fancy* is freer and more frivolous, following its whims and ranging farther from reality: unbridled *fancy;* a flight of *fancy.* Where the higher *imagination* creates vivid characters that are true to life, such as Hamlet, Falstaff, and King Lear, the *fancy* dreams up delightful, nonexistent beings, such as elves, fairies, and woodland sprites. *Imagination* and *fancy* are also used to contrast false or misleading impressions with truth or reality. [No one moved in the bushes; it was only your *imagination;* Was it fact or *fancy*?]
    Fantasy is *imagination* divorced from reality. The creations of *fantasy* may be delightfully bizarre or may be weird and grotesque, as in the case of science-fiction stories depicting monstrous men from Mars. Engaged in *fantasy,* the *imagination* projects unreal images or imaginary scenes on the screen of the mind, creating a dream world. [An amusement park full of figures from fairy tales may be called *Fantasy*land; In his *fantasies,* the meek little man was a bold, brave hero.] *Fantasy* and **reverie** both involve a withdrawal from the real world during which the

ignoble

base
beggarly
cheap
low
mean
shabby

imagination

fancy
fantasy
reverie

mind is focused on its own imaginings; but where in *fantasy* there is an element of escapism, in *reverie* the mind is not actively fleeing reality but is simply not conscious of the world without. A *fantasy* is a vivid daydream directed like a drama by the mind. *Reverie* is an undirected wandering of the mind — an abstracted, dreamlike state during which *fancies*, *fantasies*, memories, or other imaginings preoccupy the mind and free it from conscious control. See ARTISTIC, CREATIVE, DELUSION.

Antonyms: actuality, fact, reality, truth.

imitate

ape
copy
impersonate
mimic

These words refer to reproducing the style or characteristics of something taken as a model. **Imitate** is the most general and neutral of these, referring to any attempt to repeat convincingly or tellingly the recognizable features of the model; this may be done unconsciously because of a lack of originality, semiconsciously out of admiration, or consciously as satire: He hadn't realized how much he tended to *imitate* his father's way of talking; a writer who slavishly *imitated* the works of his favorite poet, Keats; a brilliant parody that *imitated* the acting of movie queens from the silent era. The word may also point to a conscious attempt at a serious resemblance for other than satiric effect: novelists who strive to *imitate* the speech patterns of real people; that phrase about art *imitating* life. The word may also suggest following some example-setting precedent: women who *imitated* the new British hair styles.

Copy stresses a conscious or at least semiconscious process; this may be done merely to duplicate information: He *copied* the relevant data out of the encyclopedia. It may also, like *imitate*, suggest following an admired or fashionable model: They *copied* in dress and speech the oldest member of their gang. Often, however, the word suggests some sort of unethical appropriation: He found himself *copying* his neighbor's answers during the gruelling exam. In a related context, the word can also refer to mere mechanical duplication: the office *copying* machine.

Impersonate exclusively concentrates on a specific aspect of *imitate*; it refers to the assuming of another person's mannerisms or appearance, either for the amusement of others or to perpetrate a real fraud: a nightclub entertainer who could *impersonate* half a dozen famous stars with amazing verisimilitude; a crime to *impersonate* a police officer. **Mimic**, in turn, concentrates on one aspect of *impersonate*, namely the acting out of someone else's mannerisms for humorous, or even satiric, effect: She savagely *mimicked* the nasal whine of their teacher; a number in which he *mimicked* the vocal styles of several famous singers. Sometimes the word is used contemptuously for any *imitating* of a style or vogue: a rash of local singers struggling to *mimic* some group of British singers.

Ape is related to this last possibility of *mimic*, but can refer either to a conscious, contemptuous caricature or to less conscious, but slavish adherence to faddish models: They howled with laughter at the way he *aped* the receptionist's dumb-broad voice; adults who desperately try to *ape* the latest dance crazes of the young. See CARICATURE, COPY, DUPLICATE.

Antonyms: CREATE, *originate.*

immerse

dip
douse

These words refer to the forceful pushing of something into water or another liquid. **Immerse** and **submerge** are the most formal of these words and are the most general in range of meaning. *Immerse* indicates the lowering of something into water so that all of it is below surface: denominations that believe a person must be completely *immersed* in order to be properly baptized; She *immersed* the cabbage in boiling water. **Submerge** also refers to putting something completely under water, but in this case, the word often suggests an object's being lowered to a greater depth than necessarily suggested by *immerse*: They weighted the old boat with rocks to keep it *submerged* at the bottom of the lake. Furthermore, the word now often suggests the self-propelled sinking that is the case with a submarine: able to fire Polaris missiles while *submerged*.

The remaining words are much more informal and refer specifically to distinct kinds of *immersing* or *submerging*. **Plunge** suggests rapid and forceful motion, but not necessarily to any great depth: *plunging* the bunch of celery in water several times and shaking it vigorously; *plunging* from the overhanging cliff in a beautiful arching dive. **Dunk** most concretely suggests a partial lowering of something into a liquid; unlike *plunge*, the motion may be slow and gentle: to *dunk* a doughnut in coffee. **Dip** may suggest any kind of partial lowering, but most often, perhaps, would suggest a cautious, tentative movement: She *dipped* a toe in the water to see how cold it was. The word may also apply to a brief but complete lowering: Easter eggs made by *dipping* them in bowls of food coloring. **Duck** now suggests the prankish forcing of someone's head under water, as when both have gone for a swim: The lifeguard warned the boys not to *duck* each other if they wished to keep their swimming privileges.

While **douse** can apply like *plunge*, it more often indicates an action in sharp contrast with those indicated by other words in this group. The liquid in this case is poured or sprinkled over something else so as to drench, soak, or cover it; the only movement involved may be the downpour of water itself. [We got thoroughly *doused* by the sudden thunderstorm; He *doused* the face of the unconscious woman with a glass of cold water.] The word can even refer to a thorough soaking, however applied: plum pudding *doused* in brandy. See PERMEATE, WET.

These words apply to what cannot or will never die. **Immortal** is the word most likely to be used in theological discussion concerning the soul or the Deity: man's *immortal* soul; the *immortal* gods of the Greek pantheon. The word is also used loosely for any human accomplishment that seems particularly durable: the *immortal* works of Voltaire. The word may also apply to the creator: the *immortal* Shakespeare; the *immortal* Jane Austen. **Deathless** and **undying** are both more lyrical in tone, but both can function in the same theological or hyperbolic ways as *immortal*. *Deathless* was popular in the Romantic Age to typify aspiration or achievement but may now sound rhetorical and high-flown; sometimes it refers pejoratively to such uses: a lady with three names who wrote *deathless* prose. *Undying* is less open to the charge of pretentiousness, partly because it is an accepted hyperbole for lasting sentiments as well as achievements: *undying* love; From that moment on he felt *undying* hatred for his oppressors.

While **imperishable** can also be used in ways identical to *immortal*, with a possible gain in vividness, the word can also indicate anything not subject to change or decay. When applied to something that is long lasting but is not, in any case, subject to physical death, *imperishable* may be more precise than the previous words: the *imperishable* Elgin marbles; the *imperishable* will of man to survive and excel; a universe in which only matter and energy can be said to be *imperishable*. See EVERLASTING, IMMUTABLE, INFINITE, PERMANENT.

Antonyms: mortal, perishable, TEMPORARY.

immerse
(continued)

duck
dunk
plunge
submerge

immortal

deathless
imperishable
undying

immutable

fixed
indestructible
unchangeable
unchanging
unfading
unvarying

These words refer to what does not change or to what cannot be changed. **Immutable** is the most formal of these words and refers strictly to what cannot be changed. The word often applies approvingly to a truth or principle that is not affected by fashion or the passage of time: the *immutable* Golden Rule; the *immutable* justice and mercy of God. In referring to things beyond the scale of human impermanence, the word need not always be approving, though it may connote humility or awe in recognizing them: the *immutable* physical laws of the universe. **Unchangeable** is a more informal substitute for *immutable*, but it also applies more widely to anything not subject to alteration: *unchangeable* hereditary traits. Often the word can be used disapprovingly of things that are too inflexible or rigid to permit vigor or growth: an *unchangeable* social order that stifled individuality.

Fixed can indicate something that appears in an *immutable* order: early astronomers who distinguished between the wandering planets and the *fixed* stars. But the word can apply within the human scale, whether positively or negatively, to anything set, predetermined, habitual, or rigid: A child's personality is *fixed* in the first five years of life; a man of *fixed* opinions; a *fixed* stare. **Indestructible**, at its most literal, refers neutrally to what can never cease to exist: earlier theories that matter was *indestructible*. As a hyperbole, the word can refer approvingly to anything that withstands decay or change: the *indestructible* pyramids; He fought on against overwhelming odds with an *indestructible* determination to win the battle.

Unfading can occasionally refer to materials that are colorfast, but much more commonly, the word refers in a general way to anything that retains its vividness over a long period of time: the *unfading* memory of their first meeting. The remaining words stress what does not change, for whatever reason, rather than something that cannot be changed. **Unchanging** can merely indicate what is lasting: *unchanging* love. But it can be more specific in a series or sequence each item of which resembles every other: *unchanging* summer days; the tenderness and simplicity with which they moved through the *unchanging* ritual of their days. The word can also be disapproving in this sense: an *unchanging* routine that made him want to scream with boredom. **Unvarying** points almost exclusively to identical items in a series. The word can be neutral or approving: He pronounced each word with *unvarying* precision. But it is often negative, with even greater force than *unchanging*: the *unvarying* daily round of their humdrum lives. See EVERLASTING, IMMORTAL, INVARIABLE, PERMANENT.

Antonyms: changing, fading, INCONSTANT, TEMPORARY.

impact

brunt
concussion
force
jolt
shock

These words refer to the energy with which objects are propelled, bear down, or collide. **Impact** is specifically restricted to an emphasis on the moment or point of contact between objects, one or both of which have been in motion: the *impact* of the meteorite on the earth's surface; the *impact* of two speeding cars. In emphasizing the contact itself, the word remains relative about the amount of stress developed: the faint *impact* of rain on his forehead; the mile-wide crater that would result from the *impact* and explosion of the bomb. The word is often used metaphorically for any effect: the *impact* of a tax cut on the economy. Here, again, the word remains relative about the amount of effect engendered. The more formal **concussion** is closely related to *impact* in stressing collision, but is even more specific, referring to the considerable destructive energy released, usually with resulting damage of a temporary or permanent nature, as in its reference to brain damage from a blow: suffered a *concussion* in the auto accident that would leave him paralyzed for life. Even outside this specific use, it suggests a violent *impact*: delicate instruments that could not survive the *concussion* of any hard landing on the moon.

Jolt and **shock** are more informal than the previous words. They are both more general than but otherwise closely related to *concussion* in stressing the giving off of considerable energy, as in a collision or blow. *Jolt* may suggest a sudden shaking motion imparted to one body by another that is in motion: thrown back in his seat with a *jolt* by the sudden slamming on of his brakes. It is widely used in a more general context for any surprising or stunning occurrence: scientific discoveries that came like *jolts* to awaken the scholastic mind of the era. *Shock* suggests an abrupt and heavy *impact* or onslaught: reeling back under the first *shock* of the attack. But the word's other meanings are inevitably present as overtones here, implying a numbed unbelieving response or physical collapse from injury: the *shock* with which she took the tragic news; a blow that sent him into a state of *shock*.

Brunt suggests an energetic bearing down that may or may not be supportable; once this may have referred particularly to abruptness of contact, much like *impact*: wiring that could not bear the *brunt* of any heavy flow of voltage. Now, more often, it refers to a steady demand that taxes endurance: the *brunt* of so many debts and so little earning power. **Force** is the most general of these words and may refer to the degree of energy with which objects make contact or to the amount of propulsion with which things move: grenades with enough *force* to blow up a well-constructed enemy bunker; applying enough *force* to dislodge the nameplate; gamma rays that strike the earth's atmosphere with considerable *force*. See BREAK (n.), BREAK (v.), IMPEL, PROPEL, WOUND.

These words refer to a lack of emotional responsiveness. **Impassive** can pertain to a total lack of sensation or feeling: the *impassive* eyes of the corpse. Used in a less extreme way, it can refer to someone who remains unmoved by an emotional appeal: The judge stared down, remote and *impassive*, while the defense lawyer pleaded for clemency. With greater suggestiveness, the word can often indicate someone who maintains a calm or unmoved exterior to conceal an emotional response: Only the faintest flicker of distaste betrayed the otherwise *impassive* expression with which she greeted the visiting head of state.

Apathetic and **indifferent** contrast sharply with this last possibility for impassive, since both point to a failure to respond. In addition, *apathetic* often carries a tone of criticism for a deplorable or pitiable lack of awareness, compassion, or empathy: students critical of parents who had grown *apathetic* about glaring social evils. Sometimes, this note of criticism may be absent: slum children already sunk in *apathetic* despair. Where *apathetic* can suggest an extreme state of anomie or listlessness, *indifferent* usually indicates a milder state of boredom or uninvolvement. Also, where *apathetic* can sometimes suggest someone dulled by adversity, *indifferent* can point to self-contentment as the motivating factor: The French ruling class had long been *indifferent* to the miseries endured by the peasants. But *indifferent* is less often condemnatory than *apathetic*; it can be neutral or even positive: people wise enough to remain *indifferent* to the exhortations of demagogues — without ever growing *apathetic* to the threat they represented.

Insensible refers to a lack of sensation or awareness that stems either

impassive

apathetic
indifferent
insensible
phlegmatic
stolid

from a physiological numbness, from a steeled and determined stoicism, or from extreme preoccupation: fingers that had grown stiff and *insensible* with the cold; Indian braves who were taught to be *insensible* to hunger, thirst, and suffering; so engrossed that he had become *insensible* to the passage of time. Less approvingly, the word can refer to a callous lack of consideration for others: *insensible* to the needs of his wife.

Phlegmatic and **stolid** most often refer to a whole cast of temperament that is unemotional. *Phlegmatic* suggests a habitually *apathetic* or wishy-washy personality, lacking in forcefulness or vividness: a *phlegmatic* dullard who was as flat as stale beer. By contrast, *stolid* suggests someone wooden, stiff, and unbending: a coarse, *stolid* jailer who could watch executions without flinching. Whereas *phlegmatic* can indicate someone weak, passive, and yielding, even to the point of suggesting physical debilitation, *stolid* suggests a sturdy or unyielding rigidity of strength that is capable of surviving challenge: *phlegmatic* intellectuals who were no match for the *stolid* mass of the dictator's adherents. See DISINTERESTED, LISTLESS, OBLIVIOUS, UNINVOLVED.

Antonyms: EAGER, HUMANE, *responsive.*

impel

drive
motivate
move
prod
prompt

These words refer to whatever causes or contributes to the starting or continuing of an action. **Impel** always suggests considerable force; sometimes this can apply to the movement of physical objects: an upward rush of sparks, *impelled* by columns of smoke that erupted from the burning buildings. More often, the word refers to people acting under strong outward constraint or inner necessity: refugees *impelled* to flee before the advancing armies; legislators *impelled* by popular opinion to campaign for the passage of a bill; *impelled* by his desire to see her once more. **Move** is much more general; it can refer to physical motion without reference to force: The earth *moves* around the sun. When applied to the behavior of people, it stresses one aspect of *impel*, namely a forceful inner conviction or depth of feeling: *moved* by her appeal to enter the fight in her behalf. Just as often, the word refers to any surge of emotion: *moved* to tears; a film that he had found very *moving.*

Like *impel*, **drive** can suggest considerable force in reference to physical objects: leaves *driven* by the wind. It contrasts with *impel* because of its greater informality. In reference to what causes people to act, it can suggest a more direct outward goading than *impel*, or a greater inner obsessiveness than *move*: Christ *driving* the money changers from the temple; *driving* off the flies with a flyswatter; a psychosis that *drove* him to act out his fantasies in reality; *driven* to drink by a nagging wife. **Motivate** is mostly restricted to expressing what causes people to act. It can be used in neutral causal explanation: What *motivated* him to commit the murder? Or it can indicate a conscious attempt to inculcate a desire for something: students *motivated* to learn by the encouragement of a good teacher.

Where all the previous words are as equally applicable to initial as to continuing action, **prod** and **prompt** both emphasize setting something into motion. At its most literal, *prod* suggests the use of some sort of tool: He *prodded* the anthill with a stick. When applied to human behavior, the word suggests a one-time impetus of any sort: a smell of smoke that *prodded* the sleeping parents into action; a book that *prodded* the nation into a belated concern for the impoverished. *Prompt* literally refers to giving a speaker a cue to his lines, as in the theater: He still had to be *prompted* after two weeks of rehearsing; a television *prompting* device for speakers delivering written speeches. In more general uses, the word is like *prod* in suggesting any sort of stimulus to action. But where *prod* often suggests a start or jolt that makes one newly aware of something, *prompt* is more like *motivate*, though less formal, in its emphasis on causation: a misstatement of fact that *prompted* him to disagree with his host for the first time that evening; What *prompted* him to behave so rudely to his guests? See COMPEL, INCITE, INDUCE, PROPEL, STIMULATE.

Antonyms: *inhibit*, PREVENT, QUELL, STOP (arrest), SUBDUE.

These words refer to the resistance of a thing to incursions upon or into it. **Impenetrable** suggests a solid mass of resistance that cannot be pierced or breached: miners trapped in the tunnel by an *impenetrable* mass of debris; rush-hour traffic that is almost *impenetrable* to the poor pedestrian; an *impenetrable* phalanx of screaming women clustered around the sale table. The suggestion of an unbroken mass, however, need not always be present; in this case the word may simply suggest the considerable resistance presented to anyone attempting to move through the medium: an *impenetrable* thicket of bramble bushes. The word may even be applied to things that permit incursions but thwart their purpose: a jungle that was *impenetrable* to a whole generation of explorers, all of whom it swallowed up with effortless ease. Used of people, their expressions, or personality, the word suggests inscrutability, lack of response, or hostility: She responded to his proposal with an *impenetrable* blankness. **Impervious** suggests even greater resistance to incursions than *impenetrable*. The failure to pierce an *impenetrable* object might still leave marks or superficial signs of damage. By contrast, *impervious* suggests something that is literally beyond showing any change whatsoever from attempts to breach or affect it: gems that are *impervious* to scratching or to wear; metals *impervious* to cold and heat. As can be seen, this word does not necessarily imply warding off efforts at piercing something so much as surviving harsh vicissitudes without change. This is even more true in the word's less concrete uses, suggesting inscrutability or hostility less than inner strength, stubbornness, or determination that cannot be swayed by externals: They led a life *impervious* to criticism; infuriatingly *impervious* to her every suggestion; *impervious* to the temptations offered him if only he would compromise his position. **Impassable** and **impermeable** are both more narrowly restricted to specific contexts of resistance than the foregoing. *Impassable* refers to any blockage that makes travel impossible: roads that became *impassable* during the rainy season; heavy snows and avalanches that rendered the mountain route *impassable*. *Impermeable* refers, even more specifically, to a membrane through which certain fluids cannot pass. The membrane itself, of course, is not the same sort of barrier to passage as those implied by these other words, since it might well be easily ruptured; also, the membrane may be selective in the substances to which it prohibits passage: tissues *impermeable* to carbon dioxide but not to oxygen. See COMPACT, HINDER, OBSTACLE, STOP (arrest).

Antonyms: *accessible, open, permeable*, VULNERABLE.

These words all refer to the absence of visible tension or excitement in persons when such reactions might well be expected by the circumstances. **Imperturbable** carries the sense of self-control based on temperament or discipline; it is perhaps most often used of a diplomatic or stately detachment and suggests more of a constitutional inability than a conscious refusal to panic: The *imperturbable* Secretary of State re-

impenetrable

impassable
impermeable
impervious

imperturbable

calm
collected

imperturbable
(continued)

composed
cool
dispassionate
sober

sponded without asperity to the severe, pointed questioning of the Congressional committee members. When applied to attitudes or conduct rather than people, *imperturbable* means unshakable, and suggests a strong, almost irrational devotion to a particular point of view: an *imperturbable* optimism that was not to be dampened by misfortune, however great.

Cool and **dispassionate** suggest a deliberate stifling of emotions in the face of disturbing influences. Where *dispassionate* emphasizes detachment and disinterestedness, *cool* points to resistance to excitability: to keep *cool* even under battle conditions; a *dispassionate* surgeon; a *dispassionate* appraisal of the state of our military preparedness. *Cool* is now used as a noun in a slang sense with the meaning of wits or composure: He completely lost his *cool* when the cop grabbed his arm.

Calm and **collected** are often paired in a phrase to suggest the complete intactness of mental resources in the face of difficulty. *Calm* stresses a quiet approach to a problem, devoid of hysterical actions or utterances, and *collected* stresses the application of appropriate mental or physical effort to the solution of the problem: to remain *calm* and *collected* in the midst of a noisy demonstration.

Composed and **sober**, in this context, suggest dignified demeanor and conduct in the midst of confusion. *Sober* suggests a reasoned, quiet, and sometimes cautious attitude; *composed* indicates an even-tempered, self-controlled attitude. [The speaker remained *composed* despite the audience's loud heckling; His *sober* approach to the crisis averted a catastrophe.] See TRANQUIL.

Antonyms: agitated, FRANTIC, NERVOUS, *shaken, touchy, volatile.*

impetuous

headlong
impulsive
precipitate
sudden

These words are applied to actions or persons characterized by a lack of forethought, warning, or preparation. **Impetuous** and **impulsive** differ from the other words in applying to both people and actions. *Impetuous* suggests more decisive or vigorous action than *impulsive*, and often implies an unfortunate outcome as a result. *Impulsive* means acting on impulse, and since impulses can be good as well as bad, *impulsiveness* is not necessarily deplorable; it may even be considered endearing or attractive. *Impetuosity*, on the other hand, implies a rather childish inability to be patient or thoughtful before taking action. [Hers was a generous, *impulsive* nature, capable of showing spontaneous affection and warmth; an *impetuous* decision that he later learned to regret; to stamp his foot in an *impetuous* rage] *Impulsive* need not always imply recklessness, and in some contexts may only imply spontaneity and the lack of premeditation: an *impulsive* urge to re-open the door and check to see if all the windows were closed before she left for the weekend.

Headlong suggests a reckless disregard of consequences along with *impetuous* haste. Unlike the other words here considered, *headlong* is used as both an adjective and an adverb; it is somewhat more formal when used as an adjective: a *headlong* advance into enemy territory; women rushing *headlong* into the store at the start of the sale; to plunge *headlong* into a new business without adequate financial backing. Where *headlong* points to a complete lack of deliberation, **precipitate** suggests that what deliberation did occur was grossly inadequate to prepare for the ensuing action; a *precipitate* action is therefore premature and rash. [The editorial called the union's rejection of management's wage offer *precipitate* and unwarranted.] **Sudden**, as here considered, suggests an abrupt or unexpected action but does not necessarily imply haste; it does point to either a spontaneous, unpremeditated act or a perception for which one is not prepared. [a *sudden* rush for the door when someone shouted, "Fire!"; His *sudden* departure from the published text of the speech caught us all by surprise; The *sudden* stop of the crowded bus threw several people to the floor.] See HEEDLESS, RECKLESS.

Antonyms: CAUTIOUS, IMPASSIVE, IMPERTURBABLE, *thoughtful*.

These words indicate the sowing or embedding of something in a receiving medium. **Implant** has the widest range of application. It can refer to a fixing or rooting in the ground: *implanting* the seedlings in a diamond pattern; *implanting* the flagpole at the top of the hill. It can refer to the inserting in tissue of a graft or device: a cutting *implanted* under the bark of the tree; *implanting* a kidney of the donor in his critically ill twin brother; *implanting* a plastic valve in the patient's heart. More generally, however, the word refers to the fixing of an idea in the mind, usually in the context of the educating of a child or student by a parent or teacher: a sense of decency *implanted* in him by his upbringing. In this use, the internalizing of rudimentary principles or attitudes is usually suggested, but rote training is not necessarily the technique by which the *implanting* is done. In any case, a deeply rooted and unshakable transfer of attitude or knowledge is implied. Such a fixing of ideas in one's own mind is not usually suggested by the word, but an unconscious process may be indicated, or even the fixing of qualities by heredity rather than environment: an innate curiosity that seems to have been *implanted* in him from birth. The word can also, at its most general, suggest the informing or propagandizing of any audience, whether overtly or subliminally: assumptions about cooperation and competition that each culture *implants* in its members.

Inseminate can still reflect its derivation by referring literally to the sowing of seed in soil. Much more commonly, however, the word refers to the introducing of semen into the vagina or to the *implanting* of ideas in the mind: studying the reproductive cycle from the *inseminating* of sperm to the birth of the child; means for artificially *inseminating* livestock; teachers who *inseminate* a respect for authority in their students.

Infuse, in its original Latin form, meant to pour in. It now carries a suggestion of that pouring in in its reference to the introduction of something, as a quality, feeling, or idea into a receiving medium. Such introduction, it is implied, lends the medium inspiration, animation, or new significance: to *infuse* life into a dull party. **Imbue** has much the same connotation as *infuse*, but whereas *infuse* may indicate a temporary or superficial influence, *imbue* more often points to a change that deeply affects the receiving medium. Another difference between the two words is the fact that *imbue* takes for its object the thing affected rather than the thing introduced: to *imbue* a man with confidence.

Ingrain means to impress firmly on the mind or character. The word, which is used almost exclusively in the passive or past participle, is like *imbue* in denoting an affecting influence that works into the inmost texture or grain of the receiving medium: a deep respect for the truth had been *ingrained* into the child.

The remaining pair are restricted solely to the context of learning. **Instill** suggests a slow, subtle, possibly gentle transfer of attitude more than facts, one that reflects its derivation from a word meaning to put in by drops. Most often *instill* suggests a conscious imparting to someone who is, at most, only partially aware of the process: striving to *instill* in her son a hatred for his father; understanding how carefully his psychiatrist worked to *instill* in him an attitude of perfect trust; seeing how blindly everything in his drab environment had worked to *instill* within him a rage against the established order; nations that, without even realizing it, *instill* in their citizens an unexamined fear of outsiders. *Instill* is the only one of these words, furthermore, that can possibly suggest the development of an attitude within oneself: a historian who has not *instilled* in himself a proper objectivity toward the period he is treating.

Inculcate limits this range of possibilities in *instill* to one situation, that in which both teacher and student are well aware of the learning process under way; a further limiting exists in that the word refers specifically to an *ingraining* of facts, ideas, or attitudes by the technique of laborious repetition: a generation of students that had not been *inculcated* with the rules of grammar. [English spelling cannot be reasoned out; it must be *inculcated*, example by insufferable example.] The word more recently has taken on a disapproving tone to refer to the deliberate *ingraining* of propaganda or flagrant falsehoods in unsuspecting subjects: *inculcating* the doctrines of race hatred in innocent children. See INSERT, TEACH.

implement

instrument
tool
utensil

These words denote mechanical and other devices for doing work. **Implement** is the most general word of this list, and can be applied to any device that is needed or useful in the performance of a task. It is specifically applied to the simple devices of farming and gardening, such as rakes, plows, hoes, and spades.

Anything operated by hand may properly be called a **tool**; one speaks of the *tools* of carpenters, masons, sculptors, mechanics, and other artisans. *Implement* and *tool* are often but not invariably interchangeable: gardening *implements* (or *tools*); a plumber's *tools* (but not *implements*). That part of a machine used directly for cutting, shaping, drilling, etc., is also called a *tool*. Delicate *tools*, such as those used by dentists or surgeons, are called **instruments**. **Utensil**, originally anything having utility, is now largely restricted to vessels or containers: cooking *utensils*; the *utensils* of a religious ceremony.

Implement, and more especially *instrument* and *tool*, are commonly used in extended senses to refer to any means by which something is accomplished or abetted. [A strong military establishment can be an *implement* of peace if used judiciously; Mathematics is the *instrument* used by the physical sciences to explore phenomena and record conclusions; Language is an *instrument* of communication; Good looks and a shrewd press agent were the principal *instruments* of her success; Among the writer's *tools*, pertinacity is at least as important as talent.] See MACHINE, MEANS.

implicit

covert
latent
potential
tacit
unspoken

These words refer to things left unexpressed, unrealized, or unacted-upon, though their existence or influence can often be detected. **Implicit** refers to something that is not revealed in words or action but that can be inferred from the evidence: an *implicit* cultural assumption that men are superior to women; riots that were merely the expression of the violence *implicit* in day-to-day ghetto life; a weakness *implicit* in his whole approach to Renaissance art. **Potential** is close to *implicit*, but stresses the capability of something to become active: on the lookout for *potential* customers; the good and evil *potential* within each person. **Latent**, by contrast, stresses something that is not conscious or acted out, with no implication that it need ever be made manifest: a *latent* homosexual; musical talent that remained *latent* through a lack of training. Occasionally the word can suggest something once in evidence but now hidden through accident or design: childhood fears that have become *latent* and fossilized in adulthood.

Covert is restricted to this last sense of *latent*, referring to something that is deliberately hidden or brought about in secret. Thus, the word may even suggest a furtive acting out of something, a possibility that is in sharp contrast to those for the previous words: *covert* assignations that brought them together often, though both remained tied to their respective spouses. The stealth implied in the word usually points to unsavory or unethical misconduct, although this is not always true: hermetic readings of scripture that saw it as a system of *covert* symbols for Gnostic doctrines; auctions conducted by means of *covert* signals between the bidders and the auctioneer. **Tacit** may apply in the same general way as *implicit*, but it does have specific relevance to agreements or understandings arrived at without verbalizing some or all of the conditions involved: a *tacit* feeling in the group that the newcomer should be watched closely; housing contracts that left *tacit* the exclusion of minority groups from the neighborhood. **Unspoken** is restricted to one aspect of *tacit*, referring more informally to things not mentioned or said aloud. Like *covert* and *tacit*, the word contrasts with *latent* in indicating things one is conscious of and acts upon, but without expressing them: eyes glinting with her evident but *unspoken* disapproval of him; sexual assumptions that were left *unspoken* out of a sense of delicacy. See INHERENT.

Antonyms: actual, DEFINITE, exposed, overt, plain.

improve

ameliorate
better
meliorate

These words mean to bring something to a higher level of quality, efficiency, etc. **Improve** is the most general word in this group; it can mean to increase, enlarge, correct, or raise, as in the following examples: to *improve* one's vocabulary; to *improve* one's understanding of world affairs; to *improve* one's habits; to *improve* one's grades. *Improve* thus refers to any means of making something higher in quality or more desirable in nature.

Better, more colloquial in tone, is in some contexts interchangeable with *improve*: to *better* (or *improve*) one's grades. But as a rule it has more narrow implications, often suggesting only a modest increase or elevation in knowledge or appreciation. Although *improve* can also be used to describe such situations, in contexts implying a profound or important elevation of status or quality, *improve* is more likely to be used: Through keen management procedures and a substantial investment the company's market potential was vastly *improved*. *Better* is often used reflexively with the sense of *improving* socially or economically. [He took the new job to *better* himself; He joined the country club with the hope of *bettering* himself.] *Better* so used often has a distinctly vulgar tone. The greater scope and importance that attaches to *improve* is immediately evident if one contrasts to *improve oneself* with to *better oneself*: He went to night school to *improve himself*.

Ameliorate is usually applied to conditions rather than to specific things, and suggests that the conditions are much in need of correction: The city council considered legislation to *ameliorate* the unsanitary conditions in slum areas. **Meliorate** has the same meaning as *ameliorate*, but is nowadays less often used. Both words, but especially *meliorate*, are extremely formal or literary: missionaries whose aim was to *meliorate* the pathetic ignorance of the indigenous peoples. See ENLARGE, REPAIR.

Antonyms: deteriorate, impair, POLLUTE, ROT, worsen.

incite

arouse
exhort
foment
instigate
provoke
rouse
stir up

The words in this list all mean to stimulate vigorously into being or action. **Incite** means to spur to action, and may be applied to measures leading to salutary as well as deplorable results, to minor as well as profound changes: to *incite* others to greater effort by setting an example with one's own conduct; to *incite* a riot by making inflammatory speeches. **Stir up** is more informal than *incite* and more often applies to less serious disturbances or to attitudes of mind: an unruly boy who kept *stirring up* trouble when the teacher's back was turned; to *stir up* indignation. When applied to mental attitudes, as in the latter example, *stir up* is close to **arouse**. *Arouse* points specifically to awakening or opening one's eyes to a certain situation or point of view, whereas the more emphatic **rouse** indicates a call to action or to vigorous opinion that is likely to lead to action. [His speech *roused* the audience to such a pitch of fury that the police were forced to escort him away hastily for his own safety; The exhibition of poor sportsmanship *aroused* a sense of disgust and humiliation in all who witnessed it.]

Instigate and **foment** usually suggest the setting in motion of events that in some way threaten or upset the status quo. They will therefore convey a negative or unfavorable connotation to the extent that one deplores violent change. *Instigate* suggests an insidious design to bring about some drastic action: to *instigate* an assassination; to *instigate* a plot to seize control of a government. *Foment*, which is derived etymologically from a Latin verb meaning to keep warm, suggests a deliberate attempt to keep people or conditions agitated in order to bring about radical change, or simply to promote dissension and discord: to *foment* rebellion; to *foment* mutiny. Whereas *instigate* emphasizes the act of initiating the design, *foment* stresses keeping it alive — fanning the fire, so to speak. *Instigate*, in addition, does have a wider range of use and can point to any design, even one of noble motive, whereas *foment* is used most often of underhanded designs aiming at radical change: to *instigate* a change in the selection of municipal judges in the cause of improving the administration of justice; to *foment* fear and discord.

Provoke, as here considered, can be used, like *instigate*, to point to a variety of results, but it does not necessarily or even commonly imply conscious design. It may on the contrary imply spontaneous reaction: The slur *provoked* a sharp retort. Like *arouse* and *stir up*, *provoke* may also be used of the stimulation of a particular mental attitude: The arbitrary police action *provoked* (or *aroused* or *stirred up*) a public outcry for an investigation. *Provoke* emphasizes more strongly than the other words of this group a direct and immediate cause-and-effect connection between the stimulus and response — the act that *incites* and the result: The outbreak of war *provoked* a call for an emergency meeting of the UN Security Council.

Exhort means to urge earnestly; it suggests an attempt to persuade someone of a course of action by emphatic and even passionate argument or by appealing to his sympathy or conscience: The senator *exhorted* his colleagues to vote against the motion to censure him for his frequent tax-supported junkets. *Exhort* often implies a degree of desperation, and can be close in meaning to beg or plead with, only more formal in tone: *exhorting* his fellow students not to expose his cheating on the examination. See INDUCE, STIMULATE.

Antonyms: DISCOURAGE, HINDER, SUBDUE.

include

These words refer to an entity that takes in two or more parts or elements. **Include**, the most general of these, can indicate clearly defined subdivisions within a whole: The health club *includes* a gym, swimming pool, sauna, and locker room. It can pertain equally well to contents that are more imponderable or less tangible: a discussion that *included* extended treatment of the two world wars, the Korean action, and the Vietnam war. The word can be useful, since it need not suggest an exhaustive listing of parts or elements: Our ten-city tour *included* a visit to Stratford. Often, the word points to an additional feature, a secondary element, or a side benefit: The second book was more useful because it *included* a detailed chronological table of the events under discussion. **Comprise** is a considerably more formal substitute for *include*, except that it most often indicates a complete or exhaustive breakdown of an entity into its parts or elements: The anthology *comprises* samples from the work of ten authors.

Most concretely, **contain** can indicate discrete things held or enclosed by a larger object: The bowl *contained* a variety of fruit. The word functions much like *include* in indicating the parts or elements making up a whole. *Contain*, however, can function only when some sense of enclosure within the whole exists. One would not, for example, speak of a tour *containing* visits to various cities. Otherwise, the word compares with *include* and contrasts with *comprise* in not being restricted to an exhaustive listing. [The dictionary *contained* biographical entries on Washington, Jefferson, and Lincoln; Does your school building *contain* an auditorium?] Where both *include* and *contain* can point to concrete or material entities and their parts, **involve** almost exclusively concentrates on less tangible things and their elements: an argument that *involved* a discussion of basic principles. In this it compares with *comprise*; by contrast, however, *involve* need not suggest an exhaustive listing: Aside from its most widely known features, his philosophical system also *involved* a belief in reincarnation. See CIRCUMSCRIBE, POSSESS.

Antonyms: exclude, leave out, omit.

These words refer to things that change frequently or rapidly or to unstable or disloyal natures. **Inconstant** and **fickle** are formal and informal terms, respectively, for unfaithfulness, usually in love. *Inconstant*, however, can apply to a single betrayal of love, whereas *fickle* applies to the habit of moving from one light or trivial infatuation to another: a fiancé who proved to be *inconstant*; career-girl hoydens who are *fickle* and promiscuous. *Inconstant* can sometimes refer more widely to anything showing variability: desert oases whose wells give an *inconstant* supply of fresh water; a politician who had been *inconstant* in his devotion to the principles of his party. In wider uses, *fickle* still applies to the basic situation of loyalty: young idealists who often prove to be *fickle* in their choice of causes to uphold.

Changeable and **erratic** are much more general than the previous pair and are less disapproving in tone. *Changeable* can register the neutral fact that something is capable of change: the *changeable* patterns of watered silk. Indeed, this capacity can be desirable: a camera with *changeable* shutter speeds. More often, however, the word carries a negative tone in reference to people who habitually and readily take up and discard attitudes or opinions: a *changeable* sort of person who favored the war one day and opposed it the next. *Erratic* points more to an uneven or arbitrary course: the *erratic* path of the rivulet; an *erratic* fellow whose actions were usually completely unpredictable.

Chameleonic is most comparable to *changeable* and **capricious** to

include
(continued)

comprise
contain
involve

inconstant

capricious
chameleonic
changeable
erratic
fickle
mercurial
protean

erratic, but both words are alike in being more vivid than the foregoing and in being more exclusively concentrated on human characteristics. *Chameleonic* refers to the chameleon's ability, as a defensive camouflage, of changing color so as to blend with its background. Sometimes the word applies to human versatility in a neutral or approving way: students who are *chameleonic* in the diversity of their extracurricular activities; *chameleonic* in the way he could make himself at home among all sorts of people. More often, however, the word suggests an insincere person willing to play any role that might be of momentary advantage to him: a *chameleonic* candidate who took pro-labor stands before union audiences and pro-business stands at chamber of commerce dinners. *Capricious*, which is exclusively negative in tone, need not suggest insincerity, like *chameleonic*, but it does stress an arbitrary and high-handed attitude in which unfair choices are made, not on the merits of a case, but on the basis of personal taste or whim: a drama critic who seemed *capricious* in the way he bestowed praise or blame; a woman who was haughty and *capricious* toward her servants.

Mercurial and **protean**, alone of these words, may suggest rapidity as well as frequency of change. *Mercurial* is most comparable to *chameleonic*, but where a negative tone preponderates in the latter's use, *mercurial* is more dependent on context to establish approval or disapproval. In favorable reference, it suggests a highly charged and energetic mental dexterity that is flexible to the demands of specific situations and responsive to opportunities for exploiting such situations to best advantage: a *mercurial* artist who completely transformed the artistic possibilities of every medium he worked in. In negative uses, the word suggests an excessively volatile quickness and impatience that results in poor control and botched efforts: too *mercurial* to sit down and do the painstaking work of revision that his brilliant first drafts sorely needed. *Protean* refers to the ability of the demi-god Proteus to change shapes as a way of eluding capture; often, *protean* can function identical to *chameleonic* in both positive and negative ways. Most often, however, the word refers favorably to someone gifted with diverse abilities and skills which are exhibited in a remarkable proliferation of accomplishments: Michelangelo's *protean* imagination. Sometimes, the word refers more neutrally to anything given to change: a period of crisis in which the same basic dilemma appeared again and again in *protean* forms. See ADAPTABLE, HESITATE, TEMPORARY.

Antonyms: EVERLASTING, *faithful*, IMMUTABLE, INVARIABLE, *loyal*, PERMANENT.

indecent

immodest
improper
indecorous
indelicate
unseemly

These words mean not conforming to accepted standards of social behavior, good taste, or propriety. **Indecent** is the strongest word in this group. Primarily it connotes condemnation of obscenity or licentiousness: *indecent* remarks directed at passing school girls; *indecent* pictures; an *indecent* proposal to engage in abnormal sexual practices. In its second meaning, *indecent* suggests a lack of decorum and a disregard for the feelings of others. [After his wife died, he remarried with *indecent* haste; His appetite for gossip is absolutely *indecent*.]

Immodest and **indelicate** are applied to that which shows little sense of what is fitting or acceptable in a society which sets a high price on propriety. In one sense, *immodest* is close in meaning to *indecent*, having long been applied, especially to women, when it is a question of revealing clothing or unrestrained behavior toward the opposite sex. [Many older people find the bikini *immodest*; My mother thinks my sister is *immodest* because she pursues boys.] *Immodest* has a second meaning of aggressive and boastful: the *immodest* self-seeking of a social climber; to brag in an *immodest* way about one's great abilities. *Indelicate* is not as strong a term as *immodest* and suggests more a lack of tact and thoughtfulness than unconventional behavior. [It is thought by many to be *indelicate* to discuss how much money one makes; Subjects fit for the smoking room are sometimes too *indelicate* to be discussed at the family dinner table.]

Improper and **unseemly** are used of actions or conduct that violate standards of good taste and the fitness of things. [It is considered *improper* for a lawyer to discuss his clients outside of his office; It would be regarded as *unseemly* and ridiculous for a well-known philosopher to endorse the qualities of a patent medicine.] Often *improper* is used as a euphemism for *indecent* in the sense of obscene: to make *improper* advances.

Indecorous is applied to conduct that does not conform to established conventions of formality and manners, conduct generally consisting of minor infractions for which any of the other words in this group would be too strong. [Loud laughter during a wedding ceremony is *indecorous*; She always felt *indecorous* when she was obliged to fasten her garter in public.] See DEPRAVED, LEWD.

Antonyms: CHASTE, MODEST, MORAL.

These words mean to make one's will or views prevail over those of another in various ways. **Induce** means to get another to do something by appealing to his reason: to *induce* a man to stop drinking; to *induce* a teen-age driver to obey the traffic laws.

Persuade is the most general term and may be substituted for any of the others. However, in its most specific sense, it means to attempt to produce a desired action by an appeal to the emotions or the will. [After he had been ill for a week, we finally *persuaded* him to consult a doctor; A newspaper article about the plight of slum children in the summer *persuaded* him to send a contribution to the Fresh Air Fund.]

In this context, **urge** is the strongest term and means to *induce* or *persuade* insistently and vigorously, usually with the strong intention of accomplishing one's goal: to *urge* a student to work harder; to *urge* an overworked mother to take a vacation.

Coax, cajole, and **wheedle** all mean to *persuade* by using gentleness, tact, and even artfulness. *Coax* implies the use of kindness and patience: to *coax* a sick child to eat by making a game of it; to *coax* a blind person to learn to cross busy streets. In an earlier sense, *cajole* meant to *coax* or *persuade* by false promises and excessive flattery, but it now suggests more the idea of being agreeable and winning in order to get a person to do something: My outgoing friends were able to *cajole* the shy newcomer into attending the party. *Wheedle* implies the use of blandishments and wiles to obtain what one wants: She always *wheedles* money out of her father by hugging him and telling him how generous he is. See IMPEL.

Antonyms: DISCOURAGE, HINDER, *repel*, SUBDUE.

These words describe events or conditions that cannot be prevented from happening. **Inevitable,** the strongest term, describes something that is bound to happen or be met with in the very nature of things. [Pain is *inevitable* when one breaks a bone; When the Japanese attacked Pearl Harbor, war with them was *inevitable*.]

induce

cajole
coax
persuade
urge
wheedle

inevitable

inescapable

inevitable
(continued)

necessary
unavoidable

Inescapable is often used interchangeably with *inevitable*, but *inescapable* suggests something which may not be completely unalterable given a different set of attitudes or circumstances. [Whereas death is *inevitable*, earning a living is *inescapable* unless one has private means or is forced to live at public expense; He felt that failure was an *inescapable* part of his lot in life.]

When used in this context, **necessary** has less impact than do *inevitable* and *inescapable*. Something that is *necessary* must logically occur because of an existing set of factors. [Hunger and disease are *necessary* concomitants of war; Crowded streets and shops are a *necessary* part of big-city life.]

Unavoidable is applied to events and conditions that are not always *inevitable*, but in specific instances are incapable of being shunned or evaded: Accidents on our highways may be *inevitable*, but a particular accident was *unavoidable* because of bad weather and heavy traffic. See COMPEL, CONCLUSIVE, INEXORABLE.

Antonyms: avertible, CHANCE, optional, preventable.

inexorable

merciless
pitiless
relentless
remorseless
ruthless
unrelenting

These words describe persons or things that do not let up or swerve from their course out of any feeling of compassion. **Inexorable** is the most formal word. It may be used of unyielding, unappeasable persons: an *inexorable* foe; his *inexorable* will. But it is more often applied to inhuman or objective forces that cannot be avoided, stopped, or changed: Oedipus could not escape his *inexorable* fate.

Remorseless, relentless, and **unrelenting** are closest in meaning to *inexorable*. All imply a powerful, driving force and unceasing progress toward a goal: driving himself at a *relentless* pace; to apply *relentless* pressure; an *unrelenting* fight against crime. But *remorseless* is the most chilling word of the three, as it may indicate utter unresponsiveness to human values: the *remorseless* progress of a fatal disease; the *remorseless* ticking of a time bomb. *Relentless* is sometimes close to *remorseless* in this sense, but it is usually less severe and is not always damning by any means. In general use, it may apply to anyone or anything that shows no mercy and cannot be stopped by entreaty or appeal: a *relentless* public prosecutor; the *relentless* passing of time. Specifically, *relentless* is sometimes used as an intensification of tireless. As such, it can imply a refusal to yield under punishing pressure: He pressed on *relentlessly*, trying to meet the deadline. Or it may focus on an implacable persistence in hounding another: the *relentless* Javert pursuing Jean Valjean in *Les Miserables*. *Unrelenting* may be less extreme in its implications, sometimes suggesting a proper rather than a cruel refusal to relent. An *unrelenting* person may not be impervious to entreaty, but he is able to resist it. He stands firm and does not give in when he might be expected or tempted to do so: The father handled his disobedient son with *unrelenting* firmness. *Unrelenting* may also suggest the unshakable resolve and fierce dedication of someone firmly committed to a cause and not to be turned aside by obstacles: an *unrelenting* crusader for equal rights.

The remaining words imply unfeeling harshness or cruelty. **Merciless,** like *inexorable*, is often used of impersonal forces: subjected to a *merciless* bombardment with noise; the *merciless* glare of the noonday sun. When it involves the agency of persons, it usually focuses on their instruments or acts rather than on their feelings: the *merciless* eye of the camera; a *merciless* beating. [A *merciless* mob of reporters descended on the bereaved family.] **Pitiless,** by contrast, is more often used to describe human beings as such. It suggests a cold, steel-hard quality: her *pitiless* eye; a *pitiless* tyrant. *Inexorable, relentless,* and *pitiless* may all imply a refusal or inability to make or allow the slightest concession: *inexorable* logic; *relentless* reason; the *pitiless* efficiency of a machine.

Ruthless conveys a greater degree of harshness than any of these other words, for it focuses on a fierce refusal to give any quarter. It is applied to persons who are so unsparing as to be cruel, driving forward single-mindedly, and sometimes savagely, with a brutal disregard for those they attack or exploit: a *ruthless* slave driver; *ruthless* in his criticism; *ruthlessly* frank. Applied to personal expression or action, *ruthless* may mean harsh, brutal, unsparing, cold-blooded, or cutthroat: *ruthless* methods; *ruthless* competition in the tournament finals. See INEVITABLE.

Antonyms: alterable, changeable, clement, humane, lenient, placable, yielding.

These words describe things which bear, bring, or involve low prices, or comparatively small amounts of money. That which is **inexpensive** costs little, but the word suggests that the product is of acceptable, or even of good quality, and is not being misrepresented to the purchaser: *inexpensive* paperback books; an *inexpensive* raincoat one may carry folded up in one's purse.

Low-priced is the most general term. It carries little connotation of true value or quality. When you say that something is *low-priced* you simply mean that it costs a small amount of money either in an absolute or a relative sense. [Wherever you may be, a packet of sewing needles is *low-priced*; Compact cars are *low-priced* as compared with cars of standard size.]

In one of its uses **cheap** has a derogatory meaning pointing to fraud, which *low-priced* and *inexpensive* do not have. The term "*cheap* labor" always strongly hints at exploitation of workers too backward or too deprived to protect their own interests. *Cheap* is applied to inferior, shoddy goods which to the inexperienced person resemble those of better quality and cost much more than they are worth: *cheap*, flashy furniture sold to the poor on the installment plan; *cheap* fur coats made of dyed rabbit skins. *Cheap* is also used to describe something that is very *inexpensive* or *low-priced* because it is plentiful, easy to produce, and useful: Soybeans are a *cheap* but excellent source of protein all over the world. In the sense of costing less in proportion to its usual value or price, *cheap* is preferable to either *low-priced* or *inexpensive*: In farm country, eggs are *cheap*.

In terms of money, **modest** means moderate or not excessive, but it also implies that the amount of money in question is more or less adequate and proper: to ask a *modest* price for a used television set; to earn a *modest* living as a small-town postmaster. See DEFICIENT, POOR.

Antonyms: EXPENSIVE.

These words refer to great quantities or to things extending without end in space, time, or number. **Infinite** is the most general here. Spatially, it refers to something that has no boundary: in a theory that space is *infinite*. It may be a less precise substitute for eternal: a kind of immortality that results if matter is finite and space *infinite*. It may refer strictly to quantity, as in mathematics, in which case it refers to a quantity that always exceeds any other. Theologically, it refers to something absolute or perfect: God's *infinite* mercy. Often, however, the word is used hyperbolically for any great amount, or simply as a superlative: an *infinite* bore.

inexpensive

cheap
low-priced
modest

infinite

boundless
illimitable
limitless

The remaining words are primarily restricted to *infinite* quantities or size, but all may refer to things whose boundaries have not yet been discovered or cannot be formulated. In addition to these possibilities, **boundless** can specifically point to something that is unconstricted or unconstrictable: his *boundless* optimism. The word often refers hyperbolically to any great amount: the *boundless* energies of our productive nation. **Limitless** suggests a situation in which no end is in sight or in which there is as much of something as could be used or desired: a *limitless* supply of drinking water; a grand jury's *limitless* freedom to move in any direction while investigating a legal issue. **Illimitable** is more formal than the previous words and suggests, in addition to its shared meanings, something to which no boundary can practically be set. [Every source of energy in the universe theoretically emits waves that travel an *illimitable* distance.] The word may also suggest *infinite* extension in one dimension: defining a line as having *illimitable* length but no width. See COUNTLESS, EVERLASTING, IMMORTAL, PERMANENT.
Antonyms: circumscribed, finite, limited, relative.

influence

affect
impress
sway

These words all mean to have an effect upon a person's behavior, thinking, or feelings. **Influence** is to bring about a change in another's actions or thoughts by persuasion, example, or action, often of an indirect sort: *influenced* by a high school biology teacher to take up the study of medicine; *influencing* workers to produce more goods by praising them and bettering their working conditions.

In this context **affect** means to have an effect on another's feelings. [He is always deeply *affected* by Handel's music; Fear *affects* some people by making them powerless to act.] *Influence* and *affect* may both be used of things that tend to respond to outside stimuli or actions. *Influence* is usually used in this sense of intangible forces, and *affect* of physical ones: to *influence* public opinion through the press; to *affect* the size of a crop by using fertilizer. *Affect* may sometimes imply an undesirable reaction: Unusual exertion may *affect* the heart.

Impress means to *affect* deeply and lastingly: *impressed* by a man's prodigious talent; *impressed* by his first view of the Grand Canyon.

Sway means to change another's opinions or feelings successfully in a deliberate way. It is a stronger word than either *influence* or *affect*. The word implies the use of control or irresistible persuasion, often combined with the weakness of the one *swayed*: to *sway* a dissatisfied minority group by impassioned political speeches full of promises; a man so *swayed* by public adulation that he snubs his old friends. See ENCOURAGE, INDUCE, MALLEABLE.
Antonyms: DISCOURAGE, HINDER, SUBDUE.

inform

acquaint
advise
apprise
enlighten
notify

These words mean to call someone's attention to something or to cause him to receive knowledge of it. **Inform** is the most general word and loosely covers the meanings of the other terms in this group. *Inform* usually points to the imparting of facts or data. [He *informed* his staff that he was going to Europe on business; This article *informs* us that the physical endurance of American school children is inferior to that of children of many European countries.]

Advise, notify, and **apprise** carry the connotation of more or less formal announcements. *Advise,* in this context, is used in the sense of giving a person facts that involve his own interests: A lawyer should always *advise* his clients as to their legal rights. *Notify* is the most commonly used term of these three, and it carries a note of urgency, demanding action or an early reply. [The girl's parents were *notified* immediately of her expulsion; He was *notified* by his draft board to report for his physical examination.] *Apprise* is the most formal of these words and can sound dated or unnecessarily fancy. It may suggest supplying an interested person with facts in accordance with regulation or agreement: Suspects must be *apprised* of their constitutional rights before being questioned.

Acquaint and **enlighten** both mean to impart knowledge of a wider scope than that suggested by the other words. *Acquaint* is to make someone familiar with facts or a situation of some complexity: to *acquaint* oneself with the details of a new job; to *acquaint* the police with the mysterious lights that appear nightly in the abandoned house. *Enlighten*, as its root suggests, means to bring information to light, usually about a particular point or situation. It carries more of an element of dispelling ignorance than does *acquaint*. [The mother *enlightened* her son as to the bad financial situation of the family; A careful daily reading of the newspaper will *enlighten* the reader as to what is happening at the United Nations.] See CLARIFY, CONSULT.

Antonyms: misinform.

These words refer to people who divulge facts to which they are privy. Among its extremely informal or slangy companions, **informer** seems formal and dignified by comparison; it is also more general than the others. It often suggests divulging secrets or information concerning illegal or scandalous behavior: turning *informer* on his cronies in the crime syndicate; encouraging children to act as *informers* against their parents. The disclosure itself may be covert or open and may be given out of vengeance, self-interest, or for pay. The *informer* may decide to disclose information he acquired in good faith, or he may have been intent at the outset on gaining and then betraying someone's confidence: an *informer* planted by the FBI to get evidence on a nation-wide narcotics ring; publicly turning *informer* at the hearing to clear himself of a charge of complicity. The disapproving tone that *informer* can give is milder than that of any other word here. It can even have a neutral or approving tone: a Nazi who turned *informer* to help the prosecutors at the Nuremberg trials.

Blabbermouth, by contrast, seldom suggests covert disclosure done in reprisal or self-interest. Instead, the word indicates general loose-mouthed behavior in someone willing to talk to anyone about anything, his own secrets as much as those of others: a *blabbermouth* who betrays his friends daily without even being conscious of it.

Tattler, talebearer, and **tattletale** all can be used to describe someone who divulges facts about someone else. Each, however, has its special area of relevance. *Tattler* in particular relates to the collecting and spreading of trivial gossip of a faintly scandalous nature: professional *tattlers* who purport to reveal the private lives of the Hollywood stars. It may also suggest the situation in which one child betrays his playmates to a teacher, parent, or other outsider; *tattletale* is perhaps more clearly related and restricted to such a context: the *tattletale* who went whining to the teacher about who had hidden the blackboard eraser. *Talebearer* suggests specifically a two-faced go-between who for reasons of his own pretends to inform each side exclusively about the other: labor mediators who lose their effectiveness as soon as either side suspects them of being *talebearers*.

Fink once was restricted to a labor context as an extremely pejora-

---

informer

blabbermouth
fink
ratfink
squealer
stool pigeon
talebearer
tattler
tattletale

tive way to refer to a turncoat who willingly informed on his fellow workers to their employer. It and the more current **ratfink** are now fad words referring to anyone who is unsavory, contemptible, ridiculous, or inconsequential: the *fink* who stole my pencil; He acts tough, but in my book he's just a spineless *fink*; My landlord is a real *ratfink*.

Squealer and **stool pigeon** are the most slangy and also the most pejorative words in this group; both may suggest a context of the criminal underworld but are widely used outside it. *Squealer* may refer to someone who divulges facts about his confederates for whatever reason: swearing that he'd never be a *squealer* no matter how long the police grilled him. *Stool pigeon*, by contrast, refers specifically to a covert *informer* who inhabits the underworld or is planted there by the police; in either case, he furtively continues to convey information to the police so long as he remains undiscovered: convinced that one of their fellow prisoners had turned *stool pigeon* and had disclosed their plans for the jailbreak. See RENEGADE.

inherent

essential
innate
intrinsic

These words refer to things that are fundamental or necessary aspects of some larger pattern. **Inherent** refers to a principle that underlies or is implicit in a manifest pattern: an *inherent* tendency to get flustered in tense situations; a respect for human possibility that is *inherent* in all the works of the Renaissance. When the word emphasizes the implicit nature of the principle, it suggests something that may not be evident but that can be inferred from the situation: a cool politeness that attempted to mask her *inherent* dislike of people. **Innate** suggests something deeply imprinted within a pattern and that may not be patently obvious, although it has its effect and cannot, by implication, be easily eradicated: gathering evidence to determine whether instincts are *innate* or learned responses; tendencies *innate* in all governmental impulses toward collectivism.

Essential does not necessarily suggest an underlying principle; something may be a quite evident and recent addition and still be *essential* if it is vital to the existence of the pattern to which it belongs: *essential* revisions in the proposed bill that made it acceptable to the necessary majority. Frequently, of course, the word does refer, like *inherent*, to fundamentals; even in this case, however, these fundamentals may be readily apparent rather than hidden or tacit: the *essential* documents on which our democracy rests. **Intrinsic** almost exclusively applies to fundamentals that underlie a larger design. The word suggests the irreducible minimum on which the design depends for its effectiveness; it also sometimes suggests that later or less *essential* excrescences may have coalesced about this minimum without necessarily impairing the functioning of the whole: the *intrinsic* decency of the common man, regardless of every failure to live up to his own promise; *intrinsic* weaknesses of design that make some automobiles deathtraps, weaknesses not likely to be overcome by a few hastily added safety features. See INNATE.

Antonyms: EXTRANEOUS.

inheritance

bequest
birthright
heritage

These words indicate property willed to someone, or anything handed down from the past. **Inheritance** is the most general of these. At its strictest, it refers to both the real estate and personal property (including sums of money) left to someone in a will. This is usually acquired upon the death of the person who made the will, although sometimes it may be reserved until the one receiving it reaches a certain age or meets certain conditions. Occasionally, the word may be used to indicate realty alone, especially an estate or family home. In a more general sense, the word refers to anything handed down by one's predecessors, from hereditary traits to cultural traditions: the *inheritance* of a recessive gene from his mother's side; the precious *inheritance* of freedom guaranteed us by the Bill of Rights. **Bequest,** by contrast, functions solely in terms of willed personal property, often a sum of money, that comes to one by formal declaration upon the death of the donor: stipulating that a number of small *bequests* were to go to several close friends.

At their strictest, **legacy** and **heritage** contrast, since *legacy* refers like *bequest* to a willed gift of money or personal property, while *heritage* refers, more like *inheritance*, to real property that goes by right to an heir. More significantly, however, both words are similar in referring generally to anything that has come down from the past. In this use, *legacy* is likely to refer to abstract things such as qualities, attitudes, principles, or rights: the *legacy* of race hatred left us by the institution of slavery; a new honesty about sexual matters, the *legacy* of Freud, Ellis, and others. *Heritage* has a particular pertinence to enduring concrete things such as monuments, buildings, or natural resources: our squandered *heritage* of untainted streams and virgin forest land; the cathedrals that are part of England's invaluable *heritage*.

In their strict senses, **patrimony** refers to an estate, usually real, inherited from one's father, while **birthright** can refer to property, real or personal, to which someone, especially a firstborn son, is entitled by birth: Esau's selling of his *birthright* for a mess of pottage. Much more commonly, however, both words are used in more general senses. Here, *patrimony* can refer to anything derived from one's father or ancestors; thus, the word is a restriction of the general sense of *legacy*, referring to family or ancestral traditions: taking up the Barrymore *patrimony* of theatrical accomplishment. Sometimes, however, the word is used even more generally, like *inheritance*: the rival *patrimonies*, still viable, of Athenian democracy and Spartan authoritarianism. In this context, *birthright* is used like *legacy*, though it is more emphatically reserved for qualities, attitudes, principles, and especially rights to which every human being is thought entitled: our inalienable *birthright* of free speech; a UN declaration naming four specific freedoms as every person's *birthright*. See BEQUEST.

These words refer to traits that are deeply ingrained as part of a functioning pattern. **Innate,** the most general of these, is the least specific in suggesting how or at what point a trait becomes of such intrinsic importance: an *innate* weakness of all electric-powered cars; an *innate* eagerness to learn that was challenging and exciting; questioning whether learned responses ever do become *innate*. **Inborn** and **inbred** are the most informal words in this group; in effect, they split *innate* into two separate halves. *Inborn* indicates those traits acquired before birth, *inbred* those traits acquired later through training: *inborn* musical ability; an *inbred* respect for other people's wishes. The split is not so neat as it appears, however, since *inborn* is not always clear about environmental influences during gestation and *inbred* is not clear about the distinction between the contingent effects of environment during infancy and later training.

Congenital presents a conflicting set of meanings that render it vague and open to misinterpretation. In its most specific sense, it refers to traits acquired during gestation and not through heredity or later training: the tragic proof that thalidomide causes *congenital* deformities. In

inheritance
(continued)

legacy
patrimony

innate

congenital
hereditary
inborn
inbred

a completely contrary meaning, however, the word refers to traits acquired any time from birth onwards: a *congenital* liar. In this instance, it would seem clearer to use habitual or some other word. In still another instance, however, the word can refer in a vague and general way to traits deeply imprinted, without specifying when the imprinting occurred; this would make it a more formal synonym for *innate*. The word is sometimes used in this context with humorous intent: the farmer's *congenital* distrust of city slickers.

In its biological sense, **hereditary** is distinguished from *congenital* in its reference to characteristics, as the color of the hair and eyes, which are transmitted or transmissible directly from an animal or plant to its offspring. In an equally specific legal sense, *hereditary* applies to that which passes, is capable of passing, or which of necessity must pass by inheritance from an ancestor to an heir: a *hereditary* estate. In a more general way the word is used to refer to anything a person possesses which had to do with or was in some way a characteristic of one or more of his ancestors: the difficulty of dealing with a *hereditary* enemy toward whom one feels no personal animosity. See INHERENT.

Antonyms: acquired.

inner

interior
internal
inward

These words refer to what lies below the surface, in the central or inside portion of something, or within its boundaries. **Inner** is the most general of these and has the widest range of meaning. It can have geographical pertinence: the *inner* regions of the island. It can refer to a side that faces in: the *inner* edge of the terrace. It can also indicate the enclosed portion of something: an *inner* room of the tavern. In addition to these physical denotations, the word suggests covert or unconscious mental activity: signs of an *inner* turbulence of emotion; an *inner* ripeness for change.

Interior also suggests the geographical context: the *interior* counties of the lake district. It has a special relevance for something hidden or obscure, suggesting enclosure: an *interior* courtyard of the Florentine variety. And it refers, most strictly, to thought processes that are carried on without being spoken aloud: *interior* monologue.

The emphasis with **internal** is on something completely surrounded and covered from view: the *internal* organs of the body; suspecting *internal* injuries. It can also refer to mental activity, relating less to *interior* in this context than to *inner*, although its point is often a distinction between feeling emotions and expressing them: an *internal* uneasiness that at last became apparent in his nervous pacing.

Inward often refers to spiritual states: an *inward* rectitude of being. Sometimes its emphasis is on invisible as opposed to visible states: his outward behavior testifying to an *inward* state of grace. On a more mundane level, the word may indicate movement toward *interior* regions: their *inward* journey up the river, tracing its course upstream through the jungle. See CENTER.

Antonyms: exterior, external, outer.

innocent

blameless
guiltless
irreproachable

These words refer to things that are perfect, free of fault or failing, or morally uncorrupted. **Innocent** pertains to freedom from immoral behavior: *innocent* children. This quality, however, may stem from self-restraint, inexperience, or lack of opportunity: chaperons who made certain that the picnic remained at a level of *innocent* fun. The word is often used more simply to denote lack of guilt for a wrongful act: pleading *innocent* to the charge of disorderly conduct.

Virginal relates to the aspect of *innocent* pertaining to freedom from immoral behavior; this word is much more restricted than *innocent*, however, in specifically referring to chastity or to sexual immaturity, especially in women: his *virginal* bride. It may have a disapproving tone when this lack might be thought no longer appropriate or inherently admirable: a *virginal* spinster. Sometimes the word suggests the limpid sweetness of youth: the *virginal* faces of young girls. **Sinless** is wider in range than *virginal*, but more restricted than *innocent* in pertaining exclusively to freedom from all sorts of behavior thought immoral: impossible to live a completely *sinless* life. The word implies a supporting theological view, since what is praised as *sinless* by one religion might seem pointless or irrelevant to another: ascetics who strove toward a *sinless* life by abjuring the eating of meat.

Guiltless functions more like *innocent*. It can refer to freedom from immorality, though without the emphasis of *innocent* or *virginal* on youth: a politician *guiltless* of the more obvious kinds of cynical dealings. The word may also refer emphatically to blamelessness concerning a specific act: *guiltless* of having murdered his wife. The word, however, never substitutes for *innocent* in legal parlance. In the context of morality, **untainted** is used more abstractly than the previous words, referring to something that has never been sullied by any sort of harmful influence; in tone it seems more passive than *innocent*: an attitude *untainted* by selfish thoughts; a life *untainted* by scandal. The word has its own concrete relevance to anything pure: water *untainted* by bacteria.

Irreproachable functions less on a theological or moral level than on the level of conduct, indicating a general propriety of behavior: an *irreproachable* teacher where her interest in the students is concerned; a formal dinner that was *irreproachable* in every respect. **Blameless** operates, like *irreproachable*, in the sphere of ethics or conduct: *blameless* manners; a *blameless* life; finding him *blameless* of having caused the accident. *Blameless*, however, is more restricted to a simple lack of fault, whereas *irreproachable* may suggest a positive attainment of excellence: *blameless* but dull acting; *irreproachable* taste that was astonishing for its flair. See CHASTE, CLEAN (adj.), GOODNESS, MORAL, NAIVE, PERFECT.

Antonyms: blameworthy, *culpable*, DEPRAVED, DIRTY, *guilty, immoral, impure,* INDECENT, LEWD, *unchaste*.

These words all mean a seeking for information or truth. **Inquiry** is the most general term and is loosely applicable to all the others. An *inquiry* may range in importance from any request for information about ordinary matters to an investigation of an official nature: to make *inquiries* at a gas station concerning road directions; an *inquiry* made by the Board of Health about a spreading epidemic of measles; an *inquiry* into alleged corruption in city government.

Examination is also a general term; but an *examination* is generally stricter or more formal than an *inquiry*, involving careful scrutiny or inspection: an *examination* of all the points in a formal argument; an *examination* of one's motives for doing something. In law, an *examination* is an *inquiry* made by direct questioning or by the taking of testimony: The suspect underwent *examination* by the grand jury.

An **inquest** is an *inquiry* or *examination*, but its meaning is now almost entirely restricted to that of a judicial or legal investigation. In its best-known sense, an *inquest* is an investigation by a coroner (often aided by a coroner's jury) of the causes of a death when there is sufficient evidence to suspect that it occurred for other than natural reasons.

innocent
(continued)

sinless
untainted
virginal

inquiry

examination
inquest
inquisition
probe
study

Inquisition and **probe** are both searching, official investigations of an individual or of a group, made in order to dig out facts proving the existence of illegal acts or of heterodoxy. *Probe* is an Americanism when used in this sense and denotes an investigation that goes deeply below the surface in a manner reminiscent of a surgeon's instrument exploring a gunshot wound. *Inquisition* is chiefly thought of in its historical meaning, that of the *examination* and punishment of heretics, as practiced by the ecclesiastical courts of Europe during the late Middle Ages and the Reformation. The term also is applied to the body of church officials engaged in this activity. In its more general sense, *inquisition* implies persecution by means of relentless investigation, and harassment by persistent and prolonged interrogation. As a proper legal procedure in modern times, *inquisition* has been largely supplanted by *examination* and *probe*. A *probe* is a thorough investigation, made either by a legislative body or by a committee set up within such a body, into alleged misconduct or illegal practices on a large scale. A *probe* is usually made into activities considered hurtful to the government and its economy or to the rights of its citizens: a *probe* into a tax evasion on the part of a large corporation; a *probe* into the misuse of welfare funds.

A **study** is an *inquiry* made by gathering information in some detail in order to arrive at certain conclusions or to obtain a body of specialized knowledge: a *study* of the habits of the mountain gorilla; a *study* of the sluggish currents of the Sargasso Sea. *Studies* are also conducted to gain an understanding of the causes of an undesirable social condition so that improvements may be made: a *study* of the traffic situation in a large city; a *study* of the incidence of relapse in mental illness. See EXAMINE, PIERCE, QUESTION (n.), QUESTION (v.).

insert

interject
interpolate
interpose
introduce

These verbs may all express the act of breaking in on a flow of words in order to make an addition, alteration, or comment. To **insert** a letter, word, or group of words is simply to put it in, often where it has a perfect right to be. Specifically, *insert* suggests that a space must be made in written or printed matter so that the addition may be fitted in: to *insert* an ad in a newspaper. A caret [∧] marks the spot where an omitted word or letter is to be *inserted* in a line. To **interpolate** a word, passage, or comment is to *insert* it where it does not belong — among words written or spoken by and attributed to another. *Interpolations* such as editorial comments, explanations, and helpful emendations are permissible if enclosed in square brackets, as in: " 'I think [Parks Commissioner William] Sanders is doing a great job,' the mayor told reporters." *Interpolations* that are not permissible are additions made by other hands that are passed off as part of the author's original, for such *interpolated* matter corrupts the original text. To **introduce** something into a speech or piece of writing is to bring it in not only as an added part, or insertion, but as a new part, a change from what is already there. [He was told that his speech would be more effective if he *introduced* examples to illustrate his points; After Shakespeare's death, lesser playwrights *introduced* changes into his plays, *interpolating* spurious passages, stage directions, spectacle, and music.]

Both **interject** and the more formal **interpose** may mean to *introduce* abruptly. These words, however, are specifically used of oral comments that break in suddenly upon an otherwise even flow of speech. What is *interjected* is simply thrown in unexpectedly and forcefully, as an exclamation arising from a natural reaction. [When that politician's name was mentioned, the doctor *interjected* an oath into the conversation.] What is *interposed* is put in as a deliberate interruption, such as a protest or digression, and is meant to halt the speech or argument going on. [A student interrupted the lecturer, ostensibly to ask a question, but actually to *interpose* his own opinion; When, in the course of his summation to the jury, the prosecuting attorney began to repeat hearsay, the defense attorney jumped to his feet and *interposed* an objection.] See ADD, MEDIATE, REVISE.

Antonyms: *abstract, detach,* ERASE, *excerpt, extract,* REMOVE, *withdraw.*

insolvent

bankrupt
broke
impecunious

These words apply to those who do not have enough money to meet their needs or to pay their debts. **Insolvent** refers to a debtor whose liabilities outweigh his assets and who therefore cannot meet the claims of his creditors. Both an individual and a business enterprise may be *insolvent.* [People thought him well-to-do, but he died *insolvent,* his estate being insufficient to liquidate his debts; Since the business was *insolvent,* it qualified as a tax loss.] In law, **bankrupt** refers specifically to a person who or business which has been judicially declared *insolvent.* When, through the operation of a *bankruptcy* law, the actual *insolvency* of a debtor has been legally determined, his assets are taken into judicial possession for equitable distribution among his creditors. The debtor, himself, is then granted by judicial decree a full discharge from legal liability for his indebtedness. For this reason, someone deeply and hopelessly in debt may choose to or have to declare himself *bankrupt.* [His business failed and he went *bankrupt*; the business went into *bankruptcy.*] Loosely, any person who is unable to pay his debts or who is devoid of resources may be called *bankrupt. Bankrupt* may also refer to utter ruin of any kind. In a figurative sense, it may mean destitute of some abstract quality, or hopelessly lacking, as in spiritual resources: a morally *bankrupt* society; a man *bankrupt* in spirit.

The remaining words focus on a lack of money rather than on indebtedness, implying empty pockets rather than red ink. **Broke** is the common, everyday word. It is sometimes used informally as a substitute for *insolvent* or *bankrupt*: The business kept losing money and finally went *broke.* But *broke* is much broader in application than the previous pair of words. A person who cannot pay his bills may claim, or be said, to be *broke*; but a person may also be *broke* without being in debt. Further, *broke* often applies to a temporary condition: a speculator often *broke* but never poor; flat *broke* the day before payday. **Impecunious** comes from Latin roots and literally means without money. It may refer to a person who never has much money or who is frequently *broke*: an *impecunious* artist living in a garret. But it is a rather high-flown, pretentious word and is often used in a self-conscious way to give a humorous, lightly mocking effect. [Sorry I can't go with you, but I'm rather *impecunious* at the moment.] See POOR, WEALTH.

Antonyms: *affluent, flush, loaded, prosperous, rich, solvent, wealthy, well-to-do.*

intend

aim
contemplate
mean

These words mean to have in mind the doing of some act or the attainment of some goal. **Intend** has the widest range of implication. It may involve no more than vague thoughts or halfhearted resolves. [I *intend* to clean out the attic sooner or later; The road to hell is paved with good *intentions.*] Or it may imply a firm decision taken with regard to an immediate or ultimate goal. [I *intend* to see to it that my son is not late again; They *intend* to work hard and save to put their children through college.]

intend
(continued)

plan
propose

Mean is synonymous with *intend* in both its strong and its weak sense, implying either a truly firm resolve or a merely professed purpose. [I *mean* to go, and nothing is going to stop me; I've been *meaning* to write to you for weeks.] But *mean* is a less formal word than *intend*, well suited to everyday speech and writing; and it is more often used than *intend* to express a dubious, weak, or unrealized resolve. [I *meant* to visit her, but I never got around to it.] *Mean* is also used to claim or give credit for good *intentions* when an action has backfired. [I'm sure he *meant* well; I *meant* no harm — I only *meant* to help.] **Aim**, like *mean*, is informal in tone. It points, though, to an actual goal, purpose, or *intention*, as distinguished from an avowed one that is open to doubt. [What do you *aim* to do?; I *aim* to succeed.] Further, *aim* may imply not only *intent* but also effort, though without the suggestion of failure often conveyed by *mean*. [I *aim* to please.]

Propose, in one sense, is closely synonymous with *intend*: He *proposes* to go on to medical school after college. But *propose* generally goes beyond *intend* and *aim* in implying that an *intention* or design has been clearly formulated in the mind, and often announced to others. [What do you *propose* to do?; I *propose* to rally the forces and attack at dawn; The chairman of the Bridge and Tunnel Authority *proposes* to build a new bridge across the narrows.] **Plan**, like *intend*, may sometimes imply only a vague goal or indefinite resolution that is not being presently acted upon: He *plans* to go to Europe someday. But *plan* may be, and often is, much more definite than *intend*, implying the taking of active steps toward the realization of an *intention*. Such *planning* involves a consideration of the ways and means of achieving a goal and the making of arrangements in advance. [I *plan* to leave on August 4, have made airline reservations for that date, and have applied for a passport.] In an intransitive sense, *plan* and *propose* may be closely synonymous. [He is always *planning* but seldom carries through with his schemes; Man never does all that he *proposes*.] *Propose* may also mean to make an offer of marriage.

To **contemplate** is to consider or anticipate, to turn over in the mind. *Contemplate* implies a greater immediacy than *intend*, *mean*, or *aim* but much less definiteness than *propose* or *plan*. [She *intends* to get married when she grows up; He is *contemplating* marriage but has not yet *proposed*; She is *contemplating* a trip to Europe, but she hasn't *planned* it yet.] See DECIDE, HOPE, MEAN, OFFER, PLAN, PURPOSE, TRY.

intimidate

browbeat
bulldoze
bully
cow
daunt
dismay
overawe
terrorize

These words mean to make submissive, compliant, or subdued by inspiring fear. **Intimidate** is the most general word, precisely directed to this concept. To *intimidate* someone is to manipulate him by using his own fear or weakness against him as a psychological weapon. The person who sets out to *intimidate* another aims to fill the chosen victim with a dread of unpleasant consequences to come if he does not comply. [The employer tried to *intimidate* his employees from forming a union by threatening to move his business away if they did; The parents were *intimidated* into paying the ransom by the kidnaper's threatening notes; The quiet leveling of the highwayman's pistol *intimidated* the driver of the stage.] *Intimidation* may involve the use of violence or coercion to influence the conduct of another or to compel his consent; but when actual force is used, it constitutes a threat of future force that would be more deadly: The syndicate *intimidated* the witness by having him worked over in a dark alley. A person may also be *intimidated* through his own shyness, cowardice, sense of inadequacy, or fear of embarrassment: so *intimidated* by the speaker's fame that they were afraid to ask him questions; *intimidated* by the surly waiter's sneer into leaving a larger tip than they had intended.

Cow and **overawe** point both to the cause and to the effect of *intimidation*. *Cow* in this sense comes from an Old Norse word meaning to tyrannize over. To *cow* someone is to reduce him to a weak, submissive state, breaking his spirit or overcoming his resistance by the use or threat of superior force: a tyrant of a father who *cowed* his children's spirits; cringing slaves, *cowed* by the overseer's whip; suddenly *cowed* by the sight of a policeman. *Overawe* does not imply the kind of fear and trembling suggested by *cow*. Instead, it focuses on reverential fear — respect that subdues or restrains one. [The peasants were *overawed* by the vastness of the cathedral; The explorer *overawed* the natives with his fine clothes and fancy equipment.]

Daunt and **dismay** deal specifically with the kind of effect caused by *intimidation*. To *daunt* is to dishearten, frighten, or otherwise discourage someone from going on; it implies a loss of the will to keep trying. [Pioneer life *daunted* her and she went back to Boston; No number of failures and disappointments could *daunt* him in his quest for a cure.] *Dismay* suggests a sinking feeling in the pit of the stomach. It points to a sense of hopeless discouragement in the face of obstacles or paralyzing fear in the face of a threat. [Their utter refusal to compromise *dismayed* him and left him at a loss; a contender in the ring, *dismayed* by the size and fierceness of his opponent.]

The remaining words all focus on the act of *intimidating* another. **Terrorize** and **bully** imply the deliberate incitement of fear as a method of *intimidation*. *Terrorize* is the more formal word and presupposes a much greater degree of violence. It has political associations, often applying to unlawful acts of violence committed in an attempt to overthrow a government: Rebels *terrorized* the countryside, staging midnight raids, planting grenades in the roads, and exacting tribute from the people. *Bully* is much more informal. As a noun, it denotes a swaggering, aggressive person who is usually cowardly at heart and who *intimidates* weaker people. Children use the word for a larger or stronger child, usually a bigger boy, who picks on smaller or weaker ones. Hence to *bully* is to push others around in this way, whether through brute force or through verbal taunts or threats: They had stood for hours, but he *bullied* them into letting him break in line in front of them. **Bulldoze** falls between *bully* and *terrorize* in force. It is a slang term that originated in the United States, pointing to *intimidation* through the use of violence or coercion or through the threat of reprisals. Now, however, it may imply force of will or exercise of abstract power rather than physical force. [They tried to *bulldoze* him, but he stuck to his guns; The president *bulldozed* the businessmen into rescinding a price increase; one holdout trying to *bulldoze* the other jurors into changing their minds] **Browbeat** implies mental harassment rather than a physical attack. To *browbeat* someone is to *intimidate* or *cow* him, or to try to do so, by means of a stern, overbearing, condemnatory manner. *Browbeat* may imply haughty, contemptuous, or rude treatment, or a bombardment of some kind that goes on without letup. [He was a meek little man, the perfect victim, *browbeaten* by his boss at the office and by his wife at home; The lawyer started *browbeating* the witness, trying to upset him and discredit his testimony.] See BELEAGUER, BRAVE, COMPEL, FEAR, FRIGHTEN.

Antonyms: blandish, ENCOURAGE, enhearten, INDUCE.

intrigue

conspiracy
machination
plot
scheme

These words refer to secret plans contrived to attain some possibly improper or illegal goal. **Intrigue** stresses behind-the-scenes manipulations, but it may or may not imply impropriety or illegality: a court rife with *intrigue* against the king's life; adept at the *intrigue* necessary to carry on a clandestine love affair; small-town *intrigue* that amounted to nothing more than trivial gossip. *Intrigue* may be a collective noun for the sum total of secret maneuvering in a given social context. **Machination** more often refers, less inclusively, to a secret or semi-secret stratagem, a devious action, or an underhand maneuver that is part of a larger plan. It usually appears in the plural and suggests, disapprovingly, some impropriety of motive: *machinations* to make it appear that the innocent girl had committed the murder.

Plot suggests a specific, inclusive plan worked out in detail by a person or group, most often to gain some improper or illegal goal: the *plot* to assassinate Caesar; a *plot* to rig television ratings. *Intrigue* or *machinations* may be resorted to as elements in furthering a *plot* or in its final carrying out. Both most often suggest subservience to the kind of master plan indicated by *plot*: certain that a *plot* of some sort was under way from the amount of *intrigue* he caught wind of.

A *plot* may sometimes be petty in scope, but **conspiracy** is applied chiefly to serious crimes, and there is something sinister about the word. Specifically, in this sense, a *conspiracy* is a *plot* involving two or more persons who plan together to commit an evil or unlawful act. [The investigative commission found no evidence of a *conspiracy* to assassinate the President; They uncovered a price-fixing *conspiracy* and indicted several industry officials.]

Scheme is much more general than the other words in this group. Nothing improper or illegal at all may be referred to; the word, in fact, might point exclusively to the devising rather than to the furthering or carrying out of a plan: suddenly coming up with a *scheme* that would solve their money problems. But *scheme*, unlike plan, often carries an unfavorable connotation, implying something underhanded and self-serving: the *scheming* Iago, devising a way to bring about his successful rival's downfall. See ACCOMPLICE, CONSPIRACY, PLAN.

invariable

constant
unchanging
uniform

These words apply to things that are not marked by change or variation. Something is **invariable** if it recurs always in the same manner or at regular intervals. The succession of neap tide and spring tide is *invariable*. Something is **constant** if it remains the same or changes at a regular rate over a long period of time. The birth rate in some countries is *constant*, and in other countries the rate of population increase is *constant*. In mathematics and science, a *constant* is a number or quantity that does not change throughout a given discussion or operation. An absolute *constant* is fixed and cannot be changed. An arbitrary *constant* can be assigned any set value. In a more general sense, *invariable* and *constant* may simply mean continual or habitual. [She *invariably* forgets to take her keys; She is *constantly* changing her mind.] And while *invariable* more often applies to routine, both words may be used of abstract qualities that are enduring or reliable: an *invariable* stop at the corner newsstand; *constant* affection; *invariable* amiability.

Something is **unchanging** in this sense if its attributes remain the same for a long period of time. Weather and climate may be said to be *unchanging* in certain areas of the world. The biological processes of life may be called *unchanging*.

In one sense, **uniform** is close to *constant*, describing something that does not undergo changes in form or character, quantity or degree: a thermostat to maintain a *uniform* temperature. In another sense, *uniform* may suggest a bringing of separate things into a state of conformity, either basically or in some salient aspect: the need for *uniform* traffic regulations throughout the nation. [The hedges were clipped to a *uniform* height; All twenty volumes of the encyclopedia were of *uniform* thickness.] See IMMUTABLE, PERMANENT, PERSISTENT.

Antonyms: INCONSTANT, *variable.*

J

jaunty

chipper
debonair
insouciant

These words are used to describe a brisk, unworried, self-assured person or the way in which he acts. **Jaunty**, which at its most positive refers to a lively, dashing urbanity, sometimes suggests a studied nonchalance — an attempt, often contrived or even forced, to be suave or sophisticated which results in a kind of aggressive good humor: struggling to look *jaunty* and interesting in his yachting outfit; the *jaunty* way he approached to ask her for a dance. **Chipper** refers more to a sprightly self-satisfaction that exudes good humor and health; the word, however, would refer to the good health of maturity rather than that of youth: Aging roués who still manage to look spruce and *chipper* are the despair of the moralist.

Debonair is more like *jaunty* in suggesting a reckless ease of manner that is filled with carefree good spirits: the typically *debonair* French lover. The word has taken on an overtone that implies worldly sophistication, as well: the eager and callow youth who for all his posturing is still naive, still far from being *debonair*. **Insouciant** translates literally from the French to mean without care; it also suggests gaiety of manner and sophistication: the *insouciant* young bohemians who travel from one party to another without a thought for tomorrow. See BLITHE, LIVELY, URBANE.

Antonyms: SEDATE.

jazz

blues
boogie-woogie
bop
Dixieland
ragtime
rhythm-and-blues
rock
rock 'n' roll
swing

These words refer to forms of popular music that ultimately derive from the folk cultures of the U.S. South. Most of them share a stress on emphatic rhythm and improvisatory melodic lines. **Jazz** is the generic word under which nearly all the remaining terms can be grouped. In itself it can apply descriptively to any such music, regardless of period, style, or the number of musicians involved: a small *jazz* combo; the influence of spirituals on the development of *jazz*; a *jazz* vocalist; big-band *jazz*; the new sounds in *jazz*. **Blues** and **ragtime** are the earliest forms of *jazz*; both were evolved by American Negroes. *Blues* typically refers to songs whose lyrics have three-line stanzas in which the first and second lines are alike. They were sung and played in a slow tempo and were in major keys (as is most *jazz*), but with unconventional scale degrees (blue notes) such as flatted thirds and certain unusual harmonies. The mood expressed was of grief, melancholy, or despair: the *blues* singing of Bessie Smith. Later, the word has been applied less exactly to any *jazz* or commercial music reflecting some of these qualities. *Ragtime* refers classically to an early form of piano *jazz*, originating in and around St. Louis, based on European marches and dance tunes but played with a characteristic syncopated Negro rhythm. The word came to be used loosely to refer to Negro-inspired popular music in general and thus was the predecessor to the word *jazz* (originally *jass*): Alexander's *Ragtime* Band (1911).

The Original Dixie Land *Jass* Band, a white group, made the New Orleans ensemble style of Negro popular music a national rage in 1917 and established the word *jazz* in popular usage. **Dixieland,** meaning New Orleans style *jazz* as played by white performers and not merely a term of geographical ascription, did not come into use until the 1940's: *Dixieland* at Eddie Condon's. **Swing** evolved in the 1930's from the ensemble *jazz* of both white and Negro groups as bands became bigger and more theatrical and orchestral arrangements more polished; it puts more stress on well-coordinated teamwork than on improvisation: Tommy Dorsey and Benny Goodman set the tone for the age of *swing*. **Boogie-woogie** is a kind of piano *jazz* in which improvisations on a *blues* melody with the right hand are played over a repetitive eight-to-a-bar figure in the left. *Swing* arrangements of *boogie-woogie* pieces were sometimes written: a *boogie-woogie* number played by Count Basie's band.

In New York City, bold Negro *jazz* experimentalists in the late 1940's developed re-bop, which became be-bop and finally **bop.** This music emphasized long-line far-ranging improvisations on standard themes set off by closely woven ensemble work that featured pungent harmonies (such as the use of chords with a flatted fifth) and polyphonic lines. This music did not become popular in turn as *swing* had been, but it was adopted by musicians, both white and black, and won the interest of an intellectual and avant-garde coterie. In contrast, **rhythm-and-blues** (often shortened to "R and B") have kept their hold on a mass audience of American Negroes since the "race records" of the 1920's; with their roots in the experience of rural Negroes moving to the great cities of the North, they are an authentic urban folk music, still meeting the needs of those for whom it is written.

In the 1950's **rock 'n' roll** fused elements of *rhythm and blues*, not yet generally popular, and aspects of Southern white "country music" to achieve such popularity as to sweep other forms of popular music and even of *jazz*, its distant relative, from public attention. This music emphasized an unvarying (even monotonous), heavy, rhythmic beat and lyrics expressive of pre-adolescent sentiments. Nearly all popular music in the 1960's had its origins in *rhythm-and-blues, rock 'n' roll*, folk music in general, or some mixture of these. In the 1960's *rock 'n' roll* was shortened to **rock** to describe a later development of this music in which as few as four musicians sing and play together in close co-ordination; *rock* stresses quite conventional harmonies, a driving but less inflexible rhythmic impulse, and free-wheeling lyrics that violate accepted *blues* or popular song patterns: folk *rock*; acid *rock*. See MELODY.

Jesus

Christ
Good Shepherd
Lamb

These words are all references to the founder of Christianity, considered by most Christians as God or one of the persons of God. **Jesus** was the name for this historical person, derived from the Greek word for the Hebrew name Joshua, meaning **Savior**. **Christ** is the English form of the Greek translation of the Hebrew word **Messiah**, meaning Anointed or Anointed King; the word was understood first as a title attached to *Jesus*' name, often with a definite article: *Jesus* the *Christ*. Here, the

Jesus
(continued)

Messiah
Redeemer
Savior
Son of God

word most clearly points to the belief that *Jesus* was the awaited king of Israel foretold by prophecy. Without the definite article, *Christ* is now attached to *Jesus* as if part of a proper name: *Jesus Christ.* This is the fullest and most formal way of referring to him. Used separately, the two words can be applied interchangeably, but by a devout Christian, *Jesus* would be felt to suggest the warm, loving, personal, and human aspect of their God, whereas *Christ* would be felt as a reference to *Jesus'* theological function as the defeater of Satan and original sin, the forgiver of sins, and the *Savior* of mankind. To non-Christians, *Christ* might be the more familiar term, since it is the basis of so many words pertaining to this religion: Christian, Christianity, Christmas.

Influenced perhaps by the captivity and scattering of the tribes of Israel, the Hebrews foresaw the coming of a king who would restore Israel and rule the Jews righteously; at times and by some prophets, an earthly king was foreseen, but in any case, this prophesied king is called the *Messiah*, still waited for by modern Judaism. From the first, as at present, Christians have believed that this foretold person was *Jesus* the *Christ* (or *Messiah*) in that they see him as having fulfilled all the particulars of the Old Testament prophecies, although he established a spiritual, not an earthly, kingdom. To Christians, **Redeemer** and *Savior* both refer to *Christ* as the one who brought salvation to the world. *Savior* suggests his saving mankind as a whole from sin and death. *Redeemer* suggests his more personal, one-to-one role as the forgiver of each person's sins.

The **Son of God** is a title for *Christ*, referring to the theological doctrine of the Trinity, held to by most sects of Christians. In this doctrine, God is indivisible but can be seen at work in three aspects, Father, *Son*, and Holy Ghost. All three have existed and will exist eternally, but the Father is seen as the creator of the universe, the Holy Ghost as His inspiriting breath or will moving through time, and the *Son* as the person, begotten by the Father, who took on human flesh in the form of *Jesus* and expiated the sins of the world on the cross. To non-Trinitarians, the term would more strictly refer to *Jesus* as deriving from God but remaining distinct from Him; non-Trinitarian Christians can, furthermore, view *Jesus* as wholly divine, wholly human, or as an amalgam of both natures.

The **Good Shepherd** is an affectionate term for *Jesus* seen as the guide and helper of his human flock; this term derives from the Twenty-Third Psalm, in which the Hebrew God was extolled: The Lord is my *shepherd. Jesus* is also called the **Lamb,** in symbolic reference to his willing sacrifice on the cross in order to redeem mankind from original sin. This term refers to the older Hebrew custom of sacrificing lambs in the worship of God; it also relates to the older Hebrew custom of selecting a ram as a scapegoat which, symbolically bearing the sins of the tribes, is sent off into the desert to die in order to expiate the sins sent along with him.

joke

gag
jest
pleasantry

These words all denote something said or done to excite laughter. **Joke** is a general term, but specifically it refers to a brief narrative or anecdote with a funny ending. A practical *joke* is an act designed to surprise or embarrass another. **Jest**, which now sounds somewhat old-fashioned except in the phrase *in jest*, usually refers to an oral remark, but may also be a playful act.

Whereas *joke* and *jest* emphasize humor, **witticism** points to a more intellectual exercise — that of wit — depending a good deal more on

joke
(continued)

quip
wisecrack
witticism

originality or irony of thought. **Quip** and **pleasantry** are, respectively, a sharp and mild instance of a comment intended to amuse, the former often imparting a sting and the latter scrupulously avoiding any painful effect. Both words stress nicety of phrasing rather than brilliance in idea.

Gag and **wisecrack** are the slang equivalents of *joke* and *witticism*, respectively. Like *quip*, but even more strongly, *wisecrack* implies a mocking or satirical motive. *Gag* often refers to a theatrical *joke*, as one prepared in advance of a performance. One speaks of the *witticisms* of statesmen, the *wisecracks* of political commentators, and the *gags* of nightclub comedians. See CARICATURE, RIDICULE.

journey

excursion
jaunt
junket
pilgrimage
tour
trip
voyage

These words refer to travel. While **journey** is the most general of these, it is now usually used of travel by land and often suggests the covering of considerable time or distance, with no necessary implication of a return: their transcontinental *journey* in covered wagons. **Voyage**, by contrast, is now usually used of travel by water: a long ocean *voyage* to England.

Where both *journey* and *voyage* are relatively formal, **trip** is the more informal substitute for either. In this case, however, the covering of a shorter time or distance is suggested and an eventual return to the starting point is often implied: He went on a *trip* to the nearest seaside resort during his vacation. In psychedelic slang, *trip* indicates an extended meditative or introspective sequence, whether drug-induced or not: He turned on and was soon off on a long *trip*; good and bad *trips*; strobes and screen projections guaranteed to send you on a *trip*.

Tour indicates a *trip* in which many places are visited, often by means of a circuitous route: a *tour* of Italy that included stops at Milan, Venice, Florence, and Rome. In a related use, the inspection of a much smaller area may be indicated: a *tour* of the castle. **Excursion** serves as a more formal substitute for *trip* or *tour*; it emphasizes a temporary departure from a given place and specifies a return to it. It can point to a sea or land *tour* or to a short outing: an *excursion* that would take us to several Aegean islands and return us to Athens after two weeks; an *excursion* to the beach, complete with picnic hampers and thermoses of cold drinks.

Pilgrimage indicates a *journey* taken to a specific place that has religious or emotional significance: the annual *pilgrimage* to Mecca; a *pilgrimage* to Kennedy's grave at Arlington. **Jaunt** and **junket**, by contrast, both suggest *excursions* for recreation or pleasure. *Jaunt* suggests a short *trip* or outing: a weekend *jaunt* to Fire Island. *Junket* is more specific in pointing to the *trip* of a public official whose expenses are paid, usually from public funds. While such *trips* may be authorized and connected with an official purpose, describing them as *junkets* often casts suspicion on this legitimate explanation and implies that these *trips* are nonessential pleasure-seeking *jaunts*: a *junket* of several Congressmen to the pleasure capitals of Europe.

joyous

ecstatic
elated
euphoric
happy

These words describe exhilarated or joyful states of mind. **Joyous** suggests a strong feeling of contentment or high spirits, often because of the expectation or realization of some good: *joyous* celebrations in anticipation of the end of war. *Joyous* is sometimes applied to people as a synonym for joyful, but is also used of something that promotes joy or is in itself an expression of joy: the *joyous* song of the hermit thrush.

Happy is the most general word of this group, but it is also the weakest, since it does not ordinarily imply the excitement and strong feeling indicated by *joyous* and by some of the other words. In social exchanges *happy* is used in mild expressions of enjoyment or willingness. [I shall be *happy* to help you find a new job; We are very *happy* to see you.] In its wider sense *happy* suggests tranquil contentment and fulfillment of one's aspirations and desires: to be *happy* in one's work; to have a *happy* marriage.

Ecstatic and **elated** both emphasize greater joy and delight than does *happy*. From its earlier meaning of being in a trancelike state of religious fervor, *ecstatic* suggests such an overpowering joy or mental exaltation that one is beside himself: a young boy *ecstatic* in his first love; a traveler *ecstatic* over the art treasures of Florence. *Elated*, less forceful than *ecstatic*, points to the great pleasure and self-satisfaction that arises from success or good fortune: a novelist *elated* over the favorable reviews of his book; a young father *elated* over the birth of twins.

A person who is **euphoric** may outwardly resemble in behavior one who is *ecstatic* or *elated*; however, upon closer observation, it will be seen that his vigor and buoyancy is exaggerated and out of proportion to the situation at hand. Although experienced at one time or another by most people, *euphoria* is commonly thought of as occurring during the course of certain mental disturbances or after the ingestion of alcoholic beverages or of certain drugs.

High and **turned on** are terms used to describe more or less artificially induced exhilaration or *euphoria*. *High* is used most commonly and colloquially of a person who is animated and talkative after drinking an alcoholic beverage. [He usually gets quite *high* on just two drinks.] *High* is also applied in a slang sense to one who has taken a narcotic drug and is experiencing the resultant *euphoria* or contented lethargy. *Turned on*, a current slang term that originated among psychedelic drug users, is more frequently found as a verb than as an adjective. In its narrowest sense, to *turn on* means either to begin feeling the effect of a marijuana cigarette or to introduce a neophyte to the practice. [Every Saturday night they and a group of their friends *turn on*; Last week his college roommate *turned* him *on*.] It may also mean to take or be under the influence of any narcotic or psychedelic drug: *turned on* with LSD. By extension, *turn on* may also mean to excite or strongly attract. [Bach's music always *turns* him *on*; Men with soulful brown eyes always seem to *turn* her *on*.] See BLITHE, CHEERFUL, LIVELY.

Antonyms: GLOOMY, *low*, MISERABLE, *morose*, SAD, *solemn*.

These words all denote a person who makes decisions in situations in which there is a conflict of views. **Judge** is the most general term. In its strictest sense, a *judge* is a government official who presides in a court of law and administers justice by hearing and deciding cases. By extension, *judge* is applied to a person who has the requisite knowledge, experience, and impartiality to make decisions or pass upon the merits of something. [Your doctor is the best *judge* of what will cure your illness; The *judges* at the fair awarded her a blue ribbon for her pie.]

Arbitrator and **arbiter** are sometimes used synonymously to denote a person, or one of several persons, chosen by disputing parties to settle their differences. However, in this sense, *arbitrator* is the preferred term. [In the labor dispute, three *arbitrators* were chosen by management and three by the workers.] *Arbiter*, a somewhat literary word, is more often applied to one who without official authorization or position has the prestige to make decisions or to set standards that others willingly follow. [Lord Chesterfield was the *arbiter* of elegant manners and good taste in his day; Dress designers are the *arbiters* of women's fashions.]

Referee and **umpire** may both mean *arbitrator*, but the two words are more likely to be used in special contexts. Many sports are presided over by official *judges* who are appointed to enforce the rules of the game or contest and to settle disputed points. In baseball, tennis, and cricket, such an official is called an *umpire*; in boxing, ice hockey, and basketball he is called a *referee*. The rules of American football call for the presence of both an *umpire* and a *referee*. Outside of the world of sports, *umpire* and *referee* have further meanings. *Referee* is applied technically to a lawyer to whom a pending legal case is referred, by means of a court order, for additional investigation and report. Although an *arbitrator*, a legal *referee* is usually appointed without the consent of the parties involved. In an important or complicated controversy, an *umpire* may be appointed to make a final decision in a case in which there is disagreement or a stalemate between the *arbitrators*. See LAWYER.

jumble

conglomeration
farrago
hodgepodge
medley
mélange
mess
mishmash
muddle
olio
olla podrida
potpourri

These words are alike in referring to a disordered condition or to a confused or heterogeneous mixture of elements. **Jumble** and **muddle** both suggest conditions of extreme disorderliness resulting in confusion. *Jumble* suggests physical disorderliness, a lack of neatness, and brings to mind objects strewn about carelessly: The room was a *jumble* of books, papers, and beer cans. *Muddle* suggests the lack of clear or coherent organization, and commonly refers to mental or intellectual disorder — confused thinking. [The club records were in a complete *muddle* — no one even knew how much money was in the treasury; Income tax returns always put him in a *muddle*; in a drunken *muddle* of misdirected antagonism.]

Conglomeration and **mélange** refer to heterogeneous collections of things. Both words often carry critical overtones, suggesting that the collection is random or inapposite: a curious *conglomeration* of witticisms, quotations, word games, and other linguistic legerdemain, entertaining enough but lacking any overall plan of organization. *Mélange* more vigorously suggests inaptness or incongruity, and is sometimes used derisively or contemptuously: a *mélange* of beatniks, middle-class matrons, and Madison Avenue executives. **Medley** and **farrago** both refer to confused mixtures or masses of elements. *Medley* emphasizes the variegated, heterogeneous nature of the elements that compose it, whereas *farrago* emphasizes the irrational or confused juxtaposition of those elements. A *medley* is necessarily various, but not necessarily composed of inharmonious or clashing elements: a *medley* of flavors. *Farrago* strikes a balance somewhere between *conglomeration* and **mess**: a *farrago* of outmoded ideas and half-understood theories.

Mess is the most general word of this set as well as one of the strongest. In the sense here considered it means a hopeless *jumble* of elements resulting in a state of confusion, or the confused state itself. It may refer either to physical disorder (After the ticker tape parade ended, the street was a *mess*), sloppiness or slovenliness (The manuscript was a *mess*, full of inkblots, erasures, and deletions), or to any thoroughly disorganized condition (He's made a *mess* of his life).

Hodgepodge (or, as it is sometimes spelled and pronounced, *hotchpotch*), **potpourri**, and **olla podrida** all refer in one sense to stews having a variety of ingredients. All also commonly refer to any miscellaneous collection of elements. *Hodgepodge*, as well as the stronger term **mishmash**, emphasize disorganization; they are the figurative analogues to an actual *jumble* of objects. [The musical comedy was a *hodgepodge* of sentimental cliché, coy sexuality, and jingoistic claptrap.] *Hodgepodge* bespeaks a lack of intelligent guidance or rational coherence.

Mishmash, the most directly contemptuous word of this group, is often used to suggest a badly mismanaged or botched undertaking, resulting in confusion and chaos: His heralded new political program turned out to be nothing more than the usual *mishmash* of stale slogans, unrealistic promises, and insincere flattery. *Potpourri*, as here considered, points to the lack of uniformity or similarity of elements, and may imply a lack of discrimination or restraint as well: The movie was a *potpourri* of slapstick, melodrama, and bowdlerized history, in spite of which it still managed to include some genuinely funny moments. *Olla podrida*, borrowed from the Spanish, and **olio**, derived from *olla*, suggest a miscellaneous collection or *medley* of elements: an *olio* of political sentiment, ranging from the radical to the reactionary. See DISPARATE, HETEROGENEOUS.

These words refer to the ability or right to rule. **Jurisdiction** is the most formal of these words and the most restricted in application. It indicates an officially or legally predetermined division of a larger whole, a division within which someone or something has the right to rule or decide: Surrogate court has sole *jurisdiction* over the execution of wills; an election in which workers were to determine what union should have *jurisdiction* to represent them; the three-nation commission that was given *jurisdiction* to govern the internationalized city. **Sovereignty** approaches *jurisdiction* in formality, but it stresses absolute or autonomous rule over something considered as a whole. In this case, the official right to rule is not stressed so much as the fact of actual ruling, however this has come about: British mercantile interests that acquired *sovereignty* over the scattering of emirates adjacent to the port; nations traditionally suspicious of surrendering the slightest token of *sovereignty* to any supranational governing body; American revolutionists who rejected England's claim of *sovereignty* over the colonies.

Dominion is less clear-cut in its implications. It can refer, on one hand, to assigned partial rule, like *jurisdiction*: a constitutional provision that gave the states *dominion* over intrastate commerce. On the other hand, it can refer like *sovereignty* to absolute control, although here it often refers strictly to the control of a superior over an inferior: the inescapable *dominion* of the rich and educated over the poor and unschooled. As an actual title for a territory, the word can suggest a colony that has gained internal self-rule but whose external affairs still come under the *sovereignty* of the colonizer: a colony that advanced to the status of a *dominion* and finally of a full-fledged republic. **Sway** can now sound old-fashioned; traditionally it has referred to a sphere in which something has absolute control: the succession of European nations that held *sway* over various portions of Africa; Aristotle held undisputed *sway* over the thinking of many medieval philosophers. As in the last example, the word is in danger of being taken in the sense of mere influence rather than absolute control; this possibility occurs because of an unrelated meaning of *sway*: a demagogue able to *sway* mass audiences to his point of view.

Authority and **Power** are less formal than the other words here and are much more general in application. *Power* refers to any exercising of control over something, often with a stress on forcefulness or strength: The monarchy won universal recognition of its *sovereignty* only after the period of its greatest *power* had begun to fade. Often, the word refers simply to the ability to choose, understand, or control: Only man of all the animals has the *power* to reason. A related use reveals the word at

jurisdiction

authority
dominion
power
sovereignty
sway

its most general in referring to any sort of mental or physical strength or force: a work of great emotional *power*; brute *power* used to put down the revolt. *Authority* can indicate an officially determined right to rule: a committee given *authority* to rule on the credentials of disputed delegations. But the word can also refer to anyone exercising power, whether assigned to do so or not: a *power* gap in the new republic that remained until several tribal leaders assumed *authority* and formed a caretaker government. The word can also indicate the taking on or delegating of responsibility: You have my *authority* to proceed with the investigation. As an abstraction, the word can indicate all sources of *power* taken as a whole: a child who always rebelled against *authority*. In related uses, the word can refer to the expert or the definitive: an *authority* on antique glass; an actor who executed the role with consummate *authority*. See LAW.

K

keen

acute
astute
penetrating
perspicacious
sharp
shrewd

These words refer to unusual mental agility or perceptiveness. **Keen** suggests both these attributes, adding to them a vigorous and forceful ability to grapple with complex or obscure problems: a *keen* mind for fine distinctions. Sometimes, by comparison to good vision, the word may suggest an ability to observe details and see them as part of a larger pattern: a *keen* understanding of the problems facing the civil rights movement. **Acute** suggests a finely honed sensitivity or receptivity to nuances that might escape others; it might also imply a high-keyed state of nervous attention that is not sustainable for long: an *acute* awareness of the slightest ambiguity in each statement made by his opponent; an *acute* alertness, heightened by the strange silence in the enemy trenches.

Penetrating relates more to the vigorous agility suggested by *keen* than the high-keyed attunement implicit in *acute*. It stresses, however, the ability to see the root causes underlying details, where a *keen* mind might see only the surface details, however clearly. The word may also suggest a brusque eagerness to get to basic principles, regardless of possible injury to the feelings of others: a *penetrating* analysis of the play's weakness that was unsparing in the harshness of its criticism. **Shrewd**, by contrast, suggests practical wisdom that does not necessarily look deeply into things at all but is wily and conscious of its own self-interest: a *shrewd* notion of how far he could go in criticizing the existing regime. Occasionally the word can be used without this overtone of self-interest, but the word still suggests cleverness rather than the impatient intensity of *penetrating*: a *shrewd* estimate of the materials the job would require.

Astute suggests a thorough and profound understanding that stems from a scholarly or experienced mind that is in full command of a given field: an *astute* assessment of the strengths and weaknesses of the plans for reorganizing the department; an *astute* evaluation of the gaps in our knowledge of how life evolved. **Sharp**, by contrast, suggests a mind that is generally well-endowed but that is not necessarily well-grounded in a given field. Its very informality suggests the practical cleverness inherent in *shrewd*, but without that word's suggestion of self-interest: a *sharp* mind for figures; a *sharp* awareness of social niceties.

Perspicacious is the most formal of these words; it stresses intensity of perception, without being very rich in other connotations: a *perspicacious* remark that illuminated the whole problem for all of them. See ACUMEN, WISDOM.

Antonyms: BLAND, *lanquid*, SLOW, STUPID.

The familiar phrase "the heart of the matter" comes pretty close to summing up the meaning of these words. **Kernel**, originating in an Old English word for corn seed, soon broadened to include any seed or cereal grain within its protective coating, then the edible inner part of a nut, and finally to its metaphorical sense as the central part of anything: The *kernel* of the prob!em is in the interpretation of the evidence.

Gist derives ultimately from a Latin word meaning to lie or rest. Its original meaning as a place of rest came to be extended to the ground or foundation on which something lay or by which it could be supported: the *gist* of an argument; the *gist* of the prosecution's case against the accused. The closely related word **substance** (from the Latin for to stand under or beneath) includes among its numerous meanings the same idea of the essential or central part of anything, of that without which it would lack stability and value. [Faith is the *substance* of things not seen; There is much *substance* in the critic's views of modern art.]

Crux, with its reference to the symbolism of the Cross, implies something pivotal, vital, and sometimes, as the word suggests, crucial: The closing of the Gulf of Aqaba proved to be the *crux* of the situation. **Nub** is an Americanism meaning very much the same as *gist*, with an informal carry-over to the idea of a point or moral: the *nub* of the story; The students cannot go far wrong if they get the *nub* of the idea in their first lesson.

Nucleus, though it comes from the Latin word for nut, has not, like the related term *kernel*, acquired currency in a figurative sense. It has been, and still is, largely restricted to technical and scientific fields, where it denotes a central part or point around which other things are gathered, as in a cell, an atom, certain complex chemical compounds, and the like. Because the ideas of movement, change, and growth have become so closely associated with it, *nucleus* serves best only where such ideas are implied in the thought expressed: The *nucleus* of Plato's philosophy was in his doctrine of the archetype. See BASIS, CENTER.

Antonyms: periphery.

kernel

crux
gist
nub
nucleus
substance

These words refer to the taking of lives. **Kill** is the most general word here, applying to any kind of death-dealing activity: a drought that *killed* our fruit trees; an insecticide to *kill* roaches; two people *killed* in a car accident; a madman who threatened to *kill* me; soldiers *killed* in action. The word's very generality allows its use in situations where cause is assigned for other kinds of death: children *killed* by neglect; the rising number of people *killed* by heart disease. The word can even apply where no life is actually lost: a veto that *killed* the bill; their decision to *kill* the news story after it had appeared in the early edition. **Murder** refers less ambiguously to the crime in which one person intentionally *kills* another: He admitted that he had accidentally *killed* his wife, but denied that he had *murdered* her in cold blood. Sometimes, the word can refer to a brutal *killing*, as in war: naked aggression in which one nation set out to *murder* the citizens of an adjoining state. Hyperboli-

kill

assassinate
butcher
dispatch
execute
massacre
murder
slaughter
slay

cally, the word can point to the mishandling of anything: expressionless actors who *murder* their lines.

Assassinate is a specific form of *murder* in which someone *kills* a public figure, usually a political leader, for whatever reason: a televised debate on whether there had been a conspiracy to *assassinate* the President or whether Oswald had acted alone. **Execute** can refer to capital punishment that a state exacts in reprisal for certain crimes: *executed* for treason; The man who *murdered* his wife was *executed* in the gas chamber. Sometimes the word can refer to an on-the-spot *killing* of enemies or prisoners by an opponent, as in a war, occupation, or insurrection; here, the notion of legal sanction may be absent: the six million *executed* by the Nazis; a brigand who ordered his captives *executed* by firing squad. **Dispatch** can function like *execute* in reference to official or formalized *killing*, although it is not restricted to this sense. In any case, the word stresses efficiency and swiftness: The emperor ordered him *executed* by slow torture, rather than allowing him to be mercifully *dispatched* on the battlefield; the Reign of Terror during which hundreds were daily *dispatched* by the guillotine. The word can also indicate the death stroke itself: a pistol with which to *dispatch* those not *killed* by the firing squad's volley.

Butcher and **slaughter** can both refer to the *killing* of animals for food. *Slaughter* is the preferred term in the meat-packing industry, possibly because *butcher* has implications of brutality or because *butcher* can also apply to the cutting or carving of meat at any point after the actual *killing*. Also, *butcher* sometimes indicates a small-scale operation, whereas *slaughter* can better suggest mass *killing*: a shed in which the farmer *butchered* livestock to feed his own family; legislation recommending humane standards for *slaughtering* cattle in packing plants. Both words take on extremely disapproving overtones when applied to the *killing* of people. *Butcher* here suggests bungling inexpertness or sadistic brutality: a rapist who had *butchered* his victim with a razor; dictators who *butcher* those foolish enough to dissent. *Slaughter* specifically suggests the *killing* of great numbers of people: Teutonic hordes who advanced across Europe, sacking and *slaughtering*.

Massacre usually applies solely to the brutal *killing* of large numbers of people. In this, it is close to one aspect of *slaughter*, but it is more specific in suggesting the wholesale and often total destruction of a group of relatively defenseless people by another, as in war, persecution, or revenge: the Incas who were *massacred* by the Spaniards; Herod ordered all infants in the land to be *massacred*. **Slay** can now sound outdated as a close synonym for *murder* or *slaughter* except in Biblical reference. [David *slew* Goliath; Charioteers were sent to *slay* the escaping Jews.] But brevity has given the word currency in newspaper headlines: Gangland leader *slain*. The past participle, in fact, is now more frequently used than other forms of the verb: a battle in which twenty were *slain*. See DESTROY, DIE, ERASE.

kin

family
kindred
kinfolk

These words refer to the people connected to one by blood or marriage. **Kin** is the general word for such people in the Southern United States. **Relatives** is the comparable word in the North. **Relations** can substitute interchangeably with *relatives*, except that it would be the word of choice to indicate humorous or serious disparagement of the people to whom one is related. Also, *kin* is more likely to concentrate on blood relationship, whereas the other two are wider in scope by including in-laws as well. *Kin* is always construed as plural.

Family is a much more restricted term, referring only to one's closest blood *relatives*, usually to those people actually living together in one household: a *family* composed of mother, father, one grandfather, and three children. The word can apply more widely to those people, past and present, bearing the same *family* name: a distinguished British *family* over three generations. **Kinsmen** often points to this same idea: He brilliantly upheld the honor of a long line of *kinsmen*. Unlike *kin*, the word has a singular form: a *kinsman* (or *kinswoman*) of mine. **Kindred** can refer to *relatives*, to lineage, or to a looser fraternal or tribal group: a clan in which the *kindred* are loyal to the same totem.

Kinfolk and **kinfolks** are informal versions of **kinsfolk** which, like **kin**, appears preponderantly in the U.S. South and has no singular form. The word suggests a good many *relatives* who keep in touch or who act together, as in a clan. By contrast, one might have relatively few known *kin* and might not be socially close to them at all. See DESCENT, FOLK.

Antonyms: FOREIGNER.

These words refer to groupings of similar things. **Kind** can indicate a grouping that has indisputable objective reality: a poker hand that contained four of a *kind*. But more informally, it can also indicate a subjective notion on the part of a speaker that two or more things are alike in some way: I don't like people of that *kind*; the *kind* of room that I can feel at home in. Often, however, the word can be used when no very serious reference to a larger grouping is actually intended: He was a friendly *kind* of person. **Sort** is even more informal than *kind*. Occasionally, it can refer to clearly defined groupings that are objectively valid: a list of the *sorts* of tree that are hardy enough to grow in cities, despite the hazard of air pollution. But even more often than *kind*, the word suggests a subjective evaluation. Furthermore, the word more often indicates a negative judgment: the wrong *sort* of person for her son to be associating with.

Type is only slightly more formal than the foregoing, but it points more clearly to objectively definable groupings: the four basic *types* of blood; *types* of world literature. But it can be used in the same indefinite way as *kind* and *sort*, although it may carry over a note of greater conviction: What an ugly *type* of building. A special use of the word refers to an individual or example as though it were the quintessence of a whole group: He was a Madison Avenue *type*; a beatnik *type*. Some careful writers avoid this informal usage — or any use of the preceding words that suggest the existence of hard-and-fast classifications where this is not the case. **Category**, the most formal of these words, applies exclusively to definable groupings, whether these reveal themselves in a material being analyzed or whether they are arbitrarily developed for the sake of order or convenience: self-evident *categories* based on the results of a single chemical test; She made *categories* of the things she wanted to take with her, things she wanted put into storage, and things to be discarded. See CLASS, PROTOTYPE.

These words relate to various ways in which something can be set on fire or made to burn, literally or figuratively. **Kindle** suggests the need for some preparatory effort or action before combustible material will start to burn. [He *kindled* a fire by setting a match to the sticks; A smoldering cigarette can *kindle* a devastating forest fire.] In reference to people, the word indicates the act of arousing, stimulating, or exciting.

kin
(continued)

kinfolks
kinsfolk
kinsmen
relations
relatives

kind

category
sort
type

kindle

fire
ignite

kindle

(continued)

inflame
light

[The boy's interest in science was *kindled* by his visit to the laboratory; The speaker's eloquence *kindled* a lively enthusiasm in the audience.]

In the sense of burning or applying great heat, **fire** has numerous applications, both technical and figurative. One can *fire* a furnace, *fire* a gun, *fire* the pottery in a kiln, *fire* a hayrick. Metaphorically, it can have much the same meaning as *kindle*, but with the suggestion of a sudden burst. [His imagination was *fired* by what he had read; The coach *fired* the team with a determination to win the pennant.] This compares with an analogous, chiefly literary use of the word **inflame** to mean exciting to violent emotion or activity: The crowd was *inflamed* by the brutality of the police. In medical usage, however, the word denotes a condition of actual heat, swelling, and soreness in some part of the body: an *inflamed* ulcer, complicated by infection.

Ignite is almost entirely restricted to the technical sense of a rapid and sometimes violent burning of something that has been exposed to a critical temperature by one means or another. [An electric spark *ignites* the gasoline in an automobile engine; A time fuse *ignited* the high explosives; Spontaneous combustion *ignited* the heap of oil-soaked rags in the cellar.]

Light has a double reference both to heat and to illumination. One can speak of *lighting* a fire or the furnace and *lighting* a lamp, with the knowledge that one result more or less accompanies the other, as when an electric current *ignites* the filament in an evacuated glass bulb, making it glow brightly. See BRIGHT, BURN, FIRE.

Antonyms: darken, extinguish, quench, smother, stifle.

knife

dagger
dirk
misericord
poniard
shiv
stiletto

These words all describe sharpened or pointed instruments commonly set in handles. **Knife** is the general term for any instrument used for cutting, piercing, or spreading, with one or more sharpened edges, and sometimes with pointed blades. A *knife*, though it may be used as a weapon, is no more essentially a weapon than is a paperweight or a pair of shears, which can also be formidable weapons. For a *knife* used as a weapon, criminals have long had a word, variously spelled but now generally rendered **shiv**. In modern criminal slang it may refer to a switchblade *knife*, but the connection is not invariable. Should switchblade *knives* be replaced by other, perhaps more ingeniously concealed *knives*, *shiv* may well make the transition as effortlessly as it has many times in the past.

A **dagger**, unlike a *knife*, is made to be used as a weapon. *Daggers* are any sharp, pointed and edged weapons for stabbing. The printing mark (†) expresses fairly well the common shape of *daggers*. All the other terms here considered are specific kinds of *daggers*.

A **dirk** is a Highland Scotch *dagger*, rather long, with a straight blade. A **poniard** is a small *dagger*, especially one with a triangular or four-sided blade. A **stiletto** is a small *dagger* with a narrow blade that is comparatively thick in cross section. **Misericord** (or *misericorde*) describes a *dagger* used in the Middle Ages to give the *coup de grâce*, or death blow, to fallen knights. See CUT, WOUND.

knit

crochet
darn

These words mean to form a fabric from threads or other strands by various methods. **Knit**, **crochet**, and **tat** are closely related in that all imply the drawing of a single strand of yarn, cotton, silk, etc., into series of interlocking loops. *Knitting* involves the use of two large, slightly pointed needles (or a *knitting* machine) on which a series of interlacing loops are made into successive rows, the fabric being transferred to alternate needles at the beginning of each new row of stitches. *Crocheting* is a type of *knitting*, but it is done with a single needle having a hook at one end. Unlike the stitches of *knitting*, those of *crocheting* are not necessarily made in successive rows. Both *knit* and *crochet* nearly always imply the direct construction of a garment or other article: to *knit* a sweater; to *crochet* a bedspread. *Tat* implies the making of an edging, as for a handkerchief, by means of a small hand shuttle that knots and loops a single thread into a lacelike strip that resembles *crochet* work.

Weave differs completely in principle from *knit*, *crochet*, and *tat*. In *weaving* fabrics, threads are entwined into a texture by interlacing on a loom two sets of strands, the warp and the weft (sometimes called woof) that are at right angles to one another. The warp threads, which run the long way of the fabric, are strung tightly on the loom; the weft threads are then passed back and forth, and over and under the warp by means of a shuttle. *Weave* is also used to describe the interlacing of straw and other pliable materials in making baskets, hats, etc.

To **darn** is to repair a hole in a garment or other cloth article by filling it in with yarn or thread, preferably by means of strands which are stitched across the hole and then filled in by transverse threads in the manner of *weaving*. See MAKE.

L

These words have to do with indicating the nature, function, purpose, disposition, etc. of anything that requires special identification, usually in the form of written or printed instructions, but also verbally or by position. At its most limited, **label** can indicate the affixing of a slip that contains a printed, written, or visual legend. In this context, **tag** indicates one form of *labeling* in which such a legend is tied or strung to something by means of cord or wire: government regulations for *labeling* canned goods; certain packages that must be *tagged* as well as *labeled*. *Tag* might also better suggest a symbolic identification rather than a detailing of information: *tagging* the diseased sheep with a red marker and healthy ones with a green marker. Used more generally, *label* has the wider range of application for any act of identifying something: a professor who got *labeled* by the students as a tiresome bore. As in this example, the word can be humorous or sarcastic, but often it points disapprovingly to unfair identifications: those who *label* as communistic anyone interested in social welfare. With fewer general applications, *tag* can suggest a looser identification: He was *tagged* by some as a miser and by others as a prudent man. Or the word may be merely a more vivid or colorful substitute for *label*: a professor who was *tagged* as a silly old bore.

Categorize is the most formal and neutral word here; it applies to the classification of something within a larger system or division: an explanation of how books are *categorized* under the Dewey Decimal System. Because of its earlier and still active use in philosophy and logic, the word can indicate an arrangement that is both imperative and final, but just as often, *categorize* can point to any arbitrary arrangement adopted for convenience in handling large masses of data or detail.

Pigeonhole suggests the same idea, but is often used, like one sense of *label*, to indicate disapproval for an attempt to fit something, in all its complexity, into simple and preconceived stereotypes: They were more concerned to *pigeonhole* a patient as a manic-depressive, schizophrenic, or what-have-you than to treat his individual illness. The word may also apply to the filing away of something to be dealt with later or forgotten: He *pigeonholed* all proposals for changing the work schedules. See KIND, ORGANIZE.

labor

drudgery
grind
toil
travail
work

These words refer to the effort required to accomplish a task, whether physical or mental. **Labor** most immediately suggests physical effort: the *labor* it would take to improvise a rope bridge across the chasm. From this sense, the word has become an abstraction for such effort: estimating that two-thirds of the repair bill went for *labor*. The word also refers to a working force, whether unionized or not: a meeting between *labor* and management. An older sense of the word refers to childbirth: attended by a nurse during *labor*. The word can, however, refer to strictly mental effort, in which case it suggests unusual difficulty: weeks of *labor* to get the accounts to balance; the grueling *labor* he put in on his master's thesis. **Work** can apply to any situation in which either a short-term or recurring task is performed: It took hard *work* to get the car out of the rutted street; depressions that throw thousands out of *work*. In a related use, the word can apply to the result of someone's *labors*: his life's *work*; a book that was the *work* of a distinguished group of scholars. It can also apply to something, as machinery, designed for a special function; this usually requires the plural: water*works*; the *works* of a clock.

Toil emphasizes the difficulty of the *work* it pertains to, but it is less often used now except for a high-toned effect, possibly specious: the *toil* of our forefathers to build a stronger nation; mothers whose *toil* to better their children often goes unrewarded. **Travail** emphasizes actual suffering, mainly because of its reference, like *labor*, to the pains of childbirth. *Travail* is, however, distinctly precious in sound and pseudo-poetical even in reference to childbirth, where the greater simplicity of *labor* gives both strength and dignity. In some contexts, particularly metaphorical, the word may nonetheless be useful: still unenlightened about the futility of war after centuries of *travail*.

Drudgery emphasizes *work* that is uninspiring, unpleasant, or arduous; it may suggest physical *work* on a menial level, but can apply to any dull and unrewarding task. Unlike some other words here, *drudgery* need not suggest hard or exhausting *labor* so much as unrelieved monotony: machines to take much of the *drudgery* out of manual *labor*; the unrelenting *drudgery* of exam week. **Grind** is in some ways an intensification of *drudgery*, but it particularly emphasizes work done under pressure in a dehumanizing routine way, whether physical or mental; it suggests the never-ending and unrelenting quality of such *labor* done over a long period of time: the twelve-hour *grind* of coal miners at the turn of the century; the daily *grind* of the office worker. See EFFORT, PROFESSION.

Antonyms: idleness, leisure, PLEASURE, *relaxation.*

laborer

job holder

These words refer to those who earn their living by physical effort, or by the practice of relatively simple skills. **Laborer** and **worker** are the most factual of these, with the least emotional tinge of one sort or another. *Laborer* specifically emphasizes physical effort while *worker* is more general in applying to a wider range of tasks and reaching higher

laborer
(continued)

proletarian
wage earner
worker
workingman
workman

up the ladder of skills. [Automation hits hardest at the completely un-skilled *laborer*, next at the blue-collar *worker*, and last at the white-collar *worker*.] By contrast with *worker*, however, **workingman** and **work-man** have a narrower or more specific range of application, *workingman* particularly being applicable at most to semiskilled labor: a full dinner pail for the average *workingman*. *Workman*, when it is not an abbrevi-ated form of *workingman*, can suggest the possession of skills approaching that of the craftsman: *workmen* who restored and refinished her parquet floors.

Job holder and **wage earner** are both ways of stressing the money a *laborer* or *worker* earns and the fact that he is, at the moment of de-scription, actually employed, that is, holding a job or earning wages. Of the two, *job holder* can apply more generally, since it stresses being in a position of employment more than the position itself, which could range from unskilled to skilled work. *Wage earner* distinguishes between some-one who gets a paycheck and someone who is self-employed.

Proletarian originally denoted a member of the propertyless, lowest class of the state in ancient Rome. The term got a new lease on life from modern political and economic theorists, particularly Karl Marx, who used it to designate that class of a state or of the world which, lacking personal means of production, is forced to sell its labor for wages in order to live. See ARTISAN.

These words all denote a deficiency or non-existence of something speci-fied or implied. **Lack** is a general term which means a total or partial insufficiency. [It was a *lack* of cash that prevented me from joining you at lunch today; A *lack* of bedding in the cabin meant that three of us had to sleep on the floor that weekend.] Although *lack* by itself can ex-press a totality of deficiency, a qualifying adjective is often used with it to avoid any possibility of confusion: The young man displayed a complete *lack* of courtesy and tact in dealing with his employer. No confusion about total *lack* is possible when **absence** is used alone. *Ab-sence* is the opposite of presence; it means non-existence: The *absence* of a chairman turned the meeting into a near riot. The difference be-tween *lack* and *absence* is apparent when we contrast "a *lack* of sugar in her diet" with "an *absence* of sugar in her diet." The former suggests that there is some sugar in the diet but not enough; the latter implies that there is no sugar at all in the diet. *Absence*, of course, can also signify the state of being away. In the example cited, "the *absence* of a chair-man" denotes the non-existence of a chairman. If the phrase were "in the *absence* of the chairman" it would be obvious that a chairman existed but was away at the time under discussion.

Shortage is synonymous with *lack* in designating a partial insuffi-ciency, but more than *lack* it suggests an insufficiency of some estab-lished, required, or accustomed amount: There was a *shortage* of dairy products in the supermarket last week because of a delivery strike. *Shortage* also means the amount by which something is deficient: The total *shortage* amounted to $500.

Dearth, in a sense no longer used, meant dearness or costliness. It came later to refer to the kind of *lack* or scarcity which makes something costly, especially food in time of famine. An extension of this sense gives *dearth* the meaning of a *lack* or scarcity of anything: a *dearth* of content in an essay; a *dearth* of oranges because of drought conditions; a *dearth* of parental affection and discipline. See REQUIRE, SCANTY.

Antonyms: abundancy, adequacy, ampleness, copiousness, sufficiency.

lame

crippled
halt
hamstrung
hobbled

These words refer to a partial or complete disablement, particularly of the legs or feet. **Lame** can refer to such impairment in a man or animal. It perhaps most often suggests a gradually worsening disablement or stiffening as from old age or arthritis. In many cases, walking might still be possible, though difficult: the *lame* old man who used a cane to get around; a horse that had gone *lame* in one hind leg and had to be shot. The word can also refer to other impairments, especially involving muscular soreness or inflammation: a *lame* back that made sitting up straight excruciating. More generally, the word can indicate something poor or awkward: a *lame* excuse.

Crippled can more often suggest an accidental impairment: left permanently *crippled* by the collision. Also, the word can more often suggest total loss of movement: telling the *crippled* man he would never gain back the use of either leg. While the word is, thus, more forceful than *lame*, it can be used for milder impairments, as well: hands *crippled* by rheumatism: a *crippled* woman who could walk by means of braces attached to her legs. **Halt** is now archaic sounding when used of a person who is *lame* or walks with a limp, except in stock phrases: a beggar who was both *halt* and blind.

Hamstrung pertains most directly to cattle or other animals when the Achilles tendons of their hind legs have been purposely cut to make them incapable of walking or escaping: *hamstrung* bulls that were left behind to be picked up by the main body of the roundup. The word can also refer to the same condition in people, usually accidental: a torn ligament that left the track star *hamstrung*. More commonly the word refers to any frustrating setback: office procedure *hamstrung* by bureaucratic complexity. *Crippled* can also be used in a comparable way: a poverty program *crippled* by cutbacks in appropriations. **Hobbled** can indicate a less drastic way of impeding the movement of cattle or horses — in which legs are tied so as to permit walking but not running or galloping: horses *hobbled* on the outskirts of the Indian camp. Metaphorically, the word also suggests reduced activity caused by some frustrating factor: a bill *hobbled* in committee by obstructionist amendments. See HURT, POWERLESS, WEAK.

lanky

angular
gangling
rangy
rawboned
spindling
spindly

These adjectives apply to leanness that is emphasized by height, length of limb, or awkwardness of bearing. A **lanky** person is tall, thin, and long-limbed, being typically loose-jointed: a tall, *lanky* fellow; a *lanky* basketball player. **Gangling** is closely synonymous with *lanky* but implies greater awkwardness, as from disproportionate growth of the limbs during adolescence: a *gangling*, ungainly girl, all arms and legs. [He hurried toward me with long, *gangling* strides.] **Rangy** carries no hint of gracelessness but stresses build. It was originally applied to animals having lengthy bodies and long limbs and therefore well adapted for roving: *rangy* cattle. Now it is also used of slim and long-legged human beings: a *rangy* cowboy; *rangy* runners on a track team.

Angular presupposes prominent bones and suggests sharp edges: *angular* features; an *angular* adolescent. Along with bony leanness, it often indicates unprepossessing stiffness — whether evinced in awkward, jerky movements or in an unbending manner. Hence when *angular* is applied to tall, thin females, it signals the absence of such womanly attributes as roundness, softness, pliancy, and grace: an *angular* headmistress with a cold eye and forbidding aspect. **Rawboned** is usually used of men and emphasizes a big, bony, often awkward frame. A *rawboned* person has a prominent bone structure and little flesh, but may be sturdily made though spare and *angular*. *Rawboned* carries the suggestion of crudity in build, of sharp or knobby bones jutting out: a ruddy, *rawboned* recruit.

The last two adjectives focus on abnormal leanness rather than a naturally *lanky* or bony build. **Spindling** describes a form that is so long and thin, so very slender, that it seems markedly out of proportion: The old man looked like an apparition — a tall, *spindling* wraith. **Spindly** adds to *spindling* the suggestion of physical weakness and frailty, describing a combination of height or length and matchstick thinness: a *spindly* invalid, pitifully wasted away; a child unable to stand on his *spindly* little legs. *Spindly* may also be used of a fragile, limblike appendage of a machine: the *spindly*, aluminum legs of the spacecraft. See BONY, CLUMSY, THIN.

Antonyms: FAT, HUSKY.

These words refer to things of more than normal size or to things of unusual mass. **Large** and **big** are both very general and very vague; both are acceptable in contexts ranging from the most informal to the most formal, although *large* would tend to be substituted for *big* in extremely formal contexts. *Big* suggests something of more than normal size, but it is particularly relevant to material or bodily mass, whereas *large* might suggest even greater departure from a norm. In this case, the word's implications are less limited to the physical: a *big* stone; a *big* bully; a *large* house; trying on a *larger* size shoe; the *large* issues confronting us.

Outsize (or its variant, *outsized*) specifically suggests something that is too *large* to conform to the norm or be accommodated by an already established measure. While the word thus suggests an object of abnormal or excessive size, unusual mass is not necessarily implied by the word: *outsize* typing paper that wouldn't fit the binder in which she kept the other reports; extra-*large* beds for *outsize* people. **King-size** (or its variant, *king-sized*) is a merchandising term that refers to a product that is longer or *larger* than the standard or usual size: *king-size* cigarettes; *king-size* beds. The use of such terminology in packaging and advertising is very prevalent, probably because it is more deceptive about value than it is informative about size.

Gigantic and **mammoth** are now mostly used as hyperboles, suggesting anything of extreme proportions. *Gigantic* derives from a word for giant; *mammoth*, of course, can refer to the prehistoric elephantlike animal. *Mammoth* in this context still may more readily suggest something physically *big*, whereas *gigantic* is more often used now for metaphorical instances: a *mammoth* skyscraper; a *gigantic* threat to our security. But this is by no means invariable: a *mammoth* weekend party; a *gigantic* brute of a man.

Giant differs from *gigantic* in often suggesting a physical change of scale or in referring to something reproduced in *outsized* dimensions: a science fiction story about *giant* cockroaches. As a mere hyperbole, it can be used indiscriminately: a *giant* protest rally. In this example, reference to a *large* rally is no doubt intended, rather than to one made up of disgruntled giants. See MASSIVE, SIZE, TREMENDOUS.

Antonyms: MINUTE, SMALL.

Laugh, the most general term of this group, describes the inarticulate, more or less explosive sounds that people make for a variety of reasons. The usual reasons given are merriment, joy, and happiness, but every

large

big
giant
gigantic
king-size
mammoth
outsize

laugh

laugh
(continued)

chortle
chuckle
giggle
guffaw
snicker
snigger
titter

school child knows that laughter is also used to conceal shyness, nervousness, or intimidation, and as a device to humiliate, deride, or ridicule. Indeed, because laughter is provoked by so many different situations, a number of words are necessary to describe the different kinds of laughter characteristic of different situations.

Giggles and **titters** denote high-pitched sounds and are usually associated with children or girls. A *titter* is somewhat breathless, as from childish embarrassment or shyness. Schoolgirls typically *titter* over any allusion to sex; perhaps this use by writers is influenced by the unrelated word titillate, meaning to excite or cause a tickling sensation in. *Giggle*, though used in similar contexts, is broader in application; it often conveys an uncontrollable fit of silly but harmless laughter — thus the colloquial expression "to get the *giggles*." One sometimes hears middle-aged or elderly women spoken of as *giggling*, just as one sometimes hears them referred to as "girls." Such uses tend to strike others as offensively coy. Both *giggle* and *titter*, but especially the latter, are often used to describe derisive laughter. [When the teacher turned his back Johnny yelled, "Hee, haw!" and the class *tittered*; The children *giggled* at the clown's antics; The girls couldn't stop *giggling* when the boy answered that Abraham Lincoln was the first U.S. president.] Both words are onomatopoetic in origin; a *giggle* is more fluid and less breathless than the staccato *titter*.

Snicker and **snigger** describe smothered or half-suppressed laughter used in derision, and while not restricted to children, they imply a juvenile temperament and a decidedly retarded if not perverted sense of humor. [The boys *snickered* as the poor dog ran about with a tin can tied to its tail; They *sniggered* when he announced that he would someday be president.]

Chuckle and **chortle** denote quiet laughter, usually harmless, pleasant, and good-natured in tone. *Chuckles* are generally low-keyed, reflective, and masculine, express satisfaction or appreciation, and are often directed at the chuckler himself. [He *chuckled* at himself for having worn two socks that didn't match; He couldn't help *chuckling* when his little boy called the Boston Strangler the Boston Snuggler.] *Chortle*, coined from *chuckle* and *snort* by Lewis Carroll in *Through the Looking Glass*, has a suggestion of high glee or impishness that is lacking in *chuckle*.

Guffaw is a loud, hearty, spontaneous roar of laughter, commonly associated with men. It is harmless and good-natured in tone, but rather gruff and rude in quality. Royalty would never *guffaw*.

All of these words can mean to say with a *laugh*, *snicker*, *chuckle*, etc. ["I've got the keys," he *laughed*; "I'm always forgetting names," he *chuckled*.] See HUMOROUS, SMILE.

Antonyms: FROWN, WEEP.

law

canon
code
commandment
constitution
ordinance

These words all denote rules of conduct or procedure which are imposed by some authority. **Law** is the broadest and most general term in this group. It designates a rule of conduct recognized by custom or decreed by formal enactment and considered by a community, nation, or other authoritatively constituted group as binding upon its members. The word also refers to a body of such rules.

A **constitution** is a collection of *laws* that establish the basic principles governing the actions of a government, corporation, or other body of persons organized for some specific purpose. The document which records such *laws* is also referred to as a *constitution*. **Code** also denotes a collection of *laws*, but these pertain to some specific subject or activity:

a building *code*; the penal *code*; a *code* of ethics for lawmaking bodies.

A **statute** is a written *law* enacted by a legislative body and duly sanctioned and authenticated by constitutional rule. An act of Congress or Parliament would be considered a *statute*. In the United States, a *statute* enacted by a municipal body is called an **ordinance**; such *laws* cover local problems pertaining to traffic, zoning, sanitation, and the like.

Regulation is a general and less formal word than the others in this group. It can designate any rule or principle, whether or not it has the effective force of enacted *law*, which is used to direct, manage, or control some system or organization.

A **canon** was originally a church *law*; it has since been extended to mean any principle which is regarded as established by common practice or by eminent authority: the *canons* of good taste. **Commandment** is found almost exclusively in religious contexts because of its allusion to the ten injunctions given by God to Moses on Mount Sinai. See JURIS-DICTION.

These words are different ways of indicating what is permitted, allowable, countenanced, or sanctioned by custom or by some recognized authority.

Lawful implies conformity with laws, statutes, canons, precepts, principles, rules, etc. intended to regulate the conduct of those coming within their particular field of action. Thus one speaks of *lawful* debts, a *lawful* claim, a *lawful* marriage, of conducting a *lawful* business or making a *lawful* decision. **Legal** has nearly the same meaning, but is restricted chiefly to statute laws as they apply at certain times and places or under prescribed conditions. [Divorce is *lawful* but subject to various *legal* requirements before taking final effect; The *legal* speed limit within the town is 15 miles per hour.]

Constitutional refers to the fundamental laws and principles that have been formally adopted to govern the efficient operations of a state acting as a unit toward those subject to its control, and in its dealings with other states. [He stood on his *constitutional* rights; A *constitutional* amendment forbids slavery in the United States.] Strict usage distinguishes *constitutional* from all the other terms because of its direct reference to a document, instrument, or body of rules acknowledged as paramount in determining what is *lawful* or *legal*: The Supreme Court dismissed the appeal on *constitutional* grounds.

Legitimate originally meant whatever was declared to be *lawful*: a *legitimate* child; a *legitimate* heir to the throne; the *legitimate* owner of the land. It is now very generally applied to anything that is recognized by custom or in popular usage as conforming to established rules or standards, being regular, orderly or acceptable in form, style, etc.: *legitimate* theatre; a *legitimate* conclusion; *legitimate* procedures. **Licit** is the adjective form in English of the Latin verb *licet*, it is permitted. It is seldom used nowadays, and then in the sense of something strictly *lawful*: a *licit* marriage; *licit* traffic in drugs or liquor. From the same root we get our *license*, *licentiate*, and *licentious*, as well as the far better known and more widely used negative form *illicit*. See PERMIT, RIGHTFUL.

Antonyms: illegal, unconstitutional, unlawful.

All these words signify an absence, disruption, or breakdown of law and order. **Lawlessness** implies either that no law exists or that the law is not being enforced or obeyed: the *lawlessness* of a frontier town without a sheriff; the *lawlessness* of a band of outlaws. In a broad sense,

lawlessness
(continued)

disorder
disturbance
riot

this word may indicate disregard of any or all restrictive regulations: the *lawlessness* of children who are allowed to run wild. *Lawlessness* may also apply to actions that are not controlled or authorized by law or in accord with it: the *lawlessness* of his behavior; the *lawlessness* of a lynching. **Anarchy** comes from Greek roots that literally mean without a leader. At its most extreme, it implies the lawless confusion and chaos that result when no central authority is exercised by anyone, either within or outside the law, and when no general rules of order are in effect: a newly independent colony plunged into *anarchy* by warring factions and a lack of central leadership; total *anarchy* after a nuclear holocaust, the only rules being every man for himself and survival of the fittest. In a general sense *anarchy* simply indicates the absence of government. Specifically, it may designate a community founded on the utopian principle that social order may exist without government, society being regulated by voluntary agreement and marked by absolute individual freedom. In a disapproving sense, *anarchy* can also imply utter license — freedom unchecked by self-regulation and unrestrained by submission to authority: the *anarchy* of rebellious youth, seeking liberty without responsibility.

Lawlessness and *anarchy* have to do with prevailing conditions. The remaining words, by contrast, apply to temporary breaches of the peace or to single incidents or outbreaks of unruly conduct. **Disturbance** is the mildest of these. A *disturbance* may be no more than a slight commotion or an annoying racket, and it can be caused by a single person or by any number of people: a drunk creating a *disturbance* in a bar; people throwing an all-night party, charged with being a *disturbance* to the peace of a quiet neighborhood. **Disorder** is the most general of all these words, but here it applies specifically to a *disturbance* of proper civic order: a man charged with *disorderly* conduct. As a noun in this sense, however, *disorder* generally implies that a number of people are involved and that there is considerably more confusion and commotion than in a *disturbance*: an outbreak of *disorder* in the gallery of the legislative chamber before the demonstrators were ejected. **Riot** indicates the largest and most violent outbreak of the three. In law, a *riot* is a tumultuous *disturbance* of the public peace by three or more assembled persons, who, in the execution of some private object, do an act, lawful or unlawful, in a manner calculated to terrorize the people. As the word is commonly understood, a *riot* involves mob action, frenzy, and often violence: a race *riot*; a long, hot summer of *riots* in the ghettos, marked by widespread vandalism, looting, and attacks on motorists. A *riot* often involves mass *lawlessness*, but it is usually not leaderless: a demagogue who deliberately inflamed his listeners to such a degree that they started a *riot*. See ANARCHISM, TURBULENT, UNRULY, UPRISING.

Antonyms: discipline, law, lawfulness, legality, order, peace.

lawyer

advocate
attorney
barrister
counsel
counselor
solicitor

These words all designate persons who have had legal training and are qualified to practice law. **Lawyer** is the general term for anyone versed in the law and duly admitted to the bar. *Lawyers* conduct lawsuits, advise clients of their legal rights and obligations, and may act on behalf of clients or plead for them in court.

Attorney, often used as a synonym for *lawyer*, in its strictest sense denotes an agent (who is not necessarily a *lawyer*) empowered to act in a legal capacity for another person: While she was living in Europe, her brother had power of *attorney* over her property. When used interchangeably with *lawyer*, the correct term is *attorney at law*.

Counselor, as one who gives advice, is the common term of address of a judge to a trial *lawyer* during court proceedings. Some *lawyers* refer to themselves professionally as *counselors at law* if the greatest part of their work is given over to court cases. **Counsel,** as well as *counselor,* is a term of address used by a judge. But *counsel* may consist of one *lawyer* only or of a legal staff working as a unit to advise a client or to conduct a case in court: After consulting with *counsel,* the defendant changed his plea.

In Britain, a *lawyer* qualified to conduct court cases is called a **barrister,** while a **solicitor** may give legal advice and may prepare court cases, but usually may not conduct them.

Advocate is used of a trial *lawyer* in Scotland and France. This term is rare in the United States except in *judge advocate* and other military usages. See ADVICE, RECOMMEND.

league

alliance
coalition
confederacy
confederation
federation
union

These words refer to a group of nations, states, or other parties that have entered into association for a common purpose. **League** is the most general word, embracing everything from private or semipublic organizations to regional, national, or international associations. It suggests, however, a specific, clearly defined area of common interest. In the U.S., the *League* of Women Voters provides civic information on issues, candidates, and voting procedures. During the Middle Ages, free towns in northern Germany and neighboring countries banded together in the Hanseatic *League* to advance and protect their commerce. The *League* of Nations, established in 1920, had as its primary purpose the preservation of world peace.

Alliance stresses common interest and the pooling of resources. It may be applied to families, referring to connection through marriage, but it is more often used of formal agreements between nations. In this latter sense, the word *alliance* implies that the nations involved surrender little or no sovereignty in banding together and that they are free to withdraw at any time. In a defensive *alliance,* all participating nations might agree to fight an aggressor if that aggressor attacked any one of them. The North Atlantic Treaty Organization (NATO) is a military and naval *alliance* of fifteen nations, organized under the North Atlantic Treaty of 1949. Presumably, a nation would remain in an *alliance* only so long as its leaders felt that this was the best form of protection.

A **coalition** is a temporary association of rival groups, such as political parties or factions. In many countries, *coalition* governments may be formed when one political party fails to win a majority of the votes cast in an election. Some members of both parties in Congress may form a *coalition* to defeat, or to secure the passage of, a particular bill.

Both **confederacy** and **confederation** refer to a formal association of states under a central government, but both imply a jealous guarding of the sovereignty or prerogatives of the separate states. The central government may be largely confined to the direction of foreign affairs. In 1781, the thirteen original American colonies adopted the Articles of *Confederation,* which bound them together in a *league* of common defense until 1789, when the ratified Constitution established a stronger federal government. Under the original *confederation,* each state retained its sovereignty, and the federal government was distinctly subordinate to the states, its powers being severely limited and restricted. Later, in 1861, the constitution of the Southern *Confederacy* was adopted; it was fairly close to the U.S. Constitution but differed in its emphasis on states' rights.

A **federation** is a *league* formed by independent states, clubs, or organizations that delegate part of their sovereignty to a central authority: the National *Federation* of Music Clubs; the American *Federation* of Labor. In political terms, a *federation* is a single government formed from separate states or from separate local governments. Although the states retain jurisdiction over their own internal affairs, the central government has stronger powers than one established under a *confederacy* or *confederation* and is able to deal authoritatively both with the state governments and with the citizens of the states.

The United States is a *federation*, and a closely knit *federation* is a **union**. *Union*, like *alliance*, may refer to marriage, but it applies to the joining together of man and wife in wedlock rather than to the consequent connection of their families. In its political sense, *union* designates a fusion of separate states in which the states have surrendered so much of their sovereignty that they are essentially one political entity: the *Union* of Soviet Socialist Republics. See ACCOMPLICE, ASSOCIATE, CLUB, CONNECT.

Antonyms: *disunion, division, isolation, secession, separation.*

leak

drip
ooze
trickle

These words apply to fluid that flows or drops little by little. **Leak** stresses the idea of accident. It refers to the unintended entry or escape of a fluid that is meant to be excluded or contained. [The roof *leaks*; Milk is *leaking* out of the carton; The faucet is *leaking*.] The noun *leak* may designate a chance opening, as a hole, crack, crevice, or faulty closure, through which fluid may pass. [The boat has sprung a *leak*; They plugged the *leak* in the dam.] In other respects, *leak* is the least specific of these words. It may apply to air, gas, light, or electric current as well as to liquid: a *leaking* balloon; a punctured tire *leaking* air. And unlike the other words, it may involve a fast, heavy, or steady flow as well as a slow, slight, or intermittent one: A *leak* in the plumbing flooded the basement.

Drip means to fall in drops or to let liquid fall in drops: rain *dripping* from the eaves; *dripping* trees; fat that *drips* from roasting meat; children *dripping* ice cream on the floor. Something that *drips* may be *leaking* or overflowing: a *dripping* spigot; a comb *dripping* with honey. A paper bag may *drip* when a container in the bag is *leaking*. *Drip* may also designate the sound of liquid falling drop by drop: the maddening *drip* of a *leaking* faucet. Where *drip* implies a broken, staccato movement, **trickle** is used of liquid that runs gently. It indicates a slow fall or slight flow of liquid, either drop by drop or in a fine, thin stream: a *trickling* spout; a rivulet *trickling* over rocks; perspiration slowly *trickling* down his back. Fluid may *drip* or *trickle* either from a *leak* that was unforeseen or from an opening designed for the discharge of liquid. And *trickle* often suggests either that a flow has not been fully started or that it is petering out: Only a *trickle* of water came out of the snakelike garden hose.

Ooze indicates a slow leakage or a sluggish flow, as of a liquid squeezing out in droplets through small openings: sap *oozing* from a sugar maple; gravy *oozing* from a hot potpie; a wounded body *oozing* blood; Sweat *oozed* from his forehead and *trickled* down his cheeks. In an extended sense, *ooze* may be applied to any similar seepage: Vapors seemed to *ooze* out of the swamp. And it sometimes refers to the unctuous flow or easy movement of a substance that is thick and slippery: the *ooze* of oil; the *ooze* of mud between the toes.

In a figurative sense, *leak* refers to an unofficial or unauthorized divulging of information. [There was a *leak* in the security system; The

news *leaked* out; An unnamed official *leaked* the story to the press.]
Trickle may indicate movement in a very small stream, one thing or person at a time: only a *trickle* of information; a *trickle* of visitors; workers *trickling* out of a building shortly before 5:00 P.M. The *trickle*-down theory presupposes that benefits bestowed on those at the top of the economic ladder will gradually make their way down to those at the bottom. *Trickle* may also apply to an uncertain, rippling sound suggestive of *trickling* water: a *trickle* of applause. *Ooze* sometimes indicates the slow, silent escape of some vital quality: His courage *oozed* away. It may also imply the exuding of something as if through the pores: a politician *oozing* confidence and affability. *Drip* suggests a being saturated or laden with something that seems to spill over in liquidlike drops: a voice *dripping* with venom; a dowager *dripping* with diamonds. See FILTER, FLOOD, FLOW, WET.

learning

erudition
knowledge
pedantry
scholarship

These words refer to the mastery of facts and concepts in a given field. **Learning** is the least formal of these words; it specifically suggests a background of orderly, prescribed instruction and study rather than a spontaneous or self-taught mastery of material: book *learning*; the *learning* required to understand the obscure references of some modern authors. A related use of the word refers to the process of acquiring mastery: patterns of *learning* in grade school children. Sometimes the word refers to the sum total of all understanding and wisdom: libraries where the *learning* of the ages accumulates.

Knowledge is more commonly used in this comprehensive way, referring to all that can be or is known: struggles to increase man's *knowledge* of the universe. *Knowledge* is more than a store of facts in the mind; it also includes the contribution of the mind in understanding data, perceiving relations, elaborating concepts, formulating principles, and making evaluations. As applied to a person, *knowledge* need not refer to information acquired through a formal education, as *learning* does; rather, *knowledge* simply points to an acquaintance with facts or an understanding of actions and concepts: a poor *knowledge* of Greek history. [She had a better *knowledge* of human nature than the cleverest psychiatrist, for all his *learning*.] *Knowledge*, thus, need not suggest an academic background at all, but can result from observation and experience. This contrasts most sharply with **scholarship**, which emphasizes exclusively that aspect of *learning* pertaining to academic accomplishment. At one level, the word may simply suggest excellent work done in school: students receiving special awards for *scholarship*. At another level, it refers to care, precision, and accuracy in searching out information and presenting facts, implying a mastery of techniques necessary for advanced research in specialized fields: the definitive book on the Medicis, marked by its authoritative mass of data and flawless *scholarship*.

Erudition refers to the personal mastery of a wide range of specialized *knowledge* in such a way as to combine both *learning* and *scholarship*. [He was not merely well-informed, but exhibited amazing *erudition* on every topic of conversation that came up; a Ph.D. candidate's dazzling display of *erudition* in his comprehensive exams.] The word suggests a detailed grasp of the most abstruse or arcane points of *knowledge*. In this it compares with **pedantry**, which is a pejorative word for the same grasp of detail, however obscure. The negative force of the word *pedantry*, of course, suggests that such details are dogmatically exploited for their own sake as a pharisaical display, without regard for their relevance to important concerns or problems: the *pedantry* of scholastics still busy refining Ptolemy, while Copernicus and Brahe were altering the whole map of the heavens. See FAULTFINDING, STUDENT, TEACH.

Antonyms: ignorance.

lease

charter
hire
let
rent

These words mean to get or grant the temporary use or possession of something, as a car, building, etc., in return for a certain payment. To do one of these things under the provisions of a governing contract is to **lease**. [I'm going to *lease* my apartment to a friend while I'm abroad next year; The land that the oilman *leased* produced a gusher that made him a rich man.] **Hire** is most commonly used in reference to paying a set sum or certain wages for a person's labor or services: a *hired* hand on a farm. [We *hired* a driver to take us on a tour of the city.] Less commonly, *hire* indicates the granting of personal service or temporary use: to *hire* oneself out as a mathematics tutor during a vacation; to *hire* out beach umbrellas to bathers. It is also employed when one wishes to designate paying for the temporary, exclusive use of another's vehicle, premises, or the like. [I *hired* a cab to take my date home from the party; The political club *hired* a hall to kick off its annual membership drive.] **Charter** is synonymous with *hire* in reference to vehicles, especially large public vehicles, as buses, airplanes, and trains: The graduating class *chartered* a bus for its trip to Mexico. *Charter*, however, also designates a specialized kind of *hiring* done in connection with a contract called a *charter party*, an agreement under which the whole or part of a vessel is *leased* for the conveyance of goods.

Rent is usually applied to the paying of an agreed amount of compensation for the use of real or personal property during a certain specified time. [My family *rented* a house at the shore for the summer; Costumes for the play were *rented* from a large theatrical supply house in New York.] *Rent* also means to grant someone the temporary possession and use of land, premises, or property; and in this sense it is synonymous with *hire* and with the chiefly British term **let**: rooms for *rent*; rooms to *let*; tuxedos for *hire*. [My aunt *rents* the top floor of her house to an old friend; Part of his estate was *let* out to tenant farmers.] See HIRE.

leave

depart
go
retire
withdraw

These words refer to the act of moving away from a previous position. **Leave**, in its generality, may stress the position that is being given up: *leaving* the office; *leaving* home; *leaving* the party early. It may also suggest, however, the casting off of something in the course of a movement: *leaving* behind a trail of banana and orange peels. Or it may simply suggest passing by something that one has not been in actual contact with at all: *leaving* one island after another in their wake. **Go** is even more general than *leave* and carries fewer connotations. In isolation, it stresses the sheer act of moving away or passing along, without reference to what one *leaves* behind: *going* forward through all sorts of terrain. It may also imply movement away from a place, position, or starting point, especially when it is used as a command or signal, as in a race: Ready, set, *go*! In contrast to *leave*, however, *go* sometimes stresses the destination of a movement rather than its point of origin: just *going* to the grocery store for some bread. **Depart**, like *leave*, emphasizes the starting point of a movement, though the destination is more often named; it is also more formal than *leave* and may suggest a planned *leaving* rather than one taken on the spur of the moment: *departing* for Europe next Wednesday; trains that *depart* (or *leave*) every hour on the hour. **Retire** stresses movement from a relatively public place to a more private one: *retiring* into the study where they could talk freely. In a special sense, it means to *go* to bed: The butler said that madame had *retired* for the evening. Its formality would make *retire* sound odd or antiquated in everyday conversation, except when it is used specifically to refer to the termination of one's active service or career: an aging opera singer who *retired* from the stage to teach. **Withdraw**, if used in a sense similar to the general meaning of *retire*, would sound even more antiquated, but it has a viable use when it suggests retracing one's steps away from a recent advance: the battalion that *withdrew* from positions they had seized the night before; *withdrawing* from her exposed vantage point at the uncurtained window. See DIE, GO, PRIVACY, QUIT, RELINQUISH, RETIRE.

Antonyms: approach, COME, REMAIN.

These verbs all mean to quit a person, place, pursuit, party, or principle. **Leave** is the most general word in the group and is relatively free of the connotations that cling to the others. It is often used noncommittally to indicate a straightforward physical departure: He *left* his hometown and moved to the big city. *Leave* in itself gives no hint as to the motives behind or consequences of a departure. One person may *leave* his country to evade prosecution for a crime, while another may *leave* it merely to seek a milder climate. *Leave* may also refer in a more abstract sense to the termination of a connection or association: He *left* school but continued to hang around the campus.

In other uses, *leave* may be closely synonymous with the other words in this group, though all of the others are more emotionally freighted. **Abandon** denotes a complete giving up, especially of what one has previously been interested in or responsible for; the word points to total relinquishment or withdrawal, sometimes under pressure of circumstances or in breach of duty. A man may, rightly or wrongly, *abandon* an attempt or an idealistic dream after encountering difficulties. A scientist may *abandon* an unpromising project to engage in more useful and rewarding research. A captain may give orders to *abandon* ship when the ship is sinking. A military commander may justifiably *abandon* an exposed position, but for him to *abandon* his troops or his post would be reprehensible. **Desert** adds to *abandon* the idea that a legal or moral obligation or trust is being violated. It means to *abandon* a post, duty, relationship, or loyalty in violation of one's faith, oath, responsibility, or orders: a recruit who *deserted* his platoon under fire; a turncoat who *deserted* his party.

Leave, abandon, and *desert* are all applied to marital or family relationships but often differ in their implications. A man who *leaves* his wife may do so openly and may still contribute to her support. A mother who *abandons* her child utterly relinquishes her personal responsibility for him, consigning his fate to chance or other people. A man who *deserts* his wife and children willfully *abandons* them, without legal justification, with the intent to renounce entirely all legal and moral obligation.

In a specific, intransitive sense, *desert* means to *leave* military service without permission and with the intention of not returning. *Leave,* by contrast, may indicate no more than a temporary departure, while *abandon* may point to a position that has been *left*. [The sentry *left* his post for a few minutes; The soldier *abandoned* his post and *deserted*.] The past participles *abandoned* and *deserted* both emphasize the result of a departure, pointing to the condition of the place *left* empty or the plight of the person *left* alone: the helpless, forlorn figure of an *abandoned* child; an outpost *abandoned* to the elements; an *abandoned* building falling

leave

abandon
desert
forsake

into ruin, *left* desolate by all its former occupants; a woman afraid to walk down a *deserted* street at night.

Forsake implies the breaking off of a close personal attachment and may refer to a spiritual as well as to a physical *desertion*. It often involves the letting down of a loved one or dependent and may point to a lack of positive action as well as to a negative *abandonment*. [She pleaded with her husband not to *forsake* her; to *forsake* one's friends by failing to go to their aid when they are in trouble.] *Forsake* may also mean to give up something that once was cherished or that formerly was freely indulged in or enjoyed. [Arthur Rimbaud *forsook* poetry at the age of nineteen; Doubts led the girl to *forsake* her faith and *leave* the church; In the marriage ceremony, the groom promised to *forsake* all others and cleave only to his wife.] See FORSWEAR, QUIT, RELINQUISH, RENEGADE.

Antonyms: keep, persevere in, stay at, stay in, stay with, stick to, stick with.

leftist

left-winger
liberal
progressive
radical

These words refer to those who favor changes, more or less drastic, in the political or economic system of a country. **Leftist** and **left-winger** arose as terms because in many European countries, conservatives are seated to the presiding officer's right while their opponents are seated on the left. Most typically, a *leftist* might be someone who favors governmental solutions to social problems, favors the working class or the disadvantaged, and opposes unregulated business or the established powers of wealth and privilege. These views may extend to a belief in public ownership of the means of production or even to the belief in the necessity of a revolution to achieve social justice, as in some forms of socialism. The emotional tone of the word would clearly depend on the persuasion of the speaker. The word was more clearly taken as a pejorative in the recent past than at present. In a negative context, the word may be used to imply that all *leftists* are revolutionists or extremists, which has given rise to such countering phrases as *democratic leftist*. At present, the word appears with greater frequency in neutral description, even by those describing themselves. *Left-winger*, by contrast, was and still is largely pejorative and would be avoided except by those who condemn such stands.

Liberal, according to its etymology, pertains to someone devoted to freedom. In actual use, as opposed to conservative, it refers to someone who welcomes constructive change as a way of solving problems. Used as a political label in the recent past, *liberal* indicated someone to the left of a moderate and as such it could be used to express distrust or suspicion, if not the disapproval often implied by *leftist*. More recently, however, *liberal* has become almost synonymous with moderate to indicate someone who favors the present tendency to solve social problems through government action, provided no drastic alteration in the social structure is contemplated. Because of this shift in emphasis and because both major U.S. parties are middle-of-the-road, many political candidates of either party refer to themselves as *liberals*. Side by side with this approving use, a new pejorative use of the word has emerged to criticize those who do not go far enough toward solving fundamental problems. This use, of course, is favored by *leftists*: His political opponent accused him of being the typical *liberal* who paid lip service to integrated education and open housing, but did nothing about them. In Britain, the word appears in the name of the moderate party, midway between right and left: the Conservative Party, the *Liberal* Party, and the Labour Party. Outside the political sphere, *liberal* can still refer in a wholly approving way to someone who favors tolerance, permissiveness, and constructive change, as in education and theology: a *liberal* who favored the new math; those cardinals at the Ecumenical Council who became known as *liberals*.

Progressive has at least twice appeared as part of a U.S. third party to the left of Democratic Party *liberals*. The term would usually imply a stance more activist than that of a *liberal* but one more moderate than that of a *leftist*. On the other hand, the word can sometimes be used simply to indicate a militance of the left: the *Progressive* Labor Party. Used more generally outside politics, the word can suggest someone who is forward-looking and dynamic: a *progressive* businessman who had contributed to many community and civic programs. **Radical** is the one word here that indicates an extremist stand, yet need not apply solely to extreme *leftists*: *radicals* of both the right and left. Often, however, particularly in historical discussion of the first half of the 20th century, the word can without qualification indicate a *leftist* who, unlike a *liberal* or *progressive*, wished to see drastic alterations in society, often by means of revolution: a freewheeling debate among Trotskyists, Wobblies, and other *radicals*. In other areas, the word indicates someone who is in favor of thoroughgoing changes in a system: *radicals* who propose that colleges abandon the grading system, the giving of degrees, and the assigning of required courses. See ANARCHISM, SOCIALISM.

Antonyms: RIGHTIST.

leftover

balance
remainder
residue
rest
surplus

These words refer to what exists as a superfluous quantity once the needed or used portion of something has been subtracted. **Leftover** is relatively informal in pointing to any such entity, concrete or abstract. Often, it suggests a survival from an earlier period: an idea that was a *leftover* from the McCarthy era. It particularly pertains to food not eaten at a given meal, suggesting something saved to be eaten later or prepared in a different way; in this use, it is often plural: observing that they'd probably be eating *leftovers* from the Thanksgiving dinner for the next month. **Residue** is much more formal and points more exclusively to actual material *leftovers*, but with the suggestion that these are wasted or unusable portions: scraping the *residue* of food from the plates before putting them under water. Most specifically, the word refers to dregs or to insoluble matter left behind by the filtration or evaporation of a liquid: hard water that leaves a chalky *residue* behind when it is boiled away. **Surplus** indicates something in excess of need, but in contrast with *residue*, this amount might be perfectly usable and possibly beneficial: agreeing to share in common any *surplus* of funds after all expenses were paid in full. The word is particularly used to indicate stored farm produce or excess military supplies: grain elevators for storing the season's wheat *surplus*; labeling the older model binoculars as *surplus*.

The remaining words are much more general, having fewer connotations about the nature of the *leftover*. **Remainder** and **balance** can both point to the amount left after subtracting one sum from another; the former often appears in the context of arithmetic, the latter in accounting. Both can be used more generally, however, to suggest a partial quantity viewed in separation from the whole for any reason: grating half the carrots and dicing the *remainder*; They burned the obviously outdated books before deciding what to do with the *balance*. The only distinction here is that *balance* has a more formal tone and can sometimes sound out of place beyond its natural context of accounting.

Rest is the most general and informal of all these words; it can refer to anything that remains outside some designated amount. [He asked

John to come with him and told the *rest* of the boys to stay where they were; I wondered how I'd live through the *rest* of the week; Only one of her reasons really mattered, but the *rest* were wide of the mark.] See MARGINAL.

lenient

indulgent
lax
merciful
permissive
tolerant

These words refer to a flexible or complaisant attitude that shuns applying rules too strictly or that is more generous than standards of discipline or conduct might allow if interpreted literally. **Lenient** indicates a generous or indifferent lowering of standards, especially in the context of discipline meted out by a superior or authority. It is the most neutral of these words in its implications, although it can easily take on a mild tone either of approval or disapproval: a prep school that was more *lenient* than most toward minor infractions of the rules; arguing that rigid regimentation militates against learning, while an atmosphere of *lenient* approval assists it; He lacked a sense of responsibility because of his *lenient* upbringing.

Merciful and **lax** are distinct from all these other words in adding to the general meaning an extreme emotional tone. They contrast sharply with each other, as well, *merciful* regarding the *lenient* attitude from a strongly favorable viewpoint, *lax* from nearly as strong a negative viewpoint. *Merciful*, furthermore, suggests compassion, *lax* laziness, indifference, or slipshod incompetence. [He begged the dean to be *merciful*; The book's worth was invalidated by its *lax* standards of accuracy; When the spirit and letter of the law appear to be in conflict, a judge is *merciful*, not *lax*, in upholding the spirit.]

Indulgent is seldom neutral. It can carry a mild positive charge, suggesting generosity, in a context pertaining to affectionate relationships; sometimes in such a context, however, and in most other uses, it is more strongly negative, suggesting undiscriminating or irresponsible complaisance: a jolly, *indulgent* uncle; too *indulgent* of her children's every caprice or tantrum; a magazine that is *indulgent* of the unexamined prejudices and meretricious tastes of its readers. **Tolerant** is far less emotionally charged, approaching neutral description in most uses. In addition to indicating a flexible attitude toward rules or standards, it can suggest approval for an open-minded reluctance to make hasty judgments or disapproval for condescending rather than equal treatment: He informed his students that he could be *tolerant* of those who fell asleep in his class provided they didn't snore; *tolerant* of the attitudes and beliefs of others; *tolerant* of but not enthusiastic about the new teen-age fads.

Permissive is a much more formal word than the others, referring descriptively to an educational approach that allows the child's interest and capacities to determine content and rate of progress: the *permissive* theories of progressive education. The word, less specifically, may refer to an extremely *lenient* way of child rearing. [The children of *permissive* parents often give their own children an authoritarian upbringing, and vice versa.] Partisans of a *permissive* approach, in either context, might use the term in neutral description, but critics of this approach may well use the word as a pejorative label: *permissive* theories that resulted, at best, in well-adjusted ignoramuses. Outside the contexts of education and psychology, the word is widely used as a synonym for *tolerant*, but goes beyond the latter in suggesting not only open-minded detachment but a passive acceptance of involvement as well: the question of how *permissive* girls should be when they start dating. See COMPLIANT.

Antonyms: exacting, rigid, severe, stern, strict.

lessen

allay
alleviate
assuage
lighten
mitigate
soften
temper

These words all indicate the act of reducing the intensity or severity of something. **Lessen** is the most informal of these and the most general, applying both to a decrease in intensity and severity. It often suggests the subtracting of a part from a whole, as in its legal use: an appeal to *lessen* the sentence of the condemned man; a higher court *lessened* the amount the defendant would have to pay. But the word can apply neutrally to any reduction in degree or quantity: The flight to suburbia *lessened* the number of middle-class families living in the city itself.

Lighten is metaphorically graphic in referring to a decrease in the weight of something; **soften** is comparably graphic in referring to a decrease in the harshness, roughness, or force of something; both are more often favorable in their implications than *lessen*. *Lighten* would apply most naturally where an existing burden is partially lifted, *soften* most naturally where the full impact of something is prevented from being felt: technology that served to *lighten* the work load of the factory employee; an attempt to *soften* the blow by telling her the good news first. In this context, **temper** refers to making something more moderate, that is, more temperate: a sea breeze that *tempered* the noonday heat. But another use of the same word gives a meaning that is diametrically opposed, referring to the act of hardening or toughening something: young bodies *tempered* by rigorous exercise. Thus, unless the context is clear, the use of this word can result in confusion.

The remaining words all emphasize a reduction in severity; they are also alike in pointing to the reduction or removal of something negative or undesirable, rather than the mere subtraction of one amount from another. **Allay** and **assuage** can both refer to the calming or satisfying of desire or appetite, but whereas *allay* can often suggest a partial lulling or pacifying, *assuage* might better indicate something approaching satiation: an attempt to *allay* their hunger by nibbling on roots and berries; a huge dinner that *assuaged* his ravenous appetite. In other uses, furthermore, where *assuage* remains more strictly tied to the notion of a need that requires satisfaction, *allay* can function more widely for any appeasing action: reassuring words that *assuaged* her fear; a codeine tablet to *allay* the pain. In the former example, *allay* would suggest less conclusive relief, whereas in the latter *assuage* would seem out of place.

Alleviate is closest to *allay* but is even more emphatic about partial relief; it is also restricted to situations in which something is made easier to bear. Thus, it is a more specific and more formal intensification of *lighten*: early attempts to *alleviate* conditions in mental hospitals that preceded this century's thoroughgoing reform in mental care; drugs to *alleviate* the pain of terminal patients. **Mitigate**, which comes from a Latin word meaning to soften, can refer more formally to the partial lessening of need, pain, or hardship: programs to *mitigate* the disruptive effects of slum living; rehabilitative therapy to *mitigate* the aftereffects of strokes and heart attacks; the judge's decision to *mitigate* the man's sentence in light of his previous record. See DECREASE, REDUCE, WANE, WEAKEN.

Antonyms: ENLARGE, ESCALATE, EXTEND, *heighten, toughen.*

lewd

lascivious
lecherous

These words all refer in a negative way to having, expressing, or arousing sexual desire. **Lewd** is the most general of these and the most negative in tone. It can equally well suggest having sexual desires, acting on them, or arousing them. Used of a person, it implies thoroughgoing immorality: *lewd* soldiers on the town. Used of thoughts or feelings, it implies coarseness of sexual appetite, untinged by affection, tenderness,

lewd

(continued)

licentious
lustful
prurient
salacious
wanton

or love, but it does not necessarily imply action: *lewd* glances at every passing woman. Used of literature or art, it implies pornographic or obscene qualities: *lewd* graffiti on the subway posters. Used of behavior, it may be considerably weaker, suggesting only a provocative or suggestive seductiveness: the *lewd* poses of the chorus girls.

Licentious and **wanton** emphasize the active satisfaction of desire, although neither word is restricted in meaning to sexual impulse alone. *Licentious* can suggest any kind of excessive freedom in behavior that goes past legal or moral bounds or violates customary standards of behavior: a *licentious* attitude toward premarital affairs. *Wanton*, by contrast, does not suggest extreme freedom so much as unruly or wasteful self-indulgence. Used of people or people's behavior it suggests sensuality more than sexuality: the *wanton*, fast-living jet set. Only in its sense of gratuitous does it suggest extreme inhumanity or cruelty: *wanton* slaughter.

Lustful and **lecherous** may suggest unacted-upon desire as well as the active seeking of satisfaction: a *lecherous* mood; a *lustful* disposition. *Lustful*, however, suggests a permanent character trait not likely to remain unexpressed. *Lecherous* can be used to refer to a momentary desire for a particular person: goaded by *lecherous* feelings for his new secretary. Neither of these words is likely to be used for pornographic materials designed to arouse desire.

Lascivious and **prurient**, unlike the other words here, tend to be restricted more specifically to having sexual desire than to acting upon it. Both words are commonly used to describe the feelings that pornography in particular is intended to incite, with *prurient* being the word favored in legal terminology: whether a book taken as a whole arouses *prurient* interests in the average person and is utterly without redeeming social importance. *Lascivious* is milder and stresses inclination, whereas *prurient* stresses susceptibility.

Salacious, alone of these words, most usually suggests the material intended to incite sexual fantasies or desires: *salacious* movies shown at stag parties.

In general, sexual impulses per se are not so widely disapproved of as formerly, and a present-day view of what should be classified as *lewd* and what as zestful high spirits would differ drastically from a 19th-century view. See DIRTY, EROTIC, INDECENT, PASSIONATE.

Antonyms: CHASTE, INNOCENT, *pure.*

lie

falsehood
fib
prevarication
rationalization
untruth

These words refer to statements or formulations that are misleading or contrary to fact. **Lie** is the most general of these, but it is exclusively restricted to a conscious and deliberate intention to distort the truth. [She told a *lie* about how much the new dress had cost her; It was a *lie* that no arms shipments were being sent to the front.] In heated debate, the word is often applied more loosely to inadvertent misstatements or statements thought to be hypocritical: It's simply a *lie* that my opponent could carry out all these campaign promises without raising taxes. Sometimes, the word can apply to masking an unpleasant situation with a pleasant exterior: She was unwilling to live a *lie* for the sake of her husband's political future. In the idiom *give the lie to*, a conclusive disproof of an assertion or theory is indicated: evidence that *gave the lie to* their claim of having remained strictly neutral during the crisis.

By contrast, **rationalization** is very specific, indicating a thought process by which one attempts to justify one's actions, either to oneself or to others, by consciously or unconsciously distorting the truth. Although psychologists may view all formulated explanations as *rationalizations*, the word has become a fad word for ingenious but specious reasoning that puts one's own behavior in the most favorable light possible: The psychiatrist works to get behind the web of *rationalizations* to the real conflicts and anxieties they conceal; his *rationalization* that being late for work was a forgivable foible, considering how indispensable he was to the office; Nazis whose *rationalization* was that they were only obeying orders.

The remaining words can all be used as euphemisms for *lie*. **Fib**, the most informal of these words, is exclusively used in this way, suggesting a trivial, harmless, or forgivable *lie*: She turned him down with a *fib* about already having a date for the evening. The word may now sound a bit dated. **Prevarication**, the most formal word here, would be taken by many as an extremely offensive and overly fancy euphemism for *lie*; as such, it might be useful as humor or irony: comforted that the commandment prohibiting *lies* said nothing about *prevarication*. The word can have a special area of meaning that refers not to bald misstatements of fact but to the deceptive statement of half-truths; this distinction would be lost on many people, however.

Falsehood and **untruth**, as euphemisms, are less formal circumlocutions than *prevarication*. *Falsehood*, however, has a legitimate reference to any incorrectness, whether intentional or not: The *falsehood* of this prevalent notion is now inescapable. *Untruth* can sometimes refer to fictions that were never intended to mislead or be taken as fact: Novelists devise *untruths* that sometimes have a greater validity than the statistical truths of the social sciences. See DECEPTION, GUILE, MISLEADING, TRICK (n.) TRICK (v.).

Antonyms: honesty, truth, veracity.

listing

catalogue
inventory
list
register
roll
roster

Listing and **list** refer to any itemized series of names, words, etc., especially when recorded in a set order: a *list* of Representatives from the state of New York arranged by county; a *listing* of drugs authorized for sale by the Food and Drug Administration. *Listing* is also used to mean an entry in a *list*: Please check your *listing* in the new telephone book and notify us of any mistakes.

Register and **roll** apply to *lists* of names. A *register* is a formal or official written record of names or transactions: a *register* of births or deaths. *Registers* are typically designed to preserve important information for future reference. A *roll*, on the other hand, is often a temporary *listing* of names, as of students in a class or soldiers in a military unit: The teacher called the *roll* every morning to see who was absent. Any *list* of names may be called a **roster**, but the word usually refers to a *list* of names of men enrolled for a particular kind of duty. In the U.S. Army and in other service organizations, duty *rosters* are maintained to assure that special duties, such as guard duty and KP, are fairly assigned to each eligible man, that is, at roughly equal intervals; the order in which names are listed on *rosters*, therefore, is all-important.

Inventory and **catalogue** refer to special kinds of *listings*. An *inventory* is a *list* of articles with the description and quantity of each. *Inventories* are periodically taken in warehouses, factories, and retail stores to record the number and kind of articles in stock. A *catalogue* (or *catalog*, the standard spelling in most libraries) is a *list* or enumeration of names or objects, usually in alphabetical order and often with some accompanying description. A card *catalog* in a library lists the title and author of the book, periodical, etc., and other useful information, such as the number of pages, the copyright date, where and by whom the work was published, an identifying number, and sometimes an indication of the subject or contents. The *catalogue* of a mail-order house lists the articles offered for sale, with accompanying descriptions and prices. Figuratively, any methodical *listing* can be called a *catalogue*: He gave me a long *catalogue* of woes: his car broke down, he had a fight with his girlfriend, he caught a cold, and so on. See ACCUMULATION, QUANTITY.

listless

lackadaisical
languid
languorous
lethargic

All of these words pertain to a lack of spirit or energy. **Listless** is the least formal of these and the most wide-ranging in application. At its most specific, the word can indicate slow or sluggish movement, at its most general a lack of the vibrance associated with good health or high spirits: He responded to my question with a *listless* shrug of his shoulders; the *listless* faces of a family of sharecroppers; a class of *listless* slum children. Most often, the word suggests a general apathy that may well be the result of disease or physical or mental fatigue.

Languid can also indicate a lack of interest or animation that may stem from poor health or fatigue, but it can also (and perhaps more often) indicate an avoidance of physical exertion as a matter of choice or temperament rather than of necessity: drooped in her *languid* pose on a bench while her friends walked from painting to painting in the exhibit. It can also suggest the affecting of a slow or lazy manner: the *languid* drawl with which he spoke. In a way that *listless* cannot, *languid* can indicate anything that is lacking in force: a *languid* wind that offered no relief from the heat. **Languorous** and *languid* both derive ultimately from the same French root, meaning to languish. *Languorous* gives a distinct and specific meaning, however, that points to the affecting of an effete or indolent dreaminess: an era of crisis in which many retired to *languorous* meditation and disengagement.

Lethargic concentrates on the aspect of *listless* that pertains to sluggish movement, but it is slightly more formal than *listless* and is considerably more critical or disapproving in tone. The word may, in fact, suggest laziness as the cause of this behavior: too *lethargic* to get his homework done on time. **Lackadaisical** concentrates on a different aspect of *listless*, the one referring to a lack of vibrance, spirit, or energy: reacting to the impassioned speech with a *lackadaisical* yawn; entrenched bureaucrats who are *lackadaisical* about proposals to make the system more efficient or humane. The word can also refer to whatever is idle, indifferent, or empty of value: a *lackadaisical* attitude toward standards of accuracy and objective scholarship. See IMPASSIVE, SLOTH, TIRED, UNINVOLVED, WEAKEN.

Antonyms: energetic, LIVELY, *spirited.*

lively

animated
brisk
buoyant
spirited
sprightly
vivacious

These words all describe people, things, or actions that are full of or display great vigor and energy. **Lively** is the most general word and suggests energy of motion and great activity: a *lively* kitten; a party that turned out to be a very *lively* occasion; a gathering in which there was much *lively* conversation.

Animated, close in meaning to *lively*, is normally limited in application to people or to behavior: an *animated* argument between a motorist and a traffic policeman; to become *animated* and talkative after drinking one cocktail.

Buoyant, **spirited**, **sprightly**, and **vivacious** all suggest a manner of speaking or acting marked by energy and good humor. *Buoyant*, which carries the suggestion of its literal meaning of floating, describes an irrepressible or resilient energy in manner or outlook: *buoyant* laughter; *buoyant* confidence in the future. *Spirited* suggests a high degree of vitality, sometimes mixed with daring. [Young stallions are very *spirited* animals; He made a *spirited* denial of having any knowledge of the crime.] *Sprightly* and *vivacious* add to the idea of energy the element of quick-wittedness and brightness: *sprightly* jokes; a *sprightly* old lady; a *vivacious* telling of a story; *vivacious* young girls.

Brisk may be applied to actions that exhibit an abundance of energy: He passed us at a *brisk* walk. *Brisk* may also describe a sharp, business-like manner that approaches curtness but also implies a controlled vitality: He always spoke to his subordinates in a *brisk* tone. See BUSY.
Antonyms: LISTLESS.

These words all mean having life or manifesting signs of life. **Living**, **alive**, and **live** may be applied interchangeably to functioning organisms in contrast to those that are dead. *Living* may sometimes refer only to the condition of not being dead. [He is the greatest *living* novelist in America; My grandfather is still *living* at the age of 93.] By extension, *living* may also describe things that are full of energy and significance or are actually operative: the *living* faith of Buddhists; *living* languages. *Alive* applies to all degrees of life, from that which is barely evident to that which implies the very utmost of vitality and power. [The mortally wounded man was unconscious but still *alive* when taken to the hospital; She is so *alive* that her presence in a room is electrifying.] *Live*, which is usually placed before the noun modified, may describe the condition of appearing in the flesh rather than being depicted in photographs, paintings, etc., or being preserved physically after death. [I was grown up before I saw a real, *live* gypsy; Having seen the stuffed gorillas at the museum, the little boy was delighted to observe his first *live* one at the zoo.] In television and radio, a *live* audience or *live* actors are actually present at the time of transmission rather than appearing in a taped performance. When applied to certain things, *live* carries over the idea of vital functioning. [A *live* wire is one charged with electricity; We broiled the steak over *live* coals; Peace talks are a *live* issue today.]

Animate carries fewer connotations than do *living*, *alive*, and *live*, and is usually limited in application to *living* organisms as opposed to dead ones or to objects, called inanimate, that do not have the property of possessing life. See EXIST.
Antonyms: DEAD.

These words refer to something that is carried or transported. **Load** is the most general word in that it may be used with any kind of carrier: a man with a *load* on his back; taking a *load* of soiled clothes to the laundry; a wagon bringing in a *load* of hay; a flatcar with a *load* of cement blocks. *Load* also refers to the quantity carried or conveyed, as measured by the capacity of the vehicle or bearer: a car*load* of frozen foods; a truck*load* of newsprint. Sometimes *load* means anything that is unusually heavy or is borne with difficulty, either in a literal sense or in a figurative one: the plum tree sagging under its *load* of ripe fruit; smarting under a *load* of monthly installment payments.

Freight and **cargo** are both applied to goods or merchandise that are carried in large quantities over long distances. Trains, trucks, wagons, and the like are usually said to carry *freight*. *Cargo* is largely restricted to commodities carried by ships, and, in more recent times, by aircraft.

living

alive
animate
live

load

burden
cargo
freight

Burden, which etymologically means that which is carried or borne, now has limited use when applied to anything physical. [Donkeys and camels are still widely used in some parts of the world as beasts of *burden*; The carrying capacity of a ship and the weight of the *cargo* are both called the *burden*.] *Burden* has greater currency in meaning something borne with difficulty or something that weighs down, especially in a mental or emotional sense: too great a *burden* of responsibility and worry; a horse quivering under the *burden* of its three-hundred-pound rider.

lodgings

accommodations
apartment
flat
quarters
suite

These words refer to living space consisting of a room or set of rooms that occupies part of a building or that exists as a unit within some larger unit. **Lodgings** and **accommodations** are equally vague in referring to any sort of living arrangements, usually temporary. *Lodgings*, especially in the United States, can sound old-fashioned; *accommodations*, while less informal in tone, is more current: troubadours who wandered through medieval France seeking *lodgings* for the night; asking him how he liked his *accommodations* at the hotel. The latter can also refer to a temporary, improvised setup, including the paraphernalia required to house a guest: setting up overnight *accommodations* for two more visitors by raiding the linen closet and calling into service the living room sofa and a folding cot.

Apartment and **flat** are much more specific than the preceding, referring to sets of rooms usually rented and occupied for a longer term. As neutral description, *apartment* is the preferred term in U.S. speech, *flat* in British speech. In U.S. usage, however, *flat* often refers to a cramped, inhospitable *apartment* without conveniences: a cold-water *flat*.

Suite is a widely applied term for any well-appointed set of rooms. It can refer to luxury *accommodations* in a hotel: the bridal *suite*. It can refer to a large or lavish *apartment*: the penthouse *suite*. It can also refer to a set of office rooms intended, not as living space, but for conducting business: an executive *suite*. **Quarters** has almost as wide a range of usage; it can refer to specified buildings within a complex of other buildings (or to a part of a building or *apartment*) where certain kinds of people live: the doctors' *quarters*; servants' *quarters*; the slave *quarters* behind the mansion. It has a particular relevance in military parlance, referring to the place where a specified group lives: officers' *quarters*; confined to *quarters*. See HOME, HOTEL, HOUSE.

loneliness

alienation
desolation
disaffection
estrangement

These words all relate to a lack or loss of friendship, love, or interrelatedness with others. **Loneliness** is the least formal and the most restricted in its application. It refers to a lack of companionship and usually implies an attendant feeling of unhappiness or unfulfillment: the stark *loneliness* of the widows and pensioners who live in resident hotels. The word may refer to a feeling rather than an actual condition of isolation: Her *loneliness* was never more acute than in a crowded theater. Occasionally, the word can refer to a welcome state of seclusion or solitude: enjoying the *loneliness* of their life on the island. Also, the word can refer to the physical isolation of anything, whether this is regarded as pleasant, factually neutral, or unpleasant: the *loneliness* of a single tree silhouetted against a prairie landscape; the *loneliness* of their cabin, high in the mountains.

One use of **desolation** can serve as an intensification of *loneliness* in referring to someone utterly alone or inconsolably forsaken: the *desola-*

tion of a Bowery derelict. Often the word can indicate an actual state of ruin or barrenness: the *desolation* left behind by the tornado; the *desolation* of Arizona's desert country. The word can also refer to intense sorrow suffered because of a serious loss: the *desolation* he felt upon hearing the news of his brother's death.

Disaffection is relatively formal; unlike the former pair, it most often suggests that an earlier fondness for someone has turned to indifference or mild distaste: She had regarded her husband over the years with a growing *disaffection*. Neither a complete separation from someone nor a transmutation of fondness into hatred need be suggested by the word. Often, however, the word has a stronger charge when it indicates someone deliberately at work to cause a more drastic change in feeling or allegiance, as in intrigues of love or politics: an envious friend who had actively promoted *disaffection* between the newly married couple; professional agitators who worked zealously to stir up *disaffection* and rebellion among the workers. **Estrangement** applies more exclusively to a voluntary *disaffection* that results in complete separation and, sometimes, a stronger feeling of dislike or hatred that replaces an earlier fondness or love: It was impossible to keep their *estrangement* secret, since they were living apart and had drawn up separation papers. Sometimes the word puts its emphasis on a process of cooling affection, without suggesting any complete break; here, it is close to *disaffection*, but it suggests a growing remoteness and lack of communication that may be involuntary: so busy with their separate concerns that neither noticed the *estrangement* that was gradually being driven between them like a wedge.

Alienation applies more widely than any other of these words. It can be used in a way resembling the last sense of *estrangement*, but with a clearer implication that no separation need take place: pressure that resulted in a feeling of *alienation* toward each other. The phrase, *alienation of affection*, implies, like *disaffection*, a deliberate attempt to bring about a reversal of feelings toward someone, but this use of the word is now less common. At its most general, the word can apply to any feeling of unrelatedness, especially a hopeless feeling of distance from society's structure and concerns: minority groups that must also cope with their own feelings of *alienation* from a society that rejects them. This fad use of the word derives ultimately from Marxism in which it is a technical term for the separation of a laborer from the fruits of his labor: Unlike the craftsman who took pride in his work, the assembly-line worker feels isolated and indifferent because of the *alienation* inherent in mass production. See LONELY, MODEST, PRIVACY, UNINVOLVED.

Antonyms: ALLEGIANCE, *camaraderie, companionship, fellowship, mutuality, reconciliation.*

lonely

forlorn
lonesome
solitary

These words are used to refer to people or places which are apart from others. **Lonely** is a broad term describing a state of mind which is induced by lack of companionship or the kind of sympathy which companionship can provide. A *lonely* feeling can range from the mild sadness engendered by a casual instance of solitude to the great unhappiness and depression one might feel after a long period of separation from or lack of meaningful relationship with other people: a *lonely* young sailor feeling sorry for himself because his date had stood him up; a *lonely* spinster whose eccentricities had robbed her of the opportunity for anything but the most impersonal kind of social contact. *Lonely* can also be used to describe an unfrequented or deserted place: a *lonely* stretch of beach where it was possible to bathe in the nude. In reference to places, **lonesome** intensifies the meaning of *lonely* to suggest a place that is not merely deserted but which has an air of melancholy about it: a house she had always thought of as overcrowded but that was *lonesome* and cavernous when her children grew up and went out on their own. In its description of people *lonesome* is again a stronger word than *lonely* but is slightly less formal in tone. It often suggests the dejection felt when one is faced with the absence of someone to whom one is or has been very close: a merchandising executive who never got over being *lonesome* when he had to leave his family for business travel; *lonesome* for a pet dog that he'd raised from a pup and that had just died.

Forlorn is more specific than either of the two preceding words in its suggestion that the person described as such is alone because he has been deserted or abandoned: wretched and *forlorn* in the sinister atmosphere of the half-empty waiting room, despairing of the arrival of a friend who had promised to meet her but who was already three hours late. The place referred to as *forlorn* seems also to have been deserted and has the air of loneliness that characterizes remote or abandoned dwellings and locales: a once fashionable resort that was now a *forlorn* ghost town.

Solitary can mean *lonely* and can describe a person or place: the *solitary* feeling one sometimes experiences in the middle of a crowded room; the *solitary* desert. But *solitary*, in a way that none of the other words in this group can, may suggest an aloneness that has been chosen rather than imposed. Thus, a person who is *solitary* by nature often prefers contemplation to companionship, and a *solitary* traveler prefers traveling alone to being with a large group on an organized tour. See ALOOF, LEAVE (abandon), PRIVACY.

Antonyms: accompanied, attended, escorted, protected.

look

gaze
glance
glare
peer
stare

These words mean to turn the eyes toward something either in an effort to see it or to convey a specific meaning or emotion. **Look** is the most general word and may mean merely to direct the eyes: to *look* out the window; to *look* at pictures in a magazine. One may also *look* in such a way as to communicate a particular feeling: to *look* wistfully at a mink coat; to *look* daggers at an intruder.

Gaze is to *look* long and steadily, often with the implication of wonder, admiration, fascination, etc.: to *gaze* at a beautiful view; to *gaze* into the eyes of a loved one.

Glance refers to the act of *looking* briefly at something when one is preoccupied or in a hurry. [On the bus I always manage to *glance* at the headlines in the newspaper.]

Peer suggests a *looking* with a narrowing of the eyes and often a movement of the head, usually forward. To *peer* may mean to *look* inquiringly or searchingly or may simply indicate difficulty in seeing clearly. [He *peered* surreptitiously into his wallet to see if he had enough money to pay the check; Nearsighted people often *peer* at you when they are not wearing their glasses.]

Stare is to *gaze* intently, especially with wide-open eyes, as in amazement, admiration, or fear: to *stare* at a drunkard reeling down the street; to *stare* in terror into the muzzle of a loaded gun. *Stare* may also connote insolence, or at least rudeness, on the part of the viewer, and may or may not be intentional. [Children should be taught not to *stare* at handicapped people; The high-school boys gather in front of the drugstore to *stare* at the passing girls.]

Glare is to *stare* fiercely or threateningly and always emphasizes hostility or fear: a trapped eagle *glaring* at his captors; to *glare* at one's opponent in an argument. See SEE, VISION.

These words refer to money, land, or goods seized by war, violence, or fraud. **Loot** in its oldest sense referred to goods seized specifically in war, especially goods of great value. More recently, it would better suggest money or goods acquired by theft: jewel thieves dividing their *loot*. Most recently, it has come to be used specifically for goods seized by rioters, roving singly or in bands: estimates of the *loot* taken in three days of rioting. In this sense, it distinguishes goods seized in this manner from ordinary stolen goods. In slang use, *loot* can refer simply to money, regardless of how acquired: How much *loot* do you have on you? By contrast, **swag** and **haul** are slang words for goods acquired by theft, although *haul* can also apply to the profits from any venture, legal or illegal: counting up his *haul* from the lemonade concession.

Spoils, like *loot*, once referred to goods seized in war, although it could refer as well to land so acquired. Occasionally it is used in the singular. Its most common meaning now, however, is money or advantages acquired through corrupt political practices: Largely honorary but highly paid appointive offices are among the *spoils* most reluctantly surrendered by machine politicians. Unlike *spoils* and *loot*, **booty** has not acquired latter-day uses and still refers specifically only to goods seized in war; in international law, it specifically applies to goods seized on land rather than at sea. It is sometimes used figuratively for any acquisition, especially one taken by violence or robbery. See PLUNDER.

These words refer to sounds of high intensity or volume, or to statements or ways of behaving that are excessive or strident. **Loud** is the most general of these, referring most concretely to sounds that are of high volume and carry considerable distances: playing his transistor so *loud* that everyone in the bus could hear it; foghorns *loud* enough to be heard nearly a mile inland; *loud* angry voices resounding down the hallway. The word may also refer to offensive behavior or appearance: a *loud* sport shirt; people with garish tastes and *loud* manners. **Noisy** and *loud*, the most informal of these words, differ in that *loud* refers to specific sources of high-volume sound whereas *noisy* refers to a general density of sound emanating from many sources: a *loud* burglar alarm ringing in the deserted street; a maddeningly *noisy* neighborhood. *Noisy*, however, need not refer to sounds of high volume: the *noisy* chirring of crickets, low but incessant. While the word has fewer applications to behavior, it suggests relentlessness or impatience: using a *loud* speaking voice to reach his *noisy* audience; hating *noisy* arguments in which everybody shouted and interrupted each other.

The remaining words all relate to specific but separate aspects of *loud* or *noisy*. **Blatant** refers most concretely to a raised insistent voice, but it gives a disapproving tone: the *blatant* hucksters of the hard-sell television commercial. More and more often, however, the word is used for any distasteful appeal or obvious and vulgar disregard for the sensibilities: *blatant* lies; *blatant* bad manners that matched his disheveled appearance. **Obstreperous** is in every way an intensification of *blatant*: the unruly screaming and shouting of her *obstreperous* children. It is also used to refer to extremely distasteful manners, with a stress on deliberate rudeness, or to behavior that is completely out of control: *obstreperous* insults; *obstreperous* guests that ruined the party.

loot

booty
haul
spoils
swag

loud

blatant
boisterous
clamorous
noisy
obstreperous
vociferous

Boisterous emphasizes, without the disapproval inherent in the previous pair of words, good high spirits that result in *loud* or *noisy* behavior: *boisterous* group singing in the ski lodge at night. **Clamorous** specifically pertains to insistent or repeated entreaties, suggesting outcries at danger or a panicked disorder: the *clamorous* cries of miners in the blocked tunnel. In this sense, the word may sound somewhat outdated, but it is still used for any general din of *noisy* voices or general outcry: a quarter of the city thick with the *clamorous* appeals of hawkers and vendors; theater lobbies filled with a *clamorous* hubbub during intermission. **Vociferous** refers to an insistent, urgent, or strident manner of speaking, sometimes suggesting anger or the determination to drive home a point: *vociferous* arguments between Freudians and Jungians; a *vociferous* outcry for a recount of the vote. See NOISE, UNRULY.

Antonyms: disciplined, peaceful, retiring, SILENT, *soft, subdued,* TACITURN, TRANQUIL.

love

affection
attachment
crush
infatuation

These words denote the emotion which a person feels for someone or something. **Love, attachment,** and **affection** are all general words which designate the kind of feeling that binds a person to another person or to a thing by ties of the heart or of the mind. *Love* goes beyond *attachment* and *affection* in intensity. Thus you would not speak of a mother's *attachment* to her baby but of her *affection* or *love*. *Love* may also imply less control or regulation of feeling than *affection* or *attachment* because it connotes the possible presence of passion in its makeup: His *love* for her, being based on physical attraction alone, could not withstand the boredom and jealousy that soon became part of it. *Attachment* sometimes suggests a warm liking: a fond *attachment* to one's pet. It can also refer to the kind of loyalty which is inspired by mental rather than emotional sympathies: He suffered from a profound *attachment* to a cause which his judgment told him was honorable but which the prejudices of his upbringing rejected as radical and morally unsound. *Affection* differs from *attachment* in that it expresses a greater depth of sentiment and is almost always directed toward a living being: the cherished *affection* of a childhood friend.

Crush and **infatuation** are alike in denoting a special kind of *affection* or *love*. Both are absorbing, extravagant, often unreasoning and unreasonable sentiments, usually as short in life as they are long on intensity. But while one can only have a *crush* on a person, one can be *infatuated* with something inanimate: When he reached middle age, my father developed an *infatuation* for gambling. There is also a difference between *crush* and *infatuation* in that the former almost always designates the feelings of a young person and the latter those of someone more mature. [Jeannie's *crush* this week is on her math teacher; The old man's *infatuation* with his nurse made her job so difficult that she asked to be taken off his case.] See EMOTION, EROTIC, PASSIONATE.

Antonyms: DISLIKE, *hate*.

loving

devoted
doting
fond

These words all convey the meaning of having a warm feeling toward or strong attachment to some person or thing. **Loving** is a broad word that refers to personal regard. It can be used in speaking of the regard itself or of its outward indications: a *loving* couple; *loving* glances. It can describe a reserved emotion or one that is notable for its demonstration: *loving* parents who would rather risk their child's displeasure than spoil him; a happy, *loving* child who seems to want nothing more than to kiss and hug anyone that comes near her.

A *loving* person whose feelings or demonstrations go beyond the bounds of good taste or good judgment is often described as **doting**: a *doting* lover whose foolish extravagances and emotional absurdities lost him his mistress; a *doting* mother who alienated her husband by lavishing too much love on their child.

Devoted and **fond**, unlike *loving* and *doting*, are used in reference to the feeling a person has toward some thing as well as toward another person. The difference between them in such usage is one of degree, *devoted* bespeaking a much greater amount of attachment to the thing involved: a student of the piano who is *fond* of all the romantic literature and especially *devoted* to that of Rachmaninoff. In characterizing emotion directed toward a person, *devoted* again is a stronger word than *fond* and often suggests the depth of feeling which is built by time-tested loyalty: a couple who were nothing more than *fond* of each other when they married but who have grown into *devoted* lovers. *Devoted*, as no other word in the group does, can refer to the enthusiasm or ardor involved in an attachment which need not necessarily have any sentimental suggestions: *devoted* to his job; a *devoted* follower of Marxist philosophy. See ALLEGIANCE, EMOTION.

Antonyms: bitter, COLD, hateful.

These words refer to a soft radiance, mostly of reflected light. **Luminous** may describe a source of light, in which case it is very general, indicating the light's brightness or clarity: *luminous* stars. Contradictorily enough, it can also specifically suggest a soft or barely perceivable radiance or one enclosed within or seen through something else: dim moonlight on *luminous* pine needles; the *luminous* dial of the radio. **Lucent** and **lucid** share in these last meanings of *luminous*, suggesting particularly refracted or suffused light: the *lucent* pool of water; a *lucid*, cloudless day. Both, but especially *lucid*, suggest clarity as a carry-over from what is now their main use, to refer to transparence. **Lambent** also suggests a radiance of refracted light: the *lambent* fog surrounding the street lamps. It has a lyrical quality that suggests gentleness or beauty, but can seem overelegant in some contexts. **Refulgent** is even more in danger of this possibility, to the point of seeming precious. It specifically indicates a reflected brightness: the *refulgent* clouds above the setting sun.

Gleaming may indicate a source of light, in which case it merely suggests brightness: *gleaming* sunlight. In this use, it seems more natural and less formal than *luminous*. More specifically, *gleaming* may suggest the brightness of reflected light: the new skyscraper's *gleaming* wall of glass. Its overtones in this case are of spotlessness. *Gleaming* may also suggest dimness: the night's darkness punctuated by faintly *gleaming* birches. **Glistening** is almost exclusively restricted to reflected light; except for this, it compares to *gleaming*, but suggests in addition to dimness an undulating reflection or a moist surface: *glistening* rain-drenched leaves. **Lustrous** suggests a more mellow reflected light than either *gleaming* or *glistening*, applying specifically to the soft shine of any smooth material: the *lustrous* gold of the wedding ring. See BRIGHT, SPARKLING.

Antonyms: dull, dusky, GLOOMY, obscure.

luminous

gleaming
glistening
lambent
lucent
lucid
lustrous
refulgent

These words all mean to move furtively or stealthily, and all express an evident desire to stay hidden or unnoticed. **Lurk** can mean to lie hidden or to exist unnoticed or unsuspected: a snake *lurking* in the grass; What evil *lurks* in the hearts of men? But its most pertinent sense here is to

lurk

creep

lurk
(continued)

prowl
skulk
slink
sneak
steal

move secretly or furtively, always with the implication of menace: assassins *lurking* among the crowd. The implied danger is often vague and ill-defined, which only increases the suggestion of menace: dark, shadowy figures *lurking* in alleyways.

Slink, creep, and **steal** all mean to move quietly or furtively, but whereas *slink* and *creep* often suggest fear as a motive for remaining hidden, *steal* may suggest other motives. *Slink* often points to a sly, guilty, or abject attitude, and suggests a cowering posture and a fairly rapid gait: The beggar, refused a handout, *slunk* away into the shadows. *Creep*, in its basic sense, means to move with the body close to or touching the ground: Marines *creeping* along through the underbrush. As here considered, *creep* often suggests timidity or fear as a cause of slow, very deliberate movement, regardless of posture: We *crept* up the staircase, our hearts pounding. But it can also mean any slow movement: The train fairly *crept* along. *Steal* emphasizes the secrecy of a mission: He *stole* over to his friend's locker when his back was turned and dropped a frog in his shoe. Both *steal* and *creep* can be used figuratively. [A note of pathos *crept* into her voice; For the first time a feeling of pity *stole* into his heart.]

Skulk, more than *slink*, suggests guilt or shame as a motive for passing unnoticed: For months after his release from prison, he *skulked* around the house, afraid to show his face during the day. But it may also suggest sober caution, and in still other contexts, menace: to *skulk* past a gang of street-corner toughs; a tough waterfront neighborhood with clusters of figures *skulking* in front of every bar. Unlike *slink* or *creep*, *skulk* does not suggest any particular gait; it may imply the hunched-over posture of one wishing to remain undetected, but no mental picture is invariably associated with it. **Sneak** gives no clue at all either to posture or gait, thus emphasizing motive — the wish to remain unnoticed — to the exclusion of manner. *Sneak* can apply to trivial or innocent events as well as serious ones: to *sneak* into a ball park; to *sneak* away from a party; to *sneak* into the kitchen for a snack. It suggests mischief or cowardliness more often than menace, and unlike *lurk* seldom or never suggests the threat of criminal acts.

Prowl means to roam about stealthily in search of prey or plunder: lions *prowling* for gazelles. When applied to people, *prowl* can suggest danger or may emphasize only the predatory instinct: would-be muggers *prowling* for victims; young men *prowling* the streets (or *on the prowl*) for girls. In the U.S., a *prowl car* is a police patrol car, so called because unless on call it typically moves slowly and in a more or less random manner, as an animal would while searching for prey. Thus *prowl*, alone of these words, may suggest a beneficial motive for stealth. See FOLLOW, HUNT, STEALTHY.

M

machine

apparatus

Machine, as here considered, is an assemblage of parts, movable and fixed, so constructed as to perform work when energy is applied to it. In size, a *machine* may vary from, e.g., a hand-operated numbering *machine* to a giant drop forge. Generally, a *machine* is thought of as more or less permanent and is expected to perform its work repeatedly or continuously over a long period of time.

Contrivance and **device** often mean a simple *machine*, sometimes improvised or makeshift, devised to perform a task once or for a short period of time. A belt attached to the rim of a drive wheel of an automobile to power a circular saw is a *contrivance* or *device*.

A **mechanism** may be a simple *machine* or one of the moving systems in a *machine*. A linotype *machine* includes a *mechanism* for spacing words evenly.

An **apparatus** is a complicated *mechanism* consisting of several separate but interconnected parts, usually constructed for a special purpose and not mass-produced. A chemist's system of tubes and flasks is an *apparatus* constructed for a specific experiment or process.

An **appliance**, in current usage, is a household *machine* such as a washing *machine*, a vacuum cleaner, an electric mixer, etc.

An **engine**, properly speaking, is not a *machine* in the sense of something that performs a specific task; rather it is a *machine* that converts energy, as heat, electricity, waterpower, etc., into mechanical power: the steam *engine*; the diesel *engine*. See IMPLEMENT, MAKE.

These words relate to the turning out of finished products by the shaping or combination of raw materials or parts. **Make** is the most general and informal of these words and can apply to any process of construction: a child *making* a paper kite; factories that *make* thousands of ball-point pens each day. **Manufacture** is narrower in scope but can range from factual neutrality in tone to disapproval for mechanical or uncreative activity: industrialized nations that can *manufacture* their own machines and equipment; an artist who doesn't *make* paintings so much as he *manufactures* them. **Produce** approaches the generality of *make*, and stresses the neutral aspect of *manufacture*. It emphasizes the amount of a product turned out, without necessarily implying a process of mass-production, as would be the case with *manufacture*: *producing* a new novel every two years; a region that has *produced* more presidents than any other area of the country; new methods that *produce* more crops from the same amount of land; an economy tied to the amount of steel the mills *produce* each year. **Assemble**, more than the other words of this group, emphasizes the combining of parts which have been *made* somewhere else: waiting for a component to arrive from the manufacturer so that he could *assemble* his hi-fi set. See BUILD, CREATE, MOLD.

These words mean to say or to write something, often misleading or false, that is damaging to a person or a group of people. **Malign** is the broadest word in the group in that the feelings which motivate a person who *maligns* another can range from the simple ill will which prompts a gossip to the bitter hatred or malicious ignorance which results in pernicious persecution: a lady author who has been much *maligned* because of her romantic indiscretions; a liberal reform candidate so *maligned* by crooked political bosses that he withdrew from a mayoralty race.

Asperse and **vilify** imply false accusations made in order to ruin someone's reputation. *Asperse*, meaning literally to bespatter, often implies indirect or vague assertions made to reduce good repute. *Vilify* usually implies violent and direct abuse, such as the calling of names. One may *asperse* a writer's integrity by suggesting indirectly that he has written lies, or *vilify* him directly by calling him a liar. *Asperse*, however, is extremely formal, and more commonly appears in the form of a

---

machine
(continued)

appliance
contrivance
device
engine
mechanism

make

assemble
manufacture
produce

malign

asperse
defame
libel
slander
vilify

plural noun: The writer accused the reviewer of casting *aspersions* on his work.

Defame can specifically indicate an attempt to destroy someone's good name. Like *vilify*, the word suggests the use of direct and harsh accusations, but *defame* is less commonly used in this way than *vilify*. Recently, it has acquired a meaning that refers to unfounded, broadside denunciations of ethnic or religious groups: the myth of ritual murder that was repeatedly used to *defame* the Jewish minority in many European countries.

In popular usage, **libel** and **slander** are applied to false accusations by any means. At their most restricted, they are legal terms that are recently being redefined by court actions and Supreme Court decisions. *Libel* invariably refers to written charges and *slander* to spoken charges. *Slander*, however, is now seldom the basis for court action. Where *libel* is concerned, proving malicious intent is paramount, but it has not always been necessary to prove that the charges themselves are false. Also, standards may be less stringent when someone is criticizing, even unfairly, the public acts of people in public life. See ACCUSE, BELITTLE, LIE.

Antonyms: PRAISE.

malleable

ductile
plastic
pliable
pliant

These words refer to things that can be molded or bent. **Malleable** and **ductile** refer most specifically to the working of metals. *Malleable* indicates a metal, such as gold, that can be beaten easily into thin sheets or other forms at will. *Ductile* refers specifically to the ease with which a metal, such as copper, can be drawn out into a continuous wire; sometimes it can also refer to the readiness with which fluids will follow a given course. In this sense, water is more *ductile* than mercury. When these two words are used to describe responsive minds, *malleable* suggests an innocent or unformed character that easily takes an impression and can be decisively altered by the conscious attempts of another person or by propaganda: the age at which a normally *malleable* student is most open to influence, whether for good or ill. *Ductile* appears less commonly in this context; when it does, it suggests the capability of being subtly led toward a not always stated goal: a demagogue flattering his all too *ductile* audience.

Pliable and **pliant** are closely related. Used of physical objects, *pliant* often suggests something that resumes its shape after being bent: a *pliant* reed. *Pliable* is often used for something that will remain in any shape given to it: a *pliable* whip; *pliable* putty. When applied to character, consequently, *pliable* should suggest a greater openness to impression than *pliant*: half-truths purveyed to *pliable* minds; a readiness to learn that was *pliant* but not incredulous. Frequently, however, these words are used with no discernible difference in meanings.

Plastic most often refers to any substance that can be molded and then hardened or set: *plastic* buttons; a *plastic* construction helmet. But the word can refer to any synthesized substance, however treated, that is initially a liquid or gel: *plastic* shower curtains. Because of its overriding use in these cases, other uses of the word may be losing ground. *Plastic* can refer to an impressionable mind when it is still moldable, unformed, or not yet fixed: the first years of life when the psyche is at its most *plastic*. The word can also refer to the creative impulse in general or to sculptural or three-dimensional qualities: the poet's *plastic* ability to find new forms for new subject matter; a building considered strictly as a set of *plastic* values; the unique *plastic* designs of the choreographer's ensemble work. See ADAPTABLE, COMPLIANT, SUPPLE.

Antonyms: inflexible, intractable, recalcitrant, refractory, rigid, STUBBORN, *unyielding.*

These words refer to people taken as a group. **Mankind** points collectively to all people, past, present, or future, as an entity about which statements can be made. The word can sometimes tend to sound high-flown or flowery, suggesting a context of formal rhetoric or solemn oratory; often the word functions as a personification that implies a unity of thought, action, and sensibility that can be generalized from the contradictory and diverse actuality. Hence, the word may be used as a quasi-poetic or persuasive term rather than as a rendering of defensible or exact observation: arguing that *mankind* has always struggled forward no matter what obstacles lay in its way; basing his politics on his view of *mankind* as insatiably greedy and intent on self-aggrandizement. The word can, of course, appear more neutrally without these liabilities: the cultures of *mankind*; a multivolumed work attempting to take in the whole history of *mankind*.

Humanity can have the same high-toned flavor as *mankind*: *humanity* in its age-old struggle for survival. By implication, however, the word points more exclusively to favorable qualities such as compassion, understanding, and the ennobling emotions: instincts of love and self-sacrifice that have always pervaded *humanity* in times of crisis. *Humanity*, in fact, can refer collectively to this bundle of ennobling or civilizing virtues, whether it is seen in a single person or in all people: a man of unmistakable sympathy and *humanity*; UNESCO's attempt to show the common *humanity* expressed in all the cultures of the earth. **Homo sapiens** is a scientific term for *mankind* as the only surviving species of the genus Homo; the term would appear in biological or anthropological discussion, particularly in making distinctions between this species and other animals: the relation of *Homo sapiens* to the other primates. The term would sound affected in a more general context. **Man** can be used as a less formal or technical term in scientific discussion: studying the evolution of *man*. This word can also be used like the first two words, however, as a personification that includes all people of all times: *man's* incessant temptation to solve his problems by using his fists instead of his brains.

Humankind, the most formal of these words, can sound even more high-flown than the first pair of words. Unlike *humanity*, however, it need not suggest only ennobling traits: the puerile attempts of *humankind* to understand the cosmos. Where *mankind* might be used to treat people collectively in narrative generalization, emphasizing a past-to-present progression, *humankind* lends itself to aphoristic statements about abiding traits, often stated in the historical present. [*Humankind* listens to the wisdom of its prophets once a week, but the bulletins of its warlords once an hour.] **Men** is like *humankind* in tending to suggest a present-tense statement about the enduring qualities of people, good or bad: pointing out that *men* are the only animals that kill for pleasure. Unlike *man*, this word would seldom be used in scientific discussion; both words, of course, include women in the implied grouping, but *men* as a collective is more ambiguous about this, since it can also be used as a collective for all human males, as well. *Men* is useful in historical discussion since it avoids the suggestion of personified unity implicit in *mankind*, applying where *mankind* cannot to point out diversity or conflict among people: the first attempts of *men* to settle disputes through reason rather than violence. See FOLK, KIN.

mannerism

affectation
air
airs
exhibitionism
pose
preciosity

These words pertain to the use of attention-getting devices or to the adoption of insincere, artificial, forced, or pretentious behavior. **Mannerism** and **affectation** both disapprovingly indicate an instance of such behavior, but *mannerism* is the milder of the two words, suggesting a noticeable but minor oddity of gesture or speech that may be either deliberate or habitual: adopting a few British speech *mannerisms* because she thought they lent her a mark of distinction; He waved his hands about as he talked — a nervous *mannerism* that he'd unconsciously picked up from his parents. Sometimes, the word can apply to any obtrusive stylistic device: coy *mannerisms* that mar her prose style. *Affectation* concentrates more exclusively on the deliberate adoption of anything that is ornate or pretentious: speech studded with faded poeticisms and other *affectations*; He thought it was an *affectation* nowadays to include finger bowls in the table settings. The word can also serve as an abstract collective for pretentiousness in general: Sincerity and simplicity are the archenemies of *affectation*.

Air and **pose** can both indicate adopting a contrived appearance or manner in order to create an effect or to impress others: She walked with an *air* of haughty disdain past the other schoolchildren; his *pose* of being one of the world's foremost authorities on contemporary art. *Air* might well suggest a momentary attempt to create a certain mood; as such, it is less disapproving than *pose*, which suggests greater contrivance and willingness to deceive. *Pose* can, in fact, extend to roles assumed by swindlers or extortionists: his *pose* of being a blind man, adopted to win the sympathy of his victims. Both words, but particularly *air*, can also refer not to deliberate role-playing but to the mood or impression that someone gives off: She faced us with an *air* of utter bewilderment; inadvertently discovered him pleading with his wife in a *pose* of genuine contrition.

Airs refers exclusively to grandiose *affectations* that do not correspond to one's real situation; the word's use is mostly restricted to a few stock phrases: giving oneself *airs*; putting on *airs*. **Preciosity** refers to striving after a rarefied refinement that might appeal to an arty or genteel coterie: stilted speech and an overall *preciosity* of manner. Often the word refers to artistic style or esthetic taste: a *preciosity* that made him prefer the Pre-Raphaelite painters to Turner. By contrast, **exhibitionism** refers to any sort of attention-getting acts. By implication these may well constitute the very opposite of refinement by being loud, garish, crude, or obstreperous: muscle boys strutting and flexing their biceps in self-fascinated *exhibitionism*; the unruly *exhibitionism* of some habitués of the discothèque. In a psychiatric context, the word can refer to a serious disorder in which someone has a compulsion to expose his genitals to a passing stranger or bystander. See CHARACTERISTIC, ECCENTRICITY, TEMPERAMENT.

marginal

inconsequential
minor
negligible

These words refer to anything that has little bearing on a given question or that is slight in quantity or importance. **Marginal** and **peripheral** both point to a small degree of value, usefulness, or importance: a *marginal* increase in pay. Of the two, however, only *marginal* can suggest something that an opposing force has almost but not quite canceled out: a *marginal* profit once costs had been accounted for; *marginal* culture traits left by an incomplete assimilation into the cultural majority.

Peripheral is more restricted to something that has slight importance; at its most specific it can point to something that may be important in itself but is not relevant to a given situation: the Civil War being of *peripheral* concern to that period of California history. Both of these words can, of course, indicate something that is distant from a center or lies at the edge of some entity: a book filled with *marginal* notations; *peripheral* vision.

Negligible adds to the general possibilities of the previous pair a particular implication of a slight amount, suggesting something so small that it can be safely ignored: arguing that only a *negligible* rise in atmospheric radioactivity had resulted from the test; a *negligible* variation that could not affect the outcome of the experiment. **Piddling** is a much more informal substitute for *negligible*, concentrating more exclusively on amount or value, particularly monetary: a *piddling* allowance. But it can also refer more vaguely as invective to weak arguments or to anything thought to be small-time: a *piddling* explanation; a *piddling* second lieutenant.

Both **inconsequential** and **minor** concentrate mainly on a lack of importance. *Inconsequential*, like *negligible*, can indicate a lack of relevance: an *inconsequential* objection to our plan. But it can function explicitly as indicating a lack of power or social status: an *inconsequential* person. *Minor* may function similarly to other words here, but unlike them it can point to something of considerably greater importance, though such a thing would still remain clearly subsidiary, secondary, or subordinate to a main point or concern: any combination of *minor* failings that could yet add up to disaster; separating those important Elizabethan poets, major and *minor*, from those of *marginal* or *negligible* interest, while ignoring completely those who have proved to be totally *inconsequential*.

All the preceding words emphasize a relative slightness of quantity or importance. **Nugatory** is the one word here that emphatically stresses an absolute and unqualified lack, in this case of worth or meaning: avant-garde experiments with language that were *nugatory* both in sense and influence. See DEFICIENT, EXTRANEOUS, SCANTY, TRIVIAL.

Antonyms: *central*, SIGNIFICANT.

marsh

bayou
bog
everglade
fen
morass
paddy
swamp

These words refer to stretches of land in which soil and water, often stagnant, are intermingled with no clear demarcations, a situation that results in unstable footing or presents resistance to navigation. **Marsh** indicates a shallow, stagnant expanse of standing water enclosed by wet and treacherous soil: a trail that swooped in a wide circle to avoid the *marsh*. **Swamp** suggests a large *marsh* that has some patches mainly of wet soil and others mainly of muddy water: They poled through the *swamp* in a flat-bottomed boat, but had to get out and drag the boat whenever it got mired. Both *marsh* and *swamp* may suggest the presence of vegetation such as grass or even trees; *swamp*, particularly, might suggest an almost impassable overgrowth.

At its most literal, **fen** can specifically suggest a *swamp* overgrown with vegetation and filled with fetid water. **Morass** more often indicates low-lying, soft, wet ground in which one can be easily mired. Both words, however, are now more often used metaphorically, *fen* for an evil or unsavory situation, *morass* for entangling complications into which it is easy to be drawn but from which it is difficult to escape, once involved: a city that was a *fen* of vice and corruption; a *morass* of work that threatened to overwhelm him.

The remaining words all suggest a *marsh* or *swamp* that has a specific locale and a particular set of topographic features. **Everglade** points to a low-lying subtropical swamp covered with tall grass: the Florida *Everglades*. **Bayou** indicates a marshy inlet or outlet of a lake or river; its root is a Louisiana French word borrowed from the Choctaw Indian word for a small stream: the *bayous* of the Mississippi delta. **Paddy** comes from the Malay, referring to flooded lowlands in the Orient where rice is grown: peasants working in the terraced rice *paddies*. **Bog** is drawn from an Irish word for soft, referring to wet, spongy soil that is overgrown with grass: peat *bogs* from which the Irish harvested a fuel for heating and cooking. *Bog* is the only one of these localized words that can apply more widely. In this case, it refers to soft, wet soil that provides only treacherous footing and from which it is difficult to extricate oneself; the metaphorical implications here are more clearly seen in the word's verbal form: *bogged* down in another useless man-to-man talk with his father. See PLAIN (n.).

masculine

male
manly
mannish
virile

These words refer to characteristics that ideally or appropriately pertain to men. **Masculine** may refer, most neutrally, to what is true for men in general, as distinguished from women: a *masculine* tendency to defer to women on such subjects. The word becomes more emphatic, however, when it evaluates men according to how near they approach some ideal for the whole group: Both men had *masculine* builds, but one of them seemed quite dull-witted; taunted because he was thought less *masculine* than the other fellows in his platoon. In this context, the word can suggest, as well, an excess of qualities normally exhibited by men: wondering if she were expected to fall over in a faint at the *masculine* charm he exuded. The word can also refer to women, with either a neutral or pejorative tone: those women's fashions that have taken on an increasingly *masculine* look; a woman rather *masculine* in appearance.

Manly is more restricted than *masculine* in applying exclusively to desirable qualities that approach those thought ideally *masculine*: a *manly* determination to fight back at his oppressors; a trim, *manly* body. It would never refer to men in general, to *masculine* excesses, or to women, whether neutrally or pejoratively. **Male** may be used, of course, merely in classification, pertaining as well to species other than human: a *male* dog; the contrast between *male* and female voting patterns; *male* hormones. Beyond this use, the word functions very like *masculine* at a more informal level: *male* attitudes that once excluded women from participation in public affairs; a perfect example of *male* stupidity. The word may be factual in qualifying something typically thought the province of women: a *male* nurse. It is less likely than *masculine*, however, to be used for unfeminine women. When the word evaluates men, its emphasis is not so much on an attained ideal as with *manly*, but on qualities that are intensely evocative of *masculine* sexuality: the coarse, *male* attractiveness of her rescuer. **Virile** is exclusively restricted to this last implication of *male*, emphasizing strength either of mind or body, but especially of sexual potency: She liked a man who felt *virile* enough to dispense with the usual *masculine* arrogance she found so tedious. *Manly* and *virile*, in comparison, might suggest a contrast between appearance and performance: husbands who appear *manly* enough but are not really very *virile*.

Just as *virile* is positive and applies exclusively to men, so **mannish** applies in an exclusive and negative way to women. The word is, thus, more heavily shaded toward the pejorative than *masculine* in referring to inappropriately *male* aspects in women: her square, *mannish* build; women's fashions that take over *masculine* styles without ridding them of their *mannish* appearance. See HUSKY.

Antonyms: FEMININE.

These words refer to things of overwhelming size, scale, or weight. Most concretely, **massive** indicates a large mass, bulk, or weight: a *massive* boulder. Weight or bulk need not be implied, however, when the word points instead to something that is imposing or impressive in scale, scope, degree, or intensity: a *massive* painting; a decision that was to have *massive* consequences throughout the succeeding century. In a medical sense, the word points to something extending over or affecting a large area: *massive* swelling.

Ponderous and **hefty** are more restricted than *massive* in that both echo the stress on weight but put less emphasis on sheer size. Relatively formal, *ponderous* points to heaviness that may be unwieldy or unbearable: pyramids made of *ponderous* stones that had to be inched into place. More often the word is used abstractly of something overserious or solemn to the point of dullness: a *ponderous* lecture on the growing immorality of present-day society. The word can also suggest a heavy sort of physical movement that is slow, tortuous, or lumbering: shuffling forward with a *ponderous* gait. Relatively informal, *hefty* can refer more readily to physical heaviness, as of a physique: a *hefty* weight lifter. Its unique area of relevance is to something that is heavy but meant to be picked up and carried: grunting as he lifted the *hefty* briefcase.

Huge and **enormous** contrast with the previous words in stressing sheer size more than heaviness per se. In this sense, both can serve as superlatives for large, with *enormous* being the more formal of the two. In itself, *huge* may suggest a looming tallness or largeness of frame: the *huge* football player; the *huge* balloon that they inflated for the Thanksgiving parade. *Enormous* suggests extension in space on a scale that goes beyond the implications of *huge*: the *huge* man dwarfed by the *enormous* room. Both words can be used metaphorically for something serious, critical, or urgent: the *huge* problems that must be faced if the population explosion is to be checked; *enormous* questions that remain to be answered. *Enormous*, however, may carry implications over from the word enormity in the sense of something abnormal, grotesque, or outrageous: *enormous* crimes committed in the name of justice.

Immense is like the previous pair in stressing size more than weight; where it refers to material masses, the word suggests something dramatically or surprisingly of large scale: an *immense* statue, a hundred times life size. But the word frequently stresses, like *enormous*, extension in space, rather than mass: early explorers who got lost in the *immense*, unchartered Atlantic. Often, the word relates to totally nonmaterial or spiritual entities, with the implication of proportions so great as to swallow up things of normal scale: the *immense* void between the Milky Way and its nearest galactic neighbor. **Vast** concentrates exclusively on extension in space, with a complete absence of implications pertaining to weight or even to measurable or definable size: the *vast* emptiness of the unending desert. In comparison with *immense*, which can suggest three-dimensional largeness, *vast* more readily suggests two-dimensional extension: the *immense* volume enclosed by the cathedral's domed nave; the *vast* lawns surrounding the Manor House. See HEAVY, HUSKY, LARGE, SIZE, TREMENDOUS.

Antonyms: MINUTE, SMALL, THIN.

massive

enormous
hefty
huge
immense
ponderous
vast

mature

age
develop
mellow
ripen

These words refer to the process of growing up or growing old. **Mature** is the most formal of these; in its most restricted sense, it indicates the natural attainment by a living thing of its adult or fullest form. [Caterpillars eventually *mature* into butterflies; Boys *mature* more slowly than girls, both physically and psychologically.] Outside this strict but neutral reference, the word can register approval for the gaining of wisdom, experience, or sophistication, particularly when this process is not necessarily inevitable: childhood hardships that *matured* in him a precocious sense of responsibility.

Age, unlike *mature*, need not refer to fruition or tempering; instead, it more often refers to the changes that result from the mere passage of time: a study of how body tissue *ages*. The word can often, in fact, refer to negative or destructive changes that occur as a living thing grows old: lines and wrinkles that revealed how much she had *aged* since I had seen her last. *Mature* is sometimes euphemistically substituted for *age* in this sense, as though the former's positive reference to fruition might soften the latter's presumed harshness in suggesting declining vigor: She had *matured* into a lovely grandmother. *Age*, however, can apply to man-made products with favorable force: whisky that has been properly *aged*. Here, it suggests valuable or desirable qualities that only time can impart. When applied to inanimate objects in general, *age* applies less positively to the attrition resulting from time's passage: unpainted houses that had *aged* because of decades of exposure to the elements.

Develop is more like the first sense of *mature* in pointing to positive change in which an existing or rudimentary form is improved, evolved, or perfected. In referring to normal biological growth and change, the word can apply more generally than *mature*, since it can be used to refer to a part as well as a whole organism, and can indicate less ambiguously other transitions than the one culminating in adulthood. [When the breasts begin to *develop*, girls are already well on their way to *maturing* into young women; The fetus *develops* lungs relatively late in the gestation period.] When the word does not refer to predictable biological change, it is more general in application, most often referring either to the improvement or detailed elaboration of something: He joined a gym to *develop* his body; a committee set up to *develop* a program for dealing effectively with air pollution.

Mellow concentrates on aspects of *mature* and *age* that pertain to the tempering imparted by time or experience. The word specifically suggests a reduction in harshness or the moderating of an extreme position: As they *mature*, many young radicals *mellow* into a more tolerant attitude toward life and society. In this sense, *mellow* is more positive than *mature* and *age*, since it gives overtones of glowing warmth, mildness, and amiability. **Ripen** is a less formal and more vivid term for *mature*, with the same reference to the attainment by something of its final or most *developed* form. At its most literal, the word applies to fruit, describing the process that brings it to its most usable or edible: Apples that were green a week ago have already *ripened*. Metaphorically, the word often refers to the filling out or enlarging of a spatial form: the girl's *ripening* body. Used in a more general way in reference to people, the word often suggests not the attainment of adulthood but a *mellowing* process in later life; here the word often points to a gain in wisdom, like one sense of *mature*, but is in less danger of being felt as euphemistic: Rembrandt slowly *ripened* into a command of the insights typical of his last great phase. Sometimes the word more simply refers to any sort of increase or growth: The reader's interest is sure to *ripen* as he gets deeper into this new suspense novel. See FINISH, FULL-FLEDGED, OLD, PERFECT, REACH.

Antonyms: regress.

These words refer to someone who is no longer a child or to something that has attained its final stage. In a biological context, both **mature** and **adult** can refer descriptively to any living thing that has completed the cycle of growth and development normal to the first stages of its existence: Peach trees are considered *mature* when they begin bearing fruit; spots that have disappeared from the coats of *mature* deer; the *adult* fruit fly. *Adult* may sometimes suggest sharp and definable differences between young and *mature* individuals, whereas *mature* can suggest that such classification is less clear-cut or is a matter of degree: the average height of the fully *mature* Sequoia. In the context of neutral classification, *adult* is more often used as a noun than as an adjective when the reference is to people. By contrast, *mature* can suggest an old person, rather than one who has just attained adulthood, although in this case the word is often a euphemism: a dialogue between *adults* and teen-agers; a dress shop for *mature* women. Both words also refer to psychological stability in adults; here, they are used interchangeably as approving fad words for sane, rational, or considerate behavior: a woman who had never learned to relate to other people in an *adult* way; Both husband and wife must be tolerant and *mature* if their marriage is to retain its vitality.

Experienced indicates someone whose familiarity with something is based on considerable actual practice. By implication, this past immersion in a subject has resulted in superior understanding: an *experienced* proofreader; an *experienced* lover; an *experienced* leader. Sometimes, no gain in wisdom need be suggested by the word so much as a piling up of involvements: She was *experienced* and worldly-wise, but had learned nothing from her many adventures. Also, the word need not be restricted to adults: already an *experienced* actress at ten years old. By contrast, **full-blown** can apply to anything that has reached its highest point of development, which may well be the point immediately preceding decay or senescence. Its literal reference is to a flower in fullest bloom, but the word applies widely beyond this situation: the starlet's *full-blown* figure; the unearthing of a *full-blown* plot to overthrow the government. Sometimes, the word can have a critical tone for something excessive or overemphatic: a *full-blown* bore.

Grown-up can be used as an informal alternative for *mature* or *adult* in reference to rational or sensible behavior: He told his daughter that she would be given *grown-up* privileges as soon as she stopped acting like a child. Like *adult*, the word often appears as a noun, particularly when used by youngsters: children who distrusted all *grown-ups*. **Full-grown** emphasizes that something has reached its normal size: a *full-grown* grasshopper; a hulking, *full-grown* adolescent. This attainment of full size may or may not correspond with the transition point at which the individual can be considered *adult*. By contrast, the phrase **of age** refers specifically to the transition point, often arbitrarily set by law, after which a person is considered to be *adult*: a young man can be drafted at nineteen, but may not legally come *of age*, at least in terms of voting, until he is twenty-one. Anthropologically, the phrase can indicate the point at which a society accepts a young person as a *full-grown* adult. See FULL-FLEDGED, OLD, SUMMIT, URBANE.

Antonyms: CHILDISH.

mature

adult
experienced
full-blown
full-grown
grown-up
of age

mean

connote
denote
imply
indicate
signify
suggest
symbolize

These words refer to the agreed-upon ideas or things that words or signs stand for. **Mean** is the least formal and the most general in embracing every kind of import a sign may have, whether explicit or implicit. [A red traffic light *means* stop and a green light *means* go; What do these symptoms *mean*?; You will have to state exactly what these terms *mean*; Does his frequent cursing *mean* he is capable of violence?] **Suggest**, by contrast, concentrates specifically on covert or implicit qualities or associations in signs or language: He claims to mean one thing, but his choice of words *suggests* quite another.

Indicate stresses a rough approximation of literal meaning, whereas **imply** stresses the unstated associative or peripheral overtones present in a sign or word: a flashing beacon to *indicate* that a stretch of road was undergoing repairs; a choice of imagery that *implied* a fear or contempt of women, whether unintentional or conscious. *Imply*, when compared with *suggest*, stresses subtlety or complexity of association; *suggest* stresses tentative alternatives in meaning or a permissible variety of interpretations: mystery plots that *imply* anyone could be guilty of the crime in order to *suggest* a bewildering array of false leads to the unwary reader.

Denote specifically refers to what a term strictly or literally *means*, while **connote** refers to all the possible associations that are *implied* or *suggested* by a term. [Scientists are interested in stripping language down to what it can exactly *denote*, while psychologists, poets, and literary critics are interested in all the hidden or penumbral associations words *connote*; Bright *denotes* intense light, but in certain contexts it can also *connote* purity or beauty or other intangible qualities.] *Connote* is closer in meaning to *imply* than *suggest*, but it is more formal and technical than either and is best reserved for linguistic or epistemological discussion.

Signify and **symbolize** stand in roughly the same relation as *denote* and *connote*, with *signify* suggesting a simple, literal meaning and *symbolize* suggesting a rich cluster of abstract concepts that are invested in a word, gesture, or object. [The legend of a map tells what each sign and abbreviation *signifies*; The cross to the Christian and the mandala to the Buddhist *symbolize* a body of doctrines and beliefs that might require volumes to spell out in explicit detail.] *Symbolize* is different from *imply*, *suggest*, and *connote* in stressing a deliberate compression of complex ideas into a concrete token that stands for them. *Signify*, like *mean*, can be used in a more general way to emphasize any aspect of conveyed understandings; sometimes the word is used especially to refer to the deepest import of an expression rather than to its more obvious or superficial aspects: analysis that gives not only the who, what, when, and where of the news, but also what these bare bones *signify*. See HINT, MEANING, SYMBOL.

meaning

implication
import
sense
significance
signification

These nouns refer to the ideas conveyed by words, phrases, symbols, actions, or events. **Meaning** has the widest range of use, embracing everything from specific, concrete denotation to a general suggestiveness. The *meaning* of a word, sign, or symbol is the idea it expresses, the object it designates, or the concept it conveys. Words may have both literal and figurative *meanings*, both of which can be expressed in definitions, but the *meaning* of a word in any given instance often depends upon the context in which the word is used. In less restricted usage, *meaning* may apply to anything expressed as a message or intent, whether verbally or in some other fashion: to look for an artist's *meaning* in his paintings. *Meaning* may also apply to motivation, purpose, consequence, or even justification. [We debated the *meaning* of his strange behavior; What is the *meaning* of this intrusion?; the real *meaning* of the cold war.] Finally, in its most abstract, connotative use, *meaning* simply indicates expressiveness, pointing to the presence of valuable insights or important intimations without specifying what they are. [His speech struck them as being full of *meaning*, in contrast to the hollow proclamations of the others.

Signification relates to specific *meaning*. It points to an official or agreed-upon *meaning*, one recognized and understood by all who are acquainted with a certain word, term, or symbol: the *significations* of standard abbreviations such as lb. and oz.; the *signification* of heraldic bearings on a coat of arms; the legal *signification* of the word incompetent. **Sense** compares with *meaning* in a broad as well as a narrow application. It often points to different kinds of use or interpretation, implying that a word has two or more *meanings* or ranges of *meaning*, or that a text has two or more levels of *meaning*: a punster playing on widely different *senses* of the same word; the symbolic *sense* of *Moby Dick*. Unlike *signification*, which is confined to a fixed *meaning*, *sense* may indicate a connotation or understanding: He is a liberal in the best *sense* of the word. It may also refer to an overall *meaning* or impression: to get the *sense* of an article written in a foreign language, even though some of the words may be unfamiliar. Something that makes *sense* conveys a clear, understandable, or logical *meaning*.

Import is less clear-cut than *signification*, indicating an intended *meaning* that may need interpretation. More than *meaning*, it indicates the grasping of an idea, pointing to someone's understanding of what has been suggested or expressed. [He stated the *meaning* of the passage in a paraphrase; Commentators explained the *import* of the president's speech; She guessed the *import* of her friend's long silence.]

Implication applies to *meaning* that may have been hinted at but that has not been actually stated or expressed in so many words. It emphasizes suggestiveness, referring almost exclusively to debatable possibilities of interpretation inherent in a statement, act, or situation. *Implication* is thus not nearly so certain as *import*, contrasting even more strongly with the precision and definiteness of *signification*. Nevertheless, the *implications* of a thing, read rightly, may be far more important to a proper understanding of it than its literal or surface *meaning*. [He was pleasant and polite, but the sinister *implications* of his remarks were not lost on his audience; She misinterpreted the *implications* of his letter and thus misunderstood his intentions.]

Significance is akin to *meaning* in its wider *sense*. It mingles *meaning* and importance, referring to the underlying ideas or *implications* that give to words, deeds, symbols, or events a special relevance. [His remarks were fraught with *significance*, but few gathered their full *import*.] *Significance* may also be used in a specific *sense*, suggesting a need to determine which of several possibilities is most relevant. [The *meaning* of their statement refusing to negotiate was never in any doubt; Its *import* of cooler relations between the two countries is also plain; But what *significance*, if any, do you place on the statement's mildness of tone?] See HINT, MEAN, SYMBOL.

These words refer to anything serving or used to accomplish a purpose. **means**
Means is the most general word. In a concrete sense, it points to a device or contrivance used to carry out an action or perform an opera-

means
(continued)

agency
instrumentality
medium

tion. [A hammer is a *means* of driving a nail; A cab was his *means* of getting to the theater.] In a broader, abstract sense, it refers to method, system, or technique: the *means* by which a politician may extend his power. [The harnessing of falling water is a *means* of generating electricity; Statistical analysis is a *means* of arriving at a fairly reliable forecast.] Ways and *means* are methods of accomplishing an end, and this phrase is sometimes specifically directed to governmental finance and fund raising: the chairman of the House Ways and *Means* Committee. *Means* may also be applied to persons and things considered in terms of their past, present, or potential usefulness. [He is the *means* of our achieving victory; art for art's sake as opposed to art as a *means* of spreading propaganda.]

   Agency suggests causation and implies active intervention. Unlike *means*, it would not be used of a passive tool employed by others in their action. Instead, it indicates a force, operation, or process that on its own produces a certain effect. [Carbon dioxide is converted into oxygen through the *agency* of plants; Corruption in government was exposed through the *agency* of the press.] Applied to persons, *agency* often indicates a deliberate working or acting on behalf of others: The dispute was resolved through the *agency* of mediators. An advertising *agency*, employment *agency*, or travel *agency* is a business that serves clients, acting in their interests and helping them attain their goals.

   Instrumentality is much more formal than the foregoing but is close to *means* in scope. It focuses on the instrument acting or being used to accomplish someone's purpose. [Through the *instrumentality* of a travelers' aid society, the lost boy was found and returned to his parents.]

   The term **medium** has the greatest number of specific senses that relate to the overall concept of *means* — all stressing the intermediate position of the *means*. Unlike *agency*, *medium* may refer to an intervening substance through which a force may act or in which an effect may be produced. [Copper is a good *medium* for the conduction of heat and electricity; Air is a *medium* of sound.] *Medium* may also designate a *means*, technique, or vehicle of expression, or the material used for such expression. [For her, poetry was a congenial *medium*; a sculptor whose favorite *medium* is stone] In a spiritualistic sense, the word *medium* denotes a sensitive, often a woman, who goes into a trance so that spirits may supposedly speak through her, using her as a mouthpiece for communication with the living. Opposed to this passive mediumship are other senses of the word that refer to a more active intermediary. Here, most commonly, *medium* is applied to modern channels of communication, often appearing in its plural form *media*. Radio, television, newspapers, and magazines are known as the mass *media*. Television is an advertising, entertainment, and news *medium*. A modern communications *medium* itself — the *means*, techniques, and effects of transmission — may seem to some more interesting and influential than the material or message the *medium* conveys. In this case, it is no longer a *medium* in the strict sense of the word, but an end in itself. See IMPLEMENT, METHOD, PERFORMER, REPRESENTATIVE, WEALTH.

meddlesome

interfering

These words describe someone who involves himself, without invitation, in the affairs of others, or who hampers them with unwelcome attentions. **Meddlesome** can suggest either of these situations; if the former, unwarranted curiosity is implied; if the latter, a self-important insistence on giving advice is masked as helpfulness: not able to tell her what had

meddlesome
(continued)

intrusive
nosy
obtrusive
officious
prying
snoopy

happened until their *meddlesome* neighbor had left; forcing upon them in the most *meddlesome* way peremptory advice about their trip. **Interfering** makes no reference to curiosity, but otherwise is close to *meddlesome*, except that it is more neutral and may suggest a less disagreeable or self-righteous approach. [A well-intentioned but *interfering* friend is better than a *meddlesome* mother-in-law.]

Prying, snoopy, and **nosy** stress offensive curiosity to the exclusion of other meanings. The extremely informal *snoopy* and *nosy* can suggest an avidity for spying on others, gathering gossip, or soliciting private information by posing leading questions. *Snoopy* may suggest a sneaky or stealthy approach in acquiring information: a *snoopy* landlady looking through her roomers' closets while they are out; a *snoopy* child, always eavesdropping. *Nosy* may indicate more forthright methods, quite literally suggesting the act of sticking one's nose into someone else's business: *nosy* neighborhood gossips. The more formal *prying*, however, goes further than either of these to suggest an absolute violation of privacy by any means whatever: *prying* questions.

Officious is now generally taken to refer to someone who, unasked, bustles about making arrangements, volunteering advice, offering unwanted services, or giving orders exactly as though he were discharging official duties. This meaning gives the word a degree of specificity none of its synonyms possess: a very *officious* woman, so bossy that no one could abide her.

Intrusive may suggest a pushing oneself in where one is not wanted, or may point to undue curiosity: an *intrusive* guest, arriving uninvited, breaking in upon their solitude. [She had always lived with them but was never *intrusive* in any way; Unknowingly *intrusive*, he had a knack for asking embarrassing personal questions.] **Obtrusive** is applied to a person who disrupts other people's affairs, either by calling attention to himself or by making self-aggrandizing suggestions or *officious* offers that are offensive and unwelcome. Where *intrusive* emphasizes the fact of a breach of privacy or other interruptive influence, *obtrusive* implies a loud, brusque, or unduly obvious way of butting in: maintaining a silent watchfulness that dampened the discussion with its *intrusive* disapproval; a member who disrupted the meeting constantly with *obtrusive* remarks and catcalls. See EFFRONTERY, ENCROACH, OVERHEAR.

Antonyms: incurious, inobtrusive, unobtrusive, unofficious.

These words refer to attempts to come between, reconcile, or compromise opposing extremes. **Mediate** is the most general of these, carrying the most overtones of meaning. The word refers to any attempt to bring extremes together or to function as a form of communication between them: *mediating* between labor and management in the dispute. In this example, the implication is that the intermediary can advise or show good will but not demand or order a settlement of differences. *Mediate* can also be applied to the divisive disagreement itself, or to its resolution: to *mediate* a dispute by seeking to find a middle ground on which the disputants can agree; to *mediate* a compromise settlement. In another use, *mediate* may simply indicate the occupying of a midway position between extremes: stable countries that have a sizable middle class to *mediate* between the extremes of wealth and poverty. The word may also be used of something that acts solely as a link or communicating agent: a church that *mediates* between God and man.

Intercede stresses a coming forward to stop a dispute in progress from continuing or getting worse, although it does not necessarily suggest that such action will solve the dispute: asking the federal government to *intercede* in the civil rights struggle before it erupted into real violence. Often the word is used to suggest a third party's being drawn into an argument in order to plead for one side or the other: asking the queen to *intercede* in his behalf.

Interpose is sharply in contrast to *mediate* in that it suggests a blockage of communication between two hostile forces. It resembles *intercede* in that no solution need be applied, but the suggestion of stalemate is stronger: an international police force that could be *interposed* along the borders between two hostile nations. Again, like *intercede*, *interpose* may indicate entrance into a dispute on behalf of one side, although in this case the act is limited, by implication, to defense: enabling the courts to *interpose* themselves between an unjust law and the rights of any individual threatened by that law.

Intervene contrasts with these other words by suggesting from the outset a more self-interested attitude in disrupting a dispute, usually to favor one side or another. The word would not be likely to refer to a mere stoppage, but does often suggest an intensification of hostilities: a nation refusing to *intervene* in the Spanish Civil War, though its sympathies lay with the Loyalists. As in the last example, the word can often suggest an unwanted meddling in other people's business, and thus can impart a pejorative tone. See INSERT, JUDGE.

mediocre

commonplace
fair
ordinary
passable
second-rate
so-so
tolerable

These words all apply to something less than good, and they all express in varying degrees a sense of disappointment or dissatisfaction. **Mediocre** is the most general, and suggests disappointment at the undistinguished quality of a thing. Calling a performance of a play *mediocre* means that the performance was neither very good nor very bad, but suggests that one had expected it to be better. *Mediocre*, then, like the rest of these words, is a relative term; and it may, like most of the others, be preceded by a qualifying adverb, such as *only* or *just*, to emphasize its disparaging implications. [Considering her reputation as a gourmet, the dinner she served was only *mediocre*.]

Ordinary and **commonplace** are probably closest to *mediocre* in meaning, but *ordinary* is broader in application and usually expresses a somewhat less severe judgment. [How was the book? Nothing very exciting, just *ordinary*.] *Ordinary* can also mean simply uneventful, in which case it connotes no disparagement at all: an *ordinary* summer day, with a cloudless sky and the hum of insects in the air. *Commonplace* stresses the disparity between one's expectation of originality or uniqueness and the disappointingly *ordinary* or vulgar reality. It often expresses the haughtiness or arrogance of one who has high standards or a keenly critical attitude. [It was a *commonplace* observation — anyone might have made it.]

Fair and **so-so** are close synonyms. Both occur rather more often in speech than in writing, and are thus somewhat more informal in tone than *mediocre* and *ordinary*. Depending on the context (or tone of voice with which they are uttered), *fair* and *so-so* can range from cautious approval to moderate disgust. They are often deliberately used in a noncommittal way, as to conceal bad news or a low opinion, often out of politeness or from the wish to keep one's own affairs private. [How do you feel now, after your operation? Oh, *so-so*; How did you like the book I lent you? It was pretty *fair*.] *Fair* is also used as a rank in a grading scale: excellent, good, *fair*, poor.

Passable and **tolerable** are both examples of damning with faint praise. *Passable* suggests bare adequacy; it expresses the attitude indicated by a shrug of the shoulders and the comment, "Well, things could be worse." If something is *passable* one is simply forced to make do with it out of necessity rather than choice. [She didn't really like the hat, but it was *passable*, and it couldn't be exchanged; The movie was just *passable* — there were one or two good scenes, but the acting was bad and the plot fell apart near the end.] *Tolerable* has a wider range of meaning than *passable*. While it may mean barely adequate, it does not always emphasize *barely*, as *passable* does, but may in fact emphasize *adequate*. [It was a *tolerable* salary, one you could live on if you knew how to keep a budget.] When used to describe someone's health, *tolerable* is informal and has a decidedly provincial or dialectal flavor.

Second-rate, when opposed to first-rate, is the most obviously derogatory of the words in this group; but when it is used in a scale of values that includes even lower categories, it joins *passable* in being a backhanded compliment. [He is definitely a *second-rate* writer, not fit to stand in the shadow of Hemingway or Faulkner; It's a good *second-rate* school, strong in some departments and weak in others, but certainly better than a great many other schools in this area.] See NORMAL, USUAL.

Antonyms: *distinctive*, EXCELLENT, *fine*, *good*, *original*, OUTSTANDING, *superior*, UNPARALLELED, UNUSUAL.

---

meet

contact
encounter
get in touch with
see

These words express the action of coming together with another or others. **Meet** is the most general word and has the widest range of application. It may mean simply to come upon: He *met* her there by chance. Or it may indicate a previous appointment: He promised to *meet* her at the restaurant at noon. In one specific sense, it may mean to go to or be at the place of a traveler's arrival: They *met* her at the station, so she didn't have to hire a cab. In some contexts, *meet* refers to a formal introduction or to the making of a new acquaintance. [Have you *met* my mother?; They *met* a very interesting couple at the beach.] Or it may indicate an assembling, as for a conference. [What time is the committee to *meet*?] In a restricted, literal sense, *meet* may stress a face-to-face approach. [He pulled out to pass and *met* another car, head on; While going to St. Ives, he *met* a man with seven wives.]

Of the remaining words, **encounter** is the closest synonym for *meet*, but it strongly implies a casual or unexpected *meeting*. [He *encountered* many interesting people on his travels and mentions a few memorable ones in his memoirs; They came sneaking around the corner and *encountered* a policeman.] *Encounter* may also mean to *meet* in conflict or face in battle. [They *encountered* one another on the dueling grounds; We *encountered* the enemy in various small border clashes.]

The phrase **get in touch with** implies the establishing or renewing of communication. It is conversational in tone. [When you are in London, you might *get in touch with* a friend of mine.] **Contact** used as a verb meaning to *get in touch with* is still regarded as informal, although it seems to be gaining more and more acceptance in the written language. *Get in touch with* and *contact* are both quite useful when the particular means of communication is not indicated. [I haven't been able to *get in touch with* him, though I've tried writing him, phoning him, and going to his office; We'll *contact* you later; I will have to *contact* my lawyer before I can give you a definite answer.]

See in one sense is close to *encounter*, referring to a chance *meeting*. [I *saw* your husband downtown the other day.] In a special sense, it refers to the granting of an appointment, interview, or date, or to the reception of guests. [The doctor will *see* you now; Her blind date asked if he might *see* her again; Madame is ill and is not *seeing* anyone today.] See MEETING.

Antonyms: AVOID.

meeting

assemblage
assembly
conclave
conference
congregation
congress
convention
convocation
council
gathering

These words are used to refer to the coming together of a number of people. **Meeting**, **gathering**, **conference**, and **assembly** are the most general and informal. As listed, these four words form a gradual progression toward greater specificity and formality. *Meeting* can apply to every situation in which two or more people come together, by accident or design, for an encounter, whether momentary or prolonged. It can range in application from trivial or everyday situations to the most portentous or official occasions: the weekly *meeting* of the cub scouts; a summit *meeting* of the heads of state. *Gathering* differs from *meeting* in its specific reference to a group of more than two people; it is like *meeting* in other respects, including its wideness of application: a chance *gathering* of people in the coffee house; the annual *gathering* of the clan. *Conference* has more formality than either of the foregoing; but, like *meeting*, it can imply a group of two people as well as of more: a *conference* with my advisor; the scheduled disarmament *conference* at Geneva. *Assembly* distinctly implies a *gathering* of many people and tends to suggest a planned *meeting* more than an unplanned one: the school's weekly *assembly*. It is also sometimes used specifically to designate the lower house in some state legislatures. [The governor was holding a *meeting* with his Senate leader to cut short the subcommittee's protracted *conference* on a bill which the *Assembly* had already passed; The *gathering* of newsmen in the corridors was tense and restless.]

Assemblage, used as an exact synonym for *assembly*, would sound archaic. Even more important, it is often used currently in a pejorative sense: an *assemblage* of hypocrites and incompetents.

The remaining words of this group are similar in being more specific than the previous words and very much more formal as well. **Conclave**, **congregation**, and **convocation** refer primarily to religious *assemblies*, though they can extend to other kinds of *meetings* as well. *Conclave*, most specifically, refers to the *gathering* of cardinals to elect a pope. Overtones of this use remain in more general applications, including solemnity, secrecy, and high purpose: political candidates elected by direct primaries or by party *conclaves*. *Congregation* is even more restricted in use, referring to the adherents of a religion who attend the same local church: the pastor's *congregation*. In a narrow sense, the word can designate those actually present at a given service, and in a broad sense, it can embrace all of a church's parishioners. *Convocation* implies a *meeting* that has been called by a higher authority: a *convocation* of Episcopal clergymen summoned by their bishop. It is also used by college social groups with no implication of being called together from above.

Congress, **convention**, and **council** often refer to governmental or political bodies. On an international scale, a *council* may include delegates from many different nations. In ecclesiastical terms, the word may refer specifically to a clerical parliament called to decide on matters of church doctrine and discipline: the *Council* of Trent; the Second Vatican Ecumenical *Council*. An international *council*, however, is more often a secular agency or body: the Economic and Social *Council* of the United Nations; the UN Security *Council*. On a national or local level, *council* usually indicates either an appointed advisory committee or an elected administrative or legislative unit: the President's *Council* on the

Fine Arts; the city *council*. In either case, it implies a small, select group, whereas *congress* and *convention* suggest larger *assemblies* or *gatherings*. A *council's* *meetings* may be closed to the public, like those of a *conclave* and unlike those of a *congress* or *convention*. Purely private organizations may also use the word in their titles: the *Council* on Equal Housing. In all but the ecclesiastical use, a *council* consists of its members whether they are gathered in a *meeting* or not.

Congress is narrower in application than *council*, being most commonly used in a governmental sense, particularly of an elected legislative body: the United States *Congress*. Another meaning survives, however, in the names of some private associations: the *Congress* of Racial Equality; the *Congress* of Industrial Organizations. *Congress* may also refer to a formal *meeting* of the representatives of sovereign nations, having as its purpose the settlement of certain questions: the *Congress* of Vienna. *Convention*, in its political sense, refers to a scheduled meeting of delegates to pass resolutions and elect leaders (or nominate candidates): the quadrennial Democratic and Republican *conventions*. *Convention* is also often used to refer to a state or national *meeting* of members from various local branches of a private organization, as a professional association, social club, or fraternal order. In this kind of *convention*, business is conducted, but many of these *gatherings* are looked on chiefly as social occasions: the Shriners' *convention* in Chicago. Where the term *convention* is typically used of national *meetings*, international *meetings*, as of scientists, are more often referred to as *congresses*: an international *congress* of geophysicists. See CONSULT, GATHER, GROUP, SUMMON.

melody

air
aria
lied
song
theme
tune

These words refer to a recognizable succession of pitches in the same voice, whether played or sung. **Melody** may refer to the pleasing or esthetically satisfying quality of such an entity: a composer noted for his exquisite *melodies*. Or it can refer neutrally to the leading voice in a musical composition: harmonizing the *melody* for a four-part choral arrangement. As a generic word, it can refer to one of the three basic ingredients of music, the one pertaining to the linear sequence of intervals: *melody*, harmony, and rhythm.

Theme refers to a *melody* or recognizable sequence that is treated in a musical composition by such means as statement, development, and recapitulation. In this case, the sequence may occur or recur in any voice or even be spread out among two or more voices: a *theme* first stated in the cellos and then referred to in fragmentary form by other sections of the orchestra.

Song in its neutral senses usually refers to a *melody* rendered by the human voice: a *song* for soprano or tenor; a popular *song* recorded by the leading crooner of the day; folk *songs* performed by the three singers to guitar accompaniment. The word can refer more widely to any rendering of *melody*: bird *songs*; whistling a *song*. In its most general sense, the word may suggest approval for any sort of lyrical intensity, as of poetry: a poetic tradition rich in *song*.

Tune is more informal than *song* and suggests a *melody* that is simple, direct, and catchy: infectious folk *tunes*. The word may refer to the music, as distinct from the words, of a *song*: stark words set to a lovely *tune*. Often, the word suggests *songs* of less than the highest esthetic rank: show *tunes*; the grating *tunes* of singing commercials.

Aria, derived from the Italian word for *song*, refers to any of the set pieces in traditional operas and oratorios. The word contrasts the formal organization and lyrical intensity of such a piece, usually a solo, with the looser, more low-key passages of recitative that surround it. *Aria* can, more generally, function like *song* to refer to any instance of lyrical intensity, but particularly those in which a single person is given the floor to express himself, often in an ornate manner: one long *aria* about how cruelly he had mistreated her.

Air is the exact English counterpart for *aria*, but it is now rarely used except in reference to early English music, often indicating the self-contained simplicity of a folk *song* rather than the ornate flourishes of a formal piece composed as part of such longer compositions as an opera: Scottish *airs* and ballads.

Lied is the comparable German word for *song*, used in English to refer to the art-song form developed by such composers as Schubert and Wolf: the Schubert *lied* about the beggar man. More often it is used in the plural, referring generically in this case to the German art-song literature or to art *songs* in general: an evening of *lieder*.

melt

dissolve
liquefy
thaw

These words refer to the process by which a solid is transformed into a fluid. **Melt** is the most general of these, referring to such a transformation of any solid: ice cubes that had already *melted*; listing the different temperatures at which various metals *melt*. Used metaphorically, the word indicates any emotional yielding, usually one in which rigidity or indifference gives way to responsiveness or affectionate concern: a story designed to *melt* the hardest heart; feeling her resistance to him *melting* away at their first touch. **Thaw** is a specific instance of *melt*, stressing the application of heat as the cause of the *melting* process, and referring mainly to the transformation of ice or snow into water: signs that the snowdrifts had begun to *thaw*; wondering when the stream would *thaw*. But the word has a special use in referring to frozen solids that remain more or less hard even after being subjected to warming: not certain whether the frozen vegetables should be plunged into boiling water or be allowed to *thaw* out first at room temperature. The word, also, can refer to any warming process: sitting by the fire to *thaw* out his cold feet. Metaphorically, the word suggests a more gradual yielding to emotional warmth than *melt*: their ceremonious reserve began to *thaw* a bit.

Dissolve may function identically to *melt*: cakes of ice slowly *dissolving* into puddles. More strictly, however, the word refers to the specific process by which a solid passes into solution in a solvent: *dissolving* the tablet in a glass of water; a cleaning agent that *dissolves* stubborn grease stains. By extension, the word is used of any supposed disappearance or eating away of solids: snowbanks that seemed to *dissolve* overnight; erosion that had *dissolved* acres of topsoil. Metaphorically, the word can suggest a collapse after having yielded to a strong emotion: *dissolving* into laughter at his discomfiture; *dissolving* into tears at the news. **Liquefy** is the most formal of these words and gives a technical or scientific tone. Its usefulness lies in referring generically to any conversion into a liquid state, whether by heat or pressure, and applies both to the conversion of solids and gases: temperatures too low for mercury to *liquefy*; using high pressures to *liquefy* nitrogen. The word is not commonly used to apply metaphorically to emotional states. See WARM.

Antonyms: crystallize, freeze, harden, jell, solidify.

merit

These words are related in meaning in that they denote in this context qualities or traits that are highly desirable and praiseworthy. **Merit** refers to attributes that are commendable, though not necessarily su-

perior, and may be predicated to that which has more favorable than unfavorable qualities: His first novel, sketchy and immature as it is, does,
nevertheless, have *merit*. When *merit* is qualified by a negative word it,
tends to emphasize a preponderance of unfavorable characteristics rather
than the presence of only a few. [As a work of serious scholarship in the
field of history, the work has little *merit*; Her singing is totally without
merit.]

merit

(*continued*)

excellence
value
virtue
worth

Excellence denotes qualities that are superior to an unusual degree,
and it is much stronger and more positive in concept than is *merit*. However, since the word does not indicate perfection, it is often modified by
an intensifying adjective. [The particular *excellence* of her cooking lies
in her skillful blending of spices; We were impressed by the technical
excellence of his draftsmanship.]

According to the meanings limited to these words as a group, **value**
and **worth** have the sense of intrinsic *excellence*. *Value*, however, points
to characteristics regarded highly for their usefulness: the *value* of a
sensible diet and exercise in maintaining good health; the *value* to a
medical student of thorough undergraduate training in the biological and
physical sciences. *Worth*, on the other hand, applies to things that are
esteemed more for their own sake than for their utility: the great *worth*
of a long, close friendship; the *worth* of being able to take pleasure in
small things.

Virtue, which in this sense has nothing to do with morality, is applied
to qualities that give a person or thing its *value* or *worth*. [The great
virtue of air travel is speed; Although this house lacks the *virtue* of architectural beauty, it is well-arranged as to space and is comfortable to live
in.] See PERFECT.

Antonyms: fault, FLAW, *unworthiness, weakness, worthlessness.*

These words refer to a set or habitual technique for doing a task.
Method suggests a fairly elaborate group of techniques and stresses
efficiency or accuracy as its goal. **Way**, by contrast, is much more general, since it can refer either to a single technique or to a complex operation; it is also more informal and carries no suggestions about the technique or operation itself, positive or negative. [The *way* most students
study is appalling; they lack any sense of *method*.] *Way* does have a
special use that refers to someone's characteristic approach to a problem:
Don't mind him; it's just his *way*. It may even suggest a whole life
style: John's *way* of doing things; a paranoid's *way* of taking criticism;
the democratic *way* of settling arguments.

method

fashion
manner
mode
procedure
system
way

Procedure and **system** relate to the elaborate efficiency implied by
method rather than to the characteristic style that may be suggested by
way. Both, however, stress an even greater elaborateness than *method*.
Procedure, the most formal of all these words, suggests an orderly cut-
and-dry set of *methods* established by a person or organization for coping
with routine or bureaucratic details: a *procedure* for withholding income
tax; a *procedure* for routing a bill through Congress. *System* may refer
to a whole bundle of *procedures* established by a person or organization,
written or unwritten; it emphasizes the meticulous working out of every
detail: the *system* for selecting draftees. Unlike *procedure*, it can be
used pejoratively, in which case it refers to a conservative, entrenched
establishment: every genius who ever had to fight the *system*. It can
refer neutrally, however, to any functioning entity: the body's circulatory *system*. It can also apply to any elaborate scheme, whether functional or not: a *system* for beating the slot machines at Las Vegas.

Manner, **fashion**, and **mode** refer more to a characteristic style than to an elaborate *method*, *procedure*, or *system*. All three may be used merely as less informal substitutes for *way*, with *mode* approaching excessive formality. Each, however, has special nuances all its own. *Manner* may suggest the good or bad carrying out of a *method* or the characteristic conduct of someone: results that depend as much on the *manner* of executing the plans as on the plans themselves; a querulous *manner* of speaking. *Fashion* may also stress execution, but is strongly influenced by its other meanings pertaining to those styles of living currently in favor: a new *fashion* of wearing her hair. *Mode* suggests the choice of one category out of many: street gangs as a *mode* of venting frustration and hostility. It is especially used in discussions of art: a *mode* of writing in which normal syntax is suppressed to give the effect of chaotic thought processes. See ACCURATE, COMPETENT, SYSTEMATIC.

migrate

emigrate
immigrate
move
travel

These words refer to the movement of people or animals from one place to another. **Migrate** suggests the movement of a large group: the Teutonic tribes that *migrated* to Britain; mallards that *migrate* south in winter. **Emigrate** and **immigrate** refer to permanent movements, mainly of people, whether singly or in small or large groups. *Emigrate* involves movement from a place; *immigrate*, movement to a place. [Irish peasants *emigrating* from their homeland during the potato famine were one of the many groups who *immigrated* to America in the nineteenth century.]

Move has a special sense of leaving one house or apartment for another: people *moving* from the city to the suburbs. Outside of this specific use, it is the most general word here, suggesting any change of locale under any circumstances: *moving* rapidly through the crowd in search of the lost child. **Travel** has a special sense of taking a relatively brief trip to a place where one does not live, without necessarily intending to stay there: *traveling* to Europe on a tramp steamer; *traveling* from one port to another in search of excitement. In more general senses, it emphasizes the mere act of getting somewhere: *traveling* to work by bus or subway. See COME, JOURNEY, LEAVE.

Antonyms: REMAIN.

mind

brains
head
intellect
intelligence
reason
wits

These words pertain to the mental capacities or qualities of people. **Mind** is the most general and most neutral. It may refer exclusively to mental facility; in this case only qualification indicates how strong or weak such facility is: challenges that stimulate those students with good *minds*; a *mind* too dull to grasp present-day scientific theories. The word can also refer to a bundle of mostly conscious attitudes (including the will), or to the whole psyche, conscious or unconscious: those who have set their *minds* against intolerance; a *mind* afflicted by irrational impulses. The remaining words are all more nearly restricted to mental ability or rational faculties alone.

Intellect and **intelligence** both refer more exactly and more formally than *mind* to mental ability. *Intellect*, the more restricted of the two, refers mostly to ratiocinative facility. It can be used informally to describe mental alertness or accomplishment: a professor with quite an *intellect*. Used more formally in description, it requires qualification to indicate degree: a mentally ill person with a relatively weak *intellect*; the highly developed *intellect* characteristic of his whole family. Of the two words, *intelligence* is the more commonly used, although it refers to a range of mental faculties wider than that suggested by *intellect*. Mental alertness, problem-solving ability, and keen perception of relationships are all implicit in *intelligence* when used without qualification: delighted to be working, at last, with students of *intelligence*. The word can also suggest, with qualification, the degree to which these traits are possessed singly or in combination: weak in mechanical skills but otherwise showing a strong *intelligence*; tests to determine the verbal *intelligence* of very young children.

Brains, head, and **wits** are all very informal words for aspects of *intelligence*. *Head*, the most restricted, usually pertains to a single faculty, often of a practical nature: a good *head* for figures; keeping a cool *head* throughout the crisis. *Brains* suggests a wider scope, like *intelligence*, but often refers to mental ability that has practical results: It takes *brains* to land a cushy job. *Wits* refers specifically to alertness or sensitivity rather than to a general mental facility: warning him to keep his *wits* about him. Like *mind*, it can also refer to the conscious or rational *intelligence*: scared out of her *wits*.

Reason refers solely to the objective, rational part of the *mind*; it is one aspect of *intelligence*. In use, it is referred to as though it were a technique, rather than a faculty: using *reason* to trace the murderer from the clues surrounding the crime. The word may also, like one use of *wits*, refer in a common-sense way to normal sanity: lost his *reason*. As an abstract noun, it can indicate a rational, unemotional, openminded approach: the hope that *reason* rather than prejudice would prevail in the community. See ACUMEN, KEEN.

These words refer to a religion's clergy — that is, those who lead a congregation in worship or belong to teaching or monastic orders. **Minister** refers exclusively to a Protestant clergyman who has been authorized to administer sacraments and conduct religious services. Even more restricted in scope, **pastor** in this context refers to those *ministers* who have churches or congregations under their official charge. Someone with such a charge may, consequently, be called either a *minister* or *pastor*, although of the two, only *pastor* is used as a title: *Pastor* Jones. By contrast, a *minister* without a charge would not properly be called a *pastor* or be so addressed or titled. *Pastor* has a further use in that it can refer to a Catholic as well as to a Protestant clergyman who is officially in charge of a congregation or parish.

Preacher and **reverend** also apply to the clergy of some Protestant faiths. *Preacher* is much more informal than the previous words and if officially sanctioned as a designation, might suggest denominations that eschew formality or ritual, or emphasize revivalism: farmers who rode into town to hear the new *preacher*; *Preacher* Smith. In other denominations, the word might be used in informal speech to refer to the *pastor*, particularly in his role of addressing a congregation in sermons; in this case, the word may have a whimsical or affectionate tone — or it may be used contemptuously, depending on context: a sedate congregation clearly displeased by this fire-and-brimstone *preacher*. *Reverend* is an informal noun derived from its more formal adjectival use in reference to Protestant or Catholic clergymen. As an adjective it may properly appear as part of a title or courtesy phrase: the *Reverend* Dr. Jones. It may appear in other set phrases before a name, such as the Right *Reverend* or the Most *Reverend*. It is often thought inappropriate or incorrect when any such title is shortened to the one word alone: *Reverend* Jones. Similarly, the word as a noun may be informally substituted for *minister* or *pastor*, but many disapprove of this usage.

minister

brother
father
monk
pastor
preacher
priest
reverend

In Catholic and Eastern Orthodox churches, **priest** designates a member of the clergy who has been authorized to administer the sacraments; if he has a parish in his charge he may be referred to as a *pastor*, but in any case, he may be addressed as **father**: *Father* Brown. [Good morning, *Father*.] The word is never used with an article, however, except to refer to the early founders of the church or, collectively, to its leaders: the church *fathers* who fought heresies on the one hand and persecution on the other; a meeting of the *fathers* of the church.

In these same faiths, **monk** refers to a man in holy orders, particularly monastic ones; such a man may or may not be a *priest* as well. If so, he would be referred to as *father*; if not, he would be referred to as **brother**. Unlike *father*, *brother* may well be used with a definite article: the poet who became a *brother* in a Trappist monastery. *Monk* and *priest* both may refer to comparable roles in other religions of the world, past or present: a Buddhist *monk*; a Druid *priest*; a Tibetan *priest*. See CLERGYMAN.

minute

infinitesimal
microscopic
miniature
minuscule

These words refer to sizes or amounts that are exceedingly small. **Minute** describes something so small as to be seen with difficulty; it can, however, refer both to size and amount: a jade carving that teems with *minute* representations of plants and animals; a *minute* trace of poison discovered during autopsy. The word may emphasize that something is small to the point of having no significance or value; it may also indicate something so small as to require careful scrutiny if it is to be understood: a *minute* amount of radioactivity that could hurt no one; a *minute* crack in the wall that led to the amazing discovery. *Minute* has a related use referring to the intensive scrutiny itself: a *minute* examination of the murder weapon.

Minuscule is derived from a word referring to an early script that used lower-case letters. While the word can still refer literally to such a script, more generally it indicates something extremely small, and as such is an intensification of *minute*. *Minuscule* can also refer both to sizes and amounts: a *minuscule* chess set with peg pieces, designed for travelers; a *minuscule* slackening of prices after active trading. When the word indicates amount, however, it is more likely than *minute* to suggest something unimportant or even petty: a *minute* inspection that turned up only the most *minuscule* defects in his argument.

Infinitesimal more commonly applies to amounts that are so small as to be incalculable and insignificant for all practical purposes; more strictly, it reflects its relation to the word infinite by referring to something that is infinitely small. The word is often used not so much literally as in exaggeration: making much of an *infinitesimal* error.

Microscopic and **miniature**, by contrast, refer most often to size. *Microscopic* literally refers to something too small to be seen without the aid of a microscope: the abundance of *microscopic* diatoms that flourish in the sea. *Miniature*, on the other hand, refers to something that is small but by no means invisible or even difficult to see with the naked eye. It suggests most strongly the scaling down of something to small size, as a model. The word relates, by derivation, to small-sized paintings and can still apply in this way. For other things, the word may carry a note of amazement or wonder at the effective job of reducing the proportions of something; it can also suggest an effect of cuteness: a *miniature* dollhouse; a *miniature* castle where children could fight out imaginary battles. See COMPACT, SMALL.

Antonyms: LARGE, MASSIVE, TREMENDOUS.

These words describe the character or behavior of a person who defies convention or authority, and are often used in reference to children. **Mischievous** is to be found in connection with the playful, teasing, but nonetheless irritating behavior that is part of every child's make-up at one time or another. It suggests that the harm done or trouble caused is neither lasting nor severe: The *mischievous* boy went through the house hanging all the pictures upside-down. When used to characterize an adult, however, *mischievous* suggests a manner or action that is more troublesome than playful, more harmful than teasing: a *mischievous* gossip who broke up her brother's marriage by spreading rumors about his wife.

Naughty is commonly used by adults when speaking of a child's misbehavior, and, sometimes, humorously, when speaking of the sexual attraction or peccadilloes of another adult. [You were a *naughty* boy, Johnny, breaking your sister's doll that way; an actress who built her reputation on being "*naughty* but nice."] Although the application of *naughty* to children is usually confined to instances of trivial breaches of conduct, it is sometimes used to refer to more reprehensible action and in such cases can be considered a euphemism for certain senses of **bad**. *Bad* is a very broad word. It can at times be interchangeable with the most innocent connotations of *mischievous*. [What a *bad* little girl you are, smearing jelly all over mummy's new dress.] But it may also describe a child (and, of course, an adolescent or adult) who is willful, intractable, immoral, or evil.

Delinquent as an adjective means neglectful in duty or obligation: a *delinquent* father who spent more time playing poker than playing with his children. This meaning is not very often found in reference to children or young people, possibly because of the very common use of the word in the expression *juvenile delinquent*, which means a young person guilty of antisocial or criminal behavior. It is unfortunate that this expression, which is specific in tone and pejorative in connotation, is applied loosely to young people who are indeed not juvenile delinquents but merely *mischievous*, *bad*, or **disobedient**.

Disobedient is another broad word. It refers simply to a failure or a refusal to obey, but its connotations when it is used to describe a child are different from those applying to an adult. Very young children who are characterized as *disobedient* might instead be called *mischievous* or *naughty*; they are rarely guilty of any serious misbehavior, and their failure or refusal to obey is more an act of will than of reason. Older children, adolescents, and adults, however, who are *disobedient* may be guilty of a major oversight or transgression: a *disobedient* student who was forced to leave boarding school; a habitually *disobedient* soldier who was finally court-martialed after he struck his commanding officer. See BEHAVIOR, BOTHER, UNRULY.

Antonyms: OBEDIENT.

These words may be applied to the personal experience of physical and mental pain or depression or to the things which cause the pain or depression. They are also used to describe things that are below average in character, condition, or performance. When a physical, mental, or environmental state causes great suffering or unhappiness it can be referred to as **miserable**. [I've been struggling along all day with a *miserable* headache; It is sometimes difficult to acknowledge that another person's lot may be more *miserable* than one's own.] The word also suggests something that is worthless or of inferior quality: to waste an

evening at a *miserable* play. **Dismal** describes something that lacks
cheer or joy, and also characterizes the gloomy, depressed feelings that
such a thing can provoke: a *dismal* day, hot and humid with threatening
clouds hanging in the sky; feeling *dismal* after reading a news account
of the latest war scare. In referring to something that is below average,
dismal hints at calamity or disaster: a new business enterprise that
turned out to be a *dismal* failure.

Sorry and **unhappy** describe unpleasant mental states. *Sorry* connotes the kind of sadness, major or minor, that is produced by loss,
injury, misfortune, or the like. It may be aroused by one's own troubles
or those of a friend, and it is often combined with a feeling of regret.
[I'm *sorry* to see my vacation end — it's been a pleasant holiday.]
Unhappy can be a weaker word than *sorry* if it merely indicates the
absence of happiness: *unhappy* about having to go to a dull party.
But it can characterize a more lasting state of discontent: a profoundly
unhappy man with no friends and no interests other than his work.
When used critically, *sorry* often gives an indication of pity, ridicule, or
concern. [What a *sorry* spectacle he made of himself when he got drunk;
The world is surely in a *sorry* state.] *Unhappy* is less general and not as
strong as *sorry* when it is used in criticism to mean unfortunate, unlucky,
not tactful, or inappropriate: an *unhappy* choice of words.

Wretched is stronger in tone than either *sorry* or *unhappy* in its indication of a severely distressed mental state but is interchangeable with
miserable in reference to physical discomfort: the *wretched* civil rights
worker whose wife was shot to death by bigots; He was feeling *wretched*
as a result of a recurrent back problem. When used to describe quality,
ability, or performance, the word is strong again in meaning unsatisfactory or worthless: The opera performance was spoiled because the
prima donna was in such *wretched* voice. See PATHETIC, SAD.

Antonyms: CHEERFUL, CONTENTED, JOYOUS.

misery

agony
anguish
discomfort
distress
passion
torment
torture

These words all denote suffering of body or mind. The suffering may be
the result of some injurious external interference, as a wound, bruise,
harsh word, etc. It may arise from an abnormality in bodily or mental
functions, as disease, envy, or discontent. It may be occasioned by the
lack of something one needs, as food or love.

Misery refers to a chronic or prolonged suffering, whether physical,
mental, or emotional. There is a suggestion of hopelessness about this
word: the *misery* of the arthritic. **Distress** is too strong a word for
little hurts, too feeble for the most intense suffering. It more often than
not is applied to mental states, referring to any deep anxiety or the external circumstances that may produce it. Very commonly it applies to
some prolonged trouble, as does *misery*, but *distress* more than *misery*
implies at least a possibility of relief: the *distress* of an underprivileged
child. **Discomfort** is the mildest of the words in this group, denoting
little more than the absence of well-being and ease: the *discomfort* of a
hot, humid day.

Agony, **anguish**, **torment**, and **torture** all refer to intense suffering
of body or mind. *Agony* and *torture* are perhaps most closely associated
with physical pain. *Agony* represents suffering, the endurance of which
calls forth every human resource. Its severity is of such extent that the
word is often used to denote the struggle and pain that may precede
death: In his final *agony* he called for the religious comfort which he had
rejected for years. *Torture* puts great stress upon the agent which causes
or inflicts it: Nazi madmen who indulged in the *torture* of their victims

before they killed them; the recurrent *torture* of migraine. *Torment* and *anguish* suggest mental suffering. *Torment* hints at repeated or continuous instances of attack: the *torment* of an alcoholic husband. *Anguish* points to the extremity of grief which so terrifies the spirit as to be insupportable: the *anguish* she knew when her husband and three children were burned to death, *anguish* so great that it turned into madness.

Passion, in the sense being compared here, is now limited to the New Testament account of the *anguish* and *agony* of Jesus Christ which culminated in his crucifixion. See HARM, HURT, PAIN.

Antonyms: HAPPINESS, PLEASURE.

These words refer to accidental losses. **Mislay** suggests the absentminded or disorganized act of putting something down where it doesn't belong, without remembering later exactly where it is: afraid that he had *mislaid* the car keys; searching frantically for the *mislaid* deed to the house. The word suggests that the *mislaid* item is of relatively small size and somewhat difficult to keep track of. **Misplace**, on the other hand, would not be so restricted: *misplaced* a whole boxcar of grain in one of the company's many railroad yards. The word, furthermore, can merely suggest bad planning: finding that the table had been *misplaced*, and was too near the open fire. The word can suggest an action that may be intentional or unwise: deliberately *misplacing* the book on a shelf where no one could find it: *misplaced* admiration for another woman's husband.

Lose is the most general of these words, suggesting any accidental failure to keep hold of something one possesses: *losing* the quarter through a hole in his pocket. Whereas *mislay* and *misplace* suggest that the desired item may eventually be found, *lose* may suggest a permanent lack: He hadn't *lost* the letter; he had simply *misplaced* it. *Lose* in its generality has a much wider range of use than these other words: *losing* his way; *losing* the account to his competitor; trying to *lose* the man in the crowd.

Miss is much more specific in this context. It points to the moment when one becomes conscious of having *lost* something: first *missing* his wallet when he offered to pay for the next round of drinks. See FORGET.

Antonyms: FIND.

These words refer to the giving or receiving of mistaken impressions. Although **misleading** is restricted to something that is apt to give a false impression, it is still the most general of these words in that it can apply to great or small potential misapprehensions, whether fostered intentionally, unintentionally, or without any intent whatever: a *misleading* advertisement that deliberately left out the drug's side effects; peace offers that were *misleading* because of inexpert translators; clouds with a *misleading* look of calm to them.

Deceiving and **deceptive** would both seem stronger than *misleading* because an actual lie is implied rather than merely a misapprehension. Nevertheless, like *misleading*, *deceptive* also restricts itself to the possibility, somewhat greater in this case, of a mistaken impression, whether intentional or not. *Deceiving*, however, does suggest both a deliberate and successful lie: vertical stripes that give a *deceptive* impression of greater height; patients who are assured by an intern's *deceiving* air of knowing what he is doing.

Dissembling refers to a deliberate pretense, whether believed or not, and **deceitful**, the strongest of all these words, refers to a constantly

mislay

lose
misplace
miss

misleading

deceitful
deceiving
deceptive
delusive
dissembling

dissembling manner and an ingrained habit of telling lies. **Delusive** functions like *deceptive* except that it suggests mistaken impressions so great as to constitute a complete derangement of mind or a flagrant departure from fact. Because delusions can be the result of mental imbalance, *delusive* often seems to suggest a self-imposed belief that corresponds to one's own wishes or needs. [With a *dissembling* diffidence, the *deceitful* Iago presents *misleading* facts, gives them a *deceptive* turn, and, with a *deceiving* concern for his victim, constructs a *delusive* theory of Desdemona's unfaithfulness.] See DECEPTION, GUILE, LIE, TRICK.

Antonyms: HONEST.

mistake

blooper
blunder
boner
contretemps
error
faux pas
goof
slip

These words denote something done, said, or believed incorrectly or improperly. **Mistake** and **error** are the most common and general words of this group. In many contexts they are interchangeable, but *error* often implies deviation from a standard or model, whereas *mistake* is preferred in the common situations of everyday life. [It was a *mistake* to suppose that George could ever get here on time; an *error* in logic or in arithmetic; a typographical *error*.] *Error* is also used in a theological sense to mean sin, since sin is perceived as deviation from the moral standards or theological truths established by religion.

A **blunder** is a blatant *error*, usually one involving behavior or judgment, and implying an ignorant or uninformed assessment of a situation. [Offering to negotiate with the enemy at that time was an inexcusable *blunder*.] **Slip** and **faux pas** (literally "false step") are minor *mistakes*. *Slip* emphasizes the accidental rather than ignorant character of a *mistake* and is often used to mean the careless divulging of secret or private information: a *slip* of the tongue. A *faux pas* is an embarrassing breach of etiquette. [He forgot that she had remarried and introduced her with her first husband's name — a *faux pas* that made everybody momentarily uncomfortable.]

Blooper, boner, and **goof** are all slang terms, and all have a somewhat humorous tone and a distinctively American flavor. Americans apparently feel that if a *mistake* is outrageous enough it is funny, and this feeling is reflected in their choice of words to describe such *mistakes*. *Blooper* is usually applied to particularly infelicitous mix-ups of speech, such as "rit of fellus jage" for "fit of jealous rage." A *boner* is any egregious and mindless *mistake*. A *goof* is an indefensible *error* honestly admitted, which contains in its admission a covert plea that the *goof* be regarded with indulgent forgiveness. [We really *goofed* this time, didn't we?]

A **contretemps**, literally "counter to or against the time," i.e. at the wrong time, refers to an embarrassing or awkward occurrence. The young girl who puts off a too-ardent admirer by saying she is quite ill and then encounters him that very night at a party has learned the meaning of *contretemps* in a way that she is not likely to forget. See FLAW, FORGET.

mixture

alloy
amalgam
blend

Mixture and **combination** are the broadest of these terms, all of which suggest the bringing together of diverse elements into a new whole. While *mixture* may apply to any materials joined in any way, it is perhaps most appropriate for the adding together of amorphous quantities in which there is no surrendering of individual particles to a new identity: a *mixture* of sand and gravel; a *mixture* of fine tobacco; a *mixture* of peanuts and cashews. Metaphorically, it may suggest fortuitous collocations, as in a *mixture* of luck and perseverance; or it may suggest a mingling of opposites, as in a *mixture* of good and bad. *Combination* suggests a closer union of mingled elements, though not necessarily their fusion: a *combination* of tested ingredients. Metaphorically, it can imply a conscious selection of elements for effect: a striking color *combination* of blues and grays. It can also imply an eclectic distillation: a *combination* of several prevailing dramatic styles; new *combinations* of proven therapeutic techniques. It is more "high-toned" than *mixture* and is often used to confer status on the user.

mixture
(continued)

combination
composite
compound

Composite is more formal still than *combination*, but tends to imply that the materials have been patched or pieced together from disparate sources; in motion pictures, for example, a *composite* is a shot that consists of several superimposed images. The word can, however, suggest a more complete fusion of elements: GI Joe was a *composite* of all the soldiers Ernie Pyle came to know as a war correspondent.

Blend suggests more fusion still and, generally, a loss of individual identity for the elements in a *mixture*: a *blend* of whiskies. The word suggests that skill, control, and conscious intention governed the making of the new whole. While many kinds of material can be used in a *blend*, the word suggests most specifically a *mixture* of fluids or gases.

Alloy and **amalgam** in their most specific senses refer to new metals made by fusing two or more metals in order to obtain valuable properties of each in the new *combination*. *Alloy* is the generic term for any such *blend*, while *amalgam* is a specific term referring to an alloy of another metal with mercury. Metaphorically, *amalgam* is loosely used to mean *combination*, but it most often suggests a confused *combination*: The child's account of what happened was an *amalgam* of fact and fancy. Metaphorically, *alloy* is often used to suggest the *mixture* of a fine quality with a baser one that reduces its purity: an *alloy* of love and possessiveness.

Compound, in its scientific sense, indicates the closest unity of any of these words; it refers to a chemical formed from two or more elements. Water, for example, is a *compound* of hydrogen and oxygen. In metaphorical uses, *compound* is less exact, meaning any *mixture* of things in fairly close relation to each other: a *compound* of wit and intelligence. See COMPONENT, CONNECT, DIVERSIFY.

These words refer to what is new or to what exists now. **Modern** suggests a historical division of time including the present and what has gone immediately before it; this can be a comparatively long or short period. [The discovery of America in 1492 demarcates medieval from *modern* history; Several *modern* schools of painting were unheard of in the 1920's.] *Modern* may also distinguish something in vogue from something old-fashioned, or a present period from an older one: *modern* furniture that looked strange against the Renaissance flavor of the room's architectural details. Like *modern*, **contemporary** may be used to refer to a historical division that includes the present, but it usually suggests a much narrower slice of time than *modern*: the trends in *modern* times that have culminated in certain *contemporary* attitudes. On the other hand, *contemporary* can suggest the mere fact of present existence, while *modern* can suggest something new or vital in spirit: a *contemporary* but hardly *modern* thinker. **Present-day** suggests an even narrower slice of time than *contemporary* but is most often used simply as classification rather than in implying a positive or negative judgment about value: arguing that *present-day* taste was evenly split between *modern* and traditional styles.

modern

contemporary
current
present-day
recent
timely

Recent and **current** stress what exists now; *recent* emphasizes factual classification of the immediately preceding past, a slice of time narrower than *contemporary* but more extended than *present-day*. *Current*, by contrast, emphasizes only those *recent* things that are still viable at this moment. [Of these three *recent* magazines, only one is still *current*.]

Timely, like *current*, refers to things of the moment, but differs from *current* in its ability to refer to things of another time that have again become fashionable or pertinent: Machiavelli's advice on the uses of power is still *timely* in the struggle for corporate leadership. See UP-TO-DATE.

Antonyms: ANCIENT, OLD-FASHIONED, *outdated*.

modest

humble
lowly
meek
retiring
shy
unassuming
unpretentious

These words refer to an absence of assertiveness, a lack of vanity or presumption, or to something moderate or small in scale. **Modest** is the only one of these words that works equally well in any of these three areas of meaning: too *modest* for the aggressiveness demanded of him; touchingly *modest* about her tremendous success; a *modest* bank account.

Meek, **retiring**, and **shy** function only in the sense of unwillingness to call attention to oneself. Whereas *modest* here suggests an inbred wish to avoid indecorousness or boastfulness, *shy* suggests bashfulness based not on decorum but on timidity or a lack of social experience, or both. *Retiring* intensifies this sense of *shy*, suggesting the habit of avoiding any sort of scrutiny altogether, though not necessarily out of fear. A *shy* person, for example, may go to parties but be afraid of taking part in them; a *retiring* person would avoid them completely for unstated reasons of his own. *Meek* suggests a tractable mildness or submissiveness, but not necessarily an avoidance of confrontation as in these other words: One girl was too *shy* to speak, but the others supplied us with *meek* answers to all our questions.

Unassuming and **unpretentious** are close synonyms to *modest* when it suggests a lack of vanity. *Modest* here refers to an understated acceptance of good fortune or recognition, or to behavior that at least acts out such an acceptance. *Unassuming* emphasizes one aspect of this, suggesting that one does not wish or demand that other people treat one in any special way. *Unpretentious* suggests having no illusions about one's relative importance or refusing to inflate one's worth out of proportion to the facts. [He was *modest* about winning the prize, *unassuming* in giving credit to those who had helped him, and *unpretentious* about the new importance it gave him.]

Humble and **lowly** relate to the meaning of *modest* that refers to something on a reduced scale. Whereas *modest* emphasizes moderate, *humble* and *lowly* distinctly suggest small. [*Humble* expectations are best; even *modest* ones are all too often disappointed.] *Lowly*, of course, suggests an even smaller scale than *humble* and is mostly used now only in jocose clichés. [Let us consider the *lowly* housewife.] Unlike *lowly*, *humble* can also suggest a lack of vanity: the great man who is also *humble*. But in either sense it has more and more acquired a patronizing tone when used of other people and an air of sanctimonious piety when used of oneself: the *humble* poor; *humble* citizens like ourselves. In the last example, calling attention so blatantly to one's supposed lack of vanity is not *unassuming*, *modest*, nor *unpretentious*. See DOCILE, SUBMIT, TIMID.

Antonyms: CONCEITED, OVERBEARING, *pretentious*, SHOWY.

mold

fashion
forge
form
model
shape

These words refer to a creative act that works some raw material into a final state of beauty or usefulness. **Mold** suggests the working of some ductile or malleable material into the desired product: *molding* the clay into little figurines; molten alloys that are *molded* into coins at the mint. *Mold* in more figurative uses retains the suggestion of a tractable material: inescapably *molding* the minds of their students, for better or worse. **Form** and **shape** are considerably more general than *mold*. They include the act of compression implicit in *mold* but may suggest many other ways of working, especially with a less tractable raw material. *Form* carries the suggestion of giving outline to something previously less well-defined; it may also suggest putting the finishing touch on a product: *forming* a strong political platform from the many proposals that were submitted, amended, and finally approved. *Shape* suggests the bringing about of a more far-reaching change than is suggested by *form*; it may also suggest an impersonal cause-and-effect relationship: *shaping* an intricate mosaic from bits of glass that lay about in seemingly confused and unrelated piles; policies that will *shape* our course for some time to come.

Forge suggests, most strictly, heated metals that are worked with anvil and hammer: *forging* pieces for a wrought-iron balustrade. In figurative uses it suggests a great expanse of labor to work out a solution against considerable resistance: negotiators who *forged* the final draft of the agreement. **Fashion** suggests none of the extremes of effort implicit in *forge*; it is very close to the literal denotation of *form* and *shape*, and is used figuratively in much the way that *mold* is, referring to the influence of instruction or conditioning on a person: *fashioning* a talented amateur into a brilliant actor. The word may sometimes suggest an improvised solution: *fashioning* from her hairpin a crude device with which to open the lock.

Model relates to *mold* in the specific sense of working a malleable raw material: children who *modeled* clay for an hour each morning. The word is more frequently used, however, in the sense of displaying an example of someone's work, especially in relation to designers of women's clothes: choosing mannequins to *model* an entirely new line-up of spring clothes. Another still viable use of this word refers to construction that is carried out along the lines of an earlier example: new countries who *model* their constitutions on ours; *modeling* his spy story on all the clichéd situations used in earlier best-sellers. See CREATE, MANUFACTURE.

These words denote pigmented or reddish marks or nodules on the skin that may be permanent and either are present at birth or develop later on in life. **Mole** refers to a type of permanent spot which may vary in color from yellowish brown to dark brown. *Moles* are usually congenital in origin and may be large or small, flat or protuberant, some having sprouting hairs. Occasionally they become malignant and are often removed either for cosmetic reasons or as a precautionary measure if they grow larger or undergo any change in appearance. At various times in history a *mole* on the face of a woman, especially on the cheekbone, has been highly prized and referred to as "a beauty mark" or "beauty spot" because it serves to set off the whiteness of the skin.

A **birthmark** is often a *mole*, but *birthmarks* may also take other forms, most commonly that of elevated pink or bright red growths (called in medicine hemangiomas), sometimes covering large areas of the skin. Popularly called "strawberry marks" or "port wine stains," such *birthmarks* are composed of clusters of small, surface blood vessels and capillaries. No effective treatment is known for this type of blemish. **Nevus** is the technical term for both *mole* and *birthmark*.

Freckle applies to one of a large colony of small, flat, brown or tan spots on the skin, which are not congenital. They tend to appear on the fair, rosy complexion of people with sandy or red hair and multiply when the skin is exposed to the sun, and often fade or disappear entirely during the cooler seasons. Unlike *moles* or *birthmarks*, freckles are rarely considered blemishes, as they are very common and often considered attractive.

Melanism is a fairly rare condition of the skin or deeper tissues in which there are abnormal deposits or patches of dark pigment, or melanin. *Melanism*, while sometimes present at birth, may arise from a disorder of pigment metabolism or as a result of constant handling of certain toxic substances, such as tar or pitch. See NEOPLASM, WART.

mongrel

cur
hound
mutt

These words are comparable in that they all are used to designate a kind of dog, and in a pejorative way, a kind of person. A **mongrel** is any animal or plant of mixed breed, but especially a dog. Since there is a strong suggestion of illegitimacy about a *mongrel*, such a dog is often looked down upon by dog fanciers. It may, indeed, be this somewhat contemptuous feeling for *mongrel* dogs which has given the pejorative connotation to *mongrel* when it denotes a person who is not of a pure race, whose parents are of different national or social backgrounds, or one whose tendencies, political opinions, religious convictions, etc., are undefined or uncertain. [Ever since the governor took office the only consistency about him has been his inconsistency; the man has proved himself to be a political *mongrel*.] **Cur** in its denotation of a dog is synonymous with *mongrel*. But whereas a *mongrel*, in spite of its questionable ancestry, can be looked on as a worthwhile pet, a *cur* is despised by the dog lover as an inferior, ugly, or unfriendly beast. The same feeling reserved for this *cur* greets the mean, malicious, cowardly, or otherwise objectionable person who is described by the same name: a man with pretensions to honor and bravery who proves himself a *cur* in the face of the slightest danger. **Mutt**, when it designates a dog, is synonymous with *mongrel* and *cur*, but, even more than is true with *mongrel*, *mutt* frequently refers to a loved pet rather than to one that is thought to be worthless. A person who is a *mutt* is stupid or doltish. Although such a person is not held in high esteem, he is usually not treated with the contempt or disdain accorded one called *mongrel* or *cur*. One might, in fact, feel the same kind of affection for the human *mutt* that is shown for the less than pedigreed dog.

Hound is, like the other words in this group, general in its designation of a dog of any breed or background. It can, however, be specific in a way the other words cannot, when it refers to any of several particular breeds of hunting dog. When *hound* denotes a person it may characterize someone who is detestable in the way that a *mongrel* or *cur* is. But it may also refer, in an informal way, to a person who is fond almost to the point of addiction of a certain pastime, activity, food, etc.: a bridge *hound*; a hamburger *hound*. See ANIMAL.

monotonous

boring

These words are all used to describe someone or something that induces a state of dissatisfaction or weariness. **Monotonous** originally meant unvaried in inflection, cadence, pitch, or tone: It was incredible that a lieder singer of her reputation should have such a *monotonous* voice. This meaning was later extended to refer to anything that is so lacking in variety as to cause fatigue or annoyance: The views from my train window grew *monotonous* after an hour or two and I found myself dozing off. **Dull** has many meanings, but in the sense being compared here, it is used to characterize a person or thing that is uninteresting, as from a lack of variety, spirit, attraction, delight, etc.: a *dull* performer; a *dull* book; a *dull* meal. That which is **boring** may be *dull* or *monotonous*: a *boring* movie unrelieved by dramatic conflict, wit, or even a decent bit of acting. *Boring*, however, more than the other words in this group, can refer to that discontent and indifference known as ennui. This feeling may be a reaction to some person or thing, but it may also be the result of spiritual torpor and a general dissatisfaction with life. **Tedious** is like the preceding words in meaning but it goes beyond them in its suggestion that monotony or inactivity causes a repression of energy and an attendant physical discomfort: The month I spent confined to a hospital bed was so *tedious* that I couldn't wait to get back to work. *Tedious* also refers to the kind of boredom one feels as a result of wordiness in speech or writing: The lecture was so *tedious* that people began to leave the auditorium before it was half over. **Tiresome**, like *tedious*, implies fatigue: a *tiresome* day filled with exhausting household chores. The word also has connotations of annoyance that are stronger than those in the four other terms: a very beautiful woman, but *tiresome* because of her bad temper. See LISTLESS, NUMB, SLOTH, STUPID.

Antonyms: diversified, exciting, interesting, stimulating, varied.

monotonous
(continued)

dull
tedious
tiresome

All these words refer to acts that are in accord with a code of right and wrong. **Moral** and **ethical**, once indistinguishable from each other, have recently taken on fine distinctions in meaning. *Moral* is now more often used in a quasi-religious sense, *ethical* in a quasi-legal sense: the *moral* rectitude of a saint; a law outlining *ethical* practices for legislators. *Moral* might be thought to include this narrower sense of *ethical*, making the one term generic, the other specific, but *moral* has more and more come to mean personal conduct as set by an external code or standard, especially when such conduct does not affect numbers of people: a *moral* standard that specified moderation in food and drink and an avoidance of worldly pleasures. *Ethical*, by contrast, is more and more taken to describe just and fair dealings with other people, not by the application of an external standard but by a pragmatic consideration of all aspects of a situation in light of past experience. To put it most extremely, *moral* can often be taken to mean private, codified, rigid, and a priori; *ethical* to mean public, improvisatory, flexible, and a posteriori: agreeing, despite differing *moral* values, on *ethical* ways to work with each other. The split between the two words, however, is by no means as sharp as this attempt to contrast them might suggest; they do overlap; they can still be used interchangeably.

Upright and decent are more informal than *moral* and *ethical*, but they shade away from each other in much the same way as the first pair. *Upright* may suggest an inner *moral* strength, *decent* an outgoing *ethical* concern for others. While *decent*, in fact, has no pejorative uses, *upright* can sometimes suggest excessive rigidity: stiff-necked, *upright* Puritans.

Virtuous and **honorable** are slightly more formal than *moral* and *ethical*, but the same contrast in shadings can be felt. Here, *virtuous* suggests a private life free of blemish, whereas *honorable* suggests *decent* and *ethical* dealings with others: a *virtuous* young girl; those businessmen who are both competitive and *honorable*.

Righteous, of course, strongly suggests someone who lives almost

moral

decent
ethical
good
honorable
righteous
self-righteous
upright
virtuous

faultlessly in accordance with strict *moral* standards. The word now is somewhat less used than previously except in such expressions as *righteous* indignation, which is indignation aroused by injustice or a lack of fair play. Otherwise, *righteous* tends to suggest priggishness, narrow-mindedness, and intolerance: an unambitious but gentle man who had the misfortune of being married to a *righteous* woman. The more common **self-righteous** is always pejorative and stresses pharisaism and an exaggerated sense of one's own moral superiority over that of others. **Good** is a vague, general synonym for any of these words and cannot be restricted to specific shades of meaning. See CHASTE, GOODNESS, HONEST, TRUST.

Antonyms: dishonorable, UNETHICAL.

moron

dope
dullard
dummy
idiot
imbecile
numbskull
simpleton

All of these words can be used as invective against someone thought to be stupid or foolish. **Moron, imbecile,** and **idiot** formerly functioned neutrally as classifications for degrees of mental deficiency, *moron* denoting a mild deficiency, *imbecile* a moderate level of deficiency, and *idiot* a degree of severe deficiency. Nowadays the phrase "mentally retarded child" (or person) preceded by a qualifying word such as mildly or severely is the preferred term, both in popular and technical writing, for any of these levels. As invective, little distinction exists between the three terms.

Dullard and **simpleton** both lack the precise denotations of the previous group, but they do refer to a slow-witted rather than to a foolish person. *Dullard* is the more formal of the two and suggests a mild degree of mental deficiency that renders one passive, unresponsive, or imperceptive: appalled to find that her class seemed to be filled with *dullards* and borderline students on probation. *Simpleton* suggests greater deficiency; it has a faintly archaic flavor that sometimes brings to mind a touching innocence or sweetness of disposition: the class *simpleton* whom we all loved for his good nature despite his inability to learn.

The remaining words all are extremely informal. **Dummy** suggests someone prone to making foolish mistakes: such a *dummy* that he kept setting himself on fire by smoking in bed. Except for its much greater informality, **dope** is like *dullard;* but as used, it suggests ill-advised or foolish behavior rather than mental deficiency: a *dope* to try swimming against such an undertow. **Numbskull** must once have seemed a vivid coinage, but now, through overuse, it has faded somewhat as a term for a hopelessly stupid person: *numbskulls* who drop out of school. See BLOCKHEAD, PSYCHOTIC, STUPID.

Antonyms: genius, intellectual, sage, savant.

motive

incentive
inducement
reason
spur

These words all denote stimuli that prompt one to action. **Motive** connotes some impulse within a person — such as love, hate, revenge, or ambition — that impels him to act with a strong sense of purpose: The police knew that the murderer's *motive* was jealousy; His real *motive* for joining the club was not to make new friends, but to try to meet potential clients.

Reason is the most general of these words, but in a specific sense it implies a logical justification, either to oneself or to others, for an action, by citing facts and circumstances. [His *reason* for entering the hospital was to undergo surgery; A severe handicap was the *reason* for his shyness.] *Reason* may sometimes hint at a contrived excuse: Although he had overslept, the *reason* he gave for his lateness was that he had been caught in a traffic jam.

Incentive and **spur** are *reasons* for undertaking action with extra zeal. *Incentive* nearly always implies a reward for such effort: prizes offered as an *incentive* to salesmen. *Spur* suggests more strongly than does *incentive* something external to oneself that causes a sudden increase in the rate of activity, as suggested by the original meaning of the word in horsemanship: Finding the cause of a disease will provide a *spur* for research on a cure for it.

Inducement denotes an attractive *reason* for choosing one thing rather than another: The promise of a yearly bonus may be an *inducement* to an executive who is considering a job offer. See STIMULATE.

These words refer to projections of earth or stone that are elevated above the surrounding landscape. **Mountain** refers to a high-rising rocky projection that is typically steep and has a narrow summit. When *mountains* occur grouped together they are collectively called a **range**: the *range* of mountains running from Alaska to the southern tip of South America. A **plateau** is a mountain that has a wide flat top, as though the peak had been sliced off or the *mountain* truncated at some midway point. *Plateau* may also refer to a much more extensive reach of highly elevated level ground that may not seem at all like a *mountain* to someone positioned on it anywhere but at its periphery: people living on the great Arkansas *plateau*. **Mesa**, a word borrowed from Spanish and used in the southwestern part of the United States, refers to a type of small, treeless *plateau*. It is a high, broad, and flat tableland with rocky slopes descending to the surrounding plain.

mountain

cliff
hill
hillock
mesa
plateau
precipice
promontory
range

Hill indicates a projection of earth that is more low-lying than a *mountain*; such a shape may be of considerable size: the Black *Hills*. Or it may point to a very slight rise of ground: the *hill* at one end of the garden. **Hillock** specifically points to such a small *hill*, typically suggesting a brief grassy rise of indefinite or ragged shape: leaving undisturbed occasional wooded *hillocks* on either side of the turnpike.

The remaining words suggest abrupt or jutting outcroppings of rocky forms that may or may not be topographically part of a *mountain*. **Cliff** indicates a high vertical shape that drops away suddenly to a lower level; it is particularly used to refer to the edges or side of a *mountain*, *plateau*, or *mesa*: a widening highway cut into the *cliff*. The word may, however, indicate a sharp break between two level stretches: sauntering out to stand on the *cliff* overlooking the ocean. **Precipice** is less general in referring almost solely to a sharply jutting vertical rise or overhang of rock or stone: the *precipice* made by the steep side of the *mountain*. **Promontory** specifically indicates a high point of land such as a *hill* or *cliff* that extends into the sea: the lighthouse set on a *promontory* that dominated the surrounding landscape.

Mountain and *hill* both have a wide range of metaphorical uses referring to great amounts, weights, or sizes. When they are not interchangeable, the preference of one word to another approaches the idiomatic: a *mountain* of work; this *mountain* of a man; a *hill* of papers on his desk. Used metaphorically, *precipice* usually suggests danger, as from falling: moving closer to the *precipice* of nuclear war. See SUMMIT.

Antonyms: PLAIN.

These words refer to the transportaton of something from one place to another. **Move** is the most general and informal of these. It can suggest the covering of slight or great distances: *moving* the desk a few inches to get better light; having the piano *moved* upstairs. As can be seen, the

move

relocate

move
(continued)

shift
transfer

word can imply great or little effort; it can also refer to the altering of position, as a part of the body, or simply an agitated back-and-forth motion: *moving* his hand to rest on her knee; *moving* about in her seat to get more comfortable; branches *moving* faintly in the slight breeze. Clearly, the word has little connotation in itself and can often be replaced with a more vivid word. It does have exclusive relevance, however, for a person's changing of residence, including the transportation of his belongings to the new address: *moving* from Baltimore to San Francisco; *moving* from a ground-floor apartment to one on the third floor.

Shift may specifically suggest a slight move: *shifting* the heavy refrigerator so that she could clean behind it; *shifting* his legs so that the latecomers could get past him to their seats. The word can also stress an abrupt or considerable change in duties, or a reorganization that results in a physical *move*: *shifted* from his position as sales manager to one of the vice-presidencies; *shifting* the state capital from an out-of-the-way town to a city more centrally located.

Relocate is like *move* in its reference to a change of location or residence. The change may be forced on one, as by a natural disaster or the condemning of one's dwelling: a tenement family which refused to be *relocated*. *Relocating* may be, however, done voluntarily in connection with one's business or job: If a better job were offered you in Chicago, would you *relocate*? **Transfer** is a more formal substitute for *move*, but it is useful to indicate change of occupation or station within the same large grouping; in this it is like one sense of *shift*: *transferred* from field work to administrative duties. The word in itself suggests neither promotion nor demotion but merely change of function. The word is also relevant for *shifting* that involves no actual movement: *transferring* his phone call to the personnel department; *transferring* the money from his checking account to his savings bank. See CARRY, GO, LEAVE, MIGRATE.

Antonyms: REMAIN, *rest*, STOP.

mutual

common
interchangeable
joint
reciprocal
shared

These words refer to something that is possessed or can be used by two or more people or in two or more situations. **Mutual** and **reciprocal** are close in meaning, suggesting most simply some interaction between two parties, in which the same thing is given and taken on both sides: their *mutual* respect for each other; a *reciprocal* lowering of tariffs between the two countries. *Reciprocal* is the more common term in official or technical contexts. Strictly speaking, neither would be used for groups of three or more unless the indicated relationship were true for every possible combination of two. *Mutual*, however, is commonly used for any similarity of interests, views, feelings, even when the relationships are not *reciprocal*: a *mutual* interest in hiking that drew the two boys together; a *mutual* excitement felt by the whole audience.

Common escapes the objections that may be leveled at *mutual*, referring widely to something possessed by two or more people: speaking a *common* language; a *common* interest in silent movies. Because the word can also mean ordinary, however, or even cheap or debased, the word's ambiguity sometimes prohibits its use, a fact which may justify the substitution of *mutual*. A *mutual* friend would unmistakably be one that two or more people were friendly with, but a *common* friend might be a vulgar or coarse person.

Joint exclusively emphasizes the actual possession of something by no more and no less than two people: a *joint* banking account. Since it suggests a unity, as of two halves within a whole, the word would not point to mere similarity of interests: a *joint* business venture in which both put up an equal amount of capital. **Interchangeable** involves a different concept altogether, applying to parts or elements that can be moved from one setting to another without loss of function or can be used one in place of the other: standardized shaving heads that are *interchangeable* from one model of electric razor to another. [Wapiti and elk are *interchangeable* words for a large North American deer.]

Shared gives a tone of even greater emotional warmth than is true for *mutual*; it also can indicate something actually divided up and used by two or more people: our *shared* lunch of bread and cheese. More generally, it can replace both *common* and *mutual* in many contexts, often with a gained clarity or sense of intimacy: our *shared* language; pointing out that *shared* interests often lead to marriage. In some cases the word would be unsuitable: a *shared* friend. Here, an odd tone of possession blurs the intended meaning. See CONNECT.

Antonyms: individual, inseparable, particular, separate, unshared.

These words have to do with matters beyond the ordinary range of one's knowledge, perception, or understanding, with the added suggestion of things kept secret or hidden from all but a favored few. **Mystical** emphasizes the idea of a direct, intuitive, deeply personal revelation, especially one of a spiritual or religious nature: the *mystical* visions of Saint Theresa; John Donne's *mystical* poems; a *mystical* belief in life after death.

An occurrence or phenomenon is **mysterious** if it contains elements that arouse one's wonder, stimulate one's curiosity, and baffle one's efforts to explain it: the *mysterious* universe; a *mysterious* ailment; the *mysterious* properties of a new drug. Here the possibility of a rational explanation remains, the obscurity being the result of inadequate rather than unobtainable knowledge.

Occult, as the word suggests, means hidden or concealed and has come to be applied chiefly to magical arts and practices, as astrology, alchemy, divination. Those who were versed in such secret matters were said to have *occult* powers, not to be freely divulged to others and exerted only under special conditions, usually determined by themselves. Thus, while one may speak of an experience as *mysterious* where the causes are unknown but ascertainable, as *mystical* when it is unique, spontaneous, and usually incommunicable, *occult* implies some agency unknown in human experience without whose deliberate intervention something would not have occurred. See BIZARRE, OBSCURE, SUPERNATURAL.

Antonyms: PLAIN.

mystical

mysterious
occult

N

Like the rest of these words, **naive** suggests either a lack of urbanity or a candid simplicity. The word also suggests a trusting innocence that has not yet been tested; *naive* ideals may be appealingly or exasperatingly out of touch with hard facts, but a *naive* person is not necessarily stupid, only limited in experience. **Unsophisticated** is more specific

naive

artless

naive
(continued)

guileless
ingenuous
provincial
rude
unaffected
unsophisticated

than *naive* in suggesting a lack of worldliness, whether one is experienced or inexperienced; the word may be used as praise or as criticism, depending on the user's attitude toward urbanity: a plain, *unsophisticated* man who can say a lot in a few words; so *unsophisticated* they didn't know what a black-tie dinner was. Unlike *naive*, *unsophisticated* does not necessarily imply a willingness to trust: carnival barkers who misjudged as *naive* their *unsophisticated* but hard-headed audience. **Provincial** suggests lack of exposure to experience, like *naive*, but implies most specifically a life remote from any metropolis or one sheltered from fashionable taste and ideas: *provincial* rednecks who guffawed to see male ballet dancers wearing tights. *Provincial*, in emphasizing remoteness of place, need not suggest innocence: Emily Dickinson and the Brontës were *provincial* but hardly *naive*. **Rude** suggests an extremely unformed taste or character, possibly as a result of a *provincial* life, but it comes near suggesting uncivilized and illiterate, except in rare instances of positive use: a *rude* but honest and stalwart people.

The remaining words deal with the manner in which *rude, provincial, naive,* or *unsophisticated* people might behave. **Ingenuous** is closest to *naive* in suggesting someone who is overly confiding, unsubtle, or unwary. Unlike *naive*, however, this need not result from a lack of experience. It may be used in a positive sense: the sweetly *ingenuous* child. It may also be used critically: so *ingenuous* as to give away your secrets to everyone at the slightest prompting.

Unaffected refers to unpretentious manners or spontaneous informality. While this word is exclusively positive in tone, what one person might consider *rude* behavior, another might think *unaffected*. Also, *unaffected* manners might be considered the very mark of urbanity, whereas *provincial, naive,* or *unsophisticated* people, by putting on airs unnatural to them, might exemplify the very opposite of *unaffected* conduct. **Guileless**, like *unaffected*, is wholly favorable in tone, but it refers less to the contrast between informality and formality than to a simple lack of deceitfulness; a person with pretentious manners might still be *guileless*. Nor does the word necessarily suggest trusting unwariness like *naive* or the eagerness to share confidences like *ingenuous*. Aside from its stress on honesty, *guileless* thus says less about a person than these other words. Similarly, both an urbane person and a *provincial* or *unsophisticated* one might or might not be *guileless*, but their way of evincing this quality or lack of it would differ markedly.

Artless once unambiguously referred, very like *unaffected*, to a winningly open and spontaneous manner. This meaning may still be intended, with its implied distrust of all art and formality as mere contrivance, but it may now often be used to mean ungraceful or awkward: a radiantly *artless* smile; the *artless* hostess who stumbled over every introduction. Unless context makes clear which meaning is intended, the word should be avoided. See GULLIBLE, SINCERE.

Antonyms: FORMAL, *pretentious, sophisticated.*

name

call
christen
designate
dub

These words mean to entitle a person or thing for purposes of identification or designation to a particular function, office, or honor. **Name**, the most general word, is to fix the thought or idea of someone or something in word form so that the person or thing may be afterward specifically known or recalled to mind. [The province was *named* Normandy; They *named* their child Janet.] *Name* also means to mention or refer to by *name* in speech or writing. [The teacher asked her pupils which one of them could *name* the presidents of the United States in five minutes.] *Name* means to identify or accuse by *name* or by *naming*. [Can you *name* that flower?; He was *named* as a murder suspect in this morning's paper.] *Name* finally means to select or nominate for or to appoint to some particular purpose or position. [July 1st has been *named* the date for the annual office picnic; My father was recently *named* to the City Council.] **Call** means to *name*: to *call* the baby Michael. It can mean to address or speak of by a specific *name*. [Don't be formal, *call* me Joe.] *Call* is also used when a descriptive word is mentioned to characterize someone. [Don't you *call* me a liar; William I of England was *called* the Conqueror.]

Designate is to *name* or entitle by some distinctive word, symbol, expression, etc.: The points of interest on the map are *designated* by letters of the alphabet. *Designate*, like *name*, means to select or appoint, as by authority, for some specific purpose, duty, etc. [Four officers were *designated* to receive the Congressional Medal of Honor; The president of the club *designated* those members he wanted to serve on committees for the charity ball.] The comparable sense of *name* differs only slightly in that it is used more often than *designate* when emphasis is placed on announcement rather than selection.

Christen is the most specialized of the words in this group since it refers to the formal Christian rite of baptism. In its original meaning, *christen* was synonymous with baptize, but it has come more and more to suggest the *naming* of a person at baptism rather than the entire ceremony: The infant was *christened* Diane. By extension, *christen* is used when inanimate objects are *named*, particularly in ceremonies analogous to baptism: to *christen* a ship.

Dub is the most informal word in the group even though it refers in its original meaning to the very formal act of conferring knighthood by tapping on the shoulder with a sword. Today *dub* means to give dignity or character to someone by means of some title or descriptive expression, or simply to nickname. [It is unfair to *dub* someone a coward merely because he refuses to fight; My friend Charles was *dubbed* "Shorty" when he was a child and he has never outgrown the nickname.] See APPOINT, CHOOSE, LABEL.

narrative

anecdote
legend
myth
saga
story
tale
yarn

All these words refer to the verbal account of an occurrence, whether real or imaginary. **Narrative** is the most formal and general of these; it can serve to categorize whatever has as its impulse the recounting of events rather than the lyrical expression of feeling or the evocation of mood, character, or place: forms of *narrative* in Elizabethan prose. More specifically, it can refer to a recitation or recounting of actual events: a day-by-day *narrative* telling his personal experiences during the plague. Sometimes it is used humorously for a long-winded telling of grievances or past miseries: a long, rambling *narrative* of the ways her various husbands had mistreated her. Often, particularly as a generic term, it appears as an adjective: *narrative* poetry; *narrative* skill in prose fiction.

Story can function as an informal substitute for *narrative* in many instances: the *story* of her narrow escape from the Nazis. Often, the word indicates an account of fictional occurrences, clearly understood as such, told for the entertainment of a hearer or reader: He improvised a bedtime *story* for his daughter. In reference to written fiction, the word serves as a literary category, indicating a compact prose form, the short *story*, or refers to the *narrative* element in any writing: reviewers who feel compelled to retell a novel's *story* before appraising it. Because of the word's reference to fictional accounts, it can be used for any explanation, possibly false, such as an alibi: a *story* she invented to explain why she was late; the suspect's *story*.

Tale can relate to this last use of *story*, applying to any exaggerated version of events, whether told to deceive or amuse: a tall *tale* about his life as a gigolo. The word can also categorize one kind of literary *narrative* — a recital by a storyteller, in poetry or prose, of actual, fictional, legendary, or allegorical events: The Canterbury *Tales*. **Yarn** is the most informal of these words and usually indicates a colorful *story* or tall *tale*, whether composed of embroidered truth or outright fiction; the word implies that the *story* or *tale* is told orally or imitates such a telling: Mark Twain's *yarn* about the Jumping Frog of Calaveras County. **Anecdote** can refer to any compact *narrative*, spoken or written, true or fictional; the word suggests greater brevity than would be the case for either a *story* or *tale*, but it is otherwise very general in its application: an *anecdote* about something that happened to her daughter at college; a novel constantly interrupted by pointless *anecdotes* and other digressions.

Myth indicates a *narrative*, in whatever form, that recounts the doings of gods, heroes, and humans before the dawn of history. The *myths* of a given culture were usually taken seriously as religious explanations of the supernatural origin of the society, although later writers and artists may elaborate upon these *myths* or create new ones without ever giving them credence: Greek *myths*; Scandinavian *myths*; Balinese *myths*. A **legend** may include elements of *myth*, but is a more extended recounting in some set form of fabulous happenings, whether these are given credence by author and audience or are accepted as fictions. Often, *legends* may derive from a period later than the creation of *myth* and may have an underpinning of historical truth: *legends* that grew up around the exploits of Richard the Lion-Hearted. Sometimes, the word can refer to present-day *stories* that have evolved to explain local events or customs: a persistent *legend* that the vacant house on the hill was haunted. **Saga** refers to an extended *narrative* that mixes *myth* and *legend* to recount the epic *story* of demigods or heroes: the Volsunga *Saga*. Less specifically, the word can refer to any epic chronicle, even of historical events: a *saga* of the Civil War. Used even more loosely, the word can refer to any long-winded oral *narrative* about past experiences. See ALLEGORY, HISTORY, NEWS, NOVEL, REPORT, TELL.

native

aboriginal
autochthonous
endemic
indigenous

These words designate persons or things that belong to the place in which they are found or in which they originated. That which is born or produced in a specific region or country is **native** to it: a *native* Californian; architecture *native* to New England; birds *native* to South America. The word may also be used of things which have been naturalized in a place for some time; thus, one may speak of the coffee plant as being *native* to Brazil, although it was introduced into that country from Africa several hundred years ago.

Indigenous is more restricted in meaning than *native* in that it excludes the possibility of introduction from elsewhere, as of a species of animal or plant, or a race of people. [The platypus is *indigenous* to Australia; Eskimos are *indigenous* to the Arctic regions.] *Indigenous* may also be applied to things that originate in a specified place. [Cliff dwellings are *indigenous* to the southwestern United States; The Irish have a rich, *indigenous* folklore.]

Aboriginal is used chiefly of primitive peoples (aborigines) having

no known or recorded ancestors and inhabiting a region at its earliest
known historical time: The Ainus are the *aboriginal* people of Japan.
Less frequently *aboriginal* is applied to *native* or *indigenous* plants and
animals.

Endemic is used of plants or diseases that are *native* to, and usually
restricted to, a specific region or part of the world because they are
peculiarly adapted to flourish there. [The maguey plant is *endemic* in
Mexico; Cholera is *endemic* in the Orient.]

Autochthonous, which originally meant "one sprung from the earth
itself," is a less common synonym of *native, aboriginal*, and *indigenous*.
It is now most often used in geology of rocks and minerals produced in
the places where they are found rather than brought in by some external
agency, such as a glacier. See ARISE, BEGIN, PROTOTYPE.

Antonyms: alien, foreign, immigrant.

These words have to do with failure to give proper attention and care
where it is due, and they are all condemnatory. **Neglect** and **negligence** are sometimes not clearly discriminated as to meaning, but
neglect refers to the act and *negligence* to the quality or trait of character
of a person who is careless and irresponsible in his actions and attitudes.
Of the two, *neglect* is the stronger word. *Neglect* of one's appearance
suggests slovenliness, while *negligence* as to one's appearance indicates
only a lack of concern for style or smartness. A child may suffer from
parental *neglect*, but it is *negligence* on the part of the parents if the child
is improperly cared for. In law, *negligence* is a violation of the obligation
to take care and caution in what one does, especially when it involves
the rights and safety of other people. A driver who knowingly operates
a car with faulty brakes, thereby causing an accident involving another
car, is guilty of gross *negligence*.

Dereliction carries a sense of greater culpability than do either
neglect or *negligence*, because *dereliction* is a deliberate and reprehensible
neglect of a responsibility, rather than merely a careless one. A surgeon
who performs an operation while intoxicated is guilty of *dereliction* of
duty toward his patient.

Thoughtlessness strongly implies oversight rather than willful
neglect. People who are usually careful to think before they act or speak
may occasionally be guilty of *thoughtlessness*. Others through lack of
imagination or understanding of the needs and feelings of other people
are to be blamed for *thoughtlessness* when they habitually cause irritation
or displeasure without appearing to realize it. See CURSORY, FORGET,
HEEDLESS.

*Antonyms: attention, attentiveness, care, concern, consideration, thoughtful-
ness.*

neglect

dereliction
negligence
thoughtlessness

These words refer to things nearby or to things that touch each other.
Neighboring is the most informal of these and suggests only that things
are close to each other but not necessarily touching: a shopping center
that drew its customers from the *neighboring* communities; no one in
the *neighboring* apartments was awakened by the sounds. In geometry,
a line that is **tangent** to a circle touches that circle at one and only one
point; this meaning is often apparent even in more ordinary uses: a
road that does not go through the city but runs *tangent* to it.

Adjoining indicates a closer relationship than the previous words,
suggesting a side-by-side placement having a common boundary: asking
the hotel for *adjoining* rooms with a door between them; French doors

neighboring

abutting
adjacent
adjoining
contiguous
juxtaposed
tangent

that revealed the *adjoining* patio. **Abutting** indicates an even closer relationship than *adjoining*, stressing an actual touching of elements, although not necessarily a side-by-side placement. The special implication here is of things driven together by force to gain strength or structural soundness: the roofbeam and its *abutting* crossbeams; a network of *abutting* boardwalks. When these implications are not present, the word functions much as *adjoining*, except that it does not necessarily suggest a side-by-side relation: a number of chapels *abutting* the apse of the cathedral. **Contiguous** is more formal than *adjoining* and *abutting* and is much less specific about the actual placement of elements that it refers to. Thus any kind of contact whatsoever can be indicated: back-door gardens that were *contiguous* to each other; a hallway that was *contiguous* to all the rooms of the apartment.

Adjacent can suggest a relationship like that indicated by *neighboring*: an explosion that brought people pouring out of the *adjacent* houses. It can also indicate the sharing of a common boundary in a side-by-side arrangement, as in the geometry term: *adjacent* angles; *adjacent* plots of land. But the word has a special use to indicate things of the same kind that do not touch but are not blocked from each other by things like them: *adjacent* islands; *adjacent* farmhouses. **Juxtaposed** also has a use distinct from those of other words here. While it can function like *neighboring* or *adjoining*, it most specifically suggests incongruous elements brought into close contact; the word often carries connotations of conflict, abruptness of placement, or surprise at contrasts: a city in which ancient and modern features are strikingly *juxtaposed*; opposing forces that found themselves *juxtaposed* the next morning on either side of the broad river. See BOUNDARY, EDGE.

Antonyms: dispersed, far-flung, scattered, separated, unattached, unconnected.

neoplasm

cancer
carcinoma
cyst
growth
sarcoma
tumor

These words refer to the development of abnormal cells, usually in tissue masses, in a living organism. **Neoplasm** is the most comprehensive term for any such development, whether malignant or benign, small or large, active or dormant, temporary or permanent. Usually the word refers to a tissue mass: *neoplasms* of the cervix, uterus, and ovaries. But the word can also refer to the abnormal production of circulating cells. [Leukemia is a malignant *neoplasm* of the blood; Hodgkin's disease is a comparable *neoplasm* of the lymph cells.]

Tumor is the medical term and **growth** the layman's term for any *neoplasm* that takes the form of a compact tissue mass. *Growth* is, of course, vague in its application to any swelling or nonfunctional mass: a *growth* on his vocal cords. *Tumor* refers specifically to a circumscribed growth that is noninflammatory, nonfunctional, and continues to develop independently of the normal rate for the tissue in which it arises: a breast *tumor*; a lung *tumor*. *Tumor*, like *growth* and *neoplasm*, need not indicate malignancy. **Cyst** refers specifically to an abnormal but not necessarily malignant sac containing fluid or semi-solid material; a *cyst* can result from the clogging of a duct and is often temporary or minor in nature: a sebaceous *cyst*.

The remaining words all refer strictly to malignant *neoplasms*. **Cancer** indicates a disease in which cells stop functioning normally, become destructive of other cells, and multiply rapidly. Most often this cellular malfunction is initially localized, becoming apparent when it produces a *tumor*, and then at last spreading or metastasizing unpredictably from one part of the body to another. Unless interrupted, as by surgery or

X-ray treatment, the result is usually fatal: lung *cancer*; skin *cancer*; stomach *cancer*. *Cancer* need not always begin as a *tumor*; sometimes leukemia and Hodgkin's disease are spoken of as *cancers* of the blood and lymph, even when no *tumor* is involved.

Carcinoma refers specifically to a malignant *tumor* of an organ's epithelial tissue, that is, the sheet-like membranes enclosing or lining it. **Sarcoma**, by contrast, is a malignant *neoplasm* of the connective tissues, particularly of the bone, cartilage, or muscles. The distinction is important since surgery is more often successful in completely eradicating the localized *carcinoma*, at least in its early stages, than the *sarcoma*, which can more readily begin metastasizing to other parts of the body. See MOLE, WART.

All of these terms imply a state of tension, anxiety, or worry. **Nervous** and **restless** are probably the most general words, but whereas *nervous* refers to an inward condition, *restless* suggests an outward manifestation of anxiety. A person can be inwardly *nervous* and outwardly calm, but if he is *restless* he shows it, as by shifting from one foot to the other, getting up and sitting down, or pacing the room. *Restless* may also be used figuratively, suggesting the free inquiring attitude of the scientist or the adventurer: a *restless* mind, never satisfied with easy generalizations; His *restless* spirit urged him on to ever greater feats. In this sense, however, *restless* often has a somewhat strained rhetorical ring. *Restless* describes a temporary condition called into play by a particular situation. A person may be *nervous* by disposition and not because of any particularly anxious situation: My mother is a *nervous* woman and always has been.

Edgy and **jumpy** both indicate an extremely *nervous* state, and are somewhat more informal than either *nervous* or *restless*. An *edgy* person is irritable and combative, ready to take offense at slight provocation, whereas a *jumpy* person is simply extremely *nervous*, literally ready to jump. In this sense *jumpy* is synonymous with **on edge**, although one is usually kept *on edge* waiting for important news, whereas one is *jumpy* because one compulsively anticipates being shocked or surprised. [The day I start catching a cold I feel very *edgy*, ready to snap at everyone; We were kept *on edge* for weeks, waiting to hear from our son in Vietnam; The war veteran still got a little *jumpy* whenever he heard a car backfiring.]

Fidgety, more than the other words so far discussed, suggests *nervous* body movements, especially small aimless gestures with the hands. It thus simply refers to an outward sign of inward nervousness or apprehension: The *fidgety* professor played with his eyeglasses as he lectured. The word usually applies to people who habitually fidget — fussy people, worriers.

Jittery, deriving from the slang expression "the jitters," is also marked by a number of body movements, but *jittery* often suggests fright as well as nervousness. A *jittery* condition may be caused by a menacing or dangerous situation: The thieves became *jittery* when they heard the news bulletin describing them accurately in detail. Animals may be *jittery* as well as people: The horses became *jittery* upon smelling the smoke.

Excitable and **flighty** are alike in suggesting enduring temperamental qualities of human beings. *Flighty* implies an inability to keep one's attention fixed in a levelheaded manner on any one particular subject. The *flighty* person keeps skipping from subject to subject in a *nervous*, virtually random manner that suggests the flitting of a butterfly.

nervous

edgy
excitable
fidgety
flighty
jittery
jumpy
on edge
restless
uptight

It often indicates a shallow mind easily distracted by inconsequential events: The conversation of the women was so *flighty* that there was simply no way to discover what they were talking about. An *excitable* person is one who is easily aroused to a high pitch of enthusiasm or emotion. *Excitable* may be applied to persons of either sex, but is usually confined to the young or inexperienced. [He was of an *excitable* nature; at the slightest hint of criticism he would stamp out the door in a rage.]

Uptight is a recent fad word for *nervous*. In its earlier slang use among jazz musicians, it referred to an opposite feeling of being so sure of oneself that one could play without sheet music. Through misunderstanding, the word now applies generally to someone who is tense, anxious, or disturbed, either because of a specific problem or a *nervous* disposition: ghetto youngsters who are *uptight* about police brutality; hippies who criticize the *uptight* world of their middle-class parents. See AFRAID, ANXIETY, FEAR, FLINCH.

Antonyms: IMPERTURBABLE, *self-controlled*, *self-possessed*, *steady*, TRANQUIL.

neutralize

counteract
counterbalance
offset

These words refer to a matching of one extreme with another so that a stable or static situation results. **Neutralize** suggests that this stability is achieved by adding a substance that will cause a change in structure: an alkali that will *neutralize* the excessive acidity of the soil; an antidote to *neutralize* the poison. The word often suggests that some danger or threat is rendered harmless: government programs to *neutralize* the effects of poverty. The word can, however, refer to the frustrating of some positive tendency: the doubt and suspicions that surrounded him and *neutralized* all his efforts to make peace.

Counteract is more forceful than *neutralize* because it suggests an act that not only restores things as they were, but that may carry the action past that point into the opposite direction: They worked vigorously to *counteract* the community's apathy; pills to *counteract* her anemia by building up her red blood cells. **Counterbalance**, however, literally suggests an equalizing of one weight by another: *counterbalancing* the demands of labor and management with a concern for the nation's welfare.

Offset suggests most specifically the replacing of something lost by a new thing equivalent to it: *offsetting* his losses at the gambling tables by his successes in stock speculations; The low selling price more than *offset* the disadvantages of the house. See BENEFICIAL, PERMANENT, TREAT.

news

data
facts
information
intelligence

These words all denote various types of acquired or derived knowledge. **News** is knowledge of recent events or developments of interest to the public at large, especially as reported in a newspaper or in a radio or television broadcast. *News* may also be the report or broadcast itself. [The *news* from Italy is that spring floods have severely damaged the crops; Each night after dinner we like to listen to the *news*.] *News* may also be something of which one did not previously know, or recent doings of which one hasn't heard. [What you have just told us about plastics being made from soybeans is *news* to me; Please write and tell me all the *news* about yourself.]

Information is the most general term and is applied to any knowledge acquired from observation, from reading or study, or from talking with others. Although such knowledge is often accepted as valid, it may not necessarily be true or accurate. [The old lady gathers *information* about her neighbors by spying on them through the window curtains; A hysterical person at the scene of an accident is a poor source of *information* as to what happened.] *Information* is also timely or specific knowledge about an event or subject of interest. [There are hundreds of sources that give *information* about the space program; Before leading his men into combat, the lieutenant called headquarters for *information* as to the enemy's position.]

Facts are pieces of *information* that are known by observation or proof to be true or real. [Research scientists must work with *facts*; A witness in a murder trial is assumed to know the *facts* in the case.]

Data (actually the plural of "datum," a Latin form, but now often used in the singular) is a formal word for a large body of facts or figures which have been gathered systematically and from which conclusions may be drawn. The amassing of *data* is usually for scientific and statistical purposes, and the *information* obtained is often fed into a computer for rapid processing.

Intelligence is now a high-flown and literary term for *information* or *news* that is communicated by or received from another: Last week we received *intelligence* of his whereabouts from the consul in Madrid. In a restricted sense, *intelligence* is the collecting of secret *information* about an enemy, as by political police, a government agency, or military authorities: an *intelligence* bureau; an officer in *intelligence*. The term applies also to the *information* or *facts* so collected as well as to the staff of persons occupied with this process: Army *intelligence*; British *intelligence*. See REPORT, TELL.

Antonyms: conjecture, OPINION.

Noise and **sound** are both general words which designate sensations excited in the ear. *Sound* is most general, embracing sensations of all qualities, whether loud or soft, pleasant or unpleasant, significant or insignificant: the soft, sibilant *sound* of two young girls whispering in class; the horrifying *sound* of a scream in the night; the different *sound* that two conductors can get out of one orchestra. *Noise*, though more specific than *sound*, is general in its application to all loud, confused, or irritating *sounds*. *Noise* may consist of high-intensity *sound* from a single source, *sound* that is loud, harsh, sharp, shrill, strident, or grating: the *noise* of a buzz saw; the *noise* of a vacuum cleaner. Or it may be a confused commingling of clashing *sounds*: the *noise* of a construction project, with all the hammering and drilling, the whine of machinery, the shouts of the men. In one sense, *noise* is part of the unnoticed natural background of existence: office *noises*. In another sense, *noise* may designate distracting *sounds* that annoy because of special sensitivity or circumstances. [The *noise* of crumpled candy wrappers spoiled the movie's most dramatic scene; I'm trying to study, please stop rocking that chair — you're making so much *noise*.] The word *noise* may also be applied to neutral *sounds* that are merely perceived and noted: the soothing *noise* of water falling; She makes little groaning *noises* in her sleep.

Din denotes loud *noise* that goes on without letup, often with maddening or deafening effect. It implies an inescapable onslaught of *sound*, sometimes involving a painful assault on the eardrums: the thunderous *din* of a gong; the earsplitting *din* of a factory. **Blare** is a loud, brassy *sound* of constant, unremitting intensity. It impinges on the privacy and preoccupies the consciousness: the *blare* of a loud radio; the *blare* of a car horn that is stuck. **Clatter** indicates a rattling *sound* or a rapid

noise

blare
clamor
clatter
din
hubbub
racket
sound
uproar

succession of short, sharp *noises*: the *clatter* of a wagon on cobblestones;
the *clatter* of a typewriter.

Hubbub designates a general, confused *noise*, as of many voices busily
talking at once: the *hubbub* in the courtroom before the judge calls for
order; the *hubbub* of the marketplace or stock exchange. *Hubbub* may
also refer to any *noise* arising from hustle and bustle: He tried to make
himself heard above the *hubbub* of a busy intersection. **Clamor** implies
a loud outcry kept up by insistent voices. It is often expressive of a
vehement public protest or demand: the furious *clamor* of the hungry
mob; the *clamor* of the press for reform; the public *clamor* for repeal
of the law. But *clamor* may also apply to any noisy commotion or confusion of *sounds*: the *clamor* of boys scuffling in the schoolyard; the
clamor of noisy bluejays and chirping chickadees. **Uproar** refers to an
unrestrained outpouring of *sound*, as in outraged shouting, clamorous
protest, or boisterous laughter. It implies the spread of turbulence, agitation, or excitement through a crowd, with a consequent eruption of
noise and disorder. [His motion threw the meeting into an *uproar*; The
class fell into *uproarious* laughter over the professor's Freudian slip.]
Racket implies *clatter*, *clamor*, or commotion — a loud, percussive *sound*
or a confused combination of *noises* that gets on the nerves: the *racket*
of hammering; The boys are making so much *racket* that I can't hear
myself think. See ACTIVITY, LOUD, MONOTONOUS.
Antonyms: calm, hush, quiet, silence, tranquillity.

normal

natural
ordinary
regular
typical

All of these words are applied to that which is usual or expected because
it conforms to a standard or rule. **Normal** implies that a particular person or thing does not exceed certain limits, or does not deviate far from
an average or a standard established for a group, class, or species.
[*Normal* body temperature ranges between 96.8° and 98.6° Fahrenheit;
Normal temperature in New York City for June is around 70°.] **Regular** implies accordance with some rule, plan, or method: to follow *regular*
army procedures.

Typical indicates possession of those properties or characteristics
that represent a particular class of things and differentiate it from all
other classes of things: the *typical* clubbed antennae of the butterfly.
Ordinary, as an equivalent for *normal* or *regular*, emphasizes commonness or usualness and often stresses the absence of superior qualities.
[An *ordinary* man is no genius; *Ordinary* ways of doing things keep
within the rules but do not initiate improvements.]

Natural emphasizes the agreement between an action and the innate character of the agent involved. Thus it is *natural* for man to seek
happiness, for birds to migrate, for the sun to set. See GENERAL, USUAL.
Antonyms: abnormal, atypical, irregular, QUEER, unnatural, unusual.

novel

fiction
romance
story

These words refer to extended works of imaginative prose. **Novel** is
the most specific and exact of these words, referring to any work that
normally has a plot, characters, action, and dialogue but that does not
refer to real people or events: best-selling *novels*; those who consider
Don Quixote the first full-length *novel*. By contrast, **fiction** is more general since it is the group word for all forms of imaginative prose, including the short story, the novella, and the *novel*. Since the *novel* is in one
sense the most important form of *fiction*, however, the group word is
often used with a special pertinence to this one form: a poor season for
fiction in that no new major *novel* emerged.

Romance is more difficult to pin down to an exact meaning. A related word in German is equivalent to our word *novel*, reflecting the development of the *novel* out of accounts of fabulous or legendary materials in the Middle Ages. In literary discussions, *romance* is often restricted to works showing this emphasis on the fabulous or legendary, or it may be used more broadly to apply to *novels* with a strong mythic or allegorical bent: Malory's gathering together and rewriting of the Arthurian *romances*; Hawthorne's *novels* seen as being essentially *romances*. Contrary to a popular misconception, the word would never in any literate use refer merely to *fiction* that concerns itself with love affairs.

While **story** most commonly is an abbreviated way of referring to an established form, the short *story*, it is sometimes used loosely and informally for any work of *fiction* with narrative thrust: novelists who concentrate on telling *stories* filled with physical violence. The word is also sometimes applied to the plot element of any *fiction*: a brief paragraph summarizing the *story* of the *novel*. See COMPOSITION, NARRATIVE, POETRY.

Antonyms: nonfiction.

These words refer to a loss of sensation, ability to move, or mental responsiveness. **Numb**, the most informal of these, is primarily related to loss of sensation that is brought about by any means whatever: hands that were *numb* with cold; her tongue still *numb* from the shot of novocaine; a leg *numb* from his having sat so long in one position. More metaphorically, the word suggests loss of emotional affect or mental alertness: tragic news that left him *numb*; looking at the questionnaire with *numb* bewilderment. **Anesthetized** is the most formal and most specific of these words, referring to loss of sensation, if not of movement or consciousness, as well; it specifically suggests a medical use of drugs to make someone incapable of feeling pain: taking a pulse count of the *anesthetized* patient; the *anesthetized* side of his mouth. Used metaphorically, it functions much like *numb*, but with greater intensity: wondering if her dull, *anesthetized* manner was the result of a tragic loss or an unhappy love affair.

Deadened may, more informally, indicate an *anesthetized* condition: working with a drill on the *deadened* tooth. In other uses it is more like *numb*, but may suggest a partial, as well as complete, loss of sensation or movement: hearing that had been *deadened* slightly by the blast; nerve damage that had permanently *deadened* both legs. In terms of mental responsiveness, the word suggests an acutely apathetic and depressed state of discouragement or hopelessness: minds *deadened* by conformity; *deadened* expectations. **Paralyzed** takes up one aspect of *deadened* exclusively, referring to a loss of ability to move: learning to walk with a brace on the *paralyzed* leg. Used of emotions or mental states, it suggests the absence of will or the inability to function: *paralyzed* with fear. It can even be used jocosely for total unconsciousness: drinking until he was *paralyzed*.

Insensible, at its most formal and precise, refers exclusively to loss of sensation: a local anesthetic to render the area *insensible* to pain. More loosely, it can simply suggest resistance to rigorous sensation: Eskimos amazingly *insensible* to cold. In another context, it refers to unawareness, rather than to sensation loss: talking on, *insensible* of her forbidding frown. It may also refer to complete unconsciousness: falling *insensible* to the floor. It has little application to mental states. This contrasts sharply with **stupefied**, which is almost exclusively restricted

numb

anesthetized
deadened
insensible
paralyzed
stupefied

to describing states of shock or incoherence: *stupefied* with disbelief; giving his alarm clock a *stupefied* scowl. It contrasts with *numb* and *anesthetized* in this context by stressing surprise or mental befuddlement rather than a draining away of feeling. It contrasts with *deadened* by stressing confusion of mind rather than dullness. And it contrasts with *paralyzed* by suggesting a partial, though bleared, consciousness rather than a nonfunctioning one. See IMPASSIVE, LISTLESS, SLOTH.

Antonyms: AWARE, LIVELY.

nurse

care for
mind
minister
tend

These words all share the meaning of looking after or taking care of someone or something. **Nurse** is specifically applied to looking after the sick, injured, or infirm: His wife patiently *nursed* him back to health after his heart attack. In this sense it implies intimate care and close, devoted supervision, although it may also refer to a more formal and professional relationship, as that between a trained nurse and a patient. **Tend** may imply devoted concern, but it is a concern based more upon one's sense of duty, charity, or religious conviction than upon one's personal feeling for the individual being helped. [It is the duty of physicians to *tend* the sick; The medic selflessly *tended* (or, more informally, *tended to*) the wounded soldiers before dressing his own wound.] *Tend* may also apply to things, thus emphasizing its essentially impersonal connotation: to *tend* machinery; to *tend* a furnace.

Minister is close in meaning to *tend* and *nurse*, but today it often sounds somewhat rhetorical or stuffy when applied exclusively to the care of the sick. It is more often applied nowadays to general wants, especially to spiritual succor, and even in such contexts it is a more formal word than *tend* or *nurse*. [An elected representative must *minister* to the needs and aspirations of his own community, city, and state; As a doctor *ministers* to the body, so does a clergyman *minister* to the spirit or soul.]

Care for is the most general term of this group. In the sense here considered, it can mean looking after all the needs of a child, *tending* an invalid, *nursing* a convalescent back to health, or *ministering* to the unwell: The foster mother *cared for* those boys as faithfully as if they had been her own natural sons.

In the sense being compared here, **mind** means to look after, watch over, or take care of. It most often suggests a temporary charge rather than a permanent devotion: to *mind* someone's children; to *mind* sheep; to *mind* a store while the owner is at lunch. See PAMPER, PROTECT.

Antonyms: SLIGHT.

O

obedient

dutiful
good
well-behaved

These words are alike in meaning morally or intellectually disposed to respect authority or custom and to follow the dictates thereof. **Obedient** stresses an acknowledgement of the authority vested in some person, organization, etc. The very common usage of *obedient* in reference to children suggests the nature of the compliance implicit in the word: a soldier who refused to be blindly *obedient* to the commands of an ignorant superior whose only saving grace was a kind of fatherly good will.

Alone among the words being considered here, *obedient* has an extended application to physical objects that respond to or act in accordance with some superior force or natural law: a ship *obedient* to the wheel. **Dutiful**, even more than *obedient*, suggests the influence of outside conditions, such as ethical demands or those of behavioral customs. *Dutiful* persons have a strong sense of respect or obligation: a *dutiful* child; a *dutiful* parent.

While *obedient* and *dutiful* connote a manner of acting that is dependent upon external circumstances, **good** refers to behavior that is the result of inner demands. Thus, a *good* child is docile by nature; he is easy to manage or teach because of his own inclination. A *good* worker, in the context of this comparison, is one who follows instructions because of a personal desire to please and do what he is supposed to do.

Someone who is **well-behaved** may be that way because of training or because of his own make-up. But the suggestion of outside influence is strong; *well-behaved* is used to characterize that kind of conduct which has standards established by the society in which a person lives: The new teacher congratulated himself on having a class that he considered more than usually *well-behaved*. See ADAPTABLE, COMPLIANT, DOCILE, MALLEABLE.

Antonyms: MISCHIEVOUS, STUBBORN.

obligation

duty
function
office
responsibility

These words are comparable in denoting that which one is bound to fulfill or perform. **Obligation** refers generally to anything that one is compelled to do, or to forbear from doing, by law, contract, promise, morality, or the like. The word often implies immediate pressure to carry out, or to refrain from, a particular action: a legal *obligation* to serve in the armed forces. **Duty** is often used interchangeably with *obligation*, but the word more often refers to that which springs from an interior moral or ethical impulse rather than from external demands: He volunteered for the dangerous mission out of a sense of *duty*. *Duty* frequently has a more general reference than does *obligation*: to put *duty* before pleasure. And the word is also applied to a particular task. **Function** refers to activity demanded by one's position, profession, or the like. It focuses on objective purpose, as discharged in the performance of particular *duties*: He mechanically performed the *functions* of a teacher but was uninspired. **Office**, as here considered, refers to the services, *functions*, or *duties* connected with a position of trust. [He swore to faithfully discharge the *office* of vice president; reconciled through the good *offices* of their clergyman.] **Responsibility** refers to any *obligation*, *duty*, *function*, or *office*, for the fulfillment of which one may be called upon to answer to a particular person, the public in general, or a Divine Being: It is the *responsibility* of the President of the United States to defend and uphold the Constitution. See COMPEL, RESPONSIBLE, STINT.

Antonyms: RIGHT.

oblivious

absent-minded
abstracted
inattentive

These words refer to a mind that is lost in thought, lacks alertness or awareness, or is given over to some matter other than the one at hand. **Oblivious** stresses lack of awareness, either because of deep thought or poor concentration: so fascinated with solving the problem that he was *oblivious* to the odd looks his fellow passengers were giving him; wandering thoughts that made him *oblivious* of the question the teacher had just asked him. **Inattentive** stresses exclusively this last possibility of *oblivious*, indicating an inability to keep the mind focused on the subject before it: *inattentive* to the demonstration the diving instructor was making of each position. This inability can be the result of restlessness, distraction, weak intellectual powers, or even a willful indifference to detail: children who grow *inattentive* during long class periods; a bored secretary, *inattentive* while taking dictation.

Abstracted stresses a mind that is far removed from mundane considerations before it, especially because of obsessive or intrusive thoughts and feelings: so *abstracted* by the beauty of the sunset that he quite forgot about the presence of his companions; the *abstracted* smile the widow gave to other mourners at the funeral. **Absent-minded** may function exactly like *abstracted* at a more informal level. More importantly, however, it is unique among these words in pointing to a fixed or ingrained tendency to lose one's bearings because of intrusive concerns: the typical *absent-minded* professor, rapt in solving an equation while crossing against a red light; An absent-minded movement of his hand caused the cup to fall. See FORGET, PREOCCUPIED.

Antonyms: AWARE, OBSERVANT.

obnoxious

hateful
odious
offensive

The words on this list are applied to a person or thing which arouses dislike, distaste, hostility, or opposition. **Obnoxious** is used to refer to that which is extremely disagreeable or even disgusting to one's personal feelings, ideas, or tastes. Very often the reasons for viewing something as *obnoxious* are largely subjective, but they are nonetheless strong enough to make one try to avoid the *obnoxious* person or thing. [I can't stand him — he's a thoroughly *obnoxious* young man who thinks he knows it all.]

Hateful and **odious** describe that which excites intense dislike or aversion, the former usually suggesting an attendant feeling of enmity, the latter associated with contempt or repugnance. Although the words are sometimes used interchangeably, *hateful* implies an angry mental response to something that outrages or arouses violent antipathy: the *hateful* animosity of resentful bigots toward civil rights workers. *Odious* often suggests something so disgusting that it evokes a physical as well as a moral or intellectual response: getting sick to one's stomach upon reading of the *odious* atrocities committed in a Nazi concentration camp.

Offensive is the mildest word in this list. It has wide application and can be used to characterize anyone or anything that is unpleasant or disagreeable: the *offensive* sight of garbage in an apartment hallway; a series of *offensive* remarks that finally led to a bitter argument. See CONTEMPTIBLE, DEPRAVED, REPREHENSIBLE, REPULSIVE.

Antonyms: HUMANE, *lovable*, PLEASING.

obscure

abstruse
arcane
cryptic
recondite

These words refer to things kept secret or hidden or to things difficult to perceive or understand. **Obscure** is the most general and least formal of these; it is now most often used to indicate things indistinct or difficult to grasp, although it still may reflect its derivation from a root meaning dark. [The letters of the sign were made *obscure* by rain; *obscure*, involuted reasoning that only served to confuse his audience; a path that grew more and more *obscure* in the fading light.] When the reference is to understanding, the word may imply disapproval because something is not clear: misled by the deliberately *obscure* language of the contract. The word may, however, refer with greater neutrality to something that is not clear, without necessarily implying any intent to confuse: references that were perfectly apparent in his own time but that have long since become *obscure*.

Cryptic and **arcane** specifically stress things that are hidden or that have been deliberately made remote from easy understanding. *Arcane* can flatly refer to something kept secret as a mystery: *arcane* religious symbols that only the high priest could interpret. More generally, it may refer to a purposely pedantic reliance on *obscure* references in order to show off one's own learning; in this sense, the word, like *obscure*, can carry a disapproving tone: *arcane* footnotes that not even a specialist in the field could be expected to understand. *Cryptic* may refer to the occult, but more generally it indicates something enigmatic or puzzling, often something deliberately made to seem meaningless, except to the initiate: *cryptic* signs and handclasps that were part of the lodge's ritual. The word may also refer to something too brief to be understood: a *cryptic*, one-word clue.

Abstruse and **recondite** may refer to things secret, hidden, or difficult to grasp, but their special area of usage here is in referring to scholarly complexity. *Abstruse* suggests a formal or learned style filled with difficulties that tax the mind: *abstruse* legal documents that supported his claim to the throne. *Recondite* is even more emphatic about the difficulty or complexity of a study or approach: needing fewer *recondite* books on the subject and more that might help a layman to understand the new discoveries. Hence, by extension, the word can refer to knowledge remote from the mainstream and available only to a few authorities: the *recondite* teachings of a minor medieval philosopher. See MYSTICAL, VAGUE.

Antonyms: CLEAR, *explicit*, PLAIN, *transparent*.

---

obsequious

abject
menial
servile
slavish
subservient
sycophantic

These words are applied to persons guilty of, or to behavior characterized by, excessive deference, flattery, imitation, or obedience. **Obsequious** shares with **abject** an awareness of low station or a feeling of low self-esteem which reveals itself in fawning behavior. *Obsequious* strongly suggests an attitude that is consciously assumed in order to placate a superior in hopes of getting what one wants, or to escape unpleasant consequences: serfs who bowed with *obsequious* politeness to members of the gentry; a failing student who was maddeningly *obsequious* to his teacher. *Abject* conveys the sense of being cast down in spirits or a loss of self-respect that results in a humiliated cringing or a pitiable fawning on others: to make an *abject* apology even though one was not at fault; a beggar so *abject* that he plucks at the sleeves of passers-by. In a related sense, *abject* designates something unusually degraded or wretched: the *abject* poverty of millions of people in the Near East and the Orient.

Sycophantic is sometimes used interchangeably with *obsequious*, but is more strongly pejorative. The word suggests a parasitical and self-seeking relationship to someone in a superior position, rather than an attitude of sincere respect: a dictator's *sycophantic* yes men; the *sycophantic* women who surround a successful movie actor.

Menial, servile, and **slavish** are applied to extremely *abject* persons or behavior. In former times, when class distinctions were more pronounced and rigid, these words were as a matter of course applied to those at the bottom of the scale: a *menial* servant; a *servile* jester; a *slavish* retainer. Nowadays these words are more likely to be applied to actions or attitudes: his *menial* unobtrusiveness; *servile* obedience; *slavish* attention to the needs of another.

Subservient is a somewhat weaker synonym for the other terms in suggesting truckling or servility. It is more often used to refer to a person who properly serves as a subordinate, or, more commonly, to a thing that has been adapted to promote some end or purpose as an auxiliary. See FAWN, FLINCH.

Antonyms: contumelious, impudent, OVERBEARING.

observant

alert
attentive
aware
discerning
perceptive

These words describe someone with a sharp eye for detail or a keen ability to detect the real meaning of a situation. **Observant** suggests someone who notices details that another person might miss: Only the most *observant* spectator would have seen which player had the ball. **Discerning** and **perceptive** take in this emphasis of *observant*, but add to it an ability to evaluate or understand the observed details. *Discerning* stresses the ability to tell apart two or more very similar things — or to evaluate slight differences by means of one's inherent good taste: the *discerning* theatergoer who shuns bad imitations of last year's hits. *Perceptive* stresses the ability to understand or make understandable the details one has observed: a *perceptive* comment on programs needed to combat juvenile delinquency.

Attentive resembles *observant* more than *discerning* and *perceptive*; it stresses the ability to concentrate on a matter without distraction or wavering of any kind: students who suddenly become *attentive* the week before exams; congressmen who are *attentive* to the needs of their constituents. **Aware** and **alert** also resemble *observant*, but they are more general than the other words here. In a different context, *aware* can point merely to being conscious; here, however, it suggests acute responsiveness to other people or to one's surroundings: discussing how they could become more *aware* of each other's problems. *Alert* is similar to, but an intensification of, *aware*; it suggests a sharp, highly receptive state of mind that is on the lookout for some event to occur, especially a dangerous or threatening event: so *alert* that not a single error in the report slipped past her; *alert* for any sign of change in the critically ill patient. See DISCRIMINATE, KEEN, VISION, WISDOM.

Antonyms: OBLIVIOUS, PREOCCUPIED, *unaware, unmindful.*

obsessed

addicted
addictive
compulsive
disciplined
obsessive

In the general sense of being independent of or contrary to a person's conscious will, these words have both a popular and a technical use.

Obsessed is to be excessively troubled, disturbed, worried, or preoccupied by virtually anything at any time, anywhere, for whatever reason or cause. [He was *obsessed* by the fear of cancer; The thought of losing the large order *obsessed* the new salesman.] **Obsessive** implies a similar mental state but carries the idea of some deep-lying character defect or personality maladjustment requiring careful, often extended psychiatric attention. Thus one may be temporarily *obsessed* by unpaid bills or a forgotten address, but have a persistent *obsessive* fear of debt or of losing one's memory.

Compulsive suggests an insistent, unwanted, and repetitive emotion, attitude, or activity that has little relation to normal standards of behavior and whose omission leads to acute mental distress: a *compulsive* need to wash one's hands or rearrange the furniture; *compulsive* eating; a *compulsive* striving for perfection. In this sense it is usually linked with *obsessive* as a psychiatric term for a large number of mental disorders: an *obsessive-compulsive* neurosis.

Disciplined is comparable to the other words in this group chiefly as it implies submission to controls imposed either by some outside authority or by one's self. The submission may be involuntary or enforced: *disciplined* prisoners of war. Or it may be consciously accepted as a means to some personal end: a *disciplined* course of action; *disciplined* behavior to one's superiors.

Addicted and **addictive** both suggest a strong attachment to or dependence upon something. *Addicted* may often mean little more than a persistent devotion to one or another form of socially acceptable activity or pursuit: *addicted* to the theater, to sports, to reading or travel. Usually, however, the word suggests an emotional or physical dependence that is not compatible with normal behavior: *addicted* to drugs or alcohol. Such dependence is emphasized by *addictive*, which has come to mean habit-forming in a bad or unhealthy sense: *addictive* drugs; *addictive* narcotics.

Antonyms: instinctive, natural, SPONTANEOUS.

These words denote anything that checks or halts progress, either in a literal or a figurative sense. **Obstacle**, **barrier**, and **hurdle** present the most trouble in overcoming. An *obstacle* is something that one must either remove or go around before being able to proceed. [The huge tree that had been blown down by the storm was an *obstacle* to traffic; Poor grades may be an *obstacle* to a boy's playing on the school team.] A *barrier* is an *obstacle* or obstruction that temporarily impedes progress, but is not necessarily impassable. [Writers never tire of depicting the *barriers* that arise between parents and growing children; The thick walls and moats of castles were built as *barriers* against attackers.] A *hurdle* is a *barrier* that one must surmount if he is to continue. *Hurdle* usually suggests challenge and a good probability of success: Every inventor faces many *hurdles* before his brain child reaches the market as a finished product.

A **bar** may be either a physical *obstacle* or a condition that prevents entry or passage: the *bars* of the lion cage; race, color, or creed being no *bar* to membership. A **barricade** is always a physical *obstacle*, and is usually conceived of as being a hastily erected *barrier* against advancing soldiers, rioters, or large crowds.

Impediment suggests something that, so to speak, entangles the feet and interferes seriously with freedom of action or movement. There is a tendency to view an *impediment* as more or less permanent. [His speech *impediment* made it nearly impossible for him to communicate with others; Legal insanity is an *impediment* to making contracts.]

Snag is literally part of a dead tree, which, lodged under the surface of a body of water, may damage boats. Figuratively, *snag* points to a hidden *obstacle* that one comes upon without warning and which is annoying or troublesome but rarely serious: Their plans for going into business sound ideal, but there is sure to be a *snag* somewhere.

Difficulty is the most general of the words in this group and may be applied loosely to any troublesome state of affairs: to have *difficulty* in learning higher mathematics; the *difficulty* of driving a car through deep mud; to have financial *difficulties*. See EFFORT, THWART.

Antonyms: HELP.

These words are applied to things or actions that do not occur often. **Occasional** means happening now and then at irregular intervals, and it carries the idea that recurrence can be expected: to make *occasional* trips to a museum; to attend an *occasional* cocktail party. **Infrequent** means occurring at greater intervals, and it neither suggests nor precludes recurrence: Total solar eclipses are *infrequent*.

Rare and **uncommon** go a step further than *occasional* and *infre-*

obstacle

bar
barricade
barrier
difficulty
hurdle
impediment
snag

occasional

infrequent
rare
scattered

occasional

(continued)

sporadic
uncommon

quent in that they are applied to that which is met with so seldom as to approach the unique. [It is *rare* to find wisdom in the young; Snow in Florida is an *uncommon* sight; The prothonotary warbler is a very *rare* bird in this state; That was an *uncommon* act of charity.] *Rare* has the added sense of precious: a *rare* medieval manuscript; a *rare* sapphire.

Scattered and **sporadic** both mean occurring in space or time in an irregular or random pattern. *Scattered* emphasizes things that are part of a group but are situated with large, unequal spaces between them: *scattered* homesteads on the Nebraska plains; *scattered* showers; *scattered* applause from a bored audience. On the other hand, *sporadic* describes things that occur here and there with little or no continuity: *sporadic* outbreaks of smallpox; *sporadic* sniper fire from roof tops.

Antonyms: frequent, INVARIABLE, *often*, USUAL.

offer

bid
present
proffer
propose
tender
volunteer

Making services available or giving suggestions is involved in all these words. **Offer** is the most general; each of the other more specialized words isolates one facet out of its total possibilities. *Offer* and **volunteer** may both refer to a generous extending of aid, services, or a desired item; this generosity may or may not follow a specific request from someone who is, in any case, free to reject or accept the gift: *offering* to do the dishes; freely *volunteering* information to the timid and bewildered tourist. When a request precedes the act of *offering* or *volunteering*, the implied situation is usually that of someone asking one or more members of a group to do a task. Those who *volunteer* agree to do the task by free choice rather than by submission to selection or command: only two trainees naive enough to *volunteer* for KP.

Offer and **bid** share the context of a competitive attempt to close a contract. Here, the very opposite of a generous and spontaneous giving is indicated: *offering* the dealer five dollars less than his asking price on the radio; *bidding* low deliberately in the hope that no one would mention a higher sum. Usually the act of *bidding* follows a request or invitation, but the *bid* would be accepted only if its terms were the most advantageous of those received. The one who *offers* or *bids*, however, is committed to the stated terms if acceptance follows.

Offer, **propose**, and **present** all share the context of putting forward ideas or suggestions in argument or discussion. *Propose* can also be used in a contractual situation, as in *proposing* marriage, in which case no previous request is implied and no following acceptance or rejection is necessarily certain. But the one who *proposes* something is bound to follow through if accepted. In the context of argument or discussion, however, *propose* and *offer* indicate a much more tentative situation, implying that a course of action has been suggested or a new idea brought forward, not so much to be accepted or rejected as to be explored and possibly shaped by still further discussion: *offering* a new slant on the problem; *proposing* several possibilities for coping with the crisis; *presenting* the pertinent facts without comment. In any case, *propose* implies at least temporary advocacy of an idea, whereas *present* suggests a much greater tentativeness still; indeed, a debater may *present* an argument only to refute it.

Present also has applications comparable to *offer* that range outside the context of discussion. Both suggest humility in certain courteous phrases: *offer* my condolences; *present* my apologies. Both may indicate bringing something forward for display or appreciation: the same producer who *offered* you last year's greatest hit; *presenting* six new productions in the fall season. Both words, here, suggest generosity, but if the

public must pay admission to see what is displayed, these words can
become unpleasantly self-congratulatory and euphemistic.

Proffer and **tender**, now going out of fashion, were once used to suggest something *proposed* or *offered* in a humble, deferential way. They
still are used in some extremely formal phrases: *proffer* my regrets;
tender my resignation. Their use in other situations might now seem
affected or coy. See TELL.

Antonyms: FORSWEAR, REJECT, *withhold*.

These words are all applied to persons who have passed youth and
middle age. **Old** is the most general word, with the widest range of
application. It may indicate strictly chronological age, referring to the
latter part of life: *old* age; an *old* woman. But it may also focus on
the negative qualities associated with *old* age, as loss of health, strength,
or motivating force: She was *old* at forty, but he still has his youthful
spirit at seventy-five. **Aged** often indicates a longer life-span than *old*,
applying to persons of very advanced years; it is more formal than *old*
as well as more limited in application. Specifically, it often points to
changes wrought by aging, suggesting a definite physical decline, though
not necessarily implying disability: an *aged* man advancing slowly, with
the aid of a cane; an *aged* crone. In a social context, the designation
"home for the *aged*" has largely replaced the plain (or blunt) term "*old*
folks' home"; the former may be preferred because it more easily suggests debilitation that might demand institutional care. **Elderly** is
more favorable than either of the foregoing. It is a polite term, often
connoting the dignity rather than the weight of years: their *elderly* parents. An *elderly* person has passed middle age but is generally regarded
as younger than an *old* person, both in age and in vigor: a resort hotel
catering to *elderly* couples; an *elderly* gentleman, silver-haired, with a
twinkle in his eye.

Superannuated and **senile** stress the negative aspects of aging.
Superannuated emphasizes the idea of being considered too *old* to continue in one's job. In a specific sense, a *superannuated* person is one who
has been retired because he has passed an arbitrary age limit, such as
sixty-five: a *superannuated* pensioner. In an extended sense, the word
means too *old* to be useful or efficient and has a disparaging tone: *superannuated* election workers, half-blind and hard of hearing but given jobs
at the polls by party officials. *Senile* implies a much more marked in-
capacity or decline. A person may be *aged* or *superannuated* without
being *senile*. *Senile* comes from the Latin word for *old* and points to
mental or physical infirmity accompanying extreme *old* age. *Senile* atro-
phy, for example, involves a wasting away of tissue and a consequent
emaciation of the body. Most specifically, however, in general use,
senile stresses the enfeebling effects of age on the mind. [She has grown
senile — her memory is going and she is in her dotage, or her second
childhood; He is as *old* as she is, but his mind is as keen and clear as
ever.]

Venerable and **patriarchal** stress the positive aspects of aging.
Venerable emphasizes the reverence, respect, and deference owed to
one's elders. It focuses on the dignity of advanced age, implying that
the person held in reverence is worthy of veneration, as because of wisdom, position, or achievement: a *venerable* father; a *venerable* sage. *Venerable* can also suggest a distinguished appearance: *venerable* white hairs.
Patriarchal means like a patriarch — the leader of a family or father of
a race. It is a close synonym of *venerable* but carries added overtones

old

aged
elderly
patriarchal
senile
superannuated
venerable

of power and authority, such as might be exercised by an ecclesiastical patriarch, or bishop. [The head of the firm was a *patriarchal old* man and struck awe into his underlings; an actor with a hoary beard and *patriarchal* bearing, often cast in Biblical epics; a *patriarchal* tribal chief.] See MATURE (v.), MATURE (adj.), REVERE, WEAK.

Antonyms: adolescent, boyish, CHILDISH, girlish, juvenescent, young, youthful.

old-fashioned

antediluvian
antiquated
archaic
obsolescent
obsolete
out-of-date
passé

These words refer to anything the times have passed by because of its age, inefficiency, or displacement by something superior, or because of changing tastes. **Old-fashioned** suggests that something has gone out of use because of an arbitrary change of custom: *old-fashioned* platform shoes for women. The word can also suggest a change in technology rather than in taste: *old-fashioned* 78 rpm records. The word, however, does not necessarily imply that the outmoded or superseded thing in question no longer exists physically: the *old-fashioned* wedding dress she had treasured for twenty years. Sometimes the word can nostalgically describe something valued for its quaintness, its formality, or its wholesome simplicity: the current rage for *old-fashioned* Tiffany lampshades; an *old-fashioned* wedding with all the trimmings; plain, *old-fashioned* home cooking.

Out-of-date and **passé** share with *old-fashioned* an emphasis on an arbitrary change of taste and style. *Out-of-date* is descriptive and neutral and may refer to a lack of factual validity as well as to a change of taste; *passé* carries a tinge of contempt for something no longer in vogue: statistics that rapidly become *out-of-date*; full of *passé* notions about what hair styles are chic and sophisticated.

Antediluvian, meaning literally before the Flood, is a hyperbole for ideas more neutrally expressed by **antiquated** and **archaic**. *Antiquated* suggests the continued existence of something very old and now functioning badly, if not also superseded long ago by a more efficient or useful arrangement: an *antiquated*, treadle-operated sewing machine. *Archaic* may also suggest something old but still surviving; in this sense, it implies a given period in the past and can be used solely to classify rather than to evaluate: the *archaic* dress of the Amish; a statue carved in the *archaic* manner. In other senses, *archaic* refers to something extremely old and not now in general use; in this case it can be a more formal or technical substitute for *old-fashioned*: many *archaic* declensions that were abandoned during the development of the language. The hyperbolic *antediluvian* is mostly used humorously for any of these meanings of *antiquated* or *archaic*, with the added suggestion, when it pertains to ideas, of an extremely conservative or reactionary temper: an economic policy as *antediluvian* as a troglodyte.

Obsolete and **obsolescent** refer to different moments in the same process. *Obsolete* indicates what has already passed totally from use or adherence or what has been completely superseded; *obsolescent* points to what is now passing away: The death penalty for theft has long been *obsolete*, but for graver crimes it is only now becoming *obsolescent*. *Obsolescent* has a special reference, as well, to arbitrary modifications of a product that are deliberately introduced not to increase its usefulness but to make earlier models seem *passé*: Automobiles, like women's clothes, are now designed to become *obsolescent* in a single year.

Obsolete, obsolescent, and *archaic* are all applied to words that are now seldom or never used. An *obsolete* word is no longer used either in speech or writing, usually because it has been supplanted by a different word. "Oscitate," meaning to yawn, is now *obsolete*. An *obsolescent* word, though still in use, is becoming *obsolete*. Much modern slang rapidly becomes *obsolescent*. *Archaic* words were current at some time in the past, and appear in literature and in the Bible; unlike *obsolete* words they are still used, either for effect, because they have an unmistakable flavor of their period or milieu, or else by persons whose vocabularies were formed in a distinctively earlier era. The word "methinks" and the phrase "I trow" are *archaic*. See ANCIENT, UNUSUAL.

Antonyms: à la mode, avant-garde, MODERN, STYLISH, UP-TO-DATE.

These words all denote an empty space or a hole in something. **Opening**, the most general of these words, refers to any vacant or unobstructed space, as a hole or passage. It can be substituted for each of the other words here considered in many contexts: an *opening* cut in a fence for passers-by to watch the construction going on in an excavation; an *opening* in the ground serving as a sump. An *opening* in a forest is a tract where few or no trees grow. Thus an *opening* may be either natural or contrived. **Gap** usually applies to a wide crack and suggests a deviation from the normal or regular conformation: a *gap* between two teeth; a large *gap* in the wall of the bombed building. *Gap* is also used abstractly, indicating a break in continuity: a *gap* in one's memory. **Aperture** is a more formal word than *opening*, and applies to any *opening* or cleft in a surface, regardless of the nature of the cause: windows regarded as *apertures* in walls; *apertures* in the leaves of a diseased tree. The *aperture* of a camera is an *opening*, often adjustable in diameter, through which light enters the lens. **Orifice**, which is derived etymologically from the Latin word for mouth, refers to an *aperture* or *opening* into a cavity or enclosed place, and therefore suggests a point of access or entry: the *orifice* of a chimney; the *orifice* of a test tube; Smoke belched from the *orifice* of the volcano. *Orifice* is much used in medical contexts in reference to *openings* into body cavities. The pulmonary *orifice*, for example, is the *opening* of the pulmonary artery into the heart. **Interstice** is a very formal word suitable only in contexts where preciseness of description is necessary. It refers to one of a series of narrow spaces or *openings* between adjoining things or parts. [The *interstices* of a sweater knitted with thick wool are comparatively large; If the *interstices* in a fisherman's net are too large, too many fish will escape through the meshes.] See CRACK, CUT, HOLE, LEAK, VACANT.

These words designate thoughts or feelings about a subject. **Opinion** ranges from purely personal prejudice to relatively authoritative judgment. At both extremes, however, it implies a prior formulation of ideas or conclusions regarding a matter in dispute or under consideration. At its most individual, it involves evaluation, indicating an expression of personal thought, feeling, preference, or taste. [What is your *opinion* of the latest styles?] In a more conclusive sense, it may represent an expert judgment in a matter of objective fact or truth. [In the *opinion* of my doctors, I should be well enough to travel by next week.] In all cases, however, *opinion* is carefully distinguished from fact. An *opinion* may be held with confidence, but it still falls short of positive knowledge and is open to challenge. [She sought the *opinion* of several experts, but even the experts disagree.] In a broader frame of reference, *opinion* may indicate prevailing ideas that many people hold in common: public *opinion*. At its most definite, it designates the formal announcement of the conclusions of a court: the majority *opinion* of the

opening

aperture
gap
interstice
orifice

opinion

belief
conviction
estimate
impression
sentiment
view

Supreme Court, citing precedents and outlining constitutional principles in support of a decision.

Sentiment and **view** relate to personal *opinion*, and both frequently appear in the plural. *Sentiment* stresses feeling rather than reason, often indicating an idealistic approach or emotional stand rather than a pragmatic one. The word is now encountered only in certain contexts. [His Fourth of July speech was full of patriotic *sentiments*; the *sentiment* expressed on a greeting card; A clever lawyer will try to assess the *sentiments* of a jury before launching his defense; I agree with you — those are my *sentiments* exactly.] *View* stresses the personal element, emphasizing an individual attitude, approach, or point of focus. [In my *view*, the scheme seems unworkable; a newsletter setting forth the congressman's *views* on Vietnam and the proposed tax cut; a naturalistic novelist's *view* of society.]

Impression and **estimate** stress the element of uncertainty in venturing an *opinion*. An *impression* arises from external factors, whether it leaves its mark on the senses or the mind. The word may indicate the first reaction of the mind, before the due consideration that warrants an *opinion*, and may imply a superficial *view* or conclusion: the danger of judging on the basis of first *impressions*. In other cases, *impression* may emphasize vagueness of recollection, or caution and unsureness in stating a *view*. [My *impression* is that she was lying, but I couldn't swear to it; He had the *impression* that they had met before.] Unlike an *impression*, an *estimate* does not reflect an uncertain memory or mind; instead, it involves a personal appraisal or a value judgment. An *estimate* is based on the pertinent facts available at the time, the implication being that other, unknown factors might enter in at a later stage. [The final bill was considerably higher than the repairman's original *estimate*.] An *estimate* also involves a consideration of the different aspects of a thing, or a weighing of pros and cons, with the attendant possibility of error in judgment. [After reviewing his first batch of work, what is your *estimate* of his ability?; a critical *estimate* of Henry James.]

Belief and **conviction** are examples of positive *opinion*. A *belief* is something accepted by the mind as being true without certain proof. It may either originate in the mind or be instilled in the mind by others: a child's *belief* that monsters lurk in the dark; a boy's *belief* in Santa Claus. *Belief* has a wide range of application, embracing ideas, theories, philosophies, religious creeds or tenets, superstitions: a *belief* that men are basically good; the Christian *belief* that Jesus was the son of God; the *belief* that Friday the 13th is unlucky. *Belief*, itself, may range from simple, unquestioning acceptance to deep emotional involvement: *belief* in a news report; *belief* in a friend's innocence. Sometimes, however, it may convey a lingering uncertainty. [It's my *belief* that she'll succeed, but only time will tell.] A *conviction* is a strong *belief* arising from a deepseated feeling of certainty. The word often implies the overcoming of previous doubt or skepticism. [Columbus' voyage to America was based on his *conviction* that the world was round; to have the courage of one's *convictions*.] See BELIEVABLE, EMOTION, IDEA, SUPPOSE.

opponent

adversary
antagonist

These words all designate a person or thing that opposes or is hostile to another person or thing. **Opponent**, the most general term in the group, designates a person engaged in some kind of disagreement, competition, opposition, or conflict. Because of the wide range of uses for this word, it cannot be said by definition that an *opponent* is hostile or not hostile; only the context in question can determine this qualification. [The two

opponent
(continued)

competitor
enemy
foe
rival

men had become fast friends when they were *opponents* in a chess tournament; *Opponents* of the proposed civil rights legislation defeated the measure in a bitter fight on the Senate floor.] **Antagonist**, unlike *opponent*, can refer to an impersonal agent: Science and superstition are eternal *antagonists*. When applied to a person, however, *antagonist* suggests more hostility or sharper opposition than *opponent* does: His political *antagonist* was determined to used every possible means to defeat the governor's bid for reelection. **Adversary**, like *opponent* and *antagonist*, is a general word with a wide range of application. [The district attorney has a kind of intuition which makes him a formidable courtroom *adversary*; Army and Notre Dame are worthy *adversaries* on the football field.] But usually *adversary* suggests a person or side that not only opposes another in fact, but does so with hostility or malignity: The two countries were ancient *adversaries* and had met more than once on the field of battle.

Rival and **competitor** both denote a person who seeks the same object or end for which another is striving; but whereas the *competitor* may be impersonal and contend with no hostility, the *rival* is usually motivated by personal feelings that can make him inimical or malicious. [The small store owner often welcomes a nearby *competitor* to stimulate business; The two men were not only *rivals* for the same job but also for the same girl, a situation which caused an extreme amount of ill will between them.]

An **enemy** is most often a person who is moved by feelings of animosity to an attempt to harm or destroy: Because of an old family feud, the two cousins were *enemies* from birth. The word can, however, suggest opposition without hostility, or merely a simple feeling of dislike. [Smog is the *enemy* of healthy lungs; She seems to have more *enemies* than friends.] In military language, all who fight on the opposite side are referred to as *enemies*, or, collectively, as "the *enemy*." No personal animosity is implicit when the word is used in such contexts; individual ill feeling may or may not exist. **Foe** is very much like *enemy* in definition, but it is distinctly more poetical or literary in tone. It suggests a hostile spirit and purpose in all contexts except the most impersonal. [The U.S. and Germany were bitter *foes* in two world wars; Ignorance is a *foe* of progress.] See COMPETE, ENMITY, OPPOSED.

Antonyms: ASSOCIATE, FRIEND.

These words refer to easy, timely, fortunate, or practical actions that promote self-interest and the hope of gain or advancement. **Opportune** has the widest range of application. It may suggest chance action that gives unexpectedly good results: an *opportune* change of plans that placed them far from the area where the disaster occurred; an accidental encounter that proved to be *opportune*. More commonly, however, the word suggests a conscious choice with an eye to suitability or timing: an *opportune* moment to bid for the vice-presidency. Often the word suggests action that is taken to ingratiate or advance oneself; a note of insincerity may sometimes be present: making *opportune* remarks that he knew would flatter the prejudices of his superior.

Advantageous lays its stress on favorable results; these may be arrived at by chance or design, but the word in any case often suggests a self-interested rather than altruistic attitude: happening on the most *advantageous* spot for viewing the sunset; seeking out the most *advantageous* positions from which to attack the enemy; driving the most *advantageous* bargain possible; lobbying for legislation that would be *advantageous* to his backers. **Convenient** suggests considerations of ease and comfort: an apartment *convenient* to the city bus lines. The word is often used, however, to suggest that these considerations have outweighed such ethical concerns as truth or fairness: telling *convenient* lies, careless of whom she hurt; *convenient* excuses; *convenient* compromises that would offend no one but accomplish nothing.

Expedient and **politic** refer much more strongly to narrow self-interest. Most neutrally, *expedient* can indicate an improvised or temporary solution taken out of necessity: an *expedient* repair job that would at least get them to the next town. The conflict between self-interest and ethics is amply apparent in most other uses, however: appealing to the city's ethnic minorities as a purely *expedient* political gesture; twisting the facts outrageously whenever he thought it *expedient*. *Politic* is milder than *expedient*, suggesting actions governed more by immediate practical considerations than by any larger view: those who think it *politic* never to disagree with their employers. The word certainly suggests insincerity and the currying of favor, if not the disregard of ethics possible for *expedient*: another excruciating attempt to be *politic* about his mother-in-law's views on current events. See BENEFICIAL, CHANCE, FAVORABLE, OPPORTUNISTIC.

Antonyms: disadvantageous, idealistic, inconvenient, inexpedient, inopportune, unseasonable, untimely.

opportunistic

ambitious
aspiring
pushy

These words are comparable in that they all refer to people who desire or are actively striving toward the attainment of some goal. **Opportunistic** is used to describe a person who takes advantage of every opportunity presented to him that contributes to the achievement of his end, and who is relatively uninfluenced by moral principles or sentiment: an *opportunistic* young man who rose in short order from office boy to office manager by callously using everyone who could further his career. **Ambitious**, like *opportunistic*, is applied to someone who purposefully utilizes opportunities but, unlike *opportunistic*, this word need not always have pejorative connotations. *Ambitious* people may or may not be principled. What they must always be is eager and active in the pursuit of the wealth, power, honors, or whatever else they have chosen as their goal: a very talented singer who was not *ambitious* enough to make the grade on Broadway. Someone who is *opportunistic* or *ambitious* might at times be described by the more informal and almost always derogatory term **pushy**. In its application to different people *pushy* may suggest offensiveness, bossiness, or crudeness: a *pushy* social climber; a *pushy* advertising trainee. **Aspiring** is a milder and more neutral word than the others in this group. It does not necessarily have the suggestions of drive and energy that are implicit in *opportunistic* and *ambitious*, and it is certainly devoid of the pejorative connotations in *pushy*. An *aspiring* person seeks something above himself, as excellence for its own sake, and the word usually implies lofty ideals: an *aspiring* politician who refused to compromise his principles in return for favors from party regulars. See BOLD, OPPORTUNE, RECKLESS.

Antonyms: indolent, lazy, TIMID, UNINVOLVED.

opposed

adverse

These words refer to unfavorable, harmful, or hostile forces, conditions, or opinions. **Opposed** is the most general word and is usually applied to persons. It refers to mental resistance or a contrary view, whether or not action is taken against anything. [All *opposed* to the motion said "no" in a voice vote; One delegation *opposed* to the amendment decided

to abstain from the vote so as not to block passage of the main bill.]
Antagonistic, when applied to persons, indicates a much deeper rancor
than *opposed*. It suggests ill feeling, whether smoldering or out in the
open: *antagonistic* rivals as contrasted with friendly opponents; a delinquent boy, highly *antagonistic* towards persons in authority. In a less
personal sense, *antagonistic* may stress basic incompatibility of aims:
Capitalism and communism are *antagonistic* economic systems. Used of
forces, it may indicate a counteracting or neutralizing effect: *antagonistic* muscular reactions.

In one sense, **adverse** is close to *opposed*, indicating disagreement:
He was *adverse* to my suggestion. More often, however, the word is
applied to inanimate forces or conditions that are unpropitious or detrimental, working against the interests of a person or thing: *adverse* winds;
adverse circumstances; an *adverse* ruling in the lawsuit, denying his claim
to compensation. *Adverse* may even point to what is ultimately disastrous or calamitous: *adverse* fortune or fate. **Inimical**, when used of
personal attitudes, implies the unfriendliness or hostility of an enemy.
[His attitude is *inimical* to our project; a former colony, now *inimical*
to the parent country.] Used of forces and conditions, *inimical* implies
a basic conflict of interest or an inherent incompatibility, as between
nature and purpose: *inimical* and irreconcilable interests; a climate
inimical to the development of an agricultural economy. See HOSTILE,
OPPONENT.

Antonyms: compatible, complementary, FAVORABLE, *friendly, well-disposed.*

These words refer to positive frames of mind. An **optimistic** person is
one who cheerfully expects things to work out all right in the future.
This attitude may be well-grounded in fact or may merely represent a
determined attempt to "look on the bright side of things" regardless of
the evidence: unofficial polls that made him *optimistic* about the election's outcome; still *optimistic* that they would be sighted, after more
than a week adrift. The *optimistic* attitude may, in fact, be grounded in
a fear of facing actualities, or in blind faith.

Sanguine emphasizes almost exclusively a habitual frame of mind
that anticipates good fortune. The word can sometimes suggest an unfounded *optimistic* view that flies in the face of fact: so *sanguine* about
the future that he didn't bother to do the work necessary to realizing his
goal. The word is more formal than *optimistic* and may seem more natural in the context of British speech.

Hopeful is not so strong as the foregoing words; a *hopeful* person may
desire a specific outcome without being certain that it will come about as
he hopes: still *hopeful* that some kind of miracle would occur, long after
her *optimistic* mood had left her. **Confident**, by contrast, stresses conviction and certainty about the future; the word, furthermore, may
imply a conviction based on a knowledge of the facts: first quarter sales
figures that made him *confident* his business venture would succeed. The
word may also suggest self-assurance: a man who walked with a *confident*
bearing. See CHEERFUL, CONFIDENCE, FAVORABLE, HAPPINESS, JOYOUS.

Antonyms: cynical, defeatist, pessimistic.

These words refer to musical groupings composed of varying numbers
of instrumentalists. Of all these words, **orchestra** can indicate the
largest group of musicians; in reference to classical music, it suggests the
full-scale symphonic group with its complement of strings, woodwinds,
brass, and percussion. While such an *orchestra* might typically have as

opposed
(continued)

antagonistic
inimical

optimistic

confident
hopeful
sanguine

orchestra

band

orchestra
(continued)

combo
ensemble
quartet

many as a hundred players, the word itself can be qualified to suggest a smaller group: a chamber *orchestra* of twelve musicians. The one strict difference between an *orchestra* and a **band** does not pertain to size but rather to the fact that an *orchestra* has a string section and a *band* does not. While a variety of music exists for performance by a *band*, the word usually suggests light or popular music: Sousa marches played by the military *band*. When the reference of both words is to popular or jazz music, performed for listening or dancing, the implications of both words change. In this case, *orchestra* can refer to a group of any size: a nightclub *orchestra*; a six-piece *orchestra*. This word is often used to give status to what is in fact a popular dance or jazz *band*, whether or not it has a complement of strings. Both words here might, most typically, refer to groups having something like twenty or fewer players.

Ensemble is the least specific of these words as to the nature and size of the group of players. Technically, two or more players can make an *ensemble*, but the word usually suggests a grouping of several players, both in classical and popular music: a chamber *ensemble*; a Dixieland *ensemble*. Since the word can refer to any group acting together in concert, it can also apply to vocal groups as well as instruments: a choral *ensemble*. **Combo** is the more informal word for a group of several jazz or popular instrumentalists: a cocktail *combo*; a bop *combo*; a rock 'n' roll *combo*. **Quartet**, of course, is specific in indicating four musicians; otherwise it is completely open to qualification by context: a string *quartet*; a woodwind *quartet*; a barbershop *quartet*; a rock *quartet*. Other words indicating an exact number of players are comparable in use to *quartet*: duet, trio, quintet, sextet, septet, octet. See JAZZ, MELODY.

orderly

natty
neat
tidy
trig
trim

These words refer to good grooming or to systematic arrangements. **Orderly** is the most general and least formal of these words. In terms of something well-cared for, it refers more to places or things than to personal appearance: an *orderly* array of law books; an *orderly* studio. The word suggests a considerable mass of details that without deliberate efforts at arrangement can easily become disarrayed. Clarity may be the motivating factor behind such an effort: an *orderly* presentation of the points to be discussed. But the word can indicate superficial rather than meaningful arrangement: an *orderly* but not very searching mind. **Tidy** need not imply the arrangement of as many details as *orderly* but it does suggest greater adherence to the arrangement chosen, even to the point of possible severity or rigidity: a pleasant, *orderly* playroom where the boys were busy building a model airplane; a room so *tidy* that it seemed doubtful that anyone actually lived in it. Sometimes, the word can suggest a happy, feminine touch, but conversely it can sometimes point to primness instead: a *tidy* bedroom with pink curtains and a simple dressing table; a school teacher who kept scolding her children about keeping their desks *tidy*.

Neat is the least formal of these words and applies much like *tidy*, but without the latter's possibly unfavorable implications. Unlike the previous pair, however, *neat* applies as well to personal appearance as to places and things. In any case it suggests careful, uncluttered arrangements or simple, fastidious good grooming: a *neat* kitchen; wearing a *neat*, newly pressed skirt; He was always *neat* in everything he did. But *neat*, like the preceding words, need not imply cleanliness, as can be seen from the common phrase, *neat* and clean. Something may be carefully arranged and yet not clean, although the two very often go hand in hand: The room was as *neat* as she had left it, although dust had settled over everything; a room that had been left *neat* and sparkling by our maid. **Trim** contrasts with *orderly* by emphasizing a sparseness rather than a quantity of detail; it also points to simplicity, compactness, and precision: the *trim* well-tailored lines of her suit; the man's *trim* haircut; a row of *trim* resort cottages. In reference to physique, the word suggests a healthy, appealing slimness: the girl's *trim* figure; the swimmer's *trim* body.

Both **trig** and **natty** apply mainly to personal appearance, particularly to clothing. Both may be more relevant to men than to women. *Natty* is often used humorously to indicate something extremely stylish, even something overelegant: a tuxedo with *natty* silk lapels; the teddy boy's *natty* Edwardian clothes. *Trig* can apply, as well, to good grooming in general: a *trig* West-Pointer; a *trig* secretary in her stylish business suit. *Trig*, in fact, can apply to something stiff and formal to the point of severity: the *trig* world of Madison Avenue with its colorless uniformity. See CLEAN, EXQUISITE, STYLISH.

Antonyms: *chaotic, disorderly, messy, untidy.*

These words refer to imposing a shape upon a mass of details in accordance with some plan or system. **Organize** indicates the most thoroughgoing shaping of materials of any of these words, since it can point to the achieving of either sequential or spatial form, or both. [He *organized* his speech so that his most telling points came last; The architect *organized* the multileveled shopping arcades around a central plaza.] In any case, while the word can imply the shifting about of given items, it more often goes beyond this to suggest an altering of each and the fusing or fitting of part to part to form a new self-contained unity. A common use applies to the shaping of work systems: a business *organized* into two separate but interlocking corporations; an administrator good at *organizing* new government programs from scratch; a union drive to *organize* unaffiliated white-collar workers.

Arrange most often indicates the shifting about of items according to a plan, but without necessarily altering the items themselves: the job of *arranging* his vast library by subject and author. While the word stresses sequence, a more complex spatial arrangement may be indicated: the painter's genius at *arranging* the graphic elements of his work within an overall design. A greater re-shaping of details is also suggested when the word refers to the creation of music to accompany a melody or singer: the composer who *arranged* her songs for voice and orchestra. **Order** can point to a thoroughgoing shaping and re-shaping of elements, like *organize*, but the word in this context is more formal and can be confused with its more common use referring to the requisition of something: catalogs for *ordering* spare parts. Nevertheless, the word can function, especially in an esthetic context, to refer to one aspect of the creative process: his ability to *order* the most disparate facets of contemporary life into a harmonious whole.

Classify refers to a categorizing process that at its most mechanical stands in sharp contrast to the creative acts that *organize* and *order* suggest. *Classify* can, however, sometimes refer to the creating of the categories themselves: Linnaeus' obsolete binomial system for *classifying* animal and plant life. At its mildest, the word can indicate the identifying of examples according to existing types, possibly with no actual *arranging* or re-*arranging* whatsoever: a walk on which he noted and *classified* every tree he came across. **Sort** suggests the selection of items according to type; this process is closely related to the categorizing process indicated by *classify*. Often, *classify* indicates a previous evaluative judgment and *sort* the disposing of items according to this evaluation: He *sorted* out the books he had earlier *classified* as worth saving. **Marshal**, the most specific of these words, serves as an intensification of *arrange*. In this case, items are brought together and *ordered* for greatest efficiency or for the most forceful effect possible: She *marshaled* example after example of job discrimination in her decisive statement before the appeals court. At its most literal, the word refers to the maneuvering of troops to greatest military advantage: an order to *marshal* troops on both sides of the mountain pass. See CHOOSE, CREATE, FORM, HARMONIOUS, LABEL.

Antonyms: bungle, dishevel, disorganize, muddle.

origin

basis
cause
root
source

These words refer to the antecedent, beginning, initiator, or motivating principle of something. **Origin** suggests a beginning of something in time or place, or something out of which another thing arises: the *origin* of the contract theory of government in the Middle Ages; the *origin* of the Mississippi; the birth trauma as the *origin* of fear and anxiety.

Cause exclusively involves time, but the span of time need not be so long as that implied by *origin*: Friction is the *cause* of the match's lighting: It also refers specifically to the notion of one thing arising out of another, rather than merely to the notion of beginning.

Basis may refer to a causal relation in time but more generally it suggests a principle that underlies some actuality: respect for law as the *basis* for a peaceful society.

Root and **source** involve metaphorical comparisons to a tree or a river. *Root* is most like *basis* and *source* most like *origin*: poor schooling that is at the *root* of the unemployment problem; Greek civilization as the *source* of our democratic ideals. The submerged metaphors in these words should be kept in mind; it might be thought ludicrous to refer to peak unemployment as the *root* of poverty, because a confusing image results. See ARISE, BASIS, BEGINNING, KERNEL.

Antonyms: RESULT.

ornament

adorn
beautify
bedeck
deck
decorate
embellish
garnish
trim

These words refer to lavish, detailed, or colorful additions to something that make it seem attractive, pleasant, or festive. **Ornament** indicates the addition of detail that makes something more picturesque: the iron deer that *ornamented* the lawn. The word is more common as a noun, referring in this case to possibly gaudier details: *ornaments* for our Christmas tree. **Decorate** is more widely used than *ornament*, applying especially to places or things: They *decorated* the bandstand with red, white, and blue bunting. Where *ornament* can sometimes suggest the addition of one or few details, *decorate* often suggests a more thoroughgoing approach which affects the whole area in question: a wall *decorated* in stripes of blue and green enamel. **Trim** is more informal than the previous pair. In the specific context of Christmas tree decorations, it can refer to everything that is added to the tree: the *ornaments*, lights, and tinsel used to *trim* the tree. In other situations, it can often refer to color or design applied to *decorate* the edges or accent points of something: a white house *trimmed* with green.

Embellish indicates the adding of flourishes or accent points, like *trim*, rather than the treatment of an extensive area, like *decorate*. The special implication of *embellish*, however, is that such flourishes are the expressions of the decorator's zest or are taken gratefully by others as making a material livelier or more interesting. Also, the flourish may be part of the material itself rather than an extraneous addition to it. [The oil portrait was *embellished* with cross-hatching of vibrant color; a speech *embellished* with amusing anecdotes.] Sometimes, the word can refer to the elaboration rather than to the decoration of something: the wealth of detail with which he *embellished* a basically simple plot line. *Embellish* can also suggest partial falsification or outright dishonesty: *embellishing* his dull life with fictitious adventures; He didn't lie so much as *embellish* the truth a little. Both *ornament* and *embellish* can also refer to musical flourishes (such as grace notes or trills, also collectively called *ornaments*, ornamentation, or embellishments): Baroque composers often expected the performer to *ornament* the melodic line as he sang or played. **Garnish** is similar to *embellish* in indicating the inclusion of accent points to make something more lively or appealing and is now most often applied to foods: an omelette *garnished* with parsley.

Adorn and **beautify** both often apply to substantial external changes that are made to give something a more pleasing appearance. *Adorn* can also apply to the adding of accents, but more often it suggests the clothing or dressing up of something in attractive materials: women *adorned* in jewels and furs. *Beautify* can sometimes refer specifically to the applying of make-up, but it can also apply very generally to any attempt to make something more attractive: mascara to *beautify* the eyes; a program to *beautify* the nation's highways. *Beautify* can also indicate *decorating* something in a garish or heavy-handed way: motels *beautified* with chrome and neon.

Deck and **bedeck** can also sound old-fashioned in reference to the adding of festive *trimming* or layers to something, though they survive in songs and poems: *Deck* the halls with boughs of holly; a garden *bedecked* with rosemary. Both can be effective as irony: a yokel whose hair was *bedecked* with hay; a dude *decked* out in his nattiest togs. See ELEGANT, GAUDY.

Antonyms: DISFIGURE, *mar*.

outrage

aggravate
bug
exasperate

These words refer to being annoyed, disturbed, or incensed by or at something. **Outrage** points to the most intense or extreme response indicated by any of these words, but it may suggest the least direct emotional involvement in that one may be merely an onlooker rather than a participant or victim: *outraged* by the international outcry against our proposal. Thus the word can suggest attitudes of moral disapproval, prudery, or haughty indignation at some displeasing display. Even where a more personal involvement is suggested in emotions approaching anger, the word applies to one's response at the actions of others, though seldom to what is done to oneself: *outraged* by his daughter's extravagance. Occasionally, the word can suggest a more direct involvement; even here, it suggests response to behavior or attitude rather than to physical or violent conflict: *outraged* by his repeated insults.

The formal **exasperate** and the slang word **bug** both introduce the personal element often lacking in *outrage*. *Exasperate* may suggest a final and complete breaking down of patience after repeated annoyance: so *exasperated* by his snoring that she went out and slept on the sofa. This notion of a build-up need not be present, however: extremely *exasperated* by the uncalled-for innuendo in the reporter's question. In any case, the word emphasizes an angry though possibly momentary loss of calm or control: *exasperated* to the point of incoherence. *Bug* may refer as a slang or informal fad word to any displeased response to something annoying, whether the annoyance is intended as such or not: *bugged* by the garish colors in the room; *bugged* by his constant snide remarks about the way I dressed. The word may suggest a process of growing annoyance, some single instance of a rising gorge, or even a continuing philosophical attitude of disapproval: *bugged* by his wife's heavy drinking month-in, month-out; an advertisement that really *bugged* me; those who are *bugged* by middle-class materialism. Also, the word can be used for a deliberate attempt to annoy someone else: trying to *bug* her about her dislike of housekeeping. The word differs in one respect from *exasperate* in that loss of control may or may not be implied by the word; it can apply equally well either to a "slow-burn" reaction that never rises above passive disgruntlement or to an *exasperated* or *outraged* response.

Aggravate focuses more directly on a slow process of growing annoyance, but without suggesting that emotions have reached their boiling point. In this use it is an extremely informal adaptation of the word, taken over from its reference to the worsening of an already bad situation: at first *aggravated* and finally maddened by the continual crying of the sleepless infant. Often, however, the word is used more loosely: so *aggravated* by the reprimand that he wouldn't speak to me for days after. See BOTHER, ENRAGE, UPSET.

Antonyms: favor, please, SATISFY, *soothe.*

outrageous

atrocious
monstrous
scandalous
shocking
unspeakable

These words refer to behavior that is intolerable or immoral, or to taste that is extremely vulgar. **Outrageous** can function in any of these ways. When its reference is to morality, it suggests irredeemable depravity: an *outrageous* distortion of truth. In reference to impropriety, it suggests extreme disapproval for conscious audacity: *outrageous* manners for which he didn't even bother to apologize. In reference to taste, it tends to be merely a vague hyperbole: her *outrageous* notion of what styles were most becoming to her. **Shocking** may apply either to an act of extreme immorality or to an unexpected or astonishing breach of manners: a *shocking* disregard for human life; his *shocking* rudeness to the elderly man. Where *outrageous* suggests an indignant response, *shocking* suggests a startled one. *Outrageous*, consequently, implies the stronger reaction of the two. Both may be used in a positive way: Tuscany's *outrageous* loveliness; the woman's *shocking* beauty.

Scandalous and **unspeakable** are more closely restricted to manners alone. *Scandalous* suggests a furor-creating breach of conduct; *unspeakable* suggests a violation of decency beyond the power of words to describe: their *scandalous* quarrels in full view of the neighbors; an *unspeakable* oaf. In a more prudish age, both words could actually refer euphemistically to anything thought indelicate: *unspeakable* frankness; the play's *scandalous* suggestiveness. *Unspeakable*, however, has maintained a wider range of viable uses than *scandalous*: *unspeakable* cruelty; *unspeakable* taste.

Atrocious, like *outrageous*, can still refer to extremely immoral acts: such *atrocious* customs as slavery and flogging. **Monstrous**, similarly, can still describe something extremely immoral, abnormal, or deformed: the *monstrous* policy of genocide. But both words have so often been used hyperbolically for anything bad or unpleasant that their original senses have been diluted: *atrocious* weather; *monstrous* luck. As hyperboles, both are commonly used to describe extremely bad manners or vulgar taste: *atrocious* rudeness; a *monstrous* style of painting. See DEPRAVED, GAUCHE, GAUDY, REPREHENSIBLE, VULGAR.

Antonyms: appropriate, commendable, decorous, discreet, HUMANE, POLITE, *tasteful.*

These words refer to statements that are simple, direct, or forceful, or to a guileless or tactless manner. While **outspoken** applies
approvingly to vigorous statements of one's position or sentiments, it
can also suggest a brusque manner or an indifference to the feelings of
others. In any case, it is the strongest word here, carrying overtones of
fearlessness and aggressiveness, as well: an *outspoken* critic of the automobile industry's standards of auto safety; an *outspoken* fool who blus-
tered and stormed but never got his facts right. Used in a more general
way, the word can indicate, with greater neutrality, a willingness to take
a stand or express oneself: He urged the timid boy to be a little more
outspoken about his needs and desires.

Where *outspoken* often implies criticism of others, **open** often suggests
someone's willingness to expose himself and his vulnerabilities to another
person: successful marriages in which both partners are *open* with each
other. The word can also refer more specifically to an unthinking
or fearless lack of secrecy, particularly in its adverbial form: They carried on their affair quite *openly*, without shame or guilt. The word can
also apply to whatever is widely known, or to public statements deliberately made for the record: an *open* secret; an *open* scandal; an *open*
avowal of their intention to compete for the government contract. By
extension, the word can indicate whatever is tantamount to a direct or
public acknowledgment: She gave me a smile that was an *open* admission of her contempt for our immediate superior.

Straightforward most often applies to a character trait; it indicates
a lack of deviousness in the way someone deals with other people.
While it suggests unflinching directness in making requests of others,
it does not need to suggest either a lack of consideration, as is possible
for *outspoken*, or a willingness to be exposed and vulnerable, like *open*:
a courteous but *straightforward* request to hear my reasons for disagreeing with him; a *straightforward* refusal to give me the facts about his
past. **Forthright** is more closely related to *open* in suggesting either a
readiness to respond to the requests of others or a sincere statement that
does not hedge or involve evasion: a *forthright* person, always willing
to give his opinion for whatever it might be worth; a *forthright* expression of his dissatisfaction with his own work on the community beauti-
fication project.

Plain-spoken is like *straightforward* in indicating directness, but
adds to this implications of simple and unambiguous utterance, as well:
She replied to their complex reasons and arguments with a *plain-spoken*
refusal to cooperate. The word can even function more emphatically to
indicate a terse or blunt statement that flat-footedly rejects circumlocutions and euphemisms: He argued that it was merely being honest
and *plain-spoken* to speak about starvation where these sharecroppers
were concerned, and not about food shortages, hunger, or malnutrition.
See BRUSQUE, CANDID, SINCERE, TRUTHFUL.

Antonyms: CAUTIOUS, *insincere*, MISLEADING, *subtle*, TACITURN.

outspoken

forthright
open
plain-spoken
straightforward

These words refer to something of unusual distinction or relevance by
reason of its excellence or motivating force. **Outstanding** is the most
general and least formal of these words; most appropriately, it suggests
excellence: an *outstanding* scientist of the nineteenth century. It may,
however, suggest a feature that is sharply distinct from its surroundings:
the *outstanding* impression of squalor that the town left us with. The
word may also refer to the most important of a number of causative
factors: frustration as the *outstanding* cause of the prison riots. **Fore-**

outstanding

distinguished
dominant
foremost

outstanding
(continued)

paramount
predominant
preponderant
prevailing
prominent

most is considerably more formal than *outstanding*, but is otherwise similar in its uses. It more strongly suggests that the excellence, distinction, or power being referred to is simply the most important of many contenders for first place: the *foremost* interpreter of Bach; the *foremost* port of the region; the *foremost* reason for the legislators' change of attitude. When referring to a person's excellence, the word may suggest formal or official recognition and approval more than actual superiority: Kozeluch was the *foremost* composer of his day despite Mozart's *outstanding* creative triumphs.

Distinguished stresses almost exclusively this last connotation of *foremost*, emphasizing merit that has been publicly recognized or honored: *distinguished* composers who, unlike their obscurer colleagues, do not have to struggle to get a hearing for their music. **Prominent** carries less suggestions of excellence than *foremost* or *distinguished*. This word may point to status gained on other grounds entirely, or suggest merely familiarity to a wide audience: socially *prominent* families; a novel that became *prominent* merely for its sensationalism.

Dominant dwells mostly on causative force or a position of power: From his *dominant* position as chairman of the board, he neglected the testimony of the *foremost* authorities; his corporation, consequently, failed to make an *outstanding* contribution to the war effort. **Paramount** strictly suggests a singular superiority rather than a most important excellence out of many — or even out of a few: lack of morale as the *paramount* cause of our defeat. The word in many contexts, however, might be thought excessively formal. **Predominant** and **preponderant**, on the other hand, imply a narrower advantage over the nearest contenders. *Predominant* suggests a recent ascendancy or points to a factor that is closely related to other, almost as important, factors; the era when religious tolerance became *predominant*; an electorate for whom the issues are the *predominant* consideration out of many extraneous factors vying for their attention. *Predominant* is less used to refer to people; in comparison to the power and control suggested by *dominant*, it suggests less clearly defined or less decisive factors: the *predominant* apathy of the people that permitted the Nazi party to gain its *dominant* position. *Preponderant* may function similarly to *predominant*, but it may specifically suggest quantity rather than ascendancy. [All kinds of trees flourish in the region, but the *preponderant* species is the elm; Caution was *foremost* in the minds of a *preponderant* number of voters.]

Prevailing is closely related to *predominant* and *preponderant* but it suggests an ascendancy that, while usual, is by no means uninterrupted or continuous: *prevailing* westerly winds. It may also suggest a consensus that is decisive but far from unanimous: the *prevailing* bipartisan foreign policy. See CONCLUSIVE, FAMOUS, GREAT, SIGNIFICANT.

Antonyms: MEDIOCRE, USUAL.

overbearing

arrogant
domineering
haughty
imperious

These words are used to describe the character or actions of persons who are possessed of an exaggerated pride or who, often because of such pride, behave in an overly determined, commanding, or even tyrannical way. **Overbearing, domineering,** and **imperious** refer to the latter group, persons in whom we can recognize a strong desire to exercise authority or at least to force their wishes on others; all three words suggest that the insistence on being dominant is based on a real or assumed superiority: an office manager who was *overbearing* in his relations with his staff; a young man who never attained any independence and initiative because he was always under the thumb of a *domineering* father; a multitude of *imperious* demands that were met with reluctance and ill will.

Arrogant means unduly proud of wealth, station, learning, achievements, etc. Because of his exaggerated sense of self, the *arrogant* person takes upon himself more power or authority than is rightly his: the generals' *arrogant* seizure of the powers of state at the end of the civil war. **Haughty** is much the same as *arrogant* in denotation, but there is in the *haughty* person more feelings of pride and less compulsion to dominate than in someone who is *arrogant*. The *haughty* man thinks highly of himself while holding others in contempt, and may be rude and boorish or at least icily reserved in his treatment of those he considers to be his inferiors: a *haughty* socialite who refused to attend her daughter's wedding because she did not approve of the groom's parents. See CONCEITED, CONTEMPTUOUS, PEREMPTORY.

Antonyms: deferential, DOCILE, MODEST, OBSEQUIOUS.

These words all refer to the action of listening in on or prying into the private conversations or affairs of others. To **overhear** is to listen to something being said without the knowledge or intention of the speaker or speakers. *Overhearing* is the most innocent action in this group because it is accidental in nature. The only time the word suggests a lack of innocence is when we know the *overhearing* mentioned went on for so long a time that the accident turned into a design. "I couldn't help but *overhear* what you said to so-and-so" is often a euphemistic way of saying "I happened upon your private conversation and stayed on to enjoy it." The word for which *overhear* would be the euphemism in this case is **eavesdrop**. To *eavesdrop* is to listen in secret to some kind of private exchange. Unlike *overhearing*, *eavesdropping* is never unintentional. Even if one were to blunder into a situation where one *overhears* something private, the *overhearing* does not turn into *eavesdropping* without thought and decision: I took a booth next to the one where Marge and Jim were dining and before long I was *eavesdropping* on their conversation.

To *eavesdrop* by means of an electronic receiver is to **monitor**. The receiver may be planted in a telephone, in the wall of a room, in a chandelier, etc., and is designed particularly to listen in on conversation with military, political, business, or criminal significance. *Monitoring* is also the word used to designate a kind of observation or surveillance kept by a person or by a camera: Police *monitored* the suspect's comings and goings with a camera planted in a building across the street from his home.

To **bug** is to put a hidden listening device in a room, telephone circuit, etc. The device, which is called a *bug*, can be so small that it might be concealed as part of a person's clothing or jewelry. Jokes and cartoons have illustrated the fact that even so harmless looking a thing as the olive in a martini might be *bugged* to facilitate a planned invasion of privacy.

To **tap** or **wiretap** is to cut into a telephone or telegraph circuit for the purpose of secretly intercepting conversations and messages. [All conversations having to do with the planned merger of the two corporations were *wiretapped* by a competitor; She hired a private detective to *tap* her husband's office phone in preparation for the commencement of divorce proceedings.]

Snoop is a general term that might be used in place of any of the

overhear

bug
eavesdrop
monitor
snoop
tap
wiretap

words in this group except the innocent *overhear*. While *snooping* has always designated a particularly sneaky, unsavory way to pry, its conversion from a personal to an electronic technique has given *snoop* much more sinister connotations than it ever had before. See ENCROACH, MEDDLESOME.

overt

open
patent
public

These words refer to things that are made amply evident by direct expression. **Overt** indicates attitudes, feelings, and behavior that are put into words or acted upon, rather than intimated or suppressed: an *overt* declaration of his desire to marry her; an *overt* homosexual; rebellious feelings that had passed the talking stage and were about to become *overt*. **Patent** stresses that something is unmistakably obvious and clear: a grasp and discrimination that is *patent* on every page of the book. The word, however, frequently carries a pejorative tone: a *patent* lie; *patent* irresponsibility; the *patent* invitations of streetwalkers in Picadilly Circus.

Open refers to things done in an honest or unashamed manner, indifferent to criticism or reproof: easy to be *open* if you have nothing to hide; arguing that the gun laws were *open* invitations to violence; an *open* declaration of their stand on the controversial proposal. While a person may be *open* with his friends about his beliefs, he might still not wish to make **public** either his affairs or his attitudes. *Public*, thus, is an extreme case among these words, suggesting a deliberate revealing of oneself to the populace at large: a *public* announcement that he would no longer be responsible for debts incurred by his wife; a *public* address on foreign policy; voracious audiences who turn the private lives of movie stars into *public* scandals. See CANDID, PLAIN (adj.), TRUTHFUL.

Antonyms: IMPLICIT, *private*, *secret*, STEALTHY.

ox

bull
bullock
calf
cow
heifer
steer

These words come into comparison in denoting domesticated cattle whether raised for milk and meat or used as draft animals. **Ox** is a general term when it is used in zoology to refer to any bovine animal, whether wild or tame. Specifically, an *ox* is an adult castrated male, once widely used to pull carts and ploughs but now common only in underdeveloped countries. **Bullock** and **steer** are also adult castrated males, but *bullock* is more closely related in meaning to *ox* in that *bullock* also suggests a draft animal while *steers* are raised, usually in large herds, for their beef and hides. When one refers to beef cattle in general, it is proper to refer to males, females, and young as *steers*.

A **bull** is an adult uncastrated male kept usually for breeding purposes only. In Spain and Spanish America special strains of cattle are bred to provide *bulls* for the ring.

Cow and **heifer** denote female bovines. The *cow* is the mature female of any variety of cattle, but the word calls to mind the familiar animal that is kept as a milk producer on most farms. *Heifer* is a young *cow*, especially one less than three years old who has not yet produced young or given milk.

Calf is the newborn or very young offspring of the cow, and the term applies to either sex. *Bull*, *cow*, and *calf* are also used to denote the male, female, and young of a number of unrelated animals, as elephants, whales, moose, walruses, and alligators.

With various implications, *ox*, *bull*, *cow*, *calf*, and sometimes *heifer* are applied figuratively to human beings. *Ox* suggests slowness, clumsiness, and slow-wittedness: as dumb as an *ox*; as big as an *ox*. *Bull* emphasizes brutish masculine strength and virility: to roar like a *bull*; a wrestler with the strength of a *bull*. *Cow* is always applied in a derisive way to an obese and coarse woman, while *heifer* suggests a young, plump, country girl. The awkwardness and bumbling of a *calf* is evoked when the term, now literary and obsolescent, is used of a gawky, callow young man.

P

These words denote sensations of discomfort or suffering. **Pain** is the most general term, and can be used in place of any of the others in this group. *Pain* can be of long or short duration, in a local or a general site, and of mild or strong intensity: anxious about an off-and-on *pain* in the abdomen. An **ache** is an often long-lasting *pain*, usually dull rather than sharp, associated with a particular organ or body part: a stomach *ache*; a tooth*ache*. A **pang** is a sudden, sharp but transient *pain* that is likely to recur: the *pangs* of hunger. A **twinge** is very much like a *pang*, but milder in intensity and often one that causes a muscle to contract: a *twinge* of rheumatism. A **throe** (usually found in its plural form) is a violent, often convulsive *pain*, such as that associated with a mortal wound, the effects of many poisons, or a violent physical process: the *throes* of childbirth. A sudden, sharp, piercing *pain*, often followed by a cramp, is called a **stitch**: a *stitch* in her side that made her wince.

All of these words except *stitch* have figurative application to mental or spiritual suffering: the *pain* of separation; the *ache* of loneliness; a *pang* of remorse; the *throes* of indecision; a *twinge* of regret. See HARM, HURT, MISERY.

Antonyms: health, PLEASURE, *well-being.*

pain

ache
pang
stitch
throe
twinge

These words refer to things, particularly complexions, that are lacking in color. **Pale** is the most general and informal of these. It is the only word here that can refer to a relative lightness of color that is permanent or natural: *pale* Scandinavians and swarthy Italians; choosing the *palest* shade of blue for the bathroom. More often, however, the word suggests a temporary loss of color because of emotion or sickness: growing *pale* with fear; looking feeble and *pale* from his long illness. In these cases, it is the change in color that the word emphasizes. The change need not be negative, however: The eastern horizon was *pale* with the first hints of dawn. Because of the word's association with illness, it can refer more generally to an undesirable weakness or dullness: a *pale* performance in an otherwise strong cast. **Ashen** is a much more restricted intensification of *pale*; it refers mainly to an extreme but possibly temporary loss of facial color and usually points to an abnormal or undesirable state: a face *ashen* with shock; troops that looked haggard and *ashen* from the long march; the *ashen*, pinched features typical of undernourished children. The word can also refer to the grayish dull appearance of something that has been vividly colored: storm clouds that turned the bright summer sky *ashen* and somber. **Cadaverous** is an even more restricted and more intense substitute for *ashen*. It refers almost exclusively to a facial or bodily state and indicates a more permanent unhealthy or deathly look. In addition to a *pale* appearance, the word sug-

pale

ashen
cadaverous
livid
pallid
wan

gests a wasted or diseased gauntness as well: the bony *cadaverous* faces of fashion models; the *cadaverous* survivors of Auschwitz. Although the word compares this kind of look to that of a corpse, *cadaverous* is usually used to describe a living person.

Pallid and **wan** are both more formal than the foregoing; both can sound somewhat archaic or precious. *Pallid* particularly has been overused as a more genteel or supposedly more elegant substitute for *pale*. In reference to facial appearance, the word concentrates on unhealthy states rather than those resulting from temporary emotional seizures: the sick child's *pallid* cheeks. It would sound incorrect or affected to describe with this word things naturally lacking color: *pallid* snow. The word is useful, however, as a disapproving word for anything that is dull, dreary, or unspirited: facing the crisis with inept formulas and a *pallid* lack of imagination. Here, the word's suggestion of preciosity is sometimes consciously brought to bear with critical intent: *pallid* Victorian poetry. *Wan* is more restricted to facial appearance and less open to criticism on the grounds of preciosity; it emphasizes a loss of vigor, temporary or permanent: the *wan* faces of coal miners who seldom saw the sun; *wan* and wasted by disease.

Livid has almost lost any usefulness it once may have had by the contradictory meanings it has gathered to itself. Coming from a root referring to the color blue, the word can refer clinically to a bruised discolored skin. Many people, however, would tend to misunderstand the word when used in this way. Parallel to this use, the word can refer to a face flushed or purplish from intense emotion, particularly rage: absolutely *livid* when he heard the news. The connection with rage has become so customary that no change in coloration whatever need be suggested by the word. In contrast to this and to the word's suggestion of a flushed or a bluish cast, *livid* can also indicate a colorless or *ashen* appearance: the *livid* lips of the corpse. Some purists insist that only this last suggestion is valid, but such a use would be widely misunderstood. See BONY, GRUESOME.

Antonyms: colorful, flushed, glowing, ruddy.

pamper

baby
coddle
humor
indulge
mollycoddle
spoil

These verbs mean to treat someone with special favor, care, protectiveness or privilege. To **pamper** someone is to cater to him, to furnish him with everything he needs for ease or comfort: to *pamper* an invalid. *Pamper* may imply treatment so tender as to be weakening or debilitating: an aristocracy so *pampered* and overprotected that it could not cope with change. Whereas to *pamper* someone is to lap him in luxury, to **indulge** him is to let him have what he wants or do as he likes. Indulgence involves making an exception, yielding to wishes or inclinations usually denied; it suggests a relaxing of normal or proper restraint and a permissive sanctioning of pleasure. A person may *indulge* himself or another person: *indulging* oneself in the luxury of sleeping late; a grandmother who *indulges* the children so much that she undermines parental discipline. Preferences, desires, and needs may also be *indulged*: *indulging* a taste for wine to the point of insobriety. One **humors** only other people. To *humor* someone is to go along with him, complying with his moods, fancies, or capricious demands, though they may seem silly. [He *humored* his wife and drove back to the house to see if the gas was turned off; Though tired, he pretended he was a comic-book hero to *humor* the child.]

To **baby** someone is to treat him like a helpless infant who can't act on his own or assume responsibility. To **coddle** a person is to treat him with much more solicitude than he warrants, going to great lengths to spare or protect him. **Mollycoddle** means much the same as *coddle*, but it is a stronger word particularly suggestive of the overprotection by which some mothers insulate their sons from experience and hardship, thus making them infantile or effeminate. *Baby*, *coddle*, and *mollycoddle* are often used sarcastically or in exaggeration. [They *babied* you in high school, but you'll have to stand on your own two feet in college; You're in the Army now, men, so don't expect any *coddling* here; He claimed people on relief were being *mollycoddled*.]

Alone among these verbs, **spoil** emphasizes effect, the damage to the disposition resulting from overindulgence. According to folk psychology, one *spoils* a child by giving in to his whims and whinings, letting him have his way, according him privileges he hasn't earned and doesn't deserve; as a result, he may well come to demand special privileges as a matter of right, and may become self-centered, conceited, and selfish. [Stop acting like a *spoiled* child; His grandparents would *spoil* him if we let them.] An adult may be *spoiled* in a different way by growing used to unaccustomed luxuries, so that he can no longer be content with what he had before. [Wintering in Palm Beach has *spoiled* me.] See CARESS, LENIENT, PLEASING, PROTECT.

Antonyms: deny, discipline, neglect, withhold.

These words refer to someone who attaches himself to someone else in order to gain a portion of the latter's money, goods, or advantages. **Parasite** and **leech** both call to mind biological organisms that attach themselves physically to a host as a source of nourishment, often harming the host's health or causing death. *Parasite* is the generic term for all such forms of life; *leech* refers specifically to a bloodsucking worm that acts in this way. As might be suspected from this, *parasite* is the vaguer of the two words when the reference is to people, and *leech* the more pejorative. *Parasite* can refer to the draining off of any sort of benefits from someone else: a gigolo who had lived as a *parasite* off rich old melancholy women; a real *parasite* when it came to bumming cigarettes from his fellow office workers. The word can suggest a weak, spineless sort of person who gains another's confidence by hypocrisy or subterfuge. *Leech*, by contrast, is much harsher in its disapproval and indicates both a more ravening and more tenacious approach: *leeches* who clung fast to him while there was the slightest advantage to be obtained from his prodigality; such a *leech* that his patron was driven into bankruptcy.

Freeloader and **sponger** are more informal than the previous pair and suggest a more hit-and-miss approach to gaining benefits from others. *Freeloader*, the most informal of these words, suggests someone who makes himself easily available to partake of someone else's hospitality, with no thought of ever returning it. The word is particularly suggestive of the hasty and voluminous dispatch of someone else's food and drink: a *freeloader* who invited himself to dinner three or four times before we got wise to him; *freeloaders* at the party who found the host's cache of expensive Scotch and made short work of it. *Sponger* refers to a person with any sort of gain in mind; the word may be especially suggestive of a one-way borrower who doesn't return borrowed items, or of a person in a public place who ingratiates himself to get free drink or food: fearing that borrowing a cup of sugar would make her new neighbor think she was a *sponger*; Soho *spongers* adept at getting Americans to buy them endless rounds of drinks. As can be seen, the word need not

parasite

freeloader
hanger-on
leech
sponger

imply a permanent relationship and is less severe in its criticism than *freeloader* and certainly than the previous words.

Hanger-on is the mildest of these words, suggesting someone who has formed a more lasting relationship with his host; rather than snatch at benefits, the *hanger-on* may simply wait timidly for benefits as they are offered: a *hanger-on* who seemed always to be present, as though in hopes of getting some dropped scrap of affection; *hangers-on* who were content to flatter him in exchange for the lavish parties he gave. See FAWN, OBSEQUIOUS.

Antonyms: host.

pardon

condone
excuse
forgive
overlook
remit

These words mean to free a person from the consequences of his guilt or to pass over a blameworthy action without censure or punishment. **Pardon** is a more formal term than **forgive** or **excuse**, and in its strictest sense implies the authority to punish in an official way: The governor *pardoned* the man unjustly convicted of murder. *Forgive* is to *pardon* with compassion, usually on a directly personal level. [A wife *forgives* an unfaithful husband; A saint *forgives* his enemies.] *Excuse* is to *forgive* a minor offense, breach of etiquette, etc.: We *excused* his brusqueness because we knew he was under a severe strain. *Excuse* may also be used of larger offenses that are not criminal nor of a personal nature: The company *excused* the watchman for falling asleep while on duty. *Pardon, forgive,* and *excuse* are all used in polite exchanges to convey regret for having caused slight inconvenience to another. In this usage, *pardon* and *forgive* tend to sound stilted and sententious and are used less often than *excuse*: to *excuse* oneself for jostling a fellow passenger on a bus.

Condone and **overlook** mean to *pardon* or *forgive* tacitly by accepting without redress actions and situations that merit censure. *Condone* suggests the toleration of more serious offenses than does *overlook* — offenses of a public nature, such as breaches of the law: Child labor is still *condoned* in some states by officials who consider themselves upright and conscientious. One also *condones* faults that are similar to one's own: A man who cheats on his income tax and on his expense account tends to *condone* these practices in his friends. *Overlook*, a less strong word than *condone*, suggests an indulgent disregarding of unimportant lapses in behavior: to *overlook* a child's sloppy table manners; to *overlook* a bright student's failure to complete an assignment on time.

Remit, once a close synonym of *pardon*, is the most formal of all these terms and its use is limited to ecclesiastical and legal contexts: to *remit* sins; to *remit* a fine for disturbing the peace. See EXONERATE.

Antonyms: condemn, convict, penalize, punish.

part

passage
piece
portion
section
segment
subdivision

These words refer to something looked at as an entity in isolation from the whole of which it is a member. **Part** is the most general of these, referring to a quantity, sometimes amorphous or unspecified, of a particular whole: asking for a *part* of his sandwich; in one *part* of the book I'm reading. It can also refer to some independently structured member of a totality: the spare *parts* needed to repair his car.

Piece and **portion** relate exclusively to that aspect of *part* suggesting a quantity drawn from a whole. *Piece* is especially appropriate in reference to flat stretches of material, such as land or cloth: a *piece* of property; a *piece* of yardgoods. The word can also be used for other quantities: a *piece* of cake. *Portion* is most appropriate in reference to servings of food or to abstract qualities: a cafeteria that serves up lavish *portions*;

a man who possesses enviable *portions* of wisdom and tolerance. *Portion*, unlike *piece*, also has a specific use in reference to a quantity of time: spending a *portion* of each summer at the ocean. **Passage** is more informal than *portion* and is even more commonly used to refer to periods of time, especially to elapsed time: a *passage* of ten years during which I did very little traveling. It also has a special use in reference to *parts* of art works, such as literature and music: a *passage* from the Second Symphony that echoed in his mind whenever he thought of Paris; the *passage* in his book in which he comes out most strongly for freedom of the press.

The remaining words all refer to clearly defined entities or groupings within a larger, structured unity. **Subdivision** is the most specific of these, suggesting a rigid logical organization of *part* to *part* within a complex framework, such as a bureaucracy, a schematic drawing of surveyed land, a legal document with numbered or lettered paragraphs, or any detailed outline or system of classification: such catalogued *subdivisions* of nonfiction as biography, history, and travel. **Segment** can refer to a specified *part* of a geometrical figure or to some natural *subdivision*: the *segments* of an orange. It can also be used as a more formal word for a *piece* of some linear quantity, such as thread or wire: laying a new *segment* of cable to connect the two stations. **Section** is the least specific of these three words; it is more closely restricted than *segment* to refer to a structured part of an organized entity, but suggests less complexity than *subdivision*: that *section* of the Justice Department dealing with civil rights infringements; a wealthy *section* of town. When it approaches *part* in generality, it suggests a definable slice of a whole, sometimes isolated for the convenience of close inspection: calling his attention to a *section* of the portrait in which a later overpainting was clearly noticeable; the *section* of her will in which she disposed of her household effects. See ADDITION, COMPONENT, FRAGMENT.

Antonyms: entirety, entity, gestalt, totality, unit, whole.

---

passionate

ardent
burning
fervent
fervid
fiery
impassioned
vehement
zealous

These words describe intense states of desire, dedication, or conviction. **Passionate** and **impassioned**, both drawn from a word meaning to suffer, are most commonly used for states of desire, with a strong overtone of sexuality. *Impassioned* is the more inward and passive and less ambiguous of the two when applied to people, suggesting deep and abiding feeling. *Passionate* is less lofty in tone and suggests that the desire is more a matter of appetite. [Their quiet hour by the fire had filled her with such *impassioned* tenderness that she was quite alarmed by his *passionate* advances.] *Passionate* may even suggest a lack of discrimination: *Passionate* as he was, he had never truly loved any of his many paramours. It may, of course, be used without suggesting such negative connotations: Lawrence preferred the *passionate* to the rational life. When applied to the effective expression of strong feeling, *impassioned* is the more usual choice: an *impassioned* speech.

Ardent, **fiery**, and **burning** describe intense feeling in terms of fire. Of these, only *ardent* is free of negative implications in describing both desire and dedication: an *ardent* lover; an *ardent* patriot. *Fiery* would not be useful to describe states of desire, except for poetic effect, in which case it might be thought cliché: *fiery* embraces. In describing dedication, it suggests angry rather than *impassioned* conviction, and even wildness or instability: *fiery* demagogue; *fiery* denunciation. *Burning*, for both desire and dedication, has become a high-level cliché, avoided by some thoughtful writers: *burning* passion; *burning* issues.

Fervent and **fervid** come from the same root, meaning to boil. Their relationship is somewhat like that of *impassioned* and *passionate*. *Fervent*, like *impassioned*, implies being filled with abiding feeling; *fervid*, an intensification of *fervent*, suggests feverish intensity and a greater compulsion to act, with the same negative overtones possible as for *passionate*. Both *fervent* and especially *fervid*, however, have become somewhat stilted in tone.

Zealous and **vehement** are both more applicable to dedication than to desire. One might perhaps speak of a *zealous* lover, but hardly of a *vehement* one. *Zealous*, most strictly, refers to intense religious conviction, although it applies as well to unwavering adherence to any set of beliefs or attitudes: a *zealous* convert; a *zealous* rock'n'roll fan. The word suggests that one is prepared to act on one's beliefs unthinkingly, without question. This gives a strong negative overtone of one-sided fanaticism: the *zealous*, witch-burning citizens of Salem. *Vehement*, even more strongly than *zealous*, implies belligerence and challenge, but unlike *zealous*, it is more often applied to things or attitudes than to people: a *vehement* reply; a *vehement* gesture; He was downright *vehement* about civil rights. See BURN, EAGER, EMOTION, EROTIC, HOT, LEWD, LOVE.
Antonyms: COLD, IMPASSIVE.

pathetic

moving
pitiable
pitiful
poignant
touching

These words refer to the compassion, concern, or empathy that can or should be aroused by viewing the situation of another living thing. **Pathetic** pertains to compassionate concern or sorrow that is or should be inspired by those less fortunate than oneself. The word stresses circumstances in which a sufferer is reduced to abject helplessness: the *pathetic* struggle of the fawn to free itself from the steel jaws of the trap; those *pathetic* cases in which a child gets little love from either parent; his *pathetic* cries for help. The word usually implies that an innocent victim has unjustly or unfairly been harmed through no fault of his own. **Pitiful** may be used exactly like *pathetic*, but it has a wider range of use beyond this context. It can, for example, be used even when the victim may have contributed to his own plight or is wholly responsible for it: the *pitiful* loneliness of the alcoholic. It may also be used of someone who may not see himself as victimized in any way and who, in fact, may seem more fortunate than oneself: the king's *pitiful* outbreaks of incoherent rage against his most loyal advisers; strutting and boasting about his virility in a most *pitiful* way.

Poignant and **touching** are closely related; they both depart from the situation of victimization or misfortune to indicate anything that arouses one's tender compassion or empathy. *Touching* is the more informal of the two, suggesting a winning appeal or inevitably affecting scene: the mother cat's *touching* zeal for the welfare of her kittens; his *touching* request that he be given one last chance to prove himself. The word most commonly suggests an audience that is actually affected by the scene, whereas *pathetic* and *pitiful* may imply no audience at all or one that is hard-hearted: a *pathetic* figure that no one in the rush of indifferent passersby found the least bit *touching*. This same distinction holds for *poignant* which emphasizes the actual arousal of a bittersweet responsiveness that mingles pity and longing or other contradictory emotions. The word once emphasized the presence of any sort of keen, sharp feelings, but it now more often points to an ambivalence inherent in subtle or gentle shades of compassion, wistfulness, or nostalgia: Her *pitiful* face had not seemed *touching* to him at the time, but recalling it now filled him with a *poignant* sorrow and delight.

Moving functions more like *touching* and *poignant* than *pathetic* and *pitiful*, but it suggests the actual arousal of stronger emotions than any of these words, applying to compassion and empathy but also to a wide range of emotions beyond them: the anger he aroused by his *moving* demand for an investigation of the tragic fire; a *moving* scene of reconciliation at the end of the short story. Except when applied to a work of art, the word often suggests an arousal to specific action: a *moving* appeal that the *pathetic* victims of the plot be compensated for the injustices they had suffered. **Pitiable** is unique among these words in stressing that someone is deserving of pity whether or not this condition is noticed by others — or even detectable by them: a *pitiable* emptiness that he kept hidden under an outwardly happy and successful life; poverty made all the more *pitiable* by the indifference of the town's more fortunate citizens. See MISERABLE, PATHETIC, SAD.

Antonyms: farcical, ludicrous, ridiculous, unaffecting.

These words refer to a voluntary self-control, restraint, or passivity that helps one to endure waiting, provocation, injustice, suffering, or any of the unpleasant vicissitudes of time and life. **Patience** is almost exclusively positive in tone. Most often it refers to a willingness to wait without becoming disgruntled or anxious: showing great *patience* while waiting to learn the outcome of the election. More generally, the word can suggest a kindly tolerance for other people's shortcomings, including a particular ability to remain unperturbed by someone else's slowness or other quirks: the *patience* with which she went over the lesson until the dullest student in the class could understand it; responding with a kind of blank *patience* to his roommate's tumultuous comings and goings. Where *patience* implies little difficulty in putting up with annoying situations, **forbearance** specifically indicates a determined struggle against giving in to negative feelings that beset one. Thus, the word's stress is on self-controlled abstinence from hasty or ill-tempered action, whatever the provocation: answering with such *forbearance* that only his flushed face showed how angry he really was. In this sense, the word is positive in tone, more strongly so than the blandness of *patience* and its implications of passivity. But *forbearance* can refer less positively to an attitude that is disposed to put up with or endure annoyance or actual harm: minority groups no longer willing to meet indignities with mealy-mouthed *forbearance*.

Sufferance and **long-suffering** both suggest the passive endurance of pain or wretchedness, and as such both emphasize passive submission. This attitude can as easily be presented as a positive virtue or as a failure of nerve. Of the two words, *sufferance* suggests a more conscious choice in indicating the ability, possibly learned, to endure pain or evil that might destroy someone else: their *sufferance* of the scapegoat's role through centuries of maltreatment. More often, however, the word may suggest a generous tolerance for the foibles of others — or an immoral or permissive failure to take a stand in the face of evil: pragmatic in his good-humored *sufferance* of his students' pranks; the average citizen's apathetic *sufferance* of the regime's repressive laws against the Jews. *Long-suffering* is more informal and less wide-ranging in usage, referring to the *patience* with which injuries or misfortunes are endured, especially over a great period of time: facing his wife's invalidism with hard-bitten grimness and *long-suffering*. The word can also be negative when it suggests a person who glories self-pityingly in his own unhappiness at great length and with much verbal ado, but without at-

patience

forbearance
long-suffering
masochism
resignation
stoicism
sufferance

tempting to alter the situation: the tedious *long-suffering* with which she recounted every failing of her husband.

Stoicism and **resignation** refer to a more profound and abiding general life-view than the previous words. *Stoicism* most specifically names the philosophy originated by Zeno, who advised men to be superior to all life's passions — joy, grief, pleasure, pain. In general use, the word is taken to refer mainly to the ability to endure pain, however. Unlike *long-suffering*, even the popular sense of *stoicism* emphatically stresses the enduring of pain without complaint or comment of any sort and usually with complete equanimity: the *stoicism* of Indians who could be tortured to death without their once crying out for mercy. Only in ethical or philosophical discussion can the word take on a critical tone, suggesting a sterile attitude in which evil is accepted as inevitable rather than actively opposed: an invidious *stoicism* that allowed otherwise decent citizens to tolerate fundamental affronts to their own self-respect. *Resignation* is much more likely than *stoicism* to be ambiguous in tone. In pointing to unresisting acquiescence and surrender to the inevitable, especially to misfortune, the word can suggest a noble or dignified response to tragedy — or a craven acceptance of an ignoble or degrading situation: the stark *resignation* with which she stood beside her husband's coffin; railing at the *resignation* with which most voters viewed the corrupt political machine that ran the city. The word also can be less charged with affect, like *patience*, when force or compulsion is present: hopeless *resignation* to his fate after twenty years of incarceration in the Bastille.

Masochism is related to the other words here in that it refers to the enduring of pain, but it is in sharp contrast to them by indicating a neurotic willingness to suffer or even the conscious or unconscious seeking out of painful experiences: the *masochism* inherent in drug addiction. The word is drawn from psychiatric terminology, where it is sometimes compounded with its opposite in the term *sado-masochism* because of the intimate connection between the neurotic pleasures of inflicting and suffering pain. But *masochism* is used widely outside the clinical context for any tendency toward assuming a martyr's role, enjoying one's own miseries, or exposing oneself to needless pain: Only a streak of *masochism* in her could have permitted her to marry such a brutal man. See ALOOF, HEEDLESS, MISERY, NUMB, PAIN, SLOTH.

Antonyms: ANGER, *impatience, militance, restiveness, sadism.*

patter

chitchat
palaver
small talk

These words refer to glib or trivial discussion or conversation. **Patter** and **palaver** are the most general of these. *Patter* emphasizes rapidity and insincerity of speech whereas *palaver* stresses a lack of content or the intent to flatter or deceive. *Patter* can indicate mechanical recitation, reflecting its derivation from a reference to the hasty saying of the Paternoster; it can also refer to rehearsed comedy routines, or to bodies of dialect or jargon. Drawing from this range of use, *patter* in its conversational context adds to the emphasis on rapidity connotations of rehearsed or at least predictable conversational patterns: the conventional *patter* exchanged at afternoon tea parties; tedious *patter* about the warm weather and high prices. A note of condescension is usually present. *Palaver* is also condescending, suggesting exchanges of gibberish that are without substance. The word can refer to a public discussion or conference, reflecting its original reference to a parley between natives and an explorer or missionary; here the condescension is quite clear. More often, however, the word can refer to an informal group talk, possibly assembled in haste to decide on a course of action: the *palaver* of neighbors gathered in front of the house from which the strange sounds were coming. It can also refer to the disorganized uproar of voices from any group, talking severally: a general *palaver* that did not die down until the overture was half over. In either case, the word has a distinctly informal tone.

Chitchat and **small talk** are both restricted to idle conversation. *Chitchat*, the most informal of all these words, combines the predictability suggested by *patter* with the lack of substance indicated by *palaver*. In contrast to *patter*, however, it may point to a slow or low-keyed tempo and, unlike *palaver*, does not suggest group discussion so much as a random exchange of banalities or gossip: the kind of *chitchat* that was a sure sign the cocktail party was dying on its feet. *Small talk*, by contrast, also refers to low-key and trivial talk but suggests, as well, that such a conversational vein may be the result of choice or inhibition and may serve as an icebreaker or a prelude to more interesting matter: waiting for the *small talk* to get over with and the real discussion to begin; rehearsing bits of *small talk* with which to worm her way into interesting conversations she might overhear at the party. See CHATTER, CONVERSATION, JOKE, RAILLERY.

These words are used to describe people who are poor, who do not have enough money to maintain a decent standard of living, or who have lost their means of subsistence. **Penniless** usually refers to someone who has undergone a sudden, calamitous loss of money and property, but who, as a result, may not actually be in real want. [At the time of the stock-market crash in 1929 many wealthy men found themselves *penniless*; His father cut John out of his will and left him *penniless*.] *Penniless* may also be applied to those who make no real attempt to be economically stable, or who are unequipped to do so: *penniless* panhandlers on every street corner; a *penniless* artist who devoted all his energies to his painting.

Poverty-stricken is the most comprehensive term and may be substituted for all of the other words in this group. It is generally used, however, to describe people who lack the material possessions to make life even passably comfortable, either through economic stress or because, as in the case of members of some religious orders, they have chosen a way of life in which they must forgo many necessities and all luxuries. *Poverty-stricken* points to a condition that is more or less hopeless and permanent, or at least tends to go on for a long period: *poverty-stricken* tenant farmers who never realize any cash profit from their crops. The word is used also to describe conditions and situations which exhibit or even cause poverty: a *poverty-stricken* country with little industry; the *poverty-stricken* homes of Indians on some western reservations.

Destitute emphasizes poverty of such severity that one is deprived of such basic necessities as food, clothing, and shelter: a *destitute* slum family evicted to the sidewalk for not paying rent; *destitute*, lost children wandering about in a bombed-out city.

Indigent indicates a state of less dire want than do *poverty-stricken* or *destitute*, and it is sometimes used in opposition to affluent. *Indigent* is applied to those suffering from a kind of "genteel" poverty in which circumstances are straitened but something of the former outward facade is preserved: The *indigent* old couple, who find it hard to make ends meet on a pension, keep their home neat and tidy.

penniless

destitute
indigent
necessitous
needy
poverty-stricken

A **needy** person is one who is certainly *poverty-stricken*, or even *destitute*, but the word implies an inability to maintain oneself without some help from public or private assistance: Christmas dinners at a mission for the homeless and *needy*; *needy* children who receive free dental care at the clinic.

Necessitous is a close synonym of *poverty-stricken* and *needy*, but it now tends to sound literary and is infrequently used today. See IN-SOLVENT, POOR.

Antonyms: affluent, moneyed, opulent, rich, wealthy, well-heeled.

people

herd
hoi polloi
masses
mob
populace
rabble

These words refer to the citizens of a country or a region when considered collectively. **People**, the most general, is usually neutral in implication; it can be used simply as the plural of person, as a reference to all the inhabitants of a given place, as a reference to public opinion, or as a way to distinguish between a group and its leaders: only two *people* in the whole bar; the *people* of Mexico; wondering what *people* would think; politicians who deliberately mislead the *people*. **Populace** is even more consistently neutral than *people* and is more restricted in meaning, referring almost exclusively to the inhabitants of a given place: Nearly the entire *populace* turned out to hear him. It is often used in statistical accounts and has consequently gained a technical flavor. The word, however, comes from an Italian pejorative and is sometimes used in this older way: too grand to be seen riding the subways with the *populace*.

All the rest of these words, with varying degrees of intensity, are pejorative ways of referring to common people or the lower classes, attributing to them vulgarity, ignorance, or gullibility, and implying in the user of these words a conscious or unconscious snobbery. **Masses** and **hoi polloi** are least pejorative of these, for differing reasons. *Masses* specifically suggests the lower classes: concocting their tawdry sentimentality for the *masses*. Leftist political thinkers, however, have sometimes used the word in a positive or outraged sense: the exploited *masses*. This has blunted the pejorative force of the word. *Hoi polloi* refers more to the ordinary citizen than to class stratification. Careful writers remember that *hoi* itself is the Greek definite article: candidates seeking the vote of *hoi polloi*. An extraneous article is frequently added by others: swilling beer with the *hoi polloi*. Mystifyingly enough, the word is sometimes mistakenly used as slang to refer to the elite rather than to the ordinary people, and this has blunted its pejorative force: hungry workers watching the *hoi polloi* drive up to the opera in their shiny limousines.

Mob in this context implies that the general public can be considered as an ignorant unity joined together by fear and anger, one easily swayed by demagogic special pleading: wit and grace too refined to be appreciated by the *mob*. **Herd** is more negative than *mob* and stresses conformity, a gullible willingness to be led, or frantic but meaningless activity: a conservative taste in clothing that set him apart from the *herd*; specious appeals for peace that won widespread support from the *herd*; the nine-to-five *herd* of commuters.

Rabble is the most pejorative of all these words; it suggests a disorganized, poverty-stricken group of ignorant people. When it is applied widely to whole groups of people, it expresses extreme contempt for democratic ideals: explanations of tax reforms that were good enough for the *rabble*. For this reason, a demagogue is often called a *rabble-rouser*. See BACKWARD, FOLK, KIN, MANKIND, POOR.

Antonyms: aristocracy, elite, nobility, royalty.

These words all mean to become aware of through one of the senses or to apprehend with the mind. **Perceive** is the most general term since it has application to all the senses: a master chef who was able to *perceive* the most subtle seasoning used in any dish; a conductor who could *perceive* even the slightest variation from true pitch in each instrument. The word is most often used, of course, in reference to the sense of sight: to *perceive* a car coming toward one. But *perceive* has definite implications of recognition that are not present in the simple verb to see. [The object I saw in the distance was too shrouded in fog for me to be able to identify it, but when our car got closer to it I *perceived* it to be an old windmill.] *Perceive* denotes mental as well as sensuous observation when it is used to mean to come to understand: to *perceive* the nuances in different philosophical propositions; to *perceive* the difficulties inherent in a projected business enterprise.

Descry and **espy** are sometimes used interchangeably because they both imply a catching sight of something that is partly hidden, in the distance, or otherwise difficult to see. But there are differences between the words that should make their usage more precise. *Descry* suggests careful observation of the distant or obscure; there is more implication of effort and attention in *descry* than in *espy*, which hints at a chance, sudden, or unexpected discovery. [A sentinel on the watchtower *descried* the approach of an enemy patrol; She turned around just in time to *espy* an old friend disappear in the crowd.] *Descry* also refers to the kind of discovery that is the property of the mind and not the eyes. In this sense, *descry* means to understand or come to realize by examination and investigation: to *descry* the true nature of a complicated crime; to *descry* the differences between two seemingly similar passages of music.

Make out is a less formal term than the others in this group. It can mean to see, but it is less simple than that verb because of its suggestion of difficulty or effort. [The room was so dark it was impossible to *make* anything *out*.] It can also denote various kinds of mental seeing, as, for example, deciphering or understanding. [Can you *make out* the inscription on this old coin? It was impossible to *make out* what she was getting at in her lecture.] See ACUMEN, LOOK, SEE, SENSATION, VISION.

Antonyms: misapprehend, misconceive, miss, overlook.

perceive

descry
espy
make out

These words refer to something that is the ultimate of its kind. **Perfect** suggests completeness and lack of blemish; it may refer to something imaginary or hyperbolically to something that exists: the *perfect* wife; having spent a *perfect* evening. It can also mean utterly typical when referring to something that exists: a *perfect* example of romanesque architecture. It may refer to negative attributes as well as positive, in this case stressing total badness: a *perfect* fool; a *perfect* villain. **Flawless** relates closely to that aspect of *perfect* which emphasizes lack of blemish: a *flawless* apple. But *flawless*, unlike *perfect*, tends only to suggest a mere absence of negative qualities. Because of this, it is not used to indicate total badness; it would make no sense to refer to a *flawless* fool. Furthermore, something can be *flawless* and yet far from *perfect*: a *flawless* but mediocre performance.

Consummate is closely related to *perfect* in its sense of ultimate completeness: a *consummate* pianist. Here it gives an added overtone of slow maturation through disciplined effort. Like *flawless*, it does not usually refer to imagined excellence, largely because it stresses actually achieved qualities. Unlike *flawless*, however, it is often used to suggest total badness, like *perfect*: a *consummate* liar.

perfect

consummate
flawless
ideal

Ideal has the most strongly positive implications of any of these words. It suggests the greatest excellence that one can imagine: an *ideal* democracy that would require *ideal* citizens. If used to describe something that exists, the resulting hyperbole invites disbelief: the divorce that ended what everyone thought was an *ideal* marriage. As with *flawless*, it would make little sense to speak of *ideal* badness. While the word can mean archetypal in the philosophy of Platonism, this specialized use does not intrude into other meanings. *Ideal*, in general, is stronger than *perfect* because something may be typical, complete, or without blemish, and still be far from *ideal*. Of course, in ordinary use, both words are interchangeably used to mean anything pleasant: a *perfect* evening; an *ideal* vacation spot. See ENTIRE, FULL-FLEDGED.

Antonyms: DEFICIENT, *flawed, imperfect.*

perform

conduct
do
execute
fulfill

These verbs all mean to carry out in action, as an assignment or a task. **Perform** is precisely directed to this concept, though **do** is the most general term. When the two words are synonymous, *perform* conveys a greater formality than *do*, or implies a greater degree of difficulty and intricacy: to *do* a trick; to *perform* a feat; to *do* odd jobs; to *perform* an operation; to *do* one's best; to *perform* a miracle. *Perform* also differs from *do* in stressing the idea of a ritual or a formal public presentation: to *perform* a christening ceremony; to *perform* a symphony. It implies the rendering of a work or the carrying out of a rite that already exists, while *do* may suggest spontaneity and improvisation: to *perform* a play or a piece of music; to *do* impressions. In another comparison, to *do* a play is to undertake it and prepare it for presentation: The repertory company is *doing* Ibsen this season. To *perform* a play is to give it before an audience: They are *performing* Shakespeare in the park tonight.

Perform can also mean to discharge an obligation, duty, or command: He wouldn't promise what he could not *perform*. In this sense, it is close to **fulfill**, which stresses the accomplishment of something pledged, hoped for, or anticipated: to *fulfill* an obligation; to *fulfill* a parent's expectations; to *fulfill* a campaign promise. *Fulfill* puts the greatest stress of all these words on completion or consummation, the realization of potential or capabilities. Hence it implies an ultimate performance: The prophecy was *fulfilled*; a novelist who never went on to *fulfill* his early promise.

Conduct is close to *perform* but stresses direction, leadership, or supervision: to *conduct* an experiment; to *conduct* a survey. In a specific sense, with reference to music, it is used of a single person and means to direct the performance of a work: to *conduct* an opera. **Execute** is like *perform* in several senses. It can suggest intricacy, meaning to *perform* something demanding expert skill or faultless technique: to *execute* a tricky maneuver; a ballerina *executing* a tour jeté; a skater *executing* a perfect double axle. Or it can point to accomplishment, meaning to follow, carry out, or put into effect: to *execute* an order. It differs from *perform* in another sense, however, implying the creation of a work according to a plan or design rather than the artistic rendering of a completed work: an artist skillfully *executing* a protrait; a seamstress *executing* a dress designer's design. See ARTISAN, COMMIT, PERFORMER, SATISFY.

performer

agent

These words refer to someone who acts for himself or others. At its most general, **performer** may indicate the one who carries out an action: the *performer* of a contract. It may also indicate someone who can accomplish goals: children who are poor *performers* in school. In these

senses, the word can also apply to inanimate objects: a report that selected out those cars that were the best *performers*. On a more specific
and less formal level, the word is much more widely used to indicate any
sort of entertainer: clowns, acrobats, and other circus *performers*. **Doer**
has no widely used specific sense, unlike *performer*, and is even less frequently used in its corresponding general sense: separating mankind
into the *doers* and the dreamers. In such uses, the word can sound like
an off-hand coinage.

Executive at its most formal can refer to someone who actually does
a job, either on his own behalf or for others; this is best illustrated by
the compound nouns of certain titles. An *executive* director is one who
actually directs the work of his group, although someone else may have
the honorary title of director. In its most common use, *executive* indicates a person who belongs to the best-paid upper bracket of a business,
the one concerned with decision-making: *executives* who rank high
enough in the firm to have a private office with a window.

Agent and **factor** refer to a person who does something on the behalf
of someone else. Businessmen, authors, and actors all may hire *agents*
to conduct their affairs. A *factor* is an *agent* in business affairs exclusively,
one who will, against a commission, finance an undertaking or carry it
out. See ACT, ARTIST, PERFORM.

These words refer to a shape's outside boundary, taken as a whole.
Perimeter can refer both to the bounding lines that enclose a plane
figure and the total length of this boundary: He posted No Trespass
signs along the *perimeter* of his estate; the ins and outs of fjords that add
hundreds of miles to the *perimeter* of the Norwegian coastline. The word
can also refer to the outer edges of something far less clearly defined:
the shifting *perimeters* of each task force in the battle zone. **Periphery**
relates most closely to this last sense of *perimeter*, referring more vaguely
to the outer edges of something, especially as seen from within: a planet
on the *periphery* of the solar system; less familiar with the paths that
ran along the *periphery* of the camping area. Sometimes the word is seen
as applying mainly to solid objects, but this is not always true. The word
does have a more generalized use to suggest something that is far from
the center of things and thus of little importance: an official position that
was on the *periphery* of the administration's center of power.

Circumference refers to the *perimeter* of a circle, both to the line
itself and to its total length. By extension, the word can refer to the
bounding line of any curved shape, plane or solid: a hundred seats along
the outside *circumference* of the amphitheatre; a barrel that was four
feet at its widest *circumference*. **Girth** refers specifically to the circumference of a curved solid, particularly the waist or belly of a person or
animal: the *girth* of a redwood at its base; a strap too short for the *girth*
of the horse; a portly man of astonishing *girth*. See BOUNDARY, CIRCUM-
SCRIBE, EDGE.

Antonyms: CENTER.

These words can serve as arbitrary labels given to sequences of time.
Period is the most general of these and **eon** the least definite. *Period*
can describe any passage of time, great or small: a rest *period* of five
minutes; the stormy *period* of adolescence. In reference to history, the
word can loosely characterize a sequence of time as a convenient aid to
discussion, without claiming that such a sequence is homogeneous or self-
contained: the *period* of artistic ferment between the two world wars.

period
(continued)

eon
epoch
era
generation

By contrast, *eon* is used, often in the plural, to indicate an immeasurably long stretch of time. While otherwise vague in reference, it does explicitly reject any notion of uniformity in the *period* alluded to: the *eons* before man's appearance on the planet; the *eons* remaining before the sun's extinction. **Cycle** is much more clear-cut at its most restricted, referring to a single and complete instance in a recurring pattern of time. [A *cycle* of the sun takes a year, while one *cycle* of the moon, revealing all its phases, takes twenty-eight days; the life *cycle* of the hookworm.] Sometimes, the word can refer to the recurring pattern itself: the business *cycle* and its alternation between the bull and bear markets.

Epoch, most strictly, indicates an event of such significance that it can be said to usher in a new *period* in history: The bombing of Hiroshima marked an *epoch* in man's history. More often now, the word is used to refer indefinitely to a compact or self-contained *period* in human history, one that is recognizable because of a consistency in its emphases or concerns: the *epoch* of Spanish conquests in the New World. **Era** refers exclusively to such a self-contained *period* of history, although the time span implied may be longer than that suggested by the extended use of *epoch*: Cubism, Abstractionism, and Pop Art have all been *epochs* in the post-realistic *era*.

Generation refers to the *period* between the birth of the parents and the birth of their offspring, sometimes calculated for human beings as twenty or twenty-five years; the word may also refer to the offspring themselves: the first *generation* of Irish to be born in the United States. More pertinent here, *generation* has become a fad word for typifying any *era*, often shorter than twenty years, in which young people coming of age seem involved in a set of concerns or sociological behavior that is more characteristic of them than of their parents: the Silent *Generation* of students during the McCarthy *Era*; hippies who consider themselves members of the Love *Generation*. Often the word is used to make dramatic sounding phrases without necessarily being apt for the members of the whole group so typified.

Age might often suggest a longer lasting *period* than *epoch* or *era*, one that could be typified in terms of some dominant interest or person: the *Age* of Shakespeare; the Atomic *Age*; the *Age* of Jackson. Some writers feel that *age* is preferable to *era* in such designations, since the former is factual in tone, whereas *era* can possibly sound pretentious or inflated.

In geology, paleontology, and archeology, the terms *era, period, epoch,* and *age* have been assigned arbitrary definitions. In paleontology, the paleozoic *era* is divided into the *age* of invertebrates, the *age* of fishes, and the *age* of amphibians. In geology, the paleozoic *era* is divided into *periods*, such as the Permian *Period*, which is further subdivided into *epochs*, such as the Thuringian *Epoch*. In archeology, the basic division is an *age*, determined by the predominant culture, as the Stone *Age*, the Bronze *Age*, and the Iron *Age*. The Stone *Age* is subdivided into *periods* or *eras*, as the neolithic and paleolithic *periods* or *eras*. See EVERLASTING, MODERN, OLD-FASHIONED.

permanent

abiding
durable
enduring

These words characterize that which does not change, pass away, or fade. **Permanent** is a broad word and means continuing in the same place or condition without change for an indefinitely long period of time: the *permanent* foundation of a building; the *permanent* effect of Latin on the English language; *permanent* damage to the spinal cord. **Lasting** is closely synonymous with *permanent*, but is used to refer to something that may end sooner or later: a *lasting* friendship; the *lasting* effects of having been in combat. **Enduring** is a stronger word than either *perma-nent* or *lasting*, as it implies great resistance to both time and change: the *enduring* grandeur of Bach chorales; the *enduring* pyramids of Egypt. **Perpetual** is perhaps the strongest word in the entire group, and empha-sizes the sense of continuing endlessly in time. It refers chiefly to an activity that is not susceptible to interruption: the *perpetual* flow of the river; *perpetual* motion. In everyday talk *perpetual* is used of things that are annoying or seem to continue for maddeningly long periods of time: a *perpetual* rain; her *perpetual* complaints. **Durable**, less closely related to the above words, describes that which is able to continue for a long time in the same state and has the power to resist change, decay, and wear: *durable* woolen cloth; the *durable* granite of the cliff; the *durable* and indomitable spirit of the old gold prospector.

Perennial differs from the other words in that it originally stipulated a set period of time — the year. In one sense it has come to mean *lasting* for one year or recurring every year: *perennial* plants. Now, by exten-sion, it means both *permanent* and *perpetual* in describing something that is unceasing and also impervious to change: the *perennial* rise and fall of the tides; the *perennial* ties between parents and children; poverty, the *perennial* problem in our cities.

Stable applies to that which has a firmness of character or position so as to resist change or displacement: a *stable* currency; a *stable* econ-omy. Alone in this group, *stable* is applied to human personality as marked by steadfastness of purpose, emotional balance, and the ability to handle stress: a nervous, excitable teacher not considered *stable* enough to continue with her work.

Indelible means permanent in the sense of not being easily erased or obliterated: *indelible* strawberry stains on a tablecloth; an old letter written in *indelible* ink; a scene of horror that left an *indelible* impression on his memory.

Abiding refers to that which has continued and will continue for a long time. It is applied mostly to feelings and abstract concepts: *abiding* love; *abiding* truth. It is now found mostly in poetry and literature of the past, and is best replaced by *lasting* or *enduring*. See EVERLASTING, IMMORTAL, IMMUTABLE, MONOTONOUS, PERMANENT, PERSISTENT.

Antonyms: brief, short-lived, TEMPORARY.

These verbs express the action of passing into and spreading through every part of something, like a liquid or a gas. **Permeate** focuses di-rectly on this concept. It emphasizes both entry and diffusion, indicating infiltration through the very pores. It may be used in a physical sense: a waterproof fabric, treated with a substance that keeps water from *permeating* it; spring rains that *permeate* the earth. Or it may apply to a sense impression: Cooking odors *permeated* the air. It is especially ex-pressive, however, in purely figurative contexts, with reference to in-tangibles. [The atmosphere of Ireland *permeates* the pub; The spirit of his times *permeates* his writings; A sense of peace and contentment *permeated* the room, seeming to fill every nook and cranny.] **Penetrate** comes from a Latin verb meaning to put within. More strongly than *permeate*, it stresses the initial entry into something, and it usually im-plies the overcoming of resistance. [A powerful headlight beam was needed to *penetrate* the fog; Here no sound can *penetrate*; *Penetrating* cold went through his coat and chilled him to the bone; tissues that allow certain liquids to *penetrate* while preventing the passage of others.] *Penetrate* is also used of a figurative breakthrough, and may sometimes

permanent
(continued)

indelible
lasting
perennial
perpetual
stable

permeate

imbue
impregnate
penetrate
pervade
saturate
supersaturate

refer to a deep or lasting effect made on the mind or emotions: a psychiatrist using hypnosis to *penetrate* a patient's amnesia; an attempt to *penetrate* the boy's protective hostility.

Pervade comes from Latin roots meaning to go through; it marks a shift in emphasis from entry to effect. Where *permeate* refers to an action like that of a gas which diffuses through all the pores or intermolecular spaces of a solid or another gas, *pervade* describes the action of a gas which fills all the open space of a chamber. Hence a gas *pervades* a room by *permeating* the air in the room. In extended senses, *pervade* is more closely synonymous with *permeate*; it may be used of any quality, idea, force, influence, or sensation diffused throughout all of a thing. [The headmaster's influence *pervades* the school; A strange stillness *pervaded* the garden, like the hush before a storm; In the eyes of the priest, God seemed to *pervade* all of creation.] **Impregnate** goes beyond *permeate* and *pervade*. It stresses the new qualities or characteristics gained by a substance through which some other substance has been diffused: air *impregnated* with poisonous gases. It is also used figuratively: Every page of his work is *impregnated* with his prejudices.

Saturate comes from a Latin verb meaning to fill up, and **supersaturate** is an intensification of it. In chemistry, a solution is said to be *saturated* when the solvent can hold no more of the solute under existing conditions of temperature and pressure: water *saturated* with salt. A *supersaturated* solution is one carried beyond the normal degree of *saturation*, made to hold more solute by a mechanical process of heating and cooling. A slight jar or the addition of one more bit of solute to such a solution can suddenly produce crystallization. When air becomes *saturated* with water vapor, having a relative humidity of 100%, the excess vapor begins to condense as dew; when *supersaturated*, the air contains an amount of moisture more than sufficient to *saturate* it, as in a fog. In general usage, *saturate* means to fill anything to the utmost extent of its capacity for absorbing or retaining. Going well beyond *permeate*, it often suggests a thorough soaking or a being thoroughly soaked. [Moisture *permeated* the wall, leaving it damp; Rain *saturated* their clothes, leaving them sodden; A swamp is land so *saturated* with water as to be unfit for tillage.] *Saturate* is also used figuratively. [His mind was *saturated* with facts after hours of cramming for the exam; She *saturated* herself in the culture and customs of her adopted land.] *Supersaturate* also has extended uses, referring to more of anything than can be absorbed or accommodated: a *supersaturated* labor market, resulting in a high rate of unemployment.

Imbue comes from a Latin verb meaning to wet, soak, or dye. In a physical sense, it suggests the imparting of a color that soaks in deep and *saturates* the whole: The dye *permeated* the cloth, *imbuing* it with a rich red. In a figurative sense, it means to fill or *impregnate*, as with emotions, ideals, or other intangible qualities. [She *imbued* her son with the principles for which his father fought; fighting men *imbued* with patriotism; a strangely sinister place, *imbued* and *saturated* with an atmosphere of evil.] See IMPENETRABLE, IMPLANT, PIERCE, WET.

permit

allow
authorize
let

These words refer to the act of not preventing. **Permit, allow,** and **let** are loosely related, *permit* being the strongest of the three. To *permit* is to grant leave to or empower by express consent; the word suggests authority that could prevent, if it so chose: The chairman recognized the delegate and *permitted* him to speak. *Allow*, used positively, means to grant as a right or privilege: a teen-ager *allowed* to stay out until midnight and *permitted* to use the family car on occasion. *Allow* and *permit* are often used interchangeably; *allow*, however, is a less formal term and often carries the idea of simply not attempting to hinder. *Permit*, by contrast, implies a greater or lesser degree of approval and may indicate official sanction. [The nurse *allowed* the visitors to remain beyond the hospital visiting hours, though it was not *permitted*.] *Let*, the least formal of these words, may sometimes suggest permission or consent, but may imply no more than a failure to prevent or restrain. [She asked her boss to *let* her leave an hour early; Don't interrupt him — *let* him speak his piece.] A person may *let* things happen passively, either through choice or through indifference, carelessness, error, or inattention. [She decided to *let* her hair grow; He *let* his insurance policy lapse; They forgot to shut the windows and thereby *let* the rain in.] As opposed to *permit*, *let* may point up a lack of, or failure to exercise, preventive authority: a timid, unassertive little man, always *letting* people take advantage of him.

Authorize is stronger and more formal than *permit* and is more limited in application. It implies positive approval of a proposed course of action by an authority empowered either to *permit* or to forbid it. [The State *authorized* the construction of a new expressway; The firm *authorized* the use of a company car by the salesman after working hours.] *Authorize* may further imply the delegation of authority: a UN delegate *authorized* by his government to conduct formal negotiations. See ENDORSE, LENIENT.

Antonyms: enjoin, forbid, interdict, prevent, prohibit.

These words all refer to something that goes on existing. **Persist** at its mildest can indicate the lingering on of something beyond the point where one would expect it to terminate: A dwindling hope of restoring the monarchy *persisted* even into our own century. At its most forceful, the word suggests a tenacious will to exist, as in a hardy or stubborn struggle against odds: a species that *persisted* despite the coming of floods, glaciers, famine, and plague. Less favorably, the word can indicate an annoying or obstinate insistence that goes on without letup. [He *persisted* in quibbling about fine points in the contract long after everyone else was satisfied; Why must you *persist* in bothering us with demands for money?]

Continue is much more general than *persist*; it is also less definite, since its neutrality is uncolored by implications of any sort. The word refers to any on-going process after its start and before its conclusion: an announcement that the bombings would *continue*; the hope that he would be able to *continue* in school; The riot *continued* to rage out of control for another day. Sometimes, the word can specifically point to a resumption after a halt: Please *continue* with what you were doing before I came in. **Last** refers specifically to something that *continues* to exist, particularly when this is not necessarily inevitable: the few masterpieces from each age that will *last* centuries. At its most literal, the word can refer to remaining viable or alive, or it can be used in connection with measuring duration: perfume with a scent that *lasts* a long time; He *lasted* out the fever but succumbed to a minor infection; an avant-garde movie that *lasts* eight hours.

Endure can be used as a more formal substitute for *last*: a body of poetry that will *endure*. The word has richer associations when it becomes transitive; in this case, the word suggests the same dauntless struggle for existence against odds that *persist* can refer to, but here no possibly interfering negative overtones of obstinance obtrude, since *endure* is almost wholly favorable in tone: a patriot willing to *endure* torture and even death to defend his country; the traditional siesta that helped us to *endure* the broiling summer days of the tropics. Intransitively, **survive** indicates *continued* existence: Somehow, we *survive*. Often, the word implies the successful overcoming of an ordeal or threat to existence: Of those wounded in the battle, only three *survived*. Transitively, *survive* compares with *endure*, except that the latter suggests a strength and permanence that can overcome obstacles intact, whereas *survive* is open to the implication of greater frailty or subsequent impairment: Although many died or *survived* only as physical or mental wrecks, a few of the hardiest explorers were able to *endure* every punishment the untracked jungles could offer them.

Weather is restricted to a transitive sense that points to the *surviving* of crises or exposures to danger. The word may apply to *lasting* out difficulty without change or impairment, but more often the word does suggest an altered state, though this may often be one of increased maturity or mellowness: She *weathered* every conflict in their marriage without the slightest difficulty; an increased sense of self-confidence among college students who successfully *weather* the trials and tribulations of their freshman year; people who *weather* a first heart attack with only slight impairment. See EXIST, MATURE (v.), REMAIN.

Antonyms: collapse, DIE, *fade*, *fail*, STOP (cease).

persistent

ceaseless
continual
continuous
incessant
unceasing
unremitting

These words refer to what continues or is repeated without letup. **Persistent** can indicate an unflagging series of efforts, favorably implying determination or unfavorably implying a meddlesome attitude: his *persistent* efforts to better himself from his first job as a bootblack to his later work as a district attorney; annoyed by the stranger's *persistent* questions. The word is very general, however, since it can also apply to anything of long duration or to any series of repetitions: finally awakened by the *persistent* ringing of the alarm clock; the *persistent* brushing of oak leaves against our bedroom windows.

Continuous refers exclusively to something that is unbroken throughout its entire length, great or small, whether its extension is through time or space: a *continuous* expanse of wall without door or window; a *continuous* hum in one of his hi-fi speakers. **Continual**, by contrast, pertains exclusively to something that, despite short or great intervals of rest, is repeated over a long period of time: the *continual* coming and going of trains in the depot; a *continual* pounding at his door; the *continual* bickering of her parents.

Unremitting is an intensification of *persistent* in both the latter's positive and negative uses. When favorable, *unremitting* can indicate earnest dedication, suggesting an undaunted or relentless series of efforts or attempts: Robert the Bruce watched as the spider tried again and again with *unremitting* patience to weave its web. When unfavorable, the word suggests inflexibility or stubbornness; in this case, it can function more like *continuous* since it suggests an unalterable or unbroken extension of something through time: an *unremitting* hatred that had not dimmed in intensity over the years.

The remaining words are all drawn from the same root meaning to delay and could thus be understood as indicating something that continues without break. While all three words can be used in this way, **incessant** is now often used particularly for anything that occurs in quick repetitions over a long time span: the *incessant* crashing of waves against the rocks. *Incessant* can also apply forcefully to annoying or meddlesome repetitions: *incessant* phone calls from the bill collector; the *incessant* whining and complaining of the little boy. **Ceaseless** and **unceasing** are close, but *ceaseless* might be the word of choice for uninterrupted action, *unceasing* for unchanging attitudes: her *ceaseless* vigil by the sickbed; the loud and *ceaseless* playing of his phonograph; *unceasing* devotion. *Ceaseless*, thus, can be a more emphatic substitute for *continuous* in its temporal application, while *unceasing* can be a milder substitute for the favorable sense of *unremitting*. See EVERLASTING, INEXORABLE, INVARIABLE, MONOTONOUS, PERMANENT, STUBBORN.

Antonyms: OCCASIONAL, *periodic*, TEMPORARY.

physical

bodily
carnal
corporal
corporeal
fleshly
fleshy
material
mesomorphic

These words refer to matter or the body as distinguished from mind or spirit. **Physical** sums up the whole range of possibilities in these words, some aspects of which each succeeding word concentrates on to the exclusion of others. It can refer to the matter and energy of the universe and the science that treats it: the *physical* sciences. Anything apparent to the senses can be described by the word: the *physical* remains of a vanished culture. It can also refer to the body: *physical* beauty; a *physical* defect. Or it can distinguish the body from the mind: tests to determine whether the heart pains were *physical* or psychological in origin. In dualistic philosophy, the word contrasts with spiritual: rejecting *physical* attachments for enduring spiritual values. Most concretely, if somewhat euphemistically, the word can refer to sexuality: *physical* love.

Corporeal more clearly contrasts with the spiritual or immaterial than *physical*: positing a spiritual basis underlying all *corporeal* things. It can also refer to anything organized into an entity: the *corporeal* law. **Material** is a less scholarly sounding term than *corporeal* in its reference to matter or to *physical* objects: the *material* universe; his *material* possessions. The word is often used to distinguish object-oriented values from more idealistic ones: the *material* greed fostered by advertising. **Corporal** now refers exclusively to the body, intensifying the negative possibilities of *physical* in this sense by emphasizing most often what is applied to or inflicted on the body: *corporal* punishment. Beyond this stock phrase, in fact, the word is less often used than the more direct **bodily**. The latter can be neutral in itself; or it can be opposed to the mental or spiritual: *bodily* sensations carried to the brain; those *bodily* appetites that are considered sinful. Related to the last possibility, *bodily* can refer specifically to sensual or sexual pleasures, possibly in a disapproving way, although this use may now sound old-fashioned: *bodily* desire.

Fleshly and **carnal** both concentrate on this last implication of *bodily*, *fleshly* appearing in a religious context and *carnal* most often in legal terminology. *Fleshly*, however, can sound even more old-fashioned than *bodily*: *fleshly* dissipations. One use of *carnal* is so familiar as to have reduced its use in other ways; this refers specifically to sexual intercourse in the phrase "*carnal* knowledge." Where it once could refer simply to sensual or *bodily* appetite, this now might be misunderstood as explicitly indicating the sexual: a *carnal* licentiousness that characterized Venetian society. **Fleshy** is useful as a neutral designation for soft *bodily* tissue as opposed to bone and sinew: wounded in the *fleshy* part of his upper arm. The word can even refer to flabby muscle or fat tissues: his torso having grown noticeably *fleshy* over the years. Although much more formal and technical, **mesomorphic** relates to *fleshy* in referring to a body in which muscular tissue has been favored by development over nervous and digestive tissue: neurasthenic, pyknic, and *mesomorphic* body types. More loosely, as a fad word, *mesomorphic* can refer merely to a substantially developed muscularity: a gung-ho *mesomorphic* platoon sergeant.

Antonyms: mental, spiritual.

pierce

penetrate
prick
probe
stab

These words indicate the forcing of a sharp, pointed instrument into something by means of a driving or cutting action. **Pierce** may suggest merely the cutting of any opening into something, though more often it is used to indicate the cutting of a hole entirely through a thin layer to its other side: a screen *pierced* to let light through; *piercing* a balloon; a hat *pierced* by a hatpin; instruments with which to *pierce* ears. By implication, the opening through the layer is made by a sharp, thin object such as a needle or lance. **Stab**, by contrast, suggests that something is merely cut into, not *pierced*; furthermore, *stab* suggests the use of a bladed instrument such as a sword or knife rather than something needlelike, as with *pierce*: *stabbing* the man with his dagger. **Prick** is more nearly comparable to *pierce*, but specifically may suggest a light, glancing thrust of a needlelike instrument to make a small opening in or through a thin layer: *pricking* the blister with a heated needle; thorns that *pricked* his skin as he ran.

Penetrate is more formal and more general than the foregoing. It may suggest the partial or complete passage made by any sort of instrument: measuring the depth to which the bullet had *penetrated* the flesh; a façade of marble *penetrated* by three rows of windows. The word may also suggest the achieving of any sort of entrance into or through something, whether along an existing passageway, through a discontinuous mass, or through a permeable membrane; in these cases, the act may by implication be difficult but it may be achieved without altering or actually *piercing* the medium itself: brave explorers who first *penetrated* the jungles of Africa; light that *penetrated* through the dusty windows; tissues that allow certain liquids to *penetrate* while preventing the passage of others. **Probe** suggests a deliberate, cautious, or exploratory attempt to *penetrate* something; the passage may already exist or may be made by the act of *probing*: carefully *probing* the cavity with a toothpick; two men sent in to *probe* the tunnels for possible survivors; scalpels with which to *probe* the tumor for signs of malignancy. See CUT, HEW, PERMEATE, WOUND.

pig

boar
hog
porker
shoat
sow
swine

These words denote a domestic mammal whose flesh, called pork, is used as food in most countries of the world. **Pig** and **hog** are the most general terms: to slaughter a *pig* every year at Christmas; to raise *hogs* for the market. Specifically, a *pig* is a young animal weighing less than 120 pounds, while a *hog* is much larger and may reach a weight of five or six hundred pounds. Perhaps the fact that *hogs* are large *pigs* explains the relative strength of these words when they are used to describe a greedy or gluttonous person. *Hog* is a more abusive term than *pig*, which is often intended half-humorously.

Swine, which is also a collective noun, has been largely supplanted by *pig* or *hog* and now has a somewhat literary sound: Circe, who turned men into *swine*; a courtesan of kings, who tended *swine* as a child. *Swine* is still commonly applied to a person and is more insulting and condemnatory than either *pig* or *hog* because it implies not only greed, but viciousness and depravity.

A **boar** is an uncastrated male *pig* of any domestic breed. It also applies to a wild *pig* of either sex which is hunted for sport in continental Europe, southern Asia, North Africa, and formerly in England. **Sow** is the correct term for a female domesticated *pig* used for breeding. Figuratively, *sow* is used contemptuously to describe a fat, coarse, slovenly woman.

Shoat, a term largely confined to farmers and experts in animal husbandry, denotes a young *pig* of either sex who has been weaned and is still less than a year old. **Porker** is applied to a *pig* or *hog* that is being fattened for slaughter. It is also a mildly humorous term for any *pig* or *hog*. See ANIMAL.

These words denote the result of processes through which things or particles are gathered together. **Pile** suggests that the things which are gathered were brought together, usually by a person, rather than accumulated by chance or natural processes. It further suggests that the accumulated things were placed in some sort of order, one on top of the others, for example, or in layers. Finally, the things in a *pile*, such as the blocks in a *pile* of building blocks, are usually all of the same kind, and, more than likely, of about the same size and shape.

Heap implies a more casual gathering of things than *pile*. The things, which eventually take the form of a mound, are thrown together carelessly or haphazardly, and there is usually no evidence in a *heap* of selection or special arrangement: a *heap* of old clothes in the attic. **Agglomeration**, even more than *heap*, suggests a chance coming together of its parts, those parts being heterogeneous and not compacted, connected, or consistent: a room that was an *agglomeration* of so many different styles of decorating that it seemed more the work of an eccentric than of an electic.

A **mass** is an assemblage of things that, together, make up a single body. There is in this word a definite indication of adherence or coherence of the individual parts or objects and a suggestion that the final accumulated *mass* has no definite shape but is relatively large in size: a *mass* of clay; a *mass* of flowers. See ACCUMULATION.

pile

agglomeration
heap
mass

These words refer to large areas of usually level country which may be farm or grazing land, or unsettled wilderness. **Plain** is the general word here for such countryside, giving no information in itself as to fertility or other topographical facts: the great *plains*; the cities of the *plain*. **Steppe** suggests a specific geographical locale — that of Russia — but is otherwise general, like *plain*, with as little indication of fertility or infertility: Mongol tribes that fanned out across the *steppes*. While **desert** suggests no geographical placement, it does specifically point to barren and infertile regions lacking in rainfall and composed mainly of sandy soil or undulating sand dunes: the Sahara *desert*; an irrigation project to make the *desert* fruitful.

All the other words here point to a specific kind of countryside and suggest, as well, a specific geographical locale. **Prairie** suggests the fertile but largely unforested *plains* of the U.S. Midwest: the rich loam of Nebraska *prairies*. **Veldt** points to the fertile *plains* of South Africa; these are by and large grassy but unforested and filled with an array of wildlife. Unlike the *prairies* of North America, much of the *veldt* has not been converted into farmland and is still wild and pristine. **Bush** suggests, less exclusively, land that is wild, unsettled, and covered with scrub growth, as in East Africa: steps taken by the Kenya government to encourage cattle-raising in the *bush*. The word is also applied to the

plain

bush
desert
outback
pampas
prairie
range
savanna
steppe
tundra
veldt

backcountry of certain other lands, especially Australia, designating an extensive, unsettled or sparsely populated region thought of as being uncivilized, rugged, or wild. The Canadian *bush* is unsettled northern forest land. **Outback** specifically indicates the backcountry of Australia and New Zealand, referring particularly to the arid and unsettled northerly regions of Australia: the vast untapped resources of the Australian *outback*.

The **pampas** are the great treeless *plains* of South America, extending from the Atlantic to the Andes, south of the Amazon River. Like the East African *bush* country, the *pampas* are used mainly for cattle grazing, the land not being fertile enough to yield much in the way of cereal crops: gauchos who ride herd out on the Argentine *pampas*. **Range** is the equivalent North American term for the same kind of countryside: cattle raised on the Wyoming *range*. This *range* country is bordered by more fertile *prairie* country on one side and mountainous countryside or *desert* on the other, intermingling features of both.

Savanna, used of country in the southeast part of the U.S., designates a tract of level, treeless land covered with low vegetation. More broadly, the term refers to a large area of tropical or subtropical grassland, as an African pasture or a South American campo, covered in part with trees and spiny shrubs, and found in regions undergoing alternate rainy and dry seasons. **Tundra**, by contrast, refers to a flat or rolling, treeless, often marshy *plain* of Arctic or near-Arctic regions, as of Siberia, the Scandinavian countries, and the Eskimo-inhabited parts of North America. The *tundras* have permanently frozen subsoil and are poor in vegetation, though they are covered with moss in summer and furnish forage for such animals as reindeer: Finns who raise reindeer on the *tundra* in northern Finland. See BACKCOUNTRY.

Antonyms: MOUNTAIN.

plain

apparent
conspicuous
evident
manifest
obvious

These words all mean readily perceived. **Plain**, the most general word of the group, means clear and understandable, and suggests strongly that there is little possibility of confusion or mistake in perceiving the object concerned. [The *plain* fact of the matter is that the man lied; His guilt is *plain* — the stolen money was found in his briefcase.]

Apparent and **evident** are close synonyms, both indicating the easily perceived or recognizable. Of the two, *apparent* is perhaps more commonly used when referring to something visible, although both words are used to describe mental perceptions as well as sensory ones. [It was soon *apparent* to the crowd that our horse was winning the race; From the quick success of the business, it was *evident* that he had invested his money wisely; He spoke with *evident* sarcasm.] Because *apparent* can also mean seeming to be, as opposed to being in fact, its use may be ambiguous (especially before nouns), and *evident* may therefore be preferred in some contexts. For example, *apparent defeat* could mean that the defeat was more *evident* than real; *evident defeat*, on the other hand, simply states flatly that the defeat was *plain*, and makes no suggestion of reality contradicting appearance.

Obvious, **manifest**, and **conspicuous** mean immediately *apparent*, unmistakably true; all imply that the issue is so unequivocal and *plain* that contradiction would be absurd. *Manifest* suggests that outward signs or actions may be taken as revealing inward character; it points to openness and explicitness as qualities that make something *plain*: *manifest* disapproval of another's actions, expressed in forthright language; The *manifest* bias of the judge, referring to the young defendant as a punk, disqualified him from presiding over the trial. *Conspicuous* implies that something stands out, unavoidably striking the eye or mind as different or irregular: a *conspicuous* defect in the cloth; a *conspicuous* typographical error, with one whole line of type printed upside-down; a discrepancy in the company accounts so *conspicuous* that no auditor could have failed to notice it. *Obvious* describes something too *conspicuous* to be concealed and too *apparent* to be disputed: an *obvious* gimmick to compensate for the playwright's flagging invention. The word is often used to point up the disparity between form and meaning in disingenuous gestures: an *obvious* pitch for maintaining the status quo concealed within the high-flown plea for law and order; Though couched in elegant diplomatic language, the note *obviously* threw cold water on any hopes Israel may have entertained for U.S. intervention in the Middle East crisis. See CLEAR, DEFINITE, FLAGRANT, OVERT.

Antonyms: concealed, hidden, imperceptible, IMPLICIT, inconspicuous, secret.

These words refer to sets of ideas developed to accomplish a desired result. **Plan** is both the most informal and the most general. It can refer at one extreme to a tentative, unverbalized cluster of notions, and at the other, to a detailed final draft stating the precise methods by which to proceed: a vague *plan* to go there sometime; *plans* for a merger that filled six filing cabinets. **Scheme** is also informal, but is restricted in meaning either to a vague, unverbalized notion or to surreptitious or unsavory ideas. Unworkability may be implied in the former case, conspiratorial plotting in the latter: coming up with *scheme* after *scheme* for getting rich quick; their carefully worked out *scheme* for assassinating the prime minister.

Design and **blueprint** both relate to that side of *plan* that suggests a detailed final draft. *Design* can suggest harmony and order as the salient feature of the *plan*; it can also suggest a symbolic rather than literal rendering of the work to be done: a building noteworthy for its simplicity of *design*; a master who made the grand *design* but left his apprentice to fill in the details. *Blueprint*, by contrast, suggests minute attention to every last detail: a complete *blueprint* for enforcing the new welfare regulations.

Proposal can suggest tentativeness, like *plan*, but it strongly implies a context of collaboration through discussion, or a hierarchic situation in which approval of a *plan* must first be obtained: a *proposal* for spending the afternoon in the park; a *proposal* approved by the Senate but defeated in the House. **Program** may suggest a detailed set of *proposals*, but alone of all these words, it most specifically suggests a *plan* that is actually being carried out: the tenth anniversary of the once controversial tax *program*.

These words refer to an inclination to take part in pleasurable activity. **Playful** is the most general of these words and the most neutral in indicating any mood of levity that does not directly contribute to the accomplishing of essential or practical tasks: distracted from her sewing by the *playful* kitten who wanted to chase spools of thread around the room; husbands who expect to return at night to well-kept homes and to lively and *playful* wives. **Frolicsome** is an intensification of *playful* in that it suggests the positive presence of exuberant high spirits that make one wish to undertake madcap or zany adventures of an unplanned spur-of-the-moment sort: a group of *frolicsome* youngsters who decided to drive to the ocean at four in the morning. The overtone of sexual

plan

blueprint
design
program
proposal
scheme

playful

frisky
frolicsome
sportive

adventurousness present in *playful* is intensified here: *frolicsome* couples in the back rows of a movie theater.

Frisky, like *frolicsome*, also pertains to exuberant high spirits, but stresses as well an extremely active physical energy that may be nervous, impatient, headlong, and irrepressible: three or four *frisky* colts cantering about the pasture; a first round of drinks that made him feel *frisky* and insouciant. The word is even more pertinent to sexual adventurousness than *frolicsome*, but may stress, more informally in this case, lusty impatience rather than good-humored desire: giving her boyfriend a swat whenever he became too *frisky*. **Sportive** may suggest an inclination to merrymaking in almost as neutral a way as *playful*, though it is considerably more formal than these other words: coffee houses that are gathering places for *sportive* teen-agers. The word may also refer specifically to an interest in games or sports: taking down his golf clubs every spring when the weather makes him feel *sportive*. More often, the word refers to a specifically sexual interest although it need not suggest either the levity inherent in *frolicsome* or the impatience possible for *frisky*: parties where *sportive* career girls can meet unattached males on the make. See LIVELY, MISCHIEVOUS.

Antonyms: LISTLESS, SEDATE.

playing

game
novelty
toy

These words refer to things designed or used for amusement. **Plaything** serves as a generic term covering the whole range of objects so used; most typically it appears in the plural to indicate objects pertaining to children's recreation: insisting that he put all his *playthings* away each night before bedtime. In the singular, *plaything* may function more specifically to suggest the ephemeral nature or triviality of an object; these implications come to the fore especially when the word is used in reference to adults. Here, *plaything* may indicate an object of idle amusement — or even a person who is subject to someone else's whims or serves as a source of merely sexual gratification: executives who can afford expensive sets of golf clubs and other idle *playthings*; treating his mistress as a *plaything* that didn't need to be taken seriously.

Toy is more restricted in reference to the *playthings* of a child. While this word can also be generic in its inclusiveness, it may suggest, particularly in the singular, a small but more complicated structure that often has moving parts and involves the child in a passive response: a *toy* that is wound up and then runs across the floor with a comical, jerking movement. In comparison, *plaything* may suggest something that is improvised or used merely as the equipment with which to carry on some more comprehensive play activity.

Game at its most inclusive can refer to play in which no *toys* or *playthings* are used whatever. In reference to objects, however, the word can refer to the set of equipment necessary to a specific kind of play; in this sense, *game* might refer to a group of objects such as a playing board, dice, decks of cards, and counters: not sure whether Monopoly, parchesi, chess, or checkers would be the best *game* to give him as a gift. Obviously the word is not restricted to the recreation of children: roulette and other *games* of chance. Recently, the word has become a fad word to refer pejoratively to typical behavior patterns that people mechanically act out without thinking: the invidious *game* of keeping up with the Joneses; Stop playing your he-man *games* with me. **Novelty** is the one word here that need not primarily suggest an amusement for children. The word can in fact refer to *playthings* designed especially for adults, in which case it may be apologetically euphemistic, as though adults might be embarrassed to think of recreational devices as being simply adult *toys*. Usually the word suggests an item that facilitates some sort of cheating or trick, some practical joke, or something that is trivial or off-color: *novelties* such as loaded dice, magic tricks, false ears, and exploding cigars. See CHILD, CHILDISH.

These words refer to a humble, deferential, urgent, or formal request for help. **Plead** may suggest a dignified humility, but in any case it stresses urgency: *pleading* for another chance. Even in legal uses, where it is now formalistic for any request or for a stating of position, as in *pleading* guilty, its implications of urgency can sometimes still be felt: *pleading* for mercy. **Beg** is much more informal than *plead* and is devoid of legal application. Furthermore, it may join to the urgency implicit in *plead* a note not so much of humility as of abjectness: *begging* with them at least to spare the lives of his children. In less extreme uses a sense of debasement may still be present, suggesting an insistent, continual harrying of someone who is in a position to grant a favor: *begging* hopelessly for another date; *begging* to be allowed to go outside and play.

Appeal may not always suggest as great an urgency as *plead*, but it suggests an even greater dignity, implying a request based on reference to moral imperatives: *appealing* to the crowd's sense of fair play. Legally, it suggests a request, in the name of justice, that one's objection be sustained or that a decision against one be reversed: *appealing* to the judge for a ruling; *appealing* to a higher court. **Petition**, like *appeal*, suggests an address to authority. It is much more formal, however, except when it refers in a political context to the backing up of a request by the signed approval of others: *petitioning* to get a separate line on the ballot. There are some situations in which this implied gathering of signatures is not present, and the word refers to a routine way of making a request: *petitioning* his neighbor to turn down the radio.

Sue is seldom used intransitively in the legal sense and is extremely formal to the point of stuffiness in more ordinary contexts, except in some set phrases: *sue* for redress. See DEMAND, REQUEST.

Antonyms: command, DEMAND.

plead

appeal
beg
petition
sue

These words are used to refer to anything that the user finds interesting and satisfying. They are, as a group, words that are associated with mild pleasures and comforts rather than with intense feelings or passionate commitments. **Pleasing** and **pleasant** are, with one exception, the mildest of these words, referring to one's positive response to a setting, person, idea, or thing. The response, however, is not so deep that one would be unable to turn away without regret. *Pleasant* suggests something that is naturally appealing because of its cheerful exterior or warm disposition. *Pleasing* may suggest, beyond this implication, a conscious attempt to please: a *pleasant* view of the harbor; a *pleasing* waitress. When *pleasing* does not refer to such a conscious attempt, it is nevertheless slightly stronger than *pleasant* in suggesting something more able to hold the attention or more satisfying; also, *pleasant* may refer more to mood, *pleasing* to comeliness: a *pleasing* figure; a *pleasant* smile. **Nice** is milder than either of the foregoing and can, of course, refer to any kind of positive response whatsoever. Having no connotations of its own, it is susceptible of any implications context may give it.

Agreeable, where it goes beyond *pleasing*, suggests something especially in harmony with the wishes of the beholder: an *agreeable* afternoon chatting with friends; an *agreeable* city for an art lover to be stranded in.

pleasing

agreeable
attractive
engaging
enjoyable
gratifying
nice
pleasant

Attractive and **engaging** are stronger than either *agreeable* and *pleasing* in suggesting something that draws or holds one's attention. *Attractive* stresses comeliness that draws attention; *engaging* suggests liveliness or some other appeal that makes it difficult to turn away from: a woman who chose her clothes to set off her *attractive* figure; valued at parties because he was such an *engaging* conversationalist.

Enjoyable and **gratifying** stress actual satisfaction rather than the ability to draw or hold attention. *Enjoyable* is of a mildness comparable to *pleasing*, but *gratifying* suggests a greater intensity of pleasure than any other word here. [The musical comedy sounded *attractive* enough to make us risk a visit, but while some of the numbers were *enjoyable* and a few of them actually *engaging*, the whole evening was far from *gratifying*.] The special force of *gratifying* lies in its suggestion that something has answered a deeper expectation or need; in this sense the word is an intensification of *agreeable*: a truly *gratifying* friendship based on many long, *agreeable* talks. See CHARMING.

Antonyms: BAD, *displeasing*, OBNOXIOUS, REPULSIVE, *unattractive*, UNGRATIFYING.

pleasure

delectation
delight
ecstasy
enjoyment
fun
glee
joy
rapture

These words all denote feelings of satisfaction or happiness. **Pleasure** is the most general term in the group. In its mildest sense, *pleasure* may be only an expression of politeness, or it may convey the mere absence of discomfort. [I have the *pleasure* of presenting our commencement speaker; The patient rallied and was able to take some *pleasure* in his surroundings.] *Pleasure* may arise from a stimulation of the mind or the senses: the *pleasure* to be found in books; the *pleasure* of watching a spectacular sunset. In its strongest sense, *pleasure* emphasizes gratification of the senses, especially of sexual appetite, or it may refer to a round of futile and frivolous amusements that exclude meaningful activity. In this meaning *pleasure* may have a pejorative implication: the *pleasures* of the flesh; a rich young man who passed all of his time in the relentless pursuit of *pleasure*.

Delight may be a strong feeling of *pleasure*, but it is likely to be sudden and transient: *delighted* cries of children on Christmas morning; to take *delight* in winning a chess match. *Delight* may also refer to that in which one takes quiet *pleasure* over a long span of time: the *delights* of spending one's childhood on a farm.

Ecstasy and **rapture** denote intense or extreme exaltation, originally that accompanying religious or creative experience, but currently that of intense *pleasure* or *delight*. From earlier usage, *ecstasy* connotes a trancelike state wherein one "stands beside himself," conscious of neither surroundings nor of self, but only of what one contemplates or feels: the *ecstasy* of a saint during a mystical experience. *Ecstasy* still implies such intensity of feeling that other perceptions are clouded over: the *ecstasy* of first love. *Rapture*, in its original sense, connotes being seized or lifted up, as by divine power. It is now closely related in meaning to *ecstasy*. Both words are commonly used hyperbolically to describe almost any degree of *pleasure* or excitement: in a state of *ecstasy* at being accepted at the college of her choice; a child *ecstatic* over a new puppy.

Joy is sometimes used interchangeably with *pleasure, delight, ecstasy,* or *rapture*, but it implies greater intensity than does *pleasure*, longer duration than does *delight*, and is seldom so intense an experience as *rapture* or *ecstasy*: the *joy* of watching the signs of returning spring after a hard winter; the *joys* of living in a warm, affectionate family setting.

Enjoyment and **delectation** may be used as mild synonyms for *delight, joy,* or *pleasure.* However, both of these words denote action accompanying these feelings rather than the feelings themselves. *Enjoyment* is the savoring of what is pleasing; *delectation* implies a giving over of oneself to something that amuses or diverts: the *enjoyment* of conversing with good friends; the *delectation* of the theater.

Fun is literally lighthearted playfulness or jesting. [He is full of *fun*; We like to insult one another in *fun*.] *Fun* is also a general term that may apply to any diversion which affords *enjoyment*, or to the *enjoyment* itself. [Picnics are *fun*; We had *fun* riding our bicycles in the park today.] It may also be applied to an activity that engages one's interest or imagination, an activity that may prove to be more than a diversion and may involve hard work: the *fun* of learning to play the piano; a lucky man who finds both *fun* and challenge in his profession; raising pedigreed dogs for *fun* rather than for profit.

Glee, once a common synonym for exuberant *joy* or for merriment, has in recent times taken on strong overtones of a malicious pleasure in another's discomfiture or bad luck: clapping their hands in *glee* at the defeat of their opponent; the ghoulish *glee* of an 18th-century crowd at a public execution. See CHEERFUL, CONTENTED, HAPPINESS.

Antonyms: AGONY, *displeasure,* MISERY, *sadness, sorrow, suffering, unhappiness.*

pledge

bail
bond
collateral
guarantee
security

These words refer to a promise that is backed up in some way and reinforced by the commitment of one's honor or material possessions. **Pledge** is the most general of these, applying in any case where someone solemnly promises to remain loyal to a principle or to undertake a given task: the *Pledge* of Allegiance to the Flag; a *pledge* of $10,000 to the Alumni Fund; a *pledge* to have the alterations completed by Friday. Only the person's honor backs up his promise in this case. **Guarantee** is like *pledge* in that it is a verbal offer, but it is often backed up by an agreement, legal or otherwise, to make good any loss from failure to perform as promised: a money-back *guarantee* to those unsatisfied with the company's product; a six-month *guarantee* on the television set for all repairs that might be necessary during that time.

Bail is a sum of money offered as a *pledge* by someone charged with a crime, assuring the court that he will appear for trial at a specified time. The alternative to posting *bail* is to remain in prison until trial; if the accused fails to appear he forfeits the amount *pledged* as *bail*. **Bond** is comparable to *bail* in that a sum of money is posted, but differs in that the sum is set aside on behalf of someone who is accused of no crime but who might, despite evidence to the contrary, conceivably make off with money or valuables he must deal with directly in his work: supermarkets that place their cashiers under *bond*; bank tellers are generally under very high *bond*.

Collateral indicates the private possessions of value that one puts up when taking out a loan and which one forfeits if the loan is not repaid: She used some stocks and some jewelry as *collateral* for the loan she was taking out. *Pledge* is sometimes euphemistically substituted for *collateral*: a loan that stipulated the *pledge* of her fur coat. **Security** can also be substituted for *collateral*, in which case it stresses the retaining of the valuables by the person making the loan. More often, the word refers to a sum of money put up upon signing certain kinds of contracts, as when one leases a house or apartment; if the conditions of the contract are not met, the sum may be forfeited: one month's rent as *security*, in addition to the first month in advance. See ASSURE.

plunder

loot
pillage
ravage
sack

The act of laying waste to something or stripping it of its valuables is suggested by all these words. **Plunder** suggests, most specifically, the roving of armed men through recently conquered territory in search of money and goods: generals who permitted the city to be *plundered* while the inhabitants cowered behind locked doors. It can also be applied, however, to the seizing of anything by force or fraud: innocent victims *plundered* of their life savings by fake cancer cures. It can suggest the devastation of something for financial gain: timber speculators who *plundered* irreplaceable forest lands. It is also used as a hyperbole for any act of depleting: recklessly *plundering* our liquor cabinet.

Pillage is less common and more formal than *plunder* and is restricted to the act of stripping conquered people or lands of money and goods during wartime: Visigoths who *pillaged* cathedral and synagogue without discrimination. In extended usage, the word may refer to any unscrupulous swindle or self-serving theft: He *pillaged* other writers and appropriated whole passages.

Sack is more extreme than *pillage*, not only implying the seizure of all valuables but usually suggesting wholesale destruction as well. A strong word, it is typically restricted to a context of war: the Greeks who *sacked* Troy; Union armies *sacking* mansion after mansion along the route of their march. **Ravage** means to lay waste or wreak havoc, as by *pillaging* or burning. The word has fewer implications of a search for valuables than *sack* and has a great many figurative uses suggesting devastation: samurai who *ravaged* the surrounding towns and farms; the disease that *ravaged* his body; open-pit mines that *ravaged* the countryside.

Loot might once have been exactly synonymous with those meanings of *plunder* and *pillage* restricted to the context of war, but it now more commonly suggests the seizing of valuables by theft or riot, especially when these forays are hasty, disorganized, or even aimless: *looting* the museum of two valuable paintings and destroying five others; bands of teen-agers who broke store windows and *looted* the displays. See LOOT, STEAL.

poet

bard
poetaster
poetess
rimer
rimester
versifier

These words refer to writers of poetry or verse. Only **poet**, however, can now refer to such a writer in a neutral or positive way; all the others would be understood mainly as terms of disapproval. Most often, *poet* implies no evaluation whatsoever: a hundred bad *poets* for every good *poet*, and a hundred of those for every great *poet*. The word is sometimes inflated as a word of vague approval: the *poet* who is often more acute in pinpointing signs of social malaise than the sociologist. Often this approving use need not imply a writer of any sort: a *poet* of the piano; housewives who bring to their work the sensitivity of a *poet*. Sometimes the word can be used in disapproval to contrast a flighty sort of mental outlook with a rational one: abuses of the scientific method that mark him as a *poet* rather than a scientist. Both approving and disapproving uses of the word may reveal more about the speaker's possibly stereotyped notions of poetry than about *poets* themselves.

A distinction is sometimes made between **versifier** and *poet*, assigning to the former all attempts to write poetry and to the latter only successful attempts: modestly insisting that he was only a *versifier*, not a *poet*; a horde of *versifiers* who could hardly be considered *poets*. This distinction is now losing ground, however, and *versifier* itself is becoming more pejorative, not in reference to a failed *poet*, but to someone whose conscious intention is to write trivial or light verse or to work in outmoded strict forms; this use classifies such a writer without reference to his success or failure at realizing his intentions: a facile *versifier* whose work appears in women's magazines.

Bard was once an approving word for *poet*, but now its only conceivable use would be to poke fun at a pompous *poet* with an uncritical admiration for his own work: shaggy *bards* who recite their poems in coffee houses. **Rimer** and **rimester** refer to the making of rhymes by bad *versifiers*; once these terms could serve as general pejoratives for all writers of bad verse. But now that a greater proportion of poetry, both good and bad, may well be unrhymed, neither word is so inclusive in its disapproval. Both now would be severely pejorative of someone who turned out doggerel or who made wooden and unimaginative use of traditional forms; of the two, *rimester* would still be felt as more severely negative in tone: poems that show him to be basically a *rimer*, still beating the heroic couplet to death; *rimesters* who write greeting-card jingles.

Poetess was once a neutral term applying to a woman *poet*. Like most feminine forms (except actress, heroine, etc.), the word has gone out of fashion; most women *poets* would now find the term offensive, if not insulting, although many people might, without understanding this change of fashion, still use the term innocently enough. The word's one viable use is as a pejorative to describe any *poet*, especially a woman, who is given to outmoded preciosity, affected delicacy, and excessive embellishments in verse: the once-common but now vanishing *poetess* who wrote of daffodils, butterflies, and unrequited love. **Poetaster** is the most clearly pejorative of all these words and has never had any uses or connotations other than those pertaining to extreme disapproval. The word indicates insincere, affected, bad writing in verse by a person of no talent, often in imitation of prevailing styles of his day, often to at least momentary critical acclaim: *poetasters* who win prizes and get fellowships, while good *poets* go begging. See ARTIST.

These words refer to verbal compositions that have greater intensity than prose or normal speech, a quality achieved by heightened language, imagery, rhythms, or sound relationships. **Poetry** and **verse** are frequently used as complements, in which case *verse* indicates all such attempts at heightened effect, while *poetry* is reserved for works in which these attempts are successful: distilling out the true *poetry* from the mass of *verse* written by Victorian poets. This use is losing ground recently, however, since *verse* all by itself can suggest work of this sort that is written in traditional forms or using traditional methods such as rhyme and meter; often the word, unqualified, can suggest light or trivial products that make no attempt at any heightening of intensity: greeting-card *verse*. *Poetry*, by contrast, is more and more used neutrally in a generic way, depending on qualifiers for any indication of success or failure: writing voluminous amounts of both good and bad *poetry* in his final phase. The word still retains, however, a positive tone when used in a wider, less exact way: a view of life touched with *poetry*. Here, it points to an indefinable emotional intensity, per se.

Doggerel refers specifically to bad *verse*, usually suggesting trivial, banal work full of clichés, inept images, and tedious rhythms: the *doggerel* scribbled on the walls of public lavatories. As a pejorative hyperbole for any *poetry* one does not like, the word still need not impugn the writer's attempt at intensified utterance — only his total failure to achieve it: critics who agreed that the most honored poet of the pre-

poetry

doggerel
jingle
poesy
rime
verse

ceding era had seldom written anything but *doggerel*. **Jingle,** by contrast, usually points to no serious attempt at intensity, but suggests instead an extreme simplicity of language coupled with singsong or monotonous rhythms. The word may have a neutral or descriptive relevance: nursery *jingles*. More often, the word suggests disapproval for tedious meter used to drive home an insipid or commercial message, often one set to music: advertising *jingles*. **Rime** once functioned much like *verse*, referring to work done in traditional form. At one point, in fact, it could be used as a generic term for all *poetry*: his essay on *rime*. The word now sounds odd and archaic and would not be used except for satirical purposes: reciting his poem, "The *Rime* of the Elder Statesmen." **Poesy** could once be used in as general a way as *poetry*, but with a more lyrical and approving tone. Now, however, the word's only use is in caustic disapproval of *verse* that is overelegant, precious, or genteel: his ladylike sheaf of *poesy* about life's trials and tribulations. See NARRATIVE, SLOGAN.

Antonyms: prose.

poison

bane
toxin
venom

These words refer to substances capable of impairing health, damaging tissues, or destroying life by their chemical action upon an organism or its parts. **Poison** is the most general of these words, being applicable to any such substance, natural or synthetic, which is deadly when swallowed, inhaled, or simply brought into contact with the skin. [Many useful drugs and medicines, when taken improperly or to excess, are *poisons*; Prussic acid and carbon monoxide gas are both lethal *poisons*.] **Toxin,** though closely related in meaning, has become a specialized term for *poisons* developed by metabolic processes in and by animal, vegetable, and bacterial organisms and capable of producing disease or serious harm. [Tetanus is caused by *toxins* formed in the body by invading bacteria; Curare, a powerful arrow *poison*, is a *toxin* extracted from a plant and is used in medicine as a muscle relaxant.]

Venom is now generally restricted to the toxic liquid secreted by various animals, especially snakes, scorpions, and some insects, and injected into their victims as an offensive or defensive weapon. **Bane,** from an Old English word meaning killer, has become archaic in the sense of *poison*, but is still found in the popular names of certain plants such as hen*bane*, wolf's-*bane*, and rat*bane*, containing substances once believed poisonous to these animals.

In figurative use, *poison, bane,* and *venom* denote that which corrupts, harms or destroys: the *poison* of malicious rumors; an alcoholic who is the *bane* of his family's existence; the *venom* of the rejected woman's spite. See DRUG, FATAL, VIRUS.

polite

civil
courteous
courtly
mannerly
well-behaved
well-mannered

These words are used to characterize a manner of social intercourse that is designed to please, or at least not to give offense. **Polite** implies punctilious observance of the forms of speech and action customary among well-bred persons: It was not *polite* of him to reply to your question so hastily and with such an obvious lack of thought. **Civil** is weaker than *polite*, suggesting nothing more than an avoidance of rudeness: a saleswoman who was *civil* but never really interested in helping her customers. To be **courteous** is to be *polite* while having also a warm regard for the feelings and dignity of others: a policeman who managed to be *courteous* to a hysterical woman who was abusing him without just cause. **Courtly** means *polite* or *courteous* in a ceremonial way, as befits a royal court; it is applied to men and implies an old-fashioned or elegant observance of formal courtesies, especially toward women: a *courtly* southern gentleman; a *courtly* foreign diplomat.

Mannerly and **well-mannered** are alike in suggesting the kind of politeness which is evidenced by strict adherence to a code of etiquette. Since there are no overtones to these words, there is no indication when someone is called *mannerly* or *well-mannered* if he is actually *courteous* or merely careful about outward appearances. **Well-behaved** can mean *mannerly* or *well-mannered*, especially when it is used to describe a young person who is well versed in social graces. But it is often used to refer to the discipline or control demonstrated by a person or, especially, by a group of persons in a situation which is difficult or trying: a crowd that was surprisingly quiet and *well-behaved* considering how long they had to wait in a hot, stuffy room. See BEHAVIOR, CONSIDERATE, URBANE.

Antonyms: GAUCHE, *rude*.

These words refer to tainting or dirtying something or otherwise impairing its integrity, purity, or effectiveness. **Pollute** now most commonly indicates a thoroughgoing physical befouling that renders something noisome or noxious to health or life: [Some factories *pollute* our water supply by dumping untreated chemical wastes into streams and rivers; The fumes from furnaces and motor vehicles have *polluted* the air we breathe and shortened our life expectancy.] Recent usage of the word has focused so heavily on such instances that other uses are taken as metaphorical extensions of this meaning: political debate *polluted* by recriminations and unfounded allegations. Actually, an earlier use of the word referred directly to any defiling of sanctity or of physical or moral purity: temples *polluted* by barbarian invaders.

Contaminate refers to the spreading of harmful or undesirable impurities through something previously free of taint. The resulting impurity may be negligible or, as is the case for *pollute*, thoroughgoing and widespread. In addition, where *pollute* often indicates readily apparent or grossly visible impurities, *contaminate* is often the word of choice where the change is slow, devious, unsuspected, or not noticeable by ordinary means: an order to burn all linen that may have come into contact with smallpox victims or have been otherwise *contaminated*; government arguments that the atmosphere had not been seriously *contaminated* by radioactive fallout from the testing of hydrogen bombs. In other uses, the word is milder than *pollute* in that it can sometimes suggest a temporary tinge rather than an irrevocable stain.

Adulterate has special relevance to food products to which harmful, low-quality, or low-cost substances have been deliberately and deceptively added in order to defraud the buyer: hamburger *adulterated* with bread crumbs and food coloring; milk *adulterated* with water. Theoretically, the word can apply to other products debased by additives, even where no intent to defraud exists, but such uses are rare. In its widest applications, the word can apply to any mixture of good and bad where the latter seems deliberately included by the producer in the hope that it will go unnoticed: academic curricula *adulterated* with courses on everything from social dancing to surfboard acrobatics.

The remaining words apply more generally than the foregoing and do not have specific applications to some concrete situation. **Pervert** indicates misdirecting something, leading it astray, or turning it in a wrong direction, as away from the good, pure, and moral, and toward what is depraved or evil: television personalities who *pervert* discussion programs into freak shows for the airing of idiot-fringe ideas; a beautiful

pollute

adulterate
contaminate
pervert
vitiate

novel that was willfully *perverted* by Hollywood into a sex-and-sadism spectacular. As can be seen, the word suggests a grotesque or hideous transformation; this makes it even more emphatic than *pollute* in comparable uses, although here complete alteration is indicated, rather than the inclusion of additives: an attempt to *pervert* the truth by appealing to dishonest, ignorant, and irresponsible bigotry. A specific sense of the word once referred to something that caused sexual deviation, but this use is more and more avoided because of its judgmental tone.

Vitiate is the most general word here, having no area of concrete reference. It applies widely to whatever can be seen as completely nullifying the value of something: an overweening arrogance that *vitiates* all his efforts to make friends. Sometimes the word is used only for impairment rather than complete destruction: an irresponsible act that to some extent *vitiates* our claim that we are seeking peaceful solutions to the crisis. More often, however, the word suggests that one thing cancels out or invalidates another: pay raises *vitiated* by the rising cost of living. See DIRTY, DISCOLOR, HARM, HURT, SOIL, WASTE.

Antonyms: CLEAN, *purge, purify,* SANITIZE.

polygamy

bigamy
polyandry
polygyny

These words refer to a married state in which someone has more than one spouse. **Polygamy** is a general term for any situation in which more than two people are knowingly joined in marriage. The word can refer to a husband with more than one wife, a wife with more than one husband, or to group marriages in which two or more husbands are married to two or more wives: a text dealing with varieties of *polygamy* in primitive cultures. Outside an anthropological context, the word is often understood to refer directly to the situation of a husband with two or more wives, since this departure from monogamy has been more widely dealt with (and perhaps practiced) than other departures: the *polygamy* of the early Mormons. **Polygyny** would be the strict anthropological term for this situation in which two or more wives are married to one husband: linking the practice of *polygyny* with cultural assumptions about the innate inferiority of women; the disappearance of *polygyny* from Turkey with the emancipation of women.

By contrast, **polyandry** points specifically to the marrying of two or more husbands to one wife: matriarchal cultures that have *polyandry* as a concomitant. **Bigamy** refers as a legal term in Western civilization to the crime of being married to more than one spouse at the same time; the word functions for either sex. At first it might seem that the term is a legal substitute for the word *polygamy*, but one can be guilty of *bigamy* without practicing *polygamy*, through discarding one spouse without a legal divorce and marrying another while claiming to be unmarried. The word usually suggests a situation in which there is deception of at least one of the spouses, since few people in a monogamous society presumably consent to marry someone already married. Even in those instances where a deceiving bigamist sets up two households and alternates visits to both, a true situation of *polygamy* does not exist, since this word most often indicates spouses who knowingly share the same household and are married to the same person as well.

Antonyms: monogamy, monogyny.

poor

disadvantaged

These words describe people who are unable to obtain sufficient money or possessions to ensure them a decent standard of living. **Poor** is the most general term and is applied to those who live in more or less constant poverty, or to anything characterized by or resulting from poverty:

poor
(continued)

hard up
lower-class
underprivileged
unemployable

poor migrant workers; *poor* housing; a *poor* neighborhood. *Poor* is often a derogatory term pointing at the squalor, ignorance, and immorality believed to exist among those who do not have enough money.

Underprivileged and the more recently coined **disadvantaged** are euphemisms employed by social scientists, welfare workers, and journalists to describe the children of *poor* parents. *Underprivileged* is vaguely and categorically applied to those who, because of economic oppression and illiteracy, are deprived of many of the basic necessities (such as adequate food, clothing, shelter, recreational facilities, and medical care) that most people take for granted as rights. *Disadvantaged* is more specific and stresses the need for granting full civil rights, effective schooling, and job training to the young who are the victims of poverty and of racial discrimination. *Disadvantaged* also suggests the psychological damage that such *poor* children suffer from.

Hard up is a colloquial term for *poor*. But to be *hard up* often implies only a temporary shortage of money rather than a state of permanent need. People who are *hard up* are not *poor* in the accepted sense of the word: so *hard up* before pay day that he had to borrow money for lunch; farmers *hard up* because of a crop failure.

Lower-class is used to describe that group of people occupying the lowest social and economic level in any society that has either a long-established caste system or one of class distinctions based on occupation, education, and income. People who are *lower-class* tend more often than not to be *poor*, but the term is frequently used nowadays in an unfavorable and snobbish way to suggest lack of ambition, crude manners, and low educational attainments.

Unemployable refers to people who for various reasons are unable to work at any job or remunerative occupation. It is now used widely of young people, especially *poor* ones, who have been so handicapped in the learning process that they cannot be trained for useful employment. In a wider sense, people who are *unemployable* may be those of advanced age or those who have physical and mental disabilities which prevent them from working. See INSOLVENT, REQUIRE.

Antonyms: privileged, upper-class, WEALTHY, *well-to-do.*

portray

delineate
depict
describe
represent
sketch

These words refer to the vivid presentation of material in the graphic arts or some other medium of communication. **Portray**, most specifically, suggests capturing a likeness, usually of a single person: a painting that *portrayed* the actress in her most famous role. It is frequently used, however, to refer to the detailed discussion of any subject, concrete or abstract: an article that attempted to *portray* the habits of the typical American family. Even in its most abstract uses, the word still suggests catching something in its most characteristic aspect. **Depict** is similar to *portray* but more general in suggesting the artistic recreation of any scene: *depicting* the landscape just at the moment of its greatest autumnal ripeness. Where *portray* suggests catching the most revealing aspect of something, *depict* suggests a choice between equally valid possibilities: *depicting* the nineteenth century in light of the Industrial Revolution. The word may also suggest a deliberate departure from reality: actually *depicting* me, without a shred of evidence, as a scheming charlatan.

Delineate, in the graphic arts, usually refers to a line drawing, but one that is subtle and careful about accuracy and detail. In other media the word suggests the same fullness and vividness: *delineating* in a magazine article the many undercurrents of dissent that affected the election; the actress *delineated* with remarkable versatility the many-faceted character of Catherine the Great.

Sketch is used in application to a quick, usually undetailed, rendering of a subject, but one that is nonetheless readily recognizable; while the word may imply haste, it does not necessarily indicate carelessness or inaccuracy: quickly *sketching* a dress that was being modeled in a fashion show; *sketching* out the main points of the subject matter which he would cover exhaustively later in the term.

Represent and **describe** are less dependent on the context of the visual arts for their implications. Of the two, only *represent* can be used in this context at all, in which case it is more like *depict* than *portray*: a woodcut *representing* the harbor as it appeared to the first settlers. In any context, *represent* can imply a symbolic or typical rather than a literal rendering: a classic statue that *represents* the human body as devoid of individuality; *representing* nuclear proliferation as the greatest threat to world peace. It can also suggest the arbitrary choosing of one thing to stand for something else, even when there is no resemblance between the two things: In describing the bombing mission at dinner, he used water glasses to *represent* enemy targets. *Describe*, most specifically, suggests the citing of details that will create a visual image in the mind of an audience; it thus suggests a context of discussion or the verbal arts: a novelist who can vividly *describe* a landscape; a patient able to *describe* his symptoms accurately to the doctor. Unlike *represent* and *depict*, *describe* necessarily suggests a literal, realistic rendering. See GRAPHIC.

position

rank
standing
status

These words refer to the relative degree of respect that someone is given by society in general or that someone attains by virtue of his accomplishments. **Position** is the most general, indicating one's relative acceptance by society, one's recognized professional attainments, or one's place in any structured order: families of wealth and *position*; a scholar of unimpeachable *position* in the academic world; assuming the *position* of treasurer for the club. **Standing** is a good deal more vague than *position*, referring to one's place, high or low, in any graduated order: people who have no *standing* in their own communities; a member in good *standing*. In the latter example, the sense is restricted to minimal acceptance that puts one on an equal footing with others of a given group.

Rank may function in the same three areas as *position*, but it tends to suggest a more definable placement, such as one indicated by a specific title given by a hierarchical order: the highest *rank* of the nobility; attaining the *rank* of associate professor that year. The word is particularly pertinent to military *positions*: the *rank* of sergeant first class. **Status** has become the most fashionable of these words to refer to all the indefinable qualities that make up social or professional success: a teacher of high *rank* but of little *status* among his colleagues. Unqualified, it suggests social acceptance: the constant striving for *status* in the middle classes. In this use, the word often has a negative tone and suggests the placing of undue emphasis on material values. See CLASS.

possess

have
hold

These words refer to the relationship between a person and his belongings or to anything and its attributes. **Possess** and **own** both stress belongings; *possess* is slightly more formal: people who *possess* large quantities of material goods; families who *own* at least one television set. *Own*, however, suggests some legal act of acquisition, whereas *possess* may simply refer to goods that now belong to someone, however acquired: time payments that allow customers to *possess* goods before they can be said to *own* them fully. *Possess*, furthermore, is often used to relate something to its attributes, while *own* is unlikely to be used in this way: a face *possessing* great strength of character.

Have is the least specific of these words and is far less clear than the rest about the kind of relationship suggested. It may be used as an informal substitute for either *possess* or *own*: a way of smiling that *has* great charm; families that *have* more than one car.

Hold and **keep** add suggestions of retention or control to *possess* or *own*. *Hold* can mean to guard something against seizure, even from someone who may rightfully *own* it: *holding* the land despite legal notices to surrender it. Compared to *have*, it stresses conviction: *have* an opinion; *hold* an opinion. It can also substitute for *own*, in which case it has a legal tone and may suggest resources not actually *used*: *holding* estates in Ireland that he had never seen. It can be used in reference to something put in trust for someone else who actually *owns* it: *holding* the monies for you until you come of age. *Keep* may suggest preventing someone else from *possessing* something: *keeping* the aspirin away from the children. It may also stress safety or emotional attachment: *keeping* the bonds in a strongbox; wishing to *keep* the program as a souvenir. See CARRY, CONSERVE, CONTROL, INCLUDE.

Antonyms: borrow, dispossess, RELINQUISH.

These words mean to put off to some future time. **Postpone** usually suggests putting something aside until something else occurs, or is done, known, obtained, etc. [The conference will be *postponed* until one week from next Friday; We are *postponing* our trip until the weather grows warmer.] However, *postpone* is often used without this limitation and may imply the intention of putting off an activity until some undetermined future time: to *postpone* planning for the future.

Adjourn is literally to *postpone* until another day or place. The word is customarily applied to a meeting of an organization or any formally constructed gathering, such as a legislative or deliberative body, which is brought to an end, especially with a view toward assembling again at a specified time or place. [The hearing will be *adjourned* until tomorrow morning at ten o'clock; Congress *adjourns* in time for the fall elections.]

Delay means to *postpone* to an indefinite future time, usually because of obstacles that impede progress. It has the strong implication of lateness or tardiness. Often such obstacles are unavoidable: Their arrival will be *delayed* because of heavy traffic. On the other hand, *delay* may suggest failure to do something at the expected or proper time through either carelessness or reluctance: to *delay* fixing the roof although it leaked badly; to *delay* having an infected tooth pulled.

The suggestion of arbitrary lateness and putting off that resides in *delay* is absent from **defer**. Etymologically, *defer* means to refrain from dealing with, and implies the intentional *delaying* of an action in a more emphatic way than does *postpone*: to *defer* payment of one's bills until the Christmas bonus is awarded.

Suspend, in this sense, is to discontinue or to withhold temporarily but indefinitely, pending the fulfillment of certain conditions. [Bus service will be *suspended* until the highway is repaired; A scientist *suspends* judgment and refrains from drawing conclusions until all the facts are in.]

Antonyms: schedule.

possess
(continued)

keep
own

postpone

adjourn
defer
delay
suspend

powerless

helpless
impotent
paralyzed

These words refer to an inability to act in one's own behalf. **Powerless** indicates an inability to act because of outside resistance. **Helpless,** by contrast, suggests someone incapable of action because of his own inadequacy, without reference to externals. These distinctions are completely at variance with what both words might seem to suggest (lack of power; lack of external help): a decision by his superiors that left him *powerless* to act; *helpless* as an infant who must be nursed and watched every second of the day. Both words can, of course, be used in the context more appropriate to the other; *helpless*, especially, can refer to someone literally without aid or assistance: a last survivor who was *helpless* to prevent the Indians from capturing the fort.

Paralyzed in this context compares an inability to act with muscular disablement; **impotent** here compares the same inability to sexual disablement. Both words suggest a will or desire to act that some other impulse has contravened: a mind *paralyzed* by its own excessively fine distinctions; embarrassment that rendered her *impotent* to speak. Both words can also refer to a will made *powerless* or a normal routine frustrated by external forces: a city *paralyzed* by the striking union; red tape that left the chairman *impotent* to innovate or experiment. *Paralyzed* is the more intense of these two words, suggesting a greater crisis and a greater difficulty of resolution. The sexual metaphor inherent in *impotent*, furthermore, is always in danger of surfacing and making the word sound unintentionally comic in this context. See WEAK.

Antonyms: HEALTHY, *potent, powerful.*

praise

acclaim
eulogize
extol
laud

These words all pertain to the act of commending someone or something. **Praise** is the most general of these and the least formal. It can refer to overall approval: He *praised* his friend as being one of the finest human beings he had ever met. Or it can refer to a specific accomplishment: All the critics *praised* the new play for its originality and emotional impact. Sometimes the word can suggest the approval of a superior: a teacher who never forgot to *praise* the slow learner who struggled to master the day's lesson. When the situation is reversed, homage to the Deity is usually involved: They *praised* God for their safe deliverance from the perils of the winter. At its weakest, it can refer to the mere paying of compliments that may or may not be sincere: Confidence men usually *praise* the shrewdness of the gullible victims they are in the process of fleecing.

Laud indicates the highest of *praise* and may suggest recognition of a special or formal kind: a citation that *lauded* him for his twenty years of service with the firm. The word can indicate excessive *praise*, as well, or *praise* formalized, officious, or ceremonious: a set of annual awards that were broken down into so many categories that even bit players stood a chance of being *lauded*. By its very formality, **extol** also suggests formal *praise*. The word's derivation from a Latin root meaning to raise up is reflected in its suggestion of an intention to elevate or magnify the recipient: The teacher was publicly *extolled* by his department head on the occasion of his promotion to full professor.

Eulogize often suggests formal *praise* given in a public speech, although the word can also apply to a written tribute. The word can imply a public or official testimonial, particularly one delivered at a funeral: friends who came forward to *eulogize* the dead hero. **Acclaim** suggests applause or vocal approval, especially by a mass of well-wishers: The convention *acclaimed* the nominee with an uproarious demonstration of their support. Used more generally, the word can suggest widespread popularity or public backing: The whole nation *acclaimed* the court's history-making decision; a singer *acclaimed* far and wide for his unique vocal style. See APPLAUSE, AWARD, RESPECT.

Antonyms: BELITTLE, *censure, condemn, discredit.*

These words refer to a stance or position that is endangered by lack of balance, solid footing, unwavering strength, or unchanging conditions. **Precarious** is the most formal of these and most restricted to the situation of a dangerous imbalance for whatever reason: the ladder propped at a *precarious* angle against the wall; his *precarious* perch on the windowsill. The word can also refer to things that can put one in danger of falling: a *precarious* path that wound its way along the mountainside; sand dunes too near the ocean and too *precarious* for building houses on. In less concrete situations, the word stresses risk or danger more than the possibility of imbalance or falling: a *precarious* theory that could only lead to war. Unless the word's concrete overtones are remembered, however, a mixed metaphor may result: his *precarious* resistance to change.

Insecure also indicates an untenable position, but it is much wider in application and less open to mixed metaphor. The word suggests exposure to threat or danger of any kind, not just that of falling: rendering *insecure* the enemy's position in the valley by capturing the foothills surrounding it. The word has also become a fad word for psychological states of uncertainty, doubt, or confusion: a child made *insecure* by the conflicting demands made on him by his parents.

Unstable and **unsteady** also refer to untenable positions. *Unstable* emphasizes impermanence, suggesting a foundation that is capable of changing or shifting: Venetian palazzos built on *unstable* islands that have been sinking for a century. It may also suggest infirm support of any kind: nailing in crosspieces to strengthen the *unstable* uprights of the bookcase. *Unstable*, in a wider context, can refer to a substance that tends to break down or change drastically: an electrically charged, *unstable* form of oxygen. It can also refer to an erratic or dangerous personality: an *unstable* eccentric who conceived of great schemes he never executed; an *unstable* sociopath who was capable of committing murder without a qualm. The more informal *unsteady* concentrates on one aspect of *unstable*, indicating a lack of firm support: a short leg that made the table *unsteady*. It can, however, also point to any sort of wavering or less-than-constant application: *unsteady* flashes of light; capable only of divided and *unsteady* attention. See DANGER.

Antonyms: firm, safe, stable, steady.

These words refer to attempts to indicate what course the future will take. **Predict** is the most commonly used in the widest variety of situations; it can range in suggestion from the mere hazarding of a guess or a wish to the making of an astute statistical estimate about the likely outcome of an event: *predicting* that he would be miserable without her; *predicting* the results of the election with amazing accuracy. As in the last example, it is commonly used to refer to the activities of professional poll-takers. Like *predict*, **forecast** can range in use from the general or vague to the specific, but in this case its most specific use — for *predicting* weather — has crowded out other uses of the word: Tiros satellites that make it easier to *forecast* hurricanes.

Divine and **foreshadow** are both concerned with suggesting rather than *predicting* the future, especially through the giving or assessing of

precarious

insecure
unstable
unsteady

predict

augur
divine
forecast
foreshadow
foretell
prognosticate
prophesy

subtle hints or clues. *Divine* implies someone capable of reading present evidence in all its ambiguity and seeing where it must lead: the first political commentator to *divine* in Hitler's threats the imminent up-heaval of Europe. The word originally suggested supernatural powers of clairvoyance, but it is now seldom used in this sense. *Foreshadow*, unlike *divine*, does not necessarily imply a shrewd reader of clues; it can refer to anyone or anything that gives an indication of what is to come: Hitler's plan of action *foreshadowed* the actual course of events so un-mistakably that anyone should have been able to *divine* it. The word is often used to refer to a storyteller's hints about what will happen eventually in his story: the novelist's skillful *foreshadowing* of her hero-ine's eventual tragic decline.

Like *divine*, **augur**, **prophesy**, and even **foretell** once suggested a supernatural ability to "read" the future. Now they have mainly lost this use, although they still suggest, unlike *predict* and *forecast*, a future that is already set and determined rather than one that can be rationally assumed from the evidence at hand. Of these three, *augur* is most like *divine* in implying a reading of subtle omens and clues as a way of pre-figuring what is to come: *auguring* from a host of economic indicators that the present boom would continue unabated. The word, like *fore-shadow*, can also refer to the sign or clue itself: a trend that *augured* well for the company. *Prophesy* is more portentous-sounding than *augur*, suggesting authoritative wisdom and acumen: the only pundit to *proph-esy* a necessary confrontation with China. Both *augur* and *prophesy* are sometimes used in place of *predict* and *forecast* to give a higher tone or to suggest unerring accuracy; many would find the uses questionable: poll-takers *auguring* a record turnout. *Foretell* now has fewer residual impli-cations of the supernatural than *augur* and *prophesy*, as well as being far less formal. It would still sound odd as a substitute for *predict* or *fore-cast*, however. Like *foreshadow*, it can refer to the clue rather than to its reader: signs of a struggle that *foretold* a violent end for the kidnaped banker. It is often used negatively in referring to the past: Who could have *foretold* that such a routine tour was to culminate is such a tragedy?

In contrast to the words just discussed, **prognosticate** comes from a different context altogether. It suggests a knowledgeable look at the symptoms of a disease in order to determine its likely outcome. This gives it a specific pertinence to medicine similar to *predict* for poll-taking and *forecast* for meteorology. Used outside this area, the word suggests inside knowledge, expertise, or shrewdness, but is often used comically or pejoratively: *prognosticating* what effect another garlic pickle would have on his digestion. See EXPECTATION, FOREKNOWLEDGE, HOPE, PRE-MONITION.

premonition

forerunner
harbinger
inkling
omen
portent
precursor
presentiment

These words refer to a sense, indication, or sign of something to come. Most, but not all, partake of the prophetic, and some directly involve superstition. A **premonition** is instinctive, based on an indefinable feeling rather than on actual information received. It may be good or bad, may come in sleep or wakefulness, and may be either borne out or proved false by later events. [A *premonition* that she would win led her to take a chance in the raffle; He had a *premonition* of his father's death.] Some *premonitions* are purely irrational or superstitious; others, possible instances of extrasensory perception. **Presentiment** is very close to *premonition* in meaning but is more formal in tone. Etymologically, where *premonition* stresses the idea of an advance warning given to the mind, *presentiment* points to a sort of inner perception, usually an instinctive feeling of foreboding, a sense that misfortune or calamity is at hand: a terrifying, but totally unfounded *presentiment* that his life was in great danger; a *presentiment* that the *Titanic* was going to sink. Like a *premonition* or *presentiment*, an **inkling** is an intimation of something yet unknown. Getting an *inkling* of something, however, does not require prophetic powers or ESP. Instead, the ability to interpret natural signs, to pick up hints, or to guess on the basis of a paucity of information is involved. [A few veiled hints she dropped gave me my first *inkling* of her purpose.] Unlike the other words, it is often used negatively in disclaiming or denying any knowledge of something. [I haven't the slightest *inkling* of what he is going to do.]

Omen and **portent** differ from the foregoing in that they designate outward and visible signs that are regarded as prophetic and are subject to interpretation. Both words strongly imply a superstitious response. To those who believe in them, there are both good and evil *omens*. A stork nesting on the roof, for example, is considered a good *omen*. A black cat crossing one's path is thought to be an evil *omen*. Unlike an *omen*, which may be favorable, a *portent* more often, though not always, indicates impending evil. A *portent* may be a sign, an event, a wonder, a natural or unnatural phenomenon: a sailor's belief in luck and in supernatural *portents*. It may be something momentous, to marvel at, as a flaming comet; or it may be something ominous and heavy with foreboding, as a total eclipse. [Calpurnia's *premonition* of Caesar's death came in the form of a prophetic dream; Casca saw a fiery tempest, a slave with a flaming, unburned hand, a lion in the Capitol, and other prodigious *portents*.] *Omen* and *portent*, modified by words like black, bad, ill, or evil, may also mean ominous significance: a bird of evil *omen*; a cloud of black *portent*.

The remaining words refer to a messenger or herald who signals the approach of a coming person or thing. Formerly, a **harbinger** was a courier who rode in advance of a party to arrange for their lodging. Now, though the word may mean anyone in the vanguard who is a preparer of the way, it is more often used figuratively of a person or thing that heralds the approach of a change. [An autumn frost is a *harbinger* of winter; The robin is a *harbinger* of spring.] Unlike the other words in this set, the designations **forerunner** and **precursor** may indicate hindsight rather than foresight, pointing to an advance sign that is seen as such only in terms of later events. Both words share the same etymological meaning, *precursor* meaning *forerunner* in Latin. They now differ somewhat in use, however. *Forerunner* more strongly retains the original sense of a person who goes ahead as a messenger to proclaim the coming of another. John the Baptist is known as the *Forerunner* since he heralded the coming of Christ. The word **precursor** was also used of John the Baptist; but where *forerunner* stresses the announcement of a more important person's coming, *precursor* implies a laying of the groundwork for a later, more significant accomplishment. Both *forerunner* and *precursor* may refer to a predecessor in a particular line of development, or an advance indication of something to come. [John Wyclif was one of the main *forerunners* of the Reformation and an important *precursor* of Martin Luther.] Used of signs or symptoms, both words may be unfavorable in tone. [Overweight and shortness of breath were the *precursors* of a heart attack; a localized border conflict that turned out to be the *precursor* of a world war; Widespread moral corruption and decadence are often the *forerunners* of national decline.] See ANXIETY, EXPECTATION, HINT, PREDICT, SYMPTOM.

preoccupied

absorbed
engrossed
involved

These words describe persons whose complete attention is held or whose total concern is aroused by a particular subject. **Preoccupied** points to a mind taken up with a certain line of thought to the exclusion of other matters which might be competing for attention. It may suggest a dedicated and voluntary concern for something: *preoccupied* with details of the merger plan. More often, it suggests an excessive or involuntary brooding about something: so *preoccupied* with his career that he was neglectful of his family; indications that thoughts of suicide had *preoccupied* him for months. The word may also simply suggest a mind lost in haphazard thought of any kind whatsoever and, consequently, inattentive to the matter at hand: a clerk who met my question with a vacant and *preoccupied* stare.

Involved pertains to commitment more than to concern, and it can be used for active behavior as well as for mental states: students *involved* in the civil rights movement; readers who can become deeply *involved* in the plot of a suspense novel.

Absorbed and **engrossed** contrast with *preoccupied* in being almost wholly positive in connotation. Both of these words refer primarily to a voluntary, almost eager, attentiveness to or interest in something. *Engrossed* suggests complete and alert intellectual concentration: *engrossed* in studying the committee's findings. *Absorbed* may suggest an emotional interest that is even more complete: utterly *absorbed* by the movie's slow unfolding. *Absorbed*, furthermore, may suggest an intensity of interest in one's own activity: so *absorbed* in his own story that he failed to notice the growing restlessness among his listeners. See BUSY. EAGER, OBLIVIOUS.

Antonyms: distracted, UNINVOLVED.

present

bonus
gift
grant
gratuity
largess
tip

These words denote something given freely to a person, group, or institution for use or pleasure. **Present** and **gift** are the most general words, and they are applied to anything, large or small, material or nonmaterial, that is given without expectation of return or compensation. *Present* and *gift* may be used interchangeably to denote things bestowed upon another: a birthday *present*; a Christmas *gift*. However, *present* is a less formal word than *gift* and is more likely to be applied to things of nominal cost, while *gift* may suggest a donation of considerable value. [Each child brought a *present* to the teacher; The foundation made a *gift* of a million dollars to the university.] An admirable quality or talent which seems to have been bestowed miraculously by nature is also called a *gift*, but never a *present*: the *gift* of prophecy; a *gift* for writing poetry.

Largess is a somewhat pompous word for a bountiful *gift* conferred in an ostentatious manner, often among many recipients. The word hints at condescension on the part of the giver and is often used ironically: a ne'er-do-well who received a government post through the *largess* of his congressman; the poor who live on the *largess* of public assistance.

A **grant** is a *gift* of money or its equivalent to a person or an institution to enable the recipient to accomplish a specific end: a *grant* to a scholar to do research; a *grant* to a technical college to develop a humanities program. *Grants* commonly involve considerable sums and are often given by public authority: a *grant* of land to establish an agricultural college.

A **bonus** is something paid or given in addition to what is usual or stipulated. An employer may give his staff a cash *bonus* at the end of the year, or he may reward a particularly valued employee with a *bonus* of an extra week of vacation. A *bonus* is also a *grant*, as of money or insurance, to citizens who have rendered military service.

Gratuity and **tip** both imply an unspecified sum of money given voluntarily in return for a service or the expectation of special attention. *Gratuity* is the more formal word and points to a more substantial *gift* than does *tip*: a *tip* to a waiter or porter; *gratuities* to servants who had been attached to the household for many years. See BEQUEST.

These words refer to something present in great quantities or something frequently met with. **Prevalent** may indicate a heavy incidence of something either in time or in place: ideas *prevalent* in the Renaissance; varieties of wildflowers that are *prevalent* in the Rockies. The word most often suggests factual observation without any attempt to evaluate the thing observed. **Prevailing** goes beyond *prevalent* to suggest that the thing observed has existed and continues to exist in such quantity as to surpass any other kind of thing that might be compared to it. This may often be a matter of subjective evaluation: discussing what he regarded as the *prevailing* theme of the modern British novel. [While many forms of life are *prevalent* throughout the world, man and the insect are perhaps the two *prevailing* forms in nearly every habitat.]

Abundant, unlike *prevalent* and *prevailing*, is mostly restricted to observations about a particular place rather than a particular time: an *abundant* harvest; a cultural life that is more varied and *abundant* than in smaller cities. *Abundant* usually suggests a valued or desirable quantity, even though the word may occasionally suggest frequency to the point of oversupply. **Common**, by contrast, shades off to suggest something that by its very frequency becomes usual or ordinary: the *common* people; an experience *common* to every traveler. *Common*, furthermore, can apply to time as well as place, much like *prevalent*: a style of dress *common* in the 1890's. Neither *abundant* nor *common*, however, suggests the notion of dominance present in *prevailing*. [Although revolutionary ideas were *abundant* and poverty was *common*, the *prevailing* temper of the times was one of sheer indifference.]

Rife and **widespread** both emphasize aspects of *prevalent*. *Rife* suggests the unchecked or unregulated spread of something: a time *rife* with conflicting theories of art and society; Bribery and corruption were *rife* in the local courts. As suggested by the last example, this word is frequently used to suggest a heavy incidence of something undesirable, thus making a sharp contrast with *abundant*. *Widespread* most specifically refers to place rather than time, suggesting something that is not so much *common* as occurring over a large area: the *widespread* misconception that Darwin had argued that we were descended from apes; paperback publishers that have had a *widespread* effect on the country's reading habits; tests to determine whether the cancer was *widespread*.

Plentiful relates, like *abundant*, to a desirable quantity or even a superfluity of something: a part of the country where work was *plentiful*; an island where edible fruit is so *plentiful* that it rots on the vine. **Copious** indicates an even greater quantity than *plentiful* and sometimes requires the interpolation of "supply of," "number of," etc., before the operative noun: The squirrel gathered a *copious* store of nuts. However, the interpolation is unnecessary when reference is made to a volume, outpouring, profusion, cascade, or flow: His writings were *copious*; *copious* tears. *Copious* can also serve as a more formal intensification of *abundant*, sometimes indicating a superfluity: a *copious* harvest; a scholarly treatise with *copious* footnotes. **Ample**, in contrast to *copious*,

prevalent

abundant
ample
common
copious
plentiful
prevailing
rife
widespread

means both just enough and more than enough, and so tends to imply an amount between enough and *plentiful*: *ample* but not generous servings; an *ample* income; *ample* room for a family of five. The word can also refer, in a humorous way, to generous or excessive size when used of a person: the matron's *ample* bosom. See GENEROUS, OUTSTANDING.

Antonyms: OCCASIONAL, SCANTY.

prevent

avert
forestall
obviate
preclude
stop

These verbs mean to keep from happening or doing. **Prevent** is the comprehensive term for the group. Used of human agency, it implies precautionary or restraining measures taken to hinder, thwart, or block a thing. These measures may involve forcible restraint. [Armed guards *prevented* us from entering the palace; They tied him up to *prevent* his escape.] Or, the measures may be positive steps taken to ward off potential trouble: concessions and reforms made to *prevent* future riots; negotiations to *prevent* a stalemate; fabric waterproofed to *prevent* permeation by rain; It is easier to *prevent* illness than to cure it. *Prevent* is also used of a nonhuman agency or chance cause that acts as a hindrance; in such cases, only the effect of the agent is stressed and no motive is attributed to it. [Rain *prevented* us from going (or *prevented* our going) on the hike; A sprained ankle *prevented* him from playing in the game.] **Stop** in this sense is more informal than *prevent* and has greater immediacy. Where *prevent* often implies forethought and advance preparation to keep something from occurring, *stop* focuses completely on responsive action to the circumstance at hand. [I'm leaving, and don't try to *stop* me from going.] Further, *stop* may refer to the halting or ending of an action already in progress. [*Stop* him from hitting me; to *stop* an alarm from ringing; to *stop* a revolt by the use of armed force.] *Prevent* also, which at first had only the anticipatory meaning, has come to apply to the *stopping* of an action at any stage, with the implication that the ultimate consequences of the act have been avoided: The enemy passed the outworks and were barely *prevented* from capturing the fortress.

To **preclude** is to *prevent* by anticipation or to rule out by necessity. This word is used not of persons but of events, circumstances, decisions, or the like. It suggests a door shut in advance, as a consequence of a prior action, occurrence, choice, or commitment. [Walls and bars *precluded* the possibility of escape; Our decision to vacation in Europe *precludes* our going to California this year; Professional duties *precluded* the doctor from accepting the invitation.] **Forestall** is like *preclude* in emphasizing anticipation, but it implies deliberate deterrence. Where *preclude* points to circumstances which make an occurrence impossible, *forestall* involves the taking of preventive countermeasures in time to turn something aside or temper its effect. [He *forestalled* the anticipated criticism by confessing his faults of his own accord; She *forestalled* my question by bringing up the subject herself; In 1933, Roosevelt closed the banks to *stop* gold shipments abroad and to *forestall* mass withdrawals by depositors.]

Avert, more strongly and more specifically than *forestall*, implies the warding off of a threat or danger. It points to the taking of effective countermeasures just in time to keep something disastrous from happening. [He swerved sharply to the right and narrowly *averted* a collision; The mayor and local leaders *averted* a riot by calming down the demonstrators at the scene of the disturbance.] **Obviate** is the most formal word in this set. It means to dispose of, referring to a risk, difficulty, objection, or the like, which is met squarely and cleared out of the way. [A settlement out of court would *obviate* the need for a long and drawn-

out lawsuit; travelers checks to *obviate* the risk of lost or stolen cash.]
See AVOID, DISCOURAGE, HINDER, STOP (arrest), THWART.

   Antonyms: EFFECT, *facilitate*, PERMIT.

These words are comparable in denoting statements of fact or generality
which are universally or widely considered to be true and fundamental.
Principle has the greatest range of meaning of all the terms in this
group, but in the context of this discrimination it refers to an elementary
proposition held to be basic in any system or chain of reasoning, conduct,
or procedure: a theological *principle*; the *principle* of self-government.
In logic, an **assumption** specifically designates the minor or second
premise in a syllogism. Less specifically, *assumption* refers to any assertion about reality which is unproved or debatable: the danger of basing
scientific conclusions upon *assumption*. **Axiom** originally denoted a
proposition, usually one agreed upon as the basis of an argument or
demonstration, whose truth was so self-evident as to be indisputable:
using the *axiom* that every effect must have a cause to prove the existence of God. In current usage, *axiom* often indicates any *principle* that
men universally receive and act upon as if it were true, rather than something deemed necessarily true. A **theorem** is a proposition that is not
self-evident but that is susceptible of rational proof. Since *theorems* are
deduced from *axioms*, *axioms* are often called first *principles*, and *theorems* are called secondary *principles*. See BASIS.

These words refer to being alone with others or by oneself, without danger of being seen, overheard, or interrupted. **Privacy** adds to this
general meaning strongly positive overtones of freedom and intimacy,
such as a person has in his own home, whether by himself, with his
family, or with chosen friends: eavesdropping devices that threaten the
privacy of the home; a Supreme Court decision affirming a married
couple's right to *privacy*. When used outside the context of the home,
the word suggests conditions approaching this state, often presented as
a luxury or added feature: the *privacy* afforded by a box at the opera; a
large ward of the hospital that permitted the patients little *privacy*; asking where they could go to talk in *privacy*. In one of its senses, **seclusion**
is an intensification of *privacy*, suggesting a situation offering even
greater protection from interference than one's own home: preferring to
work in the *seclusion* of his mountain retreat. Also, *seclusion* suggests
surroundings that protect, separate, or shield one from any sort of notice,
whereas *privacy* may give practical but not total protection: feeling free
to talk in the *privacy* of their railway compartment, though their *seclusion* was rendered incomplete by an uncovered window that looked
directly out onto the corridor. In a more specialized and not necessarily
positive sense, the word suggests a deliberate hiding from the outside
world, either to meet with, evade, or wait for someone: the grove of
trees that gave *seclusion* to the lover's lane; seeking *seclusion* from their
enemy in the hidden cave; waiting to ambush him from the *seclusion* of
the shadowed alley.

   Isolation can function like *seclusion*, but it can also stress the state
of being completely cut off from the outside world, whether by compulsion, choice, or circumstance: keeping the kidnaped family in *isolation*
by removing them to a deserted farmhouse. As can be seen, *isolation*
may suggest the condition of being utterly and involuntarily alone or cut
off from others. While the previous pair of words can suggest freedom
from interference or harm, only *isolation*, of the three, can suggest in-

principle

assumption
axiom
theorem

privacy

isolation
seclusion
solitude
withdrawal

accessibility to help or aid. Less strictly taken, the word still refers more sternly to total exclusion of the external: hoping her friends would understand her insistence on complete *isolation* during the period of mourning; erratic ferry service that contributed to the island's sense of *isolation* from the mainland; the *isolation* of the ghetto from the rest of the city.

Solitude can be a more positive and high-toned substitute for *isolation*, but mostly in the latter's voluntary senses: longing for the off-season *solitude* of a seaside resort. In an extended sense, the word can refer more generally to the stillness or peacefulness of a setting: the lofty *solitude* of the mountain peaks. **Withdrawal** places its emphasis on an act rather than a state, stressing the voluntary removal of oneself from distraction or, less positively, the rejection of the outside world: his *withdrawal* each night into the *privacy* of his home; their self-preoccupied *withdrawal* into their own affairs. The movement suggested by the word, however, need not be from public view into *seclusion*, but from one place to anywhere else: a *withdrawal* from his home life into the concerns of his hectic office life. In a psychological sense, *withdrawal* has become a fad word for any indication of introversion or introspection, even extending to catatonic or autistic states: the boy's *withdrawal* from the other students. See ESCAPE, LEAVE, LONELINESS, LONELY, MODEST.

Antonyms: company, gregariousness, publicity.

procrastinate

dally
dawdle
dilly-dally
lag
loiter
shilly-shally
stall
tarry

These words refer to the postponing of a duty or to the leisurely, aimless passing of time. **Procrastinate** and **stall** both emphasize the putting off of serious questions, but *stall* can suggest any sort of delay to gain time, whereas *procrastinate* suggests occupying oneself with other often trivial matters. *Stall*, furthermore, can indicate a brief pause, as before answering a question, while *procrastinate*, by contrast, indicates the protracted dragging out or delaying of something over a longer time. [His hemming and hawing was only a ruse to *stall* the newsmen before answering their biting questions; When faced with a deadline on a term paper, she lolls about on her bed, daydreams, goes out to movies, or does anything she can think of to *procrastinate* a little longer.] *Stall* can, however, refer to a longer delay, in which case it suggests greater ill will than *procrastinate*: legislation *stalled* in a senate subcommittee.

Dawdle may refer to a kind of *procrastinating* in which a given duty is pursued half-heartedly and phlegmatically rather than put off or put aside: She knew that if she *dawdled* over the dishes, her mother would take over in a fit of exasperation and do them herself. But the word may also refer to a leisurely passing of time, with no sense whatever of postponing a duty: In the hour between trains, he *dawdled* about in a bookstore near the station. **Tarry** means to hang behind or to stray off course; a deliberate act of *procrastinating* may be implied: Don't *tarry* on your way home from school. But the word now more often applies to aimless or leisurely stops along a course: a couple who decided to *tarry* another week in the lovely seaside village. Now the word can sometimes sound quaint or affected.

Loiter indicates standing about aimlessly or moving from place to place in a slow, rambling way: No *loitering* in these premises; a tourist who *loitered* about the town square, browsing through several of the shops. The word seldom suggests the delaying of a task, although legally it can refer to a misdemeanor and, hence, can suggest an improper or sinister motive. **Lag** can suggest something that lacks impetus or falls behind a desirable rate of progress: when interest in civil rights began to *lag*; a theory that man's social consciousness has *lagged* behind his technological accomplishments. The word may be used in a more literal way, without the disapproval inherent in the previous examples: a fifteen-mile hike during which those with blistered feet began to *lag* behind the others.

Shilly-shally suggests an evasive tactic of *stalling* for time or an attempt to avoid taking a stand: He was not one to *shilly-shally* when he disagreed with the findings of his colleagues. Most simply, the word can indicate any weak vacillating or *procrastinating* behavior: They *shilly-shallied* about technicalities while thousands of fires in the city raged out of control. **Dally** can indicate the leisurely passage of time where no postponing of duty is implied: a vacation in which they could *dally* as long as they wished in any city they found to their liking. *Dally* can also add a special note of pleasurably relaxed and even amorous *dawdling*, influenced by a related use of the word: members of the government who had *dallied* with the young woman. More disapprovingly and with no note of playfulness, the word can indicate an indecisive wasting of time: housewives who *dally* over the prepackaged cuts of meat in self-service supermarkets. **Dilly-dally**, an alternate form, more readily suggests sheer *procrastinating*: He *dilly-dallied* over what movie to go to until it was too late to go to any of them. See HESITATE, POSTPONE.

Antonyms: decide, persevere, push on, QUICKEN.

These words all refer to crude or foul language. **Profanity** emphasizes abusive vituperation or rage expressed in irreverent use of religious terms and names applied to the deity. More loosely, *profanity* may be used as the general term for any sort of habitually foul language: the *profanity* endemic to army life. **Blasphemy,** a stronger term than *profanity*, as applied to choice of language, is restricted specifically to an irreverent use of religious terms, especially the name of the deity; this may be done as a habitual mannerism of speech, to shock others, or to insult a particular person, as with *profanity*: the common speech of the waterfront, peppered with lewd remarks and casual *blasphemies*.

Cursing and **swearing** may be used loosely as general terms for crude language, but each has a more precise reference. *Cursing* refers specifically to phrases that would call down misfortunes on someone or something: the fit of *cursing* with which he punished each person who refused him the price of a cup of coffee. *Swearing* most specifically refers to *cursing* that is reinforced by an appeal to a deity to carry out the wish expressed. It is thus a specific form of *blasphemy* as well.

Obscenity refers to that element in coarse language that is lewd or suggestive in reference to sexual matters: calling out *obscenities* to every unaccompanied girl that passed the barbershop. **Vulgarity** is milder than *obscenity*, indicating reference to normally unmentioned bodily processes: speech larded with scatological *vulgarities*. In an even milder use, *vulgarity* may refer merely to blunt, tasteless, or even ungrammatical language: starlets who take crash courses to rid their speech of common *vulgarities*. See CURSE, DESECRATION, MALEDICTION.

These words refer to the long-term duties that someone takes on as a livelihood or as his main interest in life. **Profession** suggests a position that cannot be attained without a considerable amount of higher education, and that involves one creatively in mental rather than manual labor. Once the word referred mainly to the three learned *professions* — law, medicine, and theology — but it is now often used to confer status

profanity

blasphemy
cursing
obscenity
swearing
vulgarity

profession

field
job

profession

(continued)

occupation
specialization
trade
vocation
work

upon many other ways of earning a livelihood: the teaching *profession*; the acting *profession*; making his friends mostly among other members of the plumbing *profession*. Even when *profession* is used more strictly, it need not suggest dedication on the part of a given member. By contrast, one sense of **vocation** specifically stresses this dedication: finding early that he had a *vocation* for the ministry, though he ended up in the law *profession* instead. Moreover, *vocation* stresses a long-term commitment to something that is not necessarily equated with the earning of a livelihood: choosing painting as his *vocation* and earning his keep by waiting on tables. Less specifically, *vocation* can be merely a neutral reference to one's form of employment; as such, it may or may not include the *professions*, but in any case it can sound euphemistic or high-toned when so used: calling together a representative sampling of people from all walks of life and from every *profession* and *vocation*. **Occupation** is exclusively restricted to this last neutral possibility for *vocation*, though *occupation* completely escapes the danger of sounding over-elegant or euphemistic: drawn from *occupations* as diverse as medicine and carpentry.

Trade, **work**, and **job** by contrast may suggest a range of *occupations* from skilled labor to the most menial of positions. Of the three, *trade* implies the dignity of learned skills in which inventiveness and manual labor are combined: programs designed to teach high-school dropouts a *trade*; the building *trades*. *Work* is, of course, very general, and can apply to any sort of effort: the *work* of raising a child. In a professional context, it suggests the set hours of long-term employment: getting to *work* on time. Less specifically, it can point to a *vocation* or *occupation* in general: asking him what sort of *work* he did. *Job* is commonly used to refer to any sort of gainful employment, whether permanent or temporary: hunting for a summer *job*; getting *jobs* for the unemployed. The word ranges in application from a single task or piece of *work* to a regular position of employment. It may suggest either skilled or unskilled labor, for its commonness gives it informal currency in any context: the *job* of turning out first-rate psychiatrists; an editorial *job* with a publishing house; to do a good *job* of mowing the lawn.

Field is an informal and **specialization** a formal word for referring to smaller groupings within *occupations*: a medical student who intended to study in the *field* of obstetrics; a general knowledge of law but with a *specialization* in divorce cases. See ARTISAN, LABOR, LABORER, STINT.

professor

don
graduate assistant
instructor
lecturer

These words refer to academic positions or duties germane to higher education. **Professors** are the highest ranking teachers in a college or university. Usually, *professors* have tenure by virtue of status, qualification, or seniority: advancing from assistant *professor* to associate *professor* and finally to full *professor* in the shortest possible time. **Instructor**, conversely, indicates a college teacher who has not yet acquired the title of *professor* and is consequently of lower status, often without tenure: *professors* to teach the upperclassmen and *instructors* to teach freshmen.

A **graduate assistant** is a student working for an advanced degree, usually the doctorate, who is hired to teach one or more sections of a required course in his department on the freshman and sophomore levels.

Lecturer often indicates a teacher who instructs by means of formal verbal speeches, without much free exchange with his listeners. In some American colleges and universities, *lecturer* denotes a temporary or part-time appointment at various salary levels but often without standard academic rank. At other colleges, particularly in Europe, *lecturer* may be a rank in itself, and often such a person may actually be a *professor*. The word may also indicate a person invited to give a single talk or group of talks and thus is a teacher who remains outside the academic hierarchy entirely: a guest *lecturer* invited to give a term of lectures on modern art. Also, some large classes are taught by a *lecturer* and then broken down into smaller discussion groups, taught by *instructors*. **Don** indicates a teacher in British and other colleges who is neither a *professor* nor a *lecturer*, but one who instructs students individually, a technique which is the basic method of the students' education. Such a faculty member may have or may attain both rank and tenure within such systems. See LEARNING, TEACH.

These words are alike in their referral to a declaration that something must not be done or to an action which prevents something from being done. To **prohibit** is to give some formal command against or, more specifically, to make some authoritative legal enactment against. There is in *prohibit* a definite implication of readiness to use such force as may be needed to give effect to the enactment: In our city, smoking on public transportation vehicles is *prohibited* by law. **Forbid** is a less formal word than *prohibit*, and suggests a personal relationship between the people involved in the *forbidding*: Her mother *forbade* the little girl to leave the house before she had finished her homework.

> The balance of the words in this group is less general than *prohibit* or *forbid*. **Ban** and **interdict** suggest *prohibiting* by ecclesiastical or civil authority. *Interdict* is chiefly known for its ecclesiastical use: to *interdict* the administration of the sacraments to a heretical group. *Ban* frequently implies moral condemnation or disapproval: a bad movie that became an enormous box-office success because it had been *banned* in Boston on the grounds of obscenity. **Debar** means to shut out or exclude, as from some place or condition. It hints strongly at the action of an irresistible authority or inner necessity: His plea of insanity was *debarred* by his own admissions. **Enjoin** has specific application to legal contexts. It means to *prohibit* or command by judicial order or injunction: railroad workers who were *enjoined* from striking for a period of ninety days. See COMMAND, STOP.

> *Antonyms:* ENDORSE, PERMIT.

prohibit

ban
debar
enjoin
forbid
interdict

These words refer to the execution of a systematic plan for realizing an explicit objective. **Project** and **program** might both seem to refer literally to a proposed plan rather than one being carried out, but in actual usage these words can apply to such a plan at any stage of its existence, from conception to completion. *Project* is the more general of the two words and can apply equally well to the planned task of a single person or to such a task involving a number of people: a *project* to teach himself French on weekends; the government's highway construction *project*. The word is often used to refer to the end result of such work, long after its planning and completion: the six-block housing *project*. *Program* is more formal and more abstract than *project* and applies most often to group work. Where *project* might suggest a single self-contained objective often requiring physical labor, *program* can suggest a more complex set of such *projects* or the application of largely mental or administrative effort: an antipoverty *program* that would develop a number of local or neighborhood *projects*.

> **Activity** is the most general of these words. While it need not sug-

project

activity
enterprise
operation
program
undertaking

gest any plan or objective at all, it is often used to refer to the work done on a *project* or carried out by a group. It stresses the actual carrying out of something that simply continues without any point of completion: kindergartens that emphasize unprogrammed playtime *activity*; college students who slight their studies for extracurricular *activities*; settlement houses offering such *activities* as literacy training, citizenship courses, and folk dancing.

Operation is close to *activity* in its generality, suggesting continuing motion without necessarily implying the possibility of completion: studying the *operation* of the federal courts. It has come to have a special use in reference to a complex *program* designed to achieve a clearly defined goal; this use, borrowed from the military, follows the capitalized word with a colorful epithet: *Operation* Crossbow; *Operation* Headstart.

Enterprise and **undertaking** are the most formal of these words. *Enterprise* may suggest improvisation toward a less clearly defined goal and may imply an element of risk; it may also suggest boldness and strenuous endeavor: a perilous *enterprise* that few thought could succeed. On the other hand, it may simply refer to any business *activity*. [Watchmaking and banking are the chief *enterprises* of the country.] *Undertaking* is more general than *enterprise*, but unlike *activity* it suggests both considerable forethought and the possibility of completion: agreeing to the *undertaking* only after exhaustive discussion of other alternatives. It can sometimes sound like an unnecessarily fancy substitute for one of its less formal synonyms. See BUILD, CREATE, LABOR, MAKE.

propel

press
push
shove
thrust
urge

These words refer to the generation or application of force to move a thing onward or away. **Propel** is the most general word, referring to the act of driving someone or something forward by whatever means: hurried along and *propelled* through a revolving door. The word is most often used, however, of a mechanical force or a separate source of power; an explosive that *propels* a projectile from a gun; a fuel that serves to *propel* a missile or a rocket; a boat *propelled* by steam or by an outboard motor.

Push generally implies physical contact between the mover and the moved. It specifically indicates force or pressure exerted on or against one side of an object to move it forward, in the opposite direction, or out of the way. The force employed may be slight or considerable: to *push* a baby carriage; to *push* a stalled car. Applied to persons, *push* often implies impatience and consequent rudeness: to *push* ahead of someone at a counter. The word has, however, many shades of meaning depending on context: to *push* a reluctant parachutist out of a plane; to *push* a person off a diving board. **Shove** is close to *push* but is generally a stronger word, implying a greater degree of forcible pressure or physical effort: to *shove* a boat away from shore with a pole. More often than *push*, *shove* indicates exertion, as in *pushing* a heavy object along a surface: to *shove* a boat into the water. Or, used of persons, it may imply greater belligerence or determination than *push*, focusing on rough haste or blunt rudeness in *pushing* insistently: *shoving* everyone aside, elbowing and jostling his way to the front. *Push* and *shove* are often used in tandem: rush-hour commuters *pushing* and *shoving* in the subway.

To **thrust** is to *push* suddenly and forcibly, as on impulse or because of some stimulus. [The child *thrust* out his hand, asking for candy; Shy and embarrassed, the boy *thrust* the corsage at his date; Othello, in a jealous rage, *thrust* Desdemona aside.] Unlike the other words, *thrust* often specifically implies a putting of one thing into another. It may mean to put a person forcibly into some situation: to *thrust* a prisoner into a cell; to *thrust* an unwilling child onto the stage. Or it may refer to the act of *pushing* into something with a sharp or pointed instrument: to *thrust* a pin into one's skin; a matador who *thrusts* a sword into a bull. In an extended sense, it can mean to have anything forced upon one against one's will: Unwanted publicity was *thrust* upon him when he won the prize.

Press and **urge**, in this context, point to an outward influence that *propels* one toward a goal. *Urge* may be used of physical force: to *urge* a horse on with a whip or with spurs. More often, however, *urge* indicates not force but strong persuasion, the psychological exertion of a prompting or impelling influence: He *urged* them to accept the plan. *Press* refers almost entirely to psychological stress. It is stronger than *urge* in implying greater insistence and urgency, with overtones of demand: *pressing* them to meet the deadline; He *pressed* me for an answer; *pressing* hard for needed reforms. *Push* is used figuratively in a similar way, meaning to *press* persistently or to promote or advocate vigorously: to *push* for a change in the law; to *push* a new line of goods. See IMPEL.

Antonyms: DISCOURAGE, PULL, STOP.

These words mean to preserve from harm, injury, or attack. **Protect** is the most general term. It suggests from its etymology the providing of a covering or other barrier to ward off harm: to *protect* one's hands from the cold with warm gloves; to *protect* a country from surprise attack by means of an air-alarm system. **Guard** is to *protect* with extreme care and watchfulness against actual or potential danger: to *guard* a prisoner from escaping; Secret Service men who *guard* the president and his family; to *guard* against hurting someone's feelings.

Shield suggests even more strongly than does *protect* that something, as in the manner of a knight's shield, is placed between that which is to be *protected* and the impending source of harm or injury: to *shield* one's face from blows with an upraised arm; *shielding* one's eyes from strong light; overly protective parents who *shield* their children from disappointment or failure.

Safeguard implies that danger is not yet present and may even be remote, but that planning against its eventuality is prudent and far-seeing. [Vaccination *safeguards* all of us from smallpox; Saving money regularly during one's working years will help to *safeguard* one's old age from want.]

Defend emphasizes present danger and means to *protect* by the use of force or other countermeasures. [The American colonists fought to *defend* their liberties; Every child must learn to *defend* himself, when necessary, from the aggression of other children.] By extension, *defend* also means to uphold or vindicate actions, opinions, decisions, etc., against censure, punishment, or unfriendly criticism: to *defend* one's right to hold certain political views; to *defend* the reputation of a wrongly accused man; a lawyer *defending* his client in court. *Defend, guard,* and *shield* are not as complete in indicating success in warding off harm as is *protect.* One may *guard, shield,* or *defend* a person or thing in vain, but that which one *protects* tends to be secure and safe.

Shelter and **harbor** both mean to *protect* by offering or by simply being a place of refuge or safety. *Shelter* is usually applied to providing cover from inclement weather or actual physical danger or attack. [*Sheltered* from the cold in his cave, the bear sleeps until spring; They were *sheltered* from the rifle fire by a huge boulder.] *Shelter* can also, as does

protect

defend
guard
harbor
safeguard
shelter
shield

shield, convey the idea of *protecting* in a manner that serves to inhibit or keep in a state of ignorance: The Victorians believed in *sheltering* young girls and women from sexual knowledge and from other evils. *Harbor* almost always has connotations that are unfavorable or that may even suggest illegality: improperly sterilized operating rooms that *harbor* germs; to *harbor* a fugitive from justice. In its figurative use, *harbor* points to a cherishing in the mind, often secretly, of thoughts, motivations, plans, etc., that are unacceptable or hostile: to *harbor* grudges; to *harbor* a ruthless ambition that in due time may be realized. See NURSE, PAMPER.

Antonyms: ATTACK, PLUNDER.

protection

asylum
cover
refuge
sanctuary
shelter

These words are alike in denoting a place where one is guarded or defended from attack or injury; they also are used to designate the condition of safety or security which such a place provides. **Protection** is the most general and widely applied word in this group. It can refer to anything that shields from harm or destruction. [A strong defense system offers *protection* from sudden attack by an enemy; A storm cellar may provide *protection* from tornadoes.] **Shelter** usually connotes temporary *protection*, as from exposure to the elements: an awning under which we found *shelter* during the shower. **Refuge** suggests the safety one seeks when one is threatened or when one has escaped from danger or distress: a prisoner on the run who took *refuge* in an abandoned shack. Figuratively *refuge* refers to any expedient which is used to provide safety or defense: His final *refuge* was a web of lies and deceit. **Cover** is *protection* which affords safety through concealment. It can be the natural *shelter* of shrubbery or bushes used by wild animals. It can be an object, a house, etc., that serves as a shield under attack: Take *cover* in the barn as soon as you hear gun fire. It can be a military tactic used by troops, vessels, etc.: Most Allied landings in World War II would not have been possible without continuous air *cover*.

Asylum and **sanctuary** are related in meaning. *Asylum* originally designated the inviolable *refuge* from arrest or punishment offered by the temple in ancient times; *sanctuary* was the later Christian equivalent. Today such immunity from arrest, punishment, or persecution is fixed by national boundaries rather than by those of a church or temple. *Asylum* and *sanctuary* are, therefore, most often applied to the *protection* offered to a political refugee by a foreign country or its diplomatic officials: A dictator deposed by a successful revolution may find *asylum* (or *sanctuary*) in another country. *Sanctuary*, by extension, has also come to refer to those areas set apart for the *protection* and preservation of wildlife: a bird *sanctuary*. See ESCAPE, PROTECT.

Antonyms: AGGRESSION, DANGER, *distress, harm, hurt, injury.*

prototype

archetype
exemplar
ideal
original
pattern
Urtext

These words refer to the representative, perfect, or earliest form of something. **Prototype** indicates the first example of a type from which other examples are developed or after which they are modeled: the anthropoid *prototype* of modern man; The Homeric epics became the *prototypes* upon which Virgil, Milton, and others based their epic poems. The word can also indicate the first full-scale model of something: the *prototype* of his plan for urban housing projects, built to demonstrate its advantages. Less specifically, *prototype* can also indicate any sort of precursor of a later instance: Bacon was the *prototype* of the present-day scientist.

Pattern can apply to the plans for a product rather than to the *prototype* or the later creations made from its specifications; often, it suggests blueprints or templates to be followed in constructing the product: new dress *patterns* on sale. More generally, the word indicates the design or configuration that something takes in actuality: the *pattern* of imagery in *Hamlet* that pertains to bodily injury and disease; *patterns* of culture. But the word can also refer to the perfect representative of a type, or to any example thought worthy of emulation: Castiglione was the very *pattern* of the Renaissance courtier.

Original is close to *prototype* in distinguishing the first or genuine product from copies or later versions: She typed an *original* and two carbons; a painting that proved to be copied from an *original* in the Louvre; a close comparison of the two dresses, one a signed *original*, the other a mass-produced copy; a collation of all manuscript copies with the *original*. **Urtext**, the most restricted of these words, is adopted from the German and refers to the earliest version of a literary work, whether written or printed and whether extant or not: an argument that presupposed a vanished *Urtext* of the play upon which the existing version is modeled.

Archetype can also refer to the earliest version of a literary work; in this case, it refers strictly to a manuscript that no longer exists: possible to reconstruct the *archetype* from the variety of incomplete copies in existence. *Archetype* refers much more widely, however, to the abstract conception of a perfect type. In Platonism, *archetypes* are the general or pure forms of which existing things are imperfect copies: For Plato, all chairs, however various in design, can be said to reflect in their "chair-ness" the same *archetype*, just as there are *archetypes* for justice, goodness, and such institutions as a republic. A modern redefinition of *archetype* was initiated by Jung to refer to those forms and symbols in the unconscious of all men that theoretically reflect the past history of the species: a myth that deals with *archetypes* of guilt, death, redemption, and rebirth. More loosely, the word can refer to the quintessential elements that something contains: recurrent *archetypes* of conflict and resolution that can be seen in the living patterns of every family unit. *Prototype* and *archetype* are sometimes loosely substituted for one another, but strictly speaking, *prototype* suggests an early, possibly unrefined version that later versions may reflect but depart from; *archetype*, by contrast, suggests a perfect and unchanging form, real or imaginary, that existing things can more or less approach, but never equal.

Ideal is a much simpler word for some of the meanings indicated by *archetype*. But it usually suggests an imagined perfection, formulated as a goal to strive for or as a measure against which to test something that exists: describing his *ideal* of what a city should be like and comparing this to the actual monstrosities that the trend to urbanization has produced. As can be seen, *ideal* may indicate a personal rather than universal set of desirable qualities, whereas *archetype* refers to what is generally and invariably true of all examples, at least in essence. *Ideal* can also point hyperbolically to an instance seen as an embodiment of perfection: He was her *ideal* of all that was manly. **Exemplar** concentrates exclusively on this last possibility of *ideal*, pointing to an instance that seems the perfect realization of its type: a soprano who was the *exemplar* of the prima donna at her most grandiose and temperamental. See ARISE, FORM, KIND, NATIVE.

Antonyms: COPY, COUNTERPART, DUPLICATE.

These words all denote various forms of brief expressions of what are supposed to be accepted truths. A **proverb** is a homely illustration of a general truth and is couched in condensed and practical terms, as in

proverb

proverb
(continued)

adage
aphorism
apothegm
epigram
epigraph
epitaph
maxim
motto
saying

"A fool and his money are soon parted." An **adage** is a time-honored and widely known *proverb*, such as "Actions speak louder than words."

A **maxim** is a practical rule of conduct or action, such as, "Neither a borrower nor a lender be." The **motto** differs from the *maxim* in that it merely states a guiding principle or belief rather than a precept. *Mottoes* are sometimes prefixed to literary works, but commonly they are chosen by a group, an institution, a nation, etc., as an expression of a purpose or ideal. ["Semper fidelis" is the *motto* of the Marine Corps; "In God we trust" is the *motto* of the United States.]

A **saying** is a figure of speech or a remark of any type that is current among ordinary people. *Sayings* are repeated often, sometimes to the point of losing their freshness. [As the *saying* goes, "He has bats in his belfry"; As I always say, "Live and let live."] *Saying* also has the general meaning of any noteworthy or pungent observation, especially one of a group culled from the writings and speeches of well-known figures. One speaks of the *sayings* of Marcus Aurelius or the *sayings* of Benjamin Franklin.

The remaining words all refer to expressions that are more consciously literary or clever than are *proverbs* and *adages*; furthermore, their authorship is more often known. An **epigram** is a brief, pointed remark in verse, prose, or conversation that expresses a witty or even satirical observation. "The only way to get rid of a temptation is to yield to it," wrote Oscar Wilde, a composer of brilliant *epigrams*. **Epigraph** is sometimes confused with *epigram*, but it refers strictly to a brief quotation, rich in implications, that introduces a piece of writing: Eliot used a quotation from Conrad as an *epigraph* to his poem "The Hollow Men." Less commonly now, the word can also refer to the inscription of a *motto* in some material such as stone or metal: the *epigraph* on the coin. **Epitaph**, often confused with *epigram* and *epigraph*, refers to a verse or prose inscription on a tombstone. Whether signed or anonymous, an *epitaph* may be composed for the occasion or consist of a quoted *adage* or *motto*: a hobby of collecting colorful *epitaphs* to be found in old graveyards.

An **aphorism** is a thought-provoking remark that does not yield all its meaning so readily as an *epigram* and aims at profundity rather than wit. An *aphorism* may be embedded in a longer work, as the following observation from King Lear: "As flies to wanton boys are we to the gods; they kill us for their sport." In other cases, authors have deliberately written groups, sequences, or even books of *aphorisms*: the *aphorisms* of Kafka. An **apothegm** is a startling or paradoxical assertion, such as Swift's remark, "There is nothing in this world constant but inconstancy." See TRUISM.

provisional

conditional
contingent
dependent

These words refer to a tentative act, decision, or situation that is subject or subordinate to factors that are either in evidence or thought likely to come about. **Provisional** may refer merely to something adopted for the moment out of temporary necessity or until something better can be arranged: a *provisional* army. More pertinent here, the word often suggests a situation that is allowed to exist provided certain results are forthcoming: given *provisional* status as a nonmatriculated student until his first-term grades were available. The word usually suggests that the crucial factors determining ultimate status are those that lie in the future.

Dependent, by contrast, may indicate something subject to factors past, present, or future: rapid growth that was *dependent* upon the groundwork laid in the last century; a sense of well-being that is *de-*

pendent mainly on overall physical health; accepting the new liberal policies, *dependent* only upon how they worked out in practice. The word also often suggests factors that may be imposed or stipulated as part of an agreement or contract: an increased allowance that was to be *dependent* upon the uses to which it was put.

Conditional stresses almost exclusively this last sense possible for *dependent*, suggesting an agreement that will be honored by one side if its terms are held to by the other side: *conditional* approval of the book, provided certain passages were deleted. The word, less specifically, may simply mean tentative: could give only *conditional* praise to the tenor of the report, not having studied the transcript in detail. **Contingent** may refer at its least complex to something liable to happen: fearing that defeat was *contingent*. It may also indicate something unforeseen or occurring by chance or accident: *contingent* catastrophes. More pertinent here, the word suggests a cause-and-effect relationship of any sort: a political victory wholly *contingent* upon the personal popularity of the winner. The word may also suggest something *dependent* upon an uncertain event or condition. [Historical processes are *contingent* upon so many imponderables as to make untenable the approach of the scientific determinist.] See FLIMSY, SUBORDINATE, TEMPORARY.

Antonyms: CONCLUSIVE, DEFINITE, *independent*, PERMANENT.

pseudonym

alias
nom de guerre
nom de plume
pen name

A **pseudonym** is a fictitious name used in place of one's actual, or legal, name. *Pseudonym* is the most general term in this group and includes all of the others. It does not suggest any discreditable motive for concealing one's identity; a *pseudonym* may be adopted merely because it is more striking or easier to recall than one's actual name. **Pen name** and **nom de plume** (a term supposedly coined in England from French elements) both refer specifically to a fictitious name that an author signs to a book, article, or other literary work. [Voltaire was the *pseudonym* (or *pen name*) of François Marie Arouet; Mark Twain was the *pseudonym* (or *nom de plume*) of Samuel Clemens.]

An **alias** is a name taken to conceal one's identity, often for suspect purposes. An *alias* is often assumed to avoid the consequences of a criminal record or to confuse officers of the law. On the other hand, a reformed criminal or a person who has been involved in a scandal may move to another area to make a fresh start and there take an *alias* to protect himself and his family from publicity. In the strict legal sense, *alias* is not only an assumed name but may be another name by which a person is known to some people. Unlike the other words, *alias* may be used adverbially: Jason Miller, *alias* James Minton.

Nom de guerre (adopted from the French and meaning literally "war name") is a *pseudonym* adopted by a person who must conceal his true identity in order to retain freedom of action. Consequently, many persons engaged in various kinds of controversies or in political activities that are against a prevailing regime find it necessary to adopt *noms de guerre*. [Lenin was the *nom de guerre* of Vladimir Ulyanov; Currer Bell was the *nom de guerre* (and the *pen name*) of Charlotte Brontë because she found it easier to publish her works under a masculine name.

psychotic

crazy
demented

These words refer to serious disturbances of the mind. **Psychotic** is the most precise of these, being used by psychiatrists to describe someone who exhibits a total break with or withdrawal from reality; the word contrasts with neurotic, which describes someone with a distorted view of reality. A *psychotic* personality may be antisocial, violent, or merely

psychotic
(continued)

deranged
insane
lunatic
mad
psychopathic

passive: *psychotic* delusions; *psychotic* acts of cruelty; *psychotic* apathy. The word may also be used by sociologists to describe, less precisely, acts that are extreme departures from social norms: a *psychotic* split between duty and simple humanity that resulted in the setting up of the concentration camps. The word has also entered the popular consciousness, where it can be used imprecisely as a simple term of opprobrium: my *psychotic* mother-in-law.

Psychopathic is even more likely to be used in a popular context, although here it is more often a precise high-toned substitute for vicious or brutal: a *psychopathic* killer. In its strict psychiatric use, however, it refers to someone who exhibits no break with reality, unlike the *psychotic*, but who has no sense of social responsibility; while this may result in violent or criminal acts, it may also result in extreme withdrawal or passivity.

Demented at its most precise indicates someone whose mentality has degenerated from a previous level that was more nearly normal: brain damage that left him *demented*. More often, however, the word is used loosely to refer to anyone who seems possessed by odd obsessions or eccentricities: her *demented* fear of strangers. **Insane**, a word now abandoned by psychologists and psychiatrists, is still used legally to refer to someone who is so mentally disturbed as to be unable to distinguish morally between right and wrong. In popular usage, it may also refer to things that appear foolish or ridiculous: a trial that hinged on whether or not the accused could be considered *insane* at the time of the murder; an *insane* scheme for making a million on the stock market. The word can even be used as a superlative for anything intense, exciting, or fun: an absolutely *insane* beach party. **Deranged** is less likely to be used in either a psychological or legal context, but in a general way, it has validity in formal usage to refer to mental or emotional drives or balances that have become disordered: *deranged* by fever; *deranged* from a lack of food and water; She suffered a sudden shock that *deranged* her completely.

The remaining words no longer have valid uses in either psychological or legal discussion, or even in general formal use. **Lunatic**, in fact, is now less often used on any level of speech because of its old-fashioned sound; its root refers to a belief that the moon could cause mental disturbance. Sometimes it is still used comically or disapprovingly for odd or undesirable behavior: a *lunatic* notion that anyone should be able to own lethal weapons. It is also commonly found in the expression "*lunatic* fringe" which denotes those followers or devotees of a movement, idea, etc., who are extreme or fanatical in their enthusiasm. By contrast, **mad** and **crazy** are used widely to refer popularly to mental disturbance. *Mad*, the more formal of the two, may suggest profound mental disorder. More informally, the word can also refer to anything silly, flamboyant, pointless, unrealistic, or irrational: a *mad* feathered hat; a *mad* hope that help might still come; a *mad* desire to wreak vengeance on his imagined oppressor. Some careful writers avoid the word when it means angry: remarks that made her *mad* at me. *Crazy* is the most informal of these and refers popularly to someone who is extremely neurotic or *psychotic*. The word also has a wide range of additional uses to refer to the eccentric, odd, troubled, or desiring: a *crazy* collection of furniture; a *crazy* dread of failing the exam; *crazy* about sailors. It can even express approval for something that goes to extremes: a *crazy* cocktail party. See FRANTIC, FRENZY.

Antonyms: SENSIBLE.

These words refer to the action of moving something toward one or in the same direction in which one is moving. **Pull** is the most general word in the group, embracing all the other terms within its meaning: *pulling* the wagon behind him; *pulling* a straw from the broom; *pulling* the fallen climber out of the crevasse. While *pull* can suggest movement in any direction, **drag** usually refers to horizontal motion or motion up an incline; it suggests laborious effort over rough ground or against friction, resistance, or gravity: *dragging* his feet across the floor; *dragging* the body out of the airplane; *dragging* each stone for the pyramid up the long hill. **Haul** is like *drag* in suggesting laborious effort and rough going, but it is like *pull* in suggesting movement in any direction: *hauling* the loaded basket up two stories by a long, sturdy rope; *hauling* the raft over the sandbar. It also has a special use in the transportation industry for moving heavy materials or equipment: flatboats that *haul* iron ore from Duluth to the steel factories.

   Tug and **yank** both refer to intermittent or quick pulls on something: *tugging* at my sleeve to ask directions; *tugging* at his chains. *Yank* is much more informal than *tug* and might be considered slang by some. The word suggests abruptness and ill humor and, unlike *tug*, is more often used of a single motion than a series of small, quick motions: *yanking* me bodily out of my chair; *yanking* the picture from the wall. See IMPEL.

   Antonyms: PROPEL.

pull

drag
haul
tug
yank

These words refer to the result toward which one chooses to direct his activity. **Purpose** may suggest either a resolute, deliberate movement toward a result or the desired result itself: filled with high *purpose*; explaining the *purpose* of the tedious exercises. The specific overtone of *purpose* in either use is that of meaningfulness: unable to comprehend a universe without *purpose*; a cruel act done on *purpose*. The other words in this group do not carry this implication and concentrate mostly on the desired result, rather than on the manner of moving toward it. Of these, **goal** is closest to *purpose* in suggesting a deliberately selected result that can be won only with difficulty by dedicated effort: sticking stubbornly to his *goal* of prison reform. The emphasis on choice is more invariable here than with *purpose*; the latter might be supplied by someone else, but a *goal* suggests a personal determination: a tutorial system whose *purpose* was to let each student realize his own educational *goal*. Sometimes *goal* is used in a vaguer way to mean the general trend or direction a person or group takes, without implying any final result: the *goal* of a free democracy; asking himself what his *goals* in life should be.

   Aim is often used in this vague way, suggesting a general tendency: the *aims* of education; his *aim* in life. In the singular, it implies a more concrete choice than *goal*, one that could be spelled out succinctly. When used of a desired result, *aim* is most appropriate for a small or short-term *goal* and is consequently less dramatic in tone than *goal* or *purpose*: going to Venice with the *aim* of seeing as many Tintorettos as possible. *Aim* also suggests less emotional involvement in the outcome than *purpose* and *goal*, and less determination that it will be achieved. **End** is more formal than the foregoing words and is most specifically appropriate to philosophical or ethical discussions: theorizing that the *end* of exogamy is species differentiation; the *ends* of a just society. Because it has other meanings that are more common, the word in this sense is often restricted to uses in which it contrasts with the manner of achieving a given *goal*: arguing that the *end* justifies the means.

purpose

aim
end
goal
object
objective

Object and **objective** would seem too close to distinguish between, but each has a context in which it is the more appropriate of the two. Both are more formal than the other words of this group and are often used for impersonal planning of an abstract or general nature: limited desegregation as an *object* of the court's decision; economic *objectives* of the second five-year plan. *Object* would be most appropriate for an *aim* or *goal* that could be stated in a few words; *objective* suggests a wider, more intangible set of *goals* that includes a good many imponderables. *Objective*, however, has a military use for a specific or limited *goal*: naming Hill 104 as our *objective*. *Object*, by contrast, nearly always suggests specificity or singleness of *purpose*: the *object* of our search; the *object* of his fantasy life. See INTEND, PLAN, PROJECT.

puzzle

conundrum
enigma
mystery
problem
riddle

These words apply to things that are hard to solve, answer, or understand. In a limited sense, all are questions, tasks, or entertainments that have set answers or solutions and are devised to challenge the wits. A **puzzle** is a game or contrivance that tests one's ingenuity or patience. To work a jigsaw *puzzle* or a crossword *puzzle*, one must fit together pieces or words in a certain way to form a whole. A **problem** is an exercise in learning that tests one's ability to apply theory, knowledge, and technique. To work a *problem* in mathematics, one must use the given facts to find the missing ones: The *problem* is to find the average speed of a car on a trip when the distance traveled and traveling time are known. A **mystery** in this comparison is a story, novel, play, or movie that arouses one's curiosity or suspense: a murder *mystery*. To solve a *mystery*, one must follow clues and interpret evidence in order to find a plausible explanation for perplexing events. In actuality, a *mystery* story is both plotted and solved by its author, who must keep the reader guessing until the end.

Enigma, **riddle**, and **conundrum** all apply to questions or statements designed to perplex. An *enigma* is a deliberately obscure or ambiguous statement, a dark saying meant to hide as much as it reveals: The Delphic oracle spoke in *enigmas*. A *riddle* is a puzzling question stated as a problem to be solved by clever ingenuity. *Riddles* may be significant, requiring a grasp of metaphor or the ability to comprehend a paradox. The famous *riddle* of the Sphinx was an *enigma* that only Oedipus could interpret: "What goes on four legs in the morning, on two at noon, on three at night?" "Man — in infancy he crawls, at his prime he walks, in age he leans on a staff." On the other hand, a *riddle* may be merely clever, depending on a pun, as: "What is black and white and red (read) all over?" "A newspaper." A *conundrum* is a *riddle* that hinges on a pun and that involves some fanciful point of likeness or difference between things, as: "What is the difference between a floorwalker and a sailor?" "One oversees sales and the other sails over seas." *Conundrum* is an adult word for a child's game — a kind of *riddle* at best ingenious, at worst inane.

In a broader sense, all of these words may be applied to anything that baffles or perplexes. *Problem* is the most general word. Any person or thing that causes difficulty may be called a *problem*. A *mystery* was originally something beyond human understanding: the *mystery* of creation; religious *mysteries*. But the word *mystery* is now freely applied to puzzling things that have not been explained or that are not fully understood. [Her disappearance has remained a *mystery*; Why he went there is a *mystery* to me.] *Riddle* is close to *mystery* in this sense but stresses the idea of eventual solution: the unsolved *riddle* of the common cold.

An *enigma* is a tantalizing *mystery*, something darkly veiled or utterly baffling: His biographer passed over his hearty, wholesome public image to probe the *enigma* of his private life. Applied to human beings, *enigma* stresses internal contradictions, the presence of opposed traits that make a person hard to understand. *Puzzle* is close to *enigma* in this sense but is a less romantic and more pragmatic word, emphasizing the fitting together of pieces to find a solution: Though many tried to figure him out and to predict what he would do, the leader remained a *puzzle*. *Conundrum*, the most specific of these words, is the only one never applied to a person. When used in an extended sense, it means a *problem* that seems to defy solution but that invites conjecture. See CONFUSE, OBSCURE.

puzzle

baffle
mystify
perplex

These words mean to confuse or to present difficulty in understanding or solving something. **Puzzle** may suggest only a mild curiosity and therefore only a mild frustration at the inability to decipher the meaning of something: *puzzled* by his neighbor's odd looks. As in this example, the word suggests that enough hints or clues have been picked up to indicate that something is not normal, without permitting one to determine just what is wrong. On the other hand, the word can suggest merely the remarking of a situation which is unusual in some way: *puzzled* by the friendliness of the strange country's inhabitants.

Mystify suggests a greater loss of detachment than is true for *puzzle* and a greater frustration at not being able to get at the meaning of something. By implication, a person must have many more clues to be *mystified* than he needs to be *puzzled*; *puzzle* might also suggest an initial stage of investigation, *mystify* a later one: first *puzzled* and then thoroughly *mystified* as to why she had never mentioned her husband in the hundreds of diary entries she had made.

Where *mystify* most appropriately suggests astonishment in the face of an unyielding enigma, **perplex** stresses actual discomfort as the attendant emotion; it may also imply a more personal involvement with its overtones of worry and uncertainty: *perplexed* by his refusal to tell her where he was going. **Baffle**, the most intense of these words, combines the sense of astonishment implicit in *mystify* with the emotional discomfort implicit in *perplex*. It suggests someone rendered unable to act or venture hypotheses in the face of a strange or inexplicable experience: The odd noises and flashes of light in the empty house completely *baffled* him. See CONFUSE.

Antonyms: CLARIFY, INFORM.

Q

These words refer to the total size, sum, or extent of something measurable. In general use, **quantity** suggests that something is considered in its totality, in terms of mass or bulk: a sufficient *quantity* of food to last a week. *Quantity*, itself, is that property of a thing that admits of exact measurement. In order to express a *quantity* in precise terms, however, it is necessary to divide it into units of some kind, measuring it in terms of magnitude, volume, size, sum, weight, or length. A *quantity* of water in a storage tank, for example, can be measured in terms of gal-

quantity

amount
number

lons. **Amount** is often very close to *quantity* in meaning but may differ significantly in its use. It implies that the thing thought of in sum or in the aggregate can be broken down into separate units or parts that can be measured, counted, or otherwise specified: a large *quantity* of gravel; a limited *amount* of time; a large *amount* of money; a considerable *amount* of work. *Amount* rather than *quantity* is the word generally used of immeasurable or intangible things: He went to a considerable *amount* of trouble. It is *quantity*, however, and not *amount*, that is set over against quality, indicating the contrast between bulk or output and the immaterial value of excellence.

When used collectively, **number** points to a collection of individual things that can be counted, referring to things that are physically or symbolically separate, not merely separable into units. Where *amount* emphasizes the whole, *number* focuses on the parts: an *amount* of money; a *number* of coins. Where *quantity* stresses measurement in bulk, *number* stresses individual items: a *number* of peaches; the *quantity* of peaches contained in a bushel basket. *Number*, like *quantity*, may be either specific or vague. It may refer to an indefinite or unspecified *quantity*. [When he moved, a *number* of his books had to be left behind; A limited *number* of seats are still available.] Or it may refer to a specific sum or total count of units or individuals: The *number* of students absent is 6. When *number* is preceded by "the," it is used with a singular verb: The *number* of jobs is increasing. When preceded by "a," it is used with a plural verb: A *number* of graduates plan to apply. *Number*, when used with "a," and otherwise unqualified, can imply that the *amount* referred to is relatively large: A *number* of people signed the petition. Both *number* and *quantity* when used in the plural can indicate a large *amount* or group or a sizable collection. [*Quantities* of surplus materials are available; *Numbers* of people complained when the proposed shutdown was announced.] See PART, TOTAL.

queer

crazy
funny
odd
peculiar

These words all refer to behavior, appearance, or people considered out of the ordinary, strange, or unusual. Something deemed **queer** is not only strange but often bizarre and inexplicable. [It was *queer* how the TV picture kept disappearing and reappearing even though the house lights didn't flicker; a *queer* scraping sound, as though something were trying to get in the door.] *Queer* emphasizes both the singularity and strangeness of the event: a *queer* accident in which nobody was hurt but both cars were entirely demolished. (Compare "freak accident," which implies that the cause of the accident was a bizarre product of chance.) *Queer* is now often used in a slang sense in reference to homosexuals.

Odd and **peculiar** are closely allied in popular use and are interchangeable in these contexts, but the basic meaning of *peculiar* is having a unique or special character; oddness or eccentricity is neither central nor necessary to its meaning. [Great minds have a way of looking at life *peculiar* to themselves; a *peculiarly* apt choice of words] The more popular meaning of strange or *odd* has been derived from this sense: a *peculiar* habit of scratching his ear while he talked. But note that even here *peculiar* does not necessarily imply oddness; whether the habit is to be thought of as merely distinctive or as unusual to the point of being eccentric depends upon the larger context. *Odd* may be used for slight or extremely unusual qualities of behavior or appearance; it stresses deviation from the normal, ordinary, or expected: He was more than a little *odd*, very fastidious about his manners but an incredibly sloppy dresser.

Funny may be an informal word for *peculiar* or remarkable. [That's *funny*; I could have sworn I was wearing a hat when I came in here.] Sometimes *funny* suggests an endearing or cute quality: a *funny* way of wrinkling her nose. **Crazy**, a word never used by psychiatrists except in jest, means mad or insane: He was acting *crazy*, throwing up his hands and singing, then yelling that somebody was murdering him. Nowadays the word is probably more often used to mean acting as if mad, or simply unconventional, offbeat, or hard to understand: a *crazy* driver, weaving in and out of traffic; Pushing a car is a *crazy* thing to do when you have a weak heart. See BIZARRE, ECCENTRICITY.

Antonyms: NORMAL, USUAL.

These words are related in that they all mean to restore to a state of peace, quiet, or order. **Quell**, **suppress**, and **subdue** mean to put an end to a disturbance, such as a riot or a revolt, by the use of persuasion or force. To *quell* an uprising, one may employ either persuasion or force, or both; and the word suggests taking measures to discourage the participants in order to keep the situation from getting out of hand: The sergeants were able to *quell* the melee that broke out in the barracks by ordering all of the men to stand at attention. Used figuratively, *quell* may mean merely to allay or quiet, as certain feelings: to *quell* foolish fears; the mother's happiness in the event often *quelling* the pains attending childbirth. *Suppress* in this sense means to *quell* by taking specific actions that not only will put down a disturbance completely but will frustrate any attempts to revive it or to start a similar one. The word suggests a complete crushing and overpowering, often swift and violent in nature: to *suppress* a mutiny by putting half the crew in irons and hanging the ringleaders at dawn. *Subdue* takes the participants in a disturbance as its object and implies that they not only are reduced to order but, by the imposition of controls (such as curfews or threats of reprisal), are also rendered more or less incapable of resisting further. In addition to the implication of conquering completely, *subdue* also carries the idea of taming or rendering mild and gentle, often after great difficulty: The great, thundering stallion was finally *subdued* and broken in as a riding horse.

Calm and **placate** are milder in meaning than the foregoing words and apply only to the quieting of violent movement or emotion. *Calm* is the more general term here and implies causing a state of quietude which, however, may only be transient. [The nurses *calmed* the anxious patient with soothing words and small attentions; While awaiting trial, the angry prisoner *calmed* down enough to cooperate with his lawyer in preparing his defense.] *Placate* always involves appeasement and means to *calm* anger, resentment, hostility, etc., by making concessions or yielding to demands: Only by offering to do extra work at the end of the term could he *placate* the teacher who seemed determined to fail him.

Tranquilize, still a fad word after some years of use, is a back formation from the medical term tranquilizer, which is applied to a class of drugs having the property of reducing nervous tension and states of anxiety. It is rarely used in the sense of *calm* or pacify and almost always refers to the effect produced by these drugs. See DISCOURAGE, DOCILE, SUBJUGATE, VANQUISH.

A **question** is a group of words in interrogative form which calls for an answer. In this sense, **inquiry** is interchangeable with *question*: an impertinent *question* answered with steely silence; an *inquiry* to a hotel

quell

calm
placate
subdue
suppress
tranquilize

question

question
(continued)

enquiry
inquiry
query

manager about the rental rate on a suite of rooms. *Inquiry* can go beyond this simple meaning to refer to a group of *questions*, a search for knowledge or information by observing, experimenting, etc., or a full-scale, formal investigation, as that made by legal or congressional committees: the desk handling *inquiries* about stock prices; a thorough *inquiry* into the nature of a particular physical phenomenon; last year's protracted *inquiry* into the price-fixing scandal by the attorney general's office. **Query** can be used as a synonym for *question* or the corresponding sense of *inquiry*. The word, however, has a slightly formal or literary tone and is best used when the *question* being asked is an attempt to clear up some doubt or indecision, or when there is an indication of a genuine search for specific or authoritative information: to make a *query* only when the meaning of a passage is not perfectly evident; a serious *query* of such complexity that it had to be referred to the chairman of the Humanities Department. It is often, indeed, the seriousness of intent on the part of the person who poses a *question* that makes the *question* a *query*. *Questions* are sometimes designed merely to perplex, confuse, or entrap the person of whom they are asked; *queries* are never so idle or frivolous. **Enquiry** is a variant spelling of *inquiry*, used chiefly in Great Britain. See EXAMINE, INQUIRY, QUESTION (v.), REQUEST (n.), REQUEST (v.).

question

grill
interrogate
quiz

These words refer to the asking or demanding of information. Of these, **question** is the most general in meaning and the most neutral in tone. At its most restricted, it may be used as a more formal substitute for ask, in the sense of making a single or specific query: *questioning* the woman at the information desk about where he could exchange a piece of merchandise. More pertinent here, however, is its use to suggest the asking of a series of questions to bring information to light: *questioning* the witnesses for details about the physical appearance of the killer. It may suggest an informal situation: *questioning* him about why he was so late getting home from work. Often, however, the word points to an official or formal situation: The suspect was brought to the station house to be *questioned* about his connections with the deceased man. **Interrogate** is a much more formal substitute for *question* and is mostly restricted to an official examination of some sort: warning him that the prosecutor would *interrogate* him about matters that might embarrass him.

Grill, by contrast, is a much more informal word and applies specifically to intensive *interrogating* in which someone is pressured to reveal information: a dozen petty crooks who had been rounded up and *grilled* for hours about their activities on the night of the holdup. The pressure may be psychological, but can extend to physical torture: *grilling* the captured guerrilla by means of the water-torture method. **Quiz** suggests the use of much less strenuous methods than *grill* and may apply to more ordinary situations; it does, however, suggest intensive *questioning*: *quizzing* her children about every move they had made while she was gone. Often the word suggests an educational context, referring in this case to short informal tests, oral or written, conducted to determine the mastery of assigned work: *quizzing* the students twice a week on their outside reading. See DEMAND, EXAMINE, INQUIRY, QUESTION (n.), REQUEST (v.).

quick

These words refer to speed of movement. While **quick** can apply widely, it often refers less to rate of motion than to the suddenness or brief duration of a one-time action: a *quick* leap; a *quick* response to my question; The hand is *quicker* than the eye. It can also apply to a readiness to act: *quick* to take offense. When it indicates something of short duration, it often implies haste: He ate a *quick* breakfast and rushed off to work. While **fast** can also apply in a wide variety of ways, it is more apt than *quick* for referring to something in sustained motion, indicating here a high rate of speed or a capacity for such movement: a *fast* car; a *fast* getaway; You're reading too *fast* for me to follow.

quick
(continued)

fast
precipitous
rapid
swift

Rapid and **swift** are both more formal than the preceding pair and apply equally well to sudden or sustained movement: a *rapid* river; a *rapid* burst of machine-gun fire; a *swift* change of mood; a *swift* runner. *Rapid* has a special connotation relating to beneficial or advantageous speed; by contrast, both *quick* and *fast* can apply as well to catastrophic haste: a *rapid* recovery from his illness; *rapid* progress in slum clearance. A special connotation of *swift* relates to speed that is smooth, undisturbing, uninterrupted, or seemingly effortless: a *swift* transition without hesitation or awkwardness; a communications network that was *swift* and silent in operation. Also, *swift* can give a lyrical overtone: the *swift* fading of autumn into winter.

Precipitous is the one word here that stresses dangerous, undesirable, or foolhardy speed: two cars in a *precipitous* race through midtown traffic; a disguise that served him well in his *precipitous* flight from the concentration camp. The word can often suggest falling or abrupt downward movement: the *precipitous* fall of stock prices; negotiations that could not halt the two nations' *precipitous* march toward the nuclear brink. See SPEED, SUPPLE.

Antonyms: LISTLESS, SLOW.

These words mean to move or cause to move faster. **Quicken** suggests greater animation in the performance of an action, as well as a shorter time required for its completion; it is close in sense to **accelerate**, which denotes an increase in the rate of movement, growth, progress, etc., of a thing. [The dancers *quickened* their steps; Neglect has *accelerated* this building's decay.] **Speed** differs from *quicken* and *accelerate* in that it always implies rapidity of movement: The auto *sped* along the road; to *speed* production by providing better working conditions. **Hasten** indicates urgency, or sometimes a sudden and premature result. [The storm's approach *hastened* our departure; As the time for the guests' arrival approached, the housewife *hastened* her dinner preparations.] **Hurry** and **rush** are similar to *hasten*, but suggest in addition precipitous or confused motion. [The late arrivals were *hurried* to their seats; The stricken man was *rushed* to a hospital.] *Rush* suggests greater urgency than *hurry*, and sometimes includes the notion of violent action: They suddenly *rushed* pell-mell out of the door. **Expedite**, more especially a business term than any of the other words of this group, means to process quickly, as by giving special attention to, in order to save time: The delivery of your new automobile will be *expedited* by a "rush" order. *Expedite* thus has a distant and formal tone that distinguishes it from emotionally charged words like *rush* and *hurry*. See IMPETUOUS, SPEED.

quicken

accelerate
expedite
hasten
hurry
rush
speed

Antonyms: DELAY, HINDER, STOP.

These words refer to the act of giving up or withdrawing from employment, school attendance, club membership, or other activities. **Quit** and **resign** emphasize the voluntary giving up of a position, membership, or office. *Resign* usually suggests the presentation of a formal

quit
(continued)

leave
resign

letter declaring one's decision. *Quit* is a less formal word, and is likely to be applied to employment for which wages instead of a salary are paid, or to a group activity that is not highly structured: to *quit* a factory job after a row with the foreman; to *quit* playing baseball on the neighborhood team. *Quit* strongly hints at making up one's mind to go on the spur of the moment without much forethought or planning for the future. Of course in more general usage *quit* can refer to the cessation of any activity: to *quit* reading.

Leave is the most general term of this group; it does not imply much beyond the mere fact of ceasing to be part of a specific group, even in the narrower sense here considered. A person who *leaves* a job may, for instance, be planning to take a better one; he may have been dismissed; or he may have reached retirement age.

To **drop out** is to withdraw from participation or membership, usually following a period of loss of interest and of discouragement in the face of increasing competition. *Dropping out* is a more negative and passive act than are *leaving, resigning,* or *quitting.* The term is most commonly applied to adolescents who *leave* school before earning a diploma and who thereafter find it difficult to obtain employment. By extension, certain people such as alcoholics are said to be drop-outs from life itself. The word can also refer favorably to a rejection of false social values: to *drop out* of the race for material gain. See LEAVE (abandon), LEAVE (depart), RELINQUISH.

Antonyms: BEGIN, REMAIN.

quotation

blurb
excerpt
extract
quote

These words refer to short supporting passages from a longer work or another person, or to brief evaluations cited in praise or blame. **Quotation** specifically refers to a passage from another source, clearly indicated as such; it suggests an exact word-for-word rendering of what the other person said: failing to make clear in his text what was summary and what *quotation* of his opponent's argument. Brevity is usually but not necessarily an implication of this word: justifying his viewpoint by extensive *quotations* from his source material. *Quotation* can, however, apply to only a few words; **extract** and **excerpt**, in contrast, suggest longer passages from another source. *Extract* usually refers to several lines of a paragraph, especially when these are set off from the text in which they are cited by the use of indentation or smaller type: concluding his review with a twenty-line *extract* from the title poem. *Excerpt* suggests a longer passage still and may be presented in and for itself, without comment: Several magazines published *excerpts* from his novel.

Blurb and **quote** are much more informal terms than the other words here considered. *Blurb* refers to commendatory words that are cited on the dust jacket of a book or in advertisements for a play or movie. A *blurb* may consist of or include *quotations* from critics, or be an entirely anonymous account designed to persuade a customer to read or see the work. The word is often used pejoratively to refer to the extravagant and insincere praise common in such writing: a *blurb* comparing the author to Homer and Shakespeare. *Quote* is a slangy-sounding shortened form of *quotation*, used in much the same way as the more formal word. Its natural context is the field of journalism, where it suggests a brief comment by someone who has permitted its publication, either with or without attribution: Journalists and newspaper reporters were calling every Pentagon official for a *quote* on the missile crisis. See COPY, DUPLICATE.

R

These words refer to a physical and hostile entering of someone else's territory. **Raid** suggests an organized but short-range and temporary encroachment: boys planning a *raid* on the neighbor's orchard; an unexpected *raid* on the jungle stronghold of the enemy. As in these examples, stealth and surprise may be suggested as planned elements of a *raid*. The word can, however, be used humorously for less hostile acts: laying in a supply of cold cuts for the inevitable midnight *raid* on the refrigerator. **Foray** suggests a more scattered, less organized overrunning of territory than *raid*; it may be haphazard and impulsive as well and even more short-ranged and short-lived. A *foray's* sole motivation may be an intent to wreak gratuitous havoc or to plunder and pillage: students who went on *forays* in the town; a *foray* behind enemy lines.

Incursion is the most formal of these words and is often used in a technical sense to indicate a violation of a nation's territory by another nation: arguing that the overflight could be considered an *incursion* on Soviet airspace. In this sense it may suggest any encroachment: an *incursion* on Fifth Amendment rights. The word can also be used less technically for any hostile entrance, usually sudden, into another's territory: an armed *incursion* into the Gaza strip. **Invasion** resembles *raid* in suggesting an organized and well-planned violation of territory, but it specifically suggests a much more complicated and long-range operation that is usually carried out with the intention of effecting a seizure or change of a permanent sort: the massive Allied *invasion* of Normandy. Occasionally the word suggests a large-scale but unplanned *incursion*: the Danish *invasion* of Britain that occurred over several centuries and took the form of sporadic but repeated *raids* or *forays*. The word can also suggest any unwanted intrusion: an *invasion* of privacy. See AGGRESSION, ENCROACH, FIGHT.

raid

foray
incursion
invasion

These words all mean to place in a higher position. **Raise** commonly implies a physical gesture or activity, although it is often applied in figurative senses to any improved condition or motive: to *raise* one's hand; to *raise* one's spirits with encouragement and kind words. **Elevate**, when applied to a literal rise in position or altitude, sounds very formal, even pretentious, *raise* being preferred in most such contexts. When applied figuratively, however, to a rise in rank or distinction, *elevate* is commonly and easily used on a variety of levels: He was *elevated* from the rank of lieutenant to captain; to *elevate* one's goals.

Lift suggests the use of physical effort in moving something to a higher position, and **hoist** often signifies *lifting* by mechanical means. When *hoist* is used in place of *lift*, it signifies a greater expenditure of effort, as that comparable to what would be required in *lifting* something by mechanical means: to *lift* a book off the table; to *hoist* the automobile aboard the ship; The fireman *hoisted* the heavy man to his shoulder before gingerly descending the ladder. **Uplift** may be used to mean to *raise* aloft, but is more commonly used today to mean to *elevate* morally or mentally: We were *uplifted* by our audience with the Pope. See ESCALATE, IMPROVE.

Antonyms: depress, DESCEND, *lower.*

raise

elevate
hoist
lift
uplift

random

casual
desultory
haphazard

These words refer to an aimless, irregular, or erratic procedure. **Random** suggests something arrived at through accident or through arbitrary choices; it implies lack of specific direction or intent: a *random* gathering of friends and acquaintances; They followed a *random* route through the forest; having *random* thoughts on ways to redecorate her apartment.

Casual points to something that happens without intention or plan and may give a sense of freedom and ease: a *casual* meeting on the street; a *casual* question; a *casual* stroll on the lawn. On the other hand, it may also suggest the qualities of indifference or unconcern: a *casual* handshake; showing by his *casual* manner that he was unaffected by their plight.

Desultory stresses a procedure marked by stops and starts but includes the lack of plan implied by *random* and the lack of formality implied by *casual*: the *desultory* talk of old friends interrupted by long silences and lapses. Less favorably, the word can suggest wandering attention, instability, or inconsistency: his *desultory* attempts to keep his correspondence up to date. **Haphazard** is even stronger in negative implications than *desultory*; it is used almost exclusively in a disapproving way for unsystematic work or behavior that is indifferent to accuracy and efficiency: *haphazard* and slapdash experiments on which no sound conclusions can be based. See CHANCE, CURSORY, OCCASIONAL.

Antonyms: FORMAL, INVARIABLE, ORDERLY, SYSTEMATIC.

reach

accomplish
achieve
attain
earn

These words refer to successfully executing a task or arriving at a goal. **Reach** stresses arrival, regardless of whether the goal has been chosen in advance or whether great or little effort has been expended: We *reached* an unfamiliar quarter of the city after an hour of aimless walking; those few who *reach* the finish line in the hazardous obstacle course. The word can also indicate effort that expresses intention rather than successful completion: He *reached* for a book on the shelf above his head. **Earn** can point to the automatic accruing of money or benefits because on one's work or situation: How much do you *earn* a week?; stocks that *earn* a handsome annual dividend. More pertinent here, the word can suggest the struggle to acquire a special position or distinction: She worked hard to *earn* her Phi Beta Kappa key. The word can also indicate the awarding of an honor or benefit because of the excellence of some completed task: a novel that *earned* him a Pulitzer Prize. In this case, the honor cannot necessarily be foreseen or worked toward as a goal.

Achieve and **attain** can both emphasize the *reaching* of an intended goal, usually through sustained effort. But *achieve* can indicate the working out of a set or standard procedure, whereas *attain* more often applies to a goal toward which someone has aspired without being sure in advance that he would be successful: a series of experiments that *achieved* their purpose; They *attained* a decisive victory in the hard-fought battle. When these words apply, however, to the acquiring of a possibly unexpected distinction, their implications are different. In this case, *achieve* may indicate a deserved success, won because of merit or effort, whereas *attain* is open to other implications: a searching book that *achieved* an awakening of the nation's conscience to the problems of poverty; a trivial play that *attained* a successful run on Broadway.

Accomplish can stress the mere completion of a set task: He *accomplished* the building of the bookcase, although the result was a rather rickety affair. More favorably, the word can function like *attain* to indicate something executed with distinction: the first to *accomplish* the difficult work of deciphering the Minoan script. While the word always indicates success, whether minimal or exceptional, it often concentrates on interpretive or technical skills rather than creative or original work: a pianist who was able to *accomplish* the difficult passage work in the sonata with ease and brilliance. See COME, GET, PERFORM.

Antonyms: bungle, fail, fall short, miss.

read

browse
devour
leaf
peruse
scan

These words refer to the act of taking in and comprehending written or printed words. **Read** is the most general of these, yielding no more connotations beyond the shared meaning for the whole group. It is, however, the one word here that can apply to the act whether done in silence or done orally: *reading* the letter over to himself; *reading* the lesson aloud to her students. **Peruse**, by contrast, specifically means to *read* carefully and with close attention, suggesting a demanding or complicated text that requires concentration and effort: *perusing* the contract in great detail before agreeing to sign it. Sometimes the word is substituted for *read* without these implications attached, as if some sort of elegance could be achieved by using a long word where a short one will do: quickly *perusing* the road sign before applying his brake.

Devour also can refer to thorough *reading*, but it points not to a studious approach but to a zealous or enthusiastic infatuation for certain authors or genres: *devouring* every book that Hermann Hesse wrote; *devouring* at least two murder mysteries a week. Unlike *peruse*, the word can suggest rapid *reading* that may or may not be retentive, and sometimes it can point merely to a habitual or methodical total consumption of a periodical: the somber silence that always reigned in the house while father *devoured* the evening newspaper.

The remaining words point to hasty or cursory *reading*. **Browse** can indicate the act of strolling through a bookstore or library and sampling a number of books or periodicals without *reading* any, possibly as a way of selecting something to *read* more thoroughly: *browsing* through the science-fiction titles for something to *read* on the train. This meaning of the word has been extended to other kinds of shopping: *browsing* in dress shops on her lunch hour. *Browse* can also apply to the idle sampling of passages from one book or periodical: *browsing* about in the magazine without finding anything that interested him.

Leaf suggests the quick turning of pages in search of a particular item, with *reading* restricted to glimpses at key words or passages until the desired entry is found: quickly *leafing* through the phone book to find the numbers of a few restaurants. But the word can also indicate an idle looking over of a magazine or newspaper, especially one heavily illustrated, as a way of passing time; here, the word would suggest little serious purpose or little intention of *reading* much or for long: *leafing* through some old magazines until his turn in the barber chair came up. **Scan** indicates the act of quickly glancing down the body of a text so that the mind can rapidly take in the gist of what is written. Thus, this action is more methodical than the actions indicated by *browse* and certainly *leaf*: *scanning* the articles that might give the information he needed, then *browsing* about in a few related entries, and finally *leafing* past the sports and fashion sections to the television listings. See STUDY.

ready

disposed

These words suggest the accomplishment of whatever training or conditioning is necessary as a preface to action. **Ready** is the most general of these, suggesting anything from a momentary potential for a certain kind of behavior to a long period of discipline prior to an undertaking:

ready
(continued)

prepared
set
willing

ready to tell her exactly what he thought of her; *ready* to perform his first heart operation. In the first kind of use, the word suggests a ripeness for action that may have been building up for some time; in the second it suggests a delicate process of attunement. *Ready* may also suggest something that is easily available: a *ready* answer to the complex question. **Prepared** stresses that aspect of *ready* that suggests the active, conscious deliberation and effort that precede action: a student thoroughly *prepared* for the grueling examination. A more general use of *prepared* stresses a psychic resilience by which one can face alternatives not necessarily known in advance: conscientious parents whose children are *prepared* for the disappointments as well as the joys of life; *prepared* for any eventuality. **Set** suggests plans that have become definite or preparations that are complete and final: all *set* for the big party; *ready*, *set*, go.

Disposed and **willing** emphasize a different aspect of the period just before action, stressing desire rather than training or even conditioning: He was *willing* to take on the immense job, though he was poorly *prepared* for it. While *willing* implies an agreeable or voluntary choice, *disposed* suggests an innate proclivity or a settled and favorable attitude toward the impending action: *Disposed* as he was to telling the truth, he was hardly *ready* to confront her with all that he knew. In a use closer to *ready* or *prepared*, *disposed* suggests a last positioning previous to action: two battalions *disposed* for an attack on the air base. See EAGER, OBSERVANT, ORGANIZE, PLAN.

Antonyms: disorganized, inexperienced, unprepared, UNWILLING.

reasoning

deduction
induction
inference
ratiocination

These words refer to the act of exact, objective thinking that deals with provable fact and abides by the rules of logic in tracing premises to conclusions. **Reasoning** is the most inclusive and informal of the words here, indicating any attempt to draw conclusions by the use of valid methods of thought while remaining impartial and admitting for consideration only unbiased data. **Ratiocination** is a more formal word for the same concept, but it may occasionally suggest a mind moving from one conclusion to another in a long, complex, even tortuous, process: a cogent and convincing piece of *reasoning* demonstrating the common origin of man; a process of *ratiocination* that led him to several unpleasant conclusions.

An **inference** is, much more specifically, the movement from premises to conclusion; consequently *reasoning* may be said to be the attempt to make valid *inferences*, and *ratiocination* the puzzling out of a chain of *inferences*. If **deduction** is used in reaching an *inference*, *reasoning* proceeds from general premises regarded as proved or true and reaches a particular, specific conclusion. [All men are mortal; I am a man; therefore, I am mortal.] **Induction** is the opposite process in which *reasoning* collects all the particulars that relate to a problem and draws a general conclusion that explains their behavior. [Every man that he knew of had died, sooner or later. Therefore, all men are mortal.] The laws of science, such as the law of gravity, are first *inductions* from particulars. Once these laws are considered valid, however, they become the basis for any amount of *deductions* provided that these are derived according to the rules of logic. See THINK.

rebuke

These words are comparable in meaning to express disapproval, either mildly or sharply, of some fault or misdeed. To **rebuke** is to criticize or call down with sharpness, and often with abruptness, usually in the midst of some action or course of action: to *rebuke* a worker whose clumsiness was responsible for the complete breakdown of operations in his department.

Admonish and **reprove** indicate mild forms of disapproval. *Admonish* may be used in giving warning or counsel where no wrong is implied and often simply refers to duty which might have been or might in the future be forgotten: to *admonish* a student about the lateness of his assignments. *Reprove* also suggests mild or even friendly criticism designed less to chasten than to help correct a fault or pattern of misbehavior: to *reprove* a child for telling fibs.

To **reproach** is to express the kind of disapproval that arises from a personal hurt, anger, or grief at someone's thoughtlessness or selfishness: *reproaching* her husband for having forgotten their wedding anniversary.

Censure and **reprimand** agree in indicating a formal and, usually, public or official disapproval. *Reprimand* suggests a direct confrontation between the offender and his critic; one may *censure* directly or indirectly: the judge who sharply *reprimanded* a witness for being evasive and uncooperative; to *censure* a senator for flagrantly violating congressional standards of ethical behavior; a newspaper editorial that *censured* corruption among city officials. See DISAPPROVAL, SCOLD.

Antonyms: ENDORSE, PRAISE.

These words apply to persons and actions that show a heedless defiance of danger and a seeming lack of regard for consequences. **Reckless** and **rash** are applied to persons acting or actions undertaken without regard for the risks involved in terms of the end sought. *Reckless* implies wild, irresponsible action or emotion, indicating at worst a dangerous lack of self-discipline or self-control, and implying at the least a devil-may-care attitude or a frightening absence of forethought. The word indicates extreme carelessness or unconcern in respect to oneself or to others. What distinguishes a *reckless* act from a brave one is not always the action itself but rather the attitude motivating it and the circumstances behind it. A police car or fire truck may, with siren sounding, drive at great speed through the streets and through red traffic lights without being *reckless*. A joy rider doing the same thing would be guilty of careless and *reckless* driving. *Rash* is not quite so extreme as *reckless*. It points to overhasty action taken in the heat or emotion of the moment, without due caution or regard for consequences. [Quitting his job in anger was a *rash* action which he later regretted; Don't do anything *rash*.] A *rash* or *reckless* accusation is one that disregards the possible consequences to both the accused and the accuser, himself, who might be sued for libel.

Foolhardy is more informal than *rash* or *reckless*. It implies boldness exercised without consideration or judgment, pointing to action that is daringly *reckless* or downright foolish. A *foolhardy* person rushes into peril from lack of sense or forethought. Swimming out beyond one's depth when tired or after eating is a *foolhardy* action. **Daredevil** differs from the other words in indicating the deliberate taking of chances, with a certain implication of calculated risk. It points to some sort of public exhibition, often describing a professional who performs sensational feats to entertain thrill-seekers: a *daredevil* racing driver; a *daredevil* stunt pilot. *Daredevil* further suggests a certain amount of flair and debonair defiance: a death-defying aerialist performing *daredevil* feats. See BRAVE, DARING, HEEDLESS, IMPETUOUS.

Antonyms: calculating, CAREFUL, CAUTIOUS, *chary*.

rebuke
(continued)

admonish
censure
reprimand
reproach
reprove

reckless

daredevil
foolhardy
rash

recommend

advise
advocate
counsel
prescribe
suggest

These words refer to oral or written assistance given to someone who is trying to decide upon a course of action. **Recommend** indicates a positive declaration in favor of a particular alternative or set of possibilities: *recommending* a complete change of occupations that would give his life new meaning; *recommending* ten books as absolutely necessary to any understanding of the question he had raised. The word can apply equally well to situations in which help has or has not been solicited: *recommending* a walk before breakfast to everyone he met; asking her to *recommend* a good tailor. **Advocate** is the most like *recommend* of the rest of these words in emphasizing a positive declaration on the part of the person giving assistance; drawn from legal terminology, it is even stronger than *recommend* in suggesting an ardent espousal of a given course of action: *advocating* complete abstinence as the only way of combating his alcoholism. In this context, the word can imply a pugnacious tenacity or an unwelcome intrusion: *advocating* his pet theories on sexual adjustment to people far less disturbed than he. **Prescribe** compares to *advocate* and *recommend* in that a positive statement is made, but it is more specific in relating mainly to a doctor-patient relationship in which the doctor *prescribes* remedies for an ailment. In this context, the patient has sought the doctor's assistance and is usually not compelled to abide by what is *recommended*. This gives it a less ardent, more matter-of-fact tone than *advocate*, but a more authoritative cast than *recommend*: *prescribing* a good dinner and an exciting movie as the best way to cure his gloomy frame of mind.

Advise and **suggest** are much milder than the foregoing words. They do not necessarily indicate that any one alternative is *recommended* as a solution to the problem in question. *Advise* implies an extensive and detailed examination of a person's situation, however informally, with several possibilities for action opened up simply by getting another vantage point on his difficulties: *advising* me on what to expect from the college I had chosen to attend. When used as an exact substitute for *recommend*, it nevertheless adds an implication of politeness or of reluctance to seem overbearing. [May I *advise* you not to lend him large sums of money?; Would you *advise* me where I should vacation this summer?] *Suggest* implies a single, very tentative proposal that is not insisted upon: In *advising* me, he *suggested* several possibilities for revision. In some cases, the tentativeness implied by the word may result from a fear of being rejected: *suggesting* timidly that eating out would be enjoyable for both of them.

Counsel has come to have a specific reference to psychologists or guidance personnel at schools or colleges: *counseling* students on the importance of matching aptitude to vocation. In other uses, it still implies some quasi-official situation, with a stress on seriousness and formality: contending factions who *counseled* the president in secret. In ordinary uses, the word is more formal than *advise*, sometimes excessively so: *counseling* her daughter on how to behave at the prom. See ADVICE, INDUCE.

recover

reclaim
recoup
regain

These words refer to getting back something that has been lost. **Recover** is the most general; it can refer to finding a lost item by chance or accident as easily as by intention and effort: *recovering* the other overshoe while searching the attic one day for something else; only *recovering* his position of eminence among his fellow scientists in the last days of his life. **Retrieve**, most concretely, suggests something that has not so much been lost as slipped beyond reach and requires some effort to *recover*: *retrieving* the floating paddle by leaning out along the bow of the boat.

Recoup is drawn from legal terminology to mean, in ordinary use, a *recovering* of something similar to or equivalent to a disastrous or negligent loss: *recouping* his extravagance at the racetrack by embezzling funds from his bank. Like *recover*, **regain** stresses getting back the very thing lost, but in contrast it tends to be restricted to a deliberate and laborious search or effort: *regaining* the hill lost the night before to the enemy; *regaining* his eyesight after several operations; *regaining* the heavyweight championship in last week's fight.

Reclaim and **restore** both suggest bringing something back to its original condition; *reclaim* is used largely of land or large areas, *restore* of buildings or art objects: *reclaiming* good farmlands from the polluted, man-made swamps; *restoring* the house to the way it might have looked in the 1820's. *Reclaim* may also suggest an interval in which the right to a position or to a property has been transferred or disputed: *reclaiming* his title to the inheritance after a protracted legal battle. See CONSERVE, REPAIR, SAVE.

Antonyms: MISLAY.

recover
(continued)

restore
retrieve

These words mean to make or to become smaller or less, but they are not in all cases interchangeable. **Reduce** has a wider range of connotations than the other words and is also the most general. It means to make less in size, amount, number, extent, or intensity: to *reduce* household expenses; to *reduce* a labor force during a slack season; to *reduce* speed on a highway undergoing repairs; to *reduce* the acreage of a farm by selling off a field. *Reduce* further means to bring to an inferior rank, position, or financial condition: a widow *reduced* to renting out rooms to make ends meet; a sergeant *reduced* to private after a summary court-martial; a pampered woman *reduced* to doing her own housework because of a servant shortage. When applied to the losing of weight, especially when deliberate, *reduce* is popularly used intransitively: My mother and aunts are always trying fad diets in order to *reduce*.

Abate means to *reduce*, as in strength or degree, usually from an excessive intensity or amount. In this sense, it is most frequently an intransitive verb. [The anguished screams in the night began to *abate* when the police arrived; After taking aspirin, she found her pain *abating*.] In a legal sense, *abate* is used transitively and means to do away with completely or to make null and void: to *abate* a nuisance; to *abate* a writ.

Curtail is to *reduce* abruptly and radically, as by cutting off or cutting shorter than was originally intended. The word is used chiefly of non-material things and conveys the idea of the unexpected: a vacation *curtailed* by a hurricane that damaged their cottage; to *curtail* a pointless argument by turning on one's heel and leaving the room; to *curtail* useless government spending.

Diminish is a more accurate word than *reduce* when one wishes to stress the idea of removing part of something so that there is a manifest and sometimes progressive lessening, but not to the point of total disappearance. The word may suggest either the loss of something valuable or a lessening of that which is undesirable. [As people approach old age their energy may *diminish*; As his confidence in his work increased, his anxieties about it *diminished*.]

Lower is to make less, especially in value, degree, or level. It is not as emphatic or precise a word as *reduce* in this sense, although fairly

reduce

abate
curtail
diminish
lower

close in meaning: to *lower* prices on shopworn goods; to *reduce* payments on a mortgage. In extended senses, *lower* points to a lessening by undermining or weakening. [He could not bear to *lower* himself to ask relatives for help; Frequent colds *lower* one's resistance to more serious infections.] See DECREASE, LESSEN, WANE, WEAKEN.

Antonyms: enhance, ENLARGE, ESCALATE, EXTEND, *raise.*

reject

decline
refuse
repudiate
spurn

These words mean to be unwilling to accept, receive, or take into account a person or thing. **Reject** is to fail to accept or grant and carries overtones of casting aside as useless, valueless, or unsuitable. [The judge *rejected* the prisoner's appeal for a new trial; The idea that the earth is flat was *rejected* centuries ago.]

Refuse and **decline** both mean to fail to comply with or to do something. *Refuse* is the stronger of the two words and often stresses firmness and at times even rudeness: to *refuse* to obey an order. It also suggests the idea of withholding: to *refuse* money to a beggar; to *refuse* an offer of marriage. *Decline*, on the other hand, is to *refuse* politely and is applicable to invitations to social events or to a courteous offer of help: to *decline* an invitation to a dinner party; a blind man who smilingly *declined* to be helped across the street. *Decline* may be used in place of *refuse* when an atmosphere of formality prevails: The witness *declined* to answer certain questions put to him.

Repudiate and **spurn** emphasize more pointedly than the foregoing words a refusal to recognize or have anything to do with a person or thing. *Repudiate* (which once meant to cast off or divorce a wife) points to a disowning or rejection of something once held more or less dear: to *repudiate* one's religious beliefs; an author who *repudiates* the revolutionary ideas expressed in his earlier work; to *repudiate* one's relatives because of their critical attitude. Derived from an Old English word meaning to kick out, *spurn* emphasizes even more strongly the idea of driving or pushing away roughly and contemptuously: *spurning* the attentions of a man whom she despised; *spurning* the suggestion that he get his hair cut and put on a clean shirt; *spurning* a door-to-door salesman from the threshold. See DISCARD, REMOVE.

Antonyms: accept, ACKNOWLEDGE, DEMAND.

religion

belief
creed
faith

These words refer to a more or less codified set of ideas concerning the final causes of the universe. **Religion** is the most specific of these, suggesting an organized body of traditional doctrines that are reflected in a more or less complex set of institutions for fostering these doctrines: the Christian *religion*; the Buddhist *religion*; the Hindu *religion*. Within one of these large groupings, *religion* is sometimes used to refer to its denominations or sects, but this use is mostly eschewed in formal speech or writing: the Catholic *religion*; the Lutheran *religion*. **Faith** is often substituted for *religion* to put less emphasis on institutionalized tradition and more on devoted adherence: the Jewish *faith*; the Christian *faith*. Because of these implications, this word is more often used of a subdivision in one of the larger categories: the Catholic *faith*; the Eastern Orthodox *faith*.

Creed stresses an exactly delineated outline of dogma and doctrine and thus may refer to small or large divisions, even within a sect, where doctrinal differences are at issue: the several extant Mormon *creeds*; the Moravian *creed*. The word may be used outside the context of *religion* — in fact, for any codified statement of principles: a sportsman's *creed*. **Belief** is the most vague of any of these words; it may refer to groupings, large or small: a *belief* in the tenets of Islam; the *beliefs* of Taoism; the Quaker *belief*. Its stress is on wholehearted assent to details of doctrine. The word is also commonly used to indicate assent to each item of doctrine: a *belief* in life after death; the Buddhist rejection of *belief* in a supreme being. Because the word is so vague, it may point away from any organized *religion* whatsoever to a purely personal conviction about final causes: her own highly idiosyncratic *belief* in an all-powerful but not all-beneficent God; a *belief* in atheism. See CREED, DENOMINATION, SKEPTIC.

Antonyms: *atheism*, DESECRATION, *impiety, irreligion, unbelief*.

religious

devout
pious
reverent
sanctimonious

These words are comparable in that they all are used to characterize the thoughts, feelings, and actions of people, insofar as they pertain to religion. **Religious** is a general word, that embraces all the other terms in the group. It can mean simply of or having to do with religion: *religious* literature; the *religious* life. It can describe anyone, from the man who observes nothing more than the minimum obligations of his faith to a person who is genuinely devoted to a way of life that reflects a deep love of God as well as adherence to the tenets of one of the systems set up to worship God: an opportunistic businessman who found it profitable to be *religious* on Sundays; a truly *religious* man who has managed to make the Christian ideal viable in every aspect of his life.

Devout and **pious** are alike in suggesting a dedication to religion that is evidenced by the observance of established ceremonies and ritual. They differ, however, in that *devout* always implies that earnest *religious* feelings motivate the performance of *religoius* obligations, whereas *pious* may indicate the hypocrisy of one whose *religious* behavior is merely outward show: a *devout* belief in the tenets of Orthodox Judaism; a *pious* fraud whose mind is more devoted to gossip than to gospel. **Sanctimonious**, which is never used now in its original meaning of holy or saintly, is stronger than *pious* in its reference to spurious sanctity: a *sanctimonious* old man whose condemnation of other people's actions was a mask for his own immorality.

Reverent, which means feeling or showing reverence or respect, is applied to the character or actions of persons who evince great sincerity of *religious* belief and observance, and is closer in meaning to *devout* than to *pious*. See REVERE, SACRED.

Antonyms: *atheistic, impious, irreligious, irreverent*.

relinquish

abdicate
cede
renounce
resign
surrender
yield

These words are alike in meaning to let go or give up. **Relinquish** is the most general and neutral term in the group. It can indicate no more than the release of one's grasp: He *relinquished* the oars. It can denote the letting go from one's direction or possession, usually voluntarily but sometimes reluctantly. [A parent *relinquishes* control over grown children; A creditor may *relinquish* a claim in consideration of a concession.] **Surrender** means to give up under compulsion to any person, passion, influence, or power: He *surrendered* his savings to his creditors. **Yield** is close to *surrender*, but implies milder compulsion and therefore some softness, concession, respect, or even affection on the part of the person who *yields*: He *yielded* the floor to his opponent. **Cede** means to give up, usually by legal transfer or as the result of a treaty; it is most often used in reference to the concession of territory: France *ceded* Alsace-Lorraine to Germany in 1871.

Abdicate and **resign** refer to the formal giving up of some office or position along with its attendant rights, power, etc. *Abdicate* specifi-

cally applies to a monarch's relinquishment of his throne; *resign* is used
to designate the action of a president or other elected or appointed
official, or a person working in business: when George III threatened to
abdicate his throne; forced to *resign* his position as chairman of the
board because of ill health. **Renounce** means to declare against or to
give up formally and definitively: to *renounce* the pomps and vanities
of the world; to *renounce* one's citizenship. When used in place of
abdicate, *renounce* suggests that the giving up is done for something considered to be more important: Edward VIII *renounced* his throne for
the love of a woman. See ABSTAIN, FORGO, FORSWEAR.

Antonyms: cherish, claim, maintain, POSSESS.

remain

abide
linger
stay
tarry

These words all mean to continue in one place. **Remain** and **stay** are
often used interchangeably. In its narrower application, however, *remain* means to continue in one place after the removal, departure, or
destruction of other persons or things, whereas *stay* implies the temporary continuance in one place of a guest, resident, or the like. [Only the
shell of the building *remained* after the explosion; He was invited to
stay for supper.] If the fact that others have left is made explicit, either
word may be used: He *remained* (or *stayed*) in his seat after all the other
students had gone home. But if the writer's intention is to contrast
staying with leaving, *remain* has more impact. [All had left their seats
and gone home hours ago; he *remained*.]

Abide, as here considered, means to *stay* somewhere a long time, and
often connotes residing. *Abide* is a formal word, and is often used in
legal or other contexts requiring a word neutral in emotional connotation
and precise in meaning: The child *abided* (or *abode*) with his grandparents for three and a half years before being returned to his parents.

Linger implies reluctance to leave, usually because what one is doing
is pleasant; to **tarry** is to stay beyond the proper time for leaving, and
more strongly than *linger* implies excessive delay. *Tarry* is not commonly
used today apart from consciously stylized, rhetorical, or old-fashioned
contexts; it has a romantic ring to it that makes it inappropriate in
prosaic contexts. [The candidate *lingered* behind his entourage to shake
the hands of several enthusiastic supporters; *Tarry* not with your loved
ones, but join us in righteous battle.] See DELAY, RESIDE.

Antonyms: GO, LEAVE (depart).

remember

memorize
recall
recollect
remind
reminisce
retain
review

These words refer to the act of summoning up the past, to its spontaneous
cropping up in the mind, or to the fixing of present data in the memory
for future reference. **Remember** can refer generally to any mental
glance at the past, voluntary or involuntary: He caught himself *remembering* how his first wife would have cooked the same meal; struggling
to *remember* where he had been at the time the murder took place. But
often the word specifically suggests the staying power of a vivid past
event or circumstance: I can still *remember* every detail in my old dormitory room at college. **Recall** is more formal than *remember* and more
often indicates a voluntary summoning up of the past, whether silently
for oneself or verbally for others. [He *recalled* his last evening with his
fiancée whenever he felt depressed; In his closing speech to the jury,
the prosecutor *recalled* the mass of incriminating evidence he had developed during the trial.] But unlike *remember*, the word can refer to
something in the present that resembles and therefore calls up something
in the past: a view that *recalled* to him the fishing village he had stayed
in during the war. **Remind** concentrates more exclusively on this last

possibility for *recall*: a man who *reminded* her of her first lover. But *remind* can also suggest a conscious effort to insure that something will be *remembered* in the future: a note on his calendar to *remind* himself of their luncheon date; a monument to *remind* future generations of the sacrifices made in their behalf.

When used interchangeably with *recall*, **recollect** can have a regional flavor: I don't rightly *recollect* when I saw her last. But the word can apply without this flavor to the act of casting one's mind back over past events in a leisurely and ruminative manner, whether silently to oneself or verbally to others. The word can suggest the active process of piecing together dimly *remembered* and half-forgotten details: He settled back with great relish and began to *recollect* those battles in the war that he had witnessed first-hand. **Reminisce** is exclusively restricted to this last use of *recollect*, adding a positive note of pleasant nostalgia; the word may also suggest a tendency to dwell on or brood over the past: daydreams during which she *reminisced* a great deal about the life she had lived before her marriage; cronies who sit around *reminiscing* about their vanished yesterdays.

Retain can point to the staying power of a memory that often comes to mind involuntarily or without effort: He had always *retained* a picture of his father decked out in riding breeches and hunting gear. In more neutral uses, the word can involve the question of mentally holding onto facts or details that one is trying to learn: a test to measure how much of the reading exercise each person had *retained* after a given passage of time. **Memorize** is much more specifically directed to this situation, indicating a conscious and laborious effort to commit something to memory in exact detail: actors who are good at *memorizing* their speeches in short order; a last look in which he tried to *memorize* every line and angle of her face.

Review suggests an orderly summoning up of the past in summary form, applying particularly to past lessons or to facts one is trying to *memorize*: a final week to *review* the material before the exam; *reviewing* each aspect of their plan, step by step, before synchronizing their watches and setting off. See HISTORY.

Antonyms: FORGET, *ignore, repress, suppress.*

These words refer to getting rid of something or forcibly moving it to a new position. **Remove** is the most general of these and the most colorless. It ranges in tone from neutral or factual description to suggestions of rejection, disapproval, or the use of force: *removing* the phonograph record from its jacket; *removing* the sheets from the bed; *removing* a corrupt administrator from office; ordering the sergeant-at-arms to *remove* the angry man from the courtroom.

Dismiss is less likely to suggest the use of force, but otherwise is richer in connotations than *remove*. It can suggest the routine release or sending away of an inferior by his superior: *dismissing* the servant after the guests were ushered in; *dismissing* the class promptly at three o'clock. It can suggest the routine or disapproving termination of employment: *dismissing* with thanks the special consultant on the completed project; *dismissing* his secretary because of her incessant lateness. More pertinently here, the word can suggest a swift, abrupt, or final rejection. [She *dismissed* his proposal with an imperious wave of her hand; We *dismissed* the whole idea of bicycling to the west coast.]

Eliminate at its mildest pertains to the routine or methodical disposal of something: organs that *eliminate* wastes from the body; *elimi-*

remove

dismiss
eject
eliminate
evict
expel
oust

nating from the list those books she had already read. More highly charged, the word can suggest determination, if not force: *eliminating* from the club those members whose dues were in arrears. At its most extreme, the word can suggest ruthless or systematic destruction: a wave of killings as one group of gangsters set about *eliminating* its rivals; concentration camps built to *eliminate* those considered to be enemies of the state.

The remaining words are all more specific in pointing to the use of considerable force to *remove* something, although none suggest destruction like *eliminate*. **Oust** and **evict** emphasize the resistance given by the thing being *removed* from its previous position. *Oust* is restricted to those implications of the previous words pertaining to termination of employment or discharge from office: *ousted* from the party leadership by a no-confidence vote; a revolution fomented to *oust* the notorious dictator from power. *Evict* is even more specific in applying exclusively to *removing* tenants from occupancy; most often, the word suggests the gaining of legal approval to carry out this act: court-appointed officers who *evicted* the family by carrying its belongings out to the curb.

Expel and **eject** may both suggest a forcible *removing* from office or occupancy like the previous pair, but they are more general than any of these words except *remove*. *Expel*, however, has its own area of special relevance in applying to the punitive *dismissing* of a student from school for unsatisfactory behavior: students *expelled* for cheating. *Eject* is the most emphatic of this group in stressing the use of force; it pertains most appropriately to a physical or bodily removal: a spent cartridge that had been *ejected* by the murder rifle; calling the police to *eject* the demonstrators from his waiting room. See DESTROY, EXILE, MOVE.

Antonyms: POSSESS, *retain*.

renegade

criminal
crook
desperado
hood
hoodlum
outlaw
sociopath
thug

These words pertain to people, usually men, who live outside society and its laws. **Renegade** originally applied to a Christian who converted to Islam and more generally to any religious or even political apostate. Some of these general uses are still met with: a *renegade* priest who left the church to marry. But Western fiction and films have popularized the term to apply to any fugitive or lawbreaker, particularly to someone, as a member of a band of robbers, who lives outside or on the periphery of respectable society: the final scene in which the good guys shoot it out with the *renegades*. Now, the word can apply most generally to any member of a subculture of thieves or delinquents: a section of town frequented by gangsters and *renegades*. If the reference is to a young person, the word may imply that he has run away from home: *renegade* youths who gather in Haight-Ashbury and sleep in the parks.

Desperado refers most specifically to a bandit of the U.S. West or Southwest in frontier days; again, Westerns have popularized the term, but it has fewer general uses applying to other situations: the villains of the film were a band of *desperadoes* who hid out in a cave near the town. **Outlaw** can also apply within the context of the Western, much like *desperado* or *renegade*, but it has a much wider area of relevance than either of these, applying to any habitual lawbreaker, especially one who totally rejects the standards of society as a guide to conduct: a city completely controlled by *outlaws* who raked off millions from the numbers, dope peddling, loan sharking, and other kinds of racketeering. The more common use of the word, however, emphasizes that the lawbreaker is fleeing the law and has been deprived of its protection because of his crime: an *outlaw* with a price on his head.

The remaining words have no particular relevance to the Western genre whatever. Closely related to *outlaw*, **criminal** is the most general word here, referring to any hardened lawbreaker, whether he acts alone or in concert with others. Usually the word suggests someone guilty of serious and repeated offenses, whether or not he has been apprehended or punished for his crimes: kingpin *criminals* who are seldom convicted for their real offenses but are sometimes brought to justice on such relative technicalities as tax evasion; a small-time *criminal* who stole cars to support his drug addiction. Sometimes the word can be a substitute for convict or ex-convict, applying to someone who is or has been imprisoned for a serious crime: *criminals* who return to their old haunts upon parole. As penologists have shifted their emphasis to rehabilitation, this use of *criminal* has lost status.

Crook is an informal word for *criminal*. It can imply membership in a gang or a group of confidence men. It can suggest the use of deceit to fleece or defraud unsuspecting people, but at its most general, it can apply to anyone involved in any form of graft: *crooks* who ran a protection racket on the east side of the city; The mayor was a *crook* who had embezzled thousands of dollars from the city payrolls. **Hoodlum** at its most specific suggests the bodyguards or toughs who surround the leader of a gang. Where other words here carry no implications about age, *hoodlum* often suggests a brutal or coarse young man: The mobster assigned a dozen *hoodlums* to collect payoffs in his territory. In extended uses, *hoodlum* can apply to young men who belong to no organized gang but who, as small-time *criminals*, indulge in spontaneous acts of violence: a bunch of *hoodlums* who began tearing apart the movie theater out of sheer boredom. **Hood**, a shortened form, suggests even more clearly young delinquents who are anarchic and lawless in their behavior: neighborhood *hoods* standing along the sidewalk flipping coins and trying to look tough. **Thug** comes from the Hindi word for thief and originally referred to professional robbers in India who murdered their victims by strangulation. Now it can serve as an intensification of *hoodlum* in reference to burly, lower-echelon members of a gang who are coarse and brutal and who may be paid to assault or kill designated victims: an informer who had been rubbed out by one of the gang's *thugs*.

Sociopath is a recent term used to describe a mentally disturbed person, usually a young man, whose psychosis takes the form of hideous acts of gratuitous violence. Theoretically, a *sociopath* has failed to develop into a human being and cannot understand, emotionally or intellectually, human affection, compassion, or suffering: a growing number of *sociopaths* who, without warning, go on killing sprees for no apparent reason. See CONVICT, CRIME, THIEF, TRAITOR.

Central to these words is the idea or fact of a return to some previous condition usually but not always thought of as desirable. **Renewal** can apply to anything, good, bad, or indifferent, that returns, repeats, or begins again after a period of lapse: a *renewal* of the argument or discussion; the *renewal* of a lease or mortgage; an unexpected *renewal* of health and spirits.

Rebirth, in the sense of being born again, has only a figurative use. Though one can speak of a *rebirth* as well as a *renewal* of confidence, a contractual relationship of limited duration, such as a contract, treaty, copyright, or patent, is subject only to *renewal*. The distinction brings out the idea of an innate, self-sustaining vitality in something that had been or long seemed to be dead: a *rebirth* of hope.

renewal

rebirth
recrudescence
rejuvenation
rejuvenescence
renaissance
renascence

Rejuvenation and **rejuvenescence** simply mean a *renewal* of youth, with emphasis upon the recovery of lost or fading strength, vigor, alertness, resilience of body and mind. [He looked back upon his trip abroad as having provided a veritable *rejuvenation*; Disappointment followed his hopes of *rejuvenescence* after the costly operation.]

Recrudescence, derived from a Latin word meaning to become raw or to bleed again, has its primary use among doctors and surgeons to describe a breaking out afresh, as of a disease, sore, or wound that had appeared to be healing. In this unfavorable sense of a relapse, it may properly be applied to the recurrence of anything considered as evil or objectionable: a *recrudescence* of an epidemic; a *recrudescence* of Nazism.

Renaissance and **renascence** are simply formal words for *rebirth* and are given special rank as descriptive terms in the history of human culture. *Renaissance*, the more common spelling, is a French form, while *renascence* comes from Latin roots meaning to be born again. Either can be used for a widespread awakening of interest in some rediscovered aspect of life or learning, and both imply a sense of discovery and an attendant burst of accomplishment: a *renaissance* in Far Eastern studies; a literary *renascence*. The *Renaissance*, spelled with an initial capital, refers to that period of vigorous intellectual and artistic awakening in Western Europe extending from about the 14th to the 16th century. This period gave its name to the *Renaissance* man, full of fresh life, vigor, and creativity, whose interests were universal and whose accomplishments were not limited to any one field.

Antonyms: aging, loss, subsiding, termination.

repair

correct
fix
mend
rectify
remedy
renovate

These words refer to the changes made in something to restore it or to set it right. **Repair** emphasizes work done on an object that is broken, damaged, or not in proper working order: to *repair* a TV set; to *repair* shoes; the expense of having an old car *repaired*. By extension, it can refer to any effective restorative action: ambassadors who worked to *repair* the breach in trade relations. **Fix** is an informal word for the same set of meanings as *repair*: the time it took him to *fix* the flat tire. But while *repair* usually suggests a broken object to begin with, *fix* can apply to anything that needs attention or has gone awry: *fixing* curtains for the bare windows; a friend who could *fix* things between the girl and her angry parents. **Mend** suggests the *repairing* of something broken, torn, or worn threadbare: a torn page *mended* with tape; to *mend* old clothes. But it can go beyond this to suggest a growing together, a knitting and healing of injured parts in living things: tying the bent branch in place until it could *mend*; splinting the leg until the broken bone began to *mend*. Thus, it may suggest a return to health and peace in wider contexts: anxious to *mend* the rift between the two bloodthirsty factions within his party.

The remaining words apply less often to the concrete context of a broken object and are both more general and more vague in referring to steps taken to improve something imperfect or to better a bad situation. **Correct** suggests the supplying of right answers or the pointing out of errors: a special teacher to *correct* his halting mispronunciations; parents unwilling to *correct* and discipline their own children. A pedagogical atmosphere is, in fact, often suggested by the word. **Remedy** more obviously suggests a medical situation, but it appears in a wide range of contexts, implying an effort to find solutions to bothersome problems: steps taken to *remedy* the living conditions that precipitated the riot. The word may suggest alterations in a system rather than a complete reorganization: They hoped to *remedy* their lackluster performance by a few changes in personnel. The word often suggests a search for one out of many possible solutions, unlike *correct*, which gives the impression that a simple, right-and-wrong dichotomy exists.

Rectify, by contrast, stresses a more thoroughgoing change in something; one *rectifies* something wrong by setting it right, insofar as amendment is possible: to *rectify* a factual error; finally *rectifying* a miscarriage of justice. It is the most formal of these words and, in the sense discussed here, the most abstract. **Renovate** applies strictly to the *repairing* and updating of an old or run-down building: a program to *renovate* slum housing. Sometimes, the word can apply to the less desirable modernizing of a venerable or distinctive building merely because it is old or thought out of date: a committee set up to protest the proposal to *renovate* a row of 19th-century houses on the narrow street. See CONSERVE, RECOVER, REVISE, SAVE.

Antonyms: BREAK, DESTROY, REPLACE, TEAR.

replace

displace
supersede
supplant

These words refer to a situation in which the place of one thing is taken by another. **Replace** is the most informal and most neutral of these words, referring to any simple substitution for whatever reason: She *replaced* the amber necklace with a string of pearls to see which she liked better. The word, however, is especially used to indicate the substitution of something new or functioning for something old, worn-out, or lost: an offer to *replace* the missing volume of the encyclopedia; *replacing* the burnt-out light bulb; She *replaced* the old, battered throw pillows with new ones.

Displace, by contrast, indicates the dislodging or forcible removal of one thing by another, without necessarily suggesting that the first had become unusable or ineffective: republics in which new regimes *displace* old ones with wearying predictability; the growing number of employees being *displaced* by computers. **Supplant** is even more restricted than *displace*, usually suggesting that the old thing is deliberately uprooted, rendered ineffective, or wiped out so that the new thing can take over; the process, furthermore, may be immediate or gradual: Europeans who *supplanted* the indigenous Indian populations they met with; new models and fashions that vie in the marketplace to *supplant* each other.

Supersede is the most formal of these words and indicates that a substitution occurs because the new thing is better, more modern, or more effective than the old: consumers who have been taught to believe that this year's models actually *supersede* those of the year before; economic planning that would slowly *supersede* older hit-and-miss methods. The word may sometimes suggest mere substitution because of greater authority: cease-fire orders that immediately *superseded* all previous orders to attack. See CHANGE, DESTROY.

Antonyms: CONSERVE, *keep*, REPAIR, SAVE.

report

account
story
version

These words all refer to a history or statement of actual or purported events. A **report** is an official or formal statement, often made after an investigation and usually by a subordinate to his superior: a patrolman's *report* of a burglary. Whereas an **account** is a factual statement of events or conditions, usually given by an eyewitness, a *report* is an authoritative finding, often one based on interpretation and deliberation of evidence. Thus a farmer may give an *account* of a plane crash he observed; later a *report* of the crash might be drawn up by the federal agency charged with investigating aerial disasters.

Version and **story** purport to be statements of fact. A *version* is one-sided, although not always deliberately so; it merely represents one person's or one party's point of view, and always implies an alternative or several other contrasting *accounts* of the same event. Although some degree of skepticism is commonly associated with *version*, *story* is regarded with even greater doubt. *Story* may even be used to suggest a conscious distortion of the truth. [An investigation of the crime brought to light several *versions* of what took place; Good detectives can usually spot a *story* concocted to throw off suspicion.] *Story* may, however, simply mean a person's *version* of an incident, and need not imply the motive of conscious deception: His *story* is that somebody planted the stolen money in his apartment. See HISTORY, NARRATIVE.

reprehensible

blameworthy
culpable
deplorable
opprobrious
regrettable

These words all refer to undesirable acts or circumstances that are worthy either of criticism, sorrow, or pity. **Reprehensible** exclusively stresses disapproving criticism for egregiously bad behavior or character: the *reprehensible* diffidence of public officials in taking stands on the crises of the day; a *reprehensible* criminal who had robbed great numbers of people without the slightest twinge of guilt. **Opprobrious** is the strongest word in this group. It refers to something that not only merits criticism but that is looked on with disdain or scorn. There is often an implication of general rather than merely personal censure involved in anything *opprobrious*: the *opprobrious* commercialization of Christmas.

While **culpable** refers to something deserving of censure, its main stress may be on an attempt to assign guilt or blame for an accident, misdeed, or failure: *culpable* negligence; He displayed *culpable* ignorance in handling what was only a routine personnel problem. *Culpable* is milder than the foregoing words, however, in that it would not be used for outrageous or egregious violations of a legal or moral code. **Blameworthy**, like *culpable*, is concerned with assigning guilt for failure or misbehavior; the tone of the word may be factual and neutral: an investigation to determine which of the senators involved in the recent scandal were the most *blameworthy*. More generally, however, the word can express censure, although it seldom suggests the moral outrage of *opprobrious*: a *blameworthy* lack of concern for the impoverished.

Regrettable is the mildest word in this group. It need not denote a critical attitude of censure at all, but rather a sympathetic understanding of someone's failings: a *regrettable* lack of decisiveness that marred an otherwise brilliant and accomplished man. It contrasts with the previous words even more dramatically when it expresses pity for circumstances beyond human control: It is *regrettable* that such a great talent died so young. Sometimes the word is used in a polite or genteel way to express disapproval in terms of sympathetic disappointment: your *regrettable* absence from my dinner party. The word can even be used more forcefully as an ironic understatement for a severely critical reaction: I find it *regrettable* that Miss Smith chose to display her inadequacies to us so conclusively by taking on one of the most demanding roles in all of drama.

In many ways, **deplorable** is an intensification of *regrettable*. On one hand, it can express consternation and distress over what may be no one's fault: the *deplorable* accident that crippled her for life. But when it is used critically, it is harsher than *regrettable* and does not mask its criticism in irony or understatement: *deplorable* living conditions; a *deplorable* lack of human compassion. Like *regrettable*, however, *deplora-*

ble would not be used for outrageously hardened, cruel, or brutal behavior. See CONTEMPTIBLE, DISAPPROVAL, REPULSIVE.

Antonyms: admirable, EXCELLENT, INNOCENT, *praiseworthy.*

These words are alike in denoting a person empowered to take the place or position of another. **Representative** in its wider application means a person or thing that stands for, acts for, or takes the place of another. In its narrower application *representative* means a person who acts for another or others in a special capacity. [*Representatives* in Congress act for their constituents in legislative matters; American ambassadors are *representatives* of the President of the United States.]

A **substitute** is a person or thing that can be used instead of another person or thing. [Honey can be used as a *substitute* for sugar in many recipes; Men drafted during the American Civil War were allowed to hire *substitutes* to serve in their place; If an actor is ill, his understudy serves as his *substitute* in the role.]

In general, **agent** means one who acts on behalf of another person or a corporate entity by authority. [The business *agent* of a union acts on its behalf in financial matters; In a dictatorship, all government officials are personal *agents* of the dictator rather then *representatives* of the people.] In its more restricted sense, *agent* means one who acts on behalf of one of two parties. [A real estate *agent* acts on behalf of the landlord in transactions between landlord and tenant; A theatrical *agent* handles business with the producer for his actor-client.]

A **proxy** is one who acts as an *agent* for another at a ceremony or in an election. [Marriages by *proxy* were frequent during World War II: if the groom was overseas, another person would act as his *proxy* at the ceremony; Most stockholders vote for directors by *proxy*; that is, they authorize an *agent* to vote on their behalf.]

Delegate and **deputy** usually refer to *representatives* who are closely bound by instructions; the use of the title *representative* rather than *delegate* or *deputy* often implies a lack of such instructions, or less binding ones. Thus a Congressional *representative*, once he is elected, is free to vote for or against legislation as he sees fit, but a *delegate* to a presidential convention may be required to vote for the man who won the primary election in his state. A *deputy* is usually a person who acts under powers granted by a superior. A sheriff's *deputy* may have the power to arrest only if the sheriff has given it to him. See ASSOCIATE.

representative

agent
delegate
deputy
proxy
substitute

These words all pertain to what is extremely ugly, deformed, or shocking, or to anything that deserves to be hated or causes aversion or nausea. **Repulsive** can refer to visual appearance that is hideous or to behavior that is worthy of condemnation because of its crudity or immorality: a *repulsive* painting; such *repulsive* habits as belching and picking his nose. **Repellent** can refer literally to the warding off of something: an insect-*repellent* spray. But otherwise it is an intensification of the possibilities for *repulsive*: the *repellent* cruelty with which he treated his dog. Both words strongly imply a shocked or outraged reaction to the thing described, even to suggesting a physical drawing away from the object or a desire to drive it away: No matter how she tried to conquer her distaste, she found his disfigured body too *repulsive* to touch; using his cane in an attempt to smash the art object that he found so *repellent*.

Abhorrent derives ultimately from a Latin expression that refers to a horrified bristling, shuddering, or shivering action. A comparable distaste, almost physical in its intensity, may well be indicated by the word,

repulsive

abhorrent
abominable
disgusting
loathsome
repellent
repugnant
revolting

although now it applies less to visual appearance than to something that affronts one's sensibilities or moral sense: the *abhorrent* policy of apartheid. In the context of moral indignation, *abhorrent* is the most forceful word here. **Loathsome** is closely related to such a use of *abhorrent*, but where the latter might apply best as a sweeping condemnation of group action or behavior, *loathsome* applies equally well to single acts or individuals: his *loathsome* mistreatment of his wife. In reference to group action, *loathsome* is less emphatic because the word may more clearly imply a personal aversion or disapproval that is not necessarily shared by others: *loathsome* customs that the newcomer found impossible to accept.

Disgusting and **revolting** are more like the first pair in suggesting a shocked or outraged reaction that can sometimes find physical expression. *Disgusting* can suggest an actual queasiness stimulated by something objectionable, whereas *revolting* can imply physical nausea or a psyche that reacts in rebellious upheaval to such a phenomenon: He found her cooking habits to be unsanitary and *disgusting*; impossible to be polite when confronted with his *revolting* impertinence. Both words lose any suggestion of these intense reactions, however, when applied more generally, especially when used as loose hyperboles for irritation or annoyance: *disgusting* incompetence. *Revolting*, in fact, can give a tone of extreme informality when used in this way: a *revolting* development.

Repugnant also emphasizes a reaction of distaste or aversion, but is more formal than the previous pair. Also, because the word is less often used in loose exaggeration, it is considerably more forceful in effect: *repugnant* conditions in uninspected meat-packing plants; a *repugnant* indifference to human suffering. It is less forceful than *abhorrent*, however; it would show a want of feeling to speak of *repugnant*, rather than *abhorrent*, crimes against humanity, since the latter not only expresses distaste but moral outrage as well.

Abominable is closer in tone to *abhorrent* and *loathsome* in stressing that something merits severe condemnation and hatred: *abominable* working conditions. This word has suffered from overuse and exaggeration, however, to a greater degree than these other words, applying to anything that is relatively unpleasant: an *abominable* weekend of rain. Also, the word has been popularized as part of the phrase, "*abominable* snowman," referring to a legendary or imaginary man-beast reputed to exist in the mountains of Tibet; widespread humorous references to and extensions of this phrase has nearly incapacitated *abominable* itself for any serious use. See CONTEMPTIBLE, DEPRAVED, OBNOXIOUS, REPREHENSIBLE.

Antonyms: admirable, alluring, amiable, CHARMING, commendable, EXCELLENT, PLEASING, *splendid*.

request

appeal
application
invitation
petition
requisition

These words refer to oral or written statements asking someone to grant a wish or fulfill a need. **Request** is the most general and informal. Unless contravened by context, it suggests courtesy and genuine desire, but no necessary certainty that what is asked will be granted: a *request* that he be allowed to accompany her to the dance; able to supply on *request* any book in print; a disc jockey who opened his programs by playing *requests*; a written *request* that she recommend him for the fellowship. An **appeal**, if verbally made, would involve an urgent *request* for aid: *appeals* for help that rang through the burning building. It may also imply the dissatisfied seeking out of another opinion: an *appeal* to the rest of the group to settle their disagreement. In reference to written *requests*, *appeal* stresses a formal or urgent turning to a higher authority: an *appeal* to the Supreme Court for a reversal of the decision. The word may also be used to indicate the arousing of special motives in the person addressed, not necessarily by verbal means: an *appeal* to his sense of fair play; an *appeal* to the average citizen's prurient interests.

Invitation cannot suggest a *request* for aid and is completely lacking in any sense of urgency. It suggests, rather, the making of a courteous offer to someone either of hospitality or some other kindness or benefit: an *invitation* to join him for a drink after the meeting; an *invitation* to attend their wedding; an *invitation* to join the faculty as a full professor. The word has a less concrete use for an *appeal* to specific motives in the person or group singled out for attention: a look that was an *invitation* to take whatever liberties with her that he might wish; an unenforceable regulation that was an *invitation* to law-breaking.

The remaining words are mostly restricted in meaning to written *requests*. **Requisition** is the most formal of these, specifically indicating a detailed statement of the need for food, supplies, or shelter: putting in a *requisition* for new cartridge belts and canteens. **Petition** is close to *appeal* in suggesting the submission of an urgent *request* to a higher authority. In a legal context, however, it may imply simply throwing oneself on the mercy of the authority, rather than any rearguing of the case: a last *petition* to the governor for clemency. Outside the legal context, it tends to suggest the gathering of many names in support of a candidate or in requesting that a policy be adopted: the deadline for filing *petitions* to place a name on the ballot; a drive to collect signatures on a *petition* to be sent to the president. In its older sense of a simple *request*, *petition* is now seldom used and would tend to sound stuffy. **Application** suggests most strongly a routine written *request* for consideration: a three-page job *application*; turning in his *application* for a scholarship; making *application* to join the fraternity; an *application* to enter the contest. See DEMAND, REQUIRE, SEEK.

request

apply
ask
invite
seek
solicit

These words are concerned with the situation in which one person proposes the solution of a need or desire, leaving the person addressed free to decline or accept the proposal. **Request** implies the use of a courteous manner in expressing a need: *requesting* directions from a nearby policeman; He *requested* help from the librarian to locate the book he wanted. As a verb, the word remains somewhat formal and is sometimes used as a euphemism for a more imperative expression: *requesting* his immediate resignation. **Ask** is much more informal and more general than *request* and does not necessarily imply courtesy of expression at all: curtly *asking* the waiter for a glass of water. Whereas both *request* and *ask* suggest, in themselves, some unfulfilled need or desire on the part of the speaker, **invite** very often suggests that someone else is given permission to fulfill such a desire: a sign *inviting* passers-by to browse about the shop if they wished; *requesting* that he be permitted to attend the party, even though he had not been *invited*.

Seek contrasts with the foregoing words in suggesting any kind of action taken in gaining help or fulfilling a desire, without being restricted in possible meanings to the *requesting* of help in speech or writing: *seeking* approval in the faces of the audience as he spoke. Furthermore, while *request* often suggests a one-to-one relationship of an appealer and one appealed to, *seek* points to an effort to get an answer from a number of sources: *seeking* directions from everyone along the way who seemed the least bit friendly. *Seek* may also imply an insistent, rather than a courteous, manner: *seeking* the necessary document through a bureaucratic maze.

Apply, as now used, suggests mostly a written statement addressed to an institution expressing a desire to be considered for a position: *applying* for a job, a scholarship, a sabbatical, a charge account. **Solicit** suggests a canvass of likely prospects in the attempt to gain some consideration, often of a business nature: carnival hawkers *soliciting* onlookers to buy tickets to the sideshow; prostitutes *soliciting* every well-dressed man who walked their way. In more general uses, comparable to those of *request, solicit* now seems archaic, if not clouded over by unpleasant connotations from its more common use: a teacher *soliciting* the earnest attention of his students. See PLEAD.

require

lack
need
want

These words all mean to wish for or to desire something, or to consider it, for some reason, absolutely necessary. **Require** is the mildest, most formal, and most general of these. It might be used for a simple statement of things necessary for a given task: an expansion of duties that would *require* a doubling of floor space and the hiring of six more typists. It can also be used to state, somewhat dispassionately, more fundamental necessities: organisms that *require* water as surely as food and oxygen.

Need theoretically indicates the *requiring* of an absolute essential: plants that *need* sun in order to live. But the word, while more informal than *require,* can often be used for intense desire of what may not, after all, be a matter of life and death: He swore that he *needed* her love more than anything on earth. And the word can often be used hyperbolically for the slightest wish: *needing* a new hat every other week. **Lack** stresses the idea of *need* by emphasizing the absence of the thing desired: a city that *lacks* a good library; a marriage *lacking* in tranquillity and simple friendliness. On the other hand, the word can, oddly enough, be used to express the absence of negative values: a play completely *lacking* in digressions or wasted motion. **Want** is now most commonly used for the direct, personal expression of desire: the lady who *wanted* her salad without dressing; what most overindulged children *want.* In this sense, the amount of *need* expressed is not necessarily very intense. In an older use, the word can, however, express severe *need* or *lack*: a people who *wanted* for the very necessities of life; soldiers *wanting* shoes but marching on, all the same, through ice and snow. See YEARN.

Antonyms: GET, POSSESS.

resentment

huff
offense
pique
umbrage

These words are comparable in their denotation of a feeling of displeasure directed at the cause of some real or imagined wrong or injury. **Resentment** and **offense** are the terms which refer to the strongest emotions characterized by this group. *Resentment* describes a sense of grievance which is internal and suggests a persistent or recurrent brooding over injuries rather than a sudden outburst of passionate anger. *Offense* designates a state of hurt feelings less extreme than *resentment* and without the strong sense of grievance implicit in that word. There is also in *offense* no suggestion of a long-felt emotion but rather one that is transitory because less serious. [She cherished a deep *resentment* toward her employer for having denied her a promotion; Reporters and photographers alike took great *offense* at the rude way the star behaved during his interview.]

Pique, which comes from a French word meaning to prick or sting, denotes a sudden feeling of mingled pain and anger that is usually slight and transient. *Pique* often arises from wounded vanity or sensitiveness: leaving the party in a *pique* because of an imagined slight on the part of her hostess. **Umbrage** is a deeper and more persistent displeasure at being ignored or overshadowed or subjected to any treatment that one deems discourteous or disrespectful: to take *umbrage* at the criticism leveled against him because he thought it unfair and belittling. **Huff** is very much like *pique* in suggesting a petty, usually passing, sense of injury because of a blow to one's pride: in a *huff* because his boss had chewed him out in front of his secretary. See ANGER, BOTHER, ENRAGE, UNSETTLE.

Antonyms: PATIENCE, PLEASURE.

reside

dwell
inhabit
live
occupy
settle

These words all mean to make one's home more or less permanently in one place. **Reside** is the most formal term in the group and is preferred to any of the others when a legal and permanent abode is being emphasized. [When the patrolman stopped me for a traffic violation he asked me where I *resided*; A U.S. senator is expected to *reside* in the state which he represents.] *Reside* may also suggest tenancy of an elegant or imposing home: The wealthy banker *resides* in a town house on Park Avenue. **Live,** though close in meaning to *reside,* is the more general and everyday word when applied to having any established or permanent home, whether one is referring to the actual abode or a city, country, etc., in which it is located: to *live* in New York City; to *live* in the big red house on the corner; to *live* in Europe. *Live* may also mean to maintain a domicile in a specific place for the time being, either temporarily or indefinitely: President Roosevelt *resided* in Hyde Park, but during his presidency he *lived* either in Washington or in Warm Springs, Georgia.

Dwell, in the sense of *reside* or *live,* is normally limited to poetical or literary usage, especially of the past: to *dwell* in crystal palaces. In an extended sense, however, it is commonly used of states of mind or of surroundings of a particularly limited nature. [Schizophrenics *dwell* in a web of fantasy and hallucination; The philosopher *dwells* in the realm of ideas; A physician *dwells* in the world of the sick.]

Inhabit carries less of the implication of having a fixed abode than do *reside* and *live.* When used in this sense it tends to sound high-flown or archaic. Rather, it points to people or animals *living* in large areas or adapted to specific physical environments. [Before the arrival of the white man, North America was *inhabited* solely by Indians; Fishes and certain mammals, as the whale and the dolphin, *inhabit* the ocean.] *Inhabit* may also lay stress on the using of a place as a home or shelter: a huge tenement *inhabited* by families on relief; burrows *inhabited* by wild rabbits.

Occupy is applicable both to places where people *live* and to premises given over to business enterprises, and it carries the implication of taking over and holding possession. [The Lewis family *occupies* the house next door; The insurance company *occupies* a twenty-six-story building downtown.]

Settle differs from the foregoing words in that it refers to a town, country, region, etc., in which one has established a permanent home, and not to the home itself. [They *settled* in San Francisco last year and like *living* there; The Amish *settled* parts of rural Pennsylvania and usually *live* on farms.]

resolution

decision
determination
resolve

All these words can refer to the taking of a stand or to the acting out of a purpose with unflagging fixity. In the first situation, **resolution** suggests the conscious or formal spelling out of a position: a new year's *resolution*; a *resolution* adopted by the whole committee. When it refers to a manner of acting, the word still suggests a conscious choosing of goal and methods that infuses the action with vigor and, often, with ethical purpose: She administered the spanking with *resolution*; promising to weed out bureaucratic corruption with steadfast *resolution*. **Determination**, in reference to action, contrasts with *resolution* by suggesting an almost stubborn will power more than a detailed conscious spelling out of goals or principles: He drove in each nail with *determination*. *Determination*, furthermore, may suggest an undivided emotional and mental assent to the action one is performing, whereas *resolution* could suggest an intellectual choice that has actually overcome an emotional reluctance: attacking the tempting meal with lusty *determination*; They flinched at the icy water but strode into it with *resolution*. *Determination*, in the sense of choosing a stand, suggests studious investigation: arbitrators who will hear both sides before making their *determination*.

Resolve is, of course, closely related to *resolution*. In the sense of choosing, however, it does not suggest the same spelled-out complexity or formality as *resolution*, pointing instead to a single instance in which a person makes up his mind, once and for all: a *resolve* to pass the test no matter how much studying it took. In referring to action, the word also relates more to single instances of vigorous application; here the note of difficult obstacles or inner reluctance is heightened, although the ethical suggestion may be absent. [With renewed *resolve*, he tried again to climb up the sheer wall; Despite her repugnance, she flung herself into the unpleasant task with great *resolve*.] **Decision** is the least forceful of any of these words in both possible situations. In reference to taking a stand, the word can apply to any situation, serious or trivial: their *decision* to drop the bomb; a *decision* to stay home with a good book. More simply, the word can refer to a choice among alternatives: his *decision* to vote for a third-party candidate. In reference to action, the word suggests a lack of hesitation or hanging back rather than an approach based on ethical or willed conviction. The word does impart a note of acting with dispatch and, perhaps, of using an ability to improvise as one goes along without stopping constantly for a new search after methods or motives: acting with *decision* while others stood about debating. See ALLEGIANCE, OPINION, SURE.

Antonyms: DOUBT, HESITATION, *irresolution, vacillation.*

respect

consideration
deference
esteem
honor
regard
reverence
veneration

These words refer to an admiring attitude or to courteous treatment. **Respect** and **honor** can allude to both these possibilities. When describing an attitude, the words suggest an almost awed admiration for a person's views, accomplishmenst, or behavior; the person so admired is often one's superior: feeling a sincere *respect* for the old woman because she successfully met all the challenges of a very difficult life; astounded to learn that a man who had been held in such high *honor* had been dismissed from the department because of his political views. *Respect*, in a way that *honor* does not, can refer to a feeling for one's equal: a real *respect* for his opponent's intelligence. When the words refer to a manner of treatment, they suggest a courteous, sometimes humble approach: paying the old dowager every conceivable *respect*; doing *honor* to one's parents.

Regard is similar to *respect* or *honor* in that it can refer either to attitude or treatment. The attitude suggested by *regard*, however, is a warmer but less awed feeling, suggesting approving friendliness more than humble admiration. It may sometimes suggest the attitude of a superior toward a favorite: happy to have won his employer's *regard*. In any case, it is less austere than *respect* or *honor*: classmates who held him in evident *regard*. When it applies to treatment, *regard* contrasts with the two preceding words by referring to a thoughtful or attentive concern rather than humble courtesy: giving the matter my special *regard*; treating the newsmen interviewing him with unusual *regard*.

Esteem alludes only to an attitude, designating a favorable opinion of a person which is based on worth but which is joined with a feeling of warm interest in and sometimes attraction toward the *esteemed* person: hurt by the indifference of a coworker whom she had held in high *esteem*.

Reverence and **veneration** are alike in suggesting a deep, profound *honor* or *respect* for someone or something. *Reverence* implies that feelings of love are mingled with *honor* or *respect*; it can refer to an attitude or treatment, the object of which is looked on as exalted or inviolable: regarding his grandfather almost with *reverence*; to have *reverence* for the Constitution; treating a valuable piece of art with the *reverence* it deserves. *Veneration* refers more to attitude than treatment and implies *respect* mixed with awe, as for that which we consider to be not only of great worth but almost hallowed: *veneration* for a dead hero; *veneration* for the cause of civil rights.

The remaining terms almost exclusively relate to treatment. **Deference** is restricted to possibilities of *respect* in this use. The word, however, suggests an even greater formalized courtesy and need imply nothing about the true feelings of the person showing such *deference*: a briefing on what signs of *deference* the visiting head of state would expect. **Consideration**, by contrast, relates almost solely to possibilities of *regard* in this use. Here, even greater overtones of warmth are present, with thoughtfulness and concern more clearly motivated by sincere feeling: showing an unbiased *consideration* for both sides in the dispute. As with *respect* and *regard*, *deference* might be more appropriate for suggesting behavior toward a superior, *consideration* for an inferior: parents who demand to be treated with *deference* by their children, yet give very little *consideration* in return. See PRAISE, REVERE.

Antonyms: contempt, DISLIKE, disrespect, repugnance.

responsible

accountable
answerable
liable

These words refer to the agreement by which one takes on the blame or credit for the results of an endeavor over which one has charge. **Responsible** is the most general of these words, suggesting not only such an agreement but applying beyond this to anyone who is mature or able enough to discharge difficult or exacting duties, to delegate authority wisely, and to perform capably despite unforeseen obstacles. More strictly, it suggests the relationship between the performer of duties and his taskmaster: *responsible* to the people alone as to the adequate performance of his duties. It may also refer exclusively to the assignment of blame in a negative situation: a jury pondering over whom to hold *responsible* for the accident. Much more restricted in scope than *responsible*, **liable** refers exclusively to this last possibility of assigning blame; in a legal sense it can even refer, most strictly, to the payment of monetary damages in a mishap: laws that hold the driver *liable* for any injury to those riding with him.

Accountable, like *liable*, has a legal or technical sense, but in this case the word refers to the situation of stewardship in which the steward must demonstrate the wise use of things put in his trust: an administrator who is directly *accountable* to the president for the funds allocated to his department. **Answerable** has a less technical ring to it than *accountable* and can apply as well to nonlegal situations: arguing that parents were to be held *answerable* for the widespread discontent of teenagers; evolutionary changes that are *answerable* to corresponding changes in the earth's environment at the time of a species' emergence. See OBLIGATION.

Antonyms: irresponsible, unaccountable.

restaurant

café
cafeteria
coffee house
coffee shop
diner
dining room
eatery
greasy spoon
lunch counter
luncheonette

These words all denote places where refreshments or meals are provided for the public. The most widely used term in the group, and the one with the widest range of meaning is **restaurant**. A *restaurant* can be anything from a small counter operation to a very large establishment with several rooms. *Restaurants* can serve a variety of food or they can specialize in French, Italian, Chinese, Indian, Mexican, etc., cuisine. Many *restaurants* have bars or cocktail lounges where it is possible to have a drink before dining or even to have drinks without dining. At some *restaurants*, live music is played by, perhaps, a pianist or a small combination of instruments; indeed, there are *restaurants*, particularly foreign ones, where singers entertain during dinner hours and later on at night. *Restaurants* may be open for a relatively short time each day; some serve only breakfast and lunch — others serve lunch and dinner; some serve dinner only, and still others are open for dinner, supper, and late evening snacks. **Coffee shops** and **lunch counters** (or **luncheonettes**) are, for example, *restaurants* which cater to a breakfast and lunch trade. They are quick-service eating places with people seated at counters as well as at tables. When a *coffee shop* is part of a hotel, the name is used to distinguish it from the more formal and more expensive hotel *restaurant* called the hotel **dining room**.

Café is the French word for **coffee house**. In the U.S., *café* can retain that meaning and be a small place which serves coffee and other nonalcoholic beverages and simple food such as pastry or sandwiches. More commonly, however, in the U.S. such an establishment is called a *coffee house*, and often features, in addition to the same kind of refreshments, some kind of entertainment such as poetry readings or folk singing. *Café* can also designate, as it often does in Europe, an open-air eating and drinking place. In this kind of *café* it is sometimes possible to get alcoholic as well as nonalcoholic beverages and, if the *café* is part of a regular *restaurant*, a full meal. *Café* is also used to designate certain bars or nightclubs. Here, as in the case of some *restaurants* which use the word as part of their name, *café* may be thought to add a foreign flavor or at least an elegant tone to what is basically an unpretentious drinking or eating establishment.

A **cafeteria** is a particular kind of *restaurant*, the distinctive feature of which is the fact that its patrons carry their own food from the counter where it is dished out to the table at which it is eaten. *Cafeterias* may be open for part of the day or all day, and sometimes, usually in large cities, all night.

Diner originally referred to those railway cars which are equipped for the serving and consumption of food while a train is en route. This meaning is still valid, but *diner* by extension has come to denote a kind of *restaurant* which resembles a railroad car in that it is long and comparatively narrow. These *diners* are usually equipped with a counter and booths or tables, as well as, of course, an open or closed kitchen.

Eatery is an informal word for any kind of *restaurant*. It is sometimes used as part of the name of an eating spot: Mother Remer's *Eatery*. It more often appears in the writing of advertisers or columnists who may or may not be intentionally trying to match the folksiness inherent in the word. [Manhattan's newest celeb hangout is a posh new *eatery* in the east sixties.] **Greasy spoon** is slang. It graphically describes a *restaurant* whose food is cheap but no bargain and which is often as unsavory looking as the name suggests. See BAR.

These words refer to events that are caused, determined, or set in action by, or that bring to completion antecedent events of which they are the outgrowth. **Result** is the most general of these, indicating a strict causal link between the two events: unemployment that was the direct *result* of the balanced budget. The word may often suggest an earlier action that is deliberately taken to gain a particular goal: pacifying words that had their intended *result* of calming the hysterical woman. Sometimes the word may suggest earlier action taken experimentally to determine or measure what then will happen: evaluating the *results* of the double-blind cancer test. **Effect** emphasizes even more strictly than *result* the notion of causality and gives, consequently, a more objective, almost scientific tone. *Result*, furthermore, may suggest a unique or unpredictable one-time action, while *effect* emphasizes a principle that underlies a chain of events and that continues to work in other instances: a childhood familiarity with firearms that had such an unexpected and tragic *result*; the *effect* of radiation on the heredity of fruit flies.
  Consequence may refer to simple causation in a neutral way: prosperity that was the *consequence* of widely expanded governmental spending. More often, however, the word suggests a negative *result* or at least the negative concomitant of an otherwise desirable *effect*: arguing that the rise in lung cancers was a *consequence* of cigarette smoking; tolerating a measure of inflation if it was the inevitable *consequence* of full employment.
  Outcome and **dénouement** relate to *result* in emphasizing more strongly a unique or one-time conclusion to a sequence of events. The informal *outcome* suggests finality or resolution: hearing of the fight he had been in, but not of its *outcome*. The notion of causality here is far less strong than in the previous words: a tragic *outcome* for such a happy marriage. *Dénouement* is the most formal of these words; at its most restricted, it refers to the final working out of plot in a fictional narrative, especially a play: a dramatic conflict that is resolved in the surprising, but completely believable *dénouement*. This word, however, is often extended to other areas of use, where it functions as a more formal synonym for *outcome*, especially in cases where events are dramatic, suspenseful, and unpredictable: a vote of censure that came as a *dénouement* to the charges and countercharges aired during the congressional investigation; a Pyrrhic victory on the battlefield that had as its *dénouement* the inconclusive statements issued by the peace conference. See FINISH, PURPOSE.
  Antonyms: ORIGIN.

result

consequence
dénouement
effect
outcome

These words all relate to entering into or being in the state called sleep. The most formal term in the group is **retire**. It can mean simply to go to bed: We *retired* early that night because the day's activities had been so strenuous. It can, however, and often does suggest a withdrawal to a private place where one can be alone, read, write, etc., before actually

retire

fall asleep

retire

(continued)

go to sleep

grab some shuteye

hit the hay

hit the sack

sack out

turn in

going to bed: We went to see Holland after dinner, but his butler informed us that he had *retired* for the evening. **Fall asleep** and **go to sleep** are the most common terms in the group. The first stresses the natural, passive suspension of consciousness that occurs when one ceases being awake: I *fell asleep* as soon as my head hit the pillow. The second can mean the same thing: to *go to sleep* quickly. But it can also suggest the deliberate action involved in going to bed before *falling asleep*: Let's *go to sleep* now and clean up this mess in the morning.

Turn in is a colloquial equivalent for *go to sleep* in the sense which implies the action of going to bed: We *turned in* at ten and slept for twelve hours straight. It can also suggest the same kind of withdrawing that *retire* does: I *turned in* right after dinner so as to get back to the detective story I'd started the night before.

Hit the hay and **hit the sack** are both slang expressions meaning to go to bed. *Hit the sack* was widely used in the armed services during World War II, but is now known in civilian as well as in military life. **Sack out** is also Army-originated slang for go to bed, but it can mean *fall asleep* and even can suggest sleeping for a long time or at least for as long as one wishes: It's going to be great to *sack out* tonight after a whole day on K.P.

The slang expression **grab some shuteye** means to sleep. It can be used to refer to an ordinary night's rest or to even a longer than normal period. But it often indicates a short sleep or nap: I'm going to *grab some shuteye* before the party begins. See LEAVE.

revere

adore

idolize

reverence

venerate

worship

These words refer to the warm respect and honor with which one may regard an admirable person or institution. **Revere** is less formal and warmer in tone than **reverence**, which emphasizes solemnity. It is more appropriate for an institution or idea than a person, and is perhaps excessively formal in some cases: a master who still *reveres* his old teacher; the underprivileged who are asked to *reverence* the goals of a free society.

Worship and **venerate** both, of course, function directly in a religious context; in this case, *worship* might be reserved for expressing one's attitude to the divinity, while *venerate* could apply to an exemplary religious person, idea, or aspect: *worshiping* God and *venerating* the saints. More broadly, in other contexts, *venerate* is often used in conjunction with the notions of dignity and advanced age: *venerating* the old man for the wisdom and courage he had shown throughout his long career. *Worship* can be used more generally: a father who simply *worships* his children. But sometimes it may suggest an excess and uncritical respect: people who *worshiped* Mussolini as though he were some sort of demigod.

Adore suggests the most tenderness and warmth of any of these words, and while it has a religious use, it functions in other context with fewer religious overtones than its synonyms: *adoring* the name of God; boys who *adore* their mothers. The word, however, suggests the situation of love at a distance or the putting of someone on a pedestal more than it does a realistic, equal sharing of affection. **Idolize** is an extreme example of the overtones inherent in *adore*. While its pejorative possibilities should be clear in suggesting a slavish, servile, helpless love, the word is surprisingly enough often used with no negative intent whatsoever: men who *idolize* rather than attempt to satisfy their wives; a writer who simply *idolized* the novels of Dostoevski. See LOVE, RESPECT.

Antonyms: blaspheme, contemn, DESPISE, REJECT, SCOFF, SLIGHT.

These words refer to changes in an existing system, especially a written one, usually with a view to its betterment. **Revise** suggests large or small alterations, mostly in a piece of writing, in order to make it sounder or more in keeping with a given intention: *revising* the whole book to make it more compact and give it a tauter, more dramatic forward movement; ideologies that are constantly *revised* in the light of changing circumstances. **Rewrite**, by contrast, suggests a more thoroughgoing change and is more exclusively restricted in use to refer to manuscripts or documents. While it may be used in reference to a single sentence or to an entire book, major alterations in structure or theme rather than in style or expression are most often indicated: arguing that Jefferson had simply *rewritten* Paine's first attempt at a declaration of independence; the movie star who insisted that her part be completely *rewritten*; *rewriting* the conclusion of the novel in such a way as to change the theme and outcome of the whole book.

Amend indicates the change in a document by adding on new sections at the end: *amending* the Constitution so that it gave specific rules on presidential succession. While *amend*, thus, would seem to suggest less possibility for change than previous words, a document can in actual theory be *amended* so that all its provisions are nullified and replaced by completely opposite or different provisions. **Emend**, by contrast, suggests a textual change, small in extent, that is accomplished in the body of the work itself, usually by someone other than the original author: scholars who *emend* Shakespeare freely when they decide that the existing texts are garbled or unsound; lazy minds that wrench a great writer's words out of context and then further *emend* them to suit their own taste. See INSERT, REPAIR.

revise

amend
emend
rewrite

These words refer to the act of holding something up for disapproval or contempt. **Ridicule** suggests a conscious, usually verbal, attack on something so that it will be regarded as ludicrous: heaping *ridicule* on her desire to keep her job after they were married. **Derision** suggests a fiercer attack, one designed not only to prove something ludicrous, but contemptible as well; the word is often used in the context of a public display of such contempt: casting *derision* on the whole tax system; audiences who greeted her efforts at singing with catcalls and *derision*. **Mockery** may suggest a lighter, more subtle approach than *ridicule*, but it is characterized by the same motivating contempt as *derision*: stung by the note of *mockery* in his remarks. *Mockery*, however, is often used in a special way for an act that leaves a person open to intense disapproval: making a *mockery* of the whole democratic process.

The remaining three words relate more closely to the techniques for making something seem ludicrous or contemptible. **Irony** is the technique of saying the opposite of what you actually mean: his deliberate *irony* in referring to the bejeweled matrons as generous and compassionate. **Satire** suggests a less subtle assault through such techniques as overstatement, *ridicule*, or laughter-provoking *derision*: unsettling many officials with his pointed *satire* on their bungling methods for coping with the crisis. *Satire* may also refer to any work using *ridicule*: Pope's *satire* on the bad writers of his day. **Sarcasm** is most often restricted to the making of brief, unpleasant remarks that are motivated by hostility and contempt: replying with *sarcasm* to anything she tried to suggest as a solution to their difficulties. See CARICATURE, HUMOROUS, JOKE.

Antonyms: PRAISE.

ridicule

derision
irony
mockery
sarcasm
satire

right

freedom
liberty
prerogative
privilege

These words refer to the fundamental claims a person can properly make or to his unfettered ability to choose. **Right** suggests a concrete claim established by legal, ethical, or religious sanctions: the *right* to own property; the *right* of equality before the law. Although someone claiming a *right* tends to argue that it is inherent, a person's *rights* are differently spelled out in different cultures: the *right* of an Arab to have several wives; the *right* of a serf to remain immovably on his land. **Liberty**, by contrast, is a more abstract and general notion suggesting the opportunity to choose among alternatives. A document such as the Bill of Rights spells out those conditions a citizen may construe as his *rights*: the *right* to life, *liberty*, and the pursuit of happiness. *Liberty* may sometimes, in fact, refer to an unwarranted breach of someone else's *right* to consideration or privacy: taking the *liberty* of phoning you directly; unbridled *liberty* without regard for the *rights* of others. Civil *rights* is now understood to refer to racial equality, while civil *liberties* is understood to refer to all the rights enumerated in the U.S. Constitution and its amendments.

Freedom is close to *liberty* in its abstract generality but stresses a total lack of constraint more than the opportunity for choice: clothes cut to allow *freedom* of movement; rulers who took it as their right to suppress *freedom* of speech.

Prerogative and **privilege** are much more specific in their meanings than the other words here. *Prerogative* refers to a *right* that one has by virtue of his age, sex, or position: a host's *prerogative* to turn away uninvited guests; a woman's *prerogative* to change her mind; an employee's *prerogative* to receive adequate severance pay. *Privilege* suggests advantages given as favors or added luxuries rather than as necessary *rights*; a *privilege* may be given as a concession in exchange for something else. [Arriving early gave him the *privilege* of an unhurried dinner; College education is nowadays taken as a *right* rather than a *privilege*.] See BENEFIT, RIGHTFUL.

rightful

deserved
due
equitable
fair
just
merited

These words refer to anything that is fitting, proper, or called for by legal or ethical standards. **Rightful** suggests that something is in accordance with some objective set of standards: a *rightful* heir to the property; the *rightful* place of women in society. The word is often used when something thought true or fitting has been challenged: protesting that he was still their *rightful* monarch. **Just** also emphasizes an objective set of standards by which to judge whether something is fitting, but here the standards, by implication, are legal or moral ones: a *just* trial; arguing that a *just* society could not tolerate segregation of any kind.

Due emphasizes appropriateness or reasonableness: promising to answer in *due* course; a *due* punishment. In emphasizing moderation and practicality, the word can sometimes seem a denial that objective standards exist and thus imply an arbitrary judgment: asserting that there was no conflict between the censorship law and a *due* regard for civil liberties. The word can also imply something that has accrued with time or has been left outstanding: rigged juries that permit criminals to escape their *due* punishment.

Deserved and **merited** both emphasize the earning of something: a *deserved* honor; a *deserved* punishment; a *merited* award. As shown in these examples, *deserved* can be used both positively and negatively, whereas *merited* is more often used only for positive achievements. **Fair** is the mildest and most general of these words; it is also the most subjective in suggesting an appeal to reasonableness and open-mindedness:

a referee who was scrupulously *fair* in all his decisions; claiming that it wasn't *fair* that he had to do more work than his baby brother. **Equitable**, more formal than *fair*, suggests a solution that is just and reasonable to all parties concerned, but not necessarily wholly satisfactory to all. It is often used in contexts indicating an acceptable compromise rather than those susceptible of sharp distinctions between right and wrong: The wage agreement was *equitable* to both management and unions, although both had misgivings about certain aspects of the settlement. See LAWFUL, MORAL, RIGHT.

Antonyms: evil, illicit, improper, OUTRAGEOUS, *unlawful, wrongful.*

These words refer to those who in valuing the past are opposed to change in the present. **Rightist** would seem to offer a neutral description of a person with such a belief, especially in the area of politics, but in actual U.S. use, the word carries a tinge of disapproval. In other parts of the world, the word might be avowedly descriptive, but here, where both parties are middle-of-the-road and where liberal is generally a word of approval, only a candidate's opponents are likely to accuse him of being a *rightist*. **Conservative** and **traditionalist** are much more neutral and can, in addition, be used for many other areas of activity beyond the political. Especially in Britain, where it is the name for a major political party, *conservative* carries the positive implication of wishing to conserve those time-tested values handed down to us by the wise men who struggled to realize them in the past. In political discussion in the United States, however, this implication is not always present, and may suggest instead a refusal to innovate and an extreme caution toward or dislike for any extension of governmental authority. In a wider context, the word suggests a rejection of modern or contemporary styles or tastes: political liberals who are *conservatives* when it comes to their taste in art and music. *Traditionalist* is more appropriate in this wider context than *conservative*, since it cannot be confused as a reference to politics; it suggests a person who judges things in the light of clearly defined standards evolved over a long period of time: *traditionalists* whose paintings showed no influence of the current avant-garde ferment.

The rest of these words refer more exclusively to political alignment. **Tory** has been used as a generic term for any *conservative*, especially one who is a proponent or beneficiary of privilege, status, or an entrenched establishment. This word has faded from political use in the United States, although it is the popular name for the *Conservative* Party in Britain. **Right-winger** is a much more informal substitute for *rightist*; its very informality intensifies the disapproval felt in *rightist*. No *conservative* would call himself a *right-winger*: party hacks and *right-wingers* who surrounded the president.

Reactionary and **fascist** are both extremely pejorative. *Reactionary* is the milder of the two, suggesting a person who wishes to wipe out the political innovations of a previous period by returning to an older, more rigid governmental scheme: *reactionaries* who propose the abolition of Social Security. *Fascist* as a descriptive term refers to a person who espouses a strong authoritarian government based on naked power rather than on the consent of the governed; the word also frequently suggests theories that one racial or ethnic group is superior to others. In political invective, the word is used loosely by liberals for anyone who disagrees with them: *fascist* hate-mongers who voted against the bill. See OLD-FASHIONED.

Antonyms: LEFTIST, *Whig.*

rightist

conservative
fascist
reactionary
right-winger
Tory
traditionalist

rite

ceremony
liturgy
observance
ritual

These words refer to the prescribed way of conducting a formal event of significance. **Rite** now pertains mostly to a religious service, referring to the whole service as an entity: the Anglican *rite*; the *rites* of puberty in primitive societies. **Ritual** includes but goes beyond this meaning by referring to the formal manner of conducting a *rite*: Puritans who objected to the emphasis on *ritual*. *Ritual* has become popular to describe any action conducted with great formality, seriousness, or inflexibility: the opening-night *ritual* of waiting up for the drama critics' reviews; the mysterious *rituals* women undergo in beauty parlors; her little *ritual* of agreeing with everything he said. More and more the word in this context is open to a pejorative tone that disapproves of cut-and-dried ways of behaving.

Liturgy, like *rite*, pertains mostly to religious services, but it is even more restricted in use to refer solely to the body of text and actions used by a Christian denomination, especially those that emphasize *ritual*: bishops called together to codify the *liturgy*; differences in *liturgy* among the Catholic, Episcopal, Eastern Orthodox, and Lutheran Churches.

Ceremony and **observance** are not confined to a religious context. Both can refer to any stylized commemorative event: debating between a religious or civil marriage *ceremony*. *Observance* can imply the formal use of *rituals*, like *ceremony*, but it is the most general of these words in suggesting any kind of commemoration whatever, formal or informal, festive or solemn, public or private: a gala *observance* of Independence Day; a quiet *observance* of their wedding anniversary that involved a leisurely dinner for just the two of them. See RELIGION.

rob

embezzle
extort
milk

These words refer to the taking of something from someone against his will. **Rob** is the most general of these, referring to any such situation; it often suggests a one-time act involving a fairly direct use of force, as in house-breaking, or the threat of force, as in an armed confrontation: the couple whose house was *robbed* while they were on vacation; *robbed* in a holdup.

Extort and **embezzle** are more formal; each has a particular area of relevance. *Extort* refers specifically to an official who compels someone to give him something not his by right, possibly in exchange for an improper favor: fire inspectors who *extorted* bribes from landlords before declaring their buildings free of violations. Money need not always be involved: *extorted* party-line obedience from the councilmen by threatening to reveal their part in the kickback scandal. The word, thus, has a connotation that suggests any sort of shady, underhanded, or unsavory dealings, not necessarily by an official: mothers who *extort* allegiance from their children by a sort of emotional blackmail. In another related use, the word can serve as a humorous substitute for *rob*: He *extorted* my wallet from me at the point of a gun. **Embezzle** applies much more strictly to a single situation, that of covertly taking money from an employer by doctoring the relevant financial records; usually, an accountant, treasurer, cashier, or someone else entrusted with other people's money is involved in this crime.

Milk is slang for getting money or other benefits from someone by means of threats, flattery, persuasion, or any sort of unethical means; it strongly suggests the tapping of a portion of some larger amount: gangsters who *milked* protection money from every cigar store owner in Chicago. The word can also refer to small amounts acquired with difficulty: *milking* his friends for free meals and booze. Thus at one extreme, the word can be a slangy substitute for *extort*, where outright illegality is involved, and at the other indicate the mere act of freeloading, which may be annoying or unethical but certainly not illegal. See CHEAT, STEAL.

These words refer to the taking of someone else's possessions against his will. **Robbery** most often suggests a face-to-face confrontation between robber and victim in which the victim surrenders his valuables because of threat or violence. **Mugging** is a *robbery* that occurs with an actual carrying out of violence, so that the victim is rendered helpless or unconscious and then divested of his valuables. **Burglary**, by contrast, most often indicates robbing a house of its valuables, usually with the intention of avoiding a confrontation with the owners because they are asleep or absent. **Holdup** and **stick-up** approach slang in their informality; *stick-up* can function as an informal substitute for *robbery*, but like *holdup* it can also refer to the robbing of premises, such as a train or bank, when groups of people must be confronted and cowed. *Holdup* refers to this context exclusively and thus is closer to *burglary* except for its necessary implication of an intended confrontation.

Theft and **larceny** are more general and abstract than these other words; *theft* can apply to any taking of property against the will of the owner, whether by stealth, confrontation, or fraud. *Larceny* is the legal term for *theft*, but includes even the attempt to take property, whether successful or not, provided the position of the property in question has been changed, however slightly. Each State fixes a specific sum, such as $100, to measure the seriousness of this crime. If the value of stolen goods is under this amount, the *theft* is called petty *larceny* and a light sentence would apply upon conviction; if over, grand *larceny* has been committed, carrying a heavier sentence. See CHEAT, STEAL.

These words refer to the breakdown of dead organic tissues by natural bacterial processes. **Rot** is the least formal and most forceful of these words, suggesting an advanced point in this process of breakdown; the tissues at this point might or might not be foul-smelling but they would in any case be almost unrecognizable, as compared to their former state: a fear of plague that had left dead bodies to *rot* in the streets; a snail that had completely *rotted* away inside its shell; leather bindings that had *rotted* to pieces in the damp basement; leaves left to *rot* in the compost heap. **Spoil**, by contrast, refers to an earlier point in the process of organic breakdown; it is especially applied to foods that have turned "bad" or begun to turn: milk that had *spoiled* in the refrigerator; drying strips of beef in the sun so that they would not *spoil*.

Decay is a more matter-of-fact word than *rot*, and applies generally to the whole process of breakdown, but particularly to the end point of total destruction: a corpse that had already *decayed*, leaving only the skeleton intact; washed-up seaweed that lay *decaying* on the beach. **Decompose** is a more formal substitute for *decay*, but is almost clinical in its reference particularly to a point of the process between *spoil* and *rot* at which point tissues may be distended and ruptured by a build-up of gases: formaldehyde to prevent the specimens from *decomposing*; treatment plants to *decompose* sewage more rapidly.

Putrefy refers to the same point in the process as *decompose*, stressing particularly the presence of foul or poisonous gases and noxious odors: salmon that had spawned and died and now lay *putrefying* in the shallows of the stream; garbage that *putrefied* in heaps on the neglected beach. **Molder** might now be thought too precious or euphemistic a substitute for *decay*. It means to *decay* gradually and turn into dust: his remains *moldering* in the tomb; old castles *moldering* on the Rhine. See CORPSE, DEAD, DIE.

Antonyms: bloom, FLOURISH, *grow.*

rotate

gyrate
revolve
roll
spin
turn
twirl
whirl

These words all mean to have or impart a circular motion. **Rotate, revolve,** and **roll** describe three different circular motions, though they are frequently used interchangeably. A body *rotates* around its own axis or center. A body *revolves* around a center outside itself: The earth *revolves* around the sun. A body *rolls* on a plane or other surface, with which its circumference is in continuous contact: A wagon wheel *rolls* on the ground, while it *rotates* on its axle.

Gyrate is sometimes used loosely as a synonym for *revolve*. However, *gyrate* emphasizes spiral or helical movement about, or as if about, a central point or axis, while *revolve* indicates circular or elliptical movement: an eagle *gyrating* majestically up into the sky for a thousand feet before plunging down on his prey; the *gyrating* violent winds of a cyclone.

Turn is the most general word of this group, and may be used as a synonym for any of the others. It most commonly applies to rotary motion, however, and is thus most often used in place of *rotate*: The earth *turns* on its axis. *Turn* is simply more colorless and less precise denotatively than the other words; it implies nothing about speed or the complexity or course of the circular movement in question.

Spin, twirl, and **whirl** all mean to *turn* or cause to *turn* rapidly and continuously. *Whirl* usually implies greater speed than the other two words, while *twirl* often refers to a complicated series of movements of something manipulated by the hands or fingers. *Spin* emphasizes the continuity of the action, and usually the narrow compass of the circular motion; it may, however, apply to any action of *turning*: The earth *spins* on its axis. [The wind *whirled* the leaves around the yard; a drum majorette *twirling* her baton while strutting at the head of a parade; to *spin* a top] *Spin* and *whirl* may also be used for any abrupt circular motion: The car *spun* (or *whirled*) around out of control. *Whirl*, more often than *spin*, has the connotation of lack of conscious control or design: The sensations *whirled* through his mind too rapidly for him to assimilate them, much less understand his feelings. See BEND, CIRCUMSCRIBE, GO, MOVE.

rough

bumpy
crenelated
crooked
jagged
rugged
serrated
uneven

These words refer to things that are not smooth or straight. **Rough** and **uneven** are both very general and vague in their implications. *Rough* can specifically indicate a coarse-grained surface: *rough* sandpaper. At its most specific, *uneven* suggests something, as a line, configuration, or surface, that has more noticeable ups and downs: an *uneven* margin; *uneven* landscape. *Rough*, however, may also indicate irregular or *uneven* ground that is impenetrable, steep, or difficult to traverse: *rough* terrain. Less concretely, the word can indicate anything unrefined, harsh, or difficult: a *rough* sketch; *rough* treatment; a *rough* job. The last use approaches slang in its informality. In its other uses, *uneven* stays closer to its reference to something with irregular variations: *uneven* patches of shrubbery scattered across the meadow; an amusing but *uneven* play. It can also refer to something unsymmetrical, unmatched, or disarranged: a face with *uneven* features; The pictures on the walls were slightly *uneven* in placement.

Bumpy and **rugged** are much more specific in their reference to *rough* or *uneven* surfaces. *Rugged* applies mostly to landscape, stressing an extremely *uneven* topography or a resistance to smooth passage: *rugged* mountains; *rugged* waves; a *rugged* dirt road. The word carries implications of harshness or toughness, as can be seen in more general uses of the word: a *rugged*, masculine build. *Bumpy* can refer to smaller-scale surfaces as well as to landscape. In both cases, the word may suggest a generally smooth stretch that is nevertheless filled with small hollows and lumpy projections: After an hour of sanding, the boards were still quite *bumpy*. Often, the word refers to anything that results in travel that is full of jolts: a *bumpy* road enclosed by *rugged* hills; Our jet picked its way through air pockets that made the ride extremely *bumpy*.

Crooked specifically refers to undesirable departures, great or small, from the horizontal or vertical. [All the pictures on the wall were *crooked*; a *crooked* tower; The seams of her stockings were *crooked*.] In more general uses, the word can refer to anything skewed, much like *uneven*: *crooked* shelves. Occasionally, the word can be used with poetic force to describe something that is naturally *uneven* or *rugged*: a range of *crooked* mountains. **Jagged** can also be used in this way, particularly of steep or extremely *uneven* topography: the *jagged* lip of the crater. More specifically, the word refers to small-scale shapes with sharp or needle-like edges such as those that result when something brittle is broken or shattered: the *jagged* edges of the broken bone; *jagged* pieces of glass. As in the last example, the word can refer primarily to an *uneven* configuration rather than to *rough* surfaces.

Serrated and **crenelated** are the most technical and specific of these words. *Serrated* refers to any saw-toothed configuration or edge: a *serrated* knife. *Crenelated* refers most specifically to the regular notched upper edge that is typical of battlements: *crenelated* castle walls. It can apply more widely to any edge with deep notches: leaves distinguished by their *crenelated* edges. See KEEN, MOUNTAIN, STEEP.

Antonyms: even, fine, smooth, straight.

These verbs refer to movement on foot that is faster than walking. **Run** is the most general word. To *run* is to move by regular, bounding steps in such a way that both feet are off the ground during part of each step. *Running* is a rapid, continuous motion and usually implies haste. A person may *run* in pursuit, in order to escape, out of eagerness, for exercise, or towards a goal in competition: to *run* for the bus; to *run* away from an assailant; to *run* to meet a friend; to *run* in a race. To **race** is to *run* very fast, often at top speed. *Race* implies urgency in *running*. It may suggest the pressing need to reach a goal in time: They *raced* for cover when the enemy opened fire. Or it may focus on a challenge, an attempt to outstrip competition in a contest of speed: I'll *race* you to the corner. Horses and dogs are *raced* on racetracks as a form of sport. Athletes *race* in track meets, as in the 100-yard dash, the mile run, or the relay. To **sprint** is to *run* at top speed, typically for a short distance: to *sprint* a quarter mile. As a noun, *sprint* may denote a short race *run* at full speed throughout. But *sprint* may also indicate a short burst of speed in the course of a longer race, especially in the homestretch: He passed the lead runner on the outside and *sprinted* over the finish line.

Trot and **jog** emphasize the up-and-down motion of restrained *running*. To *trot* is to go at a brisk, bouncy gait midway between a walk and a run. When a horse or other quadruped *trots* he moves one front leg and the opposite hind leg together, then shifts to the other diagonal pair: The

run

jog
lope
race
sprint
trot

dog *trotted* up, wagging his tail. When a person *trots* he bobs up and down, body upright and knees lifted high, shifting his weight from leg to leg, but maintaining a quick, constant pace. [The child *trotted* obediently after his nurse; The track star *trotted* around the park to keep in condition.] To *jog* is to go at a steady, unhurried *trot*. Where *trot* may imply a need for moderate speed, *jog* suggests the slow, jolting pace of one who is in no rush. [The tireless old fellow *jogged* along, completing his first lap around the block; The water boy *jogged* back to the dugout.]

Where *jog* and *trot* denote workaday, sometimes humorous, ways of running, **lope** stresses the freedom of a leisurely and swinging gait. A person or animal that *lopes* is free from strain or pressure and is able to maintain his speed for a long time without tiring. Applied to quadrupeds, *lope* indicates an easy, bounding movement or relaxed, slow-motion *running*: the grace and ease of a fox *loping* along. A horse that *lopes* moves at a slow, easy gallop or canter. Applied to persons, *lope* suggests a long, loose, swinging stride in walking: a lanky Texan *loping* along.

In a looser sense, *run* may mean simply to hurry off: Oh dear, I'm late; I've got to *run*. *Race* may mean to rush or dash: She *raced* to the phone. *Trot* suggests determination but may imply no more than a brisk, hurried walk: I'll *trot* up there on my lunch hour. In a figurative sense, *run* may mean to be a candidate and *race* may indicate any competitive contest: to *run* for office; to *run* in a congressional *race*. *Jog*, on the other hand, suggests an utter lack of competitiveness, an easygoing indifference: He *jogs* along doing odd jobs, seemingly unconcerned about his future. *Race* may also suggest the tendency or compulsion to speed toward a goal: Her thoughts *raced* ahead, anticipating the solution. Or it may emphasize the desperate need to utilize time to the utmost: His doctors *raced* with the clock to save his life. See SKIP, WALK.

S

sacred

blessed
consecrated
divine
hallowed
holy

These words refer to things that a particular religion holds to be dedicated to its god and worthy of adoration. **Sacred** suggests something associated with a divinity as being worthy of reverence: a temple *sacred* to Apollo; a mountain thought to be *sacred* by Shintoists. In another use, the word can, however, simply mark off from everyday life a sphere of things belonging to a religion: the strict separation of *sacred* and secular laws; *sacred* and profane love. **Consecrated** may suggest, most specifically, that human beings have by a prescribed ritual recommended something to their divinity as being of special worth: the bishop who *consecrates* a king. One would, thus, say that the king was *consecrated* to his God, but not necessarily that he was *sacred* to his God. Reinforcing this distinction, *consecrated* can also mean a giving over or utter dedication to a deity or even to some other ideal: *consecrating* himself to the civil rights struggle. **Divine** is more like *sacred* but goes even further in suggesting something that is of a deity or issues from him: holding that the Pentateuch was *divine* in origin. It can, like *sacred*, also distinguish the religious realm from more ordinary ones: St. Augustine's effort to mediate between the *divine* and mundane worlds.

The remaining words, like *consecrated*, suggest something that has been made worthy of worship. Of these, however, only **blessed** may suggest the official or ritual declaration such as *consecrated* may indicate. At its most specific, *blessed* [bles'id] is the title for a deceased person who has been beatified by the Roman Catholic Church in an appropriate ceremony. More generally, the word simply indicates something worthy of reverent adoration or something given significance by the particular act of a clergyman: the *blessed* [bles'id] Bible; a crucifix *blessed* [blest] by the Pope. **Hallowed** may suggest something that has been made an object of adoration or it may, less specifically, refer to something that is in actual fact revered: the *hallowed* saints; his wish to be buried in *hallowed* ground. **Holy** is the least specific of all these words, suggesting anything dedicated to God or anything righteous or godly: the *holy* church; the *holy* days of Lent; a *holy* man from Calcutta. See REVERE.

Antonyms: lay, temporal, WORLDLY.

These words are all used of unhappy or despairing states of mind and, in some cases, of situations which cause or are evocative of such feelings. **Sad,** the mildest and most general term, is also the least explicit, as it gives no hint as to how downcast a person may be or for what reason. One may feel *sad* because of the passing of summer, or *sad* because a child leaves home to be married. A funeral may be a *sad* occasion, but so may the cutting down of a beautiful forest for timber. A monkey peering out of a cage may have the *sad* eyes of a lonely old man.

Dejected means literally cast down in spirits and suggests a temporary state of disappointment and discouragement brought on by some external event: *dejected* when she failed to win the prize; *dejected* because a friend failed to greet him on the street.

Depressed and **despondent** both apply to more prolonged states of sadness. *Depressed* describes an emotional state in which both physical and mental activity may be slowed down, sometimes to the point of apathy. The *depressed* person is flooded with feelings of hopelessness and low self-esteem, and he tends to withdraw into himself and brood. To the casual observer, one who is *depressed* often appears to be so without apparent cause or, at most, for insufficient reasons. *Despondent* is sometimes used interchangeably with *depressed,* although the former often connotes great grief and a feeling of helplessness because of some catastrophe: *despondent* because he lost all of his money in the stock market; *despondent* over the death of his wife; a patient *despondent* because his condition does not improve.

Melancholy suggests a habitual pensiveness and sadness which may not necessarily be unpleasant, and it stresses the presence of sorrow rather than of pain. [During the Romantic period it was fashionable in literature to have a *melancholy* outlook on the world and to turn one's back on liveliness and joy.] In the past, *melancholy* has been applied to persons suffering from the marked lowness of spirits associated with mental illness. It is rarely so used today, *depressed* and *despondent* having supplanted it in this sense. *Melancholy* may also describe things and places that have an adverse effect on one's good spirits: the *melancholy* sound of the whippoorwill; the *melancholy* news of a friend's bad luck; the *melancholy* beach, deserted and covered with dead seaweed and snow.

Disconsolate means refusing or unable to accept consolation or comfort, as after a loss or disappointment. *Disconsolate* is a more literary term than *despondent,* and it carries the suggestion of an outward expression of sorrow or pain rather than of listlessness: a *disconsolate* woman wailing before the smoking wreckage of her home.

sad

blue
dejected
depressed
despondent
disconsolate
lugubrious
melancholy

Lugubrious, while actually meaning *sad* or *dejected*, is now applied almost exclusively to a person or thing that is so excessively mournful or solemn as to be ludicrous. [Our Sunday school teacher used to regale us with accounts of the *lugubrious* fates awaiting bad children; A bloodhound has long ears, pendent chops, and a *lugubrious* expression.]

Blue is a loose synonym for *sad, depressed,* or *despondent*. It does not suggest the extent or depth of such a feeling except in context, and it tends to sound informal. [She was *blue* and lonely because she had no Saturday-night date; A retired person often becomes *blue* because he feels he is no longer engaged in meaningful activity.] See DESPAIR, GLOOMY, MISERABLE, PATHETIC.

Antonyms: BLITHE, CHEERFUL, *excited, exhilarated, exuberant, gay, glad,* JOYOUS, *jubilant,* LIVELY.

salary

compensation
emolument
fee
honorarium
pay
stipend
wage

These words refer to the money given for work. **Salary** and **wage** are complementary terms for the set amount of money paid periodically to an employee. *Salary* usually pertains to money received by white-collar workers or by executives in managerial positions; it implies a sum figured by the week, month, or year and paid weekly or at longer intervals. *Wage,* by contrast, usually pertains to the earnings of skilled or blue-collar workers and on down the scale to manual and menial positions; it often implies an hourly rate paid weekly or biweekly: an executive *salary* starting at $10,000 a year; a minimum hourly *wage* of $1.25; the high *wages* paid for skilled labor.

Pay and **compensation** are the informal and formal terms, respectively, for *wages* or *salary* in general: the wide gulf between the scale of *pay* for machinists and that for teachers; amateur golf competitions that rule out contestants who have played the game for *compensation*. *Pay* is the preferred term in the military for the regular amount paid to personnel, usually at monthly intervals. In any case, *pay* most often suggests a permanent, recurring amount of money. *Compensation* in some cases might sound overly formal or roundabout, but it can pertain generally to a set amount that is paid once for a given service or one-time performance.

Fee and **stipend** are specific forms of *compensation* in the last sense described above. A *fee* is usually charged by a professional person as a sum set in advance for performing a specific, one-time function: the doctor's *fee* for a general examination; asking the lawyer what his *fee* would be to take the case to court. A *stipend* is most often an allowance, also set in advance, but in this case applying mostly to students who are awarded such a grant of money in the form of a scholarship or fellowship in order to pursue their studies: a handsome *stipend* granted to him for advanced research. The word has been extended to any grant of money awarded for any reason: two geneticists, one poet, and several sociologists who were awarded *stipends* under the foundation's fellowship program.

Honorarium technically refers to the *compensation* given to a professional person for services rendered when law or custom forbids a set *fee*: an *honorarium* given a poet for a public reading of his own work. Often, however, the word can become a mere euphemism for a *fee* so low that the "honor" of doing the work must make up for the inadequate *compensation*: literary magazines that give five-dollar *honorariums* for critical articles from college teachers who must publish to further their careers. **Emolument** is the most formal of these words and would seem a needless circumlocution when it substitutes for the already formal *compensation*. *Emolument* has a unique area of relevance, however, when it suggests the money that becomes available to one upon being appointed to a particular office; often this may include, by implication, fringe benefits, an expense account, or other indirect monetary perquisites in addition to the stated *salary* or *fee*: the perfectly legal *emoluments* that sometimes go along with certain appointive offices.

These words refer to a specific thing or piece of data summoned up to represent or verify a general type or thesis. **Sample** usually indicates something that is physically present for inspection as a representative of some larger entity. [The interior decorator had brought along *samples* of the fabrics he had selected for the draperies and upholstery of the room; The enclosed essay is a *sample* of my writing.] Most concretely, **illustration** may indicate graphic material that accompanies a written text to supplement it or help explain it: a book on architecture with beautiful *illustrations*; an algebra textbook with numerous *illustrations*. But the word can refer to any citing of specific material to supplement, explain, or demonstrate a thesis or train of thought: He threw in two humorous anecdotes as *illustrations* of his main point. The word can also refer to something that is merely alluded to rather than actually presented: She cited the slaughtering of Albigensians and Incas in *illustration* of her argument that previous attempts at genocide were not uncommon.

Specimen stresses even more than *sample* the physical presence of a representative individual. The word is also clinical in tone, suggesting a laboratory or scientific context: microscopes set up with *specimens* of the four blood types; rock *specimens*; entomological display cases with *specimens* of many insect species. As in the last case, *specimen* can often imply that something is dead or has been killed, but this is not always so: cages to separate the healthy *specimens* from those that had contracted the disease. Beyond the scientific context, the word can apply to anything that seems representative of a type or larger whole: a perfect *specimen* of absurdist fiction; checking the endorsement against other *specimens* of the man's signature. When applied to a person, the word suggests someone noticeably typical, eccentric, or physically impressive; in this use, an ironic tone may be present: a standard *specimen* of the conformist, middle-class liberal; odd *specimens* of underworld life; a girl who was quite a succulent *specimen*; a real *specimen* of a man.

Example is the most general of these words. While it may indicate something physically present as a *specimen*, more often the word suggests the citing of supplementary material, comparable to the similar use of *illustration*. But *example* often implies brief citations given for clarity rather than to corroborate a thesis: a list of *examples* showing faulty and correct constructions in relation to each new grammatical rule. The implication that an *example* is an aid to learning or study comes to the fore when the context is that of discipline: a punishment that was intended to make an *example* of him before the whole class.

Instance points to a concrete *example* or *illustration* of a general thesis, particularly one drawn from the past: asked to cite *instances* of oligarchic rule in European history. The word can also refer to an isolated or minor occurrence in the present: scattered *instances* of rioting even after the major flare-ups were over. Sometimes, the word can refer to exceptions rather than typical *samples*: a few *instances* of disagreement at the otherwise harmonious meeting. Or the word can apply to details that are part of an occurrence, even when no general thesis is

sample

case
example
illustration
instance
specimen

being proven or defended: noting *instances* of the crowd's behavior as it heard the news. **Case** can function vaguely in place of other words here, but it may particularly refer to a greater body of material looked at in some detail: a presentation of *cases* in which an open conflict existed between the king and the papacy. By contrast, the word can refer to a whole argument rather than to its *examples*: his *case* for nuclear disarmament; the district attorney's *case* against the suspect. It can also refer to a specific medical or psychiatric *instance*: his analysis of some hundred terminal cancer *cases*. The word often suggests any significant or unusual body of details that is isolated for intensive study because of its puzzling or controversial nature: the strange *case* of Mark Twain; an investigation of alleged *cases* of levitation by Hindu gurus. See COPY, COUNTERPART, DUPLICATE, PROTOTYPE.

sanitary

antiseptic
aseptic
hygienic
sterile

These words refer to what is healthful, clean, germ-free, or germ destroying. **Sanitary**, the most informal of these, pertains mostly to what preserves or is favorable to health, particularly by virtue of its cleanliness. But since it has a quasi-medical tone and suggests a degree of cleanliness quite beyond that of the word clean, it can also imply a germ-free condition: A common drinking cup may be clean without being *sanitary*. **Hygienic** is much broader in scope than *sanitary*; in referring to things preserving or promoting health, it can refer more readily than *sanitary* to other aspects of healthfulness than those pertaining to cleanliness or freedom from germs: stressing that moderate exercise is *hygienic*. But it can refer generally to freedom from germs where the additional implications of extreme cleanliness in *sanitary* would be inappropriate: It is not *hygienic* to have a well situated on lower ground than a cesspool.

The remaining words relate exclusively to the absence or destruction of germs causing disease or infection. **Sterile** refers particularly to things made free of germs: *sterile* bandages; using only *sterile* instruments during the operation; precautions to make sure the wound remained *sterile*. **Aseptic** refers especially to the absence of germs from living tissue, or to the absence of putrefactive infection; in this, it is restricted to one aspect of *sterile*, with a gain in precision. This lack of infection, however, may be fortuitous rather than induced: a cut that had luckily remained *aseptic*; using *sterile* instruments so that the incision would be *aseptic*. **Antiseptic** can also refer to something kept *sterile* against germs or infection, including living tissue, though it applies to other things as well. In its particular area of relevance, however, it points to the counteracting of infections by the actual destruction of germs that may already be present: an *antiseptic* solution of sodium perborate. See CLEAN (adj.), HEALTHFUL, SANITIZE.
Antonyms: DIRTY, *noxious, polluted, soiled, unsanitary.*

sanitize

decontaminate
disinfect
fumigate
sterilize

These words mean to clean something so as to free it of germs, pests, or other unhealthful encroachments. **Sanitize** indicates thorough cleaning, with the implication that anything unfavorable to health has been removed, especially anything that might spread infection or disease: a ruling that secondhand clothes must be *sanitized* before being resold; an ultraviolet unit for *sanitizing* toilet seats. **Sterilize** specifically suggests the destruction of germs, that is, bacteria or microorganisms that cause infection or disease: the high temperatures used to *sterilize* surgical instruments; *sterilizing* the wound by applying antiseptic. **Disinfect** is even more specific, for though it indicates the same action as *sterilize*, the word implies the presence of an infection or of infection-causing germs: a liquid designed for *disinfecting* toilet bowls; an antibiotic that would act to *disinfect* the inflamed tissue.

Fumigate means to subject to smoke or fumes in order to kill germs or insect pests: to *fumigate* a sickroom to prevent the spread of contagion; to *fumigate* an apartment by spraying it with insecticides. **Decontaminate** may sometimes apply in a general way. It has gained a specific meaning, however, that refers to the destroying or neutralizing of poisonous chemicals or radioactivity that has pervaded an area: teams sent in to *decontaminate* all but the central area irradiated by the atomic explosion. See CLEAN, SANITARY.

Antonyms: POLLUTE, SOIL.

sarcastic

biting
caustic
cutting
sardonic

These words refer to sharp, contemptuous behavior toward someone, especially when it is of a verbal nature. **Sarcastic**, which comes from a root meaning to tear flesh or to sneer, describes a person, statement, expression, attitude, or tone of voice that is heavily ironic to the point of being snide. A *sarcastic* comment is generally scornful or taunting in tone, often expressing the opposite of what it literally says. The word *sarcastic*, in fact, often points to obnoxious arrogance, lacerating mockery, or wryly contemptuous teasing. By contrast, **sardonic**, which comes from a root that refers to a poison causing fatal, laughterlike convulsions, emphasizes a less direct or aggressive approach in favor of a mocking or sneering attitude that may be witty, ironic, or laughter-provoking. Where *sarcastic* suggests an attempt to express and inspire contempt, *sardonic* stresses the intent to ridicule. Also, *sarcastic* suggests single, ad hominem utterances, whereas *sardonic* may suggest a more far-reaching general attitude of somber cynicism that is not always directed at a person: his *sarcastic* remarks about the "speed" and "competence" of the waiters; his *sardonic* view of the possibilities for social reform; She kept her audience in stitches with the *sardonic* quips she tossed off half-consciously under her breath; meeting the students' brash, *sarcastic* laughter with a chilling, *sardonic* smile.

Biting refers most specifically to remarks alone, but suggests incisive or telling utterances that may express animus but need not be personal in intent: a *biting* critique of bureaucratic inefficiency. **Cutting** is close to *biting*, but here the word specifically indicates a harsh, personal rejection: a *cutting* remark on his bad manners; turning away from him with a *cutting* disdain. **Caustic** comes from a Greek root meaning to burn. It points to a critical attitude that is so sharp in its expression as to be searing, scathing, or corrosive: the *caustic* satires of an angry, embittered author; a brilliant critic whose *caustic* wit made him many enemies. See CONTEMPTUOUS, RIDICULE, SCOFF, SOUR.

Antonyms: complimentary, FAVORABLE, *flattering.*

satisfy

answer
ease
fill
fulfill
meet
palliate

These words are concerned with an adequate response to a foregoing requirement, need, or expectation. **Satisfy** can be applied in all three cases, stressing in each the completeness with which something measures up to standards set in advance: *satisfying* the requirements for a Master's Degree; unable to *satisfy* a craving for pickles; a movie that could hardly *satisfy* the claims made for it during its publicity buildup. **Fulfill** functions in all three settings and may also suggest thoroughness of response; its special overtone, however, implies a more-than-mediocre performance or one that is profound or that sets high standards: *fulfilling* the duties and obligations of his post with distinction; imaginative play projects that would *fulfill* the need for creative experimentation;

high expectations that were ultimately *fulfilled*. In each of these cases, *satisfy* might suggest adequacy, but only *fulfill* would imply going beyond set boundaries.

Answer, **fill**, and **meet** are more like *satisfy* than *fulfill* in suggesting adequacy, but no more. *Answer* suggests an exact matching of candidate and specifications: a young executive who would *answer* these requirements. If the specifications are demanding, of course, *answering* them might be a measure of excellence more than a mere proof of adequacy: a director who interviewed hundreds of ingénues before he found one who could *answer* to the special demands of the role. *Fill* applies best to the situation of eradicating a lack and may leave the question of performance entirely open: She was hired to *fill* a vacancy on the staff, but despite first-rate recommendations, it turned out that she didn't *satisfy* our expectations. *Meet*, more than any of the foregoing, may suggest a minimal measuring up to pre-set standards, or the difficulty of attaining them: They barely *met* the deadline; drinking just enough water to *meet* the minimum weight restriction for paratroopers. It may also stress reluctance or suggest an either-or conditional: *meeting* his demands with an air of unwilling surrender; They refused to negotiate unless three preliminary conditions were *met*.

Ease and **palliate** apply only to the situation of responding to a lack, both stressing that it is partially *filled* but not wholly *satisfied*: Troops were flown in to *ease* the shortage of rescue workers. *Palliate* is even more negative than *ease*, suggesting the lack has been disguised or concealed but not altered in any basic way: laws that have *palliated* the disease of segregation without curing it. See ADEQUATE, SURFEIT, TREAT.

Antonyms: miss, refuse, worsen.

save

deliver
ransom
redeem
rescue

These words are comparable in meaning to free a person or thing from some dangerous or unfavorable situation or condition. **Save** is a general word with broad application. It can refer to the help which is offered when a person or thing has already been subjected to some kind of danger or threat of injury: diving into the lake to *save* a drowning child. It can designate the protective measures taken to ward off an impending disaster: inoculating a community to *save* it from the threat of a full-scale influenza epidemic. In less serious situations, *save* can suggest the careful treatment employed to avoid fatigue, damage, etc.: Help *save* your eyesight by the use of good lighting. In all these senses, *save* goes beyond the immediate helpful action to suggest the preservation of the person or thing which is *saved* for further life or use. *Save* also has a theological reference to a freedom from spiritual death or the consequences of sin: a firm belief that his soul would be *saved* only by devoting his life to works of charity.

The sense of **deliver** being compared here is rather formal in tone and is almost never used in reference to things. Like *save*, it means to free or protect from some real or potential danger, harm, etc.: Only the most dedicated work on the part of his attorney *delivered* the condemned man from prison.

Ransom and **redeem** are alike in denoting the securing of the release of a person or thing from bondage, captivity, detention, pawn, or any like condition, upon payment of a sum of money or some figurative equivalent. *Ransom* has special relevance to the release arranged for a kidnaped person: willing to pay any price to *ransom* their infant son. *Redeem* commonly suggests the recovering of something through payment of a sum of money: to *redeem* mortgaged property; to *redeem* a pawned typewriter. In theological contexts, *redeem* has specific reference to Christ's salvation of mankind from the power and penalties of sin by his death upon the Cross.

Rescue is interchangeable with the first meaning of *save* in its implication of aid to someone who is in imminent danger: brave firemen *rescuing* people from a burning building. Less commonly, it refers to the protective measures used to *save* something that is being threatened by injury or destruction: steps taken to *rescue* the tenement from decay. See CONSERVE, HELP, RECOVER, REPAIR.

Antonyms: DESTROY, HARM, *lose*, SENTENCE.

These words all signify sharp in smell, taste, or flavor. **Savory, tangy**, and **piquant** mean pleasantly sharp in taste. *Savory* emphasizes most strongly the agreeable nature of the taste, and in a related sense means appetizing, whether sharp in taste or not: to eat every *savory* morsel of a delectable stew. *Piquant* suggests tartness and emphasizes vividness of taste and strength of flavor. *Tangy* usually implies a touch or impression of tartness rather than a heavy or long-lasting dose: a *tangy* soft drink. It is mild in force, and is more common in informal contexts than either *savory* or *piquant*. In extended senses *savory* can refer to anything eagerly received: a *savory* bit of gossip. *Piquant* suggests something that is lively and charming, and therefore of compelling interest: a *piquant* account of a contretemps with a Parisian butcher; Audrey Hepburn has a *piquant* quality that endears her to many filmgoers.

Spicy means highly flavored, and usually but not necessarily implies that the strong seasoning is pleasant: a *spicy* dish that included red pepper and horse radish; so *spicy* that we had to gulp water after every bite. In its figurative sense *spicy* means somewhat improper or risqué, and implies that certain included details are used to pique interest as spices are used to enhance flavor: a *spicy* story of the loves of a Hollywood actress.

Anything acrid or prickly to the senses is said to be **pungent**. A *pungent* odor is not only strong, but keen and penetrating: the *pungent* smell of smoking punk; The *pungent* odor of sulphur resembles that of rotten eggs. *Pungent* writing is colorful, sardonic, or sarcastic, and is characterized by a piercing or penetrating quality that is at once memorable and forceful. [The *pungent* style of H. L. Mencken left its mark on American letters; a *pungent* satire of middle-class mating customs.] See SMELL, TASTY.

Antonyms: BLAND, *insipid, tasteless*.

These verbs have to do with the utterance of words or the expression of meaning. **Say** is the least formal and most general word. It may refer either to speech or writing, and it is used both in direct and indirect quotation. ["I'm tired," he *said*; The paper *says* that it might rain.] In one sense, *say* is limited to the exact words pronounced or written: I can tell you what he *said*, but you will have to figure out what he meant. In another sense, however, *say* is not concerned with words themselves so much as with any means of conveying thoughts and feelings: *Say* it with flowers; a lot of words to *say* very little; with only a smile to *say* how much she missed him. Where *say* stresses content, **speak** is limited to vocal utterance. This verb may indicate the basic power to make sounds or utter words: A mute cannot *speak*. Or it may mean to talk or make a speech. [He *spoke* of you; What did he *say*?; The lecturer *spoke* for over an hour.] *Speak* may also imply a working knowledge of

savory

piquant
pungent
spicy
tangy

say

communicate
speak
state
verbalize

language, the ability to use words properly in conversation. [Do you *speak* French?; *Say* something in Spanish.]

State emphasizes both content and tone. It suggests a formal declaration of fact set forth explicitly in speech or writing. [*State* your name, rank, and serial number; The witness *stated* that he saw the accused at the scene of the crime; That stipulation is *stated* in the contract.] One may *state* such things as reasons, requirements, facts, claims, or conditions. [*State* your case; *State* your business here.] One may *speak* words, lines, or speeches as well as languages: words *spoken* in anger; a *speaking* part in the play; *Speak* your piece. One may *say* words or things (in general) and prayers (in particular). [If you can't *say* something nice, don't *say* anything at all; Never *say* die; *Say* the password; *Say* yes; He is *saying* his prayers.]

Where *speak* stresses the uttering of words, **verbalize** stresses the putting of thoughts into words — the ability to articulate ideas or experience. Properly used, *verbalize* implies a certain fluency, the power to pin down precisely or formulate something that is hard to express: The mystic found it hard, if not impossible, to *verbalize* his philosophical position. But the formal *verbalize* seems highly pretentious and out of place when wrongly used as a synonym for express: He found it hard to express (not to *verbalize*) his feelings for her. In another, more common sense, to *verbalize* is to speak or write verbosely, wearying the reader or listener with wordiness at the expense of wit: a pompous old windbag given to empty *verbalizing*.

Communicate focuses on the ability of one person to make contact with another and to make himself understood. Language is an effective medium of *communicating*, but only when the speaker or writer is able to convey a message, to get across what he means. A person *speaking* Spanish, for example, is unable to *communicate* with a person who *speaks* only English. And an expert who may have an impressive command of technical jargon may lack the broad-based language skills needed to *communicate* knowledge to laymen. One may *communicate*, however, not only through speech or writing but also through looks or gestures, signals or codes: prisoners who *communicate* by tapping on the walls; psychiatrists who try to *communicate* with the mentally ill. *Speak* may also imply recognition, an attempt or willingness to *communicate* by talking or making a sound. [*Speak* to me; *Say* something; They aren't on *speaking* terms and they *communicate* through an intermediary.] In a more sophisticated sense, *communicate* stresses the technological transmission of information or ideas. Men now *communicate* over long distances by means of telephone, telegraph, radio, television, and satellite. See CONVERSATION, SPEECH, TELL, UTTER.

scanty

inadequate
insufficient
meager
scarce
skimpy
sparse

All of these adjectives describe things that are limited in quantity or deficient in amount. What is **scanty** is barely adequate or not quite enough, whereas what is **meager** is not nearly enough. A *scanty* meal may be ordered by a dieter, whereas a *meager* meal suggests the pinch of poverty and may be poor in quality as well as small in amount. **Skimpy** is a more informal term than *meager*. Unlike *scanty*, *skimpy* indicates deliberate stinginess, often suggesting that more could or should be provided. *Skimpy*, thus, often implies disapproval or dissatisfaction, while *scanty* may suggest a more serious deficiency: a pretty *skimpy* serving considering that it was a $50-a-plate dinner; a *scanty* stock of emergency provisions. *Meager* is expressive of real want, implying that more is not only desirable but is badly needed: The social worker claimed that it was impossible for the old man to live on his *meager* pension.

Insufficient and **inadequate** are limited by definition to what is not enough to fill requirements or meet needs. These words are less descriptive than *scanty*, *skimpy*, and *meager*, but they are broader in application and better suited to formal contexts, being applied to abstractions as well as to material things: The urchin's *scanty* clothing was *insufficient* for the winter, affording him *inadequate* protection against the cold. Although *insufficient* and *inadequate* are often used interchangeably, *insufficient* is a purely quantitative term, being applied to what is not enough, whereas *inadequate* may be qualitative as well, being applied to what is not good enough. *Insufficient* evidence can only mean not enough evidence, but *inadequate* evidence can mean either that the evidence is *insufficient* or that it is of dubious quality.

Sparse and **scarce** also refer to what is not abundant, but they have to do with occurrence and do not necessarily involve need. *Sparse* is opposed to dense or thick, describing what is widely scattered in isolated clumps: *sparse* vegetation; a *sparse* crowd scattered thinly through the auditorium. What is *scarce* is in short supply temporarily, hard to get at a given time or in a given place: During World War II, sugar was *scarce* and was rationed. See LACK.

Antonyms: ADEQUATE, PREVALENT.

These words mean to separate and distribute widely. **Scatter** is the most general word of this group, and simply indicates the act of driving away or throwing about in different directions. [The wind *scatters* seed everywhere; With one bound the cat *scattered* the flock of pigeons.] **Broadcast** and **disseminate** both suggest the *scattering* of seed, but *disseminate* is now used exclusively in figurative senses, whereas *broadcast* retains its literal meaning of sowing by *scattering*: to *broadcast* seed. In a related sense *broadcast* and *disseminate* both mean to make public or publish: to *broadcast* gossip; to *disseminate* the Gospel. *Disseminate* is broader in scope than *broadcast* and implies a wider audience and usually a longer duration: a lifetime of *disseminating* knowledge and spiritual guidance to those in need of it. *Broadcast*, on the other hand, may indicate only a single occurrence of making something public; in the sense here considered it has a decidedly formal tone and sounds more appropriate in old-fashioned contexts than in contemporary ones: It was indelicate of the man to *broadcast* the intelligence that his wife was cuckolding him. Of course today *broadcast* has become more widely used to refer to the transmission of sounds by radio or television: a radio station that *broadcasts* news every hour on the hour; to *broadcast* a prize fight. Although *broadcast* is used of television as well as radio, "telecast," formed on analogy with *broadcast*, and the more common "televise" seem in time likely to replace it in such contexts.

Diffuse emphasizes the relationship between the area covered and the relative density of the material spread out over it: the greater the area, the lower the density of the material. [The cloud cover *diffused* the light of the sun; The *diffused* light of the candles on every table lent a pleasant, intimate air to the restaurant.] Whereas *diffused* often indicates a graduated lessening of intensity over a broad area, **disperse** suggests a wide and sometimes forcible *scattering* of elements or individual things: The mounted police quickly *dispersed* the unruly crowd. *Disperse* is often used figuratively: to *disperse* doubts and fears and instill confidence. See DIVIDE, PERMEATE, SPREAD.

Antonyms: GATHER, UNITE.

scatter

broadcast
diffuse
disperse
disseminate

scoff

gibe
jeer
sneer
taunt

These words mean to show one's disapproval or scorn by making remarks intended to belittle or disparage. To a greater or lesser extent, all of them have a hostile intent. To **scoff** is to speak slightingly and with derision of something usually accorded honor, reverence, or respect by people in general: to *scoff* at someone's fervent patriotism; to *scoff* at advice given by one's elders; to *scoff* at the teachings of a church.

Sneer carries a much stronger feeling of cynicism, superciliousness, and the deliberate wish to wound. To *sneer* is to make a contemptuous contortion of the facial muscles while uttering brief, cutting remarks that are intended to cast an unfavorable light on whatever is being attacked: to *sneer* at an adolescent's attempts to be grown-up and independent; to *sneer* at the furniture in someone's home.

Jeer means to *scoff* in a rude and open way. It carries the suggestion of mocking laughter and even shouting or booing: During the French Revolution crowds in the street *jeered* at the prisoners being driven to the guillotine.

Gibe and **taunt** mean to rail at someone with sarcastic and contemptuous remarks: During the radio interview, the critic *gibed* at the young novelist for imitating Hemingway's style in his work. *Gibe*, however, also retains some of the meaning residing in its French derivation — "to treat roughly in play" — and *gibing* may also be good-natured bantering or twitting: The two old men who met daily on the park bench constantly *gibed* at one another about their political opinions. *Taunt* is a stronger word than *gibe*. It means to insult and upbraid in a defiant way and also carries overtones of reproach: The fifth-grade pupils *taunted* the new boy because he spoke broken English and did not know how to play softball. As in *gibe*, there may be an element of teasing in *taunt*, but such teasing is likely to be harsh and cruel. See DESPISE, LAUGH, RIDICULE, SARCASTIC.

Antonyms: PRAISE.

scold

berate
chide
upbraid

These words pertain to the criticizing of one person by another. **Scold** is the most general and least formal of these. Often it can suggest an instance of reproof for misbehavior that is meted out by a superior, such as a parent or teacher: She *scolded* the child for being late to school. In this situation, the word may specifically imply a distinction between a verbal reproach and reprimands that actually involve some form of punishment. Because of this, the word can sometimes suggest ineffectual attempts at discipline: She *scolded* her children frequently, but made no attempt to correct their unruly behavior. *Scold* can even suggest continual nagging to no purpose, whether about serious faults or about trivialities; here, the relationship need not be between superior and inferior: a woman who constantly *scolded* her husband about the low pay he earned.

Chide, more formal than *scold*, is more exclusively focused on reproofs for specific failings. It can, however, suggest a wider range of emotional contexts, ranging in reference from angry rebukes or taunts to charitable efforts to help someone surmount his shortcomings: gently *chiding* his students every time they misspelled a word; the fury with which he *chided* the legislators for their lack of compassion.

Upbraid stresses the lengthy expression of displeasure or criticism, often of a total performance rather than a single failing. This may take the form of a harangue, a tongue-lashing, or less severely, a pep-talk exhorting someone toward better behavior. [He *upbraided* his wife about the sloppy way she kept track of their charge accounts; The coach *upbraided* his team for the way they had bungled play after play in the first half of the game.]

Berate can be used in a vague way for the administering of any sort of reproof, but more often it can suggest the total rejection of something or someone as being valueless, a judgment that can be delivered with no view to improving future performance. In this case, the word can also suggest an attitude of scorn or contempt for the thing being criticized, which is more often a whole pattern or way of life than a single instance of misbehavior: a young man who *berated* his parents for their middle-class values. [A teacher who *berates* and belittles his students is only admitting his inability to teach them anything.] See DISAPPROVAL, FAULTFINDING, MALIGN, REBUKE, SHREW.

Antonyms: PRAISE.

scoop

bail
dig
ladle
shovel
spoon

These verbs all describe the use of implements in moving a substance from one place to another. **Scoop** suggests a twisting or probing motion, often involving a good deal of effort, used to press into a substance and lift part of it out: to *scoop* ice cream out of a container. In informal use *scoop* is also used to mean to gather into a heap, especially hastily: He *scooped* up the coins, thrust them in his pocket, and ran away.

Dig is the most general word of this group, and can be applied to any vigorous act of pressure or penetration: He *dug* a finger into my ribs menacingly. In its primary sense, however, *dig* means to break up, turn up, or remove earth, as with an implement, claws, or fingers. [Gophers keep *digging* up the soil; He *dug* at the ground with the heel of his shoe; The workmen *dug* up the street with deafening pneumatic drills.] *Dig*, unlike *scoop*, suggests a straight thrust into a substance, and whereas *scoop* emphasizes the process of lifting out, *dig* usually emphasizes the going in. [The cook *scooped* out some sugar and sprinkled it over the cake; to *dig* up buried treasure.] Also, *scoop* suggests open or shallow indentations in a surface, whereas *dig* can apply to any sort of excavation: *digging* miles of underground tunnels.

Shovel suggests a laborious, regularly repeated *digging* motion with a long-handled implement. *Shoveling* is hard work, and typically involves the movement of something which does not easily yield or which is heavy, such as earth, rock, snow, and the like. The tools used to *shovel* vary in size from children's toys to huge, toothed, power-driven devices used on construction sites for moving mounds of earth and boulders; therefore, the word *shoveling* in isolation indicates very little about the quantity *shoveled*.

Spoon and **ladle** point to the transferal of liquids from one vessel to another, as from a pot to a bowl. *Spooning* suggests more diminutive portions than *ladling*, which can indicate gross, careless, or hasty disposal of a substance: to *spoon* out medicine in carefully measured quantities; *ladling* out soup to a mob of hungry people. **Bail**, unlike the other words here considered, indicates a particular situation and purpose, that of emptying a boat of water to keep it from becoming swamped: After each wave, all hands started *bailing* with buckets, pans, shoes — anything that would hold water.

scoundrel

cad

These words refer to unprincipled people, especially men, who are unethical or immoral in their behavior, particularly for their own gain or pleasure. **Scoundrel** is the strongest term here, referring to someone who will stop at nothing to gain his own ends. Though a *scoundrel*, by implication, often works by subterfuge, lies, and deception, the word's

scoundrel

(continued)

heel
knave
rascal
rogue
scalawag
scamp

strong disapproval suggests the actual harming of other people in cruel or needless ways: a *scoundrel* who sold substandard concrete for a school building, which later collapsed, killing numbers of school children. The word is losing some of its force, however, and can now be applied as a term of endearment for someone who is brash, dauntless, or impetuous in his life or affections: admitting that she liked the *scoundrel* for the brazen way he chased after her.

Heel has recently become the most popular informal term here for any person one disapproves of, especially one who may not act illegally but who offends common decency in some way. Heinous offenses are not necessarily implied by the word, however: acting like a perfect *heel* in promising to meet her and then standing her up cold. **Cad** now gives a nineteenth century flavor and is seldom used except comically. It once specifically suggested a man who treated women without respect: a *cad* who ruined her virtue and then refused to marry her. **Knave** is even more archaic in flavor, referring to any liar, cheater, deceiver, or *scoundrel*. Once as strong in condemnation as *scoundrel*, the word is now weak-sounding and seldom used: a sly *knave*, always scheming.

The remaining words are vague about the offenses committed by the person referred to; the words, in fact, may suggest disreputable or unfeeling people rather than those committed to outright immorality or villainy. **Rascal** suggests an amoral person, usually a man, who treats standards of conduct lightly and is inconsiderate of the feelings of others when these stand in the way of his desires: a *rascal* who went about cadging drinks from everyone at the bar. The word often suggests an appealing eccentric or curmudgeon and is often used affectionately as a way of accepting the peccadillos of a loved one: never dreaming that the handsome *rascal* she was dating would end up marrying her. The word is also used for infants or pets, implying a lovable liveliness or cuteness: obvious by his cries that it was the little *rascal's* feeding time; teaching the comical *rascal* to beg for scraps. **Scamp** suggests a high-spirited or wandering rake or good-for-nothing who seeks amusement, pleasure, or gain regardless of the consequences. Used unfavorably, the word denotes a tricky or evasive fellow — a schemer and a cheat. Sometimes, however, it is applied endearingly to a playful pet or to a person given to pranks or escapades: The puppies were happy little *scamps*.

Scalawag is now a half-admiring word for any amoral seizer of pleasures, one who may disregard niceties or decorum. The word was once more opprobrious, like *scoundrel*. It was originally a term of contempt used by Southern Democrats for native Southern whites who were Republicans during Reconstruction — thus suggesting someone who was disloyal, unprincipled, and willing to do anything to get ahead. Now, like other words here, it can be used in vague ways as an affectionate term: smiling as she upbraided the darling little *scalawag*. **Rogue**, like *knave*, was once strongly disapproving but now has chiefly an archaic flavor that makes it seldom used except comically or endearingly to describe a zesty, brawling, devil-may-care reveler: a *rogue* who could always be counted on to cut up at parties and generally cause all sorts of devilment. See DEPRAVED, MISCHIEVOUS, UNETHICAL.

Antonyms: gentleman.

section

area

These words refer to parts of geographical or demographical entities. **Section** is the most general; it can pinpoint a part of a city or country or even some natural formation: the *section* of desert surrounding the oasis. In its demographic sense, it might suggest a homogeneous population: the Spanish-speaking *section* of Harlem. But when the geographic sense predominates, no such limitations are applicable: diverse ethnic groups in that *section* of the country. In surveying, the word can specifically indicate a plot of land that is one mile square, containing 640 acres. **Area** suggests a larger, possibly less clearly defined subdividing of some entity: an *area* of the country that breaks naturally into two *sections* of opposing political attitudes; those *areas* of coastal waters infested by sharks; an *area* of the city where the wealthiest families live. The word can also refer to computed square units: suburbs taking up one-third of the state's total *area*.

Region indicates an even larger subdivision than *area*; it would not be used to refer to a *section* of a city, for example, but would most often suggest a considerable stretch of territory with some unifying principle that distinguishes it from the surrounding territory: the main dialect *regions* of the United States; the Soviet Union's arctic *region*.

The remaining words stress the pinpointing aspect of *section*, suggesting even more clear-cut or smaller subdivisions. **Quarter** refers specifically to a *section* of a city that has a noticeable homogeneity or its own identifying flavor: the French *quarter*; the bohemian *quarter*. **Neighborhood** can indicate most concretely a residential grouping in towns or cities: a friendly *neighborhood*. Its implication of communal peaceableness need not be present: a deteriorating and racially tense *neighborhood*. The word can also be used to indicate something that is merely nearby or adjacent: in the *neighborhood* of an express stop on the subway.

Locale can refer to any pinpointed environment: a *locale* in which fresh water was plentiful. More concretely it can refer to the exact place of an occurrence or event: unable to fix the *locale* where the scuffle took place. It can refer as well to the scene or setting of a work of art: The *locale* of the play was an unnamed Ivy League college; paintings that had Fire Island as their *locale*. See SITE.

These words all denote various types of passenger automobiles. A **sedan**, the most common and popular model of car, is a closed vehicle having two or four doors and a front and back seat. Depending upon its size, it may hold from four to six passengers including the driver. A two-door *sedan* has two seats in the front with folding backs and a full rear seat.

A **convertible** is an automobile with a fabric top that may be folded back in good weather. It is usually the same size as the large sedan and holds the same number of passengers. *Convertibles* differ in body structure from *sedans* or **station wagons** in that they lack the vertical posts between the sides of the body and the roof. The **hardtop**, also called the *hardtop convertible*, resembles the *convertible* in appearance and is similar in structure except that the roof is of rigid metal or heavy plastic. Some *hardtops* are so constructed that the roof may be removed entirely or lowered into a slot at the rear of the back seat.

A *station wagon* is a four-door car which also has a tailgate at the rear. It has two, and in some cases three, rows of seats and may accommodate as many as eight or nine passengers. The *station wagon* differs from the *sedan* and the *convertible* in that the seats behind the driver may be removed or folded flat to make a large level area for carrying baggage or other bulky articles.

The **limousine** is a large, luxurious car, originally having a closed compartment for from three to five passengers (two of whom sit on folding jump seats) and an open driver's seat under a projecting roof. Modern *limousines* now house both driver and passengers under the same

section
(continued)

locale
neighborhood
quarter
region

sedan

compact
convertible
coupe
hardtop
limousine
roadster
sports car
station wagon

roof, although the passengers are separated from the driver by sliding glass panels. *Limousines*, although maintained by some wealthy people who employ chauffeurs to drive them, are more frequently used to carry government officials, people in funeral corteges, etc. Another type of *limousine* is actually a small bus used to transport passengers between large cities or between a city and an airport. Popularly, a *limousine* is any large, shiny, expensive car.

A **sports car** is a low, rakish automobile, usually seating two persons, built for high speed and maneuverability. It is a car perhaps more intended for pleasure driving than for the business of getting from one place to another. *Sports cars* are seldom black.

Roadster and **coupe** are two models of cars now rarely manufactured. The *roadster* was an early type of *sports car* with a folding top and one seat, generally wide enough for only two passengers. Some *roadsters* could accommodate two extra passengers in a rumble seat which folded down into the rear compartment. The *coupe* is a type of car popular in more recent times. It is a closed, two-door automobile with one seat holding two or three passengers and a large space for luggage, either directly behind the seat or in a separate compartment in the rear. Today a two-door *sedan* is sometimes called a club *coupe*.

A **compact** is a small car that nevertheless seats from four to six people; it simply has slightly less space for luggage than conventional *sedans*, and considerably less leg room for the passengers in the rear.

sedate

earnest
grave
serious
sober
solemn
staid

These words apply to anything that lacks or eschews frivolity or merriment because of social restraint, unsparing dedication, or urgent conditions. The emphasis of both **sedate** and **staid** are on restraint in manners or behavior. *Sedate* points to unruffled self-possession and implies a flawless exterior of correctness, politeness, and propriety: a *sedate* gathering of quiet but interesting people; *sedate* matrons who sit supreme and secure in their opera boxes. The word can sometimes apply critically to people or man-made things that are genteel or too refined: the *sedate* indifference of well-bred Victorians to the miseries of the lower classes. But when applied outside the context of human affairs, the word can refer more generally to anything serene or tranquil: the *sedate* hush of Indian summer. *Staid* is now used most commonly in a way comparable to the negative possibility for *sedate*, referring to manners that are straitlaced, unbending, prim, and pompous: plays that shock the sensibilities of *staid* ladies who attend Broadway matinees.

Solemn once could refer almost exclusively to an extremely formal and awe-inspiring religious ritual: a *solemn* requiem mass. This was extended to other rituals or formalities expressing a total commitment: a *solemn* oath; a *solemn* dedication to the cause of freedom. Now the word can also refer to a person or manner that is unleavened by lightheartedness: the *solemn* faces of wives awaiting the results of the mining disaster. As a word of disapproval, it can point to someone needlessly gloomy or lacking in humor: *solemn* parents aghast at the most innocuous amusements of their children.

When applied to a lack of humor, **serious** is much more neutral in tone; depending upon context, it can be approving, strictly factual, or disapproving: a play that he spoke of as the only really *serious* attempt at contemporary drama currently to be seen on Broadway; promising to give the proposal her *serious* consideration; He couldn't bear people who were so *serious* all the time. In a comparable context, **grave** emphasizes an extremely *serious* manner that is intense and unrelieved. It may suggest a concerned, anxious, or troubled state, as well: She gave him a *grave* look that showed how alarmed she was; inspecting his son's report card with a *grave* frown. When both words apply to a state of urgency or crisis, *serious* suggests an uncertain condition that could well result in danger or failure: in *serious* condition following his heart attack. *Grave*, however, may well suggest a state too far gone to expect full recovery, although the word can be applied for emphasis to less extreme conditions: a *grave* lack of food and water on the lifeboat; a *grave* problem facing the nation. Both words can also be used for anything thought extremely bad; in this case, *grave* is again an intensification of *serious*: a *serious* lack of concern for others; a *grave* defiance of the law.

Sober and **earnest** apply more strictly than the foregoing words to human behavior and attitudes alone. *Sober* can refer at its most restricted to someone who is free of the influence of alcohol or psychedelic drugs: a test to determine whether the driver was drunk or *sober*. Used more generally, the word can suggest a wide-eyed, clear-headed approach, particularly in response to a *serious* or *grave* situation: a *sober* look at a growing political danger. It can also indicate unwavering devotion to a task: a life spent in *sober* dedication to the advancement of medicine. *Earnest* stresses this last possibility for *sober* and adds implications of zeal, selflessness, and single-mindedness: the *earnest* pursuit of his studies; *earnest* youngsters who express their idealism by joining the Peace Corps. The word can also apply to a momentary involvement in which someone is engrossed or becomes impassioned: *earnest* attention from his originally restless audience; *earnest* requests for more information during the question period. Neither *sober* nor *earnest* is useful in expressing disapproval for someone who is habitually *solemn* or overly *serious*. See DEDICATE, EAGER, FORMAL.

Antonyms: easy-going, flighty, frivolous, JAUNTY, light-hearted.

These words refer to the attentive viewing of something. **See** is the most general of these, with a wide range of uses outside this context. Here it suggests equally well an accidental or deliberate viewing of an occurrence: happening to *see* the suspect escaping down a side alley; eager to *see* the outcome of the baseball game. Because the word is so general, it carries few connotations beyond those the context may give it. **Watch** stresses attention or fascination. Whether the viewing began by accident or design, *watch* suggests the complete engagement of interest, at least while the watching continues. By contrast, one might *see* something happen and turn away without interest: breathlessly *watching* the spider attempt to spin its web for the third time. *Watch*, furthermore, is common as an imperative, whereas *see* is much less frequently so used: Just *watch* what happens when I press this button.

Look is like *see* in suggesting no particular connotations for the act of viewing something: *looking* lazily out over the city; *looking* frantically for some sign that would indicate where the lost path lay. *Look* is like *watch*, however, in being frequently used as an imperative: *Look* at that lizard over there on that rock. In this use, the word suggests the effort needed to *see* something before it disappears, whereas *watch* in the imperative might suggest a necessary attendance on a whole process about to begin. **Witness**, like *see*, is less frequently used in the imperative, but is more emphatic than *see* about an attentive viewing of a whole experience: coming in time to *witness* the changing of the guard; *witnessing* the whole gun battle from a second-story window. The word may suggest either a deliberate or an accidental viewing.

see

inspect
look
notice
observe
regard
watch
witness

All the remaining words can be used in the imperative as well as the declarative, but in either case, their emphasis on attentiveness is apparent. **Notice** suggests the taking in, almost by chance, of a small detail that may yet be important to some larger pattern: *noticing* that he kept his fist clenched in his pocket as he talked. In the imperative, the word is a call to attend to some small detail that might otherwise be overlooked: *Notice* the small scratch on the handle of this pistol. **Regard** suggests viewing at a distance in a safe, prearranged position or with a definite emotional attitude: *regarding* the movements of the man across the street with suspicion. **Observe** is like *regard* in suggesting a process of viewing something from one or more vantage points, but it implies a detached, almost clinical frame of mind, engrossed in a detailed examination: *observing* the customs of the tribe for two full years. Like *watch*, *observe* in the imperative suggests a process about to unfold. Only its slightly greater formality distinguishes *observe* from *watch* in this usage: *Observe* the expression on her face when she hears the verdict. Of this group of words, **inspect** puts the most emphasis by far on a thorough and detailed examination of something through direct handling or involvement with it: *inspecting* the child's body for any sign of the recurring rash; *Inspect* these photographs of the two murder weapons. See EXAMINE, FIND, PERCEIVE, STUDY.

Antonyms: disregard, ignore, miss, neglect, overlook.

send

deliver
dispatch
forward
ship
transmit

These words refer to the moving of objects or materials from one point to another. **Send** is the least formal and the most general of these words, carrying no implications about what is *sent* or how: *sending* my answer by return mail; *sending* half-a-dozen trunks ahead by boat. With *send*, however, the movement is viewed specifically from the point of origin rather than from its destination: wondering if he ever received the letter I *sent* a month ago.

Dispatch suggests urgency or speed: *dispatching* three fire engines to combat the blaze; *dispatching* a messenger who would give them the news before sundown. The word may also suggest a central agent who assigns vehicles to specific tasks: *dispatching* a fleet of taxicabs by radio to all points in the city. With **deliver**, the movement of an object can be viewed exclusively in terms of the point of destination: Most manufactured goods were *delivered* to San Francisco by water or stagecoach. But in the context of retail selling, the word is often synonymous with *send*: trading only with stores that *deliver*; asking that they *deliver* the groceries in an hour.

Forward and **transmit** imply a movement that is less than direct, for varying reasons. *Forward* suggests an intermediate or incorrect destination from which the object must then travel to its ultimate goal: a variety of Russian goods that are *forwarded* through Sweden; *forwarding* the letter to his new address. *Transmit* may suggest the *sending* of the contents or equivalent of a document or thing, rather than the original itself: *transmitting* the details of the high-level conference to the president himself; *transmitting* the message by ship-to-shore telephone. **Ship** indicates the moving of produce or effects by sea, air, rail, or truck. It now usually suggests a commercial operation and, if effects are involved, transportation that is unaccompanied by the owner himself: left our furniture to be *shipped* after us once we were settled in new quarters; dry goods scheduled to be *shipped* by boxcar or semi-trailers. See GO, MOVE.

Antonyms: keep, receive, retain.

These words are comparable but not closely synonymous when used to refer to a response to a stimulus or to the ability to make such a response. In a technical sense, **sensation** is applicable to an impression originating either from within or from outside of the body and conveyed to the nervous system by the organs of seeing, hearing, touching, tasting, or smelling. However, the word does not necessarily imply an identification of the stimulus: to experience a *sensation* of warmth. In general usage, the meaning of *sensation* is extended to include not only sensing but also the attendant emotional and mental responses: to have a *sensation* that everyone in the room is staring at you; a recollection that brought a *sensation* of sadness.

sensation

feeling
percept
perception
sense

Sense, as here considered, may refer strictly to the physical agencies (taste, touch, sight, hearing, and smell) by or through which a person or animal receives impressions from outside his own organism. In the plural it is applicable to the total awareness of the world around one: After the accident he came to his *senses* in a hospital bed. Whatever one experiences through the *senses* is a *sensation.*

Perception in this context involves interpretation of a stimulus and recognition of the object that produces a *sensation. Perception* is always based on earlier experience and is the process by which one becomes acquainted with his environment. Whereas a *sensation* does not suggest the agency of the mind, *perception* implies that the stimulus creating a *sensation* has been registered, however unconsciously, on the brain — checked in, as it were, like a guest in a hotel.

Percept, closely related in meaning to *perception*, is a term in psychology and is applied to the immediate knowledge and recognition of an external object gained by perceiving it. A dog will have the *sensation* of seeing or even of smelling a chair; he knows that it is an obstacle to be walked around, but he will gain no *percept* or *perception* of what a chair actually is.

Feeling, the most general term in the group, is sometimes used loosely in place of *sense, sensation,* and *perception*. More precisely *feeling* applies to the faculty by which one perceives *sensations* of pain, pressure, heat and cold, contact, etc. It may also refer to kinesthesia — the *perception* of muscular movement, tension, or tone derived from the functioning of nerves connected with muscle tissue, skin, joints, and tendons: After his spinal injury, he had no *feeling* in his legs. See AWARE, EMOTION, OBSERVANT, PERCEIVE.

These words indicate an intelligent and objective approach to problems or behavior that is temperate, fair, and sound. **Sensible** puts less emphasis on intelligence than on common sense; it suggests an attitude that is prudent, calmly controlled, considerate, understanding, and aware of consequences by virtue of distilled experience: the few *sensible* men who refused to indulge in the foolish fads of the day; a *sensible* approach to a controversial subject; the plain, *sensible* people who are the backbone of the nation. **Reasonable** is similar to *sensible* in emphasizing the value of distilled experience; but its connotations are slightly different in suggesting an approach or situation that is fair, just, objective, or unemotional in its avoidance of extremes: a *reasonable* price; *reasonable* men who eschewed the witch-hunting hysteria that was convulsing Salem; asking his son to be *reasonable* about his demands for the family car. Oddly enough, **rational** rather than *reasonable* is the word here that is most emphatic about the value of reason as a guide; this contrasts with the stress on experience implied by the previous words. Most spe-

sensible

lucid
rational
reasonable
sane

cifically, it points to a problem-solving process of thinking that employs valid or logical methods in reaching conclusions: a *rational* way of going about the vast tasks involved in city planning; a *rational* explanation for the enigmatic events surrounding the catastrophe. *Rational* may also indicate a coherent mind, one that is not mentally imbalanced or at the mercy of overpowering emotions: becoming more *rational* as the tranquilizer took effect; psychiatrists who debated if the accused man was *rational* enough to stand trial.

Lucid and **sane** are both directed to this last meaning of *rational*. *Lucid* indicates a mind free of internal pressures or distortions: *lucid* intervals between bouts of catatonic depression. It can refer to a *rational* approach or train of thought that is particularly clear, understandable, or helpful in its simplicity: a *lucid* argument against the theories advanced in the article. *Sane* is commonly used in both ordinary speech and legal terminology to refer to someone who is not psychotic; the word has no usefulness, however, to psychologists: declared to have been *sane* at the time of the murders; struggling to stay *sane* in a mad world. *Sane* also has a use akin to *reasonable* in referring to a fair, just, or *sensible* approach: *sane* legislation to deal with an increasingly urgent problem; *sane* attitudes toward disciplining their children. See ACUMEN, MIND, WORKABLE.

Antonyms: confused, impractical, incoherent, PSYCHOTIC, *unreasonable.*

sentence

condemn
convict
doom

These words have to do with judgment — the finding of guilt and the imposing of punishment. **Sentence** and **convict** are legal words, and both may be nouns as well as verbs. To *sentence* an offender is to state the penalty he must pay for a crime or misdemeanor. To *convict* (kən·vikt′) him is to find him guilty of the offense with which he is charged. A man on trial who has been *convicted* by a jury is then *sentenced* by a judge: He was *convicted* of second-degree murder and was *sentenced* to from twenty years to life in prison. The noun *sentence* denotes the penalty imposed on a defendant. A *sentence* may be pronounced (or a person may be *sentenced*) in cases where guilt is admitted by the accused, is determined by a judge, or is found by a jury: let off with a suspended *sentence* and a light fine; *sentenced* to ninety days; the death *sentence*. The noun *convict* (kon′vikt) is a term applied to a person serving a *sentence* in prison: an escaped *convict*; an ex-*convict*.

Condemn and **doom** imply severe or irrevocable judgments. Where *convict* and *sentence* are factual and neutral, *condemn* and *doom* can express emotional disapproval for excessive punishment or harsh treatment: an innocent man *condemned* to die; *doomed* by a tissue of circumstantial evidence. The connotations of these words can be misused by defense lawyers or crime reporters to win sympathy or to bolster a sensational approach. *Condemn*, however, has a more neutral use to indicate something that does not measure up to official minimum standards of health and decency: a building *condemned* as a health hazard. Sometimes, the word's disapproval in official use has advisory rather than legal force: The local bar association *condemned* the lawyer's actions but did not disbar him. *Doom*, referring originally to Doomsday, the day of the last judgment, can still sometimes suggest supernatural powers believed to determine man's fate: *doomed* to hell for his profligate life.

When *condemn* and *doom* apply more widely, *condemn* is still likely to carry implications of a conscious and overt man-made judgment that is harsh, excessive, and cruel: Jews *condemned* to concentration camps. *Doom*, by contrast, stresses hopelessness and inevitability that may be the result of deplorable circumstances as well as covert human callousness: Negro children *doomed* to ghetto life. See CONFINE, DISAPPROVAL, KILL.

Antonyms: EXONERATE, *free, liberate.*

These words refer to emotionalism that is excessive, unrealistic, false, or affected. **Sentimental** once could refer neutrally or approvingly to the capacity for feeling deeply about serious matters; it is occasionally still used approvingly, though even here it applies to more trivial emotions, particularly to nostalgia: She kept the ribbon from her corsage as a *sentimental* remembrance of her first formal dance. Otherwise, the word is widely understood as disapproving in tone, pertaining to an inappropriate willingness to be moved at the slightest prompting or by situations that do not warrant genuine feeling. The word does not censure all feeling, only that which is trivial, forced, or excessive; no one would think it *sentimental* to weep at the death of a friend; most people, on the other hand, would think it *sentimental* to supply a funeral and tombstone for, say, a pet canary that had died. **Romantic** has gone through a similar shift, although the split in meaning still exists. It once referred to the expression of deep feeling, or the valuing of feeling above form. As such, it names an artistic era or indicates works of art from any era that display this legitimate emphasis. Those who legitimately prefer a different emphasis, however, can use the word disapprovingly to point to chaotic or formless emotionality: *romantic* blithering about originality and artistic freedom. On a much less formal level, the word can refer descriptively or approvingly to things pertaining to love between a man and woman: glances that hinted of his *romantic* interest in her.

Effusive and **gushing** both refer to copious displays of any sort of emotion. *Effusive* may be approving or neutral: *effusive* in their thanks for their host's hospitality. More often, it emphasizes excessive or insincere displays: finding his *effusive* flattery unbearable. With *gushing*, only disapproval is possible, pointing with more severity to extreme or silly displays: the *gushing* sob sisters that keep alive the traditions of yellow journalism. **Mushy** at its most informal suggests contempt for *romantic* love: typical for preadolescent boys to reject any interest in girls as being *mushy*. It can also suggest a rejection of trivial or *sentimental* attitudes toward such emotions: a *mushy* love story. **Slushy** is even more critical of such attitudes toward love than *mushy*. It suggests a rejection of love seen as occasions for self-pity, weeping, and a *sentimental* evasion of reality: the standard *slushy*, sudsy soap opera.

Maudlin and **mawkish** are considerably more formal than the previous pair and more specific in meaning. *Maudlin* derives ultimately from the second name of Mary Magdalene, who was often depicted with her eyes swollen from weeping; the word now suggests strong disapproval for excessive emotionalism, especially of a tearful sort: a *maudlin* tearjerker that ran as a serial in a woman's magazine. *Mawkish* emphasizes the falsity of excessive emotions, their awkwardness and feebleness, or their offense against good taste. Unlike *maudlin*, it applies to any sort of emotion, and is even stronger in its pejorative overtones: *mawkish* appeals to the stock responses and prejudices of his audiences. See BANAL.

Antonyms: cynical, IMPERTURBABLE, *objective, realistic, sardonic, unmoved.*

These words refer to the breaking down of a grouping into smaller units. They are all alike in suggesting some division other than a splitting into equal halves. **Separate** is the most general in suggesting either a sorting

sentimental

effusive
gushing
maudlin
mawkish
mushy
romantic
slushy

separate

separate
(continued)

detach
disconnect
disengage
dismember
disunite

out of items from an amorphous mixture or the taking apart of things intimately joined or fused: *separating* the scored examination papers into percentile groupings; *separating* the whites and yolks of three eggs. Used intransitively, *separate* may also stress volition: members of the tour who wished to *separate* from the main group in order to go on side-excursions.

Detach and **disconnect** are restricted mostly to the taking apart of solid objects that retain their individual identities after the separation: *detaching* the check from its stub; *disconnecting* the lamp from the wall socket. *Detach* specifically suggests the removing of a part from a larger whole, especially when the two are designed to come apart as an added convenience in their functioning: *detaching* the bayonet from his rifle so that he could use it as a machete; *detaching* one platoon as a backstop for the rest of the company. *Disconnect* does not suggest this part-from-whole relationship so much as it indicates the separation of linked objects or components: *disconnecting* the turntable in order to plug in the tape recorder. In more general uses, *detach* may suggest simply the removal of a small part from a larger mass: *detaching* the snail from the glass wall of the aquarium. *Disconnect* may suggest any loss of contact: complaining to the telephone operator that they had been *disconnected*.

Disengage may suggest withdrawal from contact, especially from a close-fitting, interlocking, or intermingled union: *disengaging* the pieces of the puzzle; *disengaging* himself from the pressures of the crowd. It may also suggest taking something out of operation: *disengaging* the safety catch on the pistol.

Dismember and **disunite** stress a deleterious breaking apart. *Dismember* suggests removing a part from a whole, but contrasts strongly with *detach* in rejecting the implication of a designed or normal uncoupling: *dismembering* the butterfly by pulling off its wings. *Disunite* suggests most specifically the breaking up of an amorphous group so that it can no longer function as an entity, even though no visible rupture may have taken place: a political party so *disunited* from within that it was unable to agree on an election platform. *Disunite*, alone of these words, would almost always suggest a breaking down into many smaller units: internal dissension designed only to *disunite* us and turn us into a dozen squabbling factions. See SEVER.

Antonyms: combine, CONNECT, consolidate, engage.

sequence

progression
series
succession

These words are alike in denoting a group of things which come or are brought together in some particular order or according to a plan. The words are further alike in that the order they refer to is one in which the things grouped together follow each other. **Sequence** designates a following in space, time, or thought, and suggests that the things brought together are done so according to some logical system: making sure the chassis parts were added in proper *sequence*; the *sequence* of arguments in a discourse. **Succession** emphasizes the following, one after the other, of similar objects or events, without interruption. Unlike *sequence*, *succession* can, but does not necessarily, imply a logical ordering: a *succession* of hereditary kings; a *succession* of catastrophes.

Progression fixes the attention chiefly upon the act, process, or state of moving forward, and has particular reference to mathematics and music. A mathematical *progression* is a *sequence* of numbers or quantities, each of which is derived from the preceding by a constant relationship. Musical *progression* can designate either a *succession* of tones, chords, etc., or the movement from one tone or chord to another.

A **series** is a number of things ordered or arranged according to a similarity of nature or on the basis of like relationships. Although it is therefore very much like *sequence* or *succession, series* suggests the individuality of the connected things rather than the mere fact that they follow one another: a long *series* of successes in the theater. See ORGANIZE.

These words refer to the breaking or cutting apart of something by force. **Sever** is a formal term for any such action, though it often specifically suggests the cutting of a part from a larger whole: an accident which *severed* his left leg; being sure to *sever* auxiliary shoots from a plant so that they will not take strength away from the main stem. **Sunder** is an even more formal word for forceful separation, but it more often pertains to breaking something into two halves or equals. The word is now rarely used except in metaphorical senses: a civil war that *sundered* father from son and brother from brother.

sever

cleave
split
sunder

Split may suggest any forceful cutting or tearing action: *splitting* rails with a sharp ax; *splitting* his pants when he bent over. In one of it senses, however, it relates closely to **cleave**, since both words can refer to a voluntary separation within an entity, usually into equal halves: the way cells *split* during mitosis; a club that *split* up after the group's graduation. Where *split* is informal, often extremely so, *cleave* is nearly as formal as the first pair and may, most specifically, suggest a biological context: when the egg begins to *cleave* after fertilization. The word can be confusing, though, since it can apply to clinging fast as well as to breaking apart. Outside the biological context, the word, like *sunder*, is mostly used as a metaphor: the ship's prow, gaily *cleaving* the waves. More specifically, the word can refer to the cutting action of such an instrument as a meat cleaver: carefully *cleaving* the loin cuts into equal portions. See DIVIDE, HEW, PIERCE, SEPARATE, TEAR.

Antonyms: CONNECT, *fuse.*

These words refer to small groups of more than two members. **Several** emphasizes the fact that more than two are involved; **few** adds to this minimal restriction an unspecified maximum restriction, emphasizing the smallness of such a group: *several* friends dropped in during the day, but only a *few* stayed for dinner. Both words are useful precisely because they are vague, but beyond their reference to a small group, neither has any connotative richness.

several

divers
diverse
few
sundry
various

Diverse and **divers** are different in pointing to a larger, though still restricted group. Furthermore, each adds implications that make both more specific than the previous pair. When *divers* is substituted for *several*, it stresses the variety or disunity within the grouping: *divers* attitudes expressed by the panel members. The word may have an archaic sound to it, but in any case *divers* is more formal than *diverse*. The latter is even stronger in its emphasis on dissimilarities among members of a group. *Diverse* may, in fact, suggest a deliberate selection to give a representative cross section of types that are varied or diversified in form or kind: an anthology purporting to represent the *diverse* kinds of poetry being written by contemporary poets.

Sundry, in contrast with *diverse*, emphasizes the randomness of differences among members of a group indefinite in size; the word carries a tone of casual but deliberate approximation: the *sundry* skills that go into making up a musical comedy. The word can also actually suggest dissimilar things viewed in isolation rather than collected in a group: *sundry* times and places. **Various** is less formal than *sundry* but is more matter-of-fact about a wide representation of differing things, whether actually grouped together or looked at in isolation: *various* trees dotting the landscape; *various* sorts of people out for an afternoon walk. A common phrase couples this pair of words, but with little gain in specificity or flavor: *various* and *sundry* Madison Avenue types.

Antonyms: *none, one.*

shackle

chain
fetter
handcuff
manacle
tether

These words refer to being tied or bound up so that one cannot move freely. **Shackle** refers literally to the binding of ankles or wrists or both; the bands or straps used can be attached to another person or group so *shackled* or to a post or stationary object: *shackled* hand and foot to the prison wall. Figuratively, *shackle* suggests something that frustrates progress along a certain line: youthful minds already *shackled* by the prejudices of their parents; a government *shackled* by an inflexible foreign policy.

Manacle and **fetter** both deal with a separate and specific aspect of *shackle. Manacle* refers specifically to the binding of hands or wrists, *fetter* to the binding of feet. As with *shackle,* the binding may be by a band or strap; both hands or feet may be *manacled* or *fettered* together, or one of each may be attached to one of another person's: raising his *manacled* hands in protest; one hand *manacled* to the policeman who accompanied him; *fettered* so that he could walk only with difficulty about his cell; convicts *fettered* to each other by a heavy chain. In figurative uses, these distinctions are frequently forgotten and both words are used interchangeably with *shackled*; on this level, however, *fetter* suggests less loss of freedom than *shackle,* and *manacle* an even greater loss: a slow-moving program that was *fettered* by congressional caution; an apathetic populace *manacled* by gross need and squalor. In using any of these three words figuratively, one should remember that the literal image remains strong; ridiculous comparisons should be avoided. [The hand that rocked the cradle was *fettered* to the home; The current generation is *shackled* to its lust for speed and rapid changes of pace.]

Handcuff and **tether** are still more specifically restricted than the foregoing words. *Handcuff* refers exclusively to two circles of metal connected by a short chain; as with *manacle,* both wrists of a person may be *handcuffed* together or one wrist may be *handcuffed* to another person's or to a fixed object. The word is far less often used figuratively than *manacle. Tether* suggests, most specifically, an animal tied to a fixed stake by a cord or chain that is attached to the animal at the neck. This gives a limited circle in which the animal may move or graze. Figuratively, the word implies the setting of a limited area within which freedom is permitted but beyond which it is impossible to go: *tethered* within a four-year program of required courses; a group *tethered* to tedious pieties that no longer have any meaning.

Chain, while specifying the material with which the binding is done, is the most general word here in that it can refer to any manner of binding whatever. Unlike these other words, it can also suggest a more complete loss of freedom: *chained* so that he could neither stand, sit, nor lie down at full length. Figuratively, it suggests an impediment to free movement that would be difficult to overcome: *chained* to pre-Keynesian notions of economics. It is a safer word to use figuratively than *shackle, manacle,* or *fetter,* in that it less often results in a mixed metaphor. See CONFINE, THWART.

Antonyms: *extricate, free, liberate, release, unchain.*

These words refer to agitated movements that are quick, slight, or intense and are often involuntary expressions of strain or discomfort. **Shake** is the most general and is also unique in this group because it can designate something that is done to as well as by a person or object: *shaking* his fist in rage; branches *shaking* in the wind. **Quiver** is more specific in suggesting a rapid but almost imperceptible vibration: ropes that *quivered* tautly under his hands; a network of ripples that *quivered* momentarily across the surface of the still pool; her whole body *quivering* with delight. **Quake** suggests specifically a more violent upheaval: the ground *quaking* beneath them as the artillery barrage began; his heart *quaking* with panic.

The remaining words apply best to the involuntary *shaking* of a person or animal; when they are used of natural objects an anthropomorphic overtone persists. **Tremble** is like *quiver* in suggesting a quick but slight movement; to this there are added implications of uneasy or nervous discomposure: hands that *trembled* with eagerness as she opened the letter; leaves *trembling* in the faint breeze.

Shiver is like *tremble* except for specifically suggesting coldness or fear as the cause of the slight, rapid movement: beginning to *shiver* as the intense cold pervaded the room; *shivering* inwardly at the thought of having to explain to her mother why she had stayed out so late. **Shudder** suggests a more intense *shaking* than either *tremble* or *shiver*, suggesting horror, revulsion, or extreme pleasure as possible causes for the involuntary movement: *shuddering* at the touch of his leathery hand. Although *shudder* may be nearly as intense as *quake*, it may suggest movement less noticeable to an onlooker: *shuddering* breathlessly in the doorway until his pursuer had raced past. See TOTTER, VIBRATE.

These words refer to imitations or substitutes that are poorly or unconvincingly executed. **Sham** specifically suggests the hypocritical acting out of roles or the display of pretended virtues so as to result in a deliberate or unconscious travesty of the real thing: *sham* piety that sorted ill with their actual behavior; a *sham* though legally certified marriage entered into for financial gain. **Mock** is close to *sham* in suggesting an outrageously bad or hypocritical pretense to virtue, especially when done with overblown grandiosity: windy oratory full of *mock* patriotism. The word, however, has a growing use as a neutral term to describe something intended to deceive no one but having a usefulness of its own: *mock* turtle soup; a *mock* turtleneck sweater.

Fake suggests a copy or substitute which may but need not be intended to deceive: *fake* loyalty that won his boss's admiration; buying a *fake* fur to wear as a second coat along with her real mink. **Bogus** stresses the inherent worthlessness of the copy or imitation: *bogus* sentiment; *bogus* currency. **Phony**, aside from its simple pejorative use for a deliberate deception, stresses conscious hypocrisy that is never self-deceiving: a *phony* scholar who freely made up both his quotations and his sources. *Phony* is the most informal word of this group and perhaps most pejorative in its assault on priggishness and especially pretentiousness: a *phony* show-off. See ARTIFICIAL, SPURIOUS.
Antonyms: GENUINE.

These words express various shades of meaning implicit in the general idea of feeling or of making others feel uncomfortable in situations or under circumstances that involve a loss of self-esteem. **Shame**, the strongest of them, implies a painful sense of guilt or of degradation aris-

shake

quake
quiver
shiver
shudder
tremble

sham

bogus
fake
mock
phony

shame

abash

shame

(continued)

discomfit
embarrass
faze
mortify
rattle

ing from a consciousness of acting in an unworthy or dishonorable way. [They *shamed* him by their courage in the emergency; He was *shamed* by his failure to pass the final test.] **Mortify** is somewhat milder, suggesting humiliation or chagrin resulting from an unpleasant experience: The teacher was *mortified* by her pupil's poor showing. (Note that in this sense it can sometimes be replaced by *ashamed* of: *mortified* by or *ashamed* of one's behavior.) It may also signify punishment or decay: to *mortify* the flesh by fasting; the *mortification* of gangrenous tissue.

Embarrass means to make self-conscious or uncomfortable: a young lady *embarrassed* by her escort's drunken behavior at a party. It may also denote the checking or hindering of thought, speech, or a course of action: an *embarrassing* setback to his plans; to *embarrass* an opponent by awkward questions. **Abash** is to confuse or disconcert, as by arousing a sudden consciousness of inferiority. [The child was *abashed* by his mother's reproof; No amount of scorn or ridicule could *abash* him.]

Discomfit still carries its former military sense of defeating or routing an enemy: It was a great satisfaction to have *discomfited* his rival. More loosely, it can be used, instead of *embarrass* or *abash*, to suggest discomfort short of actual humiliation or defeat: *discomfited* because he forgot the address. **Faze** is a colloquial expression with the meaning to worry, vex, or disturb and is generally used only in the negative sense: He was not *fazed* by the attacks made on his character. **Rattle**, another colloquial expression, implies a state of emotional confusion or agitation: The speaker was *rattled* by constant interruptions from the audience. See EMBARRASSMENT, UPSET.

Antonyms: ENCOURAGE, UPHOLD.

shameful

disgraceful
dishonorable
ignominious
scandalous

These words all refer to conduct or a condition that violates the prevailing standards of probity or morality. **Shameful** and **disgraceful** express strong disapproval and often shock at someone else's trangressions. Both terms are commonly used for emphasis to reveal profound indignation on the part of the speaker or writer, and are more meaningful in suggesting attitude than in objectively describing shocking situations: a *disgraceful* exhibition of poor sportsmanship; a *shameful* display of ingratitude. Strictly speaking, a *shameful* act would bring shame or obloquy upon the doer, and a *disgraceful* act would bring disgrace; but this distinction is not commonly observed, and all that can be said is that *disgraceful* usually indicates a greater degree of indignation than *shameful*. *Shameful* may also suggest a note of sadness rather than contempt, as at an unfortunate condition: It was *shameful* how badly out of shape the former athlete allowed himself to become. *Disgraceful* would be too strong in this context; it is limited more usually to acts that are felt to be outrageous: a *disgraceful* misuse of company funds.

Dishonorable, though also revealing a highly critical attitude, has more objective relevance than either *shameful* or *disgraceful*, and retains more of its original sense of imputing dishonor. It is a formal word of high seriousness, and would not, as the other words here considered, ever be applied to comparatively trivial circumstances involving manners or the like. *Dishonorable* applies to one's character and to one's good name. [It was *dishonorable* of him to take credit for having written a book he had not written; The soldier was convicted of willful desertion and was issued a *dishonorable* discharge from the army.]

Ignominious and **scandalous** are both closely related to *shameful*. *Ignominious* suggests behavior that subjects one to humiliation; *scandalous* suggests sensational actions that flagrantly violate accepted standards of morality and hence stimulates reactions of intense revulsion or contempt. [She had a series of *scandalous* affairs that shocked the community; In the U.S., the fate of public officials who lose elections is often *ignominious* — they are out of work and soon find themselves forgotten.] *Ignominious* is now widely used to refer to anything that diminishes one's self-respect: He suffered through an *ignominious* silence when asked to explain his absence. See BAD, DISGRACE, EMBARRASSMENT, IGNOBLE, OUTRAGEOUS, REPREHENSIBLE.

Antonyms: exemplary, glorious, honorable, proud, reputable, upright, upstanding.

These words pertain to the coming together of two or more people to accomplish a common task or pleasure. **Share** is the most general of these and is relatively informal. It may suggest the mere dividing of a portion or activity: *sharing* the profits; *sharing* the clean-up job to make it go faster. Often, however, an added note of friendliness or warmth of feeling is present: *sharing* together an intense, unspoken sympathy. **Join** is like *share* in its informality; it may also stress good fellowship, especially in the sense of banding together for a common activity: neighbors who *joined* together in building a new house for the stricken family; spontaneously *joining* in on the refrains of the song. This note of voluntary good will, however, may be totally absent: ordering them to *join* in digging the mass grave. The word often suggests the action of a person who becomes part of an already existing group: *joining* the excursion in Rome.

Participate, although considerably more formal, is like one aspect of *join* in specifically suggesting a joining or taking part in group activity: a shy student who only with difficulty learned to *participate* in the group discussions. The word implies a more active role than is necessarily the case with *share* or *join*: members who *join* the club and *share* in its ideals but still do not *participate* in the club's programs. **Partake** is closer in meaning to *share* than to *join* or *participate*, although it is more formal than any of these words. It might, in fact, seem excessively formal in some cases. It suggests, most specifically, the receiving or taking of portions, especially of food: picnickers who unloaded their baskets and *partook* of a sumptuous though improvised feast. Sometimes the emphasis on food is felt so strongly that the word is used even for a person eating alone: *partaking* of her solitary meal.

Commune is more like another aspect of *share* in emphasizing an intense give-and-take of quiet but warm feeling: *communing* together with wordless, unhurried glances. Like *partake*, the word may be used of a single person, in which case an internal dialogue may be suggested or a silent responsiveness to one's surroundings, especially a natural setting: an old woman who sat *communing* with times long past; *communing* with nature. The last example is a stock phrase that illustrates a certain preciousness that may be present when the word appears in this context.

Relate in current usage has become a fad word referring to interpersonal relationships: an autistic child completely unable to *relate* to anyone; people who *relate* to others only on the safest and most superficial of levels. See ASSOCIATE.

These words refer to land lying along a body of water. **Shore** is the most general of these, referring to any sort of land that borders a large water mass, such as a lake or ocean: the *shores* of Lake Superior; the western *shore* of the Atlantic. As can be seen, the word most strictly regards this

share

commune
join
partake
participate
relate

shore

bank

shore
(continued)

beach
coast
littoral
strand

meeting of land and water from the view of the limit set on the water. **Coast** reverses the view, indicating the limits set on the land. Also, *coast* is most pertinent to a long stretch of land taken as a whole, making it most appropriate in reference to land masses along an ocean: the British *coast*; the states along the Pacific *coast*. One would speak of the *shore* of a very small island, rather than of its *coast*.

In contrast to these words, **bank** specifically applies to any sort of land bordering a river: the *banks* of the Wabash. *Coast* would never be used in this sense and *shore* seldom, perhaps only when emphasizing a river's width: calling to him from the opposite *shore* of the river. *Bank*, however, has an additional specific reference to a steep slope or jut of land above the water's edge: diving from the *bank* into the swimming hole. In this sense, the word would suggest a moderate jut of earth beside a pool or river; if higher land or a stony outcropping beside a lake or tidal water is in question, such words as bluff or cliff would be more appropriate in terms of connotation. **Beach** contrasts sharply with *bank*, referring to a gradual slope, especially of sand, rather than to an earthy steepness. A *beach* may exist, however, either beside fresh or salt water, lake or ocean, and even along a river: a *beach* formed along the wide bend of a river; Greek islands with naturally sandy *beaches*. Sometimes the word specifically suggests a sandy *shore* that has been designed for public use: opening two new *beaches* in the last three years.

Strand and **littoral** both apply mainly to ocean *shores*, or at least to land along tidal water. *Strand* may now sound old-fashioned or stilted, but it does refer specifically to the area of land between high and low tide: The tide being out, we walked along the *strand*. *Littoral* can refer to exactly the same area as *strand* but without risking a stilted tone: sea pools along the *littoral* where many sea creatures live between high tides. It is extremely formal and technical in tone, however, and can also refer to both the strip of land and the shallow water that lie to either side of the water line: oceanographic and ecological studies of the Aleutian *littoral*.

shorten

abbreviate
abridge
curtail
cut

These words are comparable in their denotation of reducing the length, extent, or duration of something. **Shorten** means to make or seem to make short or shorter, and can refer either to dimension or duration: angry with the demands of fashion that made it necessary for her to *shorten* so many pieces of her wardrobe; forced to *shorten* his lunch hour because of a heavy work schedule; trying to *shorten* the waiting time in his dentist's office by reading a magazine.

Curtail and **cut** imply *shortening* through removal of a part of the whole. *Curtail* suggests a lessening, as in quality or effectiveness, because of the removal of some important part: a department store whose business suffered when it *curtailed* its services to suburban customers. *Cutting*, which suggests an editing process, may or may not remove something important: Some movies seen on TV suffer when they are *cut* badly to fit into a *shortened* time slot.

Abridge and **abbreviate** both carry the idea of *shortening* so that what remains adequately represents the whole. To *abridge* suggests the *cutting* away of nonessentials while retaining the core. To *abbreviate*, generally used in reference to words or phrases, implies *shortening* by the compression or omission of parts, the remainder standing for the whole: to *abridge* a novel for its inclusion in a magazine; the *abbreviated* name of an advertising agency. See COMPACT, DECREASE, LESSEN, REDUCE.

Antonyms: ENLARGE, EXTEND.

These words refer to the revealing, demonstrating, or making clear of something. **Show** is the most informal and general of these, with an extremely wide range of possible uses: *showing* her teeth when she smiled; *showing* off his new ability on the high dive. The word is particularly useful to indicate acts that communicate an attitude or result in a visible or unmistakable sign: *showing* enthusiasm for the sketches; a gift chosen to *show* how much she cared for him.

Evince and **manifest** are the most formal of these words and are both restricted in use to suggest the giving of a sign. *Evince* may point to a subtle or slight exposure or to something that shows itself in a rudimentary or initial state: first *evincing* a grudging interest in the work project and finally becoming absorbed in it; her cool manner *evincing* a restrained dislike for their new friend; a flair for color and form that first *evinced* itself in grade school. *Manifest* indicates a much more clearcut or unmistakable revealing; unlike *evince*, it would suggest something that requires no investigation but is plainly evident to anyone: a hunger that *manifested* itself in strange ways; a country *manifesting* an unbelievable luxuriance of flora and fauna.

Display and **exhibit** both emphasize an exposure such as results from deliberately putting something on full view. *Display* may suggest a painfully obvious exposure or a flaunting one: *displaying* his drunkenness openly on the street; beach boys arrogantly *displaying* their tanned physiques. *Exhibit* may stress instead a more matter-of-fact tone, suggesting that something is almost clinically put on view for consideration or evaluation: *exhibiting* the murder weapon to the jury; a gallery *exhibiting* a new painter's work. Both words, however, can function less specifically as more formal substitutes for *show*: *displaying*, by a sign, a readiness to go away with him; *exhibiting* a slight nervousness as he read the statement. See HINT, MEAN, MEANING.

Antonyms: cloak, conceal, disguise, hide, mask, suppress.

show

display
evince
exhibit
manifest

These words refer to persons or things that are conspicuous because of their vivid or garish physical make-up or because of some striking or vulgar manner of behavior. **Showy** is a neutral term and may be used in either a complimentary or critical way. It can refer to a great or brilliant display, and in this sense may characterize such things as beauty, ability, technique, performance, or achievement: a *showy* floral arrangement, done with originality and imagination; a pianist with a *showy* technique and a mastery of the romantic repertoire. In its pejorative sense *showy* suggests a cheap display and is used to describe persons or things that in some way are offensive to good taste: a *showy* team of ballroom dancers whose performance was more gymnastic than graceful; the *showy* furniture chosen by someone whose knowledge of interior decoration was much more limited than her bankroll.

Colorful may suggest an abundance of color or colors, usually bright and vivid, often contrasting: a *colorful* afghan that had been crocheted by her grandmother and which was so beautiful that she used it as a wall hanging. *Colorful* can also describe something that is picturesque and full of variety: a *colorful* novella about life in the old West. Finally, it can characterize a person who draws attention to himself by his striking, individualistic, or even eccentric manner: my *colorful*, crotchety old grandfather; a *colorful* character actor whose off-stage life was as flamboyant as his style of acting.

Loud and **ostentatious** are more definitely pejorative in connotation than *showy* or *colorful*. *Loud*, in the sense being compared here, is sy-

showy

colorful
loud
ostentatious

nonymous with the critical meaning of *showy*. In reference to objects, it denotes flashiness and offensively bad taste: a *loud* sport shirt with clashing colors and a jarring pattern. When it describes a person or his behavior, it suggests crudity and vulgarity: a *loud*, coarse businessman whose back-slapping jocularity of manner failed to hide his ruthlessness of purpose. *Ostentatious* is not as pejorative as *loud*, but is nonetheless critical in its depiction of vain pretense or uncalled-for exhibition. It suggests the overly elaborate, flashy display that fails to impress because of its very excess: an *ostentatious* copy of an English manor house that looked ridiculous in its Midwest setting. See ELEGANT, GAUDY, VULGAR.

Antonyms: MODEST, *plain, quiet, simple*.

shrew

harridan
scold
termagant
virago
vixen

These words refer to vexatious, faultfinding, abusive, and quarrelsome women. **Shrew** is the most inclusive in the list of faults that it may attribute to such a woman. Because of Shakespeare's *The Taming of the Shrew*, the word is often used specifically to refer to a henpecking, domineering wife who nags her husband. **Scold**, by contrast, emphasizes only one fault to the exclusion of others, referring to someone who is unceasingly harsh and faultfinding. While the word often applies to a woman, and may certainly apply to a wife, it is the only word here that is not necessarily restricted to women alone: not able to decide who was the worse *scold*, his boss at the office or his wife at home. **Virago** is more like *scold* than *shrew* in emphasizing a person given to ill-tempered tirades. Here, however, the word is limited to describing a nosy, sharp-tongued woman whose talk may be harsh and incessant but not necessarily devoted solely to abuse, as is the case with *scold*: a *virago* who punished her husband with a constant volley of hysterical chatter. *Virago* comes from a Latin root referring to a mannish woman, and sometimes this is reflected in the word's use in reference to a woman of extraordinary size or Amazonian courage: often picturing Judy as a *virago* of frightening prowess and Punch as a helpless pip-squeak of a man.

With the remaining words, greater disapproval is expressed for more extremely distasteful sorts of women, often outside the context of marriage. **Harridan** refers specifically to an old woman who is hateful and vicious: *harridans* who sit bejeweled in their opera boxes but have never entertained a kind or compassionate sentiment in their entire lives. **Vixen**, by contrast, suggests animal-like ferocity not commonly associated with advanced age. The word's other application — to a female fox — supplies overtones here of a sleek, cunning woman, perhaps specifically unmarried, who is out for self-aggrandizement at whatever cost to others: a regular *vixen* who could slink about seductively one moment and lash out with tooth and claw the next. Such a woman who directs her viciousness at males is now often referred to as a castrating female. **Termagant** is the fiercest of all these words, emphasizing greater malice than *vixen* and suggesting a greater range of quixotic, bad-tempered, irrational hostility, indicating a woman who vents these qualities upon any who happen to cross her path, whether within or outside the domestic situation: a *termagant* who stomped into the meeting, pounded on the table, and insisted that her denunciation of the chairman be given instant recognition. See CONTROVERSY, FAULTFINDING, WRONG.

sickness

ailment

These words all refer to poor health or to a particular episode of bad health. **Sickness** and **illness** are the most informal of these terms; both refer to an episode of bad health, no matter what its duration. While the words are used interchangeably, *sickness* might be the more

sickness
(continued)

complaint
disease
disorder
illness
infirmity
malady
malaise

usual and general choice, *illness* the slightly more formal one. Also, since *sickness* can sometimes refer specifically to nausea alone, *illness* is sometimes used to avoid this implication when it would be inappropriate: overcome with *sickness* shortly after eating the contaminated food; an *illness* that can result in total blindness if left untreated. Furthermore, *sickness* can sometimes imply an episode that temporarily makes one unable to function, whereas *illness* can imply a longer-lasting siege that is accompanied by impairment but not cessation of normal functioning: a *sickness* that kept him in bed for two weeks; an *illness* that caused him little difficulty in his youth but began to take its toll as he reached middle age. *Sickness* can suggest external causation of the acute episode, while *illness* can suggest inherent weakness or malfunctioning as the source of chronic poor health. Also, *illness* is the word of choice for all mental disturbance, from mild neurosis through severe psychosis: the growing incidence of mental *illness*. When *sickness* is substituted for this neutral use of *illness*, an emotional coloration is added, implying greater seriousness or urgency or suggesting an attitude of condemnation: These monstrous crimes should be testimony enough to the killer's *sickness*. With a similar emphasis, *sickness* is often used in a more general way: a pervasive *sickness* in American society that predisposes us to violence as a cure-all for our frustrations and discontents.

Disease is often popularly thought to apply only to *sickness* that is infectious or communicable: *diseases* bred by poor sanitation and improper sewage disposal. But *disease* can refer as widely as *sickness* or *illness* to any kind of bad health, with the advantage that its very generality yields no implications as to whether the sickness is acute or chronic, mild or harsh, or long or short in duration: a form of heart *disease* caused by a genetic defect; a case of Parkinson's *disease*; cancer and other *diseases* whose ultimate causes are still unknown; such mild viral *diseases* as the common cold. By contrast, **disorder** usually refers to a malfunction of mind or body that may be mild or serious, infectious or inherent, but is seen in some imbalance, as a metabolic or chemical defect, or in the improper working of some mechanism: hormonal *disorders* such as cretinism; a mental *disorder* typified by delusions of grandeur and aural hallucinations. The word can be useful because it leaves the question of cause open and points strictly to symptoms indicating that something is awry.

Malady is a more formal synonym for *disease* that may seem outdated in descriptive use, although it has an emotional note of alarm that makes it useful in metaphorical situations: the denial of female sexuality that is a *malady* endemic to Western civilization. **Malaise** refers to an indefinable sense of ill-being: a predictable *malaise* that is the first sign of the onset of the *disease*. It aptly describes a psychological state in which someone feels ill at ease or disquieted for whatever reason: an abiding *malaise* that jaundiced his whole view of world affairs.

Infirmity applies most concretely to a weakness of mind or body, but nowadays it may sound too genteel as a substitute for *disease* or *disorder*; this is true, as well, in its extended uses: an *infirmity* that kept him in a wheelchair for a number of years; needless cruelty that mocks at the *infirmities* of others; his tendency to exaggerate — the one *infirmity* in an otherwise admirable personality. **Ailment** can refer to a symptom or collection of symptoms that causes noticeable discomfort to someone: What exactly is your *ailment*? This word, too, can sound outdated, although sometimes it can have an informal or regional thrust: His lumbago is the one *ailment* that keeps him on edge day in, day out. The word once more clearly focused on the enervation or depletion of one's sense of well-being. **Complaint** now functions as an informal substitute for symptom: Frequent faintness was a *complaint* she learned to live with. Sometimes, the word can specifically indicate symptoms that are confided to one's doctor: cards on which he carefully noted every *complaint* of his patients. See COMMUNICABLE, FLAW, WEAKEN.

Antonyms: health.

significant

consequential
grave
important
momentous
serious
vital
weighty

These words refer to factors that are outstanding, crucial, or that have considerable force or effect. **Significant** suggests something that is outstanding because it is especially meaningful or excellent; no urgency or forcefulness is necessarily suggested by the word, however: a *significant* trend in the public-opinion polls; a *significant* but often overlooked masterpiece of Hellenistic art. **Consequential** stresses that something is meaningful, cannot be overlooked, or has considerable impact on succeeding events, especially of a negative nature: a *consequential* contribution to the theory of cultural diffusion; a *consequential* decision to refuse the colonists representation in Parliament. In another context, the word can often refer merely to the possessing of wealth or status: the town's two or three most *consequential* businessmen.

Important, the most general of these words, is also considerably less formal than the preceding words. As its root "import" suggests, it may refer to something that is rife with meaning, but it can also suggest almost every sense that any other word here more specifically points to. In any case, the word has been weakened by overuse, especially in the superlative, referring now to anything mildly interesting, noteworthy, or of value: one of the most *important* battles of the war; an *important* new talent; an *important* trend toward smaller families.

Momentous and **vital** both refer to things that are crucial or essential. *Momentous* stresses the great and immediate impact of an event, though it also points to *significant* ramifications or results, like *consequential*, but without any suggestion that these need be undesirable: a *momentous* turning point in evolution; the *momentous* decision to drop the atom bomb on Hiroshima. *Vital*, in contrast to *momentous*, can indicate an element that is organic and essential to the well-being or functioning of the whole: a *vital* organ of the body; raw materials *vital* to the war effort. Deriving from the Latin word for life, it often means crucial or of life-and-death importance: a *vital* error; a *vital* question. It can also describe something dynamic, full of life and energy: a *vital* young executive; a fresh, *vital* work of art.

With **grave** and **serious**, the emphasis shifts to something that is urgent or crucial and that promises to have an extremely undesirable outcome. *Grave* is the more restricted of the two, specifically suggesting something that may well have a fatal conclusion: a *grave* illness; a pilot in *grave* danger. Occasionally the word can refer more generally to something ponderous or solemn, with no suggestion of a negative outcome: addressing me with a *grave* manner; a *grave* treatise on the new science of ethology. *Serious*, like *important*, is considerably less formal and more general than the other words here. It does suggest the crucial, ponderous, or solemn, like *grave*, but with less emphasis on urgency and even less on negative eventualities. Like *important*, the word has been weakened by overuse, especially in the superlative: one of the most *serious* flaws in his character. Categorically, the word can distinguish the sober from the pleasant, light, or comic: a *serious* expression on his face; a *serious* discussion. In this use, it is a milder substitute for *grave*;

here, neither word necessarily suggests something unusually meaningful or effective.

Weighty refers to factors that are not easily disregarded: *weighty considerations that militated against an immediate counterattack.* But it can also refer to a decisive preponderance or to presentations that are excessively lengthy, abstruse, or solemn: *weighty data that disproved the argument for spontaneous generation; a weighty treatment of the origins of Roman fertility cults.* See CONCLUSIVE, OUTSTANDING.

Antonyms: insignificant, MARGINAL, TRIVIAL, *unimportant.*

These words are comparable when they are applied to persons or things that make no sound. **Silent** simply means refraining from speech or being without noise; it does not necessarily suggest serenity or motionlessness: *His silent reproach was accompanied by vigorous gestures; a silent movie; a silent conversation between deaf-and-dumb people who communicated by sign language.* Because it implies only the absence of sound, *silent* can be more emphatic than any of the other words: *The vast crowd fell silent at the news that the president was dead.*

Quiet and **still**, although denoting silence, have different implications. *Quiet* implies freedom from activity or commotion; *still* suggests an unruffled or tranquil state, and often implies that the calm is an interlude between periods of noise or agitation. In most contexts, therefore, *silent, quiet,* and *still* are not interchangeable without changing the sense: *a quiet street; a quiet neighborhood; a still forest.* Note that there is a sense of permanence about *quiet* but none about *still,* which indeed suggests the potentiality of the opposite of stillness: *a still moment when the eye of the storm passed overhead.* On the other hand, when referring simply to the absence of speech, and especially if used predicatively, the three words may be interchangeable: *a child who keeps silent* (or *quiet* or *still*). Even here *still* is ambiguous, since it may simply suggest the absence of fidgeting.

Noiseless is used in commerce, usually to refer to machines that are inherently noisy, such as typewriters, air conditioners, and the like, in order to persuade consumers to purchase a particular brand that is supposed to be *quieter* than others. Like most advertising claims, it must be taken as a relative term, in this case meaning comparatively *quiet.* In more precise contexts *noiseless* means literally without any noise: *the noiseless flight of an owl; the noiseless tread of a cat.* In this sense it is synonymous with *silent.* See SPEECHLESS, TACITURN, TRANQUIL.

Antonyms: LOUD, TALKATIVE.

These words are used to describe persons or things that in some way or to some extent resemble each other. **Similar** and **alike** are close in that each means like one another in whole or part. [*My shoes are similar to the ones you had on yesterday; The two office buildings are alike in size and shape.*] The difference between *similar* and *alike* has to do with the extent of resemblance they indicate. Both words can be used in reference to a slight degree of likeness. [*I don't understand how you could have mistaken one car for the other since only their colors are similar; The cousins are alike in age, but otherwise as different as day and night.*] But when a complete correspondence is to be designated, the word with this denotation is *alike.* [*All the houses in this project are alike.*] It is interesting to note in this connection that by modifiers, *similar* and *alike* may be made to express more or less resemblance: *somewhat similar in taste; not at all alike in price.* Even with modifiers, however,

silent

noiseless
quiet
still

similar

alike
comparable
parallel

identity can only be expressed by *alike*, since we can speak of two things be ng exactly *alike* but not exactly *similar*.

Those things are **comparable** that are capable or worthy of being examined together with reference to their likeness or unlikeness, or in order to ascertain their relative excellence or defects. [The performance of this reasonably priced record player is *comparable* in quality to that of some more expensive hi-fi sets; The music of Irving Berlin is scarcely *comparable* to that of Beethoven.] **Parallel** is used when comparing things that show a great likeness, whether real or apparent, or that have great similarity in their development, construction, history, operation, tendencies, etc. [The first hundred days of President Johnson's administration were not at all *parallel* to those of President Kennedy's; Can you point out any *parallel* passages in the composer's first and second symphonies?] See COMPARE, COPY, COUNTERPART, DUPLICATE.

Antonyms: CONTRADICTORY, *contrasting, different, dissimilar, diverse.*

simple

easy
effortless
elementary
facile
simplified

These words describe things that are made, done, understood, etc., without undue difficulty, but they are not close synonyms. **Simple** and **easy** are the most general terms. In this context *simple* refers to something that is not complicated or intricate and is therefore capable of being quickly grasped by the mind. *Easy*, on the other hand, points to that which requires little effort to do: a *simple* problem in long division; the *easy* job of preparing a meal from precooked frozen foods. In popular usage, the words are often used interchangeably and their connotations tend to become blurred: twelve *easy* lessons in Italian for the tourist; a task so *simple* that a child could perform it.

In its most precise sense, **elementary** is applied to rudiments or first principles, as of a branch of learning or of a skill, and is therefore concerned with basic or introductory material which may not necessarily be *easy* or *simple*: *elementary* electronics; *elementary* Greek. By extension, *elementary* is occasionally used as a synonym for *simple* in implying the absence of complexity, but here the meaning tends to merge with that of fundamental. [Her poems deal with the *elementary* themes of the changing of the seasons and the inexorability of nature; The television drama had the usual tiresome, *elementary* story line.]

Facile and **effortless** both apply to that which is achieved, performed, or activated with apparent *ease*. *Facile* was once a close synonym of *easy* but now carries somewhat derogatory overtones. It may describe that which is superficial in a bad sense or even spurious: the *facile* smile of the hard-sell salesman. *Facile* is also used of something which shows signs of having been done with too little expenditure of effort or with undue haste. It further suggests the careless or undisciplined use of skill or dexterity: a *facile*, flowing prose style in which the author has very little to say. *Facile*, in an extended sense, also points to glibness and thoughtlessness of speech: the *facile* tongue of the born gossip. *Effortless*, while it can mean making no *effort* or being passive, is more often used to describe action or activities which appear *easy* to perform, but whose smoothness conceals a mastery achieved by long practice and control: the pianist's *effortless* playing of a difficult sonata; the trapeze artist's *effortless* somersaulting forty feet in the air. *Effortless* may also refer to natural endowments impossible for others to emulate: the *effortless* climbing flight of the eagle; the spectacular, but *effortless*, leaps of the impala.

Simplified means rendered less intricate or difficult and thus capable of being more easily understood, performed, or used. The term presupposes an original condition of complexity that has been reduced to bare essentials: *simplified* English spelling in which the words are written as they sound; the teaching of fractions *simplified* by cutting an apple into halves, thirds, and quarters; a *simplified* process for making steel. *Simplified* may also have a pejorative meaning when used to describe something that suffers from being made overly *simple* to the point of distortion or uselessness: the candidate's *simplified*, cliché-ridden suggestions for solving the complex problems of the poor. See BASIC.

Antonyms: complex, complicated, HARD, *intricate.*

These words refer to acts that violate religious, ethical, or moral standards. **Sin** has an exclusively religious connotation, referring to any act specifically proscribed by religious doctrine: a sect that considers going to a movie a *sin*. It may be used metaphorically for any act judged improper or outrageous: a *sin* to come to your party so late; a *sin* against humanity. **Transgression** is often used as a fancier word for *sin*, as though its weightier syllables more clearly indicated opprobrium. In other uses, it may suggest any violation of an agreed-upon set of rules: a clear *transgression* of the Geneva agreement.

Wrong and **misdeed** refer to evil or unjust actions; both may imply either a religious context or, more vaguely, a wider ethical context. *Wrong* suggests the giving of hurt or injury to someone: those who would unthinkingly do a *wrong* to their neighbors. The wrongful act implied by *misdeed* does not necessarily suggest hurt to others, but the word often seems euphemistic when used for *sin*: repenting his *misdeeds*.

Error and **fault** also sound euphemistic when substituted either for *sin* or *wrong*. Except in such clichés as "the *error* of his ways," *error* seems to suggest that a *sin* or *wrong* is an unintentional mistake rather than a deliberate choice. *Fault* suggests an imperfect result, a flaw or a blemish; when used euphemistically for *sin*, it seems to excuse bad conduct by suggesting that perfection, however much desired, is impossible. **Indiscretion**, most strictly, refers to an unwise or improper action, but it has become a vogue word for such *sins* as adultery, as though to minimize the *wrong* committed by attributing it to a momentary lack of judgment: a wife who was guilty of an *indiscretion* while traveling alone. See CRIME, FLAW, MISTAKE, UNETHICAL.

Antonyms: benefaction, good deed, GOODNESS, *kindness.*

These words mean free from pretense, concealment, reservation, or falsehood. **Sincere** is the most general of these and the most positive in tone, suggesting a complete absence of hypocrisy and an exact identity between appearance and reality, with added implications of friendliness, interest, and kindness: a *sincere* expression of gratitude that went beyond mere formality. **Honest** and **genuine** stress truthfulness. *Honest* may be considerably more neutral than *sincere* and may describe an isolated instance of truth-telling as easily as it suggests an unvarying character trait: Even the least *sincere* hypocrite occasionally makes an *honest* statement. *Genuine* is closer to *sincere* than *honest* in its positive warmth of tone, emphasizing that a person or thing is really what it seems: He showed *genuine* regret. In another sense, someone may be *genuine* and neither *honest* nor *sincere*: a *genuine* confidence man.

Open and **unfeigned** suggest, negatively, a refusal to play roles that might conceal one's true nature and, positively, a willingness to risk exposure and to tell all one knows. *Open* emphasizes telling the whole truth: begging her to be *open* with him, even if she disapproves of him.

sin

error
fault
indiscretion
misdeed
transgression
wrong

sincere

genuine
heartfelt
honest
open
unfeigned
wholehearted

It suggests fearlessness of the consequences and can veer over into suggesting an unnecessary or hurtful frankness: to show *open* hostility. *Unfeigned* does not necessarily suggest that the complete truth is told or expressed, but it does suggest a lack of posturing or archness: *unfeigned* delight in being with him, despite her suspicions about his behavior. Sometimes it may suggest a sudden or unwilling revealing of one's true feelings: an irrepressible outburst of *unfeigned* disgust.

Heartfelt and **wholehearted** stress that aspect of *sincere* that pertains to warmth of concern and deepness of kind or friendly feelings. *Heartfelt* can indicate a rare inward intensity that is assented to completely: giving her his *heartfelt* sympathy. The word, however, is in danger of seeming too flowery in many instances. *Wholehearted* escapes this danger, with its suggestion of thoroughgoing dedication without reservation, or an undivided response to experience: giving the proposal our *wholehearted* approval. The word also suggests emotional exuberance or enthusiasm: *wholehearted* merrymaking.

Often, *sincere* appears linked with another word here as a clarifying intensification, as though the word were limited in its force. "*Sincere* and *genuine*" seems to suggest that even sincerity by itself can be pretended; "*sincere* and *honest*" suggests that one can be *sincere* in one's intentions and yet be in error or fail to give the whole truth; "*sincere* and *open*" suggests that one could be concerned and *honest* and still be shy and reserved or hold back something of importance. Light is also cast on the felt limitations of *sincere* by another common type of doublet: *sincere* but mistaken; *sincere* but misguided; *sincere* but ill-tempered. These phrases imply that one may mean well and still fail to do the right thing, as because of a lack of knowledge, understanding, or control of one's emotions. See BRUSQUE, CANDID, GENUINE, OUTSPOKEN, OVERT, TRUTHFUL.

Antonyms: *affected, dishonest, dissembled, feigned, halfhearted, hypocritical, insincere, pretended, put-on,* SPURIOUS.

sing

chant
hum
intone

To **sing** is primarily to utter a succession of articulate musical sounds, especially with the human voice. In *singing*, the sound of the words differs from speech sound in that the vowels are lengthened and the pitches clearly defined. *Sing* has also come to mean to produce any succession of musical sounds. One says that a bird *sings*, that a brook *sings*, or that a skilled performer can make his violin *sing*. By extension, a poem or a piece of imaginative prose may be said to *sing* when read aloud, because the cadences are pleasing to the ear in the same way that music is.

To **hum** is to *sing* a tune, usually with the lips closed and without articulating the words. On the other hand, any somewhat monotonous, murmuring sound may be referred to as *humming*. [Bees *hum* as they fly from flower to flower; The flywheel in the powerhouse *hums* softly as it spins; The streets of the city *hum* with traffic.]

Chant and **intone** are closely related and mean to *sing* in a solemn and somewhat uniform cadence a piece of repetitive music such as a plainsong, a psalm, or a canticle. *Intone*, however, suggests more gravity and less resemblance to music than does *chant*. [A priest *intones* the words of the Mass, but a group of choirboys will *chant* the responses.] In its more extended meaning, to *chant* is to recite something repetitiously or monotonously in a singsong manner. [An auctioneer *chants* the amounts of money bid for items to be sold; Little girls *chant* rhymes as they jump rope.] See MELODY.

These words all denote regions, localities, or particular portions of space. **Site** is almost always restricted to an area of ground, small or large. It may be one that has been set aside for a particular use or activity: a building *site*; a factory *site*; a recreation *site*. Or a *site* may be a circumscribed locale where some event has occurred: the *site* of the battle of Guilford Courthouse; the *site* of the beheading of Anne Boleyn.

A **location** is usually a *site* considered in relation to its surroundings or noteworthy for some specific feature. [The *location* of the house is near the highway; The prison guards could not discover the *location* of the escape tunnel; A post office should be built in a central *location*.]

Place is the most general term and may be substituted in an indefinite sense for all of the others. *Place* may mean a small, circumscribed area: to take one's *place* in line; hanging one's coat in the proper *place*; to find a parking *place*. Buildings, dwellings, cities, towns, or larger localities are all loosely called *places*. [The bank is his *place* of business; We are furnishing our *place* with antiques; He comes from a small *place* in Idaho; She sent postcards from many faraway *places*.]

Setting and **scene** are both *places* or surroundings in which events (whether real or imaginary) occur or have occurred, and in this sense they may be used interchangeably. However, *setting*, rather than *scene*, is often limited in meaning to the *place* in which the incidents of a play or narrative are laid. [The *setting* of *Macbeth* is Scotland; India is the *scene* of many of Kipling's short stories.] *Scene* is more likely to be used of *places* in which actual events have occurred, but it suggests a less definite area than does *site*. [The meadow at Runnymede was the *scene* of the signing of the Magna Carta; A dark alley was the *scene* of the murder.] A *scene* may also be a wide or even panoramic landscape or view. [The wild mountain *scene* lay spread before our hotel.] In a spatial sense, *setting* suggests a scenic environment or one with special characteristics: a cabin in a woodland *setting*.

A **spot** is a specific *place*, either indoors or outdoors, of limited extent: a night *spot*; a beautiful *spot* in which to have a picnic.

In the sense treated here, a **point** is a particular *place* without reference to the size or shape of the space occupied. It suggests a fixed *location* from which position and distance may be reckoned, as when one says that he sails from *point* to *point* during a cruise. Otherwise, *point* is simply a *place* of definite, though unstated, size: to visit *points* of interest in London. See SECTION.

These words refer to taking the measure of something large or small in quantity or degree, or in a plane or solid space. **Size** is the most general, being applicable in all these situations: a country of great *size*; a small watermelon the *size* of your head; the *size* of the state's population; the *size* of the price index increase. By contrast, **area** and **expanse** restrict themselves most specifically to surface measurements. *Area* is most often used in neutral description or to focus attention on a particular region: pinpointing *areas* of discontent in Latin America; a small *area* of tenderness just behind the left ear. *Expanse* suggests a larger space than *area*: an *expanse* of virgin timberlands; an inflamed *expanse* of skin across his chest and stomach. *Area* is also used to indicate a certain portion of an abstract whole: an often overlooked *area* of anthropological research.

Volume, bulk, and **mass** all specifically refer to three-dimensional spaces. *Volume* may be used in indicating the exact amount of cubic space something takes up or the exact quantity needed to fill a container:

site

location
place
point
scene
setting
spot

size

area
bulk
expanse
extent
mass
scope
volume

a room with a *volume* of a thousand cubic feet; estimating the *volume* of water needed to fill the pool. It is also used for amplitude of sound and arbitrarily for some other measurements: an increasing *volume* of trunk calls per annum. By contrast, *bulk* does not suggest exactness of measure, but does refer to a considerable *size* that may not be proportionate to its weight: breakfast food packages of deceptive *bulk*. The word has a special use for indicating a major portion: taking on the *bulk* of the work himself. In scientific usage, *mass* refers to a quantification of matter underlying gravity and weight. In ordinary use, the word emphasizes weight, density, or quantity, and may specifically suggest a large *bulk* of uneven outline: *masses* of debris left from the explosion. Less specifically, it may suggest a great amount: a *mass* of student papers to correct and grade.

Extent and **scope** both may be used to indicate linear or plane distances like *area* or more generally to indicate degree. In surface measurement, *extent* suggests an effort to determine the distance something reaches to, especially a linear distance that is subject to change: estimating the *extent* of river made brackish by the backing up of salt water from the ocean; reports on the *extent* of the newly captured territory. Used to indicate degree, it is more flexible in application but less specific in meaning, only vaguely suggesting a metaphor of physical penetration: the *extent* to which he had plumbed his unyielding subject matter. Where *extent* implies a linear distance, *scope* implies a two-dimensional area that something has mastered or controls: bulletins on the *scope* of the flood's destructiveness. Much more commonly, *scope* is used figuratively to indicate degree of mastery or breadth of concern: a book of immense range and *scope*; the *extent* of his reach; the *scope* of his mind. See BOUNDARY, PART, SECTION, SITE.

skeptic

agnostic
atheist
doubter
freethinker
unbeliever

These words refer to people who question or reject accepted beliefs, particularly religious dogma. The relatively formal **skeptic** and the relatively informal **doubter** are alike in emphasizing someone who questions or is not sure of a given belief. *Doubter* most often refers to uncertainty about a belief already put forward; this may be a body of religious dogma or any isolated, nonreligious theory: evangelists who swept through the Midwest to convert *doubters* and harrow sinners; a detailed investigation of the assassination, with conclusions that should convince the most conscientious *doubter*. *Skeptic* can function in both these ways, but its main emphasis is on the questioning of accepted beliefs, perhaps not so much from a position of open-minded uncertainty as from one of an a priori conviction about where the truth lies: a confirmed *skeptic* about the value of any of the great religions. Most specifically, the word can refer to a philosophical belief that no final truths can be known, whether in any area of knowledge whatever or in some particular area: a *skeptic* about the validity of psychoanalytic theory. Less precisely, the word may refer to a person with a disengaged attitude of moral cynicism toward the worth or value of life as a whole: a *skeptic* who watched the fads and insanities of his time with an indifferent eye.

Freethinker and **unbeliever** are more closely tied to a rejection of religious belief than the previous pair. The first is an approving word, the second a disapproving word for the same sort of person, one who rejects the truth of a given religion or of all religions. *Unbeliever* might most often be used by a group of religious adherents to describe anyone not of their faith: a small, fanatical sect who regarded members of other religions as *unbelievers* doomed to suffer the torments of hell. More precisely, the word would indicate someone who belongs to no organized religion, or someone without religious beliefs of any sort; this sets it apart from *doubter*, which might indicate someone who belongs to a religion but is wavering in his convictions: addressing his sermons to *doubters* rather than to outright *unbelievers*. *Freethinker* emphasizes someone who has asserted the right to think and decide for himself about religious dogma; the word need not point to unbelief, but rather to a nonconforming, heterodox approach that picks and chooses from one or many religions those things, if any, that seem worthy of belief: a *freethinker* who subscribed to the Sermon on the Mount, the Upanishads, and the writings of Darwin, Freud, and Lao-tzu; a *freethinker* who objected to the attitude of most religions toward women.

Agnostic relates roughly to *skeptic* and *doubter*, while **atheist** is more comparable to *unbeliever*; both terms can be used in neutral description rather than in approval or disapproval. As widely used by the public press, political leaders, and mass-circulation magazines, however, *atheist* is a contemptuous term, as witness its common coupling with communism: *atheistic* communism. *Agnostic* suggests someone who feels that no religious certainty is possible and that no proof or disproof of such a thing as the existence of God is valid: neither a believer nor *unbeliever*, but an *agnostic*. *Atheist* is the most specific of these words in being restricted to someone who does not believe in the existence of any sort of divinity: an *atheist* with a rigorous moral code based on the Ten Commandments. See DISTRUSTFUL, DOUBT, DOUBTFUL.

Antonyms: believer, bigot, pietist, religious, zealot.

These words refer to ability that may be the result of training, talent, perceptivity, or a combination of some or all of these qualities. **Skill** is the least formal of these, the most general, and the most clear-cut in reference. It may refer, most simply, to relatively commonplace abilities gained largely through training: *skill* at taking dictation. But it may also refer to ability that training alone could not account for without considerable natural talent: the *skill* of the prima ballerina. Even in this situation, however, the word would suggest a necessary adjunct of artistic accomplishment rather than its life-blood. With **artistry**, the situation is quite the reverse. Here all the imponderables that go into exquisite performance and accomplishment are indicated, and while training, talent, and taste play their part, they work in concert with other less common qualities: the *artistry* of a great violinist. Because of the strong praise conferred by the word, it is often used hyperbolically of nonartistic acts to suggest how creatively even a seemingly mechanical task may be approached: the *artistry* with which the writer tossed the Caesar salad.

Deftness and **adroitness** are much nearer *skill* than *artistry* in their implications. *Deftness* may suggest simple manual dexterity when this natural ability has been highly trained: his *deftness* in handling the complicated tabulator. Less concretely, it can suggest a trained ability to handle any sort of difficult situation: the *deftness* of a good diplomat in avoiding embarrassing incidents. *Adroitness* also may pertain to *skill* at physical manipulation, but it is better able than *deftness* to suggest knowledgeable appropriateness of behavior in potentially charged situations: the *adroitness* of a good hostess in turning a conversation away from disagreeable topics. It is more likely than *deftness* to refer to an artistic act at a higher level than technical *skill*: the *adroitness* with which the author managed the fugal structure of his novel.

skill

adroitness
artistry
deftness
finesse
flair
mastery

Just as the previous pair are more closely related to *skill*, so **finesse** and **flair** are more closely related to *artistry*, though they suggest aspects of *artistry* rather than equivalents to it. *Finesse* pertains to unusually excellent formal technique that joins to ordinary *skill* such imponderables as exuberance, taste, perceptivity, wit, or cleverness: the chess champion's *finesse* in both defensive and offensive play. Someone crediting an artist with this quality rather than *artistry*, however, would be suggesting a lack of emotional depth or maturity: the flawless but shallow *finesse* of the young pianist. *Flair* is the one word here that need not suggest thorough training; what it points to instead is a natural talent that is surprising in its forcefulness, whimsy, colorfulness, or vivacity: a *flair* for watercolors that is all the more impressive considering his lack of experience in the medium. In reference to admittedly trained people, however, the word can suggest work with zest or dramatic impact that goes beyond mere *adroitness* or *finesse*: writing with *flair* despite the rigid limitations of the heroic couplet. Less exaltedly, the word can refer to anything that is very striking about someone's personal taste: a way of dressing that showed a *flair* for exploiting bold patterns and colors within the bounds of good taste.

Mastery is ambivalent in that it can apply to simple training, like *skill*, or to the highest of attainments, like *artistry*: *mastery* of her two-movement job on the assembly line; magnificent murals that are the apex of Michelangelo's *mastery* as a painter. See ACUMEN, ATTAINMENT, GENIUS.

Antonyms: clumsiness, incompetence, ineptitude.

skip

bound
hop
leap
spring

These words describe specific types of rapid, energetic motion of people, animals, and sometimes inanimate objects. **Skip** and **bound** both emphasize a series of motions. To *skip* is to move in a sprightly, nimble fashion by stepping, jumping lightly, and sliding on each foot in turn. It suggests lightheartedness and is commonly done by children or some young animals: to *skip* down the street to the candy store; goats *skipping* across the pasture. *Skip* is also used as a transitive verb to describe light, bouncing motions, especially across a surface: to *skip* a flat stone on the surface of the water.

Bound describes a more energetic motion than does *skip* and it involves longer and more rapid strides. *Bound* suggests high spirits and excitement: boys *bounding* down the beach after a ball; to *bound* across the room to answer the telephone. *Bound* may also imply fear or urgency: As we came near the woods, a startled deer *bounded* across the road.

Leap and **spring** are closely related in meaning and more precise than *bound* in that both involve rising and projecting oneself suddenly and vigorously upward from the ground or other supporting surface and then darting forward: to *leap* over a gate; to *spring* out of bed. However, *spring* indicates a more vigorous and catapulting motion than does *leap*. *Spring* is also used in describing the sudden elastic or recoiling action of certain devices. [The jaws of the trap *sprang* shut; The screen door *sprang* shut after the children rushed out to play.]

Hop is to move in short, often jerky *leaps* as a bird, toad, or rabbit. *Hopping* lacks the grace and speed of *skipping* or *bounding*, or the energy of *leaping* and *springing*. Of human beings, *hop* suggests limping, or jumping repeatedly on one foot as children do in certain games or in excitement. See FRISK, RUN.

Antonyms: crawl, creep, WALK.

These terms refer to congeries of specialized and nonstandard words and expressions used by a subculture or subdivision within a larger group sharing a common language, especially when such expressions would be thought illiterate, odd, or unintelligible by the average user of the language. **Slang** refers to the extremely informal language used by the members of an in-group in place of more usual expressions; *slang* may include abbreviated or made-up words, novel expressions, grammatical distortions, and other violations or departures from accepted usage. Sometimes the expressions of an in-group that gain popularity or a wider understanding are still considered *slang* by some people so long as they remain distinct from standard or even formal usage.

Argot refers to the *slang* of a very limited group which feels threatened by the hostility of society as a whole; this word was once restricted to the *slang* of criminals or thieves, but it can now apply to any use of language by minority groups that is marked by protective euphemisms and codelike secretiveness: the popular adoption of the word "camp" from homosexual *argot*; comparing the *argots* of the carnival worker and the jazz musician; Mr. Charlie and ofay are terms for the white man in the *argot* of the Negro ghetto. **Cant** once was exactly synonymous with *argot* in referring to the private language of thieves, but now it generally refers especially to the inflated, ingrown, or pompous language of a respected profession, especially in one of the social sciences: a learned paper full of sociological *cant*.

In a technical sense, **jargon** refers to a simple cross-breeding of two languages to facilitate communication, such as pidgin English. More generally, the word would be understood as referring to the extremely technical terms in use among specialists in any abstruse field: words like tweeter and woofer and other bits of *jargon* bandied about by hi-fi enthusiasts. See GOBBLEDYGOOK.

These words refer to buildings where animals are killed, butchered, and processed for market. **Slaughterhouse** may refer to a place where all these things occur in an organized way as a business endeavor, but it may also refer to a structure set aside for nothing but the killing of animals for whatever reason, though not necessarily for processing and marketing: *slaughterhouses* set up for the killing of cattle found to be infected with hoof-and-mouth disease. The word's vividness may have been thought unpalatable; in any case, the colorless term **packing plant** is now the most common way to refer to the building or complex of buildings where the killing of animals and processing of meat is carried out as a commercial enterprise: the *packing plants* of the major meat packers. **Packing house** is sometimes used instead of *packing plant*, but it can be confusing in that it might imply a small-scale, one-building operation and might indicate a place where the processing, rather than the killing, is done: delivering several sides of beef to the *packing house* for grading.

The term **abattoir** is usually confined to a place where animals are slaughtered for food and is not in wide use as a substitute for *packing plant*, except in English-speaking Canada. Because of its French root, *abattoir* might also suggest a European context; or it may be used as the basis of literary metaphors: the *abattoirs* of Belsen and Buchenwald. **Shambles**, referring exclusively to the place where animals are killed, is seldom used in this literal way in current speech; metaphorically, its reference to wholesale butchery of any kind is not even any longer felt as a reflection of the literal meaning: the smoking *shambles* of the battlefield. Killing of any sort, in fact, is not necessarily evoked by the word so much as a complete disordering of things: electricians who had made a *shambles* of the kitchen that she had just cleaned. See CLUTTER, KILL.

slave

bondmaid
bondman
peon
serf
thrall
vassal

These words refer to someone deprived of liberty, serving involuntarily, or otherwise at the mercy of a master. **Slave** is the most common of these, the one with the widest range of uses. Specifically, it refers to someone who is owned by another and has no civil rights himself, particularly someone who serves involuntarily or is given no renumeration for his services. Most countries now prohibit the possession of *slaves*, a practice endemic throughout history, as in the case of conquerors who commonly made *slaves* of conquered peoples. Trade in *slaves* still persists, however, in such places as Africa and the Near East. In a more general sense, the word is often used today in informal speech to refer to anyone victimized by someone or something: a paternalistic company that not only expected its employees to work like *slaves*, but to be grateful for the chance; a *slave* to her own narrow egotism.

Bondman and **bondmaid** are now archaic except in a historical context; they refer to a man or woman bound to serve without wages. Unlike *slave*, these words could suggest a contractual agreement which might last for a certain term only and in which a degree of freedom was permitted to the *bondman* or *bondmaid*. On the literal level, **thrall** and **vassal** are also archaic, but unlike the previous pair, both have surviving figurative uses. *Thrall* once indicated someone bound to personal service in a household; *vassal*, by contrast, indicated someone who was the master of his own affairs but pledged to serve his lord in war in exchange for protection within the lord's domain. Thus, in its literal historical meaning, *vassal* contrasts sharply with these other words, since it could apply to people of any intermediate rank between the *slave* and the absolute master: barons who rebelled against being kept as *vassals* to their king. When used figuratively, *thrall* can suggest someone intangibly bound to something, as a habit: a *thrall* to tobacco. Also, because of legends in which the use of black magic could make one an unwilling *thrall* to an evil person, the word can suggest figurative enchantment, particularly a state of involuntary fascination: held in *thrall* by the exquisite music. *Vassal*, by comparison, is more often used to refer to any kind of forced allegiance or dependency: Iron Curtain countries that are no longer strict *vassals* of the Soviet Union.

Serf, like *bondman*, is now mostly archaic except in historical reference. Under feudalism, a *serf* was bound to an estate and could not leave it; whoever owned the land was perforce his master. The *serf*, however, did have rights, unlike the *slave*, in that no one could drive him from the land nor deny his right to be there. *Serf* can be used loosely for anyone in servile subjection, but this use can sound imprecise or far-fetched. In Latin America, **peon** once referred most specifically to someone held in involuntary servitude until he had paid a debt. Since this arrangement often proved permanent in practice, the word now refers to anyone so ridden by poverty as to be virtually a *serf* or, loosely, to any poorly paid laborer. Used figuratively in English, the word refers informally but contemptuously to an underling or, in the plural, to the ordinary mass of people: a public statement full of platitudes, written strictly for consumption by the *peons*. See OBSEQUIOUS.

Antonyms: BOSS, lord.

slight

These words indicate a failure to pay the proper attention or respect to something. **Slight** makes the failure a matter of degree; the word sug-

slight
(continued)

disregard
ignore
neglect
snub

gests that whatever attention or respect has been given is totally in-adequate to the situation at hand: deliberately *slighting* the ambassador by placing him at the far end of the table; *slighting* his studies to con-centrate solely on extra-curricular activities. **Snub** is more restricted in emphasizing that aspect of *slight* that pertains exclusively to manners and propriety; in this case, however, the lack of respect is unsubtle and overt rather than implied. It also usually suggests a single, dramatic action rather than a gradual process of attrition: deliberately *snubbing* him by turning and walking away in the middle of his sentence. Whether or not a person has been *slighted* may be a matter of interpretation; there can be no doubt about someone's having been *snubbed*.

Neglect is mainly restricted to that aspect of *slight* that suggests an inequitable division of attention, except that in this case the amount of attention given is even less than is true for *slight*. The word may, how-ever, suggest either an intentional or unintentional failure of attention, unlike *slight* and especially *snub*, where the failure is most clearly con-scious and deliberate: a research project that caused him not so much to *slight* his students as to *neglect* them altogether in his usual absent-minded way. *Neglect* in its very generality can also apply to situations where courtesy or propriety is the issue: a hostess who never *neglects* the slightest expression of uneasiness on the part of any of her guests.

Disregard and **ignore** are like *neglect* in applying to the more general context of failures in attention, but both words suggest a com-plete failure rather than a partial one. In this case, *ignore* particularly stresses an intentional refusal to take account of a warning: *ignoring* the detour signs until he pulled up at the washed-out bridge. *Disregard* implies a denial of attention to something because of superior knowledge or more pressing considerations: asking the jurors to *disregard* her testi-mony as false and contradictory. While *ignore* suggests that something has been rejected without any conscious consideration, *disregard* can suggest a careful, wholly conscious evaluation that results in dismissal: eager to show that however he might *disregard* her advice, he would never *ignore* it. When these two words apply to manners, *ignore* com-pares with *snub* in stressing deliberate rudeness, but whereas *snub* refers to the commission of an offensive act, *ignore* refers to the omission of even minimal courtesies: *ignoring* the guest of honor all evening. In this context, *disregard* is unique among these words in having a use that suggests the act of deliberately overlooking someone else's discourtesy: *disregarding* her public outburst as inconsequential and unworthy of an answer. See CONTEMPTUOUS, DESPISE, FORGET, NEGLECT, SCOFF.

Antonyms: attend, cherish, consider, heed, prize, tend, value.

slogan

commercial
cry
jingle
message

These words all designate forms of advertising, the notices or announce-ments which direct the attention of the public to a product, brand, institution, or service. **Slogan** refers in advertising parlance to some striking phrase designed to catch the eye or ear and to linger as a re-minder of a product, service, etc. *Slogans* are probably the kind of adver-tisement with which we are all most familiar because constant repetition is the technique used to fix a *slogan* in the memory.

Message is the most general term in this list, denoting any group of words used by an advertiser to sell or promote something: "And now, a brief *message* from our sponsor," are familiar words to radio listeners everywhere. A **cry** is the oldest kind of advertisement under discussion. It designates the words, and hence the *message*, used by a vender in announcing his wares: the *cry* of the fishmonger in the street. Once a colorful and important selling technique, the *cry* has been all but totally displaced by modern methods of advertising and merchandising.

Commercial is the general term for any advertising *message* that is broadcast during a radio or television program, or between programs. The value of any *commercial* to the advertiser depends upon repetition and sometimes on novelty of presentation. *Commercials* may range in subject matter from a simple *slogan*, often sung, to a fairly complex "dramatic" situation involving several characters. The **jingle** is an important type of *commercial*, a short song or verse that uses a repetition of sounds, either alliterative or rhythmic, to get the attention of the listener and become impressed upon his memory. See POETRY, PROVERB, TRUISM.

sloth

acedia

anomie

apathy

autism

catatonia

indolence

torpor

These words refer to extremely dull, unresponsive, or inactive states due to laziness, sluggish health, or mental depression. Classically one of the seven deadly sins, **sloth** stresses extreme inaction due to laziness, a state amenable to a simple effort of the will. The word is sharp in its disapproval and suggests the unpleasant concomitants of sloppiness, untidiness, or uncleanliness: filthy, disheveled rooms that gave eloquent testimony to his life of *sloth* and debauchery. Unlike *sloth*, **torpor** may be applied to animals, people, or in fact to anything lying quiescent. Also, the word does not necessarily suggest a willed sinfulness and is consequently less disapproving. *Torpor* does point to a more lasting or deep-seated state near to that of sleep or hibernation and may suggest an unbroken outward uneventfulness: a *torpor* in which he merely stared out the window for days on end.

Acedia and **apathy** add to the connotations of the previous pair the suggestion of a state of mental unresponsiveness. *Acedia* (or *accidia*) sometimes replaces *sloth* in lists of the seven deadly sins, but the word is now more widely thought of as referring to a state of mental depression, implying a despair so profound that no action or attitude is thought possible or desirable: bouts of frenzied activity alternating with months of hopelessness and *acedia*. *Apathy* is a much more informal substitute for this last use of *acedia*, suggesting emotionless unresponsiveness that may stem from discouragement or low morale: looking upon his parents' quarrels with growing pessimism and *apathy*. Often the word is used sociologically to refer to a limp, passive attitude toward injustice among groups of people: slum children who face their constricted future with understandable *apathy*; the *apathy* of the German middle classes when faced with the rise of Hitler.

Anomie is specifically used in a sociological context to refer to a widespread social *apathy* that results in alienation, breakdowns in communication, hostility, and the weakening of norms of conduct; the word has recently become a fad word, used in less specialized contexts: the new delinquency among children of well-to-do parents, reflecting a widespread *anomie* among the affluent. Sometimes the word can suggest a breakdown of norms that sets the stage for chaotic or anarchic violence; in this sense, its suggestion of action puts it in sharp contrast with the other words here. By comparison, the more general **indolence** is limited to no particular technical context, and refers strictly to an aversion to exertion or work. While this could conceivably give the word a sociological context, more often it is used as a more formal substitute for simple laziness, emphasizing a deliberately chosen state of inactivity: the pampered *indolence* of the Edwardian gentry. But the word need not always be disapproving: a glorious week of *indolence* at the beach.

The remaining pair of words are both highly formal and technical terms from psychiatry. Both describe extremely withdrawn states of mental unresponsiveness. **Autism** at its most general can indicate a tendency toward daydreaming and introspection; at its most concrete it is used specifically to describe an extreme withdrawal in children that retards or destroys the development of such normal functions as speech: the years of intensive face-to-face effort involved in curing a single case of *autism*. **Catatonia** indicates a similar kind of extreme withdrawal in schizophrenic adults in which the psychosis takes the form of *apathy*, complete passivity, and inability to initiate the simplest actions: patients who, afflicted with *catatonia*, sit in the same uncomfortable positions for hours rather than shifting to a more comfortable posture. See IMPASSIVE, LISTLESS, UNINVOLVED.

Antonyms: activity, concern, diligence, industriousness, interest, involvement, liveliness.

These words are here compared as they apply to persons who do not accomplish things quickly or to actions which consume a great deal of time, often more than is thought necessary. **Slow**, the most general word, means extending or occurring over a relatively long span of time. *Slow* may be positive in its application to persons: a *slow* but meticulous craftsman; a man *slow* to anger. It may also suggest such undesirable traits as laziness or stupidity: *slow* in her work because she talks constantly to fellow workers; a person of such limited ability that he is *slow* to understand the simplest directions. Often the word indicates no more than not fast in progress or prompt in action: proceeding down the street at a *slow* walk.

Gradual and **leisurely** are never applied to persons. *Gradual* stresses advancement by *slow* or even imperceptible steps or degrees, but it involves a continuous progress: a *gradual* change for the better in one's health; to make *gradual* improvements in an old house. That is *leisurely* which is performed with no thought of a time limit and may be *slow* or simply unhurried and relaxed: a *leisurely* drive; a *leisurely* vacation.

Deliberate in this context adds the connotation of caution and care to *slow*. A person is *deliberate* if he acts after weighing all the aspects of a situation. Or a methodical man tends to plan his work in a *deliberate* manner.

Dilatory and **laggard** bring the concept of delay to *slow*. The *dilatory* person wastes time by being *slow* in doing what he could or should do promptly and procrastinates either because he is not self-disciplined or is unwilling to exert himself: a *dilatory* correspondent. *Laggard*, a stronger and more censorious word, implies lingering and falling behind in progress through laziness and a refusal to make an effort: *laggard* in paying his debt; *laggard* in finding a job, thus letting his parents support him.

Slack and **sluggish** both stress having little motion or alertness. To be *slack* is not only to be *slow*, but the word indicates negligence in the performance of one's duties: police who are *slack* in enforcing traffic rules; a *slack* housekeeper. Used of a period of time, it refers to a temporary lessening of activity in some endeavor: a *slack* season in the garment industry. *Sluggish* more than *slack* implies reluctance and sometimes an inability to move forward: a *sluggish* digestive system; a *sluggish* river. In a general sense *sluggish* is often applied to both physical and mental lethargy: to feel *sluggish* in hot, humid weather; a mind too *sluggish* to entertain new ideas.

slow

deliberate
dilatory
gradual
laggard
leisurely
retarded
slack
sluggish

At one time **retarded** meant *slow* or delayed, but it has almost completely lost its general meaning. It is now limited to describing children who are *slow* or backward in mental development and in school achievement. See LISTLESS, SLOTH.

Antonyms: agile, fast, LIVELY, *quick, rapid, speedy.*

small

diminutive
little
petite
short
squat
tiny
wee

These words refer to people or things of relatively reduced dimensions. **Small** and **little** are the most general and informal of these words. Both may be used loosely and interchangeably, but *little* without doubt suggests the most extreme departure from a norm: a *small* man; a *little* man. *Small* may suggest a slight reduction of proportions that is noticeable but not necessarily objectionable: a *small* house that would do perfectly for the two of them. *Little*, by contrast, suggests a reduction in scale that may be drastic: a *little* doll house.

When *small* and *little* refer to the physical proportions of a person, they suggest an overall reduction of scale, with *little* the most extreme. By contrast, **short** is restricted to a reduction in the scale of normal physical height: the *shortest* boy in the class; a man who appeared to be *shorter* than he actually was when he stood beside his tall wife. In this sense *short* may also be applied to parts of a human or animal body: a dwarf with *short* arms and legs attached to a trunk of normal size; The zebra has a *short* neck as compared with that of the giraffe. In reference to things, *short* is applied to that which has relatively *little* linear extension or vertical length: a *short*, dead-end street containing three houses; skirts so *short* that they resemble tunics. *Short* may also emphasize that something does not measure up to a standard or need in some way: a board that was too *short* to reach from one bank of the stream to the other; cheating by playing with a *short* deck of cards. **Squat** is an intensification of *short*, referring particularly to something that is of reduced vertical height but is not comparable reduced in its other dimensions, giving a low, wide silhouette: Romanesque churches that look *squat* beside their soaring Gothic counterparts; a heavy, *squat* man who waddled along.

Diminutive and **petite** are intensifications of the meanings implicit in *small*. Both are much more formal and both are particularly used to refer to women's figures when they are pleasingly trim and compact: a shortage of *petite* sizes in day dresses; showing off the *diminutive* figure she had earned by dieting. While *petite* would seem affected when applied to things other than women's figures, *diminutive* can be used for anything of reduced overall proportions: *diminutive* apples.

Tiny and **wee** are intensifications of *little*, suggesting such a drastic reduction of scale as to put the thing described outside established norms. *Tiny* may suggest a miniature or model of something: *tiny* toy soldiers that were exquisitely carved. In another use, the word can more simply express surprise at something extremely *small*, even when this is its normal size: a *tiny* baby; a *tiny* insect that lit on the palm of her hand. *Wee* almost inevitably sounds precious or cute, except possibly in children's literature: a *wee* lamb; a *wee* elf. Used euphemistically by adults, it suggests a humorous intent: wondering if they might have a *wee* drink, just the two of them, before going on to the party. See COMPACT, MINUTE.

Antonyms: HIGH, LARGE, MASSIVE, TREMENDOUS.

smell

These nouns denote that which is perceived through the nose by means of the olfactory sense. **Smell** is the most general word, including all the rest, and **odor** is its closest synonym. These two words are often used interchangeably, and both may be applied to pleasant, unpleasant, or neutral sensations. But *odor* is the more nearly neutral word, being freer of connotations than *smell* and better suited to scientific contexts. *Odor* tends to take its character from the words that qualify it: a pungent *odor;* a foul *odor. Smell* has a character of its own — a simple, hearty, forthright quality better suited to the kitchen than to the laboratory: cooking *smells. Odor* may sometimes signify a more delicately pleasing perception than *smell:* the clean *smell* of soap; the spicy *odor* of incense. And whereas a *smell* may sometimes be a blend of separate emanations, an *odor* is more commonly traceable to a single source: the *smell* of the sick room; the *odor* of formaldehyde.

An **aroma** is an *odor* both pleasing and distinctive, such as that given off by an appetizing food as it cooks or by good pipe tobacco as it burns. An *aroma* may be savory or smoky, permeating the air, or it may be delicate or spicy; but it is always stimulating to the senses: the *aroma* of fresh coffee. **Bouquet** is applied primarily to the delicate *aroma* that distinguishes a fine wine: He lifted the wine glass and sniffed the *bouquet* appreciatively.

A **scent** is any *odor,* natural or artificial, that is or may be faintly diffused through the air. A *scent* is always delicate and often pleasing: the *scent* of a sachet. **Fragrance** is a sweeter, fresher, more pervasive *scent:* the lingering *fragrance* of lilacs. *Scent* and *fragrance* are the words properly applied to dusting powder and perfume. *Smell* and *odor* seem inelegant and inappropriate in such contexts, except when *smell* is used with simple sincerity, as by a child: He liked the *smell* of his mother's perfume.

Applied to the natural emanations of human beings, *smell* and *odor* often signify something unpleasant or offensive, though the words are not limited in this way: the *smell* of sweat; body *odor. Fragrance* is used only of women and often occurs in popular writing, connoting a fresh, clean *smell:* the *fragrance* of her hair. *Scent* denotes the characteristic *odor* of an animal — a faint residual *odor* that lingers along the ground over which the animal has passed. A natural human *odor* is referred to as a *scent* only when the person in question is being tracked down like an animal: Bloodhounds followed the *scent* of the escaped prisoner. *Scent* and *smell* may also denote the olfactory sense itself; but *scent* is usually reserved for animals, especially dogs, and suggests an unusually sharp sense of *smell:* the keen *scent* of the foxhound.

Stink and **stench** are strong words and are applied to foul, offensive *odors, smells* that make a person hold his nose or that turn him sick to the stomach. Of the two, *stink* suggests a sharper sensation; *stench,* a more sickening one: the *stink* of sweaty feet; the *stench* of gangrene. Both words apply to what is rotting or decaying, but *stench* denotes the stronger and more overpowering *odor:* the *stench* of a battlefield after a slaughter.

Bouquet and *stench,* being the most specific of these words, are seldom used figuratively. But *odor, stink,* and *smell* are often so used. [There was an *odor* of fear in the air; He made quite a *stink* about it; It had the *smell* of foul play.] See SAVORY.

These words refer to a facial expression in which the mouth is silently widened and its corners are upturned in order to convey such emotions as affection, amusement, confidence, irony, polite approval, or disdain. **Smile** is the most general here, referring to any such expression regardless of the emotion being conveyed: giving the child a tender *smile;*

smell
(continued)

aroma
bouquet
fragrance
odor
scent
stench
stink

smile

grin

smile
(continued)

simper
smirk

swaggering down the street with a bright *smile*; unable to suppress a *smile* at his naiveté; the bitter *smile* he wore during his opponent's rebuttal. Because the expression itself suggests pleasure or approval more readily than other emotions, the word can even refer to the stereotyped mannerism that is put on automatically for other people in the absence of sincere emotion of any sort: the maddening and invariable *smile* that most stewardesses wear in response to every request or complaint.

The remaining words restrict themselves in reference to particular emotions or situations that motivate the *smile*. **Grin** indicates a greater widening of the mouth than *smile*, especially one that exposes the teeth, and suggests spontaneity, greater emotional intensity, and implies friendly warmth, pleasure, mirth, or high-spirited amusement: giving her his best wholesome, all-American-boy *grin*; the *grin* with which she greeted her old schoolfriend. The word is, however, derived from a root referring to howling or groaning, and the word is sometimes used for a less amicable or even ferocious baring of the teeth: the *grin* of a snarling wolf; the wounded soldier's *grin* of pain. In this use, the word may be a colorful substitute for grimace, which is more precise.

Simper and **smirk** are sometimes equated as indicating the same sort of silly or fatuous expression, but strikingly different connotations surround each word. *Simper* suggests smugness and self-righteousness and may even imply primness: the Wife of Bath's complaisant *simper*; a sort of mutual admiration society in which they could exchange *simpers* of superiority as they faced the uninitiated. *Smirk* may be used with precisely these same overtones. But where *simper* may suggest the reflection of an abiding inward feeling of hypocritical superiority, *smirk* suggests more often a momentary outward expression of derision or hostility: a teacher who tricks his students into giving incorrect answers and then greets them with a *smirk*; a man in handcuffs regarding his captors with a *smirk*. See LAUGH.

Antonyms: FROWN.

smutty

bawdy
pornographic
ribald

These words refer to the expression or representation of sexual desire or lust. **Smutty** is the informal and **pornographic** the formal word for frank allusions to or portrayals of sexual acts. Both can refer disapprovingly to literature or art preoccupied with this subject matter: a *smutty* series of drawings; a *pornographic* novel; a *smutty* film. Both words imply work designed to invoke a leer or outright sexual arousal, often of a neurotic kind. *Smutty* is more general and more charged with a feeling of abhorrence; it can also refer to suggestive remarks or dirty jokes: He was constantly making *smutty* comments that embarrassed everyone in the room. By contrast, *pornographic* is a more technical term referring strictly to literary or art work. Current legal attempts to define what is *pornographic* stress a work that has no redeeming social worth and is designed to arouse prurient feelings in the average person. A Supreme Court ruling has extended the definition to apply to what may be bland enough in itself but is advertised in a suggestive or titillating way.

Bawdy and **ribald** may once have been as condemnatory as the foregoing, though they have always applied more widely to actions as well as to works or remarks. Now both may sometimes be used to characterize sexual behavior or references that are frank or flat-footed, but not necessarily *smutty*. *Bawdy* derives from a word referring to a pander or prostitute, as can still be seen in the phrase, *bawdy* house. But the word refers more widely to sexual behavior that is exuberant, lively, riotous, or promiscuous: a *bawdy* novel about movie stars in Hollywood; a *bawdy*, brawling, amoral hulk of a man. While *bawdy* may suggest good humor, *ribald* specifically stresses an approach to sexuality that is both comic and *bawdy*: the *ribald* stories in Balzac's *Droll Tales*. In reference to behavior, the word adds a note of wit or merriment: a *ribald* party thrown by the jet set, at which stag movies were shown in mixed company. See DIRTY, EROTIC, LEWD, SUGGESTIVE.

Antonyms: BLAND, *bowdlerized, euphemistic, genteel*, MORAL.

These words pertain to various economic theories that propose the government ownership of a country's means of production. **Socialism**, in its generic sense, is a term of neutral force under which to group all such philosophies, but the word is blurred at the outset in that the adherents of many of these systems will argue that only their particular philosophy is the "true" *socialism*. On the other hand, advocates of an opposing economic system, capitalism, use the word *socialism* in an equally inexact way — as a general term of opprobrium for any proposal to give a government control of any aspect of a nation's economic life.

Political scientists, in attempting to keep the word useful as a neutral term of description, also must cope with the fact that *socialism* has a specific use quite different from its generic meaning. This use applies to the politico-economic systems of such countries as Britain, Sweden, Denmark, etc., in which democratic elective processes are combined with government welfare programs and government control or ownership of selected industries. This specific meaning of *socialism* (often called democratic *socialism*) is brought into play as a means of contrasting these countries with those commonly thought of as communist and in which free, elective representative government is not maintained.

Collectivism is a generic term that is useful because it does not contain the ambiguities inherent in the word *socialism*. It refers, not to a particular systematic ideology, but rather to any tendency toward the centralizing of power in the hands of a controlling bureaucracy. It can be applied with equal accuracy to any nation with a strong central government, whether democratic or totalitarian, capitalist or socialist. It is often used by the proponents of capitalism, however, in a less precise way to refer specifically to the socialistic tendencies of any government — in which case the word carries an overtone of disapproval: The century saw the rise of *collectivism* in all its variegations, with a corresponding decline in the importance put upon the worth of the individual.

All the remaining terms pertain to a particular kind of **communism**. This term itself, while the most general, is least open to a precise definition because of its constant redefinition by propagandists of all persuasions. Karl Marx and others founded **Marxism**, which advocated seizure of power by workers in violent revolution. Marx predicted that after this seizure, the state would "wither away," leaving a perfect, classless society. Until this condition of ideal *communism* could be reached, however, postrevolutionary man would approach it through the institution of a proletarian, socialist dictatorship. Because *communism* is imagined as a future perfection, some communists call their present system *socialism*, causing much confusion to those not acquainted with Marx's apocalyptic prophecies.

Nikolai Lenin, the first revolutionary leader of the Soviet Union, made basic changes in *Marxism* that gave rise to **Leninism**, or *Marxist-Leninism* as it is sometimes called. He argued that *communism* would have to develop country by country in a gradual process. Trotsky challenged this nationalistic tenet of *Leninism*, giving rise to **Trotsky-**

socialism

Castroism
collectivism
communism
Leninism
Maoism
Marxism
revisionism
Trotskyism

change. The term **revisionism**, which was first used by Lenin in criticism of the ideas of Karl Kautsky, the socialist theoretician, has recently become a term used in debates between contending groups within the communist world to refer to a doctrine which the given writer or speaker does not agree with.

Maoism is used to refer to the most militant present-day version of *communism*, as espoused by the founder of communist China, Mao Tsetung. It specifically implies a harsh intransigence in rejecting the possibility of coexistence with capitalistic states: Young radicals seem more attracted to *Maoism* than to democratic *socialism* or even the *Leninism* that has evolved in the Soviet Union.

Castroism (or sometimes Fidelism) is usually applied to the revolutionary tendency of radicals in Latin America, after Fidel Castro, the leader who established a revolutionary government in Cuba. The word carries no implication as to what brand of *socialism* or *communism* the revolutionist might prefer: He argued that *Castroism* could gain no foothold in those countries where genuinely democratic reforms were being made. See ANARCHISM, LEFTIST.

Antonyms: capitalism.

soil

  besmirch
  dirty
  smudge
  sully

These words mean to make or become unclean, impure, or stained with foreign matter. As implying the degree of uncleanness and its undesirability, **soil** is somewhat milder than **dirty** and refers largely to the inevitable staining with dust and grime, especially of wearing apparel and linens, that occurs from ordinary use: to *soil* a towel by not thoroughly washing one's *dirty* hands; a shirt collar *soiled* with sweat. In this context *dirty* is often substituted for *soil*, but *dirty* usually suggests creating an unclean condition that not only offends the aesthetic sense but may be injurious to health. Something that has been *dirtied* is often harder to clean than that which has been *soiled*: to *dirty* a neighborhood by throwing garbage on the sidewalks; to *dirty* upholstery by putting one's muddy shoes on it; to *dirty* a city's air with industrial fumes.

Smudge means to *soil* literally by begriming, as with soot, or by smearing, as with ink or dirty fingers. It often implies a degree of uncleanness as mild as, or milder than, that implied by *soil*, and suggests not making something *dirty* as much as it does spotting or staining it: Be careful not to *smudge* the drawing.

Dirty and *soil* are sometimes used figuratively in the moral context of character assassination: to *soil* a young girl's spotless reputation; to *dirty* an honored name.

Besmirch and **sully**, now found largely in literature of the past, have virtually lost all of their earlier meanings of *soiling*, *dirtying*, or *smudging* in a physical sense. Rather, *besmirch* is used as meaning to damage or dim the luster of, as one's honor or good repute: a reputation undeservedly *besmirched* by vicious gossip and slander. *Sully* is used in the same way, but carries a hint of greater injury and condemnation: his fame and standing as a diplomat *sullied* by the publicizing of his many sexual involvements. See DIRTY (adj.), DISCOLOR, POLLUTE.

Antonyms: bleach, CLEAN, *purify.*

solicitude

  care

These words agree in denoting a troubled state of mind. **Solicitude**, the most formal term, often implies anxious attention or devotion to another's welfare: The *solicitude* shown him by his neighbors after the robbery touched him deeply. *Solicitude* is especially used when the involvement of others is disinterested, stemming from feelings of charity or brotherhood rather than from intimacy or blood relationship: the *solicitude* of kings over the well-being of their subjects.

Care arises from responsibility or affection for others, and may vary from mild **concern** to profound **worry**: *care* for one's children. *Concern* is the absence of indifference, and hence implies voluntary involvement: *concern* for the nation's welfare. *Worry* implies an oppressive and fretful anxiety, and is often needless or excessive: distraught with *worry* over his daughter's late hours. *Worry* is the most personal and most intensely felt of these words, although it is sometimes used of impersonal situations to indicate irrational *concern*: burdened with all the *worries* of the world. *Care* implies an intimate and often deep attachment. *Concern* is more detached, and may only indicate a formal response to an impersonal situation: The president expressed his *concern* over the threatened railway strike. See ANXIETY, FEAR, LOVE, WORRY.

Antonyms: aloofness, indifference, NEGLECT, *unmindfulness*.

These words refer to the working out or making clear of a puzzle or mystery. **Solve** means to answer a question or work out a problem, often one deliberately set, as an exercise: *solving* the ten equations assigned for tomorrow's math class. The word can also refer to explaining any set of events by finding a workable way of dealing with them or by seeing the deeper meaning behind them: *solving* the problem of peace through world diplomacy; *solving* the dilemma of accounting for the national debt by viewing it in terms of the national accounts index. **Unravel** functions most nearly like this general sense of *solve*. The emphasis is on the untangling of a knotty problem, especially by means of research or analysis: an investigative body at work to *unravel* the motives of the assassin; an essay attempting to *unravel* the meaning of the difficult poem.

Decipher and **decode** are alike in specifically referring to the act of making intelligible a message that has been systematically garbled to confuse an unwanted reader: *deciphering* the radioed messages of the enemy; *decoding* the message by feeding it through the computer programmed to turn it into English again. In this context, *decipher* refers to translating messages scrambled according to a key or prearranged scheme, whereas *decode* refers to translating agreed-upon symbols that may be arbitrary or random. Thus *decoding* normally requires a code book in which the plain text and encoded equivalents are listed; *deciphering* only involves knowledge of the key or system, e.g. 1 for A, 2 for B, etc. *Decipher* is more often used than *decode* in a metaphorical way, in which case it refers to explaining puzzling or enigmatic signs: finally *deciphering* the odd expression he had given her a minute before. See CLARIFY.

Antonyms: baffle, CONFUSE, PUZZLE, *stump*.

These words refer to oversubtle argumentative techniques that place more emphasis on form than content, often with the intent of misleading or deceiving an audience. **Sophistry** and **sophism** both derive from a Greek word for wisdom and relate to the Sophists, a pre-Socratic school of philosophers interested in the logical expression of philosophical truth. In Socrates' day, however, the name was taken over by paid philosophers who taught logical and rhetorical techniques and were concerned more with persuasive forms of discourse than in the search for truth. Thus, both words now indicate false argument intentionally used to deceive. While the difference between the two words is slight, *sophistry* might be

solicitude
(continued)

concern
worry

solve

decipher
decode
unravel

sophistry

casuistry
hair-splitting
sophism

most useful as a generic term, *sophism* as a reference to specific examples: campaign oratory filled with *sophistry*; a statement on taxes that was a *sophism* pure and simple.

Casuistry has a Christian theological rather than classical Greek background; it refers to the science or doctrine of ambiguous cases of conscience, involving questions of moral right and wrong. The reasoning involved in this sort of argument was often so subtle and complicated that the word has come to be used with the same pejorative tone that *sophistry* has acquired. It still applies, however, particularly to disputes about ethics or morals: a governor who has abandoned the *casuistry* surrounding arguments over capital punishment. **Hair-splitting** is more specific than these other words in applying to any sort of argumentative discourse in which finicky or petty attention is given to fine points of method or substance in such a way as to lose sight of more significant questions: descending to *hair-splitting* about side issues whenever his opponent managed to present a convincing statement on the main issue. See CONTROVERSY, DECEPTION.

soup

bouillon
broth
chowder
consommé
porridge
stew
stock

These nouns denote either liquid food or food having a liquid base. **Soup** is the most general and most inclusive word. It is made by boiling meat, vegetables, or a combination of ingredients in water. *Soup* may be purely liquid — whether thick, or thin and clear — or it may consist of bits of solid food in liquid: tomato *soup*; chicken *soup*; vegetable *soup*.

Liquid that has had meat, fish, or vegetables boiled in it is called **stock** or **broth**. *Stock* stresses that the liquid is a by-product or an ingredient, not a food in itself: to strain beef *stock*; to skim off fat from chicken *stock*. *Stock* may be used as a base in making *soups*, sauces, or gravies. Beef *stock*, for example, is often an ingredient in canned vegetable *soup*; vegetable *stock* is often used as a liquid base for homemade *soups*. When *stock* is prepared as a separate liquid food — whether for use as a thin, strained *soup*, a packing fluid, or a fluid base — it is called *broth*. Beef *broth* may be made by boiling marrow bones, beef shin, vegetables, and seasonings together, then skimming and straining the *stock*: a *soup* of noodles and ground beef in beef *broth*; a can of boned turkey with *broth*. *Stock* used to make *broth* is sometimes, but not always, clarified: a chicken *soup* recipe calling for two cans of clear chicken *broth*.

Bouillon is a clear *broth* made by boiling and simmering lean beef, chicken, or other meats, then straining and clarifying the *stock*. Such *stock* may be dehydrated and sold in the form of *bouillon* cubes that are reconstituted by being dissolved in hot water. **Consommé** is a clear, strong, concentrated *soup* of meat or meat *stock* (and sometimes vegetables) boiled, strained, and seasoned: beef *consommé*; chicken *consommé*. *Consommé* is richer and more nutritious than *bouillon* or *broth*. It may be served hot, as a clear liquid; or, if it contains gelatin, it may be refrigerated, jelled, and served cold.

Where *stock*, *broth*, *bouillon*, and *consommé* are purely liquid, the remaining dishes consist of food cooked in liquid. **Stew** is a preparation of meat or fish and various vegetables simmered together gently in water or milk. Beef *stew* may contain small chunks of beef and diced vegetables in beef *broth*. Oyster *stew* may contain oysters, oyster *broth*, butter, cream, and whole milk. **Chowder** is a thick *soup* often made with milk. It usually consists of clams, fish, or corn stewed with potatoes and onions, often bacon, and sometimes other vegetables: clam *chowder*; corn *chowder*; fish *chowder* made with halibut fillets and fish *broth*. **Porridge** is a soft food made by boiling oatmeal or other meal in water or milk until it thickens. This word is used chiefly in Great Britain. It may also denote a thick *broth* or *stew* of vegetables with or without meat.

These words refer to sharp tastes or smells or to harsh dispositions and behavior stemming from them. When used of tastes, **sour** refers to the characteristic sharpness produced by acids. **Acid** itself refers more directly to such a taste. **Acidulous** indicates a taste that is partially *acid* or mildly *sour*. **Tart** refers to a sharp taste that is pleasantly *acid* or piquant in taste. **Acrid** pertains to any strong or sharp smell, but can also apply to sharp tastes produced either by acids or alkalies. **Bitter** is restricted to sharp tastes produced mainly by alkalis, but can also apply to strong unpleasant smells as well. If the *bitter* taste or smell is mild it might be regarded as savory or pleasant; if quite strong it might become wry or unpleasant, or be capable of lingering on, causing discomfort. **Caustic** suggests a sharp smell such as a strong alkali might give off; it can be used of tastes only as a hyperbole, since it also refers quite literally to alkalinity intense enough to eat away or corrode organic tissues.

On their most literal level, thus, these words are fairly clear in their neutrally descriptive distinctions from one another. In describing harsh disposition or behavior, however, their shadings of meaning are rather more blurred. *Sour* applies almost solely to mood or disposition, suggesting a pessimistic, disenchanted, or excessively solemn attitude: always wearing a *sour* expression that no pleasantry could soften; recalling her former naive idealism with a *sour* smile; having to confront the *sour* face of the superintendent. *Bitter* suggests an even fiercer gloominess that arises from a sense of having been unjustly treated or from a deep-seated anger that smolders without catching fire: a *bitter* man who saw nothing worthy of admiration no matter where he looked; *bitter* accusations concerning the unfair division of money between them. *Tart* applies more appropriately to particular instances of behavior and gives a different tone altogether; it suggests impertinence or sassiness: giving a *tart* answer to the teacher's scolding. *Acid* and *acidulous* are difficult to distinguish except for the greater formality of the latter; *acidulous* might sometimes suggest an abiding mood and *acid* an actual expression: an *acidulous* temper; an *acid* remark. In any case, *acid* seems considerably stronger in its suggestions of harsh or gratuitous hostility: *Bitter* at his own lack of success as a playwright, the critic was negative and *acid* in all his comments.

Acrid and *caustic* are the most intense of these words in pointing to harsh dispositions or expressions. *Acrid* applies best to mood: an *acrid* curtness of manner. It can also apply, however, to expressions: an *acrid* scowl disfiguring his face. *Caustic* perhaps suggests an even fiercer hostility than *acrid*, since it carries over here its implication of corrosive power: often filled with a *caustic* rage; *caustic* aspersions on his friend's abilities; answers so *caustic* as to hint at some imbalance of mind. See SARCASTIC, SAVORY, VINDICTIVE.

Antonyms: BLAND, *kind*, OPTIMISTIC, *sweet*.

These words refer to wavering coruscations of light, whether reflected from a moving surface or emitted unsteadily by the source of light itself. **Sparkling** would seem to suggest the throwing off of sparks, but as now used it is almost exclusively restricted to uneven, bright flashes reflected from light-catching objects: *sparkling* diamonds. **Glittering** is close to

sour

acid
acidulous
acrid
bitter
caustic
tart

sparkling

flashing
flickering

sparkling
(continued)

glimmering
glittering
scintillating
shimmering
twinkling

sparkling in meaning; *sparkling* perhaps suggests intenser stabs of more fleeting light, while *glittering* might suggest a larger mass of reflecting material that can be seen over a longer period of time and that casts reflections not so dependent on an exact perspective: a *sparkling* drop of dew; the whole *glittering*, rain-washed garden. In more general uses, *sparkling* suggests exuberance or animation, while *glittering* may have negative connotations of gaudiness, cheapness, or evil: her *sparkling* smile; *glittering* trinkets; *glittering* generalities; the *glittering* avarice in his eyes.

Flashing, when used for sources of light, suggests most strongly a regular on-and-off alternation of light and darkness: the *flashing* red of the traffic light. Used for reflected light, it does not suggest regularity so much as intensity; it may not even suggest wavering light at all: the *flashing*, sunlit windows. Like *sparkling*, *flashing* may suggest liveliness, but more often of an unpleasant nature: the *flashing* eyes of rage. Both **twinkling** and **scintillating** describe, most specifically, starlight that appears to waver because of the moving atmosphere through which we see it. *Twinkling* can seem coy outside its nursery-rhyme context, but may escape this in descriptive uses: the *twinkling* lights of the city far below. *Scintillating* has overtones of brilliance and has been overused in figurative contexts to suggest elegance and wit: *scintillating* conversation.

Flickering, glimmering, and **shimmering** all suggest a subdued or dim wavering of light. *Flickering* mostly relates to sources rather than reflections of light, but suggests a more sporadic or irregular wavering than the earlier words: patches of clouds that let through only *flickering* sunlight. The word has been overused to describe firelight: *flickering* logs on the andirons. *Shimmering*, in contrast, stresses reflected light that undulates quickly in a soft or dazzling blur: *shimmering* water. *Glimmering* may apply either to sources or to reflections; more than either of its two companion words, it stresses fitfulness and dimness, suggesting a source fainter than for *flickering* and slower undulations than for *shimmering*: the last coals of the *glimmering* fire; traces of moonlight in the *glimmering* darkness of the room. See BRIGHT, LUMINOUS.

Antonyms: dull, GLOOMY, LACKLUSTER.

spear

harpoon
javelin
lance
pike

These words refer to pole-like weapons, usually with pointed heads, that are thrown or used to stab. In a historical context, **spear** can indicate any weapon of this kind, from the crudest to the most highly refined; now, however, it would most readily call to mind a primitive weapon, such as one made of wood: the Roman soldier who wounded Christ's side with his *spear*; photographing a tribal dance of warriors carrying *spear* and shield. The word still occurs as a term in present-day *spear* fishing, however, where it indicates a forged, barbed instrument, usually made of steel. **Lance** and **pike** are forms of *spear* that were outmoded by the development of gunpowder. *Lance*, as it refers to the medieval weapon, suggests a long, heavy piece, one used by a mounted soldier to joust with, rather than one designed to be thrown. In the same period, *pike* indicated a larger, heavier weapon than *lance*, used by a foot soldier for bludgeoning or stabbing, rather than for throwing or jousting.

Harpoon and **javelin** both refer to specialized types of *spears* still in use. *Harpoon* can refer to a weapon particularly designed for catching fish, whether used as something to be thrown or to stab with: once it referred to a long steel-headed *spear* hurled to wound or kill such sea animals as whales; it still functions in the context of whaling and other kinds of fishing, but now it often refers to any sort of pronged instrument that may be shot, as from a gun designed for the purpose. In a context similar to that for *lance* and *pike*, *javelin* once referred to a light weapon for throwing in battle: it survives now to indicate a long, wooden-shafted *spear* that is thrown in track and field sporting events: working out with both the discus and *javelin*. See ARMS, KNIFE.

These words refer to a communication that is without ambiguity, vagueness, or evasion. With **specific**, the emphasis is on a lack of vagueness achieved by detailed rather than general treatment: *specific* instructions on how to cope with every conceivable problem that might come up during his absence. **Definite** refers either to clarity and distinctness or to expression that is conclusive or unconditional: a map that would give him a *definite* notion of his whereabouts; promising to have a *definite* yes-or-no answer within a week. As in the last example, *definite* may indicate extreme brevity, whereas *specific* tends to suggest exhaustive treatment. Something that is *specific*, furthermore, may still be unclear or inconclusive, regardless of its concreteness and detail: a study that was *specific* in listing possible alternatives but was not *definite* about which of these might give the best results.

Explicit stresses an exact spelling-out that leaves nothing to be guessed at or confused by. When instructions or description are involved, one would normally have to be both *specific* and *definite* to be *explicit*; on the other hand, if a judgment is involved, one would have to be *definite*, but not necessarily *specific*: an *explicit* list of all campaign expenditures; a brief remark that made *explicit* his dislike of Picasso. *Explicit* may tend to relate to questions, *definite* to answers: an *explicit* request that he give a *definite* reply. **Express** is similar to, but an intensification of, *explicit*. It suggests emphatic directness that avoids the tacit or evasive: unwilling to disobey an *express* command. This word, also, is often related to the posing of questions or the stating of one's desires: his *express* wish that he be cremated. See ACCURATE, CLEAR, CONCLUSIVE.

Antonyms: ambiguous, evasive, OBSCURE, VAGUE.

These words refer to someone watching any sort of event. **Spectator** can indicate someone present at a sporting event or other happening; no direct participation is implied, but the word often suggests that a *spectator* has made the effort to attend or be a member of the audience: *spectators* at the tennis match; *spectators* lined up to watch the ticker-tape parade. Less often, the word can suggest the opposite: millions of people who unexpectedly became *spectators* to the world's first televised homicide. **Onlooker**, by contrast, more often suggests an accidental or chance viewing of some event: *onlookers* who happened to be present when the Ferris wheel collapsed. The word may also suggest someone who has deliberately withdrawn from events he might well have participated in: He chose to remain an *onlooker* during most of his family's protracted quarrels.

Fan and kibitzer are more informal than the foregoing, but both specifically suggest the interested and voluntary viewing of something. *Fan* relates to *spectator* in particularly emphasizing the ardent advocacy of a given artist, performer, or team: They performed in a hall that held thousands of screaming *fans*; booed by *fans* for the home team. The word need not, however, imply a physical gathering at all: a *fan* of the prolific mystery writer; a pre-sold market of *fans* for every new record they made. *Kibitzer* relates to *onlooker* in indicating someone on the sidelines of an event, but one who in this case can't refrain from commenting on the action, or otherwise meddling in it, even to the point of being drawn into direct involvement: *kibitzers* at ringside who shouted contradictory advice to the champ; a personal argument that at first attracted *kibitzers* and finally turned into a general brawl.

Peeping Tom and **voyeur** refer to *onlookers* who deliberately spy on others. *Peeping Tom*, the more informal of the two, may sometimes suggest a devious attempt to gain information, but more often it suggests a mentally disturbed person who gets erotic pleasure from spying on unsuspecting people who are not fully dressed: a *peeping Tom* who kept watch on the apartment bedrooms across the airshaft from him. *Voyeur* is the technical psychiatric term for such a person, although here the word includes, as well, any sort of erotic pleasure derived from looking rather than active involvement, even where stealth is not present: permissive parents whose open intimacies tend to make *voyeurs* of their children.

Observer is uniquely relevant to someone specifically assigned the role of watching rather than participating, particularly someone who remains impartial and has no authority to affect the outcome: UN *observers* deployed as members of the peace-keeping mission in the truce zone. The word can also indicate the role assumed by someone, such as a commentator or critic, who is a perceptive viewer of events and reports them to or analyzes them for others: a keen *observer* of the modern art scene. In this case, it is the *observer* who may have the audience, whereas the things he reports may not. **Witness** may suggest accidental viewing, like *onlooker*: *witnesses* to the accident. It may also suggest someone who deliberately experiences something in order to report it: a crusading *witness* to racial injustice. It may, in fact, refer to the report itself: bearing false *witness*. The word, in the legal context, can refer either to *onlookers* or anyone else called to testify in court or to people called upon to observe and certify a transaction: *witnesses* who gave conflicting testimony; needing two *witnesses* to make the ceremony legal. See SEE, VISION.

Antonyms: participant, PERFORMER.

speech

address
discourse
harangue
homily
lecture
oration
sermon

These nouns apply to public speaking, denoting talks delivered before an audience. **Speech** is the most general and least formal word. A *speech* may be either extemporaneous or prepared; it may express feelings, ideas, or opinions, impart information, relate experiences, set forth a program, or outline a position: a campaign *speech*; a ghostwritten *speech*; an impromptu *speech*; an after-dinner *speech*. An **address** is a carefully prepared, formal *speech*, as one delivered by a distinguished speaker or made on a ceremonial occasion: an inaugural *address*; a valedictory *address*. Also, where *speech* emphasizes the act of talking, *address* stresses the fact that an audience is in attendance: a malcontent making *speeches* on street corners; the President's annual *address* to Congress.

An **oration** is an eloquent *address* meant to stir the emotions of a group or mass of people. It treats some important subject in a dignified style and manner, according to the rules of oratory, and is usually delivered on a special occasion, as at a celebration or a funeral: Mark Antony's *oration* over the body of Caesar; Lincoln's Gettysburg *Address* is an *oration*. Since true orators are rare, however, the term *oration* may also be applied to a pompous *speech* designed for showy, oratorical effect: an old-fashioned, small-town, Fourth-of-July *oration*. A **harangue** is a long, loud, vehement *speech*, appealing to passions or prejudices. It may be an extemporaneous tirade and is often intended to inflame those to whom it is addressed and to spur them to action of some sort: the *harangues* of a demagogue. In a looser sense, *harangue* may apply to any long, bombastic *speech*, typically a tiresome one: endless *harangues*.

Where *oration* and *harangue* emphasize the character of an *address*, the remaining nouns stress content and purpose. A **discourse** is a fairly long, carefully prepared, well-organized *speech* on a definite subject: a *discourse* on Virgil; a collection of religious *discourses*. A **lecture** is the kind of *speech* given by a teacher to a class. It is a *discourse* on a given topic, designed to inform and instruct a group of students or some similar audience: a *lecture* course in college, as distinguished from a seminar; a series of museum *lectures* on modern art. *Lecture* derives from a Latin verb meaning to read. The most effective *lectures* are not read, but giving a *lecture* does imply extensive previous preparation, including the writing down of what is to be said.

Both **sermon** (the general word) and **homily** (the more erudite term) may mean an instructive religious *discourse* delivered by a clergyman to a congregation. Originally, a *homily* was a *discourse* or *lecture* explaining a Biblical text, while a *sermon* was an *address* from the pulpit dealing with dogma or ethics. Now the opposite distinction is sometimes made — that a *sermon* takes its theme from Scripture while a *homily* gives practical ethical guidance. In the Middle Ages, *homilies* written by eloquent and learned early churchmen were often read in churches, being used as approved *sermons*. Hence the branch of theological study that treats of the art of planning, writing, and delivering *sermons* is called "homiletics."

In informal use, *lecture*, *sermon*, and *harangue* may all imply didactic moral instruction, referring to formal reproofs, stern rebukes, lengthy reprimands, or earnest exhortations to duty. [He gave the boy a *lecture* on his lateness; She was subjected to a *harangue* on her supposed ingratitude; "All right, I'll do it," he said; "you don't have to preach me a *sermon* about it."] See CONVERSATION.

speechless

dumb
inarticulate
incoherent
mute

These words all refer either to an inability or unwillingness to speak or produce sound or to be intelligible. **Speechless** often refers to a transitory inability to speak because of shock or powerful emotions: stunned *speechless* by the news. But sometimes the word can also indicate an impairment of speech functions: The brain damage resulted in an aphasia that rendered her husband totally *speechless*. Much more commonly, however, **dumb** or **mute** refer to any such sort of permanent inability to speak. *Dumb* may refer to this inability when caused by some defect of the speech organs, whereas *mute* is often the word of choice when the inability results, instead, from never having heard speech sounds, as in deafness sustained since infancy: a child who was *dumb* because of deformed vocal cords; a technique for teaching *mute* children to speak in spite of their deafness. Sometimes *mute* is substituted for *dumb*, regardless of cause, since *dumb* can also apply informally as a pejorative word for mental dullness. This linking of two unrelated deprivations may once have been deliberate but it is now felt to be both inaccurate and cruel. *Dumb* can also function like *speechless* to indicate a temporary loss of speech, though it can refer as well to an inability to make any sort of sound because of shock or emotion: *dumb* with fright. In this context, *mute* more often refers to a deliberate refusal to speak: She answered his question with *mute* contempt; a prisoner who stolidly remained *mute* under the most excruciating tortures they could devise. When the reference is not to people, *dumb* refers to a possibly natural or normal in-capacity for speech but not necessarily to an inability to produce sound: *dumb* animals. In a similar situation, *mute* may refer to complete sound-lessness: the *mute* hush of the forest at dusk. The verb form of the word is of interest here, since it refers to altered or subdued sound: *muted* trumpets.

Inarticulate can be a vague and confusing word, since it can refer to what is soundless, *speechless*, unintelligible, confused, or halting. Only context can make clear which notion is intended: His mouth worked to form words, but he remained completely *inarticulate*; gasping in *inarticulate* fright; lines in the play that were lost because of *inarticulate* mumbling; an *inarticulate* presentation of his ideas; simple lessons that help stutterers to be less *inarticulate*. **Incoherent** can sometimes be substituted for *speechless*, but most often it clearly implies confused statements or halting speech: an *incoherent* essay filled with circumlocution and digression; stammered accusations and *incoherent* outcries. See SILENT, STUTTER, TACITURN.

Antonyms: articulate, TALKATIVE, VERBOSE.

speed

alacrity
celerity
dispatch
haste
hurry
promptness
swiftness
velocity

These words refer to rapid motion or to the immediate execution of a task. **Speed, swiftness,** and **velocity** are the most general of these, with *speed* the least and *velocity* the most formal. *Speed* can be used of any rapid and continuing motion: The *speed* of the horses along the race-track was simply amazing. It is especially appropriate in referring to vehicles, machines, or inanimate projectiles: *Speed* and more *speed* is what the hot-rod enthusiast is after. It can, of course, refer to the rate of motion and not necessarily to fast motion at all: The tortoise crept along at an agonizingly slow *speed*. *Velocity* has only scientific or technical uses and would sound pretentious in other situations. It can refer to rapid, continuing motion, but is more often used for rate of motion. [The rocket attained an orbit of dizzying *velocity*; The *velocity* of sound falls far short of the *speed* of light.] *Swiftness* does not apply to rate of motion but is otherwise almost interchangeable with *speed*. It is slightly more formal, however, and would be used less for vehicles and machines than for living things. It may have a lyrical or poetic quality that is by no means necessarily trite or stilted. [The mallards streamed across the sky with a *swiftness* that dazzled every onlooker; A ballet dancer must possess both strength and *swiftness*.] Unlike *speed*, *swiftness* often also refers to a very brief interval: the *swiftness* with which she answered my question.

Haste and **hurry** both refer to a rushed manner of behavior. *Haste* is equally appropriate to formal and informal contexts and tends to imply the ineffective performance of a task, as in the motto, *haste* makes waste. When this overtone is absent, an extremely brief or partial action is still implied: Forgive the *haste* with which this note is written; I will send a long letter shortly. *Hurry* is more informal than *haste*, but otherwise similar in its possible overtone of ineffectiveness: How can you avoid mistakes when you're in such a *hurry*?

Dispatch is much more formal than either *haste* or *hurry* and is opposed to them in implying rapid action that is both efficient and thorough. It also suggests the total completion of a task. [Where could he find a secretary who took dictation with such *dispatch*?; The *dispatch* with which she finished the leftovers astonished everyone else at the table.] **Promptness**, while slightly less formal than *dispatch*, also suggests an efficient *swiftness*; it is restricted, however, to refer to punctuality or to the accomplishment of a task in a given time. [Haste simply cannot make up for your lack of *promptness*; Despite the fall of two governments, the war correspondent turned in his report with his usual *promptness*.] It can also refer to the briefness of an interval of time: He expected her to agree to his request, but the *promptness* of her reply delighted him.

Alacrity and **celerity** are the most formal of these words and apply more to readiness in a person's attitude than to *speed* of motion. *Alacrity* implies a cheerful willingness to act: The waiter's *alacrity* in greeting us and finding us a table did not match the *speed* with which he delivered the food we ordered. *Celerity* may also be used in this way but, unlike *alacrity*, it can apply simply to the *speed* of a continuing motion: The ungainly look of an ostrich is belied by the *celerity* with which it can outdistance its more graceful enemies. Both words may tend to sound pretentious or stilted. See QUICK, QUICKEN.

Antonyms: DELAY, *languor, slowness, sluggishness.*

These words refer to the extravagant or imprudent spending or use of one's resources. **Spendthrift** is the most informal of these words and the most clear and specific. It points exclusively to the spending of one's money in ways that are excessive, unwise, or unnecessary: putting their children on strict allowances to cure them of being *spendthrift*. The word by itself, however, carries no implications about the money available to such a spender or about the consequences of such spending: a legendary *spendthrift* millionaire; the penurious rich and the *spendthrift* poor. The word was once, perhaps, more disapproving than it necessarily is now: uncomplaining when he was hard up, but *spendthrift* with his windfalls.

Of the remaining words, **prodigal** is closest in meaning to *spendthrift*, though it refers beyond the spending of money to any lavish or foolish extravagance, often one of awesome proportions: a *prodigal* shopping spree; the *prodigal* extravaganzas that Hollywood turns out. The word may be used without disapproval for extreme generosity: *prodigal* in the time she spent with any student who needed extra help. In any case, the word emphasizes the quantity of expenditure involved, whereas *spendthrift* can conceivably suggest the unconcerned spending of what one has, regardless of the amount. Sometimes, *prodigal* is understood as referring to someone who, after having wasted all of his substance, returns home in repentance, after the Biblical parable of the *prodigal* son.

Improvident, the most formal of these words, indicates the unwise use of anything, with a specific emphasis on failing to foresee or provide for the future: the *improvident* grasshopper in the fable who, unlike the industrious ant, had failed to lay in supplies against the winter; *improvident* bon vivants who live only for the moment, with no thought for tomorrow. **Thriftless** relates to *improvident* in pointing to someone unable to save money or to manage his affairs economically, but the emphasis on futurity is not necessarily present: the average bachelor's *thriftless* hit-or-miss budgeting of income. The word is distinct from *spendthrift* in that no squandering need be implied in this case; an impoverished family could not be *prodigal*, though it might or might not be *spendthrift* with what resources it had. It would most likely, however, be compelled to be *thriftless*.

Wasteful is the most general of these in applying widely beyond the context of spending money; it suggests an unwise or reckless misuse of resources that fails to get the full benefit from them: *wasteful* to spend so much on a dress you'll wear only once; *wasteful* of the company's time,

spendthrift

improvident
prodigal
thriftless
wasteful

though miserly with his own; tragically *wasteful* of natural resources that can never be replaced. See GENEROUS, RECKLESS.

Antonyms: CAUTIOUS, *frugal, miserly, niggardly, thrifty.*

spontaneous

extemporaneous
impromptu
improvised
impulsive
unplanned
unpremeditated
unrehearsed

These words refer to actions that are taken on the spur of the moment or without forethought. **Spontaneous** includes both these ideas and may often include, as well, suggestions of naturalness, frankness, and good humor: the child's *spontaneous* answers to all our questions. Sometimes *spontaneous* is deliberately contrasted with such words as routinized or conformist: the *spontaneous* exuberance of teen-agers when they feel free to be themselves. In another use, the word is sometimes restricted in reference to voluntary rather than coerced action or to action that comes about by general agreement arising out of immediate circumstances: a *spontaneous* decision to vote for the insurgent candidate despite the threats of the incumbent; a *spontaneous* protest demonstration that began with a few disgruntled students and ended in a march on one of the administration buildings. **Impulsive** is far less positive in its implications as compared to *spontaneous.* It may, in fact, suggest someone governed by or at the mercy of his whims or moods without regard for others; this word, consequently, lacks the overtone of good humor present in *spontaneous* and can apply to ugly or disruptive actions as well as to pleasant ones: an *impulsive* generosity that alternates fitfully with equally *impulsive* temper tantrums. In some cases, the word can be used to describe actions occurring on the spur of the moment: supermarkets that display their wares to encourage customers to make *impulsive* purchases of items not on their shopping lists.

Unplanned is the most neutral of these words in stressing only the lack of forethought and carrying no emotional overtones about the quality of the action: an *unplanned* stopover in San Francisco because of engine trouble; an *unplanned* interview that allowed the speakers to explore questions in depth. **Unpremeditated** is the most technical of these words; in legal terminology, it refers to an *impulsive* crime committed without forethought and therefore *unplanned.* This would be less serious than the same crime devised in advance. Except in a legal context, it would sound stiff as a substitute for *unplanned* or *impulsive,* unless a comic touch were intended: a party that turned out to be an *unpremeditated* disaster.

The remaining words pertain mostly to a context of public speaking or musical and theatrical performance. **Extemporaneous** refers specifically to a speech delivered on the spur of the moment without notes, but especially without a written version of the speech to be given: ministers long used to working up overnight an *extemporaneous* Sunday sermon; the question-and-answer period of the television debate that by its very nature had to be *extemporaneous.* **Impromptu** pertains, most specifically, to a kind of musical performance in which the music played is invented as the performer goes along: an overblown piano fantasy that was surely *impromptu.* The word is also often used of speeches delivered on short notice: *impromptu* speeches tacked onto each seconding motion. In this area, the word can be distinguished from *extemporaneous* in that the latter may be a matter of choice, even when the speech has been set long in advance, whereas *impromptu* suggests being called on to speak when one is not expecting it and is therefore of necessity unprepared. [The dean gave the same *extemporaneous* reprimand, word for word, to every student caught cheating; nor did he flicker an eyelid as he listened to their *impromptu* replies.]

Both **unrehearsed** and **improvised** can be used in either a musical or a theatrical context. *Unrehearsed*, here, may suggest that a set piece is to be performed, but that the players have not previously played it through. In this context, *improvised* would suggest a basic structure within which the players have considerable opportunities for *spontaneous* invention. Although *improvised* is generally used in a neutrally descriptive way, *unrehearsed* can sometimes suggest a negative judgment: Jazz is necessarily *improvised*, but it is ridiculous to think of it as *unrehearsed*. In a more general context, *unrehearsed* approaches *spontaneous* in its implications, stressing a voluntary and *unplanned* telling or acting out: He asked bluntly if the witness's testimony was freely given and *unrehearsed*. *Improvised* can suggest a rough-and-ready substitute for something lacking or the making of decisions as one goes along: an *improvised* tent-pole made from a stripped branch; an *improvised* tour, taking them from place to place as the spirit moved them. See VAGUE, WANDER.

Antonyms: definite, forced, FORMAL, *stylized.*

These words refer to the gradual gaining of ground by something. **Spread** is the most informal and general of these, with particular usefulness in referring to the ground gained by a species, a disease, an idea, or a cultural mannerism: deciduous trees that slowly *spread* over most of the world; rats that *spread* bubonic plague throughout Europe; a rash *spreading* over most of her body; ideas that *spread* more rapidly in an age of instant communications; Carnaby Street fashions that *spread* quickly from London to America. **Propagate** also refers to something that gains ground or adherents. It suggests a conscious, laborious effort to stimulate the healthy growth of something: *propagating* a new species of seedless grapefruit. It can also apply to an insidious or harmful *spreading* of information: *propagating* the myth of racial superiority for his own devious ends.

Distribute and **circulate** lack both the negative implications possible for *propagate*. They are both most often neutral in their concentration on techniques for the wide *spreading* of something through space. *Distribute* emphasizes easy access and is particularly relevant in reference to periodicals: news trucks that *distribute* the day's papers throughout the city. The point of the word may be the availability of something to everyone concerned or the parceling out of a given quantity among a group: *distributing* a copy of the new health insurance plan to everyone in the office. *Circulate* is less concrete in reference than *distribute*; it may also refer to *distributing* periodicals: a paper that is *circulated* to the whole metropolitan area. More often, however, this word, as a verb, refers to actual movement through a mass: arterial blood that *circulates* oxygen throughout the body. The word may also point to a movement of ideas or mannerisms among a circle of people: conservative notions that *circulate* among the company's power elite. See ENLARGE, PERMEATE, ESCALATE, SCATTER.

Antonyms: ACCUMULATE, DESTROY, GATHER.

These words all denote imaginary creatures of folklore, especially European folklore, who are human in form but have no souls. They are usually invisible and are capable of working either good or evil magic against mankind. **Sprite**, which is derived from the same source as "spirit," is such a creature who is ethereal or disembodied and who lives in the air rather than on the earth, as Ariel of Shakespeare's *Tempest*.

Fairy is the most generalized term for these beings. In the narrow

spread

circulate
distribute
propagate

sprite

elf
fairy
gnome

sprite
(continued)

goblin
gremlin
hobgoblin

sense, a *fairy* is thought of as diminutive, graceful, and fair of face, but able to assume other shapes at will. *Fairies* may sometimes be masculine, but are more usually feminine. They inhabit woods, forests, and fields, but maintain a close relationship with human beings toward whom they act in both an annoying or friendly fashion. Nowadays, the word has become a pejorative slang term to describe those male homosexuals thought to be effeminate or fey in manner or appearance.

Elf is the word in English for the *fairy* of Teutonic folklore. *Elves* are popularly pictured as tiny, childlike beings with pointed ears, who are comical or quaint in appearance rather than delicate and beautiful. *Elf* suggests more of the spirit of playfulness and mischief than does *fairy*, which has a more poetical sound to it.

A **gnome** is one of a group of dwarfish *fairies* typically resembling little old men with beards. They live underground in caves to guard buried treasure or mines containing precious metals. *Gnomes* are often skilled artisans able to fashion magical weapons and armor.

Goblin suggests a misshapen *elf* of repulsive appearance who is always conceived of as being malevolent toward human beings. A night creature, he is the companion of witches and the Devil.

Hobgoblin is another word for *goblin*, although the *hobgoblin* is more often thought of as being annoying or impish in his behavior toward people rather than evil. By extension, *hobgoblin* has come to mean anything that elicits unfounded and unreasonable dread: closed-in spaces are his *hobgoblin*.

A **gremlin** is a strictly modern *fairy* or *gnome* who is a trouble-maker. The term applies especially to a supernatural being who is blamed by pilots for virtually anything that can go unexpectedly and violently wrong with or in an airplane. It is said that *gremlin* was coined after the beginning of World War II by an R.A.F. squadron leader. It has also had wide currency in the United States. See GHOST.

spur

goad
nag
needle
sting

These words refer to the act of inciting or taunting someone or something. **Spur** can refer literally to horseback riding, indicating an action of urging a horse forward by jabbing it in the sides with one's heels or with devices worn on the heels for this purpose: He *spurred* his horse forward. In other uses, the word can similarly point to anything that jogs or jolts awareness or that stimulates interest: a speech designed to *spur* the nation on toward its goal of a just peace. Unlike other words here, the word can be used with no implication of a negative or punitive act, often pointing instead to a pleasant arousal of eagerness or desire that results in speeded-up action: a lively plot that will *spur* the most lethargic reader to forge ahead to the book's completion.

Goad referred originally to a spear or pike used to drive animals forward. Unlike *spur*, *goad* seldom leaves completely behind this notion of a harassing action that forces someone or something to move forward: editorials that attempted to *goad* the government on to fulfilling its campaign promises. Sometimes the word can indicate a mere penchant for trouble-making without implying any constructive effort at reform: She constantly *goaded* her son about the largely imaginary failings of his wife. Or *goad* can indicate a being bothered and distracted by the pressure of external forces: people *goaded* by the heat; *goaded* by the demands of his job into a nervous breakdown.

Sting particularly suggests chagrin because of some external rebuff or because of the worrying action of one's conscience. [He was *stung* by his former friend's refusal to greet him on the street; Her one unfaithful-

ness to her husband *stung* her every time she returned to it in retrospect.]
Needle can also refer to the workings of conscience: constantly *needled*
by the growing conviction that he had failed his children. More often,
however, the word refers to an insistent and possibly insidious wearing
away by one person of another person's self-esteem or vanity, usually
with little attempt at constructive criticism: a playwright who loved to
needle his middle-class audiences about their values as much as his audiences loved to be *needled* about such things. Occasionally, a serious impulse at reform can be indicated: a gadfly who *needled* the administration
about its failures in urban renewal until it was *goaded* into reexamining
its whole program.

Nag stresses the repetitious insistence with which someone carries
on trivial criticisms of someone else. The word typically suggests a wife
who berates her husband for failings, large or small, but the word can
apply more widely: a *nagging* boss; leaders who know how to get results
without constant *nagging*. The word can also apply to any moderate
but annoying persistence: a *nagging* pain in his back. See BOTHER,
FAULTFINDING, INCITE, STIMULATE.

Antonyms: palliate, QUELL, *quiet*, STOP, SUBDUE.

These words refer to something that is false or worthless, particularly
when it is passed off as being genuine or valuable. **Spurious**, the most
general of these words, derives ultimately from a Latin word for bastard.
It is harshly condemnatory in tone, whether or not an attempt to deceive
is implied. It rarely now refers to illegitimacy: a *spurious* heir. More
often it refers to something that has been mistaken for the real item:
spurious paintings attributed to old masters. Often, the word leaves no
doubt that deception is involved: a candidate who made *spurious* campaign promises in order to get elected. But when the word applies to
reason or logic, a deliberate attempt to mislead need not necessarily be
involved: Invalid assumptions lead to *spurious* conclusions; an attempt
to demonstrate that his opponent's thesis was *spurious* in every detail.

Counterfeit and **forged** are exclusively focused on deliberate attempts to deceive or defraud. Most typically, *counterfeit* pertains to
false money, *forged* to false signatures, as on a check: *counterfeit* ten-
dollar bills; a *forged* endorsement on the traveler's check. Both words
can also apply to anything that is made to pass for something authentic
or of value: a *counterfeit* painting; *forged* papal decretals. Usually,
forged retains some implication of a false signature that seems to make
good a product or document, but *counterfeit* applies more widely to anything insincere: an attempt to deceive the public with their *counterfeit*
optimism over the results of the government action; the *counterfeit* concern that she lavished on her husband in public.

Shoddy can still occasionally refer to a fabric of reclaimed wool. By
extension, it now refers universally to anything that is inferior in materials or construction: *shoddy* housing developments destined to become
the slums of the future. The word can also point to any vulgar or pretentious imitation or anything cheap that purports to be of superior
quality: *shoddy* nightclubs whose meretricious glitter is designed to trap
unwary tourists. Sometimes the stress of the word is on whatever is
unsavory, worn-out, or of dubious reputation: the bum's *shoddy* clothes;
the *shoddy* red-light district of town; a *shoddy* criminal lawyer.

Apocryphal is the most restricted of these words in that it always
applies to accounts of the past whose truth or accuracy cannot be determined. In reference to disputed theological documents, the implica-

spurious

apocryphal
counterfeit
forged
shoddy

tion is that such works have been rejected from the accepted or official canon: the *apocryphal* sayings of Jesus that are excluded from the New Testament. Outside this context, the word can refer less negatively to what is legendary or unprovable: an *apocryphal* story about Lincoln as a young boy. Here, the word can refer to any body of myth and anecdote that grows up spontaneously around an object of reverence or curiosity: *apocryphal* feats attributed to John Dillinger. See ARTIFICIAL, DECEPTION, SHAM.

Antonyms: ACCURATE, GENUINE, SINCERE.

spy

agent
agent provocateur
counterspy
double agent
secret agent

These words all denote a person who secretly gathers information about persons or about countries other than his own, usually for destructive purposes. **Spy** is the most general term. In a narrow sense, a *spy* is one engaged in espionage — that is, he is sent secretly into a belligerent country to obtain military or political information wanted by his own country. If captured, especially in time of war, a *spy* is subject to be shot. In a wider sense the word is derogatory and is applied to anyone who uses underhand and furtive methods of observing the activities of others, usually for personal gain: The vice president of the firm has his *spies* in every department.

Agent and **secret agent** are now preferred to *spy* when signifying a person employed by a government to engage in espionage. An *agent* or *secret agent* enters a foreign country under a disguise and usually resides there for a time. His work is to learn the military secrets and other facts about that country which will be of use to his own government. An *agent* may also be sent within the borders of a belligerent power to commit acts of sabotage which will weaken the defenses of the enemy. *Agent* or *secret agent* may also be applied to investigators within a government who probe into treasonable activities, counterfeiting, and other infringements of federal laws: an FBI *agent*.

A **counterspy** is an *agent* who spies on the *secret agents* of the enemy, often within his own country, in order to thwart their activities and destroy their efficiency.

The **double agent**, or "double *spy*," is employed simultaneously by two opposing countries and engages in espionage against both of them while pretending to be working for only one. A *double agent* may actually be loyal to one country or he may practice deception toward both sides. *Double agents* often make effective *counterspies*.

Agent provocateur is a French term designating a *spy* who is planted in a trade union, political party, or other organization in which there are conflicting loyalties. His method is to gain the trust of the members of the group and to stir them to actions or declarations that will incur punishment. *Agent provocateur* also carries a suggestion of opprobrium, since unlike the espionage *agent*, the *agent provocateur* may be acting against and betraying his own kind. See OVERHEAR, SPECTATOR, STEALTHY.

squeal

cheep
chirp
peep
screech

These words are imitative of the shrill cries made by certain birds, insects, or animals. All may be used as either nouns or verbs, and most apply to human sounds as well, and have other, extended applications. A **squeal** is a shrill, high-pitched, somewhat prolonged nasal cry, the sort of sound that is made by a young pig. **Squeak** denotes a shorter, weaker cry — a very high-pitched, thin, sharp, penetrating sound, as the little piping noise made by a mouse. One may *squeal* out of surprise, excitement, fright, pain, anger, or protest: children *squealing* with de-

light; to *squeal* in terror at a horror movie. One may *squeak* because of
a high-pitched voice or laryngitis: The boy's voice was changing and
would go from a deep tone to a shrill *squeak* without warning.

Screech and **squawk** refer to shrill, harsh cries or to sounds that are
strident or raucous. A *screech* is a long, harsh, piercing sound — a grating scream or shriek: a small owl that *screeches* weirdly instead of hoot-
ing. One may *screech* out of pain, terror, or anguish: a *screeching* woman
trapped in a burning building. *Screech* is also disdainfully applied to a
loud, high singing voice that sounds terribly forced and strained: That
soprano isn't singing — she's *screeching!* A *squawk* is a shrill, harsh cry
such as is made by a parrot or a frightened hen. *Squawk* is also applied
to any sound reminiscent of such a cry: a *squawking* radio.

Chirp, **cheep**, and **peep** denote the high, thin, pointed sounds made
by young birds. A *chirp* is a clear, bright sound — a short, sharp, high-
pitched cry, as one made repeatedly by a bird or insect: *chirping* spar-
rows; the cricket's *chirp*. A person may make a somewhat similar sound
(or chirrup) by drawing the breath through the closed lips, as in greeting
an infant or urging on a horse. A *cheep* is a faint, shrill sound — a weak,
feeble *chirp* or *squeak*: the *cheep* of a small bat. A *peep* is the kind of tiny
cry made by a new-hatched chick: the *peep* of a frightened mouse.
Applied to human utterance, *chirp* means to talk or say in a quick, vivacious way, to cry out cheerfully with birdlike enthusiasm: "Good
morning," *chirped* the children.

Applied to things, *squeak* designates a shrill, creaking sound indicative
of stiffness or friction: the *squeak* of new shoes; a *squeaking* hinge.
Squeal refers to a loud, drawn-out, nasal sound that is reminiscent of a
hurt, protesting cry: *squealing* brakes. *Screech* implies a harsher, more
earsplitting noise: The subway train *screeched* to a stop.

In idiomatic speech, to *squeak by* or *squeak through* is to make it by
a hairsbreadth, to succeed by an extremely narrow margin: He just
managed to *squeak* through, but he passed the course. In slang usage, to
squeal is to turn informer, betraying one's confederates, as in crime:
You'd better not *squeal* if you know what's good for you. To *squawk* is
to complain or protest loudly in a harsh, shrill way: He really *squawked*
when he found the hotel didn't have his reservation. A *peep* is the slightest sound that one can make, especially a sign of dissatisfaction: I don't
want to hear a *peep* out of you. See CHATTER, CRY.

These words are comparable when they indicate a point of view or conviction about a practical matter, usually one expressed in words. **Stand**
and **position** both refer to definite, expressed convictions about single
issues that are the focal points of disagreement, debate, or controversy.
Stand often implies an emotional commitment, although it does not
exclude intellectual or rational grounds for one's feeling: to take a strong
stand in favor of amending the abortion law. *Position* implies a more
dispassionate and restrained attitude, often one decided upon after
lengthy deliberation. [My *position* on civil rights is well known; He
took the *position* that salvation depended upon good deeds as well as
piety.]

Policy implies a definite structure of convictions based on an assessment of one's needs, interests, goals, or principles: The United States
government follows a *policy* of containing Communism in southeast Asia.
In less formal contexts *policy* may mean any general rule of conduct:
It's a bad *policy* to lend money to unemployed friends. **Posture** in
recent years has come to mean *policy* in a formal sense: the defense

squeal
(continued)

squawk
squeak

stand

attitude
policy
position
posture

posture of the U.S. But *posture* may indicate also the actual disposition of forces: a military *posture* that embraced the deployment of intercontinental ballistic missiles at key places on the periphery of the Soviet Union. In its several implications, *posture* may also include the sense of **attitude**. *Attitude* is a more general term than the others here considered, and indicates a personal or institutional feeling, often unexpressed and vague in nature. In this it is at the other pole from *policy*, which represents a clearly formulated and precise enunciation of one's view: The sympathetic *attitude* of the Cuban government to rebels in South and Central America has evolved, it is charged, into a *policy* of abetting and possibly fomenting insurrection in the New World. *Posture* is therefore useful in suggesting a hardening of *attitude* without going so far as to imply a firm *policy*: the neutral *posture* of the U.S. in the Arab-Israeli confrontation; the belligerent *posture* of India toward the Chinese resulting from violent and unresolved border disputes. See OPINION.

standard

criterion
gauge
measure
test
touchstone
yardstick

These words refer to sets of rules or principles by which to evaluate the quality of something. **Standard** implies an objective, impartial rule or set of rules that have actually been spelled out in advance: the army's *standards* for physical fitness; research that does not meet our *standard* for accuracy.

Gauge and **measure** may both suggest an actual physical tool to determine the dimensions or attributes of a product: a *gauge* for determining the thickness of wire; an anemometer or other *measure* of wind velocity. Rather than the yes-or-no evaluation suggested by *standard*, these two words suggest an objective assessment of attributes. In more metaphorical uses, *measure* is the less formal of the two: agricultural production as a *gauge* of the economy's effectiveness; an honor system that will be a *measure* of our students' honesty.

Test emphasizes the act of evaluation. The previous words suggest that means for evaluation and for assessment exist, without necessarily implying that they will be used. *Test* strongly implies an actual application of these means: combat as a *test* of the soldier's bravery. [The *standards* applied so rigorously in our shoe factory are nothing compared to the real *test* to which our consumers put each pair of shoes in actual day-to-day use.]

Criterion, the most formal of all these words, suggests the independent existence of *standards* that stress excellence. The implication is less strong that the discriminations suggested by *criterion* that have been spelled out. The word, therefore, may suggest implicit taste as a more important part of the *test* than the mechanical application of an objective *measure* or *gauge*: candidates who feel that the sole *criterion* for office is the ability to win votes; a philosophy that requires each individual to state the *criteria* behind his judgments.

Touchstone and **yardstick** are metaphorical in suggesting something against which any attempt may be contrasted. *Yardstick*, the most informal of any of these words, implies a set of rules that are based on common sense, are easy to apply, and will give a cut-and-dried answer: a low rate of unemployment as the least ambiguous *yardstick* of a country's well-being. *Touchstone* gives an entirely different feeling from *yardstick*; it suggests a set of imponderable values that cannot be spelled out so much as embodied in an earlier work against which the work in question is compared: Greek and Elizabethan tragedies that are the *touchstones* for all later theatrical effort. The word suggests a rarefied level of esthetic discrimination based on tradition and precedence; it might even suggest preciosity: new artists who shattered the *touchstones* of Victorian sensibility. See CONTROL, NORMAL.

These words refer to the covert taking of property that belongs to someone else. **Steal** is the most general of these and can refer to any such act, whether done quickly or cautiously and whether a large or small amount of stolen goods is at stake. **Pilfer**, by contrast, specifically suggests a small amount of stolen goods and may even imply a series of brief forays, each netting a small amount: office personnel who constantly *pilfer* pencils from the stockroom. **Filch** also suggests petty theft, but emphasizes the furtiveness of the action: to *filch* apples from a vender occupied with a customer. **Purloin** is a formal, bookish term for *steal* or *filch*.

    Snitch, like *pilfer*, suggests the *stealing* of a small amount or of something of little value. Furthermore, it implies a relative innocence of the person who does the *snitching* and the harmlessness of the act: children who become adept at *snitching* cookies from the cookie jar between meals. *Snitch* often has a humorous or affectionate tone because of its association with children. **Swipe** may suggest a quick, brazen making off with something while the owner is not present: He had *swiped* my whole inspection display from the footlocker while I was in the shower. It is, however, often used informally among friends or intimates to suggest pique over something borrowed without permission: Who *swiped* my cigarettes? **Pinch** may suggest the stealing of something small, but by no means of something without value. It most often suggests in fact, a direct physical encounter, as on a crowded street between a pickpocket and his victim: teaching his ragamuffins how to *pinch* a gentleman's wallet without his noticing it. **Cop** suggests suddenness, and like *swipe* may be used among familiars to indicate irritation over something borrowed or taken. [Somebody *copped* my pencil; They *copped* some newspapers from the stand and disappeared in the crowd.] Both *pinch* and *cop* are now somewhat old-fashioned.

    Heist is argot among professional thieves for a complicated job involving something either of great size or value and that must be planned out in advance and in great detail: those who had planned the Brinks *heist*. **Lift** refers to the work of shoplifters who take goods from counters or shelves or remove money from momentarily unattended tills. When used more generally, its point may be, like that of *swipe*, the innocence or "borrowing" aspect of the removal: *lifting* a pencil from a neighbor's desk. See PLUNDER, ROB, ROBBERY.

These words describe things done in concealment so as not to be noticed or found out. **Stealthy** comes from an Old English word meaning to steal. It suggests the quiet of an animal moving on padded feet, slyly stealing up on its prey or warily making its way past its enemies. [The scout made a *stealthy* approach to the enemy position; The escaping prisoner moved with *stealthy* tread until he was out of earshot of the sleeping guards.] **Furtive** comes from the Latin word for thief. It suggests the quick, nervous movements of someone who feels guilty or is afraid of getting caught: the *furtive* manner of an escaped convict; A *furtive* glance confirmed his fears — he was being followed. **Surreptitious** comes from Latin roots meaning to snatch secretly. It describes something forbidden that is done or enjoyed on the sly, at an opportune moment when no one is looking: the *surreptitious* reading of a friend's private diary; a dieter's *surreptitious* snack.

steal

cop
filch
heist
lift
pilfer
pinch
purloin
snitch
swipe

stealthy

clandestine
furtive
sneaky
surreptitious
underhand

Clandestine comes from a Latin word meaning in secret. It suggests the wariness of one who hides what he is doing because of the social or political danger of discovery. What is done *clandestinely* either is illicit or is considered to be so, being kept under wraps because it is frowned on by society or forbidden by those in authority: a *clandestine* meeting of young lovers; the *clandestine* meeting of a local official with racketeers. Where a *surreptitious* act is done quickly, a *clandestine* activity may be carried on over a long period of time: a *clandestine* love affair; a *clandestine* publication put out by an underground organization.

Sneaky and **underhand** carry the suggestion of cheating, of unfair dealings and self-serving manipulations behind the scenes. Where the other adjectives emphasize the fear of detection, *underhand* suggests a sly and crafty secrecy practiced not for protection but for gain — a stooping to trickery, deceit, or fraud for one's own profit: to win an election by *underhand* means. *Sneaky* is more general and less formal than *underhand*, and emphasizes the deceitful or double-dealing nature of one's actions more than the selfishness of one's motives. It suggests a *clandestine* or roundabout manner concealing an insidious calculation: There was something *sneaky* and sinister about him, so that you mistrusted him on instinct; the *sneaky* habit of filching coins from his mother's purse. See LURK.

Antonyms: obvious, open, OVERT.

steep

abrupt
precipitous
sheer

These words refer to terrain that rises or drops away sharply or that approaches the vertical. **Steep**, while indicating a relatively sharp inclination or a considerable departure from the horizontal, is alone among these words in indicating a gradual or steadily increasing slope, usually one that is difficult to negotiate. The word's relativity can be seen by the fact that a grade that was too *steep* for a railroad locomotive might be considered a gentle rise for someone on foot; terrain that was too *steep* for a burro to climb might not be *steep* enough to interest mountain climbers. Another even more subtle connotation of the word, not always present, is its special suitability for a rise viewed from below.

By comparison, **abrupt**, while referring to a much sharper slope, very often suggests an incline viewed from above. [We were winded by our long climb upward along the *steep* path; They were confronted by an *abrupt* chasm as they emerged from the forest.] This distinction does not always hold, however. *Abrupt* suggests sudden discontinuities in a terrain rather than the gradual change implicit in *steep*; consequently, a sharp contrast with surrounding topography is a special point of the word: the *abrupt* and dramatic looming up of the giant sculpture out of nearly level countryside.

Like *abrupt*, the remaining words pertain to a nearly vertical incline. **precipitous** has special relevance to an incline viewed from above. *Precipitous* also brings to mind suddenness or unexpectedness in referring to a nearly vertical incline that is clifflike. The unique point of this word, however, may be its suggestion of an *abrupt* drop that is dangerous or perilous: a frail rope bridge over the *precipitous* chasm. The word, however, can be used without this implication: looking up at the *precipitous* rise of skyscrapers along both sides of the street. **Sheer** is related to *steep* in suggesting an incline viewed from below, but it is more intense than *steep*; *sheer* often refers to a nearly vertical slope that may be impossible, not merely difficult, to negotiate: the *sheer* face of the high wall that stood between him and his freedom. The word also has a special implication that concerns the vertical face itself, suggesting one without break, foothold, or cranny: the *sheer* surface of the cliff where not even a blade of grass had found a place to lodge. See CLIMB, DESCEND, HIGH.

Antonyms: flat, gentle, gradual, level, low, plain.

These words refer to a lack of yield or value or to the inability to have children. **Sterile** functions in all these senses: *sterile* soil; a *sterile* discussion; determining whether it was the husband or wife who was *sterile*. **Barren** is the only other word here that applies to all three situations, but it is less technical sounding and more dramatic than *sterile*: the *barren* desert; a debate that was *barren* of results; a *barren* woman. In the last sense, the word has an older, more Biblical ring and applies to women (or the union itself) rather than to men. Also, the word is less often used than *sterile* since it may seem critical rather than factual. *Sterile* itself, however, can seem overly harsh to some; this may be one reason why **infertile** is often substituted for it, although *infertile* may refer to the simple lack of success at having children for any reason, without necessarily implying that either the man or woman is biologically *sterile*. The word is also used in the agricultural sense, although its increasing use in reference to childbearing may have diminished its usefulness here: topsoil rendered *infertile* by excess alkalinity. **Childless** is the only word here that refers exclusively to people whose sexual union does not result in offspring. It points, however, to the simple fact of this lack, whether it comes about involuntarily or by choice: a *childless* couple; deciding to remain *childless* for the first few years of marriage; the adoption of children by those who are *childless* themselves.

The remaining words have no reference to childbearing, but do refer to other senses grouped here. **Arid** most concretely suggests a lack of yield because of excessive dryness or heat: miles of *arid* sand dunes; an *arid* climate. In terms of values, the word suggests dullness or lack of results: an *arid* play; an administration *arid* of new approaches. **Unfruitful** and **unproductive** are closely allied; both can apply to a lack either of yield or of value. *Unfruitful* would seem most open to the former, *unproductive* to the latter: an *unfruitful* use of land; an *unfruitful* season; mediation that was *unproductive* of changes on either side. This neat pattern is far from being the case in actual usage, however: *unfruitful* summit conferences; *unproductive* stretches of swamp land. In any case, *unfruitful* tends to sound more dramatic or colorful, and need not suggest something totally *barren* of yield or value: crop yields that doubled after *unfruitful* harvesting techniques were abandoned. *Unproductive* gives a more factual tone and tends to suggest a more nearly complete lack of any result whatever: detectives stymied by an *unproductive* search for tell-tale clues. See DRY, STERILIZE.

Antonyms: bearing, productive, VIABLE, yielding.

These words refer to the act of rendering a person or animal incapable of producing offspring. **Sterilize** is the most general of these, referring to people, animals, and even plants, and to any sort of action that makes reproduction impossible: a controversial proposal to *sterilize* mental defectives; *sterilizing* fruit flies by radiation treatment; hybrid corn that is detasseled to *sterilize* it against self-pollination. In reference to people, the word may refer to accidental or deliberate acts and to those bringing about temporary or permanent infertility in either men or women. It may also refer to an occurrence that causes no apparent alteration of the body, as with radiation exposure, or to one in which reproductive organs are altered or removed.

sterile

arid
barren
childless
infertile
unfruitful
unproductive

sterilize

castrate
emasculate
geld
hysterectomize
neuter

588 Modern Guide to Synonyms

sterilize
(continued)

spay
vasectomize

In practice, **neuter** is most often limited in reference to the deliberate removing of reproductive organs from either male or female animals: having both their male and female cats *neutered* by the veterinarian. Fix and alter are common euphemisms for this word. **Spay** functions like *neuter* but is applied exclusively to female animals: a *spayed* bitch. **Geld**, similarly, applies to the *neutering* of male animals: a *gelded* horse. Sometimes, however, *geld* can be applied to animals of both sexes, but this wider use is open to misunderstanding.

Castrate can apply both to men or male animals in specifically indicating the removal of testicles. In the case of animals, the word is clearer and more forceful than either *neuter* or *geld*: *castrating* hogs to fatten them for market. Applied to men, the word would now suggest only sadistic punishment or a surgical necessity, as to prevent the spread of a cancer; this was not always so, however: harem guards who were *castrated* to insure the inviolability of the odalisques; choirboys *castrated* to preserve their soprano voices. The word recently has become a fad word, echoing psychoanalytic theory, for any symbolic act, especially one performed by a woman, that reduces a man's feelings of manliness: women who *castrate* their husbands by humiliating them in public.

Emasculate may apply to male animals but is more commonly restricted solely to men. The word differs from *castrate* in referring more to the damage than to the actual removal of reproductive organs: *emasculated* in the war by flying shrapnel. The word, however, is sometimes used euphemistically for *castrate*. Metaphorically, *emasculate* refers, like *castrate*, to any act that reduces a man's sense of manliness. While less dramatic than *castrate* in this use, the word would seem to have greater metaphorical felicity, since no physical alteration is necessarily suggested by the word. Nevertheless, the reference to psychoanalytic theory is less apparent and may explain the faddish preference for the stronger term. *Emasculate* is also used as a generally applicable metaphor for weakening: amendments that *emasculated* the provisions for enforcing the statute.

Vasectomize and **hysterectomize**, the former applying to men, the latter to women, are medical terms for surgical operations that *sterilize* the person operated on. Actually these terms are more commonly used in their noun forms: vasectomy and hysterectomy. To *vasectomize* is to perform a simple, duct-tying operation, sometimes reversible, that is chosen specifically to make a man infertile and has no effect on body chemistry. To *hysterectomize* is to remove the uterus and sometimes the ovaries and Fallopian tubes to stop uncontrollable uterine hemorrhaging, to remove large fibroid tumors, or to eradicate a cancerous condition. The operation is never done simply to achieve infertility, as it is irreversible and can, if both ovaries are removed, have a deleterious effect on the body's chemical balance. See STERILE.

Antonyms: fecundate, fecundify, fertilize, fructify, impregnate, inseminate.

stick

adhere
cleave
cling
cohere

These words all mean to become or remain closely and firmly attached. **Stick** and **adhere** express the idea of maintaining a close or permanent union by or as if by gluing or cementing together. *Stick* is the less formal word of the two and conveys in addition the establishing of such an attachment: two young men who intend to *stick* together when they enter the armed services; to *stick* a label on a package. *Stick* may also imply perseverance, as in working at something or in keeping to an ideal, bargain, etc.: *sticking* doggedly at his physics homework until long after midnight; *sticking* to his principles of fair play; *sticking* to an agreement made in a moment of optimism. *Adhere*, which is always used intransitively, may sound formal and stiff when applied to things: a stamp *adhering* to a postcard.

Cohere, also an intransitive, refers to the *adhering* or *sticking* together of the particles of a substance, which then form a resultant whole or mass that is resistant to separation: Plaster of Paris *coheres* only when water is added. Figurative usage may indicate the achievement of logical consistency: An argument *coheres* only if it validly bridges the premise and the conclusion.

Cling is used to indicate a close attachment caused by entwining, clutching, or hanging on, rather than by gluing or otherwise causing surfaces to *adhere*: ivy *clinging* to brick walls; a baby gorilla *clinging* to its mother by clutching her fur. In the sense of holding on to attitudes, beliefs, or emotional states, *cling* used as a synonym for *adhere* often has derogatory connotations suggestive of the presence of anxiety or dependency: a widow *clinging* to her grown son; people who, despite obvious intelligence, persist in *clinging* to old prejudices.

Cleave, in the sense of *adhere* or *stick*, is now largely a literary or Biblical term for being closely attached, as in a human relationship marked by fidelity: to *cleave* to one's marriage partner through sickness and misfortune. In a few contexts, *cleave* is still used to mean literally to *adhere* or *stick* closely: In his terror his tongue seemed to *cleave* to the roof of his mouth. See CONNECT, TIE.

Antonyms: LEAVE (abandon), SEPARATE, SEVER.

These words refer, by means of a metaphor of disfigurement, to the lasting harm or discredit that may attach to someone because of an impropriety or injustice. As treated here, they all imply a distinction between such a disfigurement and those flaws that are present as an innate part of one's character. A person may acquire a **stigma** because of some improper act of his own, or, more arbitrarily, because of an unfortunate situation not of his own making: prevented from seeking office by the *stigma* of his perjury conviction; the glazed eyes and pinched minds of children who thus already gave evidence of bearing the *stigma* of poverty. Sometimes the special point of the word is the disapproval of society rather than actual injury done to the person disapproved of: a culture that put a *stigma* on anyone who was interested in the arts.

Stain, **blot**, and **taint** are almost exclusively restricted to the discredit that someone has brought upon himself; the discredit, furthermore, most often is the result of a breach of morals. Of the three, *stain* suggests the greatest or most serious breach: a *stain* on her reputation that she could never eradicate. *Blot*, by contrast, can be used almost euphemistically to extenuate a breach as accidental or slight: a record that like anyone else's showed a *blot* or two here and there. Clashing with this implication, the word appears sometimes in orotund rhetoric to mean an especially heinous disfigurement: a political machine that is a *blot* on the name of our fair city. In this sense, it is part of a common but shopworn expression: a *blot* on the escutcheon. *Taint* suggests a moral breach slighter than either *stain* or *blot*. Leaving aside the use in which it refers to a slight but innate flaw, it still stresses a vague or subtle imprint and may suggest, in fact, a less permanent discrediting than any of these other words: surrounded by the *taint* of scandal that would, nevertheless, fade with time. Even the underlying metaphor here is unique in suggesting a slight but permeating discoloration more than a single but plainly observable scar.

stigma

blot
brand
mark
stain
stigmata
taint

Mark is the least specific in this context and carries the fewest overtones. It has so many other uses that its sense of disfigurement would have to be made clear by context: a *mark* against him; accusations that left a *mark* on his reputation. **Stigmata** is the one word here that does not imply shame or dishonor, referring instead to *marks* said to appear miraculously on the hands and feet of certain saints, *marks* that correspond to the wounds inflicted at the Crucifixion.

A **brand** was originally a *mark* burned on criminals or slaves to proclaim their status; it is now an easily identifiable design put on cattle with a hot iron to indicate ownership. Figuratively used, *brand* is a close synonym of *stigma*, but suggests an even greater dishonor or notoriety, which like the burned-on *mark* is difficult or impossible to eradicate: a man bearing the *brand* of having informed against his comrades; the *brand* of illegitimacy once placed on innocent children. See BURN, DISFIGURE, ECCENTRICITY, FLAW.

stimulate

enliven
excite
galvanize
titillate
whet

These words refer to what arouses interest, motivates to action, or is satisfying and invigorating. **Stimulate** is the most general of these, applying in all three situations: a remark that *stimulated* my curiosity; a crisis that finally *stimulated* Congress into voting new funds for the beleaguered cities; a bull session that everyone present found to be extremely *stimulating*. **Excite** can also apply to the arousal of interest, but in this sense it has a more formal tone than *stimulate*: a book that *excited* a great deal of comment. More often now, the word applies to anything that brings forth an intense emotional display: They feared that the good news would *excite* the patient too much; ethnic slurs that *excited* the crowd to a violent fury.

Enliven applies solely to what is both arousing and invigorating: an outspoken couple who could always be counted on to *enliven* a dull party; open-air sculpture to *enliven* the gray uniformity of the city. **Galvanize**, by contrast, applies strictly to setting something decisively in motion, particularly after a period of vacillation or disorganization: new supporting troops to *galvanize* our flagging counteroffensive; a tragedy that *galvanized* the city government into action.

Titillate and **whet** also apply exclusively to one aspect of *stimulate*, indicating an initial arousal of interest or desire. Most concretely, *whet* applies to an appetite for food: hors d'oeuvres to *whet* the appetite. Similarly, when the word applies in other contexts, it usually suggests partaking of a small sample that leads to a desire for some larger portion: government action that only *whetted* the desires of Negroes for full equality; an opening chapter that *whets* the reader's interest in reading on. By contrast, *titillate* need not suggest any actual sampling at all. While it can operate like *whet* in the context of food, it more often suggests a tempting action achieved through allusion, insinuation, or promises of what is to come. It implies raising eager expectations of whatever kind, whether or not these promises are later fulfilled. [The appetizer was delicious and *titillated* the gourmet's palate; Rumors of secret information on the assassination *titillated* the curiosity of the public; *titillating* illustrations on the covers of pornographic novels.] See INCITE, INDUCE, KINDLE, QUICKEN, SPUR.

Antonyms: deaden, dull, enervate, QUELL, SUBDUE.

stint

These words refer to a limited, one-time, or nonrecurring piece of work. **Stint** and **hitch** are most clear about the limited or temporary nature of the work. *Stint* suggests the limited period of time in which something

stint
(continued)

assignment
chore
duty
hitch
job
task

is done. [He never starred in a long-running play, though he did several short *stints* off-Broadway; wandering from one college to another, including *stints* at Harvard and Oxford.] Where *stint* suggests a relatively brief undertaking that is voluntary or agreed-upon, *hitch* suggests a limited commitment of longer duration that may not be a matter of choice; it frequently appears in a military context: doing a two-year *hitch* in Japan before coming home to the States. In the military, *hitch* may refer to one's whole period of service, long or short: the new six-month *hitch* followed by annual summer training; NCO's who plan to do the whole twenty-year *hitch*. **Assignment** is both more formal and more general than the preceding and is applicable in a great many contexts. It indicates a limited commitment that is even more likely to be involuntary than is the case with *hitch*: chafing at the unpleasant *assignment* that had fallen to him at the behest of his employer. This need not always be so, however: offering to take on the two-week *assignment* himself. Furthermore, the word can refer to a permanent, long-term role: his *assignment* to the appellate court, where he served as a justice for twenty years. Or it may specifically apply to a student's homework: a hard arithmetic *assignment*.

Chore and **task** both indicate a circumscribed or short-term undertaking, whether voluntary or not, and suggest an undertaking that will require a relative amount of effort. The words contrast, however, in that the more general *task* is more nearly neutral in its connotations, whereas *chore* suggests something particularly onerous, arduous, or even unpleasant, despite the short duration suggested: relishing every *task* that fell to him, no matter how pesky; complaining about how much he hated the *chore* of washing dishes after every meal. Also, *task* is less specific about duration and can suggest effort arising out of personal commitment or obligation: the *task* of political reform, to which he selflessly devoted his best efforts throughout a long life. *Chore* nearly always suggests grudging reluctance: when going to parties becomes a *chore* rather than a pleasure. Used in the plural, it applies to routine household or farm duties and has a homey ring: to do *chores*.

In the context of a specific, short-term effort, **job** and **duty** emphasize different aspects of *task*. *Job* is neutral and general, open to the qualification of context: looking forward to the *job* of building the garage on his weekends; dreading the exasperating *job* of making out his income tax. *Duty*, by contrast, stresses either an involuntary or unpleasant *task* or one that calls up devoted commitment or dedication: my reluctant *duty* to set your punishment; soldiers put on KP *duty*; the painful *duty* of sorting through his father's effects; glad to undertake the *duty* of caring for the child in his wife's absence. See OBLIGATION, PROFESSION.

Antonyms: HOBBY.

stomach

abdomen
belly
guts

These words denote the section of the human or other animal body between the diaphragm and the pelvic floor. **Stomach** is the most general term; it may simply mean the external region, although specifically it is applied to the internal digestive organ. As the seat of appetite or inclination, *stomach* is used figuratively, especially in a negative sense: to have no *stomach* for strong drink; to have no *stomach* for the business of killing.

In scientific terminology, **abdomen** is the word for both the external *stomach* and for the entire internal cavity containing the alimentary canal and other organs as well: to open up an *abdomen* to remove a tumor; the enlarged *abdomen* of a woman in advanced pregnancy.

Belly was once a standard word to refer to the same region, but was later euphemistically suppressed in favor of *stomach*, which is imprecise, and *abdomen*, which to some people is less acceptable because of its technical sound. *Belly* also once meant "womb" or "uterus," as well as the organ which receives food. Perhaps for this reason it is jarring to some ears. From its original meaning of "bag," *belly* suggests both a hollow cavity and a protuberance: the *belly* of a sailing ship; his little, round *belly* tightly buttoned into his trousers.

Unlike *stomach*, *belly*, or *abdomen*, **guts** applies almost exclusively to the internal organs of the pelvic cavity. In the plural, it is a synonym for "entrails" or "intestines," and in the singular, for the entire digestive system, especially that of an animal. *Guts* emphasizes the more earthy or even revolting aspects of the intestines when they are not functioning properly or have suffered injury: the beggar's *guts* growling with hunger; a horse in the bull ring with its *guts* hanging out. *Guts* has the slang, figurative meaning of courage or effrontery: to have the *guts* to cross a field under gunfire; to have the *guts* to insult the president of one's firm. See COURAGE.

stop

arrest
block
cease
check
discontinue
halt
prevent

These words refer to the act of bringing something to an end or a complete rest. **Stop** in its generality has few specific implications, being open to any coloration context gives it: *stopping* her gently in mid-sentence with a single brush of his hand; They *stopped* the bandit dead in his tracks with a barrage of bullets.

Arrest, check, and **block** suggest a *stopping* of motion or activity by the application of a countering force: words that *arrested* his flight in mid-career across the room. All three words, however, can suggest an interruption or prevention of activity that might well begin again once the countering force is removed. [The child's development was *arrested* by an overly permissive regimen; therapy to *check* the course of the disease, although they could not cure it; *blocking* the enemy's access to the sea.] *Arrest* most specifically suggests the freezing of something just as it was at the time activity stopped. *Check* suggests keeping something hemmed in so that it cannot continue. *Block* suggests the interposition of an obstacle that cannot be got around.

Discontinue relates particularly to a manufactured item that is gradually phased out of production: a notice that they were *discontinuing* several lines of spare parts previously listed in their catalog. It may also refer to the gradual abandonment of a habitual way of doing things: The practice of binding the feet of the women was finally *discontinued*. In other uses, it may seem a rather long-winded way to say *stop*.

Cease most often suggests an abrupt *stopping*: The officer ordered him to *cease* his whistling immediately. **Halt** also suggests suddenness, but it may suggest as well a *stopping* of motion brought about by authority or force: brusquely *halting* her at the gate with a demand to see her papers. **Prevent** can apply to anything that results in *stopping* or forestalling an action by whatever means. The action, in this case, may be blocked before it has been set in motion: a thorough grounding in fundamentals to *prevent* reading difficulties from cropping up later on; a program to *prevent* drug addiction rather than treat it once it has gotten a hold on its victims. The word can also apply to a countering force, but only the potential or psychological effectiveness of such a force may be indicated: maintaining troop readiness to *prevent* being overwhelmed by surprise attack; a puritanical streak that *prevented* her from

completely surrendering herself to any momentary pleasure. See CAP-
TURE, INHIBIT, PREVENT, QUELL, SUBDUE.

    Antonyms: ACTIVATE, BEGIN, *continue*, EFFECT, IMPEL, QUICKEN, SPUR.

These words refer to the act of coming to rest or of breaking off previous activity. **Stop** is the most general, least formal, and most commonly used, yielding the fewest specific suggestions about the way in
which activity is concluded: a clock that *stopped* and started erratically;
listening with a stethoscope to find out if the old man's heart had
stopped; where the paved road *stops* and a dirt trail takes over. **Cease**
carries the specific implication of a total extinction: a newspaper that
has *ceased* publication. It may sometimes suggest abruptness: As suddenly as it began, the rain *ceased*.

    Halt is similar to *cease* but has specific reference to the abrupt, de-
cisive termination of movement: *halting* only at the edge of the cliff;
demonstrators who marched as a body into the square, *halted* in its
center, and then threw themselves down on the pavement. **Quit** may
also indicate an arbitrary *halting*, but this is usually voluntary or agreed
upon: They worked until 5:00 P.M. and then *quit*. Most often applying to work or effort, the word can sometimes suggest disgruntlement or
defeat: an administrator who *quit* his job in protest at government
policy; Battered as he was in the fight, he refused to *quit*. It may also
suggest cessation because of enfeeblement or lack of energy: The motor
coughed and sputtered, turned over a few times, and then *quit* on us.
Desist is the most formal word here. It is applied to an active agency
and implies forbearance. Specifically, it presupposes the existence of
opposition or resistance to continuance, or the presence of obstacles
that seem insurmountable: finally *desisting* in his fruitless efforts to
find the missing heir. It is often coupled with *cease* in legal parlance:
ordered to *cease* and *desist* from false advertising. See BREAK, DEMUR
FINISH, HESITATE, STOP (arrest).

    Antonyms: begin, GO, PERSIST, *start*.

These words are comparable in that each denotes a body of water flowing
in a watercourse or channel. **Stream** is the most general word in the
group, embracing all the other terms in its meaning. A **rill** is a tiny
stream, the smallest of those under discussion. A **brook** is usually a
primary *stream* emerging from a spring. A **creek** is a *stream* which is
larger than a *brook* and usually flows through a valley. A **river** is a
large *stream* of water that discharges into a larger body of water such as
the ocean, a lake, or another *stream*. In popular usage, *brook*, *creek*, and
stream are often used interchangeably.

    Of these words, only two are used figuratively as well as literally.
Stream and *river* both may refer to a continuous flow of anything, as well
as to a flow of water. [A *stream* of people issued from the theater; The
battlefield was covered with *rivers* of blood.] See FLOW, SHORE.

These words refer to open ways for public passage, particularly for the
movement of vehicles rather than of pedestrians. **Street** is a generic
term for all such public ways that lie within a town or city: the intersection of the two busiest *streets* in the neighborhood. **Avenue** can
sometimes be used more formally as a generic term similar to *street*, but
more often the word serves as a complement to a specific sense of *street*;
this sense refers to towns or cities laid out with *streets* running in one
direction, crossed by *avenues* running in the other. In this case, *avenues*

stop

cease
desist
halt
quit

stream

brook
creek
rill
river

street

alley
avenue
boulevard
highway

street
(continued)

road
throughway
turnpike

are often the wider or more important of the two intersecting systems. In other cases, however, *avenue* can refer to any sort of *street*, wide or narrow, and can form part of the name of the *street*: Garrison *Avenue*.

Alley and **boulevard** indicate sharply contrasting kinds of *streets*. *Alley* suggests a narrow, sometimes dead-ended, *street* behind or between buildings, that exists solely to permit egress for deliveries, pickups, or the parking of vehicles: carrying out the garbage to the collection cans in the *alley*. While the word may be perfectly neutral in this sense, it often has connotations of an unsavory darkness, dankness, or uncleanness: parks, rather than *alleys*, for children to play in. Sometimes the word can be used with an affected quaintness for any *street*, particularly a narrow one, even though it permits through traffic and is faced by buildings or houses: Minetta *Alley*. While *boulevard* can be applied to any city *street*, particularly a wide one, the word has connotations in sharp contrast to *alley*, suggesting a residential *street* enhanced by greenery or an intervening strip containing grass and shrubbery: expensive houses facing on a landscaped *boulevard*.

The remaining words refer mostly to public ways outside of towns and cities. **Road** here is as informal and general as *street*, with an even wider range of connotation. The word can suggest anything from a dirt path for vehicles to the most modern and sophisticated **highway**. The latter now refers to any asphalt-surfaced or paved *road* constructed for traveling motor vehicles: federal monies for building *roads*; small towns whose main *streets* are wide places in the *road*; turning off from the main *highway* onto a winding gravel *road*. Unqualified, *highway* has few imponderable connotations; *road* has many. It can refer to any course that leads to a certain destination: the *road* to nuclear disaster. In British usage, it should be noted, *road* refers specifically to a city *street*.

Throughway and **turnpike** both refer exclusively to a specific kind of *highway*. A *turnpike* is any sort of *highway*, public or private, that cannot be used without the payment of a toll: being low on money and thus wishing to avoid the *turnpike*. The word gives connotations of rapid travel, uninterrupted by stoplights or intersections, and a landscaped drive unmarred by billboards or other advertising. *Throughway* (often spelled thruway) carries none of these pleasant connotations, referring specifically to an express route built to handle capacity traffic undistracted by stops or intersections. While a *throughway* may well be a *turnpike* and vice versa, *throughway* in itself better suggests a mazed labyrinth of traffic systems built with no eye for aesthetic appeal: a six-lane *throughway* walled in from the countryside by gray concrete. See JOURNEY.

stress

pressure
strain
tension

These words are comparable in their denotation of the action or effect of a force upon a person or thing. The first term, **stress**, designates any force or combination of forces that acts on a body or part of a body, as by pressing, pushing, pulling, stretching, compressing, or twisting, and by such action causes a change in the shape or size of the body acted upon. When used in reference to a person, *stress* indicates a condition of emotional or intellectual distress. There is a suggestion in *stress* of some external stimulus, such as injury or shock, that exerts a compelling or constraining influence to which the person involved cannot adequately adjust: a serious gastrointestinal disorder which was the result of the *stress* of anxiety and grief.

Strain, when used in relation to an object, denotes the change in shape or size of that object when it is acted upon by a *stress*. A suggestion of the natural resistance an object makes to the action of *stress* is carried over to the meaning of *strain* when it pertains to persons. Resistance implies effort, and a person undergoing *strain* is subject to the physical, mental, or emotional distress that severe effort entails: the constant *strain* of trying to make ends meet on a substandard wage; the *strain* of working while suffering from a painful back ailment.

In their application to things which are inanimate, **tension** and **pressure** may be classified as types of *stresses*. *Tension* is an elongating *stress* caused by a force which pulls or stretches an object in one direction. *Pressure* is a kind of *stress* characteristically produced by fluids; its special property is that its force is the same in all directions. In designating the condition of a person, *tension* hints at a state of mental *strain* whose peculiarity is its manifestation in physical distress, as in headaches or taut muscles: a tranquilizer to reduce nervous *tension* after an unsuccessful job interview. *Tension* has also come popularly to denote any state of *strained* relations like that caused by conflict or hostility between persons or groups of persons: the dangerous *tension* existing between the U.S. and the U.S.S.R. *Pressure*, more than the other words in this group, specifically points to the things which produce a state of *strain* or *tension* rather than to the state itself. It is a general word that can apply to anything from a minor and temporary difficulty to major, continuous misfortune: the *pressure* of a too-busy social schedule; job *pressure*; the *pressures* of poverty. See ANXIETY, IMPACT, NERVOUS, PROPEL.

These words refer to what is vigorous, well-built, durable, or resistant to change or pressure. **Strong,** the most general, pertains to what has force or to what is rugged in construction or build: a *strong* headwind; a *strong* workbench; a *strong* body. It can also apply to what is vigorous, intense, vivid, or persuasive: a *strong* government; a *struck* tranquilizer; a painter who worked with *strong* colors; a *strong* argument against the proposal. At its most general, it is still relative, implying what is greater in degree than usual: a *strong* suspicion.

Powerful can function as an intensification of *strong*: a *powerful* argument. It can also indicate the ability to deliver great amounts of energy: a *powerful* turbine; a *powerful* nuclear bomb. It can particularly suggest the considerable ability to overcome resistance or opposition: a *powerful* fighter against oppression; a *powerful* army. Where *powerful* can be used to refer to someone who is physically *strong*, **muscular** is almost exclusively limited to this application, specifically suggesting a *strong*, well-built body: a *muscular* athlete. Of these three words, however, only *powerful* necessarily indicates an absolute capacity for applying considerable force: pioneer women who proved to be nearly as *strong* as the men they accompanied across the prairies; *powerful* wrists that enabled him to flick a heavy bat around as though it were a straw; a *muscular* weight lifter who couldn't have fought his way out of a paper bag.

In contrast to the foregoing, **sturdy** and **hardy** both refer more strictly to what is durable or resistant to change or pressure. But *sturdy*, like one sense of *strong*, can refer to what is well built as well: a *sturdy* footbridge that could easily support the weight of a small truck. When applied to physique, the word suggests solidity without necessarily implying the development indicated by *muscular*: a *sturdy* young boy. *Hardy* emphasizes the ability to withstand force or adversity. It is typically applied to strains of plants or animals: a *hardy* species of corn

strong

hardy
muscular
powerful
stalwart
sturdy
tough

that was unaffected by the near-drought conditions of the northern plains; sled dogs *hardy* enough to withstand the arctic weather. In application to people, it can refer to someone able to survive difficulty or to a difficult way of life itself: the *hardy* life of frenetic physical activity at summer camp.

At its most restricted, **tough** can indicate a surface or covering that is thick, dense, horny, or callous — a surface that is impervious to wear or damage: the *tough* hide of the alligator. More informally, the word can apply to physical strength or stamina, with an added implication at times of coarseness or brutality: *tough*, well-trained recruits; the *tough* bouncer that most nightclubs employ. Even more informally, *tough* can refer to what is difficult: a *tough* problem. **Stalwart** is the most formal of these words; nowadays it points more to qualities of courage and loyalty than to physical strength per se: *stalwart* Indian braves who were willing to fight the white invaders; one of his most *stalwart* political supporters. See HEALTHY, HUSKY, MASSIVE.

Antonyms: POWERLESS, WEAK.

stubborn

adamant
headstrong
obdurate
obstinate
pertinacious
pigheaded

All of these words suggest a tendency to persist in an opinion, belief, decision, or course of action, generally with more force than reason. A person may be **stubborn** by disposition, showing this quality in most of his behavior and in most situations, but may be **obstinate** in a particular instance: Dick had always been a very *stubborn* boy, but was particularly *obstinate* in his dislike of homework. **Pigheaded** usually suggests *obstinate* stupidity: His *pigheaded* refusal to accept facts makes discussion impossible. **Adamant** implies a hard and unyielding attitude that may be the result of a strongly felt or carefully thought out conviction regarding some important matter: The ambassador was *adamant* in his insistence that all the prisoners be released from the concentration camp. A similar attitude, but carrying the idea of harshness and a lack of feeling, is implied by **obdurate**: The foreman was *obdurate* in holding to rigid production schedules. Both adamant and obdurate, however, can point approvingly to a principled refusal to compromise, unlike these other words with their implications of arbitrary egocentricity.

Pertinacious, though not necessarily deprecatory, usually suggests a kind of perseverance in a course of action that can be annoying or seem unreasonable to others: The lawyer's *pertinacious* harping on the same point made the witness very nervous under cross-examination. **Headstrong** indicates a strong-willed self-direction and an impatience with restraint. A *headstrong* person cannot be held back by advice or argument and may be reckless or hotheaded in his actions: a *headstrong* impetuous youth, rushing into things without forethought; His *headstrong* attempt to seize control of the party was political suicide. See AUTHORITARIAN, OVERBEARING, PERSISTENT, UNRULY.

Antonyms: ADAPTABLE, COMPLIANT, DOCILE, MALLEABLE.

student

disciple
learner
protégé
pupil
scholar

These words refer to someone involved in studies, in attempting to gain a set of skills, or in devotion to a patron or master. **Student** is the most general word here for any such person. At its most specific, it forms a complementary pair with **pupil**. The latter now usually refers to a young person in grade school, while *student*, in this context, refers to one in high school or college: demonstrating that more kindergarten *pupils* end up as college *students* than children who enter the first grade without previous educational experience. But whereas *pupil* itself has few uses outside this situation, *student* can displace *pupil* on the one hand and refer on the other to the most advanced or specialized expert or authority in some field: a musicologist who was a keen *student* of Beethoven's later work.

Scholar can function as a more formal substitute for *student*, but the word is unique in having two special areas of relevance. *Scholar* may be used at any level for a *student* who excels in his studies: an unruly child who nevertheless turned out to be a real *scholar*. More often, the word refers specifically to an advanced specialist, without any suggestion that the person is still pursuing a course of formal education; the word, in fact, may suggest an extremely learned authority on a given subject: *scholars* who were able to test the theory by collating all existing copies of the folio text of the play. **Learner** is much more informal than *scholar* and emphasizes the other extreme—a beginner rather than an authority in some field of knowledge. The word furthermore applies less to youngsters than to adults who are purposely acquiring some new set of possibly simple skills. The situation pertains not so much to someone seeking formal education as to any sort of novice or beginner: insisting that she have a *learner's* permit before he attempted to teach her how to drive.

Disciple and **protégé** both pertain exclusively to someone devoted to a master or patron. Most strictly, *disciple* suggests a religious situation: the *disciples* of Buddha who codified his writings; the twelve *disciples* of Christ. In general use, the word refers to someone's ardent advocacy of any prominent figure or theory: an early *disciple* of Freud, though never of Freudianism per se. Often, the word has a contemptuous ring to it, suggesting someone subordinate or unimportant in himself, possibly because of his slavish devotion to or imitation of another: teen-agers who become overnight *disciples* of the newest singing sensation; business executives who pick yes-men to be their *disciples*. *Protégé* indicates a situation in striking contrast to *disciple*. Here, a young or unknown person of talent is assisted or patronized by someone else who is securely established, either as an artist or merely as a person of financial means: a wealthy benefactor who demanded nothing whatsoever in return for the money he gave to his *protégés*; a master sculptor who, seeing the boy's talent, took him on as a *protégé*. The word can have a contemptuous ring to it, like *disciple*. In this case it may suggest even greater servility in the subordinate but adds to this a suggestion of overweening vanity in the superior or benefactor; the word can even be a euphemism for a paid mistress or lover, particularly one younger than the benefactor. See BEGINNER, LEARNING.

Antonyms: master, patron, PROFESSOR, teacher.

study

consider
contemplate
ponder
weigh

These words mean to apply one's mind to a subject in order to learn about it, to resolve any questions it poses, or to reach a decision concerning it. **Study** implies a careful attempt to learn all the aspects of the subject or problem under scrutiny before making plans or taking definite action. [Meteorologists *study* information sent back to earth from weather satellites before making forecasts; A city council *studies* proposals submitted for urban renewal.]

Consider is a more general word than *study*; it can imply either momentary and casual attention given to something, or deep, prolonged concentration: *considering* whether to brave the snowstorm and drive to the movies or to stay at home; *considering* how much insurance he would need to guarantee the education of his children. *Consider* may also point to an objective judgment that has been reached after careful *study*: We are *considering* your manuscript for publication, but feel it needs extensive rewriting.

Contemplate implies thinking about something, as for a long period of time, but usually simply for its own sake and with no definite, pragmatic end in view: We have long *contemplated* the possibility of living in Europe for a year. In its related meaning of looking at intensely, *contemplate* suggests leisurely and pleasurable reflection: He *contemplated* the Unicorn Tapestries for an entire afternoon.

Ponder and **weigh** both mean to examine all sides of a question in one's own mind in order to make a careful evaluation. These words differ from *study* in that they emphasize the making of a choice between conflicting data, opposing claims, or the like, rather than the acquiring of knowledge by searching into a body of information. *Ponder* suggests that the matter is a serious one and deserves careful deliberation: Before casting his vote, a responsible, mature citizen should *ponder* his choice of candidates. *Weigh* may also be applied to important considerations: The judge advised the jury to *weigh* the arguments and testimony presented by the prosecution and the defense. When the decision to be made is of minor significance, *weigh* is to be preferred to *ponder*: to *weigh* the advantages of going to the beach or to a ball game on a hot day. See EXAMINE, READ, SEE, THINK.

Antonyms: NEGLECT, *scan*, SLIGHT.

stupid

asinine
dense
dull
dumb
obtuse
thick
unintelligent

These words refer to a lack of intellect, perceptivity, or wisdom. **Stupid** and **asinine** are the harshest of these and are more likely to be used to disapprove of rather than to describe someone. But *stupid* may suggest either a weak mentality or foolish behavior, whereas *asinine* is most often restricted to the latter: a *stupid* fellow; a *stupid* mistake; an *asinine* middle-aged woman dressing like a teen-ager. Because of this limitation, *asinine* is even more disapproving than *stupid*; its reference is to a beast of burden, the ass, traditionally considered *stupid* and obstinate.

Dense and **thick** both concentrate on the aspect of *stupid* pertaining to a weak mentality, both emphasizing an inability to understand simple facts or remember clear instructions. *Thick* may sound more formal because of its British flavor, but it is also less harsh than *dense*, which suggests an impenetrable slowness of mind. Also, *thick* may apply to a single act, while *dense* more often refers to a rooted characteristic: a bit *thick* of him not to get the point of the joke; so *dense* that he had to be talked to like a child.

Dumb in this sense is restricted to an extremely informal level when applied to *stupid* people: a *dumb* Dora; a *dumb* cluck. Purists frown on it in this use, because it means mute in other situations: the deaf and *dumb*; *dumb* animals. **Obtuse**, by contrast, is perhaps the most formal word here, referring to slow-wittedness, whether revealed by a particular act or by a person's whole character: a laughably *obtuse* misunderstanding of her request; an *asinine* television show that was specifically designed for the ignorant and *obtuse*. While the word may seem more objective at first glance, its very formality adds a note of withering scorn that is not present in the previous words.

Dull and **unintelligent** are both used more objectively to describe people or behavior revealing low mental ability. *Unintelligent*, in fact, is almost completely devoid of emotional connotations: *unintelligent* answers to complex questions. Since mental ability is a matter of degree, however, the word may mask subjective judgment, except when used comparatively: gearing her lessons to the more *unintelligent* among her students. *Dull* can be used to express simple disapproval of the *stupid* and boring: too *dull* to be able to work a beginner's crossword puzzle; a *dull*-witted fool. The word is often used more objectively, however, to refer to less than average mentality; sometimes it serves as a euphemism for the more straightforward *unintelligent*: a special class for *dull* learners. See BLOCKHEAD, MONOTONOUS, MORON.

Antonyms: BRIGHT, *clever,* CREATIVE, *intelligent,* KEEN, *smart.*

These words refer to uncertain or unsteady speech. **Stutter** is the most concrete and technical of these, referring to a chronic speech defect in which there is spasmodic repetition, blocking, prolongation of sounds and syllables, especially of initial ones; such a defect may have an organic or physiological element, but is mainly caused by a psychological disruption of normal development: therapeutic and remedial training for children who *stutter.* **Stammer** may suggest a milder degree of speech difficulty, such as halting speech, or it may apply more widely to any temporary or momentary difficulty of speaking that stems from shyness, uncertainty, or any excess of emotion: blushing and *stammering* under the attractive man's searching glance; *stammering* that he didn't know where he had put his keys; finally able to *stammer* out how much she loved him. Sometimes the word can be used in a euphemistic way to replace what may be thought of as the harsh directness of *stutter*: assuring him that many a child *stammered* a bit and that it would go away if he didn't think about it.

Whereas the previous pair emphasizes an involuntary difficulty, **hem and haw** more often suggests a deliberate reluctance to state something directly. Thus, while the word can suggest the embarrassed or halting manner of *stammer*, it more often points to someone trying to avoid answering a question or buying time until the right reply occurs to him: a question that was so surprising that he could only *hem and haw* in answer. As the amount of suggested evasiveness increases, the word can also point to someone who speaks in a slow but more particularly a roundabout or evasive manner: *hemming and hawing* about generalities instead of explaining the statistics I had cited. **Stumble** is more like *stammer* in suggesting a temporarily halting speech that is involuntary: *stumbling* over his words in his haste to tell the whole story. The reason here may be the same as for *stammer*; but the word can also suggest simple slips that are completely inadvertent: *stumbling* only once or twice in a very long speech. See TIMID.

Antonyms: articulate, enunciate.

These words refer to grooming and clothes that are fastidious, elegant, well designed, or in accordance with current taste. **Stylish** emphasizes something designed and executed so as to display a trend-setting flair for what is in vogue. In this it is close to **fashionable**, but is less formal, suggesting a more dramatic appearance, based on more transitory up-to-the-minute standards. By contrast, *fashionable* emphasizes elegance, correctness, and possibly a simplicity of expensive taste that is not likely to become dated so quickly: Leopard coats were *stylish* for a season, but mink coats will always be *fashionable*. *Stylish* is also more open to being used as a contemptuous term: beehive hairdos and other *stylish* vulgarities. *Fashionable*, however, can also be applied to transitory or disapproved-of vogues: the sack, the shift, the mini-skirt all having had their *fashionable*, tawdry, brief moment of glory. *Fashionable*, furthermore, is more likely to be applied to men than *stylish*: the

stutter

hem and haw
stammer
stumble

stylish

chic
dapper
fashionable
modish
smart
spruce

double-breasted suit that is again becoming *fashionable*. Used of men, *stylish* is likely to suggest a specialized subculture when it is not openly contemptuous: the *stylish*, bowler-hatted men of London's financial district; the dirty jeans and torn T-shirt that is thought *stylish* among motorcycle cultists.

Chic is in every way an intensification of *stylish*, except for its greater formality. Its French flavor points to that country as a source of high fashion for Western women, a fact emphasized by the word's restriction to female grooming. If anything, the word suggests an even greater concern for the last word in modernity, with a special emphasis on the exclusive and expensive: outraged to discover that her *chic* evening dress, a signed original, was being mass-produced by an American department store.

Modish sometimes concentrates on the negative aspects of *stylish*, suggesting a concern with vogue to the neglect of good taste, comfort, or decorum: women who looked like colorless cadavers in their *modish* chalk-white makeup and silver lamé dresses. By contrast, **smart** concentrates on a different aspect of *stylish*, referring to the dramatic impact of good design. *Smart*, however, puts less emphasis on vogue than any of the previous words, and suggests instead the boldness of clean lines and simple cut, particularly those conceived of as being suitable for a specific occasion: her *smart* riding outfit. Where *chic* suggests the apex of femininity, there is something of the opposite in *smart*, although its forcefulness need not suggest mannishness. The word does tend to emphasize overall appearance rather than any one isolated aspect. *Smart*, of course, can also refer to comparable aspects of male grooming without suggesting effeminacy: his *smart* Ivy-League suit. This paradox makes the word useful in joint descriptions: a *smart*, well-turned-out couple.

Dapper and **spruce**, by contrast with the previous words, are mainly reserved to describe aspects of male grooming. *Dapper* may indicate the last word in formality and correctness: looking *dapper* in his new tuxedo. More often, however, the word suggests overelegant and even prissy grooming: quipping that he reminded her of the *dapper* little gentleman on wedding cakes. *Spruce* suggests masculine neatness and cleanness, with an emphasis on simplicity and timeless correctness of costume rather than conformity to *fashionable* vogues: sailors looking *spruce* and trig in their white summer uniforms. Also, more than any other word here, *spruce* often bears directly on grooming to the exclusion of dress: coming back from the barber looking *spruce* and clean-shaven. Occasionally, the word can refer to a woman's costume; in this case, it emphasizes trimness and neatness: her *spruce* skiing outfit. See ARTISTIC, ELEGANT, EXQUISITE, MODERN, ORDERLY, UP-TO-DATE, VOGUE.

Antonyms: dowdy, OLD-FASHIONED, UGLY, *unkempt*.

subdue

check
constrain
curb
inhibit
repress

The pacification or putting down of unruly forces is suggested by all of these words. **Subdue** is the mildest of the group, suggesting a gentle but firm power exerted to moderate an impulse that might otherwise be dangerous: *subduing* his momentary impulse to tell his boss what he thought of him. *Subdue* implies that the threatening force has been put down but not necessarily altered or diminished in any basic way. **Inhibit**, consequently, goes further than *subdue* in suggesting a fundamental altering of the rebellious impulse; this is achieved, by implication, through blocking its chances for growth or decreasing the area within which it can continue operating effectively. The word often refers disapprovingly to the diminishing of natural or healthy instincts: excise laws that would fatally *inhibit* free trade; overly restrictive or permissive parents who *inhibit* the normal maturation of their children.

A similar relationship holds between **check** and **curb**. Like *inhibit*, *check* suggests the prevention of further growth; *curb*, on the other hand, suggests the moderating force implicit in *subdue*: merely wishing to *curb* some thoughtless tendencies in her pupils, while *checking* altogether any tendency toward outright hostile acts. *Check* is stronger than *inhibit*, however, in sometimes implying the complete rooting out of an impulse. Similarly, *curb* is much stronger than *subdue* in suggesting the use of considerable force, when necessary, in order to counter any threatened unruliness. Because it suggests difficulty and struggle, in fact, *curb* has greater force than *check*, even though the latter points to the complete extirpation of an impulse: A few concessions wisely made would have completely *checked* the revolution; now whole armies thrown into the breach may not be sufficient to *curb* it.

Repress and **suppress**, besides sounding so similar, are often used almost as though they were different spellings of the same word. They are differently defined by psychologists, however, and even in ordinary use a contrast in meaning can be observed. In psychology, *repress* indicates a process of returning to the unconscious mind fears and impulses so that they cannot be easily called up again; this process occurs without the subject's knowledge. *Suppress*, in contrast, relates to a single effort of will in putting away an unpleasant thought; this act may or may not be conscious, and the *suppressed* idea can more easily be recalled for consideration. The ordinary uses of these two words reflect a similar comparison; *repress* is felt as the stronger here, often implying a harsh or excessive stamping out of dissent or rebellion. Except for its greater force, it is thus similar to *check* and *inhibit*. *Suppress* suggests bringing something under control, like *subdue* and *curb*, although it suggests the use of greater force than either.

Constrain and **restrain** make a comparable pair, but they are much more clearly distinguished in common use than *repress* and *suppress*. *Constrain* indicates forcing someone else to do something against his will and carries an overtone of disapproval for such an act: *constraining* his daughter from going out on dates. *Restrain* suggests a gentler, advisory moderation and may sometimes refer to a self-imposed discipline. As such, it can often be used with a tone of approval: *restraining* himself from drinking to excess. See CONTROL, DISCIPLINE, STOP (arrest), SURMOUNT.

Antonyms: INCITE, STIMULATE.

These words refer to expression or behavior that is concerned with sexuality or bodily functions. **Suggestive** is the mildest of these words, emphasizing not frankness on these matters so much as allusions or innuendoes that are considered to be in bad taste: *suggestive* movie advertisements that are more titillating than the movies they are used to publicize. Even so distant an approach to frankness as this word can imply was once condemned by an earlier age; now the word can be used in disapproval of any leering indirectness about sex, even those cases where frankness itself might now be thought quite innocuous: that sort of parental lecture on the facts of life that is, in its embarrassed delivery, bewildering and *suggestive* rather than dispassionate and informative.

Risqué suggests a closer approach to frankness on sexual matters in that boldness of allusion is stressed. Except for someone who is extremely

subdue

(continued)

restrain

suppress

suggestive

earthy

off-color

Rabelaisian

racy

raunchy

risqué

scatological

strait-laced, this word has fewer legitimate uses in today's more tolerant atmosphere, since many kinds of direct references to sex, much less glancing allusions of any sort, are not thought particularly bold: It was once thought *risqué* for a woman to dine alone with a man in his apartment; gentlemen who traded *risqué* jokes once the ladies had retired after dinner. **Off-color** has been similarly affected, although its vagueness still permits its application, particularly to jokes of any sort that hinge on sexual matters: an *off-color* joke that was currently making the rounds of the girls' dormitory. But "dirty joke" is a more common description of this kind of humor.

The remaining words are not restricted to sexuality alone. Of these, **earthy** is the broadest in application. If once it was disapproving for something coarse or crude in reference to sexual and bodily functions, now it may be descriptively neutral or even approving: the *earthy* humor of Chaucer and Shakespeare. The word may even suggest a sentimental nostalgia for the supposedly simpler and more direct life that man lived previous to modern complexities: the trend to urbanization that has robbed man of his *earthy* acceptance of the natural processes of birth, copulation, death, and decay. **Racy** can apply to accounts that are erotic, pornographic, or *earthy*, but in this case the word suggests fast-paced action and a linguistic forcefulness gained through frank and direct expressions: a *racy* book about marital infidelity in a suburban housing development. When *racy* applies to actions it can indicate *earthy* behavior that is marked by high-spirited energy and linguistic gusto: a customer whose *racy*, pungent speech and erotic prowess would have put Don Juan to shame.

Raunchy is an informal word with a variety of applications. It can refer to personal uncleanliness or to an *earthy* disregard of hygienic niceties: He felt *raunchy* all over after three solid days of hiking in the forest; a beer-guzzling, *raunchy* brute of a husband. It can also refer to an intense but unappeased building up of sexual appetite: *raunchy* soldiers on leave in Tokyo.

Both **Rabelaisian** and **scatological** emphasize *earthy* expression or behavior. *Rabelaisian*, like *racy*, indicates high-spirited zest, but stresses a penchant for good-humored tomfoolery involving a preoccupation with sexual and excretory functions. The word refers to the French writer, Rabelais, whose work reflected such concerns: the *Rabelaisian* wit of many contemporary Southern novelists; a *Rabelaisian* rascal who delighted in playing obscene practical jokes on his friends. *Scatological* is a word of neutral description for a fascination with excrement or with the excretory functions. It is useful in discriminating work with this emphasis from other possibly obscene material that is focused on sexual functions: the *scatological* emphasis in the works of Jonathan Swift; soldiers whose language is larded with obscene and *scatological* references. See EROTIC, INDECENT, LEWD, SMUTTY.

Antonyms: BLAND, *decorous, genteel,* INNOCENT, *prissy.*

summary

abridgment
abstract
digest
outline

These words refer to a short description of the main points of a longer work or presentation. **Summary** is the most general of these words, referring to any attempt to condense into as few words as possible an extended train of thought: a day-to-day *summary* of the proceedings in the murder trial; concluding each chapter with a *summary* of its main arguments. The word implies a pithy paraphrase, with no attempt to catch the style of the original. Also, the word almost exclusively refers to something that follows after and is based on the extended presentation, or even concludes it — as suggested by the common phrase in speechmaking: in *summary*. **Abstract** and **précis** both refer to *summaries* written most often by someone other than the original author; hence they are seldom part of the original presentation, though they follow it and are based upon it. Like *summary*, they stress brevity and the schematic representation of essential points with no attempt to preserve flavor. *Abstract* most specifically refers to a scholarly or legal citation that gives the gist of what may be a complex argument or study: a quarterly containing *abstracts* of doctoral dissertations in progress; an *abstract* of the proposed legislation. *Précis* may suggest a lengthier treatment than *abstract* and one in which the exact ordering of points in the original is adhered to; also, it is not restricted to legal or scholarly fields, applying to any *summary* of thought or argument in an essay or other nonfiction prose: each sentence in the *précis* representing a paragraph in the essay; space quota that permitted *abstracts* but ruled out *précis* of research projects. The word can even refer to a skeletal list-like presentation of whole fields of knowledge: a *précis* of Renaissance art history.

Outline and **synopsis** relate to *précis* in that they both retain the point-by-point ordering of the original; they are both most often a skeletal setting down of these points, but may be drawn up either by the author or someone else before, as well as after, the writing of the original. Within these possibilities, *outline* covers a wider range than *synopsis*. It often suggests a numbered and lettered list which may contain nothing more than key words or phrases, but which may, on the other hand, present an extended prose paraphrase: a *summary* of French history written in the form of an *outline*; drawing up an *outline* of the author's arguments. *Synopsis* usually refers to a plot summary of a piece of fiction. Ordinary prose sentences are most often used, rather than the numbered and lettered list suggested by *outline*. It may tell in capsule form events treated in a completed work or those planned for a projected work: submitting the first chapter of his novel and a *synopsis* of the unwritten remainder; writing *synopses* of novels submitted as candidates for film treatment. The word may also refer to a paragraph that retells previous action and introduces an installment of a serialized work of fiction.

Abridgment and **digest** refer to more expanded treatment, suggesting condensation rather than a capsule paraphrase of the original. Consequently, what is presented after this shortening process may still be substantially in the original author's own words and style. Of the two, *abridgment* suggests the least modification of the original; it may refer, in fact, merely to the excision of a relatively few passages: an *abridgment* in which passages involving sexual frankness were omitted. The word can, however, indicate a greater amount of change: several characters and the whole subplot that did not appear in the *abridgment*; a useful one-volume *abridgment* of Gibbon. *Digest* refers to a boiled-down recasting of the original to present its essentials in shorter space. Although the original author's style and flavor may be retained at times, other passages may be rewritten on grounds of clarity or brevity: a concise *digest* of the judge's long dissent. The word may also refer to a collection of condensed pieces: a quarterly *digest* of articles pertaining to space research. In some scholarly or technical uses, the word may suggest nearly the sort of brevity implicit in *abstract*: a *digest* of all the articles presented at the annual medical convention. See SHORTEN, TERSE.

summit

acme
apex
climax
peak
pinnacle
zenith

These words refer to the highest point of something. **Summit** and **peak** both refer most concretely to mountains; *peak*, however, can indicate the whole mountain or its upper part whereas *summit* is specifically restricted in reference to the topmost surface alone: climbing the *peak* to reach the *summit*. In metaphorical use, this distinction is lost, both words referring to the position of greatest importance, intensity, or power. *Summit* is the more formal of the two and has come to refer specifically to high-level conferences, as between heads of state: the settling of nuclear policy at the *summit*. *Peak* suggests that point or moment at which something is most typical or at its best: when the Roaring Twenties were at their *peak*; a book produced when he was at the *peak* of his powers. *Summit* is less often used in this metaphorical way.

Pinnacle can refer to a turret or more commonly to a *peak* or its *summit*. It may sometimes suggest a leaner, taller silhouette than *peak*, however. Used metaphorically, it functions as a hyperbolic substitute for *peak*, often in stock combinations that approach the cliché: the *pinnacle* of success. **Acme** can theoretically refer to a *summit* but it is now almost exclusively used in a metaphorical way to refer to some abstract quality at its most quintessential; it also appears in stock combinations: the *acme* of perfection. **Apex** refers to the vertex of an angle, but can also indicate the tip or top of something or something at its maximum or its turning point: a battle that reached its *apex* the next afternoon. All three of these words can become empty metaphors, especially when used indiscriminately because of their imagined status or elegance.

Neither **zenith** nor **climax** make any literal reference to a mountain *peak* or *summit*. *Zenith* refers to the celestial point directly overhead. Metaphorically, it suggests anything at its culmination or highest development; as such it is a useful intensification of *peak*: fearing that their candidate's strength had reached its *peak* too early, before campaign intensity was at its *zenith*. Also, *zenith* is more often used to suggest something positive, whereas *peak* is not so restricted: His mastery of new painting techniques was at its *zenith* when the taste of his times had reached a *peak* of vulgarity. Most concretely, *climax* refers to the turning point of a play or a kind of rhetorical build-up in an oration. Metaphorically, the word is especially pertinent to indicate the point of fullest development in something that grows or has cyclic stages: picking only those flowers that were at their *climax*. See CONCLUSIVE, FINAL, HIGHEST.

Antonyms: base, bottom, foot, nadir.

summon

beckon
call
conjure
invoke
send for
subpoena

These words refer to an appeal for help, a mustering of forces or resources, or a request for a group or a person to gather or draw near. The most general of these words are the relatively formal **summon** and the informal phrase **send for**. Since neither word indicates what means are used to make the request, both can be convenient when only the request itself is of importance or when a variety of means is used in a gathering process. [The dying man *sent for* his only son, who was waiting outside the sick room; The cabinet was *summoned* to an emergency meeting by presidential aides who had been ordered to track down every member by any means available.] *Summon* often implies an official or formal request or demand that someone come or appear: The pope *summoned* all cardinals and bishops to the ecumenical council. The word can also apply to a mustering up of forces or resources: an attempt to *summon* up his last reserves of strength as he approached the home stretch of the race. *Send for* often implies the delegation of a task:

We stayed in our hotel room and *sent* out *for* food. The noun form of *summon* can also refer specifically to a notice to appear in court: served with a *summons*. **Subpoena**, both as verb and noun, is exclusively restricted to this sense: Both sides in a case may *subpoena* witnesses to testify.

Call can specifically indicate a *summoning* of someone by means of the spoken word or a vocal exclamation: He *called* to her from the other side of the street; the wordless wail with which she *called* for help. In other uses, the word can refer to paying a visit or the arrival of an escort: a friend who promised to *call* on us; the hour at which he would *call* for her. More pertinent here, *call* can indicate the expression of a recommendation or demand: a biting speech in which he *called* for a new approach to slum housing. With "up," the word can indicate the act of telephoning: I'll *call* you up tomorrow. Also, the same phrase can refer to *summoning* spirits or recollections — or to making any imaginative notion real and vivid by describing it in detail: a face that *called* up in his mind the image of his dead wife; He *called* up for his audience a vision of what the country might look like if the city planners were ignored. *Call* has a wide range of uses, often involved literally or metaphorically in some reference to a *summoning* process.

Beckon specifically refers to any *summoning* done by a gesture of the hand: *beckoning* me to his side; She asked them to follow her and *beckoned* them forward. **Conjure**, like one use of *call*, can specifically indicate the *summoning* of spirits or recollections, but it more often refers, like the same use of *call*, to vivid descriptions of an imagined state: a house that *conjured* up his own forgotten childhood; a senate speech in which he *conjured* up for his colleagues the grisly specter of nuclear war. **Invoke** can refer to a call for supernatural favor, particularly at the opening of a formal or official gathering: the minister who *invoked* God to guide the convention in its work. In wider uses, the word can refer to any action in which something, real or imaginary, tangible or intangible, is called into play: a plea for the proposal in which he *invoked* the memory of the late president; They *invoked* the mounting evidence of discrepancies in the report as justifying a new investigation. See GATHER, NAME, PLEAD, REQUEST.

Antonyms: *dismiss*, POSTPONE.

---

superficial

flat
obvious
shallow

These words refer to effort or understanding that is not searching or profound or that does not go deep. **Superficial** and **shallow** may both literally indicate a lack of depth: *superficial* wounds; *shallow* water. In this context, *superficial* suggests a cursory or hasty approach, an undue interest in trivialities, or a personality that by choice is not genuine or sincere: a *superficial* glance at the newspaper; a *superficial* life of self-indulgence; giving him a polite but *superficial* welcoming. In contrast, *shallow* applies not to a refusal to go into something deeply, but an inability to feel, sympathize, or understand: youngsters who rush into marriage with only the *shallowest* notions of what love and responsibility entail; a *shallow* indifference to the sufferings of others; a *shallow* anthropocentric view of the universe. *Shallow* might seem the more condemnatory of the two words, except that *superficial*, in suggesting that a better or more painstaking effort is possible, would seem to indicate less forgivable failings: a *superficial* approach to the problem that was the result of a lazy, rather than a *shallow* mind.

Obvious and **flat** more often refer to the poor results that are to be expected from *superficial* efforts or *shallow* approaches. *Obvious*, of course, is very general, with a wide range of uses. In this context, it may be pertinent to effort that attempts to go beyond the *superficial* but fails: an *obvious* treatment of problems better dealt with by other scientists; an *obvious*, if not silly, plot that vitiates the playwright's ability to create genuine conflicts. In this context, *flat* suggests an *obvious* result without any sign of ability or desire to accomplish more: the novel's *flat*, one-dimensional characters. It can also suggest something that has lost any value it once had: a story which was widely admired in the 1890's but seems *flat* to us today. As can be seen, both these words are often used to criticize works of art, particularly of a narrative sort, with *obvious* applying to action or plot, *flat* to the creation of character: The author's *superficial* approach, his *obvious* story line, and his *flat* characters all betray evidence of a *shallow* mind. See BANAL, BLAND.

Antonyms: deep, GENUINE, profound.

supernatural

magical
miraculous
preternatural
superhuman

These words refer to things and occurrences that are or seem to be breaks with the natural order, or unexplainable departures from ordinary reality. **Supernatural** would seem unambiguous in referring to anything that is literally "beyond nature" or cannot be explained by common-sense experience or the scientific method, especially to phenomena of a divine or heavenly character. However, some people would exclude the possibility of such phenomena. To them, *supernatural* might be used to express skepticism or disbelief: priestly hocus-pocus and *supernatural* rigamarole. Furthermore, *supernatural* has gathered suggestions that make it particularly relevant to the context of occultists and spiritualists; since many believers would find such interests heterodox, this flavor of the word restricts its use in a more general religious sense.

Magical has far less complicated implications; now it refers strictly to acts or things believed to confer *supernatural* powers: a *magical* charm to drive away evil spirits. This meaning makes it useful to anthropologists to describe aspects of primitive cultures whose religion is animist. More loosely, the word may refer hyperbolically to anything that is charged with meaning and emotion or that is awe-inspiring: the *magical* moment when the entire earth became visible to the orbiting astronaut. **Miraculous** is, of course, used in a religious context to refer to *supernatural* acts of saints or deities: the *miraculous* ability to levitate attributed to some Tibetan lamas; the *miraculous* changing of water into wine during the marriage at Cana. On a less elevated plane, *miraculous* is often used to refer to a last-minute or unexpected stroke of good fortune: a *miraculous* escape from their pursuers.

Preternatural puts contention to rest by specifically indicating those things that seem beyond explanation in terms of ordinary reality, but that are the result of unusual or rare causes: a *preternatural* ability to do complicated sums in his head. [Science works with *preternatural* phenomena in hopes of including them eventually within the widening circle of what we consider natural and explainable.] **Superhuman** indicates powers beyond those possessed by man, but again overtones obtrude; one might speak of the *superhuman* force of a hurricane or the *superhuman* compassion of God, but such descriptions might seem obvious, therefore trivial or irreverent. More often the word is used as a simple hyperbole for human effort that seems extreme: his roommate's *superhuman* powers of concentration. See BIZARRE, MYSTICAL, QUEER, UNUSUAL.

Antonyms: earthly, NORMAL, STANDARD, USUAL, WORLDLY.

These words suggest a smooth working of parts, especially in reference to a well-conditioned physique. **Supple** suggests a body capable of effortless movement: Unlike swimming, weightlifting does not result in a *supple* build. Used of physical objects, *supple* suggests that something can be bent without breaking or without becoming permanently distorted: *supple* branches trembling in the faint breeze. Used more abstractly, *supple* suggests something that is relaxed rather than taut or something that is smoothly articulated: the rhythmically insistent yet always *supple* music; a cool, *supple* mind able to make fine distinctions.

Lithe and **limber**, of the remaining words, are closest in meaning to *supple*. *Lithe*, in fact, is often used in tandem with *supple*: *lithe* and *supple* dancers. *Lithe* tends to suggest gracefulness and trimness of figure. *Limber* more specifically suggests a body brought into condition through training: Even naturally *lithe* and *supple* bodies need disciplined exercise to stay *limber*. While both *lithe* and *limber* are less often used of inanimate objects that can be bent, *lithe* is sometimes used, like *supple*, to describe character. Its special emphasis here is on an economic spareness: a *lithe*, understated style of writing.

Agile and **resilient** both stress quickness of response in addition to a smooth working of parts. *Resilient* specifically emphasizes a rapid rebounding into shape, *agile* the ability to move quickly yet gracefully: the *resilient* layer of pine needles under our feet; the *agile* leap of the doe. Both can also refer to qualities of mind. Here *agile* stresses the ability to think quickly without faltering: an *agile* aptness for finding the significant pattern in a mass of data. *Resilient* suggests an innovating mind that is not bound by deadening routine or habit: a *resilient* hopefulness in the face of seemingly insoluble dilimmas.

Like *agile*, **nimble** points to quickness, but here the gracefulness of movement is less emphasized than lightness and dexterity: the *nimble* fingers of a pianist. **Spry** emphasizes unexpected quickness and is often used to describe an old person who is still *agile* in movement: a *spry* old man who is still able to play tennis. See ADAPTABLE, MALLEABLE, QUICK, THIN.

Antonyms: CLUMSY, HEAVY, SLOW.

supple

agile
limber
lithe
nimble
resilient
spry

Supporter is the general term for one who allies himself with a cause or shows allegiance to its leader. [James Madison was one of the early *supporters* of the Bill of Rights; A political candidate needs the help of his *supporters* to win an election.]

Follower and **disciple** are related in that they emphasize devotion to a leader rather than to his doctrine or cause. A *follower* plays a more passive role than a *supporter* or a *disciple*. A *disciple* is one who studies under a leader or teacher of great influence and puts the leader's teachings into practice, perhaps to the point of proselytizing for him: Christ had thousands of *followers*, but it was his *disciples* who spread his doctrines.

Adherent places emphasis on support of the doctrines rather than of the leader himself. Thus, one would call Lenin an *adherent* of Marxism (not an *adherent* of Marx).

Partisan means a zealous *supporter* of a person or cause, right or wrong, sometimes to the point of wrong-headedness and obstinacy: The candidate is a strong *partisan* of the president and his domestic policy; a violent *partisan* of the conservative cause. Since World War II, *partisan* has taken on the additional meaning of a dedicated rebel who sup-

supporter

adherent
disciple
follower
partisan

ports his cause by guerrilla tactics: Italian *partisans* helped the Allies conquer northern Italy. See ASSISTANT, STUDENT.

Antonyms: antagonist, OPPONENT, TRAITOR.

suppose

assume
conjecture
guess
imagine
postulate
surmise

These words refer to the tentative adoption of an idea or interpretation in the face of incomplete evidence or uncertainty. **Suppose** and **guess** are the most informal and general of these. Both can be used, especially in speech, to present a proposal or opinion in a tentative way, making it come as a suggestion rather than as a directive. [We'd better get going, I *suppose*; It's getting late, I *guess*.] Both can also indicate any hazarding of opinion, however well- or ill-informed; but *guess* is more likely to suggest a completely arbitrary notion or a more thoroughgoing lack of information or authority. *Guess* can even suggest a bluff or a futile groping in the dark without any hope of success: multiple choice tests that allow students to *guess* at random when they have no idea of the answer. *Suppose*, by contrast, more often suggests a shrewd notion based on some evidence: able to *suppose* how upset you were just from the expression in your eyes. Also, the word can point to something adopted experimentally or to something entertained simply for the sake of argument: asking him to *suppose* what he would do if he were in such a situation. Although *suppose*, like *guess*, implies a lack of certainty, there must be some grounds for *supposing* something, however scanty. [You're only *supposing* this on hearsay; you have no proof.]

Imagine exists in a wider context, indicating either a creative act or a deliberate entertaining of something totally contrary to known fact. In the present context, the word relates more closely to *guess*, suggesting a paucity of evidence on which a supposition is based: *imagining* all the wild stories of the neighbors to be true. *Imagine* emphasizes the role of invention or fancy in influencing perception: He *imagined* that he had heard a scraping noise. Even so, *imagine* carries over from its other contexts vague connotations of sympathy, understanding, or reassurance, as in its common use as a stock phrase in speech. [You'll enjoy the movie, I *imagine*.] When related to the context of argument or reasoning that surrounds *suppose*, *imagine* indicates a more thoroughgoing fabrication: largely *imagining* the existence of such a prehistoric tribe, rather than demonstrating its existence.

Assume and **postulate** relate most closely to *suppose* in suggesting a context of argument or reasoning. *Assume* is the less formal of the two, emphasizing a conclusion based on little or no validating evidence; as such, it can suggest a general context pertaining to psychological rather than to logical mental operations: *assuming* that life owed him a living; She *assumed* he wouldn't want to know her after their quarrel. In argument, the word is even more clear than *suppose* about agreeing to adopt a tentative stance in order to test a proposition: *assuming* the report to be valid simply to see how that would affect our policies in the next decade. In the stricter context of logic and reasoning, both *postulate* and *assume* point to those things that must be accepted as given prior to the reasoning process: preferring that explanation which requires us to *postulate* (or *assume*) the fewest preconditions at the outset. *Postulate* is exclusively restricted in reference to the setting up of a theory in order to test its merit; it is therefore more precise than either *assume* or *suppose*: scientists who are traditionally driven to *postulate* a series of explanations until they find one that will stick.

Conjecture and **surmise** are comparable to *postulate* in formality, but comparable to *suppose* and *guess* in generality. *Conjecture* relates closely to *guess*, stressing the incomplete or inadequate evidence serving as a basis for judgment. A shrewd *conjecture* may include elements of intuition, extrapolations based on experience, a good sense of probability, and plain luck. When used without qualification, *conjecture* often indicates mere guesswork, unsubstantiated by any evidence and hence without much credibility: aimless *conjectures* about conspiracies organizing the assassination; *conjecturing* how long the enemy would take to zero in on his position. *Surmise* relates to the aspect of *suppose* that indicates a shrewd notion based on evidence. The word points to an ability to detect clues and to infer valid conclusions from them; its connotations suggest detachment and a cool ability to reason dispassionately: *surmising* from their looks that he had called on them at an inopportune time. *Surmise* conveys a greater degree of certainty, or at least better grounds for drawing a conclusion, than any of the other words here considered. See CONSIDER, DECIDE, REASONING.

Antonyms: actualize, execute, finalize, know, prove, validate.

These words all mean free from doubt or uncertainty. **Sure** and **certain** are used interchangeably in most contexts, but *certain* may emphasize the indisputable character of what is referred to, implying that whatever is *certain* is subject to reasonable debate. *Sure* is more indiscriminately used. [One thing was *certain*: the Democrats would never again nominate a national candidate with only a local reputation; He was *sure* that he could make the five o'clock train.] Both words, but especially *sure*, may serve as polite substitutes for a hopeful but less-than-*certain* attitude. "I'm *sure* he'll be here on time" can mean "I think (or I hope) he'll be here on time."

Positive is somewhat more emphatic than *sure* or *certain* in stressing the absolute absence of doubt and the incontestable nature of one's conviction. [I was *positive* that I had seen her face before; I could not possibly have been mistaken on that point.] **Definite**, influenced by its more basic meaning of precisely defined or limited (as in "*definite* boundaries"), is usually used in contexts that suggest a narrowing of choice or elimination of doubt, and often carries the meaning of no longer open to question, settled beyond doubt. [The president's choice of a running mate was now *definite*.]

Doubtless is more often used as an adverb than as an adjective. Indeed, its use as an adjective today strikes most ears as rather formal or dated. [It was his *doubtless* conclusion that the verdict was justified by the evidence.] As an adverb, *doubtless* often functions as a polite substitute for "one supposes," or "one would like to believe," or in contexts that show equivocation or skepticism. [*Doubtless* he had not meant to offend me, but the tone of his remarks was certainly insulting; It was *doubtless* true that the deal was technically legal, but one wondered about how ethical it was.] See CLEAR, SPECIFIC.

Antonyms: DOUBTFUL, improbable, unlikely, unsure, wavering.

These words mean to diminish, satisfy completely, or take away an appetite for something, often because of overexposure to it. **Surfeit** suggests an oversupply of something that may be appealing in itself but that causes antipathy in quantity: eating second and third helpings of the plum pudding until he was *surfeited*; a public *surfeited* to the point of boredom by the violence displayed on the television screen. **Glut** restricts itself to one aspect of *surfeit*, concentrating on the notion of oversupply without necessarily suggesting any concomitant antipathy:

sure

certain
definite
doubtless
positive

surfeit

cloy
dull
glut

surfeit
(continued)

pall
sate
satiate

a society *glutted* yet more and more avid for sexually provocative entertainment. **Sate** and **satiate** once suggested the simple appeasement of hunger or appetite, but now they suggest overindulgence to the point of discomfort. Of the two, *satiate* is the milder and more abstract and is still sometimes used for simple appeasement: gulping water from the offered canteen until his thirst was *satiated*. *Sate* almost invariably suggests the discomfort of overindulgence, especially in specifically sensual pleasures; the resulting discomfort may be felt as an enfeeblement of the senses or a sybaritic exhaustion or ennui: collapsing into sleep at last, *sated* with drink and carousing.

Dull specifically emphasizes an overtone of *sate* pertaining to sensory enfeeblement through overexposure: senses *dulled* from three days of partying; *dulling* her hunger by wolfing down half a dozen chocolates. **Pall** suggests that an attractive or desired object has lost its appeal through overexposure: a face whose beauty *palled* on him the more he looked at it; an interest in theories of conspiracy that *palled* soon after the detailed report was issued. **Cloy** suggests a sense of heavy oppression or suffocation caused by excessive gratification of an initially pleasing sensation, especially a sweet smell or fulsome manner: a strong scent of lilacs in the room that soon became *cloying*; a maternal love so strong that he found it *cloying*. See EAT, GOURMET, SATISFY.

surprised

amazed
astonished
astounded
flabbergasted
stunned

These words mean filled with wonder or incredulity because of a confrontation with something unexpected. To be **surprised** is to meet with something that momentarily, at least, sets one back and then may or may not afford pleasure: *surprised* to receive a letter from a friend she has not heard from in years; *surprised* at the drunken behavior of a business associate whom he had always looked up to. The word can also suggest a certain amount of moral condemnation, as when a person says, "I'm *surprised* at you!"

Astonished is a stronger word, indicating that a person has had more than an ordinary reaction to the unexpected: *astonished* to see how his home town had changed in the past twenty-five years.

Amazed suggests great wonder or bewilderment in the face of something that seems impossible or highly improbable: a teacher *amazed* to find that a poor student had made a mark of 100 on an important test. **Astounded** and the informal **flabbergasted** express extreme difficulty of belief. A woman may be *astounded* to learn that her dearest friend has been spreading malicious gossip about her. Describing her reaction to another friend, she might say, "I was *flabbergasted*!"

Stunned indicates shock and even speechlessness: a congregation *stunned* to hear that their pastor has just confessed to a serious crime. See CONFUSE, PUZZLE, UPSET.

Antonyms: IMPERTURBABLE.

swarthy

black
colored
dusky
mulatto

These adjectives indicate a dark or brownish coloring of the skin. Both **swarthy** and **dusky** signify skin of a dark cast, but the two words differ radically in connotation. *Swarthy* may be used neutrally in description: a tall man with a *swarthy* complexion. But it has so often been used to describe fictional characters of a romantic and sometimes vaguely sinister aspect that these associations accompany the word more often than not: a *swarthy* Spaniard or Italian in a Gothic novel. *Dusky* has exotic rather than suspicious connotations, a quality of mystery rather than menace. It seems somewhat lyrical or literary when applied to skin, suggesting a darkness of coloring that seems to have been dusted on like powder, a shadowy quality like an aura or an overlay: a *dusky* Moor; the *dusky* skin of the island girls.

Tawny and **tanned** suggest a warm coloring that falls between the extremes of dark and fair. *Tanned* describes skin that has darkened through exposure to the sun: *tanned* and healthy after a summer at the beach. *Tawny* indicates a natural coloring that is yellowish, orangish, or reddish brown. This word was once applied to persons having *tawny*-colored skin, an American Indian being called a *tawny*. But now *tawny* is seldom used of human beings except to describe the color of hair: a *tawny*-haired teenager.

Black, **colored**, and **mulatto** are racial designations, implying classification on the basis of skin color. *Black* suggests the dark pigmentation of the African Negro, and it is often used to mean Negro in the way that white is used to mean Caucasian: the so-called *black* race. *Colored* means nonwhite and may designate members of any race other than the Caucasian: *colored* people. In practice, *colored* is usually reserved for persons who are wholly or partially Negro, but the term may embrace Indians and Orientals as well, or be applied to dark-skinned South Americans or brown-skinned island peoples. *Colored*, or *coloured*, as it is so spelled there, is used in South Africa in a special sense to refer to any person who has both white and nonwhite ancestors.

Mulatto indicates the yellowish brown complexion associated with a person who has one white and one Negro parent. This term is an unpleasant carryover from an earlier era. It puts offensive stress on the idea of miscegenation, for *mulatto* derives from a Spanish word meaning "of mixed breed" that goes back to the Latin word for mule.

Many books could be written about the associations attending the word *black* in English and its cognates in European literature, and the corollary associations with the color *black* in folk myths and popular proverbs, idioms, and other homely expressions. In the literature of Western civilization, the long association of *black* with evil (*black* arts, *black*-hearted), disease (the *Black* Death), gloom and despair (a *black* future) in opposition to the associations of white with goodness, purity, chastity, and cleanliness is a fact, however misleading. With the fast-changing relationship between Negroes and whites, however, the connotations attending *black* are likewise changing. Among American Negroes, *black* is often preferred to Negro as a description of their race, Negro being considered by some as a term used mainly by white people and having disparaging or insulting overtones. This view is not shared by most white people who use it, however. *Colored* is still widely used in the U.S. to designate Negroes, but is felt by some white people to be indelicate or disparaging. Some Negroes do not seem to find *colored* so objectionable, since it is usually used simply as description.

Antonyms: fair, light, light-skinned, PALE, white, whitish.

These words agree in meaning to become or cause to become larger. **Swell** is the most general of these terms, and means to increase in bulk or dimension in any way, as by adding air or by absorbing moisture: a mosquito bite that *swelled* to the size of a quarter; a mountain brook *swollen* into a river. **Inflate**, on the other hand, means specifically to expand by filling with gas or air: to *inflate* a balloon or a tire. Both *swell* and *inflate* are commonly used in extended senses; *swell* can apply to any large increase, *inflate* always, and *swell* sometimes, applying to disproportionately large or exaggerated increases: an infant company that *swelled* into a giant corporation almost overnight; to *swell* the funds

swarthy
(continued)

tanned
tawny

swell

bulge
dilate
distend
inflate

of the charitable organization to a new high; an *inflated* sense of his own importance. *Swell* has in many contexts a suggestion of morbidity or unnatural size, illustrated by its metaphorical use in the popular expression "a *swelled* head," meaning an *inflated* self-esteem.

Bulge implies *swelling* outward, usually in one particular direction. [Sacks filled with fluid *bulge* at their weakest spots; The off-duty policeman's coat *bulged* where his service revolver was holstered on his chest.]

Distend means to expand or stretch out because of pressure exerted from within. [When you take a deep breath and hold it, your lungs are *distended*; A nursing mother's breasts are *distended* with milk.] Whereas *distend* implies an enlargement in all directions, **dilate** usually implies a two-dimensional enlargement, and is most often applied to the eyes: eyes *dilated* with surprise; Pupils *dilate* when one moves from a sunny to a darkened room. See ENLARGE, EXTEND.

Antonyms: DECREASE, *deflate, depress, extract*.

symbol

badge
device
emblem
hallmark
sign
token

These words refer to a tangible or visible indication of a detectable or agreed-upon meaning. **Symbol** is the most complex of these words in its references, emphasizing in all its uses something deliberately made to embody or constructed to communicate a certain meaning. A *symbol* may be arbitrarily arrived at: the *symbols* of the alphabet; white as the *symbol* of purity. Or it may be developed by charged circumstances: abolitionists who saw in John Brown the *symbol* of their cause. In an aesthetic sense, the word may refer to an element carefully chosen and deployed to have a desired effect: a series of unrelated misfortunes in the novel that became *symbols* for the protagonist's state of mind.

Sign is often used in place of *symbol* to refer to a simple, arbitrary representation of an agreed-upon meaning: the *sign* of the cross; waving the white flag as a *sign* that they wished to surrender. Even on the simplest level, however, the two words are often used in tandem to indicate different things; for example, letters and the words they make are referred to as *symbols*, punctuation marks as *signs*. The former yield meanings, the latter phrasings or intonations. On other levels, as well, *sign* refers to an arbitrary indication from which simple, agreed-upon meanings or instructions can be deduced. Correspondingly, *symbol* refers to an indication that embodies a greater range of meanings. These must be induced from the exact deployment of the *symbols* and cannot always be paraphrased without loss. The higher animals as well as man use *signs*, but only man creates *symbols*: the typical shriek that monkeys make as a *sign* to warn others in the tribe of an unexpected danger. [Documents such as the Bill of Rights endure as *symbols* for human aspirations that are not even necessarily enumerated in them.] More loosely, *sign* is widely used for any sort of tell-tale fact from which information can be deduced: looking for *signs* that the disease had run its course; a *sign* that more inflation was on the way.

Emblem suggests a visual *symbol* that stands as the distinctive device of a group or nation: the eagle that is an *emblem* of the United States; the hammer-and-sickle *emblem* of the Soviet Union. **Badge**, most strictly, is an *emblem* that designates membership or rank in a military or paramilitary unit or an honor given by it: the *badge* of the Second Division; a Good Conduct *badge*; a merit *badge*; the *badge* of Eagle Scout; turning back his lapel to show his police *badge*. Sometimes the word can be used as a more colorful substitute for *emblem*: wearing the scarlet letter as the *badge* of her disgrace. **Hallmark** originally referred to a distinguishing mark stamped on sterling silver; now it may refer to an *emblem* chosen to represent a group or business: the drawing of a comet that appeared as a *hallmark* on the company's stationery. Even more generally, it can refer to any unmistakable or outstanding feature by which something can be recognized: the wit and dignity that was the *hallmark* of his presidency; integrity, the *hallmark* of a gentleman.

Device, in this sense, refers to a symbolic figure or design, usually with a motto or legend, in a coat of arms borne upon a shield. It may also denote any *emblem* that has been adopted by a person or a family. By extension, the colophon of a publisher or an easily recognizable symbol used as a trade mark are sometimes called *devices*.

Token most often refers to something offered as a *symbol* or reminder of an attitude or understanding: giving her a kiss as a *token* of his love; keeping the medals as a *token* by which to remember her dead son. More recently, the word may suggest a partial effort or a minimal compliance: asking for a deposit as a *token* of his intention to buy the book; many businesses that hire one Negro as a *token* of their intention to integrate. See MEAN (v.), MEANING.

These words refer to evidence from which a whole situation, such as the presence of a disease, may be inferred. **Symptom** relates closely to a medical context, applying to any manifestations of unusual functioning that may or may not be relevant to a diagnosis: unexplained *symptoms* of dizziness and nausea. Similarly, each abnormal condition or disease gives off characteristic *symptoms*: required to name the telltale *symptoms* for hundreds of diseases. A **syndrome** is that set of *symptoms* that always occur together and are characteristic of a particular disease, whether physical or mental. A *syndrome*, however, is not the sum total of random *symptoms* detected in someone at a given checkup, but only those that fit together into the typical picture of a specific disease or ailment: the *syndrome* for one kind of hepatitis that includes yellowing of the skin, extreme fatigue, and certain digestive disorders; delusions, the hearing of voices, and a feeling of being persecuted that are an inevitable part of the paranoid's *syndrome*. This word has become a fad word for any set of characteristics commonly found in association, usually used with a negative tone: recognizing in him the whole Marxist *syndrome* after the briefest of conversations. **Prodrome**, a medical term, does not, like *syndrome*, refer to a collection of *symptoms* but to any single *symptom* that is premonitory of an approaching disease: the chronic anemia that may be a *prodrome* for leukemia.

While **indication** and **clue** may be used in a medical context, both are also used widely outside it. *Clue*, in fact, relates more directly to the field of criminology than to medicine. As such, it refers to the evidence by which a crime may be solved or from which a whole situation may be inferred: gathering *clues* at the scene of the murder that could lead them to the killer. In a wider context, the word can refer to any telltale evidence whether given intentionally or inadvertently: asking for some *clue* as to how she felt about him; noticing several *clues* that suggested he had interests similar to her own. *Indication* is the most general of these words and can point to any piece of telltale evidence in any situation or context: *indications* of the drug's effectiveness; *indications* that a quarrel had immediately preceded the murder; giving her innumerable *indications* that he enjoyed her company; some guidelines that are good *indications* of a country's economic health. See HINT, MEAN, PREMONITION, TESTIMONY.

symptom

clue
indication
prodrome
syndrome

systematic

methodical
orderly
regular

These words all imply adherence to a design, an arrangement, or a pre-meditated sequence of activities. **Systematic** implies an overriding concept or method of organization, and suggests a thoroughgoing principle that determines the operation, control, or conduct of some process: a *systematic* analysis of the effects of government spending on the gross national product; a *systematic* exposition of the relationship between urban poverty and drug addiction. **Methodical**, on the other hand, need not suggest a guiding principle or a complex organization, but only a planned, often step-by-step, arrangement or process. *Methodical* often implies routine and painstaking effort as part of a fateful or ineluctable evolution toward some end: the *methodical* process of weeding out snipers by a building-by-building search of the conquered city. In some contexts the word suggests extreme detachment to the point of ruthlessness: The murderer *methodically* bound and gagged each victim before killing him.

Orderly has a suggestion of neatness or care, and indicates an arrangement or design that is kept within predetermined limits; the emphasis is on the manner of achievement rather than on the end sought, as is most often the case with *methodical*: an *orderly* development from a predominantly rural, agricultural economy to a modern industrial economy. *Orderly* thus implies the absence of violence or disruption. **Regular** means according to a fixed rule or standard, and suggests the lack of innovation, accident, or uncertainty; it emphasizes the steadiness or continuing nature of something done according to plan: a *regular* program by which underprivileged children can be given extra remedial instruction. Perhaps these words can best be distinguished by contrasting them with their opposites, as here considered. *Systematic* is opposed to random, *methodical* to haphazard, *orderly* to chaotic, and *regular* to eccentric. See FORMAL, METHOD.

Antonyms: chaotic, disarranged, disorderly, disorganized, messy, RANDOM, UNRULY.

T

taciturn

close
reticent
secretive
uncommunicative

These words are alike in meaning restrained in speaking to others or reserved in manner. **Taciturn** characterizes a disposition to speak little, and then grudgingly; it conveys the strong suggestion of a dry-ness of manner bordering on unsociability. ["Yes," was his *taciturn* response to the complex question posed; a cold, *taciturn* nature that seldom could be aroused to the point of uttering a complete sentence] **Reticent** implies a reluctance to speak freely about particular matters, especially about one's private affairs, rather than a quality of temperament, as is the case with *taciturn*. [He became *reticent* when asked to divulge his income; *reticent* about discussing his life before his marriage] **Close**, like *taciturn*, indicates a habit of temperament rather than a particular instance. One who is *close* says little of his own affairs, perhaps because he has something to hide. **Secretive** makes the explicit accusation of knowing concealment, and is broader than the other words here considered in not necessarily applying to what is unsaid; it may apply instead to the manner of what is said: something *secretive* about him, although he answers your questions readily enough. *Secretive* implies suspicion or mistrust on the part of the observer: Why is she so *secretive* about her friends?

Uncommunicative, like *taciturn*, implies an unwillingness to speak even when speech is called for, but more strongly points to unsociableness as the underlying motive for such reluctance: police occupied with interrogating an *uncommunicative* suspect; disturbed children who were sullen and *uncommunicative*. The word may, however, also indicate a simple lack of verbal facility: high-school dropouts who are *uncommunicative* because they are unsure of themselves. See ALOOF, MODEST, SILENT, SPEECHLESS, TERSE, TIMID, UNWILLING.

Antonyms: communicative, TALKATIVE.

These words denote something that is regarded as having magical powers. A **talisman** is a material object that is supposed to work wonders because it possesses and transmits certain qualities. It is believed to have a positive power in itself. A *talisman* may be carried on the person, or, like Aladdin's lamp, simply put to use as desired or needed. Aaron's rod in the Old Testament is a *talisman*, as are the magician's wand and the cap of invisibility in folklore. In a figurative sense, a *talisman* is something that produces or is capable of producing extraordinary effects: The young queen's dignity and beauty were *talismans* against unfavorable public opinion.

In common use, *talisman* and **amulet** are frequently confused. An *amulet* is a piece of stone, metal, bone, or wood inscribed with a magic incantation. It is almost always worn on the person and is supposed to protect the wearer from danger, disease, and witchcraft, or to ensure him of success, as in love or war. Unlike the *talisman*, the *amulet* is supposed to confer passive and preventive protection and not produce active magic.

Charm is the most general word and includes anything that has occult powers. *Talismans* and *amulets* may both be referred to as *charms*. In modern times the small metal miniatures worn on chains or bracelets, and called *charms*, are no doubt a carry-over from the old or primitive custom of wearing *amulets*. But in the strictest sense, a *charm* is the uttering of words or rhymes supposed to produce magical results. By extension, *charm* is the power to allure or delight: the *charm* of a beautiful child; the *charm* of Mozart's music.

In animistic religions, a **fetish** is an object worshiped by primitive peoples because they believe it to be the dwelling of a friendly spirit. Among such objects used as *fetishes* are stones, teeth, carved bits of wood, and plants. Figuratively, a *fetish* is something to which one is excessively devoted: housewives who make a *fetish* of cleanliness. Psychiatrically, it can refer to any object or part of the body on which a deviant's eroticism is fixated: confessed to a *fetish* for women's gloves; a foot *fetish*. See SUPERNATURAL.

These words refer to the tendency or ability to talk smoothly, readily, tediously, continually, or at length. **Talkative** is relatively informal and, most often, neutral in tone. It describes a person who is easily engaged in conversation or is given to expressing himself verbally with little prompting. Context can make the word negative: a *talkative* bore. But more commonly it is descriptively neutral or even approving. When the latter is true, the word may suggest an outgoing sociable person: good to be among people who were friendly and *talkative* after facing the

talisman

amulet
charm
fetish

talkative

gabby
garrulous
glib

talkative
(continued)

loquacious
voluble

hostile silence of the villagers all day. **Gabby,** the least formal of these words, refers to a compulsive talker and as such is firmly negative in tone: a *gabby* clutch of women exchanging the latest gossip. Sometimes it can be used without harsh intent, however, when it is meant humorously or in self-deprecation: missing the *gabby* bull sessions he'd enjoyed at college; apologizing for having been so *gabby.*

Voluble and **glib** pertain specifically to the ease with which someone is able to converse or speak. Of moderate formality, *voluble* once pointed to a pleasing facility in speech, gesture, manners, and writing; now it pertains more strictly to free-and-easy verbal smoothness. It may be approving in tone or indulgently critical: a beautifully modulated baritone voice that contributed to the impression he made of being a *voluble* speaker; a *voluble* neighbor, always eager to tell me the local gossip. *Glib,* by contrast, is more harshly and consistently negative in tone, referring to a smooth, slick, and possibly vulgar way of speaking, as one adopted to mask insincerity, superficiality, or dishonesty: the *glib* flattery doled out at literary cocktail parties; a student long on *glib* answers but short on thoughtfulness; *glib* door-to-door salesmen.

Unlike the previous pair, **loquacious** and **garrulous** are less concerned with verbal smoothness than with talk that is incessant or lengthy. Of the two, *loquacious* is less clear-cut in tone. When positive, it serves as an intensification of the favorable implications of *talkative,* with a suggestion of the fluency implicit in *voluble:* an earnest and *loquacious* advocate of open housing. When negative in tone, however, it can suggest an overbearing insistence on holding forth without regard for one's listeners: *loquacious* guides who will not let you look at a masterpiece in silence; a *loquacious* public speaker who always exceeded by half the time allotted for his speech. *Garrulous* is wholly negative in tone and as such is an intensification of the negative possibilities in *loquacious.* The word suggests a nonstop talker who is rambling, wordy, possibly foolish, and usually tedious. It suggests someone who is unable to be concise or who insists on monopolizing conversations: a *garrulous* old man who kept interrupting their chat with twenty-minute accounts of his latest fishing trip. See CHATTER, PATTER, SAY, VERBOSE.

Antonyms: SILENT, SPEECHLESS, TACITURN, TERSE.

tasty

delicious
flavorful
palatable
toothsome

These words all refer to the pleasant sensations accompanying an agreeable taste or flavor. **Tasty** and **delicious** are more common in speech and less formal than the other words here considered. *Tasty* merely refers to a fine flavor; *delicious* stresses more strongly the great pleasure that attends a fine-tasting food: a *tasty* dessert; a *delicious* imported pâté that was gobbled up by the guests almost as quickly as it could be served. *Delicious,* moreover, is not necessarily restricted to pleasure induced by taste: a *delicious* silence in the park when cars are banned from the roads within it. Taste is, however, the most common association with *delicious.*

Palatable implies more modest or equivocal pleasure than any of the other words of this group. *Palatable* is now most often used to mean acceptably good or agreeable, especially when the thing tasted has not been regarded as very *tasty:* Missionaries found the native food *palatable* if not always *delicious.* In its extended senses, *palatable* refers to some saving feature that makes an otherwise unattractive thing or condition acceptable: Being sent down to the minor leagues was made *palatable* to the ballplayer by a promise that he would get to play every day.

Flavorful literally means full of flavor, but is more commonly used to mean having a strong and pleasant flavor: a *flavorful* brew of tea. **Toothsome** suggests a succulent or voluptuous quality attending a pleasant taste. In figurative uses, in which the word is perhaps more commonly used today, the quality of being appetizing or sensually attractive predominates: a *toothsome* bevy of bathing beauties. It is often thus used, as in this example, with a humorous or sardonic tone. See SAVORY.

Antonyms: BLAND, *dull, flat, flavorless, foul, inedible, tasteless, unappetizing, unsavory.*

tax

assess
impose
levy

These words pertain to a government's exacting of money or other forms of support from its citizens or those dealing with them. **Tax** is the most general and least formal of these. It refers almost exclusively to the raising of money, although this may be done through a variety of means: the average citizen who ends up being *taxed* according to his income, general purchases, real estate holdings, buying of imported goods — and even his amusements and luxuries. One of the points of *tax* is its emphasis on the actual collection of money. This contrasts with **assess**, which points to a determining of the basis for *taxing* someone; the reference of the word now is usually to the *taxing* of real estate: *assessing* his property at a higher valuation because of improvements he had made on it. In related uses, the word may also refer to determining the amount of a fine: damages *assessed* by the court at $10,000.

Impose may suggest the determining of fines, punishment, or taxes in individual cases: *imposing* stiff fines on scofflaws; *imposing* a light sentence on the first offender. More closely related to *tax*, however, is its reference to a governmental decision, general in nature, to tap new sources of revenue or support: *imposing* additional taxes on business expansion; *imposing* military service on young men of eighteen. When its emphasis is on determination rather than collection, it is like *assess*, except for its indication of a general decision. A legislative body might *impose* terms concerning the amount and source of new revenue, after which each affected person might be *assessed* and then *taxed* accordingly. *Impose* in these senses has neutral force, but it can easily be given overtones of repressive or arbitrary willfulness: a staggering burden of taxation *imposed* on those who can least afford it; a policy of *imposing* unjust taxes on the colonies. **Levy** may sometimes be used to indicate determination, like *assess* or *impose*. But more appropriately, as its root suggests, it refers to the actual raising — that is, the collection or exaction of the amount *assessed* or the duty *imposed*: a stabilizing of prices when the new tax began to be *levied*; British officers who *levied* troops and quarters from the colonists by the most arbitrary means possible. See COMPEL, DEMAND, OBLIGATION.

teach

educate
indoctrinate
instruct
school
tutor

These words refer to the process by which knowledge is imparted to students. **Teach** suggests a guided process of assigned work, discipline, directed study, and the presentation of examples. It may or may not suggest an academic context: *teaching* his son to fix a flat tire; *teaching* her pupils the letters of the alphabet. Intransitively, however, it refers to this work thought of as a profession: deciding he would *teach* after he graduated from college; *teaching* in the freshman English program. **Educate** is more formal than *teach* and is less specific; it could not substitute for *teach* in any of the examples above, referring in a more general way to a long-range, wide-scale academic process: *educating* the coming generation by means of newly discovered methods. Sometimes the word suggests the accomplishing of greater results than *teach*: schools that *teach* but simply fail to *educate* their students.

School is used rarely as a substitute for *teach*, and suggests an especially thorough process: *schooling* the class in the essentials of arithmetic; parents who had *schooled* their children in the social graces. Oddly enough, as in the last example, the word need not suggest an academic context at all, though it does indicate a special effort or training, often to master complex rather than rudimentary matters: *schooling* himself in the fine distinctions his new job would require him to make; having *schooled* herself simply to ignore his angry outbursts. **Instruct** is closer in function to *teach* than *educate* or *school*. It is more formal, however, and is mostly restricted to the specific situation of guided training or to the imparting of information or commands: one teacher to give the lecture classes, another to *instruct* the discussion groups; a manual *instructing* the buyer on the installation of an air conditioner; *instructing* the maid to come an hour earlier on Monday.

Tutor refers to a special one-to-one relationship between teacher and student: English colleges where each student is *tutored* by a don. Often, the word refers to remedial or special work done outside the classroom on a one-to-one basis: offering to *tutor* him in French in exchange for German lessons; hiring a graduate student to *tutor* him in his worse subjects. **Indoctrinate**, alone of these words, suggests the inculcation of propaganda or prejudices rather than unbiased knowledge: parents who *indoctrinate* their children with race hatred; schools that unconsciously *indoctrinate* their students with middle-class values. See IMPLANT, LEARNING, STUDENT, STUDY.

tear

rend
rip
rive

These words are comparable in that they all refer to a pulling apart of a material or an object, or to the separating of two objects that are firmly bound together. **Tear** is the most general word in the group and has the widest application. It can denote the pulling apart of a seamless piece of material, as cloth or paper, suggesting in this case that the edges of the resultant pieces are rough or irregular: *tearing* an old sheet into cleaning rags. It can refer to the damaging action of such a pulling apart: cursing under his breath when a nail *tore* a hole in his pants. It can be used in application to an injury or laceration: *tearing* her skin when picking roses. Figuratively, *tear* can mean to disrupt or distress: a political party *torn* by dissension; a sight to *tear* one's heart.

Rip has special application to the division of a fabric by *tearing* along a line of least resistance or by cutting or breaking a row of stitches: *ripping* a dress apart along its seams. It can also designate any kind of *tearing* or cutting that is accomplished with harshness or violence: *ripping* open an old wound.

Rend and **rive** have even stronger overtones of violence than *rip* in their referral to a *tearing*, splitting, or pulling apart by force: buildings *rent* by an earthquake; a tree *riven* by a flash of lightning. Figuratively, *rend* and *rive* are like *tear* in their application to dissension or painful affliction: a nation *rent* by civil war; a heart *riven* by despair. Today, however, *rend* and *rive* tend to sound lofty and poetical. See CUT, SEVER.

Antonyms: CONNECT, REPAIR, TREAT.

teem

abound

These words refer to great amounts or to dense clusters. **Teem** and **swarm** both refer to the rapid, independent movement of particles in a small space or cluster. Of the two, *swarm* is more concrete and more limited in application outside this literal situation: bees *swarming* around a hive; rush-hour traffic *swarming* over the bridges into the city; enemy soldiers that came *swarming* toward us down the hill: a section of the city that *swarmed* with hippies. *Teem* is even more emphatic about the frenetic nature of the activity referred to. While the word can have literal application, it is more often applied figuratively. Unlike *swarm*, which can often carry a negative tone, *teem* frequently suggests approval for anything that seems instinct with vibrant life: Shakespeare's *teeming* brain; a novel *teeming* with memorable characters and incidents; a new generation *teeming* with exuberance and iconoclasm. When the word applies in a more nearly neutral way, it still can have a tone of panoramic lyricism: the *teeming* slums of the city.

Overflow can specifically refer to a fluid that overruns its container: flood waters that threatened to *overflow* hastily erected sandbag barriers. In figurative use, the word suggests approval for qualities that someone or something possesses and gives off in copious amounts: a personality *overflowing* with kindness and generosity. Less often, the word can refer to any superfluity, as of emotion: pinched, bitter faces *overflowing* with sullen distrust. **Abound** is the most general of these words and the most vague in its implications; it suggests a generous portion, usually of favorable qualities: a country that *abounds* in architectural masterpieces; those of us who still *abound* in good will. Used negatively, the word can contribute an ironic forcefulness: an administration that has *abounded* in example after example of broken promises. See FLOW, GENEROUS, PREVALENT.

Antonyms: vacate, WANE, WEAKEN.

tell

convey
impart
narrate
recite
recount
relate
report

These words are comparable in the general sense of communicating with others in speech or writing. **Tell**, the least formal of the group, is applicable in many contexts where others would be more exact or pertinent, but in the sense of making something known or of disclosing or revealing, it is the word of choice: He would not *tell* who was to blame.

Narrate and **relate** both imply conscious and deliberate attention to the communication of a story, suggesting an orderly arrangement of the details with a view to continuity, completeness, and artistic effect. [Defoe skillfully *narrated* the adventures of Robinson Crusoe on his desert island; The Odyssey *relates* the misfortunes of Ulysses after the Trojan War.]

Recount carries the idea of a more careful enumeration of the particulars of whatever is being communicated: The witness *recounted* the events leading up to the crime. **Recite** may be used in the same sense but is more pertinent when it refers to something clearly remembered or repeated from memory: to *recite* the Gettysburg Address. **Report** implies giving an account of something with a more formal attention to details and to accuracy in the presentation of the relevant facts and information: The committee *reported* its findings after a thorough investigation.

Convey has the primary meaning of carry or transport from one place to another; by extension, one can *convey* information, *convey* an impression or idea. **Impart** is to make known or disclose in the sense of sharing with another person: to *impart* one's suspicions about a crime. See CHATTER, CONVERSATION, SAY, SPEECH, UTTER.

These words refer to a person's mental make-up or emotional state. **Temperament** refers most commonly to a cast of mind that is revealed by the fixed or habitual ways a person responds to life; the word may

temperament
(continued)

character
disposition
nature
personality

suggest either an innate or a learned pattern, but it does point to something deeply ingrained or unconscious rather than something reflecting an arbitrary or conscious choice. Otherwise, the word can indicate any sort of mental or emotional state: a basically frivolous *temperament*; a *temperament* marked by restless curiosity. The word can also typify a group of people: the no-nonsense *temperament* of the British. When unqualified, however, it indicates a tendency toward intense and moody rebelliousness; this is a more informal use of the word: a child full of *temperament*.

Disposition can refer to an enduring frame of mind, whether innate or learned, but it points more strictly to emotional qualities that are only one part of the more formal *temperament*: a grouchy *disposition*; the sunniness of her usual *disposition*. It contrasts most sharply with *temperament*, however, in that it can be used for transitory emotional states: coming to work in a foul *disposition*. **Nature**, in contrast to all these words, is the most emphatic about the innate and irrevocable aspect of the traits it points to. It can also point to the widest range of traits, including emotional, mental, and physical qualities: by *nature* a timid little man of mediocre intelligence; those *natures* that are unhesitatingly magnanimous and compassionate. It is also the only one of these words that is commonly used when generalizing about traits inherent in mankind as a whole: anthropologists who have successfully challenged our culture-bound notions about the *nature* of man.

Character and **personality** both point to bundles of mental and emotional traits, innate and learned, that distinguish one person from another. *Character* points to the fully developed life-style of an adult or group and often relates to moral fiber: drinking companions of questionable *character*; the stern but resourceful *character* of the Pilgrims. *Personality* pertains more to the whole indefinable emotional coloration that a specific person gives off: the young girl's winsome *personality*; a *personality* crippled by arrogance and impatience. Used without qualification, *character* suggests moral forcefulness, *personality* emotional appeal: He has *character* but no *personality*. In this use, the words can apply to anything thought to exhibit these qualities, especially when they are distinctive in their force or appeal: a face with *character*; paintings completely lacking in *character*; a striking city, full of *personality*. The latter word, used in this way, has become so popular that it is in danger of sounding trite through overuse. See CHARACTERISTIC, ECCENTRICITY, GENIUS.

temperance

abstinence
continence
self-denial
sobriety

These words refer to an avoidance of pleasurable excesses. **Temperance**, correctly used, refers to a wise moderation of indulgence in such pleasures, but as commonly used it suggests a complete rejection, especially of alcohol: a *temperance* that extended to declining drinks until four in the afternoon; the question of *temperance* that inflamed women against the evils of that devil, whisky. **Self-denial** and **sobriety** are, of themselves, vague as to the extent to which avoidance may or should go. *Self-denial* is, of course, more general than *sobriety* but is firmer in tone than *temperance* in its most general sense, suggesting specifically an attitude of refusing to give in to the demands of one's own body: a Spartan *self-denial* that made young men impervious to extremes of heat and cold, to hunger, and to the threat of death; a Victorian code of morals that stressed prudish *self-denial*. *Sobriety*, by contrast, usually applies in this context strictly to nonintoxication by alcohol. A person, of course, may be intoxicated one day and in a state of *sobriety* the next.

More broadly, *sobriety* may suggest a soberness or solemnity of mien: the grim *sobriety* in the faces of the jury.

Abstinence and **continence** are much clearer than *self-denial* and *sobriety* as to the extent of denial involved; they emphasize a total avoidance of sensation. In this they are at odds with the more general implications of *temperance*. *Abstinence*, in context, may refer to an avoidance of alcohol or sexual satisfaction or any specific named: a complete *abstinence* from salty or spicy foods. *Continence* usually is taken to mean an avoidance of sexual intercourse in particular, but at its most general it can suggest a range of possibility similar to *self-denial*: maintaining a certain *continence* toward extracurricular activities the better to concentrate on his studies. See ABSTAIN, AVOID, FORSWEAR, REJECT.

Antonyms: avidity, excess, hedonism, indulgence, intemperance.

These words refer to things that last or that remain on the scene for only a brief time. **Temporary** is the most general term, implying a measurable but limited duration. Unlike most of the other adjectives in this set, it indicates what is meant or known to last for a limited time only: a *temporary* job; a medicine that gives *temporary* relief. Further, the word often suggests makeshift arrangements made for the time being under the pressure of circumstances: a *temporary* shelter from the storm. It is also used to soften the impact of a harsh reality: a *temporary* setback, not a final defeat.

Momentary, used literally, means coming and going away suddenly, in a moment: a *momentary* misgiving. It is also used to indicate relative brevity of duration: a *momentary* delay. **Passing** emphasizes the fact that a thing does not continue to occupy the interest for very long, but runs its course fairly quickly: a *passing* fad. **Fleeting** is an intensification of *passing* in a literal sense, referring to something that passes almost instantaneously: a dilettante too preoccupied with the *fleeting* moment to settle down to serious work; I caught just a *fleeting* glimpse of my new neighbor.

Transient stresses the *temporary* nature of a stay or the brevity of a thing's duration. Though in common use as a noun, the word has formal or literary tone when used as an adjective: a *transient* joy. **Transitory**, like *temporary*, points to impermanence. It designates something destined to pass away, either fairly soon, or, at least, eventually: *transitory* pleasures as opposed to sources of enduring satisfaction; a *transitory* stage of development.

In a literal sense, **ephemeral** refers to that which lasts only a single day. It is stronger than *transitory* in indicating not only certain but speedy extinction. For this reason, that which is *ephemeral* is looked upon as slight and perishable. [Man's life is *transitory*; A butterfly's existence is *ephemeral*.] *Ephemeral* can also sometimes carry a suggestion of contempt: the *ephemeral* popularity of a pretty starlet who never learned to act. In extension, *ephemeral* denotes that which changes aspect rapidly or continuously: an *ephemeral* inspiration. *Ephemeral* is a rather literary word. **Evanescent** is lyrical and highly evocative. It refers to that which vanishes almost as soon as it appears, implying that a thing is tenuous, delicate, or unsubstantial by its very nature: the *evanescent* radiance of the sunset; an *evanescent* glimpse of the truth. See INCONSTANT.

Antonyms: EVERLASTING, IMMORTAL, IMMUTABLE, INVARIABLE, PERMANENT, PERSISTENT.

temporary

ephemeral
evanescent
fleeting
momentary
passing
transient
transitory

tempt

allure
attract
beguile
entice
lure
seduce

These words refer to things that awaken one's desires or prompt one to act upon them, possibly against one's will. **Tempt** stresses the awakening of desire despite an initial reluctance; this may result from something that is appealing by its nature or from a deliberate attempt at arousal: a steaming apple pie that *tempted* him to disregard his diet; a woman who used all her wiles to *tempt* him into following her. **Seduce** stresses someone prompted to action or permission against his will: *seduced* by the excitement of the city I had hated so at first. The sexual connotation possible for *tempt* is insistently present in *seduce*: boasting about how many women he had *seduced*. If this is not borne in mind, the word can be misleading in other contexts: not the first woman who had been *seduced* by his good looks and soft-spoken manner.

The sexual connotations of both **attract** and **allure** are less insistent and obtrusive than in the foregoing words. *Attract* may give an objective tone in pointing to the winning of notice for any reason: an eccentric costume that *attracted* disapproving comment; a bonfire that might *attract* rescuers. In the context of desire, the word suggests being drawn to something because of its intrinsic appeal; no reluctance need be implied on the part of the beholder, no design on the part of the beheld: a vivacity and beauty that *attracted* every eye in the room; *attracted* to the woman who stood alone on the observation deck. *Allure* suggests greater intensity of appeal than *attract*: *allured* by the breathtaking view that opened out as they climbed. The word may also suggest a deliberate effort to *tempt* someone against his will, even to the point of using deception: barkers who *allure* passersby into the sideshows by promising spectacles never encountered, once inside.

Lure is closely related to *allure*, but concentrates mostly on deliberate or deceptive attempts to influence someone or lead him astray, often for fraudulent or destructive purposes: cheese with which to *lure* mice into the trap; *luring* him into an alley where her confederate could rob him. The word can, of course, be used more innocently in a hyperbolic way: wondering how she could *lure* him into accepting an invitation for dinner. **Entice** also suggests a deliberate effort to *tempt* someone into action, but the word is vaguer about intent and motivation: hoping to *entice* him into joining their discussion group; psychopaths who *entice* children to come for rides in their cars. The word can also be used more simply of appeal: *enticed* by her lively interest in foreign movies. **Beguile** once referred more exclusively to deceptive attempts to lead astray for unworthy purposes: *beguiled* by his promise of a quick profit. The word has lost much of this negative force in uses that compare with *attract*: hoping to *beguile* him with her knowledge of foreign movies; an exuberance and zaniness in him that she found *beguiling*. See ATTRACTION, EAGER, EROTIC, PLEASING.

Antonyms: chill, dampen, DISCOURAGE, *dissuade, repel.*

terse

compendious
laconic
pithy
sententious
succinct

These adjectives stress brevity in speech or writing, the avoidance of any wasted words. **Terse** goes back to a Latin verb meaning to rub off or rub down. By etymology, it suggests polished style as well as pointed phrasing, implying elegance as well as economy of expression: a *terse*, vigorous style. In present use, however, *terse* emphasizes extreme compactness, concentrated force, and a strict sticking to the point: a *terse* note of dismissal with no explanation. **Laconic** literally means like a Spartan, with reference to the habitual *terseness* of Spartan speech. A *laconic* speaker is so sparing with words as to seem stingy or exceptionally self-controlled. [He was reserved and *laconic*, a close-mouthed man;

She said it with *laconic* brevity: "We've lost."] Both a *terse* and a *laconic* remark may be so brief as to seem curt. But where a *terse* remark is complete and its brevity may be due to the pressure of circumstances, a *laconic* remark may be puzzling and may suggest a deliberate taciturnity: a *terse* battlefield command; "Trust me" was his *laconic* reply. *Terse* and *laconic* imply a certain austerity of utterance, but **succinct** suggests a more reasonable rationing of words. *Succinct* comes from Latin roots meaning to gird underneath. It implies compression, the avoidance of elaboration, the exclusion of extraneous detail. Hence a *succinct* statement is brief, clear, and concise, being confined to main points or essential meaning: a *succinct* summary of a lengthy treatise.

The remaining adjectives emphasize content. **Pithy** literally means full of pith, and pith is the essential part of anything — the tissue at the center of a stem, the marrow of a bone. Hence a *pithy* remark is one full of meaning and substance; it is both brief and forceful, containing the gist of a matter in concentrated form: a *pithy* aphorism; the *pithy* couplets of Alexander Pope. **Compendious**, like *pithy*, stresses substance, but substance drawn from many sources and summarized. A *compendious* work is both brief and comprehensive, encompassing and condensing a great mass of material: a *compendious* account of the Civil War; It required a true scholar to digest so much material and organize it into so *compendious* an introduction. **Sententious** comes from a Latin word meaning opinion. It indicates the condensing of general truths or moral principles into *pithy* maxims or aphorisms: the *sententious* wisdom of the Book of Proverbs. By extension, *sententious* may connote a moralizing attitude or a pompous, all-knowing tone: a speaker too *sententious* not to be tiresome. See COMPACT, SHORTEN.

Antonyms: lengthy, TALKATIVE, *tedious,* VERBOSE.

These words may all denote statements made to a court of law. **Testimony** is any declaration made by a witness who is considered to know the facts of a case. Giving *testimony* involves the taking of an oath and the making of statements in open court in answer to questions put by a lawyer or qualified public official. *Testimony* in its wider meaning is affirmation or proof of something: The ruined buildings of the city bear grim *testimony* to the heavy bombardment by the enemy.

Both **affidavit** and **deposition** are types of legal *testimony* put into writing. Although occasionally used interchangeably, *affidavit* and *deposition* differ in several ways. An *affidavit* is a sworn document made voluntarily without cross-examination. Also, an *affidavit* may be accepted as *testimony* by a court when the testifier is unable to appear in person. A *deposition*, on the other hand, is made orally under oath in response to formal questioning, and is then taken down in writing. Unlike an *affidavit*, a *deposition* is subject to cross-examination.

Evidence is the most general term, and it includes the *testimony* of witnesses, *affidavits, depositions,* and all the facts and physical objects connected with a legal proceeding. In everyday use, *evidence* is anything that tends to prove a thing true. [Scholars have been able to unearth some *evidence* as to the true authorship of the book; Her red eyes and sad expression w re *evidence* (and also *testimony* to the fact) that she had been crying.] See REASONING.

testimony

affidavit
deposition
evidence

These words have either a direct reference to the theater or are used to describe persons and things that exhibit qualities associated with the theater. **Theatrical** is used to describe anything connected with the

theatrical

theatrical

(continued)

camp
campy
dramatic
flamboyant
histrionic

world of the theater: a *theatrical* festival; a *theatrical* booking agency. It also connotes artificiality and show: His long hair and old-fashioned attire gave him a vaguely *theatrical* air that was sometimes interesting but more often just eccentric. Since it pertains especially to actors or their performing techniques, **histrionic** has the most limited application: Her *histrionic* abilities are more at home before the camera than on the stage. The word, by extension, is used to suggest the showy or affectedly emotional qualities one thinks of in connection with actors and acting: His *histrionic* display at the funeral was in thoroughly bad taste. **Flamboyant** originally meant extravagantly ornate or elaborately styled: a house with *flamboyant* architectural detail; an essay complicated by *flamboyant* prose. In a generalization of meaning, the word came to imply brilliance or boldness and finally to suggest the same kind of affectation and showiness that *histrionic* does: the *flamboyant* foliage of autumn; a *flamboyant* style of dress; a *flamboyant* display of temper.

In its implication of an affected or showy manner, **dramatic** is like *histrionic* and *flamboyant*: She set all tongues wagging with her *dramatic* entrance at the party. But, more than the other words, it has direct pertinence to the drama and to things that are suitable to or characterize acting: a *dramatic* performance of the highest caliber; The short story was *dramatic* without being in the least sentimental.

Camp and **campy** were once restricted in use as homosexual argot to describe the supposedly tell-tale mannerisms of this in-group; the word suggested behavior that was *theatrical*, artificial, exaggerated, effeminate, or ostentatious. Recently these terms have become fad words that need not refer to homosexuality at all, but can be applied to any manifestation of popular culture that is so incredibly phoney, banal, or vulgar as to merit amazement or admiration: *campy* Joan Crawford movies from the 1930's; a *camp* feather boa that she evidently thought was the last word in chic. These words can now also describe deliberate attempts to reproduce such meretricious qualities in serious art or literature. In fact, the word is in danger of being used so vaguely and broadly as to vitiate its usefulness. See EMOTION, PASSIONATE.

Antonyms: colorless, drab, dull, prosaic, SEDATE.

thief

bandit
brigand
burglar
gangster
pirate
robber

These words refer to a person who steals property that rightfully belongs to others. **Thief** is the most general, since it can refer to any such action regardless of the means used: the *thief* who had broken into the house during their absence; the *thief* who had seized her purse and darted into the milling crowd. At its most specific, *thief* might most often suggest someone who takes property by stealth, rather than by a direct confrontation with the owner. **Robber** may be used in as general a way as *thief*, but because it relates closely to the legally defined crime of robbery, it may suggest a direct confrontation in which the victim is forced to surrender his valuables by the use of threat or violence: fearing that he might be accosted by a *robber* if he walked through the dark, deserted park. A **burglar** is one who breaks into a house to loot it, usually with the intention of avoiding a confrontation with those living there.

Brigand and **pirate** refer to members of organized bands that are devoted to robbery and live outside the law. *Brigand* would be typically applied to thieves who a rural area and terrorize the surrounding countryside; *pirates* are historically represented as having fast ocean-going ships to run down and loot other ships on the high seas. **Gangster** is the equivalent term for the member of a modern-day organized group of people based mostly in cities and set up to make money by all kinds of illegal activities.

Bandit is the most vague of these words; it is now less used as a generic term, but is sometimes used interchangeably with *brigand*, suggesting an organized group in a rural setting, as in 19th-century Italy. It may also be used of a lone marauder or *robber*, with the same sort of rural setting implied. In this case theft by the use of threat or violence is suggested. The *bandit* in a typical Western movie, for example, rides a horse and goes armed, either alone or in a group. See RENEGADE.

These words mean the opposite of fat or plump, describing persons whose weight is low in proportion to their height. **Thin** is the most general word. It suggests a lack of girth, a narrowness of frame, and may apply either to natural low weight or underweight: a tall, *thin*, distinguished-looking man; *thin* and weak after a bout of illness. *Thin* in itself is simply descriptive of appearance; but is often qualified by adverbs that express the degree of thinness or the attitude concerning it: too *thin*; terribly *thin*; pitifully *thin*. Like *thin*, **lean** and **spare** may have either positive or negative connotations. Both of these words stress the absence of fatty tissue: a *lean* and hungry look. At the same time, both imply an underlying muscular strength — a sinewy and sometimes vigorous self-discipline: a *lean*, lithe runner with great stamina; a soldier's *spare* build and fine bearing. But both *lean* and *spare* may also be expressive of hardship and deprivation, suggesting the strength to endure hard times with a minimum of sustenance: an old farmer's *lean*, hard frame; the *spare* form and weatherbeaten face of a pioneer woman. In extended senses *lean* may mean fraught with want or hardship, not prosperous or productive: *lean* years. *Spare* can mean not plentiful, meager: a *spare* meal of beans and a piece of bread.

Svelte implies trimness and elegance of figure, and is often used in a complimentary way rather than as pure description: She slimmed down tremendously and looked positively *svelte*. This use is suggested by the word's derivation from Latin roots meaning to pluck out. **Willowy** suggests a *lean* build marked by suppleness and grace: a modern dancer bending her *willowy* frame. *Svelte* is feminine in connotation and is always applied to women; *willowy* is not invariably applied to either sex, but since gracefulness is more common among women it is more often associated with them.

Slim and **slender** refer to relatively slight bodily weight, especially as it appears esthetically to an observer. *Slim*, which may apply to either sex, implies a trim figure or physique. It is most often used in the context of someone's losing or maintaining weight: She kept *slim* by dieting and by exercising diligently. *Slender*, as applied to girls or women, often connotes gracefulness, litheness, frailty, or fragility: a *slender* slip of a girl. *Slender* may also be used of men, in which case the word retains a suggestion of slightness of physique that is not, however, considered unattractive or effeminate; often the term is complimentary, but whereas *slim* suggests firmness and strength, *slender* indicates lightness: a tall, *slender* man with a sensitive face. *Slender* is often applied to parts of the body: a *slender* wrist; *slender* arms.

A person who is considered much too *thin* may be called **skinny**. *Skinny* is a rather informal term, a child's word, always blunt and sometimes humorous or touching: a *skinny* little man. *Skinny* stresses the idea that a person is underdeveloped — nothing but skin and bone: a *skinny*, knobby-kneed little girl; tall, *skinny* models. *Skinny* may also

thin

lean
scrawny
skinny
slender
slim
spare
svelte
willowy
wiry

imply a lack of strength or vigor: a *skinny* weakling who took a body-building course. **Scrawny** means small and stringy, *lean*, bony, and undernourished: *scrawny* urchins scrambling for coins. *Scrawny* is often applied to animals as well as humans: a *scrawny* chicken, too tough to eat. **Wiry** is usually used of persons, meaning *thin* but tough and sinewy. It describes one who is quite *slim* but deceptively strong: a *wiry* little man, as plucky and pugnacious as a bantam rooster. See BONY, LANKY, SUPPLE.

Antonyms: FAT.

think

cogitate
deliberate
meditate
muse
ponder
reason
reflect
ruminate
speculate

These words all mean to set the mind to work in order to seek a better understanding of something, solve a problem, or get at the truth. **Think** is the general word, and can refer to any use of the intellect to arrive at ideas or conclusions. One can *think* profoundly or superficially, seriously or frivolously: to *think* about whether man's fate is determined by his own free will or by the force of circumstances; She *thought* about dyeing her hair red. **Cogitate** is a rather pompously formal word that means to *think* seriously or continuously; it is often used jestingly: The infant seemed to be *cogitating* on the quality and depth of his navel. However, it is occasionally used soberly about a baffling problem: tax specialists *cogitating* about how to simplify instructions to the taxpayer.

Meditate, muse, **reflect**, and **ruminate** mean to *think* in a contemplative or leisurely manner. *Meditate* is the most general of these words, and implies a serious and extended period of concentration: The author *meditated* on the theme of his book before sketching out the plot and characterization. *Muse* suggests a dreamlike, aimless, or conjectural succession of thoughts. [She *mused* about whether her husband would notice her new dress; He *mused* over what he would do if he were suddenly to inherit a million dollars.] *Reflect* means to look back in a thoughtful way over what has happened: an old man *reflecting* on the changes that had taken place in the world since his youth. But *reflect* may also be used of any intellectual review: to *reflect* on the causes of urban rioting. In its basic literal sense *ruminate* is applied to certain animals and means to chew the cud (food previously swallowed and regurgitated). Analogously, *ruminate* as here considered means to turn a thought over and over in the mind: a losing candidate *ruminating* on the cause of his defeat.

Deliberate and **ponder** emphasize the slow, careful process of weighing possibilities or alternatives; *deliberate* stresses the slowness, and *ponder* the weighing of possibilities. Whereas *deliberate* suggests a methodical, rational process of decision-making, *ponder* points to the solemnness and difficulty of the problem, to which there may be no solution. [The jury *deliberated* four hours before recessing for lunch; The president *pondered* the problem of how to maintain national security without compromising individual freedom.]

To **reason** is to make logical or empirical generalizations based on evidence: The district attorney *reasoned* that the suspect's attempt to flee was ground for presuming guilt. **Speculate**, on the other hand, means to theorize or conjecture on the basis of little or no evidence: At present scientists can only *speculate* on the nature and extent of life outside our solar system. See CONSIDER, EXAMINE, IDEA, IMAGINATION, MIND, OPINION, STUDY, SUPPOSE.

throng

These words refer to large gatherings, especially of people. **Throng** and **host** are the most formal of these. *Throng* emphasizes a group in which

throng
(continued)

crowd
horde
host
mob
multitude

the members are pressed together in a crush: a *throng* of late Christmas shoppers fighting each other to the display tables of the department store. The word can also suggest a mass of tightly grouped people moving with difficulty in the same direction: a *throng* of worshipers who followed the religious procession down the narrow cobbled streets of the village. *Host*, by contrast, suggests an archaic or Biblical tone; here the group may well be spread out in space. The word may also be descriptive of an army or armed group of people: the heavenly *host* of angels who appeared to the shepherds near Bethlehem; a *host* of people spread out on the hillside in all directions; a ragged *host* of militia, falling before the gunfire of well-hidden American rebels. The word can also suggest any vast group of things: a *host* of reasons for disbanding the cavalry.

Crowd and **mob** both suggest sizable collections of people, but both are more informal than the previous pair. Like *throng*, *crowd* can suggest congestion but is even more emphatic about disorder within the group: a confused *crowd* that gathered on the sidewalk to watch the burning house. The word, however, is used informally to describe large audiences of any kind, even the most orderly: the large *crowd* that had turned out to hear the pianist's farewell performance. *Mob*, by contrast, stresses disorder in a *crowd* possessed by unruly or angry emotions and implies the erupting of potential violence or a state of riot: a *crowd* that turned into a rampaging *mob* when it learned that the boy injured by the hit-and-run driver had died before reaching the hospital. As a mere hyperbole, the word can be used informally for any great number: *mobs* of friends who came to our open-house party.

Multitude, while not sharing the quaint or old-fashioned sound of *host*, gives an elevated tone in referring to an extremely large number; when the word applies to people, it specifically implies their being spread out through space: the *multitude* gathered in Times Square to see in the new year. Like *host*, the word can also apply to any great amount: presenting a *multitude* of reasons for reopening the case. **Horde** refers specifically to a *crowd* or *mob* that is threatening, unkempt, or unpleasant in some way: a *horde* of hungry peasants who gathered before the palace. In this context, the word suggests disorganization, fierce emotion, and a motley or ragged array of people. *Horde* can also refer to a pack or swarm, as of animals or insects: a *horde* of mosquitoes that circled the night light; a *horde* of rats. Most specifically, and with a less negative tone, the word can refer to a nomadic tribe or army: the *horde* of Berbers who camped for the night just outside the desert town. See GROUP, MEETING, PEOPLE.

throw

bowl
cast
fling
heave
hurl
pitch

These words refer to sending a hand-released projectile through the air by a swing of the arm. **Throw** carries the fewest implications about the manner in which the act is done or its emotional context: taking careful aim before he *threw*; *throwing* handfuls of grass in all directions. **Hurl** suggests *throwing* something with considerable force or ferocity, **heave** the lifting and *throwing* of something quite heavy: *hurling* stones and curses at their helpless victim; seizing a boulder and *heaving* it at the advancing column of men. **Cast**, **pitch**, and **toss**, by contrast, suggest less force and greater swiftness in *throwing* lighter objects: *pitching* pennies into an upturned hat; *casting* his line downstream and reeling it in against the current; lazily *tossing* darts at a picture of his political opponent. *Cast* has fallen into disuse except in the context of fishing and in certain stock phrases such as *casting* a net, *casting* dice, *casting* bread

throw

(continued)

put
sling
toss

upon the waters. *Pitch* is, of course, specifically used in baseball to describe the *throwing* of the ball by the pitcher to the batter. Even in other contexts, *pitch* suggests care and accuracy of aim. **Bowl** as a term used in cricket means to *pitch* or *hurl* the ball to the batsman, usually on one bounce, with the arm held fully extended, not bent at the elbow as in baseball *pitching*; otherwise the *pitch* would be ruled a *throw*, which is illegal. In the U.S. *bowling* most commonly refers to the game of tenpins or similar games where the ball is *bowled* by rolling it over a level surface. *Bowl* as a general term is current in both varieties of English with this sense of rolling. To **put**, in the sense here considered, means to thrust or push forward with the arm, with the full force of one's body behind the motion. The term is now used mainly of the competitive sport of *putting* the shot (a metal ball), an event in many track and field meets: To *put* a 16-pound shot over 60 feet requires great strength, coordination, and concentration.

Toss is used almost exclusively of light objects and may suggest a haphazard movement or one in which the notion of aiming for a target is absent: *tossing* confetti pell-mell; *tossing* aside a lock of hair that had fallen over her eyes. **Fling**, unlike *toss*, does not necessarily suggest a light object, but it is otherwise similar in implying aimlessness or a forceful wildness of movement: *flinging* down his briefcase on the table and stomping upstairs. **Sling** once referred to the sudden force reminiscent of something thrown by a sling; this is less and less present as an implication of the word. It now mainly suggests inaccurate or violent movements, possibly angry ones, as in the stock phrase, *slinging* mud at your opponents. See DISCARD, PROPEL, ROTATE.

thwart

balk
foil
frustrate
inhibit

These words refer to the applying of force in a hostile way so as to repel or subdue any opposing resistance. **Thwart** suggests the outwitting of an enemy or the undoing of his plans: sending troops to *thwart* the Irish rebellion. The word often implies the use of cleverness instead of violence to attain the enemy's defeat and suggests action taken before the enemy himself has had time to move: the scheming villain whose designs on the helpless maiden were always *thwarted* before the final curtain. The word has recently appeared frequently in a psychological context, suggesting barriers that prevent the full realization of one's natural endowments: a generous and receptive intelligence that was *thwarted* from attaining its full scope by bad training, poor schools, and lack of opportunity.

Foil relates to that aspect of *thwart* that emphasizes the undoing of an enemy's plan before any damaging action has been accomplished: *foiling* the assassination plot by placing on the throne a straw dummy dressed like the king. In some modern contexts, the word may sound melodramatic and old-fashioned. **Balk** relates to that aspect of *thwart* that emphasizes the imposing of barriers, but *balk* does not necessarily suggest the interruption of an otherwise natural or inevitable process: every effort at creative teaching *balked* by the reams of paperwork that had to be filled out each week.

Frustrate in its most general context suggests the confounding of an enemy by tactics short of an open confrontation in direct battle: *frustrating* Hannibal's drive toward the sea by hemming in his troops and engaging them in inconclusive night skirmishes. Like *thwart*, it can suggest the undoing of an enemy's plans before he can execute them, although in this case the result is less conclusive than with *thwart* since here it can imply merely forcing the enemy into inaction or into holding his plans in abeyance: *frustrating* every effort the prisoner made at getting word to his confederates. When the situation of enemies is not involved, the word may suggest any sort of insurmountable obstacle that reduces someone to galling inaction: talented playwrights *frustrated* by the high cost of production and the coarse commercialism of Broadway.

Inhibit suggests, like one aspect of *frustrate*, the forcing of something into inaction rather than a complete routing of it: *inhibiting* the wage-price spiral by an increase in taxes. Both *frustrate* and *inhibit*, however, have gained currency in a psychological context for suggesting barriers that impede normal development or prevent the realization of natural desires. *Frustrate* here suggests an insoluble conflict between two forces working upon or within a person: *frustrated* by desires he believed it would be reprehensible to satisfy. *Inhibit* here specifically suggests the weakening or damaging of normal impulses: rules so rigid as to *inhibit* any calm development of self-assurance; learning to *inhibit* those anti-social impulses that would result in injury or harm to others. See CON-FUSE, SUBDUE.

Antonyms: PERMIT.

These words refer to the winding and knotting of rope or a similar material around someone to prevent free movement or to the connecting of two things by such devices. **Tie** is the most general of these words in its ability to refer to either situation with the fewest specific restrictions in meaning: He *tied* up his victims with torn lengths of bedsheets; *tying* one end of the guy wire to a low-hanging branch. **Bind** can also apply in both of these situations, but it specifically emphasizes a tight *tying*: *binding* and gagging his captive so that he could neither move nor speak; a string *binding* the rhubarb stalks into a bunch. **Truss** is considerably more informal than any of the other words here and is also alone in referring exclusively to the *tying* up of someone to prevent free movement: prisoners of war who had been *trussed* up back to back and guarded until the convoy arrived. The word goes beyond *tie* in this sense to suggest an extremely tight, careful, or uncomfortable doubling up and *binding* of the arms and legs against the body, like a fowl prepared for roasting.

The rest of these words pertain mostly to the connecting of two things by some such means as a rope or wire. Of these, **fasten** and **secure** are the most general, even when limited to connections accomplished by *tying*. *Fasten* suggests a firm *tying* in which the elements connected are made incapable of independent motion: He *fastened* an arrowhead to the shaft with a tough thong. *Secure* emphasizes the inseparability of the elements connected, but does not suggest loss of independent movement: The ends of the hammock were *secured* to two well-spaced trees.

Lash, **hitch**, and **moor** are all considerably more specific in implication. *Lash* here is similar to *bind* in its area of meaning, stressing a firm *tying* together, especially in a nautical setting: *lashing* the sail to the yardarm; He *lashed* himself to the mast so that he could not respond to the singing of the sirens. *Hitch* particularly stresses the joining together of two mobile things or vehicles: They *hitched* the stalled car to the wrecker with a long chain. *Moor*, like *lash*, has a nautical context, but it is even more specific in stressing the *tying* of a boat or ship to something immovable: *mooring* the canoe to a heavy boulder on the bank. See CONNECT, SHACKLE.

Antonyms: free, loosen, SEPARATE, SEVER, unbind.

tie

bind
fasten
hitch
lash
moor
secure
truss

timid

bashful
coy
diffident
faint-hearted
shy
submissive
timorous

These words pertain to a lack of ease in the society of others, or to fearfulness in facing new experiences. **Timid** is the most general word in the group. It points to a reluctance to assert oneself or to undertake anything new or unknown without exercising caution. [The little boy was *timid* about going to school for the first time; A *timid* driver hesitates to pass trucks and buses on the highway.] **Timorous** is a much stronger word than *timid*, although they are often used interchangeably. *Timorous* emphasizes a greater apprehension and anxiety surrounding any experience that demands daring, independence, and confidence in oneself: a *timorous* young woman unable to leave her parents and live her own life. *Timorous* may also describe one who is easily startled and seems to live in a constant state of fearfulness: a *timorous* teacher who could not control children.

Shy, bashful, and diffident share the meaning of showing unobtrusiveness and embarrassment in the company of other people. *Shy* implies self-consciousness and a fear of pushing oneself forward. The word may suggest a lack of social poise arising from inexperience: so *shy* that talking to new acquaintances made her voice tremble. *Shy* may also point to a naturally quiet and retiring nature, often not without charm: His low voice and *shy* smile soon made him a favorite among his colleagues. By extension, *shy* is used of people who because of the nature of their culture tend to live to themselves, or to animals that evade observation by man. [The Pygmies of equatorial Africa are a *shy*, primitive group; The shrew, a common field rodent, is so *shy* that even farmers rarely see one.] *Bashful* is usually applied only to children who are *shy*. The word may have somewhat humorous overtones as it suggests the awkwardness of a youngster who has been struck speechless before strangers or who shrinks from notice behind his mother's skirt. When used of adults, *bashful* tends to sound condescending: such a *bashful* man when he has to talk to women. *Diffident* stresses a want of confidence in one's abilities, point of view, or even general worth. Although the *diffident* person is *shy* with others, his main difficulty is a hesitancy in expressing himself or in trying new things.

Faint-hearted is a somewhat scornful term as it implies not only a bumbling lack of courage but also uncertainty as to how to go about getting what one wants. Formerly the word was used of a *timid* or *shy* lover held back from declaring himself for fear of being rejected. Nowadays, it may be applied to any timidity that appears to be slightly ludicrous: too *faint-hearted* to ask for a raise in pay.

Coy originally meant *shy* and was used chiefly of women who were discouraging advances from men. It now carries overtones of a feigned and consequently coquettish shyness meant to kindle amatory interest: She was *coy* over the telephone when he asked for a date, although she had flirted outrageously with him the evening before. The extended meaning of *coy* refers to a playful or sly unwillingness to reveal information or to make a statement: When I told him that I had heard rumors of his promotion, he smiled *coyly* and said nothing.

Submissive, in this context, means so *timid* or *timorous* that yielding comes more easily than resisting: a housewife too *submissive* to send the fast-talking salesman on his way. See AFRAID, COWARDLY, DOCILE.

Antonyms: audacious, BRAVE, confident, DARING, poised.

tip

These verbs mean to turn from a vertical or horizontal position. To **tip** or **tilt** something is to incline it at an angle, lowering or raising one side or end. *Tip* suggests a slight, momentary, or accidental movement away from a balanced position. It is often applied to something turned downward, thrown out of balance, or turned over. [She *tipped* the pitcher to pour out the milk; He suddenly stood up and *tipped* the boat; The vase *tipped* over.] *Tilt* suggests a more decided or more stable shift of balance — a marked, permanent, or deliberate positioning at an angle: When the restaurant was closed, the chairs were *tilted* forward against the tables.

Slant and **slope** may refer to stationary things, and both stress line rather than movement. *Slant* is the more general word. It simply indicates an oblique placement or position. *Slope* involves a change of level or direction and is most often applied to the lay of land: a *slanted* line; a *sloping* lawn. A roof or hillside may either *slant* or *slope*; but *slope* suggests the gentler, more gradual downward inclination — except when qualified to the contrary: The ground *slopes* sharply here. *Slope* is limited in application, but *slant* may be used in a figurative sense, suggesting a bias toward a particular point of view: news so *slanted* you might call it propaganda.

To **cant** something is to set it at a *slant*. *Cant* is close to *tilt* but is more formal and may imply a greater degree of permanence. An engineer *cants* his drafting table by setting one side higher than the other. To *cant* a timber is to cut off a corner or an edge of it so as to form a slightly *slanted* end: to *cant* off the end of a plank. In nautical usage, a ship that *cants* swings around, taking a position oblique to some definite line or course. In another sense, to *cant* is to pitch toward one side, and to *cant* over is to turn over in this way: a schooner *canted* by the wind; The boat *canted* over.

Careen, heel, and **list** are all nautical terms applied to vessels that lean sharply to one side. A ship, especially one under sail, *careens*, or *heels* over, from being buffeted by wind or waves. A ship *lists* when its center of gravity is displaced, throwing it out of balance: The freighter *listed* 10° to starboard. *Careening* or *heeling* is always toward one side or the other, but *listing* may be forward or astern as well. *Careen* may also apply to a stationary ship in port, turned over on one side: They *careened* the ship to clean the bottom. In general use, *careen* is applied to moving objects, as vehicles, and means to lurch or twist from side to side as if out of control: The driverless car *careened* down the embankment. See BEND, TOTTER.

These words all pertain to a lessening or depletion of strength, energy, or spirit. **Tired** is a general word and in itself indicates no specific degree of loss of vigor: *tired* from mowing the lawn; eyes *tired* from reading in a poor light; *tired* after running a 100-meter race. **Weary** is sometimes used interchangeably with *tired* to refer to a general lull in physical energy: *weary* from a long, hard day's work. However, *weary* more strongly suggests discontent and vexation arising from having put up too long with something that is, or has become, disagreeable and trying: *weary* of getting up every hour to soothe a colicky baby; *weary* of arguing with his boss; *weary* of seeing the same inane television shows every night. *Tired* may also be used in this sense: sick and *tired* of the same old, deadly routine.

Fatigued implies a painful reduction of strength, as by nervous strain, illness, or overwork. It is more precise than *tired* or *weary*: After his harrowing experience of being trapped in the mine, he became easily *fatigued*. As a symptom of a low state of health, *fatigued* is preferred to the other words: getting up in the morning as *fatigued* as he had been

tip
(continued)

cant
careen
heel
list
slant
slope
tilt

tired

exhausted
fatigued
weary
worn out

the night before. In the sense of bored or *weary, fatigued* may function in a more formal and literary way: Mozart's music gave him a sense of elation, while he was *fatigued* by Brahms' brooding lyricism.

Exhausted implies the utter draining of strength and energy, which may be restored by long rest or may be irreversible: too *exhausted* to eat his dinner; *exhausted* by the hustle and bustle of city life; on his ninetieth birthday *exhausted* and dying of old age.

Worn out carries over to this context some of its more usual meaning of having been used to the point where value or effectiveness has been lost. Here it is informal and may cover the range of meanings from *tired* to *exhausted*, but it suggests the complete depletion of energy implied in *exhausted*: *worn out* from years of toiling on a rocky, unproductive farm. Generally, the word is loosely applied to any state of lagging energy or patience: *worn out* from shooting nine holes of golf; *worn out* from listening to the constant quarreling in the apartment next door. See BORED, LISTLESS.

Antonyms: invigorated, refreshed, relaxed, rested, strengthened.

title

appellation
cognomen
moniker
name

All of these words denote a word or phrase by which a person or thing is called. **Title** has many shades of meaning; it may be the designation given to a book, painting, drama, or other creative work, or a designation that indicates office or rank, and is added to a personal name. [The *title* of Thomas Wolfe's most famous book is *Look Homeward, Angel*; Jones' formal *title* is "Professor," but he prefers to be called "Mr."]

Name is fairly general, being used of both persons and things, but it is also specific, in that we think of a *name* as being peculiarly appropriate to its object in some sense, whether familial, legal, traditional, taxonomic, etc. No such relationship is suggested between **appellation** and the thing it designates. *Appellation*, a formal term, is more general than either *name* or *title*, and can be applied to anything identifiable: No suitably brief *appellation* could be found for the organization; hence it was known by the acronym CARE. But either *name* or *title* would also fit the example just given, with a possible gain in directness.

Cognomen, originally a personal surname, is still sometimes used in the general sense of any *name*, nickname, or *appellation* — although it is very formal and, possibly, dated. In ancient Rome *cognomen* referred to the last of a citizen's three *names*, i.e. his family *name*, as Naso in Publius Ovidius Naso. **Moniker** is an old-fashioned slang term close in meaning to *appellation*; it refers to that by which a person is identified, as a *name*, nickname, signature, or the like. Perhaps because of its use in gangster movies, it has a distinctly underworld flavor. [What's his *moniker*? He's called Fatso the Greek.] See NAME, PSEUDONYM.

topic

burden
matter
subject
subject matter
theme

These words refer to the major intent of a given speech or piece of writing. **Topic** presents the greatest variety of possible meanings. It can refer to the whole intent of a complete piece or utterance or it can refer to the point of a single sentence or paragraph within such a piece: the *topic* of his commencement address; the *topic* of every paragraph being carefully introduced in its first sentence. In conversation, *topic* can refer to something of general interest to all, whether introduced deliberately or happened upon by chance: the *topic* of the week at every cocktail party I went to. In any case, the word always suggests the explicit intent toward which expression is directed.

A number of *topics*, however, may be organized into the larger concern of an overall **subject**. And whereas *topic* usually refers to what is explicit, stated, or intentional, *subject* may also refer either to what is implied by the speaker or writer or to what can be inferred by his audience: the *subject* on which he chose to speak; unconscious references to violence that were a constant *subject* of his talk. **Theme** refers more often to the emotional attitudes that underlie a chosen *subject* and that unify the *topics* selected to illustrate it: His *subject* was poverty, but the *theme* he held to was the futility of attempting to cure it through haphazard methods. *Theme*, like *subject*, may refer to something explicitly or implicitly present: asking if she were aware that all her dreams seemed an expression of the same *theme*. The word can also refer to any tone or attitude that gives unity to some variety of examples collected to make a point; this may be true of any collection, written or otherwise: a group of essays whose *theme* was the will of man to endure; a one-man show of paintings whose *theme* was the vulgarity of modern life.

Burden, by way of its reference to the refrain of a song, can indicate something frequently repeated or dwelt on as a prevailing *theme*: Antony's mocking phrase, calling Brutus an honorable man, becomes the *burden* of his oration. By way of its reference to a heavy weight, the word is often taken in the context of discourse to suggest a consequential, weighty, or solemn *topic*; even in this case, however, repetition is still implied: the needless loss of life that was the *burden* of several editorials. **Matter** and the more commonly used **subject matter** are like *subject* in designating anything which is the object of a discussion, concern, feeling, etc.: doing research on the *subject matter* which would be under discussion in his next day's philosophy class. Both are often used to distinguish the actual content of a discourse or piece of writing from its verbal decoration and rhetorical flourishes: less manner and more *matter*. See BASIS, KERNEL.

total

Total, aggregate, and **sum**, as here considered, mean a result, as a number or amount, arrived at by adding or putting together all parts or elements of a particular group or mass. They may or may not suggest that the result contains everything that should be in it. The membership of an organization may be a *total* of 150; attendance at a meeting of the organization may be a *total* of only 100. An *aggregate* of statistical samples does not cover the entire range of what is being examined; the *aggregate* of a person's characteristics is a composite picture of the entire person. The *sum* of two or more numbers is fixed and complete; the *sum* available for financing a project is merely what is on hand and not necessarily the *sum* needed.

aggregate
sum
totality
whole

Totality and **whole** indicate the same kind of result denoted by *total*, *aggregate*, and *sum*, but here the result does contain all the parts or elements that should be in it. The *totality* of a nation's productive capacity includes the *sum*, *total*, or *aggregate* of all its natural resources, productive establishments, labor force, and technical competence. The *whole* of a nation's economy is the *sum* of the value and capability of all its component parts. See ACCUMULATE, ACCUMULATION, ENTIRE, QUANTITY.

Antonyms: COMPONENT, PART.

totter

These words refer to unsteady movement resulting from insecure balance. **Totter** and **teeter** would seem interchangeably close in their referral to the in-place movement of an object that is in an unstable position: a plate that *teetered* on the edge of the table before crashing

lurch

totter

(continued)

reel
stagger
teeter
wobble

to the floor; watching nervously while the statue *tottered* on its pedestal. But *teeter* carries a suggestion of the height of an impending fall while *totter* implies that when an object falls, it falls no farther than its base: *teetering* at the head of the stairs before tumbling down; a drunken man who *tottered* to the sidewalk. *Totter* can also refer to unsteady movement along a path, especially suggesting the instability resulting from old age or weakness: the old man who came *tottering* along; the *tottering* steps of a baby learning to walk.

Lurch can suggest one sudden, violent movement through space, especially a shift in the rate or direction of movement already underway: expecting the airplane to *lurch* as it hit the pocket of warm air. The word can also suggest the irregular movement or walk of a person who is drunk, disabled, or disoriented in some way: *lurching* dizzily up the stairs. **Reel** can indicate an irregular motion, like *lurch*, or a recoil from an impact that causes one to sprawl out or fall back: a *lurch* of the train that sent me *reeling* across the aisle; *reeling* under the enemy's counterattack. Like *totter*, **wobble** can suggest both the unsteady in-place motion of an object and an ungainly walk. Used of an object, however, the word need not suggest the precarious placement implicit in both *totter* and *teeter*; it can refer, instead, to a slight back-and-forth rocking motion resulting from uneven support: a short leg that caused the table to *wobble*. The word can also suggest any irregularity of continuing motion: a turntable that *wobbled* badly at low speeds. Where *totter* suggests age as the possible cause of an unsteady walk, *wobble* tends to suggest fatness or a misproportioned squatness of build: a fat man who *wobbled* slowly down the street. **Stagger**, like *reel* and *lurch*, can refer to an abnormal or grotesque walk, suggesting the unsteady gait and uncertain balance of some one who is drunk or semiconscious: sleepily *staggering* to the ringing telephone; addicts who *stagger* into a hospital asking for help. See PRECARIOUS, VIBRATE, WALK.

tradition

convention
custom
ethos
folkways
manner
manners
mores
practice

These words refer to established patterns or instances of typical behavior of a group, community, or culture. **Tradition** in its broadest sense refers to knowledge and doctrines as well as patterns of behavior transmitted from generation to generation. More specifically, *tradition* means a particular observance so long continued that it has almost the force of law: the *tradition* calling for the Queen to declare Parliament in session. **Custom** refers to the habitual pattern of hehavior of a community or people. A *custom*, while well established in usage, does not have the force of a *tradition*; *tradition* emphasizes more strongly historical significance: the *custom* of shaking hands; the *tradition* by which the bridegroom places the wedding band on the finger of his bride.

A **convention** is a rule or approved technique, and is applied to the arts as well as to conduct: the *convention* in the Elizabethan theater of employing boys to enact the roles of women; the *convention* of wearing a jacket and tie to business; hippies flouting *convention* by carrying signs displaying obscene words. Whereas *custom* suggests a long-standing cultural habit relatively independent of the influence of ephemeral fashions, a *convention* might be considered an expression of the **manners** of a people, *manners* in this sense referring not to etiquette but the modes of social behavior prevailing in a group during a particular period. Observing *convention* therefore implies a measure of conformity, even if unconscious, whereas observing a *custom* implies only the enacting of a habit shared with a great many other people. *Manners* in the sense here considered is often applied to literary works; a novel of *manners* is a novel describing the social attitudes and behavior of a group of people — often a stratum of society — in a given place at a given time. **Manner**, on the other hand, refers to a typical or customary way of doing something, especially a characteristic style used in one of the arts: painted in the *manner* of Rubens. **Practice** refers to a usual way of acting, working, or behaving — in short, a *custom* — but, unlike *custom*, implies a voluntary choice: the whalers' *practice* of discarding the fins; the traditional medical *practice* of charging patients fees according to their ability to pay. In a related sense *practice* refers to individual habit: it was his *practice* to read several books a week on a variety of subjects.

Ethos, mores, and **folkways** are terms most often encountered in sociological contexts. *Ethos* means the underlying and distinctive character or spirit of a people, group, or culture. The *ethos* of a group is seldom recognized by the members of that group; it is nevertheless implicit in their *manners* and finds expression in their *folkways*. *Folkways* is not restricted to behavioral patterns, but applies also to patterns of thought and emotional attitude, and is thus more closely allied to *tradition* than to *manners*. *Mores* refers to the established, traditional *customs* or *folkways* regarded by a social group as essential to its preservation and welfare: the Christian *mores* of marriage and family life; ascetic Puritan *mores*. *Mores* is often used, however, to refer to any prevalent moral attitudes or social *customs*: teen-age *mores* placing a high value on "going steady." See HISTORY, RITE, USUAL.

These words are compared as they denote repeated action. **Training**, the general word, means the systematic development of the body or mind for the purpose of acquiring proficiency in some physical or mental pursuit. [The *training* of troops prepares them for combat; A medical student faces years of *training* before he is qualified to specialize in one area.]

Practice is the putting into action of what one has learned in theory, in order to gain skill and facility: gunnery *practice*; daily *practice* at the piano. **Exercise** is primarily physical action to gain strength and vigor. By extension, it becomes *practice* to maintain a facility already acquired: the operatic soprano who sings the scales as a daily *exercise*. **Drill** is systematic and rigorous *practice* under a teacher or commander; the object of a *drill* is to be so proficient that the desired action becomes virtually automatic: fire *drills* to insure orderly evacuation of the building in an emergency.

Discipline, in this sense, adds to *training* the idea of the control — often self-control — needed to achieve proficiency at anything. *Discipline* strongly suggests dedication and firm commitment. [He had talent to spare, but he lacked the *discipline* to practice the four to eight hours a day that a concert pianist must devote to his craft.] See SKILL, TEACH.

training

discipline
drill
exercise
practice

These words are comparable in that they all refer to someone who violates or forsakes his allegiance to a government, political party, faith, or other belief. **Traitor**, in its specific denotation of a person who commits treason, is the strongest, most derogatory term in this group. It designates one who makes war against his own country or gives aid and comfort to its enemies: a *traitor* who, without putting up a fight, surrendered his army to an enemy force much smaller than his own. In a less opprobrious but still disparaging way, *traitor* refers to anyone who for any cause betrays a trust, a responsibility, a position, etc.: held to

traitor

apostate
deserter
turncoat

be a *traitor* to the upper class because he so eagerly embraced a socialist doctrine. Interestingly enough, this most critical of the four words under discussion is the only one used to express displeasure in informal situations: Imagine that *traitor* leaving the cast just before dress rehearsal.

An **apostate** is one who forsakes his religion, party, or principles. It is applied especially to a person who has given up his religious faith or, even more particularly, his allegiance to some special church. In *apostate* there is no definite suggestion of the active hostility which is implicit in the strongest sense of *traitor*: an *apostate* Catholic who was never able to shake off doubts about his separation from the Church.

Turncoat, more than the other three terms, hints that opportunism rather than a heartfelt change of persuasion is responsible for the actions of the person who abandons an allegiance. Since personal gain or convenience is his motivation, a *turncoat* is likely to treat an allegiance lightly and change it with little or no thought and concern: a political *turncoat* who left his liberal comrades in the lurch when a conservative mood hit the country.

Deserter particularly applies in the case of a soldier who violates his military obligations. He may run off from the place to which he has been assigned, or he may "desert to the enemy" — one of the most serious of military offenses. See HERETIC, LEAVE (abandon), RENEGADE.

Antonyms: SUPPORTER.

tranquil

calm
placid
quiet
serene
still
undisturbed
unruffled

These words all denote freedom from violent movement or emotion. **Tranquil** and **calm** both describe an absence of turmoil and agitation. However, *tranquil* implies an enduring condition, while *calm* points to a more transient one: a long, *tranquil* life; a *calm* interlude during a hurricane. In terms of personality, the words retain much of this same distinction: a *tranquil* mind given to reflection; remaining *calm* and in command of himself during the crisis.

Quiet and **still,** as here considered, imply an absence of bustle and commotion as well as the secondary suggestion of consequent silence. *Quiet* is the more relative of the two terms and describes that which is peaceful and is characterized by little excitement, but which is not necessarily silent: a *quiet* fishing village; a *quiet* evening spent at home; a *quiet* little man who does his work unobtrusively but well. *Still* may verge on the absolute. On the one hand it emphasizes a contrast with motion: the *still,* humid air of an August night; the *still* face of the dead woman. It may also point to the overcoming of an inherent tendency toward movement: On Sundays the great flywheels of the power station are *still;* The child sat *still* through the long, boring sermon.

Serene suggests that which is elevated above earthly turmoil: a *serene* blue sky. In referring to persons, the word implies the presence of an almost otherworldly calm and peace of spirit which has been reached through self-fulfillment and a philosophical acceptance of what life brings, or through religious faith: a *serene* old age passed in puttering about in his garden; the *serene,* kindly face of the mother superior.

Placid, when used to describe persons, indicates an untroubled, even temperament that is little given to anger or other strong emotions. The word tends to have an unfavorable connotation in suggesting an unimaginative, bovine dullness of personality: a large, *placid* girl who seemed to pass unmoved through the uncertainties of adolescence. In referring to things, *placid* points to that which is prevailingly *calm* and *tranquil*: a *placid* little lake hidden among the hills.

Undisturbed and **unruffled**, being negatives, are usually applied to the absence of superficial agitation rather than to the lack of turmoil implied by the other words in this group: The senator appeared to be *unruffled* by the biting criticism of his opponents and *undisturbed* by their open hostility. See BLAND, IMPERTURBABLE, SILENT.

Antonyms: *agitated*, *disturbed*, *excited*, FRANTIC, NERVOUS, TURBULENT.

These words refer to materials that obstruct total or perfect vision but through which light can penetrate. **Translucent** may refer either to something that permits an imperfect view or to something that merely allows the passage of light with little or no view possible: the *translucent* silver of the brook through which the pebbled bottom could be seen; partitions made of *translucent* panes of frosted glass to give the occupants of each cubicle complete privacy. **Blurred**, by contrast, usually specifically indicates a particular point between a near-perfect view and none. This would be that point at which figures or images could be seen hazily or, possibly, distortedly through the refracting medium: wiping his hand across the *blurred* windshield. In metaphorical uses, the word emphasizes distortion or lack of soundness: a deliberately *blurred* treatment of the issues.

The remaining words all suggest vision that is *blurred* because of thin intervening layers or tissues, whether spread evenly or in distorting folds. **Diaphanous** indicates the least obstruction, suggesting an extremely thin or delicate gathering of folds: a formal dress with a *diaphanous* outer sheath of organdy; *diaphanous* wisps of clouds that did nothing to mask the full force of the sun. **Filmy** suggests a greater obstruction of vision than *diaphanous*, but may apply either to an even layer or a gathering of folds: a *filmy* glaze of condensation on the cold pitcher. When the word refers to cloth, it resembles *diaphanous* but is less formal: stitching together yards of *filmy* chiffon. With **veiled**, the emphasis is on a greater obstruction of vision than *diaphanous* or *filmy*, with particular reference to a cloth designed for partial concealment, as of the face: thick clouds that *veiled* the sun. In metaphorical uses, a deliberate partial disguise may be implied: a *veiled* hint. See BRIGHT, FOGGY, LUMINOUS, TRANSPARENT, VAGUE.

translucent

blurred
diaphanous
filmy
veiled

These words refer to materials that not only permit the passage of light but present no obstruction to vision. **Transparent** is the most matter-of-fact of these words, giving a tone of technical precision: a roll of *transparent* tape; frosted glass in the lower part of the window and *transparent* glass above. In metaphorical uses, the tone of the word shifts drastically to emphasize what is obvious, especially when a poor attempt at deception is referred to: a *transparent* falsehood she didn't even bother to justify. **Clear**, in reference to unobstructed vision, emphasizes freedom from blur or blemish: letting the water run until it turned *clear*; a *clear* day. In this sense, it is often simply a more informal substitute for *transparent*. In metaphorical uses, however, the word is in sharp contrast to *transparent* and its suggestion of obvious deception; in this case, *clear* means lack of obscurity: arguments that were *clear* and concise.

Limpid, **pellucid**, and **crystalline** are more lyrical in tone than *clear* and *transparent*. *Limpid* suggests a view through a refracting medium, particularly water, that is utterly unclouded and untroubled: the stillness of the *limpid* water on the inland side of the reef. In metaphorical uses, the word suggests simplicity or serenity: the *limpid* love-

transparent

clear
crystalline
limpid
lucid
pellucid

liness of her smile. *Pellucid* is lyrical, sometimes to the point of preciosity, and its stress may be on the umblemished fragility of the refracting medium: a *pellucid* soap bubble. In metaphorical use, the word is perhaps even in more danger of preciosity, referring to a remarkably *clear*, sweet, or delicate quality: a choir boy's *pellucid* soprano. *Crystalline*, in this sense, conveys the sparkling *transparent* quality of quartz or of flint glass: the *crystalline* air of mountain regions; the *crystalline* lens of the eye. In an extended sense, *crystalline* may refer to that which is either literally or figuratively clear-cut and distinctly outlined: a leafless tree standing in *crystalline* sharpness against the sky; the *crystalline* clarity of his prose.

Lucid is almost never used nowadays to refer in a literal sense to something that is so *clear* or *transparent* as to permit unobstructed vision. Once it was widely employed in this way in literature and poetry. Its application now is principally to treatments that are understandable and unambiguous: a *lucid* explanation of evolution; a *lucid* prose style. *Lucid* may also refer to mental processes which are *clear* and rational, especially in persons who may experience periods of remission from a mental illness: From time to time he would be free of delusions and hallucinations and be *lucid* for days. See FLIMSY, TRANSLUCENT.

Antonyms: FOGGY, OBSCURE, VAGUE.

treacherous

disloyal
false
hypocritical
specious
traitorous
treasonable
unfaithful

A betrayal of trust is implicit in all these words. **Treacherous** implies strong moral condemnation. It refers to a tendency or a disposition to imperil or betray another to whom one has shown apparent loyalty and good will: a *treacherous* coworker who denounces one to the boss; a *treacherous* dog who bites his master. *Treacherous* may also mean simply dangerous or unreliable, especially when applied to things: roads that become *treacherous* during the spring thaw; *treacherous* times in our history. **Disloyal** is the most general word, suggesting either frank or covert hostility toward anything one has paid allegiance to: *disloyal* to the standards of his profession; situations in which political dissent is thought *disloyal*. **Unfaithful** narrows its implications to one possibility in *disloyal*, being now used mainly for personal situations. A person would be *disloyal* to his country, but *unfaithful* to his wife. One aspect of **false** relates to these words, especially in the phrase, *false* friend. Here, it suggests a total or irreparable breach, as in the case of a *treacherous* friend. A *disloyal* or *unfaithful* friend, unlike a *false* friend, could conceivably have temporarily or accidentally erred and yet repent of his action later.

Specious and **hypocritical** both suggest a misleading contrast between appearance and reality or between stated beliefs and actions. *Specious* once suggested no more than a pleasing appearance, but now it is taken most often to mean a deliberately dissembling manner or to suggest something that seems true but proves *false*: *specious* reasoning; *specious* declarations of friendship. *Hypocritical* suggests either a conscious or unconscious discrepancy between what one claims to be and what one does. In the context of betrayal, the stress would fall on conscious dishonesty: *hypocritically* promising the voters lower taxes.

Treasonable is closely related to the aspect of *disloyal* that refers specifically to betrayal of cause or country; the word is more likely to be applied to acts, however, than to people, and sometimes suggests behavior approaching or tantamount to treason rather than outright betrayal: insisting that the protest demonstration was not *treasonable*, either in effect or intent. **Traitorous**, the most formal of these words, may now sound slightly old-fashioned to some ears. Like *treasonable*, it is also most often restricted to betrayal of one's country. In contrast, it is most appropriately used to describe people, although it can be used of acts as well. In any case, it suggests deliberate betrayal rather than a close approach to it: a *traitorous* officer who relayed war secrets to the enemy. See CRIME.

Antonyms: CANDID, HONEST, *loyal*, MORAL, SINCERE.

These words all mean to restore to health or soundness a diseased or injured condition, especially by means of medical attention. **Treat** is the most general word. To *treat* medically is to accept someone as a patient, to diagnose his illness, and to help relieve it. [After the accident, the truck driver was *treated* for cuts and bruises; Some skin diseases are difficult to *treat*.] *Treating* may specifically involve the prescribing of drugs, special diets, exercises, etc., or simply advice on habits of living. But all of these measures involve the overall effort to restore a sick or injured person to health.

treat

cure
heal
mend
remedy

Cure usually applies to diseases, **heal** to injuries. [Penicillin *cured* him of pneumonia. The cut on his finger *healed* quickly.] *Cure* is sometimes used to suggest a sudden and dramatic improvement. [The blind man was miraculously *cured* at the shrine; At any moment someone may discover how to *cure* cancer.] **Healing**, on the other hand, is usually a slow process, sometimes of very long duration. It is never quick or dramatic: His injured back had been *healing* nicely until he wrenched it again yesterday. In this sense *mend* is a close synonym, but suggests, in accordance with its literal meaning, a drawing together of parts, whereas *heal* implies simply a return to a healthy condition: His fractured wrist is *mending* (or *healing*) rapidly.

In some contexts *heal* does suggest the charlatan or quack, possibly from the application of the term "healer" to medical poseurs. In other cases *heal* sounds pretentious and highflown: A physician's sacred duty is to *heal* the sick. *Cure* and *heal* are sometimes used figuratively: to be *cured* of coming late to breakfast; to be *healed* of old regrets.

Remedy may also mean to *cure* or *heal* by medical treatment. Aspirin may *remedy* a headache, or specially fitted shoes *remedy* fallen arches. However, you are more likely to say that aspirin *cures* a headache and that special shoes correct fallen arches. In its wider sense, *remedy* means to overcome a defect or undesirable state of affairs not necessarily having to do with health. See ALLEVIATE, NEUTRALIZE, RECOVER, REPAIR.

Antonyms: neglect.

These words denote types of agreements or political adjustments between two or more nations. **Treaty** is the general term for a formal, signed contract that is drawn up after diplomatic negotiations and in accordance with the rules of international law. *Treaties* may end wars, provide for the purchase of territory, or contain provisions to ensure peace. Many *treaties* are named for the places in which they are ratified: the *Treaty* of Westphalia; the *Treaty* of Versailles.

treaty

coexistence
détente
entente
pact

In recent times, **pact** has been frequently substituted for *treaty*: the Kellogg-Briand *Pact*; the Locarno *Pact*. However, in general, *pact* often suggests a less important and less binding agreement than does *treaty*. One would always refer to a decision to cease international hostilities as a *treaty*, but one to regulated trade between otherwise friendly countries is likely to be called a *pact*. In its wider meaning, *pact* is any covenant made between two or more persons or groups in which each agrees to carry out a certain action: a *pact* between owners of rival stores to charge fair prices; a suicide *pact*.

Entente, a shortened form of "*entente* cordiale," a French term meaning understanding, is an informal compact, rather than a *treaty*, between governments with reference to the conducting of foreign affairs or cooperation in the event of military aggression from without. An *entente* may or may not be set down in the form of a document; it may simply be a pledge made between heads of states.

Détente suggests a more negative situation than does *entente*, as a *détente* is a lessening in or a suspension of strained relations between governments, especially after a military crisis has been narrowly averted. A *détente* may be uneasy and temporary, or it may lead eventually to an *entente*.

Coexistence, a fairly new word in diplomacy, is the simultaneous existence, through a policy of mutual noninterference, of two or more nations differing widely in ideology. *Coexistence* differs from an *entente* in that it is a more or less neutral state of affairs, often implying mere forbearance for the sake of preventing outright war. *Coexistence* may come into being after a *détente*; on the other hand, it may be the forerunner of an *entente*. See COVENANT.

tremendous

colossal
herculean
prodigious
stupendous
thumping
titanic
whopping

These words refer to anything that is extremely great in size, scope, scale, intensity, or importance. **Tremendous** not only suggests something extraordinarily large or vast but something that is unusual, striking, or astonishing in its magnitude: a *tremendous* skyscraper; issues of *tremendous* consequence for every citizen. The word is often used loosely as a hyperbole for anything one thinks of as interesting or pleasant: a *tremendous* party. **Prodigious** can refer to sheer size, but more particularly it suggests anything that is preternatural to the extent of being a prodigy or marvel; it also can be used vaguely in hyperbole: a basketball player of *prodigious* height; a *prodigious* blow to the economy. The word may also refer to something achieved with effort, or to precocious development: a *prodigious* space-age triumph; the boy's *prodigious* ability at working differential equations. **Stupendous** could once refer to any phenomenon that staggered the mind, but it has suffered more from overuse than the previous pair and now may seem mere overstatement: a *stupendous* movie.

Colossal and **titanic** both derive from references to large bodies. *Colossal* comes from the Colossus of Rhodes, a huge statue that was one of the wonders of the ancient world. *Titanic* refers back to the Titans, a race of giants in Greek mythology. Some echo of these origins remains in that *colossal* may stress monumentality, while *titanic* may stress force and power: a *colossal* façade of windows blocking the sky; a *titanic* effort to arm the nation following the sneak attack. Both are overused as hyperboles. Like the previous pair, **herculean** has a classical origin, referring back to the hero Hercules. The word suffers less from loss of meaning through overuse, however, and can still refer not only to a powerfully built man, but to selfless labor dedicated to accomplishing seemingly insuperable tasks; this shade of meaning is also a reference to the *prodigious* feats of Hercules: *herculean* athletes; the *herculean* job of combating the upsurge of crime in recent times.

Thumping and **whopping** have a colorful, informal, or slangy sound that saves them from the gray vagueness that some of these words have been reduced to through overuse. *Thumping* hints at the physical sound that a large or plump object might give off or, less concretely, suggests ripeness, health, or perfection: a *thumping* ten-pound baby. *Whopping* may deliberately suggest an awareness of overstatement in someone else's hyperboles or outright lies, as in a tall tale: a *whopping* excuse for being late; a *whopping* lie. In a more general way, it can refer to anything that seems forceful or decisive: a *whopping* landslide election victory over his opponent. See HUSKY, LARGE, MASSIVE, SIZE.

Antonyms: MINUTE, SMALL, TRIVIAL.

All of these words involve the intention to deceive. **Trick** is the most general, and may apply to any device used to fool someone, whether in earnest or in fun: a mean *trick* to obtain money; prankish schoolboys' *tricks*.

Artifice has a general meaning of artistic skill or even the created work itself. One of its meanings, however, relates it to this set of words describing expedients used to gain an end. In this sense *artifice* means something contrived especially to win out in a given situation. It has connotations of cleverness and may or may not suggest an unethical approach. [The labyrinth was an *artifice* created by Daedalus to imprison the violent Minotaur; Pretending to be a sightseer was a harmless *artifice* if it permitted him to speak to the beautiful woman in the piazza.]

In **blind** and **subterfuge** the element of an unethical deception or disguise is stronger. A *blind* usually involves out-and-out role-playing, whereas a *subterfuge* can be a momentary deception which invites the onlooker to mistake a person's real intentions. [His job as a bartender was simply a *blind* for conducting an illicit traffic in narcotics; Her sudden illness was a *subterfuge* to prevent her son from leaving home.]

Both **wile** and **ruse** imply cunning pretenses in order to persuade, but *ruse* may be more innocuous than *wile*, which suggests taking unfair advantage. [The *ruse* of having a later appointment permitted her to escape from the aggressive bore; All his *wiles* could not persuade her to entrust him with her money.]

Dodge and **evasion** are much more harmless in tone, implying the avoidance of a confrontation rather than the active initiation of a false situation. [The actress changed the subject quickly, a skillful *dodge* to avoid admitting her actual age; She had built her career on a succession of such *evasions*.]

Stratagem and **maneuver** are drawn from military parlance to describe carefully plotted offensive or defensive tactics. Both imply conscious, calculated planning. [His *stratagem* for winning her approval was to agree with everything she said; Announcing his candidacy was only a *maneuver* to prevent his enemy from gaining the nomination.] See CHEAT, DECEPTION, LIE, MISLEADING, TRICK (v.)

trick

artifice
blind
dodge
evasion
maneuver
ruse
stratagem
subterfuge
wile

These words all mean to use secret or underhanded devices to make someone believe something that is not true or to accept as real or worthwhile something that is false or valueless. **Trick** suggests the accomplishment of such a purpose by means of a plot, maneuver, artifice, wile, etc.: to *trick* a fugitive into believing that he had eluded his pursuers. To **deceive** is to *trick* by the distortion of truth or reality: a bookkeeper who *deceived* his employer by manipulating the accounts of the business.

To **delude** or **mislead** is to lead into error, as by a series of deceptive or alluring utterances or demonstrations. Both words suggest evasion

trick

deceive
delude
dupe
hoodwink
mislead

or avoidance of the real facts of a matter rather than deliberate misrepresentation: propaganda designed to *delude* the public about the true extent of civilian casualties during a month of heavy bombing; unethical teachers who *mislead* untalented, gullible students into thinking they can become successful musicians.

To **dupe** is to take advantage of a victim's naiveté or credulousness in *deceiving* him about the reality, truth, or value of something: country bumpkins being *duped* by shills at a county fair. **Hoodwink** means to befuddle the mind to the point at which truth and falseness are indistinguishable: a crooked attorney trying to *hoodwink* a jury by confusing the issues. See CHEAT, DECEPTION, MISLEADING, STEALTHY, TRICK (n.).

trite

cliché
hackneyed
shopworn
stale
stereotyped
stock
threadbare

These words refer to expressions or ideas that have lost freshness and meaning through overuse and consequently insult good taste by their superficiality, obviousness, or banality. **Trite** and **cliché**, while firmly negative in tone, can be used in simple description or classification, without the same degree of opprobrium suggested by the rest of these words. *Trite* is milder than *cliché*, but more general, referring to overused expressions, obvious ideas, or a style that relies on either or both of these: a *trite* simile comparing her teeth to pearls; a story that is beautifully written but is concerned with the *trite* theme of adolescent loneliness; the standard Independence Day speech, *trite* in both delivery and sentiment. *Cliché* (or clichéd) in contrast more often refers to expression alone: coinages such as "promotionwise" that can become *cliché* almost overnight. Occasionally, it goes beyond these restrictions: *cliché* characters that marred an otherwise good play. In any case, the fault of overuse indicated by *cliché* is more serious than that suggested by *trite*.

Hackneyed and **shopworn** are the most critical of these words. *Hackneyed* points to expression, style, and content that befit a hack writer, that is, someone hired to do routine and commercial, if not trashy, writing: the *hackneyed* jargon of movie romance magazines. Extreme cheapness or vulgarity of expression is often indicated by the word, and possibly dullness and lack of any serious intent. Expressions might become *trite* or *cliché* by striving pathetically for elegance or loftiness: no longer possible to speak of rosy-fingered dawns without being *cliché*. *Hackneyed*, however, suggests low, narrow meanness undiluted by striving of any kind. *Shopworn* gives less opprobrium than *hackneyed*, but it vividly characterizes anything whose appeal and interest have worn out through overuse: *shopworn* political talk about a candidate's image, his ethnic appeal, and other claptrap.

Stale and **threadbare** emphasize that something, now overused, might once have been fresh or novel. Both, like *shopworn*, apply here metaphorically. *Stale* suggests comparison to perishable food, *threadbare* to the wearing out of cloth. *Stale* is unique in that it suggests a process of dating that need not result through overuse: *stale* Victorianisms that are mercifully disappearing from the language. When overuse is suggested, the emphasis is on a lack of liveliness: a campaign speech that was a *stale* reiteration of respect for God, country, and motherhood. *Threadbare* points to overuse that results in an expression's ultimate meaninglessness: *Threadbare* metaphors like "kick over the traces" no longer have any meaning for most people. It should be pointed out in passing that, because of their metaphorical colorfulness, *shopworn*, *stale*, and *threadbare* are themselves in danger of becoming *trite* through overuse.

Stock and stereotyped suggest things mass-produced, struck from a mold or deliberately made to resemble forerunners. *Stock* may suggest a situation in which originality is not expected or desired: *stock* formulas according to which hit musicals are constructed. *Stereotyped* suggests oversimplification of complexities to the point of caricature, however recognizable: the *stereotyped* figure of the Negro butler in whisky ads. Both words, however, can refer to an audience's expectation of being given the comforting or the usual, or even the desire to see or understand something according to standard patterns: the *stock* response when the image of a cooing baby is flashed upon the screen; *stereotyped* attitudes toward minority groups that persist even in the face of plain evidence to the contrary. Of the two, *stereotyped* is more critical and severe in this situation. See BANAL, BLAND, OLD-FASHIONED, SUPERFICIAL, TRUISM.

Antonyms: CREATIVE, UP-TO-DATE.

trivial

measly
paltry
petty
picayune
puny
trifling

These words are comparable in that they all mean small or insignificant. **Trivial** is used to characterize that which is ordinary or commonplace and hence of no special value or import: to interject a *trivial* remark. The word is not always opprobrious, and may sometimes be used in reference to something which is unimportant because it is easy to deal with: to dispose of *trivial* business in the morning. That which is **trifling** is so *trivial* as to be unworthy of notice: a *trifling* distinction. The word is also applied to small amounts of money: The cost of the required books would have been *trifling*.

Petty and **picayune** are alike in their implication of small-mindedness, but *petty* has overtones of meanness and spite while *picayune* has special relevance to a narrow or rigid point of view: a *petty* gossip who delighted in breaking up her sister's romance; a *picayune* politician who hadn't expressed a new idea in ten years of campaigning. *Petty* can also be used to describe any small, minor, or subordinate person or thing: a *petty* irritation; a *petty* officer. *Picayune* is much like *trivial* when it refers to something small: Why should we quibble about such a *picayune* sum? And it can be like *petty* in expressing a carping or fault-finding meanness: It was *picayune* of him to criticize his secretary in front of the other girls.

Paltry and **measly** are derogatory, and are applied to that which is contemptibly small. *Paltry* suggests that the thing it describes should be larger or greater: a *paltry* contribution to the charity. *Measly* hints at scantiness and stinginess: a *measly* serving of stew for a hungry, hardworking man.

Puny specifically refers to a person whose body is feeble, underdeveloped, or weak: Poverty with its attendant miseries and inadequacies had turned a perfectly normal baby into a *puny*, neurotic child. By extension, *puny* can apply to anything that is insignificant or enfeebled: a *puny* attempt to solve a problem that was too big for his knowledge and experience. See EXTRANEOUS, MARGINAL, SCANTY.

Antonyms: SIGNIFICANT.

troops

army
forces

These words refer collectively to the men that make up a military contingent, as distinguished from their arms and material. **Troops** is relatively informal and refers to the whole body of men in a unit or to fighting men in general. The word is most often used for land detachments rather than for naval or air units, and it also is sometimes used exclusively to apply to enlisted men as distinct from their officers: sending

troops
(continued)

personnel
soldiers

troops into the off-shore island; officers trying to quiet the grumbling of the *troops*. **Army** clearly distinguishes land *troops* from naval or air units, but unlike *troops*, it clearly includes both officers and enlisted men: joining the *army* as a second lieutenant; an *army* sent to put down the rebellion. **Soldiers** may loosely refer to all the men in an *army*, but more specifically it refers to enlisted men, and sometimes even more strictly to men enlisted in the infantry: invading *soldiers* supported by massive artillery detachments.

Both **forces** and **personnel** are more formal, more inclusive, and more abstract than the other words here. *Personnel* refers collectively to all the men in a unit, whether of an army, navy, or air unit. It can, in fact, refer collectively to the men in all these groupings: the cancelling of leaves and discharges for all military *personnel*. The word is used in distinguishing men from arms or materiel. In a wider context, of course, this word can refer to the members of any kind of group or business whatsoever: the factory's *personnel*. **Forces** specifically considers collectively all the men in all branches of the military: asserting that our *forces* in the present struggle were adequate to the task at hand. The word differs from *personnel*, however, in viewing *soldiers* and officers in the context of all their supporting armament and supplies: building up their military *forces* into the best-equipped and most modern in the world. See GROUP.

truism

bromide
platitude
saw

These words refer to sayings that express self-evident truths or oft-repeated assumptions. **Truism** is the most neutral of these: the *truism* about the fool and his money being soon parted. Often, however, the word refers to statements widely regarded as true or accepted as fact: setting out to disprove the *truism* that the world was flat. Since it is needless to point out what is obvious, the word can also carry a critical tone: lectures that were a mere collection of *truisms*.

In the case of **platitude** and **saw**, the tone is decidedly critical. Unlike *truism*, the statements referred to by these words need not be self-evident or even true; the words do suggest ideas that have been repeated so often as to be no longer vivid or meaningful. *Platitude* suggests an attempt at wisdom that expresses, instead, a commonplace sententiousness: weather that made a mockery of the *platitude* about March coming in like a lion; fathers who wish to be helpful concerning their sons' problems but can only spout embarrassed *platitudes* to them. *Saw* refers to any well-worn saying whose point may be wit rather than wisdom, but that has become pointless through repetition or misapplication: countering her *saw* about a penny earned by quoting the one about being penny-wise but pound-foolish.

Bromide is the most disparaging of all these words. It denotes a stereotyped, inane remark made as though it were an original idea or observation. *Bromides* are usually uttered by people who exhibit a lack of imagination and intellectual perception: the *bromide* that it's not what you learn in college that counts but the friends you make there. See BANAL, PROVERB, TRITE.

Antonyms: witticism.

trust

confidence

These words denote the feeling that a person or thing will not fail in loyalty, duty, or service. **Trust** and **faith** suggest the greatest degree of conviction in this context. *Trust* indicates a feeling of certainty that someone or something will not fail in any situation where protection, discretion, or fairness is essential: their *trust* in us to defend them if they are attacked; placing her *trust* in him to keep her secret; unwilling to put any *trust* in banks. The word emphasizes this feeling of certainty whether it is justified or misguided: an investigation proving that their *trust* in him was warranted; misplaced *trust* in a man who turned out to be a charlatan. *Faith* is an intensification of *trust*, suggesting an even deeper conviction of fidelity and integrity, often in spite of no evidence whatever or even in the face of contrary evidence: *faith* in her son's goodness despite innumerable examples of his inability to keep out of trouble; blind *faith* in his wife's loyalty; an unquestioning *faith* in the curative powers of psychiatry. The word emphasizes such a deep-seated conviction that it is appropriate in a religious context to refer to belief that is based on steadfast loyalty rather than on demonstrable evidence: a simple, pious *faith* that remained unshakable in the face of every misfortune.

Confidence and **reliance** more often suggest *trust* based on the proven reliability of someone or something. One can intuitively *trust* someone at first glance, rightly or wrongly, but *confidence* suggests a conviction borne of time-tested familiarity; it also pertains specifically to a feeling that someone or something will not fail or behave differently than it has in the past: a voting record that merits the *confidence* of minority groups; *confidence* in his ability to survive the crisis, based on his many narrow escapes in the past; a diabetic's *confidence* in the efficacy of insulin. Sometimes the word is detached from any notion of evidence as a basis for *trust*: a buoyant *confidence* that things would somehow work out all right in time. *Reliance* is even more specific than *confidence*, pointing to an actual dependence on something else, whether out of choice or necessity: speeding along with complete *reliance* on the effectiveness of his brakes. Often it suggests the need for protection of the weak by the strong: the *reliance* of emerging countries on the foreign-aid programs of the world's affluent nations. Sometimes *reliance* indicates something that is resorted to as a solution to a specific problem: the administration's *reliance* on increased taxes to bring in more revenue to support the space program. See ALLEGIANCE, ENTRUST, MORAL.

Antonyms: ANXIETY, *distrust*, DOUBT, UNBELIEF.

These words characterize personal qualities of people in whom one has great confidence. **Trustworthy** is the strongest word, implying that one's confidence is complete and profound: a *trustworthy* friend. **Reliable** suggests competence and consistency: A *reliable* judge is one who has a record of sound opinions. A *reliable* person can be counted on to do what he has promised or been told to do: a *reliable* baby sitter. When applied to things, *reliable* means adequate, serviceable, or true; a reference book, for example, might be called *reliable* if the information it presents is accurate. **Dependable** is akin to *reliable*, but is a little more subjective; *reliable* is often used of relationships based on service between superiors and inferiors, whereas *dependable* more often suggests an attitude of personal allegiance rather than one of honesty or scrupulosity in the performance of a duty. One goes to a *dependable* person confident of receiving loyalty, support, or aid: a *dependable* ally. When applied to things, *dependable* suggests stability and consistency of performance: a *dependable* drug.

That which has been found *reliable* in the past is **trusty**, though it may not merit as much confidence as something *trustworthy*: a *trusty* prisoner; a *trusty* sword. See ALLEGIANCE, SURE, TRUST, TRUTHFUL.

Antonyms: HEEDLESS, INCONSTANT, *irresponsible*, *negligent*.

trust

(continued)

faith
reliance

trustworthy

dependable
reliable
trusty

truthful

good
honest
reputable
veracious

These words all refer to estimable qualities. **Truthful** and **veracious**, stemming respectively from the Old English and Latin words for true, are close synonyms that mean habitually telling or disposed to tell the truth. *Veracious* is considerably more formal and more limited in application; it is used principally of a person's habitual tendency rather than of particular instances of truth-telling: a *veracious* (or *truthful*) man; a *truthful* remark. **Honest** and **good** are of course rich with connotations; as here considered, *honest* means not given to lying, cheating, or stealing, and stresses the virtuous and worthy motivation and principles of a person to whom the word is applied. *Truthful* and *veracious*, by contrast, while usually complimentary, since truth after all is highly valued, do not necessarily suggest an accompanying nobility of character: a *truthful* but malicious retort; He was *veracious* but unkind. *Honest* in this sense implies holding nothing back; it suggests an extreme candidness, even when at one's own expense: an *honest* admission of his failure. *Good* may suggest honorable motives and noble character even more strongly than *honest*, but unless placed in a limiting context suffers from vagueness. By itself it is little more than a reflection of the high opinion of the writer: a *good* reporter; a *good*, straight answer. **Reputable**, although it refers specifically to a *good* reputation, implies that the reputation is justified. *Reputable* may be used of a solid, respectable, dependable person highly regarded by the community, or it may be applied to a firm known for the consistent good quality of its goods or services: a *reputable* doctor; a *reputable* department store. On the other hand, *reputable* may simply mean famous or greatly esteemed for one's achievements: a *reputable* physicist. See CANDID, DISINTERESTED, MORAL, SINCERE.

Antonyms: bad, cheating, corrupt, *lying,* TREACHEROUS, *underhanded, venal.*

try

attempt
endeavor
strive

All the words in this group mean to make an effort to do or accomplish something. **Try** is the most general term, and in its wider application suggests the expenditure of physical or mental energy to get something done, but with the implication that success is likely. [She always *tries* to finish her housework before noon; *Try* to get your assignments in on time.] *Try* may also imply that one will use other means or search into other ways if not at first successful: Since exercise hasn't helped you to lose weight, have you *tried* to cut down on starches? In another sense *try* indicates making use of something in order to test its properties or to see if it functions properly: to *try* out a new recipe for pot roast; to *try* a window that is hard to open; to *try* driving a car with an unfamiliar type of gearshift.

Attempt may serve as a more formal synonym for *try*; but in general it has its own special connotations. It sometimes puts an emphasis on beginning or embarking upon something rather than on the energy expended toward accomplishing it: The ex-convict went to another part of the country to *attempt* to lead a new and law-abiding life. *Attempt* may also imply that the desired or expected result is not always forthcoming. [The hysterical woman has several times *attempted* to kill herself in order to get attention; We have *attempted* to reach him by mail and by phone, but apparently he is out of town.] In idiomatic usage *attempt* means to *try* to make an attack or an assault, and it is used elliptically without the infinitive: to *attempt* (to climb) the Matterhorn; to *attempt* (to take) the life of a hated dictator.

Endeavor and **strive** suggest the use of great exertion, especially in the face of difficulty. *Endeavor* is to *try* to do something requiring unusual and earnest effort: an alcoholic *endeavoring* to stop drinking. *Strive* puts the emphasis on the toil and strain involved in doing something rather than on the result achieved: *striving* to make ends meet on a small, fixed salary. Both *endeavor* and *strive* tend to sound somewhat pompous today when used arbitrarily in place of *try* or *attempt*. [I shall *endeavor* to do my job well in order to deserve the trust you have placed in me; He will *strive* to be a better husband and father in the future.] See INTEND.

    Antonyms: drop, LEAVE, QUIT.

tryst

assignation
date
rendezvous

These words refer to prearranged meetings of an intimate nature, often secret, illicit, or amorous in intent. **Tryst** is the most specific of these; it points almost invariably to a secret prearranged meeting, often at night, in a hidden place. The word hints at furtiveness and so strongly suggests a meeting of lovers that it could sound odd when used of any other encounter: a midnight *tryst* in the garden under an old oak tree. **Assignation** specifically indicates secrecy as well, but it also strongly suggests an illicit meeting. A *tryst* might be perfectly innocent, one that would cause no surprise or alarm if known about by others. In contrast, *assignation* denotes a meeting with an amorous or sexual purpose: arranging an *assignation* with the attractive widow while his wife was out of town.

    Rendezvous emphasizes prearrangement, but it may or may not be secret or unsavory in implication. Often, the word can suggest a simple matter of synchronizing independent movement so as to coincide at a planned time and place. It appears in contexts of romantic love, conspiracy, and military tactics: a dimly lit cafe where the lovers held their *rendezvous*; the crowded bus depot where the addict and his connection made their *rendezvous*; a *rendezvous* of the two patrols in Zone A at 0600 hours. **Date**, by contrast, is the most general and informal of these words and is not often likely to suggest either a secret or illicit meeting. Most commonly, the word suggests an evening of shared entertainment between a man and woman who are not married: college students who confine their *dates* to weekends. The word can apply, however, to any sort of prearranged meeting at any time for any purpose: a luncheon *date* with another secretary in her office; a *date* with her hairdresser. See MEETING.

turbulent

blustering
riotous
stormy
tempestuous
tumultuous
violent
wild

These words refer to extreme agitation, either of external physical forces or of internal emotional states. **Turbulent** suggests troubled, tumbling, erratic, chaotic, or confused activity or a whirl of uncontrolled emotion: *turbulent* anxieties that drove her to suicide; the *turbulent* airflow around a badly streamlined airplane; a *turbulent* mob of jostling, jeering workers. As in the last example, the physical and emotional applications of the word may often coalesce.

    Violent and **wild** are the most general of these words. *Violent* stresses destructive or uncontrolled physical force: a *violent* hurricane. In reference to human action, it stresses extreme agitation and often harmful or vicious behavior: the *violent* manner in which he pounded the podium with his fist; trying to keep the *turbulent* crowd from becoming *violent*; a *violent* person capable of killing anyone who got in his way. *Wild* suggests an untamed state of nature: the Lewis and Clark expedition over *wild*, uncharted prairies and mountains. Used of a person, the word can suggest uncontrolled, uncivilized behavior: cursing and stomping about like a *wild* man. It can also suggest derangement or immorality: a woman who went *wild* and stabbed her three children; staggering from the lifeboat with *wild* eyes; a *wild* party.

Stormy and **tempestuous** can refer to *turbulent* weather, but also to human emotion. In either case, *tempestuous* suggests greater force or intensity: *stormy* weather that had run its course by morning; *tempestuous* barrages of wind and rain that hammered the island for three days without let-up. Used of emotions, *stormy* indicates great agitation, but there is no necessary implication of potential harm or of an unpleasant outcome: *stormy* lovers' quarrels that end in lovemaking. In this context, *tempestuous* suggests forceful or disordered emotional intensity, but like *stormy*, no necessarily harmful or lasting result: a *tempestuous* six-month love affair. The word can suggest the running of a range of emotions at their highest pitch; consequently, the word sometimes is used in descriptions of art, particularly works from the romantic era: a *tempestuous* piano concerto. **Blustering** is related to *stormy* and *tempestuous* in that it can refer to weather, but by contrast it suggests erratic stop-and-start gusts of wind or rain. As applied to emotions, however, the word has a drastically different set of connotations, usually suggesting hasty, rash, angry outbursts of uncontrolled speech or action: *blustering* about the office and breaking out in fits of *violent* fury that he directed at his amazed secretary.

Both **riotous** and **tumultuous** can apply to *turbulent* or *violent* groups of people. In this use, *tumultuous* is like *turbulent*, while *riotous* is even more forceful than *violent*. *Tumultuous* stresses noise, mass crowding, and erratic activity, but does not necessarily suggest potential danger or destructiveness; the word can, in fact, indicate the opposite: *tumultuous* crowds that gathered to hail the astronauts; *tumultuous* applause for her performance. A *riotous* crowd, by contrast, is by implication one verging on angry mob action: an orderly meeting that became *riotous* as more and more people cried out in favor of lynching the suspect on the spot. *Riotous* can refer to any sort of bewildering array or profusion: a field *riotous* with colorful flowers. It is less likely to describe emotions than *tumultuous*, however. In this context, the latter suggests an extreme upheaval accompanied by surges of contradictory feelings during which the rational mind cannot sort out or control the developing confusion: a *tumultuous* state of both anger and fear. See LAWLESSNESS, UNRULY.

Antonyms: TRANQUIL.

U

ugly

homely
plain
unattractive
unsightly

These words all refer to people or things that are esthetically displeasing or objectionable. **Ugly** is the strongest and most unfavorable word and is broadest in application. It may refer to morally repulsive behavior as well as to people or things that are distasteful in appearance: an *ugly* hat; an *ugly* tenement building; in an *ugly* mood. Because of the blunt force of *ugly* when applied to people, **homely**, **plain**, or **unattractive**, which have softer or more diffuse impacts, are often preferred in describing someone of unpleasing appearance.

Homely, influenced by its basic sense meaning familiar or everyday in character, implies ugliness by reason of a common, dull, or gross appearance entirely lacking in any appealing or distinguishing feature. *Plain* also emphasizes a lack of distinction that would lend interest or appeal, but is somewhat gentler in tone than *homely*. [The older sister was unfortunately rather *homely*, and was never married; The girl, though *plain*, had a good, kind face.] *Unattractive* is more diffuse and vaguer than *plain* or *homely*, and may be applied to things and behavior as well as to personal appearance: an *unattractive* habit of cracking his knuckles; a pimply, *unattractive* child; an *unattractive* neighborhood, with rundown transient hotels and squalid walk-up flats. A person or thing considered *unattractive* is not necessarily *ugly*. Whereas *ugly* usually implies inherent form or nature, *unattractive* may refer to a superficial or temporary aspect or condition: an *unattractive* window display; He considered Byzantine architecture *ugly*.

Homely and *plain* usually apply specifically to facial appearance, and since women are commonly judged on the basis of personal beauty, these terms, as well as *unattractive*, are more often applied to women than men. Indeed, when a man is far from handsome no one hesitates to call him *ugly*, because the word's force seems masculine in strength, and few men have such a great stake in their looks that they would regard *ugly* as shocking or excessive, especially when the word is applied to someone else. But to call a woman *ugly* is like calling a man pretty; it can hardly be taken as other than a deliberate insult.

Unsightly means offensive to the sight, and is most often used to describe an aspect rather than a person: Johnson made an *unsightly* appearance in his tiny, ill-fitting wig and loose black breeches; shampoos designed to rid one of *unsightly* dandruff. *Unsightly* suggests more elegant standards than the other words discussed here; it has a prim quality that implies a failure to measure up to some standard of visual decency, decorum, or propriety. It does not indicate ugliness as such, but rather the visual pain of observing a breach of taste or manners: an *unsightly* stain on his tie. See GRUESOME.

Antonyms: attractive, BEAUTIFUL.

unbelief

disbelief
incredulity

These words are comparable in that they each denote a chronic tendency or temporary disposition to withhold belief. **Unbelief** refers to the absence of positive belief, especially the lack of belief in God and any of the religious faiths based on a belief in God. It, more than the other two words in this group, suggests a chronic mental quality rather than a particular instance of doubt: the impossibility of trying to harmonize the *unbelief* of an atheist and the conviction of a Catholic dogmatist. In theological usage, *unbelief* has condemnatory force, since it implies the willful rejection of manifest truth.

Disbelief refers to a positive conviction that a particular act, statement, doctrine, etc., is untrue, even in the face of its asserted validity. It hints at a one-time or temporary rejection instead of a continuously doubting state of mind: so committed to his point of view that he dismissed with *disbelief* all evidence of his error; A look of *disbelief* replaced the smile on his face.

Incredulity is a disinclination to accept as true whatever has been suggested as such; it is based on skepticism and a disposition to criticize or object. The word indicates a set frame of mind more than does *disbelief*, but less so than *unbelief*: extravagant claims for a product that were met with *incredulity* by a knowledgeable group of buyers. See DOUBT, DOUBTFUL, SKEPTIC.

Antonyms: credulity, OPINION, RELIGION.

unethical

amoral
immoral
nonmoral
unmoral
unprincipled
unscrupulous

All these words can apply to acts that go against the codes which society sets up to regulate social behavior. **Unethical** in its generality has the widest range of uses, applying particularly to any act that harms another person: *unethical* campaign practices such as bribery, appeals to bigotry, and anonymous pamphleteering. The word has a popular connotation, as well, that suggests a milder sort of breach, one that is unfair but not so apparently harmful to someone: insisting that it was *unethical* to curry favor with an instructor. By contrast, **immoral**, at its most general, can point to much more grave or serious harm: believing that it was *immoral* to sanction violence in the midst of ghetto unrest. Here, *unethical* would seem a hair-splitting way of typifying the action under discussion. In popular usage, *immoral* more concretely points to sexual misbehavior: parents so hopelessly old-fashioned and puritanical that they forbade dancing to their children as an *immoral* activity. *Immoral*, of course, can be applied like *unethical* to whatever one disapproves of: sects that view movies and dancing as *immoral*.

Unscrupulous and **unprincipled** both apply to people willing to do anything for their own gain, regardless of whom they harm. *Unscrupulous* is the less condemning of the two, suggesting someone who would commit any venial breach of taste, conduct, or manners to advance himself, though perhaps stopping short of anything outright illegal or at least anything that would get him into trouble: an *unscrupulous* office manager who would betray any confidence in his vain hope of ingratiating himself with the front office. *Unprincipled*, by contrast, suggests an even more rapacious attitude: an *unprincipled* dope peddler who made a fortune by ruining hundreds of lives.

Amoral points to behavior that is at variance with society's codes of behavior because of ignorance, indifference, or a more or less principled rejection of these values: the *amoral* lives of new bohemians who see old values as nothing more than institutionalized cruelty. **Unmoral** and **nonmoral** mean not within the realm of morality. [A baby is *unmoral*; Meteorology is a *nonmoral* study.] See DEPRAVED, SIN, WRONGDOING.
Antonyms: MORAL, *principled, scrupulous.*

uninvolved

apathetic
bored
indifferent
unconcerned
unmoved

These words suggest a lack of participation in an activity, or a lack of sympathy for it. **Uninvolved** is the most general as well as the most neutral in tone. It suggests an attitude of standing apart from an activity as well as from its benefits or consequences: preferring to remain *uninvolved* in the counterfeiting scheme; seeking Negro jurors *uninvolved* in the civil-rights struggle. One may have strong feelings about an activity but choose to be *uninvolved* because of fear or other pressures. **Unconcerned**, however, stresses lack of interest or sympathy: those citizens totally *unconcerned* by the deepening missile crisis. The word may even suggest carefree abandon: blithely *unconcerned* about the piling up of his debts.

Indifferent and **unmoved** are intensifications of *unconcerned*, suggesting a complete lack of feeling. *Indifferent* might especially apply to an uncaring attitude about the outcome of something when faced with two or more alternatives: equally *indifferent* to every entrée on the menu. It can also suggest a lack of response to an emotional appeal: *indifferent* to his passionate advances. *Unmoved* is an intensification of this last sense of *indifferent*, referring particularly to a situation designed specifically to elicit a given reaction: a maudlin play that left me completely *unmoved*. The word also suggests a refusal to perform a suggested action: a pep talk on enlisting that left the team *unmoved*.

Apathetic and **bored** suggest even more resistance to arousal than *unmoved*. *Apathetic* suggests a general lethargy or dullness of feeling in a person or a group: teen-agers awakening from an *apathetic* acceptance of injustice and prejudice. *Bored* is more narrowly specific in meaning, suggesting an *unmoved* response to a particular event; the word does not necessarily imply the inactivity of *apathetic*: *bored* and restless children; members of the audience so *bored* by the tedious play that many left before the first-act curtain. See ALOOF, DISINTERESTED.

Antonyms: concerned, engaged, interested, moved.

These words all refer to the bringing or coming together of several different elements to form a whole. **Unite**, stemming from Latin *unus*, meaning one, emphasizes the completeness of the process and the singleness of the resulting entity: to *unite* forces to overcome a common enemy; to *unite* two families in marriage. **Combine** means to bring together into close union; it is more general in application than *unite*, and does not emphasize so strongly the completeness of the process of coming together; to *combine* military forces, for example, would not exclude the possibility of each force's retaining a separate command, but to *unite* forces would imply the formation of a single force under one command. *Combine* is used in a wide variety of contexts. [To succeed as an artist one must *combine* talent and discipline; To get gray, one *combines* black and white.] Thus *combine* may suggest mixing or compounding, a connotation lacking in *unite*. **Blend**, even more strongly than *combine*, suggests a mingling of different elements; unlike *combine*, it specifically refers to the obscuring or harmonizing of various components: to *blend* modern and medieval architecture; to *blend* sugar and egg whites to make a meringue. **Merge**, like *blend*, suggests the loss of separate identity of ingredients, but does not imply the physical act of mixing or mingling together different elements: The two railroad companies *merged* to cut costs.

Join, the broadest term of this group, can mean to become part of, to bring together or connect, or to put together in close contact: The path *joins* the road; to *join* two wires; to *join* hands. **Fuse** means to *join* by or as if by melting together. Whereas *fused* wires, therefore, are connected by being melted together, *joined* wires might be attached with solder or by simply being intertwined. *Fuse* in other contexts implies a solid, lasting connection: The feeling of persecution and a sense of defeat became *fused* in his mind. **Coalesce** suggests a gradual or natural growing or coming together, as the segments of a broken bone. [The operation set the bones in position to *coalesce*; The sections of a baby's skull are not fully *joined*, but *coalesce* after a few years.] In extended senses *coalesce* suggests two separate courses that gradually *merge* into one: The idea of nationalism and the traditional American mistrust of foreigners *coalesced* to form a policy of isolation. See CONNECT, GATHER, MIXTURE.

Antonyms: SCATTER.

These words are used to describe someone or something that differs from the ordinary or the usual. That which is **unparalleled** is different in that it has no parallel or equal; it is unmatched. It suggests not so much a uniqueness of kind as an overwhelming superiority or quantity: his *unparalleled* achievements in the field of astrophysics. That which is **special** has some distinguishing or individualizing characteristic: These machines are all identical in their surface design but each one is *special*

unite

blend
coalesce
combine
fuse
join
merge

unparalleled

extraordinary
singular
special

in its interior construction. Something *special* might be designed for or concerned with a specific purpose: The hospital has over fifty *special* diets for different kinds of illnesses. *Special* can mean peculiar or even unique: Each problem that crosses my desk is *special*. It is often used to refer to the exceptional in amount or degree: a *special* fondness for French cooking. *Special* is the most comprehensive term in this group; anything described by one of the other words could certainly be called *special* as well. **Extraordinary** means greatly beyond the ordinary or usual. It is a neutral word that can function in either a complimentary or a critical description: *extraordinary* kindness; *extraordinary* wickedness. It can also, like *special*, be used to refer to something that is employed for a specific purpose: an envoy *extraordinary*. **Singular** has a wide range of meaning. In the most precise usage, it implies that whatever is being described is the only one of its type: a phenomenon *singular* in the history of this experiment. In an extension of this sense which is less limited in application, *singular* refers to the uncommon, the rare, or the *extraordinary*: a woman of *singular* grace and charm. Finally, *singular* has to do with the kind of difference from the usual that is characterized as odd or eccentric: It is difficult to excuse her *singular* behavior at the funeral. See BIZARRE, ECCENTRICITY, QUEER, UNUSUAL.

Antonyms: GENERAL, NORMAL, USUAL.

unruly

intractable
recalcitrant
refractory
restive
uncontrollable
ungovernable
unmanageable
wayward

These adjectives apply to persons or things that rebel against restraint or defy control. **Unruly** stresses a boisterous quality — the tendency to burst free from restrictions or to get out of line. An *unruly* person or thing is disposed to resist discipline but can be brought under control: *unruly* boys at a party creating a momentary disturbance; to plaster down an *unruly* cowlick. **Wayward** goes beyond *unruly* in indicating willfulness and immorality. It suggests a straying from the straight and narrow, and sometimes connotes potential delinquency or sexual promiscuity: a home for *wayward* girls. Like *unruly*, *wayward* may be applied to a piece of hair that will not stay in place: a *wayward* curl.

Restive emphasizes impatience and irritation — a chafing under restraint and a struggle against coercion. A *restive* horse impatiently resists control or struggles to break free. A *restive* area is not disposed to "rest" but is ready to rebel: a *restive* ghetto, ripe for a riot. By extension, *restive* has come to mean restless or fidgety, discontented with the status quo: an inattentive, *restive* audience, impatiently waiting for intermission.

Intractable, refractory, and **recalcitrant** are more formal words that indicate an obstinate refusal to yield. An *intractable* person or animal stubbornly resists all efforts to lead, guide, restrain, or influence him: The boy was shy and quiet, yet strong-willed, independent, and *intractable*, as stubborn as a mule. Applied to things, *intractable* means difficult to manipulate, treat, or work: The source material was *intractable* and there was little the librettist could do with it. *Refractory* implies more activity of resistance, suggesting a positive rather than a passive disobedience. *Refractory* persons are both obstinate and rebellious, determined to protest the dictates of authority: a *refractory* child, doing just the opposite of what he is told. A *refractory* metal or ore is one that resists heat or ordinary methods of reduction. [Fire clay is a *refractory* material used to make crucibles and furnace linings; it resists the highest temperatures of the blast furnace without melting.] *Recalcitrant* comes from Latin roots meaning to kick back. It is close in meaning to *refractory* but more extreme, implying uncompromising resistance or a disposition to be defiant: A *recalcitrant* student who wanted to drop out of school not only refused to obey the rules but threatened a teacher with violence.

Unmanageable, **ungovernable**, and **uncontrollable** apply to things that are hard to handle or impossible to control. An *unmanageable* person or animal will not submit to guidance or direction. An *unmanageable* thing is incapable of being handled or dealt with successfully: a heavy but not *unmanageable* work load. That which is *ungovernable* cannot be regulated by rules or agreed-upon restraints; it defies any attempt to tame it or to bring it under orderly, rational control: an *ungovernable* land, beset with warring factions and internal strife. *Ungovernable* often suggests a loss or lack of self-control: an *ungovernable* temper. *Uncontrollable* is the most extreme of these words. It applies to that which goes beyond the bounds of control, as by being involuntary, instinctive, irrepressible, or wild: *uncontrollable* muscular spasms; *uncontrollable* anger. See LOUD, MISCHIEVOUS, STUBBORN.

Antonyms: ADAPTABLE, COMPLIANT, DOCILE.

These words refer to an uneasy or exasperated response to external factors or causes. **Unsettle** is the least intense of these, suggesting someone who has been unnerved or vaguely disquieted by something; the cause may be a specific distraction or a more indefinable mood or atmosphere: *unsettled* by the constant wailing of an infant in the next apartment; *unsettled* by the institutionalized coldness of the office. Even in the active voice, the word does not suggest an intentional attempt to unnerve someone so much as a subjective or intuitive response to an existing state of affairs. One would not be likely to say: He deliberately *unsettled* me. But one could say: Oddly enough, his presence in the room *unsettled* me. In contrast, **annoy** can indicate both an intentional disturbance and a disturbed response. [Why do you insist on *annoying* her?; I was *annoyed* by the way he kept mumbling something over and over to himself.] In any case, *annoy* indicates a greater degree of emotional upset than does *unsettle*: His whistling *unsettles* me a bit, but it doesn't really *annoy* me all that much.

Irritate suggests a repeated, abrasive action that *annoys* one by draining him of patience or good humor; nothing is too trivial to *irritate*, if the temper of the observer is highly strung or petulant: Her habit of tapping her fingers on the chair while she read the newspapers *irritated* him. **Nettle** suggests being temporarily aroused to anger or pique, often because of something considered damaging to one's self-respect: *nettled* by her willful disregard of his advice; *nettled* by the critic's casual rejection of his arguments. *Nettle* often implies, as in these examples, a sense of indignation occasioned by a real or fancied slight.

Rile is in every way an intensification of *annoy*, but it is also more informal; it might, in fact, be considered dialect by some, although Western movies have made it widely familiar. Also, the word emphasizes response without suggesting an intended cause: *riled* by his unthinking rudeness; I didn't mean to get you all *riled* up over nothing. **Put out** is related more closely to *unsettle* than to the previous pair. It points to the vague dissatisfaction of someone who has been displeased, inconvenienced, or disappointed. [He was *put out* by the way everyone at the party ignored him; She tried to get her work done but was terribly *put out* by the constant interruptions of the workmen; Only a sullen silence suggested how *put out* he was over not getting his promotion.] As in the

unsettle

annoy
irritate
nettle
put out
rile

last example, the word can imply a minimal, passive, or withdrawn response; this may also be true for *unsettled*. In contrast, *annoy* and *irritate* suggest a more agitated or noticeable response. In the active voice, *put out* refers more exclusively to inconvenience: I hope we haven't *put* you *out* by staying so late. See ANGER (v.), BOTHER, INCITE, OUTRAGE, UPSET.

Antonyms: calm, relax, relieve, soothe, tranquilize.

unusual

exceptional
offbeat
rare
unique

That which is **unusual** is something that varies from the ordinary, the expected, or the commonplace: It was an *unusual* day for summer, damp and chilly, with a biting wind more reminiscent of January than July. *Unusual* is a neutral word; it can be used to describe something thought of as good or something thought of as bad: a gift expressing her *unusual* generosity; an act that evidenced *unusual* malice. **Exceptional**, like *unusual*, describes something that departs from the usual; it too can function in either a complimentary or a critical description. [He treated his employees with *exceptional* kindness; She showed an *exceptional* disregard for detail in her work.] *Exceptional*, however, in a way that *unusual* cannot, may suggest excellence or superiority. If one speaks of a singer's *unusual* voice, there is no implicit indication of quality. But a reference to a singer's *exceptional* voice would almost certainly be a compliment. *Exceptional* is also applied to children who are mentally or physically gifted, as well as to those who are retarded to the extent that they require special education and psychological aid.

One says of a thing that it is **rare** when one wishes to describe it as something that is found or occurs but seldom, whether or not it once was common: *rare* moments of quiet in the midst of a loud debate; a *rare* out-of-print book which is the only one remaining out of thousands that were printed. That which is *rare* may be ordinary, but it is usually *exceptional*, and the word can be employed to identify something that is superlative or excellent: a gem of *rare* beauty and worth; a *rare* ability for handling personnel problems. While something that is *rare* is infrequent of its kind, something that is **unique** is alone of its kind. [Great poems are *rare*; "Paradise Lost" is *unique*.] *Unique* was once limited in definition to this sense, but usage has extended its meaning to *unusual* or *rare*, often preceded by a qualifier: a *unique* opportunity; a rather *unique* situation.

Offbeat is slang and means differing from the usual. It implies a departure from the familiar, the orthodox, or the conventional, and so it is often used to describe something of which the speaker or writer is critical: a really bad novel, full of violence and *offbeat* sex. However, since the *unusual*, the unorthodox, and the unconventional are often the forerunners of popular fashions and trends, *offbeat* may be complimentary in tone in some contexts: Her boutique specializes in *offbeat* clothes and has become one of the most talked-about fashion spots in town. See OCCASIONAL, UNPARALLELED.

Antonyms: established, GENERAL, INVARIABLE, NORMAL, USUAL.

unwilling

averse
disinclined
hesitant

These words indicate the refusal to assent to something or a cautious, grudging, or indecisive attitude toward it. **Unwilling** points to a flat rejection and is the most forcefully negative of these words: *unwilling* to lend him the money and *unwilling* even to discuss it. The word can also indicate someone involved in something contrary to his wishes: the ancient mariner's *unwilling* listener. **Loath** (or, as it is also spelled, *loth*) can be taken as having negative force equal to or surpassing that of *unwilling*; this may stem from overtones supplied by its near relative, loathe: *loath* to do anything detrimental to her reputation. In common use, however, the word can suggest resistance to or distaste for something without implying the adamant refusal inherent in *unwilling*: *loath* to go to the opera, but doing so to please his wife. This is especially true where one feels compelled to do something whether one likes it or not: *loath* to acquit the man, though the lack of conclusive evidence left the judge no other choice. To illustrate the contrast with *unwilling*, it can be said that most draftees are probably *loath* to enter military service, but only pacifists are *unwilling* to be inducted. On the other hand, one might not be *loath* to do something and yet remain *unwilling*: keenly interested in the assignment but *unwilling* to do it for so little money. **Averse** suggests distaste that may be innate but that in any case is so strong as to be unalterable; this deep-seated distaste, however, may or may not result in an *unwilling* response: so *averse* to crowds that he habitually went to any lengths to avoid them; *averse* to the idea of his wife's working, but agreeing to it because of their desperate financial situation. **Reluctant** may sometimes suggest firm resistance to something: insisting that he was and would remain *reluctant* to vote for any bill liberalizing the divorce law. More often the word indicates a grudging or provisional consent: finally giving his *reluctant* permission to test the drug on human beings, but only under a program of strict control. **Disinclined** is similar to *loath* and even more to *averse* in suggesting distaste for something. It suggests a weaker resistance than these words, however, and may point to a cautious or prudent attitude that is habitual or is based on past experience or present evidence: *disinclined* to opt for an all-out attack on the enemy. *Disinclined* is alone in this set of words in applying to opinions, views, or judgments as well as to consent or action: *disinclined* to believe the man's story; *disinclined* to take the reports of flying saucers very seriously. Sometimes the word is used as a circumlocution for a more direct word of disapproval. **Hesitant** suggests the least resistance of any of these words. It can, in fact, refer merely to indecisiveness or immobilizing cautiousness: so many confusing alternatives that he was *hesitant* to commit himself to any one choice of action. See OPPOSED, STUBBORN.

Antonyms: EAGER, FAVORABLE, *inclined*, READY, WILLFUL.

These adjectives are low-keyed, unemotional words used to call the wisdom of actions or decisions into question without giving offense. All are politely or mildly critical, emphasizing the absence of a positive attribute rather than the presence of a negative one. And all may be used either to express disapproval or to convey a word of warning. **Unwise** is the most general word and may serve as a less precise substitute for the others. When used in expressing an opinion on something already done, it implies a preferable alternative that would have been considered wiser: an *unwise* choice. When used as an advisory or precautionary word, it may sometimes imply considerable risk and possible danger: To make speculative investments without adequate savings is *unwise*. **Injudicious** is a milder word, suggesting not so much a lack of basic good judgment as a failure to exercise the best possible judgment in a certain sensitive situation. Where *unwise* may refer to something foolish or risky, what is *injudicious* is simply ill-considered or indiscreet. [The official made some hasty, *injudicious* remarks; Her *injudicious* eagerness to buy the antique encouraged the dealer to raise the price.] *Unwise*, *injudicious*, and **imprudent** all point to a lack of foresight, a failure to think ahead and anticipate consequences. But *imprudent* emphasizes a lack of discretion, implying that greater precautions might be taken or that greater circumspection might be shown. [The doctor thought it *imprudent* for his patient to take a long trip; The teacher's colleagues felt that it was *imprudent* of him to overpraise his students.]

Ill-advised is perhaps the least offensive of these inoffensive terms. It tends to shift responsibility or blame from the person himself to his actual or supposed advisors. Where *unwise* might imply a personal failure in judgment, *ill-advised* suggests that a person was acting or that a project was undertaken in accordance with bad or inadequate advice. [You were *ill-advised* to sell the stock, as it has good growth potential; an *ill-advised* strike that forced their employer to go out of business] *Ill-advised* may also be used to warn someone against taking action without getting enough sound advice beforehand: It would be *ill-advised* to abandon the project now before all of the preliminary reports are in. See ABSURD, HEEDLESS, RECKLESS, STUPID.

Antonyms: CAREFUL, CAUTIOUS, CONSIDERATE, *judicious, provident,* SENSIBLE.

uphold

back
champion
defend
maintain
support
sustain

These words are concerned with protection or assistance given in the face of difficulty or hostility. **Uphold** specifically suggests an active attempt to prevent something from giving way or from falling into danger or neglect: an innate pride that *upheld* her during the worst of the crisis; *upholding* the sport's tradition of fair play. **Back** can also apply to the protection of principles or ideas, but it is very often used in a more personal way, suggesting that one person stands behind or subscribes to the efforts of another who has exposed himself to danger or disapproval. The word can therefore suggest a more passive role than *uphold*: careless of his own safety in *upholding* the cause because he was confident that others in the community would silently *back* him up. *Back* may also specifically suggest the choosing of sides in a contest: voters who had *backed* the less popular candidate.

Defend and **champion** suggest action in the face of hostility. *Defend* is smaller in scope than *champion*, stressing the protection of a challenged right or position. The extent of the action taken, however, may be slight or great: *defending* her reputation with a well-placed word or two; *defending* his friends from injury by throwing himself on the falling grenade. *Champion* specifically stresses a more active, offensive role and may suggest taking the place of someone less able to act. It may also suggest a single-handed offense, as opposed to most of these other words which imply that many could conceivably cooperate in protection or assistance: the only newspaper that insistently *championed* the right of the convicted man to a new trial.

Support and **sustain** are like *back* in suggesting the assistance of something that is in an exposed or endangered position. *Back*, however, suggests more determination than either of these words in themselves. *Support* states the mere fact of aid or favor, without any implications of resoluteness or permanent commitment: *supporting* his candidacy in the primary but not in the general election. Unlike *back* and *support, sustain* cannot apply to the choosing of sides in a contest. It can go beyond *support* in other situations to suggest a continuing loyalty: *sustaining* his interest in their plight over more than a decade. In another use, it can suggest the granting of a point or the giving of peripheral aid, without taking sides on larger issues: asking the judge to *sustain* his objection concerning the tactics of his opponent; friends who helped to *sustain* his morale during exam week by popping in often with coffee and sandwiches.

Maintain may suggest resoluteness in the context of advocacy: *maintaining* that the boy's confession had been coerced. In other situations, it may suggest continuing *support* that may be, however, minimal or less than adequate: The absent father *maintained* the payments over many years, but they were never enough to *sustain* the whole family. See ENCOURAGE.

Antonyms: betray, DESTROY, *drop.*

These words all denote some kind of effort to defy or overthrow a government or other form of authority. **Uprising** is the broadest term and may be substituted in a general way for any of the other words. Specifically it may refer to a minor or unsuccessful act of popular resistance: an abortive *uprising* of the slaves on a Georgia plantation. It can also apply to those localized signs of unrest and discontent which indicate the imminence of widespread conflict: the first short-lived *uprisings* in Germany and Austria which led to the Peasants' War of 1524–1526. **Rebellion** is an armed resistance or *uprising* against a government, often on a large scale and frequently doomed to failure. If successful, however, a *rebellion* may become a full-scale **revolution**, which involves the overthrow and replacement of a government or political system by those who are governed. In a wider sense, *revolution* can denote any extensive or drastic change in economic institutions, in ideas, or in mores: the Industrial *Revolution* that began in England in the mid-18th century; the *revolution* in manners and morals that followed World War I.

Insurrection points to an organized effort to seize power, especially political power, while **revolt** emphasizes protest against oppression or other intolerable conditions. Unlike *insurrection*, *revolt* has the extended meaning of any refusal to go on tolerating an allegiance or a powerful authority: a *revolt* within an established church.

Insurgency has almost the same meaning as *insurrection*, but it usually designates a better organized kind of *revolt*, and is often used today to refer to revolutionary activity which is aided by foreign powers. **Counterinsurgency**, a word most common in current news and propaganda media, is any measure designed to combat revolutionary activity or guerrilla warfare.

If an *uprising, insurrection,* or *insurgency* continues for a long period of time without being effectively countered, the country of its origin may be said to be in a state of **civil war**. *Civil war* is armed conflict openly carried on between parties or sections of the same country, whether or not both parties involved are legally recognized as belligerents. In the usual sense of the term, *civil war* involves factions (generally two), each of whom is trying to gain control of the existing central government. In this way, a *civil war* differs from a *revolution* in that the emphasis is not on overthrowing a regime. The American *Civil War* differs from the above concept in that the South seceded and wished to become a separate nation. See CONSPIRACY, CRIME, INTRIGUE, LAWLESSNESS.

These words refer to acts that cause or result in emotional upheaval. **Upset** is the most general and the least formal, stressing a complete or sudden loss of mental equilibrium, although this may or may not be accompanied by an outward show: finally admitting that she was deeply

uprising

civil war
counterinsurgency
insurgency
insurrection
rebellion
revolt
revolution

upset

agitate

upset
(continued)

demoralize
disconcert
disturb
exacerbate

upset; ridicule deliberately designed to *upset* him. Usually the word suggests a temporary state of mind from which one can normally recover in time: *upset* all morning until her usual sense of calm returned. Although *upset* can imply a more permanent derangement, **disturb** is now more frequently used in this sense: juvenile delinquents who are emotionally *disturbed*. In this case, *disturb* suggests a mental disorder that may verge on psychosis. When the word refers to a momentary upheaval, it suggests a milder anguish than *upset* and possibly one more gradual in onset. It might also imply a deepening uneasiness difficult to objectify: She was growing more and more *disturbed* that he had neither arrived nor phoned to explain the delay. **Agitate** is more like *upset* in suggesting a sudden upheaval, but it contrasts with the latter in specifically suggesting an unavoidable outward show of one's turbulent state of mind: so *agitated* that he stalked about the room muttering incoherently to himself. On the other hand, the turbulence may be the intensified expression of a chronic nervousness rather than the result of deep emotional shock.

Demoralize and **disconcert** indicate a less intense upheaval than the foregoing words, suggesting that something has reduced one to a state of complete ineffectiveness. Of the two, *disconcert* more nearly resembles *upset* in implying a sudden onset accompanied by no necessary outward show, but resulting momentarily in mental disarray and confusion. In contrast, it most often suggests an upheaval that results from some specific confrontation: *disconcerted* by the salesclerk's snide remarks about her taste. Although *demoralize* may indicate the slightest emotional upheaval of all these words, it nonetheless suggests a gradual and long-term exhaustion or sapping of the will because of a hopelessly snarled situation or the unremitting pressure of hurtful hostility: bureaucratic inefficiency and wasted effort that had thoroughly *demoralized* the whole staff; *demoralized* and embittered by the platoon sergeant's constant harassment.

Exacerbate refers to the worsening of anger, irritability, pain, etc. In this context, it can function as an intensification of any of these other words: first *upsetting* her with the news that he was leaving her and then *exacerbating* the hurt by proceeding to call her names. *Exacerbate* may also mean simply to exasperate or irritate, but this usage tends to sound informal. See COMPLAIN, CONFUSE, DISTRESS, EMBARRASSMENT, ENRAGE, FRENZY, OUTRAGE, PUZZLE, SHAME, SURPRISED, UNSETTLE.

Antonyms: calm, relax, relieve, soothe.

up-to-date

fresh
modernistic
new
novel

These words are alike in applying to conditions, events, or things of the present time. **Up-to-date** usually means keeping abreast of recent developments or accurately reflecting the modern world: an *up-to-date* encyclopedia, revised thoroughly every year. It can also mean being in step with contemporary life, and in this sense is the opposite of old-fashioned: Get with it, be *up-to-date*, smoke Whamo for that cool taste. But note that *up-to-date* does not necessarily mean fashionable in the sense of stylish: Though the woman's suit was hardly a Paris original, it was well-tailored and *up-to-date*.

Fresh emphasizes originality and the absence of prejudice or preconceived notions: The president convened a high-level committee of diplomats to take a *fresh* look at our foreign policy in southeast Asia. A *fresh* look may result in the confirmation of old policies; it is nevertheless **new**, in the sense that the old assumptions and reasons have been critically reexamined from a disinterested point of view.

New is the broadest term of this group. It may mean keeping up with the times, being contemporary, and in this sense it is synonymous with *up-to-date*: a *new* (or *up-to-date*) method of testing for vocational aptitudes. But perhaps its most common meaning refers to being recent or original; here it is applied to something just invented, created, or developed: a *new* can opener, based upon an entirely different mechanical principle; a *new* book, just published. In this sense the phrase "brand new" is sometimes used to emphasize the recentness of the action referred to, e.g., A brand new pair of shoes refers to a pair of shoes which has just been bought. *New* is also used synonymously with *fresh* in the sense of unprejudiced: a *new* (or *fresh*) approach to the problem of urban poverty.

Novel is close to *new* but stresses the ingenuity and difference that characterize new things. A *new* idea may be original, but a *novel* idea is sparkling and ingenious. *Novel* suggests more originality and creativity than any of the other words here considered, and it is therefore sometimes used with a degree of mistrust or with a suggestion of impracticality. [It was a *novel* arrangement, but it just didn't work; She just purchased a *novel* device for slicing onions.]

Modernistic means tending to be modern or giving the appearance of being modern in style, as furniture, architecture, or art. It may be used neutrally, but often connotes superficiality and sometimes cheapness: a *modernistic* painting that demonstrates no real understanding of contemporary art. In connotation the word is close to streamlined; it often suggests the deliberate intention to be modern rather than the simple fact of being modern. See MODERN.

Antonyms: ANCIENT, OLD, OLD-FASHIONED, *timeworn*.

---

urbane

cultivated
genteel
sophisticated
suave

These words all deal with qualities of mind or manner characteristic of well-bred, worldly-wise, or educated people. Virtually every one of the words here discussed is sometimes used in a derogatory, disapproving, or humorously condescending way.

Urbane means having a refined or polished manner, such as befits one who is well-traveled, well-bred, or long habituated to the society of **cultivated** people; an *urbane* conversation about continental cuisines. *Cultivated* indicates a sophistication acquired through formal education or purposeful experience: a *cultivated* appreciation of abstract art. *Cultivated* speech is educated speech, as distinguished from the speech of the ignorant, untutored, or illiterate. When applied to people, *cultivated* often stresses knowledge and the appreciation of the arts, whereas **sophisticated** can suggest superficiality, indicating overly polished manners and sometimes a skeptical or jaded attitude toward life: Too *sophisticated* for plain fare, she frowned in disgust at the simple food humbly placed before her. *Cultivated*, however, can also be used derogatorily to mean contrived or affected: a carefully *cultivated* British accent designed to impress her friends.

When *sophisticated* is positive in tone, it points to advanced perception and an appreciation of culture which comes with study or experience; in such contexts even the toughness or worldly-wise quality the word connotes may be viewed with admiration: Although the play was considered strong stuff by small-town audiences, the *sophisticated* New York playgoers found it weak tea, and the show closed in three weeks. When applied to things, *sophisticated* often means using advanced and complicated technological techniques: a very *sophisticated* anti-missile missile defense system. In its association with scientific achievement, the word acquires a wholly positive character; there are few things more highly valued in twentieth-century America than modern technology.

Genteel conveys derogatory or humorously condescending connotations in most uses today. *Genteel* formerly meant simply well-bred or refined, but nowadays it usually means too consciously *cultivated*. To call a person or his manners *genteel* implies that he is defensive and unsure of his own social background or status, and therefore so anxious to prove himself *cultivated* that he succeeds only in making himself pretentious or ridiculous: Her *genteel* manners made it impossible for her to grasp a coffee cup without elevating two fingers, even though the coffee frequently sloshed out onto the floor as a result. Buildings are sometimes described as being "shabby *genteel*," indicating a ludicrous incongruity between the once splendid decor and its present, poorly maintained condition or old-fashioned style. The personification suggests someone who has seen better days and is now trying with only moderate success to appear respectable.

Suave means smoothly pleasant or ingratiating; it may be purely descriptive and quite neutral in tone, and in this sense is close to *urbane* in meaning: a *suave* and masterfully executed bow. But it may be associated with a surface politeness, an oily manner, and glibness in speech: At first she found him attractive and *suave*, but she soon recognized his phoniness and basic vulgarity. See BLITHE, EXQUISITE, GREGARIOUS, POLITE.

Antonyms: BRUSQUE, GAUCHE, NAIVE, VULGAR.

use

consume
employ
expend
utilize

These words refer to putting something to work, with or without altering it in the process. **Use** is the most general and informal of these, and there is no context within which it would not be suitable for expressing this activity, whether or not the object involved is altered in the process: *using* a dictionary as a check against his spelling; *using* about a ton of coal a month. When the word is applied to a person, however, a strong note of disapproval for the act is evident: the egotist who *uses* other people as if they were doormats. When the word occurs with the preposition "up," the word refers to the total depletion of the thing in question and often suggests waste or extravagance: *using* up the last of his water supply; *using* up his gifts in a brief burst of youthful profligacy.

Consume and **expend** emphasize the alteration or depletion of the thing *used*. At their most concrete, however, the words contrast sharply in that *consume* refers to the taking in of something, as in eating, and *expend* refers to the paying out of something: asking how many bushels of fodder his herd *consumed* in a day; *expending* no more than a quarter of your earnings in rent. *Consume* particularly emphasizes the total depletion or destruction of something: the amount of trees *consumed* to make the newsprint in one Sunday edition of your newspaper. Destruction need not be the word's main point, however: the energy *consumed* in debating the project. Related uses cast light on the word's connotations in this context: ravenously *consuming* a full four-course dinner; a building *consumed* by fire; *consumed* with envy. None of these connotations of haste, waste, or destruction is present in one of the most popular meanings of the word, referring in business or economic parlance to the purchase or turn-over (and presumably *use*) of goods: a more sophisticated public that *consumes* an ever greater variety of products. Beyond its references to depletion or the paying out of money, *expend* can point, like *consume*, to the using of nonmaterial things: *expending* a good deal of effort on the term paper. In the parlance of military supply, it functions exactly like *consume* in its business sense, but in this case the word suggests the actual *using* up, wearing out, or destruction of perishable military goods: not required to account for helmet straps and other items that are considered *expended* upon issue; *expended* rounds of ammunition.

Employ has a legitimate use to refer to the *using* of hired workers of any kind: a corporation that *employs* many thousands of people. In other situations, it can seem a needless substitute for *use*, perhaps resorted to in the hope that its greater formality will lend status or objectivity: *employing* a spatula to turn the eggs. Here, the clarity and brevity of *use* would prevent pretentiousness. Similarly, *use* can in every instance be substituted for **utilize,** with an invariable gain in directness and clarity. But like *employ*, *utilize* has a distinct sphere of meaning all its own, referring to the conversion necessary to make something useful, a meaning now largely ignored: underwater oil deposits that had no value before science taught us how to *utilize* them. More often, the word appears indiscriminately in place of *use*: *utilizing* a chafing dish to serve the casserole. See WEAKEN.

Antonyms: CONSERVE, *waste.*

These words are used to describe things that happen in the everyday course of events or are accepted by most people as normal and natural rather than as novel or strange. **Usual** is applied to whatever recurs frequently, steadily, or with relative constancy. Unlike some of these words, it may be applied to natural happenings as well as to occurrences based on the customs of a community or the habits of an individual. [Thunder is the *usual* sign of an approaching storm; Flowers are the *usual* gift for a convalescent; Playing chess is his *usual* pastime.]

Regular, ordinary, and **common**, in the sense of *usual*, have equally wide applications. *Regular* emphasizes a conformity to the established or natural order of things. [Overtime work is work in excess of the *regular* weekly schedule; Most of us thrive on *regular* meals and *regular* hours of rest.] *Ordinary*, implying such comformity less strongly, connotes an absence of exceptional or striking characteristics: An *ordinary* work day is eight hours. *Common* also emphasizes the unexceptional, but may in some usages suggest somewhat less frequency than does *usual*: the *common* household accident of slipping in the bathtub; the *usual* congratulations one extends to the parents of a new baby.

Customary, habitual, wonted, accustomed, and **conventional** seldom refer to natural occurrences except metaphorically. In most cases they indicate what is *usual*. *Customary* is applied to something that characterizes a given community or person. [It is *customary* for Tibetans to put yak butter into their tea; It is *customary* for our family to sleep late on Sunday mornings.] *Habitual* refers to acts or qualities in individuals that have been strengthened by constantly repeated actions: a *habitual* chain-smoker; a *habitual* liar. *Wonted*, a word that now sounds bookish and quaint, emphasizes habituation, but is applied to both personal habits and to social customs when less stress is being laid on their fixity: returning home each evening at his *wonted* hour. *Accustomed* is often used in place of *customary* or in place of *wonted*, but suggests fixed custom less strongly than does *customary* and is less stilted than *wonted*. It often implies simply getting used to something: *accustomed* to reading the paper at breakfast each morning; her *accustomed* attitude of optimism. *Conventional* is the strongest of these words in suggesting the following of established custom or usage, and it emphasizes the general

usual

accustomed
common
conventional
customary
habitual
ordinary
regular
wonted

agreement accorded to it: It is *conventional* for men who are friends to shake hands when they meet on the street. See DAILY, GENERAL, MEDIOCRE, NORMAL, TRADITION.

Antonyms: OCCASIONAL, SPECIFIC, UNPARALLELED, UNUSUAL.

usurp

appropriate
arrogate
confiscate
pre-empt

These words are comparable in that they all mean to claim or take possession of something. To **usurp** is to seize and hold in possession something, such as a position or status that belongs to another person and to which one has no legal right, and to exercise the authority and enjoy the privileges which stem from such a position. *Usurp* pertains especially to the forcible seizure of kingly power: an upstart pretender trying to *usurp* the throne.

Appropriate, as here considered, denotes the lawful or unlawful acquisition for one's own use of something originally belonging to another or to no one in particular. Thus, a farmer may legitimately *appropriate* water for irrigation form streams running through his farm; if unscrupulous, he may also *appropriate* parts of his neighbors' land.

Arrogate means to claim, demand, or take that which belongs to another. It differs from the other words in this group in one particular way, that is in its suggestion of the overbearing or haughty manner which accompanies *arrogating*: a university chairman who *arrogated* the right of deciding how each person on his staff should set up his teaching program.

Confiscate means to *appropriate* by authority something that belongs to another, but not necessarily for one's own use: Customs officials have the right to *confiscate* goods being smuggled into their country.

Originally **pre-empt** referred to the securing of the right of purchase of public land. In general usage, *pre-empt* means to establish a prior claim to something which is sought by others: arriving early at the theater so as to *pre-empt* the best seats. See GRASP.

Antonyms: RELINQUISH.

utter

express
pronounce
voice

These verbs all refer to the communication of facts, thoughts, feelings, etc., especially by the medium of speech. **Utter** can apply to the making of any audible vocal sound, and is thus not confined to those disciplined sequences of sound called speech: to *utter* a cry of warning; to *utter* a scream of terror; to *utter* a loud oath. *Utter* often emphasizes the violence or suddenness of the sound produced, as in these examples. It may also apply to normal speech, but it is used only to describe or summarize discourse, not in direct or indirect quotations. [He *uttered* what we were all thinking; He *uttered* the opinion that not all men were equal in ability.] One would not say, however, "He *uttered*, 'I will go'," nor "He *uttered* that he would go." *Utter* may be used, as exemplified by the sentences in brackets above, to contrast speech with silence and to suggest a bold speaking out. In this sense the word is close to **pronounce** in meaning, but *pronounce* is more solemn in tone and more suitable to formal proceedings than ordinary discourse: The justice *pronounced* his opinion with a grave and impressive air; to *pronounce* judgment; to *pronounce* her guilty. Influenced by its phonetic sense of articulating sounds in producing speech, *pronounce* may suggest an orotund or dramatic manner of delivery.

Voice, more informal than either *pronounce* or *utter*, means to put into words, especially a feeling or opinion rather than facts or statements: to *voice* the suggestion that club members owing dues be suspended. *Voice* thus means literally to give voice to something thought or felt, and is synonymous to one sense of **express**, a much broader term: to *voice* (or *express*) an unpopular opinion. *Express*, however, is not limited to oral nor even to verbal communication; it may refer to any means of exposing feelings, ideas, etc. [a musical theme that *expresses* melancholy; Picasso's painting entitled *Guernica expresses* a profound horror of war; to *express* anger by frowning; The habitual dress and habits of hippies may be interpreted as *expressing* contempt for middle-class values.] See ASSERT, DECLARE, SAY, VERBAL, VOCAL CORDS.

V

These words all refer to conditions characterized by the absence of people or things. **Vacant** and **empty**, the most general in this sense, can both mean containing or holding nothing: a *vacant* lot; an *empty* hallway. But *vacant* is usually restricted to the absence of people occupying a place whereas *empty* has a much wider range of application, and may refer to anything that does not have the usual or proper contents. An *empty* theater may have a few people in it; a *vacant* theater, however, is one wholly without occupants and probably not in use. *Vacant* implies longer duration or a more settled state than does *empty*. A *vacant* apartment is one that is not presently occupied by tenants and is available for rent; an *empty* apartment is simply one that does not have people in it at a given time: Burglars broke into the *empty* apartment while the tenants were away on vacation. Both *vacant* and *empty* are used in extended senses that imply the lack of essential qualities. *Vacant* can mean uninspired, dull, vapid, or listless, and suggests a lack of intelligence or point: a *vacant* stare. *Empty* can mean hollow, meaningless, or bland, and suggests a lack of significance or substance: *empty* promises; *empty* dreams.

Unfilled and **open**, in the context of this comparison, are alike in meaning available or not taken: both refer to the absence of a person or persons from some specific position: The office manager's job is still *unfilled* (or *open*) after three months.

Unoccupied is like *vacant* in its reference to a state created by the absence of people, but does not so strongly suggest, as *vacant* does, that the absence of occupants is temporary: an old, *unoccupied* house alleged to be haunted.

Devoid, from the past participle of an obsolete word that meant to empty out, means emptied, not possessing, or destitute, and is used with "of": *Devoid* of hope, the shipwrecked sailors resigned themselves to the promise of never again seeing their loved ones. *Empty* can also be used in this way: The poem was *empty* of beauty, and without any moral grandeur. In this sense **bereft**, the past tense and past participle of *bereave*, is also commonly used as an adjective meaning deprived: *bereft* of joy. *Devoid* and *empty*, however, unlike *bereft*, are used to describe the absence of physical things: a lake *devoid* of fish owing to the pollution of the water; sidewalks *empty* of people.

Free, in the sense here considered, means cleared or *devoid* of something, and is used with "of" or "from": *free* from any taint of scandal; *free* of infection. See LACK.

Antonyms: filled, full, occupied, replete.

vacant

bereft
devoid
empty
free
open
unfilled
unoccupied

vague

dim
hazy
indefinite
indistinct
obscure

These words all refer to that which is not clear to the senses or to the mind. To be **vague** is to fail, whether intentionally or accidentally, to state precisely what one means or to make oneself clearly understood. [He had only *vague* memories of his early childhood; The senator was *vague* about his plans, saying only that he would not refuse to run again if nominated.]

Indefinite means not precisely defined or limited; **indeterminate** means not definite in extent, amount, or nature: *indefinite* frontiers; an illness with *indeterminate* symptoms. In short, *indefinite* means *vague*, but with the emphasis on blurred outlines or a lack of focus; that which is *indeterminate* may be quite definite, such as specific symptoms accompanying an illness that nevertheless give no clear indication as to the nature of the underlying disease. An *indeterminate* number may be definite, but simply cannot be known: An *indeterminate* number of rioters dispersed to their homes before the police could arrive.

Obscure, indistinct, hazy, and **dim** refer to various ways by which something is blurred or hidden. *Obscure*, the strongest word, may suggest a difficulty in perception caused by a murkiness of the atmosphere; or it may suggest a difficulty in understanding caused by the complex, abstruse, or ambiguous nature of the material presented. In either case the result gives only an *indistinct*, partial view of something still very much hidden from sight or sense: *obscure*, muffled sounds; an *obscure* outline; an *obscure* passage of the Bible. *Indistinct* emphasizes the faintness of the impression on the senses or mind as well as the blurred outlines of the whole; it is thus synonymous with one meaning of *vague*: *indistinct* (or *vague*) memories. *Hazy* and *dim* suggest different ways in which perception may be rendered *indistinct*. *Hazy* implies a glary atmosphere impenetrable to sight; *dim* points simply to darkness. Whereas *hazy* conveys a strong sense of confusion, uncertainty, and blurred impressions, *dim* stresses simply the difficulty of seeing or perceiving. [Though heavily sedated, she had a *dim* awareness of what was happening; His wife had only the *haziest* of notions about what he did on the job.] See DOUBTFUL, FOGGY, MYSTICAL.

Antonyms: CLEAR, DEFINITE, PLAIN, SENSIBLE.

valet

batman
flunky
lackey
orderly
servant

These words are comparable in that they all refer to someone who works for someone else, particularly in the capacity of a personal or household attendant. **Valet** denotes a man who performs such services as taking care of clothing and laundry for another man. A *valet* is often called a gentleman's gentleman, and this designation accurately reflects the true nature both of the man who is so employed and of the position itself. For although it is true that any man of means can employ another male to act as his *valet*, the traditional *valet* in fact and fiction has been in service with a man of high social status. And the *valet*, probably because of the enforced intimacy of association with his gentlemanly employer, has always conducted himself, at least in fiction if not in fact, in the manner of a gentleman. (It is this customary intimacy with its inevitable destruction of dignity that made Madame Cornuel's "No man is a hero to his *valet*" so pertinent.)

While one thinks of a *valet* in terms of devoted, deferential service, there is no implication of servility in the word *valet* as there is in **flunky** and **lackey**. Originally, *flunky* was a contemptuous term for a liveried manservant, especially one who served as a footman. Today *flunky* designates any person who behaves in an excessively attentive, compliant, or sycophantic way toward a person of superior rank, social position, wealth, etc. *Lackey*, like *flunky*, first denoted a footman, but the word had no pejorative connotation. Today's *lackey* is the same kind of hanger-on as the modern *flunky*, but his role is more demanding in that it calls for him to do work of an unattractive nature: a TV star followed by the usual entourage of *flunkies*, each trying his best to be ingratiating; the Congressional hack whose *lackeys* did all the low-level politicking that kept him in office year after year.

Servant is a broad, neutral word with none of the connotations implicit in *flunky* or *lackey*. It can refer to a personal or domestic attendant: a large household made up of a family of six plus two *servants*. It can denote any person who is employed by another: A policeman is the *servant* of the people. Finally the word can be used in impersonal contexts to mean anything that is used to serve the purpose or interests of something else: Science is the *servant* of mankind.

Orderly and **batman** both have special reference to military service. An *orderly* is a private or noncommissioned officer detailed to carry orders, take messages, or do other service for an officer. The word is also applied to a male attendant at any hospital. *Batman* originally designated a soldier in the British army who was in charge of a bathorse, that is, a horse which carried baggage, especially in a military campaign. Today *batman* can refer to any personal *servant* of an officer in the British Army. See ASSISTANT.

These words all mean to get the better of, especially by using physical force in battle. **Vanquish** means to defeat utterly in battle, while **conquer**, though also implying victory, gives greater emphasis to gaining mastery or control over the defeated and their territory: to *vanquish* the enemy; The Romans *conquered* parts of Britain in the 1st century B.C. *Conquer* may apply to geographical area or to a political entity, whereas *vanquish* refers specifically to military forces. Both words may be used in extended or figurative senses: to *vanquish* fear; to *conquer* disease; to *conquer* one's shyness.

Overpower and **overwhelm** imply a disastrous defeat in which the defeated are rendered helpless by a sudden onset of superior power. *Overpower* stresses greater strength, as in numbers or weaponry; *overwhelm* implies complete and utter dominance, a one-sided victory that virtually constitutes a **rout**. *Rout* strictly speaking, implies that the defeated are put to flight. [An army which has been *overpowered* or *overwhelmed* may either surrender or be *routed*.]

To **overthrow** is to defeat an opponent so thoroughly that he is deprived of his position or power: a government *overthrown* by an adverse vote; a champion prize fighter *overthrown* by a challenger.

Surmount literally means to rise above, and is now used chiefly to refer to getting the better of difficulties, obstacles, or the like: Peace negotiators must *surmount* mutual suspicion and resentment. **Overcome** suggests *overpowering*, as in *overcoming* one's enemies, but now the word is applied chiefly to getting the better of something nonmaterial: to *overcome* temptation. See DEFEAT, DESTROY.

Antonyms: capitulate, ESCAPE, *lose,* SUBMIT, *succumb.*

vanquish

conquer
overcome
overpower
overthrow
overwhelm
rout
surmount

Central to this group of words when considered as verbs is the idea of confronting an uncertain or precarious situation with the intention or hope of obtaining a satisfactory outcome.

When the purpose is to show courteous disagreement or resolve, **venture** is preferred. [I *venture* to contradict you; He *ventured* to insist

venture

bet
chance

venture

(continued)

dare
gamble
hazard
risk
stake
wager

on certain changes]. But if the emphasis is on challenge or defiance, the otherwise closely synonymous **dare** is more often used. [I *dare* you to do it; He wouldn't *dare* to cancel the contract.]

Bet, gamble, and **wager** carry the suggestion of pitting one's wits, knowledge, and resources against a set of equally probable events, only one of which is or can be favorable: to *bet* on the races; to *gamble* away a fortune at roulette; to *wager* that a certain candidate will win an election. *Gamble*, though applicable in virtually every situation covered by the others, implies a more reckless commitment under less favorable circumstances: to *gamble* (not *bet* or *wager*) on the stock market. **Stake** also has the same general sense: to *stake* one's reputation on the outcome. More specifically it means giving money or assistance in advance to further a venture, on condition of sharing in any gains. [He *staked* a large sum on his friend's new factory.]

Chance means to happen or come about accidentally: She *chanced* to find her sister at home; it may also refer to a more or less deliberate attempt to bring some desired but problematical event to pass: I'll *chance* it. In this latter sense it is nearly interchangeable with **risk,** but *risk* contains an added suggestion of damage, loss, or injury not to be lightly ignored: The general *risked* his whole campaign on the outcome of one battle. **Hazard** points up the same distinction: to *hazard* all his winnings on the next fall of the dice. But it may also substitute at a milder level for *venture*: to *hazard* a guess. See DANGER, DOUBTFUL.

verbal

oral
spoken
vocal

These words relate to various forms of utterance. In strict usage, **verbal** refers to the actual words used, and does not exclude the possibility of a written communication: a *verbal* dispute; *verbal* translations from the Greek; He gave his *verbal* consent to the proposals.

Oral and **spoken** mean uttered or communicated by mouth: an *oral* examination in defense of one's Ph.D. dissertation; the *oral* tradition of epic poetry; a spoken account of his adventures. The distinction between these two words and *verbal* is often blurred by a tendency to confuse a written (or printed) communication with one that is only *spoken*. *Verbal*, in short, can mean *oral* or *spoken*, but is simply less precise when so used: *verbal* testimony.

Vocal retains its original and primary meaning of voice, and means having or endowed with the power of utterance: *vocal* cords; *vocal* music; *vocal* creatures. As such it refers to anything from meaningful speech to a confused murmuring or shouting. [He was very *vocal* in his objections; The crowd was *vocal* in its welcome of the new President.] See SAY, UTTER, VOCAL CORDS.

verbose

diffuse
pleonastic
prolix
redundant
repetitious
wordy

These words refer to the use of more words than necessary to make a statement. **Verbose** is formal, **wordy** informal, but both are similar in pointing to the mere fact of an excess of words in speech or writing, without specifying further: a *verbose* chapter on foreign affairs; a *wordy* poem on a familiar subject. *Verbose* is more general than *wordy*, however, since in addition to describing a specific example of excessive wordage, it is the more likely of the two to typify a writer or speaker, particularly the latter, who habitually uses more words than necessary or is extremely garrulous: a *verbose* story-teller who left his captive audience stony-eyed with boredom.

Redundant and **pleonastic** can pertain to a particular example or a whole statement, but rarely to a writer or speaker. In any case, they both refer to excessive wordage that results from tautological or unnecessary expressions. *Redundant* is of moderate formality and is restricted almost completely to indicating an excess caused by tautology: *redundant* phrases like essential requisite or fundamental basis. It is also more likely to pinpoint specific examples than to typify a whole style. *Pleonastic*, by contrast, is the most formal of these words; it can refer to specific *redundant* examples: a speech full of *pleonastic* phrases. But it is more general in pertaining, as well, to a whole speaking or writing style that is *wordy* or riddled with *redundant* expressions, especially when the style is complicated or pretentious: the *pleonastic* superelegance of the standard Victorian sermon.

Except for *wordy*, **repetitious** and **diffuse** are the least formal of these words. Both specify a particular fault that results in a *wordy* or *verbose* style. *Repetitious* points to excess because of the needless restatement of already established points: *repetitious* commericals that relentlessly hammer home their slogans. The word can refer to the speaker or writer himself: a *repetitious* debater whose arguments approached the simple-mindedness of propaganda. *Diffuse* suggests an excess of words that results when a piece of discourse is spread out, rambling, or poorly ordered in its movement from statement to statement: an essay so *diffuse* that it becomes almost impossible to grasp the points the author wishes to make.

Prolix approaches *pleonastic* in formality, but is somewhat different from the rest of these words in indicating a piece of discourse that is both unnecessarily long and tedious, with the suggestion that the whole approach is excessively intricate or complicated: a *prolix* contract unintelligible to anyone but a legal expert. The word can also refer to specific examples of involuted syntax. [When too many phrases interrupt the normal flow from subject to verb, a *prolix* sentence can result.] See CHATTER, CIRCUMLOCUTION, MONOTONOUS, TALKATIVE.

Antonyms: SILENT, SPEECHLESS, TACITURN, TERSE.

These words refer to a line that stands so as to form a ninety-degree angle with a flat, level surface. **Vertical** may stress an exact ninety-degree alignment: Because the floors slanted, a level had to be used to make sure the supports for the bookcases were *vertical*. But the word is often used to indicate approximate alignment as well: the *vertical* shafts of young birch saplings. It can apply, even more vaguely, to any upward motion: airplanes capable of *vertical* take-off; setting off a *vertical* escalation of stock prices.

In cases where *vertical* might suggest an approximation, **perpendicular** itself stresses an exact ninety-degree angle: *vertical* rays of sunlight falling across New York's *perpendicular* canyons of glass and steel. *Perpendicular* can apply to upward motion, but may be preferred over *vertical* for describing sharp downward motion: climbers trying to scale the almost *perpendicular* mountainside; tons of water falling in a *perpendicular* line from the cliff's edge.

Upright is less formal than either *vertical* or *perpendicular* and stresses an approximate rather than exact up-and-down alignment, with an implied comparison to something that leans or has fallen: several columns among the ruins that still stood defiantly *upright*. In figurative uses, moral decency or resoluteness may be suggested. **Plumb** is related to a context of building or carpentry, in which it suggests that an exact *perpendicular* alignment has been achieved by use of a *plumb* line: tapping the bottom of the two-by-four until it was *plumb*. See HIGH.

Antonyms: flat, horizontal, prone, prostrate, supine.

vertical

perpendicular
plumb
upright

vessel

boat
craft
ship

These words denote types of hollow structures, capable of floating and of carrying considerable weight, that are used to move goods and people over water. **Vessel**, in accordance with its original meaning of a hollow receptacle, suggests a large structure, especially in terms of its function of carrying goods or people or of being engaged in a specific type of commercial enterprise: a merchant *vessel*; a passenger *vessel*; a whaling *vessel*.

Ship is applied to large seagoing *vessels* when the type of propulsion is being stressed: a steam*ship*; a motor*ship*; a sailing *ship*. *Ship* also carries the implication of a *vessel* that has distinctive and even personal qualities for the men who sail it, and is traditionally referred to by the feminine form of the personal pronoun. [The captain and the crew all went down with the *ship*; The Bounty was a notorious *ship*; She was a gallant *ship*.] In literature and in figurative uses, *ship* suggests poetic and emotional overtones that are not inherent in any of the other words here considered. ["I have seen old *ships* sail like swans asleep"; "Sail on, O *Ship* of State!"; Pray for our *Ship*, the Church.]

Boat and **craft** may both be used as general designations for all of these structures. *Craft* is more generalized than *boat* in that it does not have any specific connotation as to size, use, or means of navigation. Although it is somewhat indefinite in meaning, *craft* may be used in the singular: Our *craft* was moving at nine knots. More commonly *craft* is a collective noun: hundreds of sailing *craft*; a lake full of small *craft*; a fleet of fishing *craft*. *Boat* is applied loosely to water*craft* of any size: to cross the river by ferry*boat*; to go to Europe by *boat*; to race a sail*boat*. In a narrow sense, *boat* is applied to any small, open craft propelled by oars, sails, or a portable engine: a row*boat*; a speed*boat*; a life*boat*. According to an old naval rule, if a *vessel* can be hauled out of water it's a *boat*; otherwise it's a *ship*.

viable

fecund
fertile
fruitful
proliferous
prolific

These words are comparable as they denote a capacity to produce or the power of producing, either in the biological or medical sense, or figuratively. The distinctions relate chiefly to the particular context in which they are used, although some hints are given by their etymology.

Viable, from the French word *vie*, means capable of living and developing normally: a *viable* seed, egg, or newborn child. It has also been applied to anything thought of as being able to continue an independent existence, and in this sense has the meaning of workable or practicable: a *viable* plan or project; a *viable* arrangement.

Fertile goes back to the Latin *ferre*, to bear, carry, or bring, and means capable of producing or reproducing, whether in a material or figurative sense: a *fertile* woman; *fertile* soil; a *fertile* breed of cattle; a *fertile* imagination; *fertile* in ideas; a *fertile* resoucefulness in the face of difficulties. Note, however, that what is *viable* is not necessarily *fertile*: a seed or newborn child is *viable* but can become *fertile* only at a certain stage in its own development.

By extension, **fecund** suggests the actual productivity or yield of any *fertile* person or thing. [Queen Victoria was a very *fecund* woman; a *fecund* crop; *fecund* with ideas] **Fruitful**, though often a close synonym of *fecund*, carries the idea of something that in and of itself promotes further productivity along similar or related lines. [A well-fertilized soil is *fruitful* in crops; Newton's laws were *fruitful* for the future development of science; The lecture led to a *fruitful* discussion.]

Prolific is a contraction of a medieval Latin word with the literal meaning of to make offspring or progeny. It is more widely used than *fecund* or *fruitful* to emphasize a rapid and abundant production of anything. [Rabbits are *prolific* animals; He comes of a *prolific* stock; Zola was a *prolific* writer of naturalistic novels.] **Proliferous**, having the same root as *fertile*, is generally restricted to biological and medical contexts: a *proliferous* growth of cells, buds, branches, or new tissue. See PREVALENT, WORKABLE.

    Antonyms: aborted, jejune, STERILE, *stillborn, untenable.*

These words refer to back-and-forth motion. **Vibrate** is the most general of these, suggesting a rapid continuing pulsation: feeling the train begin to *vibrate* with the monotonous roll of wheels along the track. **Oscillate**, a more formal word, often used in scientific contexts, applies to any regular shifting back and forth, as of a pendulum, or to any uncertain change of position: common stocks that *oscillate* in a predictably cyclical way; attitudes that *oscillated* between extremes of despair and hope. Apart from technical contexts and especially where uncertainty rather than regularity is intended, *oscillate* may sound stiff or ambiguous.

    Swing, while much more informal, relates closely to *oscillate* in suggesting motion like that of a pendulum or of anything stationary at one end and free at the other: *swinging* apelike from vine to vine. Unlike *oscillate*, the word may suggest a curving movement, like that followed by a pendulum's weight: *swinging* the car around sharply to void being struck.

    Undulate and **sway** are more specific than the foregoing words. *Undulate* suggests the slow, irregular alternation of swells and hollows in an elastic surface: smooth waves *undulating* across the bay. Unlike the other words treated here, *undulate* can also be applied to things completely at rest but composed of gentle swells and hollows: foothills that *undulated* gently along the highway. *Sway* may suggest the swelling and hollowing of a surface, like *undulate*, but most specifically it suggests the slow back-and-forth movement of something standing upright: trees *swaying* in the first gusts of the storm. This contrasts with *swing*, which strongly suggests the movement of something attached at the top and free to move at the bottom, rather than vice versa.

    Fluctuate and **waver** refer less to physical motion than to shifts in rate or changes of mind. *Fluctuate* suggests an irregular up-and-down motion or an uncertain or erratic course: stock prices that *fluctuate* for no apparent reason. *Waver* stresses indecisiveness or purposelessness: *wavering* between going to a movie and staying home. *Waver*, in referring to observable motion, suggests a faltering, unsteady course: the ragged caravan that *wavered* across the last mile of desert. See BOUNCE, ROTATE, SHAKE, SKIP, TOTTER.

These words express some of the least attractive aspects of human nature. **Vindictive** means spitefully vengeful, and suggests the harboring of grudges for imagined wrongs until the *vindictive* person, with satisfaction and perhaps even enjoyment, sees the object of his hatred suffer. **Spiteful** and **rancorous** emphasize the bitterness that attends feelings of malice and hate. *Rancorous* suggests a festering ill will, perhaps stemming from resentment over some real or fancied wrong. It does not, however, like *vindictive* and *spiteful*, necessarily imply a desire to hurt — only a deep-rooted malice. **Resentful** is less intense than *spiteful*, since the *spiteful* person is actually prompted to vengeful acts, whereas the *resentful* person's indignant anger may be suppressed or inhibited. Indeed, resentment often arises from feelings of frustration

vibrate

fluctuate
oscillate
sway
swing
undulate
waver

vindictive

malevolent
malicious
mean
rancorous
resentful
spiteful

vindictive
(continued)

splenetic
venomous

akin to envy. [The boy was *resentful* when the teacher selected another to be valedictorian; The *spiteful* girl deliberately broke the doll when she was told she couldn't keep it.]

Mean is applied to base or ungenerous feelings or actions. A *mean* person or attitude is small-minded, petty, and lacking in those qualities of human consideration and fair play that we tend, perhaps too hopefully, to regard as natural attributes of most people. [Her failure to invite the Harrises simply because they were not wealthy was a *mean* gesture.] Related to this sense is the informal use common in the U.S., meaning vicious, ill-tempered, or dangerous: a *mean* horse, ready to buck and throw you if you're not careful.

Venomous and **splenetic** refer to feelings of malignant spite. *Venomous* retains some of its basic serpentine sense of able to give a poisonous sting, and thus stresses effect as well as motive. A *venomous* review of a book suggests sharp, biting, painfully acute criticism. It also suggests a personal and possibly *vindictive* motive, since the attack is too strenuous to issue from impartiality. *Splenetic* means fretfully *spiteful* or peevish. It of course relates to the traditional sense of spleen as the seat of various emotions, among them ill temper, spite, and melancholy. Thus *splenetic* acts are moody and unpredictable, and stem from someone's nature or condition rather than from external causes. [The last words of the dying man were characteristically *splenetic*: "Hope to see you soon."]

Malicious and **malevolent** both imply the intent to do evil or to harm. *Malicious* is applied chiefly to actions and motives, *malevolent* to personal disposition. *Malevolent* has more sinister implications than *malicious*, implying a deep-seated irremediable antipathy that is manifested by wishing another ill: the *malevolent* nature of a miser; a cunning, *malevolent* smile; the *malicious* destruction of school property by vandals; a *malicious* lie. See ENMITY, RESENTMENT.

Antonyms: benevolent, friendly, GENEROUS, genial, gracious, HUMANE, kind, well-meaning.

virus

animalcule
bacillus
bacterium
germ
microbe
microorganism
pathogen

Virus, a Latin word for "poison," is the technical name of a large class of protein substances so small that only the electron microscope can make them visible. Capable of existing indefinitely in the form of crystals, they are seemingly lifeless until contact with the appropriate cells of a living organism triggers them into a reproductive activity whose power, subtlety, and virulence have given us such infective and frequently epidemic diseases as polio, smallpox, influenza, rabies, and the still unpreventible common cold.

The general term for all typically one-celled forms of life is **microorganism**, a word that includes both plants and animals. **Microbe** was popularized by Pasteur, who applied it to all forms of *microorganisms*, replacing the much older word **animalcule**, restricted to animals and now only rarely used. Because Pasteur's work was so largely concerned with harmful varieties, *microbe* came to suggest only those disease-producing organisms of which the correct scientific name is **pathogen**. In this sense it is still colloquially used: *microbe* hunters; the *microbe* of tuberculosis. **Germ**, as in the expression "*germ* theory of disease" made popular by the work of Koch and others, acquired a similar meaning, though strictly it refers to the living part of a seed or to any minute, not necessarily harmful, organism: a wheat *germ*; *germ* cell; *germ* plasm.

Bacterium (the singular of the better-known plural **bacteria**) is the inclusive term for any of numerous, widely distributed *microorganisms*

exhibiting both plant and animal characteristics. Though most of them
are harmless to man, and many are essential to the processes of life, some
are *pathogens* that cause serious, often fatal diseases, such as cholera,
diphtheria, tetanus, syphilis, and botulism. **Bacillus**, meaning "a little
rod," denotes a member of one of the three broad classes of *bacteria*
identified by characteristic shapes and modes of action. See COMMUNI-
CABLE, SICKNESS.

These words refer to seeing, whether in a literal or a metaphorical way.
Vision, at its most limited, can refer to the proper functioning of the
eyes: 20-20 *vision*; cataracts that blurred her field of *vision*. This
extends readily to sharpness of understanding: a man with keen *vision*.
In this sense, it can indicate thoughtfulness, foresight, or acuity. **Sight**
is a less formal term for the same concept, except that it cannot refer by
itself to understanding: injury that resulted in a complete loss of *sight*.
Both these words can also apply to something seen. *Vision*, here, would
indicate something seen in a dream or hallucination, or something that
may be illusory, imaginary, ideal, or supernatural: a *vision* that came to
him in his sleep; a medium who summoned up a *vision* of his dead wife;
his *vision* of a world free of war. *Sight*, here, may be a neutral reference
to a look at something real: catching *sight* of the Statue of Liberty; the
first *sight* he saw on debarking. More informally, it can indicate anything that looks odd or extraordinary: a badly overdressed woman who
thought she looked a *vision* but was merely a *sight*.

    Perception can refer, like *vision*, to seeing, but it is more general in
referring to the action of any of the other senses, as well: lacking *perception* of greens and reds; a sharp *perception* of mold and darkness in
the unlit room. The word emphasizes not merely the registering of a
phenomenon but the interpreting of it by the mind, often instantaneously: His trembling hands and blank stare confirmed her earlier *perception* that he was extremely ill at ease. Carrying this tendency further,
the word can indicate, like *vision*, any sharpness of understanding: a
critic of keen *perception*.

    Eyesight would seem to add nothing to the idea of *sight* itself, since
no other organs than the eyes are able to see. Yet the word is firmly
established in usage: insured against the loss of *eyesight*. The word does
select out the strict reference to seeing from *sight's* other reference to
whatever is viewed. See LOOK, PERCEIVE, SEE, SENSATION.

These words all apply to organs or parts of the human body used in
the production of speech. Voice is produced when air is drawn from the
lungs and forced between two bands or ribbons of muscle (**vocal cords**),
causing their tense edges to vibrate. The *vocal cords* are located in one
part of a cartilaginous box (**larynx**), which is in the upper part of the
windpipe, or trachea. When seen from without, the *larynx* — or more
particularly the thyroid cartilage, the part of the *larynx* to which the
vocal cords are attached — appears as an irregularly shaped prominence
in the throat that moves when one swallows or yawns. It is especially
noticeable in men; hence its popular name **Adam's apple**. In nontechnical use the *larynx* is known simply and accurately as the **voice
box**.

    The space between the *vocal cords* is called the **glottis**. For ordinary
breathing the *vocal cords* are relaxed and widely separated. For voiced
sounds, including all vowels and some consonants, such as the initial
sounds of "bin, zip, and this," the *vocal* cords are pressed lightly together;

vision

eyesight
perception
sight

vocal cords

Adam's apple
glottis
hard palate
larynx
palate
pharynx
soft palate
uvula
velum
voice box

gether; the air forced between them produces vibration and thus voice. In whispering, the main part of the *glottis* is tightly closed, but two movable cartilages (arytenoids) which form one end of the *vocal cords* are drawn slightly apart, and the air is forced out between them, thus producing voice of a different sort from that of ordinary speech.

The **palate** refers to the roof of the mouth, and it is commonly thought of as consisting of two parts, the **hard palate** in the forward part, and the **soft palate**, or **velum**, in the rear part. The *velum*, consisting of muscular tissue, acts as a valve for the production or suppression of nasality; when a nasal sound (such as the initial sound in "mouse") is to be produced, the *soft palate* moves forward so that the stream of air, whose exit through the mouth is blocked elsewhere (in the case of mouse by closed lips), is forced up and out through the nose. Otherwise the *velum* is moved back to block a nasal exit, and the air is forced out entirely through the mouth. Of course, in reality there are many gradations between nasal and oral sounds, and a certain degree of nasality is present even when one does not intend it.

That part of the alimentary canal behind the mouth and nasal passages and extending down to the esophagus and trachea (or windpipe) is called the **pharynx**, after the Greek word for throat. The *pharynx* is the passageway for both food and air.

The **uvula** is the soft, fleshy appendage hanging in the back of the mouth. It is part of the *soft palate*. Its chief function so far as most speakers of English are concerned seems to be to get red and inflamed when one gets a "sore throat," but in other languages and in some dialects of English it is used in the production of speech sounds. See UTTER.

vogue

fad
fashion
rage
trend

These words all refer to the prevailing acceptance or usage of things that are subject to change in form or style, as dress, décor, manners, etc. **Vogue** and **fashion** are sometimes used synonymously but *vogue* is a more limited word than *fashion* in its stress on the amount of acceptance or usage of a way of dressing, decorating, etc. *Vogue* can designate a person or thing that enjoys temporary public approval: the comedian who became a *vogue* after one lucky break on TV. It can refer to the approval itself: back in the twenties when short hair and short skirts were both in *vogue*. It can also denote the period of the *vogue*: during the recent *vogue* of rock-and-roll music. *Fashion*, more than *vogue*, is concerned with the clothing, furniture, behavior patterns, etc., in and of themselves. [Women's *fashions* of that era were unflattering and unfeminine; It has become the *fashion* for royalty to appear as democratic and folksy as the average politician.] In reference to attire, *fashion* sometimes retains its original meaning of shape, mold, style, or make: I don't like the *fashion* of that coat. It also suggests the high social standing of people who are influential in establishing customs, making a style of dress popular, etc.: to be seen at the right places with people of *fashion*. A *fashion* that has a short but very active life is a **fad**. It is the rapidity with which many people become interested and then lose interest in the *fashion* that distinguishes a *fad* from a *vogue*: The question in so many clothing manufacturer's minds is whether short skirts are to be a passing *fad* or a long-lived *fashion*. A **rage** is a *fad* which is attended by violent enthusiasm and, quite often, a lack of taste or judgment: a folk-rock quartet that was a *rage* one week and a forgotten name the next. **Trend** literally means the general course, direction, or line of movement followed by a coastline, river, etc. By extension, the word refers to any general course, inclination, or tendency: to evaluate the *trends* in modern education. More pertinent to this comparison is the meaning of a style or *vogue*: the *trend* toward bright colors and wild patterns in today's men's wear. See DRESS, STYLISH, UP-TO-DATE.

These words all mean to put an end to something. **Void, abrogate,** and **cancel** are often used interchangeably with **invalidate** and with each other in specific contexts. To *invalidate* is to bring to an end the effectiveness of documents or claims. A faulty signature may *invalidate* a check. Evidence shown to be false may *invalidate* a claim in court. Negotiators may *void* a disputed clause in a contract, thereby *invalidating* its provisions. A government may *abrogate* a treaty, thus in effect *invalidating* it by declaring it no longer in force. A landlord may *cancel* a lease, thereby *invalidating* his tenant's claim to shelter and his own claim to payment.

void

abolish
abrogate
annul
cancel
invalidate
negate
nullify
repeal
rescind
revoke

  Abolish is applied to practices, conditions, or social institutions. [The Emancipation Proclamation *abolished* slavery; Modern educators have for the most part *abolished* corporal punishment.]

  To **nullify** is to prevent or end the effectiveness of some condition or activity. Often it means to counterpose an action or a condition that renders the original action or condition futile or inoperative: Counterintelligence seeks to *nullify* the enemy's espionage efforts. To **negate**, as here considered, is to prove an assertion false and thus render ineffective a claim based on it: The testimony of eyewitnesses *negated* the accused's alibi. To **annul** is either to end something existing or to declare that it never really existed. A municipality may *annul* a charter and thus *abolish* its provisions. A court may *annul* a marriage, thus declaring that it never existed, rather than declaring a valid marriage at an end. To **repeal** and to **rescind** are to bring to an end the effect of a law or an order, respectively, and by depriving them or the authority behind them, *invalidate* them. The Twenty-first Amendment to the United States Constitution *repealed* the Eighteenth Amendment by declaring it no longer in effect. When issuing new regulations, a military headquarters may *rescind* earlier regulations governing the same subject.

  To **revoke** is to bring to an end something that has been authoritatively given, permitted, or granted. [Evidence of forgery *revoked* the Donation of Constantine, which purported to establish that the Emperor Constantine the Great gave the Western Roman Empire to the Papacy; King Louis XIV of France *revoked* the Edict of Nantes, in which King Henry IV had granted religious liberties to the French Huguenots; His license was *revoked* for drunken driving.] See ERASE.

  Antonyms: ENDORSE, *establish, legalize,* PERMIT, RECOVER, *renew, reinstate,* UPHOLD, *validate.*

These words are comparable in that they are all used when one wishes to describe the character, speech, or actions of people who have in some way offended one's sensibilities or moral standards. **Vulgar** and **obscene** are similar in their suggestion of indelicacy or indecency. But *vulgar* points more to a lack of refinement or good taste while *obscene* suggests a preoccupation with the pornographic: displaying shockingly *vulgar* table manners; a madwoman shouting *obscene* epithets.

vulgar

coarse
crude
gross
obscene

  Literally, **coarse, crude,** and **gross** refer to physical properties and carry the idea of an absence of fineness or delicacy. *Coarse* suggests roughness: a *coarse* fabric. *Crude* points to rawness or a lack of preparation: *crude* oil. *Gross* is used in reference to excessive fat: *gross* features. In their figurative meanings, the words are applicable to persons and their behavior. *Coarse* and *crude* are like *vulgar* in indicating a lack of refinement, as in manners or language: *coarse* behavior that was a reflection of a complete absence of training in the rudiments of social conduct; a group of schoolboys making *crude* jokes about their teachers. *Gross*, the strongest of these three words, suggests a reversion to animal instincts: the *gross* behavior of an invading army. See INDECENT, LEWD, PROFANITY, SMUTTY, SUGGESTIVE.

Antonyms: EXQUISITE, POLITE.

vulnerable

defenseless
exposed
untenable

These words refer to something open to attack or left unprotected from possible harm. **Vulnerable**, the most wide-ranging of these, comes from a Latin root meaning to wound; reflecting its derivation, the word can literally refer to the danger of physical wounding: the boxer's lowered guard left him *vulnerable* to his opponent's jab. *Vulnerable* always stresses a lack of protection against physical or mental harm: an uncritical admiration of her husband that made her *vulnerable* to his every whim. The word also is relevant to the context of argument, where it applies to an assertion that cannot be supported or corroborated or that is easily rebutted: a new foreign policy statement that was *vulnerable* to attacks from both the hawks and the doves. In military strategy, it suggests a position that is liable to capture or encroachment by the enemy: attempts to lure the guerrillas into the open countryside where they would be most *vulnerable* to air attack; a *vulnerable* nest of machine guns.

Defenseless refers strictly to an undesirable inability to ward off harm or danger. In this sense, it is more extreme than *vulnerable*, since it suggests an utter lack of protection or precaution, whereas *vulnerable* can suggest defenses inadequate to some danger or threat. [The most massive defense system would still leave the nation *vulnerable* to nuclear attack, though it might comfort the average citizen to think that he was not *defenseless*.] *Defenseless* also adds a note of complete helplessness: a *defenseless* child. **Exposed** emphasizes a lack of protection that might shield one from discomfort, harm, or danger: broken windows that left them *exposed* to the sub-zero temperatures; a battle plan that left their left flank dangerously *exposed* to attack. Sometimes the word can suggest an actual testing of something, whether or not the possibility of harm is involved: experiments in which rabbits were *exposed* to the drug as a way of checking its suitability for use by humans. Sometimes it is the risk rather than the harm that is emphasized: an attempt to track down everyone who had been *exposed* to the bacillus; his odd ideas, which left him *exposed* to ridicule.

Untenable reflects its derivation from a French word in referring to what cannot be "held," — that is, defended or maintained. In the context of argument, the word refers not only to a statement that may be refuted, as in the case of *vulnerable*, but to one that is inherently unsound. [Although the prosecution's case was *vulnerable*, the defense had chosen a line of reasoning that was inept and *untenable*.] In terms of military strategy or, by extension, any form of competition, the word suggests a precarious position or deployment of forces that cannot resist attack: an *untenable* beachhead, *exposed* to attack from high ground on all three sides. The word suggests a greater certainty of defeat than *vulnerable* and almost as much as *defenseless*. See POWERLESS, PROTECT, UPHOLD, WEAK.

Antonyms: fortified, guarded, IMPENETRABLE, impregnable, invincible, protected, unassailable.

W

These words all refer to emerging from sleep. Four of these verbs, **wake, waken, awake, awaken**, are so closely connected that their inflected forms are, for the most part, used interchangeably. Certain distinctions of taste can be felt in some cases, however. A tendency has been noted to prefer *awake* and *awaken* in figurative use: His suspicions were *awakened*; a country *awakening* to new challenges. *Awake* may be preferred in referring to the condition of wakefulness or alertness: I am fully *awake*. In reference to the emergence from sleep itself, *wake* is most common: I *wake* at seven each morning.

In other cases, little distinction exists among these four words. Thus, one may say I *woke*, *awoke*, *wakened*, or *awakened*. The forms I *waked* and I *awaked* are also heard, although much less commonly; *waked* is sometimes reserved for transitive constructions: I *waked* him at noon. All these forms are acceptable; all mean the same thing. The most common past tense, however, is *woke*. *Wakened* and *awakened* are usually felt to be more formal, although they seem to be the preferred forms for passive constructions: I was *awakened* by a loud noise. *Woke* and *woken* as past participles occur in the United States primarily in dialectal speech, but they are accepted as standard forms in British English. *Awoken* is seldom used. For the past participle, *waked* is probably the simplest and most direct, but many people avoid this form as questionable or uncomfortable and shift to the more natural-sounding *awakened*. [I generally *wake* early, but yesterday I *woke* two hours later than usual. In fact, I have not *awakened* so late in years.]

Wake up gives the most informal or emphatic tone of any of these forms. [She had to *wake up* several times a night when their baby was ill; *Wake up*!] It retains its informal flavor in transitive use: I volunteered to *wake* her *up*.

Rise is most often used to refer strictly to the daily act of *waking* and getting out of bed. [They *rose* early that morning; *Rise* and shine!] Sometimes it can make a distinction between *waking* and getting up. [She *woke* at dawn but didn't *rise* for another hour.] Unlike *rise*, **rouse** cannot be used intransitively, although in reflexive constructions it can suggest a difficult or slow act of *awaking* or emerging from a quiescent state: He struggled to *rouse* himself from sleep. By contrast, the word can suggest, in the passive, an easy *waking*, as from a light sleep: *roused* by the birds singing outside his window. In the active voice, the word can stress the effort to *awaken* someone else: trying unsuccessfully to *rouse* him from his nightmare. See INCITE, STIMULATE.

Antonyms: lull, RETIRE, sleep, slumber.

These words relate to ways people move on foot. All are of moderate informality. **Walk** is the most general and neutral of these, encompassing all manner of moving on foot short of running or leaping. **Stride** refers to a swift, purposeful way of *walking*; it suggests long steps and an energetic rhythm: *striding* through the depot a few minutes before the train's departure. **Amble, stroll,** and **saunter**, in sharp contrast with *stride*, suggest a slow, wandering movement without a clear-cut goal;

wake

awake
awaken
rise
rouse
waken
wake up

walk

amble
saunter
stride

walk
(continued)

stroll
strut
swagger
waddle

each may furthermore suggest laziness, leisure, indecisiveness, or simply the enjoyment of *walking*. *Amble* emphasizes a leisurely but even movement, smooth and uninterrupted: *ambling* along without stopping at any of the displays. The smooth, swaying motion suggested derives from a horse's *amble*, in which two feet on one side are lifted together, alternately with the two feet on the other side. *Stroll* emphasizes a slower movement, more wandering and aimless, with suggestions of many starts and pauses: *strolling* through the park with many a rest on any secluded bench he came across. *Saunter* suggests an even movement, like *amble*, but it emphasizes ebullience of mood as well. One might *stroll* while attending to disagreeable thoughts, but one would hardly *saunter* in such a state of mind: whistling as he *sauntered* along the beach.

The rest of these words describe the manner of a person's walk rather than commenting on its larger intent. **Strut** and **swagger** intensify the cheerfulness of *saunter*. *Swagger* suggests showy overconfidence or inflated egotism; it applies mostly as a negative comment: *swaggering* through crowds of autograph-seekers. *Strut* is even more disapproving in tone than *swagger*, suggesting an affected posture of bombastic self-importance: the candidate who *strutted* about the room like a latter-day Napoleon.

Waddle means to *walk* with short steps, swaying from side to side like a duck. When applied to people it suggests an awkward, laborious gait, such as that of a very fat person. See RUN, TOTTER.

wander

meander
ramble
range
roam
rove
stray

These words refer to motion or to travel that is slow, aimless, pointless, or without purpose or goal. **Wander** suggests a slow but possibly steady rate of movement. It usually indicates action that is idle or without purpose and is often applied to the movement of water, to travel, or to verbal discourse: a stream that *wandered* through the hilly countryside; nomadic tribes that *wander* through the desert from oasis to oasis; a disorganized speech that *wandered* badly from example to example without ever coming to the point. As can be seen, the word acquires a severely negative tone when applied to verbal discourse, emphasizing confusion or ineptness.

In the same context, **meander** might suggest an amused rather than a disapproving tone: an old backwoodsman whose anecdotes seemed to *meander* on without end. More concretely, *meander* suggests the movement of water: brooks *meandering* through verdant meadows. The word is less often used for travel, although here it can give a tone of amiable idleness: *meandering* around the theater district like a stage-struck kid. When used in the context of travel, **ramble**, like *meander*, usually refers to a specific occasion rather than a habitual way of life. It can give a tone of pleasant relaxation, like *meander*, but is more concrete in suggesting a particular manner of walking, one in which a sauntering gait is linked with a start-and-stop unevenness of speed: We went *rambling* through the park every weekend; a couple who liked to *ramble* about the antique ruins in search of a secluded picnic spot. When used of discourse, however, the word takes on a negative tone like that of *wander*, referring specifically to any presentation in language that is lengthy, poorly organized, and full of digressions: yawning while his wife *rambled* on about one trivial grievance after another; an essay that *rambles* too much to have any persuasive force.

Unlike the previous words, **roam** and **range** may both suggest a more serious purpose behind the uneven or circuitous movement. [He *roamed* through six states in search of his vanished father; The student's report *ranged* through a dozen cultures to cite examples supporting his thesis.] *Roam* can, like *ramble*, be used to describe a pleasant stroll: *roaming* about the hills and picking a bouquet of wildflowers. The implication of making a thorough search or having some other specific purpose in mind is seldom completely absent, however: *roaming* about dusty museums in search of unauthenticated paintings. *Roam* is furthermore the only word here that is specifically associated with the grazing or foraging activity of horses and other animals: letting his horse *roam* free so that she could eat her fill of prairie grass. *Range* implies a thorough or systematic movement over a wide area: His search *ranged* over three continents and twice took him across the Pacific Ocean. More often it refers to a sorting through or presenting of diverse ideas. More formal than *roam*, the word also suggests more certainty of purpose, a deliberately various course, and a wide grasp of far-flung materials: books *ranging* from popular fiction to learned treatises.

Rove and **stray** both most readily suggest negative aspects of idle movement. *Rove* can sometimes indicate, with an effect of cuteness, the pleasant overtones of *meander* or *ramble*. Often it suggests a greater intensity or a more clearly defined goal, but particularly a more fickle attitude toward the experience at hand. As such, the word often suggests a cynical inconstancy in love: always on the go, *roving* from one woman to another, never satisfied for long. *Stray*, by contrast, is the one word here that specifically emphasizes someone who has lost his way or inadvertently drifted off-course; with this sense, it can apply in any context, including those that circumscribe other words here: constantly *straying* from the main point of his talk; to *stray* from the prescribed route laid down by one's guide   Like *rove*, *stray* may refer to unfaithfulness in love; more generally, the word refers to outright sinfulness of any sort: wives earnestly trying to win back husbands who have *strayed*; inevitable that humanity would *stray* from its ideal standards of conduct. See CIRCUMLOCUTION, EXTEND, WALK.

Antonyms: REMAIN, *rest, settle.*

These words refer to a person who has no fixed home and who moves sporadically from place to place for short or indefinite stays. **Wanderer** stresses movement from place to place: social welfare schemes that are inhospitable to migrant workers and other *wanderers*. **Drifter**, by contrast, stresses the aimlessness of such movement. A *wanderer* might have definite reasons for his movements; a *drifter*, by implication, has none — or at least no very compelling ones. Furthermore, while a *wanderer* might be part of a group and move about with it, *drifter* introduces an implication of solitary movement: There were signs that a *drifter* had built his campfire there, stayed a day or two, and then moved on.

Nomad and **fugitive** both carry suggestions as to the reason for the homelessness or restlessness in question. *Nomad*, most strictly, refers to one of a group that moves about together for hunting or trading or in accord with the seasons: Asiatic *nomads* who brought strange cultural artifacts with them into Europe; *nomads* who take their herds into the mountains during the summer. In less restricted use, *nomad* may refer to anyone who moves frequently for any reason: the phenomenon of the transfer student as a sort of academic *nomad*. *Fugitive* suggests secretive movement to escape capture: detectives who traced the trail of the *fugitives* across four states.

Transient stresses a short or temporary stay at one place and is a

wanderer

drifter
fugitive
hobo
nomad
transient
vagabond
vagrant

term used by the hotel business to distinguish temporary from permanent lodgers. It may also be used to describe a locale's idle or newly arrived strangers: rounding up the town's *transients* for questioning. **Hobo** specifically suggests a lone man with no monetary resources who floats around the country, living off odd jobs and handouts: the grizzled old *hobo* in tattered clothes who knocked on the screen door and asked if he could chop some wood in exchange for his breakfast. **Vagrant** may be a more formal term for *hobo*, but this meaning is sometimes obscured by the fact that the word can also be a legal catch-all for a person committing any of a number of minor offenses completely unrelated to sporadic movement from place to place. Sometimes *vagrant* can suggest someone who wanders in search of work: *vagrants* who went from farm to farm and worked wherever day-laborers were needed. **Vagabond**, when it is not used interchangeably with *vagrant*, suggests a lazy, cheerful *drifter*: heavily romanticized portraits of gipsy *vagabonds*. See HIPPIE.

Antonyms: habitant, homesteader, resident, settler.

wane

ebb
fade
slacken

These words refer to a gradual decrease in quantity, size, rate, or intensity. **Wane** is most concretely used to describe the slow decrease in the lit portion of the moon, following its full phase. It is widely used as well, however, for any process of attrition: watching the patient's stamina *wane* from day to day; hoping that the enemy's morale would *wane* as the siege continued. In such uses there is no implication of a cyclical recovery, as is true of the moon. **Fade** implies even more strongly an irreversible process. Most concretely, it refers to a loss of intensity or distinctness in a color or marking. The process suggested, in any case, might be more drawn out than for *wane*: a memory that *faded* year by year. *Fade*, in fact, is often used to suggest attrition caused by the passage of time: a striking beauty that the years had *faded*. **Ebb** refers to the running out of a tide; even in other uses, the reference is often to a diminished rate of flow: a pulse that *ebbed* and became almost indistinct. In general, *ebb* suggests a shorter period of time than *wane*, thus contrasting strongly with *fade*. On the other hand, both *ebb* and *fade* refer most often to a decline from a better to a worse state, whereas *wane* can be applied more widely: waiting for his anger to *wane* and his good humor to return. Inconsistently enough, however, *ebb* is sometimes used to suggest a slow recovery: feeling his strength *ebb* back.

Slacken is far less concrete than the previous words, referring neutrally to any slow decrease. *Slacken* suggests a decrease in rate, volume, or pressure: in the summer when the hectic pace *slackened* a bit. *Slacken*, unlike the foregoing words, may suggest a voluntary adjustment: *slackening* my stride so that she could catch up with me. See DECREASE, LESSEN, REDUCE, WEAKEN.

Antonyms: brighten, ENLARGE, mount, multiply, rise, wax.

want

beggary
destitution
indigence
pauperism

These words refer to a lack of what is desirable for or necessary to a decent standard of living. **Want** is the most general of these; as an abstract noun, it indicates an unwilling and harmful lack of the necessities of life: faces pinched by *want*; the two-thirds of the world that are at present doomed to disease-ridden lives of *want*. *Want* can also be used apart from an economic context to refer to any sort of desire, whether momentary or abiding, whether deeply felt or trivial: returning to his homeland became for him a lifelong *want*; a husband who could cater to her every *want*. **Pauperism** and **beggary** concentrate on economic *want*, but both have become dated, since the forms of hardship they refer to are now less common. *Pauperism* refers to someone who, utterly without resources, has become a public charge; *beggary* refers to such a person who, while not a public charge, makes public appeals for money or handouts. Nowadays, the pauper would more likely be called a welfare client, the beggar a bum or panhandler. Similarly, their condition would be referred to by one of the following words. Either term, however, may still be used for its strong connotation of helpless dependence on others: fearing that his daughters would reduce him to *pauperism* (or *beggary*).

Of the remaining words, **indigence** indicates the mildest degree of economic *want*, referring to someone who is poor and lacks ordinary comforts but is not desperate for the means to sustain life: a recession that reduced many families to a state of *indigence*. **Poverty** can indicate a more severe state of economic *want* than *indigence*: those who, living in *poverty*, seldom have the means to acquire adequate food, clothing, shelter, and medical care. *Poverty* can, however, function as a generic term that includes all forms and degrees of economic *want*: the federal government's war on *poverty*. Economists sometimes find it convenient to name an arbitrary income figure and consider those who earn less to be living in *poverty*.

Penury indicates a state of *poverty* that cramps or hampers normal life; thus it points specifically to a severer degree of *want* than *indigence*. Even more severe is the state indicated by **privation**, in which the economic hardship has become painful or harmful: a life of ignominious *penury* wherein the loss of a few pennies was tantamount to disaster; permanent damage to the body and brain because of malnutrition resulting from extended *privation* in childhood.

Destitution is the most severe of all these words in pointing to a state of *poverty* so harsh as to endanger life: the utter *destitution* of the peasants on the eve of the French Revolution. *Destitution* can also sometimes refer to what has been abandoned, particularly to face unfavorable conditions: fatherless children left in *want* and *destitution*. See INSOLVENT, PENNILESS, POOR.

Antonyms: affluence, opulence, plenty, prosperity, solvency, wealth.

These words refer to feelings of need for some sort of object or satisfaction. **Want** is the most general and informal of these. It can range in intensity from expressing a weak preference or inclination to the most extreme states of need or passion: asking if he *wanted* more butter; *wanting* very much to go to a movie; *wanting* the new sports car more than anything in the world; gasping out how desperately he *wanted* her. The word can also express, more simply, a lack of the necessities of life, whether consciously expressed or not: peasants who *wanted* food, clothing, and decent homes.

Wish is also very general and wide-ranging in application. It can suggest mental fantasy, as in a daydream, and can express regret for past action or hopes about the future, whether they be realistic or not: *wishing* that a Prince Charming would come along and rescue her from her drab existence; *wishing* that he hadn't made such a fool of himself the night before; *wishing* to do well on the exam tomorrow; *wishing* that one day he would be a millionaire. *Wish* can also be used as a slightly more formal equivalent of *want*: Do you *wish* another helping of meat?

Desire can also function as a more formal substitute for *want*: ask-

want
(continued)

penury
poverty
privation

want

covet
crave
desire
wish

ing if he *desired* another drink; the many people who *desire* better working conditions and more education for their children. The special province of the word, however, is in referring to sexual or sensual appetite
or need: a growing sexual hunger that more and more *desired* expression;
desiring her more intensely than any woman he had ever known; *desiring* all sorts of sybaritic pleasures.

Crave, in its most restricted use, relates most concretely to hunger:
surprised to find himself *craving* a taste of Mexican food. The word is
widely used in other ways, however, to suggest either a mild hankering
or a gnawing inclination: *craving* a change of pace in their humdrum
life. It can even, by an analogy comparing hunger to sexual appetite,
refer unambiguously to intense erotic need: *craving* another long kiss and
close embrace. In this case, it stresses mere appetite, whereas *desire*
might sometimes more inclusively suggest a tincture of love and affection
as well. **Covet** most specifically refers to a longing to possess the material goods or anything that rightfully belongs to someone else: *coveting*
his neighbor's land; *coveting* his friend's wife. As now used, the word
may suggest a feeling as weak as that indicated by *wish* or as persistent
as that suggested by *craving*. It may suggest harmless envy or a poisonous determination to possess: *coveting* the unrestrained exuberance of
the other people at the party; *coveting* the jewels that lay unattended
on the table. See EAGER, EMOTION, EROTIC, GREEDY, HOPE, YEARN.

warm

lukewarm
muggy
stuffy
tepid

These words suggest a temperature midway between cold and hot.
Warm is the most general of these and is extremely relative. It can
have positive, neutral, or negative force, depending on context: pointing out that the champagne was still *warm*; offering to heat up the
warm coffee; a *warm*, cheery fire; an uncomfortably *warm* room. In
reference to emotions, the word has an exclusively positive tone, indicating sincere interest or affection: our *warmest* regards.

Lukewarm and **tepid** at their most literal refer more neutrally to
things that are not too hot. Of the two, *lukewarm* is less formal and
more clear in its neutral emphasis on description: fabrics that must be
washed in *lukewarm* water. *Tepid* more readily permits implications
that something is too cool: water that had become too *tepid* to wash
dishes in. Both may refer to halfhearted or indifferent feelings. *Lukewarm* suggests interest that remains mild: *lukewarm* reviews of the play.
Tepid is more emphatic in suggesting a lack of animation or enthusiasm:
tepid evenings spent with dull people.

Muggy and **stuffy** both refer mainly to an unpleasantly warm atmosphere or weather. *Muggy* emphasizes warmth accompanied by oppressive humidity: staying *muggy* for days after the hot spell was over.
Stuffy is restricted specifically to an over*warm* and poorly ventilated
area, usually indoors: becoming *stuffy* in the crowded lecture hall; the
stuffy, airless bedroom. See HOT, HUMID, PASSIONATE.

Antonyms: COLD.

wart

boil
carbuncle
cold sore
fever blister

These words denote various types of localized swellings or inflamed
places on the skin that are caused by certain microorganisms. **Wart**
refers to a hard, nonmalignant lump formed on and rooted in the skin,
usually somewhere on the hands or feet. Although caused by a virus,
warts are not inflamed or purulent and sometimes remain for long periods
without treatment only to disappear spontaneously.

Pustule is the general medical term for any small, rounded swelling
on the skin with an inflamed base containing pus, whether occurring

singly or over wide areas of the body, as in certain infectious diseases. A **pimple**, which is an inflammation of a sebaceous gland, appears most commonly on the face, especially during adolescence. A **boil** (in medical terminology, a **furuncle**) is larger and more painful than a *pimple*, as it involves not only the skin but, to a greater extent, the tissues directly beneath it. *Boils* have a central core of dead tissue surrounded by pus. A **carbuncle** is similar to a *boil*, but is much larger, more serious, and may be accompanied by fever. **Sties** appear only on the edge of the eyelid and, like *pimples*, arise from infected sebaceous glands. The **cold sore** (or **fever blister**, as it is sometimes called) is an eruption of small blisters on or near the lips and is caused by a virus. *Cold sores* frequently accompany a cold or a fever. See MOLE, NEOPLASM.

These words refers to castoff remains or leavings. **Waste** is the most general, referring to anything left over from some process, regardless of whether it can or cannot be used in some other process: bundling and selling the piles of newspapers as *waste*; more sophisticated sewage plants to process human *wastes*. **Refuse** suggests an accumulation of broken or unusable objects, especially bulky ones: a once-limpid pool filled up with old tires, tin cans, and other *refuse*. **Rubbish** suggests a collection of less bulky items than *refuse* and may imply, as is not necessarily so with the former word, used-up remnants collected specifically to be disposed of: shoving sacks of *rubbish* down the incinerator. Sometimes *rubbish* is distinguished from *refuse* as being burnable, but this is not universally true. **Garbage** is the most specific of these words, referring almost exclusively to uneaten or inedible remains from the kitchen that must be disposed of before they spoil and become a sanitary problem. By contrast, *rubbish* does not imply the same necessity for disposal since it refers largely to incorruptible materials.

Pollutants refers specifically to motor or industrial *wastes* that are emptied into waterways or the air and result in the fouling of these elements: *pollutants* from the exhausts of cars and buses; chemical *pollutants* from a single factory that can kill thousands of fish annually. **Debris** refers to the random piling up or scattering of extremely bulky remnants or pieces of wreckage: a plane crash that scattered *debris* over a full half-mile; *debris* from the construction job that was never hauled away. It can be used like *refuse* for less sizable items, but in this case it still implies a random or bit-by-bit scattering: *debris* carelessly tossed into the ditches along our highways.

Junk and **trash** can both refer to worn-out or worthless castoffs. In an industrial context, *junk* can refer to old cars and other large machines collected for the reusable parts or metals in them. In a housekeeping context, *junk* can refer to smaller items of little or no value: broken teacups, jars of mismatched nuts and bolts, and other *junk*. *Trash* is close to *refuse* in its generality, but it suggests a collection of heterogeneous items of small size: After cleaning up the attic, we swept up the *trash* and put it into the *garbage* pail and hauled stacks of *junk* out to the dump.

These words are compared as they denote upheaval of the ocean's surface. **Wave** is the general term, applying to any ridge or undulation moving on the surface of a liquid. A **ripple** is a very small *wave*, such as might be produced by a light breeze, or by an object dropping into still water. A **chop** is one of many small, irregular *waves* produced by opposing forces, as tide and wind. **Billow** is a poetic word for any *wave*,

wart
(continued)

furuncle
pimple
pustule
sty

waste

debris
garbage
junk
pollutants
refuse
rubbish
trash

wave

billow
breaker

wave
(continued)

chop
comber
ripple
roller
surge

but especially for a *wave* of great height. A **roller** is one of the long, irregular *waves* that move swiftly outward from a storm center. High, curling *rollers*, such as those that produce whitecaps, are called **combers**. A *wave* that curls over into a mass of foam as it strikes the shore is a **breaker**. **Surge** is the vaguest of these words; it is sometimes applied to a series of *breakers*, and sometimes to the rise and fall of the water's surface under any kind of *waves*.

Wave, of course, has other uses that depend on particular aspects of its basic sense. The visual aspect is emphasized, somewhat poetically, in the word's application to any series of curves suggesting *waves* of the ocean: *waves* of grain. The turbulent power and regularity of *waves* are emphasized in the word's application to a period of excitement or activity: A *wave* of enthusiasm swept the nation.

waylay

ambush
surprise

To **waylay** and to **ambush** are to attack suddenly from a place of hiding. *Waylay* is generally used when a person is set upon by robbers, assassins, etc., who have been lying in wait for him: armed bandits *waylaying* travelers in a deserted stretch of the valley. *Ambush* suggests that the object of attack is a military enemy: In the French and Indian War, British soldiers were frequently *ambushed* by Indians.

In the context of this discussion, **surprise** means to attack an enemy without warning, often but not necessarily from a place of hiding: Washington's purpose in crossing the Delaware was to *surprise* the British at Trenton. See ATTACK, CAPTURE, GRASP.

weak

debilitated
decrepit
feeble
frail
infirm

These words refer to lack of strength or health or to an inability to bear strain or pressure. **Weak** is the most general of these, carrying no implications as to how the lack of strength came about. It may be used in a purely physical sense: *weak* and dizzy after a fainting spell; born with *weak* eyesight; walls that without buttressing would have been too *weak* to bear their own weight. Or it may refer to a lack of mental or moral strength, indicating instability of character or deficient will power: a *weak* youth, easily led astray by bad associates. Sometimes, however, *weak* simply points to a lack of influence or authority: a government with a *weak* executive branch and a strong legislature. Or, generally, it may refer to any lack of normal power, strength, or potency: a *weak* voice; *weak* coffee; a *weak* heart; a *weak* link in a chain.

Frail, when used of a person, stresses an extremely slender, delicate, or sickly physique: *frail* and undernourished children who stared out from the windows of the tenement. In other situations, the word suggests something easily broken or unable to resist an opposing force: *frail* porphyry columns long since snapped in two; a *frail* theory that even the average person could refute. **Infirm** concentrates on a lack of soundness that is either inherent or that results from aging, illness, or the like: an *infirm* constitution inherited from his father's side of the family; a mind that had grown *infirm* with poverty, sickness, and old age. Used more abstractly, the word suggests a thoroughgoing faultiness resulting from incorrect methods of working: *infirm* conclusions based on deliberate distortions of the evidence. It may also point to a lack of stability or firmness, meaning irresolute or insecure: *infirm* of purpose; an *infirm* prop.

Feeble suggests a lack of strength that results in a fitful but always subnormal performance marked by a pitiable lack of alertness or resilience: a hand so *feeble* that it could scarcely lift the cup from its saucer;

feeble-minded. When used of the human body, it generally suggests that a process of attrition has occurred. Used literally of things, it may mean faint or inadequate: a *feeble* light; a *feeble* cry; a *feeble* defense system. Used of abstract things or of ideas, it points to ineffectualness, pointlessness, or pitiable performance: a *feeble* effort at courtesy; a *feeble* joke; a *feeble* interpretation of the play.

Debilitated and **decrepit** specifically suggest the sapping of strength formerly present. *Debilitated* is more general in applying to any result of such a process: a body *debilitated* by the ravaging disease; a house *debilitated* by its long exposure to the elements. *Decrepit* specifically restricts itself to a loss of strength or usefulness because of advanced age: *decrepit* dodderers in the rest home; musty stairs grown so *decrepit* that they groaned under a child's weight. See BONY, FLIMSY, FRAGILE, POWERLESS, SICKNESS.

Antonyms: energetic, hardy, HEALTHY, HUSKY, resolute, stout, strong, sturdy, tough.

Weaken, the most general word of this group, refers to the lessening of strength or power of a person, organization, or force. [The Democratic Party was *weakened* by the defection of several leading senators; He was so *weakened* by the disease that he could barely stand up.] **Enervate** and **sap** both mean to lessen the vitality or strength of; both are applied only to people. *Sap* implies a gradual or insidious loss of strength; *enervate* focuses on a loss of vitality and a general lassitude, as after an illness, during a spell of hot weather, or because of a loss of moral fiber. [The emotional strain of attending to his dying mother *sapped* all his strength; After his illness, he felt *enervated* and listless; The youth was *enervated* by dissipation.] **Enfeeble** is like *enervate* and *sap* in being used chiefly of human beings. It differs, though, in indicating an extreme *weakening*, as through long, debilitating illness or serious deprivation, and in suggesting a resultant helplessness: *enfeebled* by the insidious spread of cancer; prisoners of war *enfeebled* by chronic undernourishment.

Exhaust means to use up and to empty utterly, while **deplete** means to lower the resources of a thing. To *deplete* one's store of ammunition is to lower it to the point of danger; to *exhaust* it is to have none left. *Deplete* is often used of natural resources to express alarm at the reckless or wasteful use of unrecoverable materials: a bill that would prevent our shrinking preserve of virgin timberland from being further *depleted*. Where *deplete* refers to quantities, *exhaust* may also refer to qualities that cannot be measured. **Spend** is close to *exhaust*, but shares with *sap* the connotation of gradual exhaustion, a using up by degrees. [The candidate's energy was *spent* after the long and arduous campaign.] *Spend* and *exhaust* may apply to anything giving power. [The fuel was *spent* (or *exhausted*).] *Sap* and *enervate*, on the other hand, are always associated with life or with the life-giving spirit, and cannot be used of nonvital processes. [The constant battle to protect his reputation from the envious taunts of petty people *sapped* his strength and *enervated* his spirit.] See DECREASE, HARM, LESSEN, LISTLESS, REDUCE, TIRED, WANE.

Antonyms: energize, invigorate, replenish, revitalize, strengthen, vitalize.

These words refer to what one owns or has, as money, land, or other possessions of value. **Wealth**, considered in its concrete rather than its abstract sense, is a broad word meaning a store or accumulation of any-

weaken

deplete
enervate
enfeeble
exhaust
sap
spend

wealth

wealth
(continued)

assets
chattels
estate
goods
means
property
resources

thing that men desire to possess. It is used especially of material things having economic utility or monetary value, and may be applied to individuals, groups, or inanimate entities: a man of *wealth*; a nation's *wealth*. In a broader sense, *wealth* may refer to the possession of non-material things of value and may indicate a great abundance of anything: a *wealth* of experience; a *wealth* of learning.

The other words in this set are used to denote specific kinds of *wealth*. **Property** and **estate** generally refer to material possessions. *Property* is the broader term, referring to any object of value that a person or group may lawfully acquire and own: private *property*; government *property*. *Property* may be either real or personal; that is, it may consist of *wealth* regarded as immovable or permanent, as land or tenements, or of *wealth* regarded as movable or temporary, as jewelry, books, furniture, and the like. *Estate* may refer to a usually extensive piece of landed *property* or to the residence built upon it: a country *estate*. In another sense, the term designates the entire *property* and possessions of a dead person or of a bankrupt: to settle creditors' claims against a millionaire's *estate*. Certain intangible rights are also referred to as *property*, as copyrights, patents, and the like, and may be included in a deceased's *estate*.

Assets is a legal and commercial term used to designate sources of *wealth* as opposed to liabilities. The *assets* of a person, partnership, or corporation are all of the real and personal *property* that could be converted into money if necessary for the payment of debts or legacies. In a literal sense, land, buildings, furniture, supplies, equipment, stocks, bonds, and savings are *assets*. By extension, useful characteristics and attributes are often referred to as *assets*: An outgoing personality is a definite *asset* to a salesman.

Means and **resources** are *wealth*, particularly material possessions, that can be readily utilized for general or specific purposes. A man of *means* is presumed to possess money or negotiable *assets* sufficient to procure satisfactions in excess of bare necessities. The word *means* is sometimes qualified to indicate strictly limited funds: working girls of slender *means*. Or it may simply refer to one's budget, or money available for spending: an expenditure beyond her *means*; to give children equal opportunity for education, regardless of their families' *means*. The term *resources* implies the existence of a reserve supply of *wealth* or *assets* that can be drawn upon when needed. An individual's *resources* may include his bank account, his business, and his credit standing. A nation's natural *resources* include its raw materials, as water, oil, metals, and fertile soil, as well as its human *wealth*, as its scientists, artists, and technicians. *Resources* can also refer to a person's skill and ingenuity in handling problems and dealing with situations: a man of many *resources*, invaluable in an emergency.

Goods is a limited term, referring to personal and movable *property*. It is usually reserved for merchandise or other salable wares. **Chattels** is a broader word than *goods* but is generally limited to legal use nowadays. *Chattels* include *goods* and such other forms of *wealth* as promissory notes, mortgages, bonds, and the like. See CREATIVE, MEANS, POSSESS.
Antonyms: debts, liabilities, WANT.

wealthy

affluent

These words are all used to characterize people who possess a large share of money, real-estate holdings, and other things of value. **Wealthy** and **rich** are the most general of the terms that specifically apply to owning goods or having money. To call a person *wealthy* often suggests that he is an established and prominent member of the community:

one of our most *wealthy* citizens. *Rich* is blunter in tone, and indicates only the possession of many goods or much money; it is therefore more forceful and impressive when the object is to emphasize the great extent of someone's wealth. [He was not merely *wealthy* — he was *rich*; By cunning manipulation of his stocks he became a *rich* man before he was forty.] *Wealthy* can be used flexibly to describe various levels of wealth: a moderately *wealthy* family. *Rich*, on the other hand, is an either-or word; one is either *rich* or not *rich*; although one can be very *rich*, seldom is one spoken of as being moderately *rich*. *Rich*, unlike *wealthy*, is widely used in extended senses to mean full, pregnant, or abundant: a *rich* find of rare minerals; a full, *rich* voice; an experience *rich* with meaning.

Affluent and **opulent** are formal words derived from the Latin words meaning, respectively, to flow and power or wealth. *Affluent* thus suggests an abundant flow of goods or riches, wheras *opulent* has a strong connotation of ostentation or showy display of wealth: an *affluent* community where every family owned two cars; an *opulent* tapestry woven with gold and silver threads. *Opulent* most often refers to things, i.e. the products of wealth, whereas *affluent* describes people or human societies that possess wealth.

The less formal **flush** and the slang **loaded** mean having plenty of money, especially money on hand at a particular time. [*Flush* with his race-track winnings, he went on a spending spree; We just got paid so we were all *loaded*.] *Loaded* may also mean simply *rich*, in the sense of having a lot of money. Both these words differ from the others here considered in referring specifically to money, to the exclusion of other forms of wealth.

Prosperous and **successful**, while implying the acquisition of wealth, do not indicate simply the possession of money and goods. *Prosperous* means thriving or flourishing, and suggests a temporary or developing state of affairs: a *prosperous* farmer; a *prosperous* period of industrial growth; a *prosperous* business community. A *prosperous* person or group need not be *rich* nor even moderately *wealthy*, but only one whose economic situation is relatively good or on the rise: The vagrant felt himself *prosperous* when he found a dollar in the gutter. *Successful* moves one step further in broadening the context to include wealth as just one facet of meaning. As here considered, *successful* combines the sense of *prosperous* with the fulfillment of certain goals or ambitions, independent of wealth, and thus connotes a greater degree of stability or permanence than *prosperous*; a *successful* banker, for instance, is one who has achieved prominence in his field, whereas a *prosperous* banker is simply one who is doing well financially. Nevertheless, since success is often measured by one's wealth, the role of wealth in determining what *successful* means is not to be minimized; it is hard to conceive of a *rich* man who will not be considered *successful* by most people, but it is not hard to imagine someone or something that is *successful* but not *rich*: a *successful* business in which his profit margin was small but reliable; A *successful* character actor for many years, he managed to live on his income by careful frugality. See OUTSTANDING, PREVALENT.

Antonyms: destitute, INSOLVENT, *penurious*, POOR.

These words all describe the inarticulate sounds and shedding of tears indicative of grief, pain, or other strong emotions. **Weep** and **cry** are close synonyms, and are often used interchangeably. *Weep*, however, is more often used in writing than in speech, and gives greater emphasis to

wealthy
(continued)

flush
loaded
opulent
prosperous
rich
successful

weep

blubber

weep

(continued)

cry
sob
wail
whimper

the shedding of tears than to the accompanying sounds. *Cry*, on the other hand, usually gives primary emphasis to the sounds, although, paradoxically, it may also describe the act of silently shedding tears. [She *wept* copiously over the death of her dog; She *cried* loudly in despair; The child *cried* himself to sleep.] *Cry* does not always indicate depth of feeling: The baby *cried* loudly when he had emptied his bottle. Babies never *weep*. Both words can describe a variety of emotions: to *weep* with joy; to *cry* with fright; to *cry* from exhaustion.

Sob and **whimper** describe different varieties of *weeping*. To *sob* is to *weep* with audible convulsive catches of breath and the heaving of one's chest. *Sobbing* is usually accompanied by gasps and is akin to sighing. *Sob*, more than *weep* or *cry*, implies pathetic circumstances: The movie ends with the heroine *sobbing* desperately as her lover walks away resolutely. To *whimper* is to *cry* or whine with plaintive broken sounds; *whimper* introduces the suggestion of defenselessness or timidity, and is most often associated with fright: a lost child *whimpering* for his mother. But the word can also criticize ill-humored, unfounded, or self-pitying complaints: those who *whimper* about high taxes.

Blubber and **wail** stress the sounds accompanying *weeping*. *Blubber* means to *weep* or *sob* noisily; the word reflects an attitude of ridicule or contempt on the part of the person using it, and is thus more abusive than descriptive, although in some contexts it may be used humorously to emphasize the inappropriate loudness of the *weeping*. [I just *blubber* like a baby at the movies; A child your age shouldn't sit around *blubbering* over a lost toy.] *Wail* suggests a loud, unbroken, usually high-pitched *cry*. *Wailing* is traditionally associated with grief; a *wail* is a formal *cry* of mourning. Nowadays, however, *wail* is most often used to describe any sad or melancholy sound, whether in grief or not. Otherwise it is used more informally, like *blubber*, as a term of contempt, implying a weak, self-pitying attitude: *wailing* as though he were dying every time he stubbed a toe.

All of these terms are also used to mean to say while *weeping*, *crying*, *sobbing*, etc. ["I don't have a home," she *wept*; He *blubbered* something about a package he'd lost.] See GRIEVE, SAD.

Antonyms: LAUGH, rejoice.

wet

dampen
drench
moisten
soak
steep

These verbs mean to cover, fill, or permeate with water or other liquid. **Wet** is the most general word and may indicate all degrees of this condition. When not otherwise qualified, *wet* generally implies the agency of water. [*Wet* a corner of the washcloth; The girl *wet* her hair before setting it.] But any liquid can *wet*, and in a special sense the word refers to urination: The baby *wet* his diapers.

To **moisten** or **dampen** is to make or become somewhat wet. *Moisten* stresses the act of *wetting* slightly: to *moisten* the lips with the tongue while speaking; to *moisten* a gummed label. *Dampen* emphasizes the moist condition that results: to *dampen* a shirt before ironing it. Both words may imply diffusion of moisture, but *moisten* more often indicates a localized *wetting*. [He *moistened* the soil around the plant; The morning dew *dampened* the ground.] In a figurative sense, *dampen* means depress: He was a *wet* blanket, *dampening* everyone's spirits.

Soak and **drench** mean to *wet* thoroughly. *Soak* often implies immersion. To *soak* something is to place it in liquid and leave it long enough for the liquid to act upon it: to *soak* dirty dishes in warm, soapy water to loosen the food particles; to *soak* a sprained ankle in Epsom-salt water to lessen the swelling. *Drench*, on the other hand, typically involves the pouring down of liquid from above. It is a stronger word than *soak*, emphasizing the cause or instant effect of *wetting* where *soak* stresses the final result: *drenched* by a sudden downpour; *soaked* to the skin. When *drench*, like *soak*, involves immersion, it implies an excessive rather than a normal *wetting*: *soaking* in a warm bath; a guest in evening dress *drenched* and bedraggled by a dunking in the swimming pool. Both *soak* and *drench* may mean to leave sopping wet: *drenched* with sweat; *soaking* wet with perspiration. But *soak* stresses permeation or absorption, a passing through the pores of something: Water *soaks* into the soil. *Drench* suggests that excess liquid is running off, not sinking in: *drenched* and dripping trees. In a figurative sense, *drench* suggests a flood of something spilling over everything like liquid — drowning, saturating: a hill *drenched* with sunlight; a room *drenched* with color. *Soak* focuses on absorption, meaning to take up eagerly or readily, as if by drinking in through the pores: to *soak* up knowledge like a sponge; a sunbather *soaking* up the sun.

Steep, more strongly than *soak*, stresses immersion in a liquid and *wetting* for a purpose. One may *soak* or *steep* a thing to soften, saturate, or cleanse it; but *steeping* may also have a more radical effect: to *soak* black-eyed peas before cooking them; to *steep* barley in water until it starts to germinate. *Steeping* frequently involves the extraction of some constituent. [In making cornstarch, kernels of corn are *steeped* in a weak solution of sulfur dioxide in order to loosen the hull and remove the germ containing the corn oil.] Specifically, in general use, *steeping* often indicates the extraction and *soaking* up of an essence: tea leaves *steeped* in hot water. Figuratively, *steep* implies saturation through *soaking*, a making something part of the self, as if by total immersion in it: a scholar *steeped* in medieval lore; a child *steeped* in his parents' prejudice. See FILTER, FLOOD, HUMID, LEAK, PERMEATE.

Antonyms: dehumidify, dehydrate, desiccate, dry.

Whim, caprice, and **vagary** are all sudden and sometimes irrational notions, especially impulses to do something. A *whim* is a passing fancy or wish, often fantastic or odd. [On the first day of spring, the *whim* struck him to wear a huge rose in his hatband; Queen Elizabeth I, although an expert in statecraft, tended in private to indulge in foolish *whims*.] *Caprice*, stemming from the Latin word for goat, is a sudden change of mood, opinion, or purpose without apparent motivation. As implied by its etymology, *caprice* suggests an insistence upon having one's own way: a governess trying to control the *caprices* of a willful little girl; a patient whose various *caprices* against obeying the doctor's orders delayed his recovery. *Vagary* originally meant a journey or a rambling about and still suggests strongly unpredictable, erratic, or even irresponsible behavior: the *vagaries* of an employee who is always late and frequently lazy. It is a stronger term than either *whim* or *caprice*. *Whim, vagary*, and *caprice* may also be used in figurative senses: to sail at the *whim* of tide and wind; the *caprices* of fortune; the *vagaries* of April weather.

A **crotchet** is a perverse idea or opinion, about a particular subject, held obstinately despite its obvious untruth or contradiction to common opinion. [Mr. Midwick was well off, but his *crotchet* was that skimping on butter was a virtue.] *Crotchets* often concern minor points of doctrine or belief or merely trivial matters. [There is no *crotchet* so ridiculous nor any idea so silly that it cannot find acceptance somewhere.]

Whimsy, once considered a synonym of *whim*, now is applied almost

whim

caprice
crotchet
vagary
whimsy

exclusively to an odd, fanciful style of humor that delights and astonishes. *Whimsy* may appear in speech or actions, but it is more likely to occur in literature: the *whimsy* of Lewis Carroll; the whimsy of *The Wind in the Willows*. *Whimsy* may range from charming fancy to tongue-in-cheek drollery. See ECCENTRICITY, HOPE.

wild

feral
ferocious
fierce
savage

These words describe actions, appearances, or living things that display brutality, violence, or lack of restraint.

Wild is sometimes used loosely as a substitute for the other words in this group: a *wild* tiger; *wild* eyes; a *wild* rage; the *wild* man of Borneo. Strictly speaking, that which is *wild* is simply unrestrained and often implies no anger or harshness: *wild* delight; *wild* terror; the *wild* west wind.

Feral, from its original application to an undomesticated or untamed animal, carries the suggestion when applied to people of the behavior of a beast of prey: the *feral* attack of an assassin in a dark alley; the *feral* appetites of those who enjoy watching public executions.

Fierce, in this sense, is applied mostly to people or animals who are frightening to others because of a forbidding aspect or the violence of their actions. [An angry gorilla has a *fierce* roar; My grandfather became *fierce* when he lost his temper; To be a good watchdog, a dog must be *fierce* toward strangers.]

Ferocious always denotes a tendency to violence or viciousness. It is more distinctly bloodthirsty than is *fierce*: the *ferocious* crocodile; a *ferocious* killer whale. Whereas *fierce* suggests vehemence and lack of control, *ferocious* implies an animalistic wildness that is extremely menacing: a *ferocious* man-eating tiger; a *fierce* dog. *Fierce* may also describe actions: a *fierce* battle in which both sides suffered heavy losses.

Savage emphasizes lack of training and a lack of those restraints practiced by civilized people in controlling their aggressive impulses toward others: to make a *savage* attack against a political opponent; to be *savage* in one's revenge. More basically, it means not domesticated: *savage* animals.

Ferocious, *fierce*, and *savage* are all used in an exaggerated and sometimes playful sense to describe things that cause discomfort or excite anxiety: the *ferocious* heat of a July day; a *fierce* final examination; the *savage* crowding in a city slum. See CRUEL, UNRULY.

Antonyms: DOCILE, *domesticated, gentle, harmless,* TIMID.

willful

firm
hard-headed
hard-nosed
no-nonsense
strong-willed
tenacious
tough

These words all describe more or less uncompromising or fixed states of mind. The differences between them reveal that obstinacy in itself can be adjudged either good or bad, depending on the motive behind it and the uses to which it is put.

Willful means bent on having one's own way, and therefore careless or indifferent of other people's feelings or wishes. It has critical if not damning implications, but is somewhat mitigated by its common association with children: A *willful* child, she insisted on wearing yellow socks with her maroon smock. When applied to adults it may be considered a sign of immaturity or unreasonable conceit: a *willful* decision, taken without regard to the well-being of the community. **Strong-willed**, on the other hand, is usually taken to be complimentary, especially if the person indicated is a man: a *strong-willed* leader of men. It is also used, however, to imply criticism less strong than *willful*, perhaps mixed with a certain degree of admiration. [Robert is a very *strong-willed* person; once he has made up his mind, he won't change it.]

Firm is decidedly favorable in tone. It means fixed and unshakable, and often implies deep commitment to a moral principle: a *firm* resolve to spend two hours each evening at study; a *firm* commitment to civil rights. *Firm* is also commonly used as a euphemism for obstinate, because it substitutes the motive of high moral dedication for willfulness or self-seeking; indeed, whether one calls someone *firm* or stigmatizes him with a less attractive adjective depends upon whether one happens to share his convictions. Politicians are famous for being *firm* (believers in democracy, supporters of the president, upholders of free enterprise, etc.). **Tenacious**, meaning tending to hold strongly, as opinions, rights, etc., is also much favored by men and women in the public eye: a *tenacious* defender of states' rights. *Tenacious* has the implication of hanging on, refusing to let go no matter what the odds against eventual victory. This can be interpreted as blind stubbornness or as fierce devotion to right principle. Nevertheless, the word always conveys some respect; a *tenacious* adversary, for instance, may be disliked but he is certainly not to be taken lightly.

Hard-headed, hard-nosed (or its variant *hard-nose*), **no-nonsense**, and **tough** all describe practical, businesslike, or ruthless attitudes. All are on the whole favorable in tone, since all suggest that the people so characterized are doers, people who care primarily about results rather than about the means by which they are achieved — an attitude evidently highly valued by most Americans. *Hard-headed* means having a shrewd and practical mind; a *hard-headed* businessman is not given to sentiment or to much thought about human feelings, although he is not necessarily unkind or inhuman. He simply regards such considerations as unimportant or boring, in any case not worth thinking about. *Hard-nosed*, as reported in the journal *American Speech* of February 1928, was originally carnival slang and meant stubborn. In recent uses it appears to mean experienced, hard-bitten, unyielding, even ruthless in the pursuit of a practical objective: a *hard-nosed* approach to government spending; the stereotyped *hard-nosed* Marine sergeant. *No-nonsense* means without time-consuming formalities or the rigmarole of polite intercourse, and indicates a straight, blunt, even gruff approach, with the aim of getting things done quickly and efficiently even at the price of wounding someone's feelings or offending protocol. **Tough** in its primary sense means capable of sustaining great tension or strain without breaking. If one thinks of emotional rather than physical tension or strain, one has an excellent definition of its common colloquial use applied to people who are deemed shrewd and canny, not easily fooled or worn down by argument: a *tough* negotiator; a *tough* competitor. *Tough* and *no-nonsense* often appear together in informal or self-consciously modern writing: a *tough, no-nonsense* strongman of the Middle East; A *tough, no-nonsense* "take-charge" guy was needed to head the local anti-poverty program. See IMPERTURBABLE, OPPORTUNISTIC, STUBBORN.

Antonyms: accommodating, ADAPTABLE, COMPLIANT, DOCILE, *easygoing*, NAIVE, *tender*, TIMID, WEAK.

Wind and its synonyms are terms for natural movements of air. **Windstorm** is a general term for movements of air that are so strong as to be a source of concern.

Breeze is a general term for a light *wind*; it is also, as are some of the other words treated here, defined precisely by the Beaufort meteorological scale, which is used by the U.S. Weather Bureau. The Beaufort

wind

blizzard
breeze

wind
(continued)

cyclone
gale
hurricane
squall
storm
tempest
tornado
twister
typhoon
whirlwind
windstorm

scale defines a *breeze* as a *wind* having a velocity of between 4 and 31 miles an hour; *breezes* are further defined as "light" (4–7 miles per hour), "gentle" (8–12), "moderate" (13–18), "fresh" (19–24), and "strong" (25–31).

Gale is a general term for a very strong *wind* capable of doing considerable damage to property and usually regarded as hazardous for small craft at sea. The Beaufort scale defines a *gale* as a *wind* having a velocity of between 32 and 63 miles an hour; *gales* are further defined as "moderate" (32–38 miles per hour), "fresh" (39–46), "strong" (47–54), and "whole" (55–63).

Storm is a general term for any atmospheric disturbance, especially one marked by a great whirling motion of the air and accompanied by rain, snow, hail, etc. The Beaufort scale defines a *storm* as a *wind* having a velocity of between 64 and 75 miles an hour, thus placing it between a "whole *gale*" and a **hurricane**, which is defined as a *wind* having a velocity of over 75 miles an hour.

Whirlwind, tornado, twister, cyclone, and **typhoon**, as well as *hurricane*, denote winds that whirl helically around a central axis. Though *whirlwind* is the general name, this word is chiefly used as a synonym for *tornado*, an extremely violent vortex of small diameter. A *tornado*, visible as a funnel-shaped cloud of dust which moves in a relatively narrow path, can be devastating in its destructiveness. In certain parts of the United States, a *tornado* is popularly called a *cyclone*. *Twister* is also a common popular name for a *tornado*, especially in the central plains. Technically, a *cyclone* is a vortex, usually hundreds of miles in diameter. In the northern hemisphere, the *wind* of a *cyclone* spirals counterclockwise around an area of low barometric pressure. A *cyclone* that originates over tropical seas deposits driving rain as it advances; such a *cyclone* originating in the West Indies is called a *hurricane*, and in the western Pacific, a *typhoon*.

A **squall** is a sudden and violent *wind* of short duration, and is often accompanied by rain or snow. The word is perhaps most commonly used to describe *storms* at sea. A **blizzard** is a high, cold *wind* accompanied by blinding snow that accumulates to a considerable depth. **Tempest**, nowadays a somewhat poetic term, can be applied to any *storm* of great violence, especially one involving both wind and rain, snow, or hail. See FLOOD.

wisdom

discernment
discrimination
judgment
sagacity
sense

These words are comparable in denoting mental qualities that have to do with the ability to understand situations, anticipate consequences, and make sound decisions. **Wisdom** is a broad term, embracing the meanings of all its synonyms in addition to outranking them all in suggesting a rare combination of discretion, maturity, keenness of intellect, broad experience, extensive learning, profound thought, and compassionate understanding. In its full application, *wisdom* implies the highest and noblest exercise of all the faculties of the moral nature as well as of the intellect: A great jurist bases his decisions on a *wisdom* gained from far more than his study of the law.

Sense is also very general in meaning. It can refer to rational perception accompanied by feeling. Used this way it suggests an intense awareness and realization of the stimuli to which it is responding: a highly developed *sense* of right and wrong. The word is commonly applied to the ability to act effectively in any given situation. It is very close in this meaning to **sagacity**, both terms suggesting the kind of knowledge or know-how which is the result of broad experience and the thoughtful evaluation of such experience: a politician who showed good *sense* in avoiding the mistakes he'd made in a previous campaign; a *sagacity* that was reflected in all his business dealings. But *sagacity* is more formal and can also suggest a searching profundity, like *wisdom*: the old man's *sagacity* about the dilemmas of life.

Discernment and **discrimination** are alike in denoting an analytic ability that allows one to see things clearly. *Discernment* is applied to the evaluation of character and is concerned with the kind of accuracy of observation that finds the real behind the apparent: With *discernment* a lawyer can screen a jury panel in such a way that he will secure impartiality for his client. In another meaning, *discernment* can refer to making distinctions; in this usage it suggests the power to recognize quality or worth, as in a work of art: a music critic whose *discernment* of great talent has been proved time and time again. *Discrimination* is very closely allied to the second meaning of *discernment*, denoting an ability to perceive very subtle distinctions, even when they might be blurred to ordinary observation: a chef with such gustatory *discrimination* that he could recognize any seasoning, no matter how delicate, that had been used in the preparation of a meal.

Judgment is *sense* applied to the making of decisions, especially correct decisions, and thus it depends to some degree upon the exercise of *discernment* or *discrimination*: the dangerous fallibility of a man with a good heart and poor *judgment*. See ACUMEN, DISCRIMINATE, KEEN, OBSERVANT.

Antonyms: folly, foolishness, imprudence, indiscretion, miscalculation, misjudgment, senselessness, silliness, stupidity.

These words refer to an introspective frame of mind that is sad, thoughtful, or intense. **Wistful** stresses sadness that is mild and bittersweet, often suggesting a light, wishful longing after something past or impossible: a *wistful* hour spent remembering her childhood dream of becoming a great writer; giving his friend's wife a *wistful* look. Sometimes, the word suggests an aura of not unpleasant sadness that is not attached to any specific aspiration: feeling tipsy and *wistful* as the last guests left the party. **Nostalgic** specifically applies to a longing for familiar or beloved circumstances that are now remote or irrecoverable. *Nostalgic* thoughts focus on events or people that actually happened or lived, whereas *wistful* thoughts may center on far-fetched hopes or past illusions. A *wistful* feeling may be casual or fleeting, but a *nostalgic* feeling is usually deeply felt and is often suggestive of a mood lasting some time. [She opened the photograph album whenever she was in a *nostalgic* mood; *nostalgic* memories of boyhood street games whenever he passed through a lower-class neighborhood] *Nostalgic* suggests both satisfaction and regret, and usually implies a warmth and intensity of feeling lacking in *wistful*.

Plaintive may stress any sort of longing, sorrow, or wish expressed in words or song: a *plaintive* request that he call her up some time; a *plaintive* melody. But as now used, the word has drawn closer to *wistful* in not necessarily indicating utterance at all: looking after him with a *plaintive* smile. The emotion suggested here, however, is a shade more intense than that of *wistful*, with a possible suggestion both of greater hopelessness and greater need or desire: the *plaintive* cry of a kitten who had got separated from the rest of the litter.

Pensive, strictly speaking, can refer solely to a musing, reflective thoughtfulness: *pensive* chess-players bent over the board. Very often,

wistful

moody
nostalgic
pensive
plaintive

however, the word is felt to imply a state of mind that is also tinged with sadness or resignation: feeling *pensive* and lonely as he watched the boat fading away in the distance. **Moody**, by contrast, can refer to a wide variety of emotions, including sadness, sullenness, or anger. Most typically, it might suggest any dark, depressed, and withdrawn state of mind, one considerably more intense than would be true for other words here: He would slouch about for days in a *moody* silence. The word often implies a petulant or uncertain disposition: a *moody*, sulky child. See CONSIDERATE, IMAGINATION, SAD, SENTIMENTAL, THINK.

Antonyms: airy, FLIPPANT, HEEDLESS.

withstand

bear
cope
defy
endure
manage
put up with
resist

These words all mean to tolerate, undergo, sustain, or oppose, as a trying or painful experience or the weight of superior authority. **Withstand** means to hold out against someone or something, and usually implies that the initiative for the action was taken by the opposing side: to *withstand* an enemy siege. It also suggests strong moral or physical qualities in the person or group doing the *withstanding*: to *withstand* forceful arguments because of firm conviction. *Withstand* may be used, too, in contests where the opposing force is a strong influence or attraction: Nobody can *withstand* her charms.

Put up with is informal and is used in reference to unpleasant or mildly harmful situations. [Our office manager couldn't *put up with* his secretary's irritability and complaints so he fired her; If you can *put up with* a bit of cold air, I'd like to ventilate this room.] In some cases, **bear** is synonymous with *put up with*. [She can't *bear* her sister; For a long time, I couldn't *bear* living alone.] But usually, *bear* refers to a burden that weighs one down, as pain, sadness, or responsibility, and is suggestive of a test of one's physical or moral strength. [She *bore* the pain of childbirth without complaint; Of all the sorrows I have had to *bear*, none was so great as the loss of my father.] **Endure** is very much like *bear* in its pertinence to serious physical or mental hardship, but *endure* goes beyond *bear* in its suggestion of lasting strength in the face of a continual series or an unbroken period of trials. [That couple has *endured* so many emotional and financial crises it is amazing their marriage has lasted.]

One **manages** or **copes** in situations that require some searching for ways and means to overcome whatever problem or difficulty has been encountered. [The family *managed* by constant denial and rigid budgeting; My sister had to learn to *cope* with complicated social situations when she married a man who was much wealthier than she.]

Resist and **defy** imply more active opposition than the other words treated here. *Resist* means to act counter to or fight against in order to stop, prevent, or defeat: to *resist* aggression by armed force; *resisting* the impulse to sleep by reminding himself of the severe penalty for falling asleep while on guard duty. *Defy* implies even more open and bolder opposition, and may convey a sense of daring or bravado if not outright belligerence: He *defied* the government's rule against traveling to Communist countries. *Defy* is usually used in connection with a superior authority: teen-agers *defying* their parents by smoking marijuana. See COMPETE, CONTROL, FIGHT, PERSIST.

Antonyms: FORGO, RELINQUISH, submit.

wording

Wording refers to the particular words a person uses in a certain bit of speech or writing and the manner in which he uses them: The *wording* of the proposition is simple and direct. **Verbiage** is sometimes used as

wording
(continued)

language
verbiage
vocabulary
wordage

a synonym for *wording*, but it more often designates an excess of words in proportion to the ideas which they express: The author's *verbiage* produced a document of mammoth size and microscopic import. **Language**, in one sense, denotes all sounds spoken and combined into words and sentences that human beings use for the communication of ideas or emotions. In a more limited sense, *language* refers to those words and combinations that have been systematized and confirmed by usage among members of a certain nation, people, or race at a given period: the French *language*. In its widest sense, *language* signifies expression of thought by any means: the *language* of the eyes; the *language* of flowers. The words or expressions used in a specific business, science, etc., are also referred to as *language*: the *language* of mathematics. **Vocabulary** is the sum of words used or understood by a certain person, making up a particular *language*, or employed in some specific business, science, etc.: the immeasurable contribution of Greek to the English *vocabulary*; a lawyer's *vocabulary*. It refers, by extension, to a person's preference in the area of *language*: Hardy's *vocabulary* was largely Anglo-Saxon. **Wordage** is a formal and not widely used term meaning words collectively. But *wordage* can refer to the amount of words allotted for or taken up by a piece of writing, as a newspaper article: an analysis that was inevitably superficial, considering the compressed *wordage* he was permitted. See CONVERSATION, SAY, SPEECH, WRITE.

These words refer to what is useful, sensible, suitable, or capable of being realized. In its most restricted application to an idea or proposal, **workable** indicates simply that something can be carried out in reality: a committee that presented several *workable* plans, though it didn't claim to know which of them would be most effective. The word can, however, include in its meaning a proposal's likelihood of being effective as well: While both plans were perfectly sensible, only one seemed *workable* in terms of actually reducing delinquency. The word can also apply to methods, plans, or systems already underway, in which case it refers strictly to proved ability to accomplish set goals effectively: many employee suggestions that proved to be *workable* once they were adopted. **Possible**, while very general and wide-ranging in application, is restricted in this context to the most limited meaning of *workable*, suggesting something that can actually be carried out: the pair who first proved that it was *possible* for man to fly. But the word can point merely to the chance that something may occur or to whatever is not ruled out as an eventuality by the nature of reality: vaguely *possible* that he could still win the election.

Feasible is more formal than the foregoing, but is otherwise like *workable* in pointing either to something's capability of being realized or to its success, once carried out. It is distinct from *workable* in that the latter views effective operation as if in a vacuum, whereas *feasible* may suggest a variety of impinging external factors that qualify performance; a design, for example, may prove *workable* under ideal conditions and yet not be *feasible* for ordinary use.

Practicable is the most restricted of these words in meaning. It compares to *possible* in pointing solely to proposals that can be realized, but it is more limited in eliminating notions of mere occurrence or likelihood to concentrate instead on what can be produced, created, built, or put into effect. It compares naturally with and complements **practical**, which points mainly to something of proven effectiveness. Thus this pair relates like *workable* and *feasible*, but with a much more clear-cut set of distinctions in meaning. While there would be a *practical* use for a robot that could, for example, clean the house on command, the manufacture of such a device is not yet *practicable*. It is *practicable* to make phonograph records three feet in diameter, but the user would not find them convenient or *practical*. See SENSIBLE.

Antonyms: DOUBTFUL, *impracticable, impractical, impossible, unlikely, unworkable.*

worldly

earthly
mundane
profane
secular

These words refer to things of the world rather than of the spirit, or to things pertaining to public, ordinary, or everyday life. **Worldly** indicates a liking for the goods and pleasures of the world; it often points with disapproval to such a liking when it is stronger than any interest in spiritual matters: a *worldly* prelate; a minister whose sermons attacked the godless and *worldly* members of the community. *Worldly* suggests, as well, a particular kind of sensualist, one who is cosmopolitan and sophisticated. Thus, a farmer with a zest for good food and drink would less likely be called *worldly* than a city dweller with the same appetites. In one sense, in fact, *worldly* can be neutral or even approving of such urbanity, suggesting someone who is well-informed, discriminating in taste, and wise in the ways of the world: Benjamin Franklin's ambassadorship to France brought no quaint rustic to the fleshpots of Paris but rather a clever and cultured man in the grand style, both *worldly* and *worldly*-wise.

Secular and **profane** are neither condemnatory nor approving but strictly neutral in classifying those things that pertain to a totally non-religious sphere: a *secular* drama; *profane* art. *Secular* can also indicate something pertaining to the laity rather than the clergy: *secular* resistance to the church's attitude toward birth control. Most specifically, *secular* can refer to a clergyman not bound by monastic vows: a *secular* priest. **Mundane** refers to things belonging strictly to the ordinary world of everyday affairs, suggesting something practical, routine, or dull: idealistic students who criticize their affluent parents for having no concerns beyond the *mundane* worlds of the office and home. **Earthly** remains largely confined to religious use, and is directly opposed to heavenly: this *earthly* paradise; *earthly* joys.

Antonyms: SACRED.

worry

brood
care
fret

These words are used in relation to interested, concerned, or troubled states of mind. **Worry** and **care** both express a wide range of emotional involvement. One may be said to *worry* when the feeling described is as mild as uneasiness: Don't *worry* if you're late for the meeting. On the other hand, *worry* is frequently used to convey a sense of deep anxiety: I'm *worried* sick about her driving the car tonight on the icy roads. *Care*, in a way that *worry* can not, denotes a purely objective interest: It is impossible that a man who is otherwise so involved with contemporary problems should not *care* at all about the civil rights issue. It can designate sorrow: to *care* about a friend's being out of work. It can, finally, indicate serious concern or anxiety: It was obvious from the press conference that the prime minister *cares* deeply about the recent worsening in the relations between East and West.

Brood, like *care* and *worry*, denotes a concern about some person or thing, but more than the other two words, it implies a thoughtful and sometimes morbid dwelling on the object of concern, often to the point of moodiness or depression. [She *brooded* so long on her mother's illness that she sank into a state of melancholia; He *broods* continuously about the wrongs he claims were inflicted on him by his late employer.] **Fret**, like *brood*, suggests a lingering state of mind, with the governing emotion being that of anxiety, grief, or unhappiness: Since her husband's death, she has done nothing but *fret*. Often with this word, however, there is a suggestion of whining and complaining that is not present in *brood*: I pity his hypochondria, but I pity more the poor wife who has to put up with his continual *fretting*. See AFRAID, ANXIETY, BOTHER, SOLICITUDE.

wound

bruise
cut
lacerate
scar

These verbs pertain most strictly to external physical injury, though all of them are used widely for other sorts of damage. **Wound** most often indicates a relatively serious external breaching of the flesh, possibly by a piercing or gouging action, one that may go deep: *wounded* in the fall, but escaping permanent injury; *wounded* by machine-gun fire. Often the word is used to contrast the injured and the dead: ten people killed and two *wounded*. The word also refers to emotional injury, whether serious or trivial: *wounded* by her sharp retort.

Cut and **lacerate** both are restricted to specific kinds of *wounding*. *Cut* suggests the stabbing or slashing action of a sharp instrument; where *wound* may suggest a cleavage or gash, *cut* suggests a slitlike opening, whether shallow or deep: *cutting* her finger by accident with the paring knife. More generally, *cut* may suggest any severing or paring action: *cutting* off the gangrenous limb; *cutting* the paper in two. *Lacerate* is more restricted, like *wound*, to bodily injury, but it specifically suggests a jagged *cutting* or the making of a group of cuts, as by an abrading action: *lacerating* his hand on a crooked piece of glass; *lacerated* by the pavement as he was dragged helplessly along by the speeding car. In metaphorical uses, the word suggests a savage or vehement *wounding*: an acerbic review that *lacerated* the author.

Bruise is distinct from the other words in indicating an injury of the surface flesh, caused by a blow that does not necessarily break the skin and that typically results in a black-and-blue swelling of the affected area: *bruising* himself by stubbing his toe in the dark. The word can also suggest the tendency to turn black-and-blue from small impacts, as in the quip, "I *bruise* easily."

Scar, most strictly, refers to the forming of a mark over a healed wound: permanently *scarred* by the acid thrown in his face. Sometimes, however, the word is used less precisely as a harsher, more emphatic substitute for *cut* or *lacerate*: instantly *scarred* by the breaking pane of glass. Used of the emotions, the word suggests the doing of damage that will leave a lasting mark: *scarred* by the constant hostility of his father. See DISFIGURE, HURT.

wriggle

slither
squirm
wiggle
writhe

These words refer to convulsed or contorted movements within a body. **Wriggle** can suggest a deliberate shaking or shuddering not intended to result in motion along a path: *wriggling* uncomfortably in his wet clothes; *wriggling* with delight as the waves broke over her. More often, the word does suggest forward movement achieved by a crawling or creeping action: *wriggling* into the tunnel with a flashlight in one hand; a caterpillar that *wriggled* down the girl's back. **Slither** points exclusively to this sort of movement, but where *wriggle* may suggest jerking, awkward, or ungainly motion, *slither* implies a sinuous and graceful sliding of an elongated body, such as that of a snake: pythons *slithering* noiselessly over rock; a rope that *slithered* unseen down the prison wall.

Squirm is nearly identical to *wriggle* in suggesting either in-place shaking or a forward crawl. In both cases, however, a greater amount of internal undulation is suggested by *squirm*, as well as more thrashing about: watching the stranded octopus *squirm* each time they stabbed at it; trying desperately to *squirm* free from the tangled bedclothes. In contrast to the foregoing words, both **writhe** and **wiggle** point primarily to in-place motion. *Writhe* would suggest a slower, less voluntary shuddering than *squirm* and even *wriggle*; it often describes the throes of someone in pain: bodies *writhing* in agony. But the word can also suggest other kinds of contorted movement: *writhing* teen-agers dancing the frug. *Wiggle* suggests a side-to-side or back-and-forth motion: proving to them that he could *wiggle* his ears; the woman who seemed unaware of how much she *wiggled* as she walked. As in the last example, if forward movement is indicated, the word points to incidental motion rather than to motion that contributes directly to the gaining of ground. See BEND, ROTATE, SHAKE, VIBRATE.

write

inscribe
jot
pen
scribble

To **write** is to make, form, or trace letters, numbers, words, etc., as with a pencil or pen. In this basic sense *write* is the most general of the words being compared here and can be used as a synonym for any of them. *Write*, of course, has many more applications than the other terms because of its variety of specialized meanings, all of which are extensions of the basic sense. *Write* can mean to describe, communicate by letter, be the author of, and draw up or draft: to *write* one's impression of an art show; forced to *write* from Europe to ask her family for money; a famous statesman who has *written* his autobiography; the lawyer who *wrote* my will.

    Inscribe suggests *writing* for some solemn or official purpose. It can refer to the putting down of a person's name in a formal list or register: to *inscribe* a student's name in his school's permanent honor roll. It can denote the marking or engraving of words, characters, names, etc., as part of a conspicuous or permanent record: to *inscribe* a name on a public monument; to *inscribe* a ring with a personal message. It can also designate the signing or dedication of a book, photograph, etc.: to *inscribe* a volume of poetry to an old friend. To *write* something brief and do it in a hasty way is to **jot**. There are suggestions of a lack of forethought or preparation about this word: to *jot* down an idea on a paper napkin; a telephone number *jotted* down on the back of a matchbook cover. **Pen** means to *write* with a pen: to *pen* a letter to a friend. By extension it means to *write* in any way, but it often has connotations of composing with great care and thought: the enormous difficulties involved in *penning* a really fine short story. The word now has a formal, old-fashioned tone that may appear stuffy or pretentiously quaint in some contexts. **Scribble** is like *jot* in its implication of *writing* with haste and a lack of care: two young schoolgirls *scribbling* notes to each other during class. *Scribble* also refers to the making of illegible or meaningless marks: The two-year-old laughed happily after having *scribbled* all over the walls with his mother's lipstick. See SAY.

wrong

abuse
maltreat
mistreat

These verbs all refer to acts that are unjust or that harm other people. To **wrong** is to treat unjustly or harmfully without good cause: a man who *wronged* his wife by mistakenly accusing her of infidelity; an innocent man *wronged* by being sent to prison. **Abuse**, the most general term in this group, covers all injurious use or treatment by word or act; it does not, however, always connote a deliberate act: an overweight woman whose severe self-imposed diet *abused* her health; a policeman who *abused* his authority by searching a house without a warrant.

Maltreat and **mistreat** are close in meaning; both usually imply base motivation for the actions concerned. *Maltreat*, however, suggests harsher or more consciously cruel treatment than *mistreat*, which can apply to acts whose chief effect is psychological rather than physical: accused of *maltreating* the dogs in his kennel; an author who felt *mistreated* by his agent on the grounds of neglect and indifference. *Mistreat* is thus more general than *maltreat* and need not imply physical abuse or even the desire to harm.

To **persecute** is to *maltreat* because of race, religion, or beliefs. **Oppress**, the strongest word of this group, implies the harsh and unjust use of force in keeping someone in subjugation. *Persecute* implies a deliberate, systematic, and often ruthless attempt to harm; *oppress* emphasizes action rather than motive, and suggests the weighing down or crushing by the might of irresponsible authority. [The Puritans, *persecuted* for their religious beliefs, fled to America; The American colonies, feeling themselves *oppressed* by taxes and without due political representation, revolted.] To *oppress* a people is to deprive them of their liberty and often of their hope; to *persecute* them is to inflict suffering upon them. See DESTROY, HARM, UNSETTLE.

Antonyms: favor, help, NURSE, PROTECT, UPHOLD.

Y

These words refer to a strong inclination toward something or an unfulfilled want that one may or may not take action to fill. **Yearn** points to an inclination that is continually present as a gnawing or unhappy feeling of lack for something, either for a clearly defined object or for something more abstract, less definite, or beyond one's reach: *yearning* for one look from her; *yearning* to have a girlfriend of his own. The word must be used with care, since it can give a tone of sentimental overstatement: *yearning* for self-fulfillment, she knew not how. This tone can be deflated in brusque usages: *yearning* for a cold glass of beer. The likelihood of such a sentimental tone is even more heavily incurred by **pine**, which would now be thought old-fashioned in most situations. It can give an implication of long-term *yearning* so intense as to result in a wasting away of physical or mental health, as in folk ballads: missing her dead lover so much that she *pined* away and died. **Moon** informally satirizes such excessive grieving or *yearning*: all this adolescent *mooning* after a girl who is nothing but a tramp; teenage girls *mooning* over the latest pop-cult heroes.

Long is less open than *pine* or *yearn* to the charge of sounding high-toned, though such a tone is possible: man's age-old *longing* for freedom. More often, the word points to a weaker, more enduring, or more hopeless want, if not to one totally impossible or contrary to fact: *longing* to be as attractive as the most popular girl in her class. It can apply informally to less extreme situations, however, pointing to any sort of emotional want: telling him how much she *longed* simply to lie in the sun for a solid week. **Hanker** specifically suggests sexual desire of a trivial, momentary, or frivolous nature: *hankering* after the woman at the bar who kept looking at him in the mirror. The word can also suggest any mild desire, impulse, or inclination: *hankering* to see a good movie. See EAGER, EMOTION, EROTIC, GREEDY, HOPE, WANT.

yokel

hayseed
hick
rube
rustic

These words refer unflatteringly to rural, provincial, uncultured, or unsophisticated people. **Yokel** and **hayseed** are contemptuous informal terms for a person from a rural or farming background who is uncultured or ignorant. The main difference here is that *hayseed* is more vivid and even more withering in its scorn: stuck off-season in a resort filled with country *yokels*; a *hayseed* who didn't seem able to understand the simplest request for directions. Also, *yokel* can refer to any noncosmopolitan audience: taking a program of hackneyed piano pieces on tour, since they were sure to please the local *yokels*. Both terms seem old-fashioned today; they have the ring of a bygone era.

Hick can apply to someone in a provincial setting, as well, including those from towns or even cities considered to be removed from the center of things: attacking him for sneering at so-called *hicks* in Chicago and San Francisco who wanted to build their own cultural centers rather than depending on road companies from New York. Where *yokel* and *hayseed* usually place the provincial person in his home town, *hick* can apply to someone who appears to be newly arrived in a cosmopolitan setting and is still unfamiliar with its ways: *hicks* who come to Greenwich Village to look at the hippies.

Rube, another old-fashioned abusive term for a person from a rural area, was originally carnival slang for any patron, viewing him contemptuously as being easily gulled, duped, or conned: the *rubes* who came to see the heap of plastic bones they believed to be the skeleton of Goliath. **Rustic** is the most formal of these words — and the least uncomplimentary as well. It suggests a colorful, possibly even likable country eccentric who is set in his ways or appears to be quaint in his tastes: sketching the old *rustic* who sat whittling on the wharf. While all these words, by implication, indicate men, *hick*, *rube*, and possibly *rustic*, may refer to both men and women when pluralized: the dumb *hicks* in that town; an audience of *rubes* willing to believe anything; a quaint village peopled by genuine *rustics*. See BLOCKHEAD.

youth

adolescent
teen-ager
young man
young woman

These words denote young people of the ages between childhood and maturity. **Youth**, now a rather old-fashioned word, is applied to young males almost exclusively, especially those in their teens or early twenties: a callow *youth*; to go to sea as a *youth*. As a collective, *youth* denotes young persons as a group, both male and female: the *youth* of a nation; the flower of American *youth*.

Adolescent and **teen-ager** both designate a person from the age of thirteen through nineteen. *Adolescent* is a more formal term than *teenager* and may simply be used in the chronological sense: a course in safe driving for *adolescents*; to have three *adolescent* daughters. In an extended sense, *adolescent* connotes the awkwardness, the rapid growth, and the emotional upheavals of this period of life. When used of an adult of any age, *adolescent* is a disparaging term and emphasizes immaturity in behavior or thinking. *Teen-ager* has gained wide acceptance since World War II, especially as exploited in the advertising world and in the press. Whereas *adolescent* points to the period approaching young adulthood, *teen-ager* emphasizes an age group which more and more deliberately sets itself apart from the adult world and which has its own standards of conduct, its own fashions, its own entertainments, and even its own argot.

Young man and young woman tend to be relative terms, as their use sometimes depends upon the age of the person who says or writes them. However, in general, it may be assumed that a *young man* and a *young woman* are persons roughly between *adolescence* and the age of thirty-five. In a playful or scolding way, *young man* is frequently used in addressing small boys: *Young man*, wash those dirty hands. "*Young lady*," rather than *young woman*, is used of girls in the same way. See CHILD, HIPPIE.

Antonyms: adult, adulthood, grown-up.

Z

zero

aught
cipher
naught
null

These words come into comparison as verbal equivalents of the symbol for nothing, 0. The choice of which one to use depends upon a context that may range from the archaic and informal to the mathematical and scientific.

Zero and **cipher** both come from the Arabic word *sifr*, meaning empty. In this sense *zero* has come to be the most commonly used to indicate the absence or negation of something. [Subtracting any number from itself gives *zero*; The results of all the tests were *zero*.] It is also regarded as the standard reference point in any scale of values, quantities, magnitudes, dimensions, etc. [The temperature was 10 below (or above) *zero*; The gambler bet on *zero* at roulette; Heavy fog reduced visibility to *zero*.] *Cipher*, though literally synonymous, cannot replace *zero* in any of the above examples. It is still thought of as representing any numeral from 0 to 9, a use carried over from the verb form meaning to count or calculate. We can, of course, increase the value of any whole number by adding *ciphers* at the end of it, but the distinction is recognized by saying that the enlarged number, say 643,000, contains three *zeros*, not *ciphers*. However, the idea of nullity or nonentity is usually clear from the context, especially if we are using the word in a figurative sense: Man is a mere *cipher* in the universe.

Naught (sometimes spelt *nought*), an Old English word for nothing, doubles for *cipher* in its literal sense. [This number has a lot of *naughts* in it; Let's play at *naughts* and crosses.] But this use is rare and mostly colloquial, though less so than its clipped version **aught** (a *naught* taken as an *aught*). As an epithet for a person or thing devoid of merit or value, *naught* still has poetic force. [All his plans came to *naught*; There was *naught* to be done in the emergency but wait.]

Null is best known to us in the reduplicated legal phrase "*null* and void," meaning without force or effect, or invalid. But it also serves a useful purpose to indicate a negative result or outcome, especially in certain types of scientific work. [All the Geiger counter readings were *null*; The results of the first experiments to prove the value of the new drug were *null*.] See LACK, VACANT.

zest

brio

These words all denote states or attitudes of keen enjoyment, invigoration, or vitality. **Zest** expresses dynamic vigor along with uninhibited sensuous delight: The remarkable aspect of the life of Don Juan was not the number of women he seduced but the *zest* with which he seduced

zest
(continued)

dash
drive
energy
gusto
panache
pizazz
verve
zip

them. In some contexts **gusto** and *zest* are interchangeable: He ate with *zest* (or *gusto*). But *gusto*, while intensely felt, is commonly associated with single events of short duration, whereas *zest* may signal a more profound or enduring characteristic. [After his illness he lost his *zest* for life; They traded insults with *gusto*.]

Energy emphasizes the vigor of physical action rather than a dynamic motivation. To eat with *energy*, for instance, suggests nothing more than the expenditure of a good deal of effort in hastily transferring food from plate to mouth, whereas eating with *zest* or with *gusto* expresses keen appreciation of the food. *Energy* is often used, however, as an enduring quality: A man of considerable *energy*, he took a brisk stroll every morning before breakfast.

Drive is an informal word used mainly in the U.S. to denote *energy* stimulated by ambition: He has lots of *drive* to get ahead in his work. This use of *drive* may have been influenced by the word's psychological meaning of a strong, motivating power or stimulus: the sex *drive*.

The U.S. Post Office rejuvenated **zip** by adopting the acronym *ZIP* Code (for *Z*one *I*mprovement *P*lan) for its numerical system designed to speed the delivery of domestic mail. *Zip* means *energy*, get-up-and-go, vitality, zing: a song with plenty of *zip*. Apart from Post Office use it has a slightly dated quality, reminding one of other obsolescent words like *roadster* and *rumble seat*. The verb meaning to go at great speed does not always share the archaic flavor of the noun; jets can still *zip* along. A new fad word replacing *zip* in many contexts is **pizazz** (also spelled *pizzazz, pzzazz, pazazz,* and many other ways). The best current translation seems to be "that extra something" — an unnameable quality that invests someone or something with *zip*, vitality, and irresistible appeal. As one might have guessed, the word, like so many other slang expressions, has been adopted by advertising and fashion writers because of its attraction to young buyers: a miniskirt with *pizazz*! When applied to people *pizazz* means something like charisma. [The crowds gape wherever he goes; he has, in a word, *pizazz*.] Fad words change so rapidly that it would be foolhardy to predict what this word will mean in one year or five years from now, or whether it will be used at all.

Brio, meaning spirit, suggests exuberant, often careless, vitality. [He spoke with tremendous *brio*; his speech, always loud no matter where he was, was punctuated with brilliant but unrepeatable oaths and cheerful slanders, and his gestures were appropriately flamboyant.] As a musical direction, *con brio* means with spirit, in a lively manner.

Dash and **verve** both emphasize a great and vigorous *energy*, but *dash* points more particularly to a brilliant or flamboyant style carried out with sophistication and speed, whereas *verve* stresses the enthusiasm and untiring nature of the effort. [Ethel Merman sings with *verve*; He toasted our health with exquisite courtesy and entertained us with considerable *dash*.] **Panache** is derived from the Latin word for feather, and its literal meaning is a plume or bunch of feathers, especially when worn as an ornament on a helmet. *Panache*, in its more common sense, is thus a fancy equivalent of *dash*, even more strongly emphasizing the flourish of wit or brilliance of style with which something is done or said: the aristocratic jewel thief who pulls off his jobs with elegance and *panache*. *Dash* and *panache* both suggest an elegant independence of spirit amounting to an indifference to or contempt for popular manners or morals. See EAGER, LIVELY, PASSIONATE.

Antonyms: blandness, dullness, exhaustion, hebetude, insipidity, lethargy, listlessness, weariness.

INDEX

alive LIVING 349
allay LESSEN 345
allege ASSERT 24
ALLEGIANCE 12
ALLEGORY 12
alleviate LESSEN 345
alley STREET 593
alliance LEAGUE 337
allocate DIVIDE 172
allot DIVIDE 172
allow PERMIT 440
alloy MIXTURE 382
allure TEMPT 622
ally ASSOCIATE (n) 25
ALOOF 12
alter CHANGE 81
altruism BENEVOLENCE 47
amalgam MIXTURE 382
amass ACCUMULATE 3
AMATEUR (n) 13
amazed SURPRISED 610
AMBASSADOR 13
ambiguous DOUBTFUL 175
ambitious OPPORTUNISTIC 414
amble WALK (v) 674
ambush WAYLAY 682
ameliorate IMPROVE 299
amenable DOCILE 173
amend REVISE 513
amiable GREGARIOUS 256
amid BETWEEN 48
amidst BETWEEN 48
among BETWEEN 48
amongst BETWEEN 48
amoral UNETHICAL 650
amorous EROTIC 195
amount QUANTITY 481
ample PREVALENT 465
amplify ENLARGE 190
amulet TALISMAN 615
amuse ENTERTAIN 192
ANARCHISM 13
anarchy LAWLESSNESS 335
anathema CURSE 141
ANCESTOR 14
ancestry DESCENT 156
ANCIENT 15
ancillary AUXILIARY 29
androgynous BISEXUAL 50
anecdote NARRATIVE 393
anesthetized NUMB 401
ANGER (n) 15
anger ENRAGE 191
angst ANXIETY 16
anguish MISERY 380
angular LANKY 332
animadversion DISAPPROVAL 163
ANIMAL 15
animalcule VIRUS 670
animate LIVING 349
animated LIVELY 348
animosity ENMITY 191
animus ENMITY 191
annals HISTORY 277
annex ADD 8
annihilate DESTROY 159
annotation EXPLANATION 203
announce DECLARE 146
annoy UNSETTLE 653
annul VOID 673
anomie SLOTH 562
ANSWER (n) 16
answer SATISFY 525
answerable RESPONSIBLE 509
antagonism ENMITY 191
antagonist OPPONENT 412
antagonistic OPPOSED 414
antediluvian OLD-FASHIONED 410
anticipate HOPE 279

anticipation EXPECTATION 202
antipathy DISLIKE 168
antiquated OLD-FASHIONED 410
antique ANCIENT 15
antiseptic SANITARY 524
ANXIETY 16
anxious AFRAID 10
apartment LODGINGS 350
apathetic IMPASSIVE 293
apathetic UNINVOLVED 650
apathy SLOTH 562
ape IMITATE 290
aperture OPENING 411
apex SUMMIT 604
aphorism PROVERB 475
aplomb CONFIDENCE 115
apocryphal SPURIOUS 581
apologia EXCUSE 200
apology EXCUSE 200
apostate TRAITOR 635
apothegm PROVERB 475
apparatus MACHINE 356
apparel DRESS (n) 176
apparent PLAIN 446
apparition GHOST 248
appeal PLEAD 449
appeal REQUEST (n) 504
APPEARANCE 18
appellation TITLE 632
append ADD 8
appendage ADDITION 8
appendix ADDITION 8
APPLAUSE 18
appliance MACHINE 356
application REQUEST 504
apply REQUEST 505
APPOINT 18
apportion DIVIDE 172
appreciative GRATEFUL 253
apprehend CAPTURE 73
apprehension ANXIETY 16
apprehensive AFRAID 10
apprentice BEGINNER 41
apprise INFORM 306
approach COMPARE 106
approbation APPROVAL 19
appropriate USURP 662
APPROVAL 19
approve ENDORSE 189
approximate COMPARE 106
APPROXIMATELY 19
appurtenance ADDITION 8
aptitude GENIUS 245
arachnid BUG 69
arbiter JUDGE 321
arbitrator JUDGE 321
arcane OBSCURE 404
archaic OLD-FASHIONED 410
archetype PROTOTYPE 474
ardent PASSIONATE 429
arduous HARD 264
area SECTION 532
area SIZE 555
argot SLANG 559
ARGUE 20
argument CONTROVERSY 127
aria MELODY 373
arid STERILE 587
ARISE 20
armada FLEET 222
armament ARMS 21
ARMS 21
army TROOPS 643
aroma SMELL 564
around APPROXIMATELY 19
arouse INCITE 300
arousing EROTIC 195
arraign ACCUSE 4
arrange ORGANIZE 417

arrest CAPTURE (v) 73
arrest STOP (arrest) 592
arrive COME 102
arrogant OVERBEARING 422
arrogate USURP 662
arsenal ARMS 21
arteriosclerosis HEART ATTACK 266
arthropod BUG 69
article COMPOSITION 111
artifice TRICK 641
artificer ARTISAN 22
ARTIFICIAL 21
artificial ARTISTIC 23
ARTISAN 22
ARTIST 22
ARTISTIC 23
artistry SKILL 557
artless NAIVE 391
arty ARTISTIC 23
ascend CLIMB 97
ascertain FIND 218
ascribe ATTRIBUTE 28
aseptic SANITARY 524
ashen PALE 425
asinine STUPID 598
ask DEMAND 151
ask REQUEST 505
aspect APPEARANCE 18
asperity BITTERNESS 51
asperse MALIGN 357
aspersion DISAPPROVAL 163
aspiring OPPORTUNISTIC 414
assail ATTACK 26
assassinate KILL 325
assault AGGRESSION 10
assault ATTACK (v) 26
assemblage MEETING 372
assemble GATHER 241
assemble MAKE 357
assembly MEETING 372
assent CONSENT (v) 118
ASSERT 24
assess TAX 617
assets WEALTH 683
asseverate ASSERT 24
assiduous DILIGENT 161
assign APPOINT 18
assign DIVIDE 172
assignation TRYST 647
assignment STINT 590
assimilate ABSORB 1
assistance HELP 269
ASSISTANT 25
ASSOCIATE (n) 25
association CLUB 98
assuage LESSEN 345
assume SUPPOSE 608
assumption PRINCIPLE 467
ASSURE 26
astonished SURPRISED 610
astounded SURPRISED 610
astute KEEN 324
asylum PROTECTION 474
atheist SKEPTIC 556
atherosclerosis HEART ATTACK 266
atrocious OUTRAGEOUS 420
attach ADD 8
attach CONNECT 117
attachment ADDITION 8
attachment LOVE 354
ATTACK (v) 26
attack AGGRESSION 10
attain REACH 488
ATTAINMENT 27
attempt TRY (v) 646
attend ACCOMPANY 2
attentive CONSIDERATE 120
attentive OBSERVANT 406
attire DRESS (n) 176

confidant FRIEND 237
confide ENTRUST 194
CONFIDENCE 115
confidence TRUST 644
confident OPTIMISTIC 415
configuration FORM 232
CONFINE (v) 116
confines BOUNDARY 62
confirm ENDORSE 189
confiscate USURP 662
conflagration FIRE 219
conflict CONTROVERSY 127
conflicting CONTRADICTORY 125
conform ADAPT 6
confound CONFUSE 116
CONFUSE 116
confusion CLUTTER 100
congenital INNATE 309
conglomeration ACCUMULATION 3
conglomeration JUMBLE 322
congregate GATHER 241
congregation MEETING 372
congress MEETING 372
congruent DUPLICATE 178
conjecture SUPPOSE 608
conjure SUMMON 604
CONNECT 117
connote MEAN 366
conquer VANQUISH 665
conscientious CAREFUL 74
conscious AWARE 31
consecrate DEDICATE 147
consecrated SACRED 520
CONSENT (v) 118
consequence RESULT 511
consequential SIGNIFICANT 550
conservative RIGHTIST (n) 515
CONSERVE (v) 119
CONSIDER 120
consider STUDY 597
CONSIDERATE 120
consideration RESPECT 508
consign ENTRUST 194
CONSOLE (v) 121
consommé SOUP 570
conspicuous PLAIN 446
CONSPIRACY 122
conspiracy INTRIGUE 316
conspirator ACCOMPLICE 3
constant INVARIABLE (adj) 316
constituent COMPONENT (n) 111
constitution LAW 334
constitutional LAWFUL 335
constrain COMPEL 107
constrain SUBDUE 600
constricted COMPACT 106
construct BUILD 69
CONSULT 122
consume EAT 180
consume USE 660
consummate PERFECT (adj) 435
contact MEET (v) 371
contagious COMMUNICABLE 105
contain CIRCUMSCRIBE 90
contain INCLUDE 300
contaminate POLLUTE 455
contemplate INTEND 313
contemplate STUDY 597
contemporary MODERN 383
CONTEMPTIBLE 123
CONTEMPTUOUS 123
contend COMPETE 108
content CONTENTED 124
CONTENTED 124
contention CONTROVERSY 127
contiguous NEIGHBORING 395
continence TEMPERANCE 620
continent CHASTE 84
contingent CHANCE 80

contingent PROVISIONAL 476
continual PERSISTENT 442
continue PERSIST 441
continuous PERSISTENT 442
contour FORM (n) 232
contract COVENANT 134
CONTRADICT 124
CONTRADICTORY 125
contrary CONTRADICTORY 125
contravene CONTRADICT 124
contretemps MISTAKE 382
contribute FURTHER 241
contributory AUXILIARY 29
contrivance MACHINE 356
contrive DEVISE 160
CONTROL (v) 126
CONTROVERSY 127
controvert CONTRADICT 124
conundrum PUZZLE 480
convene GATHER 241
convenient OPPORTUNE 413
convention MEETING 372
convention TRADITION 634
conventional USUAL 661
CONVERSATION 128
convert CHANGE (v) 81
convertible SEDAN 533
convey CARRY 76
convey TELL 619
convict SENTENCE (n, v) 538
conviction OPINION 411
convincing BELIEVABLE 43
convivial BLITHE 53
convocation MEETING 372
convoy ACCOMPANY 2
convoy FLEET 222
CONVULSION 129
cool COLD 101
cool IMPERTURBABLE 295
cop STEAL (v) 585
cope WITHSTAND 692
copious PREVALENT 465
COPY (n) 130
copy IMITATE 290
cordial GREGARIOUS 256
core CENTER 79
coronary HEART ATTACK 266
corporal PHYSICAL 443
corporeal PHYSICAL 443
CORPSE 131
corpulent FAT 210
correct ACCURATE 4
correct DISCIPLINE 164
correct REPAIR (v) 500
correlate COUNTERPART 131
correspond COINCIDE 100
correspond COMPARE 106
corrupt DEPRAVED 154
costly EXPENSIVE 203
costume DRESS 176
coterie CLIQUE 98
council MEETING 372
counsel ADVICE 9
counsel LAWYER 336
counsel RECOMMEND 492
counselor LAWYER 336
count CONSIDER 120
counteract NEUTRALIZE 398
counterbalance NEUTRALIZE 398
counterfeit SPURIOUS 581
counterinsurgency UPRISING 657
COUNTERPART 131
counterspy SPY 582
COUNTLESS 132
coupe SEDAN 533
couple CONNECT 117
COURAGE 133
courageous BRAVE 65
courteous POLITE 454

courtly POLITE 454
COVENANT 134
cover PROTECTION 474
covert IMPLICIT 298
covet WANT 679
covetous GREEDY 255
cow INTIMIDATE 314
cow OX 424
COWARDLY 134
cower FLINCH 223
co-worker ASSOCIATE 25
coy TIMID 630
cozy COMFORTABLE 104
CRACK (n) 135
crack BREAK (v) 66
craft GUILE 262
craft VESSEL 668
craftsman ARTISAN 22
craftsman ARTIST 22
crave WANT 679
craven COWARDLY 134
crazy PSYCHOTIC 478
crazy QUEER 482
crease fold (n, v) 227
CREATE 135
CREATIVE 136
creator ARTISAN 22
creator ARTIST 22
creature ANIMAL 15
credible BELIEVABLE 43
credit ATTRIBUTE (v) 28
credulous GULLIBLE 262
CREED 137
creed RELIGION 494
creek STREAM 593
creep LURK 355
crenelated ROUGH 518
crevice CRACK 135
CRIME 138
criminal RENEGADE 498
cringe FLINCH (v) 223
crippled LAME 332
crisp DRY (adj) 177
criterion STANDARD 584
critical CRUCIAL 138
criticism DISAPPROVAL 163
crochet KNIT 328
crony FRIEND 237
crook RENEGADE 498
crooked ROUGH 518
crotchet WHIM 687
crow BOAST 56
crowd THRONG (n) 626
CRUCIAL 138
crude VULGAR 673
CRUEL 139
crush BREAK (v) 66
crush LOVE (n) 354
crushing HEAVY 268
crustacean BUG 69
crux KERNEL 325
CRY (n) 140
cry SLOGAN 561
cry WEEP (v) 685
crypt GRAVE 253
cryptic OBSCURE 404
crystalline TRANSPARENT 637
cuddle CARESS (v) 74
cuff BLOW (n) 55
cull CHOOSE 89
culpable REPREHENSIBLE 502
cult DENOMINATION 153
cultivated URBANE 659
cunning GUILE 262
cur MONGREL 386
curb SUBDUE 600
cure TREAT (v) 639
current MODERN 383
CURSE (n) 141

EAGER 179
earn REACH 488
earnest SEDATE 534
earthly WORLDLY 694
earthy SUGGESTIVE 601
ease COMFORT (n) 103
ease SATISFY 525
easy SIMPLE 552
EAT 180
eatery RESTAURANT 510
eavesdrop OVERHEAR 423
ebb WANE (v) 678
ebullient BLITHE 53
ECCENTRICITY 181
ecclesiastic CLERGYMAN 96
ecstasy PLEASURE 450
ecstatic JOYOUS 320
EDGE (n) 181
edgy NERVOUS 397
educate TEACH 617
efface ERASE 195
EFFECT (v) 182
effect RESULT (n) 511
effeminate FEMININE 215
efficient COMPETENT 108
EFFORT 183
effortless SIMPLE 552
EFFRONTERY 183
effulgent BRIGHT 67
effusive SENTIMENTAL 539
EGOISM 184
egotism EGOISM 184
egotistical CONCEITED 113
eject REMOVE 497
elaborate ELEGANT 185
elastic ADAPTABLE 7
elated BLITHE 53
elated JOYOUS 320
elderly OLD 409
elect CHOOSE 89
ELEGANT 185
element COMPONENT 111
elementary SIMPLE 552
elevate RAISE 487
elevated HIGH 272
elf SPRITE 579
eliminate REMOVE 497
elongate EXTEND 205
elucidate CLARIFY 93
elude AVOID 30
emaciated BONY 59
emanate ARISE 20
emasculate STERILIZE 587
embarrass SHAME 543
EMBARRASSMENT 186
embellish ORNAMENT 418
embezzle ROB 516
emblem SYMBOL 612
embolden ENCOURAGE 188
embolism HEART ATTACK 266
emend REVISE 513
emerge ARISE 20
emergent BACKWARD 32
emerging BACKWARD 32
emigrate MIGRATE 376
eminent GREAT 254
emolument SALARY 522
EMOTION 187
employ HIRE 276
employ USE (v) 660
empty VACANT 663
enchanting CHARMING 83
encircle CIRCUMSCRIBE 90
enclose CIRCUMSCRIBE 90
encompass CIRCUMSCRIBE 90
encounter MEET 371
ENCOURAGE 188
encourage CHEER 86
ENCROACH 188

encumber HINDER 273
end FINISH (v) 219
end PURPOSE 479
endeavor TRY (v) 646
endemic NATIVE 394
endless EVERLASTING 197
ENDORSE 189
endowment BEQUEST 48
endure PERSIST 441
endure WITHSTAND 692
enduring PERMANENT 438
enemy OPPONENT 412
energy ZEST 699
enervate WEAKEN 683
enfeeble WEAKEN 683
engage HIRE 276
engaged BUSY 72
engagement FIGHT 216
engaging PLEASING 449
engine MACHINE 356
engrossed BUSY 72
engrossed PREOCCUPIED 464
engulf FLOOD (v) 224
enigma PUZZLE 480
enjoin PROHIBIT 471
enjoyable PLEASING 449
enjoyment PLEASURE 450
ENLARGE 190
enlighten INFORM 306
enlist HIRE 276
enliven STIMULATE 590
ENMITY 191
enormous MASSIVE 363
enough ADEQUATE 9
enquiry QUESTION 483
ENRAGE 191
ensemble ORCHESTRA 415
entente TREATY 639
enterprise PROJECT 471
ENTERTAIN 192
enthusiastic EAGER 179
entice TEMPT 622
ENTIRE (adj) 193
entrancing CHARMING 83
ENTRUST 194
enunciate DECLARE 146
envelop CIRCUMSCRIBE 90
envious GREEDY 255
envoy AMBASSADOR 13
eon PERIOD 437
ephemeral TEMPORARY 621
epicene BISEXUAL 50
epigram PROVERB 475
epigraph PROVERB 475
epitaph PROVERB 475
epoch PERIOD 437
EQUIP 194
equitable RIGHTFUL 514
equivocal DOUBTFUL 175
equivocation DECEPTION 145
era PERIOD 437
eradicate DESTROY 159
eradicate ERASE 195
ERASE 195
erect BUILD 69
EROTIC 195
erratic INCONSTANT 301
error MISTAKE 382
error SIN 553
ersatz ARTIFICIAL 21
erudition LEARNING 339
erupt EXPLODE 204
ESCALATE 196
ESCAPE (v) 197
escape AVOID 30
eschew AVOID 30
escort ACCOMPANY 2
espy PERCEIVE 435
essay COMPOSITION 111

essential INHERENT 308
estate CLASS 94
estate WEALTH 683
esteem RESPECT (n) 508
esthetic ARTISTIC 23
estimate OPINION 411
estrangement LONELINESS 350
eternal EVERLASTING 197
ethical MORAL 387
ethos TRADITION 634
eulogize PRAISE 460
euphemism CIRCUMLOCUTION 89
euphoric JOYOUS 320
euphuism CIRCUMLOCUTION 89
evade AVOID 30
evanescent TEMPORARY 621
evasion TRICK 641
everglade MARSH 361
EVERLASTING 197
everyday DAILY 143
evict REMOVE 497
evidence TESTIMONY 623
evident PLAIN 446
evil DEPRAVED 154
evince SHOW 547
exacerbate UPSET 657
exact ACCURATE 4
exact DEMAND 151
exact DUPLICATE (adj) 178
examination INQUIRY 311
EXAMINE 198
example SAMPLE 523
exasperate OUTRAGE 419
excavation HOLE 278
excellence MERIT 374
EXCELLENT 199
exceptional UNUSUAL 654
excerpt QUOTATION 486
exchange BARTER (v) 36
excitable NERVOUS 397
excite STIMULATE 590
exculpate EXONERATE 202
excursion JOURNEY 320
EXCUSE (n) 200
excuse PARDON (v) 428
execrable CONTEMPTIBLE 123
execration CURSE 141
execute KILL 325
execute PERFORM 436
executive PERFORMER 436
executor ARTISAN 22
exemplar PROTOTYPE 474
exercise TRAINING 635
exertion EFFORT 183
exhaust WEAKEN 683
exhausted TIRED 631
exhibit SHOW (v) 547
exhibitionism MANNERISM 360
exhilarate CHEER 86
exhort INCITE 300
EXILE (v) 200
EXIST 201
EXONERATE 202
expand ENLARGE 190
expanse SIZE 555
expatriate EXILE (v) 200
expect HOPE 279
expectancy EXPECTATION 202
EXPECTATION 202
expedient OPPORTUNE 413
expedite QUICKEN 485
expel REMOVE 497
expend USE 660
EXPENSIVE 203
experienced MATURE 365
expire DIE 160
explain CLARIFY 93
EXPLANATION 203
explicate CLARIFY 93

GREEDY 255
GREET 256
GREGARIOUS 256
gremlin SPRITE 579
GRIEVE 258
GRILL (v) 258
grill QUESTION 484
grim DISMAL 169
grim GRUESOME 260
grimace FROWN (n, v) 239
grin SMILE (n) 565
GRIND (v) 259
grind LABOR (n) 330
grip GRASP (v) 252
gripe COMPLAIN 109
grisly GRUESOME 260
grit COURAGE 133
gross FLAGRANT 220
gross VULGAR 673
grotesque BIZARRE 51
grotto CAVE 78
ground BASIS 37
GROUP (n) 259
group CLIQUE (n) 98
grouse COMPLAIN 109
grovel FLINCH 223
grown-up MATURE 365
growth NEOPLASM 396
GRUESOME 260
gruff BRUSQUE 68
grumble COMPLAIN 109
guarantee ASSURE 26
guarantee PLEDGE (n) 451
guard PROTECT 473
guarded CAUTIOUS 77
guess SUPPOSE 608
guffaw LAUGH (n, v) 333
GUIDE (v) 261
GUILE 262
guileless NAIVE 391
guiltless INNOCENT 310
GULLIBLE 262
gush FLOW (v) 226
gushing SENTIMENTAL 539
gusto ZEST 699
guts COURAGE 133
guts STOMACH 591
gyrate ROTATE 518

habitation HOME 278
habitual USUAL 661
hack HEW 272
hackneyed TRITE 642
haggard BLEAK 53
hail GREET 256
hair-splitting SOPHISTRY 569
hale HEALTHY 265
hallmark SYMBOL 612
hallow DEDICATE 147
hallowed SACRED 520
hallucination DELUSION 150
halt LAME 332
halt STOP (arrest) 592
halt STOP (cease) 593
hamper HINDER 273
hamstrung LAME 332
handcuff SHACKLE (v) 542
handsome BEAUTIFUL 39
hanger-on PARASITE 427
hanker YEARN 697
haphazard RANDOM 488
HAPPEN 263
HAPPINESS 263
happy CHEERFUL 87
happy FAVORABLE 213
happy JOYOUS 320
harangue SPEECH 574
harass BOTHER 60

harbinger PREMONITION 462
harbor PROTECT 473
HARD 264
hard-headed WILLFUL 688
hard-nosed WILLFUL 688
hard palate VOCAL CORDS 671
hardtop SEDAN 533
hard up POOR 456
hardy STRONG 595
HARM (v) 264
harmonious ARTISTIC 23
harpoon SPEAR (n) 572
harridan SHREW 548
harshness BITTERNESS 51
haste SPEED 576
hasten QUICKEN 485
hasty CURSORY 142
hateful OBNOXIOUS 404
hatred ENMITY 191
haughty OVERBEARING 422
haul LOOT (n) 353
haul PULL (v) 479
have POSSESS 458
hayseed YOKEL 698
hazard DANGER 143
hazard VENTURE (v) 665
hazy VAGUE 664
head BOSS 59
head HIPPIE 275
head MIND 376
headlong IMPETUOUS 296
headstrong STUBBORN 596
heal TREAT 639
healthful BENEFICIAL 45
HEALTHY 265
heap PILE (n) 445
heart CENTER 79
HEART ATTACK 266
hearten ENCOURAGE 188
heart failure HEART ATTACK 266
heartfelt SINCERE 553
hearty HEALTHY 265
HEATHEN 267
heave THROW 627
HEAVY 268
heckle BELEAGUER 42
hectic FRANTIC 236
hector BELEAGUER 42
HEEDLESS 268
heel SCOUNDREL 531
heel TIP (v) 630
hefty MASSIVE 363
heifer OX 424
heinous DEPRAVED 154
heist STEAL 585
HELP (n) 269
helper ASSISTANT 25
helpful CONSIDERATE 120
helpless POWERLESS 460
hem and haw STUTTER 599
herculean TREMENDOUS 640
herd PEOPLE 434
hereditary INNATE 309
HERETIC 270
heritage INHERITANCE 308
hermaphroditic BISEXUAL 50
heroic BRAVE 65
hesitant UNWILLING 654
HESITATE 270
HETEROGENEOUS 271
HEW 272
hick YOKEL 698
hideous GRUESOME 260
HIGH (adj) 272
high JOYOUS 320
HIGHEST 273
high-priced EXPENSIVE 203
highway STREET 593
hill MOUNTAIN 389

hillock MOUNTAIN 389
HINDER 273
HINT (n) 274
HIPPIE 275
hipster HIPPIE 275
HIRE 276
hire LEASE 340
HISTORY 277
histrionic THEATRICAL 623
hitch STINT 590
hitch TIE (v) 629
hit the hay RETIRE 511
hit the sack RETIRE 511
hoard ACCUMULATE 3
hoard CONSERVE 119
hoary ANCIENT 15
hobbled LAME 332
HOBBY 277
hobgoblin SPRITE 579
hobo WANDERER 677
hodgepodge JUMBLE 322
hog PIG 444
hoi polloi PEOPLE 434
hoist RAISE (v) 487
hold DELAY (v) 150
hold POSSESS 458
hold-up ROBBERY 517
HOLE 278
hollow HOLE 278
holy SACRED 520
HOME 278
homely UGLY 648
homily SPEECH 574
homograph HOMONYM 279
HOMONYM 279
homophone HOMONYM 279
Homo sapiens MANKIND 359
honest SINCERE 553
honest TRUTHFUL 646
honor AWARD (n) 30
honor RESPECT (n) 508
honorable MORAL 387
honorarium SALARY 522
hood RENEGADE 498
hoodlum RENEGADE 498
hoodwink TRICK 641
hop SKIP (v) 558
HOPE (v) 279
hope EXPECTATION 202
hopeful OPTIMISTIC 415
hopelessness DESPAIR 157
horde THRONG (n) 626
horror FEAR 214
HORSE 280
host THRONG 626
hostel HOTEL 282
HOSTILE 281
hostility ENMITY 191
HOT 281
HOTEL 282
HOUND (n) 282
hound BELEAGUER 42
hound MONGREL 386
HOUSE (n) 283
household HOME 278
housing HOUSE 283
hovel HOME 278
hub CENTER 79
hubbub NOISE 399
huff RESENTMENT 506
hug CARESS (v) 74
huge MASSIVE 363
hulking HUSKY 287
hum SING 554
human HUMANE 283
HUMANE 283
humanitarian HUMANE 283
humanity MANKIND 359
humankind MANKIND 359

inquisition INQUIRY 311
insane PSYCHOTIC 478
inscribe WRITE 696
insecure PRECARIOUS 461
insect BUG 69
inseminate IMPLANT 297
insensible IMPASSIVE 293
insensible NUMB 401
insensitive HEEDLESS 268
INSERT (v) 312
insight ACUMEN 6
insinuation HINT 274
insipid BANAL 34
insolent CONTEMPTUOUS 123
INSOLVENT 313
insouciant JAUNTY 317
inspect EXAMINE 198
inspect SEE 535
inspire ENCOURAGE 188
instance SAMPLE 523
instigate INCITE 300
instill IMPLANT 297
instinct GENIUS 245
institute BEGIN 40
instruct TEACH 617
instruction COMMAND 104
instructor PROFESSOR 470
instrument IMPLEMENT 298
instrumentality MEANS 367
insufficient SCANTY 528
insure ASSURE 26
insurgency UPRISING 657
insurrection UPRISING 657
intact ENTIRE 193
integrity GOODNESS 251
intellect MIND 376
intelligence MIND 376
intelligence NEWS 398
INTEND 313
intensify ESCALATE 196
intent EAGER 179
intercede MEDIATE 369
interchangeable MUTUAL 390
interdict PROHIBIT 471
interest ENTERTAIN 192
interfering MEDDLESOME 368
interior BACKCOUNTRY 32
interior INNER 310
interject INSERT 312
interlude BREAK 65
interminable EVERLASTING 197
intermission BREAK 65
intern CONFINE 116
internal INNER 310
interpolate INSERT 312
interpose INSERT 312
interpose MEDIATE 369
interpret CLARIFY 93
interpretation EXPLANATION 203
interrogate QUESTION 484
interstice OPENING 411
intervene MEDIATE 369
intimate FRIEND 237
intimation HINT 274
INTIMIDATE 314
intolerance BIGOTRY 49
intone SING 554
intractable UNRULY 652
intrepid BRAVE 65
INTRIGUE (n) 316
intrinsic INHERENT 308
introduce INSERT 312
intrude ENCROACH 188
intrusive MEDDLESOME 368
inundate FLOOD 224
invade ENCROACH 188
invalidate VOID 673
INVARIABLE 316
invasion RAID 487

invent CREATE 135
invent DEVISE 160
inventive CREATIVE 136
inventory LISTING 347
investigate EXAMINE 198
invitation REQUEST 504
invite REQUEST 505
invoke SUMMON 604
involve INCLUDE 300
involved PREOCCUPIED 464
inward INNER 310
ire ANGER (n) 15
irony RIDICULE 513
irrational ABSURD 2
irrelevant EXTRANEOUS 206
irreproachable INNOCENT 310
irritate UNSETTLE 653
isolation PRIVACY 467
issue ARISE 20

jabber CHATTER 84
jagged ROUGH 518
jail CONFINE 116
jargon SLANG 559
jaundiced DISTRUSTFUL 171
jaunt JOURNEY (n) 320
JAUNTY 317
javelin SPEAR 572
JAZZ 317
jeer SCOFF 530
jejune BANAL 34
jeopardy DANGER 143
jest JOKE (n) 319
JESUS 318
jewel GEM 243
jewelry GEM 243
jibe COINCIDE 100
jingle POETRY 453
jingle SLOGAN 561
jittery NERVOUS 397
job PROFESSION 469
job STINT 590
job holder LABORER 330
jocose HUMOROUS 285
jocular HUMOROUS 285
jog RUN (v) 519
join CONNECT 117
join SHARE 545
join UNITE 651
joint MUTUAL 390
JOKE (n) 319
jolt IMPACT 292
jot WRITE 696
JOURNEY (n) 320
jovial BLITHE 53
joy PLEASURE 450
JOYOUS 320
JUDGE (n) 321
judgment WISDOM 690
JUMBLE (n) 322
jumpy NERVOUS 397
junk DISCARD (v) 164
junk WASTE (n) 681
junket JOURNEY 320
junta CONSPIRACY 122
JURISDICTION 323
just RIGHTFUL 514
juvenile CHILDISH 88
juxtaposed NEIGHBORING 395

KEEN 324
keen EAGER 179
keep DELAY 150
keep POSSESS 458
KERNEL 325
kibitzer SPECTATOR 573
kick the bucket DIE 160

KILL (v) 325
KIN 326
KIND (n) 327
KINDLE 327
kindness BENEVOLENCE 47
kindred KIN 326
kinfolk KIN 326
kinfolks KIN 326
king-size LARGE 333
kinsfolk KIN 326
kinsmen KIN 326
knack GENIUS 245
knave SCOUNDREL 531
KNIFE (n) 328
KNIT (v) 328
knock BLOW (n) 55
knowledge LEARNING 339

LABEL (v) 329
LABOR (n) 330
LABORER 330
laborious HARD 264
lacerate WOUND 695
LACK (n) 331
lack REQUIRE 506
lackadaisical LISTLESS 348
lackey VALET 664
laconic TERSE 622
ladle SCOOP (v) 531
ladylike FEMININE 215
lag PROCRASTINATE 468
laggard SLOW 563
Lamb JESUS 318
lambent LUMINOUS 355
LAME (adj) 332
lament DEPLORE 154
lament GRIEVE 258
lance SPEAR (n) 572
language WORDING 692
languid LISTLESS 348
languorous LISTLESS 348
LANKY 332
larceny ROBBERY 517
LARGE 333
largess PRESENT 464
larynx VOCAL CORDS 671
lascivious LEWD 345
lash TIE (v) 629
last FINAL 217
last PERSIST 441
lasting PERMANENT 438
latent IMPLICIT 298
laud PRAISE 460
LAUGH (n, v) 333
launch BEGIN 40
lavish GENEROUS 244
LAW 334
LAWFUL 335
LAWLESSNESS 335
LAWYER 336
lax LENIENT 344
lead GUIDE (v) 261
leader BOSS 59
leaf READ 489
LEAGUE 337
league CLUB 98
LEAK (n, v) 338
lean BEND 44
lean THIN 625
leap SKIP (v) 558
learn FIND 218
learner STUDENT 596
LEARNING 339
LEASE (v) 340
LEAVE (abandon) 341
LEAVE (depart) 340
leave QUIT 485
lecherous LEWD 345

PASSIONATE 429
passionate EROTIC 195
pass on DIE 160
pass out FAINT 208
pass over DIE 160
pastime HOBBY 277
pastor MINISTER 377
patent OVERT 424
paternalistic AUTHORITARIAN 28
pathogen VIRUS 670
PATHETIC 430
PATIENCE 431
patriarchal OLD 409
patrimony INHERITANCE 308
patronize CONDESCEND 114
PATTER (n) 432
pattern PROTOTYPE 474
pauperism WANT 678
pause BREAK (n) 65
pause HESITATE 270
pay SALARY 522
peak SUMMIT 604
peculiar QUEER 482
peculiarity CHARACTERISTIC 82
pedantic FAULTFINDING 211
pedantry LEARNING 339
pedigree DESCENT 156
peep SQUEAL (n, v) 582
peeping Tom SPECTATOR 573
peer LOOK (v) 352
pellucid TRANSPARENT 637
pen WRITE 696
penetrate PERMEATE 439
penetrate PIERCE 444
penetrating KEEN 324
pen name PSEUDONYM 477
PENNILESS 433
pensive WISTFUL 691
penury WANT 678
peon SLAVE 560
PEOPLE 434
people FOLK 228
PERCEIVE 435
percept SENSATION 537
perception ACUMEN 6
perception SENSATION 537
perception VISION 671
perceptive OBSERVANT 406
percolate FILTER 217
perennial PERMANENT 438
PERFECT (adj) 435
perfected FULL-FLEDGED 240
PERFORM 436
performance ACT 5
PERFORMER 436
peril DANGER 143
PERIMETER 437
PERIOD 437
peripheral MARGINAL 360
periphery PERIMETER 437
periphrasis CIRCUMLOCUTION 89
perish DIE 160 ·
PERMANENT 438
PERMEATE 439
permissive LENIENT 344
PERMIT (v) 440
perpendicular VERTICAL 667
perpetrate COMMIT 105
perpetual PERMANENT 438
perplex PUZZLE 481
perplexing HARD 264
perquisite CLAIM 92
persecute WRONG 696
persevering DILIGENT 161
PERSIST 441
PERSISTENT 442
personality TEMPERAMENT 619
personnel TROOPS 643
perspicacious KEEN 324

persuade INDUCE 303
pertinacious STUBBORN 596
peruse READ 489
pervade PERMEATE 439
perverse BISEXUAL 50
pervert POLLUTE 455
pester BOTHER 60
pet CARESS 74
petite SMALL 564
petition PLEAD 449
petition REQUEST (n) 504
petty TRIVIAL 643
phantom GHOST 248
pharmaceutical DRUG 177
pharynx VOCAL CORDS 671
philanthropic HUMANE 283
phlegmatic IMPASSIVE 293
phony SHAM (adj) 543
PHYSICAL (adj) 443
physician DOCTOR 173
picayune TRIVIAL 643
pick CHOOSE 89
pictorial GRAPHIC 252
picturesque GRAPHIC 252
piddling MARGINAL 360
piece PART 428
PIERCE 444
PIG 444
pigeonhole LABEL (v) 329
pigheaded STUBBORN 596
pike SPEAR 572
PILE (n) 445
pilfer STEAL 585
pilgrimage JOURNEY 320
pillage PLUNDER 452
pilot GUIDE (v) 261
pimple WART 680
pinch STEAL 585
pine YEARN 697
pinnacle SUMMIT 604
pious RELIGIOUS 495
piquant SAVORY 527
pique RESENTMENT 506
pirate THIEF 624
pit HOLE 278
pitch THROW (v) 627
pithy TERSE 622
pitiable PATHETIC 430
pitiful PATHETIC 430
pitiless INEXORABLE 304
pizazz ZEST 699
placate QUELL 483
place SITE 555
placid TRANQUIL 636
plague BOTHER (v) 60
PLAIN (n) 445
PLAIN (adj) 446
plain UGLY 648
plain-spoken OUTSPOKEN 421
plaintive WISTFUL 691
PLAN (n) 447
plan INTEND 313
plastic MALLEABLE 358
plateau MOUNTAIN 389
platitude TRUISM 644
plaudit APPLAUSE 18
plausible BELIEVABLE 43
PLAYFUL 447
PLAYTHING 448
PLEAD 449
pleasant PLEASING 449
pleasantry JOKE 319
pleased CONTENTED 124
PLEASING 449
PLEASURE 450
pleat FOLD (n, v) 227
PLEDGE (n) 451
plenipotentiary AMBASSADOR 13
plentiful PREVALENT 465

pleonastic VERBOSE 666
pliable MALLEABLE 358
pliant MALLEABLE 358
plot INTRIGUE (n) 316
plotter ACCOMPLICE 3
pluck COURAGE 133
plucky BRAVE 65
plug HORSE 280
plumb VERTICAL 667
plump FAT 210
PLUNDER (v) 452
plunge IMMERSE 290
plutocratic AUTHORITARIAN 28
poach BOIL 57
poesy POETRY 453
POET 452
poetaster POET 452
poetess POET 452
POETRY 453
poignant PATHETIC 430
point SITE 555
pointer HOUND 282
poise CONFIDENCE 115
POISON (n) 454
policy STAND 583
polished EXQUISITE 204
POLITE 454
politic OPPORTUNE 413
pollutants WASTE 681
POLLUTE 455
polyandry POLYGAMY 456
POLYGAMY 456
polygyny POLYGAMY 456
polymorphous perverse BISEXUAL
    50
pompous FORMAL 233
ponder STUDY 597
ponder THINK 626
ponderous MASSIVE 363
poniard KNIFE 328
pony HORSE 280
POOR 456
poor DEFICIENT 148
popular GENERAL 244
populace PEOPLE 434
porker PIG 444
pornographic SMUTTY 566
porridge SOUP 570
portent PREMONITION 462
portion PART (n) 428
portly FAT 210
PORTRAY 457
pose MANNERISM 360
POSITION 458
position STAND 583
positive SURE 609
POSSESS 458
possible WORKABLE 693
POSTPONE 459
postulate SUPPOSE 608
posture STAND 583
potential IMPLICIT 298
potpourri JUMBLE 322
pour FLOW 226
pout FROWN (n, v) 239
poverty WANT 678
poverty-stricken PENNILESS 433
power JURISDICTION 323
powerful STRONG 595
POWERLESS 460
practicable WORKABLE 693
practical WORKABLE 693
practice TRADITION 634
practice TRAINING 635
prairie PLAIN 445
PRAISE (v) 460
prate CHATTER 84
prattle CHATTER (v) 84
preacher MINISTER 377